Flawed Giant

FLAWED GIANT

Lyndon Johnson and His Times
1961–1973

ROBERT DALLEK

New York   Oxford
OXFORD UNIVERSITY PRESS
1998

Oxford University Press

Oxford   New York
Athens   Aukland   Bangkok   Bogotá   Bombay
Buenos Aires   Calcutta   Cape Town   Dar es Salaam
Delhi   Florence   Hong Kong   Istanbul   Karachi
Kuala Lumpur   Madras   Madrid   Melbourne
Mexico City   Nairobi   Paris   Singapore
Taipei   Tokyo   Toronto   Warsaw

and associated companies in
Berlin   Ibadan

Copyright © 1998 by Robert Dallek

Published by Oxford University Press
198 Madison Avenue, New York, New York 10016

Oxford is a registered trademark of Oxford University Press

Library of Congress Cataloging-in-Publication Data
Dallek, Robert.
Flawed Giant:
Lyndon Johnson and His Times, 1961–1973 /
Robert Dallek.
p.   cm.   Includes bibliographical references and index.
ISBN 0-19-505465-2
1. Johnson, Lyndon B. (Lyndon Baines), 1908–1973.
2. Presidents—United States—Biography.
3. United States—Politics and government—1961–1963.
4. United States—Politics and government—1963–1969.
5. United States—Politics and government—1969–1974.
I. Title   E847.D26   1998
973.923'092—dc21   [B]   97-39084

3   5   7   9   8   6   4   2

Printed in the United States of America
on acid-free paper

For Geri
Who Makes It All Possible

Contents

Preface

Like Lyndon Johnson's contemporaries, historians disagree about his presidential standing. A 1996 assessment of his White House record by thirty-two scholars was notable for its differences: fifteen historians saw him as a near great President; twelve thought him only average; and five described him as either below average or a failure.

I wish this second volume on LBJ's life, which principally focuses on his presidency, more clearly defined his place in history. But it doesn't. His contradictions—flaws and virtues, successes and failures—are on full display and will both enhance and detract from his historical reputation.

More important than the book's impact on Johnson's presidential ranking is its contribution to our understanding of the man and his actions. Presidential standing, especially of recent Presidents, is subject to constant change; explanation has a more enduring influence.

As in his pre-presidential career, Johnson was an outsized character who did his utmost to hide his intentions. Believing that understanding was power and that uncertainty about his views shielded him from opposition, he worked to baffle his contemporaries. He remembered FDR's comment to Treasury Secretary Henry Morgenthau, Jr.: "You are my right hand, but I always keep my left hand under the table."

Unpredictability was a political weapon. Occasionally, when reporters got advanced word on a presidential appointment, Johnson would name someone else to throw the press off-balance. Trip itineraries were kept from journalists until the last possible minute and changes along the way were commonplace. Task force reports describing domestic problems and remedies were "state secrets"; premature revelations of presidential intentions were "impediments" to the Great Society.

Outlandish comments and behavior were other parts of Johnson's political calculations. Urinating in a sink, inviting people into the bathroom, showing off a scar, exposing his private parts—after a while nothing surprises the biographer. For Johnson, they were meant to shock and confuse and leave him in control.

Johnson was an actor, a role player who in turn could be courtly and crude, gentle and overbearing, magnanimous and vindictive. There was no trusting anything he said or did on a given day, recall those in constant attendance at his White House. Posturing was a device for extracting information and influencing political friends and foes.

The events described in my first volume about Johnson's rise to prominence as a congressional secretary, National Youth Administration director, congressman, and Senate Majority Leader are a prelude to understanding his more consequential actions as President.

There is no question but that LBJ wished to be the greatest presidential reformer in the country's history. In his first State of the Union message in January 1964, he asked Congress to do "more for civil rights than the last hundred sessions combined," and "to build more homes, more schools, more libraries, and more hospitals than any single session of Congress in the history of the Republic."

The war on poverty and the Great Society flowed from Johnson's impulse to transform the nation's domestic life. But we have been left with numerous questions as to how Johnson intended to reach "the promised land," as he called it. The many laws passed in 1964 and 1965 were works in progress, not finished acts of calculation defining LBJ's welfare state. Thirty years later, the opening of presidential records gives us insights into Johnson's intentions that we hadn't fully understood before.

Beginning in 1965, the Vietnam War slowed and sidetracked LBJ from implementing and adding to the domestic changes of his first two years in office. Whatever his public rhetoric about having both guns and butter, the war decisively shifted his focus and energies from altering America to shaping events overseas.

Vietnam is a particular conundrum. From the first, Johnson knew that the war was a potential disaster for the country and his administration. He was far more anguished by the conflict and much less certain about how to proceed than we have previously thought. And yet he pursued the conflict with a determination that defies good sense. The sources of Johnson's commitment to fighting the war are among the principal questions I address in this book.

The 1968 election is another part of the story that yields to greater understanding than we have had—about both Johnson's motives and actions, which he obscured during the campaign.

Most of all, though, this is a biography about a brilliant, highly effective, but deeply troubled man. At times, Johnson came frighteningly close to clinical paranoia. His presidency raises questions about executive incapacity that can neither be ignored nor easily addressed.

For all my research effort, the book is hardly the last word on so important a twentieth-century President. The release in coming years of some 6500 taped conversations will be an inducement to future biographers to recount Johnson's presidential career. As with the approximately 3700 tape recordings that the LBJ presidential library has already made available, I expect that the unprocessed materials will add rich detail to the story rather than fundamentally alter it. Nevertheless, I hope that this study will lay the groundwork for others in trying to understand and measure as complicated and controversial a character as ever sat in the White House.

Washington, D.C.   R.D.
September 1997

Acknowledgments

This second volume on Lyndon Johnson's life completes fourteen years of work on the man and his times. As with *Lone Star Rising*, this book is a collaborative effort of the author with participants in the administration, archivists, other scholars, journalists, editors, my family members, and personal friends.

The Lyndon B. Johnson Library in Austin, Texas, is a model of what a presidential library should be: an even-handed facilitator of scholarship on LBJ and his presidency. The tone is set by Harry Middleton, the library's director, who has devoted the last twenty-five years to opening the vast collection of manuscripts and now tape recordings for use by anyone with an interest in studying Johnson and his times.

Others at the library have been equally forthcoming: I am indebted to Tina Houston, the archivist, Charles Corkran, Allen Fisher, Kathy Frankum, Regina Greenwell, David Humphrey, Michael Parrish, Lawrence Reed, E. Philip Scott, Robert Tissinger, John Wilson, and Gary Yarrington for their help. Four others at the library earned my special appreciation. Linda Hanson answered my requests for materials and my many questions with unfailing good humor and made access to the millions of documents in the library a feasible enterprise. Claudia Anderson, Mary Knill, and Ted Gittinger were more than helpmates in climbing the mountains of paper records and oral histories; they are dear friends who made my visits to the library more a pleasure than a chore.

Robert Divine, James Galbraith, Lewis L. Gould, Dagmar and Robert Hamilton, Sanford Levinson, and Thomas D. Russell at the University of Texas endured my ramblings about LBJ and made wise suggestions which in one way or another were incorporated into this second volume.

I am indebted to the numerous people who agreed to share their recollections of LBJ with me, including Lady Bird Johnson, McGeorge Bundy, William P. Bundy, George Christian, Murray Fromson, Robert Hardesty, Nicholas Katzenbach, Robert McNamara, Harry Middleton, Bill Moyers, George Reedy, Walt and Elspeth Rostow, and Larry and Luann Temple.

Several people read parts of the manuscript or contributed useful suggestions for revision and correction through conversations about the manuscript: Joel Aberbach, Irving Bernstein, Michael Beschloss, William P. Bundy, Matthew Dallek, Elias P. Demetracopoulos, Jeffrey Frieden, Edward A. Goldstein, Max Holland, Robert Jervis, Stanley I. Kutler, Lawrence W. Levine, Peter Loewenberg, Arthur Schlesinger, Jr., Bruce Schulman, Martin Sherwin, Jeff Shesol, Martin and Susan Tolchin, Richard Weiss, and John Wright. William C. Gibbons kindly let me read the proofs of the fourth volume of his magisterial Vietnam study. W. Thomas Johnson gave me access to his valuable oral histories. Diana Claitor did the photo research for the book. Roger E. Sandler generously helped with selecting and organizing the book's illustrations.

Stephen J. Solarz, Geraldine Dallek, and Brian VanDeMark read the entire manuscript and provided invaluable suggestions for improvement. I am greatly in their debt.

My editor and dear friend Sheldon Meyer at the Oxford University Press has been a mainstay in seeing both LBJ volumes to completion. His masterful reading of the manuscript for this book, with excellent suggestions for cuts and additions, makes him a kind of co-author. Sheldon's forty-year career at the Press has given us more valuable studies of U.S. history than that of probably any other editor in this century. The historical guild looks forward to the additional contributions to scholarship he will surely be making in retirement.

I am indebted to several other people at Oxford University Press for their help in publishing this volume: Joellyn Ausanka, John Brehm, Laura Brown, Ellen Chodosh, Mary Ellen Curley, Susan Day, Marjorie Mueller, Vera Plummer, Susan Rotermund, Brandon Trissler, and Jonathan Weiss. Stephanie Sakson did a first-rate job of copyediting, saving me from more errors than I can count.

I am grateful to Tony Smith at the University of Minnesota for help with the Hubert H. Humphrey Papers and to Carol Ebert for help with the Richard Russell materials at the University of Georgia. The UCLA Academic Senate supported my research with several grants. Jack Bresch and Jaime Steve helped by reading page proof.

Most of all I am grateful to my wife, Geraldine Dallek, who took time from her full professional life to help with my work, and to our children, Matthew Dallek and Rebecca Dallek, for their understanding and support.

Flawed Giant

1

"The Most Insignificant Office"

THE morning of January 20, 1961, dawned cold and clear. The eighteen-mile-an-hour wind gusts and the seven inches of snow that had fallen on Washington, D.C., the previous day gave way to bright sunshine and a twenty-two-degree noontime temperature. On the east wing of the Capitol, where an inaugural platform and temporary wooden grandstands had been erected, thousands had gathered to witness the swearing-in of the new President and Vice President. As Lyndon Baines Johnson, the Vice President-elect, walked onto the platform, a Texas partisan rose to his feet, waved his ten-gallon hat, and shouted, "All the Way with LBJ," Johnson's campaign slogan in his 1960 bid for the presidency. Johnson waved and smiled.

His look of pleasure at the friendly reception masked the mixed feelings he had had since accepting John F. Kennedy's proposal to become his running mate. At 12:40, as he shed his overcoat and stepped forward to take the oath of office, Johnson was nervous and distracted. During the singing of "The Star Spangled Banner" by Marian Anderson he had stood glum and silent. Speaker of the House Sam Rayburn, Johnson's fellow Texan and strongest supporter in Congress since LBJ had entered the Lower House in 1937, administered the oath. Despite the brevity and familiarity of the pledge, Johnson stumbled over its closing words.[1]

He was a reluctant Vice President. He had hoped and planned for the presidency, but fate or the limitations of his time, place, and personality had cast him in the second spot. And he despised it. From his earliest days in the Texas Hill Country, he had aspired to be the best, to outdo friend and foe. He needed to win higher standing, hold greater power, earn more money than anyone else. Some inner sense of want drove him to seek status, control, and wealth. Being less than top dog made him feel rejected and unworthy.

It is never easy to identify the origins of such strivings. In Johnson's case, nature and nurture surely played their parts. Sam Ealy Johnson, LBJ's father, was a hard-driving, grandiose character whose two terms in the Texas lower house and activism in local politics only partly satisfied his reach for public influence. Rebekah Baines, LBJ's mother, took pride in her prominent Texas ancestors, and expected her oldest son to reach heights worthy of her family's heritage.

If success and prominence were Johnson and Baines bloodlines, LBJ's childhood also contributed to his larger-than-life personality. Johnson was an emotional orphan. He was the offspring of "absent" parents: his father was a self-absorbed character who was often away from the household, and his mother was usually too depressed to fill her children's emotional needs. LBJ's childhood is an object lesson in the formation of a narcissistic personality. Yet it does not explain how so self-centered a child, adolescent, and mature man was able to translate his neediness into constructive achievements that were the envy of healthier personalities. LBJ is also an object-lesson in the complexity of human behavior. He may have been, as *New York Times* columnist Russell Baker says, "a human puzzle so complicated nobody can ever understand it."

How, for example, are we to explain Johnson's misery during the 1960 campaign? Running for Vice President hardly seems like a punishable offense—unless you were Lyndon Johnson. His sense of defeat at having to take second place expressed itself in "the heaviest period of boozing" in his life. At times his staff "had to lift him physically out of bed and pump his arms up and down to stimulate breathing and make him functional." One night "he went on an incredible toot... wandered up and down the corridors" of the hotel and crawled into bed with one of the secretaries, where he tried "to snuggle into her arms the same way a small child will snuggle into its mother's arms."[2]

Throughout his life Johnson had demonstrated a compensatory grandiosity that spawned legends. In one of them, German Chancellor Ludwig Erhard asked Johnson whether he had been born in a log cabin. "No, no, no," LBJ answered, "you're confusing me with Abe Lincoln. I was born in a manger."

Political rivals, collaborators, and journalists all felt the energy of his drive. He was a human dynamo, one childhood friend remembered. Fellow senator Hubert Humphrey compared him to "a tidal wave.... He went through the walls. He'd come through a door, and he'd take the whole room over. Just like that.... There was nothing delicate about him." Bending people to his will became an art form

Washington journalists Rowland Evans and Robert Novak called "the treatment." Meeting Johnson reminded Ben Bradlee of the *Washington Post* of going to the zoo. "You really felt as if a St. Bernard had ...pawed you all over.... He never just shook hands with you. One hand was shaking your hand; the other hand was always someplace else, exploring you, examining you."[3]

Johnson's behavior largely came from the conviction that intimidation was indispensable in bending people to his will. It was gratifying to have people love you, but it was essential to overpower them if you were to win on controversial public issues. Johnson's more than thirty years in politics told him that people did not act out of affection for others but rather for reasons of self-interest or concern that you had the capacity and will to help or hurt them.

The economist Gardner Ackley remembers a meeting in LBJ's office with Roger Blough, the chairman of U.S. Steel. Johnson wanted Blough to hold the line on steel prices. And so he "just started working him over and asking him questions and lecturing him. I have never seen a human being reduced to such a quivering lump of flesh. ...But it wasn't really what he said, it was the way he just leaned over and looked at him."[4]

Robert Strauss, the Texas Democratic party power broker, was an intimidating figure in his own right. Yet he recalls being no match for Johnson. "Lyndon Johnson just towered over me and intimidated me terribly," Strauss said. "He's the one person who had my number all his life. Even when he was a sick old man, out of office, whenever he called, perspiration broke out on the top of my head. He was the best I ever saw. Tragic, but the best I ever saw. I remember once asking him, 'Why did you cast that vote, Mr. President?' 'Bob,' he said, 'one thing you'll learn someday is that you have to be a demagogue on a lot of little things if you want to be around to have your way on the big things.' I'll never forget him saying that. A lesson in primer politics from the Master."[5]

In the fifty-two years before he became Vice President, Johnson had converted his ambition into a series of political triumphs. As secretary to a wealthy, self-indulged south Texas congressman, he had taken over the duties of the office, making it responsive to depression-ridden farmers, businessmen, and Army veterans. In the mid-thirties, he became the youngest and best state director of FDR's National Youth Administration, a Texas *wunderkind* who at age twenty-eight beat several better known opponents for a south-central Texas congressional seat. After eleven years in the House, where he established himself as a supremely effective congressman with powerful White

House ties, he defeated, by fair means and foul, one of the most popular governors in Texas history for a U.S. Senate seat. Twelve years in the Senate, where he became the most effective Majority Leader in American history, made him a viable but unsuccessful candidate for President.[6]

Johnson's reach for power and influence rested on more than a desire for personal gain. Although self-serving ends were always a prime concern, he was never happier than when he could marry his ambition to some larger design. He associated his attainment of high office with the delivery of "good works." He told his biographer Doris Kearns: "Some men want power simply to strut around the world and to hear the tune of 'Hail to the Chief.' Others want it simply to build prestige, to collect antiques, and to buy pretty things. Well, I wanted power to give things to people—all sorts of things to all sorts of people, especially the poor and the blacks."

Johnson had a keen sense of identification with the needy. Throughout his life he had suffered from feelings of emptiness, which he answered with constant activity: "I never think about politics more than 18 hours a day," he joked. He filled himself with excessive eating, drinking, and smoking, and an affinity for womanizing—sexual conquests gave him temporary respites from feeling unwanted, unloved, unattended.

His strivings also translated into efforts to fill the poor with the material possessions and psychic well-being he wanted for himself. It was as if the disadvantaged were extensions of himself; his yearning for recognition, for concrete and symbolic demonstrations of his worth expressed itself in helping others, but especially those most in need. For Johnson, gaining the presidency meant fulfilling fantasies about becoming a great man who gave all Americans a richer life. The recipients of Johnson's largesse were understandably indifferent to what propelled him, and any final assessment of his work does better to focus on the consequences of his actions than their origins. His motives are essentially a matter of analytic interest to biographers and historians.[7]

Pained by childhood poverty in rural Texas, educated by national deprivation during the depression, and inspired by FDR, the greatest liberal reformer in the nation's history, Johnson had indeed produced "good works." His commitment to New Deal, Fair Deal programs, the liberal nationalism of the 1930s and 1940s, helped transform America, particularly his native South and West. Aid to education, dams providing flood control, conservation, and cheap rural electrification, public works modernizing the nation's infrastructure, low-cost public housing sheltering millions of poor Americans, Social Security benefits, minimum wages, and farm subsidies serving the elderly, unskilled workers, and farmers, black civil rights, and space exploration through a National Aeronautics and Space Administration (NASA), all had benefited from LBJ's public service.[8]

And now after thirty years of accomplishment, as Vice President, he found himself in a dead-end job. Or so the 172-year history of the office suggested. There were no notable achievements by a Vice President to give him comfort, and no Vice President had succeeded to the presidency by election since Martin Van Buren in 1836. Johnson was mindful of the observation made by Thomas R. Marshall, Woodrow Wilson's V.P., that the Vice President "is like a man in a cataleptic state. He cannot speak. He cannot move. He suffers no pain. And yet he is conscious of all that goes on around him." John Adams, the first occupant of the office, wrote: "I am Vice President. In this I am nothing, but *I may be everything.*" Johnson recalled: "Every time I came into John Kennedy's presence, I felt like a goddamn raven hovering over his shoulder."[9]

John Kennedy added to Johnson's sense of being eclipsed and useless. The son of a famous father, Joseph P. Kennedy, Harvard-educated, handsome, charming, urbane, a northeastern aristocrat with all the advantages, JFK appeared to be everything LBJ was not. As painful to Johnson, Kennedy's claim on the presidency seemed unmerited alongside of his own. "It was the goddamnedest thing," Johnson later told Kearns, "here was a whippersnapper.... He never said a word of importance in the Senate and he never did a thing. But somehow ... he managed to create the image of himself as a shining intellectual, a youthful leader who would change the face of the country." Behind Kennedy's back, Johnson called him "sonny boy," a "lightweight" who needed "a little gray in his hair."

When the forty-three-year-old Kennedy, the youngest man ever elected to the presidency, declared in his Inaugural speech that "the torch has been passed to a new generation of Americans," Johnson saw the reference as applying not only to Eisenhower, at age seventy, the oldest man then to have served in the White House, but also to himself. To be sure, he had established a record as an exceptional Senate leader and had made a significant contribution to JFK's victory in November 1960, helping him carry Texas and six other southern states. But whatever his political savvy as a legislator and a campaigner, he was now an outsider, a marginal figure in a Kennedy White House taking its distance from familiar faces and programs as it sought to conquer "the New Frontier."[10]

Defining the Job

Johnson had no intention of remaining a fringe player in a Kennedy administration. He had left the Senate in part because he believed he would not be able to sustain his influence as majority leader: the bipartisanship of Eisenhower's presidency, a necessary condition of LBJ's influence, seemed certain to disappear; a Democratic or Kennedy White House also seemed likely to diminish Johnson's importance in the 87th Congress beginning in 1961.

In accepting the vice-presidential nomination, he had high hopes of transforming the office. Presiding over the Senate and casting rare tie-breaking votes—a Vice President's only constitutional duties—were not Johnson's idea of how to achieve a second four years as Vice President and a record to win the presidency. A promise from Jack Kennedy to Sam Rayburn that he would give Lyndon "important domestic duties and send him on trips abroad" was music to Johnson's ears. During the 1960 campaign one of Johnson's aides told him that the Founding Fathers "intended the Vice President to be the number two man in the government" and that a larger executive role for the Vice President should complement a significant part for him in rallying Congress behind the President's program. Johnson wanted the memo published in a national magazine.[11]

Johnson's plan to make himself a powerful Vice President ran into insurmountable obstacles. On January 3, seventeen days before taking office, he tried to assure himself of an unprecedented congressional role. At a Democratic Senate caucus, Mike Mansfield of Montana, Johnson's hand-picked successor as Majority Leader, asked the 63 Democratic senators to let Johnson preside over future caucuses. The proposal angered several senators, who saw this as a power grab and a challenge to the traditional separation of congressional–executive authority. Liberal Senator Albert Gore, Sr., of Tennessee spearheaded the opposition: "This caucus is not open to former senators," he declared. Although a vote of 46 to 17 gave Johnson a large majority, it left no doubt in his mind that most senators opposed the plan. "You could feel the heavy animosity in the room, even from many who voted for Lyndon," Gore asserted. The reaction of his Senate colleagues humiliated and enraged Johnson. "I now know the difference between a caucus and a cactus," he told someone who leaked his remark to reporters. "In a cactus all the pricks are on the outside."[12]

Johnson suffered another humiliating defeat within days after becoming Vice President. In his eagerness to establish an important role for himself, Johnson proposed that Kennedy sign an Executive Order giving the Vice President "general supervision" over a number of government agencies, including NASA, and directing Cabinet heads and department chiefs to give Johnson copies of all major documents sent to the President. Knowing a power grab when he saw one, Kennedy simply ignored the memo. But White House aides, determined to put Johnson in his place at the start of the new administration, leaked the incident to the press and compared Lyndon to William Seward, Lincoln's Secretary of State, who had made a similar unsuccessful proposal.[13]

Yet in turning aside Lyndon's reach for power, Kennedy did not want to alienate him and destroy his usefulness to the administration. Indeed, Kennedy was sensitive to Lyndon's plight: the powerful Majority Leader of 1955–60, whom the younger, less experienced JFK had to court for favors, was now the supplicant asking for a share of power. Kennedy had no intention of letting Lyndon become a dominant figure or more than a well-controlled functionary in his government. But neither did he wish to provoke him into becoming a covert opponent, as John Nance Garner, FDR's first Vice President, had been. "I can't afford to have my Vice President, who knows every reporter in Washington, going around saying we're all screwed up, so we're going to keep him happy," JFK told White House aide Kenneth O'Donnell. Having won the presidency by a paper-thin margin over Nixon and needing southern Democratic support to pass significant legislation and win reelection to a second term, JFK saw LBJ as a useful political ally.

Kennedy tried to assuage Johnson's huge ego with the trappings of power. He raised no objection to letting Lyndon hold on to his Majority Leader's office, a seven-room suite across from the Senate floor, known as the "Taj Mahal" or the "Emperor's Room." Decorated in royal green and gold with crystal chandeliers and plush furniture, the office featured a lighted full-length portrait of Johnson leaning against a bookcase and two overhead lamps projecting "an impressive nimbus of golden light" as Lyndon sat at his desk. In addition, although Kennedy rejected a request from Johnson for an office next to the President's, he assigned him a six-room suite on the second floor of the Executive Office Building (EOB) next to the White House. Since many, including Presidents Truman and Eisenhower, believed that the Vice President was a member of the legislative rather than the executive branch, Johnson's presence in the EOB had significant constitutional implications. Kennedy also invited Lyndon to attend Cabinet meetings, weekly sessions with House and Senate Leaders, pre-press conference briefings, and National Security Council meetings, as required by law.[14]

Kennedy insisted that his staff treat Johnson with the same

respect they would have wanted shown him were their positions reversed. "You are dealing with a very insecure, sensitive man with a huge ego," JFK told O'Donnell. "I want you literally to kiss his fanny from one end of Washington to the other." Kennedy also asked Angier Biddle Duke, White House Chief of Protocol, to take care of the Johnsons. " 'I want you to . . . see that they're not ignored, not only when you see them but at all other occasions.' " Kennedy explained that everyone in the administration eventually would be so busy they would forget about Johnson, and he wanted Duke "to remember." And so during White House photo sessions, when Lyndon "would always hang in the back as if he felt he was unwanted," Duke "would say in a loud voice, 'Mr. Vice President, Mr. Vice President,' and then the president would look around and say, 'Where's Lyndon? Where's Lyndon?' Johnson liked that, and he'd come up front."

New York Times columnist Arthur Krock remembered Kennedy's "often" expressing concern about Lyndon, saying, " 'I've got to keep him happy somehow.' " To appease Johnson, who would descend on him with personal complaints, Kennedy worked out a routine with O'Donnell. JFK would first hear Lyndon out, and then call in O'Donnell for a tongue-lashing about Johnson's problem. Johnson would then "go away somewhat happier." Johnson told Secretary of State Dean Rusk that he "had been treated better than any other Vice President in history and knew it."[15]

Johnson's satisfaction was hardly Kennedy's first priority. His problems with the Soviet Union, Cuba, Southeast Asia, the domestic economy, black pressure for equal rights, and the political survival of his administration left him little room to fret over a discontented Vice President. Yet he had genuine regard for Johnson as a "political operator" and even liked his "roguish qualities." More important, he viewed him as someone who, despite the limitations of the vice presidency, could contribute to the national well-being in foreign and domestic affairs and, by so doing, make Kennedy a more effective President.

JFK gave some careful thought to Johnson's role in the administration. He did not want him managing its legislative program and creating the impression that the President was following the lead of his Vice President, a more experienced legislator. Kennedy was happy to have Johnson gather intelligence on what senators and representatives were thinking, but he had no intention of allowing him to become the point man or administration leader on major bills. Besides, he understood that Johnson no longer had the means he used as Majority Leader to drive bills through the Senate. Instead, he wanted Johnson to head a new Committee on Equal Employment Opportunity (CEEO), chair the National Aeronautics and Space Council, and represent the United States on trips abroad.[16]

Kennedy knew that civil rights was going to be a major issue during the next four years. The campaign in the fifties by Martin Luther King, Jr., and the Southern Christian Leadership Conference against racial segregation made civil rights a compelling question for JFK's administration. He doubted, however, that a cautious Congress dominated by southern Democrats would be favorably disposed to a bill assuring black Americans the right to vote and access to public facilities across the South. Consequently, he planned to rely on executive action as an immediate device for advancing black equality. He wanted the CEEO to combat discriminatory hiring practices in the federal government and by private businesses with federal contracts. Lyndon was to be one of the principal figures implementing this strategy. As a southern moderate who had led a major civil rights law through the Congress in 1957 and believed the national well-being required equal treatment for blacks, Johnson could be invaluable in advancing a rational response to a highly charged issue and preventing southern alienation from the administration.

At the same time, Kennedy wanted Johnson, the legislative father of NASA, to have a significant part in shaping space policy. Again, he would not let Lyndon eclipse him on an issue given high public visibility by Soviet space shots, but he was eager to use Johnson's expertise on a matter of vital national concern. Moreover, in giving Johnson some prominence as an architect of America's space program, Kennedy was making him a political lightning rod. Should an effort to catch and pass the Soviets in space technology fail or suffer a well-publicized defeat, Lyndon would be out front taking some, if not much, of the heat. As for trips abroad, this was a ceremonial given of the Vice President's office, but Kennedy also saw them as an outlet for Johnson's restless energy.[17]

None of what Kennedy asked him to do made Johnson happy. He resented the President's unwillingness to rely on his legislative expertise, telling people that his knowledge and contacts on the Hill were not being used. "You know, they never once asked me about that!" he complained privately about administration dealings with Congress. He had little enthusiasm for foreign travels that would be more symbolic than substantive. Although he saw some political benefits coming to him from chairing CEEO and the Space Council, he also saw liabilities that could work against his having another vice-presidential term or ever getting to the presidency. As important, he viewed both jobs as relegating him to a distinctly secondary role in the administration, which, of course, they did.

Goodwill Ambassador

Initially, one of the hardest assignments for Johnson to accept was that of goodwill ambassador. In the nearly three years he served as Vice President, he spent almost two and a half months making eleven trips to thirty-three foreign lands. Most of it consisted of showing the flag. But Kennedy saw it as a good way to fill Johnson's time and improve his disposition. Kennedy told Florida Senator George Smathers, "I cannot stand Johnson's damn long face. He just comes in, sits at the Cabinet meetings with his face all screwed up, never says anything. He looks so sad." Smathers suggested that the President send Johnson "on an around-the-world trip . . . so that he can get all of the fanfare and all of the attention and all of the smoke-blowing will be directed at him, build up his ego again, let him have a great time." Kennedy thought it "a damn good idea," and in the spring of 1961 he sent Johnson to Africa and Asia.[18]

Johnson was reluctant to spend his time on what he saw as mostly frivolous business. But his craving for center stage, which he could have traveling abroad but not at home, quickly made him an enthusiast of foreign trips. Indeed, they became a kind of theater in which he could act out his zany, irreverent, demanding, impetuous characteristics that amused and pleased some and offended and amazed others. They also gave him an opportunity to bring a message of hope to needy people in distant lands. In Africa and Asia his trips partly became a crusade for the New Deal reforms that had transformed America. Eager to combat Communist appeals to poor developing nations, Johnson pointed to economic change in his native South as a model for Third World advance.[19]

A four-day trip to Senegal in April 1961 was part comic opera and part serious diplomatic mission. Kennedy's decision to send Lyndon there largely rested on a desire to compete with Communist efforts to woo emerging nations. For Johnson, it immediately became a chance to play the great man offering enlightened guidance to an impoverished people. He insisted that a seven-foot bed to accommodate his six-foot-three-and-a-half-inch frame, a special shower head that emitted a needlepoint spray, cases of Cutty Sark, and boxes of ballpoint pens and cigarette lighters with L.B.J. inscribed on them travel with him to Dakar.

There, he ignored the diplomatic niceties urged upon him by

the U.S. Embassy. One morning at 4:30 he and Lady Bird traveled to a fishing village, where the American ambassador refused to leave his limousine. "It was too smelly a town for him," a Johnson traveling companion recalls. The ambassador counseled Johnson against any contact with these people, whom he described as dirty and diseased. But the Vice President strolled among the villagers handing out pens and lighters, shaking hands with everyone, including a few fingerless lepers, and advising the bewildered natives that they could be like Texans, who had increased their annual income tenfold in forty years. Back at the ambassador's residence he kept the household up most of the night sending and receiving cables and irritating the ambassador's wife, who clattered up and down the stairs in a long robe and slippers bringing refreshments on a great silver tray. When he returned to the United States, Johnson told black civil rights leader Roy Wilkins that Senegalese mothers, into whose eyes he looked, were just like Texas mothers; all of them wanted the best for their children. The trip was a microcosm of Johnson's career: a grandiose, temperamental man doing outlandish things simultaneously to get attention and improve the lot of the poor.[20]

A two-week trip to Asia in May had a similar design. With Communist insurrections threatening to overturn pro-Western governments in Southeast Asia, Kennedy sent Johnson and Jean and Stephen Smith, JFK's sister and brother-in-law, to visit government chiefs in Laos, South Vietnam, Taiwan, the Philippines, Thailand, India, and Pakistan. The principal business of the trip was in Saigon, where Johnson was supposed to encourage Ngo Dinh Diem, the President of South Vietnam, to introduce social reforms and increase his military effort against the Communists.

Most recollections of this trip, however, focus on Johnson's outlandish behavior. While crossing the Pacific he exploded at long-time aide Horace Busby for some omission, ordering him off the plane. "But we're over the ocean," Busby replied. "I don't give a fucking damn!" Johnson shouted. Mrs. Johnson's intervention restored peace. In Saigon, while security people responsible for the Vice President's safety fretted and everyone sweated in the stifling heat, Johnson repeatedly stopped a motorcade from the airport into the city to shake hands with South Vietnamese onlookers and give them pens, cigarette lighters, and gold and white passes to the U.S. Senate gallery. "Get your mamma and daddy to bring you to the Senate and Congress and see how the government works," he told bewildered children. In downtown Saigon he made a passionate arm-waving speech in which he called Diem the Winston Churchill of Asia. "He was totally carried away by the occasion," one journalist remembered. The next day, in a suburb of Saigon, when he discovered a herd of Texas cattle bred on the King ranch, he chased them around a pasture until the photographers could get a good picture of him with the steers. Back at the hotel, during a press conference that included several foreign correspondents he didn't know, he disrobed, toweled himself off, and climbed into fresh clothes.[21]

In Bangkok he held a press conference in his pajamas at three in the morning to respond to some misinformation published by a newspaper. The next night Johnson aides announced a 7 a.m. tour of the Klongs, the water market. One journalist then received a call in the middle of the night canceling the trip and a second call at 6:30 in the morning saying that Johnson had already gone. Cautioned that touching people, and particularly anyone's head, would offend the Thais, Johnson strolled the streets of Bangkok shaking hands and jumped on a bus, where he patted children on the head. Entering a store full of Chinese customers, Johnson lectured the non-English-speaking crowd on the virtues of democracy and the dangers of Chinese Communism. In a meeting with the Thai Prime Minister, a military dictator, Johnson repeated assurances stated in a letter from JFK of American concern for Thai security, and advised that "now is the time to separate the men from the boys." One American diplomat who accompanied the Vice President cabled the State Department: "Saigon, Manila, Taipei, and Bangkok will never be quite the same again."[22]

India was next on Johnson's agenda. John Kenneth Galbraith, the Harvard economist who had become JFK's Ambassador to New Delhi, gave the President a sample of his famous wit in a note about Johnson's arrival. "Lyndon . . . arrives next week with two airplanes, a party of fifty, a communications unit, and other minor accoutrements of modern democracy. I . . . will try to make him feel good that he was on the ticket. His trip may not be decisive for the peace of Asia. The East, as you know, is inscrutable." In New Delhi Johnson had what he called "a belly-to-belly talk" with Prime Minister Jawaharlal Nehru, a neutralist in the Cold War. A want of "appreciable business" between the two produced long silences on Nehru's part until Johnson hit on the subject of rural electrification, a matter on which they were in fervent agreement. The conversation impressed Galbraith as innocuous: "Both Nehru and Johnson spoke rather formally on education, which they favored; poverty, which they opposed; freedom, which they endorsed; [and] peace, which they wanted."[23]

The rest of Johnson's stay in India consisted of brief trips outside New Delhi, where he campaigned as if he were running for Congress. Galbraith told a translator: "If Lyndon forgets and asks for votes, leave that out." Johnson rode on a bullock cart, drew water from a well, laid a cornerstone at an engineering institute, shook hands all around, handed out pencils with the inscription, "Compliments of your Senator, Lyndon B. Johnson—the greatest good for the greatest number," and recounted the triumphs of electrification in rural America. Galbraith advised the State Department that Johnson "carries all precincts visited and would run well nationwide." At the Taj Mahal in Agra, he tested the monument's echo with a Texas cowboy yell and poked fun at the Kennedys' wealth by suggesting that one day Jean might want to build such a monument for her husband Steve.[24]

In Pakistan Johnson made headlines with his campaign-style diplomacy. On his way into the city from the Karachi airport, he stopped to shake hands with some of the applauding, enthusiastic crowd lining the streets. Spotting a barefoot man standing with a camel at an intersection, a man with a fine, cherubic face, Johnson stepped across a muddy ditch to greet him and urge, as he had done repeatedly on the trip, "y'all come visit me in the United States." The next day a Karachi newspaper lauded Johnson for reaching out "to the man with no shirt on his back" and for inviting Bashir Ahmad, the camel driver, to come to America and stay at the Waldorf-Astoria Hotel in New York. Not long after Johnson returned home, the American Embassy in Pakistan reported that Bashir's visit to America had become a cause célèbre and that, if it didn't happen, "the Vice President was going to look like the biggest four-flusher in history." Before Johnson could arrange the trip, however, the Pakistani government, fearful that Bashir, an illiterate peasant, would embarrass it, had him arrested and hidden by the police. A direct appeal by Johnson to the President of Pakistan freed Bashir to come to the United States, where with the help of a sophisticated Pakistani translator, who turned much of what Bashir said into "beautiful little homilies," the camel driver made a triumphal tour and received a pickup truck donated by the Ford Motor Company.[25]

Johnson's behavior abroad makes it easy to poke fun at him as a comic figure or some sort of fabulous Texas character, a man with a monumental ego whose priority was more the selling of Lyndon Johnson than the advancement of any foreign policy goal. There is, of course, a certain truth to this. Johnson was a larger-than-life character with self-serving impulses that entered into everything he did. Yet he was also someone who never lost sight of bold public designs.

Johnson's trips to Africa and Asia, and especially Vietnam, where the competition with the Communists had turned violent, was a kind of New Deal crusade. It was an attempt to get out and meet the people and sell them on the virtues of American democracy and free enterprise. For Johnson, Vietnam, and Southeast Asia more generally, was less a geopolitical balance-of-power contest with Communism than a giant reclamation project—a campaign to sell his beloved New Deal liberalism to Asians as superior to Communism's economic and political command systems or even their own less productive and less stable economic and political institutions. When Johnson defied the advice of American diplomats not to touch Thais, he was not simply thumbing his nose at conventional wisdoms, he was also affirming his belief in American democratic habits. However parochial it may have been, Johnson, like Woodrow Wilson and other evangels of democracy, was a crusader for the American dream, an exponent of the idea that inside of every impoverished African and Asian there was an American waiting to emerge.

Johnson thought of his trips abroad, and particularly the episode with Bashir, as a welcome contrast to what he called "Cadillac diplomacy," the failure of U.S. representatives to get out of their limos and meet the people. On a later trip, as they drove from the airport to a hotel, a diplomat "methodically instructed him, as if he were some sort of uncouth backwoodsman, on how to behave. Johnson listened to this singular performance with unaccustomed patience. When they arrived ... the diplomat said, 'Mr. Vice President, is there anything else I can do for you?' The Vice President, looking stonily up and down at his model of diplomatic propriety, replied, 'Yes, just one thing. Zip up your fly.' "[26]

Kennedy, most professional diplomats, and journalists saw Johnson's behavior as cornball diplomacy that had limited value in foreign relations. Kennedy lodged no protest against Johnson's actions—and in fact was happy to see him so cheerfully occupied—but it confirmed Kennedy in an impulse to keep Johnson at arm's length in the management of foreign affairs. Indeed, during the Bay of Pigs crisis in April 1961, when CIA-supported anti-Castro Cubans staged an abortive invasion of their homeland, Johnson, at JFK's request, had entertained West German Chancellor Konrad Adenauer at his Texas ranch. Moreover, Kennedy had systematically excluded Johnson from any part in the operation.[27]

Johnson was so frustrated at being ignored in these deliberations that he had a secretary ask a Kennedy friend to lobby the President for more of a Johnson role in making foreign policy. When the friend asked JFK why he didn't lean more on Lyndon, Kennedy replied: "You know, it's awfully hard because once you get into one of these crunches you don't really think of calling Lyndon because he hasn't read the cables.... You want to talk to the people who are most involved, and your mind does not turn to Lyndon because he isn't following the flow of cables." Of course, Kennedy could have arranged to make it otherwise, but he obviously had no desire to give Johnson a more central part in shaping foreign policy.[28]

Nevertheless, Johnson had some influence on foreign affairs. His trip to Vietnam gave him a chance to speak his mind on what the administration saw in 1961 as the threat to U.S. interests in Southeast Asia. French defeat at the hands of the Viet Minh in 1954 had stirred American fears of Communist gains throughout the region and moved the Eisenhower administration to back the pro-Western Diem government in South Vietnam. A civil war in neighboring Laos heightened concern at the start of the Kennedy presidency that Communist-sponsored wars of national liberation in Asia would represent a major challenge to the United States in the next four years. If America faltered, Kennedy warned, "the whole world, in my opinion, would inevitably begin to move toward the Communist bloc."

Yet Kennedy's actions in Vietnam contrasted sharply with his rhetoric. Although he encouraged the U.S. military to develop a program of counterinsurgency warfare, he was reluctant to make any significant commitment of American forces to Laos or Vietnam. Consequently, he struggled to find a middle ground between a significant U.S. military effort and noninvolvement that might allow Communist success. The failure at the Bay of Pigs and the reluctance of the administration to do more than negotiate a settlement in Laos, however, joined with Diem's stumbling efforts against the Viet Cong to encourage some stronger action by Kennedy in Vietnam.[29]

Johnson's trip to Saigon in May was meant to reassure Diem and the South Vietnamese people that the United States would not abandon them to the Communists. Johnson carried a letter from Kennedy promising more military advisers and aid which would allow Diem to increase the size of his forces. On his return to the United States Johnson pressed the case for a greater commitment to the defense of South Vietnam. "I cannot stress too strongly the extreme importance of following up this mission with other measures, other actions, and other efforts," LBJ told JFK. The trip had "sharpened and deepened" his basic convictions, Johnson added. "The battle against Communism must be joined in Southeast Asia with strength and determination ... or the United States, inevitably, must surrender the Pacific and take up our defenses on our own shores." Without America's "inhibitory influence, ... the vast Pacific becomes a Red Sea."

This did not mean an American commitment to send troops other than advisers on training missions, although open attack by the Communists "would bring calls for U.S. combat troops.... The basic decision in Southeast Asia is here," Johnson asserted. "We must decide whether to help these countries to the best of our ability or throw in the towel in the area and pull back our defenses to San Francisco and a 'Fortress America' concept." Though Johnson did not mention Munich, memories of appeasement in 1938 echo through his advice to Kennedy on Vietnam. Failure to take a stand would mean retreat and defeat and greater ultimate dangers to the national security.[30]

Kennedy had other advice. John Kenneth Galbraith, who described himself as "sadly out of step with the Establishment," warned against an expanded U.S. role in Vietnam. Spending "our billions in these distant jungles" would do the U.S. no good and the Soviets no harm. "Incidentally, who is the man in your administration who decides what countries are strategic? I would like to ... ask him what is so important about this real estate in the space age." Galbraith also advised seizing the opportunity to make "any kind of a political settlement." Though it would bring political attacks, these would be better than "increasing involvement. Politics is not the art of the possible. It consists in choosing between the disastrous and the unpalatable. I wonder if those who talk in terms of a ten year war really know what they are saying in terms of American attitudes."[31]

But Johnson's view of Vietnam represented the prevailing wisdom in the administration, the Congress, and the press. Defeat in Vietnam would mean the loss of all Southeast Asia and worse. In the grip of the World War II experience, when one uncontested Hitler aggression led inevitably to the next, most Americans, including JFK, shared Johnson's exaggerated fear that a Communist victory in Vietnam would become the prelude to a Red tide sweeping across the Pacific. In consequence, between 1961 and 1963, the Kennedy administration expanded the number of U.S. military advisers from 692 to 16,700 and increased materiel aid to a level that marked a "transition from advice to partnership" in the war. When Diem's repressive rule in his country produced ever greater instability in South Vietnam, the Kennedy administration, accepting Galbraith's proposition that "nothing succeeds like successors," acquiesced in a military coup that toppled Diem's rule and took his life. Johnson thought the decision to oust Diem "very unwise," but, as with other foreign affairs questions, he had no significant impact on administration actions. Johnson's voice on Vietnam was no more than an echo of what other, more influential advisers were telling JFK.

Nothing underscored Johnson's limited role in foreign policymaking more than his silence during White House deliberations on the Cuban missile crisis in October 1962. During the two weeks that JFK held meetings on how to settle the greatest post-1945 crisis in

Soviet-American relations, LBJ was a shadow figure, expressing few opinions and asserting himself only on the afternoon of October 27, when the President was not present. Johnson kept his silence, not because he lacked opinions or conclusions on how to respond to the Soviet challenge, but because he felt compelled, as Vice President, simply to follow JFK's lead. Johnson said later that he followed a "general policy of never speaking unless the President asked me." Since Kennedy asked his opinion only once during the discussions, Johnson assumed that the President wanted him to be no more than a silent partner.[32]

The one instance in which LBJ played more than a peripheral role in foreign affairs was during a crisis over Berlin in August 1961. An exodus of many of the best-trained citizens from East Germany through Berlin moved the Communists to build a wall sealing off the eastern part of the city. Unclear as to whether this was a prelude to more aggressive action against West Berlin, unwilling to order an assault against the wall, as some in Germany asked, and eager to counter demoralization in the American, British, and French zones, Kennedy ordered Johnson to make a symbolic trip to Berlin.

Johnson was reluctant to go. He believed that such a journey might produce more recrimination over U.S. weakness than hope that America intended to stand up to Soviet expansion. If he were right, as the President's representative, he would then take some, if not much, of the heat for a gesture that was too little and too late. Kennedy ordered 1500 U.S. troops to move from West Germany to West Berlin as a show of American determination. But believing this was insufficient to boost morale in West Berlin, he wanted Johnson to make a very public appearance in the city as a demonstration "to the Russians that Berlin was an ultimate American commitment."[33]

Despite his doubts, Johnson took on the assignment with characteristic energy and preparation. He stayed up all night on his trans-Atlantic flight discussing his itinerary and speeches that would give meaning to his trip. Landing in Bonn, where West German Chancellor Konrad Adenauer met him, Johnson refused to be drawn into the current election campaign between Adenauer and West Berlin Mayor Willy Brandt. He refused Adenauer's request to travel together to West Berlin. Instead, he focused on giving the West German crowd greeting him a message from President Kennedy that America was "determined to fulfill all our obligations and to honor all our commitments." We will "dare to the end to do our duty."

Johnson's trip to West Berlin was a triumphal tour. After an eighty-minute flight to Tempelhof Airport, LBJ rode to the city center in an open car cheered by 100,000 spectators. Stopping repeatedly to shake hands with the people lining the curbs, he was greeted with unmistakable enthusiasm. At City Hall, where 300,000 Berliners had gathered, he declared himself in Berlin at the direction of President Kennedy to convey the same commitment that "our ancestors pledged in forming the United States: 'Our lives, our fortunes, and our sacred honor.'" The wall, Johnson presciently declared, was a testimony to Communism's failure. This was not a time for despair, but for understanding that "in the long run this unwise effort will fail. . . . This is a time, then, for confidence, for poise, and for faith—for faith in yourselves. It is also a time for faith in your allies, everywhere throughout the world. This island does not stand alone."

The next day, Sunday morning at 9 a.m., Johnson and General Lucius Clay, former High Commissioner for Berlin, who Kennedy had asked to join the Vice President, went to the Helmstedt entrance to West Berlin, where they waited the arrival of the 1500 troops traveling along a 104-mile stretch of Autobahn. President Kennedy, who normally spent his summer weekends in Hyannis Port, stayed in Washington to await word of the convoy's unimpeded arrival. When the column of tanks and troops reached the city at 10 a.m., Berliners greeted them with shouts, tears, and flowers. The commanding officer remembered the occasion as "the most exciting and impressive thing I've ever seen in my life, with the possible exception of the liberation of Paris." The moment was the capstone of what LBJ saw as his most successful vice-presidential mission abroad.[34]

Outer Space

Space policy was another matter. During the 1960 campaign Kennedy had attacked the Eisenhower administration for allowing the Soviets to get ahead of the United States in missile technology and the space race. The issue to JFK and most Americans was not just a concern that the Soviets were gaining a military advantage but the sense that America was losing the global contest for "hearts and minds." In 1961–63 few things in the Cold War counted more to Kennedy and Johnson than the wish to convince people everywhere that America's institutions and industrial and scientific capacity—its standard of living—were superior to Russia's.[35]

In April 1961, after a Soviet cosmonaut became the first man to orbit the earth and the failure at the Bay of Pigs had embarrassed the United States, JFK asked Lyndon to make "an overall survey of where we stand in space. Do we have a chance of beating the Soviets by putting a laboratory in space, or by a trip around the moon, or by a rocket to land on the moon, or by a rocket to go to the moon and back with a man? Is there any other space program which promises dramatic results in which we could win?"

Johnson replied that the Soviets were ahead of us "in world prestige attained through technological accomplishments in space." And other nations, identifying space gains as reflections of world leadership, were being drawn to the Soviets. A strong effort was needed at once to catch and surpass the Russians if we were to win "control over . . . men's minds through space accomplishments." Johnson recommended "manned exploration of the moon" as "an achievement with great propaganda value." The control of outer space was going to "determine which system of society and government [would] dominate the future. . . . In the eyes of the world, first in space means first, period; second in space is second in everything." When people complained about the cost of space exploration, Johnson replied: "Now, would you rather have us be a second-rate nation or should we spend a little money?"[36]

Kennedy needed no prodding from Johnson to make the case for some dramatic space venture. At the end of May, he told a joint session of Congress: "If we are to win the battle that is now going on around the world between freedom and tyranny, the dramatic achievements in space which occurred in recent weeks [a sub-orbital flight by astronaut Alan Shepard] should have made clear to us all . . . the impact of this adventure on the minds of men everywhere, who are trying to make a determination on which road they should take. . . . Now it is . . . time for this nation to take a clearly leading role in space achievement, which in many ways may hold the key to our future on earth." Kennedy asked the country to commit itself to the goal of landing a man on the moon and returning him safely to earth before the decade was out.[37]

Yet Kennedy worried that a highly publicized American space effort that ended in failure would further damage the nation's prestige and inflict a political wound that could jeopardize his hold on the presidency. Shepard's flight had encouraged Kennedy's hopes that America might catch and pass the Soviets, but he remained concerned about future mishaps. In June, when Shepard drove with the President, LBJ, and Newton Minow, head of the Federal Communications Commission, to speak before the National Convention of Broadcasters, Kennedy poked Johnson and said: "You know, Lyndon, nobody knows that the Vice President is the Chairman of the Space Council. But if that flight had been a flop, I guarantee you that everybody would have known that you were the Chairman." Everyone laughed, except Lyndon, who looked glum and angry, especially after Minow chimed in: "Mr. President, if the flight would have been a flop, the Vice President would have been the next astronaut."[38]

The possibility that he would be a sacrificial political lamb for a faulty space effort did not dampen Johnson's enthusiasm for a manned mission to the moon. His commitment partly rested on his faith in liberal nationalism, the ability of government to assure economic and social progress through the use of its largesse. For Johnson, whose whole career had been built on the assumption that federal monies well spent on infrastructure, social programs, and defense could serve the national well-being, especially in the less affluent South, the space program was a splendid way to bolster the country's defense, expand the domestic economy, and advance scientific understanding.

In 1963, when criticism from academics, journalists, and political conservatives began to be heard against "the moon-doggle," Johnson told Kennedy: "The space program is expensive, but it can be justified as a solid investment which will give ample returns in security, prestige, knowledge, and material benefits." During a plane trip to visit various space installations around the United States, Johnson gave "a very impassioned talk" to Newton Minow for about an hour on the virtues of communications satellites in advancing education in underdeveloped countries and educational television in the United States.[39]

Johnson saw other, more selfish benefits flowing from the space program. Convinced he was backing a winner, he made strong efforts to identify himself with every aspect of its work. Not only did he crisscross the country in publicized visits to space installations, he also gave a series of "factual space reports to the public" on the work of NASA and his space council. The ostensible objective was to educate the country, but it had the added advantage of keeping his name in the news.[40]

Then there were the pork-barrel gains that served the economic interests of Texas and the South and strengthened his political hold on the state and the region, especially at a time when his support of civil rights for blacks was undermining it. Although he denied any part in the selection of southwestern companies receiving Apollo or moon program contracts or in shifting half of space operations from Cape Canaveral in Florida to a command center in Houston, Senator George Smathers knew better. "He and I had a big argument about it, big fight," Smathers says. "Johnson tried to act like he didn't know. ... It never has made sense to have a big operation at Cape Canaveral and another big operation in Texas. But that's what we got, and we got that because Kennedy allowed Johnson to become the theoretical head of the space program." Indeed, with Robert Kerr of Oklahoma, a Johnson friend, running the Senate Space Committee, Texas Congressmen Overton Brooks and Olin Teague the House counterpart, Albert Thomas, another Texas representative, chairing the Appropriations Committee, and James Webb, Johnson's nominee, directing NASA, the Southwest generally and Texas in particular profited most from Kennedy's accelerated space program.[41]

In 1962, when lobbyists and congressmen from outside the South began to complain about a southwestern monopoly on NASA contracts, Kennedy made Richard L. Callaghan, a congressional staffer, an assistant administrator to Jim Webb. Callaghan's job was to arrange for a more equitable distribution of contracts, which would relieve congressional pressure on Kenny O'Donnell, and find out whether Kerr and Johnson were pulling strings for their friends at NASA.

As Callaghan later told Robert Sherrod, a *Time-Life* reporter: " 'Kenny O'Donnell wasn't only interested in getting the contractors off his back. He wanted to satisfy himself about the Kerr-Johnson influence on the Space Agency. He wanted to find out who was getting what—wanted to satisfy himself that the organization was honest.' " According to what Sherrod later learned from O'Donnell, there was no evidence to prove any wrongdoing by anyone at NASA. Nor could they find anything on LBJ that might have made him a potential liability to the administration.[42]

Johnson's thousand days as Vice President demonstrated his effectiveness in building a national consensus for a space program. As James Webb later said: "When President Kennedy asked him [LBJ] to prepare a memorandum as to what our space program should be, ... he called in some businessmen.... Then he called in Werner von Braun and General Schraver from the Air Force and a large number of technical people and sort of had hearings." After that "he called in the political leaders ... in Congress and ... said to them: 'We ought to go forward but we don't want to go forward unless you are going to commit yourself to stay with us.' ... So he developed this commitment of certain leaders ... and this ... made it a lot easier for the rest of the country to come along. They saw that these very powerful, responsible people ... believed this should be done," and so the mass of Americans accepted a manned mission to the moon as a wise national goal.[43]

The Committee on Equal Employment Opportunity

Johnson's greatest challenge as Vice President was chairing the CEEO. The goal of helping black Americans win equal access to jobs appealed to his sense of fairness and compassion for a disadvantaged minority, concerns dating from early in his political career. To be sure, his congressional voting record on civil rights before 1957 in no way distinguished him from southern segregationists. But his inner convictions were different: for the South to come into the mainstream of the country's economic and political life, it would have to abandon the separation of races that consigned blacks to second-class citizenship and barred them from the economic gains sought by whites. As National Youth Administration Director in Texas during the thirties, Johnson had quietly tried to improve the lot of black youngsters. As a congressman and a senator, he had helped black farmers, provided low-cost housing to blacks and Hispanics, and slightly reduced legal roadblocks to black voting in the South through the 1957 and 1960 civil rights laws.

During the 1940s and 1950s he had said more than once: "The Negro fought in the war, and . . . he's not gonna keep taking the shit we're dishing out. We're in a race with time. If we don't act, we're gonna have blood in the streets." His aide Horace Busby remembers that during the 1948 Senate campaign, in a small town Johnson had no hope of carrying, he refused to speak until blacks in the audience stood on the same side of the railroad tracks with whites. Later, he asked Busby: " 'Buzz, Buzz . . . how many votes you think I'll get here?' I held up both hands: ten votes. He said, 'Oh, no,' and held up two fingers."[44]

The CEEO chairmanship had the added advantage of disarming northern liberal hostility, which Johnson saw as a potential obstacle to a presidential bid in 1968. His presidential ambitions partly account for his support of the 1957 and 1960 civil rights bills; it was a means of establishing himself as more of a national than a regional figure. He once told Bill Moyers, his press secretary, that Senator "Pitchfork" Ben Tillman of South Carolina "might have been president. I'd like to sit down with him and ask how it was to throw it away for the sake of hating." He felt much the same about his old friend Georgia Senator Richard Russell. When Johnson was President, he told Moyers: "God damn it. Jim Crow put a collar on more smart men as sure as if they were sentenced to a chain gang in Georgia. If Dick Russell hadn't had to wear Jim Crow's collar, Dick Russell would be sitting here now instead of me."[45]

Yet Johnson also feared that chairing the CEEO might trap him into antagonizing northern liberals, who would complain he did too little, and southern conservatives, who would attack him for doing too much. At the start of Kennedy's term all agreed that civil rights was a political liability. Kennedy, who had backed the Democratic party's platform of equal access to "voting booths, schoolrooms, jobs, housing, and public facilities" and seemed ready to put a major civil rights bill before the Congress, initially did almost nothing about the problem, except to promise action through Johnson's Committee. "I have dedicated my Administration to the cause of equal opportunity in employment by the government or its contractors," JFK announced in March. "I have no doubt that the vigorous enforcement of this order will mean the end of such discrimination." Whatever the committee might achieve—and few were optimistic that it would be much—Kennedy was primarily using it as an expedient between advocates of bold legislative proposals and southern defenders of the status quo.

Reluctant to put himself between the clashing forces on the most visible domestic problem of 1960–61, Johnson didn't want to take the job, telling Kennedy: "I don't have any budget, and I don't have any power, I don't have anything." Johnson had a point. The committee he inherited from the Eisenhower administration, which Vice President Nixon had chaired, depended for funding on Executive agencies, including the Labor Department, and had authority to act only when victims of discrimination brought complaints. Kennedy, however, wouldn't let Johnson off the hook, saying, "You've got to do it because Nixon had it before, even though he didn't do anything; you're from the South, and if you don't take it, you'll be deemed to have evaded your responsibility. And so you've got to do it."

But fearing that Attorney General Robert Kennedy, the President's brother, who had opposed his selection as Vice President and helped limit his influence in the new administration, wanted him to take the heat on civil rights, Johnson tried again in February to avoid the assignment. He argued that taking the job would exceed the Vice President's constitutional powers, and he proposed instead that the Secretary of Labor replace him. After the Deputy Attorney General refuted Johnson's reading of the Constitution, JFK issued an Executive Order setting up the committee and announced his and Johnson's dedication "to the cause of equal opportunity in employment by the government or its contractors."[46]

Although he saw political liabilities resulting from almost anything he did at the CEEO, Johnson was determined to get something done. This was partly a matter of personal temperament and ego; the assignment was a fresh challenge, a test of Lyndon Johnson, a questioning of his capacities as a leader, a politician. As with every job he ever confronted, it triggered his competitive urges, driving him to do his best, disarm critics, and win praise for a gold medal performance.

At the same time, he believed that racial discrimination had no legitimate place in American life. When Harris Wofford, an early supporter of JFK's and a leading civil rights advocate in Kennedy's White House, tried to persuade Roy Wilkins of the National Association for the Advancement of Colored People (NAACP) to back Kennedy in 1960, Wilkins said that "of all the men in American political life, I would trust to do the most about civil rights,... it would be Lyndon Johnson. And," Wofford added, "I think Roy was not too far wrong on that. Civil rights really was something that, by this time, was burning pretty strongly in Johnson." James Farmer, of the Congress of Racial Equality (CORE), who risked his life in 1961 by leading a small group of black and white freedom riders challenging segregation on interstate carriers across the South, met Johnson after he became head of the CEEO. "He was sincere, he was very interested, almost a passionate concern came through. My view of him changed as a result of that meeting," Farmer says. "He came through as one who was not merely working on this because it was politically expedient but because he had a strong belief in it. And I was convinced of that."[47]

Charles Boatner, a Johnson aide, remembers that the Vice President collected statistics on the number of black college graduates working in their fields. When he learned that practically none were— that a black B.A. in electrical engineering had to work as an electrician—he described it "as a tremendous waste of manpower ... we were just throwing aside, through prejudice, one of our great assets, ... brainpower. Here were these educated people ready to move out into the world, and the white world wouldn't let them, closed down on them, blocked the door."

Elizabeth Gatov, Kennedy's Treasurer, recalls being asked by Johnson: " 'How many minority members do you have on your staff and what are their grades?' " Her answer provoked a strong response: " 'A very poor showing. They're all in the lower grades. What have you done about recruiting for higher grade jobs? If you haven't done anything, please do, and tell us what you're doing.' "[48]

Kennedy and Johnson believed that the CEEO could make a difference in giving blacks a fairer chance at more and better jobs. A federal work force of over two million and government contracts paying the salaries of another 15.5 million Americans gave the government considerable leverage to advance the interests of black wage earners.

JFK asked Johnson to draft an Executive Order that would set the CEEO in motion. Relying on his old friend Abe Fortas, a prominent Washington attorney, Johnson pushed to have "this Executive order go as far as an Executive order could go." When Kennedy pressed Johnson through White House aide Richard Goodwin to get the order out, Lyndon replied: "We are trying ... to make [the committee] more workable and more effective ... we don't think it has produced much results in eight years." In particular, Johnson insisted that all contractors doing business with the government sign statements denying discriminatory practices and that the committee be free to cancel contracts with businesses violating their commitments.[49]

At the same time, though, Johnson was the soul of caution. Discrimination against "Negroes" was wrong; it violated the spirit and letter of American ideals; it limited the country's economic output and injured its prestige abroad. But it was part of the southern landscape, and moving too vigorously to break old habits would produce social divisions and political losses that neither Kennedy nor Johnson were prepared to accept, at least not in 1961–62.

In the first half of 1961, when a black professor of surgery from Howard University in Washington, D.C., and the Ghanian Ambassador to the United States had difficulty getting reservations at the Hilton Hotel in Houston, Johnson interceded. Although he headed off actions that threatened to undermine African-American relations and bring "great grief" to Hilton and himself, the most visible Texan in the administration, his private discussions reveal how uncomfortable he was in pressing fellow southerners into equal treatment for blacks.

"You will have to do just like we did when we were in Africa," he told a Hilton executive in Texas. "The President [of Senegal] wanted Mrs. Johnson to sit next to him at the head table. She did, and it didn't hurt her." If the ambassador wanted to eat in the dinning room, he should be given "a nice little separate table. ... Because if you have a hotel in Ghana, you can't afford to hurt his feelings—it would take a lot of white people to fill up a hotel in Ghana." If he wanted to go swimming, "let him." "I would give anything if he weren't coming, but he is," Johnson said. "The best medicine you can take ... is to lean over backwards to be cordial. ... If word gets out that the Hilton hotels are segregated, Hilton hotels all over the world are in trouble—the Jews, etc., all of them won't like it."[50]

Johnson was also reluctant to compel southern accommodation to his committee's equal employment demands. "This is not a persecuting committee or prosecuting committee," he announced in March 1961. "In most cases, we believe and hope the situation can be straightened out through persuasion and ... appeals to good will."

Johnson had an excessive faith in volunteerism. In a meeting with forty-eight of the nation's largest defense contractors in May, he described the urgency of the situation. Discrimination was a reality of American life, and sympathy for its victims was an inadequate response. "They need jobs—and it is not enough to tell them that if they are patient their children or their grandchildren will have justice. We must act now." His committee had considerable power to force nondiscrimination, Johnson pointed out. "But I do not think this problem will be solved by threatening people or bullying them. . . . We are going to operate on the rule of good faith." Lyndon's inclination to rely on the goodwill of defense contractors in the South had less to do with their demonstrated readiness to respond than his reluctance to force an issue that could hurt him and the administration.[51]

To increase black employment, Johnson principally relied on "Plans for Progress." The scheme originated with Robert Troutman, an Atlanta attorney and businessman reacting to a series of complaints by the NAACP against the Lockheed Aircraft Corporation plant in Marietta, Georgia. Lockheed was eager to reach an accommodation with the NAACP and avoid jeopardizing its agreements with the Air Force, which made it the federal government's largest contractor. Likewise, Georgia officials and New South entrepreneurs like Troutman, who had helped make Lockheed the largest employer in the state and saw desegregation of businesses in the South as essential to the region's economic well-being, were eager to resolve the conflict.

When Lockheed removed "White" and "Colored" signs from its Marietta plant and promised more and better jobs for blacks, Troutman hailed it as a model of what could be done with other corporations across the South. Moreover, using his ties to the White House, which included an acquaintanceship at Harvard with the late Joe Kennedy, Jr., and an early commitment to JFK in the 1960 campaign, Troutman won appointment as chairman of a CEEO "Plans for Progress" subcommittee.

A great self-promoter and charming personality with a knack for negotiating deals and ingratiating himself with influential people, including the President, Troutman quickly persuaded dozens of the country's major defense contractors to join "Plans for Progress." He described the operation as based on voluntary agreements that would open "doors of job opportunity" without making the CEEO into "an employment agency or a policeman with a nightstick chasing down alleged malefactors." Troutman also emphasized his opposition to quotas, hiring people for reasons of "race, creed, color, or national origin." The objective was to remove all such considerations from job selection and use merit as the only criterion. Troutman himself, however, acknowledged that such an approach promised little change:

blacks, he said, lacked the training to qualify for the best jobs or even good ones.[52]

Johnson was not especially happy about Troutman's central role at CEEO. He was Jack Kennedy's man, who had opposed LBJ in the 1960 campaign, and with his talent for self-advertising he seemed likely to win credit for gains that Lyndon craved. On the other hand, he also served Johnson's purposes: should things go wrong, he could be a lightning rod protecting JFK, Lyndon, and the CEEO from critics; he also had a moderate, voluntary program that Johnson warmly favored; and he provided a counterbalance to two other CEEO officials, Jerry Holleman and John G. Feild, early Kennedy supporters with roots in the Texas and Michigan labor movements, respectively, who wanted to replace Troutman's volunteerism with an aggressive policy of mandatory compliance.[53]

By the summer and fall of 1961, tensions inside the CEEO over the value of "Plans for Progress" had become an open secret. The New York Times reported that, despite White House ceremonies lauding voluntary agreements with contractors, solid evidence of greater black employment was hard to come by. Privately, Feild told Holleman that changes in corporate hiring resulted less from "Plans for Progress" than pressure generated by the committee's affirmative action requirements. Moreover, he warned that White House praise for Troutman's program carried "the danger of public suspicion that these statements are mere words."[54]

To the White House's discomfort, the debate over CEEO policy intensified during 1962. Despite a growing list of corporations joining "Plans for Progress," civil rights advocates within and outside the administration disputed the CEEO's "gains." One CEEO staff member described some of the agreements as not "worth the paper they were written on, they were just absolutely meaningless documents." Kennedy himself was fearful that Troutman's program "would turn out to be a fraud or a delusion or an illusion, that there were a lot of plans signed and then no Negroes would be hired." Johnson himself acknowledged that "it is difficult, if not impossible, to measure progress in this field in terms of numbers or percentages." When NAACP leaders publicly complained that corporations signing the plans saw themselves as insulated from penalties for job discrimination and pointed to a black unemployment rate double that of whites, the Kennedy White House welcomed Troutman's offer to resign.[55]

Johnson was relieved to see him go. Even before he had decided to quit, LBJ, distressed by the committee's poor press and stumbling efforts, had asked Theodore Kheel, a prominent New York labor negotiator and civil rights advocate, to survey and evaluate the CEEO's activities. In his report to Johnson in July, he recommended a shift from voluntary to compulsory compliance and a staff reorganization that would include appointment of an executive vice chairman who eliminated internal squabbles and ran day-to-day operations. Johnson seized upon Kheel's suggestion to force Feild's resignation. Since Holleman had also resigned in the spring after newspaper stories tied him to Billy Sol Estes, a Texas cotton broker accused of fraud and influence peddling, Lyndon was now liberated from the Troutman–Feild–Holleman division. Moreover, he assured his future control of the committee by making Hobart Taylor, Jr., a black Michigan attorney and son of a longtime Texas friend, executive vice chairman.[56]

But Johnson had won a Pyrrhic victory. His more direct control over the CEEO came at a time when nothing his committee did could satisfy explosive pressure for genuine advance toward black equality. In 1962–63 Lyndon used the CEEO to expand black job opportunities in the government and the private sector. Federal jobs held by blacks increased 17 percent in fiscal 1962 and another 22 percent in fiscal 1963. In addition, Johnson's committee directed private contractors to correct nearly 1700 complaints lodged against them by black employees, doubling the rate at which the CEEO had required "corrective actions" in one year. Yet these CEEO gains barely made a dent in black unemployment or satisfied the demand for comprehensive civil rights legislation that would challenge the whole Jim Crow system of segregation across the South.[57]

Civil Rights

By 1963 the pressure to do something about black rights in the South had reached fever pitch. In the spring of 1961 black and white freedom riders challenging segregated transportation in Alabama suffered beatings at the hands of mobs unrestrained by local police. When Bobby Kennedy asked civil rights leaders for a "cooling-off period," which could save the President from embarrassment on a European trip, James Farmer of CORE replied: "We've been cooling off for 100 years. If we got any cooler we'd be in a deep freeze." In the summer and fall, Martin Luther King led an unsuccessful campaign to desegregate public facilities in Albany, Georgia, where the local police chief averted violence by jailing civil rights workers who had broken no laws. In 1962 James Meredith's effort to become the first black to enroll at the University of Mississippi in Oxford resulted in mob violence that forced the dispatch of hundreds of federal marshals, the federalizing of the Mississippi National Guard, and the deployment of U.S. troops. Meredith's registration left two people dead and numerous injured, including several marshals attacked with bricks and bottles.[58]

In response to the strife, the Kennedys exercised greater executive leadership in behalf of civil rights than any administration in American history. They won judicial orders enjoining local police forces and anti-civil rights groups like the Ku Klux Klan from interfering with interstate travel. They persuaded the Interstate Commerce Commission to end segregation in interstate bus terminals. They filed forty-two lawsuits in behalf of black voting rights, and helped win congressional approval of the Twenty-fourth Amendment to the Constitution—anti-poll tax. They also appointed forty blacks to important administration posts, and put Thurgood Marshall, the winning counsel in the landmark 1954 school desegregation case, *Brown v. Board of Education*, on the federal Circuit Court of Appeals in New York.[59]

Yet most civil rights advocates saw the Kennedy administration's response to the struggle for black equality as inadequate. Above all, Kennedy refused to take on the Congress, and particularly its southern power brokers, by asking for a major civil rights law. The Kennedys justified their inaction by pointing out that not even a 1962 literacy bill guaranteeing voter registration for anyone with a sixth-grade education could overcome a southern filibuster. The argument carried little weight with civil rights advocates, who pointed to JFK's timidity in issuing an Executive Order desegregating federally supported housing. When the President finally acted in November 1962, making the simple "stroke of a pen" he had promised in the 1960 campaign, his order was limited to future housing. Moreover, his refusal to lobby the Senate for a change in Rule 22 from a two-thirds vote to a three-fifths vote to end filibusters confirmed the view that he would not risk any part of his legislative program for the sake of civil rights.[60]

Lyndon adopted the same strategy. When newspapers reported that he was dissatisfied with the way Kennedy had handled the Mississippi situation, he told the President that neither he nor his staff had discussed Mississippi with newsmen and that the conflict "had been handled better than he could ever have thought of handling it." He also reminded the President that when he and the Attorney General had requested his advice, "he had asked not to be consulted concerning Mississippi." Likewise, Lyndon refused to inject himself into the Senate fight over Rule 22. Asserting that he had no right as presiding officer to decide the constitutionality of a Senate rule and that it was up to a majority of the Senate to make its own rules, Johnson angered liberals, who wanted him to throw out the two-thirds requirement for cloture on debate as unconstitutional.[61]

In the spring and summer of 1963, the pressure on Kennedy to provide bold leadership on civil rights became irresistible. In February, JFK had asked Congress for limited reforms affecting voting rights and school desegregation. But there was little indication that the White House would make a strong push for even these modest proposals and no one in the civil rights movement anticipated significant gains without a renewed crisis in the South.

As a consequence, Martin Luther King launched a campaign in April to desegregate Birmingham, Alabama—the largest segregated city in America. The response by police chief Eugene (Bull) Connor shamed the nation. Showing no regard for the constitutional rights of demonstrators, Connor's men beat protestors with nightsticks, herded them into vans with the help of electric cattle prods and snarling police dogs, and turned high-pressure fire hoses on them that ripped the bark off trees. Kennedy told a delegation of Democrats at the White House that the scenes he witnessed on television made him sick. When a confrontation with Governor George Wallace over admitting black students to the University of Alabama at Tuscaloosa coincided with continuing turmoil in Birmingham, Kennedy gave an emotional speech to the nation decrying the oppression of its black citizens a hundred years after emancipation and asked Congress to enact the most comprehensive civil rights law in history.[62]

Kennedy's decision represented a turning point in his presidency. As Theodore Sorensen, White House aide and later JFK biographer, said: "The decision to ask for legislation . . . was a very, very important decision for him. . . . He knew that it would tie up the Congress for the rest of the year, at least; he knew that it would make some other legislation impossible; . . . and he knew how much was riding on it for him, politically and historically. He knew all of that."

The extent of the risk came home to the White House during the next three months when Congress showed little disposition to act on or even take up other administration bills. And Kennedy's popularity showed a steady decline during these months, with people complaining that he was pushing integration too fast and expressing increasing preference for Republican Governor George Romney of Michigan as the next President.[63]

Robert Kennedy

No one in the administration was more upset by developments than Robert Kennedy. Bobby was fiercely loyal to Jack; he was like "a tigress protecting her cubs," JFK Assistant Secretary of State Averell

Harriman remembered. Columnist Joseph Alsop said: "Bobby never diverged for one instant from his brother's views, nor did he ever really consider anything except his brother's interest." In 1960, at a meeting in New York with a reform group that included Eleanor Roosevelt and Senator Herbert Lehman, Bobby declared, "I don't give a damn about anybody in this room, [I] only want to elect my brother President of the United States." Robert's biographer Arthur Schlesinger, Jr., describes him during the campaign as a "tireless invigorator and goad.... He became the man to do the harsh jobs, saying no, telling people off, whipping the reluctant and the recalcitrant into line." When it came to serving JFK's needs, Bobby displayed "a brusqueness or abruptness or roughness that would have offended anyone," said Lee C. White, chief White House aide on civil rights.[64]

In 1963 Bobby Kennedy believed that unless the administration delivered on greater equality for blacks it would miss a chance to advance simple justice for an oppressed minority, lose liberal support, and put off the mass of voters by appearing ineffective and weak. Convinced that the administration needed to prevent racial tensions from exploding into further violence and that his brother's reelection was at stake, he began pressuring everyone on civil rights. Deputy Attorney General Burke Marshall says that Robert Kennedy "fussed and interfered, if you want to put it that way, with almost every other department of the government in 1963 on that issue, on their employment policies, and on whether or not Negroes were allowed to participate in federally financed programs."[65]

Few got more heat from Bobby Kennedy than Lyndon Johnson. But more than civil rights was involved. There was bad blood between them going back to 1955, when Joe Kennedy unsuccessfully offered Lyndon financial backing if he ran for President with Jack as his running mate. The go-between on the proposition remembered that the twenty-nine-year-old "Young Bobby ... was infuriated. He believed it was unforgivably discourteous to turn down his father's generous offer." In 1959, during a visit to Johnson's ranch to ask whether he was running for President against Jack, Bobby was knocked to the ground and cut above the eye by the recoil of a powerful shotgun Johnson had given him to hunt deer. Reaching down to help Bobby up, Johnson said: "Son, you've got to learn to handle a gun like a man." The incident was an indication of Johnson's small regard for Jack's claim on the White House.

In the spring of 1960, Peter Lisagor, a *Chicago Daily News* reporter, enflamed Bobby's antagonism to Lyndon by repeating a conversation he had with Johnson on a plane. "All of the enmity and hostility he held for the Kennedys came out." Johnson described Jack as "a 'little scrawny fellow with rickets' and God knows what other kind of diseases." Johnson predicted that Jack's election would give Joe Kennedy control of the country and would make Bobby Secretary of Labor. When Lisagor finished, four-letter words and all, Bobby turned to the window and said: " 'I knew he hated Jack, but I didn't think he hated him that much.' "[66]

"No affection contaminated the relationship between the Vice President and the Attorney General," Arthur Schlesinger writes. "It was a pure case of mutual dislike. . . . Johnson was seventeen years older, six inches taller, expansive in manner, coarse in language, emotions near the surface. It was southwestern exaggeration against Yankee understatement; frontier tall tales, marvelously but lengthily told, against laconic irony. Robert Kennedy, in the New England manner, liked people to keep their physical distance. Johnson, in the Texas manner, was all over everybody—always the grip on the shoulder, tug at the lapel, nudge in the ribs, squeeze of the knee. He was a crowder, who set his great face within a few inches of the object of his attention and, as the more diffident retreated, backed them across the room in the course of monologue."[67]

Johnson, whose fierce competitiveness and habit of abusing subordinates and opponents made him many enemies, couldn't stand to be disliked. He understood, of course, that no one he intimidated would love him for the abuse. But once he dominated someone, he quickly made amends with extravagant demonstrations of affection and regard, which he assumed would be reciprocated. But unable to master Bob Kennedy, Lyndon complained to several Kennedy associates about Bobby's antagonism to him. He wanted to know why Bobby disliked him and what might win him over.

One night in 1962, after a social event at the White House, Johnson confronted Kennedy directly: "Bobby, you do not like me. Your brother likes me. Your sister-in-law likes me. Your daddy likes me. But *you don't like me*. Now, why? Why don't you like me?" A witness to the performance said it "went on and on for hours." Finally, Johnson supplied the answer: Bobby thought he had attacked his father at the 1960 convention and had tried to deny Jack the nomination. When Johnson denied both facts, it incensed Bobby, who later complained that Johnson "lies all the time. . . . In every conversation I have with him, he lies. . . . He lies even when he doesn't have to."[68]

For all their differences, Kennedy and Johnson shared characteristics that made them antagonists. In 1968, after years of rivalry, Lyndon told Bobby in their last meeting, "Bobby, you and I weren't made to be Vice President," alluding to their similar temperaments.

Both men were powerful, at times overbearing, tyrannical characters who did not treat opponents kindly. They were alley fighters,
knee in the groin, below-the-belt punchers, hell-bent on winning at
almost any cost. Dirty tricks, intimidation, hard bargains were weapons in their political arsenals they carried into campaigns for high
office and for legislative and political gains needed to keep them or,
in Bobby's case, Jack there. They also shared bold, indeed, noble
dreams for the country of better race relations, less poverty, and more
security from external threats. They held a common regard for the
national system that had allowed them both to gain prominence and
power. But each self-righteously saw the other as less capable of
achieving the great ends bringing them together in the same party
and the same administration.[69]

The issue dividing them in 1963 was Johnson's performance at
the CEEO. In the first five months of the year, when the press prominently and repeatedly reported that "Plans for Progress" was "largely
meaningless," the President urged Johnson to "keep after the companies" and to publicize what had been achieved.

Although the compliance rate was much higher than indicated
in the newspaper accounts, Robert Kennedy believed the stories, and
they enraged him. He saw Johnson's committee as "mostly a public
relations operation" with no real leadership from the Vice President.
There was no "adequate follow-up" to the "Plans for Progress" agreements, and the head of the staff Hobart Taylor "was an Uncle Tom."
In the end, Bobby believed that the President, not the Vice President,
would pay the price for the committee's failure: "I could just see
going into the election of 1964, and eventually these statistics or
figures would get out. There would just be a public scandal." It was
bad enough that blacks weren't getting jobs but "what concerned me,"
Bobby said, was the thought of "this coming out in 1964." When
Bobby spoke to his brother about the situation, Jack "almost had a
fit." He said: "That man can't run this committee. Can you think of
anything more deplorable than him trying to run the United States?
That's why he can't ever be President of the United States."[70]

Bobby gave clear expression to his feelings about Lyndon's performance at the CEEO. In May and July, he attended the committee's
meetings, where one high administration official remembers Bobby
treating Lyndon "in a most vicious manner. He'd ridicule him, imply
he was insincere." Secretary of Labor Willard Wirtz shuddered "at
the way those two men would cut each other up in meetings." At
the May session, in the midst of the Birmingham turmoil, Kennedy
"asked a lot of questions that were impatient, very impatient; I could
see," Burke Marshall said, "it made the Vice President mad." Armed

with the information that fewer than 1 percent of federal employees in Birmingham were black, in a city that was 37 percent black, Kennedy went after Johnson and Hobart Taylor. "Bobby came in the other day to our Equal Employment Committee," Lyndon said a few days after the meeting, "and I was humiliated. He took on Hobart and said about Birmingham, said the federal employees weren't employing them down there, and he just gave him hell."

At the July meeting, with the civil rights bill before Congress and the issue hotter than ever, Kennedy went after Johnson again. He turned his fire on James Webb, the head of NASA, for failing to have information about black employment in his agency. "It was a pretty brutal performance, very sharp," one participant recalled. "It brought tensions between Johnson and Kennedy right out on the table and very hard. Everybody was sweating under the armpits.... And then finally, after completely humiliating Webb and making the Vice President look like a fraud and shutting Hobart Taylor up completely, he got up. He walked around the table ... shook my hand ... and then he went on out."[71]

Johnson felt unfairly abused. The CEEO's record wasn't as bad as some made it out to be. Moreover, the voluntary approach, which was receiving such bad press, had originated with Jack's man, Troutman. "Bobby Kennedy was probably tougher with Johnson than he needed to be and should have been," Lee White said. Nevertheless, what Bobby and the White House saw was a Vice President unable to convince people that his effort to advance black job equality was anything more than a sham.

LBJ also resented the fact that he received no credit for having gotten out front on civil rights in a series of public addresses that sounded a moral call to change. At Wayne State University in Detroit in January 1963, he had said: "To strike the chains of a slave is noble. To leave him the captive of the color of his skin is hypocrisy." Later in the month before a largely black audience in Cleveland, he called for a national agenda that would solve the problems left unresolved by Lincoln's Emancipation Proclamation. At Gettysburg, Pennsylvania, on Memorial Day, he declared: "One hundred years ago, the slave was freed. One hundred years later, the Negro remains in bondage to the color of his skin. Until justice is blind to color, until education is unaware of race, until opportunity is unaware of the color of men's skins, emancipation will be a proclamation but not a fact."[72]

Johnson also felt that he had been ignored and then unappreciated for what he had done in behalf of the 1963 civil rights bill. The bill had been drafted without consulting him, and he resented it. He was also angry that, despite JFK's injunction to Lee White to include Johnson in White House discussions with congressional leaders, he was rarely invited. Johnson was so much on the fringe of things that White usually forgot to ask him to meetings. "He called me," White recalled, "in sort of a hangdog expression saying, 'What the hell! I heard the President had a meeting and I didn't know about it.'" On June 3, after newspapers reported that Kennedy would send a civil rights bill to Congress, Johnson told Ted Sorensen in a telephone conversation: "I don't know who drafted it. I've never seen it. Hell, if the Vice President doesn't know what's in it how do you expect the others to know what's in it? I got it from the *New York Times*."[73]

Unable to get in to see the President about the bill, Johnson used his conversation with Sorensen and discussions with two Justice Department officials to say his piece. He believed it a mistake for Kennedy to put legislation before the Congress without first doing more homework. If he sent a bill up now, it wouldn't be enacted and would be "disastrous for the President's program."

Besides, the real issue wasn't a bill that would get "a little thing here ... or vote or something," but an equal chance at jobs and education and housing. True, a civil rights law was essential in 1963, but that would require a strategy different from the one currently being followed. Kennedy first needed to appear personally in the South. "If he goes down there and looks them in the eye and states the moral issue and the Christian issue, and he does it face to face, these Southerners at least respect his courage." He needed to tell them that it was plain wrong to expect black citizens to die for their country and be denied access to a public lunch room in Mississippi to have a cup of coffee. Then the President needed to call in black leaders and persuade them that he was a genuine "moral force" on their side. After that, he could bring the necessary pressure to bear on congressional leaders as a prelude to presenting a bill.[74]

Believing it "a very wise suggestion" to do some more work in Congress, the White House delayed sending up the bill for nine days. Then it arranged a series of meetings with influential groups to generate support in the country and pressure on Congress to pass the law. The President, Vice President, and Attorney General were the principal figures at these sessions, and many of the participants—educators, labor leaders, businessmen, civil rights advocates—remembered Johnson as the strongest, most passionate voice for the legislation. "Johnson was extremely effective at those [meetings], and at the one or two I attended," Arthur Schlesinger recalls, "I thought more effective than the President or the Attorney General."[75]

Yet none of this sat very well with Bobby Kennedy. Although

he acknowledged the wisdom of Johnson's advice on dealing with Congress and the support he gave the bill after it went forward, he saw the Vice President as "opposed to sending [it] up" and as generally unhelpful. He later said: "The President was rather irritated with him at the time because he was opposed to these things—this and a good number of other measures—but did not come up with alternative suggestions."

Without question, Johnson underestimated the importance of Kennedy's civil rights proposal compelling equal access to public accommodations. He minimized the need to force an end to legal segregation as a prelude to economic and educational gains. Injured pride or his absence from the drafting process may partly account for his coolness to the bill. He also was insensitive to how besieged the Kennedys felt about the civil rights struggle. Robert remembered that Jack thought the 1963 bill might "be his political swan song. We used to discuss whether what had been done was the right thing to do, just the fact that I'd gotten him into so much difficulty. We used to talk about it every three days, because there was so much attention focused on it at that time in an unpleasant way." Nevertheless, for the Attorney General to see Johnson as more of an obstructionist than a facilitator in the battle for civil rights is a distortion that tells more about the animus between the two than Lyndon's part in trying to advance the cause of black equality.[76]

Scandals and Politics

More than civil rights or personal differences, however, had Bobby on edge about Lyndon. In 1962–63 public scandals involving Billie Sol Estes, a Texas wheeler dealer, and Robert G. (Bobby) Baker, the secretary to the Senate Majority Leader, threatened to reveal unsavory connections to Johnson that would embarrass the administration and make it vulnerable to charges of corruption in the 1964 campaign.

Both scandals occurred against a backdrop of longstanding allegations that Lyndon had won his Texas elections to the House and the Senate by exceeding campaign finance limits and stuffing ballot boxes. His victory in 1948, when he had defeated former Governor Coke Stevenson for the Democratic Senate nomination by eighty-seven votes, was particularly suspect. There were also questions about the Johnson family fortune. Many folks wondered how a career politician could have accumulated radio, television, real estate, and bank holdings worth nearly $15 million. The Johnsons' 414-acre ranch in Texas, with a 6300-foot landing strip for two planes, and a sumptuous mansion in northwest Washington, "The Elms," purchased in 1961 from Perle Mesta, the "hostess with the mostest," added to the speculation. Although Johnson had cut numerous corners, engaged in various improprieties, and committed legal transgressions to win elections and become rich, he had escaped prosecution by cleverly obscuring his actions.[77]

John Kennedy had taken account of Johnson's reputation before offering him the vice presidency and had concluded that Lyndon would be more of an asset than a liability. Nevertheless, given Johnson's public image as a Texas wheeler-dealer, any fresh hint of corruption was bound to make the Kennedys take notice and prepare themselves for the worst.

During the spring and summer of 1962, the Billie Sol Estes case triggered their concern. In March, the FBI arrested Estes, a generous contributor to the Democratic party and a pillar of his community in west Texas, on fraud and theft charges. Estes's multi-million-dollar dealings in storage tanks, phony mortgages, and cotton allotments forced the dismissal of Agriculture Department officials in Washington. It also focused attention on allegations that the Johnsons had joint business ventures with him and that Lyndon had lobbied the Agriculture Department in his behalf, tried to impede the FBI's investigation, and been the recipient of gifts, including an airplane. The Attorney General and the President kept close tabs on these rumors, including one that a Republican congressman was preparing impeachment proceedings against the Vice President. Robert Kennedy insisted that the FBI make a thorough investigation of the charges, despite strong denials from Johnson and his staff.[78]

The death of Henry Marshall, an Agriculture Department official in Texas who was investigating Estes's operations, made the case all the more sensational. Although Marshall had bruises on his face, arms, and hands and had been shot five times with a bolt-action rifle that had to be pumped each time to eject a shell, his death had been ruled a suicide. The *Dallas Morning News* reported that "President Kennedy has taken a personal interest in the mysterious death of Henry Marshall" and that Robert Kennedy was prodding "the FBI to step up its investigation." During the eleven-day grand jury inquiry into Marshall's death, Bobby called the judge ten or twelve times to keep abreast of developments.

There is no evidence that the Kennedys anticipated Billie Sol's assertion twenty-two years later that he, Lyndon, and Cliff Carter, a vice-presidential aide, arranged for Mac Wallace, a convicted murderer, to kill Marshall. Estes claimed that Marshall had information tying LBJ and Carter to his fraudulent dealings. Although a Texas grand jury ruled in 1985 that Marshall's death was a murder rather than a suicide, the prosecutor conducting the grand jury inquiry found "no corroboration of Estes's charge" against Johnson. The grand jury concluded that those responsible for the slaying were dead. Estes's allegation against Johnson had no more credibility than all the rumors about Johnson and Estes; the FBI's investigation of these charges turned up nothing. As Johnson later said, "the damn press always accused me of things I didn't do. They never once found out about the things I did do."[79]*

The Bobby Baker case was more of a problem for Lyndon and gave the Kennedys greater concern. Robert G. Baker had come to the U.S. Senate as a page from Pickens, South Carolina, in 1942. Twenty-one years later, at the age of thirty-four, he had been Secretary to the Majority Leader for eight years and had established himself as a power to be reckoned with on Capitol Hill. Some called him the 101st senator. In the fifties, Baker was known as LBJ's protégé or "Little Lyndon." And even after Johnson became Vice President, they remained close. In January 1962, after Baker had sent LBJ a condolence note about the death of one of Johnson's sisters, Lyndon replied: "You have been on the mountain peaks with me and down in the valleys with me. I do not know what I would do without Bobby Baker and I do not want to find out."

Like Johnson, Baker was a man of enormous energy and guile. Johnson's aide Harry McPherson remembers Baker as "very smart, very quick, and indefatigable. Just worked all the time. He was always running some place to make some kind of deal." One senator said: "If you wanted to know what was going on, Bobby was the guy you called. He had the head count. He knew who was drunk, who was out of town, who was out sleeping with whom."[81]

By 1963, he had used his connections to become a millionaire. In 1962 his business dealings attracted the attention of the FBI. A part owner of a luxury motel in Ocean City, Maryland, described as a "high-style hideaway for the advice and consent set," Baker was believed to be in partnership with some unidentified "hoodlums." In October 1963, when a vending machine firm named him as a defen-

---

*It is conceivable that J. Edgar Hoover suppressed information linking Johnson to Estes's wrongdoing, as Athan Theoharis and John Cox suggest in *The Boss: J. Edgar Hoover and the Great American Inquisition* (New York, 1988), 345–46. It is also possible, as Curt Gentry asserts in *J. Edgar Hoover: The Man and the Secrets* (New York, 1991), 558, that, as President, Johnson later destroyed incriminating files. But the FBI material I read suggests that the bureau made a serious effort to learn the truth about Johnson and Estes and found no significant ties.[80]

dant in a $300,000 civil suit charging that Baker had forced them out of a defense contractor's plant over a kickback dispute, questions about his integrity forced him to resign his Senate post.

An investigation of his wheeling and dealing immediately provoked speculation about Johnson's involvement in Baker's business affairs. Lyndon had been a prominent guest at the opening of Baker's motel in July 1962. Although Johnson had nothing to do with Baker's questionable practices after 1960, he and Baker had some tainted dealings in the 1950s that came to light in 1964. Baker had arranged for Don B. Reynolds, an insurance agent, to sell Johnson $200,000 in life insurance. Johnson aide Walter Jenkins had pressed Reynolds into using part of his commissions to buy $1200 in advertising time on LBJ's Austin television station. Then, under prodding from Baker, Reynolds gave the Johnsons a $542 stereo as a gift. Johnson later claimed that the gift came from Baker himself.[82]

The Kennedys paid close attention to the allegations about Johnson and Baker. Larry O'Brien, JFK's special assistant for congressional relations, remembers that the President had a "keen interest" in the Bobby Baker case. The Attorney General closely followed the Justice Department's investigation, including inquiries into Johnson's possible part in Baker's corrupt dealings. In November 1963, when a reporter privately asked Bobby Kennedy about the investigation, he replied that "he had a lot of stuff about what Baker had done, investments he'd made and this money, loans, et cetera, but he said he didn't think it really tied into Johnson at all. He said that very flatly."[83]

Despite wrongdoing on Baker's part that would eventually send him to prison, Johnson believed that Bobby Kennedy instigated the investigation in hopes of finding something that could knock him off the ticket in 1964. There is no question but that Kennedy disliked Johnson and saw him as less helpful to the administration than he might have been and as a potential impediment to JFK's reelection. In 1963, Bobby went to Texas to plan a presidential visit. An aide to Democratic Governor John Connally remembered him as "the most arrogant person I had ever met." At the airport, the aide handed Kennedy a memo on what they wanted the President to say about oil and gas. After reading it, Bobby tore it up, threw it on the ground, and said, "We're not going to say anything like that. We put that son of a bitch on the ticket to carry Texas, and if you can't carry Texas, that's y'all's problem."[84]

Johnson saw abundant evidence that Kennedy was trying to get him. He believed that Bobby began tapping his phone in 1961 after LBJ agreed to see an Israeli political leader JFK refused to meet.

During a trip to Greece in September 1962, Johnson complained to the American Ambassador about an interview Edward (Ted) Kennedy, Jack and Bobby's younger brother, gave a Greek journalist a few days before Lyndon arrived in Athens. Johnson saw it as Bobby's way of undermining him. In January 1963 Harry McPherson further enflamed Johnson's suspicions by advising that anti-Johnson Democrats saw the Rule 22 fight as "a predicate for dumping you in 1964." Then, after his direct confrontations with Bobby at the CEEO in 1963, Johnson got reports of Bobby's saying, "As soon as we get rid of that oaf from Texas." Johnson also noted the fact that newspaper articles about Bobby Baker's problems initially came from reporters at the Justice Department rather than from those on the Hill.

In the fall of 1963, when the press began reporting that JFK was considering a replacement for LBJ, it confirmed what Johnson had been convinced of for over two years. "President Kennedy worked so hard at making a place for me, always saying nice things, giving me dignity and standing," Johnson later told the journalist Helen Thomas. "But . . . in the back room they were quoting Bobby, saying I was going to be taken off the ticket."[85]

Jack and Bobby Kennedy emphatically denied that they ever had a plan to drop Lyndon. Privately, JFK told journalists and political associates that it "was preposterous on the face of it. We've got to carry Texas in '64 and maybe Georgia," he said. When Florida Senator George Smathers told JFK that everyone on the Hill was talking about Bobby's desire to get Johnson off the ticket, Kennedy sarcastically said: "George, you have *some* intelligence, I presume. . . . Now who's Bobby going to put on the ticket, himself?" If he dropped Lyndon, it would mean losing the South and would suggest that they had a serious scandal on their hands in the Bobby Baker case. "I don't want to get licked," JFK added, "and Lyndon's going to be my Vice President because he helps me!" At a press conference in October, Kennedy stated his determination to keep Johnson on the ticket. Likewise, Bobby denied that he had initiated the Bobby Baker investigation to get something on Johnson or that he and Jack had ever had any discussions about dumping Lyndon.[86]

Was there any basis to Johnson's suspicions? Despite inquiries by many researchers, no one has found Robert Kennedy wire taps on Lyndon's phone. The taps of course could have been destroyed or they may still exist in a closed file, but until someone comes up with something more concrete than suspicions, the taps can be seen as nothing more than Johnson's imaginings. As for Bobby Kennedy's instigation of the Baker probe, an investigation in the late sixties by Ramsey Clark, LBJ's Attorney General, established that revelations about Baker's corruption rather than anything Kennedy did touched off the inquiry.[87]

The question of whether Robert Kennedy or people close to him discussed throwing Johnson off the ticket is open to dispute. In 1964 the U.S. Attorney in Minneapolis, an ally of Minnesota Senator Hubert Humphrey, told the FBI that a group he called the "Kennedy crowd" at the Justice Department had discussed with him their efforts in 1963 "to use the Baker issue as a means of freezing Mr. Johnson out as Vice President." Humphrey said that he also had reports of Robert Kennedy's friends plotting Lyndon's ouster. He didn't think Bobby himself would have gone along with the idea, since "it would not have been intelligent to dump Johnson as Vice President." Humphrey's rivalry with Bobby Kennedy to become LBJ's choice as Vice President in 1964 may account for these assertions by Humphrey and his supporter.[88]

Yet in 1968, Evelyn Lincoln, JFK's secretary, published a book in which she recounted a conversation with the President on November 19, 1963, three days before his death. Kennedy told her that he intended to replace Johnson with Governor Terry Sanford of North Carolina as his running mate, saying, "it will not be Lyndon." When Arthur Schlesinger alerted Bobby to Lincoln's revelation, he said: "Can you imagine the President ever having a talk with Evelyn about a subject like this?" Stephen Smith, JFK's brother-in-law and political confidante, also denied the existence of any plan to drop LBJ. Several prominent journalists thought it unlikely that Kennedy had any plan to do this. Tom Wicker of the *New York Times* said: "I never believed that.... I felt that Kennedy still had his same problem with the South, worse than ever probably, so I never bought the idea that he was dumping" Johnson.[89]

Yet there are reasons to believe that the Kennedys discussed replacing Johnson. With the Bobby Baker case on the front pages and links to LBJ a distinct possibility, it seems reasonable to assume that the Kennedys considered contingency plans for 1964. There was also the fact that when JFK made his alleged remarks to Lincoln, he was in a foul mood about Johnson. On November 20, the day before Jack was scheduled to make a political trip to Texas, he told Bobby "how irritated he was with Lyndon Johnson who wouldn't help at all in trying to iron out any of the problems in Texas, and that he was an s.o.b. ... because this was his state and he just wasn't available to help out or just wouldn't lift a finger to try to assist."

Kennedy's remarks to Lincoln (if he actually made them) may have been no more than a spontaneous expression of his anger toward LBJ. His larger design, especially once it seemed likely that Johnson would ride out the Baker scandal, was to do the politically necessary thing and keep Johnson in place. Moreover, denials by the Kennedys of plans to dump Lyndon was also good politics. While public speculation on dropping Johnson helped make it possible, denials that it was intended served the greater likelihood that Lyndon would again be Jack's running mate.[90]

Hidden Misery

By the fall of 1963, Johnson was largely a forgotten man in the country. An article in the *Texas Observer*, "What Is an LBJ?," reported that comedians and newspapers were having a field day with Johnson's obscurity. When the popular CBS-TV show *Candid Camera* asked a random sample of Americans, "Who is Lyndon Johnson?" the on-camera replies demonstrated LBJ's public invisibility. "No, I don't know him," one man said. "I'm from New Jersey." Another replied: "There's a lot of Johnsons around here." One woman answered: "He's not president. Am I getting close?" A man working in a warehouse said he didn't know him and suggested that they look him up in the phone book.[91]

As the reality of Johnson's eclipse registered on him, he had become sullen and depressed. When his former Senate aide Harry McPherson went swimming with him one afternoon at his home, McPherson thought he "looked absolutely gross. His belly was enormous and his face looked bad, flushed, maybe he had been drinking a good deal. ... His life was not causing him to come together physically, morally, intellectually, any way. On the contrary, ... it must have been a tremendous frustration."

Johnson's unhappiness registered on Frank "Posh" Oltorf, a longtime Texas associate, when he came to former Senator Tom Connally's funeral in Marlin, Texas. Oltorf remembered LBJ as "very despondent" and angry that he was the only national official there. Connally "did a lot of great things for this country," Johnson said. "There's so little gratitude." When Elizabeth Wickenden told Abe Fortas, both old Johnson friends, that Wilbur Cohen, a prominent New Dealer, thought Lyndon would succeed JFK in the White House, Fortas said: "Oh, get on the phone. Call him up right away and tell him because he's so depressed." Johnson himself made no bones about the vice presidency. He later described the office as "filled with trips around the world, chauffeurs, men saluting, people clapping, chairmanships of councils, but in the end, it is nothing. I detested every minute of it."[92]

His attitude expressed itself in a kind of sullen reserve at most White House gatherings. At legislative strategy sessions and breakfast meetings preparing the President for press conferences, Johnson sat in silence, his face "vacant and gray," looking "discontented and tired." When asked directly by Kennedy to give an opinion, he mumbled, "his words barely audible to the person sitting beside him. On rare occasions when he was particularly excited or perturbed, he would suddenly raise his voice for a few moments to its customary shout, only to let it quickly sink again into an unintelligible murmur."[93]

Yet he never gave public expression to his disgruntlement. As he had told JFK almost a year after their inauguration, "Where you lead, I will follow." And he did. Although he disagreed with Kennedy on a number of issues that arose during his presidency, Lyndon had swallowed his objections. He would not let on to reporters that there was ever the least difference between him and the White House or would he speak in other than "measured phrases" about the President in private. During Cabinet and National Security Council meetings he had invariably backed Kennedy's policies. He cleared all major speeches at home and abroad with the White House. When his old friend, journalist William S. White, visited him at his office, Johnson suggested that they see less of each other as a way to avoid suspicions that any critical White column originated with him. "Johnson showed great self-discipline and strength" during his vice presidency, Dean Rusk said. "I think it was a major effort of self-control to fit into that role—with all that volcanic force that was part of his very being."[94]

But Johnson was containing that "volcanic force" in hopes of using it another day. His self-discipline partly stemmed from the conviction that a Vice President owed his President full loyalty. It was an unspoken contract Johnson had accepted when he signed on as Kennedy's second-in-command. But beyond that there was the hope that after eight years of unstinting service he would have Jack Kennedy's backing for his own presidential term. As Vice President, he had continually worried about his public image, working with his aide George Reedy, a former journalist, and Phil Graham, publisher of the *Washington Post*, to encourage views of himself as "really deep." "The objective here is not to get a newspaper story," Reedy had told him, "but to build up among the newsmen the attitude that you are a thoughtful man." Johnson understood that any number of things could sidetrack his ambition, including a shift in political circumstances that would lead Kennedy to drop him from the ticket or JFK's defeat in 1964. Both these possibilities nagged at him, but he had tried to forestall them and advance his prospects for 1968 by being as disciplined and devoted a member of the Kennedy administration as he could.[95]

Dallas

On November 21, 1963, the President traveled to Texas on a trip he had been planning for over a year. In 1961–62 very little Texas money had come into the Democratic National Committee, and Dick Maguire, the party's financial chief, had pressed JFK to attend a fundraiser in the state. In August 1962, when Kennedy asked Lyndon's advice, Johnson urged the President to check with John Connally, LBJ's former aide and JFK's Secretary of the Navy, who had given up his post to run for Governor of Texas. Connally, who didn't want Kennedy siphoning off money from his campaign and saw JFK's presence in the state as doing Connally's liberal opponent more good than him, convinced Kennedy to delay coming.

At a meeting between Connally, LBJ, and the President in June 1963, however, JFK declared his intention to come to Texas in the fall. He wanted to raise money for the national party and polish his image in a state he feared losing in 1964. Texas voters were increasingly drawn to Republicans opposing Kennedy on civil rights, and the Democratic party was badly divided between conservatives led by Connally and liberals led by Senator Ralph Yarborough. Though the split in Democratic ranks went back to 1940 and JFK and LBJ had managed to mute it enough in 1960 to win the state, intra-party tensions had reached new heights by 1963.[96]

Johnson accepted Kennedy's decision, but he saw little gain to Kennedy or himself from a visit. Lyndon believed that Kennedy would find it almost impossible to draw the competing Democratic factions together. Kennedy himself was increasingly identified with the Yarborough liberals, and the ongoing struggle over civil rights, especially the pending bill in Congress, undermined the likelihood that the President could engineer some kind of compromise between the two sides. Johnson also saw the trip as likely to underscore his ineffectiveness in holding his own state Democratic party together. Lyndon's support of civil rights had put him at odds with his old friend and ally John Connally, and a series of patronage and policy fights with Yarborough had brought him into sharp conflict with the senator's liberal camp.[97]

Once Kennedy decided to come to Texas, though, Johnson wished to give him a gala reception, especially at his ranch, where he and Lady Bird planned to entertain Jack and Jackie Kennedy on the night of November 22 and the next morning. Lady Bird went home a week before the Kennedy's arrival, and Johnson came down on the 19th to prepare for their guests. Lady Bird and Lyndon tried to anticipate all the Kennedys' needs, from the President's favorite Scotch and a bed to support his ailing back to Jackie's preference for terry-cloth hand towels and a well-groomed walking horse she might wish to ride.[98]

On the afternoon of the 21st, Lyndon stood at the head of a huge crowd greeting the Kennedys at the San Antonio airport. Only the refusal of Senator Yarborough to ride in the same car with Lyndon in the motorcade to the city marred the occasion. Informed that Governor Connally intended to ignore him during the ceremonies at a fund-raising dinner in Austin on Friday evening, Yarborough retaliated by refusing to share Lyndon's car. When he repeated the performance on the ride into Houston from the airport later in the afternoon, reporters saw the day's story as the division in Democratic ranks.

That evening, in his hotel room, before speaking at the Houston Coliseum, Kennedy gave Johnson an earful about Connally's treatment of Yarborough and instructed him to solve the problem. After Johnson left, Jackie, who was in the next room and heard raised voices, asked: " 'What was that all about? He sounded mad.' 'That's just Lyndon,' " Kennedy replied. " 'He's in trouble.' " When one journalist greeted Johnson the next morning at a hotel in Fort Worth, he seemed "dour, mechanical, perfunctory." At the same time, JFK ordered his aides Larry O'Brien and Kenny O'Donnell to make Yarborough ride with Johnson during the motorcades scheduled for the 22nd. Though stories surfaced later of Kennedy's telling Yarborough that he would either ride with Johnson or walk, the issue was resolved by other means. O'Donnell remembers that Texas Congressman Albert Thomas, "a great pal of the President's, . . . knocked their heads together." He persuaded Connally to show Yarborough the deference due him, and O'Brien convinced the senator that his continued refusal to ride with the Vice President would hurt the President.[99]

When the President's party landed at Love Field in Dallas on the morning of the 22nd, Lady Bird "had some apprehension about an ugly show of bad taste." During the 1960 campaign right-wing demonstrators had verbally abused Lyndon and Lady Bird on a visit to the city, and four weeks before JFK's visit Adlai Stevenson, Kennedy's Ambassador to the U.N., had been heckled and physically attacked by radical-right zealots.

Riding in the fourth car of the procession behind the Kennedys and Connallys and two cars of security people, the Johnsons, Ralph Yarborough, and Rufus Youngblood, a Secret Service agent, heard an explosion as they reached the intersection of Houston and Elm Streets in downtown Dallas. It was 12:30 p.m. Youngblood observed abnormal movements in the President's car and saw Kennedy fall to his left. Reaching back with his left hand to grasp Johnson's right shoulder, he shouted, "Get down! Get down!" as he forced the Vice President to the floor. Youngblood swung his body across the back seat and sat on top of Johnson as two more explosions in rapid succession rang out. Yarborough, who smelled gunpowder, shouted, "My God! They've shot the President." Lady Bird answered, "No, no, no—that couldn't be." Youngblood remembers a message from one of the security cars, saying, "The President's been hit. Get us to a hospital, fast but safe."[100]

At Parkland Hospital Secret Service agents hustled the Johnsons through the emergency entrance along a series of corridors to a small room with hanging sheets and muslin curtains the agents closed. As they had come past the President's car toward the hospital entrance, Lady Bird saw a blur of pink in the back seat. It was Mrs. Kennedy lying over the President's body. During the forty-five minutes the Johnsons spent in the tiny room, a succession of people entered and left. The head of JFK's Secret Service detail informed Johnson that the President's condition was quite serious and urged the Vice President to make immediate plans to return to Washington, where he would be safer from a conspiracy that might be behind the attack on the President. Johnson thought Ken O'Donnell should be consulted before making a decision. Ten minutes later, at 1:13 p.m., the agent returned with the news of the President's death. Two minutes after, O'Donnell told Johnson, "He's gone."[101]

Response to the Assassination

The nation and people around the globe fell into a state of grief and anguish. The loss of someone who was so vibrant, so brimming with hope for the future of his presidency, his country, the world made his death inexplicable. "In Washington grief was agony," a White House aide later wrote. "It was all so grotesque and so incredible. . . . The people of the world grieved as if they had terribly lost their own leader, friend, brother."[102]

Johnson remembered himself in a state of shock with a rush of emotions ranging from anguish, bewilderment, and distress to compassion and deep concern for Mrs. Kennedy and her children. He later said that it was "impossible for me to re-create the thoughts and emotions that surged through me during the forty-five terrible, interminable minutes that we spent in Parkland Hospital." Some of those thoughts and feelings came from a sense of loss over the death of someone so young and vital, so magnetic and charming, and so full of promise and hope for the betterment of his country.

Yet Johnson must have felt some guilt as well. But not because, as some books, dramas, and films would later allege, he was part of a conspiracy to kill the President. He had absolutely nothing to do with JFK's assassination. It was more the guilt of a competitive older brother, a sibling or close associate who suddenly displaces his younger, more successful rival. For all his genuine regard for Jack Kennedy and sense of terrible loss at the President's demise, Johnson surely felt some elation at having gained the office he had said he deserved more than JFK. Five days later, when he spoke before Congress, he began, "All I have I would have given gladly not to be standing here today." It was the new President's way not only of expressing his grief but also of publicly unburdening himself of the inner guilt he felt at having eclipsed his great collaborator and rival.[103]

Although Johnson's ambivalent feelings toward JFK and all his associates partly shaped his actions in the immediate aftermath of the assassination, larger public affairs held first place in his mind. He immediately insisted on presidential prerogative by taking JFK's plane, Air Force One, for the return to Washington and arranging a swearing-in ceremony before taking off. Although Johnson's rush to take command offended JFK's associates, one of them says it "came, not from unseemly haste to grab the perquisites of office, but from compelling desire to calm a frantic people and reassure a shocked world." Indeed, Johnson's first concern on hearing of JFK's passing was to return to Washington and provide the country and the world with a sense of stability. Since he suspected a conspiracy behind the assassination, it seemed doubly important that he get back to the nation's capital, where he could preside over a smooth transition and an inquiry into Kennedy's murder. At the same time, however, he felt it was impermissible to leave Mrs. Kennedy and the President's body behind. Consequently, he ordered that he and Lady Bird be taken to Air Force One and that their departure be delayed until Kennedy's body and Jackie were on board.[104]

He also decided not to leave until a swearing-in ceremony had established his legitimate hold on the presidency. Although he had actually succeeded to the office on JFK's death, Johnson wasn't sure of this. And if there were a conspiracy that required immediate counter-action on his part, he did not wish to be without authority to act for the few hours it would take to return to Washington.

In addition, the constant compelling need to have approval and esteem—to be assured of everyone's regard, especially from those who seemed most likely to doubt him—drove Johnson to insist on the collaboration and backing of the Kennedy family and friends in giving him legitimacy as President. In an act of considerable insensitivity, he called Robert Kennedy for legal advice on the taking of presidential power. To be sure, he offered him heartfelt condolences, but he also asked for Bobby's approval of an immediate swearing-in and for information on who could administer the oath and its wording. Bobby, of course, *was* the Attorney General, but the details of this business could have been handled by subordinates, as indeed they were. But Johnson was asking Kennedy less for legal advice than for expressions of support.

Similarly, Johnson insisted that Jackie Kennedy stand next to him at his swearing-in. Kenny O'Donnell urged Johnson not to subject her to what he believed would be a painful moment. But Johnson was determined to have her by his side. When everyone was assembled and she hadn't arrived, Johnson said: "We'll wait for Mrs. Kennedy. I want her here." He asked that someone get her, but then announced that he would go himself. Having decided that she owed it to the country to endorse the transition of power by her presence, Jackie arrived before Lyndon came after her.[105]

Robert Kennedy was less cooperative. In a state of profound shock and grief, he was in no mood to indulge anyone's needs beyond those of his immediate family. When Air Force One landed at Andrews Field in Maryland, Bobby, "his face ... streaked with tears," hurried by the Johnson party to Jackie's side. "He ran," Johnson later complained, "so that he would not have to pause and recognize the new President." Arthur Schlesinger says: "Perhaps some such thought contributed to Robert Kennedy's haste. But a man more secure than Johnson would have sympathized with the terrible urgency carrying him to his murdered brother's wife." Johnson lacked that inner security. "I took the oath," he later told Kearns, "I became President. But for millions of Americans I was still illegitimate, a naked man with no presidential covering, a pretender to the throne, an illegal usurper."[106]

Other concerns tore at Johnson as well. He believed it essential to provide the nation with a convincing explanation of why and how Kennedy was killed. "A troubled, puzzled, and outraged nation wanted to know the facts," he writes in his memoirs. But on November 24, when Jack Ruby, a Dallas nightclub operator, shot Lee Harvey Oswald to death in the garage of the Dallas jail on his way to a court hearing, the incident, Johnson said, turned the nation's "outrage to skepticism and doubt."

Suspicions now abounded about a conspiracy perpetrated by right-wing fanatics or Russia or Cuba or the CIA or the FBI or the Mafia or even Johnson himself. To quiet these rumblings and to investigate the President's death, on November 29, Johnson appointed a bipartisan panel that included Chief Justice Earl Warren, former CIA Director Allen Dulles, former U.S. High Commissioner of Germany and prominent foreign policy adviser John J. McCloy, Democratic Senator Richard Russell of Georgia, Republican Senator John Sherman Cooper of Kentucky, Republican Congressman Gerald Ford of Michigan, and Democratic Congressman Hale Boggs of Louisiana. They were all men with reputations for integrity and devotion to the country. They inspired confidence in the belief that an honest assessment of what happened would result from their work.[107]

During the next ten months, while the Warren Commission studied the information put before it by government investigators, Johnson pressed for a report as soon as possible so as to quiet public suspicions of a conspiracy. The commission operated in an atmosphere of concern from high government officials, including Johnson, the Justice Department, the FBI, and the CIA, that its report point to Oswald as the sole assassin and refute suggestions that any official in the United States or in any other country had planned Kennedy's death. When it delivered its findings in September 1964, the commission said just that: Oswald and Ruby each acted alone, "without advice or assistance," and that no conspiracy determined the actions of either man.[108]

Whatever the accuracy of the commission's report, Johnson, like a majority of Americans, then and since, did not take its findings at face value. He knew that the CIA and the FBI, the principal investigative arms of the commission, held back information that could damage their reputations. The CIA hid its part in plots to assassinate Cuba's Fidel Castro, information that would have enflamed suspicions of a Cuban hand in killing Kennedy. Nor did the FBI provide the full story of Oswald's ties to the Soviets and the Cubans; to do so would have meant acknowledging the bureau's failure to monitor the activities of someone it considered a subversive and a security risk.

Johnson believed that suggestions of Cuban or Soviet involvement in Kennedy's death would provoke an international crisis. His appeal to Warren to head the commission included a statement of how disturbed he was by rumors of Castro's and Khrushchev's involvement in a conspiracy; he feared "that it might even catapult us into a nuclear war if it got a head start." It was enough to convince Warren, who doubted the wisdom of a Chief Justice serving on such a commission. Johnson's appeal brought tears to Warren's eyes, Johnson told California Senator Thomas Kuchel. When Richard Russell resisted joining the commission, Johnson told him that 40 million American lives might be lost in a nuclear war if a trustworthy commission did not refute charges that Khrushchev or Castro had killed Kennedy. When Russell proved less vulnerable to this appeal than Warren, Johnson told him: "I can't arrest you and I'm not gonna put the FBI on you, but you are goddamn sure gonna serve I'll tell you that." And, of course, he did. Johnson also assumed that any conspiracy theory about JFK's assassination would eventually point to him. Within days of Kennedy's death, the FBI was being flooded with correspondence from people alleging an LBJ role in killing the President.[109]

Yet Johnson himself believed that Oswald had not acted alone. Aside from the facts in the case, Johnson had a suspicious cast of mind that caused him to see a conspiracy behind every major mishap. He was so given to political manipulation and back-room dealings that he tended to see public affairs as principally shaped by preplanned designs. During his presidency, he told a number of people that JFK's death was the result of a conspiracy. In 1967, he told a White House aide that the CIA had something to do with JFK's killing.

He apparently also had suspicions about the Secret Service; a week after Kennedy's death he asked J. Edgar Hoover to help assure his safety. He advised Hoover that he intended to take every precaution he could, and told him that "I was more than head of the FBI—I was his brother and personal friend; that he knew I did not want anything to happen to his family; that he has more confidence in me than anybody in town; that he would not embroil me in a jurisdictional dispute; but that he did want to have my thoughts on the matter [of his security] to advocate as his own opinion."[110]

It is difficult to put too much credence in Johnson's suspicions of the CIA or Secret Service. If he truly believed they had conspired to kill a president, would he have failed to mount a serious investigation of both agencies? His safety alone would have dictated such action.

He was more convinced of a Vietnamese or Cuban role in the killing. During Johnson's presidency, he shifted back and forth between blaming Vietnamese backers of Diem and Castro Cubans for murdering JFK. Shortly after the assassination, Johnson told Hubert Humphrey that "we had a hand in killing him [Diem]. Now it's happening here." At about the same time, Johnson told a small group, which included a high official of the CIA, that "Kennedy's murder was an act of retribution ... by unnamed persons seeking vengeance for the murder ... of ... Diem."[111]

In time, Johnson settled on the idea that Castro Cubans were responsible. LBJ told his domestic affairs chief Joe Califano, "President Kennedy tried to get Castro, but Castro got Kennedy first." He repeated his suspicions to journalists, telling one, "We had been operating a damned Murder Inc. in the Caribbean." He pointed out that Kennedy had been killed a year after a CIA-assassination team had been picked up in Havana. Although he ordered an end to such assassination plots, Johnson feared a Cuban attempt against him. In February 1964, after FBI reports reached him that Cuban "kamikaze" pilots might try to shoot down his plane on an upcoming trip to Florida, he held a meeting in the family quarters of the White House with the highest government officials. The FBI found no substantiation of the rumor. The meeting was additional evidence of his conviction that more than a lone gunman was behind Kennedy's death.[112]

Johnson feared that he would also be assassinated. Bill Moyers remembers LBJ's anxiety. During the 1964 campaign, "there were times," Moyers says, "when he did not want to step off the plane in front of that crowd. It took a lot of guts. And once he did, he was exuberant; he felt liberated." After an appearance in Denver, "we had a huge reception there; he'd gotten up in the back of the car and just would make speeches with a bullhorn and then throw himself into the crowd. We got back to the plane, and I forget what I said to him, but his answer was, 'Nobody shot at me.' "[113]

Johnson wanted no public discussion of his concerns. Not because, as Anthony Lewis of the *New York Times* said, "The search for conspiracy only increases the elements of morbidity and paranoia and fantasy in this country.... [and] obscures our necessary understanding ... that in this life there is often tragedy without reason." Rather, Johnson believed that increased speculation about a conspiracy could threaten international stability and undermine his authority by encouraging allegations about his possible role in killing JFK. Instead, he thought it better to repress such divisive discussions and concentrate on bold domestic reforms, which he instinctively understood could now be made in Kennedy's name. And once he had paid proper homage to the fallen President, he wanted to seize the opportunity that had unexpectedly come to him and turn the country in directions few expected him to take.[114]

2

From JFK to LBJ

O NLY one other President in the century, Theodore Roosevelt, had come to power after an assassination. And the passive, unspectacular William McKinley, T. R.'s predecessor, was no John Kennedy. Lyndon Johnson faced the toughest transition since Harry Truman succeeded the legendary Franklin Roosevelt. "I always felt sorry for Harry Truman and the way he got the presidency," Johnson told an aide two days after Kennedy's death, "but at least his man wasn't murdered."

Johnson had to confront the grief and despair many people felt over the loss of a beloved leader and their antagonism toward someone who, however much he identified with JFK, seemed like a usurper, an unelected, untested replacement for the man the country now more than ever saw as more suitable for the job. In the first days of his presidency, only 5 percent of the public felt they knew very much about LBJ, while 67 percent said they knew next to nothing about him. Seventy percent of the county had doubts about how it would "carry on without" Kennedy.[1]

Johnson, like T. R. and Truman, understood the essential need for continuity, for reassuring people at home and abroad that the new President would be faithful to the previous administration. The death of a President was trauma enough, but Kennedy's assassination made his passing a national crisis in self-confidence, a time of doubt about the durability of the country's democratic system and its tradition of nonviolent political change. "A nation stunned, shaken to its very heart, had to be reassured that the government was not in a state of paralysis," Johnson later recalled. "I had to convince everyone everywhere that the country would go forward.... Any hesitation or wavering, any false step, any sign of self-doubt, could have been disastrous.... The times cried out for leadership."[2]

Johnson remembered himself in the first days of his presidency
as "a man in trouble." He feared that "the enormity of the tragedy"
and "the tide of grief" following Kennedy's death might "overwhelm"
him. He might "become immobilized . . . with emotion." The responsibilities of the office frightened him, as any sensible person would
have been. But the self-doubts that had been the engine of his ambition now also agitated him. Could he possibly measure up? Was he
smart enough? Knowledgeable enough? He was a Texan, a southerner, a man on the fringe with no hold on the imagination of the
country and limited experience in world affairs.

The possibility of failure troubled his sleep. On the night of
November 23, after his first full day in office, he was so anxious he
could not stand to be alone. It was not enough that Lady Bird shared
his bedroom; he insisted that Horace Busby, his old friend and aide,
spend much of the night in an armchair watching over him. Twice
during the night, when Busby thought Johnson had fallen asleep and
tried to tiptoe out of the room, the President cried out to him not to
go: "Buzz, are you still there?" he asked. Only toward morning, when
Johnson had fallen into a deep sleep, was Busby able to leave.[3]

Despite his private fears, Johnson was an inspiration to the country. His public appearances, his use of language, his management of
the press promoted feelings of continuity and unity. To be sure,
traditions of political stability and shared assumptions about cooperative efforts to advance the national well-being eased Johnson's burden. But an almost uncanny feel for the appropriate word and gesture
honed by thirty-two years in the political arena were as important in
making him equal to the task.

His self-conscious effort to overcome a reputation as an overbearing egotist who believed himself more deserving of the presidency than JFK is a case in point. In his first meetings with Kennedy's
aides, he said that "he did not have the education, culture, and understanding that President Kennedy had . . . , but he would do his
best." "I want you to draw the threads together on the domestic
program," he told Ted Sorensen. "But don't expect me to absorb
things as fast as you're used to."

It was false modesty on Johnson's part. His brain power or force
of intellect was the equal of any President's in the century. His real
message was: I won't let my outsized ego, my need to control and
dominate, keep me from listening to and relying on others to do my
job. Or, stated another way, Jack Kennedy was open-minded, surrounded himself with talented people, and made effective use of their
advice; I'll try to do the same.[4]

In the difficult days after Kennedy's death, words were Johnson's weapons in a war on uncertainty and gloom. Like a master therapist, the new President soothed the nation with language that conveyed sincerity and wisdom. Proclaiming a national day of mourning on November 23, Johnson invoked the martyred Kennedy as a source of national strength: "As he did not shrink from his responsibilities, but welcomed them, so he would not have us shrink from carrying on his work beyond this hour of national tragedy." Two days later, speaking to the states' governors at the White House, Johnson urged "continuity without confusion."

The next day Johnson described a meeting with representatives of Latin American countries as "a family gathering," and declared that nothing in President Kennedy's public career meant more to him than the ties uniting our countries. Johnson asked that the Alliance for Progress, which JFK had launched nearly three years before in the room where LBJ spoke, become Kennedy's "living memorial."[5]

Few things contributed more to Johnson's successful transition than a national address on the evening of November 27. Speaking to a joint session of Congress from the rostrum of the House, where he could remind Americans that he was a seasoned and successful political leader with thirty-two years of experience on Capitol Hill, Johnson's demeanor and language struck exactly the right tone. Dressed in a dark suit and tie reflecting the country's somber mood, he humbly asked the help of all Americans in shouldering "the awesome burden of the Presidency," which "I cannot bear ... alone."

Invoking memories of FDR, who in another time of crisis began his administration with a call for action, Johnson urged the country "to do away with uncertainty and doubt" and show "that from the brutal loss of our leader we will derive not weakness, but strength; that we can and will act and act now." Johnson described Kennedy's dreams of a better America and a more peaceful world and reminded the country of JFK's words, " 'let us begin.' Today, in this moment of new resolve, I would say to all my fellow Americans, let us continue." Thirty-four bursts of prolonged applause interrupted Johnson's twenty-five minute speech. The enthusiasm for his words in Congress reflected the national response.[6]

Fearful that Kennedy's Cabinet and aides would do him and the country harm by resigning their posts, Johnson used all his powers of persuasion to retain them. "I want you all to stay on. I need you," he told the Cabinet at a brief meeting on November 23. If many, or even some, of JFK's principal appointees left, it might be seen not as an expression of regard for the new President, who was entitled to have his own handpicked staff, but as a repudiation or an indirect statement of no confidence in him.[7]

No one was more important to Johnson in this regard than Robert Kennedy. As the second-in-command during JFK's term, Robert was more the direct heir of his brother's political legacy than LBJ. Understanding this, Johnson kept his negative and competitive feelings toward Bobby in check and pressed him to remain as Attorney General. "I need you more than the President needed you," LBJ told him on the morning of the 23rd. Robert didn't want to discuss the matter, and Johnson came back to it again on the 27th after his speech in the House. By then, new tensions between them made the meeting awkward and unpleasant. Robert was unhappy about what he and some JFK aides felt had been Johnson's unseemly haste in taking over Kennedy's plane and moving into the President's office. Johnson resented the fact that Bobby came late to the Cabinet meeting on the 23rd. He believed that Robert had deliberately tried to spoil the meeting's effect, and Johnson quoted Kennedy as telling an aide: "We won't go in until he has already sat down."

On the 27th, after Johnson received a memo from his aide George Reedy about someone in the Justice Department whom a newspaper quoted as calling LBJ a "wheeler-dealer," he told Kennedy: "People around you are saying things about me. . . . you can't let your people talk about me and I won't talk about you." Robert didn't remember what he said in response, but with Johnson promising to fulfill his brother's legacy and asking his continuing counsel and support, Bobby stayed at his post. "He saw himself," his biographer writes, "as yoked with Johnson in the execution of a legacy and the preservation of a party."[8]

Although many of Kennedy's people would play a significant part in Johnson's administration, especially in foreign affairs, Robert Kennedy was not one of them. There was already too much between them for an effective working relationship to develop. For the immediate future Bobby was useful to Johnson as a symbol of continuity. But even this wouldn't last. In January 1964, Johnson aide Walter Jenkins told Cartha DeLoach, FBI Director J. Edgar Hoover's liaison to the White House, that "the President was not yet quite ready to take on Bobby," but he was planning to oust some of his close associates soon.[9]

The comment was a signal to Hoover that he could ignore the Attorney General and deal directly with the President, as had been his habit until JFK dictated otherwise. In fact, as one of Robert's aides told DeLoach in March, "the President's body had not even become cold before you [Hoover] started circumventing the Attorney General and dealing directly with the President." Hoover, who wanted to force Bobby Kennedy's resignation as a way to prevent his own retirement from the FBI, fed Johnson unflattering stories about Robert. In particular, he alleged that Bobby's friends planned to make Johnson take Kennedy as his running mate in 1964 by using the Bobby Baker case against the President. Though none of this was true, Johnson was a receptive audience. Jenkins told DeLoach that Johnson "was shocked over this matter." It fit in with Johnson's feeling that Bobby would not give him his due as President, and "acted like *he* was the custodian of the Kennedy dream, some kind of rightful heir to the throne."

Early in 1964 Johnson and Kennedy had a face-to-face blowup. Paul Corbin, a friend of Jack's and Bobby's at the Democratic National Committee (DNC), was saying unpleasant things about LBJ that got back to him. Much worse from LBJ's perspective was a Corbin effort to promote a vice-presidential write-in for Kennedy in New Hampshire. The possibility that he might get more votes for V.P. than Johnson running for President particularly troubled LBJ. Though Corbin was doing this without Kennedy's permission or support, Johnson thought otherwise. He wanted Corbin fired from the DNC. When O'Donnell, who believed Johnson justified in doing this, told Bobby, the Attorney General said, "Tell him to go to hell." O'Donnell told Bobby to do it himself.

Kennedy and Johnson went head to head over the man in a meeting at the White House. " 'I want you to get rid of that Paul Corbin,' " Johnson told Kennedy. " 'I don't think I should,' Bobby replied; 'he was appointed by President Kennedy, who thought he was good.' 'Do it. President Kennedy isn't president anymore. I am.' 'I know you're president, and don't you ever talk to me like that again.' " Robert rose abruptly and walked out of the office.

In a telephone conversation, Johnson described the meeting differently: When Kennedy said the President, meaning JFK, "liked the work he [Corbin] did, I said, I know it, Bobby, but I'm President, and I don't like what he's doing." After Bobby complained that Corbin wasn't getting a fair hearing or a fair deal, LBJ described himself as saying, "we'll give him a fair hearing and we'll give him a fair deal. But we're not gonna have him going around operating independently."

In subsequent meetings, "their relationship was correct," O'Donnell says. But both were only hiding their animus. LBJ's description of their meeting about Corbin was a muted version of what occurred. Johnson now intended to wait until after the 1964 election to deal with someone he considered a nemesis.[10]

In the meantime, Johnson focused his efforts on soothing the country's sense of loss and rekindling hope that it could deal effectively with domestic and foreign problems. In meetings with the press and leaders from every walk of life, Johnson reminded audiences of John Kennedy's achievements and all that remained to be done in his name.

His objective, LBJ candidly told a press conference, was to create a sense of continuity and unity in the country. By the first of the year, Johnson could not have been more pleased with his success. The press, George Reedy told him, had never before been so completely on his side: "They are in a mood now where they are merely looking for historical indications that you are going to be a good President and a strong President." Gallup polls showed Johnson with a 79 percent approval rating, with only 3 percent disapproving of his performance. In December, Johnson topped the list of the ten most admired men in the world; Eisenhower, Churchill, humanitarian Albert Schweitzer, Bobby Kennedy, Evangelist Billy Graham, Adlai Stevenson, Pope Paul VI, Charles de Gaulle, and Richard Nixon stood next in line.[11]

The Kennedy Legacy

Cynics at the time and since credited Johnson with a good but largely contrived performance. By their lights LBJ was a "wheeler dealer" who launched his 1964 election campaign the day after becoming President. His appeals for continuity and unity were good politics aimed more at serving himself than the national interest. Johnson's affinity for cutting corners throughout his political career make such suspicions understandable. And indeed, considerable manipulativeness—a substantial gap between what he said in public and what he worked toward privately—would characterize much of his presidency beginning in 1965.

But this was not the case with the transition from JFK to himself and to much of what he initially did in domestic affairs. True, he could not help thinking about the election that was only eleven months away. What career politician, who had spent much of his life running for office, could have, or even should have, done otherwise? Attending to the public's needs to gain votes is central to the country's democratic system. But Johnson's first year in office was a period of largely honest dealings: He genuinely aimed to help the country recover from its sense of loss over JFK's murder, and he was passionately committed to the domestic gains he asked from the Congress.

Between November 1963 and the 1964 election, LBJ identified himself with JFK not only as a means of winning public support but also because he saw Kennedy's unfinished liberal agenda as essential to the national well-being. In his November 27 address, for example, he had told the country that "no ... eulogy could more eloquently honor President Kennedy's memory than the earliest possible passage of the civil rights bill for which he fought so long. We have talked long enough in this country about equal rights. We have talked for one hundred years or more. It is time now to write the next chapter, and to write it in the books of law." Johnson also urged passage of JFK's $11 billion tax cut, a measure "designed to increase our national income and Federal revenues, and to provide insurance against recession."[12]

In pressing the case for JFK's domestic reforms, Johnson was on comfortable ground. His idea of the presidency was picking up where FDR's New Deal had left off—expanding prosperity, opening doors of opportunity to poor folks, and honoring the country's rhetoric about equal treatment under the law. Shortly after becoming President, Johnson had several old New Deal friends over for dinner. Elizabeth Wickenden, who was there, remembers the occasion as a moment when Johnson was reconnecting with his liberal past and charting a course for the future. On the evening of November 25, when he met with his principal economic advisers, "the confident way in which he approached the whole problem" of economic advance greatly impressed one of them. Johnson told Walter Heller, chairman of the Council of Economic Advisers, to get his "liberal friends ... to lay off ... to quit lobbying. I'm for them. I know they have good programs. ... They don't need to waste my time ... with their memorandums and their phone calls."[13]

Johnson had already stated his eagerness for reform in a private conversation with Heller two days before. Heller had told Johnson that Kennedy had asked for a plan that would help the 22 percent of Americans living in poverty. JFK's visit during his 1960 campaign to West Virginia shantytowns with poorly nourished children had shocked him. The publication of Michael Harrington's small but powerful book, *The Other America*, and literary critic Dwight Macdonald's review of it, "Our Invisible Poor," in *The New Yorker* had spurred interest in the issue in 1962–63.

The President was already mindful of the many Americans, especially the elderly and blacks, who lived "on the outskirts of hope" in "inherited, gateless poverty." He had told Heller about antipoverty plans: "That's my kind of program. We should push ahead full-tilt on this project." Moreover, as Heller was about to leave, at the end of an exhausting day, the President stopped him at the door "to say something about all this talk that I'm a conservative who is likely to go back to the Eisenhower ways or give in to the economy bloc in Congress. It's not so, and I want you to tell your friends—Arthur Schlesinger, Galbraith and other liberals—that it is not so. I'm no budget slasher. I understand that expenditures have to keep rising to keep pace with the population and help the economy. If you look at my record, you would know that I am a Roosevelt New Dealer. As a matter of fact, John F. Kennedy was a little too conservative to suit my taste."[14]

An attack on poverty had much appeal to LBJ. Not only was it his kind of program, it also gave him a platform for 1964. During the dinner with New Deal friends he told Wickenden, " 'I've got to be thinking about my future.... I have to carry out the Kenendy legacy. I feel very strongly that that's part of my obligation, and at the same time I've got . . . to put my own stamp on this Administration in order to run for office.' So he came to this poverty program— making it nationwide. He didn't go into what it would do specifically."[15]

Johnson's eagerness for a poverty program did not mean that he or anyone else had a well-formulated plan. Within days after Kennedy's death, some of his close associates publicly revealed that he intended to attack the causes of national poverty in a second term. They acknowledged that he had no precise blueprint and did not expect to get a bill through Congress until after the 1964 election. Nevertheless, public discussion of Kennedy's interest in an antipoverty crusade increased Johnson's desire to do something at once.[16]

But what? Johnson initially thought of such a program as a revival of FDR's National Youth Administration. The attack on poverty would focus on poor youths in inner cities and depressed rural areas, where inadequate schooling and limited opportunity had made for unemployment and delinquency. Heller's idea, drawn from a study made by a Robert Kennedy aide in the Justice Department, was to ease poverty by relying on "Community Action." Poor people knew what was best for themselves and should be given command of federal educational and jobs programs.

In a series of meetings at Johnson's ranch during the Christmas holiday, Johnson at first rejected and then accepted Heller's proposal. Johnson didn't see how Community Action would provide education and create jobs, the essentials for any successful attack on poverty. Elizabeth Wickenden and Busby also cautioned him against signing on to something they thought could cause political problems with Congress, local officeholders, and middle-class Americans. Federal and local officials would object to a program that bypassed them, and middle-class taxpayers would resent shouldering the costs of what would be attacked as new handouts to the undeserving poor. "America's real majority is suffering a minority complex of neglect," Busby told Johnson. "They have become the real foes of Negro rights, foreign aid, etc., because, as much as anything, they feel forgotten, at the second table behind the tightly organized, smaller groups at either end of the U.S. spectrum."[17]

Despite the uncertainties, a war on poverty, as they agreed to call it, excited Johnson's attraction to grand visionary plans. "We were moving into uncharted territory," Johnson later wrote. "Powerful forces of opposition would be stirred.... But the powerful conviction that an attack on poverty was right and necessary blotted out any fears that this program was a political land mine." Johnson wanted something that would "be big and bold and hit the whole nation with real impact." "When I got through," he told a journalist, "no one in this country would be able to ignore the poverty in our midst."[18]

Announced with a flourish in his January 1964 State of the Union message, the War on Poverty was pure Johnson—bigger, bolder, grander in concept than any reform proposal in the country's history. "This Administration today, here and now, declares unconditional war on poverty in America.... Our aim is not only to relieve the symptoms of poverty, but to cure it and, above all, to prevent it," he said. He wanted Congress to pass a parcel of laws that would give the government the wherewithal to fight and win the war.

However much eliminating poverty exceeded political capacity, Johnson wasn't alone in seeing it as within reach. In 1962 a group of University of Michigan social welfare experts predicted that it would be relatively easy to end poverty in America at a cost of $2 billion a year, less than 2 percent of GNP.

Johnson's pronouncement on curing poverty was of a piece with other bold proposals he urged on Congress. He asked the next session to do "more for civil rights than the last hundred sessions combined"; to enact "the most far-reaching tax cut of our time"; to achieve "the most effective, efficient foreign aid program ever; and ... to build more homes, more schools, more libraries, and more hospitals than any single session of Congress in the history of our Republic. All this and more can and must be done. It can be done by this summer," Johnson said. It would be no more than fulfilling the faith that John Kennedy had in his fellow Americans to create "a nation that is free from want ... for our time and for all time to come."[19]

The Legislator

Although Congress and the public gave Johnson's speech a warm reception, no one familiar with the slow almost tortuous means by which major bills become laws expected Johnson to get most of what he asked. Johnson himself had few illusions about the difficulties he faced in Congress. As he told one aide shortly after becoming President, "Everything on my desk today was here when I first came to Congress" twenty-six years ago.

But in calling for so much reform so quickly, Johnson wasn't posturing for history. In January, Hubert Humphrey responded to Republican attacks on the Democrats by declaring that "the issues are ... set out already; they include war on poverty, economic growth, world peace, security and medicare, human dignity, human rights, education, opportunity for the young. The issues of smear and fear are not worthy of this republic. . . . The Republicans want to spent a lot of time on that, and while they're digging there we will just be building a better America." Johnson told him: "Goddamn, that couldn't be better; that's as fine a statement as I ever saw of that view in a few words."

Johnson had every hope that JFK's tax cut, the civil rights bill, and the war on poverty would translate into concrete laws. He believed that the sympathy for proposals identified with JFK would make them irresistible. When Florida Senator George Smathers suggested that LBJ put aside JFK's tax cut as a way to win quick passage of the appropriation bill, Johnson told him: "No, no, I can't do that. . . . We can't abandon this fellow's program, because he is a national hero." Years later, Johnson told Doris Kearns: "Everything I had ever learned in the history books taught me that martyrs have to die for causes. John Kennedy had died. But his 'cause' was not really clear. That was my job. I had to take the dead man's program and turn it into a martyr's cause." In addition, he believed that a tax bill that would spur a sluggish economy, a rights law that would end the injustices of southern segregation, and an attack on economic suffering that might benefit all Americans made his appeal a realistic call to congressional action.[20]

As important, he had every confidence that these were the right proposals at the right time and that he was the one who could enact them. In dealing with Congress, he had three decades of experience and the knowledge that as Senate Majority Leader he had exercised more effective control in the Upper House than any senator in American history. This had not been the result of chance or circumstance but of considered actions and hard work. Though it was clear to

Johnson that his role as President was different from that of Majority Leader, he nevertheless saw useful similarities that could help him pass laws.

In the Senate he had exchanged favors for votes. As President, he had a greater variety of gifts that could be traded for congressional backing. Further, he had asserted his power in the Senate by learning the needs and wants of his colleagues and playing to them at every turn. As President, he had greater means to measure legislators' wants and more ways to satisfy them; he expected the Johnson "treatment" to be more effective than ever in bending Congress to his will.

"There is but one way for a President to deal with the Congress," Johnson later told Doris Kearns, "and that is continuously, incessantly, and without interruption. If it's really going to work, the relationship between the President and the Congress has got to be almost incestuous. He's got to know them even better than they know themselves. And then, on the basis of this knowledge, he's got to build a system that stretches from the cradle to the grave, from the moment a bill is introduced to the moment it is officially enrolled as the law of the land."[21]

One aide recalls: "The best liaison we had with the Congress was Lyndon Johnson. He spent an enormous amount of time persuading congressmen to vote for particular issues." Columnist Drew Pearson, in a memo he wrote to himself, marveled at all the personal attention Johnson was giving to congressmen. "He phones them, writes them notes, draws them aside at receptions to ask their opinions, seeks them out to thank them for political favors. Almost every Tuesday and Thursday he invites a group of congressmen over for an evening at the White House. While Lady Bird shows the wives around the upstairs living quarters, the President talks policies and politics with the men."

When Larry O'Brien reminded the President that there was to be an evening legislative gathering at the White House, Johnson urged him " 'to get a good afternoon nap so that you can dance with those big fat women over there.' . . . 'I bet you're not too displeased that this is the last one tonight,' " O'Brien said. " 'They talk about how I love this dancin',' " Johnson answered. " 'I wish those sons of bitches writers would come take my place.' " But Johnson knew that these socials built up a measure of goodwill that was invaluable. He even wanted O'Brien to consider arranging an evening for legislative aides, who did so much of the work on the Hill.

Labor leader George Meany believed that Johnson "had a greater knowledge, current knowledge, day-to-day knowledge, of what was going on over on Capitol Hill than any other President ever had." Director of the Budget Bureau Charles Schultze remembers Johnson's unrelenting absorption with getting bills passed. Never let up was LBJ's motto: "Don't assume anything; make sure every possible weapon is brought to bear ...; keep everybody involved; don't let them slacken."[22]

Kermit Gordon, Schultze's predecessor, was "in awe" of LBJ's understanding of the legislative process, the principal figures in the Congress, and how to manipulate them. In 1964, after an earthquake and tidal wave in Alaska, Johnson decided to set up a commission to supervise the use of federal reconstruction funds in the state. At Johnson's request, Gordon suggested names of people who might direct the commission. Ignoring Gordon's list, the President pressured New Mexico Senator Clinton Anderson into taking the assignment. Gordon was mystified: "A senator running an Executive Branch Commission? Anderson was ill—very reluctant to do it—but the President was marvelously persuasive, used humor and mutual recollections of episodes they'd been through together. . . . And Anderson agreed."

Gordon left Johnson's meeting with Anderson doubting the President's wisdom. He couldn't see letting a senator that close to administrative decision-making. But in no time at all he viewed it as "a brilliant decision." It was Johnson's way of preventing Alaska's senators from raiding the federal treasury. Johnson knew that Anderson was one of the few people in the country with the clout to sit on the two Alaskans. LBJ displayed a keen understanding of "what motivates senators and how you play off one ... against another," Gordon said.[23]

Johnson also understood that mastering Congress meant having a first-rate staff. As President, he could not interact with senators as he had as Majority Leader, though this was difficult for him to accept. One aide remembers holding the President back from involving himself too much in the hour to hour management of pending bills. "There was no time day or night he wasn't prepared to charge in." Early one morning, after a losing all-night struggle in the House, the aide called Johnson to report the defeat. "When did this happen?" Johnson asked. In the middle of the night, the aide replied. "Why didn't you call me?" Johnson said. "You should have called me and told me about it. You know, when you're up there bleeding, I want to bleed with you. We have to share these things."[24]

Initially, Johnson's legislative staff consisted of the Kennedy aides manning the office of congressional relations. Lawrence F. O'Brien, a public relations expert who had worked for JFK since 1952, was its principal figure. An amiable and soft-spoken man with roots in the liberal wing of the Democratic party, O'Brien shared with the Kennedys an Irish background, a warm sense of humor, and an unsentimental astuteness about politics that had made him an effective campaign organizer and a skilled liaison with Congress. By the time Johnson had become President, O'Brien and his staff had become more effective in dealing with issues on the Hill than at the start of Kennedy's term. "When Lyndon Johnson came to us for help," one of them says, "we were ready to provide it."

O'Brien and Johnson got along exceptionally well. "I enjoyed him," O'Brien recalls. "I hadn't known him well, but in very short order I liked his openness."

Johnson saw him as highly effective in dealing with Congress, and as someone with whom he could have some fun. After an agriculture bill passed in April 1964, the President puzzled over having so many textile manufacturers at the signing ceremony. He doubted "the wisdom of having all these damn textile rake offs in here for this signing," he told O'Brien. "I'd get every . . . goddamn farmer I could . . . I'd get . . . senators and make 'em bring a whole bunch of horny handed sons of toil in here for the picture. . . . If he [Agriculture Secretary Freeman]'s got one goddamn dirty tobacco chewin' farmer that's for this bill get him in here. I don't think he has. I think they're all towel manufacturers. . . . Just tell him that in that kind of language. Can you Irish talk that kind of language?" Johnson asked. O'Brien confessed to having tried it a couple of times. "I don't want you to try it on me," Johnson told him. Try it "on Freeman. We bled for him. I don't want to bleed for him any more."

The only problem between Johnson and O'Brien was their shared verbosity: "a matter that could have been resolved in five or ten minutes could result in an hour of discussion."[25]

Johnson never confined legislative work to designated specialists. "The Johnson people, no matter what their assignments were," O'Brien says, "joined me at his urging in participating in the legislative effort. That applied to every Johnson person in the White House over the years that I was there." The principal Johnson men were four Texans and a midwesterner whom Johnson liked to describe as "valuable chunks of humanity who can do anything." They were men of exceptional energy and devotion to a boss who had no qualms about calling on them any hour of the day or night.[26]

Johnson had no official chief of staff. He "ran the White House as he had his Senate office, under his hat," one aide said. Though no assistant had overall supervisory powers, Walter Jenkins was the first among equals. The forty-five-year-old Jenkins had been with Johnson since graduating from the University of Texas in 1939. Described as gentle, quiet, and the only one who had "total rapport" with the President, Jenkins was a man Friday who enjoyed everyone's trust and presided over the details of daily operations at the White House. Historian and special consultant to the President Eric Goldman remembered him sitting "in his big office in the West Wing, suit baggy, his middle collecting fat, his dark hair graying and his face turning the more florid the wearier he became, endlessly doing a sweeping variety of tasks. . . . Jenkins rode herd on things President Johnson wanted done, finding out why the expected had not happened and why the unexpected did."[27]

George Reedy was Johnson's second longest serving aide. The son of a Chicago *Tribune* crime reporter, Reedy was something of a child prodigy who attended the University of Chicago, where he became a socialist and developed an interest in journalism. After college and a stint in the Army Air Force as an intelligence officer during World War II, he became a Capitol Hill reporter for United Press International. In 1951 he gave up journalism for a job on Johnson's Senate staff. Asked by a friend how he could leave reporting to work for a politician, Reedy replied: "Because Lyndon Johnson is a first-rate man. He's the senator who's going to get useful things done, and he will be President someday. I'm hitching my wagon to a star."

The forty-six-year-old Reedy was a shrewd political analyst who counseled Johnson on everything from his public image to legislative maneuvers and election campaigns. His work for Johnson as Vice President focused on press relations, and when Pierre Salinger, JFK's press secretary, left that post in March 1964, Reedy replaced him. Johnson had enormous regard for Reedy, but he sometimes became impatient with his philosophizing. "You ask him what time it is," LBJ once said, "and he discusses the significance of time before he tells you it's eleven-thirty."[28]

Horace Busby was another "triple threat man," as Johnson liked to describe his aides. At the University of Texas in the 1940s Busby, or "Buzz," as his friends called him, established a reputation as a crusading student journalist devoted to reform politics. In 1948, Busby worked in Johnson's Senate campaign and then served him on and off over the next fifteen years as a speech writer and legislative and political analyst. As soon as LBJ became President, the forty-year-old Busby became an official member of Johnson's staff. His duties were speech writing and "special projects," which meant feeding the President ideas about domestic change and the political repercussions of anything he might attempt. Johnson, one White House observer recalls, liked having Busby around him. More than any other staff member, Busby "thought and felt like" Johnson. And so in the opening months of LBJ's presidency, "Busby was most often the man who served as LBJ's other self."[29]

Bill Moyers was the youngest, and in many respects the most extraordinary, member of Johnson's staff. A poor boy from Marshall in northeast Texas, Moyers began his forays into journalism as a student at the University of Texas that won him a job at LBJ's Austin television station KTBC. After study at the University of Edinburgh and at Baptist Theological Seminary in Fort Worth, Moyers had worked for Johnson in his 1960 vice-presidential campaign. During the next three years, he had served as deputy director of the Peace Corps, where he functioned as an "idealist-operator," mixing "the nineteenth-century American missionary instinct with twentieth-century managerial attitudes and cynicism." The twenty-nine-year-old Moyers entered Johnson's White House as an appointments and scheduling secretary and part-time speech writer. But his talent and devotion to the President quickly projected him into the front rank of Johnson's aides. "That boy has a bleeding ulcer. He works for me like a dog, and is just as faithful," Johnson said. Like the President, Moyers had a "natural . . . zest for politics, as well as LBJ's tendency to talk about it in uplifted phrases."[30]

Jack Valenti, a forty-seven-year-old Houston advertising man, whom one journalist described as "the most enigmatic and the most omnipresent of the Johnson men," had first met LBJ in 1956 at a businessmen's reception. Impressed with the strength of the senator's personality, Valenti had written a flattering column about him in the *Houston Post* and then in 1960 managed the Kennedy-Johnson advertising campaign in Texas.

During LBJ's vice presidency, while courting and then marrying Mary Margaret Wiley, Johnson's secretary, Valenti had seen a lot of LBJ. Johnson enjoyed his exuberance, charm, and intelligence and saw him as a "can do man" with a prodigious appetite for work. The two men also shared an affinity for the sentimental. The President, Valenti said approvingly, "doesn't like cold intellectuals around him. He wants people who will cry when an old lady falls down in the street." After Kennedy's assassination, Johnson had asked Valenti to fly with him to Washington, where he began serving the President as everything from a "glorified valet" to a chief of staff. He did "whatever needed to be done." He "was a major liaison with Senate Minority Leader [Everett] Dirksen; soothed the feelings of congressmen whose districts had lost an appropriation; moved projects through the bureaucratic web; [and] functioned as President Johnson's ambassador in telling important people things they did not want to hear."[31]

All Johnson's aides were put in the service of his principal goal—to pass laws that would make a difference in people's lives.

That had been his work as a congressman and a senator. Now, as President, he intended to do the same—only from the other end of Pennsylvania Avenue.

His agenda was so ambitious he needed a "two-shift day" to achieve it. Rising at 6:30 or 7:00 each morning, he began his workday in bed, where he read newspapers, the *Congressional Record*, and documents prepared by aides who conducted early morning business in the bedroom. Johnson thought nothing of placing early morning phone calls to congressmen and senators. "I hope I didn't wake ya," LBJ told Ohio Congressman Wayne Hayes one morning at 6 a.m. "Oh, no," Hayes replied. "I was lying here just hoping you would call." Reaching the Oval Office at about nine, Johnson worked until 2 p.m., when he exercised by vigorously walking around the White House grounds or taking a swim.

The second half of his "day" started at 4 p.m. after a nap in his pajamas, a shower, and fresh clothes. It lasted until at least midnight and often until one or two o'clock in the morning. Sometimes the two shifts turned into an uninterrupted fourteen or sixteen hours. It was his means for not only doing good but also making a record that served his sense of self. If he could get Kennedy's program passed, he said, "Kennedy would live on forever and so would I."[32]

From the start of his presidency, Johnson had focused on asserting his control over Congress as a prelude to getting major legislation. Although JFK had managed to win passage of some significant laws in 1961–62, Congress had refused to act on federal aid to elementary and secondary education or Medicare, a program of health insurance for the elderly under Social Security. In 1963, a coalition of conservative southern Democrats and Republicans blocked passage of all reform proposals, including the tax cut, which seemed likely to increase the federal deficit, and civil rights, which would force desegregation on the South. The stalemate in Congress had extended to appropriation bills; unable to agree on how to balance the federal budget, Congress had passed continuing resolutions to finance current expenses. "This Congress has gone further than any other within memory to replace debate and decision by delay and stultification," one columnist said.[33]

Johnson believed that Kennedy had been too passive in dealing with Congress. James H. Rowe, Jr., a White House aide to FDR and an old LBJ friend, expected Johnson to be more aggressive. "When Kennedy died and Johnson came into office—I used to say my boss Roosevelt had both style and substance. And Kennedy had style. And this fellow Johnson has substance.... Kennedy looked fine, made nice speeches, but he didn't get much done.... The difference between

Kennedy as president and Johnson as president. A senator would come
to Kennedy and say, 'I'd love to go along with you, Mr. President,
but it would give me serious trouble back home.' Kennedy would
always say, 'I understand.' Now Johnson knew damn well the senator
was going to tell him that, and he never let the senator get to the
point of his troubles back home. He would tell him about the flag,
and by God, the story of the country, and he'd get them by the lapels
and they were out the door."[34]

The day of Kennedy's funeral Johnson set to work mastering
Congress. The issue was a foreign aid bill, which included a provision
to finance the sale of surplus wheat to the Soviet Union. Led by
Republican Senator Karl Mundt of South Dakota, conservatives proposed amending the bill to bar loan guarantees facilitating trade with
Communist countries. "We could not afford to lose a vote like that,
after only four days in office," Johnson believed. "If those legislators
had tasted blood then, they would have run over us like a steamroller
when they returned in January, when much more than foreign aid
would depend on their actions."

Two days of hard work that went late into the night of November 26 gave Johnson a twenty-one-vote margin of victory in the Senate. When Minnesota Senator Hubert Humphrey called LBJ to report
the outcome and urge an end to the congressional session as a way
of suspending tension between the two ends of Pennsylvania Avenue,
Johnson refused. He described a need for a significant victory in Congress to restore confidence in the country and pass his legislative
program in the coming year.[35]

And the bill he wanted was foreign aid. If he tried for something
more important like the tax cut or civil rights, he would be stymied.
"We have been a year in doing it [the tax cut]," he told congressional
leaders at a breakfast meeting on December 3. "[We] can't expect
better results in a week. Civil rights has been there since May," and
the committee responsible for it wouldn't even schedule hearings until next year. The leadership thought the President could get a cotton
bill passed, but Johnson didn't "want to launch my administration
with a Cotton Bill."[36]

Foreign aid seemed like a better choice. Unlike the tax cut and
civil rights, an aid bill was a sure thing; only the level of funding
and executive freedom to support Soviet wheat purchases were in
dispute. But Johnson knew that a victory for the White House on
these particulars would be significant. And so when the House insisted
on including the Mundt Amendment in the bill and Johnson's hopes
of excluding it evaporated with the departure of reliable supporters
for the Christmas holiday, the President decided on a showdown.

First, he called Arthur (Tex) Goldschmidt, an old friend who was part of the U.S. delegation at the U.N., to Washington to discuss the bill. Playing devil's advocate, he pressed Goldschmidt as hard as possible to make an effective case for foreign aid. "He kept whamming away," Goldschmidt remembered. "Oh, what a miserable time I had in that office! I was just sweating, because he's such a bully physically—I'm a little guy and he's a big guy, and he really does put you through the wringer."

Goldschmidt wrote a memo that Johnson used for marching orders to his aides. Insisting that absent House Democrats sympathetic to his position return to Washington, Johnson invited them and congressional opponents to a December 23 Christmas party at the White House. During the course of the evening, Johnson courted Republican Minority Leader Charles Halleck, a principal opponent, and made an impassioned plea for support in a talk he gave standing on a velvet upholstered gold chair in the State Dining Room. Acknowledging the need to make foreign aid programs less expensive, he agreed to appoint a committee to make foreign economic and military assistance more efficient and less costly. The next day, when the House voted his way, Johnson believed that "the power of the federal government began flowing back to the White House.... We had finally begun to break up the stubborn legislative barriers behind which so much serious and vital legislation had languished. The major battles lay ahead, but we had won our first big test with the Congress."[37]

The Tax Cut

The accuracy of Johnson's assessment initially depended on enactment of JFK's $11 billion tax cut. A debate between conservatives and liberals had kept it bottled up in the Senate for ten months. Conservatives, complaining that federal budget deficits were a drag on the economy and would become more of an economic impediment with a tax cut, dismissed liberal arguments that lower taxes would fuel an economic expansion and "full employment." Liberals also asserted that growth and fewer tax loopholes, including a reduced oil depletion allowance, would provide additional revenues to cut deficits. As Vice President, Johnson had been publicly silent on the bill, but his orthodoxy about balanced budgets and sympathy for oil and gas made him unsympathetic to JFK's proposal.[38]

As soon as he became President, however, he changed his mind. If he were to make his commitment to Kennedy's legacy believable, he needed to sign on to the tax cut. Moreover, the argument of distinguished economists that cutting taxes would mean a $30 billion expansion of the gross national product in 1964 rather than $12 billion made the reform almost irresistible. A warning from economic advisers that without a tax cut a slowdown and a rise in unemployment would occur next year clinched the argument.

The implications for the 1964 presidential campaign were clear. But just in case Johnson needed schooling on this count, one adviser explained: "The rise of income associated with the tax cut must be financed by adequate supplies of money.... In 1956 and 1959–60, restrictive monetary policies and very large increases in the rate of interest occurred. In 1956, this did not matter, for Eisenhower had a large lead. But [in 1960] it was very costly to the Nixon candidacy, for it greatly increased unemployment." In 1964, they urged him to avoid Nixon's error.[39]

On November 25 Johnson told economic advisers that he accepted the need for a tax cut to spur the economy, but emphasized the political necessity of spending reductions that would hold the 1965 federal budget under $100 billion. "What about your tax bill?" he asked Treasury Secretary Douglas Dillon. Before Dillon could reply, Johnson answered his own question: "We won't have the votes to get it to the floor unless we tell them the budget will be about $100 billion."

During a discussion of various senators' views on the bill, Johnson demonstrated "pretty clear knowledge of every vote. He said he had been checking up on it ([but] not too directly—that would be beneath the dignity of the President!).... 'Unless you get that budget down around $100 billion,' " Johnson said, " 'you won't pee one drop.' " The reduced budget would "buy off" Senator Harry Byrd, the conservative chairman of the Finance Committee. Besides, Dillon pointed out, once you have the tax bill, "you can do what you want. Like Ike did, the President said—talked economy and then spent." Throughout the discussion, Johnson showed no equivocation; he was "in command—not necessarily implying that he knew the answers, but that he knew the score, and that the problem could be solved. All we had to do was to decide how to tackle it."[40]

Johnson had that sorted out as well. He mapped out a plan for expediting the Senate Finance Committee's deliberations, assuring daily quorums, proxies, afternoon meetings to "maximize progress," and agreement not to load the bill down with amendments that would alienate supporters. At the same time, Johnson rallied business, labor, agriculture, educators, the elderly, and other groups of organized opinion to pressure Congress. "I need your cooperation," he told the Business Council in December. "I need it now. I need it tomorrow, next week, next month to win the tax cut, to help you widen your opportunity for your company's expansion. . . . I am the only President you have. If you would have me fail, then you fail, for this Nation of yours fails. If you would have me succeed, then you benefit, and the country benefits." Johnson told various citizens committees for tax reduction: "Every single month that we delay on the tax bill makes more than $550 million worth of difference to America's economy" in less monthly take-home pay and purchasing power.[41]

Privately, Johnson converted Senator Harry Byrd into a supporter and arranged a last-minute defeat of a potentially disruptive amendment. The President invited Byrd to the White House for lunch. Jack Valenti remembers it as the only time LBJ ever ate in the small room off the Oval Office. Johnson "personally . . . supervised the setting and the menu." During lunch he told Byrd: "This tax cut is vital to my program. I've got to have it." Byrd didn't think it could be done with so large a budget deficit. Johnson replied that he didn't see how he could get the budget below about $102 or $104 billion. But if he managed to get it beneath $100 billion, would Byrd let the tax bill out of his committee and onto the floor? Byrd said, "We might be able to do some business." When Johnson came in with a $97.9 billion budget, he called Byrd back to the White House to give him the good news. Delighted at the President's fiscal responsibility, Byrd said: "I'm going to have to vote against the [tax] bill, [which he did both in his committee and on the floor of the Senate] but I'll be working for you behind the scenes."

As the tax bill was about to leave the Finance Committee, Louisiana Democrat Russell Long convinced colleagues to adopt an amendment reducing excise taxes on luxury goods, an alteration that could have killed the bill. The President personally lobbied all seventeen members of the Committee.

His telephone conversation with Abraham Ribicoff of Connecticut was typical: "Abe, can't you go with us on this excise thing and let us get a bill? We were all ready to report this bill to the Senate, and now we got it just good and screwed up." Ribicoff, who said it would mean giving up "something for my home state," worried about "how I can save my face." Johnson: "You save my face this afternoon and I'll save your face tomorrow. You just work it out. I don't give a damn about the details. I just want you to work it out. Will you?" Ribicoff promised to do his best.

After Ribicoff and eight other Democrats changed a 10 to 7 favorable committee vote to a 9 to 8 negative one, Johnson called to congratulate him. "You did a great service for your country, and a bigger one for your president. . . . They would have riddled us if it weren't for you. You're a team man, and I'll bet on your team." LBJ told Harry Byrd, who also sided with him: "You're a gentleman, and a scholar, and a producer, and I love you." A lopsided Senate margin of 77 to 21 on the tax cut was a prelude to congressional approval at the end of February.[42]

Johnson's victory was not an occasion for gloating over the defeat of opponents in and out of Congress. On the contrary, it became an opportunity to create additional momentum for the administration's legislative program by conciliating conservatives and stroking congressional supporters. In nationally televised remarks, the President praised House and Senate leaders for their support, including Harry Byrd, "who, though he was very much against the bill, . . . saw to it that the majority was allowed to work its will." Johnson then pledged to keep faith with Byrd and other conservatives by cutting government spending and promoting free enterprise. Indeed, if the tax cut worked as anticipated, "then the federal government will not have to do for the economy what the economy should do for itself." Whatever the actual impact of the tax bill, Johnson seized on it as a chance to portray his administration as a nonpartisan agency benefiting all Americans.[43]

The War on Poverty

In encouraging views of himself as no group's special advocate, a President above the battle working only for the national interest, he had his eye on the anti-poverty campaign. If he were going to sell Congress and the country on fighting poverty, he believed it essential to advertise it as of benefit to all Americans—not just the poor and especially inner city blacks, who made up a significant part of the country's disadvantaged.

From late November to the middle of March, when he put a poverty bill before Congress, Johnson's several public references to fighting poverty emphasized that this was a "sound investment: $1,000 invested in salvaging an unemployable youth today can return $40,000 or more in his lifetime." Poverty was costing the government billions of dollars annually in welfare costs and the lost tax revenues of unproductive citizens. In private, Johnson cautioned aides against including anything in the poverty program that could be seen as a "dole" or an attempt at redistribution of wealth. He wanted the program to be seen as a "hand up" not a "hand-out."

The columnist Walter Lippmann saw clearly what Johnson

intended: "A generation ago it would have been taken for granted that a war on poverty meant taxing money away from the haves and turning it over to the have nots.... But in this generation a revolutionary idea has taken hold. The size of the pie can be increased by intention, by organized fiscal policy and then a whole society, not just one part of it will grow richer."[44]

Establishing the ultimate goal of an antipoverty crusade—abolishing poverty—was much easier than figuring out how to make it work. "I'm gonna put $500 million in this budget for poverty, and a good deal of it ought to go to your people," Johnson told Roy Wilkins in January. "But we ought to have some better ideas about how" to do it. "These boys are pretty theoretical down here, and if I get it passed, I'm gonna have to have more practical plans."[45]

Johnson first had to decide whether to turn the program over to a Cabinet member and an existing government agency or set up a special anti-poverty office with a separate director and budget. Several liberals urged him not to bury the program in any of the Cabinet departments, but to keep it at the White House, "where people will know what you are doing, where it can have new staff and a fresh man as director." Robert Kennedy, who apparently wanted to head the war on poverty, advised Johnson to coordinate the many federal, state, and local programs aimed against poverty by putting them under "a Cabinet-level committee with one of the members as chairman." Unless the President followed this approach, Kennedy warned, "the anti-poverty program could actually retard the solution of these problems."[46]

Johnson preferred to give the program an independent base, making it like the National Youth Administration or Civilian Conservation Corps, separate New Deal agencies that made significant gains for the needy in the thirties. Johnson believed that if you put a new agency into an old-line bureaucracy, it would kill it. He remembered how "FDR always put new ideas into new hands, in new bureaucracies, to give them freedom, running room, a chance to be creative." But even if he had thoughts of putting the poverty fight under a Cabinet officer, Kennedy's advice was enough to make Johnson do otherwise. To his thinking, "a Cabinet level committee with one of the members as Chairman" meant Kennedy as anti-poverty director. Johnson had no intention of giving Bobby the prestige that could come from such an assignment and could be used in a campaign for the vice-presidential nomination. Still, Johnson wanted to keep John Kennedy's name associated with the poverty struggle.

The perfect man, therefore, to head the war on poverty was Sargent Shriver, JFK's brother-in-law. Shriver had much else to recommend him. He had convinced LBJ that there was no love lost between him and Bobby. In the days after JFK's assassination, Shriver had kept Johnson informed through Bill Moyers of what Kennedy was saying about LBJ. Moyers denies that Shriver was anything but loyal to the Kennedys, but Johnson put an interpretation on Shriver's action that made him acceptable to LBJ.

More important, as head of the Peace Corps, Shriver had turned what many, especially in Congress, thought would be an overly idealistic crusade for foreign hearts and minds into a practical, highly appealing program for aiding Third World countries. " 'When we started the Peace Corps in 1961,' " Shriver told a reporter, " 'many were worried that it would be a tutti-frutti organization, a lot of kids bouncing around the world in Bermuda shorts.' . . . As he talks," the reporter noted, "one begins to understand how he took the infant organization scoffers had dubbed 'Kennedy's Kiddie Korps' and built it into the most universally respected of New Frontier innovations." Shriver impressed Johnson as a sensible idealist who knew how to get along with Congress, make the Peace Corps work, capture the public imagination at home and abroad, and counter Cabinet officers who would try to keep a poverty agency from taking away any of their authority.[47]

On Saturday, February 1, Johnson phoned Shriver at his home, where he had just returned from an overseas mission for the President. "Sarge," Johnson said, "I want to announce you as the new head of the War on Poverty." Shriver asked if the President couldn't wait until next week for an answer; he wanted to talk to his wife and people in his office. " 'No,' Johnson replied, 'we've got to get on with that war against poverty. So please talk to Eunice now, and I'll call you back.' I couldn't believe my ears," Shriver recalled. "The next thing you know, the phone rang again. 'What have you decided?' " Johnson asked. Shriver explained that it would be much better for everyone if they could hold off until next week. An announcement would bring immediate inquiries about what he planned for the new agency, and, since he wouldn't know what to say, "that will be a source of embarrassment to me and maybe not so good for you."

Johnson said he'd call back, which he did in twenty minutes. In a very low, confidential sounding voice, the President explained that he had the Cabinet with him and had to keep his voice down. "You just have to understand, Sargent, this is your President speaking, and I'm going to announce you as the head of the war against poverty. Boom," Johnson hung up. Shriver turned to his wife and said: "Looks as if I'm going to be the new head of the war against poverty."[48]

In a follow-up letter, Johnson made less than clear how Shriver would carry on the fight. Shriver was to direct the activities of all executive departments involved in the program, and he was to act as Johnson's representative to Congress in advancing necessary legislation. He was also to coordinate all government and private activities across the nation and attend Cabinet meetings, where the war on poverty was to become a regular part of their business. Invoking FDR's memorable observation about one-third of the nation, Johnson asked for maximum effort to assist the "ill-housed, ill-clad, ill-nourished." Johnson left it up to Shriver to implement his directive. Specifically, Shriver was to design a program described in a bill Johnson wanted before Congress by the middle of March.[49]

In selecting Shriver, Johnson had made the right choice. They shared an evangelical enthusiasm for conquering seemingly insoluble problems. Like Johnson, Shriver believed that "if you do good, you'll do well"; both wanted to be remembered as men who did their "best for folks who couldn't do theirs."

Also like Johnson, Shriver had a huge appetite for work, sometimes calling aides at three and four in the morning. He told the chairman of AT&T that he imagined a telephone system that "had us all plugged in like an umbilical cord so we could never get away." Lest enthusiasm for the job at hand flag, Shriver hung motivating mottos on his office walls. "There is no place in this club for good losers," one said. "Bring me only bad news; good news weakens me," another advised.[50]

Shriver faced a daunting assignment, as discussions about the content of the poverty program made clear during February and March. A task force of advisers, which Shriver began assembling twenty-four hours after being appointed by Johnson, experienced "chaos and exhaustion," or what one participant called "the beautiful hysteria of it all." One member of the Council of Economic Advisers remembered how "bewildered" they were "by the complete disarray of the nominal professionals in the field of poverty."

Shriver struggled to make sense of his assignment. On Sunday, February 2, the day after Johnson announced his appointment, Shriver spoke to Frank Mankiewicz, Peace Corps Director in Peru, who was in town for two days. Shriver asked him if he knew anything about the question of poverty. Mankiewicz said yes and talked about Harrington's book. Later that day, Shriver invited him to attend an evening meeting. To Mankiewicz's surprise, Shriver introduced him to other participants as his executive assistant for the war on poverty. Everyone at the meeting, except Shriver, Mankiewicz, and Adam Yarmolinsky, a special assistant to Defense Secretary Robert McNamara, favored a community action approach to the problem. "We weren't even sure what should go in" the poverty program, Mankiewicz said, "but we thought it shouldn't be just that." Nothing was settled that night, but Mankiewicz agreed to stay in town for six weeks to sort out what they would do.

At a Monday luncheon with Michael Harrington, Shriver said: "Now you tell me how I abolish poverty." Harrington replied: "You've got to understand right away that you've been given nickels and dimes for this program. You'll have less than a billion dollars to work with." Ever the optimist, Shriver saw the glass as half-full: "I don't know about you, Mr. Harrington, but this will be my first experience at spending a billion dollars, and I'm quite excited about it." When Shriver convened representatives of the federal agencies listed in a three-inch book identifying government programs to aid the poor, "the infighting over who would do what got so bitter that it appeared the whole project might be wrecked. 'Sometimes the walls dripped with blood as the empire-builders clashed with the empire-wreckers,' " one official recalls.[51]

Johnson wasn't much help to Shriver. Mankiewicz remembers a meeting with the President and Shriver. "We went over and outlined some of the things we had. And as I recall, he listened rather impassively and didn't object to anything." Then, less than a month before they were scheduled to put a poverty bill before Congress, the President proposed that Shriver consider organizing the program along the lines of "the National Foundation for Infantile Paralysis—with a National Headquarters of professional paid workers and a chapter in each city of each state made up of volunteers serving as an Executive Board for that county." The local boards would "feed in ideas and facts on needs to National; pass on feasibility of program as handed down from National; and recruit volunteers for local work."

Johnson's suggestion was his only attempt at designing the poverty war. And it disappeared without a trace. His contribution instead was to ride herd on Shriver's proposals. A week after he suggested his own plan, he responded to a Shriver draft message to Congress by asking for "more logic and less rhetoric." Moyers explained that Johnson wanted "to point out—with facts and figures—how the obligation to help the poor goes beyond even the fundamental moral obligation we have; in other words, eliminating poverty will have what substantial effects on the total American economy."[52]

Johnson's interest was principally in having a bill he could sell to Congress. He had a general preference for a program that would focus on helping young people through education and job training. But beyond that, he wanted Shriver to manage the details of how the program would be organized.

During a Cabinet meeting in February, Secretary of Labor Willard Wirtz, "a big, ponderous, humorless man," bypassed Shriver to sell Johnson on a $3 billion to $5 billion jobs program financed by a cigarette tax and run out of his department. Johnson wanted no part of a proposal that would alienate Congress by being so expensive and be unpopular with tobacco state senators and organized labor, which disliked government jobs programs. Nor did he want to get in the middle of the debate over how to fight the war on poverty. As Wirtz made an impassioned plea, Johnson ignored him by making phone calls. Then, when Shriver spoke up, Johnson made his feelings clear without saying a word: "I have never seen a colder reception from the president," one observer noted. "He just—absolute blank stare—implied without even opening his mouth that Shriver should [ignore Wirtz and] move on to the next proposal."[53]

The Economic Opportunity Act (EOA) Johnson sent to Congress on March 16 was a blend of several things. It proposed the creation of a Job Corps and work training and work-study programs—all aimed at giving impoverished youngsters the opportunity to complete their education and develop salable skills. It outlined a Community Action Program, which would "give every American community the opportunity to develop a comprehensive plan to fight its own poverty—and help them to carry out their plans." Third, it asked funding for VISTA, Volunteers in Service to America, a domestic Peace Corps for those ready to enlist in the war against poverty. Fourth, it proposed a loan program to provide incentives for those who would hire the unemployed. And last, it urged the creation of the Office of Economic Opportunity as a vehicle for coordinating the war on poverty.

Johnson's message to Congress asking passage of the poverty law obscured the details of the plan. It told Congress and the country that, however innovative it might seem, the program aimed to serve the traditional American goal of opportunity for everyone. "It is a struggle to give people a chance.... We do it also because helping some will increase the prosperity of all."[54]

Johnson's appeal was four parts evangelical conviction and one part guile. He unquestionably had a passion for liberating the poor from the shackles of poverty. If he could save just some of the 35 million American families earning less than $3000 a year, if he could rescue even a small number of the 17 to 23 million children, some of whom were third-generation relief recipients, Johnson could feel that he had made a beginning on slowing and maybe even eradicating a national plague. Some poor folks would be helped, the nation would be well served, and Johnson would be remembered as a great benefactor.

At the same time, however, Johnson, like everyone else, had no clear idea how to overcome poverty. Neither he nor Shriver had much faith in Community Action; when Shriver heard the suggestion during the task force deliberations, he said privately: "It'll never fly." But he and Johnson were sold on the idea by the prevailing wisdom of poverty experts, who believed strongly in overcoming the "culture of poverty" by the largely untried but promising means of "maximum feasible participation."

In trying to sell Congress on legislating a fight against poverty, Johnson could rationalize his public rhetoric by private hopes that, even if what he proposed now did not work, there would be ample opportunity in the next eight years to find the means that would. Moreover, he understood from past experience that, once a major government program had been put in place, it would be easier for supporters to modify its workings than for opponents to dismantle it.[55]

The Great Society

On March 15, the day before he sent the poverty bill to Congress, Johnson gave an interview to representatives of the three television and radio networks. Eric Sevareid of CBS asked whether the President had settled on a catch phrase like the New Deal or New Frontier to describe his administration. Johnson answered that he had been too busy to think of "any slogan, but I suppose all of us want a better deal, don't we?" Although saying he didn't believe in labels, Johnson described himself as a prudent progressive.[56]

A better deal and a prudent progressive were two of the phrases Johnson had come up with in an avid search for a "big theme" to characterize his presidency. Despite his protestations about being too busy and not believing in labels, Johnson had been "badgering" Richard Goodwin, a JFK aide and now LBJ speech writer, to find a popular slogan that would resonate with voters in the 1964 campaign and give his administration its historical identity.

In February, Johnson had summoned Goodwin and Moyers to join him in the White House swimming pool. "We entered the pool area," Goodwin recalls, "to see the massive presidential flesh, a sun bleached atoll breaching the placid sea, passing gently, sidestroke, the deep-cleft buttocks moving slowly past our unstartled gaze. Moby Dick, I thought. . . . 'It's like going swimming with a polar bear,' Moyers whispered." Without turning his body, Johnson called across the pool: "Come on in, boys. It'll do you good." Stripping on the spot, they joined the President in the pool, where he "began to talk as if he were addressing some larger, imagined audience of the mind." He declared his intention to go beyond Kennedy and create a "Johnson program, different in tone, fighting and aggressive." Suspended almost motionless in the water, Goodwin "felt Johnson's immense vitality" as he enunciated a vision that could move the nation "toward some distant vision—vaguely defined, inchoate, but rooted in an ideal as old as the country."

Goodwin then consulted with Eric Goldman, the Princeton historian who had joined Johnson's White House in December as the organizer of a "quiet brain trust." Goldman's duties included suggesting goals and specific programs. He thought that the President should use "a full-dress speech to place his Administration in the perspective of the long-running American experience." Goldman believed that Johnson's presidency could mark the transition from a generally affluent America to one in which the nation attended "not only to the quantity but to the quality of American living.... I suggested," Goldman recalled, "that in terms of a popular slogan, the goal of 'post-affluent' America was probably best caught by the title of Walter Lippmann's book of some years back, *The Good Society*."[57]

Preferring "the Great Society" to describe Goldman's idea, Goodwin used the phrase and concept in a draft speech marking the presentation of the first Eleanor Roosevelt Memorial award to a New York Judge. Johnson and Jack Valenti liked the feel and language of Goodwin's draft so much that they wanted "to build a whole speech around it." They believed they "could fit a lot of what we were trying to do within the curve of this phrase." They soon fastened on a May 22 commencement address at the University of Michigan in Ann Arbor as the occasion for using it. In the meantime, though, Johnson, "sort of fondling and caressing this new phrase, surfaced it" several times in other talks.

Goodwin drafted a speech that Moyers and Goodwin felt embodied Johnson's program, aspirations, and "undying philosophy"; it was "a statement of national purpose, almost prophetic in dimension, that would bind citizens in a 'great experiment.' " They were confident it would make American intellectuals "sit up and say: 'This President is *really* thinking about the *future problems of America*.' " They believed it would create a momentum for a Johnson program in 1965 and beyond. Johnson agreed. It "bespoke what he felt about this society, that it told in clear, and sometimes ringing, tones what he felt was the direction he wanted to take in this country."[58]

The speech appealed to the best in the American temperament. "For a century," Johnson said, "we labored to settle and to subdue a continent. For half a century we called upon unbounded invention and untiring industry to create an order of plenty for all of our people. The challenge of the next half century is whether we have the wisdom to use that wealth to enrich and elevate our national life, and to advance the quality of our American civilization. . . . For in your time we have the opportunity to move not only toward the rich society and the powerful society, but upward to the Great Society. . . . It is a place where men are more concerned with the quality of their goals than the quantity of their goods."

To reach this promised land, Americans would have to rebuild their cities, eliminating urban decay and providing modern housing and efficient transportation for all and a renewed sense of community. They would also have to recommit themselves to "America the beautiful," the preservation of the country's natural splendor and an unpolluted environment with clean air, clean water, green forests, and usable seashores. Third, they would need to rededicate themselves to educational reform, building school systems across the nation that would offer an escape from poverty and stimulate a love of learning. In the service of these goals, Johnson promised "to establish working groups to prepare a series of White House conferences and meetings—on the cities, on natural beauty, on the quality of education, and on other emerging challenges."

Johnson called upon his audience and Americans everywhere to pledge themselves to a crusade for excellence. "For better or for worse, your generation has been appointed by history . . . to lead America toward a new age," he said. "So, will you join the battle to give every citizen the full equality which God enjoins and the law requires, whatever his belief, or race, or the color of his skin? Will you join in the battle to give every citizen an escape from the crushing weight of poverty? Will you join in the battle to make it possible for all nations to live in enduring peace—as neighbors and not as mortal enemies? Will you join in the battle to build the Great Society?"[59]

The twenty-minute speech before more than 80,000 people in the university's stadium on a warm sunny day was a great hit. The jubilant crowd, grateful for the President's attendance at their children's graduation, sensing that they were hearing a landmark address, and, stirred by the President's words, interrupted him for applause twenty-nine times. For Johnson the approval and enthusiasm were intoxicating. On the plane ride back to Washington, he was "manic" or "just . . . absolutely euphoric." Violating a self-imposed rule, he had a scotch highball and joined the pool reporters in the back of the plane. Asking them what they thought and warming to their positive assessment, he "read, with emphasis, portions of the speech to us. He wanted to make sure we got the story. He'd say, 'Now did you get this?' and 'Back here I said this and that.' "[60]

Johnson's euphoria rested not only on the reception of his speech but the sense that he was fully in command of the nation's support—that his appeals for a war on poverty and a Great Society were being met with enthusiastic anticipation of better times and greater achievements for the country.

Few Americans took Johnson's rhetoric at face value. When the Gallup poll asked whether people thought poverty would ever be done away with in the country, only 9 percent said "yes" and 83 percent said "no." Moreover, hardly anyone expected Johnson's Administration or subsequent ones to reach the utopian goals LBJ outlined in his Great Society speech.

Johnson himself had little idea of what a Great Society or a war on poverty meant beyond "fulfilling FDR's mission." His objective, Bill Moyers says, was to finish the Roosevelt revolution. Johnson "never really liked the term Great Society," Moyers adds. "It didn't come easily to him." But it gave the press a "bumper sticker. He didn't like it as much as he liked the New Deal. That's really what he saw himself doing." He kept saying to Moyers, "I'm going to be President for nine years and so many days, almost as long as FDR" or second only to FDR, and he saw it as a chance to finish what Roosevelt had begun.[61]

Though there were no polls saying start a war on poverty or a community action program or environmental protection, people didn't object to Johnson's grand designs. To the contrary, his positive outlook on the nation's future was a welcome antidote to the grief and dejection so many Americans continued to feel over Kennedy's assassination. In short, Johnson's enthusiasm and confidence that the country could reach unprecedented heights made Americans feel better about themselves. Never mind that he was overstating and overselling his vision of where he hoped the country would go. It was enough that he forecast a better day when pride in the nation's accomplishments would replace recrimination and doubt about a violent America doomed to national decline.[62]

Johnson's appeals answered another felt need in the country for less materialism and more spirituality. The consumerism and private absorptions of the fifties had left the country feeling somewhat jaded and hungry for renewed public crusades. JFK's popularity had partly come from idealistic calls for self-sacrifice that would advance the country and the world toward the noble dreams of greater equality and social justice Americans had advocated throughout their history. Johnson's emphasis on similar ends resonated more strongly than ever with national sentiment. In the first half of 1964 the country gave him consistent approval ratings of about 75 percent, with only some 10 percent expressing doubts about his job performance and policies.[63]

The Irony of Fate

The principal area in which Americans had doubts about their new President was foreign affairs. From the start of his term, commentators saw him as uncomfortable with overseas questions and less adroit at juggling international challenges than domestic ones.

In January, the first direct public criticism appeared in a *New York Herald Tribune* article citing "mounting evidence" that LBJ had not yet developed "an effective technique for the day-by-day conduct of foreign affairs." Instead of a "systematic," long-term approach to world conflicts, he had displayed a tendency to be reactive, dealing "with international trouble only after it has occurred." In May, six months into his term, *New York Times* columnist James Reston described Johnson's relations with the "diplomatic community" as "insecure." At the same time, political scientist John Roche, the president of the liberal Americans for Democratic Action, told Bill Moyers that "the intellectual community's 'major concern about Mr. Johnson' is a feeling that we may revert to the FDR emphasis on domestic affairs at the expense of foreign affairs. People . . . in the ADA are waiting to see if the President is going to develop a positive foreign policy."[64]

The initial concerns about Johnson as an effective foreign policy leader seem puzzling. Compared with several other White House predecessors, including Harry Truman, whose presidency was largely given over to managing world crises, Johnson came to the Oval Office with a significant track record in international affairs. As a congressman, he had served for almost twelve years on the House Naval Affairs and then on the Armed Services committees. During his twelve years in the Senate, he had sat on its Armed Services committee, chaired a preparedness subcommittee during the Korean War, participated in the Senate investigation of General Douglas MacArthur's dismissal by President Truman, and been the architect of legislation creating NASA and advancing the space program. Furthermore, during his congressional service he had traveled to Mexico, the southwest Pacific, and Europe, and then, as Vice President, he had been to almost every corner of the globe.[65]

At the start of Johnson's term, moreover, some experienced foreign policy leaders had every confidence that LBJ would be highly effective in dealing with the world beyond our shores. During the 1960 campaign, for example, President Eisenhower thought that "Lyndon Johnson ... would be the best Democrat of them all as President from the viewpoint of responsible management of the national interest." Ike later told Johnson, " 'You were my strong right arm when I was President.' [You] made it possible for ... [me] to carry forward a[n effective] foreign policy."

Walt W. Rostow, head of the State Department's Policy Planning Council under JFK and LBJ, believed it was "palpable nonsense" to think that Johnson "neither knew nor cared much about foreign policy.... As the minority and majority leader of the Senate, he was in the middle of all the great foreign policy decisions in the 1950s. ... It's clear that he knew a great deal about foreign policy." Likewise, National Security Adviser McGeorge Bundy, responding to a reporter in March 1964, said: "If you mean to suggest that this is not a man who understands the world, or if above all you meant to suggest that the President is not aware of the danger to which he and the other holder of strategic power in the nuclear age have a shared responsibility, then I would say that is not so."[66]

Because Johnson's experience and the opinions of Eisenhower, Rostow, and Bundy were of little consequence in shaping initial public thinking about the President's competence in foreign relations, Johnson searched for ways to convince the press of his effectiveness. He and Busby discussed having press secretary Pierre Salinger give "background" briefings to improve the President's "image": He was to emphasize that Johnson's affinity for personal, or "Texas Hill Country," diplomacy was an effective means for getting close to other world leaders.

In January, Johnson himself was advised to tell reporters: "I am spending more time on foreign affairs than on any other subject. I have had 175 separate meetings ... [and] I have made 188 telephone calls.... I've met twice with the National Security Council. I've had Secretary McNamara at the White House 30 times. I've met with the Joint Chiefs of Staff three times in 60 days. I've had Secretary Rusk here 51 times.... I have instructed my staff to notify me immediately when something important happens anywhere in the world.... I am often called in the middle of the night ... with late information on developments abroad."[67]

However much he tried to put a positive face on his handling of foreign affairs and publicly discount criticism, he was furious at what he saw as unwarranted carping. He described Douglas Kiker, a *Herald Tribune* reporter who was in the forefront of Johnson's critics, as "a little dirty son of a bitch." He wanted press secretary George

Reedy to tell reporters that the White House saw "bigotry in the north against a southerner on questions that involve his ability to handle foreign relations. . . . We think it shows some of the same attitude toward a southerner that Mississippi shows toward Harlem."[68]

However skewed press judgment on Johnson's foreign policy leadership may have been, it had little or nothing to do with an antisouthern bias. LBJ's personal style offended the journalists, but it hardly added up to a vendetta against a southerner. His impulse to attribute criticism to regional differences made it too easy for him to dismiss press complaints about his direction of overseas affairs.

Despite the substantial time and energy Johnson gave to foreign issues, he could not mask his preference for and greater competence in domestic matters. Like Woodrow Wilson, who believed "it would be the irony of fate if my administration had to deal chiefly with foreign affairs," Johnson hoped that external demands would not distract him from what needed to be done at home. As one aide put it, LBJ "wishes the rest of the world would go away and we could get ahead with the real needs of Americans." Mrs. Johnson was soon saying: "I just hope that foreign problems do not keep mounting. They do not represent Lyndon's kind of presidency." Johnson himself said half-jokingly: "Foreigners are not like the folks I am used to."[69]

Johnson's congressional service had not given him a sure feel for mastering overseas events the way it had for legislative challenges. Nor had his travels abroad given him a clear sense of what he should aim for there. To be sure, containing Communism and avoiding a nuclear holocaust were obvious goals. But beyond these generalizations Johnson did not have the sort of keen interest in the world Kennedy brought to the White House. Kennedy's residence in England during his father's ambassadorship in the late thirties and his writings on foreign affairs were a prelude to an inaugural address that focused on international challenges.

The foreign crises of 1961–63 had done little to hone Johnson's judgment on foreign policy as they had JFK's. Kennedy had stumbled badly in the Bay of Pigs fiasco at the start of his term, but by November 1963 he had weathered a series of challenges, including the Cuban missile crisis, and made sufficient gains in world affairs, especially in Soviet-American relations, so that he could approach a second four years with great confidence in his ability to handle almost any international threat.[70]

Not so with Johnson. Here, he could not exercise the same control he asserted over Congress and domestic politics. Other governments, other heads of state could not be manipulated or subjected to the "treatment"—stroked, humored, pressured, or cajoled—the way

American political leaders were. Foreign policy was an abstraction: a scheme for working your will in international affairs with economic and military might and political prestige. It didn't have the sort of hands-on quality Johnson always associated with internal politics. Johnson's idea of a successful diplomatic demarche was an early encounter with German Chancellor Ludwig Erhard, whom he described as "all over me. He was ready to go in the barn and milk my cows, if he could find the teats. There's only one way to deal with the Germans," Johnson told an aide. "You keep patting them on the head and then every once in a while you kick them in the balls."[71]

Nothing probably added to Johnson's shaky start on foreign affairs as much as his memories of the Cuban missile crisis. In a meeting during the crisis with CIA Director John A. McCone, Johnson had opposed the President's decision to blockade Cuba, expressing "displeasure at 'telegraphing our punch'" and saying "the blockade would be ineffective because we in effect are 'locking the barn after the horse was gone.'" Johnson "favored an unannounced [air] strike rather than the agreed plan." Since Kennedy's blockade had resolved the crisis in America's favor and since an air strike might have led to a nuclear war, Johnson's response to the most dangerous Soviet-American confrontation of the Cold War undermined his confidence in his capacity to assure the national security and international peace.[72]

His uncertainty about charting the right course for the varied and confusing challenges pressing in on him daily from all over the world made him dependent on JFK's foreign policy advisers, especially Secretary of State Rusk, Defense Secretary Robert McNamara, and, most of all, McGeorge Bundy, the National Security Adviser.

Rusk was an enormous comfort to Johnson. He was almost the perfect man in the right place at the right time. He was a rock-solid adviser on foreign and national security policy. After serving as an army colonel in the China–Burma–India theater in World War II and a staff officer in the Pentagon, he was Assistant Secretary of State for United Nations Affairs and then for the Far East during Truman's presidency. In 1952 he had become head of the Rockefeller Foundation in New York, where he was serving when he became JFK's compromise choice for the State Department. As secretary, he had been a tireless and generally faceless diplomat, working, as one colleague in the Kennedy administration described him, "as long and as hard as anyone in Washington. In negotiations with foreign countries, he was vigilant, impassive, patient and skilled. He displayed the same qualities in his relations with Congress and proved the most effective Secretary of State on the Hill since Cordell Hull."

There was much else in Rusk's background and personality that appealed to Johnson. A Georgian with a soft southern drawl, Rusk was a self-made man who shared LBJ's passion for helping the poor, ending segregation, and opening avenues of opportunities for all peoples regardless of race or social background. Johnson, a graduate of Southwest Texas State Teachers College in San Marcos, loved associations with the academic elite, men and women he enviously called "the Harvards" and at the same time admired for having obtained something he valued and craved. Rusk's attendance at Oxford University as a Rhodes scholar, his professorship of government at Mills College in California, and his service as president of the Rockefeller Foundation also gave him standing with LBJ.

He instantly became a loyal number two, a superb technician who comfortably stood in Johnson's shadow while providing the information and support for their shared views on how to counter the Communist threat and advance "the cause of freedom" around the globe. There was, Bill Moyers says, a "kinship, a kinetic energy between Johnson and Rusk on the issue of the right wing and the injury done to the body politic by that right wing attack over China and Korea." If all this were not enough to recommend him, his deference toward LBJ during Kennedy's presidency, which included regular briefings, gave him a connection to the new President that would blossom into a fuller collaboration on foreign affairs than anything he had under JFK.[73]

Robert McNamara's presence in the Defense Department also reassured Johnson, who viewed him as an ideal complement to Rusk. The forty-seven-year-old McNamara held degrees from Berkeley and the Harvard Business School, where his brilliance as a student had won him a faculty position teaching accounting. During World War II he had served as an officer in the Air Force, applying "proven business methods to war" and making a reputation that landed him a postwar job at the Ford Motor Company. By 1961 his managerial skills had made him the chief executive officer. His talent for administering a huge bureaucracy persuaded Kennedy to appoint him Secretary of Defense. McNamara's faith in rational solutions to vexing problems gained him the title of "the can-do-man in the can-do society in the can-do era." After Johnson met McNamara for the first time, he described him—"that fellow with the Staycomb" in his slick black hair—as Kennedy's smartest Cabinet member: You could almost hear the computers clicking away, Johnson said. Like Johnson, he loved the idea of using power to do good.[74]

During Johnson's first year in the White House his admiration for and trust in McNamara became almost worshipful. Over time the relationship would change, but in the beginning Johnson found him to be "enormously energetic and enormously loyal and enormously reliable." Johnson told a reporter: "He has exceeded my expectations. ... He is an expert on economic matters, prices, strikes, taxes and other things as well as defense. He is the strongest poverty and Head Start man except Shriver. He is the first one at work and the last one to leave. When I wake up, the first one I call is McNamara. He is there at seven every morning, including Saturday. The only difference is that Saturday he wears a sport coat."[75]

The third member of Johnson's foreign policy and defense triumvirate was Mac Bundy, as his friends called him. He was a descendant of the Boston Lowells, who made a fortune in New England textiles and played a central part in the development of Harvard. He was a man of impeccable background and supreme self-confidence. At Groton, a leading prep school, his brilliance and self-assurance moved a fellow student to say he was ready to be dean of the school at the age of twelve. An essay he wrote as an undergraduate at Yale was, in the judgment of his teacher, a distinguished historian, better than anything all but a few faculty members could have achieved. After Yale, he became a Junior Fellow at Harvard, an appointment reserved for those identified as too gifted to bother with a normal Ph.D. After service in the Army during World War II and a brief period teaching in the Harvard government department, Bundy, at the age of thirty-four, became the youngest Dean of Faculty in Harvard's history. Despite his youth, during the next eight years he dominated both the faculty and president of the university as few men have in Harvard's history. Then, as Kennedy's Special Assistant for National Security Affairs, he became a dominant figure in a universe of powerful, brilliant men.[76]

Even Lyndon Johnson, the most imperious of men, could not entirely resist Bundy's natural impulse to dominate and lead. Though Johnson, according to one observer, really didn't like Bundy, "sensing at times a patronizing attitude," he took special satisfaction from having the former Dean of Harvard College, the most thoroughgoing symbol of New England Brahmins, the leading figure among "the Harvards," working for him. He so delighted in "Mac's style—Mac briefing, tidying up a complicated question, so professional, so clean— that a small amused smile would come to his face, like a hitting coach watching a fine hitter or a connoisseur watching a great ballet dancer. Mac was dancing, and dancing for him."

But it was more than that. Johnson also needed Bundy. And

Bundy, in Schlesinger's words, "forever sustained by those two qualities so indispensable for success in government—a deep commitment to the public service and a large instinct for power"—
answered Johnson's need. His memos to the President in the first
months of his term counseled Johnson on how to deal with Rusk,
McNamara, the press, congressional leaders, foreign visitors, Panama, Cuba, Cyprus, Vietnam, Laos, Soviet Russia, NATO, and outer
space.

It is not surprising that Bundy's advice reached across so wide
a spectrum. As National Security Adviser, most of this was in his
province. What is striking, though, is the didactic tone of the memos.
They were never disrespectful or patronizing, but, like a teacher's
instructions to an eager student, they advised Johnson on what to say
and how to orchestrate every detail of foreign policy. Before Johnson's
first month in office was over, U.N. Ambassador Adlai Stevenson and
Under Secretary of State Averell Harriman were warning Johnson
against allowing Bundy too much control over international relations.
They believed it "vital for you to make clear that Bundy speaks as
your Assistant and not as the President." In 1961, Sam Rayburn had
sent up a different warning signal about the Kennedy men: "They
may be every bit as intelligent as you say," Rayburn told Johnson,
"but I'd feel a whole lot better about them if just one of them had
run for sheriff once."[77]

Yet despite his reliance on Rusk, McNamara, and Bundy, Johnson wouldn't let on that he was anything less than their boss. As
Bundy puts it, Johnson's "problem in foreign affairs at the beginning
was . . . 'I'm going to show these guys I'm not a Texas provincial. I'm
a world statesman. I can talk to De Gaulle.'" But Johnson found it
difficult. Foreign affairs "wasn't his own home country in the same
way that proving to Larry O'Brien that he could count the Senate
better than O'Brien. That was easy," Bundy said.

Nevertheless Johnson was determined to set his own course in
world affairs. "You couldn't tell what he thought about . . . [the
memos given him on foreign policy] except by what he did," Bundy
asserts. "He didn't want to talk about the pluses and minuses of a
paper. . . . My experience with him was very much trial and error. He
wouldn't say what he wanted to do. . . . You had to find out by doing
it or not doing it." It is "total baloney" that we, Rusk, McNamara,
and Bundy, were running the government, Bundy adds. We "understood that we were working for a President who . . . insisted on making his own decisions. It's baloney that we were running, defining"
Johnson's actions abroad.[78]

The Perils of Foreign Policy: Latin America

However much Johnson preferred to focus on domestic issues, he knew that foreign affairs were going to play a significant part in the life of his administration and that he would do well to establish his mastery of overseas challenges at the first opportunity. As with JFK's economic and social proposals, Johnson wanted to carry Kennedy's foreign policy to a successful conclusion, demonstrating once again his regard for JFK and his own special capacity for getting things done. If he could make some notable achievement here, it would also help quiet the feeling that he was less than well qualified to assure peace and national security.

Not the least of Johnson's concerns was to convince the Soviets that he was a firm defender of U.S. interests and would not be passive toward any Communist aggression. In February 1964, after Havana cut off water supplies to the American naval base at Guantanamo over a dispute about Cuban fishing boats in U.S. waters, Johnson ordered the navy to make the base water supply self-sufficient. "I had no doubt about Castro's purpose," LBJ said later. "He had decided, perhaps with Soviet encouragement, to take the measure of the new President of the United States, to push me a little and see what my response would be." His impulse to see Cuba's response as a Soviet test of his mettle was more a demonstration of his insecurity about foreign affairs than a realistic assessment of Moscow's intentions.[79]

By the third week of his term, Johnson had decided to focus his efforts on Latin America. His choice rested on the conviction that JFK's much-publicized Alliance for Progress was sputtering and that his Tex-Mex connections gave him a special feel for the hemisphere. Johnson called JFK's Latin American policy a "thoroughgoing mess," complaining that it was too ideological, too antibusiness, and too unrealistic. He thought he could do better. "I know these Latin Americans," he privately told a group of reporters shortly after becoming President. "I grew up with Mexicans. They'll come right into your yard and take it over if you let them. And the next day they'll be right up on your porch, barefoot and weighing one hundred and thirty pounds and they'll take that too. But if you say to 'em right at the start, 'hold on, just wait a minute,' they'll know they're dealing with somebody who'll stand up. And after that you can get along fine." Whether dealing with Soviets or Cubans, Mexicans or Germans, the Munich analog was central to LBJ's thinking about challenges abroad.[80]

Johnson aimed to rescue the Alliance for Progress by shifting its focus. JFK's goal of "peaceful revolution" or democratization through economic development was nowhere in sight in 1963. To the contrary, during Kennedy's thousand days in the White House, Latin America had seen a series of military coups that "depressed" Kennedy and discouraged his hopes for greater economic and political democracy. An additional problem was his failure to create a coherent chain of command for Latin American policy. The White House, State, and the Agency for International Development vied within and among themselves for control. After the Bay of Pigs, for example, Kenny O'Donnell and Larry O'Brien asked Ralph Dungan, another Kennedy aide with some foreign affairs experience, to keep a watch on that "Goddamned [Richard] Goodwin and [Arthur] Schlesinger, crazy nuts on Latin America." At the time of his death, JFK was moving toward a consolidation of authority.[81]

Johnson decided to implement Kennedy's administrative reform and more. In December, he appointed Thomas C. Mann director of the Alliance, special assistant to the President, and Assistant Secretary of State for Inter-American Affairs. A fellow Texan and professional foreign service officer who was then Ambassador to Mexico, Mann shared Johnson's impulse to make the Alliance less a vehicle for advancing democracy than a means for promoting private investment and backing anti-Communist regimes. "Everybody in Latin America is scared of this fellow Mann," Johnson told Dick Russell. "They highly regard him because he's a tough guy."

Though Johnson's public rhetoric would echo Kennedy's talk about transforming the hemisphere "into a vast crucible of revolutionary ideas and efforts," Johnson wanted to blunt Communist appeals for revolutionary change with limited New Deal–style reforms that raised standards of living. As LBJ speechwriter and aide Harry McPherson later said, Johnson's "passionate" description of the Alliance "that seemed to welcome revolution ... at the same time we were dealing on behalf of our businessmen" was a "lot of crap."[82]

Johnson's selection of Mann and shift in Alliance goals signaled his determination to chart his own course in foreign affairs. Schlesinger told Robert Kennedy that Johnson's appointment of Mann was "a declaration of independence to show that this is *his* administration and that he is master in his own house and strong enough to take charge in a field that has been of special concern to President Kennedy.... He [LBJ] has shown his power to move in a field of special concern to the Kennedys without consulting the Kennedys."[83]

But Johnson's maneuvers on Latin America netted him very little. Kennedy's spectacular success in the Cuban missile crisis and with the Test Ban treaty made it difficult for Johnson to establish himself quickly as a comparable foreign policy leader. Unlike domestic reform, where Kennedy had been stymied and Johnson was able to show to good advantage, foreign affairs frustrated Johnson's hopes. There was nothing in the many challenges abroad that he could use quickly to boost his standing.

On the contrary, a crisis in Panama beginning in January 1964 made Johnson seem out of his depth. Panama was essentially a no-win situation for him and would probably have frustrated Kennedy as well. But since it was Johnson's first major test in external affairs, it had far more importance to him than it would have had to Kennedy. Moreover, no matter how well Johnson performed, it was impossible for him to appear heroic in a confrontation with tiny Panama, a country he derisively described as "no larger than the city of St. Louis."[84]

The crisis erupted out of long-standing Panamanian discontent with U.S. control of the Canal Zone "in perpetuity." On January 9, 1964, when Zonians—U.S. citizens working and living in Panama—demonstrated against allowing Panama's flag to fly alongside the American flag over civilian institutions in the zone, fighting broke out between Panamanian students and U.S. residents. Disorders during the next three days cost twenty-four Panamanian and four American lives. The riots persuaded Panama's President Roberto Chiari to break diplomatic relations with the United States.[85]

Johnson understood that Chiari reflected nationalistic sentiments in his country that could not be ignored or easily accommodated. He also believed that Chiari hoped to win a May election by turning the crisis to his advantage. As Tom Mann told the President after a trip to Panama in mid-January, during which he confronted hostile demonstrators, Chiari and his supporters "put on quite a show—I think . . . designed to impress us that this was a very serious situation," which endangered the Canal Zone and showed "that the Panamanian people were determined to take over. . . . I'm convinced myself . . . that the crisis was largely inspired by the government for domestic political purposes in the hope that the United States would become frightened and cave under that kind of pressure."[86]

Johnson refused to be intimidated. Chiari's insistence that the United States renegotiate the 1903 treaty granting American rights in the zone was a condition Johnson would not accept. He shared Bundy's conviction that "we cannot let our foreign policy be governed by Molotov cocktails." When Richard Russell told LBJ that somebody has "got to play the part of ole Andrew Jackson," Johnson replied: "I'm not about to get on my knees and go crawling to him [Chiari] and say I want to apologize to ya for shooting my soldiers. . . . I wasn't raised in that school."

For Johnson to begin his administration by bending to violence from a small country seemed likely to encourage other foreign explosions of hostility to the United States and certain to undermine his domestic support. Telegrams to the White House ran at between 10 and 15 to 1 in favor of a hard line, while a Gallup poll showed only 9 percent of Americans attentive to the crisis favoring concessions. Johnson was mindful of this political reality and sensitive to congressional demands for a firm stand, especially from Senate Republican Minority Leader Everett Dirksen, who said: "We are in the amazing position of having a country with one-third the population of Chicago kick us around. If we crumble in Panama, the reverberations of our actions will be felt around the world."[87]

Johnson also feared that Panama's tiny Communist party, supported by Castro's Cuba, might take advantage of the crisis. Although the Panamanian government, the Organization of American States, and the U.S. Army commander in the zone gave little or no credence to the Communist threat or to Castro's involvement, Johnson shared a widespread feeling in the U.S. government that the upheaval represented another testing of America's resolve to resist Communist expansion around the globe. "I think the damn Communists are gonna cause trouble every place in this country they can. I think we got to get a little bit hard with them," he told Mike Mansfield. "I think Dick Russell may be right. He says that they're gonna do this in every damn nation they can." Remembering how U.S. planners had underestimated Castro's popularity before the Bay of Pigs invasion, Johnson and his advisers intended to err on the side of caution in assessing Communist influence in Panama.

Rusk, McNamara, Bundy, Mann, and CIA Director McCone had no doubt that Communist subversion was at work in Panama and threatened the United States with another Cuba in Central America. Johnson himself expressed concern to these advisers that "the Administration would be accused of knowing exactly what was going to happen and not doing anything." Bundy assured him that the intelligence community had not predicted the Panama outbreak and that except for Bolivia no other leftist challenge to a Latin American government seemed likely.[88]

Johnson handled the crisis with an impressive measure of restraint. He ignored demands from right-wing critics in the United States, who urged a get-tough response to the Panamanians, including the seizure of additional land from Panama to strengthen canal defenses. When his old Texas friend George Brown urged him to follow a hard line with Panama, LBJ told him: "That's what all these gringos say all the time, . . . 'give 'em hell, they'll love it, rub their nose in it, they'll like it. . . . ' Most of Latin America is against us," Johnson said. "And we did act a bunch of damn fools with our kids up there at the flag." Believing that the toppling of Diem in Vietnam had made matters worse, Johnson feared that excessive pressure on Panama would overturn its government and create greater instability.

Instead, in a telephone conversation with Chiari, Johnson urged that everything be done to restore calm, after which they could "talk over differences and find solutions." Johnson warned that there were "elements unfriendly to both of us who will exploit this situation." Though Johnson was ready to consider amending the 1903 treaty, he would not agree to a review of existing agreements until peace and full diplomatic relations had been reestablished. "I sure don't want to imply that I'm gonna sit down and talk to them about changes that I'll make in the treaties and revise the whole thing, and that all they got to do is burn a U.S.I.S. embassy and then we'll come in hat in hand and say, 'come on boys, we'll let you write your ticket,' " LBJ told Mann. In the three months it would take to restore full relations, Johnson refused to be provoked into either a harsh response or concessions to Chiari's demands for immediate commitments to a larger Panamanian role in controlling the canal.[89]

Yet Johnson did not win high marks for his handling of the dispute. His lack of finesse or sensitivity to diplomatic conventions and his erratic behavior during the crisis provoked criticism. Johnson "was not interested in the diplomatic approach," Senator J. William Fulbright of the Foreign Relations Committee said, "because it was unfamiliar to him." Accounts of a phone call to Chiari on January 10 demonstrated his indifference to diplomatic niceties. " 'Get me the President of Panama—what's his name—on the phone,' " Johnson was reported as saying. " 'Mr. President,' " the aide replied, " 'you can't do that. It isn't protocol. You just can't do things like that.' 'Why in hell can't I? Come on now, get him on the phone.' "

On February 29, when he compared Panama, a sovereign country, to St. Louis in a press conference, it angered Latin American diplomats. Moreover, in mid-March, after the Organization of American States (OAS) announced that the United States and Panama had agreed to name ambassadors for "discussions and negotiations," Johnson abruptly reversed course. Angered by Panamanian radio accounts of the "agreement" describing it as a Panamanian victory and warned by Senate Armed Services Committee Chairman Richard Russell and Republican leaders that agreeing to "negotiations" would make him appear "weak," Johnson ordered his press secretary to deny that any agreement had been reached.

The next day Johnson compounded the problem by impromptu

comments to Latin American diplomats at a ceremony marking the
third anniversary of the Alliance for Progress. Pointing out that there
had been no genuine meeting of minds between himself and Chiari,
Johnson denied that the United States had committed itself to a revision of the 1903 treaty and would not do so until "diplomatic relations are resumed." According to two journalists, Johnson's remarks
infuriated and appalled the Latins. The unhappiness of the OAS with
his performance led Johnson to say of the organization, knowing his
words would be repeated: "It couldn't pour piss out of a boot if the
instructions were written on the heel."

Despite these missteps, which moved some critics to say that the
crisis "had been very badly handled," Johnson reached a settlement
with Chiari in April. It committed them "to review every issue which
now divides us." By agreeing to "review" rather than "negotiate"
differences, Johnson was able to begin discussing the possibility of
treaty revision without the political reverberations that would flow
from an open commitment to do it.

In December, eight months later, when the crisis had passed,
Johnson announced that the U.S. and Panama would negotiate a new
treaty. Though Johnson's management of the conflict now seemed
sound, his earlier actions had heightened doubts about his diplomatic
skills.[90]

Johnson's reputation for effective leadership abroad also suffered
from a mid-March meeting in Washington with his ambassadors to
Latin America. The gathering aimed to demonstrate his concern with
hemisphere affairs and his intention to shift the emphasis in the
Alliance for Progress. A speech by Mann to the diplomats stressed
the administration's determination not to intervene in the political
affairs of the Latin republics by refusing to recognize military regimes. The United States would now maintain relations with any
government in control. As a consequence of a leak, the speech became
headline news, with liberals loudly complaining that the Johnson
policy was a betrayal of Kennedy's efforts to discourage military
coups.[91]

In fact, in the last months of his presidency, Kennedy was moving toward the acceptance of military regimes, particularly in Hon-
duras and the Dominican Republic, that he thought we should
support. Nevertheless, because people tended to remember Kennedy's
rhetoric more than his actions, Johnson and Mann came across as
much, rather than somewhat, less liberal than JFK toward Latin
America. In April, their quick recognition of a military government
in Brazil, which replaced the left-leaning Joao Goulart regime, added
to the conviction that Johnson was all too ready to accept any anti-

Communist government in the hemisphere, regardless of how it came to power.[92]

"The *New York Times* to the contrary notwithstanding," a corporate business chief wrote Johnson, "our deep knowledge of the Brazilian situation leads us to the conclusion that you and Secretary Rusk made exactly the right kind of statements at exactly the right time about the recent political developments in Brazil." However much Johnson wished to discount the *Times* and see the businessman's view as more representative of national sentiment, he could not ignore the fact that his initial forays into foreign affairs were controversial at home and producing mixed results abroad.

Despite Johnson's concerns, hardly anyone was describing his actions as disastrous or as anything resembling Kennedy's failure at the Bay of Pigs. Indeed, the overall picture of accomplishment during his first months in office allowed Johnson to put aside criticism of his foreign policy as not mattering "a damn." With "voices . . . comparing the President to Andy Jackson or to Teddy Roosevelt" and predictions that he would sweep every part of the country in the November elections, Johnson was confident that his handling of foreign affairs would not cost him more than "a bushel of votes."[93]

Vietnam: Opening Moves

In the first months of his presidency Johnson put a brave face on his handling of foreign affairs. As far as the world could tell, he was confident about the good sense and effectiveness of his foreign policies. But privately he was much less sure of himself and frustrated by criticism that made telling points about his shaky approach to overseas events.

His frustration expressed itself in a confrontation with Under Secretary of State George Ball during the Brazilian crisis in April. When Ball, as acting secretary, issued a directive recognizing the new government without consulting the President, Johnson was "furious." He demanded to know why Ball hadn't let him know. "It was three o'clock in the morning," Ball replied. But Johnson saw this as no excuse: "Don't ever do that again. I don't care what hour in the morning it is, I want to know. I'm not saying that what you did wasn't right, but after this I want to know."

Johnson's insistence on being called is reminiscent of what he told Larry O'Brien about dealings with Congress. In both instances, he insisted on presidential prerogative and control. But because he felt genuinely on top of domestic affairs, his response to O'Brien was

benign. With Ball, however, he was "really angry." And not because
Ball did anything contrary to administration policy; Ball's action
closely followed Johnson's design.

But his small show of independence agitated Johnson's feelings
about foreign affairs; it was an arena in which he had only limited
control or capacity to dictate the course of events. And for Johnson,
who could not stand to be dominated by anyone or anything, foreign
policy was a constant irritant he could neither ignore nor relieve. It
agitated his feelings of inadequacy or long-standing concern that he
was not the powerful, competent, can-do person he wanted everyone
to see him as but a Texas hick, a provincial who could not compare
to John Kennedy as a world leader respected by heads of government
abroad and foreign policy makers at home.[94]

Vietnam had heightened Johnson's feelings of frustration about
external challenges during his first months in the White House. As
in domestic affairs, Johnson saw a need initially to continue Kennedy's policy. But just what that meant was difficult to know. Kennedy had repeatedly stated his determination in public to prevent a
Communist takeover in South Vietnam. He had backed this up by
increasing arms shipments to Saigon and expanding the number of
military advisers from 685 to 16,700. Moreover, he had deepened
American involvement by acquiescing in the military coup that toppled Diem. Once the U.S. government played a part in determining
who ruled in South Vietnam, it assumed an additional responsibility
for the life of that nation.

Yet at the same time, Kennedy gave strong indications that the
American commitment would go only so far. Repeated requests from
U.S. military chiefs for combat troops in Vietnam had received a
blanket refusal from JFK. Further, he had told a number of political
associates that he intended a total withdrawal of American military
personnel from Vietnam after the 1964 election. In the fall of 1963
he had begun giving concrete expression to this policy by ordering
1000 advisers home by the end of the year. Yet this decision was
made at a time when the U.S. military in Vietnam was predicting a
victory that would allow American withdrawal. In addition, there is
some reason to believe that Kennedy's order was a ploy meant to
scare Diem into reforms that could help preserve political stability.
Only one thing, then, seems certain about Kennedy's future actions
toward Vietnam; we do not know what he would have done in changing circumstances.[95]

Nevertheless, judging from Kennedy's temperament and record,
it is reasonable to assume that, if he had expanded U.S. military
involvement in Vietnam, it would have been a restrained escalation

that left open the possibility of withdrawal without the appearance of defeat. "No one can say what JFK would have done" in Vietnam, Mac Bundy says. "But that it would have been different and it would have been less [than Johnson] are I think safe generalizations."

Larry O'Brien convincingly states: "I know Kennedy reflected on Vietnam a good deal, but . . . whatever he might or might not have done if he were reelected none of us will know." Yet O'Brien believes that if Kennedy had stayed the course after November 1964, this would not have led to a political trap. "I think he would have found a way of disengaging before it became all-out."[96]

The same cannot be said of Johnson. A different man facing different circumstances, Johnson charted his own course. Was Johnson's policy in Vietnam a continuation of Kennedy's? I asked Robert McNamara. How could it have been? McNamara answered. Johnson "inherited a mess." Between the time the administration announced the withdrawal of U.S. advisers from Saigon and JFK's death, Diem had been killed. "And that changed the dynamics," McNamara said. "Now I'm not going to suggest to you what I think Kennedy would have done had he lived. All I want to say is that he didn't live after we decided to withdraw the 1000 troops. Diem was killed and Johnson inherited that. And it was a mess. It was a hell of a mess."[97]

Despite the change in circumstances, Johnson saw his actions as largely in line with Kennedy's. To be sure, he believed Kennedy erred in agreeing to the coup against Diem. But he was confident that Kennedy's response to post-coup developments would have been similar to his. In a conversation on November 24 with Ambassador to Saigon Henry Cabot Lodge, McCone, Rusk, McNamara, and Bundy, Johnson received mixed assessments of conditions in South Vietnam. In response, he expressed a determination to maintain JFK's policy of aiding Saigon against the Viet Cong and the North Vietnamese. But to get this done, he believed we needed to end the bickering among Americans in Vietnam and to back away from trying to do too much—namely, trying "to immediately transform . . . [Vietnam] into our image." It would be enough just to "win the war—he didn't want as much effort placed on so-called social reforms." He also expressed concern that "strong voices in the Congress felt we should get out of Vietnam."[98]

According to one of the participants in the meeting, Johnson also said in response to Lodge: "I am not going to lose Vietnam. I am not going to be the President who saw Southeast Asia go the way China went. . . . I don't think Congress wants us to let the Communists take over South Vietnam." Johnson urged people at the meeting "to devote every effort" to the war. "Don't go to bed at night until you have asked yourself, 'Have I done everything I could to further the American effort to assist South Vietnam?' "[99]

Mac Bundy remembers that Johnson was "simply not going to accept the notion that he's going to be the man who can't hold the Alamo.... [It's an] unfair jump in the sense he knows it's not the Alamo, but the judgment he's going to have rendered on him is not going to be that he lost [Vietnam]. He's going to hold it with everybody, and he's going to organize—he's not going to command it—he's going to Senate Majority lead it."[100]

Bill Moyers remembers Johnson telling him after the meeting: Lodge " 'says it's going to be hell in a handbasket out there.... If we don't do something, he says, it'll go under—any day.... They'll think with Kennedy dead we've lost heart. So they'll think we're yellow and don't mean what we say.' 'Who?' " Moyers asked. " 'The Chinese. The fellas in the Kremlin. They'll be taking the measure of us. They'll be wondering just how far they can go.... I'm not going to let Vietnam go the way of China. I told them to go back and tell those generals in Saigon that Lyndon Johnson intends to stand by our word, but by God, I want something for my money. I want 'em to get off their butts and get out in those jungles and whip hell out of some Communists. And then I want them to leave me alone, because I got some bigger things to do right here at home.' "[101]

The conversations are a window on Johnson's initial thoughts about Vietnam. First, he was concerned about eliminating American differences. Without unity among U.S. officials in Saigon, the South Vietnamese would falter. Second, he intended to inhibit a missionary impulse, particularly his own, to turn Vietnam into an Asian United States. Third, he feared that a larger U.S. involvement in Vietnam might divide Congress and keep him from working his will on domestic reform. Yet he had no intention of letting Vietnam succumb to Communism; it would undercut him at home the way China's "loss" had plagued Truman and the Democrats. Finally, he felt compelled to stand fast, because he had to prove his mettle in foreign affairs. Kennedy had demonstrated his toughness in the Cuban missile crisis, and now Johnson, a new President, would have to show the Chinese and the Russians that he was as ready to stand up to them.

In sum, Johnson saw Vietnam as a test of American resolve abroad. But he also thought it had the potential for disturbing consequences at home. He wanted quick and effective action against the Communists in Vietnam as a way to head off losses overseas and stalemate on domestic reform. But the whole business unnerved him. "Right now I feel like one of those catfish" in your part of Texas, LBJ also told Moyers. "I feel like I just grabbed a big juicy worm with a right sharp hook in the middle of it." The bait was so tempting, but was he the one being hooked?[102]

Even if Johnson had answered "yes," it is nearly inconceivable that in 1963–64 he would have walked away from Vietnam. Given existing assumptions about the Cold War—about a long-term struggle between capitalism and Communism, between democracy and totalitarianism—and public feeling in America about the imperative of meeting global challenges from Moscow and Beijing to assure the survival of the United States, no President, especially an unproven, unelected one, could simply have withdrawn without some real hope that the South Vietnamese could have held off a Viet Cong–North Vietnamese takeover. Retrospective thinking, colored by later results, should not ignore or distort this reality.

Johnson's views expressed themselves in a National Security Action Memorandum (NSAM) he approved on November 26. It declared the "central object of the United States in South Vietnam [is] to assist the people and Government of that country to win their contest against the externally directed and supported Communist conspiracy." It reaffirmed the objective of withdrawing 1000 advisers by the end of 1963, but promised to maintain programs of military and economic assistance at the same level as during Diem's rule. It also called for planning "of possible increased activity." At the same time, Johnson sent memos to Rusk, General Maxwell Taylor, Chairman of the Joint Chiefs, and McCone asking them to "put our blue ribbon men on this job at every level."[103]

The NSAM, which was largely like one drafted by Bundy on November 21, encouraged Johnson to believe that he was essentially following Kennedy's lead. JFK's three principal foreign policy advisers echoed each other's advice on Vietnam as if it were the received wisdom. "We are heavily committed in South Vietnam . . . , and we should all of us let no day go by without asking whether we are doing everything we can to win the struggle there," Bundy told Johnson. "We have to live in the same world with the Soviet Union, but we do not have to accept Communist subversion."

In late December, after a two-day visit to Vietnam, McNamara advised the President that "the situation is very disturbing. Current trends, unless reversed in the next 2–3 months, will lead to neutralization at best and more likely to a Communist-controlled state. . . . We should watch the situation very carefully, running scared, hoping for the best, but preparing for more forceful moves if the situation does not show early signs of improvement."[104]

McNamara's report made a strong impression on the President. Johnson told a journalist at the beginning of February: "There's one of three things you can do [about Vietnam]. One is run and let the dominoes start fallin' over, and God Almighty what they said about us leaving China would just be warmin' up compared to what they'd say now. I see Nixon is writin' about it today and Goldwater, too. You can run or you can fight, as we are doin', or you can sit down and agree to neutralize all of it, but nobody's gonna neutralize North Vietnam. So that's totally impractical; so it really boils down to one or two decisions: gettin' out or gettin' in. . . . We can't abandon it to them, as I see it. And we can't get them to agree to neutralize North Vietnam. So I think old man DeGaulle [who was urging neutralization] is puffin' through his hat."[105]

Some in Congress counseled Johnson against any deeper involvement. Richard Russell, Johnson's mentor in the Senate, urged him to "spend whatever it takes to bring to power a government that would ask us to go home." Russell was opposed to helping a country like Vietnam, which was "not willing to lift their finger or suffer even a pin prick in their own behalf." The "general willingness in Congress to support the Vietnamese to the hilt" mystified him.

Yet Russell was cautious in his advice to the President. He worried that, if the U.S. simply walked away from Vietnam, it would injure American prestige, shake international confidence in our reliability, and embolden our enemies. "I didn't want to go in there, but now that we're in there, I don't know how to get out," Russell told the President in March. A few months later, with Vietnam becoming ever more of a problem, Russell declared: "I didn't ever want to get messed up down there. I do not agree with those brain trusters who say that this thing has got tremendous strategic and economic value and we'll lose everything in Southeast Asia if we lose Vietnam. I don't think that's true. But as a practical matter, we're in, and I don't know how the hell you can tell the American people you're comin' out. . . . They'll just think that you've just been whipped and you've been run; you're scared. It'd be disastrous."

Senate Majority Leader Mike Mansfield was less ambivalent about Vietnam. In December and January, he cautioned Johnson against expanded commitments that could lead to "massive costs," which the American people would be reluctant to bear, a situation similar to Korea in the fifties. Mansfield feared that "we are close to the point of no return in Viet Nam," and he suggested a diplomatic offensive that might lead to the neutralization of Southeast Asia, limiting the roles of both the U.S. and China in the region. Johnson responded that "we do not want another China in Viet-Nam," meaning a Communist victory with painful political repercussions in the United States.

Asked by Johnson for their views of Mansfield's proposal, Rusk, McNamara, and Bundy emphatically rejected it, calling neutralization a prescription for a Communist takeover and the same sort of political fallout we had over China. "The stakes in preserving an anti-Communist South Vietnam are so high," McNamara replied, "that, in our judgement, we must go on bending every effort to win."[106]

The only note of dissension in the administration came from Ted Sorensen, JFK's closest White House aide. Sorensen acknowledged the wisdom of the Bundy–McNamara–Rusk warning against following Mansfield's lead. Nevertheless, he thought Johnson should publicly espouse a neutralization scheme that would emphasize Communist responsibility for continuation of the war. He also urged him to "continue to emphasize that the South Vietnamese have the primary responsibility for winning the war—so that if during the next four months the new government fails to take the necessary political, economic, social, and military actions, it will be their choice and not our betrayal or weakness that loses the area." Like Kennedy, Sorensen saw the need to hold the line in South Vietnam, but simultaneously wished to plan an escape from what might turn out to be a losing cause.[107]

But Johnson was reluctant to say anything that could be interpreted as defeatism by the South Vietnamese or the Communists. Instead, he wanted everyone to adopt a "can-do" attitude. Throughout his political career, he had made a habit of berating aides who voiced reservations about any of his marching orders, saying, "Don't tell me what you can't do, tell me what you've done."

Vietnam now became a matter that Johnson wished to subject to his irresistible political will. Shortly before McNamara went on his December trip to Saigon, Johnson gave him "quite a lecture on South Viet-Nam and expressed concern that we as a government were not doing everything we should." Shortly after McNamara returned with a downbeat assessment, Johnson sent Lodge and General Duong Van Minh, Diem's successor, letters urging them to get on with the job of beating the Communists. Johnson didn't have much confidence in Lodge. He thought he was "dumb" and a poor politician to boot. And so he felt compelled to light a fire under Lodge, telling him his "energy and leadership" were "indispensable to an effective performance by our government in Saigon." Likewise, it was up to Minh "to act now to reverse the trend of the war."[108]

A coup at the end of January, in which General Nguyen Khanh replaced Minh, opened the way to yet greater instability and likelihood of Communist success in Vietnam. But it did little to discourage Johnson from a growing resolve to meet the Communist challenge.

He immediately sent word to George Ball that he wanted to hold a press conference to counter negative newspaper reports, and "any positive statement he could make on Vietnam would make him happy." Bill Moyers urged Johnson to instruct American officials in Saigon "to get the Vietnamese moving against the Viet Cong—to launch an offensive before the Communists launch one." Believing the message should be more direct, Johnson himself told Khanh of "the necessity of stepping up the pace of military operations against the Viet Cong."[109]

He also tried to strengthen America's effort in the war by organizational changes and rhetoric. He laid plans to speed the replacement of General Paul Harkins, the chief of the U.S. military mission, with General William Westmoreland and to set up an all-agency working group on Vietnam headed by William Sullivan, a veteran diplomat with special knowledge of the country.[110]

In March, Johnson sent McNamara back to Vietnam to make clear that Khanh was now "our man," and we wanted no more coups. In addition, McNamara was to discuss increased assistance to the South Vietnamese and explore with Lodge what stronger measures might be taken if the situation went from bad to worse. Johnson was convinced, as he told Mac Bundy, that with "15,000 advisers and 200,000 people [Republic of Vietnam troops, we could] maintain the status quo for six months; I just believe we can do that if we do it right." From Johnson's perspective, this meant being able to put Vietnam on hold until after the November election, when other decisions could be made.

A major McNamara speech on Vietnam at the end of March indicated what these might be. McNamara emphasized America's determination to keep helping South Vietnam. The country and the region were described as having "great strategic significance in the forward defense of the United States." Further, McNamara pictured Vietnam as "a test case for the new Communist strategy"—wars of national liberation or "covert aggression or insurgency." In a meeting the following week with congressional leaders, the President and McNamara explained that they were considering "taking the war to . . . North Vietnam," a policy the Joints Chiefs believed essential for success in the south.[111]

Johnson worried about congressional support for a more aggressive policy, but Arkansas Senator J. William Fulbright, chairman of the Foreign Relations Committee, eased his concern with a March 25 speech entitled "Old Myths and New Realities." Though he urged greater flexibility in dealing with the Communist world, Fulbright saw only two options in Vietnam. Because withdrawal or a negotiated settlement were out of the question, our only current choices were continued support for Saigon's anti-guerrilla struggle or a wider war fought by U.S. troops and marked by an invasion of the North. Fulbright did not say which option he preferred, but asserted that "it should be clear to all concerned that the United States will continue to meet its obligations and fulfill its commitments with respect to Vietnam."[112]

During April and May Johnson confronted a growing crisis when Communist aggression in Laos and Cambodia joined with continuing advances by the Viet Cong in Vietnam. Johnson pressed McNamara to find a military man who could come up with a plan that would let us win the war. "Let's get some more something, my friend, because I'm gonna have a heart attack if you don't get me something," Johnson said. "Let's get somebody that wants to do something beside drop a bomb that can go in and take out after these damn fellas and send them back where they belong. . . . What we got is what we've had since '54. We're not gettin' it done; we're losin'. We need something new."[113]

McNamara and Bundy agreed. "What is at stake overall is whether the Communists will take over Southeast Asia—by a process of subversion and terror and general nibbling," Bundy urged the President to tell a group of Republican senators on May 26. LBJ now asked Congress for an additional $125 million in military and economic assistance to Vietnam, and the White House called a meeting of top advisers on Vietnam in Honolulu for June 1–3. Johnson instructed the participants to discuss plans for "selected and carefully graduated military force against North Vietnam . . . after appropriate diplomatic and political warning and preparations."[114]

The officials also were to consider asking Congress for a resolution supporting future military actions. Jack Valenti remembers that Johnson "was very, very disgruntled and discontented with the fact that we were messing around in Southeast Asia without congressional approval." On several occasions in the spring of 1964, he told Valenti: " 'By God,' and he quoted [Michigan Senator Arthur] Vandenberg, 'if you want us in on the landing, we sure as hell better be in on the take-off.' " He wanted "something in writing at some point. He wanted to go to the Congress and get the Congress to approve and to authorize the Southeast Asia adventure. . . . He intimated to me that when he was majority leader the idea of some president doing this without getting the Congress to come aboard—by God, Lyndon Johnson would have torn his balls off." Johnson also told Valenti that Bill Bundy was drafting a congressional resolution that could take care of the problem.[115]

Although an air of gloom and apprehension about Vietnam surrounded the Honolulu meeting, several considerations worked against immediate implementation of the military and political steps under discussion. First, the crisis in Vietnam had not reached a point that cried out for action. Second, without a public sense of urgency about confronting the North Vietnamese, the administration believed it would be difficult to make a compelling case for a resolution. Johnson had little doubt that he could arouse the Congress and the public to back military pressure on Hanoi. But he and his advisers saw this as a thin reed to lean on. In the spring of 1964 a Gallup survey showed 63 percent of the public giving little or no attention to the fighting in Southeast Asia, while in another opinion poll 25 percent of Americans had heard nothing about the conflict. Although a majority of those attentive to the problem favored stronger action, this amounted to only a small percentage of the public.[116]

The strongest inhibitions Johnson saw on pushing a resolution were the 1964 election and pending bills in Congress. Fulbright was opposed to a congressional resolution before the November election. He believed "it would create a kind of war fever on the Hill" that would open the administration to charges of having "mishandled the situation up to this point." He declared himself eager "to do everything that keeps the maximum freedom of maneuver for the President—which distinguishes him from some of his colleagues."[117]

Johnson believed that a war fever in Congress and the country would undermine his chances of getting the civil rights bill passed and might cause his defeat in the presidential election. Johnson "was not so stupid that he didn't know that he was pushing his problem ahead of him," Mac Bundy said. "And he knew that it was going to be there as a great big nuisance." But for the moment, he thought it wiser to continue with undramatic pressure "to strengthen the effectiveness of Khanh and his colleagues, at *every* level and by *every* means."

He also wanted to intensify administration efforts to educate Americans about the stakes in Vietnam as preludes to a resolution and greater involvement in the war. The White House needed to convince the American people that it would ultimately be cheaper in U.S. blood and treasure to "CONTAIN the Communists in the Viet Nam area. [The] KEY POINT in this course of action: Communication with the public so they understand what we are doing and why." On June 22, Johnson signed NSAM No. 308 declaring "domestic understanding and support ... essential to the success of United States operations in Southeast Asia." In the meantime, Johnson pushed for bigger things at home.[118]

The Economic Opportunity Act

In the spring of 1964 Johnson's focus was principally on winning passage of the EOA and JFK's civil rights bill. Johnson and Shriver had prepared the way for the EOA by consulting businessmen, labor leaders, economists, state and local officials, welfare workers, and just about anyone with an interest in the legislation. In March, when Johnson sent the poverty bill to Congress, the White House released "a partial list of [137] people Mr. Shriver had consulted in developing the poverty program." Shriver himself said: "Wait 'til I show them [the congressmen] the list of businessmen who've helped us with this program."[119]

Yet however many and varied the people consulted, Johnson and Shriver knew that if Congress made a careful assessment of the poverty bill, especially the community action provision, it would jeopardize its passage. They had little confidence that a genuine debate about the EOA would improve the bill and lead to a more effective war on poverty. Any extended discussion seemed more likely to raise questions about the effectiveness of their plans and the wisdom of fighting an unwinnable war.

Their strategy was to get Congress and the country to focus on the plight of the poor rather than on proposed remedies and create a climate of sympathy for doing something—never mind just what—to help the needy in our midst. Shriver, for example, arranged to blitz the House committee considering the bill with witnesses testifying to the moral need for a solution to the problem. Of the seventy-six people who appeared during twenty days of House hearings, only nine opposed the bill. But the evangelical fervor of proponents describing the urgency of helping the poor drowned them out.[120]

The point man in the campaign was the President. "The master chef who compiled the ingredients and supervised as they were blended into one *chef d'oeuvre* was Lyndon Baines Johnson," one commentator wrote. Before the Society of Newspaper Editors in mid-April, Johnson declared: "For the first time in American history, poverty is on the run and . . . its elimination is no longer impossible, because it is right. We are fighting this war because it is wise."[121]

Between the end of the month and early May Johnson made two trips to Appalachia, where poverty among rural whites was a way of life. His objectives were, first, to arouse nationwide support for an anti-poverty crusade, and second, to encourage the belief that an attack on poverty would do as much or more to help whites as blacks. It is "time for this great and strong and good-hearted and rich Nation to give attention to the needs of its own cities who have been passed by, and . . . its own people," he said. Like an evangelist spreading the Word, Johnson summoned audiences to join him in a crusade "to free 30 million Americans from the prison of poverty. . . . It is not enough for the Congress to pass laws," he asserted, making approval of the EOA seem like a small step in a revolutionary struggle to eliminate deprivation across America.[122]

During the spring and summer of 1964 the country was "deluged with vivid descriptions of the life of the poor." Discussions of poverty became fashionable, with even the conservative *Saturday Evening Post* running a lead article entitled "The Invisible Americans." Senator Hubert Humphrey published a book endorsing the current belief that a culture of poverty in American had made it an "almost genetic certainty" that poverty would be transmitted between generations unless the government took rigorous measures to break the cycle.[123]

Despite the national mood, Johnson did not take congressional action for granted. As early as February, he and Larry O'Brien had worked out a strategy for blunting opposition. The term " 'War on Poverty' is a terrific slogan," one Republican complained. "It puts doubters under the suspicion of being in favor of poverty." Johnson saw the management of the bill as even more crucial. The President, O'Brien, and Henry H. Wilson, one of O'Brien's aides, cooked up the idea of asking Philip Landrum, a conservative House Democrat from rural Georgia, to sponsor the measure. Landrum, who believed this would sit well with the many poor whites in his district, readily agreed. As opponents and supporters in the Congress recognized, it was a master stroke. With northern Democrats and Republicans likely to back the President, Landrum's support promised to disarm enough southern opposition to pass the bill.[124]

Opposition surfaced nevertheless. Republicans complained that a poverty war would duplicate existing programs, undermine the authority of the states, and create a new, inefficient bureaucracy. But such objections to a federal effort in behalf of disadvantaged folks was familiar rhetoric and had little resonance.

Opponents made more headway with assertions that the poverty war was essentially a smokescreen for forcing racial integration on the South and helping blacks. When an administration spokesman presented Wilbur Mills of Arkansas, chairman of the House Ways and Means Committee, with a document supporting the legislation, Mills threw it across the room, and "said a few choice words about how he was not going to be involved in any program to help a bunch of niggers and threw me out of his office."

One Georgia congressman, who was a warm Johnson supporter and liked the idea of a poverty war, told a White House aide that he and others in the "Southern bloc" feared the bill as "a deliberately disguised attempt to further racial integration." It's a measure, "suggested by the Negro leadership," that will "be implemented by devious sinister individuals who believe in government by decree and not by the democratic legislative process."[125]

When opponents didn't make much headway by pressing the race issue, they raised a religious question. Republicans encouraged an amendment assuring that poverty funds would go to parochial school children. It provoked a storm of protest, especially from southern Baptists, who complained that the Pope was shaping the antipoverty plan. Damn it, Johnson told Speaker John McCormack and two Catholic congressmen, Charlie Halleck and the Republicans are "promotin' all this stuff. He's the one that started it. First he [said], we're gonna do too much for Nigras. He thought that would run the southerners off. And it didn't do it.... Now he's tryin' to do it with the Pope. And if they get through with the Pope, they'll do it some other way. They're tryin' to beat this bill and divide this party. Now, we gotta outsmart 'em." When a Baptist preacher called Bill Moyers to complain about Catholic influence, Moyers told him that he couldn't interrupt the President now because he was meeting with the Reverend Billy Graham. Johnson convinced Catholic supporters that unless they got the amendment out of the bill, it wouldn't have a tinker's chance of passing.[126]

The bill also came under fire for threatening traditional lines of political authority. In May, Elizabeth Wickenden wrote Walter Jenkins about mounting opposition in the House committee to the way community action funds would be distributed. She predicted that "a majority of Congress simply will not vote for a much publicized program without some method of protecting themselves against the expectations of their constituencies. And since the President has put so much of his own enthusiastic interest behind this bill, its defeat or substantial modification by Republican action could be seriously damaging to him."[127]

Johnson would not let any of these differences stand in the way of the bill. In early July he told Larry O'Brien to ask House leaders to take necessary procedural steps to get an early committee vote on poverty. "This bill means more than any other in our program. Please do your best." O'Brien and Shriver and Moyers did. "When you talk about Bill and Sarge on the Hill," O'Brien says, "I'm sure they wore out a couple of pairs of shoes in the process." But "no one did as much legwork on the Hill as Sarge," O'Brien adds. "He was indefatigable," spending a lot of time selling "the enemy, . . . recalcitrant Southerners and some Republicans."

At the same time, Harlem Congressman Adam Clayton Powell, who chaired the House hearings, played hardball with opponents, scheduling meetings at irregular hours without sufficient notice and gaveling down committee members raising hard questions. When one Republican complained of being "stampeded," Powell replied: "I am the chairman. I will run this committee as I desire."[128]

Yet the White House also made its compromises. It agreed to minor revisions in the bill to assure the support of some fence-sitters: It abandoned a program to help create family farms or promote what critics called "collective farming" and incentive loans to businesses to hire hard-core unemployed.

More important, the White House won some southern votes by promising to drop Adam Yarmolinsky as Shriver's second-in-command. Described as a "leftist" who as a member of the Defense Department had forced integration of off-base military facilities in the South, Yarmolinsky was anathema to southerners desperately trying to preserve their region from swiftly moving currents of change. After Landrum announced on the House floor that "I have been told on the highest authority that . . . he will not be considered if he is recommended for a place in this agency," Shriver advised Yarmolinsky: "We've just thrown you to the wolves, and this is the worst day of my life."[129]

Administration tactics worked. At the end of July the Senate approved the bill by a two-to-one margin, and in early August the House followed suit by a 226 to 184 vote. In a signing ceremony at the White House Johnson told Americans that "for the first time in all the history of the human race, a great nation . . . is willing to make a commitment to eradicate poverty among its people." He assured the country that the EOA would "offer the forgotten fifth of our people opportunity and not doles."

But thoughtful commentators at the time had their doubts. Pointing to the "lack of research," one poverty expert asserted, "we don't know enough. . . . we are flying blind." *Time* saw the law as reflecting "the uniquely American belief . . . that evangelism, money and organization can lick just about anything, including conditions the world has always considered inevitable." Even the liberal *Nation* thought the war originated in "an almost mystical belief in the infinite potentials of American society. Poverty, like polio, will be defeated when the right vaccine is found."

Johnson himself was clueless as to just how the program would work. Shortly after the bill passed, Moyers told Yarmolinsky, "the

President thinks that community action will be a publicly managed program like the old National Youth Administration he administered in Texas in the 1930s." Nevertheless, Johnson was optimistic that good things would come of the poverty war. The relief and reconstruction fostered by new Deal programs gave him an abiding faith in the capacity of the government to change things for the better. True, the initial attack on poverty might be highly imperfect, but he had no doubt that in time ways could and would be found to make the poverty war work. For the moment, the objective was simply to begin.[130]

Twenty years later, a historian reflecting on the poverty law said: "When the Economic Opportunity Act was enacted, neither the President who sponsored it, the director-designate who would administer it, nor the congressmen who passed it really knew what they had done. Indeed, a history of the legislation might well be entitled ... 'How Not to Fight Poverty.' "

The alternative, he believes, was to have given serious, extended thought to what should be done, which would have raised the possibility of more radical action. But how many in America were ready for that? And so, as with many of the other big problems the country had addressed in its history, the practical solution became a program notable more for its rhetorical appeal than its commitment to significant change. Since some good seemed a likely outcome nevertheless, it made more sense to act than to wait. As important, by pushing the poverty war only so far, in spite of all his overheated rhetoric, Johnson left himself free to reach for bigger gains elsewhere.[131]

Civil Rights

Unlike his uncertainties about the poverty war, Johnson knew what he wanted to do about civil rights. From the moment he assumed the presidency, he saw a compelling need to drive Kennedy's bill through Congress with no major compromises that would weaken the law.

As a southerner who had accommodated himself to segregation through most of his career, Johnson seemed like an unreliable advocate of a civil rights statute that would force an end to the system of racial separation in public facilities across the South. He could not fully divest himself of attitudes instilled by a southern upbringing. In January 1964, he told a Texas friend: "I'm gonna try to teach these nigras that don't know anything how to work for themselves instead of just breedin'; I'm gonna try to teach these Mexicans who can't talk

English to learn it so they can work for themselves . . . and get off of our taxpayer's back." However patronizing to both minorities, Johnson was determined to rise above his own limitations on race and to bring the country with him. "I'm going to be the President who finishes what Lincoln began," he said to several people.

A few days after he became President, he asked Senator Richard Russell of Georgia, an unyielding segregationist, to come talk to him about the civil rights bill. "The President sat in a wing chair. The Senator sat at one end of a small couch. Their knees almost touched." As Jack Valenti remembered it, Johnson said: " 'Dick, you've got to get out of my way. I'm going to run over you. I don't intend to cavil or compromise.' 'You may do that,' he replied. 'But by God, it's going to cost you the South and cost you the election.' 'If that's the price I've got to pay,' said the President, 'I'll pay it gladly.' "

The following week Johnson told labor leaders that "the endless abrasions of delay, neglect, and indifference have rubbed raw the national conscience. We have talked too long. We have done too little. And all of it has come too late. You must help me make civil rights in America a reality." Two days later, in a well-publicized meeting at the White House, he gave the same message to the country's principal black leaders. "This bill is going to pass if it takes all summer," he told them. "This bill is going to be enacted because justice and morality demand it."

His initial impulse had been to meet with the black leaders at his ranch. But Lee White, JFK's special assistant on civil rights, urged Johnson not to do something that would be seen as "so damned phoney." Though Johnson followed White's advice, he told him on the phone from Texas: "I live down here. This is my home, and I ought to be able to invite people to my home." He was determined to show that black leaders would be treated the same as whites.[132]

He had several reasons for wanting to make good on civil rights. First, he felt that passing Kennedy's bill would help heal the wound opened by his assassination. To Johnson's thinking, the President's murder resulted from the violence and hatred dividing America and tearing at its social fabric. Roy Wilkins, one of the civil rights leaders who had met with LBJ in December, remembered that the tragedy of Kennedy's death hung over the civil rights bill and influenced Johnson's view of it. "And it was on this note that he [Johnson] felt the federal government had to take a stand to halt this schism between people—violence, bloodshed and that sort of thing."[133]

As important, there was the moral issue or the matter of fairness that Johnson, the great political operator, felt with a keenness few could fully understand. Johnson—the prominent politician, the great

Majority Leader, the Vice President, the all-powerful President—was at the same time Johnson the underdog, the poor boy from Texas struggling to emerge from the shadows and win universal approval. Johnson identified with and viscerally experienced the suffering of the disadvantaged.

He repeatedly told the story of Zephyr Wright, his cook, "a college graduate," who, when driving the Vice President's official car with her husband from Washington to Texas, couldn't use the facilities in a gas station to relieve herself. "When they had to go to the bathroom," Johnson told Mississippi Senator John Stennis, "they would . . . pull off on a side road, and Zephyr Wright, the cook of the Vice President of the United States, would squat in the road to pee." He told Stennis: "That's wrong. And there ought to be something to change that. And it seems to me that if people in Mississippi don't change it voluntarily, that it's just going to be necessary to change it by law."[134]

His sense of outrage was even more pronounced toward Alabama Klansmen who had killed four black youngsters by setting off a bomb at a Birmingham church in September 1963. He urged FBI Director J. Edgar Hoover to leave no stone unturned in finding the perpetrators. He also asked Hoover to step up his investigations of several other Birmingham bombings tied to racial intolerance. Hoover, a political chameleon with a keen feel for what served his interests, gave Johnson a detailed accounting of expanded bureau efforts to solve the crimes.[135]

Yet all Johnson's rhetoric could not entirely disarm the suspicions of civil rights advocates. If he had felt so strongly about the issue, why had it taken him so long to act on it? Why was he going to make an all-out fight for the civil rights bill now? Roy Wilkins asked him at their December meeting. Johnson thought a minute, wrinkled his brow and said: "You will recognize the words I'm about to repeat. Free at last, free at last. Thank God almighty, I'm free at last." Borrowing from Martin Luther King's speech to the civil rights advocates who had marched on Washington in the summer of 1963, Johnson was describing himself as liberated from his southern political bonds or as a man who could now fully put the national interest and moral concerns above political constraints imposed on a Texas senator.[136]

At the same time, Johnson saw civil rights reform as essential to the well-being of his native region. He had known for a long time that segregation not only separated blacks and whites in the South but also separated the South from the rest of the nation, making it a kind of moral, economic, and political outsider, a reprobate cousin or embarrassing relative the nation could neither disown nor accept as a respectable family member. An end to southern segregation would mean the full integration of the South into the Union, bringing with it economic progress and political influence comparable to that of other regions. And though many in the South would abandon their roots in the Democratic party in response, Johnson was determined to administer the unpleasant medicine that would cure the region's social disease. The election of Presidents from Georgia, Texas, and Arkansas during the next thirty years testifies to the region's renewed influence in the nation anticipated by LBJ.[137]

Johnson also saw personal political gain from pressing ahead with civil rights legislation. In the fall of 1963, 50 percent of the country had felt that Kennedy was pushing too hard for integration. Only 11 percent wanted him to go faster, while 27 percent were content with his pace. By February 1964 the number opposing more vigorous civil rights efforts had dropped to 30 percent, and the percentages favoring more aggressive action and what Johnson was doing had increased to 15 percent and 39 percent, respectively. By the last week of April, 57 percent of the public said they approved of the way Johnson was handling the civil rights problem, and just 21 percent disapproved.

It was welcome news to LBJ, who believed his election to the presidency depended in significant part on his firm advocacy of a civil rights law. "I knew that if I didn't get out in front on this issue [the liberals] would get me," he later told Doris Kearns. "I had to produce a civil rights bill that was even stronger than the one they'd have gotten if Kennedy had lived. Without this, I'd be dead before I could even begin." Richard Russell understood Johnson's dilemma: "If Johnson compromises," Russell told a reporter, "he will be called a slicker from Texas."[138]

Yet Johnson also had reason to think that a forceful stand on civil rights might ruin him politically, as Richard Russell had warned. Black civil rights leader Andrew Young said that, while Johnson knew that support of the civil rights bill was the way to assure his place in history and "the way to really save the nation, he knew it was not politically expedient."[139]

Johnson also worried that an all-out push for a bill that didn't pass could be a serious blow to his political standing. And he saw defeat as a distinct possibility. When he asked Hubert Humphrey to lead the civil rights act through the Senate, Johnson said: "This is your test. But I predict it will not go through." Partly because he believed it and partly to light a fire under Humphrey, Johnson launched into a diatribe about the ineffectiveness of Senate liberals.

"You bomb-throwers make good speeches, you have big hearts, you believe in what you say you stand for, but you're never on the job when you need to be there. You spread yourselves too thin making speeches to the faithful."

Because they would be up against Richard Russell, who knew all the Senate rules better than the liberals, Johnson expected Humphrey to lose the battle. It was a "speech" Humphrey had heard repeatedly from Johnson, but it was less a cry of despair than a summons to do better. He firmly promised to back Humphrey to the hilt. "As I left, he stood and moved toward me with his towering intensity: 'Call me whenever there's trouble or anything you want me to do,'" Johnson said.[140]

To guard against some of the political fallout from a possible congressional defeat, Johnson told Robert Kennedy: "I'll do ... just what you think is best to do on the bill. We'll follow what you say. ... I'll do everything that you want me to do in order to obtain passage of the legislation." Johnson sent word to Senate Democratic leaders to get Bob Kennedy's approval on everything. Why did he do that? an interviewer asked Kennedy. "He didn't think ... we'd get the bill," Bobby answered. And if that were the case, "he didn't want ... to have the sole responsibility. If I worked out the strategy, if he did what the Department of Justice recommended ... —and particularly me—then ... he could always say that he did what we suggested and didn't go off on his own." Kennedy believed that "for political reasons it made a great deal of sense." Johnson couldn't lose this way, because if the bill passed, he would still get "ample credit."[141]

With this safeguard in place, Johnson made every effort to get congressional action. He "wanted to make it very clear—and did— right at the outset of his administration that this was something he was going to move forward in every possible way and with much more than deliberate speed," Deputy Attorney General Nick Katzenbach recalled. "There was nobody more ardent in his espousal of civil rights legislation than Lyndon B. Johnson," Larry O'Brien says.[142]

At the outset, his legislative strategy was the same as Kennedy's: first, get a bill through the House. In the five months before his death, JFK had convinced House leaders from both parties to agree on a compromise law that concentrated its fire on giving southern blacks access to public accommodations and public schools and all citizens equal employment opportunities. This bill had received the approval of the House Judiciary Committee in October and was before the Rules Committee in November when Johnson became President.[143]

On November 25, Johnson told the nation's governors that he expected bipartisan approval of the bill in the House. "The real problem will be in the Senate," he advised congressional leaders. But he took nothing for granted in the House, where Howard Smith of Virginia, Chairman of the Rules Committee, seemed determined to delay matters as long as possible. To put some heat on Smith, Johnson launched a campaign for a discharge petition that would bypass his committee. Republican supporters, seeing this as a liberal Democratic bid to take exclusive credit for the bill, resisted Johnson's pressure. Moderate Democrats, eager not to jeopardize bipartisan support, did the same. "I have talked to them all and don't get that do-or-die attitude out of them," Johnson told Senate Democrats. On January 30, after he had agreed to drop the petition, the Rules Committee approved the bill by an 11-to-4 vote.[144]

Although Johnson and Larry O'Brien were fairly confident that the bill would pass the House, they worried that some of the Republicans might not stay committed and that various amendments, which could dilute the bill, might pass. Consequently, during the next eleven days, Johnson was constantly on the phone, bargaining with Democrats and Republicans alike. "We let them [the Congressmen] know that for every negative vote there was a price to pay," Jack Valenti recalls. "There were many times on that floor when even [Republican leader Charlie] Halleck, in spite of his commitment, would vote for crippling amendments, which we had to beat down," civil rights leader Clarence Mitchell remembers. "And there were many times when if it had not been for the Johnson intercession, we wouldn't have had enough votes on the floor to hold things."

On February 10, within minutes after the bill passed the House 290 to 110, Johnson was on the phone to congressmen praising their action. "We're rollin' now with tax and civil rights if we can just get this through the Senate," he told one of them. "I don't know how we'll ever do it, but we sure gonna try."

He also called Clarence Mitchell and Joe Rauh, a prominent civil rights attorney. "The phone rang in one of those booths over there in the House wing," Mitchell says, "and to our amazement it was the President calling—I don't know how he ever managed to get us on that phone, but he was calling to say, 'All right, you fellows, get on over there to the Senate and get busy because we got it through the House and now we've got the big job of getting it through the Senate.'"

At about 2 a.m. the next morning, Johnson reached Texas Congressman Jake Pickle, one of only six southerners to vote for the bill. "I didn't want to let the night go by without my telling you how proud I am of you," Johnson said. He reflected on the fact that, as a member of the House, he had lacked Pickle's courage to vote for a civil rights bill.[145]

Johnson carefully considered his role in trying to win Senate approval of the bill. "A President cannot ask the Congress to take a risk he will not take himself. He must be the combat general in the front lines. . . . I gave to this fight everything I had in prestige, power, and commitment." But he understood that it would be a poor idea to become too involved in the day-to-day tactics on the Hill. It was unbecoming to a President, and senators would resent it as an inappropriate Executive intrusion on their legislative function. Also, "I deliberately tried to tone down my personal involvement in the daily struggle so that my colleagues on the Hill could take tactical responsibility—and credit." Nevertheless, he had no intention of leaving anything to chance or letting Senate allies design a strategy. The evening of February 10 he told Robert Kennedy and Nicholas Katzenbach how Senate Majority Leader Mike Mansfield should proceed in leading the bill through the Upper House. The following afternoon he gave Mansfield marching orders on the telephone and kept in close touch with him on evolving strategy.[146]

Johnson believed that he could best help advance the bill by repeated public appeals. At a February press conference he made clear that he expected a filibuster in the Senate, but that he would oppose any attempt substantially to change the House bill. During the next five months, while the Senate debated civil rights, hardly a week went by without a restatement of Johnson's conviction that a law should be passed just like the one approved in the House. We are "committed" to the bill with "no wheels and no deals," he said. He also made clear that, having won most of his legislative agenda for the session, he was ready for a long filibuster. "They can filibuster until hell freezes over," he declared. "I'm not going to put anything on that floor until this is done."[147]

Johnson used the prestige of his office in other ways to advance the cause of civil rights. In June of 1964, after three young men, two northern whites and a southern black, disappeared in Mississippi, Lee White pressed Johnson to accept a request from the parents for a meeting. The President was reluctant to set a precedent, which might force him to see other parents in the future. When White, however, pointed out that the newspapers might make much of his refusal to meet, he gave in. And once committed, he turned the occasion to effective account, using the meeting to suggest that the full majesty of the government was behind the search for these young men and equal treatment under the law a civil rights bill would assure.[148]

Yet Johnson did not confine his efforts to public statements and symbolic gestures. Behind the scenes he continually gave direction and energy to the Senate battle for a bill. In January, he told Roy Wilkins "to get on this bill" and get twenty-five Republican votes for cloture. "You're gonna have to persuade Dirksen why this is in the interest of the Republican party," LBJ said.

He believed that the key to overcoming a filibuster and winning approval for the principal features of the House measure was to weaken resistance among southern senators and to enlist Dirksen in the fight. Kenny O'Donnell remembers Johnson telling the southerners, "You've got a southern president and if you want to blow him out of the water, go right ahead and do it, but you boys will never see another one again. We're friends on the q.t. Would you rather have me administering the civil rights bill, or do you want to have Nixon or [Republican Bill] Scranton? You have to make up your minds."[149]

Johnson's appeal was effective. Clarence Mitchell remembers the pained expression on one southerner's face when he described the pressure Johnson put on him. While this senator would never have voted for the bill, "he could have hurt us in a lot of ways that [he] didn't hurt us." Johnson's point registered on Richard Russell as well. "Now you tell Lyndon," Russell told Bill Moyers, "that I've been expecting the rod for a long time, and I'm sorry that it's from his hand the rod must be wielded, but I'd rather it be his hand than anybody else's I know. Tell him to cry a little when he uses it."[150]

Whatever gains he made with the southerners, Johnson saw Dirksen as the lynchpin in the fight. "They say I'm an arm-twister," Johnson told Roy Wilkins, "but I can't make a southerner change his spots any more than I can make a leopard change 'em. . . . I'm no magician. I'm gonna be with ya, and I'm gonna help everywhere I can." But others needed to join in, especially Dirksen, whom he told could establish a special place for himself in history by recognizing that civil rights reform was inevitable. He used the example of Senator Arthur Vandenberg of Michigan, whose shift from isolationism to internationalism during World War II won him a historical reputation as a statesman. At the same time, Johnson told Humphrey: "Now you know that this bill can't pass unless you get Ev Dirksen. You and I are going to get him. You make up your mind now that you've got to spend time with Ev Dirksen. You've got to let him have a piece of the action. He's got to look good all the time."[151]

Humphrey, having arrived at the same conclusion, flattered and courted Dirksen at every turn. "I began a public massage of his ego," Humphrey writes, "and appealed to his vanity. I said he should look upon this issue as 'a moral, not a partisan one.' The gentle pressure left room for *him* to be the historically important figure in our struggle, the statesman above partisanship, ... the master builder of a legislative edifice that would last forever. He liked it." Humphrey, as he said later, was ready to kiss "Dirksen's ass on the Capitol steps." Yet Humphrey also felt that as much as Dirksen liked the stroking, his "sense of history and his place in it" would ultimately be the difference in winning his support. Johnson agreed and egged Humphrey on.[152]

Humphrey, in fact, had a better sense of how to manage Dirksen and other senators than Johnson. When Dirksen wanted to schedule a cloture vote at the end of April, after a month's debate, Humphrey, with Johnson's help, convinced him to wait. No Senate filibuster had ever been ended before by cloture, and Humphrey foresaw that additional weeks of debate would be needed before such a groundbreaking development could occur. In addition, against the judgment of Johnson and liberals in and out of the Senate, Humphrey agreed to several amendments Dirksen proposed as a prelude to getting his support on cloture. Since the amendments did nothing to weaken the provisions of the bill as they applied to the South, civil rights proponents accepted them as a necessary but small compromise.[153]

On June 10, after seventy-five days of debate, the Senate took a cloture vote. The night before, Johnson called Humphrey to ask whether he had the sixty-seven votes, or two-thirds needed to end the debate. "I think we have enough," Humphrey replied. Johnson wasn't satisfied. "I don't want to know what you think. What's the vote going to be? How many do you have?" Confident of only sixty-six supporters, Humphrey spent the evening working on three southwestern Democrats whose votes were not certain. Though Johnson largely left the lobbying and head counting to Humphrey, he had promised a Central Arizona water project to Carl Hayden for his backing—a vote which seemed likely to tip several other senators to the administration's side, including the two from Nevada.[154]

Dirksen, who "had a magnificent sense of drama, loved the center stage, [and] loved the sound of his mellifluous ... voice," had the last word before a vote. Taking his text from Victor Hugo, Dirksen, who was suffering from a peptic ulcer and whose "face looked like a collapsed ruin, drawn and gaunt," intoned: "Stronger than all the armies is an idea whose time has come. The time has come for equality ... in education and in employment. It will not be stayed or denied. It is here."

Predicting that they would get sixty-nine votes, Humphrey followed the proceedings with keen anticipation. Senator Clair Engle of

California, who was dying of a brain tumor and could not speak, arrived in a wheelchair and pointed to his eye when called to vote. The final tally of 71 to 29 exceeded Humphrey's expectations. He "involuntarily" raised his arms over his head at what he saw as the culmination of a lifetime in politics fighting for equal rights.[155]

Johnson took great satisfaction from this historic gain. Should we have a major signing ceremony or should we do it quietly? Johnson asked legislative aide Lee White. "It's so monumental," White answered. "It's equivalent to signing an Emancipation Proclamation, and ought to have all the possible attention you can focus on it." In a simple, dignified ceremony in the East Room of the White House attended by government officials, foreign diplomats, and black and white civil rights advocates, Johnson signed the bill before a national television audience on the evening of July 2. One panoramic photograph of Johnson at a small table before the more than 100 dignitaries seated in long rows conveys the sense of importance Johnson and his audience attached to the occasion.

"We believe all men are entitled to the blessings of liberty," Johnson said. "Yet millions are being deprived of those blessings— not because of their own failures, but because of the color of their skin. The reasons are deeply imbedded in history and tradition and the nature of man. We can understand—without rancor or hatred— how this happened, but it cannot continue. . . . Our Constitution, the foundation of our Republic, forbids it. The principles of our freedom forbid it. Morality forbids it. And the law I will sign tonight forbids it."[156]

Yet Johnson also had his doubts and anxieties about an act of law that was about to change the social structure of the South. He told Hubert Humphrey in May: "The thing we are more afraid of than anything else is that we will have real revolution in this country when this bill goes into effect. . . . It took us ten years to put this Supreme Court decision into effect on education. . . . Unless we have the Republicans joinin' us and helpin' put down this mutiny, we'll have mutiny in this goddamn country. So we've got to make this an American bill and not just a Democratic bill. . . . It doesn't do any good to have a law like the Volstead Act if you can't enforce it."[157]

The evening Johnson signed the bill, Bill Moyers visited him in his bedroom, where he found Johnson seated on his bed with several newspapers headlining the civil rights act spread around him. Johnson seemed deflated. Sensing his mood, Moyers asked why he was so glum. "Because, Bill," he replied, "I think we just delivered the South to the Republican party for a long time to come."[158]

Johnson remained concerned that the South might resist the law.

He feared it would lead to violence, bloodshed, public anarchy, economic dislocation, and defeat for his administration and the Democratic party in the 1964 campaign. In fact, nothing of the kind occurred, as Richard Russell predicted to Clarence Mitchell after his defeat on cloture. Because the civil rights bill was an act of Congress rather than "judge or court made law," Russell expected the South to accept the outcome with little trouble. It did. By the 1980s access to public facilities across the South for blacks was so commonly accepted that youngsters born in the 1970s could not imagine the segregated society of pre-1964.[159]

But Johnson could not know this at the time. And so civil rights was an uncertain element in the presidential campaign, which by the summer of 1964 was the focus of Johnson's political life.

3

"Landslide Lyndon"

FRANKLIN Roosevelt's idea of the presidency was himself in the White House. Lyndon Johnson's idea of the presidency was FDR, Truman, Eisenhower, and even Kennedy in the office. But LBJ? Despite much talk about eclipsing "the whole bunch of them" as a reformer and a vote-getter, Johnson found it difficult to see himself as Chief Executive. He knew he was as smart, and maybe even smarter, than most of his predecessors. He had no doubt that his thirty years in Washington made him as well prepared to be President as anyone else. But he couldn't shake a constant, nagging concern that he didn't quite measure up, that he didn't belong or wasn't legitimate or hadn't won "real" acceptance from the people, the press, the Kennedy "crowd," the "liberals," the northerners, the business establishment, the "eastern intellectuals," or anyone who criticized him or challenged his judgment on even the smallest thing. Yet his conviction that others doubted him told more about his own uncertainty than any public reluctance to see him in the Oval Office.[1]

Throughout his career, inner doubts translated into worries about losing elections, even when every political calculation suggested otherwise. His fears made him back and fill and agonize over withdrawing from races he badly wanted to run and seemed almost certain to make. And when he ran, he was unrelenting, pressing himself and everyone in the campaign into ceaseless, frenzied, exhausting efforts. It was as if his survival depended on winning; defeat seemed to threaten his identity, not just his professional life but his reason for existing. The loss of political office would have consigned him to the emptiness he had struggled with throughout his life. His hold on his House seat in 1941 made his loss to "Pappy" O'Daniel in a special election for a U.S. Senate seat bearable. His eighty-seven-vote victory out of nearly a million cast for the same Senate seat in 1948 rested on a no-holds-barred strategy that permanently cost him his reputation for political probity. His manipulation of the Texas legislature in 1960, allowing him to run for the vice presidency and his Senate seat at the same time, guaranteed that he would remain in office.

The 1964 election put Johnson's self-doubts on display to everyone around him. A constant refrain during his first nine months in the presidency was his uncertainty about running for a full term. Most everyone thought he was being too clever by half. There was no chance Johnson wouldn't run. He was playing a political game, or so they believed. But "he wasn't just playing games with his intimates," his old friend Abe Fortas said. "He was playing games with himself, too. That is to say he was constantly rearguing the question with himself, constantly saying to himself, 'This is not the right thing to do. Maybe . . . the convention won't really want me, and even if they do want me, I . . . shouldn't do it.' " He feared rejection by the party's liberals: "[T]o them my name is shit and always has been and always will be," he complained. "I got their goddamn legislation passed for them, but they gave me no credit."[2]

The day after the Democratic party convention opened in August, he drafted a withdrawal statement. "Our country faces grave dangers. These dangers must be faced and met by a united people under a leader they do not doubt. . . . The times require leadership . . . and a voice that men of all parties, sections and color can follow. I have learned after trying very hard that I am not that voice or that leader."[3]

During a two-hour walk around the south lawn of the White House, he showed George Reedy his statement and scared him into thinking he might not run. "I got home that night in a nervous funk," Reedy says, "thinking, My God, he's going up there tomorrow and resign; the convention will be thrown into chaos. . . . There wasn't any good reason for him to quit," Reedy adds.[4]

Invariably, in a kind of ritualized game, Lady Bird and others close to him would talk Lyndon out of quitting. In response to his statement, Mrs. Johnson soothed him with assurances that he was "as brave a man as Harry Truman—or FDR—or Lincoln." She told him that "to step out now would be *wrong* for your country, and I can see nothing but a lonely wasteland for your future. Your friends would be frozen in embarrassed silence and your enemies jeering." She declared herself unafraid of the press "or lies or losing money or defeat. In the final analysis I can't carry any of the burdens you talked of—so I know it's only *your* choice. But I know you are as brave as any of the thirty five. I love you always." When Johnson told Richard Russell that he had decided against running, Russell, "begging forgiveness for frankness, ... told him he was talking like a child—and a spoiled one at that. ... [I] knew he was not serious and my advice was to take a tranquilizer and get a couple of hours sleep."[5]

Johnson's fears of being seen as unpresidential or unworthy of the office partly rested on realistic concerns. He was right about some of the liberals: No matter what he did they could not accept him or generate genuine enthusiasm for him as President. "The real liberals—never truly accepted Johnson," New York attorney and old Johnson friend Ed Weisl said. "I don't know why, because he was more liberal than the most liberal of them. ... It's partly style, partly the fact that he's from Texas. ... They would tell you, 'He's good and he's wise and he's effective, but well, he just isn't our kind of a guy. ...' They never truly accepted him, except the old-time liberals, you know, like [New York Senator Herbert] Lehman ... [or] Mrs. Roosevelt." It made Johnson angry and bitter: "What's the difference between a cannibal and a liberal?" he would ask. "A cannibal doesn't eat his friends."[6]

Johnson also worried that his affinity for what others considered crude, inappropriate presidential behavior might do him in. If the press began publicizing his vulgarity, which was an open secret in Washington and Texas, he believed it could drive him from office. His abuse of aides, shouting at them in public and calling them into the bathroom while he "sat on the throne," was well known to reporters. Moreover, during the first months of his presidency he had shocked journalists visiting him at his ranch by graphically describing the sex life of bulls, urinating on his grave site, and belching between gulps of highballs.

Columnist Stewart Alsop had LBJ's unrestrained behavior in mind when he predicted that "Only Johnson could beat Johnson" in 1964. It was impossible to give flat-out assurances that Johnson would be elected, because he was such "an unpredictable man," Alsop said. He imagined Johnson losing his temper at a press conference and the anger rushing out of him "like some dark and elemental force of nature" that would ruin him. This side of Johnson's character had already registered on the public: Voters surveyed in five states said that Johnson was "several steps down the social ladder" from John F. Kennedy.[7]

To counter a picture of him as a Texas primitive and back-room operator, Horace Busby suggested that Johnson be seen in photos strolling hand in hand with Mrs. Johnson in the White House gardens or sitting with her in the White House quarters reading books. He also might want to be seen wearing a cap as an effective counter to his Texas image in five- and ten-gallon hats. A portrait of him bowling with one of his daughters would convey a wholesome father-daughter closeness.[8]

Johnson took Busby's advice, but he couldn't escape his real self. In late March, during an Easter holiday at the LBJ ranch in Stonewall, the President treated the Washington press corps to some Texas-style drinking and driving. Inviting four reporters to join him in his Lincoln Continental for a tour of his "spread," Johnson, sipping Pearl beer from a paper cup, led a caravan of journalists and photographers along Hill Country roads at speeds of up to ninety miles an hour. When *Time* published a detailed account of Johnson's recklessness, it strengthened impressions of him as a Texas wheeler dealer who played fast and loose with the rules and gave less thought to the national well-being, which would suffer terribly from the loss of another President, than to his own self-indulgence.

White House denials that Johnson had exceeded the speed limit or done anything wrong deepened rather than countered feelings of distrust. Coming only two weeks after Johnson had publicly denied that Bobby Baker, who was then being investigated by a Senate committee, was his protégé, and a week after the *Wall Street Journal* published an exposé about the Johnson radio and television properties, reports of the high jinks in Texas gave Johnson reason to fret about his appeal to voters in a national campaign. And if all this weren't enough to raise his negative ratings with the public, descriptions of him lifting two pet beagles by the ears made him appear cruel as well as coarse.[9]

The criticism enraged Johnson. When Senate Republican minority leader Everett Dirksen declared that he wouldn't treat his dogs the way Johnson treated his, LBJ told Mike Mansfield that Dirksen is "acting like a shit ass. . . . It's none of his damn business how I treat my dog," Johnson said, "and I'm a hell of a lot better to dogs and humans, too, than he is." Johnson complained that his critics didn't know a damn thing about hounds, but they had "every dog lover in the country raisin' hell, thinkin' I'm burnin' them at the stake."[10]

Also giving Johnson pause about a presidential race were allegations in the hands of the FBI of ties to the extreme left and the extreme right. A Bureau memorandum in February 1964 about a National Committee to Abolish the House Un-American Activities Committee noted that Aubrey Williams, "a Government official and a 'New Dealer,'" who "has spoken before and supported a number of left-wing and communist-led organizations," had ties to the President. The bureau not only had a 1959 photograph of Williams and then Senator Johnson but also evidence of LBJ's wish to recommend Williams's appointment to the Peace Corps in 1961. Almost as worrisome, between January and April, the FBI investigated false allegations that Johnson had been a member of HYKERS, a Texas branch of the Ku Klux Klan.

Johnson had no intention of letting J. Edgar Hoover undermine his election to the presidency by leaking this or other derogatory information in his FBI file gathered over the years. Hoover, who would be turning seventy, was scheduled for mandatory retirement on January 1, 1965, but Johnson decided to extend his service. At a news conference on May 8, 1964, he told the press that Hoover was "a hero to millions of decent citizens, and an anathema to evil men." Hoover was to be exempted "from compulsory retirement for an indefinite period of time."

Though pleased about the reprieve, Hoover worried that Johnson could show him the door whenever he liked. At the end of May, however, Hoover received additional assurance from the President. " 'Mr. Hoover has never been wrong, especially on the subject of the Communist Party and their activities,' " Johnson told a luncheon guest, who passed the word on to Hoover. "He went on to state that many left-wingers wish to see you out of the F.B.I. but that he, the President, stated that you would be there long after most of them had departed from the scene." When an aide questioned Johnson's decision to extend Hoover's term as director, he replied: "I'd rather have him inside the tent pissing out than outside the tent pissing in."[11]

Johnson's sense of vulnerability was exaggerated; through the spring of 1964 national opinion was decidedly in his favor. In January he told Richard Russell that in Pennsylvania "I beat [Republican Governor Bill] Scranton 79 to 20; I beat Goldwater 82 to 17." Russell assured him that "the people of this country are one million percent back of your position." In late March, pollster George Gallup told a White House aide that "the President is doing a fantastic job. We all thought that the honeymoon would last 30–45 days and then the polls would drop off sharply. But this has not been the case. The President still has a fantastically high national rating, and it looks like that rating is going to continue."

Similarly, Senator Abe Ribicoff of Connecticut sent word after a trip through several western states that the President would be "overwhelmingly elected." People across the country had "enormous respect . . . for the President's dedication and the way he has handled the job." He also urged Johnson to ignore the Bobby Baker story, which was "of no consequence whatever outside of Washington." A statewide poll in Minnesota confirmed Ribicoff's assessment: while

80 percent of those surveyed had heard of the Baker case, only 4 percent said it made a difference in the way they viewed the President.

In April, Johnson complained to Mac Bundy that liberal Kennedy supporters demeaned him and his staff as "buffoons and corn pones and not interested in [foreign] affairs and not being able to get any job done and demeaning the presidency . . . , but the polls show us 81 percent in the east" and 77 percent nationally. "Our problem," Johnson said, "is trying to keep some of the big, mean, rich, fat Republicans from being too strong for us." The only place poll numbers showed the slightest problem was in the South, where LBJ had a 13 percent disapproval rating.[12]

Despite all the good news on his popularity, Johnson believed that if he were going to win in November he needed, first, to enact the liberal agenda—the tax cut, war on poverty, and civil rights—and, second, to demonstrate that he was a President who could rise above politics to serve the national interest.

The perfect opportunity presented itself in April when the railroad brotherhood threatened to stage a nationwide strike in response to attacks on "featherbedding." Determined to head off a national economic slowdown, the likely outcome of an extended strike, and to duplicate JFK's success in a 1962 dispute with the steel industry, Johnson summoned negotiators from both sides to the White House in a last-minute attempt to stop the walkout. Five hours of the Johnson "treatment"—urging, warning, pleading, persuading—produced an eleventh-hour agreement to postpone a strike for fifteen days. Confronted by an appeal to avoid a disastrous downturn in the economy, a request to give "the only President you have" a chance to settle the dispute, and a warning about the potential damage to themselves, both sides gave in.[13]

During the next two weeks, Johnson micromanaged the negotiations. Insisting that discussions take place at the Executive Office Building, where he showed up repeatedly, the President barraged negotiators with demands for a settlement. Armed with memos from his Council of Economic Advisers and Secretary of Labor, he emphasized anew the cost to the economy, to himself, and to them from an ongoing dispute and the benefits to the country from a compromise. After considerable horse-trading, especially with the carriers, who won promises from the President to press Congress for greater freedom to set rates and the Internal Revenue Service for more liberal depreciation allowances on tunnel and bridge construction, Johnson got an agreement.

His "joy at settling the railroad dispute was so great he could hardly wait to share the good news with the country," UPI reported. " 'Where are we going?' a motorcycle policeman shouted at a Secret Service agent . . . as the President's motorcade roared out of the White House gate, carrying Johnson to the CBS television studio." There, flanked by representatives of labor and industry, a beaming President announced the settlement to the country, depicting it as a triumph of American industrial democracy and saying "the needs and demands of the people's interest . . . come first. For, says the Old Testament, 'he that keepeth understanding shall find good.' "[14]

By May, Johnson's success in mediating the rail dispute seemed to give him an unshakable hold on the presidency. A political cartoon caught the mood of the moment: Depicting LBJ seated at a card table with a deck in the middle and "tax cut" cards tucked in the brim of his ten-gallon hat, "R.R. Settlement" and "Boom Times" cards coming out of his sleeves, and "Common Touch" and "Poverty Fight" cards in the cuffs of his pants, the drawing showed a smiling Johnson asking: "Now Who'd Like To Play?"[15]

Johnson had the additional advantage of having mapped out a campaign since the first of the year. He had seen effective management of domestic and foreign affairs as his best strategy for winning in November. But designing a plan to meet the challenge from a particular Republican opponent did not lag far behind.

Johnson's initial list of GOP candidates included Nixon, New York's Governor Nelson Rockefeller, Ambassador to Vietnam Henry Cabot Lodge, Pennsylvania Governor Bill Scranton, and Arizona Senator Barry Goldwater. Until June, the White House, like most political pundits, found it difficult to say who would become the nominee. Roy Roberts, publisher of the *Kansas City Star*, whom Averell Harriman described to the White House as "one of the best weathervanes of midwestern pit-of-the-stomach opinion around," dismissed the chances of Rockefeller and Lodge. The former "has never got off the ground [as a candidate] and never will," and the latter would never pass muster with party bosses who saw him as too aloof. Roberts would not count Goldwater out, but he expected the nomination to go to Nixon or Scranton.[16]

Despite his defeat in a 1962 gubernatorial race in California, Nixon also stood high on LBJ's list of likely competitors. At least Johnson was worried enough about his potential candidacy that in January he considered making plans to hold a summit conference with Soviet leader Nikita Khrushchev as a way to blunt Nixon's greater experience in foreign affairs. Johnson also asked the Democratic National Committee to prepare a memo on Nixon's inconsistencies in his eighteen-year political career.[17]

But others in the administration did not think Nixon would emerge as the nominee. In 1963, when the principal Kennedy advisers began talking about the election, they had focused on Rockefeller, Scranton, and Goldwater. By February 1964, they had found no reason to change their minds. Moreover, one report coming out of New York, where "the real center of the controlling group of the GOP" resided, predicted "a tremendous play in the press" for Scranton in the coming weeks. A moderate who "gave the impression of being reasonable, sincere and thoughtful," Scranton was described as "the most dangerous kind of opponent for Democrats to handle."[18]

Predicting the Republican outcome became more complicated in March, when Lodge won a surprising write-in victory in the New Hampshire primary. Rockefeller and Goldwater, who were the front-runners in the state, seemed badly hurt by the result, especially Rockefeller. A hard-liner on foreign policy, a moderate on domestic affairs, and a man with exceptional name recognition, Rockefeller, JFK believed, could have beaten him in 1960. But 1964 was another matter. In 1961, a divorce from his wife of thirty-one years and his remarriage in May 1963 to someone perceived as having abandoned her own marriage to wed Nelson tarred him with a "scandal" that undermined his candidacy. Only 19,500, or 22 percent, of the voters in New Hampshire chose Rockefeller. Goldwater did a little better with 20,700 votes.[19]

Because he found it difficult during the spring to anticipate his opponent in the fall campaign, Johnson tried to prepare himself for a race against either a moderate or a conservative Republican. He thought all of them, as he told Hubert Humphrey, would be vulnerable to the argument that "the reason the Republicans haven't won any elections [since Hoover] except Eisenhower ... is because they spend all their time on Roosevelt's boy Jimmy and on his dog, and ... on Truman and Margaret and the music critics and ... on Kennedy and his religion ... and ... if they don't stand for something, hell, if they just come out here and talk about revival of the corn tassel or come out for Tom Watson watermelons, it'd be something. But they just, by God, [are] against things, against everything and trying to smear and fear."[20]

In April, when Oliver Quayle, LBJ's pollster, assessed the President's strength in six states in the West, Middle West, and East, he pitted Johnson against three moderates and one conservative, Rockefeller, Nixon, Michigan Governor George Romney, and Goldwater.

Johnson decisively beat all of them. And though some voters were suspicious of him as a "southern conservative, and some find his less sophisticated appearance and personality lacking," Quayle saw "no serious weaknesses" in his candidacy.[21]

Nevertheless, Johnson acted to blunt a likely GOP attack on his administration regardless of the nominee. His greatest concern was Republican "smear and fear" tactics over the Bobby Baker case. During the first five months of 1964, he complained repeatedly about newspaper stories and Republican efforts to "link" him to the scandal by suggesting that he had enriched himself through influence-peddling. He had dozens of conversations about how to meet this onslaught from "mean-spirited" political enemies desperately searching for something that could ruin him.[22]

At the same time, he moved to counter predictable Republican complaints that he was a spendthrift, wasteful Democrat who never met a government program he didn't like. "Fiscal frugality," paring department and agency payrolls, was a White House refrain. Turning out the lights in the mansion became a symbol of Johnson's determination to reduce government costs. "The light bill on the White House a few months ago was $5,000 a month," Johnson told a gathering of IRS officials in February. "This month it is $3,000." Later in the year a reporter asked Reedy: "George, could you tell us or ascribe some reason to this heavy concentration on fiscal matters and government economy? . . . Is it preliminary to the work on the new budget or could it have something to do with the forthcoming election campaign?" Oh, no, Reedy answered. Ever since he had known Johnson in 1950 he had been "wedded" to government economies and increased efficiency.[23]

Johnson also worried that the Republicans might score points against him by criticizing his management of foreign affairs. To blunt such complaints, Horace Busby told the press that there were few indications of Republican gains from suggesting that Johnson was "soft" in dealing with the "East." The "harshest critics . . . can't convince [the] public" of this. And even if Johnson's track record overseas had no dramatic gains comparable so far to those at home, his "effectiveness and experience . . . in handling domestic matters" was being transferred "as a major plus to international affairs." Moreover, Busby told reporters, as soon as Johnson began acting openly as a candidate, the GOP would find itself in a "more difficult position than was first expected after November 22." But Johnson didn't need to counter the Republicans in the first half of 1964; their intra-party strife was doing it for him.[24]

Barry's the One

Only sixteen states held primaries in 1964, with the rest choosing delegates to the national conventions at local and statewide party caucuses. Despite his defeat in New Hampshire, Goldwater's supporters, led by F. Clifton White of New York, a superb political organizer, won most of the state contests. By mid-April, some estimates gave Goldwater nearly 450 of the 655 delegates needed to win the Republican nomination. Though losing to Rockefeller in Oregon on May 15, Goldwater all but assured his candidacy by winning the California primary on June 2. When Texas added fifty-six delegates to his column in the middle of June, Goldwater was only sixty-seven votes short of victory.[25]

Barry Morris Goldwater was the envy of a fiction writer's imagination. Born in the Arizona territory in 1909, he was the offspring of Jewish and Protestant pioneers who built the two biggest department stores in the area and played leading roles in the public life of the territory and state beginning in 1912. During World War II Goldwater left the family business for service in the Air Force as a pilot flying cargo planes across the Himalayas between India and China. After the war he became a leading figure in the struggle to reform a corrupt city administration in Phoenix. In 1952, he won a U.S. Senate seat and immediately became an outspoken advocate of ultra-conservative ideas that put him at odds with not only most Democrats but also the Eisenhower administration, which he called "a dime-store New Deal."

A blunt man with little feel for the nuances of traditional American politics, Goldwater did nothing to hide or shade his political views. Well before he began his presidential campaign, he had put himself on record as favoring the withdrawal of recognition of the Soviet Union, freedom for local military commanders to use atomic weapons against the USSR—"Let's lob one into the men's room of the Kremlin," he had said—the sale of FDR's Tennessee Valley Authority, and abolition of the graduated income tax. During the New Hampshire campaign, he had urged that Social Security be made voluntary, described welfare recipients as people with low intelligence and little ambition, decried government interference in the economy and federal aid to education, defended his opposition to civil rights legislation, and advocated the bombing of North Vietnam. "I followed him about for several days ... to observe the [Barry] phenomenon, and it was quite clear he did not know what he was doing," the journalist Theodore White said.[26]

Democrats watching the rise of Goldwater's candidacy were

gleeful. "It begins to look as though the Republicans are really going on a Kamikaze mission in November," ADA president John P. Roche wrote Bill Moyers in June. "This puts the President in a wonderful strategic position: he can play the campaign with lofty statesmanship ignoring the fact that Goldwater exists. At the next level we can really run a savage assault: A billboard, e.g., can be devised reading 'Goldwater in 64—Hotwater in 65?' with a mushroom cloud in the background."

On the eve of the Republican convention in July, Lou Harris released a national survey showing that "on eight out of 10 issues facing the country, the American people feel they are in sharp disagreement with the Arizona senator. . . . Rarely has a man in such a commanding position for a major party Presidential nomination found his political positions—as understood by the public—to be so diametrically opposed by the voters themselves."[27]

But in 1964 conservative Republicans, who had seized control of the party machinery and assured Goldwater's nomination, were more interested in trumpeting their ideology than in winning an election. At the Cow Palace in San Francisco, where the Republicans began their convention on July 14, Goldwater's supporters showed no mercy for their political enemies—the liberal press, moderate Republicans, and Great Society Democrats. When former President Eisenhower lambasted "sensation-seeking columnists and commentators . . . who couldn't care less about the good of our party," and attacked indulgent liberals and weak-minded judges for "maudlin sympathy" toward criminals "roaming the streets with switchblade knife and illegal firearms," the delegates exploded in a display of raw emotion that offended some and frightened others.[28]

But it was mild compared with the reception given Nelson Rockefeller. Speaking against extremism or the "kooks" he saw lined up on Goldwater's side, Rockefeller's words were the equivalent of a red flag to a bull. The Goldwaterites jeered and yelled, shook cowbells, blew horns, and beat drums in a concerted attempt to drown him out. Warming to the challenge, Rockefeller derided them for "Communist and Nazi methods," which provoked them all the more. A tall, thin, blonde woman in the galleries, incensed by Rockefeller's words, made an indelible impression on one reporter. She stood, "her fists upraised and shaking, screaming at the top of her lungs: 'You lousy lover, you lousy lover, you lousy lover!' " The journalist added, "As the TV cameras translated their wrath and fury to the national audience, they pressed on the viewers that indelible impression of savagery which no Goldwater leader . . . could later erase."[29]

Goldwater himself saw no reason to mute his message or hold

back from the conservative vision that had carried him to victory over the party's moderates. He chose as his running mate William E. Miller, an obscure, fiercely conservative upstate New York congressman who echoed Goldwater's commitment to an uncompromising right-wing ideology.

Goldwater's acceptance speech at the convention underscored his determination to make his campaign "a choice not an echo," as his supporters advertised. The speech was not a traditional appeal for conciliation and party unity but a preaching to the converted, a call to the faithful to stand with him against "collectivism" and Communism, against "bureaucratic make-work" and the "bread and circuses" their opponents were inflicting on the nation. The current administration wasn't guilty of "mere political mistakes," its errors were "the result of a fundamentally and absolutely wrong view of man, his nature and his destiny." The Republican party's goal above all, Goldwater asserted, was "Freedom"— "Freedom" from the misappropriation of power by the federal government and "Freedom" from the threat of Communism, which is the enemy of "every man on earth who is or wants to be free." There could be no compromising these goals. "Extremism in the defense of liberty is no vice! . . . Moderation in the pursuit of justice is no virtue!" Goldwater declared. "My God," one reporter remarked, "he's going to run as Barry Goldwater."[30]

Johnson and his closest advisers puzzled over how to react to Goldwater's nomination. There was an impulse to see Goldwater's candidacy as "absurd" and the Republican party as conceding the election. It was difficult to believe that so right-wing a candidate, espousing such extreme views on both domestic and foreign affairs, could marshall a significant challenge to a popular incumbent, as Johnson was in the summer of 1964.

At the same time, one White House aide cautioned against complacency. "It is time someone said to the President what apparently no one has yet said to him—that he could lose this election, and that he could lose it despite having lined up all the press and the television networks, all the top labor leaders, most of the top business leaders, all of the Negro vote, and perhaps even Lodge and Rockefeller." A Goldwater campaign based on "three potent commodities: Race prejudice . . . Chauvinism . . . [and] Simple answers to complicated questions" could produce surprising results. Of the three, Johnson and everyone around him worried most about a white backlash against black advances under the civil rights bill. In the spring of 1964, Governor George Wallace of Alabama, an outspoken segregationist, won between 30 and 43 percent of the votes in the Wisconsin, Indiana, and Maryland Democratic presidential primaries.[31]

Johnson, taking nothing for granted, insisted on a tough, hard-driving campaign. He saw "Goldwaterism" as "the outgrowth of long, long public unrest with Big Government, Big Spending, . . . and feeling that 'Washington doesn't understand our problems.' " He wanted to broaden the Democratic party base by reaching out to Independents and Republicans. Moreover, he wanted the Democratic National Committee, Democratic congressmen, senators, and governors, and administration figures to carry the fight to Goldwater and the conservatives. He asked the DNC to prepare a line-by-line refutation of the Republican platform, and agreed to Bill Moyers's suggestion for a "topic-a-day attack on Goldwater's main positions." Though he would be his own campaign manager and insisted on involving everyone at the White House in the election, he intended initially to act presidential and avoid taking on Goldwater himself.[32]

When a series of riots in the black ghettos of East Coast cities began on July 16 with the slaying of a teenager by a police officer, Johnson confronted the first direct test of his strategy for defeating Goldwater. The senator asked for a meeting at the White House to discuss the crisis in the cities. Johnson was reluctant to raise Goldwater's "stature and prestige by bringing him in for a summit meeting with the President . . . on a matter of important national policy." Moreover, it seemed likely to blunt Goldwater's image as an extremist and give him cover against charges that he was anti-black and anti-civil rights. At the same time, however, saying "No" would open the White House to the complaint that the President "will talk to Communists, have a hot line to Khrushchev, but won't talk to Goldwater about keeping peace in the streets."[33]

Johnson felt compelled to see Goldwater, but he and his aides outlined a plan to limit any political gain he might get from the meeting. At a press conference shortly before he saw Goldwater, Johnson said he had no intention of taking the civil rights issue out of the campaign. But if the senator agreed to follow his course in "rebuffing and rebuking bigots and those who seek to excite and exploit tensions, then it will be most welcome and . . . a very fine contribution to out political life." At their meeting, Johnson stressed the need to enforce the civil rights law and to respect court decisions. He also urged the avoidance of statements that might add to tensions and increase rioting. Such explosions could "be exploited by . . . racist groups and communists who do not have the best interests of the Negro people or the United States at heart." Seeing Johnson's request as a challenge to his patriotism, Goldwater agreed to eliminate any appeal to racial passions in the election. With the riots petering out in the next month, Johnson had managed to shelve the "backlash" as a Goldwater advantage in the campaign.[34]

The "Bobby Problem"

Despite initial maneuvers against Goldwater and the Republicans, Johnson wasn't yet ready to focus his full attention on the fall campaign. Since early in the year he had been wrestling with questions about who would be his running mate. Initial soundings indicated warm support for Robert Kennedy. National polls showed Bobby holding a four-to-one edge over Hubert Humphrey, his closest rival. Moreover, syndicated columnist Stewart Alsop argued that it would "be remarkably hard for President Johnson to turn him [Bobby] down if he wanted the vice presidency." To do so could mean losing Catholic, black, and pro-Kennedy votes in big northern states, which Johnson must have in November. One astute political observer told Alsop: "Lyndon is boxed in—if Bobby really wants it, he can have it."[35]

But did Kennedy want the vice presidency? He wasn't sure. Early in December 1963, after being told that some party members favored him for the second spot on the ticket, he spoke to Arthur Schlesinger. Schlesinger counseled him against running, for, in Kennedy's words, "he did not like the idea of taking a job which was really based on the premise of waiting around for someone to die." In February, when Paul Corbin and some New Hampshire Democrats organized the Kennedy-for-Vice-President write-in, Bobby spoke to a New Hampshire national committeeman, asking how he viewed "this thing and was it going to be something that he would get seriously embarrassed on"? A few days before the primary vote, Kennedy decided to announce that the President "should be free to select his own running mate," but he rejected the idea of categorically taking himself out of contention. The election gave him just 3700 fewer votes than Johnson and a big measure of satisfaction.[36]

Johnson felt frustrated and trapped by the prospect of having Kennedy on the ticket. It was an open secret that they disliked each other. Someone "very close" to Johnson told Alsop "categorically that Johnson will never under any circumstances choose Robert Kennedy." Three weeks after JFK's death, Johnson himself had told Ken O'Donnell: "I don't want history to say I was elected to this office because I had Bobby on the ticket with me. But I'll take him if I need him." Johnson had also said: "If I don't need him, I'm not going to take him. I don't want to go down in history as the guy to have the dog wagged by the tail and have the Vice President elect me, because that's what they're going to write."[37]

Johnson didn't want Kennedy and hoped he wouldn't need him. "That upstart's come too far and too fast," Johnson told Eric Goldman. "He skipped the grades where you learn the rules of life. He never liked me, and that's nothing compared to what I think of him."

The New Hampshire campaign for Kennedy enraged Johnson. It "drove Johnson up the wall," O'Donnell says. He was certain that Bobby was behind the whole thing. Kennedy remembered their conversation about Corbin and the New Hampshire primary as mean and bitter. "It was the meanest tone that I've heard," Kennedy said. "If he really wanted to organize a campaign for Vice President," he told friends, "it certainly would be a great deal more effective and professional than the slapdash New Hampshire effort." Johnson didn't believe him. He told a Texas friend, "If they try to push Bobby Kennedy down my throat for Vice President, I'll tell them to nominate him for the *presidency* and leave me out of it."[38]

Through the first half of 1964 Johnson maneuvered to find a way around the "Bobby problem." He tried to ease matters with Kennedy by "establishing a considerable amount of contact" with Massachusetts Senator Ted Kennedy, Bobby's younger brother. Johnson talked to Larry O'Brien several times about his difficulties with Robert. He wanted to know "why Bobby had this attitude . . . toward him when he and Teddy had this pleasant relationship." O'Brien thought that Johnson "was making a real effort to see if he couldn't bridge this. And he felt that having this pleasant relationship with Teddy would lead to Bobby not having that glare on his face all the time."[39]

But when it came to Robert Kennedy, Johnson couldn't restrain himself. At the same time he was trying to soften differences, he was also exacerbating them. In the spring of 1964, he told Pierre Salinger, who predictably repeated it to Bobby, that JFK's assassination was "divine retribution" for "his participation in the assassinations of Trujillo [of the Dominican Republic] and President Diem." Since JFK had no direct connection to either killing, it made the assertion all the more galling to RFK.[40]

Throughout the spring Johnson explored possible alternatives to Kennedy as a running mate. Partly, this was an exercise in creating interest in what would otherwise be a cut and dried Democratic convention. Mostly, though, it was a serious attempt to jettison Kennedy. In a "philosophical" moment, as Bill Moyers puts it, Johnson said, he "couldn't have Bobby because it would create a divided presidency.

It just wouldn't work. It would be wrong for him; it would be wrong for me."[41]

First, Johnson floated Sargent Shriver's name. A Catholic, a member of the Kennedy clan, Shriver seemed like a good substitute for Bobby. Johnson told Moyers, who had suggested Shriver, to leak the idea to the press. The Kennedys vetoed it. O'Donnell told Johnson: "If you're going to have a Catholic then you're going to go first-class, take the best Catholic, not somebody's brother-in-law because he's a nice-looking fellow. You're talking about a man who may be President of the United States. . . . We want someone who's qualified to run this country. Religion really doesn't interest us." On consideration, Johnson didn't like the idea either. Shriver's presence on the ticket would still have raised questions about LBJ's capacity to win on his own.[42]

At a White House meeting in April with several politicians and aides, Johnson went around the room asking who the Vice President should be. Everyone but Walter Jenkins voted for Hubert Humphrey, who argued for Eugene McCarthy, the junior senator from Minnesota. Jenkins produced a poll, which O'Donnell says was cooked up about fifteen minutes before the meeting and showed that LBJ needed a Catholic running mate to beat Goldwater. O'Donnell thought it was a lot of "hogwash" and told Johnson so: "Whoever gave you that poll, you ought to get your money back." Everyone in the room, except Jenkins, continued to recommend Humphrey over McCarthy.[43]

Johnson was reluctant to take Humphrey. He told Moyers: "I don't think Hubert would be happy as my VP. Moreover, I would have lots of problems with him: He's so exuberant, so enthusiastic, he'd get off the reservation all the time. He talks too much to be Vice President."[44]

Johnson also considered Robert McNamara. He was close enough to the Kennedys to make him a worthy substitute for Bobby; but he was also distant enough from them to quiet talk that Johnson couldn't win without a Kennedy. McNamara, a lifelong Republican, had the additional virtue of being attractive to independents and businessmen. Democratic bosses, however, opposed him as a slight to party regulars and as someone who would not help Johnson with liberals, where he was weakest. The press put McNamara on Johnson's short list of candidates, but he didn't want the job. "You could never take at face value what he said," McNamara told me about Johnson. "I don't mean to say he was duplicitous. He was a very shrewd guy. . . . He said to me, 'Bob, I haven't selected my running mate and I'd like you to run with me.'" McNamara, who had never run for office and believed himself unsuited to do it, said, "Absolutely not!" But even if he had said yes, McNamara doubts that it would have settled anything. Johnson "would have said, 'I'm delighted to know that' and then left matters open."[45]

Johnson wanted Kennedy to take himself out of the running, but Bobby wouldn't do it. He had no illusion about Johnson's wishes, nor did he find the job all that appealing. True, it would make him an heir apparent to the presidency, but it carried a price he didn't want to pay. As Johnson himself had found out, the vice presidency was an inconsequential office that inevitably frustrated anyone eager to shape national affairs. Worse yet, a Johnson Vice President would need to be a "yes man" who conformed to LBJ's every wish. "Whoever he is," Johnson told people in 1964, "I want his pecker . . . in my pocket."[46]

In May, Kennedy privately told an interviewer about Johnson's vice-presidential dilemma: "The one thing Lyndon Johnson doesn't want is me as Vice President, and he's concerned about whether he's going to be forced into that." He mentioned that Lyndon had already tried and failed to solve the problem by getting Shriver or McNamara. Now "he's hysterical about how he's going to . . . avoid having me or having to ask me. That's what he spends most of his time on, from what I understand: figuring out how he's going to avoid me. . . . I'm just trying to make up my mind what I'm going to do." If he stayed in the race and got the job, he saw himself losing "all ability to ever take any independent positions on matters." Johnson had this ability "to eat people up, even people who are considered rather strong figures. . . . He's mean, bitter, vicious—an animal in many ways."

Knowing all this, Kennedy still wouldn't drop out of the race. The allure of the second spot as a stepping stone to the first remained, but there was also some satisfaction in making Johnson squirm. Even if Bobby didn't run, he wanted to be asked.[47]

By June, however, after Goldwater's victory in California, Johnson began to feel that the vice-presidential nomination would be of little consequence in determining the outcome of the election. Polls early in the month showed him with a 74 percent approval rating and a 77 to 18 percent margin over Goldwater in a trial election. As important to Lyndon, polls began to show that none of the vice-presidential candidates would do anything to strengthen his candidacy. And the one candidate who seemed likely to hurt him was Robert Kennedy, who would weaken the Democratic ticket in the South and among businessmen.

"I was constantly having conversations with the President on the results of all the polls that were being conducted," Larry O'Brien recalls. "He'd pull them out of his inside pocket, and we'd go over them one more time. Of course the polls were simply showing what obviously they would, that of all these various candidates none of them strengthened Johnson's position, and Hubert Humphrey was a wash." One night over coffee, showing his brother Sam Houston one of the polls, Johnson declared: "Look here. I don't need that little runt to win. I can take anybody I damn please."[48]

Yet Johnson couldn't just put Kennedy to one side. In June, Bill Moyers heard from a reliable source in Atlantic City that "Bobby's boys are all over the place . . . making plans to stage a kind of 'Stevenson in 1960' rally here in an effort to steamroller the convention." During the last week of July, a month before the Democratic convention, Johnson worried that a twenty-minute film tribute to JFK on the first night might stir emotions that would lead to Bobby's nomination against his wishes. Despite a state-by-state analysis of convention delegations showing that, even with a big push, Kennedy would fall well short of a vice-presidential nomination, Johnson had the convention's arrangements committee shift the film to the last night when it couldn't affect anything.

By the end of July, however, Kennedy had decided to resign as Attorney General and run for a U.S. Senate seat from New York. After he described his plans to five friends and relatives, Kenny O'Donnell persuaded him to hold off announcing it so that liberals could use the leverage of a possible Kennedy bid to force Johnson into taking Humphrey.[49]

Despite everything working against Kennedy's nomination, including a presidential veto over who held the job, Johnson couldn't abandon the thought that the convention might spontaneously choose him. "What Lyndon Johnson and his associates went through in the . . . Convention reflected absolute paranoia on their part regarding Bobby Kennedy and people like me," Larry O'Brien says. Though O'Brien calls Johnson's concerns "ridiculous" and "ludicrous," Johnson saw Bobby's public silence on the vice presidency as a demonstration of ongoing hope that he might be chosen against the President's wishes.[50]

Johnson now developed a plan to eliminate Kennedy from the running. On July 27, he called him and arranged a meeting at the White House on July 29 at 1 p.m. The care with which Johnson prepared for their talk testifies to how much importance he placed on it. He discussed the matter at length with Jim Rowe and Clark Clifford, both old friends and two of Washington's most seasoned attorneys and Democratic party war-horses. Clifford gave the President a memo of talking points, which lay on Johnson's desk as he and Kennedy spoke. Instead of sitting on a sofa by the fireplace, his

usual custom for making a guest feel relaxed and welcome, Johnson
sat formally at his desk with Bobby in a straight-back chair alongside
it. By conducting the talk at his desk, Johnson not only established
his dominance—a sort of teacher-to-pupil relationship—he was also
able to tape the discussion and, he believed, bar Kennedy from putting out a version that would be too self-serving or in any way injurious to him. Convinced that Johnson was taping the discussion,
Kennedy later dictated his own record of the talk.[51]

Johnson's memorandum of what he said emphasized his regard
for Kennedy, his belief that he had a bright political future, which
he wished to further, and his willingness to appoint him Ambassador
to the U.N. or another government job in which he would be hap-
piest. Johnson made clear, however, that he would not ask him to be
Vice President. The decisive consideration was Goldwater's nomination, which made it imperative that the ticket counter his strength
in the South, Southwest, Border States, and Middle West. Johnson
also recorded himself as asking for Kennedy's help leading up to the
convention on August 24 and during the subsequent national campaign. In his memoirs, Johnson said he told Kennedy that no member
of the President's Cabinet should be considered for the vice-
presidential nomination. Johnson also remembered that as they
walked to the door Bobby "said words to this effect: 'Well, I'm sorry
that you've reached this conclusion, because I think I could have been
of help to you.' I said: 'Well, I think you *will* be of help to us—and
to yourself too.' "[52]

Kennedy's recollection of the conversation stressed other things.
He remembered that it went on for about forty-five minutes, the first
three of which were given over to Johnson's explanation of why he
didn't want him as Vice President. Bobby also recalled Johnson's
hopes for his future and the President's offer to give him any other
job he wished, but urged him to stay on at the Justice Department,
where he had such a good staff. Kennedy was "shocked" to hear him
speak critically of his own staff, "of people who had been so loyal to
him. Just as much as anything else, it convinced me that I could not
have worked closely with him." Kennedy said that Johnson then
spoke to him about running the campaign and that he declined, explaining that it would be inappropriate for an Attorney General to
do so. The rest of the conversation was largely focused on the Bobby
Baker case, which Kennedy raised.[53]

For twenty-four hours after their talk, Johnson explored ways
to make Kennedy's exclusion public. He wanted Bobby to announce
that he was taking himself out of the race. Johnson sent Mac Bundy
to ask Kennedy to make such a statement. But Bobby wouldn't do it,

saying "it wasn't true" and would upset those who had been urging him to run. The next day, Johnson asked Ken O'Donnell about a withdrawal statement from Kennedy, but O'Donnell repeated Bobby's response to Bundy. Consequently, at 6 p.m. that evening, Johnson put out his own statement, declaring that no one in the Cabinet or who met with the Cabinet, meaning Adlai Stevenson and Sargent Shriver, would be considered for the vice presidency. Johnson said it would be too great a distraction from running their respective departments.[54]

Robert Kennedy made light of his conversation with Johnson, joking with disappointed associates, "Aw, what the hell, let's go form our own country." That weekend, he was " 'very matter of fact' about the Johnson meeting and 'quite funny' about the subsequent stages. He set forth a number of possible comments if reporters asked about the exclusion of the Cabinet: 'I am sorry that I had to take so many fellows down with me' or ... 'I swear to the best of my knowledge I am not now and have never been a member of the Cabinet on the ground that it might tend to eliminate me.' "

Yet he was also angry at being turned aside by Johnson and at the thought that the President may have taped their conversation. After the meeting, when he ate lunch at the Sans Souci restaurant with O'Brien and O'Donnell, he said: " 'He told me he wouldn't take me under any circumstances and that's it.' He [Bobby] was kind of laughing. He was mad but laughing." When Bundy presented Johnson's request for a statement, Bobby became angry at Bundy for what he saw as an act of "inexplicable disloyalty."[55]

Kennedy's anger expressed the feelings of a proud man who was locked in an unresolvable feud with a powerful enemy. Yet he should not have been surprised at LBJ's rough treatment. He surely understood that for Johnson this was payback time, the chance for a thin-skinned adversary who remembered all their differences, imagined and real, to retaliate. Indeed, up to this point, Bobby didn't have much to complain about. True, Johnson's ploy about the Cabinet was silly, and his fears that Bobby would be nominated against his will also made little sense. Yet Bobby was intentionally provoking him: He knew Johnson would never put him on the ticket and that his refusal to step aside was a thorn in Johnson's side.

If the matter had ended with Johnson's announcement on July 30, neither man would have had much of a case against the other. But Johnson's exaggerated concern with Bobby moved him to inflict a public humiliation on Kennedy that would ill-serve him. Having consigned him to the outer circle or put his ambitions on hold while Johnson ran the government, the President, who was seventeen years older and held the upper hand politically, could have now put the vice-presidential issue and tensions between them to rest at no cost to himself. Indeed, had he acted generously toward Kennedy at this point, it would have registered on the press and the public as acts of decency by a large-hearted man.

Instead, Johnson, with a vindictiveness that spoke poorly of himself and demeaned the high office he held, ridiculed Bobby in the press. On July 31 he invited three Washington reporters from the *New York Times, New York Herald Tribune*, and *Washington Post* to have lunch with him in his private quarters at the White House. During four hours of drinking and eating, the President held forth on the vice presidency and the difficult decision he faced. Johnson acted as if he had carried off a coup that had restored his political control. Showing the reporters telegrams from the fifty state Democratic party chairman endorsing his announcement about the Cabinet, Johnson emphasized their support for what he had done.

He then recounted his meeting with Kennedy. It was an enthralling tale performed with facial expressions, gestures, and mimicry. For his audience, it was like an afternoon in the theater. Bobby's pained expression at hearing the news, his bobbing Adam's apple, which "bounded up and down like a yo-yo," his "funny voice," which reminded Johnson of how he must have sounded when he was in a similar situation to Bobby's in 1960, were presented in graphic detail.

Johnson's account of events immediately became the lead topic of discussion among Washingtonians and a prominent item in the press. It understandably enraged Kennedy, who, at their next meeting, objected to Johnson's breach of confidence. When Johnson denied talking to the reporters, Bobby accused him of lying. Johnson said he would check his calendar to see if he had forgotten such a conversation.[56]

Johnson had no regrets about getting rid of Bobby or settling accounts with him. "Now that damn albatross is off my neck," he told an aide after disposing of the "Bobby problem." Though this issue was settled, Johnson would spend the rest of the campaign and his presidency trying to emerge from the Kennedy shadow. Indeed, with Goldwater as his opponent, Johnson's campaign was as much an effort to separate himself from the Kennedys and establish himself as the country's and his party's leader as it was to defeat the Republicans.

More immediately, an end to Bobby's candidacy freed Johnson to encourage speculation about the vice-presidential nominee. His conversation with the three reporters included a lengthy discourse on the virtues and defects of the various candidates. Adlai Stevenson would be best for the job, but by the end of eight years he would be seventy-two. Johnson said he had polls showing that every one of the many candidates he was considering, and whose names he ticked off, "would hurt him in some way. In other words, he would do better in the November election if he had no running mate." Having freed himself of Kennedy and the fear that he might lose control of his party, he couldn't resist the grandiose conclusion that no one deserved to be his second-in-command. It was also a way to baffle reporters, get them writing about Johnson's problem in choosing a Vice President, and stir public interest in what would happen at the Democratic convention beginning on August 24. But before he got to the convention and subsequent campaign, Johnson felt compelled to answer doubts about Vietnam.[57]

The Tonkin Gulf Resolution

By June of 1964 Vietnam had become a constant low-level irritant to Johnson. At home, the public and many in the Congress seemed indifferent or bewildered by the war; a few senators cautioned against deeper involvement; and Barry Goldwater complained about the administration's weak response to the Communist challenge. In Vietnam itself there was no immediate prospect of a stable regime capable of resisting attacks without continuing and probably greater U.S. military and economic support.

Johnson's preference in the middle of June was to put the problem on hold until after the November election. He had no intention of letting Vietnam go, but he hoped for a respite from politically distracting decisions during the campaign.

Bill Bundy, State's Assistant Secretary for East Asian Affairs, drafted a memo, "Alternative Public Positions for U.S. on Southeast Asia for the Period July 1–November 15." It was agreed that the U.S. would need "to make its position on Southeast Asia as clear and strong as possible in the next five months." But "the immediate watershed decision" was whether to seek a congressional resolution giving the President "general authority . . . to defend the peace and security of the area."

Johnson's answer was "No." He wanted to keep the issue out of the campaign. To be sure, ongoing efforts to educate the American public to the importance of the struggle and support for Saigon against its foes might produce unanticipated developments, but Johnson hoped that none of this would compel a more assertive policy or force a domestic debate.[58]

In April 1964, Johnson had moved Michael Forrestal, a member of the National Security Council staff, to the State Department as a special assistant to Dean Rusk on Vietnam. At that time, Johnson "did everything to convey to his associates that their principal job in foreign affairs was to keep things on the back burner." Because he didn't trust the State Department, Forrestal says, Johnson "wanted his own man over there to be sure those damned fools didn't do something stupid while he was out in the hustings trying to get elected. And the instructions were 'Keep the lid on. I don't want to have headlines about some accident in Vietnam. And if I do, Forrestal, it will be your fault.' "[59]

Yet, however much Johnson wished to deemphasize the issue, Vietnam was not a problem that would even temporarily go away. If, for example, the North Vietnamese thought his administration was immobilized during the presidential campaign, Johnson believed it could mean the demise of South Vietnam. Nor did he dare risk having American voters view him as ineffective in dealing with the Communist threat. At the end of May, during a meeting in the Cabinet Room, he scribbled on a paper: "Do all we can to stabilize strengthen effective and efficient resistance to Viet Cong envelopment. Appeal to UN, appeal to SEATO, appeal [to] all allies."[60]

At the same time, he resisted advice for prompt, greater U.S. efforts to save South Vietnam. His objective was not to abandon the fight but to put decisions on hold. To this end, he told U.N. Ambassador Adlai Stevenson at the end of May, "I shudder at getting too deeply involved there and everybody thinks that's the only alternative." Stevenson replied: "Well, I've been shuddering on this thing for three years, and I'm afraid we're in a position now where you don't have any alternative, and it's a hell of an alternative. It really gives me the shakes."[61]

Johnson asked Richard Russell for his advice as well. Russell said, If you asked me to settle the Vietnam problem "as I saw fit, I would respectfully decline.... It's the damn worse mess I ever saw. ... I knew we were gonna get in this sort of mess when we went in there, and I don't see how we're ever gonna get out without fightin' a major war with the Chinese.... I just don't know what to do." Johnson declared: "That's the way I've been feelin' for six months." Russell thought that the South Vietnamese could not be relied on to fight for themselves; he expected conditions to deteriorate and didn't think the American people would agree to send U.S. troops. Russell suggested finding a South Vietnamese leader who would ask us to leave.

Johnson asked: "How important is it to us?" Russell answered: "It isn't important a damn bit," except maybe from "a psychological

standpoint." Johnson agreed and launched into a defense of U.S. involvement. "From the standpoint that we are party to a treaty
[SEATO], and if we don't pay any attention to this treaty, why I
don't guess they think we're payin' attention to any of them." Russell
agreed that honoring our word and saving our face were important.
Johnson said his advisers thought that "we got to show some power
and some force." They didn't think we had "much choice. We're
treaty-bound; we're there; this'll be a domino that'll kick off a whole
list of others; we just got to prepare for the worst." Johnson was
worried that the American people would rebel against having our
boys killed in a war they didn't understand.

Johnson saw nothing to do but hold the line. It chilled him to
think of sending American boys to die in Vietnam. But arguments in
behalf of neutralization or appealing to the United Nations or holding
an international conference impressed him as unrealistic. And Russell,
who believed it a terrible mistake to get more deeply involved, didn't
know what to do. "I wish I could help ya," Russell concluded. "God
knows, I do. It's a terrific quandary that we're in over there. We're
just in the quicksands up to our very necks." Johnson wanted Russell
to stand up in the Senate and urge U.S. withdrawal. If he did that,
LBJ told Moyers, it "could protect me against Goldwater throughout
the South," and it would help him if he ever had to get out. But
Russell, who was genuinely torn about what to do, wouldn't go on
record.[62]

Later that day, Johnson covered the same ground with Mac
Bundy. He pressed Bundy, who was urging stronger action, for constructive answers. "The more I stayed awake last night thinking about
this thing," Johnson said, "the more ... it looks like to me we're gettin' into another Korea. . . . I don't think it's worth fightin' for and I
don't think we can get out. And it's just the biggest damn mess. . . .
I look at this sergeant of mine this morning; he's got six little ole
kids and ... what in the hell am I ordering him out there for. What
in the hell is Vietnam worth to me. . . . What is it worth to this country?" But Johnson immediately acknowledged that we had a treaty
and "of course, if you start running [from] the Communists, they may
just chase you right into your own kitchen." The dilemma, Bundy
said, "is what that half of the world is going to think if this thing
comes apart on us." Johnson agreed. Mansfield's proposal for neutralization, he said, showed "no spine at all."[63]

On June 1, George Smathers told Johnson that nobody he spoke
to in Congress thought "we ought to fight a war in that area of the
world. To start committin' more and more is just got everybody really
worried." Johnson quoted the Republican answer: "We can't retreat,

because . . . it'll be very disastrous to the United States to give up all of our interests in Southeast Asia. . . . The Chinese are very aggressive, and, if you run from 'em, why, we'd of run out of Greece and Turkey a long time ago. . . . If we show some strength, we may have a chance to hold on."

On June 12, Johnson made clear that he had no intention of leaving or expanding the war in Vietnam. He seized upon a visit by Germany's Chancellor Ludwig Erhard to announce their mutual opposition to Hanoi's aggression against Saigon and determination to support the South Vietnamese against the Viet Cong.

Privately, Johnson asked *New York Times* columnist James Reston what he would do about Vietnam. Nothing big can be done there over the long haul, Reston replied, without the acquiescence of China. In the short run, however, he saw no choice but to do what we had been doing. "We can't get out and we can't go smashing into China à la Mr. Goldwater." Johnson agreed: "That's exactly the way I look at it," he said. "We won't abandon Saigon, and we don't intend to send in U.S. troops." Instead, he was working day and night to hold the line and keep the South Vietnamese government as stable as possible.

At a news conference on June 23, when Johnson announced General Maxwell Taylor's replacement of Lodge as ambassador, he reiterated America's determination to stand fast against aggression in Southeast Asia. Assuring the world that the United States "seeks no wider war," he also emphasized that we would not be weak or timid in meeting our obligations to a besieged ally. During the last week in June, when Republican senators and congressmen attacked the administration for a no-win policy in Vietnam and journalists described the United States as vacillating between a tough and a soft line, Johnson urged an aide to make clear to reporters that "we are where we were on November 22" and to get "appropriate experts" to come up with "new projects" that affirm "our determination not to retreat from this area."[64]

In the first half of July, Johnson considered making a nationally televised talk on Vietnam that, in Bill Moyer's words, "could de-fuse a Goldwater bomb before he ever gets the chance to throw it." Moyers reminded Johnson that they had "talked for some time about your making a special 'Report to the Nation' on Viet-Nam, particularly if some action were needed to enlarge the scope of the war." But Moyers thought Johnson should do this before the Republican convention met in mid-July and Goldwater introduced his "strategy of *forcing you to talk about Viet-Nam* and also, in effect, actually admitting that Viet-Nam is a political issue."[65]

At the same time Johnson worried about meeting a Goldwater challenge to his Vietnam policy, General Khanh in Saigon pressed him to step up efforts against Hanoi or to "go north." Maxwell Taylor was so fearful of a Khanh resignation and South Vietnamese overtures to the Communists for a negotiated settlement that he proposed joint contingency planning for bombing North Vietnam. Taylor also asked for several thousand additional military advisers, which Johnson agreed to send.[66]

Worse yet from Johnson's perspective was a growing feeling of discontent in the United States about his Vietnam policy. In late July a Gallup poll recorded 58 percent of Americans as favoring a U.N. army to deal with the problems of Southeast Asia. Fifty-two percent of the sample said they thought the United States was handling affairs in Vietnam as well as could be expected, while 38 percent believed matters were being "badly" handled. A Lou Harris poll was even more discouraging to the White House. Fifty-eight percent of the country was negative and only 42 percent positive about the job the administration was doing in Vietnam. Moreover, where Harris found a 64 to 36 percent lead for Johnson in the presidential race against Goldwater, he saw a five point drop in support for LBJ or a 59 to 41 percent split on who voters trusted more to deal effectively with the conflict in Southeast Asia. "Vietnam was clearly an issue working for Goldwater," Harris said.[67]

By the end of July, Johnson was eager to bolster South Vietnamese morale, put Hanoi on additional notice of U.S. determination to stand fast, and deprive the Republicans of any advantage they hoped to gain from Vietnam in the campaign. To help advance the first two goals, the administration increased secret military efforts known as Operation 34-A, raids on the coast of North Vietnam by South Vietnamese commandos and U.S. advisers, and DE SOTO patrols by U.S. destroyers gathering electronic and other military intelligence and making a "show of force" to Hanoi.[68]

During the night and early morning of July 30–31, a 34-A operation took place against two North Vietnamese islands in the Gulf of Tonkin. The following day the USS *Maddox*, an American destroyer, began a DE SOTO patrol in the same area. On Sunday morning, August 2, three North Vietnamese torpedo boats attacked the *Maddox* in international waters sixteen miles from the coast. The *Maddox*, supported by planes from the aircraft carrier *Ticonderoga*, hit back, sinking one and damaging another of the North Vietnamese boats.[69]

George Ball and Senator J. William Fulbright later said that the stepped up operations in July and August were meant to provoke

Hanoi into a response that would allow the United States to begin air attacks on North Vietnam. Fulbright, in fact, held this view at the time of the attack. In a telephone conversation on the morning of August 3, Fulbright told Ball that "he was a little suspicious and thought probably that the incident was asked for."[70]

But McNamara and the Bundys dispute that. MacNamara told his biographer Deborah Shapley: "I don't believe that the president, or I, or Dean Rusk, or Mac Bundy were planning, in the sense of anticipating or embarking upon 'overt war' with North Vietnam in 1964. I know that the president didn't intend 'overt war' and I didn't intend 'overt war' in 1964. Johnson didn't have plans for military action other than to continue on as we were."

Likewise, Mac Bundy told Shapley, Johnson "didn't want to take decisions on this issue [Vietnam] in an election year. He was extremely careful about timing and speeches. There was great frustration [among the advisers] because you couldn't get a decision out of him." At a 1991 roundtable discussion on Vietnam, Bundy remembered telling a CIA official in 1964: " 'We know we're not going to do a goddamn thing [about Vietnam] while this goddamn election is going on. Can we make it that far?' " The CIA man remembers Bundy asking: "Can we get through this goddamn election without making a big thing out of Vietnam?" The official predicted that "we will just barely squeak through if we're lucky."

Bill Bundy remembers that on August 1 he began a ten-day vacation with the understanding that Johnson "would not make any new major decision, or . . . seriously consider expanding the war, at least until after the election." Bundy believes that his "state of mind was a full reflection of the Washington policy circle. Trouble was the last thing we expected. We were muddling through with our fingers crossed."[71]

Johnson's response to the August 2 attack in the Gulf bears out the assertions of MacNamara and the Bundys. Though Johnson was determined to show Hanoi that the United States would not be intimidated, his initial impulse was to play down the incident and keep it from escalating into a confrontation that would agitate unwanted questions about military action during the presidential campaign.

On the morning of August 2, when he met with State Department and military advisers, he "sounded bewildered about what had happened; he couldn't understand why they [the North Vietnamese] had done it. . . . He certainly didn't say, 'The sons of bitches, what do they think they're doing?' . . . He changed the subject to the postal pay bill. We spent about fifteen minutes discussing the postal pay bill, this unique group of advisers on postal pay. The President turned to General Earle C. Wheeler [Chairman of the Joint Chiefs] and said: 'General, you are my chief strategic adviser. If you saw this postal pay bill marching down Pennsylvania Avenue, how would you handle it?' ... We all felt greatly relieved," Tom Hughes, State's director of intelligence, recalled, "that we'd been at one high point of history or another, though we didn't know whether it was the attack on the Gulf of Tonkin or the postal pay bill."[72]

The conversation was Johnson's way of saying that he didn't want to turn the August 2 attack into anything more than it was: an incident in the ongoing struggle between Hanoi, Saigon, and Washington over the fate of South Vietnam. Johnson "was a chess master, although he didn't play the game," Jack Valenti says. "Johnson was always five moves down the board, and if he says to General Wheeler, 'What do you think about the postal thing?' it's because he's already playing the fifth move."[73]

On August 2 and 3, when the North Vietnamese said nothing in public about the attack, Johnson assumed that they also wanted to keep the incident from ballooning into something more. The President and all his principal advisers concluded that Hanoi had made a false connection between the 34-A operation on July 30–31 and the subsequent *Maddox* patrol. Believing that the *Maddox* had been part of the attacking force against their Tonkin Gulf islands, the North Vietnamese had felt compelled to attack the destroyer.

Seeing the incident as an error by Hanoi, the White House wanted to let the episode fade from view. At a meeting Johnson insisted not be seen as "high-level" with Rusk, McNamara, and Wheeler on the 3rd, it was agreed that no further immediate action was required. Moreover, to counter Hanoi's belief that the *Maddox* was part of the 34-A attack, McNamara, Bundy, and Ball discussed leaking information to clear up the mistake. To assure against additional problems of this sort, future patrols were to be more distant from where 34-A operations occurred. Confident that they were solving the problem, the administration, Bill Bundy says, made no plans "for the contingency of a new attack, no working groups were set up, and the general supposition was that this had been a one-shot event most unlikely to be repeated in the face of the clear and firm U.S. posture." To that end, Johnson announced on the 3rd that the Navy would continue patrols in the Gulf, now with two destroyers instead of one, and that U.S. forces would meet any future attack with the intent of destroying the attackers.[74]

Johnson and his advisers read Hanoi wrong. They could not believe that the North Vietnamese would be so foolish as to challenge U.S. military power head-on. Everyone from Johnson on down saw the destroyers in the Gulf as an intimidating force that would discourage Hanoi from further aggression or at least put them on notice that they would have to deal directly with American power if their campaign of subversion continued against the South. The North Vietnamese viewed the American ships not as a deterrent but rather as a target or an opportunity to tell Washington that it would not be inhibited by U.S. power in pursuit of its vital national interest, the unification of all Vietnam under its control.

The American ship commanders in the Gulf had a clearer understanding of Hanoi's intent. The commander of the *Maddox* reported on the morning of August 4 that intercepts of North Vietnamese communications showed that a 34-A operation on the previous night made all U.S. ships in the gulf, though some sixty miles out in international waters, belligerents in the eyes of Hanoi. At 7:40 p.m. that evening (7:40 a.m. in Washington) the *Maddox* reported preparations by North Vietnamese torpedo boats to attack it and the *Turner Joy*, its companion destroyer.

When Democratic congressional leaders met with the President for a weekly legislative breakfast discussion, Johnson told them about the possible attack. They agreed that military action and a congressional resolution supporting the President should be the response to any clash. After the meeting, Johnson and Kenny O'Donnell discussed the political consequences of military retaliation, and they agreed that unless Johnson acted forcefully he would open himself to charges of weak leadership by Goldwater and the Republican right.

Johnson then conferred with House Majority Leader Carl Albert of Oklahoma, whom he asked to stay after the other leaders left. During their discussion, McNamara phoned the President with a report that the two destroyers were under attack by torpedo boats. Albert heard Johnson say: "They have? Now, I'll tell you what I want. I not only want those patrol boats that attacked the *Maddox* destroyed, I want everything at that harbor destroyed; I want the whole works destroyed. I want to give them a real dose."[75]

After Albert left, Johnson went to see Mac Bundy in his office. "You know that resolution your brother's been talking about for the past few months?" Johnson said. "Well, now's the time to get it through the Congress." Bundy didn't think it wise to move so fast. He remembers saying "something like, 'Mr. President, that seems too fast to me' [or] 'Mr. President, let's think about this.'" But Johnson had made up his mind and didn't want any discussion. He told Bundy: "'I didn't ask you that question,'" or "'No, I'm not asking for a discussion; I want you to do it.'" But whatever the President's exact words, it was clear to Bundy that Johnson "had already decided the other way," and he wanted him "to climb on board." Either before or right after seeing Bundy, Johnson arranged for the television networks to give him time in the evening to announce his response to the North Vietnamese attack.[76]

During two midday meetings with his principal national security and foreign policy advisers, Johnson mapped out a military response. They agreed to an air strike against North Vietnamese torpedo boat bases. The discussion, Mac Bundy told George Reedy, "was marked by thoroughness, clarity, and an absence of significant disagreement." By now, everyone was "on board," and Johnson was fully in command. "How is his nibs taking it?" James Reston asked George Ball on the phone the next day. "Extremely well," Ball replied. "He is the kind of guy that thrives on crises in the sense that he seems more cool and relaxed when he has real decisions to make than he does otherwise."[77]

The straight line toward retaliation hit a snag in the afternoon of the 4th when the *Maddox* commander raised doubts that an attack had taken place. At 1:27 p.m. the ship sent word that "a review of the action makes many reported contacts and torpedoes fired 'appear doubtful.' 'Freak weather effects' on radar, and over-eager sonarmen may have accounted for many reports. 'No visual sightings' have been reported by the *Maddox*, and the commander suggests that a 'complete evaluation' be undertaken before any further action."[78]

Though the commander of U.S. Pacific forces quickly assured Washington that an attack had taken place, despite some inaccurate sonar reports, Johnson and McNamara wanted guarantees that they were not responding to a phantom battle. What added to the uncertainty were doubts that Hanoi would open itself to retaliation by again attacking U.S. ships in international waters. At a meeting early the next morning, Mac Bundy expressed bewilderment at North Vietnam's motives. Walt Rostow described Hanoi's action as "extremely difficult to explain."

Likewise, when Ball and Reston discussed the Gulf clash on the telephone, they saw no rational basis for North Vietnam's attack. "Let's don't bring reason into this," Reston said. "What we are seeing now makes no sense for them to move from the kind of war where they had all the advantages to the kind of war where we have all the advantages. This seems to me very puzzling." Ball thought they might just be acting "irrationally. That they have these boats and they misjudged the American psychology as to some extent Khrushchev misjudged the American psychology in placing the missiles in Cuba. It seems such an irrational act."[79]

On the afternoon of the 4th, Johnson asked McNamara for a

prompt report on whether the attack had occurred. Shortly after 4 p.m. McNamara spoke with Admiral Sharp, the commander of Pacific forces in Honolulu. Sharp summarized "the latest dope we have" as "a sort of ambush attempt by the PTs," and "it [the report] said initial ambush attempt was definite." When McNamara asked if there was "any possibility there was no attack," Sharp said, "Yes, I would say there is a slight possibility. . . ." McNamara explained that "we obviously don't want to do it [retaliate] until we are damn sure what happened." Sharp promised to get him a "definite" report by 6:00 p.m.

During the next two hours, McNamara met with the Joint Chiefs "to marshal the evidence to overcome lack of a clear and convincing showing that an attack on the destroyers had in fact occurred. They conclude[d] that an attack had taken place." Their evidence was: illumination from automatic weapons fired at the *Turner Joy*, cockpit lights seen by one of the destroyers, shots fired by a North Vietnamese boat at two U.S. aircraft; a Hanoi announcement "that two of its boats were 'sacrificed,' " and "Sharp's determination [which came in to the Defense Department during the meeting] that there was indeed an attack."[80]

In meetings with the National Security Council and congressional leaders during the evening, Johnson treated the attack as a given and stated his determination to retaliate and eagerness for a supporting congressional resolution. "Do they want a war by attacking our ships in the middle of the Gulf of Tonkin?" Johnson asked the NSC. "No," CIA Director John McCone replied. "The North Vietnamese are reacting defensively to our attack on their off-shore islands. They are responding out of pride and on the basis of defense considerations. The attack is a signal to us that the North Vietnamese have the will and determination to continue the war. They are raising the ante."

Johnson saw no reason to back down. He asked: "Are we going to react to their shooting at our ships over 40 miles from our [sic] shores? If yes, we should do more than merely return the fire of the attacking ships. If this is so, then the question involves no more than the number of North Vietnamese targets to be attacked." Carl Rowan, the director of the U.S. Information Agency, tried to shift the discussion to proof that the attack had occurred. "Do we know for a fact that the North Vietnamese provocation took place? Can we nail down exactly what happened? We must be prepared to be accused of fabricating the incident." McNamara responded: "We will know definitely in the morning."[81]

Johnson's subsequent discussion with congressional leaders and public remarks during the next twenty-four hours assumed the reality of an attack, which U.S. forces had done nothing to provoke. Rusk, speaking for the President, declared to the leaders that "This was a serious decision to attack our vessels on the high seas.... It was planned to take place forty to sixty miles away from port.... We should not look on anything as accidental." If we don't respond, "they would misinterpret" our position in Southeast Asia.

Johnson asked congressional support not only for military action but also for a resolution backing a more general policy of firmness in Southeast Asia. "I don't think any resolution is necessary," Johnson said, "but I think it is a lot better to have it in the light of what we did in Korea." Remembering the growing opposition to Truman over the Korean fighting, which had gone forward without formal congressional endorsement, Johnson wanted to forestall any possible dissent by making Congress a collaborator on future steps in Vietnam. He also wanted assurances that the Congress would support a resolution without embarrassing debate. Republican House leader Charles Halleck predicted that it would pass "overwhelmingly," and Republican Senator Ralph Aiken said, with perhaps unintended irony, "By the time you send it [the resolution] up, there won't be anything for us to do but support you."[82]

Later that night, Johnson told the country in a televised speech about the "attack" in the Gulf and America's response. He described the assault as "a number of hostile vessels attacking two U.S. destroyers with torpedoes.... Aggression by terror against the peaceful villagers of South Viet-Nam has now been joined by open aggression on the high seas against the United States of America." The next day in a speech at Syracuse University, Johnson said: "The attacks were deliberate. The attacks were unprovoked. The attacks have been answered.... Aggression—deliberate, willful, and systematic aggression—has unmasked its face to the entire world."[83]

The same day Johnson sent the Tonkin Gulf Resolution to Congress. The document, which partly rested on resolutions passed in 1955, 1957, and 1962 backing executive policies toward Formosa, the Middle East, and Cuba, respectively, laid out the current challenge to peace and security in Southeast Asia from Hanoi and what seemed essential to combat it. The resolution gave congressional approval and support for all measures deemed necessary by the Commander in Chief to repel and counter future attacks on the Armed Forces of the United States. Further, it endorsed whatever the President believed necessary to assist members of SEATO asking help to defend their freedom. And third, it provided for expiration of the resolution when the President declared the peace and security of the area reasonably assured or when Congress passed a concurrent resolution repealing it. On August 7, after two days of hearings and brief debate, the resolution won unanimous approval in the House and passage in the Senate with only two dissenting votes.[84]

The two dissenters and some other senators who voted for the resolution worried that they were giving the President a blank check or a pre-dated declaration of war. When Senator Wayne Morse of Oregon, the most outspoken opponent of the resolution, told a Senate colleague his doubts, the latter replied: "Hell, Wayne, you can't get in a fight with the President at a time when the flags are waving and we're about to go to a national convention. All Lyndon wants is a piece of paper telling him we did right out there, and we support him, and he's the kind of president who follows the rules and won't get the country into war without coming back to Congress."[85]

Johnson entirely agreed. Though he described the resolution as being "like grandma's nightshirt—it covered everything," he had no intention then of using it to take the country into an undeclared war. He saw the bombing raid against North Vietnam and the resolution as principally serving two short-term purposes. They put both Saigon and Hanoi on notice of American resolve to stay the course in preserving an independent South Vietnam, and they deprived Goldwater of the chance to make Vietnam an issue in the campaign. Seizing the political advantage coming to him from the crisis, Johnson called Goldwater to ask his backing. Though he believed that Johnson might have invented the whole episode, Goldwater saw nothing to do but issue a statement saying "we cannot allow the American flag to be shot at anywhere on earth if we are to retain our respect and prestige."[86]

At the same time Johnson wanted Goldwater's support on the resolution, he also wished to sustain the belief that the senator was a reckless war hawk, while he was a prudent leader assuring the national security without rushing into a limited or full-scale war. During the campaign in September and October, he took pains to tell voters that he wasn't "ready for American boys to do the fighting for Asian boys." He was trying "to get the boys in Viet-Nam to do their own fighting with our advice and with our equipment. . . . So we are not going north and drop bombs at this stage of the game, and we are not going south and run out and leave it for the Communists to take over."

He had no intention of fighting against China's two-million-man army or of getting tied down in a land war in Asia, he added. When Moyers and Mac Bundy gave him the phrase, "We seek no wider war," for inclusion in his campaign speeches, Moyers recalls that LBJ was euphoric and never "more kindred with me." He called me at home and said: "That says exactly what we are going to do." As a demonstration of his balance, Johnson also declared that we would not withdraw. The goal remained to preserve South Vietnamese independence by providing materiel and advice.[87]

Johnson's statements provided an effective contrast to Goldwater. But they also expressed LBJ's genuine hopes for a limited part in Vietnam's conflict. He balanced these hopes, however, against the possibility of a wider role in the fighting, and he partly saw the Tonkin Resolution as an endorsement of that end. But his assessment of the resolution's use in the long run was badly skewed. Despite a sense of elation at having effectively handled a foreign crisis, the realm in which journalists were saying he didn't excel, his response to the August 4 episode was a time bomb waiting to explode.

First, there was the possibility of accusations that the attack in the gulf had never occurred. To be sure, with his Pacific commander and his Secretary of Defense assuring him that it had, Johnson had every reason to assume this was the case. Nevertheless, he had his doubts. As he later told George Ball "with disgust . . . , 'Hell, those dumb, stupid sailors were just shooting at flying fish!' "[88]

Though more than thirty years later no one can state with absolute certainty that an attack occurred, the bulk of the recent evidence suggests it did. Still, Johnson couldn't have known the full details of the case at the time. And so he went ahead, knowing full well that he might be acting on a false premise. But once the report of the attack had come in and he had asked the networks for air time and decided that now was the moment to get the congressional authorization he wanted on Vietnam, he wasn't going to back down.[89]

As Mac Bundy puts it: "Lyndon Johnson didn't want to fight a war without congressional authorization. He was a past master at questions of when and how you pass something through Congress. It was plain to him and to whomever he talked with about it on the Hill that attacks on ships on the high seas were a perfect reason for getting a resolution through. He'd made that decision without asking, 'Are you absolutely sure?' " And so when McNamara pressed Sharp for an answer, "it was McNamara asking on behalf of a president who had already committed himself to having a resolution and a speech and had the air time." Johnson had "made a political decision, confirmed it with Senator Russell, and the last thing he wanted to do was reexamine that."[90]

At the same time Johnson authorized air strikes against North Vietnam and won an endorsement from Congress over an incident he knew was in doubt, he also misled the public about American actions in the gulf. In describing Hanoi's attacks as deliberate, un-provoked aggression, he was conveniently omitting the 34-A opera-tions, which CIA Director McCone had told him were the basis for North Vietnam's attacks.

An even greater mistake on Johnson's part was assuming that the Tonkin Gulf resolution gave him congressional or any other kind of backing for a potentially wider struggle in Vietnam. It is true the resolution gave him a formal endorsement for using American power against Communist subversion in South Vietnam. But there had been no actual debate about committing substantially more American blood and treasure to a war in Southeast Asia. And as a keen student of American politics, who remembered the great debate of 1939–41 over America's response to the European war and FDR's reluctance to do anything without a stable consensus, Johnson should have known that a resolution rushed through Congress under crisis con-ditions could not be a firm basis for future escalation in an undeclared and ill-defined war.

"The real question of whether you wanted to stay and fight in Vietnam is much wider and deeper than what happens in the Gulf of Tonkin," Mac Bundy said later. "What we have here is a crossroads of the extraordinary qualities of Lyndon Johnson. It's nobody's busi-ness what you have to do to get a law; if you get the law, that does the job. Now that isn't true really, and he found it out to his great pain later because it was too easy for people to duck and bug out and find excuses, and say there wasn't a second shot or the torpedoes were going in a circle or whatever the hell they did say. Therefore, there's great imperfection in this enterprise, but it is a part of this extraor-dinary man's way of operation. There is no point in our ducking away from it."[91]

Johnson knew that all the most effective political leaders of his era cut corners—FDR, Truman, Eisenhower, Rayburn, JFK, and Nixon saw behind-the-scenes machinations as essential to some of their success. But knowing when political stealth would and would not work was central to their survival in high office. Beginning with the Tonkin Gulf resolution, the Vietnam conflict would test Johnson's judgment on the political limits of secret operations in foreign affairs.

Choosing a Vice President

The immediate response in the country to the bombing of North Vietnam and the Resolution elated Johnson. Eighty-five percent of Americans endorsed his actions, with 71 percent saying they thought the United States was handling affairs in South Vietnam as well as could be expected. Forty-eight percent of the country favored stronger measures, while only 14 percent wanted to negotiate a settlement and leave.[92]

Johnson now felt temporarily free to ignore Vietnam and focus his attention on the presidential campaign. With the Democratic convention opening on August 24, he wanted to savor the formalities leading up to his nomination and the attention his choice of a running mate commanded from the press and the public.

After the announcement that Robert Kennedy and the Cabinet were out of the running, Hubert Humphrey became the odds-on favorite. "Hubert, it's you," Adlai Stevenson called to say. Despite what Johnson had told Moyers, he and Humphrey had good relations dating from the 1950s when they had created a bridge between conservative and liberal Democrats. More important, Humphrey's presence on the ticket would give the country a competent second-in-command and would strengthen Johnson's electoral appeal in the Midwest and industrial Northeast.[93]

Humphrey had been campaigning for the job for months. The day of JFK's funeral he had told a friend that he might try to run with LBJ in 1964. Shortly after, he had told his closest advisers: "I want to become president, and the only way I can is to become vice president." All of his associates urged against tying himself to Johnson, warning that "he'd lose his freedom. We said Johnson would cut his balls off." But Humphrey saw the vice presidency as his only route to the White House and convinced his friends to begin a quiet campaign.

In January, Johnson had encouraged Humphrey by saying he "could take confidential soundings and scout for support for the vice presidency." Humphrey began asking for political and financial help and made himself Johnson's most reliable Senate ally. Johnson sent Jim Rowe to see Humphrey seven times about the vice presidency, assuring him, " 'Everything being equal, you're the candidate.' " Rowe subjected Hubert to what he called "the horse shedding." Johnson wanted to know: "How much money does your family owe? Where are the mortgages? Are there other women in your life?" Humphrey exploded at Rowe: "My God, I've been in public life twenty years. Everybody must know everything about me. Why do you ask these things?" Rowe answered: "Hubert, you're in the big leagues now. Every question I ask, the Republicans are going to be asking also."[94]

But Johnson already knew the answers. Hubert had no hidden liabilities. Johnson's objectives were to assure his control over Humphrey and create some drama at the Democratic convention by holding off a decision until the last minute. Despite his private messages to Humphrey, Johnson kept floating other names to the press during strenuous walks around the White House grounds in the summer heat. The physical stamina on display in his walks also helped him refute lingering doubts about his recovery from a 1955 heart attack.

As his friends had anticipated, Humphrey had to pay a high price for the privilege of becoming Johnson's lieutenant. Two weeks before the convention, Eric Goldman watched Humphrey eating lunch at the White House mess: "His face was that of a man who was being drained. These days he was telling friends the sad story of the girl whose hero was the handsome captain of the football team. He would keep phoning her—always to ask her opinion of some other girl and never for a date." In public, he handled his awkward situation as unrequited suitor with self-effacing good humor. "Nobody has to woo me," Humphrey told reporters. "I'm old reliable, available Hubert."[95]

Johnson kept Humphrey on tenterhooks until the last possible minute. Shortly before the convention, he sent Jim Rowe to grill him again about possible skeletons in his closet and to emphasize the President's insistence on absolute loyalty. At the end of their talk Rowe called Johnson and put Humphrey on the line: "You can rely on me," Humphrey said. "I will be loyal." Johnson thanked him, but made no commitment in return.[96]

On August 24, the first day of the convention, Johnson finally sent word through Rowe that Humphrey was his choice. But Rowe was instructed to reiterate Johnson's demand for unflagging loyalty. "You can be against me in our conferences until . . . I make up my mind," Rowe quoted the President, "then I want you to follow my policies." Rowe invited Humphrey to his room to await a call about plans to meet with Johnson at the White House the next day. When Walter Jenkins phoned to say that they would have to wait until tomorrow to fly to Washington, Humphrey, whose patience with Johnson's delaying tactics was exhausted, "blew his top . . . raised hell. Swore." Rowe calmed him down by saying: "Hubert, tonight you're just a senator from Minnesota but this time tomorrow night you'll be a candidate for vice president and then we can both tell Johnson he's a shit." At 1 a.m. Rowe called Humphrey to warn him that any leak would doom his candidacy.[97]

Humphrey's ordeal extended through most of the next day. At breakfast, he learned that Gene McCarthy, Hubert's ostensible rival for the job, had withdrawn his candidacy during the night. Johnson never forgave McCarthy's unwillingness to play out the game to the end. The President now convinced Senator Thomas Dodd of Connecticut to join Humphrey on the plane to Washington and encourage the illusion that Johnson was trying to decide between the two of them. "Is Tom Dodd being considered, too?" an exasperated Humphrey asked Rowe. No, no, Rowe assured him, "this is just a cover. It will keep the press off balance and continue the speculation. That's what the President wants." In Washington, Jack Valenti met them in a limousine, which drove aimlessly around downtown until television gave full coverage to Lady Bird's arrival at the convention. Then, they drove to the White House, where Dodd went in to see LBJ, while an exhausted Humphrey napped in the back of the limousine.[98]

At 5 p.m. a knock on the car door awakened Humphrey, who was taken to the Fish Room, outside the President's office. When Johnson appeared, he suggested they talk in the Cabinet Room, where, unknown to Humphrey, Johnson could tape their conversation. Johnson now went over the ground Humphrey had discussed repeatedly with Rowe about loyalty. Johnson emphasized what a terrible job he would be taking on and how the office would get in the way of their friendship, as it had with other Presidents and Vice Presidents. He wanted Hubert "to understand that this is like a marriage with no chance of divorce. I need complete and unswerving loyalty," Johnson said. Humphrey repeated his vows of fealty, and the bargain was finally sealed.

The hectoring and humiliation Johnson forecast began at once. "If you didn't know you were going to be vice president a month ago, you're too damn dumb to have the office," Johnson told him. He then suggested calling Muriel, Hubert's wife, to fill her in. "Muriel, how would you like to have your husband be the vice-presidential nominee?" Johnson asked. After she expressed proper enthusiasm and appreciation for the President's largesse, Johnson, in what an irritated Humphrey described as "his Texas idiom and style," said, "We're going to nominate your boy."

Johnson then ordered Humphrey, who was aching to tell the world, not to say anything to anyone. In effect, he had "to continue the charade of doubt, my words had to deny what was clearly on my face." Not until the next day, while Humphrey was being interviewed on a Minneapolis radio station, did the White House announce that the President was going to Atlantic City to recommend Humphrey's nomination. "Johnson had drained every bit of juice out of the nomination," Humphrey wrote later, "and he had drained a good deal out of me."[99]

Johnson's obsession with assuring Humphrey's obedience and conformity to his designs had some basis in political reality. A frus-

trated Vice President, as with John Nance Garner of Texas, FDR's
first number two, can be a burden to an ambitious President with
large plans. But Garner was the exception to the rule. Though no
Vice President had ever found much satisfaction in the job, they had
nevertheless kept their counsel and served in relative obscurity,
buoyed by thoughts of gaining the highest office at the end of their
terms. Johnson's insistence on "loyalty," however, had little to do with
fears that Hubert would become a political rival. Johnson knew that
Humphrey would warmly support almost everything he favored in
domestic affairs and that his ambition to be anointed as LBJ's successor would also keep him in line.

Something else was at work here. Johnson hated criticism or any
challenge to his authority. Everyone who worked for him was expected to be 100 percent a Johnson man, a loyalist who, whatever his
inner thoughts, would subordinate his views and ambitions to Johnson's. This is not to say that Johnson wanted only ciphers around
him. To the contrary, he valued having the services of "the best and
the brightest." But at the same time, he wanted them to bend the
knee, to take a back seat, to subordinate themselves to the President,
as aides had subordinated themselves to Johnson, the state director of
the Texas NYA, the congressman from the Tenth Texas District, and
the Senate Minority and Majority Leader.

Johnson knew that Humphrey's exceptional talents and experience made him an excellent President-in-waiting. He also understood
that Humphrey would be miserable, as he had been, in the do-
nothing job of Vice President. And so he wanted to be absolutely sure
that Hubert understood the ground rules. Working for Lyndon Johnson meant complying with his every demand. "I want people around
me," Johnson said repeatedly, "who would kiss my ass on a hot summer's day and say it smells like roses."

Humphrey accepted Johnson's conditions because he believed it
would make him President. The week after he was nominated, Humphrey told his brother that he wished their father, who had predicted
he would become President, were still alive. As his biographer puts
it, "that was the closest he came to saying what was on everybody
else's mind: that he was not only advancing to an office a heartbeat
away from the presidency but to four years as second man to a President whose heart had already once nearly stopped beating."[100]

Johnson's orchestration of Humphrey's nomination was reflective of his overall handling of the Democratic convention. He micromanaged everything. When he concluded that housing arrangements
in Atlantic City, for example, were being mismanaged and might
provoke antagonism among delegates, he ordered Walter Jenkins to

take charge of convention politics and brought old Texas friend Marvin Watson to the White House to oversee "all the housekeeping chores—the housing, getting people to and from places and the general operational aspect of the convention." Johnson "was like the mother of the bride," Eric Goldman remembered, "considering, controlling, fussing over every detail. This was to be *his* convention, leading to *his* triumph. He personally chose where his aides would stay . . . , and he supervised bloc by bloc the allotment of spectator's seats in the auditorium. He specified that a forty-foot photograph of himself would flank the stage; that he would be nominated," in unprecedented fashion, by "co-nominators" Pat Brown, the Catholic Governor of California, and John Connally, the Protestant Governor of Texas. And he arranged for the theme song of the convention, "Hello Lyndon," sung to the tune of "Hello Dolly." He also planned his acceptance speech for August 27, his fifty-sixth birthday, and a $1000-a-ticket party in his honor in the ballroom of Convention Hall.

Hubert Humphrey later said that the convention was, for all practical purposes, Johnson's production. "He wrote the music, choreographed the action, chose the stars, and virtually wrote their lines. What Lyndon wanted, Lyndon got. He accepted every cheer as adulation, and when it reached a crescendo, it seemed to erase the ghost of John Kennedy's presidency from his mind." Only later did anyone in the White House worry that Johnson's self-promotion might have produced a picture of an immodest President that could hurt him with the electorate.[101]

Humphrey's assumption that Johnson's triumph allowed him to emerge from JFK's shadow and see himself as President in his own right underestimated LBJ's enduring preoccupation with Kennedy's challenge to his legitimacy. The painfully insecure Johnson could not let go of the feeling that people were always comparing him to JFK and the Kennedy clan and finding him wanting. One can well imagine that if Jack Kennedy had not existed, Johnson would have invented him. In short, if it wasn't Kennedy—Jack or Bobby—Johnson would have found someone else to assign the role of a popular, self-confident rival directly or indirectly questioning Lyndon's right to hold the highest office.

Johnson's ongoing concern with the Kennedys expressed itself at the convention through his lingering fear that Bobby might yet steal the show and become the recipient of a spontaneous nomination to the vice presidency. To keep track of Kennedy's doings and bottle him up, Johnson asked the FBI to send a team of men to Atlantic City. Ostensibly, the thirty agents assigned to the squad were "to assist the Secret Service in protecting President Johnson and to ensure that the convention itself would not be marred by civil disruption."

The reality was different. The existence of the squad was hidden from the Secret Service and especially Attorney General Kennedy, whose "activities [in Atlantic City] were of special interest, including his contacts with [Martin Luther] King." When an FBI agent assigned to Kennedy arrived in Atlantic City, Cartha (Deke) DeLoach, Hoover's deputy overseeing operations there, told him: "There's some thought that Attorney General Kennedy might try to stampede the convention.... If he does that and he's got an FBI agent by his side, the President will not be too happy with the FBI organization, so you're to immediately leave Atlantic City."[102]

The objects of scrutiny were not only Bobby Kennedy but also civil rights activists who might disrupt the convention to force a stronger rights plank in the platform and the seating of a Mississippi Freedom Democratic Party (MFDP) delegation trying to displace a lily white, segregationist one. Though Kennedy and civil rights demonstrators were the initial focus of White House concern, by the time the convention began it had fixed on the conflict over who legitimately represented Mississippi. The White House feared a floor fight that would embarrass the party and the President and intensify a backlash that could cost the Democrats all over the country.[103]

Eager to show Johnson, who seemed likely to be in power for at least another four years, how effective the FBI could be, DeLoach left nothing to chance. For seven days beginning on August 22, the squad kept "the White House apprised of all major developments during the Convention's course." Using "informant coverage ... various confidential techniques," a wiretap on King's hotel room, and "a microphone surveillance of SNCC and CORE," and "infiltration of key groups through use of undercover agents, and ... agents using appropriate cover as reporters," DeLoach provided Jenkins with "44 pages of intelligence data" and "kept Jenkins and Moyers constantly advised by telephone of minute-by-minute developments."

DeLoach later claimed that the information he provided convinced the White House to "make major changes in controlling admissions into the Convention Hall and thereby preclude infiltration of the illegal ... MFDP delegates in large numbers into the place reserved for the regular Mississippi delegates." DeLoach also said that FBI counterintelligence gave the White House advance notice of all major MFDP, CORE, and SNCC plans, which was of "prime importance" in helping it deal with the problems they posed.[104]

The White House was understandably grateful for the bureau's work. After a telephone conversation with the President, Richard

Russell recorded: "Hoover has apparently been turned loose and is tapping everything—...He [Johnson] stated it took him hours each night to read them all (but he loves this)." Walter Jenkins called Hoover to convey the President's thanks, saying, "the job the Bureau had done in Atlantic City was one of the finest the President had ever seen." Jenkins also added: "There were a lot of bad elements up there, and because of the work some of the Bureau people did they knew exactly where they were and what they were doing and consequently, they were not able to be very effective."

Johnson commended Hoover for keeping "Walter Jenkins and Bill Moyers...constantly alerted to the actions of certain personalities and groups who, if left unchecked, would certainly have proved far more disruptive. The presence of your men, although completely unobserved by all except my immediate assistants, contributed tremendously to the successful outcome of the Convention." After Moyers sent DeLoach a "very thoughtful and generous note concerning our operation in Atlantic City," DeLoach expressed pleasure at having been "able to come through with vital tidbits from time to time which were of assistance to you and Walter."[105]

DeLoach and Jenkins later denied any wrongdoing on the FBI's part. The thirty-man squad had been sent to Atlantic City not to gather political intelligence but information "which would reflect on the orderly progress of the Convention and the danger to distinguished individuals, and particularly the danger to the President of the United States, as exemplified by the many, many references [to possible civil disturbances] in the memoranda furnished Mr. Jenkins." Jenkins said he didn't know about the wiretapping or bugging by the FBI and DeLoach had no memory of telling him about it.[106]

Nine months after Kennedy's assassination, it is understandable that the White House wished to take every precaution against dangers to the President. It was also accepted procedure for Johnson, who had limited trust in the Secret Service after Dallas, to rely on the FBI to assure his safety. But for anyone to argue that there was no political side to what DeLoach's men were doing in Atlantic City defies logic. Johnson surely hoped the FBI would provide an added measure of security and would help reduce chances of civil unrest at the convention. But he, Jenkins, Moyers, and other White House aides understood that the FBI's work in Atlantic City was partly helping Johnson head off political trouble from dissident civil rights activists at the convention, and especially from the MFDP.

Johnson was almost hysterical over the threat he believed the MFDP posed to the smooth functioning of the convention and the unqualified triumph he wanted. Before the convention began he had assigned Humphrey and Walter Reuther, head of the United Auto Workers, to resolve the problem without a public battle that would embarrass him and the party.

Liberal Washington attorney Joseph Rauh, who was representing the MFDP, got call after call from Humphrey and Reuther. Humphrey would say: "Joe, the President is very concerned about this, and I've got to tell him something." Rauh would reply: How can you seat a delegation headed by a governor who described the NAACP as "niggers, alligators, apes, coons, and possums?" Reuther, speaking for LBJ, began to predict that, if you force a floor fight, "we're going to lose the election." Rauh was incredulous, replying: "Are you serious? I mean, Goldwater has been nominated. How can you lose it?" Reuther, answering for himself and Johnson, said: "We both think the backlash is so tremendous that we're going to lose the election if you go through with this. You can't possibly win, but if you should win, the pictures of all the black delegates going in to replace the white is going to add to the backlash, and we are convinced that Goldwater will be president."[107]

Johnson kept close tabs on the developing debate. He "went right up the wall" over testimony before the convention's Credentials Committee from MFDP delegates Aaron Henry and Fannie Lou Hamer; they described beatings inflicted on them by civil rights opponents that won national attention. Johnson "told Humphrey bluntly that he was doing a lousy job." When an aide suggested that he could get around the problem by having some of the Mississippi delegates say they were ill and give their seats to MFDP replacements, Johnson talked to Jenkins in Atlantic City "in 'what if' ways, planting the idea of seeing if a substitution could be made."[108]

Although many of the FBI's reports to Jenkins focused on the MFDP problem, the information it provided was of little help in resolving the dispute. To be sure, the FBI summaries of wiretaps revealed the frustration of Martin Luther King and other civil rights leaders over the President's acceptance of the "legally" chosen Mississippi delegates, but they contributed little to the compromise that resolved the problem on the second day of the convention.

White House pressure on the Credentials Committee not to side with the MFDP was much more important in shaping the outcome of the conflict. An agreement required all regular Mississippi delegates to pledge allegiance to the ticket, to make two MFDP leaders delegates at large with full voting rights, and to agree to bar future delegations "from states where the Party process deprived citizens of the right to vote by reason of their race or color."[109]

The agreement allowed Johnson to turn the convention into the personal triumph he craved. Only the appearance of Bobby Kennedy on the last day detracted in his mind from the full measure of adulation he wanted and felt he deserved as President. Scheduled to introduce a film about his brother on Thursday evening, Kennedy and John Seigenthaler, an aide at the Justice Department, were led quietly into a small room under the platform, where they could see and hear nothing. Kennedy understood fully the challenge his appearance, despite its unimportance in the substantive decisions of the convention, presented to Johnson. Bobby said, "Would you check on the program? We can't hear anything back here. . . . I think Lyndon may just have put us back here with orders to forget us. They'll probably let us out day after tomorrow." When they got to the runway behind the platform, none of Lyndon's handpicked backers "was enthusiastic about coming and saying 'hello.' "

After a few minutes, Senator Henry (Scoop) Jackson, the presiding officer, motioned Kennedy forward. Seigenthaler remembered that "when Scoop introduced him, it hit. I mean it really hit. . . . It just went on and on and on." Seigenthaler stood in the midst of the ovation watching it reach "a new intensity every time that Robert Kennedy, standing with a wistful half-smile on his face, tried to bring it to an end. As Kennedy once more raised his hand to still the uproar, Jackson whispered to him, 'Let it go on. . . . Just let them do it, Bob. . . . Let them get it out of their system.' " After twenty-two minutes, he began what became the most memorable speech of the convention, particularly its ending quote from *Romeo and Juliet* Jackie Kennedy had given him:

> When he shall die
> Take him and cut him out in little stars
> And he will make the face of heaven so fine
> That all the world will be in love with night,
> And pay no worship to the garish sun.

Arthur Schlesinger wondered whether either Jackie or Bobby had "consciously noted the thrust of the last line."[110]

Johnson was absent during the JFK film and Bobby's speech. He was busy putting the finishing touches on his acceptance address. He showed up to hear Humphrey accept his nomination, with an attack on Goldwater's record that delighted the audience. Ticking off the important bills most Senate Democrats and Republicans had voted for, Humphrey repeatedly intoned, "but not Senator Goldwater," until the audience took up the chant of complaint against Goldwater's extremism.

Johnson followed with a speech that some have described as one of the worst of his political career. Eric Goldman, who helped write it, later said, "It contained not a single memorable phrase, no tang or vault, little to pull the delegates or the television audience out of their evening lethargy." An overnight telephone survey of reaction to the speech showed that it had been met with general indifference and had done nothing to hurt the President's image. Moreover, it did not dampen the enthusiasm of 4000 guests attending Lyndon's birthday party or the thousands more participating in a parade that ended at one o'clock in the morning with a huge fireworks display that lit the skies with a red, white, and blue portrait of LBJ.[111]

The Campaign

At the beginning of September, as the presidential campaign shifted into high gear, polls showed Johnson with a decisive lead. George Gallup's soundings of voter sentiment from late July to the end of August gave the President a consistent two-to-one advantage over Goldwater. In the middle of September, Gallup found that Johnson had an astonishing 69 percent to 31 percent lead. By the first week of October, a month before the election, the President continued to command twice as many votes as his seemingly hapless opponent.[112]

The polls were a source of satisfaction to LBJ. They fed fantasies of winning the greatest popular victory in presidential history, larger than the 60.3 percent won by Warren Harding in 1920 and the 60.8 percent won by FDR in 1936. And there is no doubt that Johnson badly wanted the record. But when it came to setting campaign strategy, Johnson's highest priority was to assure a victory that not only reduced conservative influence in the country but also gave him an identity as a President in his own right. He wanted an endorsement from the electorate that said we are voting for Lyndon Johnson not because of his connections to John F. Kennedy but because he is someone whose attributes seem likely to make him a great President.

Though every political indicator pointed to Johnson's election, he refused to take anything for granted. Quite the contrary, he assumed the worse. Instead of fixing on the evidence suggesting a big victory, he seized upon every hint of trouble and every pessimistic or cautionary analysis projecting a close and possibly even a losing race. "I don't think we ever really relaxed in that campaign," Jack Valenti says. "I know the President didn't. He felt like that anything could go awry.... We knew that the other side was getting increasingly desperate, and when an opponent is desperate they'll do anything to win, so that worried us.... I would say that there was never a real feeling of 'Well, we've got it won, we can relax now.'... Just the opposite happened; as any wily, experienced politician knows, you always run scared and Johnson did that."[113]

Besides, the Johnson camp believed that Goldwater and his backers were extremists who would do terrible things to the country if they won. In mid-July, immediately after the Republican convention, Cornelius Vanderbilt, who had sat through the "well-rigged" proceedings, urged Valenti to tell Johnson that *"the entire buildup of the GOLDWATER group follows the line of the Nazis, pre-WWII. ... The President has got to know the kind of enemy we are fighting. ... These people will stop at nothing.... There is only one way of getting rid of this pest and that is to ... attack him as he is attacking Mr. Johnson, and we liberals.*" Others echoed Vanderbilt's concerns. Republican Senator Margaret Chase Smith of Maine, an old Johnson friend and Goldwater rival, expressed outrage at Goldwater's tactics in San Francisco and at his intention to "purge" a moderate Republican ally who had opposed him. The political journalist Richard Rovere described the Goldwaterites at the convention "as hard as nails. The spirit of compromise and accommodation was wholly alien to them." They aimed at "a total ideological victory and the total destruction of their critics.... They wished to punish as well as to prevail."[114]

A California "advertising man" who "studied" the Goldwater-Rockefeller primary in the state, confirmed White House opinion that the President was up against an unbalanced character who would do almost anything to win. *"I'm afraid Democrats don't realize that unless President Johnson fights a tough, no-holds-barred campaign, he's going to lose the election,"* this man wrote Valenti in late July. In California, the "Goldwater people fought with a TV campaign that was masterful, with door-to-door organization, with some of the most distorted appeals I've ever seen or heard, and with fanatical zeal.... President Johnson cannot, as Rockefeller did, settle for vague words, and campaign quietly as the President of all the people.... He's got to get out and fight."[115]

Additional confirmation of Johnson's concerns came from other sensible people who could not be seen as alarmists. They feared Goldwater's extremism and worried that he might find a way to win. In September, a survey of the nation's 12,000 psychiatrists revealed that only 657 of them saw Goldwater as fit to be President, with 1,189 saying he suffered from paranoia and was unfit to serve. The distinguished historian Richard Hofstadter gave credence to these fears by urging Americans to view right-wing "agitation as a kind of vocational therapy" or the product of nonrational thought. Ed Weisl, a staid New York attorney with a reputation for moderation, warned LBJ that a rising backlash against the administration's stand on civil rights made polls an unreliable measure of voter feeling and urged him not to take New York or any other state for granted.[116]

In deciding on how best to win in November, Johnson also took account of specific information on what Goldwater intended to emphasize in his campaign. Relying on an inside report of thinking in the Republican high command, Johnson learned in August that Goldwater would push four themes: "race, corruption, nostalgia, and nationalism."

Goldwater was planning "a passive exploitation" of the race issue, which, in a time of prosperity, might allow him to break Johnson's hold on the northern workingman's vote. Second, he would emphasize the President's ties to Bobby Baker and try to take advantage of Johnson's reputation as someone who had used political power for self-serving purposes. Third, Goldwater would appeal to the "little people" or the "forgotten majority" who belonged to none of the organized pressure groups representing "Big Business, Big Labor, and Big Government. . . . There will be the usual laments for the old, simpler America." Finally, he would try to exploit disenchantment with foreign aid and foreign policy and general antagonism to the outside world, particularly Communism. In short, Goldwater intended to attack Johnson personally, his commitment to government intrusiveness in private life or the welfare state, and his inability to master the Communist threat.[117]

Johnson saw two possible ways to deal with Goldwater. He could answer him with primarily a positive campaign, pointing to the accomplishments of his brief time in office and the promise of more to come in a four-year term. Or he could subordinate this to a largely negative assault on Goldwater's "extremism" and the dangers he posed to national political traditions and world peace.

Beating up on Goldwater seemed the safest course. A survey of public opinion in August showed Johnson that his accomplishments in office would give him only a limited advantage in the campaign. A majority of Americans *were* positively disposed toward Johnson's performance in the White House, seeing him as a highly effective leader who had managed "to get stalled legislation through Congress." Majorities also gave Johnson credit for prosperity—the forty-three-month, longest business expansion since World War II, limited inflation, and a good tax program.

At the same time, however, more than half the voters surveyed were unhappy with or indifferent to the $4.5 billion increase in Johnson's federal budget, the administration's civil rights program, its handling of medical care for the aged, which was stalled in Congress, problems of the big cities, and the war on poverty, which only 34 percent believed would work as Johnson had promised. The administration's overall rating was also well below what Johnson himself registered in straw votes against Goldwater. Nine percent thought the White House was doing an excellent job, 44 percent said it was good, 38 percent rated it as only fair or poor, and 9 percent had no opinion.[118]

In deciding how to beat Goldwater, Johnson also harked back to his experience in earlier campaigns, especially in Texas, where mud-slinging, hidden machinations, and illegal vote-getting were common practice. Johnson found additional encouragement to take the low road in JFK's 1960 race for the presidency, with its vote-buying in West Virginia that beat Hubert Humphrey in the Democratic primary and the narrow victories against Nixon in Illinois and Texas, where questionable practices, or so Johnson believed, made the difference.

But nothing was more important in encouraging Johnson to mount negative attacks on Goldwater than the likelihood that they would give him a big advantage in the campaign. On September 7, Jack Valenti told the President that, based on polls and conversations with newsmen and state political leaders, "our main strength lies not so much in the FOR Johnson but in the AGAINST Goldwater. Therefore: We ought to treat Goldwater not as an equal, who has credentials to be President, but as a *radical*, a preposterous candidate who would ruin this country and our future."

The method for bringing Goldwater down was "humor, barbs, jokes, ridicule." Goldwater was to be made "ridiculous and a little scary: trigger-happy, a bomb thrower, a radical" who "will sell TVA, cancel Social Security, abolish the government, stir trouble in NATO, be the herald of World War III." The central point was not to take Goldwater and Miller seriously but instead as some kind of April Fool's gag. When Goldwater attacked the President's morals, the campaign needed to hit "hard" at the Republicans for their "immorality." Above all, though, the Democrats needed to "keep fear of Goldwater as unstable, impulsive, reckless in [the] public's mind. This is our strongest asset."[119]

Goldwater's continuing political recklessness during the campaign gave Valenti's strategy added appeal. The journalist Theodore White said: "No man ever began a Presidential effort more deeply wounded by his own nomination, suffering more insurmountable handicaps. And then . . . he made the worst of them." Instead of trimming sail and trying to find a middle ground, where he could broaden his appeal to voters from both sides of the spectrum, he pressed the case for a moral regeneration in America that would eliminate traditional special interest politics and the symbol of the country's corruption, Lyndon Johnson in the White House.[120]

Goldwater emphasized Johnson's immorality by pointing out that he visited "city after city in a political travesty of the Lord's day" and turned "Sunday into a day of campaign chaos." "There was so much dirt swept under the carpet of the White House," Goldwater declared, "that it could qualify for the soil bank." And "Lyndon Johnson had so much power and wanted so much more power that Democrats didn't know whether to vote for him or plug him in."[121]

To underscore his alienation from conventional politics, Goldwater declared that he had purposely gone into "the heart of Appalachia" and attacked the administration's "phony war on poverty"; he had gone into "the heart of Florida's retirement country" and "warned against the outright hoax of this administration's medicare scheme." He took pride in having attacked TVA in the Tennessee Valley and denounced agricultural subsidies in the heart of America's farmland.

On foreign affairs, he also made no concession to campaign realities. His message throughout the election remained the one set forth in his 1963 book, *Why Not Victory?* There could be no compromise with Communism. Either the United States was prepared to risk a showdown with Moscow and Peking, including the possibility of nuclear war, or it would have to accept the ultimate sacrifice of freedom around the globe to Communist authoritarianism. In a speech in Hammond, Indiana, where he was supposed to put the "bomb issue" to rest, Goldwater promised liberation of Eastern Europe and issued "a thoroughly bellicose call to man the ramparts."

A campaign stressing moral principals over practical political considerations, Goldwater's crusade was symbolized in the bumper stickers displayed proudly by supporters: "IN YOUR HEART YOU KNOW HE'S RIGHT!" and "A CHOICE NOT AN ECHO." Opponents, capturing the spirit of Johnson's campaign, responded, "YES, FAR RIGHT" or with bumper stickers saying, "IN YOUR HEART, YOU KNOW HE MIGHT," "IN YOUR GUT YOU KNOW HE'S NUTS," "STAMP OUT PEACE—VOTE GOLDWATER," and "GOLDWATER FOR HALLOWEEN."[122]

Johnson's assault on Goldwater was a masterpiece of both covert and overt negative campaigning. It actually began in July when Jim Farley, FDR's Postmaster General, released a statement approved by Johnson attacking Goldwater and his supporters as extremists with little regard for traditional American politics and an affinity for "hatred and bigotry" that might incite "insurrection and civil disorder." Later that month Bill Moyers learned from a psychiatrist friend that a magazine was polling mental health practitioners about Goldwater's emotional stability. "This really hits below the belt," the psychiatrist told Moyers. "I hope most psychiatrists won't answer it." Moyers expressed no concern, especially since *Medical Tribune*, a professional journal, had already found that psychiatrists favored LBJ over Goldwater by ten to one.[123]

At the beginning of August, the White House prepared a secret rebuttal to the Republican platform, blasting the GOP's attack on Johnson's policies as "false and misleading." Eager to show the President as above the battle, the White House misled the *Washington Post* into believing that the "analysis" came from the research staff of the Democratic Senatorial Campaign Committee.

The following week, when a Republican Unity Conference—including Goldwater, Eisenhower, Rockefeller, Scranton, and others—staged a "closed session meeting" in Hershey, Pennsylvania, the White House obtained a copy of the "confidential proceedings" from a *Newsweek* reporter. At the same time, to counter suggestions that he should debate Goldwater, Johnson arranged to kill a congressional resolution suspending the "equal time" provision of the Communications Act requiring a part for minor candidates in debates. At the end of the month, while the Democrats met in Atlantic City, the White House drew up "Guidelines for Handling Major Goldwater-Miller Speeches." Effective responses depended on obtaining advance copies to see what "major" charges were being made against "key" administration policies or officials.[124]

Johnson's campaign began in earnest in September, when he started devoting himself tirelessly to the details of the race. Publicly, Johnson presented himself as a Chief Executive who was so busy—so presidential—that he could not get out on the hustings until the end of the month or involve himself in day-to-day campaign operations. Only the Democratic National Committee and citizens eager for his election were supposedly attending to these matters. It was a public relations ploy to enhance Johnson's image.

In the first days of September, word reached Johnson that the Democrats had not yet begun to fight. "Where is the Democratic campaign?" one party leader asked. "Where are the bumper stickers and other paraphernalia? Are the Democrats organized? Why has Goldwater been permitted such opportunity to close ranks? If there is a fear about the President's campaign among the active Democrats I have talked with,... it is not of the backlash or of a 'hidden vote,' but of failure to get the President's campaign *organized* and *operating*."[125]

In response, Johnson lit a fire under party and administration officials that he stoked constantly during the next two months. Aides not only had to develop the details of his speaking schedule and keep him posted on the daily attacks on Goldwater, they also had to report from the field on what they found in every region and state and on the status of campaign materials. He wanted to know how many buttons, posters, mailing labels, bumper stickers, decals, and books of matches promoting his candidacy had been manufactured and distributed.

Nor did this information cross his desk unattended. All you ever heard from Johnson, Kenny O'Donnell says, were complaints "that he hadn't seen any stickers; it was just like a guy running for the House of Representatives. . . . He used to do the silliest things in the world." When a campaign button featuring equally proportioned likenesses of Johnson and Humphrey came to hand, Lyndon blew up. He insisted that buttons giving him greater prominence and relegating Humphrey to the background replace the unsatisfactory ones.

When anything went slightly wrong in the campaign, he would be all over his aides. "He treated them awful," O'Donnell says. Nor did he treat Mrs. Johnson "a hell of a lot better," screaming at her in front of O'Donnell one day that she was "working for Goldwater . . . but this was Lyndon. He's up and down."[126]

Led by Johnson, everyone at the White House saw the principal work of the campaign as emphasizing Goldwater's extremism and the danger of trusting him with the powers of the presidency. The first objective was to give "maximum exposure" to Goldwater's past "outrageous statements." One aide compiled a short list: "Doggone it, I'm not even sure that I've got the brains to be . . . President"; "Sometimes I think this country would be better off if we could just saw off the Eastern seaboard and let it float out to sea"; the radical anti-Communist "John Birch Society policies and philosophies are fine." And on foreign policy and nuclear weapons, Goldwater could be damned by his admission, "I possibly do shoot from the hip."[127]

As important as nailing Goldwater on past statements were attacks on his current campaign statements and actions. On September 2, for example, after Goldwater voted against a Medicare bill, Moyers informed Johnson that he had urged Ken O'Donnell "to pull out all the stops among organizations of older Americans. . . . This is a great opportunity for us to beat him to death among these older people if we just play it right. I suggested a number of alternatives, including

some form letters, advertisements, perhaps a pamphlet, etc."
O'Donnell "agreed to get right on it."[128]

A principal technique for attacking Goldwater was through the
press. The White House knew that Goldwater frightened most of the
newspapers and magazines, which wanted to help Johnson defeat
him. Johnson and his aides had no hesitation about undermining the
supposed impartiality of the press. "Reporters are puppets," Johnson
said. "They simply respond to the pull of the most powerful strings.
... Every story is always slanted to win the favor of someone who
sits somewhere higher up. There is no such thing as an objective
news story. There is always a private story behind the public story.
And if you don't control the strings to that private story, you'll never
get good coverage no matter how many great things you do for the
masses of the people."[129]

Journalists, editors, and publishers confirmed Johnson's cynicism
about the press by aiding his campaign. On September 5, for instance,
after Goldwater and Miller had attacked Johnson and Humphrey as
"misfits" and Humphrey in particular as a draft dodger, Moyers and
Jenkins spoke to Drew Pearson, Kay Graham, and Al Friendly at the
Washington Post, William S. White and James Reston at the *New
York Times*, and Walter Lippmann about answering the "degrading
way the Republican campaign has opened." Most of them promised
to take Goldwater to task for his irresponsible statements. The following week, CEA Chairman Walter Heller persuaded syndicated columnist Sylvia Porter to write a critical piece on a Goldwater tax cut
plan, while Walter Lippmann agreed to consider doing a column and
the *Washington Post* prepared "a *stinging editorial*," which was "being watered down."

The White House also tried to get reporters covering Goldwater
to supply detailed accounts of what the senator was saying off the
record. In mid-September, when Cliff Carter at the DNC gave Valenti
one such report, he wrote: "The attached was written by a reporter
traveling with Senator Goldwater. We're trying to make connections
so that we can always have him thusly covered."[130]

More important to the White House than having reporters spy
on Goldwater were editorial-page endorsements and anti-Goldwater,
pro-Johnson material in the news columns of the papers. Leonard
Marks, a Washington attorney who had represented the Johnsons'
radio and television stations and would become the director of the
United States Information Agency in 1965, worked "to secure editorial
endorsements from newspaper friends and clients." Once papers
agreed to back Johnson, a member of the DNC was assigned to keep

in touch with their editors and publishers and supply them with
campaign materials.

The White House also closely followed "how Mr. Johnson's
speeches, utterances or releases were carried across the country. . . .
We had reporters in about fifty major cities that would call in during
the night and report what placement in the paper Mr. Johnson's
speech got," a campaign aide recalls. Johnson himself, who closely
followed these efforts, held meetings with Washington bureau chiefs
of leading papers to help knock down Goldwater and improve his
image. The objective was to "convey a picture of a President calm,
concerned, busy at his Presidential business, but eager to win a decisive mandate in November."[131]

Johnson saw the press as essential in helping him defeat Goldwater, but he wanted a more systematic and reliable mechanism for
using it and other means to win the election. Valenti reflected Johnson's view when he told Moyers and other aides on September 14
that "if we are not careful, the Goldwater image will get all smoothed
up to our detriment. Right now, the biggest asset we have is Goldwater's alleged instability in re atom and hydrogen bombs. We MUST
NOT let this slip away."[132]

To answer Johnson's concern, the White House organized a six-
teen-man committee presided over by aides Myer Feldman and Fred
Dutton. It included people from a number of government agencies
and Clark Clifford's Washington law firm. The committee met twice
a day, 9:30 in the morning and 6:00 in the evening. They began
developing books that would demean Goldwater: *You Can Die
Laughing, Goldwater Versus Republicans*, and a book of cartoons.
They prepared statements on major issues on which Goldwater had
made himself vulnerable, and distributed them to people who could
"get them into the papers in the right places at the best time." They
assigned one staffer to feed negative information to LBJ supporters,
who would get it in the local press prior to or during Goldwater
visits. They prepared rebuttals of Goldwater-Miller statements and
assigned committee members to get them published. They fed hostile
questions to reporters traveling with Goldwater; they wrote letters to
popular columnists like Ann Landers; they made lists of columnists
they knew and lobbied them regularly for articles critical of Goldwater; and they pressured mass magazines like *Look, Saturday Evening Post*, and *Parade* to attack Goldwater's views on nuclear
weapons.[133]

The "anti-campaign" or "five o'clock club," as the committee
was called, was directly under Johnson's control. Feldman reported to
him almost every day on its activities. The committee was a deep,

dark secret, which only came to light after the conclusion of the campaign. "No political operation in history was ever conducted with such secrecy," journalists Evans and Novak wrote later.[134]

As a major supplement to the "anti-campaign" of the "five o'clock club," Johnson assigned Richard Goodwin, Jenkins, Valenti, and Moyers to work with the ad agency Doyle Dane Bernbach (DDB) in preparing television and radio spots that Valenti believed can "be a heavy weapon for us ... our real attack on Goldwater without involving the President." Johnson agreed to devote considerable financial resources to an electronic media campaign—$3 million for local spots and another $1.7 for network programs. The objective was to convince as many people as possible that Goldwater was an extremist who could do some terrible things. Moyers suggested television ads, saying: If Goldwater became President he could take us out of the United Nations; he "could have his finger—or that of some field commander—on the nuclear trigger; ... he could ... destroy the nuclear test-ban treaty; ... he could ... make the social security program voluntary. ... He *could* do these things—But only if we let him. Vote for President Johnson on November 3. The stakes are too high to stay home."[135]

The DDB ads destroyed any slight hope Goldwater might have had of overcoming Johnson's lead. On September 7, the Johnson campaign broadcast the "Daisy" spot, the most famous political ad ever made. It began with a little girl in a field of flowers picking petals off a daisy while she counted to ten. As a man's voice counted down from ten to one, the film showed a startled look on her face and then a close up of her eye, which dissolved to black and then an atomic explosion. As viewers watched the mushroom cloud, Johnson declared: "These are the stakes—to make a world in which all of God's children can live, or to go into the dark. We must love each other, or we must die." An announcer's voice then urged: "Vote for President Johnson on November 3. The stakes are too high for you to stay home."[136]

The ad was slated to run only once. The White House had a number of others they wanted to use and didn't think repetition was a good idea. The response to the ad convinced Moyers and Valenti to stick to their plan. Moyers remembers that the White House switchboard "lit up with calls protesting it [the ad], and Johnson called me and said, 'Jesus Christ, what in the world happened?' and I said, 'You got your point across that's what.' ... Johnson was very pleased with it," but he had "a wonderful time putting on an act. He said, 'What in hell do you mean putting on that ad? I've been swamped with calls, and the Goldwater people are calling it a low blow,' and on and on and on. . . . His voice was chuckling all the time. He said, 'You'd better come over here and tell me what you're going to do about this.' "

When Moyers arrived, Johnson complained about the ad in front of eight or nine people who were with him. Moyers said it was a good idea to remind people that we need "an experienced hand on the button." He also emphasized that the ad wouldn't be shown again. Then he "turned and went back to the elevator, which is in a little alcove on the second floor." Johnson called out for him not to leave, and "came down to the alcove with his back to the group. He said, 'You sure we ought to run it just once?' I said, 'Yes, Mr. President.' "[137]

The hullabaloo raised by the "Daisy" ad did not deter Johnson from using other negative spots attacking Goldwater. A few days after the "Daisy" ad, the Democrats ran another showing a little girl licking an ice cream cone. A woman's voice related the dangers from nuclear explosions in the atmosphere to children and everyone else. She further explained that a nuclear test ban treaty had begun to make the radioactive poisons go away. "But now, there is a man who . . . doesn't like this treaty. He's . . . voted against it. He wants to go on testing more bombs. His name is Barry Goldwater, and if he's elected, they might start testing all over again." The ad closed with the same appeal as in the "Daisy" spot for people to vote for Johnson, with the admonition, "The stakes are too high for you to stay home." DDB created variations on the "Daisy" and test ban spots that were shown during the campaign, and the DNC ran a half-hour network film on election eve sponsored by Scientists, Engineers, and Physicians for Johnson-Humphrey and entitled, "Sorry, Senator Goldwater, We Just Can't Risk It."[138]

Other DDB ads depicted Goldwater's domestic radicalism. One quoted his wish to "saw off the Eastern seaboard"; another focused on Republican divisions over Goldwater's candidacy; and a third, far harsher spot pictured Ku Klux Klansmen burning a cross and quoted an Alabama Klansman's remark: "I like Barry Goldwater. He needs our help." The most effective and heavily used ad described Goldwater's threat to the Social Security system. It showed two hands ripping up a Social Security card, while an announcer warned that on at least seven occasions Goldwater had declared his intention to change the present Social Security set up. It ended with the reassurance that "President Johnson is working to strengthen Social Security. Vote for him on November 3."[139]

Johnson had no compunction about hitting Goldwater so hard, partly because the negative attacks seemed to be so effective. In late

September, a Gallup poll found that Johnson had a three to one advantage over Goldwater when Americans evaluated their qualifications for the presidency. Moreover, where only 2 percent of the public thought Johnson was reckless, 24 percent described Goldwater that way. During the first week of October, after Interior Secretary Stewart Udall had visited most of the Western states, he reported that Johnson had a commanding lead, even in "hard-rock 'Goldwater country' states as Utah and Wyoming," where the President showed "margins of 60% or better."

In the last days of October, a report from the University of Michigan Survey Research Center showed that many voters, including Republicans who were deserting to Johnson in unprecedented numbers, thought that Goldwater was a "terrible" candidate who made his party look like "a gang of nuts and kooks." A poll coming to Johnson four days before the election showed him with a 61 percent to 39 percent lead. Everything suggested that he and his aides had made all the right choices in the campaign.[140]

If Johnson had qualms about running so negative a campaign against Goldwater, they were diminished not only by the conviction that this was the sure road to victory but also by the ugly attacks and innuendos Goldwater and the Republicans used against him. Between March and August a series of articles appeared in the *Wall Street Journal*, the *Washington Star*, and *Life* raising questions about how Johnson had amassed a fortune of between $9 and $14 million. After the *Emporia (Kansas) Gazette* wrote a scathing editorial describing Johnson as "the most corrupt man ever to enter the White House" in modern times, the Republicans began running it as a campaign ad in newspapers.[141]

As distressing to Johnson, the Republicans began distributing, especially in the South and the West, copies of *A Texan Looks at Lyndon* by J. Evetts Haley. The book was a vicious attack on Johnson, bringing together every negative story ever told about him and questioning his right to be President. It was the most prominent of several right-wing tracts, which Drew Pearson said in August 1964 were outselling lurid novels. In October, the abundance and growing impact of this smear literature became a topic of discussion at the White House. After a tour of Western states, Larry O'Brien reported to the President that "these books are being distributed by the Republican Party as well as by John Birchers and other right-wing organizations. They are available at all newsstands. They are being read and having some impact. At every meeting our campaign leaders agreed the books are hurting ... some weapons should be placed in the hands of our people to counteract the effect of the books." Other observers gave Johnson similar reports, and expressed concern that "the smear campaign" was helping Goldwater win votes.[142]

In addition to the outright attacks on Johnson, there were rumors of hidden corruption that Republicans encouraged as a way to undermine his public standing. A former congressional staffer spread the story that the State Department arranged for LBJ to receive a large sum in counterpart funds for his personal use when he visited Hong Kong in 1961. The rumor was so persistent that the department "urgently" asked the Consul General there in October 1964 to provide a full report. And though no evidence of wrongdoing was found, J. Edgar Hoover obtained copies of the department's cables for his Official and Confidential File.[143]

At the same time, rumors also began to circulate that Johnson had kidney tumors that were much more serious than his heart condition. Two Navy radiologists told this to someone who passed it on to an associate of Drew Pearson's. Texas newspapers carried ads about Johnson's medical history and the odds of his surviving another term.[144]

In mid-October Johnson was also concerned about an "Opinion Research Poll" showing Goldwater catching up in various states. Johnson asked the New Jersey state Democratic chairman to talk to the Gallups in Princeton. Ted Gallup sent word through Jim Rowe that either the Republicans or Opinion Research, a polling group working for Goldwater and using the same raw figures and computers as Gallup, were faking the results. Gallup "*emphasized* this is *confidential*, because he must be protected for tattling on his colleagues and competitors."[145]

All the rumors and smear books bothered Johnson less than Goldwater's attack on his morals. A spot ad the Republicans ran during the last month of the campaign featured an announcer saying: "What has happened to America? We have had the good sense to create lovely parks—but we're afraid to use them after dark. We build libraries and galleries to hold the world's greatest art treasures—and we permit the world's greatest collection of smut to be freely available." Pictures of an empty park and a seedy newsstand emphasized the points. A cartoon of Bobby Baker and a photo of Billie Sol Estes formed the backdrop to the observation that "the highest echelons of government are embroiled in scandals—that are cynically swept under the rug." A tape of Goldwater speaking to the camera followed: "The national morality, by example and by persuasion, should begin at the White House, and have the good influence to reach out to every corner of the land. Now this is not the case today because our country has lacked leadership that treats public office as a public trust."[146]

The Republican National Committee also wished to run a half-hour film called *Choice*. It showed "urban riots, a woman in a topless swimsuit, and a Lincoln Continental speeding down a dirt road with beer cans flying from the windows." NBC president Robert Kintner, who was strongly for Johnson and joined his administration as a special assistant in 1966, called the film an "appallingly tasteless production." When others complained of its racism, Goldwater told Republican officials, "I'm not going to be made out as a racist. You can't show it." If the Republicans showed the film, Johnson and the Democrats planned to attack them for running down America and to praise the accomplishments of the American people and their free enterprise system.[147]

The Republican assault on Johnson's morals got a big boost during the campaign when a scandal involving Walter Jenkins became public in mid-October. On October 7, after attending a cocktail party at *Newsweek* in downtown Washington, Jenkins was arrested in a nearby YMCA men's room on a charge of indecent sexual behavior. Although rumors of the incident circulated in Washington during the next week, nothing became public until a *Washington Star* reporter discovered Jenkins's name on a police blotter. When an editor at the paper called the White House with the information, he was told that Jenkins would call back with a denial. Instead, Jenkins went to see Abe Fortas and Clark Clifford, who lobbied the editors of Washington's three newspapers to get more evidence before printing a story that could devastate Jenkins and his family. Jenkins was now so agitated that a doctor hospitalized him.

That evening, after reporters discovered a similar undisclosed charge against Jenkins dating back to 1959, the press published the story. When Johnson, who was campaigning in New York, learned of these developments from Reedy, he responded with glacial calm and instructed Jenkins to resign. The same evening Mrs. Johnson, without consulting Lyndon, gave a heartfelt statement to the *Washington Post* describing the extraordinary burdens Walter had been shouldering since Kennedy's death, offering her prayers for him and his family, and expressing her hopes for his recovery.[148]

The episode bewildered everyone who knew Jenkins. An FBI investigation to determine whether Jenkins had been blackmailed and the source of any security leak turned up only expressions of amazement at Jenkins's behavior. Most everyone the FBI talked to speculated that Jenkins had cracked under the strain of eighteen-hour workdays. When George Reedy saw him in the hospital, Jenkins said he had no recollection of anything that had happened between the time he left *Newsweek* and the time he found himself at the police station. One man the FBI interviewed remembered having lunch with Jenkins on the 7th and being troubled by his behavior. "Jenkins ordered a drink, which he did not touch, and later ordered food which he did not eat. . . . Jenkins was not as coherent or [did not] express himself as well as he generally did on that particular day. . . . His face was beet red." A suggestion that he should go home brought the reply that "he did not feel well but had too much work to do and had to go back to the office."[149]

Johnson and most top campaign aides believed that Jenkins had been entrapped by a Republican dirty trick. George Reedy later said that Jenkins, overwhelmed by the pressures on him, may have committed "a form of suicide," but he could never understand why three policeman were waiting in the men's room where Jenkins was caught. He also asserted that some of the rumors preceding the press stories and a number of phone calls to reporters came from the Republican National Committee.

Kenny O'Donnell also believed that Jenkins "got framed." O'Donnell couldn't understand why the police didn't call the White House after Jenkins was arrested. "It's just automatic," O'Donnell says, "when a guy comes in with a White House pass they call the Secret Service," which they never did. O'Donnell also says that the RNC kept calling the police and asking why they hadn't notified anybody, meaning the press. "I talked to the Washington police, . . . I've got some friends over there," O'Donnell asserts. "And every one of them was convinced it was a frame, every one of them!"[150]

Johnson also saw a Republican conspiracy behind Jenkins's arrest. He later told Doris Kearns: "I couldn't have been more shocked about Walter Jenkins if I'd heard that Lady Bird had killed the Pope. It just wasn't possible. And then I started piecing things together. The Republicans believed that the question of morality was their trump card. This was their only chance at winning. . . . Well, the night of October 7, the night of the arrest, I had been invited to a party given by *Newsweek*. . . . I couldn't go, so I asked Walter to go in my place. Now the waiters at the party were from the Republican National Committee, and I know Walter had one drink and started on another and doesn't remember anything after that. So that must be the explanation."[151]

It is difficult to believe that the whole episode was a "frame." Logic suggests that Jenkins cracked under the pressure of work, as he had apparently done once before in 1959. It also seems likely that Johnson had been told of Jenkins's arrest on October 7 and had made every effort to keep the matter quiet. The police never informed the White House—and O'Donnell in particular—because Johnson had already been told. Moreover, Reedy's and Valenti's descriptions of Johnson's reaction to the news on October 14 suggests that he already knew about the incident.

Johnson's inability to keep the lid on the scandal resulted from an aggressive rumor campaign by the RNC to alert reporters to the arrest. Undoubtedly having received information about the incident from a Republican in the police department, the RNC encouraged an investigative journalist to get at a record that could not be hidden from a good police reporter. And once the Washington papers had the story, it was not difficult for them to track down Jenkins's earlier arrest. In April 1961, after the Secret Service had asked the FBI for a routine investigation of Jenkins in response to a request for a White House pass, the bureau reported the 1959 arrest on a charge of "investigation of a suspicious person."[152]

Republican success in getting the Jenkins story before the public frustrated and angered Johnson, but it did not surprise him. He had assumed throughout the campaign that just as he would exploit Goldwater's every weakness, so the Republicans would attack his. Yet he could not dismiss the Jenkins revelation as inconsequential, and so he immediately instructed his private pollster to sound out public opinion. The initial results showed no significant shift in feeling toward the President. But even if there had been more of a response to the Jenkins story, news in the next two days that Nikita Khrushchev had resigned as Soviet Premier, a Labor government had taken over in Britain, and the Chinese Communists had exploded their first nuclear bomb would have eclipsed it.[153]

Goldwater himself refused to say anything directly about the Jenkins incident. When reporters on his campaign plane pressed him for a comment, he would only speak "off the record." "What a way to win an election," he said, "Communists and cocksuckers." Goldwater publicly ignored the scandal, but his campaign chiefs had high hopes that it would seriously wound Johnson. When CBS correspondent Murray Fromson, who was covering Goldwater, told one of Barry's principal aides about the spectacular developments in Moscow, London, and China, Fromson remembers that the blood drained from his face.[154]

What the nonreaction to the Jenkins case should have told Johnson was that negative information did not necessarily serve either Goldwater or himself very well in the campaign. Unquestionably, Goldwater's defects worked strongly against him. But his affinity for overstatement and conservative positions had fastened themselves clearly on voters before he entered the fall campaign. Consequently, Johnson could have decisively beaten Goldwater without the emphasis the Democrats placed on his failings in the months leading up to November 3.[155]

As the campaign progressed, some Democrats began to tell Johnson that he would do better accentuating the positive. On October 1, the diplomat John Bartlow Martin told Bill Moyers that so far Johnson "has given the people something to vote against—Goldwater. Perhaps now he should give them something to vote for." Martin believed that too much name-calling and too little substance were undermining rather than arousing interest and enthusiasm for Johnson. "Many people think this a 'strange' campaign, as though the nation was going through a meaningless dumb show. They don't like it."

Larry O'Brien and Ken O'Donnell saw the same thing. O'Brien recalls that we began getting "requests in almost every state for more positive material in our television spots." And by the third week of October, O'Donnell was urging the President to shift gears from negative attacks to "a strong, issue-oriented, high-level program." He described the television spots as having "outlived their usefulness," and he suggested ads that presented the administration's past achievements and future programs.[156]

If Johnson needed more direct evidence of the wisdom of being positive, he could have found it in what he saw and heard on the campaign trail. At the end of September, for example, he went to New England, where he received as warm a reception as he could have wished. Huge crowds in Providence, Hartford, Burlington, Portland, Manchester, and Boston greeted his motorcades and shouted their approval at everything he said. Jack Valenti remembers how they "were mobbed. It was like trying to pull your way through a big mass of molasses, it was so thick and friendly." Johnson knew that this was not the result of some "advance operation. This was the people responding to the President." They were showing their affection for someone who had masterfully managed the crisis following JFK's death, and now, in his own right, was forging a consensus for progressive advance aimed at serving all the nation. They were expressing appreciation for his balance and common sense, his affinity for the political center, alongside an opponent who seemed like less a spokesman for the great American middle than a representative of a radical right fringe.[157]

Similarly, in early October, when Johnson spoke about civil rights in New Orleans, he encouraged a view of himself as more of a statesman than a barnstorming politician. Though advance men and political aides traveling with him counseled against saying anything on blacks and civil rights—"the less said the better," he was advised—Johnson believed it essential to advocate something that would serve the well-being of Louisiana, the South, and the whole nation. On his arrival at the train station, he told a huge crowd of blacks and whites: "I am going to repeat here . . . what I have said in every State that I have appeared in. . . . As long as I am your President, I am going to be President of all the people," whose constitutional rights he promised to protect.

Later that night at a fund-raising dinner, he was more specific: "If we are to heal our history and make this Nation whole, prosperity must know no Mason-Dixon line and opportunity must know no color line. . . . Whatever your views are, we have a Constitution and we have a Bill of Rights, and we have the law of the land, and two-thirds of the Democrats in the Senate voted for it [the civil rights bill] and three-fourths of the Republicans. I signed it, and I am going to enforce it, and . . . any man that is worthy of the high office of President is going to do the same thing."

Departing from his text, he then told an anecdote about Sam Rayburn's going to see Senator Joseph W. Bailey of Texas, who talked to him about southern economic problems and northern exploitation of the South's rich resources. Bailey explained that the South could make great progress if it could avoid being distracted by racial matters. " 'Sammy,' " Johnson quoted Bailey as saying, " 'I wish I felt a little better. I would like to go back to old [Mississippi, where Bailey was born and grew up] . . . and make them one more Democratic speech. . . . The poor old State, they haven't heard a Democratic speech in 30 years. All they ever hear at election time is nigra, nigra, nigra.' "[158]

Johnson could not doubt that he had struck the right chords with his speech. Horace Busby, after talking to the press, told him: "The New Orleans (Negro, Negro, Negro) speech captured them. . . . There is enthusiasm (for the first time) for your speeches. . . . Why? The New Orleans speech was courageous—and, most especially, *courageous politics.* . . . Overnight, they are speaking of you—as once of FDR—as the 'master,' 'the champ.' "[159]

The outcome of the election left no doubt that Johnson was now indeed "the champ." Winning forty-four states to Goldwater's six, five in the South and Arizona, Johnson held a 486 to 52 margin in the electoral college. Only FDR's advantage of 523 to 8 electoral votes in 1936 was larger. Johnson's victory was record-breaking in every other respect. His 43,129,484 popular votes against Goldwater's 27,178,188 represented the largest vote, the greatest margin, and the biggest percentage (61 percent) ever received by a President to that point in U.S. history. In addition, voters gave him the largest majorities in Congress since FDR's election in 1936—a Senate with 68 Democrats and 32 Republicans, two more than before, and a House favoring the Democrats by a 295 to 140 margin, a gain of 37 seats.[160]

Would Johnson have done as well if he had run a less combative campaign? Perhaps not. But the election drew a smaller percentage of eligible voters—62.1 percent—than Kennedy and Nixon did—63.8 percent—in 1960. Moreover, where the Kennedy-Nixon campaign had produced a 10 point increase in the percentage of voters going to the polls, the Johnson-Goldwater contest saw a drop of nearly 2 percent. Neither Goldwater nor Johnson generated the degree of enthusiasm that JFK and Nixon had stirred four years before.[161]

Still, Johnson hardly saw that as a blight on what everyone agreed was a spectacular success. Most important to LBJ, he now believed that he had an endorsement for his Great Society, the War on Poverty, and a tough, but not reckless, hold-the-line policy against any Communist advance, particularly in Vietnam. He saw the victory as *his*; he had carried it off without a Kennedy on the ticket. Now he was free to launch a Johnson administration that was much less in the shadow of JFK.

As many supporters recognized, though, the decisive result was more the product of anti-Goldwater than pro-Johnson or pro-administration sentiments. If there was a mandate in 1964, it was for avoiding extremism of any kind at home and abroad. By failing to make explicit where he intended to take the country in the next four years, Johnson won less than a solid consensus for bold change in either domestic or foreign affairs. But he refused to see it that way. For the moment, he assumed he had national backing for major reforms equal to anything in our history.

4

King of the Hill

THE autumn and winter of 1964 were a happy time for Lyndon Johnson. He was fulfilling every imaginable fantasy in his political life: He was a highly popular President winning passage of ground-breaking laws, describing broad plans for bold advances in American life, and gaining election in his own right with an unprecedented number of votes. If success gave him a temporary sense of repose, a feeling that at age fifty-six he had indelibly stamped his mark on history and could enjoy the prospect of another four and possibly even eight years achieving great things for the country, it was not evident to anyone around him. Johnson, Bill Moyers says, had "an exquisite hole at his center, which was an unfillable void." He was an inveterate malcontent, a man constantly reaching for new goals.

He was, as someone said of Napoleon, a tornado in pants. In August, after his nomination, and again in November and December, after his election, he spent weeks at his Texas ranch, where he was supposed to be relaxing. But a vacation from work, even a brief respite from his normally arduous schedule, was impossible. "Rest for him," Hubert Humphrey said, "was controlled frenzy."[1]

Watching Johnson on the plane flying to Texas after the Democratic convention in August, Humphrey felt that "if the plane had run out of fuel in mid-air, President Johnson's frenetic energy and excitement would have kept it flying."

At the ranch, he was in constant motion. It was not enough that he attended to the daily business of government, he also had to micromanage the affairs of his "spread." As Humphrey remembered, "If a fence was falling, he'd call his ranch foreman by phone from the car to report it. If a gate was loose, that word would go out. He would check cattle, looking for an injured or diseased one. When nothing caught his eye, he worried about dinner, calling the cook at the ranch house, asking, 'What's for supper?' If it was early enough, he'd help plan the menu. And all this at the wheel of his speeding white Lincoln. He drove as if he were a test driver or a Demolition Derby fanatic."[2]

In his relations with everyone he remained as overbearing, controlling, and needy as ever. No amount of success or personal gain could salve his ego or ease his need for deference. He had to bend everyone to his will. When *Washington Post* publisher Katharine Graham ran into him at the Atlantic City airport after the convention, he insisted that she accompany him and Lady Bird to Texas. Never mind that she was on her way to her farm, where she expected weekend guests; she was under presidential command. Likewise with the Humphreys, who were given virtually no notice and whose plans were a matter of indifference to Johnson.[3]

Visiting Johnson's ranch, Humphrey said, was to be an actor on Lyndon's stage. As his "guest, you did things his way." He made Hubert kill two deer, which repelled him. And Johnson humiliated him by making him don a cowboy outfit many sizes too big and insisting he ride a large, spirited horse to which he clung "like a tiny child on his first merry-go-round ride." No one escaped Johnson's abuse. He berated Lady Bird for getting him into an appearance at Stonewall he didn't want to make, and he lit into Graham for coming to Mrs. Johnson's defense. During one of his joyrides at breakneck speeds across rough country with no roads, he stopped to relieve himself. One of the Secret Service men standing near him "felt warm water on his leg. He looked down and said, 'Mr. President, you are urinating on me.' And Johnson's response was, 'I know I am . . . it's my prerogative.'" The reporter who recounted the story wasn't sure it was true, but, having covered Johnson as a senator and Vice President, he found it believable.[4]

Although Johnson had a reverential regard for the presidency, often telling people who tried to resist his demands, "I'm the only President you have," he didn't see his personal crudeness as demeaning the office. As throughout his Senate and vice-presidential years, he remained an exhibitionist and a philanderer who didn't mind flaunting his conquests. When a woman reporter at a private session with several journalists asked him a tough question, he "reached down and pulled his crotch and said, 'Well . . . I don't know.' And he was scratching himself, it was terrible."

During his vice presidency, the press called his Senate office "the nooky room." It was well known that he had ongoing affairs with a secretary, a beautiful Hispanic woman people called the "chili queen" and a woman at his ranch dubbed "the dairy queen." In addition, he wanted beautiful women working for him and viewed them as fair game. In January 1964, he complained to John Macy, the director of White House personnel, about the inefficiency of his secretaries. He told Macy to get him "the five smartest, best educated, fastest, prettiest secretaries in Washington." He didn't "want any broken-down old maids. I want them from 25 to 40," Johnson said, and expected them to work nights and weekends.

When the wife of television newscaster David Brinkley accepted an invitation to visit Lyndon and Lady Bird at the ranch on a weekend her husband couldn't be there, Johnson tried unsuccessfully to get her into bed. A journalist friend told Johnson that he had a beautiful new bride. Johnson asked to meet her, and the journalist agreed. But he candidly said, " 'I'm scared to introduce her to you.' " Johnson replied, " 'You don't need to be scared of me, sweetheart. I'm here at the office and I'm working.' "[5]

Lady Bird shut her eyes and ears to some of his behavior. What she didn't know or acknowledge preserved her from painful offenses. Yet she was mindful of and troubled by his crudeness and intemperateness, saying that Lyndon was often his own worst enemy. But she was a large-hearted person whose generosity and sense of humor gave her some detachment from her husband's shortcomings. Years later, when someone told her that Governor John Connally's memoirs described an affair Lyndon had with Alice Glass, Lady Bird, after a brief silence, declared: "I would have thought that Alice Glass was a bit too plump for Lyndon." Instead of dwelling on Lyndon's failings, Lady Bird principally fixed her attention on his virtues and took satisfaction from being an anchor in his life, a steadying force that helped give him the wherewithal to achieve as much as he did.

More than one observer at the White House has described to me Johnson's unhappiness—sense of abandonment or loss—whenever Lady Bird was away. One journalist remembered how Johnson would seek out the press for solace in her absence. Two aides recalled that LBJ was "like a caged tiger" when Mrs. Johnson was gone; he would drink to excess and invite himself to someone's home for dinner. He'd call up and ask you to eat with him at the White House, a friend recalls. If you were already going somewhere, he'd complain that he hadn't been invited. "If they knew you were free, I'm sure you would have been asked, too," the friend would reply. "Great," Johnson would answer, "I'll be there." Friends would suddenly find the President at their dinner table, where he would wolf down his food and begin working on the plate next to his. Afterward, he would press friends to spend the night with him at the White House.

National Security Advisor Mac Bundy remembers Johnson going

off on "tantrums" and becoming "very difficult to manage" when Lady Bird wasn't there. Moreover, if he became angry with you, he would cut you off. It was a hell of a way to run a government, Bundy says. But after a while Lady Bird would patch up differences by extending an invitation to dinner or some other social event that would bring Johnson and the exiled adviser back together. She was the civilizing force that checked Lyndon's erratic, intemperate behavior and helped him channel so much of his raw energy into making the government work as well as it did.[6]

Johnson's neediness and abuse of people around him was not the sum total of the man. Indeed, people close to the Johnsons have told me that it is unfair and inaccurate to describe Lyndon as essentially a difficult character who made life miserable for everyone who worked for him. To the contrary, they describe Johnson as a wonderfully funny, almost zany character, who loved his friends and associates and took pains with their well-being. He had an exceptional gift for storytelling and mimicry, which made him a superb entertainer. He was also a highly sentimental and emotional man whose compassion for human limitations and suffering made him especially generous toward people less fortunate than himself.

Johnson aides took special exception to descriptions of Mrs. Johnson as a long-suffering wife who sat on her feelings, passively accepting a painful fate as Lyndon's spouse. To the contrary, they believe she greatly enjoyed being married to someone as dynamic and successful as Lyndon. Indeed, they think that Johnson's extraordinary career greatly enriched her life, opening opportunities for personal connections to fascinating people from a variety of fields and for public service that she found highly rewarding.[7]

Almost all of Johnson's outrageous personal behavior was hidden from the public. In the sixties, journalists largely kept their knowledge of presidential transgressions of the sort Johnson committed to themselves. And not just because current mores dictated such journalistic restraint; reporters and publishers, who had been a partisan force against Goldwater, were reluctant to undermine someone as progressive as LBJ. True, privately, he was sometimes a Neanderthal whose crudeness offended them, but in public he was an unflinching advocate of social reforms that promised large improvements in the lives of all Americans, particularly minorities and women. And the media, reflecting the current national mood, found much to say for a President with a genuine passion for righting historic wrongs.

Yet Johnson did not see himself getting a free ride from the press. As Jack Valenti told him a few days after the election, "Many of the report[er]s are ready to turn on us now that the right-wing dragons have been slain. Others like [Douglas] Kiker and his kind (thankfully small in number) are meanly determined to assault us. These types will not be trying to instill glory in us—but in extracting gore from us."

To counter press attacks, Valenti proposed a "carefully considered plan" to give certain writers and photographers special access to the President. "This will allow us to create a lasting image of the President that emphasizes his assets and diminishes imagined liabilities." John F. Kennedy had begun "the creation of the Kennedy legend" by courting particular newspapers and magazines. Johnson could "do the same and do it better. . . . If the President will allow the construction and execution of carefully prepared programs of public imagery we can begin now to establish the real and enduring Lyndon Johnson instead of the callous and spiteful sketching that will spill out from cynics in the White House lobby." Johnson thought it an "excellent" suggestion. But he had no intention of creating an image without substance. Valenti's public relations campaign would rest on a bedrock of achievement that would be the true basis for "the Johnson legend."[8]

Creating the Great Society: Ends and Means

After announcing the Great Society in May 1964, Johnson had set his sights on defining just what his grand design would entail. He had little patience with the vague hopes of doing good that he associated with traditional liberals. He had wanted concrete ideas that could be translated into legislative proposals on matters like education, housing, health, transportation, and the environment.

In July, he had told the Cabinet that he was setting up fourteen task forces made up of small groups of experts who would identify and describe national problems and propose practical solutions. He hoped this would lead to "a tremendous infusion of objective thinking of new ideas, and new approaches." Moreover, he insisted that the entire procedure and the results of task force deliberations be kept secret. During JFK's presidency, leaks to the press about domestic proposals had provoked public debate which, Johnson believed, made it harder to win legislative gains. The task forces "will operate without publicity," Johnson said. "It is very important that this not become a public operation. The purpose of these task forces is to come up with ideas, not to sell those ideas to the public."[9]

Most members of the task forces were academics, "idea men" who would propose bold answers to difficult questions. Traditional interest groups were purposely shunned, though Johnson assured enough "representativeness" in each group so that its proposals would enjoy a good chance of winning congressional and public support. Still, the premium was on getting innovative suggestions that Johnson would arrange to turn into federal laws.[10]

Johnson's landslide election gave a degree of viability to his task force procedure that he could not have fully anticipated. As Clark Clifford told him: "1. You have been elected by the largest majority in modern political history. 2. You carried into office with you senators, congressmen, and governors who would not have made it without you. 3. You wear no man's collar. You have come through without any restricting commitments to any individual group. This gives you complete freedom of decision."[11]

Johnson was not so sure. He doubted that his smashing victory was a mandate or an unqualified national commitment to any specific legislative program. To be sure, the country understood that he intended to "move ahead," but it hadn't endorsed a particular set of bills or given him unqualified support for bold measures advancing radical change. He believed there was "too much glib talk about the ease" with which he could get legislation passed. He thought it would be "a hard fight every inch of the way."

Look, he told his congressional liaison men in January 1965, "I was just elected President by the biggest popular margin in the history of the country—16 million votes." But he was convinced that he had already lost about three million of those supporters now that Barry Goldwater wasn't around to scare the hell out of people. "After a fight with Congress or something else, I'll lose another couple of million. I could be down to 8 million in a couple of months." In addition, Johnson expected Congress to assert itself against him in due course. "I've watched the Congress from either the inside or the outside, man and boy, for more than forty years," he told presidential adviser Eric Goldman, "and I've never seen a Congress that didn't eventually take the measure of the President it was dealing with."[12]

For all his caution, Johnson nevertheless saw his electoral victory and current popularity as an unusual opportunity to get a lot of important bills through Congress. "I worked like hell to become President," he also told Goldman, "and I'm not going to throw it away." The pollster Elmo Roper encouraged Johnson's hopes of doing big things: "Having won, if not a mandate on the issues, a clear vote of confidence in his ability to handle them, he can proceed with a full sense of having earned his position of leadership. . . . He will have the greatest opportunity to put across his program granted to any President since Roosevelt in 1936." Johnson described Roper's assessment as "excellent."[13]

The initial key to building a Great Society, Johnson believed, was managing and controlling the 89th Congress. He was gleeful at the challenge; he felt as if he had spent his career preparing for it. His nearly twenty-four years in the House and the Senate gave him a special advantage. As one long-term Senate aide described it, Johnson was one of the "Old Bulls" that still dominated both sides of Congress: "He had . . . a perfectly beautiful, symbiotic relationship with Congress. . . . It was all very cozy."[14]

But Johnson knew that these friendships would go only so far; taking Congress for granted would be a mistake. It would have to be stroked, cuddled, made to feel that it was the center of the political universe. "The most important people you will talk to are senators and congressmen," Johnson told Jack Valenti. "You treat them as if they were president. Answer their calls immediately. Give them respect. They deserve it." Texas Congressman Jake Pickle says Johnson had a rule that aides had to return a congressman's or senator's call in "ten minutes or else!" Johnson himself, "contrary to almost any president I've ever heard of, was on the phone constantly, talking to members of the House and the Senate. It would be nothing for him to talk to fifteen, twenty, or thirty different congressmen or senators during a day about some matter." And he was "awfully persuasive. He's about the best close-in, eyeball salesman that you'll run across."[15]

The effort to sell Congress on the Great Society began in the summer of 1964, well before a single proposal went to the Hill. In August, he held a "Salute to Congress" at the White House for all members of both Houses and their wives. "This is the first recognition of this kind ever given by a President to the Congress and its members," House Speaker John W. McCormack wrote him afterward. "A large number" of those present told McCormack how much they appreciated the recognition.

Johnson had applied the same treatment to individual congressmen and senators. In December 1963 he had called Republican Silvio Conte from Massachusetts to thank him "on behalf of the nation for your vote." Conte "damn near collapsed right on the spot. . . . It's the only time since I have been in Congress that a President called me. I will never forget it," Conte said. Similarly, Johnson took pains to assure that the most conservative members of Congress would not be too antagonized by his Great Society proposals. He instructed Larry O'Brien, for example, to send an aide to the Hill to tell Mississippi Senators Jim Eastland and John Stennis that the President was ready to see them "any time a serious problem arises."[16]

Yet not everyone succumbed to Johnson's wooing. Missouri Republican Thomas Curtis, who had served in the House since 1950 and was a member of the Ways and Means Committee, had little patience with Johnson's methods of winning congressional support. He remembers being called to the White House to receive the "treatment." When "Lyndon sat down right next to me and started out, 'Now, Tom, your President wants to go over some matters with you,' I interrupted rudely and said: 'Come off it Lyndon, my President your ass, what do you want to talk about?'" Despite investing half an hour, Johnson made no substantive gain with Curtis.[17]

A crucial element in getting congressional cooperation was to keep anyone from getting "mad." To this end, Johnson wanted no talk of a miracle "Hundred Days," a whirlwind of activity producing a host of major bills that would challenge Congress to do more than seemed achievable. In December, Johnson told *New York Times* editor Turner Catledge that he did "not expect a large legislative program in this first session." He declared himself "very determined... to avoid a major clash with Congress." He wouldn't repeat the mistake FDR had made after his great landslide in 1936. "He broke his leg on the Supreme Court bill," and "'he couldn't get Congress to pass the time of day.'"[18]

Despite what he told Catledge, by mid-November Johnson had already set plans in motion for big legislative gains. Reluctant to give too much advance notice of his agenda, which might stir organized opposition, LBJ muted his plans for as long as possible. He called Speaker McCormack and Majority Leader Carl Albert of Oklahoma to the White House, where they discussed the President's program. And Albert then briefed the press. "President Johnson's legislative program is expanding like a batch of yeasty bread in a warm kitchen," the Associated Press reported. Albert told reporters that in addition to medical care for the aged and federal help for the eleven-state Appalachian region, the President might propose several other major actions, expanded Social Security benefits, immigration reform, federal aid to education, and redevelopment for areas with high unemployment.

Albert emphasized that no details had been discussed, but that if these proposals turned into full-blown bills, Congress would have a substantial part in shaping them. The bills would be not simply administration measures but laws closely identified with particular congressmen and senators and especially chairmen of various congressional committees. Johnson's objective, as he later told Doris Kearns, was "to crack the wall of separation enough to give the Congress a feeling of participation in creating my bills without exposing my plans . . . to advance congressional opposition before they even saw the light of day."[19]

Privately and publicly, Johnson stressed the cooperative nature of the legislative effort about to occur and the high regard he had for Congress. On November 19, he had told his Cabinet how important it was for each of them to "get to know personally the new members of Congress, Republicans as well as Democrats." A "personal relationship between senior members of the administration and new members of Congress will return handsome dividends." In his State of the Union address on January 4, he was almost shameless in his appeal to congressional vanity: "I am proud to be among my colleagues of the Congress whose legacy to their trust is their loyalty to their Nation." These were "men whose first love is their country, men who try each day to do as best they can what they believe is right." He had "total respect" for "this Hill which was my home," and where he was "stirred by old friendships."[20]

Later that year Johnson stated his regard for congressional leaders in a private conversation with the historian William E. Leuchtenburg. "I revere 'em." Johnson said: "I am not for denouncing Congress all the time. I am not like [Arthur] Schlesinger and you writers who think of congressmen as archaic buffoons with tobacco drool running down their shirts . . . I got up at seven this morning to have breakfast with them. I don't have contempt for them." Neither did Schlesinger and Leuchtenburg, but this was Johnson's way of saying that liberal intellectuals lacked the practical know-how or couldn't compete with a Lyndon Johnson in getting legislation passed.[21]

Johnson's concern with holding congressional support was a constant refrain; he came back to it time and again. Since he saw his administration as a kind of four-year campaign to pass bill after bill after bill, he gave everyone around him periodic refresher courses on how to deal with Congress.

In the fall of 1965, after almost two years of remarkable success in getting laws passed, Johnson told the Cabinet: "I have encouraged each one of you, and your deputies and key assistants, to meet frequently and informally with members of Congress. . . . It is vital to everything we do. Make an effort to get to know the men who sit on the committees that oversee your operations. . . . The job of day-to-day contact with Congress is the most important we have. Many battles have been won, and many cases settled 'out of court' by the *right* liaison man being there at the *right* time, with the *right* approach."

By now, any Cabinet member who hadn't acted on this advice would have been long gone from Johnson's White House. But past success was no guarantee of future achievement, and Lyndon, never content with past victories, prepared for the next challenge with reminders of the fundamentals that allowed him to bend legislators to his will.[22]

Johnson's State of the Union message was partly a testimony to his skill at managing the Congress. It was largely an appeal for action on Great Society measures—laws that would enrich the quality of life of all Americans. Though he spoke of the cities, the environment, the schools, the arts, and the people's health, he avoided the sort of details that arouse opponents to action. He emphasized his eagerness for government savings that would exceed the $3.5 billion in eliminated waste his administration had achieved last year. He promised a cut in excise taxes and a balanced budget that would free up money for his national agenda. But he alone would "not shape a new and personal vision of America." It would be collected from "the scattered hopes of the American past." The Great Society, in short, was not simply Lyndon Johnson's program; it was the fulfillment of the American dream, of the promise of American life.[23]

Johnson believed rhetorical flourishes of this sort essential to advance his program. But he considered it no substitute for the nuts and bolts work that inevitably went into passing a law. His first priority was to assure that the principal committees of the House—Appropriations, Rules, and Ways and Means—were receptive to his designs. In its first piece of business the House, partly responding to liberal victories in the election, used new criteria to assign members to Appropriations and Ways and Means. As a result, Johnson loyalists dominated both committees. "This change means that half the battle of enacting the Johnson program is over," Larry O'Brien said.

At the same time, the White House helped break the power of the Rules Committee to prevent bills from reaching the House floor or going to House-Senate conferences. To bypass conservative Virginia Democrat Howard Smith, who chaired Rules, the House agreed to let the Speaker force a vote on a bill twenty-one days after reaching the Rules Committee and to send a measure to a two-House conference without approval by Rules. The situation in Congress "could be better," Johnson now said, "but not this side of heaven."[24]

Yet Johnson took nothing for granted. Influence over the three crucial House committees was only a first step. As he told Kearns, he "insisted on congressional consultation at every single stage, beginning with the process of deciding what problems and issues to consider for my task forces right up to the drafting of the bills."[25]

As bills made their way through committees and reached the House and Senate floors, Johnson followed their every twist. He received daily reports from aides on their contacts with representatives and senators, with special emphasis on anything that might be considered an impediment to enactment of a law.

White House aides not only listened to what legislators had to say, they also made regular inquiries about what the White House could do for them. Explicit promises of rewards for votes were rarely given, but it was an unspoken assumption of the process that cooperation with the administration would lead to White House favors that would serve the legislator's interests.[26]

Senate Republican Minority Leader Everett Dirksen, for example, worked through Jack Valenti, sending the President sheaves of paper about appointments to judgeships, ambassadorial offices, and administrative posts, and asking attention to the interests of various industrial and agricultural constituents he represented. Dirksen, who did much to facilitate Johnson's legislative requests, got most of what he wanted.

Valenti recalls how Johnson and Dirksen would sit in the living quarters of the White House, "their knees almost touching," sipping refreshments. " 'Now, Mr. President,' the organ tones would pour forth like melodic molasses flowing over tiled slopes, 'there is that matter of . . . ' And here Dirksen would mention some regulatory agency or commission, and inevitably the minority leader would have on the tip of his tongue the names of several people who were, in Dirksen's words, 'ably suited. . . . ' " Johnson "would pretend mock outrage" at the incessant demands for appointments and long lists of candidates. But by the close of their meeting, "a deal had been sealed. Dirksen would have an appointment of one of his friends and the president would have a commitment on some piece of legislation."

By contrast, uncooperative legislators paid a price for their independence. Democratic Senator Frank Church of Idaho, who went against the President on a major bill, defended his vote by saying that noted columnist Walter Lippmann shared his views. Johnson replied: "I'll tell you what, Frank, next time you want a dam in Idaho, you call Walter Lippmann and let him put it through for you." When Democratic congressmen persisted in defying the President's wishes, John McCormack arranged to strip them of committee seniority, a substantial blow to the influence of long-term members.[27]

Federal Aid to Education

Johnson's highest Great Society priority was to broaden educational opportunities and enrich the quality of school offerings. He had an

almost mystical faith in the capacity of education to transform people's lives and improve their standard of living. He shared with earlier
generations of Americans an evangelical faith in educational opportunity as a public good. "He was a nut on education," Hubert Humphrey said. "He felt that education was the greatest thing he could
give to the people; he just believed in it, just like some people believe
in miracle cures."[28]

Public education had been Lyndon's ticket out of poverty in
rural Texas, and he wanted all children in the country to have the
same chance to advance themselves. He was confident that federal
funds could make a significant difference in expanding and improving
education at every level. Indeed, with the postwar baby boom causing
overcrowded classes in rundown schools short of competent teachers,
Johnson believed that there was no choice but for Washington to take
the initiative in meeting the problem. The increase in school population had created an unusual opportunity: Middle-class parents in
every region of the country would welcome federal efforts to improve
education for the poor as well as their own children.

On November 1, 1964, as a prelude to legislative proposals to
the 89th Congress, Johnson issued four Presidential Policy Papers on
Education, Health, Conservation of Natural Resources, and Farm Policy.

Education was no. 1: "Nothing matters more to the future of
our country," LBJ declared. The nation's military strength, economic
productivity, and democratic freedoms depended on an educated cit-
izenry. In the coming decade, 30 million boys and girls were slated
to enter the job force: 2.5 million would never see the inside of a
high school; 8 million would never earn a high school diploma; and
more than a million qualified for college would never go. All this
would occur "unless we act now [to] broaden and improve the quality
of our school base, . . . concentrate our teaching resources in the urban
slums and poor rural areas, [and] . . . expand and enrich our colleges."
While education was primarily the responsibility of states and localities, the federal government needed to assure that these basic needs
were met. Every President from FDR to JFK had worked toward that
goal. "I plan to get on with the task."[29]

Johnson said nothing about the frustration all Presidents had
suffered since Roosevelt when asking for federal aid to education. To
be sure, the Lanham Act in 1940 had begun support for school districts with military bases or "impacted areas," the G.I. bill had helped
World War II veterans attend colleges, the National School Lunch
Act in 1946 had provided a hot meal for school children, and the
Cold War had promoted science, math, engineering, and foreign lan-

guage study through the National Science Foundation and National Defense Education Act; but more general attempts to aid elementary and secondary education had repeatedly failed.

The three R's—race, religion, and Reds—had blocked action: To many Americans, federal aid meant enforced integration, unconstitutional support of parochial schools, and excessive government control of people's lives.[30]

Johnson needed a strategy that could overcome the three R's and neutralize conservative Rules Chairman Howard Smith, whose committee was known for its "no rules for schools." The House reform diluting Smith's power took care of the latter. Further, the 1964 civil rights bill, barring segregation in federally supported programs, eliminated race as a reason to oppose federal aid to education. Moreover, two-to-one margins in both houses of Congress for Democrats espousing a liberal faith in government activism weakened the appeal of objections to federal interference in local affairs.[31]

The church-state issue, however, remained a formidable stumbling block to a schools bill. In the fall of 1964, as aides worked to find a solution to the problem, Johnson told Assistant Secretary of Health, Education and Welfare (HEW) Wilbur Cohen: "By the way, Wilbur, be sure ... you don't come out with something that's going to get me right in the middle of the religious controversy. I don't want to have the Baptists attacking me from one hand and the Catholics from another."[32]

After consulting administration officials and educational and religious leaders, Commissioner of Education Francis Keppel found an answer. Instead of proposing general aid to public schools, which would reignite "a bitter battle" over helping parochial students, Keppel suggested "categorical aid" to poor children in city slums and depressed rural areas. Partly inspired by *Everson v. Ewing Township*, a 1947 U.S. Supreme Court ruling that federal aid to parochial students was constitutional if it went to children rather than schools, Keppel urged help to needy children regardless of whether they attended public or private schools. The money, moreover, was to go to impacted districts described in the 1940 Lanham Act, assuring the distribution of federal funds to well-off and impoverished schools.

Understanding that Keppel's approach would mute debate over aiding parochial schools and help generate a national consensus for federal aid to education, Johnson warmly endorsed it. In addition, Johnson resisted proposals from HEW, the Bureau of the Budget, and the Office of Education to assure that money under Lanham would go more to poor than prosperous school districts, which had been receiving the lion's share of the grants. Although advertising the bill

as aimed at educating the underprivileged, Johnson believed it would
have a better chance to pass if it also gave substantial sums to middle
class and well-to-do children.[33]

Johnson's keen feel for domestic affairs told him that the time
was ripe for a major education bill. Though Keppel had taken the
lead in proposing categorical rather than general aid, LBJ knew that
the initiative had a broader authorship and commanded substantial
support in Congress and the country.[34]

On January 11, Johnson told the Cabinet, "Tomorrow I am sending to the Congress the Message on Education.... I want—and I
intend—education to be the cornerstone on which we build this
administration's program and record.... I consider your first priority
of responsibility to support education—not merely the legislation, but
the cause itself."[35]

In his message, Johnson described education as "the number one
business on this Nation's agenda ... 'the guardian genius of our democracy.' " He announced "a national goal of Full Educational Opportunity," reminded Congress that the country spent "seven times
as much on a youth that has gone bad" as on one who stayed in
school, and asked for a doubling of federal spending on education
from $4 billion to $8 billion, with $1 billion going to elementary and
secondary students.[36]

Later in January, Keppel remembers being in the Fish Room at
the White House "with a bunch of other fellows who had bills that
the President wanted to go through. He [LBJ] came in, looking cheer-
ful as can be, and said,... 'Look, we've got to do this in a hurry.' "
He predicted that his majority support in the country would start
eroding by about a million a month, and he wanted these aides to
get their " 'subcommittee hearings going. Keppel, when are you starting yours?' " he asked. "And he turned around with that characteristic
gesture and said,... 'I want to see this coonskin on the wall,' banging
away with his hands at it, you know—wonderful gesture!"[37]

The reaction to his message on education was everything Johnson could have asked. Leading newspapers warmly endorsed the President's proposal. The *Washington Post* praised LBJ's "genius for
finding a way out of blind alleys." Johnson's bill reflected "political
realism at its pragmatic best." It attacked "the most glaring and urgent aspects of the country's educational problem," and "without im-
periling vital constitutional principles."[38]

Yet Johnson knew that Congress, not newspapers, passed laws
and would not act on a ground-breaking measure without constant
pressure. His aides would need to monitor the many twists and turns
the Elementary and Secondary Education Act (ESEA) seemed certain

to take in Congress, and he would have to lobby or stroke pivotal congressmen and senators.

The work of persuading Congress to approve ESEA began the day after Johnson sent his message to the Hill. Bill Moyers and Douglass Cater, the White House point man on the bill, had lunch with Oregon Congresswoman Edith Green, a House leader on education with a reputation for political independence. Moyers reported to Larry O'Brien that they had "massage[d] her ego" and tried "to feel out her position" on the bill. Although she seemed warmly disposed to the measure, the President asked her to come to the Oval Office, where he urged her to "help Larry O'Brien and the Leaders move on this."[39]

Meanwhile, Larry O'Brien developed a detailed strategy. Doug Cater would lead the way, having already helped formulate the bill and the President's message and shown it to the committee and subcommittee chairmen. He would now have to ride herd on committee witnesses by helping prepare their testimony. He would also be responsible for monitoring the reactions of committee members and figuring out how to defeat opposition proposals.[40]

By the first week of March, the House Labor and Education Committee had approved the President's bill. But, as O'Brien told LBJ, neither the press nor the public understood "the magnitude of your victory . . . and the difficulty in obtaining it." During the two weeks after Johnson submitted the bill, everything had gone "beautifully," with the House subcommittee ready to vote 6 to 3 in favor.[41]

In early February, however, trouble erupted. Adam Clayton Powell, the chairman of the House Education and Labor Committee, promised to take up the bill in full committee on February 8. But Powell canceled the meeting, went to Puerto Rico, and refused to answer phone messages from either O'Brien or Speaker John McCormack. Under suspicion of improper use of expense money, Powell, in return for ESEA approval, wanted administration pressure to reverse Rules Committee votes reducing funds for his committee. But a White House promise to help was not enough to get action from Powell.

In response, O'Brien arranged for a resolution to keep the committee in session until it reported the bill. But committee members, only two of whom were southerners, were reluctant to act unless the North got more money and the South got less. Then, other "special considerations" arose that also threatened prompt action. Members demanded and got an additional $63 million for city school districts, and Edith Green agitated the religious issue, telling Protestant leaders that "this bill will put Catholic priests in the public schools." Though the committee passed the bill by one vote at the beginning of March, O'Brien believed that potential religious and racial problems made quick approval "as compelling as ever." He told the President, "We're devoting the major part of our time to contacting members, stimulating pressure groups, and putting out the fires we discover on this bill."[42]

Johnson now involved himself directly in the fight. In February, after he met privately with National Education Association (NEA) leaders, they voted to endorse ESEA. At the end of the month, he made a symbolic visit to the Office of Education. "Nothing in the world could have done our cause more good or raised morale higher," Keppel told Jack Valenti. Johnson then invited 200 NEA officials to the White House on March 1 to underscore his eagerness for federal aid to education.[43]

Over the next six weeks, while Congress completed its work on the bill, Johnson pressured House and Senate leaders with a series of phone calls, and kept tabs on the likely congressional votes. The House rewarded his efforts with a margin of 263 to 153 on March 26. He now insisted that the Senate enact the same law and avoid the need for a conference committee, which might cause mischief. Republican Senator Winston Prouty of Vermont complained that the issue before the nation was not education, but "the future of the Senate as a co-equal partner in the legislative process." Ignoring Prouty, the Senate passed the House bill by 73 to 18 on April 9.

Eric Goldman described Johnson's performance as an astonishing piece of political artistry. In only eighty-seven days, "the Congress had passed a billion-dollar law, deeply affecting a fundamental institution of the nation. . . . The House had approved it with no amendments that mattered; the Senate had voted it through literally without a comma changed."[44]

Johnson was euphoric. He said: "Since 1870, almost a hundred years ago, we have been trying to do what we have just done—pass an elementary school bill for all the children of America. . . . We did it, by all that's good we did it, and it's a wonderful proud thing. . . . This is the most important bill I will ever sign."

On April 11, in a ceremony outside a dilapidated little building a mile and a half east of his ranch, where he had first gone to school, Johnson signed the law in the presence of Katie Deadrich Looney, his first teacher; a classmate; some of the Mexican-Americans he had taught in Cotulla, Texas, in 1927–28; four debate team members he had coached in Sam Houston High School in 1929–30; and a number of Washington dignitaries. "Take it from me," he declared at a White House ceremony two days later, "I worked harder and longer on this measure than on any measure I have ever worked on since I came to Washington in 1931—and I am proud of it."[45]

Johnson knew that enactment of ESEA was only the beginning of wisdom. At the signing ceremony, he quoted Thomas Jefferson: " 'Preach, my dear sir, a crusade against ignorance; establish and improve the law for educating the common people.' We have established the law," Johnson declared. "Let us not delay in putting it to work." As he told congressional leaders two days later, he was moving immediately to prepare the Office of Education "for the big job that it has to do."[46]

Yet Johnson's reach in administering the law was limited. Beyond delegating the work to administration officials, his preoccupation with passing other bills and managing foreign affairs left him little time and inclination to pay close attention to how ESEA was working. More important, the bill dictated that local school districts rather than the federal government have the greatest say in spending ESEA funds. And they chose to use them on conventional ends and means. Moreover, Federal spending under Johnson's reform amounted to only 6 percent of the cost of elementary and secondary education.

"Lyndon Johnson thought Title I [of ESEA] was an antipoverty program," historian Allen J. Matusow writes. "Local officials made sure it never was. A 1977 sample survey revealed that nearly two-thirds of the students in programs funded by Title I were not poor; more than half were not even low achievers; and 40 percent were neither poor nor low achieving." Eight years later, and twenty years after ESEA had passed, the National Institute of Education estimated that about half the funds spent under the law had gone to children living above the poverty line.

Moreover, as studies shortly began to make clear, Johnson's hopes that education could improve the lives of poor youngsters far outran the reality. Educators found that poverty had more to do with family background and general social context than the quantity and quality of education a child received. And even where studies suggested initial improvements for poor kids helped by ESEA reading and math programs, later assessments indicated that benefits faded quickly and left students little better off than those not in the programs.[47]

Still, as Johnson anticipated, the aid to education mandated under ESEA contributed to the national well-being. Though the law never provided either the equal education or the educational opportunity Johnson hoped it would, it went far to spur state governments to become more involved in educational questions, shape new teaching techniques such as small-group instruction, fix attention on the importance of early childhood schooling, benefit students at near-average achievement levels, speed desegregation of schools, and assist handicapped and non-English-speaking pupils who previously had received no special attention. Finally, it led to the creation of a Cabinet-level Department of Education in 1980 and the enduring hope that additional studies and efforts may yet bring our understanding of elementary and secondary instruction to a point that will more fully assure the educational opportunity Johnson considered a birthright of all Americans.[48]

In November 1965 Johnson signed a Higher Education Act (HEA) at his alma mater, Southwest Texas State University in San Marcos. The law established college and university community service programs designed to assist in the solution of urban and suburban problems. It provided monies to support library acquisitions at colleges and universities and to train librarians and specialists in information sciences. It instituted a program for "strengthening developing institutions," which meant aid to poor black colleges. Its Title Four, the law's most important and expensive part, provided scholarships, loans, and more spending on federal work-study programs to aid students.

By 1970, in five years, one out of every four college students in America was receiving some form of financial assistance provided by HEA. The law facilitated a huge expansion of college enrollments. In 1970, 34 percent of the eighteen-to-twenty-one age group in America attended some college degree credit program; up from 15 percent in 1950. By 1990, the number had grown to 52 percent.[49]

In 1993, the Organization for Economic Cooperation and Development issued a report card on the educational systems of the world's industrialized nations. The OECD found that "the United States does a reasonably good job of educating its citizens and preparing them for work." It also offered a statistical portrait of American education that was "far more favorable than several studies undertaken in recent years by American educators." Ninety percent of American five-year-olds attended early childhood programs, and a significantly higher percentage of American youngsters were enrolled in college than their counterparts around the world. The United States spent about twice as much per student on higher education than most other industrialized countries. "Thirty-six percent of Americans between the ages of 25 and 64 held college degrees—among the highest in the world." Though the report found much to complain about in American education—the limited number of weekly hours students spent in classrooms and the excessive spending on noninstructional personnel—it nevertheless gave American education pretty good grades.[50]

The fact that the country's educational system works as well as it does has something to do with the federal support Johnson initiated in 1965. If his educational reforms did not lead to a Great Society, they have at least made for a better society. It is an achievement for which Johnson deserves the country's continuing regard.

Medicare

For Johnson, there could be no Great Society—no improved quality of national life—without greater access for all Americans to health care and special efforts to conquer the country's most disabling diseases and common killers, heart attack, cancer, and stroke.

As with all the major reforms he backed throughout his political career, he was most ardent and effective when he could see a public problem as an enlargement of a personal concern. A war on poverty, government programs to eliminate individual and family need, resonated with his own memories and enduring feelings of deprivation; equal rights and opportunities for minorities was an indirect assault on prejudice against a Lyndon Johnson, the southerner or southwesterner from rural Texas whose regional identity partly kept him from a presidential nomination in 1960; federal aid to education meant increased opportunity for the schooling Lyndon had used to pull himself up the economic and social ladders.

Johnson's family history sensitized him to the losses inflicted by heart attack, cancer, and stroke. His father had died at sixty-three from coronary disease; his mother had succumbed to cancer; and he remembered a grandmother immobilized by a stroke. His own heart attack in July 1955 at the age of forty-six, from which he had made a strong recovery, raised doubts about his longevity. " 'I don't like to sleep alone ever since my heart attack,' " Johnson told an aide. "If Lady Bird was away, the President would often call friends . . . and ask them to stay at the White House in the room next to his. . . . 'The only deal is,' he would say, 'you've got to leave your door open a crack so that if I holler someone will hear me.' " A war on heart disease was a possible vehicle for extending his life.[51]

But, of course, it was much more than that. Johnson had been an advocate of federally supported health care delivery and research since the 1940s when he had backed the Hill-Burton law assisting states to build hospitals. In 1956, he had attached an amendment to a Social Security bill making it possible to provide federal health insurance to the elderly.

At the same time, Johnson had become a warm friend of Mary Lasker, a wealthy supporter of health care research, who had borrowed advertising techniques her husband Albert had pioneered to create public backing for federally financed studies of cancer and heart disease. "Mary and her little lambs," as Lasker's backers were called, had persuaded Congress to create the National Institutes of Health (NIH). In 1959, Johnson, who had told someone that there was probably "no more important problem facing us than finding the solution to the dread diseases," allied himself with Lasker in overcoming White House opposition to increased funding for medical research.[52]

In the first months of his presidency, Johnson sent a message to Congress announcing his determination to make "the wonders of modern medicine" available to all Americans. He urged hospital insurance for the aged, more modern hospitals, increased and better medical manpower, and greater spending on mental health and ways to prevent and cure heart disease, cancer, and strokes, the country's leading causes of death.[53]

Johnson's highest initial health care priority in 1964 was not Medicare or hospital insurance for the elderly but the creation of a Commission on Heart Disease, Cancer and Strokes (HDCS). "Two-thirds of all Americans now living will ultimately suffer or die from one of them," he told the Congress. He asked the commission to submit recommendations by the end of the year for combating these diseases.[54]

In April, when he introduced the members of the commission in a White House ceremony, he announced his "keenest," "greatest," and "most personal interest" in their work, and urged them to spare no effort in bringing America's three great killers and cripplers under control. He expressed full confidence in their ability to meet this challenge before the end of the decade: "When this occurs—not 'if,' but 'when,' and I emphasize 'when'—we will face a new challenge and that will be what to do within our economy to adjust ourselves to a lifespan and a work span for the average man or woman of 100 years."[55]

Buoyed by Johnson's evangelism and by the medical advances of the 1940s and 1950s that had produced cures for infectious diseases, especially polio, the commission issued a report in December that promised "miracles" in the near future. A $2.8 billion program implemented over five years could bring the "ultimate conquest" of heart disease, cancer, and strokes. Swept up in the euphoria of overcoming the diseases that had accounted for 71 percent of the country's deaths in 1962, Johnson declared the world on "the threshold of a historic breakthrough. Heart disease, cancer, and stroke *can* be conquered—not in a millennium, not in a century, but in the next few onrushing decades."[56]

To fulfill the commission's promise, Johnson asked Congress for money to set up the Regional Medical Program (RMP), a network of hospitals in which research and practice would be federally funded. The President's proposal met insurmountable opposition. "This country of ours can declare war on poverty, war in Viet Nam, but *not* war on cancer or strokes or heart attacks," a physician declared. "It just doesn't work this way, and I think it is cruel to so mislead the American people." The American Medical Association (AMA) protested against a government-operated system of hospitals that would threaten to replace the world's most advanced health care delivery system with an American form of socialized medicine. Responsive to these pressures, Congress agreed to a watered-down RMP that barely resembled the original plan.[57]

During 1964–65 Johnson's interest in mounting a war on heart disease, cancer, and stroke had waned as the political realities of what he confronted became clear. Instead, he increasingly focused on hospital insurance for the aged under Social Security. Although it had been on liberal reform agendas since the 1930s and had failed to win passage in four successive Congresses beginning with the 85th in 1957, it had gained widespread public appeal by the summer of 1964 as the most desirable change in the country's system of financing and delivering health care.

Partly responding to opinion surveys by pollster Oliver Quayle of the most important election-year issues, Johnson publicly made Medicare a high legislative priority in the 1965 congressional term. In November, on the eve of the election, when asked by a reporter whether Medicare would be a "must" bill next year, Johnson answered: "Just top of the list." Two weeks later, the President told HEW Assistant Secretary Wilbur J. Cohen, who was the administration's principal advocate of Medicare, that he would make it our "number one priority." He asked Cohen to "touch base with everyone concerned," keep Cabinet members abreast of developments, and put his "full energies" behind the bill.[58]

A prime Johnson concern was to assure that a Medicare law would pass the 89th Congress. With two-to-one margins in both Houses, it seemed likely that some kind of hospital insurance for Americans over sixty-five would be approved. Larry O'Brien believed that passage of a Medicare bill was "as inevitable as tomorrow morning's sunrise." But Johnson, always reluctant to take Congress for granted, wanted nothing left undone to assure passage. Cohen consulted congressional and AFL-CIO leaders and reported through HEW Secretary Anthony Celebrezze that the President's "continued cooperation" would bring success during the first few months of the new Congress. In December, Larry O'Brien made a head count of the Senate, where he predicted a favorable vote of 55 to 45. If Richard Russell could be added to the majority, it would make for a more secure and larger margin. Johnson passed the information along to Cohen and asked Valenti to "talk quietly with Sen. Russell."[59]

The key figure in passing Medicare was Arkansas Congressman Wilbur Mills, the chairman of the Ways and Means Committee. Mills and his committee had been staunch opponents of government-sponsored hospital insurance. A fiscal conservative, Mills worried that Medicare would lead to large federal deficits. He was also reluctant to back any controversial legislation that might fail or pass by a small margin. In July 1964, when Cohen had asked the President to get a commitment from Mills on Medicare, Johnson replied that "he hadn't been successful in getting Mills committed to anything." Johnson didn't like Mills, whom he later described to Doris Kearns as a "prissy, prim and proper man" who "worried more about saving his face than ... saving his country. He was afraid to put his reputation behind a risky bill," Johnson said. "But when you run around saving your face all day, you end up losing your ass at night."[60]

For all Johnson's vaunted talent at persuasion, Mills was not susceptible to presidential pressure. Nor was he very responsive to national opinion favoring Medicare legislation. Holding a safe seat and seeing himself as a man of principle who would not jeopardize the country's fiscal future for the sake of a social reform, however worthy, Mills and his committee had been an insurmountable obstacle to Medicare in 1961–64. In 1962, for example, when the Kennedy administration had encouraged public rallies by senior citizens backing Medicare, it had learned how tough Mills could be. The rallies "made little or no impact," Larry O'Brien recalls. To the contrary, they "antagonized" Mills.[61]

Yet, as Johnson appreciated, Mills was a political realist. With the Democratic landslide in November 1964, Mills understood that he would no longer command a conservative majority on Ways and Means and that it would be difficult, if not impossible, to resist passing Medicare. Consequently, on November 11, 1964, and again on January 1, 1965, he publicly acknowledged that his committee "would be able to work something out" on Medicare, though he continued to insist on the importance of a sound financing plan.[62]

Mills's comments convinced Johnson that he could get a Medicare law passed in the first session of the 89th Congress. In his State
of the Union address on January 4 and more fully in a special message
to Congress on the 7th, Johnson made the case for hospital care under
Social Security: Since "four out of five persons 65 or older have a
disability or chronic disease," since hospital stays and costs for folks
over sixty-five are twice what they are for younger people, since
"almost half of the elderly have no health insurance at all," and since
"the average retired couple cannot afford the cost of adequate health
protection under private health insurance," the President asked that
Social Security "be extended to finance the cost of basic health services" through "regular, modest contributions during working years."
In this way, the government would lift the specter of catastrophic
hospital bills from the lives of the elderly.[63]

Johnson was so confident now that he could get Medicare passed,
he agreed to put the bill at the top of his legislative agenda; the
House and Senate labeled the bill H.R.1 and S.1. But to assure against
creating new grounds for opposition, he proposed a narrowly focused
bill, which would cover the aged for hospital, but not physicians' costs.
By omitting doctors' fees, Johnson hoped to avoid charges of "socialized medicine."

As designed by Mills and Wilbur Cohen and approved by the
President, Medicare provided 60 days of hospital coverage, 180 days
of skilled nursing home care, and 240 days of home health visits for
Social Security recipients sixty-five and older. A Hospital Insurance
Trust Fund created with small payroll deductions and employer contributions amounting to 0.076 of 1 percent of wages was to finance
the program. The outlook for the bill seemed so bright that seventy
House members and forty-three Senators offered themselves as co-
sponsors. Moreover, Speaker McCormack advised the White House
that Mills and the House leadership saw no need for hearings.[64]

Yet it quickly became apparent that conservative Republicans
and the American Medical Association might be able to sidetrack the
administration's bill with alternative proposals. John Byrnes, the senior Republican member of Ways and Means, introduced "Bettercare,"
a voluntary plan providing federal payments of insurance premiums
for older persons with low incomes. The Byrnes plan covered both
doctors' and hospital fees, with some cost sharing. Federal monies for
the program were to come out of the general fund. The AMA proposed a variation on the Byrnes plan called "Eldercare." It promised
to cover all medical costs of the indigent elderly by expanding an
existing medical welfare program administered through the states
since 1960. Though the Byrnes and AMA plans would leave most

elderly Americans uncovered, their more comprehensive coverage for
qualified recipients and the absence of a new special fund for financing made them appealing.[65]

Because Mills feared an effective Republican attack on the administration's bill as less generous than "Bettercare" and "Eldercare,"
he proposed incorporating their principal features into Medicare. At
a closed session of his committee on the afternoon of March 2, Mills
made the "ingenious" suggestion that Medicare become "a three-layer
cake": hospital insurance under Social Security; a voluntary insurance
program for doctors' bills subsidized out of general federal revenues;
and an expanded medical welfare program for the indigent administered through the states and known as Medicaid. As Cohen told
LBJ, Mills was "almost certain that nobody will vote against the bill
when it comes on the floor of the House." Mills thought it would be
"unassailable politically from any serious Republican attack."[66]

Johnson needed no prodding to accept Mills's proposal. He saw
it as a significant advance on the administration's bill and as certain
to fly through the House. When Cohen told him that Part B insurance
for doctors' bills would cost the government about $500 million a
year, Johnson dismissed the cost as cheap for so desirable a reform.
" 'Five hundred million. Is that all?' Johnson exclaimed with a wave
of his big hand. 'Do it. Move that damn bill out now, before we lose
it.' " When Ways and Means reported the bill and the House passed
it on April 8 by a 110-vote margin, a group of senior citizens feted
Mills at a luncheon. "We've seen the promised land," the delegation
chairman told the gathering.[67]

But "the promised land" lay through the Senate. And despite
every expectation that the upper House would also pass a Medicare
bill, Johnson still took nothing for granted. In January, after Medicare
had been introduced in the House, Johnson had invited House and
Senate leaders to the White House for "an extremely important, very
sensitive meeting." They had no idea that they would be reviewing
the status of the bill before television cameras.

Johnson saw this as an opportunity to win a public commitment
from conservative Senator Harry Byrd, Sr., the chairman of the Finance Committee, not to sidetrack Medicare, as he had in the past.
The President surprised Byrd by asking him to commit his committee
to prompt hearings. "I will see that adequate and thorough hearings
are held on the bill," Byrd replied. Johnson wasn't satisfied: "You
have nothing that you know of that would prevent that coming about
in a reasonable time?" he asked. "There is nothing ahead of it in the
committee?" Byrd answered: "Nothing in the committee now." Johnson wouldn't let go: "So, when the House acts and it is referred to

the Senate Finance Committee, you will arrange for prompt hearings and thorough hearings?" "Yes," Byrd said. As he left the White House, Byrd told one of LBJ's aides, if he had known he was to appear on television, he would have dressed more formally.[68]

Though Byrd was true to his word, Russell Long of Louisiana, a fellow committee member, was not so accommodating. Eager to show his independence of Johnson after having voted with him on civil rights, Long, who shared conservative concerns about government interference in health care, proposed a catastrophic insurance amendment that fundamentally transformed the bill. Moreover, he persuaded committee members, who had not read his proposal, to vote for it by misrepresenting what it included. Only after a series of telephone calls rebuking committee members for their votes and vigorous lobbying by Medicare advocates was Johnson able to reverse the committee's action. Even then it took over 500 minor Senate amendments and some hard bargaining in a conference committee before Congress passed Medicare on July 28.[69]

Johnson's central concern now was to assure that AMA members would not refuse to participate in the Medicare and Medicaid programs. He believed "the medical profession's cooperation was absolutely crucial to Medicare's success." But "predictions that hospitals, clinics, and doctors' offices would be flooded with hordes of elderly patients, [and] that the system would collapse under its own weight," discouraged health professionals from cooperating. Worse yet, some conservatives, like the actor Ronald Reagan, saw Medicare as the advance wave of socialism, which would "invade every area of freedom in this country." Reagan predicted that Medicare would compel Americans to spend their "sunset years telling our children and our children's children what it was like in America when men were free."[70]

Some members of the administration were so worried about winning the cooperation of the AMA that they opposed a Medicare signing ceremony featuring Harry Truman; it seemed likely to evoke memories of Truman's preference for a more comprehensive insurance program and might suggest that LBJ now had this on his agenda. They also urged a meeting with AMA leaders at which the President appealed to doctors to support a law favored by the people and worked out "in the most painstaking way in accordance with the exacting rules of our democracy."[71]

Johnson did not think that the AMA and most physicians would find it easy to oppose Medicare without serious damage to their public standing. When labor leader George Meany told Johnson of his concern about the AMA, LBJ replied: " 'George, have you ever fed chickens?' 'No,' " Meany answered. " 'Well,' " Johnson said, " 'chickens are real dumb. They eat and eat and eat and never stop. Why they start shitting at the same time they're eating, and before you know it, they're knee-deep in their own shit. Well, the AMA's the same. They've been eating and eating nonstop and now they're knee-deep in their own shit and everybody knows it. They won't be able to stop anything.' "[72]

Nevertheless, Johnson saw a meeting with AMA leaders as an opportunity to both stroke them and compel a public acknowledgment of support for Medicare. On July 30, in a discussion with eleven AMA officers at the White House, Johnson, quoting Republican Congressman John Byrnes, emphasized that it was time to abandon past animosities and make the new Medicare program work as well as possible.

Johnson then went on to ask the physicians for help in getting doctors to rotate in and out of Vietnam for a few months to serve the civilian population. Appealing to their patriotism, Johnson declared, "Your country needs your help. Your President needs your help." The doctors responded almost in unison with promises to start a program immediately. "Get the press in here," Johnson told press secretary Bill Moyers. When they arrived, Johnson described and praised the AMA's readiness to help the Vietnamese. But the reporters, probably primed by Moyers, wanted to know whether the doctors would support Medicare. Johnson, with mock indignation, said: " 'These men are going to get doctors to go to Vietnam where they might be killed. Medicare is the law of the land. Of course, they'll support the law of the land. Tell him,' " Johnson said, turning to the head of the delegation. " 'You tell him.' 'Of course, we will,' " the AMA president responded. " 'We are, after all, law-abiding citizens, and we have every intention of obeying the new law.' " A few weeks later the AMA announced its intention to support Medicare.[73]

Within a decade Medicare had become a widely popular entitlement that no President dared oppose. During his eight years in the White House from 1981 to 1989, Reagan, despite vigorous efforts to contain Medicare and Medicaid costs, never proposed the dismantling of either program. The elderly, who had become a powerful voting bloc and had reduced their chances of falling into poverty with the help of Medicare, were ready to punish anyone at the polls who attacked a program they cherished almost as much as Social Security.[74]

Yet all was not perfect with the health care reforms Congress and Johnson had put in place. Eager to assure the cooperation of hospitals and physicians, they took pains to assure their support. Wilbur Cohen had promised the Ways and Means Committee "that there would be no real controls over hospitals or physicians." Hospitals were entitled to be reimbursed for reasonable costs, which was whatever hospitals said they were. Physicians were to be paid customary fees, which would be based on past billing history. There was no inhibition on the freedom of doctors to raise charges each year and submit their higher fees as "billing history."

The results of this generosity were staggering increases in medical costs to the entire society. Where total Medicare expenditures were $3.5 billion in the first year of the program, they had risen to $144 billion by 1993, despite repeated attempts by the government to rein them in. The approximately 5 percent of gross national product Americans spent on health care in 1965 had increased nearly threefold by the early nineties. Though advances in medical technology drove some of this expense, much of it resulted from the increasing availability of insurance and lack of medical cost controls. The benefits to the elderly and the indigent from Medicare and Medicaid are indisputable. But they did not solve the problem of care at reasonable cost for all Americans. Johnson's reforms were only a partial and imperfect solution to a dilemma that other industrialized societies had addressed more successfully.[75]

Selma and Voting Rights

Johnson's vision of a Great Society included an unprecedented degree of racial harmony, with blacks granted equal opportunities to advance their well-being. He hoped that the 1964 civil rights act would begin the process of integrating African Americans into the mainstream of southern life. At the very least, he hoped that all sides in the region's racial strife would give the act a chance to work and relieve the federal government of the need to take new steps to right historic wrongs. This meant not only southern acceptance of desegregation in public facilities but also full participation by blacks in southern politics. In Johnson's view, allowing blacks to vote and hold local, state, and federal offices would give them the same political influence other groups had used to serve their interests.

In a conversation with *New York Times* editor Turner Catledge in December 1964, Johnson stated his wish for an Attorney General replacing Robert Kennedy who "will not be vindictive or punitive against the South. He wants to avoid rubbing the South's nose in its own troubles," Catledge recorded. "He thinks the 'good people' of the South have suffered quite a bit." He didn't want to force acceptance of the civil rights act through "trial and punishment." When Catledge asked "whether it might not be better if the leadership of the civil rights movement would concentrate entirely on voter registration and leave the other things less active for a while," Johnson "bolted out of his chair waving his hands: 'That's exactly what I tell 'em! You know I'm thinking of a scheme to register 'em for federal elections at the post offices.' "[76]

Yet Johnson knew that southern accommodation to desegregation under the 1964 law might not be enough to give blacks, who had been systematically excluded from the polls, the franchise. In Mississippi and Alabama, for example, only 6 and 19 percent, respectively, of voting-age blacks were on the rolls, and office-holders, whose power rested on the existing political customs, would not voluntarily alter a system that served their interests.

To make southern leaders understand that the alternative to regional reform was federal intervention, Johnson demanded an end to unconstitutional limits on black voting in his January State of the Union message. He asked for the elimination of "every remaining obstacle to the right and the opportunity to vote" and declared that "opportunity for all" must include the end to "barriers to the right to vote" by "Negro Americans." At the same time, he privately asked Nicholas Katzenbach, the acting Attorney General, to draft legislation that would enforce constitutional guarantees to vote.[77]

Johnson was ambivalent about putting a voting rights bill before Congress early in 1965. Not because he doubted the value of giving blacks the ballot. He considered such a law "in many ways ... even more critical than" the civil rights act. "Once the black man's voice could be translated into ballots," he said later, "many other breakthroughs would follow." Rather, he saw prospects for congressional passage as "unpromising," and he was reluctant to force another confrontation with the South.[78]

He was also concerned that another major civil rights drive might injure the movement. During 1964 he had read transcripts of FBI recordings of Martin Luther King's "personal activities," or womanizing, which the bureau hoped to use to discredit King. Bill Moyers remembers Johnson as "appalled at the possibility of the movement being collapsed because of this. I shared ... his concern," Moyers says. "There was nothing beyond what Stennis and Eastland and that crowd" might do to undercut King and the whole civil rights effort.[79]

Despite the FBI, in the first three months of 1965, King and the Southern Christian Leadership Conference masterminded a campaign in Selma, Alabama, that persuaded Johnson to sponsor a voting rights act. King and the SCLC leadership saw no prospect of black enfranchisement flowing from recent laws and actions. Efforts by a variety of civil rights organizations to register black voters under the "Freedom Summer" project in 1964 had brought little more than violence and intimidation. King saw black enfranchisement in the South coming only when the federal government made it happen. And this would require another Birmingham or some fresh demonstration of repressive police action against black demonstrators peacefully asking for the vote.

Selma, the "most oppressive" city in the South, where less than 1 percent of potential black voters was registered, became the focus of King's campaign. It also had a law enforcement officer who was a caricature of himself. Pinning a "Never!" button to his lapel, surrounding himself with deputies carrying electric cattle prods, Jim Clark, a heavyset, jowly man who called blacks "the lowest form of humanity," lived up to his advanced billings as a violent southern sheriff. After an attack on demonstrators that aroused national sympathy for their campaign and stiffened their resolve to fight on, civil rights organizations voted Clark "an honorary member of SNCC, SCLC, CORE [and] the N-Double A-C-P."

In a speech on January 2 at Selma's African Methodist Episcopal church, King declared that, if state and county authorities did not meet black demands for the vote, "we will seek to arouse the federal government by marching by the thousands to the places of registration." And if this didn't work, there would be another march on Washington "to appeal to the conscience of the Congress." King received an answer of sorts to his demand when he tried to register at a local segregated hotel. Egged on by a white woman yelling, "Get him, get him, get him," a twenty-six-year-old member of the National States Rights party hit King in the head and kicked him in the groin.[80]

Beginning on January 18, a series of demonstrations by black residents asking to register captured national attention. Jim Clark played into King's hands by arresting numerous protestors, including hundreds of school children, and committing acts of violence that made the front pages of newspapers across the country. On February 3, King sent Johnson a message asking him to send a personal emissary to Selma to evaluate the situation, make a statement supporting the voting drive campaign in Selma, and take appropriate legislative and executive action to secure the right to vote in all elections, including those controlled by individual states.[81]

Johnson responded cautiously. At a press conference on February 4, he urged all Americans to "be indignant when one American is denied the right to vote. The loss of that right to a single citizen undermines the freedom of every citizen. This is why all of us should be concerned with the efforts of our fellow Americans to register to vote in Alabama." He explained that the government was "using the tools of the Civil Rights Act of 1964 in an effort to secure [Negroes] their right to vote." He also cited federal efforts to use the courts to eliminate voting discrimination. When a reporter asked whether he intended to send federal marshalls or military personnel to Selma or do anything else, Johnson restated his intention to use the civil rights act and the courts to assure the right to vote.[82]

Because Johnson evaded the issue, King now publicly declared his intention to press for a voting rights law. The following day, February 6, Johnson announced through his press secretary that he would ask Congress for such a bill. Though its content was yet to be determined, the White House indicated that it would go to Congress "this year." Before the administration acted, however, civil rights advocates in the House introduced two bills on February 8. "I had hoped that we could wait until we had an opportunity to see the Civil Rights Act in operation before we took up new legislation," one of them said, "but the events of recent weeks have made this impossible."[83]

Despite these developments, Johnson was still not ready to act. He did agree to a fifteen-minute meeting with King at the White House on February 9, after King had seen Katzenbach and Vice President Humphrey. As a condition of the meeting, Johnson insisted that King issue a statement emphasizing the President's commitment to voting rights and intention to propose legislation. King, in fact, told reporters that the President planned to do this "very soon," though he did not repeat Humphrey's expression of doubt that Congress was ready to pass a law. King, a biographer notes, "returned to the South knowing that further interest in voting rights problems and the Selma campaign needed to be stirred."[84]

Violent confrontations over the next several weeks, including the death of a twenty-six-year-old demonstrator shot in the stomach by a state trooper, and King's announcement on March 3 that he would lead a walk from Selma to the state capital of Montgomery beginning on March 7, sustained discussion in the administration and Congress of enacting a rights bill. At another meeting on March 5, LBJ and King renewed their discussion of legislation, but, according to King, Johnson did not tell him "exactly what would be in the voting proposal and had offered no promises." Johnson also apparently warned King against mistakes by civil rights groups that could drain off national interest in voting legislation.[85]

All the mistakes now came from Alabama officials. On March 6, Governor George Wallace banned the March 7 walk as likely to endanger the public safety. But 600 demonstrators, without King, who remained in Atlanta after being warned of a plot against his life, set out on the march anyway. After crossing the Edmund Pettus Bridge over the Alabama River, they confronted some fifty state troopers and dozens of Clark's deputies barring their path on U.S. Highway 80. After warning the marchers to disperse and giving them two minutes to leave, the troopers rushed forward, beating them with clubs and driving them back across the bridge into town. Besieged by tear gas, clubs, whips, and mounted horsemen, seventeen marchers needed hospitalizing and forty required treatment for minor injuries and tear gassing.[86]

The national reaction to what the press called "Bloody Sunday" was everything advocates of a voting rights law could have wished. Television provided graphic descriptions of the police actions, and newspapers all over the country featured the story on their front pages. Johnson himself issued a statement "deploring the brutality with which a number of Negro citizens of Alabama were treated when they sought to dramatize their deep and sincere interest in attaining the precious right to vote." He also announced his intention to send a voting rights bill to Congress in the following week.[87]

In the meantime, he focused his efforts on trying to head off more violence in Alabama. When King announced that he would begin another march to Montgomery on March 9, the White House urged him to avoid a fresh confrontation. With a federal judge issuing a temporary order barring all marches, King was reluctant to defy the very authority he was trying to enlist in his campaign. Consequently, he agreed to a compromise worked out by a mediator the President had sent to Selma. King led 2000 marchers, including 200 religious leaders from all over the country, across the Pettus Bridge, where Alabama troopers once again blocked the way. After singing "We Shall Overcome," the anthem of the civil rights movement, and kneeling in prayer for several minutes, King led the marchers back to Selma without incident.

King's restraint contrasted dramatically with the actions of local whites the next day. They beat up the Reverend James Reeb, a white minister from Boston, who died in a Birmingham hospital the following night.[88]

Johnson now came under strong pressure to intervene with federal troops. Sympathy marchers in cities around the country urged the President to protect the protestors in Alabama, while pickets outside the White House carried signs denouncing Johnson's inaction: "LBJ, just you wait . . . see what happens in '68."[89]

Johnson was pained at the attacks on his commitment to support black voting rights. "Once again my Southern heritage was thrown in my face. I was hurt, deeply hurt," he wrote later. But he was determined "not to be shoved into hasty action." Though he had put 700 troops on alert during the second march on March 9 and though federal attorneys, marshalls, and FBI agents had been sent to Selma to keep the peace, Johnson was reluctant to publicize his actions. Southern obstructionists eager to show the South as a victim of overbearing federal power might use them to their advantage. If he acted too aggressively, Johnson believed it would alienate southern moderates, antagonize centrists everywhere, and block passage of a voting rights act. On the other hand, if he did nothing to protect the marchers, it would deepen the rift between North and South and undermine his ability to lead a law through Congress.[90]

Johnson needed the cooperation of George Wallace, who also wanted to prevent further bloodshed. Wallace had national ambitions and the sense to see that more violence would mark him as simply a racist rather than an opponent of federal authority, which he rightly believed could be made into a popular political issue. "Now that Wallace, he's a lot more sophisticated than your average southern politician, and it's his ox that's in the ditch, let's see how he gets him out," Johnson said at a meeting convened to discuss the crisis.

To escape his dilemma, Wallace asked Johnson to see him. Johnson agreed at once, and they met at the White House on the afternoon of March 13. The meeting provided the occasion for what one aide called possibly LBJ's finest performance. Johnson's objective was to put Wallace on the spot, to make clear that he would back the legitimate demands of the marchers and insist that Wallace protect peaceful demonstrators from police violence.[91]

Johnson orchestrated every aspect of the meeting. He received Wallace in the Oval Office, where he sat him on a couch with soft cushions that placed him some three or four feet above the floor. Johnson positioned himself in a rocking chair "and leaned toward the semi-recumbent Wallace, his towering figure inclined downward until their noses almost touched." After Johnson let Wallace say his piece against outside agitators stirring up trouble and his opposition to federal intervention in the affairs of his state, Johnson gave him the "treatment." "I know you're like me, not approving of brutality," Johnson said, and handed the governor a newspaper with a picture of a state trooper kicking a black protestor who had been knocked to the ground. Johnson waved aside Wallace's explanations that the troopers were only doing their duty, that it was an isolated incident, and that they didn't start the ruckus. Johnson pressed Wallace into acknowledging that there was "brutality."

Then raising the issue of black disenfranchisement, Johnson asked Wallace to persuade Alabama registrars to give blacks their constitutional right to vote. Wallace protested that he didn't have the wherewithal to sway these local officials. "Don't shit me about your persuasive power, George," Johnson replied. "I saw you . . . attacking me [on television], George. And you know what? You were so damn persuasive that I had to turn off the set before you had me changing my mind."

But Lyndon wanted Wallace to understand that he was the great persuader, who would bend Wallace and the South to his will. " 'Why don'tcha just desegregate all your schools?' " he asked Wallace. " 'You and I go out there in front of those television cameras right now, and you announce you've decided to desegregate every school in Alabama.' " Wallace replied: " 'Oh, Mr. President, I can't do that, you know. The schools have got school boards; they're locally run. I haven't got the political power to do that.' Johnson said, 'Don't you shit me, George Wallace.' "

After nearly three hours of hammering at the governor, Johnson appealed to his sense of history. He urged Wallace not to "think about 1968; you think about 1988. You and me, we'll be dead and gone then, George. Now you've got a lot of poor people down there in Alabama, a lot of ignorant people. You can do a lot for them, George. Your president will help you. What do you want left after you when you die? Do you want a Great . . . Big . . . Marble monument that reads, 'George Wallace—He Built'? . . . Or do you want a little piece of scrawny pine board lying across that harsh, caliche soil, that reads, 'George Wallace—He Hated'?" After their meeting, Wallace remarked: "Hell, if I'd stayed in there much longer, he'd have had me coming out for civil rights."[92]

At a subsequent press conference, Johnson left no doubt about his intentions. He wanted to eliminate "a deep and very unjust flaw in American democracy" by sending Congress a voting rights law that would enforce the constitutional guarantee against barring people from the polls because of race or color. As for his meeting with Wallace, Johnson described the governor as eager for law and order. To that end, Johnson said he had suggested three actions: that Wallace declare his support for universal suffrage in Alabama, that he assure the right of peaceful assembly, and that he call for a biracial meeting to promote greater unity among all Alabamans.

Johnson said nothing about an agreement with Wallace on how to keep the peace. When Wallace thought it necessary, he would ask the President for help, and Johnson, according to one aide, "would help him save his political ass by accepting the subterfuge." Conse-

quently, after a federal court had agreed to an SCLC plan for a march
to Montgomery beginning on the 21st, Wallace wired Johnson that
Alabama lacked the funds to protect the marchers and asked the
President to use federal means to do the job. Johnson replied on
March 20 by calling 1800 Alabama national guardsmen into federal
service.[93]

Johnson's immediate concern was to mobilize congressional action on voting rights. He didn't think it was enough simply to send
a proposal to the Hill with a special message describing the historical
record of constitutional violations of black rights. Rather, he felt compelled to go before Congress, where he could command the attention
of the nation and the world and emphasize the importance and urgency of remedying this national insult to law and democracy. "I
wanted to use every ounce of moral persuasion the presidency held,"
Johnson wrote later. "I wanted no hedging, no equivocation. And I
wanted to talk from my own heart, from my own experience."

Though Richard Goodwin wrote the speech, it was, in Goodwin's
phrase, "pure Johnson. . . . It was by me, but it was for and of the
Lyndon Johnson I had carefully studied and come to know." Other
aides also had a go at drafting, but, Eric Goldman says, "to an extraordinary extent the final manuscript was Lyndon Johnson in Lyndon Johnson's own language."[94]

It was Johnson's greatest speech and one of the most moving
and memorable presidential addresses in the country's history. Comparing Selma to Lexington and Concord, to Appomattox, Johnson
described it as "a turning point in man's unending search for freedom.
. . . Rarely in any time does an issue lay bare the secret heart of
America itself. . . . Rarely are we met with a challenge . . . to the values
and the purposes and the meaning of our beloved Nation. The issue
of equal rights for American Negroes is such an issue. And should
we defeat every enemy, should we double our wealth and conquer
the stars, and still be unequal to this issue, then we will have failed
as a people and as a nation."

The issue, Johnson said, was democracy, the right of the individual, regardless of race or color, to vote. "There is no constitutional
issue here," Johnson asserted. "The command of the Constitution is
plain. There is no moral issue. It is wrong—deadly wrong—to deny
any of your fellow Americans the right to vote in this country. There
is no issue of States rights or national rights. There is only the struggle for human rights."

And, Johnson declared, measuring every word, "what happened
in Selma is part of a far larger movement which reaches into every
section and State of America. It is the effort of American Negroes to

secure for themselves the full blessings of American life. Their cause must be our cause too. Because it is not just Negroes, but really it is all of us, who must overcome the crippling legacy of bigotry and injustice. And," Johnson paused, raising his arms for emphasis, "We shall overcome."

A moment of stunned silence followed, as the audience absorbed the fact that the President had embraced the anthem of black protest. And then almost the entire chamber rose in unison, "applauding, shouting, some stamping their feet." Tears rolled down the cheeks of senators, congressmen, and observers in the gallery, moved by joy, elation, a sense that the victor, for a change, was human decency, the highest standards by which the nation was supposed to live.

Johnson did not wish to conclude before giving African Americans their full due. "A century has passed, more than a hundred years, since the Negro was freed. And he is not fully free tonight.... A century has passed, more than a hundred years, since equality was promised. And yet the Negro is not equal.... The real hero of this struggle is the American Negro," the President added. "His actions and protests, his courage to risk safety and even to risk his life, have awakened the conscience of this Nation.... He has called upon us to make good the promise of America. And who among us can say that we would have made the same progress were it not for his persistent bravery, and his faith in American democracy?" Martin Luther King, watching on television in Birmingham, cried.

Johnson was not content to confine his speech to a request for voting rights. He linked this civil right to his larger purposes: the war on poverty and the building of a Great Society. It was not enough to give people full rights, Johnson asserted; it was also essential "to open the gates to opportunity." He did "not want to be the President who built empires, or sought grandeur, or extended dominion. I want to be the President who educated young children to the wonders of the world. I want to be the President who helped to feed the hungry and to prepare them to be taxpayers instead of taxeaters. I want to be the President who helped the poor to find their own way and who protected the right of every citizen to vote in every election. I want to be the President who helped to end hatred among his fellow men and who promoted love among the people of all races and all regions and all parties. I want to be the President who helped to end war among the brothers of this earth."

Idealism has been common in American political oratory, but Johnson carried the art to heights not heard since Woodrow Wilson promised to end war and make the world safe for democracy. As with Wilson, Johnson meant every word of it. "I never thought ... that I would be standing here in 1965," Johnson told Congress. "It never even occurred to me in my fondest dreams that I might have the chance to help the sons and daughters of those [poor Latino] students [I taught in 1928] and to help people like them all over this country. But now I do have that chance—and I'll let you in on a secret—I mean to use it." The speech was Lyndon Johnson at his best.[95]

First, though, he intended to shepherd the voting rights bill through Congress. Designing a constitutionally sound bill was a considerable challenge. The voting provisions of the earlier civil rights bills had placed the burden of enforcement on the courts with little positive result. Now, the administration decided to propose an automatic formula that would do away with literacy tests and rely on federal examiners to register voters in unresponsive districts. Specifically, the administration bill stated that literacy tests would automatically be suspended if less than 50 percent of voting-age citizens in a state or any of its political subdivisions were registered or voted in the 1964 elections. Further, if elimination of literacy testing did not raise the percentage of voters to 50 percent, the Attorney General could then send federal examiners into the offending state or district to register voters.[96]

Johnson had every indication that the bill would pass both houses quickly by wide margins. Though administration representatives in the Senate had to break a conservative filibuster and fend off liberalizing provisions that jeopardized the bill, by May 26, after only two and a half months, the Senate passed the bill by a lopsided 77 to 19 count. In the House, where conservative maneuvering presented a challenge, the bill won passage on July 9 by an overwhelming 333 to 85 vote. A conference committee spent all of July throwing out House and Senate additions, largely restoring the bill to what the White House had initially proposed. On August 6, in remarks in the Capitol Rotunda, Johnson emphasized the historical importance of the measure he was about to sign and promised that he would move swiftly to enforce its provisions.[97]

The impact of the law across the South was evident at once. By the end of 1966, only four states of the old Confederacy had less than 50 percent of their voting-age blacks registered, and in three of these, registration had reached 47 percent. Only Mississippi, with 33 percent of blacks on the voting rolls, was well short of the law's requirement. At the end of 1967, Georgia, Louisiana, and Virginia had also exceeded the 50 percent target, and Mississippi had 45 percent of its black citizens registered. By the 1968 election, Mississippi was up to 59 percent, and black registration in the eleven Confederate states averaged 62 percent. In 1980, ten million blacks were on the nation's voting rolls, only 7 percent less than the proportion of voting-age whites.

Black office-holding now also expanded dramatically, with the number of black officials multiplying in six Deep South states during the next four years nearly sixfold. Between 1968 and 1980, moreover, the number of southern black elected state and federal officeholders nearly doubled. As important, white politicians seeking black votes abandoned the region's traditional racist demagoguery. In the words of one historian, "a new generation of moderate governors, putting aside the ancient obsession with race, gave the South enlightened leadership." The act also made a large difference in numbers of black elected officials nationally; by 1989, the few hundred black office-holders of 1965 had grown to 6000.[98]

Backlash

The moral and legal gains to the nation from enfranchising blacks was paramount in Johnson's mind. But he also calculated the advantages to himself and the Democratic party from a substantially enlarged black vote. It would be a way to offset the loss of white voters in the South, who responded to the 1964 civil rights and 1965 voting rights laws by shifting political allegiance from the Democrats to the Republicans.

Johnson knew that southern senators, reflecting the change in regional political temper, were furious at him for his passionate embrace of the civil rights movement. At a breakfast meeting the day after Johnson's voting rights speech, Florida's Spessard Holland "asked angrily: 'Did you hear ol' Lyndon say we shall overcome?' The moderate Lister Hill, of Alabama, turning to Richard Russell, asked, 'Dick, tell me something. You trained that boy. . . . What happened to that boy?' The Georgia senator responded, 'I just don't know, Lister. . . . He's a turncoat if there ever was one.' "[99]

Johnson's combination of moral fervor and practical politics had also moved him to press the case for African Americans in a speech at Howard University in June 1965. In May, Johnson received a copy of a report on the black family by Assistant Secretary of Labor Daniel Patrick Moynihan. Describing the breakdown of black families in ghettos across the nation, Moynihan stressed the need for a stable family life as essential to economic and social advancement. The coming challenge would be to assure that blacks had the means to convert opportunities opened by the civil rights revolution into genuine equality. Moynihan saw the heart of the problem as "the systematic weak-

ening of the position of the Negro male." The solution to the problem
was jobs. "We must not rest until every able-bodied Negro male is
working," Moynihan advised.[100]

Moynihan's analysis of the African-American plight stood at the
center of Johnson's Howard University commencement speech on
June 4. Moynihan and Dick Goodwin collaborated on the drafting of
the address, which Martin Luther King, Jr., Roy Wilkins of the
NAACP, and other black leaders enthusiastically endorsed before
Johnson delivered it.

Describing American Negroes as "another nation: deprived of
freedom, crippled by hatred, the doors of opportunity closed to hope,"
Johnson declared that freedom now was not enough to remedy black
suffering. "You do not take a person who, for years, has been hobbled
by chains and liberate him, bring him up to the starting line of a
race and then say, 'you are free to compete with all the others,' and
still justly believe that you have been completely fair. Thus it is not
enough just to open the gates of opportunity. All our citizens must
have the ability to walk through those gates. This is the next and
the more profound stage of the battle for civil rights. We seek . . . not
just equality as a right and a theory but equality as a fact and equality
as a result." More than thirty years later, Johnson's faith in "equality
as a result" of affirmative action seems excessively hopeful, if not
naive.

Johnson described the widening economic gap between whites
and blacks and attributed it to the "centuries of oppression and per-
secution of the Negro man" and the resulting collapse of the black
family, which must be made whole again to break the cycle of despair
and deprivation. Johnson announced the convening of a fall conference entitled, "To Fulfill These Rights." It would assemble scholars,
experts, and government officials aiming "to help the American Negro fulfill the rights which, after the long time of injustice, he is
finally about to secure." It was to be the beginnings of a campaign
for affirmative action—an effort to find ways to help blacks compete
for jobs and admission to the country's best institutions of higher
learning.[101]

The momentum for black advance generated by Birmingham,
Selma, and King's brilliant campaign of nonviolence ground to a halt
in August 1965 with five days of rioting in Watts, the black ghetto
of Los Angeles. Outwardly the most benign black inner city in the
country, Watts, with its tree-lined, unlittered streets and neat single-
family cottages, seemed like an unlikely place for an explosion of
protest against the conditions of deprivation and despair LBJ had
described in his speech. But it was as full of joblessness, crime, suf-

fering, and hopelessness about escaping the miseries of black urban life as any other ghetto in America.

Because the disorders, which cost thirty-four lives and $35 million in property damage, agitated fears that black anger would now turn into mass upheavals in the country's cities, white America responded to Watts with diminished sympathy for black suffering and LBJ's agenda. In California, a widespread increase in gun sales to suburban whites and a rise in the political fortunes of conservative movie actor Ronald Reagan signaled fear of black violence and antagonism to government programs serving poor blacks.

Lyndon Johnson "could see as clearly as Ronald Reagan or anybody else the effect of the Watts riot on the American people, the fear that it caused and the hatred that flowed from the fear," then Deputy Attorney General Ramsey Clark said later. Initially, though, the riots stunned Johnson. He could not square them with the great 1964 and 1965 advances in civil rights. "How is it possible," he asked, "after all we've accomplished? How could it be? Is the world topsy-turvy?" Johnson wasn't the only one surprised by the riots. When an assistant came running into Ramsey Clark's office to report that a major riot was going on in Los Angeles, with hundreds of cars being burned, he replied: "That can't be. There must be a great distortion in the communication of the facts, and that just can't be."[102]

Joseph Califano, LBJ's principal coordinator for domestic affairs, who had joined the White House staff in July after Reedy had resigned and Bill Moyers had become press secretary, tried unsuccessfully to speak to the President for more than two days after the riots began. When Califano finally reached him, Johnson emphasized his eagerness to avoid any "federal presence in Los Angeles" and, by implication, any indication that his administration had contributed to the upheaval by indulging black anger.

He feared, Johnson told Califano, that " 'Negroes will end up pissing in the aisles of the Senate,' and making fools of themselves, the way . . . they had after the Civil War and during Reconstruction. He was worried that just as government was moving to help them, 'the Negroes will once again take unwise actions out of frustration, impatience, and anger.' He feared that the riots would make it more difficult to pass Great Society legislation and threaten the gains we'd already made." The President's words gave Califano a grasp of "how acutely Johnson feared that the reforms to which he had dedicated his presidency were in mortal danger, not only from those who opposed, but from those he was trying to help."[103]

Despite his worries about a white backlash, Johnson had no intention of turning his back on Watts. Within days of the riots, instructions went out to almost every federal agency to help ease black problems in Los Angeles. By the end of the month, more than $29 million had been allocated to the job. At the same time, however, Johnson had insisted on "total secrecy" about the federal effort to assemble a program for combating the underlying causes of the Watts upheaval. "LBJ worried about how the American public would react to putting any more social programs into Watts," Joe Califano recalls. "He didn't want to do anything that might lay him open to charges of encouraging others to riot." A few days before he announced the federal program, he declared the rioters no better than Ku Klux Klansmen, all of whom were "law-breakers."[104]

Johnson's concern to accommodate to the emerging backlash against federal support of blacks registered in his dealings with both Hubert Humphrey and the fall conference "To Fulfill These Rights." In February 1965, Johnson had made Humphrey chairman of a President's Council on Equal Opportunity (PCEO), a body brought into being to coordinate the jumble of government agencies tripping over each other on civil rights. Hubert took up the assignment with his customary enthusiasm and energy. Moreover, his long-standing identification with the crusade for black equality symbolized Johnson's determination to make civil rights a major priority of his administration.[105]

After Watts, however, Johnson felt compelled to mute his public commitment to black rights and opportunities. While he wished to sustain the fight for legal and de facto equality he had spoken of so warmly in his Howard University speech, he now wanted to give it less notoriety. To this end, he decided largely to eliminate Humphrey's role as the administration's point man on civil rights. Shifting his voluble, garrulous Vice President to the sidelines signaled his sensitivity to the changing political mood in the country on aid to African Americans.

Joe Califano recalls a lunch meeting in mid-September with LBJ, during which the President described a conversation with Walter Reuther, president of the United Auto Workers. Reuther had pressed Johnson to launch a massive program of urban renewal, warning that without it blacks would burn America's cities to the ground. Johnson then said, "You know the difference between Hubert and me? When Hubert sits across from Reuther and Reuther's got that limp hand [maimed by a would-be assassin's bullet] stuck in his pocket and starts talking about burning down the cities if billions of federal dollars aren't poured into them, Hubert will sit there smiling away and thinking all the time, 'How can I get his hand out of his pocket so I can shake it?' Well, when Reuther is sitting in the Oval Office telling me that, I'm sitting in my rocker, smiling and thinking all the time, 'How can I get that hand out of his pocket—so I can cut his balls off!' "[106]

Johnson saw Humphrey's demotion as good politics, but he also worried about an outcry from civil rights advocates complaining that the President had lost his nerve. Johnson wanted to reduce public visibility of administration efforts, but he didn't want significant substantive cutbacks in support of black advance or pickets again protesting in front of the White House against administration foot-dragging.

To strike the right balance between competing pressures, Johnson insisted that Humphrey publicly take the lead in shunting himself to the sidelines on civil rights. At a meeting with the Vice President, Johnson said that people keenly interested in the issue believed that greater progress would result from shifting programs under the control of Hubert's PCEO to the departments directly responsible for them. Though Hubert gasped and blanched at what Johnson was saying, he acceded to his wishes, saying that he remained committed to doing whatever the President wanted him to do.

To make the change appear as much Humphrey's as his own, Johnson insisted that the Vice President sign a memo suggesting the civil rights reorganization and then announce it at a press conference at the White House. In his memoirs, Humphrey blamed the change on Califano, who "liked power, and did not want to share it." But the initiative in fact came from LBJ, who sacrificed Humphrey to political needs and the wish to demonstrate that black extremism would make the country and his administration less rather than more ready to address the problems of black America.[107]

At the same time Johnson was demoting Humphrey, he was also postponing and downgrading the fall conference. During the summer, as plans went forward for the meeting, Johnson took a keen interest in its agenda and attendees. In early August, in talks with King and other civil rights leaders, Johnson discussed holding the conference in the middle of November with as many as 4000 participants. Watts, however, made the idea of such a conference less palatable to LBJ. And then the reaction in August and September to the release of the Moynihan Report made a highly publicized White House meeting on civil rights unacceptable to him.

Moynihan's description of black difficulties angered many black and white civil rights leaders. They saw his analysis as patronizing, a case of blaming the victim rather than the perpetrator—white America—for black suffering. Since the conference now seemed likely to make the President, whose Howard University speech had rested so much on Moynihan, a target of liberal hostility and since inflammatory rhetoric at a meeting sponsored by the White House seemed certain to deepen white opposition to the administration's civil rights efforts, Johnson wanted to delay and deemphasize the conference.

Consequently, he worked out a plan to turn the November meeting into a planning session for a June 1966 conference that would be organized and run by conservative black business executives. Though Johnson was far from abandoning his civil rights campaign, he now approached the issue of black rights with greater caution than had been the case in the first two years of his term. He wanted the discussion of black rights, and particularly of affirmative action to advance black opportunity, temporarily put aside. He intended to come back to these matters, but he believed that a tactical pause would now serve the larger cause of long-term advance.[108]

The Many Paths to a Great Society

By slowing administration efforts for civil rights and making them less visible, Johnson hoped not only to get more done for blacks in the long run but also to free himself to advance the many other programs he believed essential to a Great Society. If the country was to reach the promised land he had described in his Ann Arbor speech, it would have to expand its commitment to the war on poverty, eliminate "shameful" ethnic barriers to immigration, make its cities more livable, good housing more accessible, the environment cleaner and more attractive, the consumer less vulnerable to false claims, and the fine arts and humanities a larger part of the nation's life.

By the beginning of 1965, the Office of Economic Opportunity was actively fighting poverty through community action, the job corps, work training, work-study, adult education, the Neighborhood Youth Corps, Volunteers in Service to America (VISTA), and Aid to Families with Dependent Children (AFDC).

As Johnson told the Congress in February, forty-four states had local antipoverty programs and the other six would join them by June. Fifty-three job corps centers were being established around the nation, where nearly 6000 applications were arriving each day; members of 25,000 welfare families were receiving work training; 35,000 college students were on work-study programs; 35,000 adults were being taught to read and write, and as many as 90,000 adults were ready to enroll in basic education programs; Neighborhood Youth

Corps had been set up in forty-nine cities and eleven rural communities, where youngsters between the ages of sixteen and twenty-one had jobs to help them stay in or return to school, or receive training that could prepare them for permanent positions; 8000 volunteers had joined VISTA; and over 4 million people were receiving AFDC benefits.[109]

But to Johnson this was only the beginning of wisdom. In February, he asked Congress to double expenditures for the war on poverty. He urged a commitment to continue poverty programs for the next two years, with an appropriation of $1.5 billion to pay for them in the current fiscal year. His objective now was to fund not only those programs in place but new ones that would increase the likelihood of productive schooling for poor children and teenagers, assure legal services to the indigent, and set up public works projects that could help revitalize the economies of impoverished small towns and rural areas.

During 1965, the 89th Congress, with its liberal majorities and a passion for an antipoverty crusade comparable to the President's, gave Johnson almost everything he asked. It backed Project Head Start for preschool children who had "never looked at a picture book or scribbled with a crayon." The goal was to enroll economically and culturally impoverished kids in programs that would allow them "to enter school on an equal footing with their more fortunate classmates." Congress agreed to Upward Bound, a program designed to provide college preparation for poor teenagers. It also signed on to Legal Services, a nationwide federal program staffed by attorneys offering free counsel to people too poor to hire a lawyer.

Congress also passed a Public Works and Economic Development Act aimed at restoring economic opportunity to folks in "the fishing villages and the old textile towns of New England; . . . the railroad centers of Pennsylvania where the coal trains no longer run; . . . the small areas of Arkansas and Oklahoma and east Texas; [and] . . . the mountain towns of Utah and Idaho, the timber settlements of the Far West."[110]

At the same time, as a matter of simple justice, Johnson pressed Congress to make fundamental changes in the National Origins Act of 1924. Basing migration to America on someone's ethnic origins was as unpalatable to Johnson as prejudice against anyone because of their regional background. As a Texan, who despised the national bias against southerners, he urged an end to "what has been alien to the American dream." Johnson told Speaker John McCormack: "There is no piece of legislation before the Congress that in terms of decency and equity is more demanding of passage than the Immigration bill."

Though polls showed that a third of the country wanted no change in the ethnic quota system and that another 17 percent were indifferent to the matter, Johnson pushed an immigration reform bill that he insisted "not be changed by one comma." The law made skills and family ties the priorities for admission to the United States. In a ceremony at Liberty Island, Johnson described its passage as repairing "a very deep and painful flaw in the fabric of American justice."[111]

Johnson felt as passionately about making the country's cities more habitable. He declared it time to give America's urban centers an enlarged voice in the federal government. With more than two-thirds of Americans living in cities and that population likely to double in the next thirty-five years, Johnson saw a compelling need for a Cabinet Department of Housing and Urban Development. He wanted a department that would take a broad approach to urban problems, "combining [housing] construction with social services and community facilities." As LBJ conceived it, HUD would work to "develop unified transportation systems," assure adequate water supplies and up-to-date sewage services, create a sense of neighborhood through community centers, build "adequate housing for low- and middle-income families," rehabilitate slums, assure enough recreational space, and beautify cities.[112]

The bill passed by Congress and signed by Johnson on September 9 gave the President "enormous organizational latitude," permitting him to bring a variety of issues under the department's control. To decide how to organize HUD, Johnson set up an urban task force at the end of September. He wanted the group to describe how he could use federal resources more effectively in the service of the cities without antagonizing interested parties in and out of Congress. Though a provision of the law said that he had to appoint a secretary, or at least an acting secretary for the department by November 9, Johnson refused to act.[113]

Ostensibly, he was waiting for his task force to report. But, in fact, Watts had created political problems Johnson felt compelled to solve before he chose a secretary and launched the department on a course of urban reform. Everyone had expected the President to make Robert Weaver, the administrator of the Housing and Home Finance Agency, the first black Cabinet member. But Johnson worried that the Senate might see Weaver's appointment as too radical or too much like an attempt to appease black rioters. Moreover, Weaver did not enjoy much influence on Capitol Hill. In mid-October, after the

House rejected rent supplements for the poor because he had published regulations that Republicans called too generous, Johnson was doubly cautious about naming him to the post, privately lambasting his "political stupidity."[114]

Johnson decided to wait until January when excitement over Watts had subsided before announcing his HUD appointee. In the meantime, he played a cat and mouse game with Weaver, encouraging him to withdraw his candidacy one minute and urging him to stay in the running the next. As Joe Califano recalls the episode, Johnson left Weaver "numb. He made it clear he could break or make Weaver—by doing both. He gave me a glimpse of the trait that sometimes drove him to crush and reshape a man before placing him in a job of enormous importance, much the way a ranch hand tames a wild horse before mounting it. To Johnson, this technique helped assure that an appointee was his alone."

At the same time he manipulated Weaver, he allowed black and liberal leaders to lobby him for Weaver's appointment, creating the impression that they were indebted to the President for something he intended to do anyway. While all this was going on, he lined up Senate support. When he announced Weaver as his choice, the Senate took only four days to give unanimous consent.[115]

A desire to clean up and beautify the environment matched Johnson's eagerness to end poverty, expand educational opportunities, assure access to medical care, reform immigration restrictions, and improve urban centers. Though he made much of how important each of these programs was to him, he had no real priority among them; he wanted them all. Johnson said later that had there been nothing for his administration to do but reduce pollution and restore the country's natural beauty, he would gladly have been "a conservation President." Johnson would never have been content with only one great challenge during his term, but it is clear that environmental protection commanded his attention and aroused his best instincts.

In a series of speeches and messages during 1965, he declared his determination to reduce air and water pollution not only by cleaning up the country's atmosphere and waterways but by setting air and water quality standards that would prevent pollution before it occurred. The objective was "to restore as well as to protect." At the same time, he asked Congress to pass a Highway Beautification Act that would curb billboard advertising, eliminate junkyards, and improve landscaping, opening more attractive vistas to motorists as they drove across the United States.[116]

His proposals ran into stiff opposition from the automobile, chemical processing, and billboard advertising industries. Larry

O'Brien remembers that "it was our conviction through the New Frontier–Great Society period that what was needed was dramatic and drastic action" to improve the country's air and water quality. But "up to this time, there hadn't been any major effort to impose rules and procedures on the auto industry, which is contributing tremendously to the problem of our air. Now you're getting into big lobbying, a powerful group with supporters in the Congress."

Likewise, effective opposition to the water and highway bills forced the White House into arm twisting of reluctant congressmen and senators. "These measures met with considerable resistance," LBJ recalled. "Powerful special interest groups, particularly in industry, foresaw that it would be expensive to change their methods of operation in order to meet strict new federal pollution standards."[117]

Though Johnson won passage of his air and water quality and highway beautification bills, they were less than what he wanted. When he signed the Water Quality and Clean Air acts in October, for example, he called the laws a "beginning" in the assault on pollution. "Today, we begin to be masters of our environment," he declared. But he had no illusion that these laws would "completely assure us of absolute success. Additional bolder legislation will be needed in the years ahead." This was especially true of the Highway Beautification Act, which Mrs. Johnson had made, along with Head Start, major First Lady projects.[118]

Johnson's commitment to environmental reform amazed some people who, remembering his Senate career, thought of him as a captive of big oil interests. Similarly, his reputation as an earthy powerbroker seemed to make him an unlikely advocate of the arts. At the start of his presidency, few political observers would have predicted that Johnson would do as much for the arts and humanities as any modern President. But Johnson understood that "artists and scholars . . . are the creators and the keepers of our vision." Moreover, he recognized that "the creative and performing arts constitute a real national treasure" and that a nation's most enduring legacy was usually the product of its humanists. Johnson's commitment to the arts translated into legislation establishing the National Endowments for the Arts and the Humanities.[119]

As the congressional session came to a close in the fall, Johnson took great satisfaction in the record of major reforms sponsored by his administration. Yet in spite of his success, he lived with nagging doubts that he would get credit for what he had achieved or that something wouldn't come along to sweep away his Great Society. Throughout his life he had seen past gains as insufficient and future challenges as promising greater fulfillment. There was always a higher mountain to climb, a greater prize to be won. He loved the challenge, the prospect of yet another battle for some seemingly impossible goal that others had failed to attain. Yet the sense of incompleteness also frustrated and angered him, making him feel as if there was no end to his quest for recognition and approval, no way ever to win the love and esteem that he craved.

Johnson's doubts had some basis in fact. When the historian William E. Leuchtenburg attended a convention of the American Political Science Association in September 1965, he "thought speakers underestimated not only the originality of the Great Society but also Johnson's contribution to getting the programs enacted. They assumed that the great spate of laws could be wholly explained by the 1964 election, which had so greatly swelled the Democratic margin in Congress, but Franklin Roosevelt had enjoyed an even bigger advantage in 1937 and had not achieved nearly so much that year. The country, I firmly believed, did not properly appreciate Lyndon Johnson."

Senate Majority Leader Mike Mansfield shared Leuchtenburg's belief. He told Leuchtenburg later that month: "Johnson has outstripped Roosevelt, no doubt about that. He has done more than FDR ever did or ever thought of doing."[120]

Johnson shared their conviction about his accomplishments and fretted over the muted response to them. He "ached over the lack of appreciation from the people for his achievements and longed to find a way to gain their recognition," Joe Califano remembers. "I am willing to let any objective historian look at my record," Johnson said privately in the following year after he had put other landmark laws on the books. But he believed that the principal historians in the country were all Kennedy liberals like Arthur Schlesinger and would never give him his due.[121]

On September 22, when Leuchtenburg, who was preparing to write an article on the origins of the Great Society, interviewed Johnson at the White House, the President "appeared morose, even ill-tempered." Seeing Leuchtenburg as a stand-in for Schlesinger, Johnson tried to set these "liberal" historians straight with a recitation on his unprecedented accomplishments. Leuchtenburg attributed Johnson's hyperbole to a self-aggrandizement bordering on egomania. And that was surely part of the explanation, but Johnson was also giving vent to his anger at the insufficient appreciation of his leadership. He wanted to be recognized as the greatest presidential legislator in U.S. history.[122]

Fortas and the Supreme Court

Johnson believed that the courts might be a principal agent in any future attack on Great Society laws. The memory of FDR's struggle with the Supreme Court and Congress in 1937 over the constitutionality of principal New Deal measures was never far from his mind. At a Cabinet meeting in September 1965, Johnson said: "I saw FDR sweep everything before him in Congress. His majorities were greater than ours. There were no distractions abroad. He seemed able to get anything and everything he wanted. Then he lost the Court bill. . . . And from that Congress to this, no really major social legislation was enacted."[123]

Johnson and leading aides saw the achievements of the 89th Congress as bolder than Roosevelt's in 1933–35 and, as a consequence, even more open to constitutional challenge. "There has never been an era in American history when so much has been done for so many in such a short a time," Johnson believed. Larry O'Brien said later: "My God, civil rights, Medicare, education legislation, highway beautification. . . . Now you get to this point . . . this was revolutionary, and it disturbed a lot of people on the Hill and in the private sector."[124]

In August 1965, Johnson's concern about a constitutional challenge to his War on Poverty–Great Society efforts found its way into a speech. "With the support of Congress," he declared, "we have really begun to open the gates of opportunity for the very poor people of this country. [But] every time we try to do that, there are many obstacles. There are suggestions made as to why this is unconstitutional, we are doing it too fast, we are doing it the wrong way. I have never seen a real comprehensive effort made to help the very poor that there weren't apostles of greed who would find reasons why it couldn't be done." Privately, Johnson told Bill Moyers that he expected court challenges on the blurring of church-state separation in the education law and over community action.[125]

Remembering what a terrible time FDR had over his conflict with the Supreme Court, Johnson wanted to prevent a recurrence of any such development. To be sure, Johnson understood that the Court under Earl Warren in 1965 was a much more liberal institution than the Court of the thirties. The record of the Warren Court on civil rights, for example, gave Johnson little reason to think that it would stand in the way of desegregation and black voting. But Johnson also knew that the Court, and especially particular justices, had sometimes surprised the country with independent judgments that ran counter to administration policies and accepted wisdom. And even if such a development was unlikely in the mid-sixties, Johnson's fear that it might occur made him eager to do something to forestall it.

Specifically, Johnson wanted someone on the Court who would keep him informed of its thinking and might deter rulings against Great Society laws. Johnson was familiar with traditional ideas about separation of the branches. But he also knew that justices were not strictly apolitical animals who steered clear of private political discussions. Indeed, Associate Justice Hugo Black had saved Johnson's political life in 1948 with a ruling that partly rested on political considerations. When Lyndon sent Black a greeting on his seventy-ninth birthday in February 1965, he added a handwritten postscript: "And I need not remind you that I have been the recipient and beneficiary of your courage and wisdom."[126]

To assure himself of an insider on the Court—of a "mole" who could keep him abreast of Court thinking and help anticipate Court decisions—Johnson wanted to make Abe Fortas an associate justice. Fortas was perfectly suited to the job. Their friendship dated from 1937, the beginning of Johnson's service in Washington as a congressman, and had been cemented in 1948 when Fortas took the lead in Johnson's successful court fight to run for the U.S. Senate. Johnson thought of Fortas as "the wisest man I have ever known." Moreover, he was "Lyndon Johnson's insider." During the first two years of Lyndon's presidency, Fortas had performed a variety of legal and political tasks for Johnson, usually in secret and with the single-minded goal of serving the President's interests.

In July 1965, when Justice William O. Douglas, a twenty-six-year veteran of the Court, urged LBJ to appoint Abe Fortas, he bluntly advised: "I need not tell you what a superb choice Abe Fortas would be. . . . I hope you feel free to release him for that post. He can still serve you and the country, too." In short, Abe can still advise you on both personal and political matters while acting as an associate justice. Johnson also wanted Fortas on the Court because he would be an excellent justice and would receive the reward Johnson wished to give a deserving friend.[127]

But Fortas had resisted taking a government post. He was content earning a lot of money in his private Washington law practice while quietly serving the President at the same time. In August 1964, after Robert Kennedy resigned, Johnson had "moved heaven and earth" to make Fortas Attorney General. But Fortas had refused, saying Carol Agger, his wife, wouldn't hear of it. Johnson and Agger argued the question for over an hour on the telephone, with Johnson lamenting "that not even his dog would do anything for him." Johnson's complaint aroused no sympathy in Agger, and the President gave in, telling Fortas, "Well, if Carol says no, I won't try to put myself ahead of her."[128]

Besides, Johnson preferred to have Fortas on the Supreme Court rather than as Attorney General. And so, in the spring of 1965, after Johnson had begun making plans to shift Secretary Anthony Cele-brezze from HEW to the U.S. Court of Appeals, the President saw an opportunity to put Fortas on the Court. He considered moving Associate Justice Arthur Goldberg, a former counsel for the United Steel Workers of America and Secretary of Labor, from the Court to HEW, leaving a vacancy for Fortas. On May 10, Johnson asked the FBI for background checks on Goldberg and Fortas for presidential appointments. But Goldberg, who described himself as "happy on [the] Court," was reluctant to take the job.[129]

Adlai Stevenson's death on July 13, however, opened the U.N. ambassadorship, a job Goldberg found more appealing. Johnson understood how to sell Goldberg on the appointment. "He's the sort of man who would cry if he saw an old widow woman and some hungry children," LBJ said a few days before he pressed Goldberg to take the assignment. "He feels that quality would be useful in dealing with underdeveloped countries and poorer nations."

Moreover, to assure Goldberg's transfer, Johnson held out the possibility that he might later run for Vice President. "Goldberg is vastly ambitious ('he wants to be the next Vice Presidential nominee') he will take any orders you give him," columnist Joe Alsop told Johnson. Johnson flattered Goldberg with the suggestion that he might become the first Jewish Vice President of the United States. "You never know what can happen, Arthur," LBJ told him. "You're over there on the Court, isolated from the action, and you can't get to the Vice Presidency from the Court."

Goldberg agreed to go to the U.N., saying later, "Have you ever had your arm twisted by Lyndon Johnson?" He also remembered it was "because of vanity. I thought I could influence the President to get out of Vietnam," an idea Johnson himself planted by suggesting that as ambassador Goldberg would have a prominent say on foreign policy.[130]

Arranging Fortas's appointment was also a challenge for Johnson. The principal impediment was Carol Agger, who believed it was premature for her husband, at age fifty-five, to go on the Court. She thought it would be better if he waited five or six years, when he might gain appointment as Chief Justice; she and Abe would have a larger nest egg; and his law firm would be on a surer footing. Besides, she did not want any change in their lives at a time when they were both happy and prospering. Johnson "didn't believe that Abe Fortas did not want to be on the Supreme Court," Mrs. Johnson says. LBJ was right. Fortas shared Agger's views about timing, but he very much wanted to become a Supreme Court justice, and he was reluctant to let this opportunity pass. As his biographer Laura Kalman says, Fortas "was a pragmatist who knew that history could be managed only up to a point. The opportunity had arisen now, and it might not occur again."[131]

Fortas nevertheless felt compelled to pretend that he resisted taking the appointment and only Johnson's insistence forced him into it. Fortas entered into a conspiracy of sorts with Johnson. The object was to convince everyone, especially the press and Agger, that Fortas had to be dragged kicking and screaming into the position. Fortas sent Johnson a letter on July 19, saying he declined the offer "with a heart full of gratitude," explaining that he would be better able to serve the Johnson family and his law firm by remaining off the Court, and falsely asserting that "Carol thinks I should accept this greatest honor that a lawyer could receive."

As Johnson and Fortas recounted the story, the President wouldn't take "no" for an answer. On July 28, Johnson asked Fortas to come to the White House, where he told him he was about to announce the sending of 50,000 troops to Vietnam and his appointment to the Court. Fortas needed to follow the lead of these men by making a sacrifice for his country. Johnson remembered that Fortas now gave in and accompanied the President to a press conference. "That was the only way I managed to get him on the Court," Johnson said. Fortas complained that Johnson informed him of his intention only on the way to the press conference and never even gave him the chance to respond.[132]

Such a picture of Fortas's appointment made Johnson seem like a great persuader. Try as people might, they could not resist the President. It salved Johnson's ego and served his political purposes. Press and public would see LBJ as an extraordinary leader who almost always got what he believed was good for the country.

As for Fortas, the picture of the captive candidate gave him cover with his wife, who was furious at Abe's appointment. She hung up on Johnson, when he called to explain why he had to have Abe on the bench. "You don't treat friends that way," she told him. "What are you trying to do, destroy Abe?" she asked. Fortas later told one of his law partners that he had "never heard anybody talk to the President like Carol did." Johnson told a secretary, "Oooh boy, Carol was furious with me." She privately complained to others about the "dirty trick LBJ played" on Abe, calling it "the goddamnest thing." Fortas's biographer writes: "She would not talk to Johnson for the next two months, and her relationship with her husband during that period was also tense. Eventually, however, she forgave Fortas."[133]

Fortas's confirmation hearings in August were brief and uneventful. He skillfully downplayed his relationship with the President, which some senators feared might compromise his judicial independence. "There are two things that have been vastly exaggerated with respect to me," he said. "One is the extent to which I am a Presidential adviser, and the other is the extent to which I am a proficient violinist. I am a very poor violinist but very enthusiastic, and my relationship with the President has been exaggerated out of all connection with reality." Fortas was misleading the committee, but it took him at his word, unanimously confirming his appointment. There were only three votes against him in the final Senate tally.[134]

With Fortas on the bench, Johnson believed he had taken another stride toward a Great Society. The rush of legislation Congress was then in the midst of passing combined with steps to make the judicial and executive branches supportive of the Johnson reforms added up to an extraordinary first year in his own full term.

Johnson's success rested on a unique set of circumstances that will probably never recur. First, there was the man himself. No one with the combination of Johnson's legislative experience, understanding of how to move Congress, and ambition to pass so many major laws had ever been President. Second, a President with two-thirds of both Houses strongly on his side is a rarity Johnson was able to use to his advantage.

Third, and perhaps most important, in 1964–65 there was an uncommon national receptivity to righting historic wrongs and using federal power to improve people's lives. Johnson's Great Society laws may be seen as a surge of evangelical faith in the nation's capacity to make up for past mistakes—segregation and black disenfranchisement—and benefit all citizens through federal programs of education, environmental protection, urban renewal, medical care for the elderly, and cultural enrichment.

John F. Kennedy's assassination played a large part in creating a national mood of eagerness for reform. It was as if the country wished to purge itself of feelings that it was a sick society that fostered violence instead of healing and education and uplift. Johnson with his evangelical fervor for social change and ability to speak to the country and the South in particular about its past failings and past successes in restoring itself to economic health and social stability was the right President in the right time.

But the elation Johnson and the country felt at the historical advances his administration was making at home was in competition with disquieting developments abroad. As has so often been the case in American history, overt movement in one direction obscured underlying changes shaping a very different future—a time in which criticism and division over public policy would show Johnson why Thomas Jefferson had described the presidency as "a splendid misery."

5

Foreign Policy Dilemmas

THE Gulf of Tonkin Resolution in August 1964 gave Johnson a temporary respite from unpleasant choices in Vietnam. Having hit back at the North Vietnamese and having rallied Congress and the country behind a promise not to abandon South Vietnam, he wished to mute discussion about Southeast Asia. But he knew the problem would not go away. On August 10, he told national security advisers that the next challenge from Hanoi, which he expected soon, would have to be met with firmness. He had no intention of escalating the conflict "just because the public liked what happened last week," he said. But he wanted planning that would allow us to choose the grounds for the next confrontation and get maximum results with minimum danger.[1]

Still, he wanted no significant change in policy before the November election. Having "stood up" to Communist aggression, he now wished to sound a moderate note. In speeches during the campaign, he emphasized giving Vietnam limited help: He would "not permit the independent nations of the East to be swallowed up by Communist conquest," but it would not mean sending "American boys 9 or 10,000 miles away from home to do what Asian boys ought to be doing for themselves."[2]

Coups and counter coups in Saigon during August and September made it difficult for Johnson to hold to his word. Under Secretary George Ball told James Reston on August 29 that things were "very serious" in Saigon, and substantial doubts existed about the future "authority and stability" of the central government. On the 31st, Mac Bundy advised Johnson that the situation in Saigon "could hardly be more serious."

Contingency plans for limited escalation—"naval harassments, air interdiction in the Laos panhandle, and possible U.S. fleet movements"—were being considered as ways "to heighten morale and to show our strength of purpose." Thoughts were also being given to setting up a U.S. naval base in South Vietnam or sending in a limited number of Marines to guard installations. Bundy himself proposed the "more drastic possibility which no one is discussing" of using "substantial U.S. armed forces in operations against the Viet Cong. ... Before we let this country go we should have a hard look at this grim alternative, and I do not at all think that it is a repetition of Korea."[3]

In early September, Pentagon and State Department planners settled on steps to bolster Saigon and deter Hanoi. They included additional U.S. naval patrols in international waters, South Vietnamese operations along the coast of North Vietnam and in the air over Laos, and responses to Communist attacks on U.S. forces and to "any special DRV/VC action against SVN." The planners also discussed deliberately provoking Hanoi into a clash that would allow the United States to relieve Communist pressure on Saigon.[4]

At a meeting on September 9 with national security advisers, Johnson anguished over what to do. First, he wanted to discuss stronger actions than those proposed by the planners. Vietnam Ambassador Maxwell Taylor, CIA Chief John McCone, and Secretary of State Dean Rusk argued against doing more than recommended. "Rusk said that a major decision to go North could be taken at any time—'at 5 minutes' notice.'" Johnson agreed, saying that attacks against the North should wait until "our side could defend itself in the streets of Saigon." He didn't "wish to enter the patient in a 10-round bout, when he was in no shape to hold out for one round. We should get him ready to face 3 or 4 rounds at least."

Johnson then questioned the value of staying in Vietnam. Taylor, Rusk, McCone, and Chairman of the Joint Chiefs Earle C. Wheeler repeated the now familiar case for holding fast. A retreat would undermine our overall position in the area and the world. Losing South Vietnam would mean losing Southeast Asia. Communist China would dominate the region. In sum, retreat was unthinkable. Johnson concurred. He declared his readiness "to do more, when we had a base" or when Saigon was politically more stable.[5]

Johnson was not happy about his choices in Vietnam. None of them seemed quite right. His only certainty in the summer of 1964 was that election politics dictated an image of himself as a firm but cautious defender of the national security. At a background meeting with the press in mid-September, he restated his determination to sustain the Eisenhower-Kennedy policies of providing measured support for Vietnam while avoiding another Korea. But privately he worried about involvement in an unpredictable struggle, a conflict that might require greater commitments than he wished to make. He had a sense of foreboding about Vietnam—a feeling that no matter what he did things might end badly.[6]

On September 18, when he received reports of another attack on U.S. destroyers in the Tonkin Gulf, he refused to let it turn into a crisis. He told advisers that "he was not interested in rapid escalation on so frail evidence and with a very fragile government in South Vietnam." Additional reports the following day increased his skepticism about the "incident." When Rusk stressed "the importance of not seeming to doubt our naval officers on the spot," Johnson "replied somewhat sharply that he was not planning to make a radio broadcast on the matter.... He refused to give a public statement." Moreover, he rejected McNamara's request for a continuation of patrols in the Gulf, saying: "We won't go ahead with it, Bob. Let's put it on the shelf."[7]

Between September 20 and the end of October the situation in Vietnam deteriorated further. On October 1, Mac Bundy asked the President to "give a hint of firmness" in public. Seeing a better than even chance that they would have to act against North Vietnam in the next two months, Bundy did "not want the record to suggest even remotely that we campaigned on peace in order to start a war in November." But during the remainder of the campaign, Johnson refused to go beyond what he had been saying about holding to a middle ground.[8]

On November 1, a Viet Cong attack on Bien Hoa air base in South Vietnam tested Johnson's determination. The attack killed five U.S. servicemen, wounded seventy-six, and destroyed twenty-seven of thirty planes, which were there to signal Hanoi that escalation would bring U.S. air retaliation. Understanding that Johnson would be reluctant to respond during the election, the Communists saw the planes not as a deterrent but an inviting target.

Taylor and the Joint Chiefs urged Johnson to respond with air strikes against the North. But the President, backed by Rusk and McNamara, decided against a retaliatory attack. He feared reprisals against U.S. dependents in South Vietnam and worried that increased military action might do more to weaken than strengthen Saigon.

But his reluctance to face a public crisis over Vietnam on the eve of the election and to increase America's role in the fighting were more important in restraining him. He feared charges of political cynicism—that he had manufactured a crisis to win a campaign advantage—and he worried that air strikes would seem to commit the United States to "a systematic bombing program." On the day of the attack, Johnson asked pollster Lou Harris whether a failure to respond would undercut him with voters. When Harris answered no, it confirmed Johnson's decision to avoid a military response.[9]

Vietnam: The Fork in the Road

On November 2, the day before the election, in response to the Bien Hoa assault and predictions of a South Vietnamese collapse, Johnson asked an NSC committee to begin "intensive planning." The following day, the group discussed how the United States should answer Hanoi's next attack. They assumed that "overt military pressures against North Vietnam probably would be required." As historian William C. Gibbons puts it, "the planning process in November was action-oriented—not whether to act, but what to do." There was little, if any, discussion about leaving Vietnam, "or whether the U.S. could succeed where the French had failed. It was generally assumed that the U.S. was already committed to stopping the Communists, and that this required the use of U.S. forces."[10]

On November 19, the Working Group gave LBJ an interim report. Three options were under consideration: (1) Continuation as at present, while working toward a negotiated settlement; (2) a sharp increase in military pressure on Vietnam, with negotiations a long-term goal; or (3) a slow increase of military operations against Hanoi, with simultaneous efforts to begin peace talks. A "devil's advocate" proposal by George Ball making the case for negotiations and withdrawal was also in the works.

Johnson's only recorded comment was a request that no firm decision be made without consulting the military; "he could not face the Congressional leadership on this kind of subject unless he had fully consulted with the relevant military people." Johnson wanted cover from possible future political attacks. You must "sign on" the Joint Chiefs to any decision, Jack Valenti told LBJ. "That way . . . our flank will have been covered in the event of some kind of flap or investigation later."[11]

Johnson responded cautiously to the planners' recommendations. He did not see his landslide victory as a mandate for anything in Vietnam, and he was as uncertain as ever about what to do. In December, he rejected suggestions that he announce a greater military effort. Moreover, he would agree only to a limited increase in military pressure on Hanoi.

At a White House meeting on December 1, he focused on promoting unity among the South Vietnamese and winning commitments from America's allies for more help to Saigon. "Most essential is a stable govt.," he said.

Johnson also worried that we had "oversold them [the Vietnamese] on our necessity of being [a] power in the Pacific. 'Are they drunk on [Joe] Alsop?' " who was consistently urging stronger U.S. action. LBJ then said: It's "easy to get in or out. [But] hard to be patient." He didn't "want to send [a] widow woman to slap Jack Dempsey." But he saw the day of reckoning coming, and he wanted to be sure "we've done everything we can" to assure stability in Saigon.

Johnson summarized matters by saying: "Purpose of this mtg: . . . To pull stable govt together. . . . Before Wh[eeler and the military] saddle up, try anything. . . . Hesitant to sock neighbor if fever [in Saigon] 104. Want to get well first. We've never been in position to attack. Easy to sock. Easy to follow [Senator Wayne] Morse [in pulling out]. They [Congress]'ll be back in January. We want to be prepared to answer the questions. If need be, create a new Diem, so then [we] tell Wh[eeler] to slap, we can slap back." As the Defense Department history, *The Pentagon Papers*, later concluded, "It is clear that the President didn't make any commitment at this point to expand the war through operations against North Vietnam."[12]

True, he approved additional support of South Vietnamese naval raids, 34-A actions, and bombing runs against North Vietnamese movements in Laos, but he was not ready to commit himself to the use of sustained force against Hanoi. Moreover, on December 3, he sent instructions to Maxwell Taylor that echoed his belief that "we should not incur the risks" involved in expanded hostilities against North Vietnam until there was a government in Saigon that could survive a wider war. The government would have to "be able to speak for and to its people," and "be capable of maintaining law and order in its principal centers of population."[13]

Johnson's caution reflected his reluctance to do anything abroad that might distract domestic attention from Great Society reforms. He saw Vietnam as a potential trap that could frustrate his principal goals and politically injure him. Privately, he compared the situation of the South Vietnamese government and himself to a man standing on a newspaper in the middle of the Atlantic Ocean. There was no escape from disaster: If he moved left or right or just stood still he was going to sink. It was an apt metaphor: He saw Vietnam as a sea in which he and his highest hopes could be lost. Yet his fundamental belief that U.S. national security dictated against abandoning Vietnam meant that he would risk the adverse consequences of a larger war.[14]

Events in Saigon during the rest of December deepened Johnson's skepticism about larger military commitments. Continuing political turmoil, marked by threats of a new military coup, made South Vietnamese unity more elusive than ever. Consequently, when Taylor and American military chiefs urged retaliatory air strikes against North Vietnam for a Christmas eve attack on a U.S. officers' billet in Saigon, Johnson, supported by Rusk and McNamara, refused.

Johnson told Taylor: Before he would take such action, he wanted to remove U.S. dependents from South Vietnam, improve security arrangements for Americans, expand efforts to ease South Vietnamese divisions, and make greater use of U.S. ground forces. "Every time I get a military recommendation it seems to me that it calls for large-scale bombing," Johnson said. "I have never felt that this war will be won from the air." Johnson, Bill Moyers says, knew about studies questioning the effectiveness of World War II strategic bombing and doubted the efficacy of sustained air strikes in Vietnam.

He was ready, however, to look with favor on ground action, despite the realization "that it may involve the acceptance of larger American sacrifice. We have been building our strength to fight this kind of war ever since 1961, and I myself am ready to substantially increase the number of Americans in Vietnam if it is necessary to provide this kind of fighting force against the Viet Cong."[15]

But Johnson still refused to commit himself. "I am not giving any orders at all in this message," he told Taylor. He was betwixt and between. He didn't really care much about Vietnam per se. To him, it was a remote, backward place dominated by squabbling factions unresponsive to political reason. Few there seemed to understand the great American traditions of compromise and consensus, of getting on with business by accommodating to political, economic, social, and military realities.

In December, Mike Mansfield wrote Johnson that we were on a course in Vietnam "which takes us further and further out on a sagging limb." In time, he predicted, we could find ourselves saddled with "enormous burdens in Cambodia, Laos, and elsewhere in Asia, along with those in Viet Nam." In reply, Johnson said: "I think we have the same basic view of this problem, and the same sense of its difficulties." He objected, however, to Mansfield's suggestion that "we are 'overcommitted' there. Given the size of the stake, it seems to me that we are doing only what we have to do."

During a conversation in December with columnist Walter Lippmann, who was advocating a negotiated U.S. withdrawal from an unwinnable struggle, Johnson complained that he was not eager for American involvement, "but this is a commitment I inherited. I don't like it, but how can I pull out?" Lippmann repeated what De

Gaulle had told him: Even with a million Americans in Vietnam, a lasting military victory would be impossible.

De Gaulle's opinion carried little weight with LBJ. However strong his reservations about expanded U.S. involvement in Vietnam, French defeat and judgments did not add greatly to them. In Johnson's view, a powerful anti-imperialist America was not like a divided France, which had tried to preserve colonial rule in Saigon. America's involvement in Vietnam was a defense of the free world against Communist advance, not an exercise in outdated imperialism.[16]

In the winter of 1964–65, Johnson felt pressured much more by hawks than doves. He complained to some liberals "that all the [military] chiefs did was come in every morning and tell him, 'Bomb, bomb, bomb,' and then come back in the afternoon and tell him again, 'Bomb, bomb, bomb.'" His principal advisers also favored using force to resist a Communist takeover in South Vietnam. To be sure, they argued about the means and timing of attacks on the North Vietnamese and Viet Cong, but they believed it had to be done. Moreover, though polls revealed no well-defined majority in favor of escalation, a substantial plurality supported military action against the Communists, with only between 26 percent and 30 percent opposed.[17]

Joe Alsop and conservatives in Congress also urged stronger measures. In December 1964, Alsop staged a one-man campaign to force Johnson's hand. In a column on December 23, he described Americans in Saigon as convinced that the President was "consciously prepared to accept defeat here." And if it occurred, it would "be his defeat as well as a defeat for the American people." In another column on the 30th, Alsop compared LBJ to JFK in the Cuban missile crisis. "If Mr. Johnson ducks the challenge [in Vietnam] we shall learn by experience about what it would have been like if Kennedy had ducked the challenge in October 1962."

The suggestion that he lacked Kennedy's guts and strength enraged Johnson. He was also incensed at congressional conservatives, who saw a larger military effort in Vietnam as not only an essential response to the Communist threat but also a way to derail Great Society reforms. Or so Johnson believed. He said that conservatives intended "to use this war as a way of opposing my Great Society legislation. . . . They hate this stuff, they don't want to help the poor and the Negroes but they're afraid to be against it at a time like this when there's been all this prosperity. But the war, oh, they'll like the war."[18]

Yet whatever his irritation with Alsop and conservatives, Johnson also shared their concern about not losing Vietnam. He was as much a believer in the need to stand up to the Communist threat as anyone in America. Throughout the Cold War he had consistently backed strong Truman, Eisenhower, and Kennedy actions against Communism. Nor, as President, was he loath to follow in their footsteps. Remembering Munich, he saw weakness overseas as leading to World War III. Moreover, if he held his hand and South Vietnam fell, it could work havoc with his political influence and power to achieve domestic advance. A new Joe McCarthy might come on the scene to pose rhetorical questions about how Vietnam had been lost.[19]

Still, in the closing days of 1964, despite his national security and domestic political concerns, Johnson had doubts that restrained him from more decisive action. Would the country be better served by throwing itself into a possibly unwinnable fight or by delaying defeat, holding back from full-scale involvement, and using our resources to meet the Communist threat on more manageable ground? John Corson, a Johnson friend from NYA days and the head of a task force on income maintenance, remembers a White House meeting of task force chairman at this time. "The most impressive thing of the evening" was the President's discussion of Vietnam, which lasted between one and two hours, "and his seeming involvement in Vietnam to the exclusion of almost everything else." Johnson said: "I've tried this to get out of Vietnam; I've tried that; I've tried everything I can think of. What can I do next?"[20]

With still no clear answers to his question, Johnson followed his political instincts. When confronted by sharp divisions of opinion throughout his career, he had almost always adopted a moderate position, identifying himself as an accommodationist who reflected the national desire for compromise rather than ideological rigidity. Since abandoning Vietnam seemed unthinkable and since public and congressional support for a full-scale conflict seemed unlikely to outlast substantial human and material costs, he chose measured increases in U.S. military action with continuing efforts to negotiate a settlement.

Achieving his goals depended on unlikely developments: unity among the South Vietnamese, North Vietnamese acceptance of Saigon's autonomy, and American acceptance of an open-ended limited war. But Johnson prided himself on being a can-do leader, the man who had made extraordinary breakthroughs on civil rights, had won a landmark electoral victory, and now confidently expected to enact bold domestic reforms that had eluded predecessors, including FDR. Against this backdrop, compelling an acceptable settlement in Vietnam did not seem out of reach.

"We are in bad shape in Vietnam," Johnson told Turner Catledge of the *New York Times* in December 1964. "Uncertainties in that area are far more than the certainties. Yet we can't afford to, and we will not, pull out. We must find some way to bring the job off even if we have to set it up so that a withdrawal would have a better face."[21]

Yet Johnson was not convinced by his own analysis. His fear of escalation and sustained involvement outran his calculations of what would work. "I knew from the start that I was bound to be crucified either way I moved," he later told Kearns. "If I left the woman I really loved—the Great Society—in order to get involved with that bitch of a war on the other side of the world, then I would lose everything at home. All my programs. . . . All my dreams to provide education and medical care to the browns and the blacks and the lame and the poor. But if I left that war and let the Communists take over South Vietnam, . . . there would follow in this country an endless national debate—a mean and destructive debate—that would shatter my presidency, kill my administration, and damage our democracy."[22]

During January 1965 Johnson remained guarded and hesitant about how to proceed. A report from Bill Bundy on the 6th deepened his concern. Morale in Saigon was now more shaky than ever, partly because of "a widespread feeling that the US is not ready for stronger action and indeed is possibly looking for a way out." Bundy saw this producing a serious loss of U.S. prestige in Asia, with the likelihood that Thailand and other nations would soon fall into the Communist orbit. Stronger American action now "would have some faint hope of really improving the Vietnamese situation, and, above all, would put us in a much stronger position to hold the next line of defense, namely, Thailand."[23]

Bundy's warning did not convince Johnson "to make any new decisions." On the 7th and again on the 14th, when he cabled Taylor in Saigon, he still refused to commit himself to a bombing campaign against the North, which Taylor believed could have a significant impact on Saigon's morale.[24]

The decision for stronger action Johnson had been creeping toward came in the last week of January when another change of government occurred in Saigon. On January 26, the day of the coup, Douglass Cater told Johnson that Peter Grose, the *New York Times* correspondent in Vietnam, believed "the next six months may mark the end of the road and urges that we be exploring every opportunity to withdraw with honor."

The next day, Mac Bundy and McNamara told Johnson that "our current policy can lead only to disastrous defeat. . . . Bob and I believe that the worst course of action is to continue in this essentially passive role which can lead only to eventual defeat and an invitation to get out in humiliating circumstances. . . . The time has come for harder choices. . . . Dean Rusk does not agree with us. He [believes] that the consequences of both escalation and withdrawal are so bad that we simply must find a way of making our present policy work. This would be good if it was possible. Bob and I do not think it is."[25]

Johnson agreed to follow a more aggressive policy. The combined pressure of events in Saigon and the unequivocal advice that he needed to act decisively persuaded him to strike at the North Vietnamese. " 'Stable government or no stable government,' " he said, " 'we'll do what we ought to do.' I'm prepared to do that. We will move strongly. [General Nguyen] Khanh [head of the new government] is our boy."

He sent Bundy to Vietnam to discuss ways to help stabilize South Vietnam. He also agreed to a resumption in early February of an American naval patrol in the Tonkin Gulf. It would demonstrate U.S. resolve and might provoke a North Vietnamese attack, which could then become the basis for U.S. retaliation. After hearing the news, Taylor cabled Washington: A North Vietnamese attack "followed by immediate strong and effective U.S. retaliation would offer a priceless advantage to our cause here."[26]

Johnson's commitment represented a striking shift in judgment. His concern about having a stable regime in the South before attacking the North gave way to the hope that increased pressure on Hanoi could somehow bolster Saigon. Johnson had no evidence to support his altered assumption. But fear that a pro-Western South Vietnam would become first a neutralist and then a Communist regime drove him to expand American efforts to defend Saigon.

After a three-day visit to South Vietnam at the beginning of February, Mac Bundy confirmed Johnson's belief that "without new U.S. action defeat appears inevitable." Bundy also told him that "there is still time to turn it around" and that U.S. action would have the effect of blunting "the charge that we did not do all that we could have done, and this charge will be important in many countries, including our own." By fighting in Vietnam, "it should . . . somewhat increase our ability to deter such adventures" elsewhere.[27]

Bundy's views reflected prevailing ideas in Washington. On February 6, after the Viet Cong killed eight U.S. advisers and wounded dozens of others in an attack on an American base at Pleiku in the central highlands, Johnson decided to retaliate. In a National Security Council meeting that included congressional leaders, he announced plans for an air attack against army barracks in southern North Vietnam.

When he asked for judgments on his decision, only Mike Mansfield, urging negotiation, dissented. Johnson's reply, according to Bill Bundy, was "terse and quite biting." Johnson remembered himself saying: "They are killing our men while they sleep in the night. I can't ask our American soldiers out there to continue to fight with one hand tied behind their backs." He believed that the air strike would show North Vietnam that it "could not count on continued immunity if they persisted in aggression in the South." Johnson also asserted that neither the Soviets nor the Chinese "wanted direct involvement" in the fighting, and would not intervene.[28]

This retaliatory attack did not signal the beginning of a sustained air war against North Vietnam. When McNamara reported that weather conditions had allowed only one of four targets to be hit and that we would not stage a new raid to take out the other three, George Ball endorsed McNamara's recommendation, saying that to do otherwise would signal that we were "launching an offensive." The President agreed to McNamara's recommendation.[29]

But on February 8, after reading Mac Bundy's report on his visit to Vietnam, Johnson decided on systematic bombing of the North. He would now order continuing air attacks. He wasn't happy about it; he wasn't even sure it was the right decision. But since abandoning Vietnam was unacceptable, his only alternative seemed to be forceful action. But he didn't want to make this evident to the Congress or the press or the public. At an NSC meeting that morning, McNamara declared that it was not necessary to bomb every day; once a week would be "enough to keep morale up in Saigon." Johnson then said: "We face a choice of going forward or running. We have chosen the first alternative. All of us agree on this but there remains some difference as to how fast we should go forward."[30]

Shortly after, when congressional leaders joined the meeting, Johnson declared that last December we had agreed on a program of further pressure on North Vietnam but had not implemented the policy. "We are now ready to return to our program of pushing forward in an effort to defeat North Vietnamese aggression without escalating the war." When Congressman Gerald "Ford asked whether all we intended to do was to react to Viet Cong provocations," Johnson "replied that all Viet Cong actions did call for a response but we did not intend to limit our actions to retaliating against Viet Cong attacks." He closed the meeting by asking that no one describe our actions in public as a broadening of the war.[31]

Johnson stated his intentions in a cable to Taylor that afternoon. "I have today decided that we will carry out our December plan for continuing action against North Vietnam with modifications up and down in tempo and scale in the light of your recommendations... and our own continuing review of the situation." Since Saigon seemed likely to take heart from "private assurances... that we do now intend to take continuing action," Johnson authorized Taylor "to convey this in general terms to key leaders and political figures as you see fit."[32]

Though Johnson had made up his mind to initiate sustained bombing, he did not wish to launch the campaign until Soviet Premier Aleksei Kosygin, who was visiting Hanoi, had left. Consequently, on February 10, when the Viet Cong struck another U.S. base at Qui Nhon on the central coast of South Vietnam, killing twenty-one Americans, Johnson authorized only a retaliatory attack. No mention was to be made of "continuing action" for the time being.[33]

"Rolling Thunder," as the sustained bombing campaign was named, was initiated on February 13, after the Joint Chiefs had identified a series of targets to be attacked during the next eight weeks. "We will execute a program of measured and limited air action jointly with GVN against selected military targets in DRV," the White House cabled Taylor. "We will announce this policy of measured action in general terms." In fact, no public statement was issued. As columnist James Reston described it in the New York Times the following day, the United States had entered "an undeclared and unexplained war in Vietnam."

Johnson's refusal to make the expanded air war clear to the public partly rested on a concern not to distract Congress and the country from his reform agenda. But ambivalence about the policy also motivated him. The possibility that this was the beginning of ever larger commitments troubled him. Was this the start of something that would take on a life of its own and ultimately overwhelm him? Not going public with the bombing campaign was a form of denial; no announcement was a way not only to mute the reality of the fighting but also to keep it from gaining an importance Johnson did not wish it to have.

"He had no stomach for it," Mrs. Johnson told me, "no heart for it; it wasn't the war he wanted. The one he wanted was on poverty and ignorance and disease and that was worth putting your life into. ...And yet every time you took it to the people, every time you said anything in a speech about civil rights your audience would begin to shift their feet and be restive and silent and maybe hostile. But then the moment you said something about defending liberty around the world—bear any burden—everybody would go to cheering."[34]

"A Cloud of Troubles"

In agreeing to an air campaign against the North, Johnson had only vague hopes of what would be gained. The most optimistic proponents of bombing believed it would immediately boost Saigon's morale and stiffen its resolve to fight. There was also an expectation that steady escalation would force Hanoi to rein in the Viet Cong and ask for a halt to the attacks. The United States could then continue air raids until the North ceased backing the Communist insurgency in the South. Initially, however, it was assumed that bombing would increase the level of Soviet and Chinese aid to North Vietnam and provoke Hanoi and the Viet Cong to intensify the war. But if the U.S. stuck to a campaign of slow escalation, it could force a settlement on terms favorable to itself and the South Vietnamese.[35]

At the same time Johnson heard positive estimates of what an air campaign could achieve, he also received warnings that it would lead only to more fighting. The Joint Chiefs themselves, mindful that they were bombing a country without an industrial infrastructure or a capacity to produce its own war materiel, doubted that air strikes could significantly alter Hanoi's behavior. George Ball and Ambassador to Moscow Llewellyn Thompson urged Johnson to understand that Hanoi would never give up the struggle for control of South Vietnam unless it faced "a crushing military defeat." The bombing would raise the possibility of a confrontation with China and the Soviet Union without compelling North Vietnamese agreement to an independent South Vietnam.[36]

Johnson himself had substantial doubts that an air campaign would force Hanoi to end its aggression. But he saw immediate gains. It could forestall a Communist victory in South Vietnam and the rest of Southeast Asia and a domestic ruckus over who "lost Vietnam."

As for long-range effects, no one could offer guarantees. Ball remembers that Mac Bundy refused to be pinned down as to the ultimate outcome of an air war. Bundy told him: "Since 'we did not know what the answer [would] be,' we did not have 'to follow a particular course down the road to a particular result.' He was, in other words, . . . opting to leave our objective unformulated and therefore flexible." Ball himself at the time supported the systematic bombing campaign as the only means by which the United States could achieve "an international arrangement that will effectively stop the insurrection in South Vietnam and deliver the entire country south of the Seventeenth Parallel to the government in Saigon free and clear of insurgency."[37]

Short-term rather than longer-term results convinced Johnson to begin sustained bombing. Holding off a South Vietnamese collapse and a distracting domestic debate were irresistible attractions. Ball recalls that on February 13, when he gave the President his and Thompson's memo about the dangers of bombing, Johnson asked him "to go through it point by point. He thanked me and handed the memorandum back without further comment. Why he followed that uncharacteristic course I do not know."[38]

Later in February, Ball made another try at deterring Johnson from greater commitments in Vietnam. He gave LBJ a document he had written in October 1964 challenging assumptions that losing Vietnam would undermine America's world position and predicting that an air campaign would not deter Hanoi but provoke it to expand the ground fighting in the South.

Johnson called a meeting to discuss Ball's memo. He took issue with specific points in his paper, even remembering "the page numbers where those arguments occurred." McNamara, who was also present, "responded with a pyrotechnic display of facts and statistics to prove that I had overstated the difficulties we were now encountering. ... Secretary Rusk made a passionate argument about the dangers of not going forward. The meeting, though lasting a long while, ended on an inconclusive note. I had made no converts."[39]

Despite rejecting Ball's advice, Johnson didn't see himself as committed to an all-out struggle that would become the country's principal concern during the next four years. On February 15, for example, after agreeing to Rolling Thunder, Johnson gave Bundy and McNamara the impression that he was still less than committed to a continuing air war.

"I have been brooding about our discussion of yesterday," Bundy wrote him on the 16th. He was concerned about "the firmness of your own decision to order continuing action; [and] ... the wisdom of a public declaration of that policy by you." Because the air attacks represent "a major operational change ... , there is a deep-seated need for assurance that the decision has in fact been taken. When you were out of the room yesterday, Bob McNamara repeatedly stated that he simply has to know what the policy is so that he can make his military plans and give his military orders. ... Thus it seems essential to McNamara—and to me too—that there be an absolutely firm and clear internal decision of the U.S. Government and that this decision be known and understood by enough people to permit its orderly execution."[40]

But this is exactly what Johnson did not want. On February 16 and 17, when he held additional meetings about the air campaign, he manifested continuing doubts. On the 16th, he renewed his commitment to go ahead with the bombing, saying, "I'm just hoping out of hope that they'll draw people in Saigon together." On the 17th, he turned to former President Eisenhower for reassurance that he was doing the right thing. Ike gave him emphatic support, but it would be seven more days, punctuated by another coup in Saigon and a forceful plea from Rusk, before Johnson gave the final approval for Rolling Thunder.[41]

Although he agreed to let the military bomb North Vietnam on a regular basis, he still didn't see himself as committed to a war in Southeast Asia. The U.S. was now clearly doing more than before, but he didn't want to describe it that way. He wanted the freedom to turn the air campaign off when he saw fit, and, if need be, take the United States out of the conflict without any sense that there had been an embarrassing defeat.

On February 11, when Senator Fulbright spoke privately with Arthur Krock of the *New York Times*, he complained that it was "impossible to tell" what was in LBJ's mind about Vietnam. At meetings with congressional leaders, there was no discussion of the subject, only announcements of executive decisions, which Johnson hoped they would accept without objection. In short, Johnson wanted the freedom to push ahead and pull back in Vietnam as he believed necessary without interference from Congress or the public or the press.[42]

To assure himself of the greatest possible flexibility, Johnson insisted on saying little in public about what he was doing. Others told him this was a bad idea. They wanted him to prepare the country for substantial sacrifices by publicly stating what an air campaign might mean.

Bundy, for instance, urged LBJ to understand that "at its very best the struggle in Vietnam will be long. It seems to us important that this fundamental fact be made clear ... to our own people and to the people of Vietnam. Johnson made clear to Bundy, however, that there would be no "loud public signal of a change in policy," that White House aides would say little or nothing to the press, and that statements about Vietnam would be confined to general remarks by Rusk and Stevenson.[43]

Hubert Humphrey also tried to persuade Johnson that he might be making "the most fateful decisions of your Administration" and needed to assure public backing. "There has to be a cogent, convincing case if we are to enjoy sustained public support," he wrote LBJ on February 15. "In World Wars I and II we had this." Even in Korea, where "we could not sustain American political support for fighting Chinese," the public had a better understanding of what we were doing than in Vietnam. Humphrey predicted that if "we find ourselves leading from frustration to escalation and end up short of a war with China but embroiled deeper in fighting in Vietnam over the next few months, political opposition will steadily mount." Humphrey warned that it would come from "Democratic liberals, independents, [and] labor" and would gain a hold "at the grassroots across the country."[44]

Johnson was not happy with Humphrey's criticism and warnings. He did not want to confront the issues Hubert was raising. When Fulbright told the President that Humphrey had introduced him to men who believed that the problem in Vietnam "could get started toward solution if we would replace our military provincial pro-consuls and advisers with civilians who knew the peasants and village people," Johnson responded: "In a choice between Humphrey and General Taylor as our major strategist I am disposed toward Taylor."

Humphrey's warnings made him persona non grata to Johnson. As Humphrey described it, he contributed little to discussions on Vietnam in the next several months. Johnson sent him into "limbo," with his access to the President "limited" and his "counsel less welcome." It wasn't Humphrey's misreading of Vietnam, but other considerations that motivated Johnson's response.[45]

The warnings from Bundy and Humphrey that escalation posed potential problems for Johnson heightened rather than weakened his determination to say little publicly about the expanding war effort. First, he couldn't bring himself to acknowledge that the bombing made an ever larger U.S. role in the struggle inevitable. Such a development, with potentially disastrous consequences for his administration, was so unpalatable to him that he didn't want to discuss its eventuality. Second, since the question of America's role in the fighting remained opened, he shunned discussion of commitments that could easily distract Congress from passing landmark reforms. Third, opinion polls suggested to him that for the time being he didn't need publicly to discuss escalation.

February surveys showed 75 percent of Americans favored "negotiations to settle the war." At the same time, though, the country doubted that discussions would work: 68 percent of a survey predicted that the Communists would violate a negotiated cease-fire. More important, 83 percent favored bombing North Vietnam; 79 percent saw an American withdrawal leading to Communist domination of Southeast Asia; 79 percent believed it "very important" to prevent that from happening; 48 percent supported "sending a large number of

American troops to help save Vietnam"; and 60 percent gave the President positive marks for his handling of the problem.[46]

It was clear to Johnson and others at the White House that these "opinions" partly reflected a temporary surge of patriotism in response to an international crisis. Moreover, it was evident that public sentiment was mercurial and could turn against the administration if it involved the country in a dead-end struggle costing significant numbers of lives. Nevertheless, for the time being, Johnson felt he had sufficient support for what he was doing and saw little need to explain his actions.

Johnson "is particularly sensitive to charges that he is not talking enough to the American people about the complexities and risks of the Vietnam war," James Reston wrote at the end of February. "He carries around in his pocket a series of private polls that purport to show that the vast majority of the people not only know what he is doing but approve what he is doing." Johnson understood perfectly that this could change. In politics, he liked to say, "overnight chicken shit can turn to chicken salad and vice versa." For the moment, however, he believed it sound policy to keep his counsel. If and when developments dictated otherwise, he would consider shifting ground.[47]

From late February to the end of March, while he continued to say little publicly about the war, he searched for additional means to influence developments in Vietnam. Now that he had agreed to sustained bombing, he wanted everyone in the government to figure out how to make it work. He proposed to Carl Rowan, the director of the United States Information Agency, that he have CBS President Frank Stanton travel to Saigon to evaluate a USIA "psychological program" aimed at developing "among the South Vietnamese people a sense of national unity and a determination to fight off Communist aggression."

He was trying everything he could think of, Johnson told congressional leaders on February 25. "We are doing the best that we know how to do, with ... the best men we know how to get." "We have given them complete authority and they have the first priority on our time. And I would say we spend five or six or seven hours a day and night. And we'll be awake a good deal tonight after we leave you, on this problem."

The following day LBJ ordered Army Chief of Staff Harold K. Johnson to make an on-site evaluation in Vietnam. He made clear what he wanted. "Bomb, bomb, bomb. That's all you know. Well, I want to know why there's nothing else. You generals have all been educated at taxpayers' expense, and you're not giving me any ideas and any solutions for this damn little piss-ant country. Now, I don't need ten generals to come in here ten times and tell me to bomb. I want some solutions. I want some answers." As the general was about to leave, the President poked his finger in his chest and said, "Get things bubbling, General."[48]

But as LBJ understood, injunctions to his generals and advisers were not enough to change conditions in Vietnam. "Light at the end of the tunnel," Johnson told Bill Moyers about the bombing. "Hell, we don't even have a tunnel; we don't even know where the tunnel is."[49]

On March 6, Bundy, McNamara, and Rusk gave him the bad news that "chances of a turn-around in South Vietnam remain less than even; the brutal fact is that we have been losing ground at an increasing rate in the countryside in January and February. The air actions have lifted morale, but . . . there is no evidence yet that the new government has the necessary will, skill and human resources which a turn-around will require."

When McNamara's principal aide on Vietnam, who had just returned from a fact-finding trip, underscored the worsening situation there, the President said that, after fifteen months of trying to stabilize Saigon, he didn't feel he could get out; "we all agree we have to do more." Lady Bird confided to a diary that "Lyndon lives in a cloud of troubles, with few rays of light. . . . In talking about the Vietnam situation, Lyndon summed it up quite simply, 'I can't get out. I can't finish it with what I have got. So what the Hell can I do?' "[50]

Military and civilian advisers answered: more force in the air and on the ground. On March 15, when General Johnson reported on his trip to Vietnam, he recommended increased bombing of North Vietnam, with attacks occurring further north, additional covert operations by U.S. Army and CIA forces, and consideration of deploying a U.S. Army combat division in the central highlands and an international force of four divisions along the North-South border to prevent infiltration. Two days later, the Joint Chiefs recommended deploying two American divisions and one South Korean.

Mac Bundy now also urged consideration of sending in ground forces. American air operations alone, he counseled the President, would not stop Hanoi's aggression against the South. It was essential that the United States show the Communists that it was not a paper tiger. Moreover, with conservatives vocally warning against the abandonment of Vietnam, Bundy cynically declared: "in terms of U.S. politics[,] which is better: to 'lose' now or to 'lose' after committing 100,000 men? Tentative answer: the latter."[51]

Johnson was ready to accept some of this advice. He approved more bombing of the North and the covert operations. But deploying ground forces was another matter. He was not adverse to doing it. To the contrary, he believed that ground troops would do far more good against the Viet Cong and North Vietnamese than air strikes and would not directly risk a confrontation with Peking or Moscow, which an error in the air war might provoke. And so at the end of February, he had agreed to send U.S. Marines to guard an American air base at Danang. But he was not ready to put them directly into combat and risk the casualties that would expand U.S. involvement in the war. Only defensive operations on the perimeter of the base were permitted.

The deployment at Danang marked a significant step beyond what the 23,000 military advisers in Vietnam were doing. Moreover, General Johnson had the impression that the President was receptive to putting in additional ground forces. At least, he conveyed that belief to the American military in Saigon, telling them, " 'Gentlemen, as you know, I don't come as the Army Chief of Staff. I am here as the representative of the President of the United States. Mr. Johnson asked me to come and tell you that I came with a blank check. What do you need to win the war?' "[52]

In suggesting ground forces, the President's advisers were responding to his insistent demands that they give him answers to his Vietnam problem. In a meeting with Rusk, McNamara, and Bundy on March 16, he asked for "more ideas and more horsepower and more imagination." He wanted every able-bodied South Vietnamese man under forty enlisted in the army to "fight" and "kill" the Communists. "Get off that gold watch, Phi Beta Kappa key," he demanded. *Let's get going.*"

At additional meetings during the next three weeks, Johnson asked, "Where are we going?" and reiterated his demand for effective plans. His advisers now flooded him with proposals, most of which he approved: a forty-one-point program of nonmilitary actions, continuing expansion of the air war, an increase in logistical troops of between 18,000 and 20,000, the deployment of two additional Marine battalions and a Marine Air Squadron, planning for the deployment of two more divisions, and, most important, a change in mission for all Marines battalions from defensive to offensive operations.

Johnson also repeated his determination to avoid "premature publicity" of the additional deployments and the shift in mission for the Marines. He wanted no indication of sudden changes in policy. Everything they were doing "should be understood as being gradual and wholly consistent with existing policy." When a reporter at a press conference on April 1 asked him if "dramatic" proposals were in the works on Vietnam, he asserted that there was "no far-reaching strategy that is being suggested or promulgated." As for reporters who speculated on such things, he declared: "God forgive them for they know not what they do."[53]

Vietnam: Peace on Our Terms

In March, Johnson told Eric Goldman that Rolling Thunder, about which he had so many doubts, would force North Vietnam into a settlement in twelve to eighteen months. He compared it to a "fili-buster—enormous resistance at first, then a steady whittling away, then Ho [Chi Minh] hurrying to get it over with."

Johnson's bold prognosis was all part of the ambivalence and contradictions that characterized everything he did about Vietnam in the sixteen months after he became President. From the first, he said he wouldn't walk away from the conflict, but didn't want to become too deeply involved, partly rationalizing this middle ground by the conviction that this was where the great majority of Americans stood. He decried Barry Goldwater's hawkishness, but seized upon the Tonkin Gulf clash to bomb the "aggressor" and pledge himself and Congress to the defense of the South. He insisted on stability in Saigon before committing to attacks on the North and then began bombing to stabilize the South. He resisted sending in ground forces, but believed they would probably be essential to a winning strategy. He saw a compelling need for congressional and public support but didn't want to make overt efforts to assure it.[54]

The fog of uncertainty that plagued Vietnam policy-making troubled Johnson. As his remarks to various advisers demonstrated in March 1965, he was impatient for clarity on how best to proceed or find a strategy that would bring the conflict to a rapid conclusion and allow him to keep his focus on domestic challenges. He also believed that the confusion surrounding Vietnam opened him to criticism and encouraged the Communists. A column in March by the journalist Joseph Kraft describing his foreign policy as largely based on presidential whim intensified his concern to set a fixed course in Vietnam. Indeed, by the spring of 1965, Johnson's highest priority for Vietnam was to settle on a well-defined, consistent policy that held out prospects of ending the conflict and convincing people that he knew what he was doing.

Public opposition to administration policy following the onset of retaliatory bombing and then Rolling Thunder heightened LBJ's sense of urgency about resolving the crisis. In the weeks after the bombing began, criticism erupted in Congress, the press, on university campuses, and in White House correspondence. Opponents complained that the United States had no vital interest in Southeast Asia, where we were involving ourselves in a civil war, and that bombing would expand the fighting in Vietnam, increase tensions with China and Russia, and sidetrack Johnson's domestic reforms. The U.S. government had shown itself too quick to fight and too reluctant to negotiate a regional neutrality pact.[55]

The attacks on his policy surprised and pained Johnson. Mac Bundy remembered that Johnson "underestimated and I think we all did, the virulence and the earliness of the opposition to the war. The notion that people would get tired of it if nothing happened in three years I think was never far from his mind. . . . But the antiwar movement as such I think was a surprise." Bundy believed that, even without Vietnam, as in France, a cresting of social and political forces made an explosion of domestic opposition a force to reckon with in the sixties.

Bundy was right; something more than Vietnam was at work here: Antagonism to established authority, a preference for curing domestic ills, and a growing cynicism about Cold War homilies are some of the tensions that agitated protestors during the decade. But it was difficult to look beyond Vietnam in the spring of 1965 to see what else was going on. What possible complaint could liberals have against a President who was breaking new ground by embracing civil rights and a reform agenda that touched everything from poverty to education, medical care, the environment, and peace? Johnson understandably saw the protests as strictly aimed at his actions in Southeast Asia.[56]

And the criticism angered him. Johnson never did well with opposition. He always personalized attacks on his policies, feeling as if his self-worth were under challenge. Public objections to what he did, especially from people he thought beholden to him, like liberals, greatly bothered him. "He is a highly sensitive and vain individual who reacts quickly to pressures," the journalist Tristram Coffin wrote Drew Pearson in March. "Now, in Vietnam, . . . [the] major need is for the President to think out thoroughly alternative courses to war. . . . He will only do this under pressure of criticism, for he needs the warmth of public approval."[57]

On April 3, after Canada's Liberal Prime Minister Lester B. Pearson had given a critical speech in Philadelphia about the President's Vietnam policy, Johnson invited him to Camp David, where he vented his frustration. Johnson did all the talking. "If there had not been a kind of 'et tu, Brute' feeling about the assault, without any personal unpleasantness of any kind," Pearson writes in his memoirs, "I would have felt almost like [Austria's Kurt] Schuschnigg before Hitler at Berchtesgaden!"

Pearson was reluctant to reveal how overbearing the President had been, even, one eyewitness said, grabbing the Prime Minister by the lapels. When asked at a Cabinet meeting what had really happened, Pearson recounted "the story of a British policeman giving evidence at a murder trial. 'My Lord,' the policeman told the judge, 'acting on information received, I proceeded to a certain address and there found the body of a woman. She had been strangled, stabbed and shot, decapitated and dismembered. But, My Lord, she had not been interfered with.' At Camp David, Pearson explained in conclusion, he had at least not been 'interfered with.' "

The burden of Johnson's complaint was that Pearson "had joined the ranks of the domestic opponents of his Vietnam Policy: [Senator Wayne] Morse, [Walter] Lippmann, the New York Times, ADA [Americans for Democratic Action], the ignorant liberals, the 'know nothing,' 'do gooders,' etc." Johnson seemed "forlorn at not being understood better by friends." He impressed Pearson as being "tired, under great and continuous pressure, and ... more worried about U.S. policy in Vietnam than he was willing to show. His irritation at any indication of lack of full support for his policy; his impatience of criticism and his insistence that everything is working out in accord with a well-conceived plan; all these really indicate a feeling of insecurity about the situation, rather than the reverse. As the President said: 'It's hard to sleep these days.' 'I'm beginning to feel like a martyr; misunderstood, misjudged by friends at home and abroad.' "[58]

Johnson was determined to disarm his critics and unify the country behind his Vietnam policy. His objective at the beginning of April was to answer complaints about American resistance to a negotiated settlement by proposing talks on terms the North Vietnamese would find hard to resist. Johnson doubted that Hanoi would come to the peace table. How dare his critics call him a "war-monger," he told Pearson, when it was the Communists who wouldn't negotiate.

The President "gave me a frank and revealing exposition of U.S. plans," Pearson recalled, "told with great vehemence, many short and vigorous vulgarities at the expense of his opponents, and a few Texas illustrations." Johnson saw three possibilities. Former head of the Strategic Air Command General Curtis LeMay and other "hawks" advocated wiping out "Hanoi, Haiphong, even Peking, and other Asian Communist centers by using the Strategic Air Force; in short, all-out war." Johnson vowed to continue his eighteen-month resistance to this policy: " 'Not bad, for a warmonger,' " he said. At the other extreme was a "lock, stock, and barrel" pullout "back to the

continental USA and to hell with Asia and Vietnam." European and
Asian countries, as well as the United States, viewed this as impermissible.

The only alternative was *his* policy: "Helping South Vietnam in
spite of its political confusion and military unreliability; step up
American military aid, which would mean more troops; kill more
Viet Cong, really go after them; follow through on the planned bombing of the North." This did not mean "unlimited bombing," Johnson
explained, but rather "the progressive destruction, if necessary, of
military installations, communications and industrial facilities important in the assistance North Vietnam was giving the South. . . . They
would also do everything possible to avoid killing civilians, for which
restraint, the President repeated with the bitterness he had previously
shown on this matter, they would get no thanks from their friends."
Pearson "thought everybody would be relieved, to hear of the careful
character of this planned retaliation."[59]

Pearson's support encouraged Johnson to pursue the policy he
described. But no more so than an opinion poll three days later: 60
percent of Americans felt that only U.S. troops would be able to stop
the Communist infiltration of South Vietnam. Forty-six percent of
the sample wanted Johnson to "hold the line" in Vietnam, "doing
what we need to do in order to maintain strength for the democratic
position." An additional 20 percent wanted an expansion of the war
in the North. But 31 percent favored negotiations, "with a view to
getting out." The country was evenly split for and against sending in
large numbers of U.S. troops.[60]

In late March Johnson decided to give a speech at the Johns
Hopkins University, which had three aims. First, it would demonstrate that administration policy toward Vietnam was not confused
and erratic but in line with what had been in place for ten years.
Second, it would offer "unconditional discussions" for peace that
would silence critics calling the President a "warmonger." Third, if
there were no productive result from a proposal for talks, it would
clear the decks for a steady escalation acceptable to most Americans
and likely to force a negotiated peace assuring independence for South
Vietnam.

Johnson's speech before a university audience critical of an expanded effort in Vietnam began with the background and basis for
American involvement in the struggle. A ten-year pledge to South
Vietnamese independence dating from the Eisenhower presidency and
running through Kennedy's meant that the Johnson administration
had "a promise to keep." The loss of Vietnam would be a prelude to
new aggressions in Asia and across the world. Consequently, in the

struggle for Vietnam, Johnson said, "We will not be defeated. We will not grow tired. We will not withdraw, either openly or under the cloak of a meaningless agreement."

Because "our patience and our determination are unending" in defense of Vietnam, Johnson urged Hanoi to begin peace talks before thousands more died and North Vietnam suffered the devastation of what it had "built with toil and sacrifice." If Hanoi guaranteed South Vietnamese independence, it could look forward to a cooperative effort, backed by a billion-dollar American investment, to develop all of Southeast Asia. "The vast Mekong River can provide food and water and power on a scale to dwarf even our own TVA. The wonders of modern medicine can be spread through villages where thousands die every year from lack of care. Schools can be established to train people in the skills that are needed to manage the process of development."

Johnson's appeal convinced neither critics at home nor opponents abroad. His assumptions that a Communist victory in Vietnam would extend to all of Southeast Asia, that the area was vital to U.S. security, and that a failure to fight in Vietnam would undermine our influence around the world and might even lead to a war with China and Russia seemed no more persuasive after his speech than before.[61]

Moreover, though Johnson told Bill Moyers that "Ho will never be able to say, 'No,'" to a billion-dollar development program, the North Vietnamese leader did just that. Johnson's New Deal evangelism, his experience with the transformation of rural Texas and the South, and his underestimation of Ho's commitment to the unification of all Vietnam and distrust of what he saw as neo-colonialism, a Western capitalist state exploiting Vietnam, clouded Johnson's judgment about Ho's response. Yet Johnson himself, in a moment of greater realism about Southeast Asia, had declared: "If I were Ho Chi Minh, I would never negotiate." Ho, in fact, said the same thing. The war could end only if the United States totally withdrew from the South and ceased attacking the North, and Saigon shared political power with the Viet Cong.[62]

If Johnson didn't get the response from Hanoi he wished, his speech nevertheless put him in a stronger position with Congress, the press, and the public. In the main, all responded positively to what the *Washington Post* called the "skillful brandishment of both the sword and the olive branch," and Senator George Smathers of Florida described as "the glint of iron" alongside "the velvet in the speech." A State Department survey of American opinion concluded that the President's "adroit exposition of U.S. policy" received "wide acclaim." And though some like Walter Lippmann saw little gain resulting from Johnson's speech, Johnson himself believed that the address now gave him a stronger basis on which to fight a wider war.[63]

The Dominican Republic

In the spring of 1965, the domestic opposition to Vietnam and possible wider war set Johnson on edge and troubled his sleep. While a crisis in the Dominican Republic at the end of April temporarily diverted Johnson's attention from Vietnam, it added to tensions that shortly raised concerns among White House intimates about the President's emotional stability.

In 1961, the assassination of Rafael Trujillo had ended a thirty-one-year military dictatorship and led to the election of Juan Bosch in December 1962. The Bosch regime lasted only seven months, when a coup replaced him with a military junta. Bosch's departure produced few regrets in Washington, where he was viewed as "a dangerous demagogue" who might inadvertently open the way to a Communist government.

The Johnson administration, especially Thomas Mann, in charge of Latin America, was far more comfortable with the "nontotalitarian" dictatorship of Donald Reid Cabral, a pro-American businessman, whom U.S. Ambassador William Tapley Bennett, "a courtly southern gentleman [and] career foreign service officer of the old school," called "Donny." Under Bennett's and Mann's guidance, the Reid Cabral government received more money, $100 million, in direct and guaranteed loans than any regime in Dominican history.[64]

The eruption of a constitutionalist countercoup on April 24, 1965, discomforted the U.S. Embassy in Santo Domingo and the State Department. Initially, Washington adopted a wait-and-see policy. Reluctant to abandon the existing regime and convinced by the embassy that the rebels were too weak to win control, the U.S. government did nothing. As the uprising gained strength in the next twenty-four hours, the embassy held to its advice that the U.S. not intervene. This rested on the mistaken assumption that the coup was no more than a case of the "outs" against the "ins." The rebels were seen as disgruntled military chiefs who would simply establish another junta little different from the existing government except for personalities.[65]

Over the next three days, however, it became clear to the embassy and Washington that the rebellion was a "countercoup" aimed at restoring constitutional rule and possibly the presidency of Juan

Bosch. The embassy, seeing this as against U.S. interests, began encouraging the Dominican government's military chiefs "to forestall a leftist takeover." When attacks on the 27th threatened to overwhelm the rebels, they asked Bennett to mediate an end to the crisis. But he refused, lecturing them on the Communist danger to which they had exposed the Republic.

Bennett's refusal partly rested on the belief that the constitutionalists would be defeated and a new pro-U.S. government would gain control. But the embassy once more miscalculated: Between the evening of April 27 and the morning of the 28th, the rebels, in what some described as a miraculous turnabout, regained the initiative and threatened to rout loyalist forces. An alarmed Bennett cabled the State Department on the afternoon of the 28th: "The issue here now is a fight between Castro-type elements and those who oppose. I do not wish to be over-dramatic but we should be clear as to the situation." Four hours later, he reported a rapid deterioration in the situation and urged landing U.S. Marines to protect American lives, which he believed were in danger. He saw no need for a discussion of political goals. "*If Washington wishes*, they can be landed for the purpose of protecting evacuation of American citizens. I recommend immediate landing."[66]

Throughout the crisis, Johnson had remained closely in touch with developments. He told the State Department to keep him "constantly informed" of what was happening. One high-ranking Pentagon officer recalls that the President "was immediately drawn into that and took a very active and vigorous stand." Ambassador John Bartlow Martin remembers that "the President was running the Dominican intervention like a desk officer in the State Department." Johnson had numerous reports from the CIA on concerted efforts by three organized left-wing groups in Santo Domingo to advance the possibility of a "Castro-type government." He also had reports of anarchy and violence that was claiming hundreds of lives and threatening the safety of U.S. citizens.[67]

Consequently, on the afternoon of the 28th, when Bennett cabled his request for Marines, Johnson saw no alternative to sending them. At a meeting with congressional leaders two hours later, he stressed the threat to American lives as the basis for his action. But when CIA Director Admiral William Raborn reported a "positive identification of three ring-leaders of the Rebels as Castro-trained agents" and Senator Dirksen and House Speaker McCormack expressed concern about the Communist threat, the President replied that "there was no alternative to the actions being taken by the United States in view of the unanimous recommendations received from all responsible officials," and "observed that we can't waste one moment in taking action." In a public statement later that evening, Johnson explained his use of troops as necessary to assure the safety of Americans.[68]

The next evening, in a meeting with *New York Times* journalist Charles Mohr, Johnson emphasized his concern to save lives. "I had made a journalistic mistake in my first-day story on the Marine landing in not giving more emphasis to the guarded report by Mann and Ball that some Communists had been identified among the rebels," Mohr told LBJ. "Johnson disagreed, saying it was hopeless to think that anyone would ever believe him but that he had not landed Marines to put down a communist threat."[69]

Already under sharp attack for his actions in Vietnam, Johnson didn't wish to open himself to additional criticism as a knee-jerk anti-Communist who saw a military solution to every left-wing threat around the globe. But, in fact, he was greatly concerned about the possibility of a Communist takeover in Santo Domingo. When former Ambassador to Santo Domingo John B. Martin told Johnson the last we want to have happen is for U.S. troops to start shooting up a capital city, LBJ replied: "No, it isn't. The last thing we want to have happen is a communist takeover in that country."[70]

In an early morning meeting with his national security advisers on April 30, Johnson described continuing violence and instability in the Dominican Republic as the prelude to a Communist regime.

Mac Bundy believed that a Castro victory in the island would be "the worst political disaster we could possibly suffer. But in order to quash Castro in D.R. we need above all else to get hemisphere public opinion on our side." Bundy urged a press conference at which "indisputable evidence that Castro-communists are in control in D.R." would be provided. "We *must* lay the public opinion base—a *clear choice—freedom vs. Castro.*"[71]

Johnson tried to establish a consensus for his policy with a live radio and television broadcast on the evening of the 30th. He explained that violence and disorder were increasing in the island, that foreign nationals and Dominicans themselves remained in danger, and that "people trained outside the Dominican Republic are seeking to gain control." He announced an OAS mission to the island to arrange a cease-fire and help promote a democratic solution to the conflict. He pledged U.S. backing for the right of all "free people of this hemisphere to choose their own course without falling prey to international conspiracy from any quarter."[72]

Two days later, with no letup in the crisis, Johnson increased the number of troops to the island and stepped up his efforts to convince people at home and abroad that he was doing the right thing. At a congressional briefing on May 2, he reviewed developments in the crisis, explaining that the "Embassy has been under constant fire," and action was taken only when the Dominican "authorities washed their hands and said it is up to us to protect our people." Fulbright then asked: "Is Bosch a Communist?" Johnson replied: "Doesn't make any difference—His own people got sidetracked. The other folks have come to the top. Our position, we are not supporting *either* side. We are trying to stop murder. We hope OAS can come up with the answer."[73]

A few hours later, the President took his case to the public. "At stake are the lives of thousands, the liberty of a nation, and the principles and the values of all the American Republics," he declared. He then reviewed the events compelling U.S. intervention, saying some people were objecting that "we should have waited, or we should have delayed, or we should have consulted further, or we should have called a meeting," but when the entire nine-member U.S. team in Santo Domingo advised that without U.S. forces " 'men and women—Americans and those of other lands—will die in the streets'—well, I knew there was no time to talk, to consult, or to delay."

Meanwhile, Johnson said, the revolt "took a tragic turn. Communist leaders, many of them trained in Cuba, ... took increasing control. And what began as a popular democratic revolution ... was taken over and really seized and placed into the hands of a band of Communist conspirators." For anyone who cared to know the facts, there was "firsthand evidence of the horrors and the hardship, the violence and the terror, and the international conspiracy from which U.S. servicemen have rescued the people of more than 30 nations from that war-torn island." As for the outcome of the crisis, Johnson declared the United States committed to an end to violence and the establishment of a freely elected non-Communist government.[74]

Although the mass of Americans approved of the President's policy, influential critics in Congress, the media, and the universities disputed his description of events. They did not believe that the Communist threat in the island was what Johnson represented it to be or that the U.S. government was so ready to stand aside while the Dominicans determined their political fate. Their skepticism was warranted.[75]

Johnson, in fact, shared his critics' doubts. He knew that the evidence of Communist subversion was less clear and the dangers to foreign nationals less pronounced than he said. But he believed domestic pressures compelled him to act as he did. "If I send in Marines,

I can't live in the Hemisphere," he told congressional leaders on May 2, "if I don't, I can't live at home."[76]

With the embassy in Santo Domingo warning of dangers to Americans and a Communist threat and pressing for troops to solve both problems, Johnson couldn't say no. If a number of Americans were killed and/or a left-wing government came to power, conservative critics in the United States would have denounced his "failure" to act. He found it much more palatable to follow the embassy's lead regardless of the facts. And once he did, he wished to carry the country and the hemisphere along with him.

But the situation in the Dominican Republic was too murky to lend itself to clear demonstrations of any kind, which left Johnson vulnerable to criticism he couldn't refute. As a consequence, he began to overstate the case for intervention. Just as he used his towering physical presence—his characteristic clutching and holding—to overwhelm a political opponent, so he engaged in verbal overkill to persuade critics that his Dominican policy was a necessary response to circumstances beyond presidential control.

In meetings with reporters in the Oval Office or during walks on the south lawn, he described embassy warnings that without U.S. troops blood would have run in the streets. In fact, he said, "some 1,500 innocent people were murdered and shot, and their heads cut off, and six Latin American embassies were violated and fired upon over a period of 4 days before we went in. As we talked to our Ambassador to confirm the horror and the tragedy and the unbelievable fact that they were firing on Americans and the American Embassy, he was talking to us from under a desk while bullets were going through his windows and he had a thousand American men, women, and children assembled in the hotel who were pleading with their President for help to preserve their lives." Since none of this was strictly true, it deepened rather than eased doubts about Johnson's response to Dominican developments. Moreover, when the Santo Domingo Embassy released a list of fifty-four "Communist and Castroist leaders" of the rebels, some of whom turned out to be conservatives, it further undermined Johnson's case for intervention.[77]

Johnson's hyperbole won few converts and provoked additional criticism of him as either misinformed or a "liar." This in turn stimulated further attempts on his part to refute criticism and justify his policy. He scrutinized press accounts and public statements throughout the spring and summer, instructing members of his administration to counter this criticism as vigorously as possible. "I don't like people calling me a liar," he told Ambassador Bennett. "I want you to go down there [to Santo Domingo] and see if you can find some of those people who were beheaded." When Max Ascoli, the editor of *The New Leader*, published a conversation with LBJ about "the unpopularity of being anti-Communist," Johnson wanted "some good liberal Senator to speak on this and insert it in the *Record*." When reporters complained about the quality of press briefings at the Santo Domingo embassy, Johnson wanted "the best press man we have" to spend some time on the island helping out. Johnson also considered releasing a White Paper that would "make people aware of the damage done by irresponsible reporting in a time of crisis."[78]

Happily for Johnson the Dominican crisis lasted only a short time. Under prodding from the OAS and the U.S. government, the Dominican factions signed a cease-fire agreement on May 5. Two days later a Dominican General set up a five-man "Government of National Reconstruction." But the rebels refused to accept it as a legitimate expression of the popular will. They did, however, agree to cooperate with an OAS committee in trying to arrange for a democratically elected regime. While negotiations proceeded, the OAS sent in an Inter-American Peace Force, which included U.S. troops, to prevent a renewed outbreak of fighting. On August 29, the OAS committee won agreement to an "Act of Dominican Reconciliation" providing for a provisional government and the promise of free elections within nine months.

On June 1, 1966, after a period punctuated by continuing acts of violence, particularly against the left, Joaquin Belaguer defeated Juan Bosch by a vote of 57 percent to 39 percent in an election largely free of fraud. Though the left saw the outcome as the product of U.S. intimidation, the Johnson administration hailed the result as a victory for constitutional government.[79]

Johnson also took satisfaction from a poll in August showing that 69 percent of the American people approved his decision to send in the Marines. But Oliver Quayle, Johnson's pollster, advised the White House to "tell the President that while this is highly favorable, he should not kid himself into thinking it was overwhelming. The truth is that one in five disapprove of sending Marines to the Dominican Republic. The main reason is that we're butting into other people's affairs."[80]

More important to the President, the crisis seemed to deepen the feeling in the press and among the public that he was out of his depth in foreign affairs. The exaggerated explanations for his decision to send in troops and the questions raised about his candor and dispassion in the crisis caused *Newsweek*, for example, to describe the President as "touchy, bitter and exasperated" by the complexities and unmanageability of foreign events. Worse yet, from Johnson's perspective, the doubts raised by the Dominican problem translated into additional questions about the wisdom and likely outcome of policy toward Vietnam.

One of the chief consequences of the Dominican crisis for Johnson was a heightened sense of urgency about identifying and following an unwavering course in Vietnam. He believed it essential if he were to convince supporters and opponents at home and abroad that he had an effective strategy for meeting the challenge in Southeast Asia.[81]

Vietnam: "The Winning Strategy"

Even before the crisis in Santo Domingo intensified Johnson's desire for a long-term solution to the problem of South Vietnam, he had begun moving toward the only means he saw for rescuing the country from Communist control—great numbers of American ground troops who could inflict substantial losses on the Viet Cong and North Vietnamese regulars. His agreement at the beginning of April to broaden the mission of the Marines from strictly defensive to offensive operations and to plan for the introduction of two additional divisions had opened the way to the escalation of the land war. Between April 12 and 14 he advised U.S. senators that the aggressive use of American Marines in Vietnam was producing three times as many Communist casualties as before. If we were to sustain this and bring peace to the South, he would need to send Army forces.[82]

On the 15th, Johnson approved the deployment of two Army brigades to guard bases in Vietnam. When Ambassador Taylor, who believed U.S. troops would be bogged down in an unwinnable land war, challenged the decision, Johnson suspended his order until advisers could evaluate the deployment at a Honolulu conference on April 20. On the 21st, McNamara reported that the Honolulu conferees had agreed not only to the need for two Army brigades but also three more Marine battalions and logistical troops to prepare for the two divisions. By the middle of June, the total of U.S. ground forces in Vietnam was to be 82,000, a 150 percent increase.

Only George Ball took exception to the proposal, and Johnson, who was ready to sign on to the escalation, gave Ball until the following morning to come up with "a settlement plan. If you can pull a rabbit out of the hat, I'm all for it!" the President said. Ball had no such magic at his command, and Johnson approved the additional troops.

As concerned as ever not to stir public debate, which could distract Congress from Great Society bills, Johnson hid his decision, pre-ferring "to announce individual deployments at appropriate times." Yet the escalation was an open secret. On April 21, Hanson Baldwin, the military correspondent of the *New York Times*, published an account of the Honolulu recommendations and reported that U.S. ground forces were shifting from defensive to offensive operations. Dean Rusk had tried and failed to squelch the *Times* story. Johnson complained that Rusk had been "too gentle" in trying to kill it.[83]

Yet the President had no intention of unilaterally escalating the American ground effort in Vietnam. He believed it essential to have congressional support, but he wanted no debate that might distract Congress from domestic business and allow the Communists to see emerging divisions over his policy. Consequently, on May 2, in the midst of the Dominican crisis, he told congressional leaders that "Congress ought to show the world that it really backs up his policies." Two days later, he told the six most important congressional committees that he wanted a supplemental $700 million appropriation for Vietnam and the Dominican Republic. This was "no ... routine appropriation," he said. "For each member of Congress who supports this request is voting to continue our effort to try to halt Communist aggression." A failure to stop the Communists in Vietnam would "show that American commitment is worthless," and then "the road is open to expansion and to endless conquest."[84]

A special message to Congress later that day emphasized that "this is not a routine appropriation." Moreover, he offered no "guarantee [that] this will be the last request." If ensuring the safety of South Vietnam required more of a commitment, he would "turn again to the Congress."[85]

The Congress, where voices of dissent over the escalating war had been heard in greater numbers since March, was surprisingly pliant. In two days, with next to no debate and no amendments in either chamber, the House approved the request by a 408 to 7 vote and the Senate by a margin of 88 to 3. With U.S. forces already in the field, the congressmen and senators saw no way to deny them what Senator John Stennis of Mississippi described as "the tools with which to fight." Senator Mansfield, an unbending opponent of escalation, asked that "no one misunderstand this vote.... There is not a Senator who would not prefer, with the President, that a decent peace might be achieved quickly in Vietnam. But we will vote for this measure because there is not one member of this body who does not desire to uphold the President and those who are risking their lives."[86]

During the rest of May, while the Dominican crisis played itself out, Johnson made no additional commitments to expand the war in

Vietnam. This was in spite of growing concern about Saigon's capacity to survive. Political instability brought the collapse of a civilian government and the return in early June of military rule under Nguyen Van Thieu as Chief of State and Nguyen Cao Ky as Prime Minister. Ky, who declared he had only one hero, Adolph Hitler, "because he pulled his country together," made American rhetoric about preserving South Vietnamese freedom seem ridiculous.[87]

At the same time, a Communist offensive beginning in mid-May inflicted a series of defeats on South Vietnamese forces and threatened a military collapse. By the beginning of June, Ambassador Taylor was reporting that the bombing offensive against North Vietnam was changing nothing in the South, where we faced an impending disaster. He now came to the reluctant conclusion that "it will probably be necessary to commit U.S. ground forces to action." Bill Bundy says: "Almost with the suddenness of a thunder clap, it sank in to American military men, and through them to Taylor and Washington, that ARVN, or at least much of it, was outclassed and in danger of collapse."[88]

Johnson, who was now spending more and more of his time on Vietnam, intensified his efforts to find a workable formula. On June 3, he discussed a wider air campaign with congressional leaders, but made clear that he opposed "an irreversible extension of the war" through attacks on Hanoi and Haiphong.[89]

A larger ground war in the South held more appeal. On the 5th, he joined Rusk, McNamara, Ball, and the Bundys for lunch at the State Department. "Lady Bird is away, I was all alone, and I heard you fellows were getting together, so I thought I'd come over," he said.

Bill Bundy recalls that the meeting "developed into a reflective discussion of where we were headed, with no attempt to decide anything, but with much light on the basic approach." When the discussion turned to troops, "Johnson pitched in. Would more Americans, he asked, mean that the Vietnamese would do less? McNamara said there was no sign of this reaction now." Johnson then asked, "How do we get what we want?" Rusk, McNamara, and Ball ventured answers that rested on "the rational belief that a frustrated and pained Hanoi must in time call it off."[90]

For the time being, however, the North Vietnamese and Viet Cong seemed more likely than ever to sustain their war effort. On June 7, the U.S. military command in Saigon reported the disintegration of ARVN and the likely collapse of the government unless U.S. and third-country forces came to the rescue. General William Westmoreland asked for an increase of U.S. troops from 82,000 to

175,000—41,000 immediately and another 52,000 over the next several months, a total of forty-four battalions. He wanted to abandon
a "defensive posture" and "take the war to the enemy."[91]

In three meetings over the next seventy-two hours, Johnson
struggled to define a response. He settled on the idea that an increase
to about 100,000 men would allow the South Vietnamese to hold the
line through the summer without turning the conflict into an American or, as George Ball put it, "a white man's war." Ball emphasized
that, once you got above 100 to 150,000, you would end up going to
300 to 400,000 men and a shift from South Vietnamese reliance on
themselves to dependence on America to fight and win the war.

"At the end of the meetings on both the 10th and the 11th,"
Bill Bundy recalls, "the President made remarks suggesting strongly
that he accepted the recommendation [of 100,000] but he obviously
wished to mull it over further and to put it into an overall plan that
included congressional consultation, some careful explanation to the
country, and perhaps a renewed form of congressional authority."[92]

Whatever Johnson's caution, he had already made up his mind.
During a conversation with Henry Graff, a Columbia University historian writing an article for the *New York Times Magazine* on how
Johnson made foreign policy, LBJ described himself as boxed in by
unpalatable choices: between sending Americans to die in Vietnam
and giving in to the Communists. If he sent additional troops, he
would be attacked as "an interventionist," and if he didn't, he risked
being "impeached." Phrased in these terms, could any one doubt what
Johnson's decision would be? The real choice he was making was
between "What will be enough and not too much?"[93]

This is not to suggest that Johnson did not anguish over the
decision. A *New York Times* reporter, who saw him privately on June
24, spent most of the session on foreign policy. He got the "impression
of [a] deeply frustrated man. [LBJ] says he doesn't know what to do."
The thought occurred to the reporter that this may have been Johnson's way of creating sympathy for himself. But the "thought also
flashed through my mind the way he was twitching and fidgeting
when he talked about Vietnam, maybe he wouldn't last. . . . Overall
impression: The man is deeply worried about Vietnam and sees no
way out. Desperate for workable plan. His wife is worried about
him."[94]

Only the belief that he was not making irreversible decisions
eased Johnson's concerns. In a memo Ball sent him on June 18, he
cautioned Johnson against being drawn into "an endless flow of forces
to South Viet-Nam," which might become bogged down in the jungles and rice paddies and, like the French, end up suffering defeat

"after seven years of bloody struggle." Instead, Ball urged the President to limit the number of U.S. troops to 100,000, while telling his "top advisers . . . that you are *not* committing U.S. forces on an open-ended basis to an all-out land war in South Viet-Nam; that instead you are making a *controlled commitment* for a *trial period* of three months." If after this time, the U.S. faced a "vast protracted [war] effort, we would do better to cut our losses and reach a political solution, which would surely fall short of our objectives. A larger commitment of troops than the 100,000 would make disengagement far more difficult and costly should the war go badly."[95]

Johnson signaled his sympathy for Ball's short-term approach at a meeting on June 23. Ball urged the 100,000-troop limit and consideration of shifting our attention to Thailand in three months should conditions in Vietnam not improve. Rusk and McNamara predicted the collapse of Southeast Asia to Communism from such a strategy, and McNamara argued the case for greater troop commitments if conditions required them. Johnson "let the discussion rage around him without interjecting his own views." He then asked Ball and McNamara to prepare "studies covering military and political moves over the next three months and beyond." He wanted the studies in a week but gave "no assurance that the issue [of larger troop commitments] would then be decided."[96]

During the next two weeks, the struggle over Vietnam policy raged more intensely than ever. McNamara, Rusk, Ball, both Bundys, and former President Eisenhower weighed in with a variety of proposals ranging from Ball's renewed emphasis on reaching a compromise solution to McNamara's recommendation for substantial expansion of the ground and air wars.

Except for Ball, all agreed on the necessity of preserving the independence of South Vietnam from a Communist takeover. At a meeting on July 2, Johnson made clear that he wanted to postpone final decisions until the end of the month. He ordered McNamara to go to Saigon in mid-July to discuss Westmoreland's military plans; he directed Averell Harriman to travel to Moscow to discuss a possible reconvening of the Geneva Conference; and he asked Ball to explore possible contacts with the North Vietnamese and Viet Cong as a prelude to negotiations. Johnson wanted bold actions on Vietnam to wait until the voting rights and Medicare bills had been passed.[97]

As part of the delaying process and effort to build a broad consensus, Johnson asked the counsel of the "wise men"—ten prominent, former foreign policy officials, including Dean Acheson and Clark Clifford. On July 8, they advised Johnson that he had no choice but to expand the war to prevent a Communist victory that would jeopardize America's national security around the world. He also needed to create national backing for the war by publicly explaining his decisions.

When Johnson began lamenting his predicament, complaining "how mean everything and everybody was to him—Fate, the Press, the Congress, the Intellectuals & so on," Dean Acheson blew his top and told him that he had no choice but to press on. "With this lead my colleagues came thundering in like the charge of the Scots Greys at Waterloo," Bill Bundy says. The President "probably expected that *most* of the Panel would be *generally* in favor of a firm policy," Bundy adds. "What he found was that *almost all* were *solidly* of this view."[98]

Bundy considered this " 'quickie' consultation with outsiders" a poor way to proceed. These elder statesmen may have had the wisdom of their experience but they had done "very little in terms of a really hard look at the difficulties of the particular case." George Ball shared Bundy's reservations about the casualness with which these elders gave their judgment. "You goddamned old bastards," he told Acheson and one other member of the group after the meeting, "you remind me of nothing so much as a bunch of buzzards sitting on a fence and letting the young men die. You don't know a goddamned thing about what you're talking about.... You just sit there and say these irresponsible things!"[99]

Though Ball's remarks "shook the hell" out of Acheson, they were not repeated to Johnson, who accepted the advice of the elders as a confirmation of his own views. At a news conference on July 9, he stated that casualties were increasing in Vietnam on all sides and that things were likely to get worse before they get better. "Our manpower needs there are increasing, and will continue to do so." Seventy-five thousand U.S. troops "will be there very shortly. There will be others that will be required. Whatever is required I am sure will be supplied." He predicted that "understanding and endurance and patriotism" would be needed in the future, but he had no "plan to let up until the aggression ceases." Four days later, in another press conference, he declared that increased aggression from the North may require a greater American response on the ground in the South. "So it is quite possible that new and serious decisions will be necessary in the near future."

At a Rose Garden gathering of Rural Electric Cooperative officials on the 14th, the President predicted that long debates and criticism of him were in the offing over Vietnam. But "our national honor is at stake in southeast Asia, and we are going to protect it, and you might just as well be prepared for it." Despite "some dark days" ahead, he expected the country to continue to live up to its responsibilities abroad.[100]

The question he posed to himself in the second half of July was not whether to put in additional troops but how many and at what pace. He wished to send enough men initially to prevent a South Vietnamese collapse and then to change the course of the war. But he also intended to make a commitment that would be compatible with domestic goals. On July 16 he told Deputy Defense Secretary Cyrus Vance that he could not submit a supplementary budget request to Congress of more than $300 to 400 million before next January; he believed an earlier and "larger request . . . will kill [his] domestic legislative program." Johnson took comfort from Mac Bundy's advice on the 19th that no additional appropriation was needed now, because "there are other ways of financing our full effort in Vietnam for the rest of the calendar year, at least."[101]

Johnson was reluctant to make new commitments without another review of his choices. At a White House meeting on July 21, he asked McNamara for his judgment. After McNamara urged an increase in troops to between 175,000 and 200,000 and a reserve callup of 235,000 men, Johnson warned against "snap judgments"; he wanted careful consideration of "all our options." Did we want simply to come home? Johnson thought not. "The negotiations . . . , the other approaches have all been explored," he said. "It makes us look weak—with cup in hand." He wanted this option and all others discussed nevertheless. "Is anyone of the opinion we should not do what the [McNamara] memo says—If so I'd like to hear from them."

It was an invitation to George Ball to restate his case for withdrawal. Ball did so guardedly, saying that "if the decision is to go ahead, I'm committed." Johnson pressed him to make his case anyway, though expressing the belief that there was "very little alternative to what we are doing. . . . I feel it would be more dangerous for us to lose this now, than endanger a greater number of troops." Still, he wanted another meeting that afternoon to consider Ball's alternative.

Joseph Califano explains that, even after Johnson had made up his mind on a major question, he "continued to consult and ferret out opposing views . . . because he didn't want to be surprised by any opposition, fail to muster all possible support, or miss any opportunity to overwhelm or undermine an opponent he could not persuade."

Ball obliged the President. "We can't win," he declared when the group reconvened. He anticipated a "long protracted" struggle with a "messy conclusion." The war would produce serious problems at home and abroad. As casualties mounted, Americans would demand a strike at North Vietnam's jugular. The war would also encourage the view that "a great power cannot beat guerrillas." Ball had serious doubts that "an army of westerners can fight orientals in [an] Asian jungle and succeed." Ball recommended abandoning South Vietnam to its fate.

Johnson objected that we would lose credibility; "it would seem to be an irreparable blow." Yet Johnson wondered whether "Westerners can ever win in Asia," and he doubted the viability of fighting a war for a country "whose government changes every month." But McGeorge Bundy, McNamara, and Rusk countered that Ball was underestimating the consequences of an American withdrawal and making too little of North Vietnamese costs from a larger U.S. effort. The President needed to make clear to the public that America was being asked "to bet more to achieve less," Bundy said, and if that didn't pay off, there would be time to withdraw after we had "given it a good try."

At the end of the meeting, Johnson summed up: "Withdrawal would be a disaster, a harsh bombing program would not win and could easily bring a wider war, and standing pat with existing forces ('hunkering up'—as he called it) was only slow defeat. Only . . . doing what McNamara urged was left. . . . It was the end of debate on policy," Bill Bundy says, "and the beginning of a new debate on tactics and above all on presentation to the country. In his own favorite phrase, the President had decided to 'put in his stack.' "[102]

Though Johnson continued the behind-the-scenes debate over escalating or getting out for several more days, his focus was now on how to put the decision for a wider war before the country. "How would you tell the American people what the stakes are?" Johnson asked his military chiefs in a meeting on the 22nd. "The place where they will stick by you is the national security stake," one general replied. "Do all of you think the Congress and the people will go along with 600,000 people and billions of dollars 10,000 miles away?" the President asked. "Gallup poll shows people are basically behind our commitment," Army Secretary Stanley Resor declared. "But if you make a commitment to jump off a building, and you find out how high it is, you may withdraw the commitment," Johnson said. "I judge though that the big problem is one of national security. Is that right?" he asked rhetorically. No one disagreed.[103]

At a smaller meeting three hours later, Johnson searched for a formula to announce escalation without suggesting a major change in policy. He feared it would agitate Congress and the public and encourage Moscow and Peking to increase support of Hanoi. "I don't think that calling up the reserves in itself is a change of policy," LBJ said. "Moving from 75,000 to 185,000 men is a change of policy," Rusk declared. "Much is to be said for playing this low key." Bill Moyers said: "I don't think the press thinks we are going to change basic policy, but the requirements to meet that policy." "That's right and we ought to say it," Johnson exclaimed. Rusk suggested that Johnson advise congressional leaders of his decision on July 27 and announce it publicly the following day. Johnson agreed, but asked, "Is the message a personal talk to the Congress or a normal message? Possibly a normal message," he answered himself.[104]

Years later Johnson remembered that as he decided how to reveal his decision on escalation, he "could see and almost touch [his] youthful dream of improving life for more people and in more ways than any other political leader, including FDR. . . . I was determined to keep the war from shattering that dream, which meant I simply had no choice but to keep my foreign policy in the wings. I knew the Congress as well as I know Lady Bird, and I knew that the day it exploded into a major debate on the war, that day would be the beginning of the end of the Great Society."[105]

The President was determined to avoid a public explosion over Vietnam. At a National Security Council meeting on the 27th he explained that he could ask Congress for "great sums of money, [to] call up reserves and increase [the] draft." He could put the country on a war footing and declare a state of emergency. But he didn't "want to be dramatic and cause tension." He thought "we can get our people to support us without having to be provocative." He planned to send more troops to Vietnam "out of forces in this country" and to "use his transfer authority to get the money we need until January." At a meeting with congressional leaders immediately after, Johnson repeated his determination to avoid dramatics and asked the leaders not "to talk about what is going on. The press is going to be all over you. Let me appeal to you as Americans to show your patriotism by not talking to the press."[106]

To mute his decision, Johnson announced the expansion of the war at a press conference rather than in a speech to a joint session of Congress. Moreover, all he would say was that troop commitments were going up from 75,000 to 125,000, with additional forces to be sent later when requested. Nor would he call up reserve units now, though he would give it careful consideration in the future. His decision did "not imply any change in policy whatever," he also told reporters. To further downplay the action, Johnson surrounded it with talk of his Great Society goals, which he would not allow to be "drowned in the wasteful ravages of cruel wars," and announcements of Abe Fortas's nomination to the Supreme Court and John Chancellor's appointment as director of the Voice of America.[107]

"If you have a mother-in-law with only one eye and she has it in the center of her forehead," Johnson joked privately, "you don't keep her in the living room." Yet Johnson knew that he could only hide the full meaning of his larger military commitment for so long. For he had no illusion that his administration was undergoing a sea change resembling FDR's shift in the 1940s from Dr. New Deal to Dr. Win-the-War.[108]

Dr. Win-the-War

Johnson did not reach his decision casually to fight a land war in Asia. He and his advisers had made exhausting reviews of their options. The defeat of the French in a similar struggle, the difficulty of fighting a guerrilla war with conventional forces, the determination of the North Vietnamese to make it long and costly, the likely hesitation of the American public once the price in blood and treasure began to register, and the likelihood that a protracted conflict would divert resources from the Great Society all gave Johnson pause.

But the conviction that a Communist victory would have worldwide repercussions for America's national security, especially in Southeast Asia, and would provoke a right-wing reaction in the United States that would wreck Johnson's administration overwhelmed his doubts. Moreover, he and most of his advisers thought it unlikely that the Viet Cong and North Vietnamese would be able to hold out forever against America's massive air, land, and sea power. True, it was going to cost American lives to accomplish the goal, but the extent of that sacrifice was not assumed to be large or anything like the Korean losses, which ran to 30,000 men. Before any such development, the Communists would have to come out and fight, and when they did, American forces, in the words of one general, would "cream them."

Were these considerations enough to trigger Johnson's escalation of the war? Yes. But something else was at work here that helped clinch the decision: ego or personality or Johnson's lifelong compulsion to be the best, to dominate and win. It seems worth repeating that few people were more competitive than Johnson. He could not bear to lose or take a back seat to anyone. As senator, he had to be the leader; as Vice President, he was a miserable second fiddle. Once he held the presidency, it wasn't enough to be *the* Chief Executive; he needed to be the best or, at a minimum, one of the best Presidents in American history. In particular, he saw Franklin Roosevelt as the President to measure himself against. FDR, the winner of a historic landslide election in 1936 and the most successful reform leader and greatest war President of the century, was Johnson's model and target to surpass.

This was not some casual game Johnson played with himself. His competitiveness and need to be top dog were at the core of his being. It translated into wanting unsurpassed reform accomplishments. He wanted to improve "life for more people and in more ways than any other political leader, including FDR," he later told Kearns.

When the historian William E. Leuchtenburg interviewed him about the Great Society in September 1965, Johnson gave him a glimpse of his reach for presidential greatness. " 'Mr. President,' " Leuchtenburg began, " 'this has been a remarkable Congress. It is even arguable whether this isn't the most significant Congress ever.' ... Before I could add one more sentence to frame a question, Johnson interjected, 'No, it isn't. It's not arguable.' I grinned, then realized he was dead serious—even a little angry. It was my first indication that he believed his accomplishments were the most important in all our history. 'Not if you can read,' he snapped. 'You can perform a great service,' the President continued, 'if you say that never before have the three independent branches been so productive. Never has the American system worked so effectively in producing quality legislation—and at a time when our system is under attack all over the world.' "[109]

Johnson had few illusions about what escalation of the war would mean at home. He knew that wars had sidetracked Populism, Progressivism, and the New and Fair Deals. "Losing the Great Society was a terrible thought," Johnson later told Kearns, "but not so terrible as the thought of being responsible for America's losing a war to the Communists. Nothing could possibly be worse than that."

Yet at the time, Johnson had every hope that escalation would not mean the end of reform. On the contrary, by the time Johnson was "putting in his stack," his legislative program was largely in place. True, he would put additional reforms before the second session of the 89th Congress, but it did not match the proposals of the first in importance. Johnson's comments to Leuchtenburg in September 1965 about the unprecedented achievement of the government was a statement of his belief that, even if future reforms were sidetracked, he had already gained enough major legislation to put foreign affairs on an equal and possibly even higher footing than domestic ones.[110]

Harry McPherson, one of LBJ's principal White House aides, says that "by the end of 1965 Johnson had passed almost everything that anyone had ever conceived of. It was hard to imagine any other federal program in any field." Johnson seemed to agree when he told McPherson: "You know, you only have one year. No matter what your mandate is you have one year, and you've got to get everything done in that year." Given Johnson's continuing domestic initiatives, there is some exaggeration in his statement about one year. Still, it seems fair to say that he was now ready to focus as much and, if necessary, even more on Vietnam as on domestic advance.[111]

But if Johnson had largely created the legislative framework for his Great Society and was ready to devote himself to Vietnam, why was he so reluctant to speak more openly to the country about expansion of the war? Because until October 1965, Congress was still at work on his reforms. After that, however, he was ready to see the war come front and center. By then, the most important Great Society laws would be fixtures on the national scene. World War II had not destroyed the major elements of the New Deal, and Johnson expected it to be the same with the Great Society and Vietnam. True, some of the programs would not get the full financing they needed, but this would come in time, when the struggle in Vietnam ended. And so to Johnson, fighting in Vietnam meant not destroying the Great Society but delaying its full impact on American life.

Indeed, for all his anguish over Vietnam, Johnson saw positive developments flowing from the war: It was an opportunity to combat Communist hopes of advancing their cause through wars of national liberation. It was also another in a series of brave responses to Cold War challenges faced by America since 1945. It was one more opportunity to show the Chinese and the Soviets that we could not be intimidated. They would then be more receptive to detente or a peaceful standoff with the West.

As he saw matters in the summer and fall of 1965, he was meeting the challenge to presidential greatness at home and now he hoped to do the same abroad. For the war in Vietnam was a chance not only to promote long-term international stability but also to allow Johnson to make a great mark in foreign affairs. He had not gone looking for a fight. He was not contriving an international conflict for the sake of his historical reputation. But confronted by a foreign challenge that seemed to pose a major threat to the national well-being, Johnson intended to do his duty. If it added to his presidential greatness, all to the good. But it was no more than a secondary, comforting reason to fight.

Yet however many constructive reasons Johnson saw for fighting, he could not quiet a fear that the war might ultimately ruin his presidency. There were no guarantees that U.S. military pressure would bring the Communists to negotiate a settlement or that the American right wouldn't mount an effective attack against a political compromise in Vietnam or that the domestic left wouldn't be able to stir mass opposition to a long war.

In 1965, Johnson was more concerned about the right than the left. "George," he told Ball, "don't pay any attention to what those little shits on the campuses do. The great beast is the reactionary elements in the country. Those are the people that we have to fear."[112]

But he could not ignore the power of antiwar dissenters to sway public opinion. True, opinion polls in the spring and summer of 1965 showed the country to be generally sympathetic to his course in Vietnam. In mid-May, Americans favored the use of military force in Southeast Asia by a two to one margin, 52 percent to 26 percent. At the end of June, 62 percent of the country thought the President was doing a pretty good or excellent job in Vietnam.

Yet at the same time, the public was sharply divided over the fighting. At the end of April, 20 percent supported carrying the war to the North, while 28 percent wanted negotiations and 43 percent urged holding the line. In July, a quarter of the country supported a complete withdrawal or a halt to fighting and the start of negotiations. A like number wanted stepped-up efforts and/or a declaration of war. Sixteen percent were content to continue on the present course, but the largest number, 33 percent, had no set view of how to proceed. The uncertainties were reminiscent of the discontent during the Korean war, which had eroded Truman's public standing.[113]

In this context, Johnson feared the damage opposing voices in the press and among the country's intellectuals might have on the war effort. "Every student anti-U.S. policy demonstration is priceless gold for the Viet Cong," Jack Valenti told LBJ in April. In May, Valenti and Douglass Cater suggested that Johnson use a press conference "to bring up the problem of [U.P.I. reporter Peter] Arnett who has been more damaging to the U.S. cause than a whole division of Vietcong. (His stories on defective ammunition, antiquated aircraft, use of 'poison gas.')"

The campus teach-ins, columnists, and public marches denouncing the bombing of a weak third-world country greatly troubled Johnson. Attacks on him personally for a "credibility gap"—for exaggerating the dangers in the Dominican Republic and for failing to tell the truth about America's growing involvement in Vietnam—further incensed him. "How do you know when Lyndon Johnson is telling the truth?" a joke began to make the rounds. "When he pulls his ear lobe, scratches his chin, he's telling the truth. When he begins to move his lips, you know he's lying." The journalist Hugh Sidey said that to Johnson "the shortest distance between two points was a tunnel."[114]

A White House Festival of the Arts Eric Goldman organized for June 1965 increased Johnson's anger. When the poet Robert Lowell's acceptance and then withdrawal from the festival made the front page of the *New York Times*, it infuriated the President. He was especially hurt by the personal disdain academics and intellectuals seemed to have for him. "I look at that Texas cowhand and listen to him mangle the language," one professor told Goldman, "and I say 'No, dammit, go fight your own war.'"

Johnson responded to the flap over the festival by saying "within earshot of the press . . . , 'Some of them insult me by staying away and some of them insult me by coming.' Privately, he added, 'Don't they know I'm the only President they've got and a war is on?'" He described these intellectuals as "sonsofbitches" and "fools" and close to being "traitors."[115]

Richard Goodwin believes that these attacks on Johnson and his foreign policy made him "paranoiac." Goodwin describes several monologues by Johnson in the spring and summer of 1965 which represented a break with reality. "I am not going to have anything more to do with the liberals," he quotes LBJ as saying. "They won't have anything to do with me. They all just follow the communist line— liberals, intellectuals, communists. . . . I can't trust anybody anymore. I tell you what I'm going to do. I'm going to get rid of everybody who doesn't agree with my policies."[116]

Others shared Goodwin's concern. Hugh Sidey told him that "there was an increasing worry about the president around town. A fear that his personal eccentricities were now affecting policy." Likewise, Moyers called Goodwin one evening at midnight to say that "he was extremely worried, that as he listened to Johnson he felt weird, almost felt as if he wasn't really talking to a human being at all."

Goodwin says that "Johnson began to hint privately . . . that he was the target of a gigantic communist conspiracy in which his domestic adversaries were only players—not conscious participants, perhaps, but unwitting dupes. . . . On July 5, Johnson interrupted our conversation on domestic matters to confide: 'You know, Dick, the communists are taking over the country.'" Johnson complained to Moyers "that the communist way of thinking had infected everyone around him." He also told his staff that "the communists already control the three major networks and the forty major outlets of communication."[117]

Johnson was particularly concerned about criticism in the *Washington Evening Star*. He asked J. Edgar Hoover to find out "what might be behind" criticism of the President published in the paper. Johnson described how he had "spent considerable time" trying to disarm the *Star*'s hostility, and he expressed the belief that "Bobby Kennedy had bought considerable stock in the *Star*." The FBI's investigation showed that Kennedy had no investment in the paper and that *Star* opposition rested on conservative antagonism to big government.[118]

Johnson wasn't the only one who saw Communists manipulating the antiwar movement. A number of congressmen and senators shared his concern. They took their lead from a Senate Judiciary subcommittee report, which said that control of the antiwar movement was in "the hands of Communists and extremist elements who are openly sympathetic to the Vietcong . . . and . . . call for massive civil disobedience, including the burning of draft cards and the stopping of troop trains."[119]

Yet Johnson's reactions went much beyond any reasonable response to criticisms. Bill Moyers described Johnson to me as not only paranoid but deeply depressed. Even in the best of times Moyers remembers Johnson as given to paranoid outbursts and depressive reactions. But it was "never more pronounced than in 1965 when he was leading up to the decision about the buildup in Vietnam." Moyers attributes it to "the realization about which he was clearer than anyone that this was a road from which there was no turning back." Johnson saw the decision to send in troops as marking the potential demise or "end of his presidency. . . . It was a pronounced, prolonged depression," Moyers adds. "He would just go within himself, just disappear—morose, self-pitying, angry. . . . He was a tormented man," who described himself to Moyers as in a Louisiana swamp " 'that's pulling me down.' When he said it," Moyers remembers, "he was lying in bed with the covers almost above his head."

Were others in the White House as troubled by Johnson's behavior as you and Goodwin? I asked Moyers. Yes, Moyers replied. And "when they were deeply concerned about his behavior, they would call me—Cabinet officers and others. Rusk would call me and tell me about some exchange he just had with the President that was very disturbing, and he would say that he seemed to me to be very depressed."

On one occasion Johnson asked Rusk to leak some material to the diplomatic press that "shouldn't have been leaked." Rusk had no problem with ignoring the President's request: " 'I can afford to ignore it,' " he told Moyers. " 'I don't have a problem with that. But

I'm more deeply concerned about the state of mind of the man who would ask me to do it.'.... It wasn't the secretary's offense at that," Moyers says. "It was a highly agitated state of mind that he read in LBJ which caused him to wonder at that moment about his stability."

Moyers says he went to see Mrs. Johnson about the President's "paranoia, which made him irascible...suspicious...inconsistent" and "created a very uneven persona." He is "not at liberty to talk about that conversation," Moyers states. "But I came away from it knowing that she herself was more concerned, because she was more routinely and regularly exposed to it."

Mrs. Johnson remembers the President's pain over the war: "It was just a hell of a thorn stuck in his throat," she told me. "It wouldn't come up; it wouldn't go down.... It was just pure hell and did not have that reassuring, strong feeling that this is right, that he had when he was in a crunch with civil rights or poverty or education. It didn't have that: we'll make it through this one: Win or lose, it's the right thing to do. So, uncertainty... we had a rich dose of that. ... True, you can 'bear any burden, pay any price' if you're sure you're doing right. But if you do not know you're doing right—" she ended, and her voice trailed off.

There seems little question but that the decisions to bomb and put in a large number of ground forces combined with the antiwar dissent to greatly upset LBJ. His agitation partly stemmed from the anguish he felt over putting so many boys in harm's way. He lived with constant anxiety about the loss of American lives in the war. One White House aide recalls Johnson's descriptions of American losses in Vietnam as intensely personal. "I lost 320 of my boys this week," he would say. Where the military around the President discussed "body counts," Johnson always referred to "my boys," as if they were family members. "The worst time was the boxes coming back on the train," Mrs. Johnson says, "the dead soldiers heading for their final resting place back home in Texas, or in Arlington or Alabama."

There was also the conviction that the war would destroy his presidency. "Lyndon could see pretty far down the road most of the time," Mrs. Johnson remembers. The French "did not lose their war on the battlefields," she adds. "They lost it on the streets of Paris. And I think that possibility hovered over Lyndon early on, and he just didn't think the American public would have the stomach or the desire" to keep fighting. "So early on he wanted to get out but he couldn't find any gettin' out place." It is small wonder that his decisions for a wider war greatly agitated him.

Was Johnson continuously depressed and incapable of rational policy judgments? I asked Moyers. No, he answered. He was erratic. One day he would be in a down mood and the next he would be quite upbeat. He could be in a deep depression, and then "24 hours later no one who had seen him this way would ever have suspected it." He would convince himself that he could win the war, or the passage of a bill would brighten his mood or "be an antidote. But always when he returned to the subject of Vietnam this cloud in his eyes and this predictably unpredictable behavior" would recur.[120]

If Johnson's agitation skewed his judgment about anything, it was over the domestic politics of Vietnam. His reluctance to openly discuss escalation, and by so doing build the necessary consensus for the fighting, was a grave error. Part of this reluctance stemmed from the political conviction that fully describing the escalation would play havoc with the Great Society reforms. But even when these were secured, Johnson couldn't bring himself candidly to discuss the step-by-step expansion of the fighting. It was as if facing up to escalation publicly would have confirmed his deepest fear that he was committing himself to a long struggle that would eventually bring him down. It was less troubling to avoid confronting that reality and operate on the assumption that he was fighting a relatively brief war that he didn't need to explain and wouldn't ruin his presidency.

Vietnam: Hearts and Minds

In the four months after Johnson made his July 28 announcement, he focused on the need to solidify support for the war effort in Vietnam and the United States without public debate.

With over 200,000 U.S. troops deployed by the end of October, he believed that the conduct of the war would now take care of itself. Unlike the bombing, which Johnson constantly worried might provoke the Chinese and Soviets into a confrontation with the United States, LBJ largely left the U.S. military to determine how ground forces were to be used in the war. By contrast, he paid substantial ongoing attention to targets and the minutiae of bombing as a way to guard against a wider conflict.

In the autumn of 1965 Johnson's principal focus was on signs that the Communists would now limit or even end their aggression in Vietnam. There was a belief among Johnson and his associates, Bill Moyers says, "that if we indicated a willingness to use our power, they [the Communists] would get the message and back away from all-out confrontation.... There was a confidence ... that when the chips were down, the other people would fold."

General Maxwell Taylor told LBJ: "By the end of 1965, the North Vietnamese offensive will be bloodied and defeated without having achieved major gains. Hanoi may then decide to change its policy. 1966 could be a decisive year." In short, the very presence of so much U.S. power in Vietnam was enough to do the job without additional planning on Johnson's part as to exactly how those forces would be used. Indeed, the President assumed that the next big decision about land forces in Vietnam would not be how they would operate but whether more would be needed to achieve our ends.[121]

Johnson was more focused now on encouraging political stability in a country where divisions and coups had become a way of life. He partly took his cue from an August 1965 paper on "Politics and Victory in Vietnam" by Walt W. Rostow, the head of the State Department's Policy Planning Council. Success in the war, Rostow argued, required "some effective political expression of South Vietnamese anti-Communist nationalism. . . . We must turn to the problem of the political life of South Vietnam with a seriousness which matches that now accorded to military and diplomatic aspects of the crisis." All America's efforts in behalf of the South Vietnamese, Johnson believed, would come to naught unless we effectively encouraged the development of a viable political system commanding the loyalty of the people.[122]

The summer and fall of 1965 was a particularly satisfying time for American officials who emphasized the importance of "pacification" or "development." Henry Cabot Lodge, who had been Ambassador to Saigon in 1963–64 and returned to the job in August 1965, was a strong believer in the importance of "nation building."

He preached the idea to anyone who would listen and relied on Edward Lansdale, a CIA official, to make the program work. Though some officials warned against the dangers of taking too much responsibility for South Vietnamese affairs or becoming an occupying force that did little to advance national autonomy, Johnson, Lodge, and Lansdale gave high priority to "pacification," including proposals from John Paul Vann, a former U.S. Army officer who had returned to Vietnam in 1965 as a civilian advocate of U.S. measures to turn the Saigon government into a genuine democracy. Fearful that pushing "pacification" too hard would provoke charges of American colonialism, the White House and U.S. Embassy in Saigon endorsed policies that promised cooperative actions between U.S. and South Vietnamese officials.[123]

Yet the struggle for hearts and minds in Vietnam commanded much less of Johnson's attention in the summer and fall of 1965 than the one he fostered in the United States. Accurately believing that a stable consensus at home was essential for a sustained war effort, he mounted an unacknowledged campaign to refute the arguments of war critics and discredit them as sensible exponents of America's national interest.

In the second half of 1965 the White House expanded upon steps begun in the spring to justify the war in general and Rolling Thunder in particular. The State Department and national security advisers had taken the administration's case to campus teach-ins; friendly academics and journalists had been enlisted to write favorable articles; Hubert Humphrey and Averell Harriman had been sent to speak to university audiences as well as gatherings of business and labor leaders; national organizations had been lobbied to pass approving resolutions; a committee of prominent citizens had been set up to speak out in defense of the war in newspaper ads and letters to the editor; and a White House speechwriting team had begun "to provide the fodder for congressional support for Vietnam policy."[124]

To win the political war over Vietnam at home, Johnson took aim at three targets: the media, Congress, and the mass public. He saw the press as particularly troublesome. "We are getting only bad things from the press," he told a National Security Council meeting on August 5. A U.S. Information Agency officer replied that only "a minority of the correspondents cause trouble," and he thought this could be taken care of if editors were pressed to "present a balanced picture in their news reports."[125]

Johnson was not convinced. That night, CBS broadcast a report by Morley Safer with film of a U.S. Marine using a Zippo lighter to burn a thatched hut in the village of Cam Ne, while an old peasant woman pleaded for her home.

Safer's report, which emphasized Vietnamese casualties and said nothing about Marine losses, infuriated Johnson. He woke up CBS President Frank Stanton to complain that the network had "shat on the American flag." Johnson wanted to know why CBS would use a story by Safer, a Canadian with "a suspicious background." He also asked: "How could CBS employ a Communist like Safer, how could they be so unpatriotic as to put on enemy film like this?" CBS executives ordered their correspondent Murray Fromson back to Washington to explain the story to the White House. In a conversation with Bill Moyers, Fromson explained that Safer's nationality was irrelevant to a story that poignantly showed Vietnamese peasants fleeing huts burned by U.S. troops.

Moyers, whom Fromson describes as unconvinced by his explanation, devoted himself to repairing American prestige. "I have been working the past few days on steps we can take to improve coverage of the Vietnam war—steps in Saigon and Washington," he wrote Johnson. "We will never eliminate altogether the irresponsible and prejudiced coverage of men like Peter Arnett [a New Zealander] and Morris [sic] Safer, men who are not Americans and do not have the basic American interest at heart, but we will try to tighten things up." "Good!" Johnson scribbled on Moyers's note.[126]

In general, the media supported Johnson's decisions to fight. Like most Americans at this time, they believed the national interest required an independent South Vietnam. But this was not enough for Johnson. He wanted to control the flow and content of the news and bend the media to his designs. After all, the White House had done this during the 1964 campaign when the great majority of reporters, columnists, editors, publishers, and television networks had lent themselves to defeating Goldwater. Now, in a war against the Communists, Johnson found it hard to believe that the media would shift ground.

Johnson was mindful of the fact that an adversarial relationship was normal between Presidents and the press. As James Reston told Moyers, "the White House press corps has a built-in, philosophical suspicion of Presidents and Press Secretaries and will never come to trust them, . . . and . . . the best course for Presidents and Press Secretaries . . . is to give out all the spot news possible and worry as little as possible about the private prejudices and opinions of the journalists." Johnson's old friend Jim Rowe also counseled him not to be "too disturbed about the press. The country is behind you, your friends are behind you and the others don't count. (I hope you will keep repeating that last sentence to yourself regularly!)"[127]

Joseph Alsop considered Johnson's attempts "to be the source of all information in Washington" by closing off the middle level of government to the press to be "silly." Chief executives, Alsop said, "are generally pretty awful in their relations with the press. Johnson is much worse." Another White House reporter complained that "with Johnson, it's a one-man government."[128]

Johnson refused to be passive toward media criticism. He and his principal press aides believed that "poisonous and sour" reporting seriously undermined the war effort. Johnson suspected that "subversives" had "infiltrated the press corps." "The Viet Cong atrocities never get publicized," he complained. "Nothing is being written or published to make you hate the Viet Cong; all that is being written is to hate us."

The White House also saw attacks on the President's war policies as encouraging the Communists to think that America would not stay the course. It repeated Averell Harriman's story about the Viet Cong representative in Warsaw who "brandished copies of Walter

Lippmann's and other columnists' articles, saying that there was only confusion in America about the Viet Nam war, no widespread support, with the implication that shortly American opinion would force our troops to withdraw."[129]

The media's antagonism enraged Johnson. "We treat those [critical] columnists as whores," he told historian William E. Leuchtenburg. "Anytime an editor wants to screw 'em, they'll get down on the floor and do it for three dollars. That's the price of [naming to Leuchtenburg two of the best-known Washington correspondents]. We don't pay any attention to it."[130]

But, of course, he did, taking pains to assure as far as possible that news out of the White House was only what he wanted it to be. Managing the news by invoking national security, planting questions at press conferences, encouraging publishers to print prowar columns, and making life as difficult as possible for unfriendly reporters became standard operating procedures. Woe unto any administration official who provided the press with an unauthorized leak. To intimidate aides and reporters, Johnson directed White House switchboard operators to record all outside calls to staff members. Reporters beat the system by using fictitious names.[131]

Johnson also saw Congress as vital to any successful war effort. And not primarily because they controlled the purse strings. He knew that, once U.S. forces were deployed, Congress would feel compelled to provide the funding, which, in fact, it did. More important, the President understood that a congressional majority would consistently support the war but that some of it would be grudging or soft. And this worried him.

Richard Russell, for example, privately told a friend in August 1965, "I was opposed to our entering Asia to fight a land war . . . , but it is too late to debate this question now. We are in Viet Nam, our flag is there,—and, above all, American boys are under fire there, and I am supporting all of the President's efforts there to the hilt." Johnson understood that Russell's doubts would be an open secret in Congress and would indirectly encourage congressional opponents to speak their minds.[132]

Johnson accurately saw congressional opposition as a spur to press and public skepticism about the wisdom of fighting. Consequently, in September 1965, when Fulbright raised his voice against Johnson's actions in the Dominican Republic and Vietnam, it sent a chill through the White House. Though Fulbright wrote Johnson that he believed his dissenting view would help the administration and the country come to grips with foreign policy questions, Johnson saw it only as an impediment to a successful war effort.

Up to that point, Johnson had kept Fulbright informed about Vietnam, even arguing with him privately about the war. But Johnson now complained to an aide in February 1965 that Fulbright "is a cry baby—and I can't continue to kiss him every morning before breakfast." Once Fulbright went public with his criticism in September, Johnson "never after that had another private conversation with me," Fulbright said. When one of Fulbright's aides attended a White House function after the September speech and "sought to shake hands, Lyndon looked at me, right through me, and said: 'What are you doing here?' I was never invited back."[133]

If Johnson needed any other reason to shun Fulbright, he found it in a report the FBI passed along to him early in 1966 about Everett Dirksen, Fulbright, Wayne Morse, and Dominican Communists. Dirksen told DeLoach that Dominican land owners had tried to draw him into the role of political mediator between the country's warring factions, even offering him the services of "a very attractive young lady." On the advice of LBJ and Hoover, he had steered clear of entanglements with the Dominicans, but he asserted that the same was not true of Fulbright and Morse, whom he described as "deeply involved and very much obligated to Communist interests." He said that if the information given him by the FBI were furnished to the American public, it "could obviously ruin Senator Morse." Johnson may have been tempted to bring down two of his greatest tormentors in the Senate, but apparently his better angels, recognizing how unfounded these charges against Fulbright and Morse were, convinced him to keep Dirken's allegations quiet.[134]

Besides, Johnson believed that an intensive public relations campaign in the United States could help hold public support for the war without trying to ruin two prominent senators. In early August, the administration's principal public affairs officers began to discuss "the information problem," as they euphemistically referred to the difficulty of selling the country on the war. They asked themselves four questions: How could they get "the private sector" to release the kind of information that would serve the war effort? "How can we do a better job of creating an image of a President who has something besides Vietnam on his mind? How do we convey to the American people the concept of the twilight" or limited war in which there weren't the pitched battles of World War II and Korea that the country found more understandable? And, last, how could they "coordinate and manage more effectively our information effort?"

They found no easy answers. Despite setting up committees, holding regular meetings, relying on professional publicists, and devoting considerable resources to the campaign, they were confronted with what one of them called "a non-packageable commodity." A whirlwind of behind-the-scenes activity in support of the war—newspaper leaks, prowar publications, group endorsements, manufactured displays of patriotism, attacks on war critics—could not stem the tide of doubt and opposition to the conflict.

To the contrary, in November, Eric Goldman told the President that administration pressure was counterproductive. It was being labeled "liberal McCarthyism," which expressed the belief that "the Administration is not doing enough to check a tendency to associate criticism of the Vietnam policy with pro-Communism and an accompanying tendency to seek to cut down on the Constitutional rights of opponents of the Vietnam policy to express themselves.... This uneasiness is decreasing the vigor of the support for your Vietnam policy."[135]

Goldman's advice didn't sit well with Johnson, though there was much to indicate that the White House didn't need to worry so much about antiwar advocates. Polls, for example, were showing a consistent pattern of strong support for administration policies in Vietnam. In June, Lou Harris pointed to a 69 percent popularity rating for LBJ and a 65 percent approval mark on Vietnam as evidence that the President had "a clear mandate." In August, Harris reported "a notable rallying behind the President on Vietnam." He saw an "overwhelming mandate to send as many U.S. troops there as necessary to withstand the Viet Cong attacks during Monsoon season."

In mid-September, moreover, the *Washington Post* reported that Johnson had "more solid support for his policies in Viet-Nam than at any other time since the fighting began to escalate in February." Seventy-five percent wanted Johnson to hold the line or carry the war north, and only 25 percent, a drop of 11 percent from May, preferred negotiations.

In November, the Gallup poll reported that, "in sharp contrast to recent public demonstrations, survey evidence indicates that American public opinion is moving toward greater support of U.S. military action in Vietnam." Sixty-four percent, compared with 52 percent in May, believed the U.S. should have become involved in the war, and only 21 percent thought not. Harris's November survey continued to give Johnson a 66 percent approval rating. In December, Harris recorded a ten-to-one margin against withdrawal from Vietnam.[136]

Yet all this "scientific sampling" did not convince Johnson that the public was reliably behind the war. One NSC staff member had it right when he declared in December: "The polls give the President high marks on Vietnam—but I have a vague feeling that this support may be more superficial than it is deep and committed (many people probably do not even understand what it is that they are support-ing)."[137]

Like the NSC official, others in the administration, including Johnson, had a sense of unease about the national commitment to the fighting. The President and others around him couldn't put their finger on it, but they knew this wasn't like World War II, with a powerful and transparently immoral enemy opposed to fundamental American values. Nor was it the same as Korea, which had occurred at the height of the Cold War and seemed a more serious test of American resolve to meet the Communist challenge in Asia and around the globe. True, the rhetoric about preventing Communist expansion and assuring allies of America's commitment to their se-curity was much the same as in the early 1950s. But changes on the world scene—the Sino-Soviet split, the successful confrontation with Moscow over Cuba, the Test Ban Treaty, the balance of nuclear terror, which made a full-scale war so impermissible, and a war against a guerrilla army—made Americans less susceptible to appeals for sac-rifices in a conflict that just might not be as important to the national security as conventional wisdom said it was.

When dissenters raised questions about the wisdom of fighting Third World Communists who had no power to directly injure the United States, it registered on Americans in ways that made Johnson and his advisers uncomfortable. For they also sensed that Vietnam did not have the hold on the public imagination that would allow for a long war. Hence, the administration's impulse to press the case for Vietnam regardless of what the polls said.

In these circumstances, why didn't Johnson seek some alterna-tive other than escalation? Historian Ernest May and political scientist Richard Neustadt posed a similar question in a study of the decision twenty years later. "The more often we review the case," they con-cluded, "the harder we find it to outline what LBJ could have said in 1965 to explain to the American people why he was dropping JFK's South Vietnamese allies or, alternatively, why he was beginning all-out war against *Hanoi* because of what impended in *Saigon*." In trying "to outline the speech Johnson could have given over televi-sion," they gravitated "toward a conclusion that LBJ's one real alter-native was one scarcely hinted at even by Ball, namely, another dose of the 1963 medicine: engineering a change of regime in Saigon, but this time to bring in a clique that would call for neutralization and American withdrawal.... But when journalists picked up the scent, as they undoubtedly would, what then?"[138]

One can imagine another scenario. If Johnson had encouraged a wide-open debate in Congress and the press on what to do about

Vietnam, it would, judging from the polls, have also led to escalation. Perhaps some Great Society legislation would have been shelved as a consequence, but given liberal majorities in Congress it is hard fully to credit Johnson's fears.

What seems reasonably sure, however, is that an expanded war following a debate would have meant a stronger, more stable commitment to the fighting. This by no means guaranteed an enduring consensus in the face of stalemate, defeat, and substantial casualties, but it would have put Johnson in a much stronger political position. Complaints about his credibility, objections to "Lyndon Johnson's war," with all the political difficulties these attacks entailed, could have been avoided. More important, escalation of the fighting by national agreement rather than Johnson's unilateral decisions would have placed him in a position to escape the war if and when it turned sour. As matters stood at the end of 1965, Johnson had committed the prestige of the country and his administration to a conflict that great numbers of Americans now felt we could not afford to lose.

6

Retreat from the Great Society

BY the winter of 1965–66 Johnson had a government in place of his own making. A number of Kennedy's appointees still held high office, most notably, Rusk at State, McNamara at Defense, and Larry O'Brien as principal legislative liaison. But no one could doubt that the Kennedy officials had now become Johnson's men, officeholders who worked comfortably in behalf of the President's domestic and foreign policies.

Most of the aides Johnson had appointed in November 1963 were still at their posts two years later. But Jack Valenti and Bill Moyers had become firsts among equals. Valenti continued to be a man Friday. He kept the President's calendar, coordinated work on presidential statements, prepared LBJ's correspondence, and oversaw "special presidential projects," which meant everything from liaison with Senators Dirksen and Mansfield to day-to-day dealings with the State Department. Valenti was as loyal to Johnson as anyone in the administration: "I sleep better at night knowing Lyndon Johnson is President," he told the press. But two and a half years with LBJ had exhausted him, and in April 1966 he decided to accept appointment as president of the American Motion Picture Association of America.[1]

Bill Moyers would also leave at the end of 1966, complaining later that "after you've worked with LBJ, you can work with the Devil." The strains of serving Johnson and a chance to return to journalism decided him to become the publisher of the Long Island newspaper *Newsday*. But for three years he had been one of Johnson's most devoted special assistants. And Johnson had rewarded him: In October 1964 he had become Chief of Staff with responsibility for task forces that had shaped so many of the landmark reforms during 1965. In July 1965, Johnson had made him George Reedy's successor as press secretary. Though Moyers's principal activity was the care and feeding of the press, Johnson had announced that he would also "be working on anything I want him to from time to time."[2]

As press secretary, Moyers struggled with a number of problems. Johnson was never happy with his media coverage, and Moyers became the object of LBJ's hostility for not getting the press more fully behind the administration on Vietnam. Johnson and other aides saw the credibility gap as the consequence of Moyers's deviousness rather than the President's. "Bill was never overly scrupulous about the truth," George Reedy said later. "It was no accident that the President's popularity started to fall very abruptly as soon as Bill took over." Jake Jacobson, another White House aide, shared Reedy's judgment: Moyers answered too many questions, Jacobson believed, and never replied, "I don't know. . . . Whether it was the President's answer or him, you never did know that." However much Moyers may have contributed to the credibility gap, it was the President's own deceitfulness that stood at the center of the distrust that congressmen and senators, journalists, and ultimately people all over the country felt toward him.

Moyers's difficulties with Johnson also stemmed from what the President saw as the excessive press attention given to a member of his staff. Other aides complained that Moyers was ready to step over them and the President in the service of his own ambitions. If all these in-house problems were not enough to drive Moyers to retire, he also had to cope with journalists who saw him as the President's defender and an obstacle to information he denied them. When he took the press secretary's job, Moyers remembers telling his wife, "This is the beginning of the end, because no man can serve two masters," meaning Johnson and the press. By the summer of 1966, all these burdens put Moyers in the hospital with a case of bleeding ulcers.[3]

During 1966, as Valenti and Moyers made their exits, other aides filled the vacuum. Domestic affairs became the principal responsibility of Joseph Califano. When Moyers began his press duties, he recommended that Johnson shift Califano to the White House from Defense, where he was serving as McNamara's special assistant. A graduate of the Harvard Law School and a brilliant systems analyst, the thirty-four-year-old Califano was asked to take on Moyers's job of preparing and coordinating domestic legislation.[4]

On the first day in his new position, Califano learned what working for LBJ would mean. Getting up at 3 a.m. to fly to the President's ranch, he joined the President at his pool for a swim. "Are you ready to come help your President?" Johnson shouted at him from one end of the pool. Saying it would be an "honor and a privilege," Califano plunged into a three-and-a-half-year whirl-wind of activity. Day and night, Califano ate more meals with Johnson than his own family, frequently seeing him "early in the morning in his bedroom and late at night as he fell asleep. He barked orders at me over the phone at dawn and after midnight, in the formal setting of the Oval Office and as he stood stark naked brushing his teeth in his bathroom."[5]

Califano was such a quick study and so devoted to the Great Society programs that, within six months of coming to the White House, he sometimes became a surrogate President. Early in 1966, as Johnson was about to go abroad, he called Califano to his bedroom, where he said: " 'You're going to be the President. . . . We have to get all this legislation passed. We have to do this, we have to do that.' And then he . . . gave me cufflinks. He gave me an electric toothbrush with the Presidential seal on it. He gave me a tie clasp, he gave me cigarette lighters and I ended up walking with my arms full of all these presents, to say goodbye to him. . . . I don't think I slept . . . for all the time he was away. I worked so hard because all these bills were on the Hill," and Johnson called him every night at three in the morning.[6]

The other principal figure to join Johnson's domestic staff was Marvin Watson. A Texas businessman and wheelhorse in the state Democratic party, Watson was a Johnson loyalist who in 1960 had established one of the first Johnson-for-President clubs. In 1964, he had served as LBJ's coordinator at the Democratic Convention. The following January, Johnson made him a special assistant in charge of appointments, management of the White House office, and liaison with Democratic governors, the Democratic National Committee, and various state and local political groups. One journalist described him as the "White House's No. 1 Hatchet Man." Responding to Johnson's insistence on a leak-proof administration, he required that White House operators record all incoming and outgoing calls, including the names of the parties speaking to each other. He insisted that White House chauffeurs report on the destination of any staff member using official transportation.[7]

Watson also served as Johnson's liaison to the FBI, which led some reporters to call him a "mystery man" or "gum shoe" opera-tor. Watson denied that he was any sort of mystery man, just a faithful presidential servant. One White House coworker described him as a stickler for details, "the greatest nit-picker around," "the master of the paper clip." Judging from the FBI record of a meet-ing on White House physical security, Watson deserved his repu-tation. He provided Deke DeLoach with the precise number of

White House guests during 1965 and the fact that 65,873 trades-
men or workmen also came to the mansion during that time. He
passed along detailed information on how many White House, Executive Office, and press passes had been issued and the number of
times the building had been picketed last year. Watson was Johnson's bureaucrat par excellence.[8]

The greatest change in Johnson's foreign policy staff was the
replacement of Mac Bundy by Walt W. Rostow as National Security Adviser. In the spring of 1965, as Johnson expanded American
commitments in Vietnam, Bundy urged a public debate to convince
the country that the administration was following the right course.
In April, Bundy agreed to debate Hans Morgenthau, a prominent
international relations expert from the University of Chicago.
When Johnson learned this, he sent Bundy to the Dominican Republic to report on the crisis. Later that year, when Bundy resched-
uled the event, the President sent word through Moyers that he
didn't want Bundy to debate. Believing that he had lost the President's confidence and doubting the wisdom of escalation based
largely on the Gulf of Tonkin Resolution and questionable public
opinion polls, Bundy decided to resign. He asked Harvard President
Nathan Pusey about a professorial appointment, but, before Pusey
could reply, Bundy agreed to become president of the Ford Foundation beginning in April 1966.[9]

The forty-nine-year-old Rostow was seen as a strong choice for
Bundy's post. Rostow had been a Rhodes Scholar at Oxford; held a
Ph.D. in economics from Yale; had taught at MIT's Center for International Studies for ten years; published a famous book, *The Stages
of Economic Growth: A Non-Communist Manifesto*; and served since
1961 as the head of the State Department's Policy Planning Council.
In 1964–65 he had helped persuade the President that only a strong
public stance, including direct military pressure, against North Vietnam could stop the insurgency in the South.[10]

Johnson saw Rostow as the right man for the job in all respects
but one. He was too prolix, too verbose. Johnson instructed Valenti
to talk to Rostow about how he liked to work with an adviser. Valenti
sat down with him before LBJ announced the appointment and told
him how to write a memo and how to conduct himself in a meeting
with the President. Valenti explained that Johnson liked the crispness
with which Bundy or MacNamara presented a case. "I told him that
... if he were opening a meeting to state the issue and briefly, very
briefly, maybe state the pros and cons and then shut up." Memos
"ought to be very spare, very lucid." Rostow took Valenti's instruction

"with amazing good grace and great humility," and largely gave Johnson what he wanted.[11]

As with all his aides, Johnson began their new relationship with some abuse, which was calculated to intimidate and subordinate someone whose natural talents might make him too independent. The President never wanted toadies working for him but he wanted people who were entirely responsive to presidential commands. A press leak about Rostow's appointment threw Johnson into a rage, or at least Johnson acted as if it did. He called Rostow late at night to chide him for abusing the President's confidence. Rostow, who had done no such thing, emphatically denied the charge. Johnson slammed the phone down with no indication of whether this meant he had changed his mind about appointing him. Without further discussion or notice to Rostow of his intentions, he announced the appointment the next day to the press.[12]

It is more than likely that Johnson himself was the source of the leak on Rostow's selection. Califano recalls more than one instance in which Johnson orchestrated a situation that subjected an aide to a presidential tirade. "With the guy that was something before he came to him," Califano says, "he [LBJ] always seemed to have to break him in some way or get him to agree to do something, or even in the worse sense he'd humiliate him in some way to make him totally his man, ... to make sure he was totally loyal."[13]

The cast of characters close to Johnson at the White House included three other highly talented men who worked tirelessly to make the Great Society a reality. Douglass Cater, a forty-one-year-old Alabaman with two degrees from Harvard, joined LBJ's administration in 1964 after serving for fourteen years as the Washington and national affairs editor of the *Reporter* magazine. Initially hired as a speech writer and "idea" man whom the President instructed to "think ahead," Cater focused his attention on health and education issues. By the beginning of 1965 he had become Johnson's "expert" on these matters and played a central role in shaping and passing some forty health and education bills in the next two years.[14]

Harry McPherson, a thirty-six-year-old native Texan and University of Texas law graduate, joined Johnson's staff in August of 1965. His acquaintance with the President dated from 1956 when he had worked as assistant counsel to the Senate Democratic Policy Committee. A thoughtful and well read man, McPherson served as assistant secretary of state for educational and cultural affairs from July 1964 to August 1965. With Bill Moyers's support he became counsel to the President for six months, succeeding to the post of special counsel in the following February. Though he worked as the President's personal lawyer for the next two years, he principally served as Johnson's top speech writer. An evocative writer with a keen feel for Johnson's style of speaking and desire for terse, spare prose that included "a little poetry" and some alliteration, McPherson crafted all the President's major addresses beginning in the summer of 1966.[15]

The oldest and most famous of Johnson's special assistants was Robert Kintner. Born in 1909, by the time Kintner had come to the White House he had established himself as a prominent journalist and network television executive. In the 1930s he had been a reporter for the *New York Herald Tribune* and had coauthored the widely read column "Capitol Parade" with Joe Alsop. After service in World War II, he had become a vice president at the American Broadcasting Company, succeeding to the presidency in 1950. In 1956, he had left ABC for NBC, where he was president from 1958–65, and chairman of the board in 1966.[16]

Kintner and Johnson had a friendship dating back to the late thirties. As someone who had "no political ambition, no need for money and no desire for publicity," the fifty-six-year-old Kintner was, according to one journalist, "better geared psychologically to serve the President than any member of the inner circle." Kintner's assignment was to advise on top-level appointments, help Democratic candidates in 1966, and improve the President's public image.

John Roche, a political scientist who succeeded Eric Goldman as White House intellectual, didn't think well of Kintner or what he did. "When I arrived at the White House there was a guy sitting in the basement in the corner room whom I took to be the White House bookmaker. His name was Kintner, and he sort of sat in there. I figured he was taking bets. I didn't know what else he did. He looked like a bookie. He was in my judgment a thoroughly unpleasant man," who used to write memos in the third person."[17]

But Kintner played a much more valuable role than Roche allowed. He was one of the few independent voices on Johnson's staff who freely criticized "the President's liabilities, including his sensitivity to what was printed about him, the shutting out of individuals who didn't agree with him, the lack of pre-planned press conferences, and a poorly organized White House staff." Kintner decried Johnson's overexposure in the media, counseled against televised meetings with reporters, and urged a regular schedule of better managed press conferences every ten days. Kintner tried to soften his advice by telling Johnson: "At least you are getting honest opinions from one in support and no axe to grind."[18]

The State of the Union

In the winter of 1965–66, Johnson struggled to define what the coming political year would bring. He had no doubt that Vietnam would dominate his conduct of office, but he had no intention of saying so publicly or of acknowledging that the surge of domestic reform would now have to take a back seat to the war. Though he understood the impossibility of maintaining the momentum of domestic change while fighting so large a war in Vietnam, he refused to acknowledge this publicly.

His eagerness to do right by the nation and political calculation convinced him to promote the fiction that the country was rich enough and committed enough to have guns and butter. We knew, Califano says, that "we had to pay incredible attention to the economy both to figure out what was ... right ... but also [to] do it in a way that did not jeopardize the continuation of the Great Society programs."

At the end of the 1965 congressional session Johnson had written Mike Mansfield to praise him and Congress for their great accomplishments, but he also pointed to "23 major items of legislation" that were still to be enacted. Mansfield responded by recommending a slow down in 1966 and an emphasis on implementing the many major bills just passed. Harry McPherson urged much the same, proposing the creation of a commission to assure the proper administration of the new laws.

Johnson was of two minds about how to proceed. He knew Mansfield and McPherson were giving him sound advice, but he couldn't let go of a determination to make the second session of the 89th Congress another watershed moment in the country's history. Nor did he believe it made good political sense for him to shift his emphasis from enacting laws to administering existing ones.[19]

His State of the Union speech on January 12, 1966, reflected the dual commitments he urged the nation and Congress to reach for in the coming year. He acknowledged at the start of his address that Vietnam "must be the center of our concerns." But he refused to accept that the Communists in Vietnam could "win a victory over the desires and the intentions of all the American people. This Nation is mighty enough, its society is healthy enough, its people are strong enough, to pursue our goals in the rest of the world while still building a Great Society here at home."[20]

Johnson challenged the country and Congress "to carry forward, with full vigor, the great health and education programs that you enacted into law last year." He urged Americans to "prosecute with vigor and determination our war on poverty" and to "rebuild completely, on a scale never before attempted, entire central and slum areas of several of our cities." He asked a commitment to attack the poisons in our rivers, with an eye to "clean completely entire large river basins." He called for an expansion of federal efforts against crime in the streets; he decried the continuing abuses of civil rights, asking for additional legislation to ensure nondiscrimination in federal and state jury selection and in the sale and rental of housing; he recommended modernizing and streamlining "the federal government by creating a new Cabinet-level Department of Transportation and reorganizing several existing agencies," including reforms in the civil service to make it more efficient and productive; he recommended consumer protection bills requiring truth in selling and truth in lending; and he suggested a constitutional amendment extending the terms of congressmen to four years, concurrent with the President's.[21]

"Because of Vietnam," which took up half of his speech, Johnson said that "we cannot do all that we should, or all that we would like to do." But he outlined how much could be accomplished nevertheless. By attacking government waste and inefficiency, preventing labor strikes, holding down inflation, and maintaining the economic growth of the last five years, which had raised after-tax wages by 33 percent, corporate earnings by over 65 percent, and farm income by nearly 40 percent, the administration could find the means to continue building the Great Society.

In an emotional appeal that brought the largely liberal congressmen and senators to their feet, Johnson asked "the representatives of the richest Nation on earth, you, the elected servants of a people who live in abundance unmatched on this globe, . . . [to] bring the most urgent decencies of life to all of your fellow Americans." He urged Congress not "to sacrifice the children who seek the learning, or the sick who need medical care, or the families who dwell in squalor" to false economies not required by the war. The *Washington Post* described the President's message as, "U.S. Can Continue the 'Great Society' and Fight in Vietnam . . . —LBJ Hands Congress Massive Work Load."[22]

Despite his rhetoric, Johnson was too much of a political realist to think that he could achieve all this. But he saw three reasons to try or at least give the appearance of trying. First, he genuinely wanted to ease suffering among the poor and enrich the lives of the middle class. And even if he couldn't do as much as he liked in 1966, bold pronouncements about marching toward Eden would increase the likelihood that he could get part of what he put on the agenda. Second, he believed it politically essential to declare his determination to reach the promised land. He saw any indication of a slowdown in reform efforts as an invitation to conservatives to attack the whole enterprise as unaffordable and unreachable. Third, it was remotely possible that a series of administration actions affecting the economy might provide enough money to combat the Communists in Vietnam and public problems in the United States.

Nevertheless, Johnson knew his public appeal for fresh crusades was most likely to be more rhetoric than reality. Consequently, he had been unclear on how to pitch his State of the Union message. Should he simply declare his intention to fight on two fronts—against poverty at home and Communism abroad? Or should he give more emphasis to Vietnam and press the case for some domestic programs over others? His discussions with aides about the speech had revealed his inner tensions.

Califano remembers that Johnson "turned preparation of the State of the Union message into a wild melee of conflicts over ideas and even writing styles." In mid-November, Johnson had asked government departments to send Califano suggestions about domestic proposals to be included in the speech. Simultaneously, Valenti had worked on the foreign policy part of the address.

At the end of November, Valenti had sought LBJ's permission to ask Richard Goodwin, who had resigned a few months before, to help draft the speech. Johnson had "flatly refused." He was angry at Goodwin for resigning. Anyone who left LBJ's orbit without permission made Johnson feel betrayed; he took it as an affront, an implicit statement that Lyndon Johnson wasn't worth working for. It was as if Goodwin's resignation had diminished him, and Johnson could neither forget nor forgive.

But the resistance to relying on Goodwin ran deeper than Johnson's personal pique. Goodwin had written three of the President's most successful speeches: the Great Society, Voting Rights, and Howard University talks. If the President had wanted another landmark address, he surely would have brought Goodwin into the picture at once. But he had waited a month while Califano and Valenti put a series of unsatisfactory drafts before him. Only then did Johnson agree to Goodwin's participation, though he refused to meet with him and proposed to edit closely everything he produced.

Johnson was torn about what to say. On one hand, he badly wanted to propose another massive set of Great Society measures that would even go beyond the achievements of the previous year.

At a meeting with Califano on December 29, for example, he approved "a massive second-year program that would astound the Congress and the country when he unveiled it" on January 12. But Johnson was uncomfortable about letting matters rest there. Between January 5 and 11 he drove his aides to distraction over the speech, rejecting numerous drafts as not expressing what he wanted to say.

At 4 a.m. on January 12, Goodwin, Califano, and Valenti sent what they hoped would be the final draft to Johnson's bedroom. At 7:15 a.m. Johnson summoned five aides, but not Goodwin, to discuss the draft in his bedroom. He remained unhappy with the size and substance of the speech. He ordered a complete reorganization of the draft and a reduction by a third. The work went on until almost the last minute, with the President calling for final changes an hour and a half before delivering the address.

And even with all this effort, it was one of Johnson's less impressive speeches. Califano later described it as "a short, dull message, primarily concerned with foreign policy." Historian Irving Bernstein said it was "a very bad speech. It reads as though it had been composed by a harried committee, which, of course, was the fact. It was too long, repetitious, disorganized, and impossible to believe." Indeed, as Califano remembered, after the address, several congressmen asked him: " 'Is he really serious? Are we really going to do this?' " Bill Barrett from Pennsylvania, a key House figure on urban affairs, said, " 'Joe, you can't be serious. How can you push this program? Where are we going to get the money?' "

That was exactly the point. No one, including Johnson, knew where they were likely to find the money to fund the expanding costs of the war and a massive second-year set of Great Society reforms. Since a substantial tax increase was out of the question, Johnson tied the program to the unlikely assumption that a growing economy, largely free of strikes and inflation, combined with a streamlined government eliminating all waste, would generate enough money to fight the war and sustain the Great Society. He predicted that in spite of an increase of $5.8 billion in Vietnam spending, federal outlays would grow only by $600 million, with a budget deficit of just $1.8 billion, "one of the lowest in many years." This was "because of the stringent cost-conscious economy program inaugurated in the Defense Department, and followed by the other departments of Government." The numbers Johnson cited, as with his whole economic plan for fighting the war and advancing the Great Society, were illusions that the realities of 1966 would largely dispell.[23]

Saving the Great Society: Wages and Prices

In the second half of 1964, after the tax cut had passed, Johnson's economic advisers had been full of optimism about the economy. Walter Heller, head of the Council of Economic Advisers, had told the President in June that the economy was "showing new vitality and promise," with "no inflation in sight." A year later, however, some experts began to see disquieting signs of overheating that could end in an economic collapse like that of the thirties. Federal Reserve Board Chairman William McChesney Martin, for example, began signaling the need for interest rate hikes that would cool a booming economy. The CEA staff disagreed, expressing concerns about slower economic growth that might compel an additional tax cut.

The expansion of the war in July 1965 did not alter thinking at the CEA. To the contrary, Gardner Ackley, Heller's replacement, saw the increased defense spending as a stimulus to the economy, which would reduce the need for another tax reduction. By November, however, the CEA had begun to have second thoughts, expressing the belief that the war might create "a significant and undesirable acceleration in the pace of overall economic activity." Martin had no doubts about where the economy was heading. On December 6, the Federal Reserve announced an increase in the discount rate banks paid on loans from 4 to 4.5 percent.[24]

Though Johnson publicly objected to the rate hike, saying it would have been better if the Fed had waited until the administration budget estimates had been announced in January, he was already deeply concerned about the dangers the expanding war posed to the economy. Indeed, as early as the previous August, after deciding substantially to expand U.S. ground forces in Vietnam, Johnson had begun working to compel labor and industry to adhere to wage and price guidelines that would head off inflation.

This was no small matter to LBJ. There was a quality of hyperbole to everything he did. And when he turned his attention to a problem, it became the center of his universe: The difficulty had to be mastered or his world would collapse. Controlling inflation took on that dimension. He had to hold down prices or they would become an avalanche burying his administration.

The first great challenge to wage and price settlements of 3.2 percent, the estimated annual growth rate in productivity, came from the steel industry and the United Steel Workers of America. Contract negotiations in the summer of 1965 left the two sides far apart. I. W. Abel, the newly elected president of the union, demanded wage increases of about 5 percent, with industry offering half that amount.

Giving in to the union, steel executives predicted, would force a jump in steel prices well above the 3.2 percent guidelines. Abel, who had won his union presidency promising wage increases comparable to those given by the can and aluminum industries, refused to compromise. The steel companies, mindful of Johnson's determination to prevent a strike and the pressure he would put on labor for a settlement, also dug in their heels.[25]

Johnson, who saw a steel settlement as crucial to wage agreements in other industries, pressed both sides to give ground. On August 17, he worked on Abel at the White House. "I made commitments to the members who elected me," Abel declared. "You're starting to sound just like Dick Russell," Johnson replied, knowing that the comparison to the segregationist Georgia Senator would bother Abel. "He sat on that very couch talking to me about my civil rights bill in 1964. I asked him not to filibuster. 'We've got to make a stand somewhere,' he said. He sounded just like you."

Johnson, ever the great persuader, softened his criticism of Abel with an anecdote meant to amuse and instruct him. "I told Dick Russell the story about the Negro boy in bed with the white gal" whose husband unexpectedly arrives home. " 'Hide. Hide,' " she whispered. " 'He'll kill you and then he'll kill me.' " Johnson described how the Negro boy hid in the closet. "At this point," Califano recalls, "Johnson bolted from his rocker, stood upright, arms stiff at his side, legs straight, tight together, back and shoulders ramrod straight." Johnson, with appropriate gestures, described the husband shouting that someone was in the bedroom and "furiously opening doors" until he found the young man. " 'What the hell are you doin' here?' this little white gal's husband shouts, fire in his eyes. 'Everybody's gotta stand somewhere, boss,' this Negro boy answers."

Califano remembers the burst of laughter and Johnson looking into Abel's eyes. " 'Everybody's gotta stand somewhere,' he repeated slowly and softly, leaning into the labor leader and reminding him that 'like that Negro boy he wanted to keep down,' Russell stuck himself in a closet with nowhere to go on civil rights. 'Mr. Abel, I know you gotta stand somewhere. But you gotta stand where you can move around a little. Not just pinned in the linen closet.' "[26]

Johnson instructed his Secretaries of Labor and Commerce, William Wirtz and John Connor, to negotiate a settlement. But believing that Wirtz was too sympathetic to labor and Connor too ready to allow steel price increases above the guideposts, Johnson decided to mediate the negotiations himself or at least through former Florida Governor Leroy Collins, a successful conciliator of civil rights disputes, and Wayne Morse, a sensible leader in the Senate on labor issues. Despite Morse's outspoken opposition to the Vietnam fighting, Johnson knew he could rely on him to serve the national well-being in the steel negotiations.[27]

On August 30, after Collins and Morse found themselves unable to win an agreement, Johnson directly entered the talks. During breakfast at the White House, Wirtz, Connor, Collins, and Morse were pessimistic about reaching a settlement within the 3.2 percent guidelines. "We'll never settle the steel case on that basis," Morse said. The four were divided on whether Johnson should exert direct pressure on the parties.[28]

Johnson relished the opportunity to join the discussions. He called both sides to the White House, where in front of reporters and cameramen, he demanded "a non-inflationary settlement." Convincing labor to postpone a strike for eight days, he bought time to mount additional pressure on the principals. He told Califano to contact U.N. Ambassador Arthur Goldberg, a former attorney for the steel unions, and Clark Clifford, the counsel to Republic Steel. Both men, without the knowledge of Wirtz or Connor, were asked to arrange a settlement. At the same time, Johnson urged Wirtz and Connor to believe that he was relying solely on them to achieve an agreement. He also told union and steel representatives "that everything depended on them—and them alone."

Over the next few days, as the negotiators struggled to find a compromise, they pressed Johnson to allow some selective price increases above the guidelines, which would then permit the companies to increase their wage offer to labor. But the President wouldn't bend. "No price increase. None. Zero," he told Califano, making a circle with his thumb and forefinger. Believing the key to the situation was through his Cabinet secretaries, who had largely become advocates for their respective sides, Johnson told Califano to compel Wirtz and Connor to reach an agreement within the guidelines, sign it, and present it to the opposing parties. Through nonstop negotiations over five days that exhausted Wirtz and Connor, Califano got what Johnson had asked. And as he had anticipated, the union and companies quickly followed the recommendations.[29]

On September 3, Johnson gleefully announced the settlement live on network television. His success confirmed White House convictions "that the President could get anyone to agree and that we could exert enormous influence over labor negotiations in the future," Califano said. Walter Heller wrote Johnson: " 'Masterful' is the word for the way you brought the steel crisis to a successful solution. You struck a key blow for continued cost-price stability and the country's economic health."[30]

Yet the President's success was short-lived. During the next year he repeatedly spoke out in behalf of the administration's guidelines. "No challenge cries out for greater cooperation than the need to preserve the stability of prices and costs," he declared in December 1965. In January, he underscored the point in his State of the Union message, a press conference the following day, and his economic message on January 27. Tying the guideposts to the conflict in Vietnam, he declared: "When 200,000 of our fellow citizens are risking their lives in the defense of freedom overseas, the Government's duty is to ask those who enjoy a comfortable prosperity at home to exercise responsibly their freedom to set prices and wages."[31]

Johnson was even more aggressive in private trying to hold the wage-price line. Hardly a day passed without a meeting, a call, or a discussion about business and labor restraint to avoid inflation. The White House generated constant pressure on labor leaders and individual companies to toe the line. Aluminum, copper, sulfur, steel, chemicals, airlines, automobiles, railroads, construction, lumber, industry by industry, heard from the White House about the need for consideration of the national interest in reaching for greater profits. Likewise, union officials, beginning with representatives of federal employees and running through the leadership of most of the major private labor groups, got the same message from either Johnson himself or high-ranking administration figures.

In May 1966, when the *New York Times* reported that the White House was changing its price policy, Califano instructed Moyers to tell reporters that the story was untrue.[32]

Administration appeals ultimately fell on deaf ears. In January 1966, John V. Lindsay, the newly elected liberal Republican Mayor of New York, agreed to give transit workers a 6.3 percent pay raise. Construction workers in the Northeast also began to win pay increases that breached the guidelines. The indifference to the administration's demands for wage and price restraints produced more presidential jawboning. "Irresponsible action," Johnson warned, "can only bring on an inflation that would damage all—labor, business, and the national interest." "These were grave challenges," he said.[33]

But the pressures to raise prices and increase wages above the 3.2 percent level became irresistible in the second half of 1966; economic realities eclipsed presidential demands. In the summer, steel ignored the President's wishes by breaching the guidelines. Despite a statement by Gardner Ackley that "the action of these companies can only be characterized as irresponsible" and a blow to "the public interest," they refused to roll back prices. Johnson put the best possible face on the outcome, but he had to admit that "we have not been effective" in urging them to reconsider their decision.[34]

A settlement between the International Machinists and Aerospace Workers (IMA) and the country's airlines largely made the guidelines irrelevant. When the union asked for a 5 percent increase and industry proposed 2.8 percent, Johnson urged a compromise agreement. But when neither side would budge, he delayed a strike in the spring by invoking a sixty-day cooling-off period under the Railway Labor Act. The efforts of a mediation board and a personal appeal from the President at the end of July could not prevent a strike or achieve a satisfactory settlement. A new agreement gave the union a 4.9 percent raise and, in the words of the IMA president, "destroy[ed] all existing wage and price guidelines now in existence."

At a Cabinet meeting Johnson bitterly remarked, "Secretary Wirtz and his group worked their hearts out with the airline machinists, whose whole purpose in life seemed to be to shatter the guideposts. . . . As we all know, we had no power to tell either party what they had to take. . . . This is a complicated and difficult problem." For Johnson, it was an uncharacteristic understatement.[35]

Saving the Great Society: The Limits of Fiscal Policy

In the winter of 1965–66 public attention had focused on the tension between financing the war in Vietnam and domestic reforms. In December, a reporter asked Joe Califano's view of "the stories that the Great Society is being drastically cut back to accommodate the war budget in Vietnam." In January, Richard Russell told the Georgia General Assembly that he was "one of those who has questioned whether this nation, for all its wealth and resources, can fight a war of the magnitude of Vietnam and carry on a broad range of domestic spending—without a tax increase or a dangerous deficit. The President apparently believes that we can. For the sake of the country and the soundness of the dollar, I hope and pray that he is right."[36]

Califano emphatically denied that Vietnam would change any of the administration's domestic plans. Even if nothing were being spent on Vietnam, Califano said, the Great Society programs would receive "very little more." There was no way they could accommodate more spending in their initial phase.[37]

Califano's explanation reflected LBJ's thinking. Johnson saw the war as a drain on Great Society resources. But he wouldn't acknowledge it. When he asserted that we could have guns and butter, it was not simply a case of deceiving the public or even himself. Rather, his optimism rested on some hope that modern tools for controlling the nation's economy would allow him largely to deliver on domestic promises despite the billions required to fight the war.[38]

Johnson had little expectation that a strong economy would mean much in the way of additional Great Society reforms. His goal was to maintain the economy at a level that would fund the war in Vietnam and domestic programs in place. If he could get any other major reforms passed, all the better. But this was a third priority. His public rhetoric gave no hint of this: Calls for additional reforms now muted the importance of the war, kept conservatives on the defensive, and established an agenda for the future.

Johnson hoped to sustain the Great Society through a balanced budget and low inflation. His budget message at the end of January proposed outlays of $112.8 billion, an increase of $6.4 billion over the previous year: $600 million more for the Great Society and $5.8 billion additional for Vietnam. Spending on the war, which the administration saw ending in June 1967, totaled $10.5 billion. A deficit of only $1.8 billion would mean little inflation. Johnson warned that none of this was in concrete: As a result of events in Southeast Asia, spending could be higher or lower than currently assumed.[39]

Johnson's caveats about more spending on Vietnam masked doubts about the budget that had begun to agitate him and economic advisers. In December 1965, Ackley had warned Johnson that a $115 billion budget would mean "an intolerable degree of inflationary pressure" and would require "a significant tax increase."[40]

By the end of December, Ackley and Budget Director Charles Schultze were urging a tax hike. When Wilbur Mills, chairman of the House Ways and Means Committee, indicated that he "had no appetite for a tax increase bill in 1966" and warned that any such proposal could lead to a budget fight, with negative consequences for Great Society programs, Johnson put the question aside. Instead, his budget message raised the possibility of more spending on Vietnam and asked for a $4.8 billion tax rise through accelerated collection of corporate and individual income taxes and a delay in scheduled reductions of telephone and excise taxes.[41]

During the first three months of 1966 the administration aggressively defended its budget against charges of being "misleading" or "gimmicked," despite evidence to the contrary.[42]

Indications that inflation was mounting and that tighter money and tax increases would be necessary made Johnson all the more eager to press for his fiscal policies. The CEA told him that "inflationary psychology and inflationary symptoms are taking root." He wanted no public discussion of the problem, for fear that it would do more to spur than inhibit it. Moreover, he saw no way to win a tax increase, which could hold down inflation.[43]

Johnson also thought it too soon to press for a tax rise. His experience taught him to be skeptical of economic experts. Put two economists in a room and you'll get three opinions, he would complain. He remembered Harry Truman's observation: "Just once in my life, I'd like to meet a one-armed economist." Johnson told Califano: "I've been in this town for 35 years, and I've seen every President put the brakes on too long or too soon. The result was recession. I am not going to make that mistake." Besides, he believed that only an economic crisis would persuade Congress to raise taxes. Without a crisis, conservatives would see more taxes as simply financing more social programs, while liberals would object to them as a means to finance the war.[44]

But war costs and the domestic economy began forcing Johnson's hand on taxes. In mid-March he arranged a $4.8 billion supplemental appropriation for Vietnam. Though he hoped this would finance the war for the rest of the year and limit the need for more government revenues and restraints on costs, he couldn't be sure.[45]

In a speech at the end of March, he spoke publicly and with considerable candor about uncertainties in deciding economic policy. He emphasized that the administration's actions had brought widespread prosperity with the lowest unemployment rate in twelve years and the highest after-tax corporate profits in the country's history. Yet he acknowledged that this could be too much of a good thing and that additional restraints might have to be applied.

For the moment, however, he saw higher interest rates and the speedup in tax collections doing the job. He thought the economy might be slowing. Yet at the same time, labor shortages were showing up in several industries, capital investment was over $2 billion higher than estimated in January, and consumer prices were increasing at a rate of more than 5 percent a year, the highest inflation in ten years.[46]

He hated the uncertainty. It left him feeling out of control, a prisoner of circumstances. But the economic news in April temporarily encouraged him. Interest rates on bonds dropped, suggesting slower economic growth, while larger tax collections promised a smaller federal deficit and less inflationary pressure. His economic advisers, however, quickly dampened his optimism by remaining divided over a tax increase.

Developments in May and June gave resonance to their uncertainty: At the same time inflation accelerated, economists predicted that the national business expansion was "ready to take a breather."[47]

By early September rising interest rates and doubts about the economy had driven down stock prices and created a sense of national crisis. After Senator George Smathers had spoken to leading economists and businessmen, he told Johnson that there was a "crisis in confidence" in the country. "The President of the United States . . . has suddenly begun to appear as though he has no program or suggestion to make, even in the face of what is obviously a worsening economic situation. . . . Any program which you announce is better than the present no-program and aimless drift." On September 2, in a rare show of unanimity, Johnson's principal advisers recommended a statement of intention to ask for tax increases, an immediate additional budget reduction of $1.5 billion, another $2 billion cut later, if necessary, and the suspension of a 7 percent tax credit to slow capital spending.[48]

Johnson responded on September 8 by announcing "additional steps we consider necessary to assure the continuing health and strength of the economy." He promised "to cut all federal expenditures to the fullest extent consistent with the well-being of our people." In particular, he proposed cuts in federal spending on structures and equipment, but promised not to "make the poor carry the burden of fighting inflation."

As for a surcharge on corporate and individual income taxes, he said nothing. Though it left open the possibility of a future request, he refused to force unpalatable action on the Congress in an election season. Moreover, he remained unconvinced that the duration and cost of the war would make this absolutely necessary. He saw his current actions as enough to meet present problems. The next three or four months would show him whether he needed to do more.[49]

But rather than clarifying matters, events in the last months of the year further complicated the issue. The economic numbers in late September indicated rapid growth with significant weak spots in housing and autos. Prices were also mixed: sharp declines in some industrial materials were offset by a spurt in farm and food prices. By the middle of October evidence of slower-paced growth convinced some economists that there should be no tax increase.[50]

The slowing had become more pronounced by the first week of November. Still, the CEA found it difficult "to get a precise reading on economic activity today. There are some weaker signs along with stronger ones." The conclusion: "Policy will have to be made carefully to avoid the dangers on both sides—a new inflationary surge or an excessive slowdown."[51]

Johnson's meetings with his economic advisers at this time were exercises in gloom. Piling uncertainties about Vietnam on top of a rudderless economy made Johnson irritable and difficult to deal with. He was relieved when the need to announce a budget in January 1967 forced him to decide the tax question. A prospective budget deficit of $10 to $11 billion, fueled by some $20 billion in spending on Vietnam, persuaded him to ask for a tax increase.

But exactly how much and when to implement it remained unanswered questions. Walter Heller told Johnson of his hope that "you will get Divine guidance on the question of a 1967 tax increase, since economic guidance gives you no very firm answer at the moment." Indeed, with the economy giving clear signs in December of "a loss of forward momentum," Johnson was reluctant to ask for a tax rise. To the contrary, the CEA saw a "need for new stimulus, both from fiscal and monetary policy, to minimize the risk of a dangerous stall." It advised "the maximum degree of flexibility to back away from a tax increase."[52]

Johnson's budget message to Congress on January 24, 1967, was an exercise in tightrope walking. He declared his intention to hold the annual deficit to $2.1 billion; to permit a higher deficit would risk choking off lower interest rates and renewing inflationary pressures. But a lower deficit would be "self-defeating under present economic conditions." He had rejected a large tax increase or "large slashes in military or civilian programs," he told the nation. Instead, he recommended a temporary 6 percent surcharge on corporate and individual income taxes, which would take effect on July 1, 1967, and remain in effect for two years.[53]

No one could be certain where the economy was heading at the start of 1967. Uncertainty about the duration of the war and the force levels required to win it made federal expenditures, deficits, and inflation estimates little more than guesswork. Only one thing seemed certain: For all Johnson's good intentions and rhetoric about helping the poor and funding and expanding the Great Society, commitments to new domestic programs all but disappeared, while support for existing ones slackened.

Advancing the Great Society: The Department of Transportation

Johnson loved the idea of being the most prolific reform leader in presidential history. Giving help to the poor, making life better for all Americans was a constant preoccupation. The second-year Great Society agenda he had unveiled in his State of the Union message consisted of 113 separate measures on everything from child, consumer, and environmental protections to urban renewal. It was a grand follow-up to the stunning achievements of the first session of the 89th Congress.

It also commanded his determination to get it passed. At the end of May, after most of the agenda had been introduced, the President called in the Cabinet Secretaries. The job now, Johnson told them, was to raise "legislative promises into full-grown realities.... If we approach it half-heartedly or over-confidently, we will fail.... I do not intend to fail. I do not intend to waste a single chance, or break the smallest promise." At the same time, he instructed all Cabinet officers to cut their "travel plans to the bone. This legislation will not be passed unless you are up on the Hill—working for it every day."

Yet for all Johnson's devotion to another round of reform legislation, his 1966 proposals were a pale imitation of those of 1965. To be sure, Congress would approve 97 of LBJ's 113 bills. But compared with the educational, health, and voting rights acts of 1965, the reforms of 1966, with two exceptions, were relatively limited. Child nutrition, truth in packaging, rent supplements, the teacher corps, clean rivers, child, mine, and tire safety, and the Freedom of Information Act did not have the impact that the earlier laws had on the country. This is not to say that they were inconsequential; each of them had a significant effect on various groups, but none of them had the reach and resonance of the earlier measures.[54]

Even before the 1966 legislative session began, Johnson signaled that his second-year program would not enjoy the same degree of personal involvement he had previously shown. After telling Califano in August 1965 to develop the second-year agenda with the help of "the finest minds in the country," he uncharacteristically "offered little guidance." Further, in December 1965, when the press reported Hubert Humphrey as saying LBJ was considering an urban rebuilding or demonstration cities program, Johnson upbraided Califano for letting Humphrey sit in on the urban affairs task force. He told Califano he didn't "need the Vice President to try to commit him to some crazy, Goddamned expensive idea that Congress would never approve anyway."[55]

During 1966 he was more focused on holding down spending on the 1965 reform programs than on passing new ones. "We're going to have to take our time on everything, except Vietnam," he told Califano in March. Califano said later: Johnson "launched major Great Society programs with minimal amounts.... Johnson's extravagant rhetoric announcing new programs belied the modest funds he requested to begin them."[56]

By early August some observers concluded that the administration was "suffering from a feeling in the nation that the domestic program had lost its momentum." To reinvigorate the Great Society, Doug Cater and Bill Moyers wanted Johnson to consider announcing a "Spirit of 1976" as "a basic theme for the fall's campaign."

Johnson ignored the suggestion. And the belief that the Great Society was stalled continued to grow. In September, a liberal congressman complained of the administration's failure to deliver on its promises. He inserted a newspaper column in the *Congressional Record* saying that "the Great Society had begun to ring hollow.... The most marked social change in America since war was declared on poverty has been the further enriching of the rich by higher interest rates and tax benefits.... The impression that the Great Society is drifting in a wrong direction is not just due to bad articulation. It is real." Though Johnson scribbled in the margin, "I can prove him wrong," his budget cuts and legislative record in 1966 did little to change this perception.[57]

Only two new programs in 1966 commanded Johnson's strong interest: the creation of a transportation department, with, among other things, a responsibility for highway safety, and the rebuilding of inner cities.

The role of the federal government in managing the country's transportation systems was a microcosm of Johnson's view of federal authority. Since the start of the Republic, the government had played a significant part in drawing the nation together through road, canal, railroad, and airport construction. By the 1960s more than thirty agencies, most of them under congressional control, regulated the nation's road, river, sea, and air transit. In a country as vast as the United States, with a mid-sixties population of nearly 190 million people, Johnson, ever the New Dealer faithful to the conviction that consolidation of control in the executive assured greater economy and efficiency, intended to create a Department of Transportation responsible for all phases of national mobility and safety.

Beginning in 1965, Johnson had made clear to his task force on transportation that he wanted a program that would improve conditions "radically, looking not only to next year, but to 1980, the year 2000 and beyond." Johnson saw a transportation department as not only a chance to "invigorate" and "modernize" the country's transit systems but also to do "major things" without costing much money. In December, he gave a reporter for *Forbes Magazine* the impression that he had "a greater grasp of the transportation situation than any one else in this country," and that he intended "to put the transportation house in order." Talking to this journalist was part of a concerted presidential effort to sell a department to government agencies responsible for transportation and safety programs and to representatives of the automobile, truckers, railroad, airline, and maritime industries.[58]

Aware that a transportation department might arouse strong opposition, Johnson had White House aides talk to as many interested parties as possible. When Califano reported that the head of the American Trucking Association was an enthusiastic supporter, the President brightened and said: " 'Joe, we're going to get our Department of Transportation! You know why?' I had no idea. He gave me a patronizing look, and almost whispered, 'Because of the truckers. When the truckers deal on the Hill, they deal one on one'—Johnson paused for effect and leaned toward me—'and only in cash.' He slapped his leg approvingly."[59]

On March 2, Johnson sent a bold transportation message to Congress outlining what he saw as the problems and solutions. The country's expenditures on transportation accounted for one-sixth of the American economy—$120 billion. But there was terrible waste caused by time-consuming road, airport, and harbor congestion, highway accidents costing 50,000 lives a year; a reliance on "aging and often obsolete plant and equipment, networks chiefly designed to serve a rural society"; and "the failure to take full advantage of new technologies." The country needed an enlightened government agency that would serve "as a full partner with private enterprise in meeting America's urgent need for mobility."

The new department was to be a catch-all agency. It was to include the Commerce Department's office of transportation, the Bureau of Public Roads, the Federal Aviation Agency (FAA), the Coast Guard, the Maritime Administration, the safety functions of the Civil Aeronautics Board (CAB) and the Interstate Commerce Commission consolidated under a new National Transportation Safety Board, and the agencies responsible for the Great Lakes, the St. Lawrence Seaway, and the Alaska Railroad. In addition, the new department was to assume shared responsibility with the CAB for subsidies to local airlines, with the Army Corps of Engineers for river and harbor construction projects, with the State Department and the CAB for international aviation routes and fares, and with Housing and Urban Development for urban transportation.

Johnson also asked Congress to pass a Traffic Safety Act to reduce the carnage on America's highways. Since the introduction of the automobile, 1.5 million Americans had died in car crashes—"more than all the combat deaths suffered in all our wars." Under the act, the President proposed to increase federal grants to the states for highway safety, compel improved auto safety performance, and create a national highway safety research and test center.[60]

Despite considerable enthusiasm in most quarters for a department performing the functions Johnson described, the legislation ran into objections threatening its passage. In the Senate, where John McClellan of Arkansas chaired hearings on the bill, questions were raised about shifting the Coast Guard and the FAA into the new department and the criteria that would be required for approval of new Corps of Engineer navigation projects. Under a new rule, some $3 to $4 billion in projects might be sidetracked.[61]

McClellan, who saw the new standards blocking projects he favored, resisted the change. The President was willing to accept his demand for the old standard on advancing river construction, but he didn't want to write it into the bill.

To force McClellan's hand, Johnson told Califano to leak a rumor to the press that McClellan was holding up the transportation act " 'because he wants the Corps of Engineers to build a dam on land he owns so he'll get a lot of money when the government buys the property.' 'Is that true?' " Califano asked. Johnson leaned back in his chair and described how his former boss Congressman Dick Kleberg publicly accused a competitor for his House seat of taking " 'female sheep up into the hills alone at night. Well,' the President said, 'I jumped up and shouted, Mr. Kleberg, Mr. Kleberg, that's not true. And you know what Mr. Kleberg did?' Johnson asked . . . 'He just looked down at me and said, "Then let the son of a bitch deny it." ' Johnson and I both laughed, then he paused and said quietly, 'You just let John McClellan deny it.' "[62]

Though no such pyrotechnics were necessary to bring McClellan into discussions of passing the bill, some tough negotiations followed on the language that went into the act on navigation projects. After Califano thought he had reached an agreement with the senator, he brought it to Johnson, who dismissed it as no bargain at all. Johnson told Califano to check under his fly, " 'because there's nothing there. John McClellan just cut it off with a razor so sharp you didn't even notice it.' "[63]

Though McClellan and the White House reached a compromise that assured Senate passage of the bill, the House leadership frustrated Johnson by excluding the Maritime Administration from the new department. Shipowners and maritime labor unions supported by a bipartisan majority in the House wanted to create an independent Maritime Administration that would give special attention to the problems of an ailing industry.[64]

Johnson tried to prevent a development that he thought would seriously undermine the proposed Cabinet office. If maritime interests could preserve their autonomy, it would boost the case for an independent FAA. "Altogether," Budget Director Charlie Schultze told him, this could "begin a wholesale gutting of the Department bill." To counter such a result, the President promised to give a maritime administrator in a transportation department authority to build "a modern, efficient merchant marine fleet." If the maritime industry went its separate way, it "would be the only major transportation mode not represented in the new Department" and would "not have a voice at the Cabinet table or as a powerful voice in the policymaking councils of Government."[65]

Johnson instructed Califano to work out a settlement with the shipping interests urging maritime autonomy. Promises were made to include a maritime subsidy board and give "a special statutory delegation of authority" to a Maritime Administration in the department. But this still failed to meet labor and industry objections, and AFL-CIO President George Meany effectively pressured House members into excluding merchant shipping from department control. Senator Henry Jackson told the White House that if the maritime provisions had remained in the bill, "the House would have rejected the conference report and 'there would be no Department of Transportation during this Congress.' "[66]

In a signing ceremony at the White House on October 15, Johnson celebrated the birth of a department that would untangle America's lifeline. "Today we are confronted by traffic jams. Today we are confronted by commuter crises, by crowded airports, by crowded airlanes, by screeching airplanes, by archaic equipment, by safety abuses, and roads that scar our nation's beauty." The department "we are establishing will have a mammoth task—to untangle, to coordinate, and to build the national transportation system for America that America is deserving of."

Johnson was incensed at the exclusion of the Maritime Administration and refused to invite representatives of the shipping industry and unions to the bill signing. He also urged Congress to "reexamine its decision to leave this key transportation activity alone, outside" the jurisdiction of the Department. Fifteen years later, in 1981, the Congress saw the wisdom of Johnson's advice and moved the Maritime Administration into the department.[67]

The month before the transportation bill became law, Johnson had signed the National Traffic and Motor Vehicle Safety Act and the Highway Safety Act. Together with the new Transportation Department, the clean air and water acts of 1965, the 1966 clean rivers law, the Fair Packaging and Labeling Act, and the other safety laws for children, mines, and tires, Johnson began a process of regulation that improved the environment and reduced the hazards that had injured and killed millions of Americans. At the same time, it touched off an ongoing debate about the value of government intrusion into people's daily lives and demands for greater freedom from government controls. Did the gains in safety and product quality outpace the costs and problems generated by regulation? There are no simple answers to these questions. Johnson himself, when signing the transportation bill, felt compelled to declare: "Our transportatation system was built by the genius of free enterprise. And as long as I am President, it will be sustained by free enterprise."[68]

Yet one thing seems clear: The failures of a free enterprise system provoked an outcry for tough regulations, which, according to safety experts, have played a crucial role in reducing highway deaths and injuries. Since the safety and regulatory measures Johnson put in place more than thirty years ago have largely remained and been expanded, despite creating some limits on economic growth, it seems reasonable to conclude that the reforms of 1965–66 did significantly more good than harm.[69]

Advancing the Great Society: Model Cities

There are many who would not say the same for model cities. The program originated in the belief that the Watts riots in August 1965 demonstrated the crisis in America's inner cities and the fact that existing solutions—urban renewal, public housing, the war on poverty, and federal urban aid or categorical grants—could not solve the problems of crime, poverty, failed schools, slum housing, pollution, and congestion. Model cities also originated in the view that the success of the new Department of Housing and Urban Development depended on finding a fresh way to overcome urban difficulties.[70]

A model cities bill took shape from a recommendation by United Auto Workers President Walter Reuther and a presidential task force asked to study urban problems. Speaking for himself and the task force, Reuther asked Johnson to create a TVA for the cities. Just as TVA had become "a worldwide symbol to combat erosion of the land," so the President should create an agency that would "stop erosion of life in urban centers among the lower and middle income population." Specifically, a demonstration cities program, operating in six "big urban centers"—Washington, Detroit, Chicago, Philadelphia, Houston, and Los Angeles—was to rebuild the economy, transportation and health care systems, schools, housing, policing, and recreational facilities of neighborhoods with some 50,000 people. The job was to be done through a cooperative effort of the community and all levels of government.[71]

Under Johnson's watchful eye, the suggestion evolved into a "Demonstration Cities Program" he put before Congress in January 1966. The goal was to "offer qualifying cities of all sizes the promise of a new life for their people." The proposal was a fitting follow-through on the President's determination to conquer poverty and build a Great Society. It was the ultimate in social engineering. Johnson recommended "massive additions to the supply of low and moderate-cost housing," combining "physical reconstruction and rehabilitation with effective social programs . . . , new flexibility in administrative procedures," and a focus of "all the techniques and talents within our society on the crisis of the American City."

To qualify for the program, a city would need to demonstrate its readiness "to arrest blight and decay in entire neighborhoods" and "make a substantial impact within the coming few years on the development of the entire city." Indeed, the result of this effort should be nothing less than "a change in the total environment of the area affected."

And the prescription for achieving such lofty goals? The cities winning federal backing for the reforms had to "make use of every available social program." Maximum use of local residents in all phases of the work was mandatory, as well as "local and private initiative." The participating cities would rely on "modern cost-reducing technologies without reducing the quality of the work," "make major improvements in the quality of the environment," provide relocation housing to displaced residents at no cost to them, place the program under a single city authority, present agendas "consistent with existing development plans for the metropolitan areas involved," and complete the project in six years.

Johnson expected the total cost to be about $2.4 billion, an investment of some $400 million a year. If the project realized its full potential, the result would be "a sense of hope:—that the city is not beyond reach of redemption by men of good will—that through wise planning, cooperation, hard work, and the sacrifice of those outmoded codes and practices that make widespread renewal impossibly expensive today, it *is* possible to reverse the city's decline. That knowledge, that confidence, that hope can make all the difference in the decades ahead." Though Johnson counseled Congress not to "underestimate the problems involved in achieving such a plan," he declared his belief that it could mean "the rebirth of our cities."[72]

Many in Congress did not share Johnson's evangelical faith in overcoming urban blight through a federal program that sounded more like a summons to a crusade than a realistic blueprint for a major undertaking in social reform. In February, the *New York Times* predicted that the cost of the program would be at least twice Johnson's estimate. Liberals complained that the administration was shortchanging the proposal. Given the gravity of the problem, how could it expect to solve anything with just $2 billion? New York City alone needed $6 billion now.

Conservatives thought the White House wanted to spend too much on a will-o'-the-wisp. One Republican saw the President pouring "good money after bad—proposing an expensive new urban renewal program without requiring reform in the old"; another objected to spreading the program so "far and thin," saying it "would do nobody much good." Democrats and Republicans alike complained that this was a presidential program put forward without consulting congressmen, senators, or mayors.[73]

By the beginning of April, HUD Secretary Weaver did not think demonstration cities would be enacted. Southerners in the House and Senate objected to provisions requiring desegregated housing; the title "demonstration cities" evoked complaints of appeasing demonstrators and rioters; few groups in the country seemed actively disposed toward the legislation; small- and medium-sized cities believed that only big cities would benefit from the measure; and neither the House nor the Senate was particularly well disposed toward a bill that seemed to duplicate other programs and might end up costing a lot for very little gain. By the middle of May, the *New York Times* declared the proposal "dead." At best, the President's men on the Hill told him, Congress would pass a watered down measure providing only $12 million for planning.[74]

To salvage the bill, the administration proposed a competing draft measure asking $100 million for planning grants, but no money for implementation until reports were provided on total costs. Johnson, however, refused to back away from his original request, telling Califano and Larry O'Brien to "get the Vice President and Weaver out there revving up the interest groups. Turn the House committee around and get them to report out our bill. Then, tell them to hold it, because the House won't want to take up any legislation this controversial in an election year unless they're sure the Senate will act. So we'll have to get the Senate to act first."

As the House subcommittee was about to vote out the revised administration bill, Hubert Humphrey persuaded its chairman to postpone a vote for three weeks. Using the time to mount an effective lobbying effort, including word from Johnson that Demonstration

Cities was "the most important domestic measure before the Congress and to the future of the American cities," the administration won majorities at the end of June in the House subcommittee and committee for the original bill.[75]

But getting the President's proposal to the floor of the House was only a first step in the legislative dance. The Senate seemed no more likely than the House to pass the bill. Its subcommittee considering the measure was rudderless. Alabama Senator John Sparkman, its chairman, faced a reelection fight and wanted nothing to do with a law promoting integrated housing. Paul Douglas of Illinois, the second-ranking member, was enthusiastic about the bill, but a tough reelection campaign also put him on the sidelines.

Johnson pressed Ed Muskie of Maine, a warm supporter of urban reform, to take up the cause of model cities. A senator from a largely rural state with little to gain from the legislation, Muskie was just the man Johnson wanted to lead the fight. When Califano pointed out to the President that Muskie didn't have a single city in his state that would qualify for the program, Johnson replied, " 'Well, he has one now.' "[76]

Muskie, however, had questions about the bill's financial provisions and the capacity of government agencies to administer a model cities program. He was also reluctant to commit himself to a losing fight. In response, the White House agreed to modifications in the language of the bill, especially muting provisions for desegregated housing.

The administration also accommodated Thomas McIntyre of New Hampshire, another member of the subcommittee up for reelection. McIntyre feared antagonizing voters by backing a bill of little consequence to them and costing over $2 billion. To win McIntyre's support, Johnson agreed to downplay the closing of Portsmouth, New Hampshire's, Navy base, provide photos of himself and McIntyre for his campaign, and cut the cost of model cities by limiting initial authorization to $900 million for two years. McIntyre, after introducing the amendment cutting the appropriation, helped win subcommittee approval on July 23 by a 6 to 4 vote.[77]

Senate committee hearings beginning in mid-August on "the crisis in the cities" and urban violence fueled opposition to the bill. Throughout the summer the country's major eastern and midwestern cities saw a series of riots that raised additional questions about the value of "demonstration cities." Led by Ribicoff, Robert Kennedy, and Jacob Javits of New York, the hearings posed hard questions to administration officials about the adequacy of what they were doing to meet urban blight. Robert Kennedy complained that model cities was "a drop in the bucket" and that "a domestic Marshall Plan" was essential to deal with the crisis of the cities, "the central problem of American life."

Johnson saw the Kennedy-Ribicoff attack as a prelude to a Kennedy bid for the White House, and scoffed at suggestions that Congress would appropriate large amounts of money to combat urban ills. In a speech in Syracuse, New York, he challenged Congress to "Give us action. Give us progress. Give us movement. And American cities will be great again." Because a majority of senators saw a compelling need to do something about the cities at once, demonstration cities became a kind of stop-gap or halfway measure that would explore possible ways of meeting the crisis. Despite the criticisms leveled at the measure during his committee's hearings, for example, Ribicoff said that, "the cities bill was the most imaginative proposal in the whole area and he did not want to do anything to injure it."

Conservatives, however, remained unconvinced. Many of them saw the program as only "something for blacks" or a way of appeasing ghetto protesters. Consequently, on August 19 the Senate passed the President's bill with only fifty-three supporting votes. Twenty-five senators absented themselves from the voting.[78]

In September and October, the struggle over the bill resumed in the House, where the responsible committees agreed to make revisions in line with Senate changes and reduce the initial funding to $900 million. But even this less ambitious proposal confronted difficulties. Members complained that it would spur inflation, become the private preserve of black power advocates, compel school busing, and jeopardize the reelection chances of freshman Democrats in closely contested districts.

White House aides, seeing a close division in the House, where "50–60 Democratic votes have to be shored up to insure passage," urged a fresh presidential endorsement and additional pressure from the private sector on Congress. Johnson didn't hesitate. At a press conference on October 6 he declared no domestic problem "more critical than rebuilding our cities and giving our people who live in the cities opportunities to develop as healthy, educated, productive citizens of our society." He described demonstration cities as "one of the most important pieces of legislation for the good of all American mankind that we can act upon this session." At the same time, Califano convinced a group of prominent businessmen to endorse the bill as an imaginative and humane response to "the single most important domestic proposal before the Congress."[79]

On October 14, a week before adjournment, the House narrowly approved the bill by 178 to 141. After a conference committee report smoothed out differences between the two chambers, the bill came up for final votes. A 38 to 22 margin in the Senate and a 142 to 126 vote in the House demonstrated how many representatives and senators were away campaigning and what limited enthusiasm existed for a law that few expected to make the sort of difference Johnson said it would.[80]

Johnson nevertheless had high hopes for what he insisted now be called "Model Cities" instead of "Demonstration Cities." "Don't ever give such a stupid Goddamn name to a bill again," the President told Califano after signing the law.

Changing names did nothing for the success of the measure. Twenty-two years later, the *New York Times* pronounced the program a failure. The principal problem was not in its name or even the substance of the law. The *Times* believed that model cities never got a fair chance: "As envisioned, the program would have concentrated billions in huge demonstration grants to a handful of cities. Such grants would have tested whether comprehensive aid could create a realistic chance of eradicating blight. It didn't, because such aid never materialized. Every legislator had to have a slice of the pork. The few cities became 75, then 150. Eventually the money was shoveled around only a half-inch deep anywhere. The program was destined to fail."[81]

Yet within the limits under which it operated the program had its gains. As Charles Haar, one of its architects, writes, model cities had "real and lasting" accomplishments. It encouraged cities "to reappraise many of their programs seriously, to change hiring practices, to regularize social service planning, and to extend public services to disadvantaged areas." But, most important, it contributed "the vision of a systematic, concentrated use of resources to achieve the best possible urban life.... Dead before reaching maturity, the program nevertheless did its best to create an opportunity for exchange of ideas, challenge, stimulus, and diversity."[82]

The Great Society in Retreat: Civil Rights

As the war in Vietnam expanded and resources for Great Society–War on Poverty programs diminished, Johnson had to confront the problem of what more his administration could do to advance civil rights for blacks and open wider avenues of opportunity. The riots in Watts followed by upheavals during the summer of 1966 in thirty-eight cities, including Chicago, Cleveland, Milwaukee, Atlanta, Philadelphia, and Minneapolis, aroused concerns that black militants were intent on driving the country into a race war. Television pictures of black youths shouting "burn, baby, burn" sent waves of fear through suburban America and turned sympathy for helping an oppressed minority into hostility toward suggestions of making additional special efforts to right past wrongs.

In July 1966 one congressional survey of 12,000 constituents revealed a majority in favor of cutting poverty programs, welfare, urban renewal, and rent subsidies to finance the Vietnam War. Strong support was voiced for pollution programs and safety legislation, but an amazing 90 percent opposed additional civil rights legislation. In September 1965, when Gallup asked white Americans how blacks could improve their lot, 88 percent favored self-improvement, more education, and harder work, as opposed to government help.

A *U.S. News & World Report* article in December on "Negro Progress in U.S." described significant black gains in education, jobs, income, and life expectancy. The article acknowledged that great disparities remained between whites and blacks, but asserted "that the American Negro is winning his fight." The implicit conclusion was a diminished urgency about meeting black needs or less reason to be sympathetic to ghetto protesters, who were seen as rebels with a questionable cause. A year later, in a Gallup survey 52 percent complained that LBJ was going "too fast" on integration, 29 percent viewed his policies as "about right," while only 10 percent said they were "not fast enough."[83]

The riots and the rise of black militancy puzzled and troubled Johnson. He couldn't understand how black agitators could be so indifferent to the legal and legislative advances his administration had provided. Though he understood that the ghetto explosions weren't strictly rational expressions of black sentiment, he marveled at the political insensitivity of militants to how they undermined White House efforts to win public and congressional backing for appropriations and new laws to serve black interests.

As so often during his political career, Johnson saw himself as holding a middle ground on black rights between reactionaries antagonistic to government support of any kind and radical "bomb throwers" too impatient to let the rule of law and national regard for fair play ease the plight of African Americans.

During 1965–66 Johnson tried to sustain black gains through the courts and additional legislation that would require little or no increases in spending. He also tried to keep the political costs to a minimum. In the summer and fall of 1965 he had pressed the case for school integration, ordering daily reports on the progress of southern school districts in complying with requirements that they submit desegregation plans. Holding out the prospect of federal monies under ESEA to cooperative districts, the President made Education Commissioner Francis Keppel the instrument of his policy. By September 1965, Johnson could point to 88 percent compliance in the South, with a threefold increase in black students attending desegregated schools.

Though Johnson was ready to push desegregation across the South, where he felt he now had little left to lose politically, he had no intention of pressing the issue beyond the bounds of political reason in the North, where he feared provoking more of a backlash than was already evident.

When Keppel, without consulting the White House or Mayor Richard Daley, cut off funds to Chicago schools because of noncompliance with the 1964 Civil Rights act, Johnson confronted a political firestorm that he quickly doused. Daley, who had repeatedly delivered Illinois's congressional delegation to Johnson in House fights, saw the decision as an impermissible assault on a political ally. Johnson would not let Daley entirely off the hook, but he had no intention of making him comply fully with the letter of the law. Since Keppel had failed to follow proper procedure in giving Daley and the school district a chance to desegregate, the White House restored the funds and arranged a voluntary compliance plan with the Chicago school board.

Shortly after, Johnson announced a request to the Civil Rights Commission for "a study of racial isolation as a barrier to quality in education." The President explained that "racial isolation in the schools persists—both in the North and the South—because of housing patterns, school districting, economic stratification and population movements." Because the problems were "more subtle and complex than those presented by segregation imposed by law," Johnson believed it essential to get the facts before the nation as a prelude to reasoned remedies. For people intent on quick change, Johnson's actions looked like foot-dragging. To a seasoned politician like the President, it was his way of signaling a continuing desire to help and a sense of limitations imposed by conditions beyond his control.[84]

Despite the landmark civil rights laws of 1964 and 1965, Johnson believed that significant legislative reforms further assuring equal treatment and expanding federal jurisdiction to combat civil rights crimes were possible at small cost to the government. Since all-white southern juries continued to ignore miscarriages of justice in race crimes, the President believed that Congress would give a sympathetic hearing to a civil rights bill including provisions for impartial jury selection. Second, since bias in the sale and rental of housing had contributed to the creation of black ghettos, where festering problems erupted in riots, Johnson hoped Congress would agree to prohibit housing discrimination. Finally, Johnson wanted Congress to expand the Attorney General's authority to bring suits to desegregate schools and public facilities and to protect civil rights workers.[85]

The most controversial part of another civil rights bill was the attack on housing discrimination. In October 1965, Califano told the President that there was "tremendous pressure from civil rights leaders" to take additional executive action on the issue. If he acted without Congress, Califano told him, he might provoke a drawn out court fight and "be accused of over-extending your authority." If he asked for legislation, it would have the advantage of reducing a possible defeat in court, would be more broadly applicable than an Executive Order, and would put the political burden as much on Congress as himself. On the other hand, a legislative proposal would confront strong congressional opposition fueled by constituents fearful of reduced property values following integrated housing.[86]

Johnson chose the politically more expedient and legally surer course. In his State of the Union message, he urged Congress to enact a civil rights bill with housing, jury selection, and crime enforcement provisions. Everett Dirksen immediately announced his opposition to the ban on housing discrimination. During the first four months of 1966 Johnson struggled to find ways to build support for his proposal. In early March, White House aides felt that congressional contacts were still "inadequate" and that more time was needed to discuss matters with Dirksen, who, as with the 1964 and 1965 acts, seemed likely to be crucial to Senate passage. Though Dirksen would not endorse the fair housing provision and one legislative aide told the President that the "housing proposal will be impossible to enact," Johnson refused to abandon what he saw as the core of the bill.[87]

At the same time, however, he felt compelled to deemphasize the importance of another civil rights act. To be sure, his message to Congress on April 28 rang with strong language about injustice, equality, opportunity, and fairness. Moreover, he did not mince words about the extent and destructiveness of unfair housing codes. "The time has come for the Congress to declare resoundingly that discrimination in housing and all the evils it breeds are a denial of justice and a threat to the development of our growing urban areas. . . . The truly insufferable cost of imprisoning the Negro in the slums is borne by our national conscience. When we restrict the Negro's freedom inescapably we restrict a part of our own."[88]

But the President also wanted to make clear that no civil rights act at this time would make a definitive difference in solving the problems of racial discrimination. Johnson asked that several paragraphs be added to his message to make clear that "no amount of legislation, no degree of commitment on the part of the national government, can by itself bring equal opportunity and achievement to Negro Americans. It must be joined by a massive effort on the part of the states and local governments, of industry, and of all citizens, white and Negro." It was now up to black Americans "to take full advantage of the improved education and training . . . to use the opportunities for orderly progress that are now becoming—at last—a reality in their lives."[89]

To underscore the limited importance Johnson attached to the bill, he considered releasing his civil rights message to Congress when he was out of town. "It will be difficult to get any decent coverage for the message because the White House Press Corps will go with you," Joe Califano told him. "Who wants more coverage?" Johnson asked rhetorically.[90]

Johnson knew that getting the bill through Congress intact was a long shot. A White House poll of Democratic congressmen and senators in the spring on what they considered the most important issues in their districts and states put civil rights well down the list behind Vietnam, inflation, and the war on poverty. The housing section of the bill was so controversial that the House subcommittee separated it from the rest of the proposal. The full committee defeated a motion to kill the housing provision by only 17 to 15. A coalition of liberals and southerners then defeated several amendments that would have weakened the bill.

Southerners believed that a strong law would not pass the House. To their surprise, the House approved the legislation on August 9 with limitations on what constituted housing discrimination. The President issued a statement praising the House action and putting the best possible face on the fair housing provision.[91]

The Senate could not be persuaded to act. The Judiciary Committee bottled up the bill. When one liberal senator tried to put the measure on the Senate's calendar for floor action, it was blocked. A motion to set aside consideration of a pending bill and begin discussion of the civil rights act produced a twelve-day filibuster. Cloture petitions in September netted only 54 and 52 of the 60 necessary votes. Dirksen, despite pressure from Attorney General Katzenbach and Johnson himself, refused to back a bill with a housing title, and predicted that even a change in his position would not assure the votes for cloture. Katzenbach advised against seeking a bill without the housing provision, which civil rights groups and House conferees insisted remain in the law. He also urged the President to see Dirksen as a way of making "it clear that we had done everything we could to get a civil rights bill and that our failure to do so was the responsibility of the Republican leadership."[92]

Johnson now decided to abandon the fight for the time being. And even if he had wanted to continue the struggle, it was clear to him that the summer riots and divisions in the civil rights movement between traditional leaders like A. Philip Randolph, Roy Wilkins, Whitney Young, and Martin Luther King and younger leaders of CORE and SNCC, like James Farmer, Floyd McKissick, Stokely Carmichael, and H. "Rap" Brown, made the task very difficult.[93]

At the same time, he understood that he himself remained closely identified with civil rights and that he could not simply stand aside and let differences between blacks and whites deteriorate into a race war. As Harry McPherson told him, "you cannot shake off that leadership. You are stuck with it, in sickness as in health. The very fact that you have led the way toward first-class citizenship for the Negro, that you are identified with his cause, means that to some extent your stock rises and falls with the movement's." The President needed more than ever to point the way toward "peaceful change" by helping pass social reforms that opened additional opportunities to blacks and by persuading moderate black leaders to "speak out for order."[94]

Johnson didn't need prodding to remain attentive to civil rights issues and search for strategies that could promote integration and black gains. A Gallup poll in September, as the civil rights bill failed, described "racial problems" as America's biggest domestic issue.

But even before the poll came to hand and the 1966 bill was lost, Johnson had sent "a top-level team of White House aides to at least four major cities in the North and one in the South, to discuss education, employment, housing—and the racial crisis—with university and political experts." He had also set up a committee to consider what civil rights legislation to propose in 1967. In August, Katzenbach had been asked to chair the task force that was to develop "a vigorous and imaginative program" to address "our deep concern with the many problems remaining in the civil rights field." Katzenbach's group was to consider ways to expand equal employment opportunities, improve fair housing laws, compensate victims of racial violence, shift civil rights cases from state to federal courts, and coordinate more effectively the work of federal civil rights agencies.[95]

The task force was largely a response to the White House civil rights conference of June 1–2, "To Fulfill These Rights," and the summer riots. After the planning session in November 1965, at which critics of the administration had complained of excessive caution and limited funding in dealing with black problems, the White House had tried to assure that the June meeting focused on constructive ways to provide jobs, education, and housing. It had also intended to educate ghetto dwellers about the opportunities for self-improvement and to "mobilize them to do it."[96]

As the meeting approached, the White House had worried that radicals would disrupt the conference by saying that Vietnam was destroying the war on poverty and using more militant tactics. By putting the conference under the control of black moderates, however, the administration assured against attacks on its policies and managed to keep discussion on ways to "move beyond opportunity to achievement." As one aide told the President, "the conference, while sitting on a number of kegs of dynamite constantly, was a strong plus." The "highlights of the meeting" were a Johnson speech with "twenty interruptions for applause and standing ovations in the twenty minutes you spoke."[97]

Johnson's speech emphasized the idea that the administration could not do it all. "The dilemma that you deal with is too deeply rooted in pride and prejudice, too profound and complex, and too critical to our future for any one man or any one administration to ever resolve," he said. "No matter how committed to its resolution, this issue is beyond the mastery of one man or one group of men. . . . No national government, however enlightened, can by itself change the conditions of Negro life in America."

Nevertheless, Johnson counseled against the loss of hope and arguments of those urging separation of the races, whether coming from southern advocates of continued segregation or black power proponents preaching a "go it alone" strategy. The best choice, Johnson asserted, was to move the nation "towards civil peace and towards social justice for all of its citizens." The key was job opportunities, decent housing, and a good education for everyone—the paths out of poverty.[98]

But there were limits now to what he felt free to do. He did not want to bury the conference report, which a twenty-nine-member council had issued at the end of June. The report called on state and local governments, businesses and unions, and civic and religious groups to help ease the plight of black Americans. But it also asked for the introduction of new federal programs and a substantial expansion of existing ones to do the job.[99]

Johnson struck all the right symbolic chords in response to the proposals. He agreed to have the report presented to him personally and to "consider its recommendations in a vigorous, visible, and aggressive way." To that end, he set up a Cabinet Council to examine the proposals for federal action, asked council members to appoint someone full-time to study how each of their departments could respond to the conference recommendations, and promised to develop ways to demonstrate federal interest in having federal, state, and local officials do all they could in behalf of civil rights and equal opportunity.

At the same time, however, he saw no way to fund the conference suggestions. Against a backdrop of a growing war and rising white antagonism to federal programs that many believed encouraged rather than reduced black violence, Johnson, despite continuing genuine concern about black suffering and alienation, refused to give civil rights the priority it had in 1964–65.[100]

The Great Society in Retreat: The War on Poverty

During 1966 the War on Poverty faltered. It was a victim of expenditures on Vietnam, threatened inflation and economic disarray, and its own internal contradictions.

Johnson could not admit publicly that the antipoverty crusade was in trouble. He knew full well by the end of 1966 that his public pronouncements trumpeting the coming end of want in America were unrealizable. If he still had hopes of reaching that exalted goal, Harry McPherson urged him to see matters as they were. "There is no real agreement on how to go about improving the job situation, or education, or family income in the slums," McPherson told him in December. "I think we have about all the social programs we need— already authorized. We may have too many. ... You need to ask: What is this program trying to accomplish? How well has it done? What *should* we be trying to accomplish in this area?"[101]

Johnson wished to level with the public about the limitations of the poverty war. "I wish the public had seen the task of ending poverty the same way as they saw the task of getting to the moon, where they accepted mistakes as a part of the scientific process," he later told Doris Kearns. "I wish they had let us experiment with different programs, admitting that some were working better than others. It would have made everything easier. But I knew that the moment we said out loud that this or that program was a failure, then the wolves who never wanted us to be successful in the first place would be down upon us at once, tearing away at every joint, killing our effort before we even had a chance."[102]

Yet Johnson himself didn't think of the overall war on poverty as a "failure," certainly not in 1966. In public, he had nothing but praise for the achievements of OEO and the whole poverty fight. And he had reasons to believe that much good was being done. At the end of 1965, Walter Heller had urged him not to skimp on the Great Society: "A billion or two extra invested in better training, education, and housing—especially for the poor and the Negro—will give America a *far bigger payoff than if we add that billion or two to already-swollen private consumption and investment*," Heller told him.[103]

But even without the additional money, by the beginning of 1967 Johnson saw a record of accomplishment that spelled much more success than failure. For one, federal spending on the poor had increased in every relevant category—education and training, health, and cash benefits like social security and unemployment insurance—and government services provided by the OEO and the Community Action Program (CAP) had raised government outlays for the poor from nearly $13 billion in 1963 to almost $20 billion in 1966.

In December 1966, budget analysts told the President that the administration's best weapon in the poverty war was jobs. An increase in employment of 8.4 million from 1960 to 1966 helped explain why the number of poor Americans had declined from 22 percent to 17 percent. In addition, the government's policies and general prosperity had helped keep a "large number of people . . . from falling into poverty" and raised the standard of living for even those who remained below the poverty line. "*What have we learned?*" a paper presented at a Cabinet meeting asked. "*Poverty in America Can Be Eliminated.*" The 38 million poor of 1959 had come down to 25.9 million by 1967; the 14 percent of whites and 47 percent of nonwhites in poverty had declined to 10 percent and 35 percent, respectively.[104]

Johnson spoke repeatedly in public during 1966 about the gains being made against want. Spending on Great Society programs had nearly doubled in three years: Federal outlays for health and education were up 59 percent; spending on cities had leaped 76 percent; and unemployment was sharply down, by 32 percent for whites and 34 percent for blacks.[105]

Nevertheless, it was an open secret that the President's commitment to Great Society–War on Poverty programs had waned and that hopes were being disappointed. In November 1966, Charlie Schultze told Johnson that "states, cities, depressed areas and individuals have been led to expect immediate delivery of benefits from Great Society programs to a degree that is not realistic. This leads to *frustration, loss of credibility, and even deterioration* of State and local services as they hang back on making normal commitments in order to apply for federal aid which does not materialize."[106]

Johnson did all he could to combat the impression of a slowdown in the antipoverty campaign. "We just have to keep hammering home our side of the question every time we get a chance," Bill Moyers told the President. But Johnson knew that there was a gap between his public declarations and private actions. For one, he was at war with the Community Action Programs around the country. Under the flag of "maximum feasible participation," CAPs challenged local political leaders for control of poverty funds. They put the poor on local poverty boards, "neighborhood service centers," which fought with established institutions—schools, welfare agencies, and housing authorities—about the ways in which they served inner city residents. "Local governments didn't bargain for all this—being sued, being demonstrated against, having sit-ins in their offices," one proponent of CAP said.

Local officials began complaining to Washington that Marxists intent on a class struggle were organizing the poor into tenant unions, welfare protesters, and political action groups seeking to overthrow local authorities. Mayors Richard Daley of Chicago and Sam Yorty of Los Angeles persuaded the U.S. Conference of Mayors to condemn CAP for promoting "class struggle" and insist that local programs remain under the control of local officials.[107]

The growth of community action challenges to local political organizations worried Johnson. During 1964 and much of 1965, however, he had been reluctant to intervene. He took some pleasure in seeing poor folks have a say in local affairs and bend political machines to their will. He believed that the pressure generated by the CAPs might make the war on poverty more effective. As long as squabbles between city officials and CAPs didn't endanger other Great Society programs, Johnson was content to placate complaining politicians with sympathetic words about the difficulties of reining in out-of-control agencies.

By late 1965, however, with congressmen and senators growing reluctant to provide money for activities challenging local political allies, and an emerging White House conviction that organizing efforts among the poor would become a launching pad for a Robert Kennedy presidential campaign, Johnson took steps to check "maximum feasible participation." When he was told about an attack on Democratic party leaders in the District of Columbia by CAP protesters, for example, he instructed Bill Moyers: "For God's sake get on top of this and put a stop to it at once." As other complaints came in, Johnson told his aides to quash the political organizing of CAP radicals.

A Shriver memo in October 1965 pressing the case for an enlarged poverty fight fanned Johnson's suspicions about Bobby Kennedy. The Vietnam War alone was enough to deter Johnson from committing greater sums to antipoverty programs, but his belief that Shriver intended to leak his memo to the press as a demonstration that he and Kennedy wanted to favor social action at home over a distant war abroad moved LBJ to launch a counter-strike. Under Hubert Humphrey's prodding, Budget Director Schultze told the President that OEO was more concerned with organizing the poor than getting them jobs and should be deterred from setting up "competing political groups." Johnson agreed, and Schultze tried to curb Shriver's agency.

But OEO and the local CAPs were not so easy to control. Shriver and Schultze got into a public war of words over appropriate actions by poverty fighters. Shriver gave vent to his irritation in a letter to the President, who saw Shriver's undiplomatic memo as additional evidence of his disloyalty and commitment to help Bobby run for President in 1968.[108]

Johnson's conflict with OEO now extended to some of the local CAPs. In particular, he fell into a struggle with the Child Development Group of Mississippi (CDGM), which had set up eighty Head Start centers in forty communities staffed by poor blacks. John Stennis, who chaired the Appropriations Committee and had a large say in funding Great Society programs, complained that CDGM was not a legitimate arm of the OEO but a black nationalist front organizing civil rights actions. Stennis also charged that CDGM was violating OEO procedures. Rather than cross Stennis, the White House cut off CDGM funds, but relented when the National Council of Churches picketed OEO offices and an ad appeared in the *New York Times* titled, "Say It Isn't So Sargent Shriver," and demanded an explanation. After arranging for Mississippi Action for Progress (MAP), a moderate group of blacks and whites, to join with CDGM in running the Head Start centers, the White House restored some of its funding.[109]

Similarly, an OEO plan to put $1 million a year into a literacy project sponsored by James Farmer, the head of CORE, provoked a new outcry from Daley and Yorty. Warned that funding Farmer's project would lose OEO forty votes in the House, Johnson persuaded Adam Clayton Powell to block the proposal in his Education and Labor Committee. Under other circumstances, Johnson would have been avid to back a literacy campaign helping poor blacks gain the sort of basic skills they could turn into productive work. But given the political muscle aligned against the proposal, Johnson made expediency his guide.[110]

By the end of 1965, the President had considered reorganizing the OEO and shifting its functions to "existing departments and agencies." The Job Corps and Neighborhood Youth Corps would go into the Labor Department; HUD would take over CAP; VISTA would become part of the Peace Corps; Rural Loans would join the Agriculture Department; while the rest of the War on Poverty, Head Start, Work Study, Adult Literacy, and Migrant Workers would come under HEW. Shriver, who would then be out of a job, could become the new HUD Secretary.

When Califano warned the President that this was "potentially the most politically explosive act the administration could take," though "it makes good organizational sense," Johnson backed down. "He didn't want to precipitate a nasty bureaucratic war within his administration or a political brouhaha on Capitol Hill," Califano says. "He did not wish to give Shriver's brother-in-law Robert Kennedy and congressional liberals any ammunition to accuse him of shorting the needs of the poor because of the Vietnam War."[111]

A year later, a White House task force on reorganizing HEW recommended shifting all of the OEO programs to appropriate Cabinet Departments, except community action. OEO would then "be set up as a separate agency outside the Executive Office of the President to run CAP and to develop and demonstrate new programs which would be ultimately turned over to on-going departments as they matured."

Johnson was clearly looking for a way to neutralize the OEO. He saw everybody at OEO as "disloyal to him." He complained repeatedly to Wilbur Cohen at HEW that "the OEO people were always trying to undermine him." Shriver, who now offered to resign, urged Johnson to replace OEO with a domestic National Security Council chaired directly by the President and including the Vice President and all the major Cabinet officers. Shriver wanted his departure to give no suggestion of bad blood between himself and the White House, or so he said. Concerned that the reorganization of OEO and Shriver's resignation would be seen as a downgrading of the whole War on Poverty, Johnson persuaded Shriver to stay as head of the OEO, which was also to remain intact.[112]

Yet in spite of maintaining the status quo, Johnson was in fact crimping the war on poverty. Throughout 1966 his struggle to hold down federal expenditures partly revolved around trimming antipoverty costs and discouraging Congress from adding funds to his appropriation requests.[113]

Advocates for the poor pressed him not to make cuts. In March, Whitney Young of the Urban League urged the President to promise black leaders that "you will fight any cutbacks in funds for the War on Poverty in a forceable way." Johnson refused. Dick Lee, the mayor of New Haven, complained that urban poverty programs, despite administration promises, were not being funded. "The war against poverty should not become a casualty of the war in Viet Nam," he told Califano in November. Califano asked Secretary Weaver what he could say in reply to Lee. "The answer is obvious," Weaver said, "and it relates to the budgetary pressures on the administration and the competing requirements for public expenditure."

In December, when the White House learned that the National Urban League planned protests in seventy-five cities against reduced antipoverty payments and heard rumors of a poor people's march on Washington, OEO increased spending in D.C. "to try to decrease the agitation."[114]

By the beginning of 1967, Johnson had few qualms about holding down antipoverty spending. But not because he was ready to give up the fight against want. On the contrary, as far as he could tell, the War on Poverty was succeeding with only modest expenditures of $1.5 to $1.75 billion. All the statistics he saw indicated a steady decline in the numbers of indigents. Just how this was happening was not clear to him, though he understood that this was partly the consequence of an expanding economy generating more and better-paying jobs.[115]

Less obvious was the fact that community action programs across the country, but particularly in major cities, were promoting greater awareness of welfare rights, which brought substantial numbers of poor onto the welfare rolls. "Since the federal government picked up half the tab for Aid to Families with Dependent Children (AFDC)," one analyst says, "welfare was often the cheapest way to give poor blacks something they needed— ... money. Nor were there powerful white voting blocks competing for welfare dollars or resisting black demands, as there were in education, housing, and employment."

Between 1960 and the early 1970s, there was a fourfold increase in AFDC, with much of the expansion coming after 1964. "The federal government accomplished little in the ghetto save opening up the welfare rolls," this analyst concludes. Some of the Great Society programs gave modest numbers of poor a hand up rather than a handout. "But in the ghetto—where schooling was poor, where the family was already in serious trouble, and where crime was becoming a way of life for many young men—the successful policies were irrelevant. The real impact was on welfare, and thus on dependency and on the black family."[116]

The Elections of 1966

The domestic difficulties, coupled with growing frustration about Vietnam during 1966, spelled trouble for Johnson and the Democrats in the congressional and state elections. Even in good times, the incumbent party and President usually suffer some losses in mid-term contests. And with the uncommonly large margins the Democrats held in the House (295 to 140), the Senate (68 to 32), and the state-houses (33 to 17), they seemed certain to lose some ground.

For more than a year before the November voting, the White House had been tracking the decline of Democratic party fortunes. As early as the summer of 1965, Hubert Humphrey had begun helping seventy freshmen congressmen prepare their reelection fights. In November, local elections, led by Republican John Lindsay's mayoral victory in New York City, boosted GOP hopes of additional gains in 1966. The results led Democratic party analysts to predict a loss of between twenty and thirty-six House seats. By January, one party appraisal cautioned against a naive faith in breaking the mold of traditional off-year election results. Moreover, the Democratic party structure was seen as "in bad shape," and the Republicans seemed certain to win several gubernatorial campaigns. Johnson and the party received more bad news in February and March when polls showed a decline in the President's popularity to 56 percent, a drop of five points in just one month and the lowest level since he had assumed office in November 1963.[117]

Johnson now considered what role to play in the upcoming campaign. His identity as a lifelong Democrat encouraged him to fight for his party. In addition, Democratic defeats would be seen as partly a personal repudiation and would weaken his ability to lead in the next two years.

At the same time, however, he had an aversion to excessive partisanship. In the fifties, during Eisenhower's presidency, he had built his national reputation as a moderate southerner and an advocate of bipartisanship, particularly in foreign affairs. His appeal in the 1964 campaign had been to both parties, urging Democrats and Republicans alike to join him in opposing extremism of the left and the right. Johnson also had a history of tension with northern Democratic party leaders and labor unions, whom he described as "a bunch of damn crooks" and "racketeers." As for the Democratic National Committee, he considered it largely superfluous. Hubert Humphrey said, "Legend to the contrary notwithstanding, when it came to party politics, he [LBJ] was not good."[118]

Johnson approached the 1966 elections with great caution. Re-

membering FDR's failure in the 1938 primaries to oust conservative
Democrats and seeing it as accepted "policy" to remain neutral, he
made clear to party candidates that he would "stay completely away
from any of the [primary] campaigns until these are over and the
General Contest is on."

As for the fall elections, he took a wait-and-see attitude. If he
were to involve himself in the campaign and the Republicans made
significant gains, he would be the biggest loser. If he largely stood
aside, he would likely shoulder less of the responsibility for Democratic defeats. One aide advised him in early May that if things took
"a turn for the better in Vietnam, you should go on the campaign
trail. . . . If, however, things get worse, . . . the best policy would be for
you to remain in the White House." Horace Busby urged him to
remain above the battle. "The political role for a President is treach-
erous in times like these." Busby reminded him how poorly Woodrow
Wilson's campaigning had served him in 1918. "Your posture and
image has been above partisanship; any change, at this time, could
carry a very costly backlash."[119]

At the end of May Johnson saw reason to sit out the elections.
A chart on results from presidential efforts in off-year campaigns gave
no reason to get significantly involved. Moreover, current polls suggested little that he could do to reverse party fortunes. His popularity
continued to fall. Worries about inflation, Vietnam, and his proposal
to bar racial discrimination in the sale or rental of private housing
were further reducing his attractiveness to voters. Likewise, the Democrats, who had a twenty-one-point advantage over the Republicans
in November 1965 as the party best able to handle national problems,
held only a seven-point edge over the GOP in May. It was the closest
the margin had been since August 1960, when the two parties had
been nearly even. The results of this question over the years had been
a good indicator of voter sentiment and suggested that the Republicans might gain as many as fifty or even sixty House seats and two
in the Senate, where there were thirty-five races.[120]

When the President's approval rating slipped to between 46 and
50 percent in June, the White House began focusing not on how to
cut Democratic losses in Congress but how to improve Johnson's public appeal. "Our standing is down and likely to drop further," Bill
Moyers told Johnson on June 9. In the face of this, Bob Kintner
privately told reporters that the President had no plans for the fall
campaign, or at least Kintner didn't know of any. In fact, Johnson
had instructed Kintner to develop a "program for me." But it was
not to include special efforts to save the seventy-five Democratic congressmen who were "most vulnerable in their reelection bid." When

Cliff Carter at the DNC asked the President to film one- to five-minute conversations with these congressmen for use in their campaigns, Johnson refused.[121]

Instead, the White House began an intense effort to staunch the President's political bleeding. Though in February he had declared himself "sick of having to offset any [unfavorable] image," Johnson now instructed aides "to disseminate more affirmative polls" and arrange to enter positive editorials in the *Congressional Record*. At a meeting of the President's top staff members, they discussed speech themes and other means of boosting his standing. All agreed that Vietnam, peace, inflation, and agriculture were the concerns of the moment. But the real problem was not finding themes but humanizing a President who seemed too humorless and too intent on a search for consensus. Greater candor and consistency also seemed essential to creating some momentum for his political resurgence.[122]

In July, Johnson took up the challenge by making two trips to the Midwest and holding background meetings with journalists. By the middle of the month, the President's aggressive defense of his administration and stepped-up bombing against North Vietnam caused a surge in his popularity, jumping ten points to 56 percent from his low point in June. Johnson's second tour demonstrated to the columnist Marianne Means that he had not "lost his fire on the stump nor his ability to mesmerize a crowd, particularly when he discusses such dramatic events as the war in Viet Nam."[123]

Yet in spite of this surge, Johnson continued to keep his distance from the congressional campaigns. When Tommy Corcoran suggested that the DNC turn the election into a referendum on LBJ with the slogan, "A vote against Johnson is a vote for Hanoi," he vetoed it. He also rejected a suggestion to bring in the freshmen Democrats for a meeting and pictures. A proposal that he campaign for "a number of marginal Democrats" in Pittsburgh and Dayton or Cincinnati on his way to Indiana in late July was no more convincing to him. To be sure, Johnson agreed to a private meeting with the 16 Democratic senators up for reelection, but this exposed him to no public risks.[124]

Though the President made two more "nonpolitical" trips in August to the Northeast and West, his public standing took another downturn. By September, his approval rating had fallen back to 48 percent, with people expressing diminished confidence in his ability to manage the economy in general and inflation in particular. A trial presidential heat between LBJ and Michigan Governor George Romney gave Johnson a slight 51 to 49 advantage. A Harris poll also showed the Democrats losing more ground in the congressional and gubernatorial races.

Because Johnson now feared losing as many as sixty seats in the House and 6 to 8 seats in the Senate, he approved a plan for some sixty administration officials—the Vice President, Cabinet, and sub Cabinet Secretaries—to coordinate visits to congressional districts across the country. The worst thing that could come out of this, Kintner told Johnson, were newspaper stories saying "the President fears a major defeat in the election and has rallied his appointees to political activity to try to offset it." Johnson now also agreed to meet with Democratic incumbents at the White House and make a three-and-a-half-minute film for use by Democratic candidates.[125]

Yet at the same time, the President continued to refuse to become overtly partisan. In late September, he told reporters that he had no plan to travel widely in the states before the election. He also refused to get into a public dispute with the Republican House leadership over Vietnam. And when he did get out on the hustings, he said, "We haven't been talking party matters. We have been talking people matters; problems of people."

On financial support for Democratic candidates as well, he was not very forthcoming. Because of Republican accusations that big contributors to Johnson's principal fund-raising committee, the President's Club, were receiving favored treatment for government contracts, Johnson largely closed down the operation in the last months of the campaign, when money was badly needed. Partly to distance himself from the election, Johnson decided to make a seventeen-day trip to Asia from October 17 to November 2. Shortly before he left, he said that he had no plans to campaign when he returned.[126]

In October, Marianne Means told readers of her column that the President has "displayed an indifference toward practical politics which dismayed and perplexed party leaders. He seldom left the White House. He sharply restricted money-raising endeavors and forbade solicitation of new members for the President's Club. He let the Democratic National Committee flounder uselessly."[127]

Privately, Johnson was torn about what to do. He saw a substantial Republican victory coming, and he wished to insulate himself from it as much as possible. As important, he saw some advantage to replacing liberal Democrats with Republicans. True, it would make it harder, if not impossible, to win significant legislative victories. But it would give him stronger support in Congress to fight in Vietnam. And by the fall of 1966, this was his highest priority. Indeed, the periodic reports he requested from aides on the congressional races during 1966 included assessments of candidates' views on Vietnam as the lead item.[128]

Still, Johnson didn't want to let the Republicans win without a fight. It galled him to think that a President with his record of achievement should be identified with any kind of political defeat. "I am willing to let any objective historian look at my record," he told aides in an Anchorage, Alaska, hotel room the evening before he returned to Washington from Asia. "If I can't do more than any- [one else] to help my country, I'll quit. FDR passed five major bills the first one hundred days. We passed 200 in the last two years. It is unbelievable. We must dramatize that."[129]

The week before he left for Asia he mapped plans for a four-day campaign blitz carrying him to eleven states all over the country. During his Asia trip, six more states were added to his itinerary. More important, detailed plans were made for Johnson to sign various bills in appropriate settings.[130]

But sensing a strong Republican showing, regardless of what he did, Johnson canceled the trip at the last minute. When he publicly denied that he had ever planned such a campaign swing, it hurt him and the Democrats more than if he had followed through on his plan. On November 8, the Republicans gained 47 House seats, reducing the Democratic margin to 248 to 187, three Senate seats, making the division 64 to 36, and eight governorships for a 25 to 25 split of the states.[131]

As the year ended, Johnson's credibility, his willingness to be honest with the press, the public, and Congress, had become a bigger issue than his extraordinay legislative gains or Democratic party defeats. And central to so many doubts about the President's reliability was his direction of the war in Vietnam, which was becoming the country's greatest concern.

7

"Lyndon Johnson's War"

BY the winter of 1965–66 nearly 60 percent of the country saw the Vietnam War as America's most urgent problem. The number had more than doubled since the presidential campaign in 1964. Two out of three Americans considered it essential to take a stand in Vietnam, with only 20 percent favoring a pullout over an expanded role for U.S. forces. Seventy-five percent of a sample poll viewed the war as "part of our worldwide commitment to stop Communism."[1]

There were also growing indications that as the war went, so would Lyndon Johnson's public standing. At the end of 1965, his approval rating remained impressively high at 64 percent. Moreover, for the third year in a row, Americans chose him as the most admired man in the world, with Dwight Eisenhower second and Robert Kennedy third. Some three-fourths of the country endorsed the President's handling of Vietnam and expressed antagonism to antiwar demonstrators.

Yet at the same time, the public's support had distinct limits. It had little appetite for a long, expanded war. Bill Moyers told Johnson in December that most Americans hoped that stepped-up military actions would facilitate "a negotiated, compromise peace." Escalation was acceptable because it would bring "peace more quickly." But impatience and frustration were also evident: Only 25 percent of the country thought "we are making any progress" in Vietnam and 43 percent complained that the administration was not doing enough to end the fighting.[2]

Sentiment in the United States, although important, was only one element shaping Johnson's judgments on the war. In November, Vietnam Ambassador Henry Cabot Lodge told the President that "we are beginning to master the technique of thwarting and eventually overcoming the Viet Cong main force units and military redoubts."

Lodge warned against a cease-fire or anything that might demoralize Saigon and collapse the government.[3]

Johnson didn't have much regard for Lodge. He had little confidence in his brain power or judgment. But in this instance he shared Lodge's resistance to even temporarily reducing pressure on the Communists. A recommendation from U.S. military and State Department officials in October that the administration test Hanoi's interest in negotiations with a bombing pause had little appeal to Johnson. He had limited faith in the wisdom of his national security advisers. It was becoming increasingly clear to him that their advice rested on guesswork or trial-and-error experiments in war making. But with growing convictions that additional troops and expanded bombing of the North would be necessary in 1966, Johnson saw some advantage to a temporary bombing halt. At a meeting on November 11, he declared himself "60–40 for it about Thanksgiving." The pause would be "preparatory to knocking Hell out of 'em."[4]

The "60–40" preference for the pause was like everything Johnson now did about Vietnam: He agonized over every decision. He doubted that a pause would change anything in the fighting, but it might help with domestic opinion, especially after a report that the administration had rejected a North Vietnamese overture for peace talks in 1964. The story provoked complaints that "The U.S. is . . . incessantly proclaiming its desire for peace in Viet Nam, while first concealing and then giving the brushoff to Hanoi's overtures for talks."[5]

The Joint Chiefs urged LBJ to expand the American military effort. On November 10, they asked for an additional 113,000 troops to shift from phase I of the fighting, in which U.S. forces had stopped "losing the war," to phase II, in which we would "start winning it." They also recommended intensified bombing, highlighted first by strikes against petroleum, oil, and lubricant facilities and electric power installations and then military targets in the Hanoi-Haiphong area.

According to Marine Lieutenant General Charles G. Cooper, the Joint Chiefs put their case before the President at a meeting in the Oval Office in early November. Speaking for the Chiefs, Wheeler warned that unless we began "using our principal strengths—air and naval power— . . . we would risk becoming involved in another protracted Asian ground war with no definitive solution." The chiefs urged "isolating the major port of Haiphong through naval mining, blockading the rest of the North Vietnamese coastline, and simultaneously beginning a B-52 bombing offensive on Hanoi."

Johnson didn't want any part of a policy that might provoke a wider war. He didn't think the Chiefs had a clue as to what they were proposing. He responded with an explosion of invective that stunned them. "He screamed obscenities, he cursed them personally, he ridiculed them for coming to his office with their 'military advice.' . . . He then accused them of trying to pass the buck for World War III to him. It was unnerving. It was degrading," Cooper says. "He told them he was disgusted with their naive approach toward him, that he was not going to let some military idiots talk him into World War III. It ended when he told them to 'get the hell out of my office.'"

Johnson's response partly rested on messages from Peking that China would join the fighting if Washington supported a South Vietnamese invasion of the North. As disquieting, it was clear to American analysts that Chinese leaders saw the war in Vietnam as a means of stimulating their people to back Mao's Cultural Revolution. Johnson could not ignore the fact that unstable domestic conditions might move Peking to use expanded U.S. military operations in Vietnam to fight a unifying war.

Yet at the same time, Johnson's intemperate response to the Chiefs demonstrated how anguished he remained about the conflict. As in the spring and summer of 1965, when Moyers and others saw him agitated by the belief that Vietnam might destroy him, so in November he viewed the recommendations of the Chiefs as leading to an international and personal catastrophe.[6]

Robert McNamara's evolving view of the fighting underscored the President's dilemma. At the beginning of November, McNamara had told Johnson that the Communists had matched U.S. troop deployments since July and unless the U.S. chose to abandon Vietnam and allow China a victory in its planned mobilization of Asia against the West, we would need to deploy additional forces. He recommended a bombing halt to test Hanoi's interest in talks and to demonstrate America's commitment to peace.

At the end of the month, after his seventh visit to Vietnam, McNamara concluded that the administration would have to increase troop strength in 1966 to 400,000 and possibly to 600,000 in 1967. None of this guaranteed "success" or "victory," but it seemed likely to forestall a Communist takeover of the South or a "no-decision," with U.S. killed in action running at as many as 1000 a month. "Any prospect of military success" would then be "marred by the chances of an active Chinese intervention." In short, McNamara saw no military solution to the conflict, only a political one, which he viewed as the containment of Asian Communism. Beginning to be even more skeptical than Johnson of what could be achieved in a limited war, he saw a need for the quickest possible exit from the conflict. In a private conversation with a group of liberal friends, McNamara defined America's "objective in South Vietnam as 'withdrawal with honor.' "[7]

Johnson shared McNamara's outlook; he hoped for a negotiated settlement rather than a military victory. But he saw peace only following a sustained, strong military effort. He saw no sensible alternative to expanding America's combat role. To step out now made no sense to him. Despite Hanoi's strong response to American escalation, he still believed it necessary to show the Communists that America would not be intimidated by aggression, even if it meant fighting a limited war at considerable cost in lives and dollars. He would commit himself to a pause only, therefore, if it facilitated America's war effort.[8]

Bundy and McNamara gave him reason to think it would. Since they faced "a pretty grim year" of fighting at heavy budget costs, Bundy told him, it argued for "one further demonstration that our determination to seek peace is equal to our determination on the battle field."[9]

Johnson was unconvinced. At meetings in early December, he resisted a pause. Once we stopped bombing, he thought it would be difficult to resume. He focused on deploying 15,000 troops a month instead of announcing a decision to send another 100,000 or more men. He wanted to make the "steady increase of pressure on the ground . . . as undramatic as possible."[10]

Johnson was now all doubts about the wisdom of a pause. "We mustn't take off into the wild blue yonder," he said in a December 7 meeting with advisers at his ranch. "I don't want to take off till I know I can get back." He asked whether there was any evidence the Communists were "getting ready for a peace offer." Rusk and McNamara thought not.[11]

In a meeting with senior advisers on December 17, Johnson stated his willingness "to take any gamble on stopping the bombing" if there were any chance of a result. But he didn't think it would have an impact, either on the Communists or "the Fulbrights and Lippmanns. They're not coming aboard."

If there were to be a pause, a Mac Bundy proposal for a halt from December 24 to January 2 most appealed to LBJ. But he wanted it done without announcements. If questions were raised, the Pentagon could use "weather as an excuse and Christmas as a factor." It could also point to America's allies, who were saying "we are not doing enough to find peace." As for the Joint Chiefs, McNamara could tell them: "We've got a heavy budget, tax bill, controls, danger of inflation, kill the great society. With all these things, we've got to make sure the diplomats can talk. They claim they can't talk with bombs dropping." The pause could last a month, from December 22 to January 22.[12]

Johnson was still fretting about what to do when he saw his advisers again the next day. He thought a pause contained "serious military risks." It also rankled him "that we have to prove again to Congress we are striving for peace. We've done that again and again." In addition, he feared that a pause that failed and weakened America's military position would bring on "a deadly crisis.... When we suffer reverses, it will be attributable to this. The support we have will be weak as dishwater."

McNamara saw a case for a pause in the fact that a military solution was unlikely. "Then, no matter what we do in military [field] there is no sure victory," Johnson said. "That's right," McNamara replied. "We have been too optimistic." Abe Fortas and Clark Clifford, who Johnson had invited to the meeting, spoke forcefully against a pause. "There is danger Hanoi would greet a pause as possible evidence that protests have had effect on the U.S. Government," Fortas declared. Clifford predicted that North Vietnam would not talk peace until they believed they couldn't win the war.

Johnson agreed. He thought a pause would make the Communists "doubt . . . our will to see this thing through." After saying this, Johnson "looked solemnly at the men around the table. Then he casually addressed McNamara. 'We'll take the pause.' With a slight wave of the hand, he strode from the room." It was another demonstration of Johnson's uncertainty about what to do in Vietnam and of the shaky resolve behind his every decision on the war.[13]

The President's commitment weakened during the next few days. When he met again with his advisers on December 21, he declared a pause "more a sign of weakness than anything else. All we'll get is distrust from our allies, despair from the troops, and disgruntled generals."[14]

Johnson's advisers were now thoroughly confused as to what he intended. Nevertheless, on the following day, Washington and Saigon announced a thirty-hour Christmas truce, suspending all air and ground action. Though nothing was said about an extended bombing pause, no one in the U.S. government was clear on when air attacks would resume. Johnson had left his subordinates in the dark, partly because he himself was so unsure of how to proceed. But he was also concerned not to show the depths of his own confusion. He was determined to guard against stories that he was hesitant and the government without firm leadership.

It was clear to Bill Bundy that "the war . . . was beginning to get to him." And why not? No one he looked to, neither the brilliant civilians nor well-trained military around him, had anything resembling a solution to the Vietnam problem. The debate over the pause was symptomatic of Johnson's larger dilemma.

Johnson now saw the pause as a way to fend off "a hard look" by Congress at the war and steps toward "new authorizing action." Bundy speculates that Johnson considered whether "a frontal confrontation with Congress, laying all the cards face up, would be helpful." But, as in July 1965, the President concluded that such an open discussion of war needs would give the conflict a centrality in public affairs that would become a reason to starve and dismantle the Great Society. Consequently, Johnson again chose to be less than candid about what would be required to fight the war.[15]

It was a tragic error. Instead of openly confronting the hard choices the country now faced in Vietnam and encouraging a national debate, he obscured the harsh realities—planning, for example, to expand troop commitments month by month without acknowledging that decisions had been made for a doubling of forces by the end of 1966. For the second time in six months he had a chance to rally a generally receptive public to fight a difficult limited conflict and make Vietnam America's war. Instead, he chose the path of indirection, which irrevocably made the struggle Lyndon Johnson's war and all that would mean for a President presiding over a potentially losing cause.

A national debate was no guarantee that the country wouldn't first support and then later want to abandon a costly limited war. But it would have given Johnson political protection from charges that he escalated without giving Congress and the public their democratic right to choose. Moreover, it would have given him greater political and psychological freedom to alter policy in response to developments at home and in Vietnam. It seems fair to say that Johnson's political instincts failed him or that his imperious self eclipsed his accommodating side in making war policy.

The can-do, grandiose part of Johnson didn't anticipate insurmountable political liabilities in identifying Vietnam as his war. Exaggerated optimism about the conflict was a counterpart to his fears that the war would surely ruin him. In the winter of 1965–66, when the press described the conflict as "McNamara's war," Johnson told Califano, " 'That man is under a terrific strain and he can't take that. I've got to make this my war. I've got to stop the press from calling it McNamara's war because it will break him. And I need him and want him here.' "[16]

Johnson finally agreed to a bombing pause on December 27. But it was fraught with uncertainty. The day before, after a Christmas truce ended on the ground, Johnson considered whether to resume bombing as well. Rusk and State Department subordinates wanted renewed air strikes and a pause later after the White House had made clear to Moscow that a major peace effort was under way.

Mac Bundy, McNamara, Jack Valenti, and Bill Moyers counseled otherwise. The latest polls showed 73 percent of Americans eager for a cease-fire, with 61 percent favorable to "all-out bombing" of the North if no negotiations followed a pause. Moyers and Bundy warned that a resumption of bombing before the New Year would result in attacks on the pause as "half-hearted." General Maxwell Taylor also urged a longer halt as a way to show "the American public that we have left no door to peace untried." McNamara, who spent three hours talking to the President at his ranch on the evening of the 27th, pressed the case for a longer pause. He and Taylor saw little, if any, negative military consequences resulting from an extended bombing halt.[17]

In response, Johnson agreed to begin a "peace offensive." He was skeptical that it would come to anything, but he hoped it would refute Communist propaganda and prepare the country for a larger war: "The prospect of large-scale reinforcement in men and defense budget increases of some twenty billion for next eighteen-month period requires solid preparation of American public," Rusk told Lodge. "A crucial element will be clear demonstration that we have explored fully every alternative but that aggressor has left us no choice." Johnson himself told Averell Harriman: "We don't have much confidence that much will come out of this but that is no reason not to try. . . . I think with your friends Fulbright, Scotty Reston, Mansfield, Arthur Krock and the *New York Times*, all these people thinking there could be peace if we were only willing to have peace, we ought to give it the old college try."[18]

Now that he had agreed to make another effort for peace, Johnson intended, as he told George Ball, to make "sure we have bled it for all it is worth." The President instructed him to coordinate a worldwide campaign and explained that he "wanted him here because he was inspiring, stimulating and 'shoving.' " Johnson also explained that he wanted no time limit set on the pause, and concluded with another admonition that "Ball was not to let 'them' talk him out of anything."

Johnson's advice to Ball sounds like what he must have been telling himself: Having signed on to the pause, he would not let the military chiefs or conservative war hawks or his own doubts deter him from an all-out push for peace.[19]

Beginning on December 28, messages went out to dozens of countries, and personal envoys flew to European and Asian capitals to press the case for talks with Hanoi. Humphrey carried the word to Tokyo, Manila, and New Delhi; Harriman traveled to Warsaw for talks with the Polish government; U.N. Ambassador Goldberg went to the Vatican, Paris, and London; while America's Ambassador to Burma informed North Vietnam's Consul General in Rangoon of the pause and our eagerness for a reciprocal response. The President's envoys informed 115 governments around the world of America's peace blitz.[20]

To assure that "we come through loud and clear" to Americans as well as other governments, Rusk held a press conference in which he emphasized America's eagerness for a settlement that would grant South Vietnam self-determination and initiate a process of development for all of Southeast Asia. The President also asked Ball to talk to Fulbright, Mansfield, and conservative Senator Bourke Hickenlooper of Idaho. Johnson wanted Ball to assure Fulbright that the President was not slighting him and that the peace initiative "is just an execution of what Fulbright has talked about." He wanted the same done with Mansfield, explaining that we "are doing what Mansfield has said." The message to Hickenlooper was different. Ball was not to "let Hickenlooper think we are retreating. Re the bombing nothing much could be gained bombing during Holy Week; the weather is not good; and we are just telling everybody about our position."[21]

All the President's pushing and hauling produced no significant results. Hanoi gave no sign of agreeing to negotiate; they were letting "us stew in our own juice," Johnson said. He also had reports that the Communists were taking advantage of the pause to strengthen their military position.

Nevertheless, he put the best possible face on the peace campaign. He said privately that the bombing pause had created "a better basis to call on the U.S. people not only for their sons, but also their treasure. Americans feel better if they know we have gone the last mile." Rusk now told Lodge that "Lyndon Johnson understands power and its use. He is now gathering his political forces at home and abroad. He is not going to give away South Vietnam and he is not going to fail to meet the commitment of the U.S. Indeed if I were a leader in Hanoi and not prepared for peace, I would be a very worried man."[22]

But it was the President who should have been worried. His talk about American readiness to expand the war was largely wishful thinking. True, military chiefs and Senate hawks like Stuart Symington and Dick Russell urged prompt renewed bombing "with additional target license." But other congressmen, journalists, and many ordinary citizens found it difficult to understand Johnson's policy in Vietnam and doubted the wisdom of a larger war.

Jack Valenti drove home the point to him in January. "We have to, simply, logically and honestly, tell the people why we fight, and how enormous are the stakes in their future," Valenti wrote the President. "One reason for some unpopularity of the war is the queasy notion that we ought not be there since our vital interests are not really involved." When Valenti suggested a presidential statement "of the 'why' and the 'where,' " Johnson agreed and asked him to "draft it in a hurry."

Ball also gave the President reason to believe that his policy rested on shaky support. After testifying before the House Foreign Affairs Committee, Ball reported a shift from being "gung ho" about Vietnam to wanting "a way out." Johnson expressed concern that the House would become more skeptical as he expanded U.S. commitments and that the "Senate will be worse than the House." He feared that divisions in Congress and a critical press would upset the "people." He "felt it was a very difficult problem to steer a course which would be reasonably acceptable to diametrically differing forces."[23]

The Senate Foreign Relations Committee particularly worried Johnson. As Ball prepared to go before Fulbright's committee on January 12, the President told him to stress that the door was "open for any of their suggestions." But he wanted the committee to understand that debate and opposition to the war would "destroy the morale of our people." After testifying, Ball reported that the committee didn't "see any solution other than the course being followed." Nevertheless, they still weren't convinced this was a wise policy. They couldn't see any "permanent advantage" for us at the end of the fighting.[24]

But Johnson couldn't understand the committee's confusion over American goals. He thought the matter pretty straightforward. Communist North Vietnam was trying to destroy South Vietnamese independence and bring Saigon under its control. The Chinese supported Hanoi as part of a drive for a Communist Asia. America's national interest dictated the containment of Asian Communism as it had blocked Soviet expansion in Europe and the Middle East.

The antiwar opposition read Hanoi's actions differently. This was essentially a civil war, with North Vietnam sustaining a long-term anticolonial struggle to free all of Vietnam from Western control. As for China, it saw America's war in Vietnam aimed as much against Peking as Hanoi. The struggle in Vietnam was part of a larger

American campaign not simply to contain Communism but to destabilize and defeat it everywhere.

In short, Johnson and the antiwar opposition did not speak the
same language. Moreover, he was uncomfortable with congressional
hawks who wanted to unleash U.S. power to end the war quickly,
but showed little concern for the dangers involved. Consequently,
when the Foreign Relations Committee asked the President to hold
direct discussions with its members about Vietnam, he wanted no
part of it. Neither committee hawks nor doves would change his mind
about what needed to be done; nor did he believe he could alter their
thinking on Vietnam. Instead, he met with Democratic congressional
leaders on January 24 and a larger bipartisan group of representatives
and senators on the next day.

Both meetings confirmed his feeling that there was an unbridgeable gap between himself and congressional critics. On the 24th,
Mansfield argued against a resumption of bombing and warned
against a conflict with China. Louisiana Congressman Hale Boggs
cautioned against an indefinite pause, and House Speaker McCormack
thought the suspension was making the U.S. and the President look
weak.

At the meeting on the 25th, with Fulbright present, a sharper
debate erupted. Fulbright and Mansfield urged a continued lull, since
the "best chance of getting to [the] peace table is to minimize our
military action." Fulbright asserted that we were now "properly accused of taking the place of the French." We should "try to find a
way out" before we found ourselves at war with China. By contrast,
Dirksen urged the President to "do what is necessary to win." Russell
echoed the point: "For God's sake, don't start the bombing halfway.
Let them know they are in a war. We killed civilians in World War
II and nobody opposed. I'd rather kill them than have American boys
die. Please, Mr. President, don't get one foot back in it. Go all the
way."[25]

Johnson was unhappy with both sides in this debate. He saw
the Fulbright-Mansfield policy as a strategy for defeat, both in Vietnam and at home, where he thought conservatives would destroy his
administration for having given in to Communist aggression. But the
win-or-leave approach didn't hold much appeal for him either. He
shared Fulbright's concern that it could precipitate a war with China,
which might then escalate into a nuclear confrontation with Moscow.
Partly based on private polling results, he believed that the majority
of the country favored his middle-ground course: a measured escalation of pressure on Hanoi aimed at forcing peace talks and the
preservation of Saigon's independence.

Despite the general national support for his policy, he knew, as the polls showed him, that there were "a lot of uneasy people" on whom he might not be able to count in a drawn out, costly conflict. A late January opinion survey on renewed bombing, for example, revealed a deep national division: 44 percent favored resumption; while 42 percent wished to give negotiations more time to develop. Nevertheless, Johnson saw no alternative to the steady escalation he now believed essential on the ground and in the air.[26]

By late January, his first order of business was to resume bombing North Vietnam. But he struggled with questions of when and how to do it. He wanted to extend the pause, but with "no indication of any success at all," he couldn't see imposing "hardships on our soldiers much longer."

With all his advisers urging a resumption, except Ball, who believed bombing the North gave little help to the South and threatened to provoke a war with China, Johnson declared: "We haven't bombed in thirty days. But they have done nothing. They are reinforcing— rebuilding—reinfiltrating— . . . We have gone longer than anyone thought necessary."[27]

Though Johnson had doubts about the military value of renewed bombing and offered no effective public explanation of how the bombing would shorten the war, he believed it essential for South Vietnamese morale and to show North Vietnam that we would not give up the struggle. Between January 26 and 30 he held five private discussions on ending the lull. He believed it essential to "emphasize how sorrowful we are" as a way to blunt Fulbright and Mansfield. He also expressed concern about provoking Chinese intervention and wanted suggestions on how to prevent it.[28]

But he saw no alternative to renewed air attacks. "The only way to get a fellow to talk to you is to show strength," he declared in one meeting. "If you stop bombing they will go for something else. If you let them run you out of the front yard, they'll run you out of the house. I don't want war with Russia or China. . . . [But] I don't want to back out—and look like I'm reacting to the Fulbrights. We must realize the price we pay for going back in. We will lose a good part of the Senate."[29]

Johnson kept coming back to the domestic opposition that he faced in fighting the war. He told advisers and a group of "wise men,"—Clark Clifford, Arthur Dean, Allen Dulles, and John J. Mc-Cloy—"I see each day serious difficulties, mounting of pressure. It may result in deep divisions in our government. A year ago, by 504 to 2, the Congress told the President to do what was necessary in Vietnam. Today they [war opponents] could muster probably forty

votes. The Majority Leader and the Chairman of the Foreign Relations Committee are against the general policy of that resolution."

The President wanted some assurances on how long it would
take to break the Communists' will. General Earle Wheeler thought
"within the next two years we ought to get favorable results." But
Max Taylor believed that Hanoi would keep going as long as they
saw divisions in the United States that might force us out of the war.
"Our enemy gets great encouragement from the opposition voices
here. Is that right?" Johnson asked. "Yes. It's true," Taylor replied.
Dean and Clifford urged the President to stand firm and convince
the North Vietnamese that we would not relent. "They will never
talk until they are so convinced," Clifford said. The President replied:
"I am not happy about Vietnam but we cannot run out—we have to
resume bombing."[30]

At the same time he announced renewed bombing on January
31, he said that the end of the pause did "not mean the end of our
pursuit of peace." Johnson asked for an immediate meeting of the
U.N. Security Council to discuss means of getting to the conference
table. He also expressed "full sympathy" with a renewed peace appeal
by Pope Paul.

In meetings with advisers leading up to his announcements, he
said: "We have to demonstrate to people that we are not Goldwater.
. . . We can't talk about peace on [just] Saturday morning. We must
do it all the time." He was worried that the renewed bombing would
put "the Fulbrights and the Morses under the table and the hard
liners will take over—unless we take initiatives. I can see a lot of
things developing in the future to distress us. So let us keep peace
emphasis on."[31]

The Honolulu Conference

The renewed bombing provoked fresh expressions of dissension in the
United States. Hawks, as militants now began to be called, complained that Johnson had set back the war effort by the pause, and
it was about time he gave Hanoi a full dose of U.S. firepower. House
Armed Services Committee Chairman Mendel Rivers warned the administration that the war was "getting very unpopular the way we
are conducting it." Limiting targets and slow escalation was playing
the Communists' game. It wouldn't faze them to wait ten years,
Rivers said. "They would wait 100 years. That is their business. And
furthermore they are Orientals, add another 100 years for Orientals,

they will wait you out. The American people want this thing over yesterday."

Doves, as antiwar activists were described, protested against the expansion of an immoral and unwinnable war. They warned that Johnson was going to increase troop commitments to 500,000 men and was leading the country into "a cataclysmic world conflict." At a Senate Foreign Relations Committee hearing on January 28, Fulbright said he had never seen so much apprehension in the country over a military involvement. On February 4, Fulbright's committee began hearings on the war that attracted widespread public attention generated by unprecedented live gavel-to-gavel coverage from the three television networks.[32]

Disturbed by the criticism, Johnson wished to offer fresh dramatic proof that renewed bombing and increased troop commitments were in the service of long-term peace and development in Vietnam. On February 4, as the Fulbright hearings began, the President announced that he was going to Honolulu for three days to meet with Lodge, Westmoreland, the Vietnamese Chief of State Nguyen Van Thieu, and Prime Minister Nguyen Cao Ky. He stressed that the discussions would cover military and nonmilitary matters, particularly agricultural, educational, and health-care reforms in Vietnam. Secretary of Agriculture Orville Freeman and HEW Secretary John W. Gardner would be going with him to help advance these ends. Johnson's message was clear: He was a man of peace who wanted a speedy end to the war in order to build a secure and prosperous future for all of Southeast Asia.[33]

At the same time, the President tried to blunt the impact of the Foreign Relations Committee hearings. He told reporters that Rusk, McNamara, and General Wheeler would not appear before the committee because public testimony might aid the Communists. The way to avoid such problems was through private hearings, with appropriate parts of them released to the press.[34]

Johnson now saw Fulbright, Morse, and other members of Congress as unwitting Communist dupes. He asked the FBI to study comments made at the hearings to see if they reflected Communist views. Though Hoover was unable to show that Communists or other subversives were influencing Johnson's Senate critics, the President asked the FBI to keep a close watch on Communist diplomats in the United States to see if they were "making contacts with senators and congressmen and any citizens of a prominent nature." The President believed that "much of this protest concerning his foreign policy, particularly the hearings in the Senate, had been generated by [Communist officials]."[35]

Johnson's belief that subversives were the hidden authors of war criticism gave him license to dismiss antiwar opponents and counter their "propaganda" by fair means and foul. Consequently, he asked the FBI to spy on Congress, and used the Honolulu conference first to divert attention from the Fulbright hearings and then to suggest that future American efforts in Vietnam would be focused as much on "pacification" or winning the battle for hearts and minds as on fighting a larger air and land war.

Johnson believed that his presence at a conference in the Pacific was the most effective way to sell American and world opinion on his Vietnam policy. Jack Valenti had urged him to meet with Ky and show everyone the "cordial relations" between them and their "combined faith in the kind of world that can be built without fighting in South Vietnam."

Johnson was also responding to a recommendation from Bill Moyers that he publicly explain the war. "No one has ever had greater success with the direct approach to people than yourself," Moyers wrote on January 25. "A television image coming forth with another statement from Washington" simply lacked the impact that an appearance "in front of the people" had. Johnson was convinced: "Let's go somewhere every Fri & Sat," he jotted on Moyers's memo. He also wanted to take the initiative away from critics like Bobby Kennedy, who publicly said on January 31 that military action alone in Vietnam would assure nothing. Rather, "new programs of education, land reform, public health, [and] political participation" offered the best hope of "achieving our aims in Vietnam."[36]

Though the conference was to stress "pacification," the President's first order of business on arriving in Hawaii was to discuss the military situation with Westmoreland and McNamara. The President wanted Westmoreland to tell him about possible plans for a stepped-up offensive and whether he needed more manpower. "At present pace, how long will this war last? Must the U.S. take over control of the war, advancing beyond the support role? . . . What effect does our bombing actually have on infiltration? On Hanoi's capacity to wage war?" Johnson also wanted to know whether Westmoreland saw Washington as too controlling of bombing targets in North Vietnam, and what the general hoped would come out of this meeting.[37]

At the same time, however, Johnson believed that social change in South Vietnam could go a long way toward defeating Communist subversion. Pickets at the Honolulu airport carrying signs—"Vietnam for the Vietnamese" and "Protect what freedom in Vietnam?"—heightened Johnson's determination to identify his Vietnam policy with democratic reforms. At the opening conference session he told Ky that "the struggle in your country can finally be won only if you are able to bring about a social revolution for your people."[38]

Ky was more than ready to accommodate himself to the President's requests. Johnson's notes on Ky's response described him as largely parroting the President's call for social reform: "1. *Coop of People* 2. Establish mod society in country side—carry Social Rev from bottom not from top. 85% of population are peasants in countryside. They have suffered for 100 years—Must have *support of people*—3. Must have good well trained honest dedicated cadre. 4. Destruction of all VC Infrastructure."[39]

Ky's comments won high praise from the President. "When you talk about giving land instead of taking food from the land, and when you talk about building schools instead of beheading teachers, and when you speak of erecting clinics instead of firing mortars and destroying them, you speak our language," Johnson said. "We applaud your statement. When you talk about defeating the Viet Cong and social misery and establishing a stable economy and a democratic government, you speak our platform."

Johnson was not willing to leave the matter there. He wanted concrete suggestions for attaining these goals. "I hope every person here from the United States side," he said, "will bear in mind that before I take that plane back, I want to have the best suggestion obtainable as to how we can bring better military pressure on Hanoi and from the pacification side how we can bring a better program to the people of South Vietnam."[40]

Johnson's insistence on prompt action extended to the Vietnamese. Though he publicly assured Thieu and Ky that how they accomplished their social revolution "must be your decision," he privately pressed the Vietnamese leaders to develop specific economic, social, and political steps for implementing the program of reform.[41]

In his closing remarks the next day, Johnson explained that he had not gone into questions about "growing military effectiveness" because he didn't "want to overshadow this meeting here with bombs, with mortars, with hand grenades, with masher movements." The objective had been to talk about "building a society."[42]

The final conference communiques reflected the President's concerns. In a joint statement by Johnson, Thieu, and Ky and in "The Declaration of Honolulu," the two sides described the purposes of the South Vietnamese and the United States in fighting the war as "defense against aggression, the work of social revolution, the goal of free self-government, the attack on hunger, ignorance, and disease, and the unending quest for peace."[43]

Despite the knowledge that the conference and its final pronouncements were essentially exercises in rhetoric crafted by the
President's advisers on the plane to Hawaii, Johnson and his aides
treated the meeting and its high-minded declarations as realistic solutions for transforming South Vietnam into a stable, popular democracy that could win the war against the Communists. Johnson
told the conference that the final communique "will be a kind of
bible that we are going to follow."[44]

After the conference, Johnson cabled Lodge: "I was particularly
impressed with the apparent determination of Thieu [and] Ky ... to
carry forward a social policy of radical and constructive change." He
intended to do everything possible to make it work, and he wanted
Lodge to give "a clear and visible sign to the Vietnamese and to our
own people that the Honolulu Conference really marks a new departure."

Auto-intoxication is the only way to describe what LBJ and his
aides said about the meeting. Rusk characterized the talks as "not a
stunt" but "hard-working and successful." Mac Bundy, who went to
Saigon after the conference, told Johnson that "the general atmosphere here is enormously better than it was a year ago." Bundy saw
"the change from 1965" as "fantastic." Valenti, who was with Bundy,
cabled the President that press skepticism about the meeting, "which
was high at first, is now diminished. General reaction is that conference did truly focus on defeating social misery."[45]

The idea of winning in Vietnam by transforming the country's
economic and social life had great appeal to LBJ. Like the antipoverty
crusade in the United States, this was a war Johnson could readily
understand. Because he didn't want to lose momentum and wished
to keep the spotlight off the Foreign Relations hearings, he asked
Humphrey to meet him in Los Angeles on February 8, where he
announced that the Vice President would go to Saigon and other
Asian capitals to implement the work of the conference.[46]

Humphrey, who was a standing symbol of reform energy in
Johnson's White House, accepted the assignment with much pleasure
and determination to fulfill the President's noble aims. He soon compared the Honolulu Declaration to FDR's Atlantic Charter, saying it
represented a Johnson Doctrine for "realizing the dream of the Great
Society in the great area of Asia, not just here at home." Privately,
he told Johnson that he could "cut the Gordian Knot by a stroke of
history as significant as the Emancipation Proclamation by a massive
land reform program. This would leave the Viet Cong without a cause
and would provide an economic underpinning for a democratic government."[47]

Humphrey's trip lasted two weeks and took him to nine countries, including South Vietnam. The problem, as Jack Valenti described it to Johnson, was "to come up with meaningful and newsworthy events" that the "unusually large" and "high level" press contingent could translate into appealing stories for consumption in the United States.

On February 24, the day after Humphrey returned, he briefed the President and congressional leaders at the White House. He saw no "easy solution" nor a "speedy end" to the conflict, but he was confident that "aggression can be defeated, subversion could be stopped, [and a] social revolution can be started." The only concern the Asian leaders showed about U.S. policy was over "our perseverance to stick it out."

Johnson promised not to cut and run. He said the SEATO agreement, in which we promised to resist aggression, should be enforced. Also, he had asked and received a congressional resolution of support before he had begun to bomb and send in ground forces. "If you choose, you can repeal the resolution. I think I have the authority without the resolution." House and Senate leaders assured the President that repeal "wouldn't get to first base. Repeal wouldn't get four votes," Dirksen said.

Johnson expressed puzzlement over "why Americans who dissent can't do their dissenting in private. Once we are committed to a program of action, there has never been public dissent." Forgetting the divisions in the United States over the Korean fighting and World War I, Johnson said, "You have to go back to the Civil War to find this public dissent. . . . Our men understand why we are in Vietnam even if senators can't." Johnson also complained about suggestions to bring the V.C. into the Saigon government: "To treat VC, who are murderers and assassins, as legitimate government would disintegrate all that we have in Vietnam." The Honolulu meeting had "focused attention on the 'other war.' Now the eyes of a major campaign have been opened to ending poverty."[48]

The war now so engaged Johnson, Humphrey, and most other foreign and defense policy makers in the administration that they could no longer respond unemotionally to criticism of their actions. Having committed American lives, prestige, money, and their political fates to the struggle, Johnson and most everyone else in the government who had urged greater U.S. involvement felt a keen need to see it through. They had come too far to turn back. They could no longer be reasonably objective about the outcome of the fighting. They clutched at anything that hinted of success or seemed like a program for "holding the line," "turning the tide," or preventing

South Vietnamese collapse. There was a quality of illusion to every-thing they now said and planned for Vietnam

As Humphrey's aides prepared a report on his trip, for example, Jack Valenti told them: "The President wants optimism; the President wants optimism." And Humphrey, honoring his promise to be a com-pliant Vice President, gave it to him. The "tide of battle, which less than a year ago was running heavily against the Government of South Vietnam, has begun to turn for the better," he wrote LBJ. "The Honolulu Declaration emphasizing the defeat of aggression and the achievement of a social revolution could represent a historic turning point in American relationships with Asia."[49]

Humphrey's positive picture of developments did not square with what war critics saw as the harsh reality of an unwinnable war propping up an unpopular government at the cost of more and more American lives. A private discussion between Humphrey and Ful-bright became so heated and the questioning so sharp that Humphrey is supposed to have cried. "You know we all love you," Fulbright reassured the Vice President.

A public exchange between Rusk and Fulbright revealed similar tensions. To the Secretary, the war was a simple matter of repelling Communist aggression and honoring our commitments. Fulbright, by contrast, described the conflict between North and South Vietnam as "a civil war" lacking the sort of vital interest worth the cost of many lives and much money. He also believed that a compromise settle-ment would not hurt but rather enhance America's world prestige as a self-confident, strong, magnanimous country. When Fulbright as-serted that "there is something wrong with our approach," Rusk coun-tered: "Senator, is it just possible that there is something wrong with them [the Communists]?"

At a closed session of the committee, McNamara and Fulbright squared off on American strategy. Fulbright pressed McNamara to say what we would do if the North Vietnamese kept fighting despite increases in U.S. force levels. After all, they had been continuing the struggle for twenty years. Though McNamara privately had been predicting such a stalemate, he refused to acknowledge that possibility to Fulbright.[50]

Tensions over the war now made for adversarial conditions that discouraged reasoned discussion of an escape from the fighting. The traditional middle ground of American politics was giving way to ideological strains that left little room for maneuver between "hawks" and "doves." "You are either with us or against us" became the pos-ture both sides adopted toward the war. After retired General James Gavin testified against the war, Johnson, or so Gavin believed, arranged an IRS audit of his tax returns. When retired Ambassador George Kennan, who was also critical of the war, appeared before the committee, CBS President Frank Stanton, a friend of LBJ's, decided to show reruns of *I Love Lucy* and *The Real McCoys*. News division head Fred Friendly resigned in protest.

Johnson now saw no reason to hold additional discussions with war critics. Advice that he talk to Gavin and Kennan about the conflict and that he reconcile differences with Fulbright and Mansfield fell on deaf ears.[51]

With diminishing prospects for some sensible consensus on what to do about Vietnam, each side waited on events to prove that their judgment on the war was right.

Reality Bites

Beginning in March and on through the spring of 1966, war critics had much the better of the argument. The hopes generated by the Honolulu declarations rested on illusions that could not withstand conditions in South Vietnam. A French journalist conversant with the country's political life asserted that the Hawaii meeting had "exposed the nearly total failure of a great Western power to understand public opinion in a small country.... In organizing the conference Washington had hoped not only to strengthen Ky's position but to encourage him to be more flexible politically and to undertake social reforms. However, so far as most Vietnamese were concerned, Washington had already shown unprecedented contempt for their country by imposing Premier Ky on them in the first place; to them, the meeting was no more than a summons from a foreign general to a cocky lieutenant—a glaring example of Saigon's 'abject' dependence on Washington."[52]

In fact, the dependence was a two-way street: Washington needed Ky's government almost as much as Saigon needed Johnson's support. Without a stable regime in South Vietnam, U.S. ability to combat a Communist takeover seemed certain to collapse. Consequently, in February and March, when Buddhist leaders allied with General Nguyen Chanh Thi, Commander of the Central Highlands, pressed for an end to the fighting and internal reforms repugnant to Ky, the State Department privately warned against "any actions that would weaken or bring down the present government and with it the military and development efforts which have been so laboriously brought to at least the beginning of hopeful stage."[53]

On March 10 the Saigon government moved to blunt Buddhist

pressure by dismissing Thi and forcing him to leave the country for four months. Since Ky and Thieu assured Washington that Thi's removal would solve their problem, Johnson and his advisers accepted the action without protest.[54]

Thi's dismissal sparked protests in Vietnam that included dissident takeovers in Danang and Hue. The upheaval shook Johnson's confidence about Vietnam and intensified his fears of Communist gains. On March 12, he told a group of state governors that "our country is constantly under threat every day—Comm[unists] working every day to divide us, to destroy us. Make no mistake about the Comm[unists]," he said. "Don't kid yourself a moment. It is in the highest counsels of gov[ernment]—in our society. McCarthy's methods were wrong—but the threat is greater now than in his day."[55]

Who was Johnson thinking of? Were his remarks just hyperbolic rhetoric meant to scare war critics into "getting on the team"? Or did he actually believe that congressmen, senators, and journalists were intent on overturning the country's traditional institutions? It is difficult to take his comments at face value. Whatever his propensity for suspicion—even paranoia—it is hard to imagine that he genuinely saw high government officials and prominent reporters as secretly promoting Communism at home or abroad.

Yet at the same time, he could not accept the view that his opponents were expressing independent judgments. From his perspective, anyone in America who thought carefully about the war would see the need to resist a Communist advance. Johnson believed that some academic critics were "gullible" men mesmerized by romantic assumptions about the virtues of Communism in Vietnam. Their naivete made them vulnerable to the Communists, who, he believed, skillfully encouraged and orchestrated their opposition to the war.

Four days after his meeting with the governors, Johnson told Lodge to warn the Buddhists against overturning everything we have been working toward. They were creating "chaos and anarchy" which made U.S. support ineffective.[56]

Though the political crisis continued in Vietnam through March, Johnson behaved as if the United States had no choice but to fight on. Planning for economic, political, and social change proceeded as promised in Honolulu, while the President agreed to deploy another 65,000 men by August 15, bringing the total to 325,000.

At the same time, the White House expanded its campaign to unite Americans behind the war. Nothing was to be said about troop increases until the additional forces arrived in Vietnam. Nor were there to be any indication that we were taking more control of Saigon's domestic and administrative affairs; any hint of this seemed certain to provoke additional war protests in the United States.[57]

Despite all our efforts, Johnson wondered whether we could prevent a Communist victory. At a meeting with advisers on April 2, he stated his intention to "make every effort to keep Ky. But be ready to make terrible choice. Perhaps take a stand in Thailand—or take someone else other than Ky." At another meeting two days later, Johnson took a more determined stand. He was worried about a constitutional assembly Ky agreed to call to blunt Buddhist demands. Johnson said he would "rather have someone we can control . . . than a communist takeover at the Assembly." Max Taylor warned against "a Tri Quang government. He will tear down everything." Johnson urged "more planning on how to pick a man before he takes over so we won't have to get out when the wrong man gets in . . . The way I see it," the President said, "Ky is gone, the last gasp. Doubt he can pull it off. When he goes, there'll be hell in this country. Let's get a government we can appoint and support."[58]

The President's concern with how to interpret these developments was well founded. During March he saw a steady erosion of support for himself and his Vietnam policy. Poll results released early in the month showed Johnson's approval rating at 46 percent, its lowest level since he had taken office. The survey also registered a sharp jump in public disapproval to 34 percent. Pollsters agreed that the cause was frustration over Vietnam.[59]

One prowar congressman warned that the President was piling up a lot of trouble for himself by not being honest with Congress. At the White House briefing on February 24, the President had given "no indication whatsoever that any substantial troop increases were being contemplated for the immediate future. . . . Then just a very few days later the announcement came that 20,000 more US troops were on their way. This . . . had created considerable disillusionment . . . and . . . raised the question of the credibility of the administration." Johnson rejected the complaint as unwarranted. He circled the beginning of a sentence—"If the President had frankly said they would have to send more troops"—and wrote in the margin: "I say this every time I open my mouth."[60]

Likewise, Johnson rejected the advice of Fulbright, John Kenneth Galbraith, and Jack Valenti that it was time to get out of Vietnam. Fulbright urged negotiations to neutralize Vietnam and all of Southeast Asia. Johnson replied that Hanoi and Peking would not negotiate, and, besides, our experience in Laos suggested that the North Vietnamese and Chinese would not honor an agreement, even if they signed it. Galbraith told Johnson that Ky's fall would provide "an opportunity only the God-fearing deserve and only the extremely lucky get"—namely, to make "an orderly withdrawal." Valenti also sent a heartfelt plea "to find some way out of Vietnam. All that you strive for and believe in, and are accomplishing is in danger, as long as this war goes on." Valenti saw "no reasonable hope. All your military advisors assert you must double your force, and still they give you no prophecy of victory. . . ." Johnson made no written reply to either Galbraith or Valenti.[61]

Instead of withdrawal, he signed on to greater U.S. involvement. On April 2, when Ky asked Lodge to help suppress the rebels in Danang and Hue by providing transport planes, Lodge agreed. Though Johnson did not reverse his ambassador's decision, he told Lodge "to keep our troops and equipment out of riot area. We don't want to become involved."

Political pressure, however, was another matter. Johnson wanted the embassy to help arrange a solution to the crisis "as quickly and as peacefully as possible." He instructed Lodge to have "substantially more contact with GVN and with opposing and other political elements than has hereto seemed wise either to you or to us." The Buddhists were to be told "that present situation represents grave danger of simply handing over country to VC and that they must cease to insist on unrealistic demands." Pressure was also to be applied to General Thi, and should he resist advice not to become a candidate, "we may have to face up to it and consider how we would handle."[62]

Partly driving the reach for greater control in Vietnam was the belief that U.S. military power was beginning to be decisive. Since 1961 the Viet Cong had allegedly suffered three times as many battlefield deaths as South Vietnamese and U.S. forces and four times as many wounded. Moreover, on April 8, Deputy Defense Secretary Cyrus Vance reported after a trip to Vietnam that "we are doing well militarily and are continuing to impose heavy losses on both the VC and North Vietnamese."

Maxwell Taylor also urged an expanded air war. "In the eyes of the Hanoi leaders, the ground war in South Viet-Nam must now appear to be going rather badly," Taylor told the President, "and it is important that they receive an equally discouraging impression from the air war. Not until they get a gloomy composite from both is there much hope of bringing them to negotiations."[63]

Walt Rostow held a similar view. If Saigon got through the current political crisis intact, he advised, "we will have passed a great turning point." The Communists would see "it as a major defeat. Then will be the time to pour it on and see if we can't force, in the months ahead, a resolution of the conflict. The strain on our political *and economic life and the strain on the South Vietnamese is all but intolerable.... We've got to try to shorten this war without doing unwise or desperate things."*[64]

Though Ky wanted to unleash his military against the rebels in early April, the White House discouraged him. An unsuccessful use of force would reflect badly on the United States, which had abetted the campaign through an airlift and supplies of heavy armor. Johnson believed it essential to precede any attack with political steps aimed at greater democracy. Only by this means would the United States be likely to preserve its influence with "major [political] elements" in Vietnam.[65]

While Johnson struggled to find a way to resolve the political crisis in Saigon, he grew more confident that the U.S. would achieve its ends in the war. An opinion poll in New York reaching him on April 11 showed a resurgent approval rating of 67 percent compared with only 53 percent for Bobby Kennedy, the state's junior senator. Better yet, 78 percent of a Massachusetts poll said that the government's handling of Vietnam was "satisfactory." The President heard additional good news from Bill Moyers, who reported that prominent columnists "from Reston to Russ Wiggins to David Lawrence are quietly applauding the reserve and patience you are showing in the midst of so much flux in Vietnam."[66]

At the same time, Johnson received fresh news of military gains that heartened him. Robert Komer, Johnson's deputy on pacification, returned from Saigon in mid-April to report that "our splendid military effort is going quite well." On the 20th, an estimate of Communist casualties showed startling results: Where from November 1965 to February 1966 the enemy had suffered total loses of between 8,700 and 12,000, the numbers for March alone were between 11,000 and 15,700. In early May, Johnson received a report from the Rand Corporation "on the extensive damage done to the Viet Cong and North Vietnamese during the past three months." As Rostow told him, "It is distinctly encouraging, but does not indicate a decisive break in VC morale yet."[67]

Moreover, as one national security analyst cautioned, "you can make a case for a somewhat less optimistic view of VC casualties than ... presented." Estimating total losses for March at between 6600 and 7500, this analyst thought "there might not be any erosion at all" in Communist strength. Since the VC/DRV buildup might be larger than estimated, the enemy might have ended the month with more troops in the South than assumed.[68]

With so much uncertainty over Vietnam's political future, Johnson and his advisers decided to make some "basic" policy decisions.

At a meeting on April 25, Johnson agreed "to continue roughly along present lines. . . . We shall stay on course and explore with Lodge a cautious Track B," meaning an attempt to draw the Viet Cong into talks, with an eye to causing divisions among them. The embassy was also to reiterate to the Saigon government "that our continued support is contingent upon adequate unity and effectiveness on the part of the Vietnamese."[69]

But all the discussions in Washington and verbal pressure on Saigon couldn't shape affairs in Vietnam. The State Department believed that the election of a constitutional assembly was essential for domestic and international "support of our Vietnam policy." Ky, however, put this in jeopardy by announcing on May 6 that he would hold power until elections in 1967. Rusk wanted to threaten to leave Vietnam if Ky didn't give control to an assembly before then. Johnson rejected the suggestion: He told the National Security Council on May 10 that "we are committed and we will not be deterred." In other words, even if democracy were deferred in Vietnam, it was essential that we prevent a Communist take over in Saigon.[70]

American incapacity to shape events in Vietnam made itself clearer in mid-May, when Ky unilaterally decided to end the political crisis by forcibly retaking control of Danang. Rusk saw it as "intolerable" that Ky had acted "without consultation with us." The challenge now was "to pick up [the] pieces and prevent a major debacle."[71]

Johnson was determined to carry on as before and try to persuade the Vietnamese to end their internal divisions before they lost their country to the Communists. Lodge, who was back in Washington for consultations, declared: "Damn the torpedoes! The hell with it. Even if we haven't got a government in Saigon, let's keep going." Johnson tried to put the best possible face on the difficulties. At a press conference on May 21, he defended the South Vietnamese, saying, "They are trying to build a nation. They have to do this in the teeth of Communist efforts to take the country over by force. . . . There is . . . no instant solution to any of the problems they face."[72]

Though Ky succeeded during May and June in suppressing the rebels in Danang and Hue, the crisis took a substantial toll on American public confidence. As Wheeler told Westmoreland, "even if we get some semblance of solidarity and common purpose among the contending factions, . . . we have lost irretrievably and for all time some of the support which until now we have received from the American people. In other words, regardless of what happens of a favorable nature, many people will never again believe that the effort and the sacrifices are worthwhile."[73]

The War at Home

The political crisis in Vietnam in the spring of 1966 intensified divisions in the United States over the war. Where about half the country believed it best to continue the current policy, 35 percent wanted to withdraw, a 15 percent increase over the previous year. The most striking feature of the polls in the midst of the political divisions in South Vietnam was American confusion and frustration. Our inability to force Hanoi to the peace table or into submission bewildered Americans. How could a country as powerful as the United States be unable to work its will on so weak and undeveloped a nation as North Vietnam?

The impulse was to blame LBJ. It seemed up to him to find a way out of the mess by either applying more power or relying on diplomacy to end the fighting. People didn't want to hear about the way in which a limited jungle war against a determined adversary operating under favorable circumstances blunted the effectiveness of U.S. power. Richard Russell reflected the national mood when he declared that it was time to "get it over or get out." By June 1966 only 41 percent of Americans approved of the job the President was doing in Vietnam, with 37 percent disapproving.[74]

Public attitudes toward the war, in turn, bewildered Johnson. He had made sincere efforts to negotiate but the Communists would not talk. He believed it was going to take more troops, more bombs, and more enemy losses before they came to the peace table. But there was no shortcut to doing this. If he expanded the war too much—striking at targets indiscriminately in the North or invading with ground forces—it might lead to a wider war with China and/or Russia. The need was for patience and moderation. But U.S. losses in the fighting and pessimism about getting results from a policy of measured force heightened American impulses either to "declare victory and leave," as one senator counseled, or "bomb 'em back to the stone age," as an air force general advised.

The divisions and uncertainty frustrated no one in the United States more than Johnson. As he told the press conference on May 21, "the longer we are there [in Vietnam], the more sacrifices we make. The more we spend, the more discontent there will be. The more dissatisfaction there will be, the more wish and desire there will be to get out. Leading that parade is the President. If you want to feel that it troubles you 100 percent, just double that and make it 200 percent for the President."[75]

Since Johnson believed it irresponsible to withdraw or escalate too much and since he had no magic bullet for ending the conflict quickly and in line with what he saw as U.S. interests, he renewed his efforts to educate the public and strengthen support for his policy of limited but unrelenting military pressure on Hanoi. "We are trying to provide the maximum deterrents that we can to Communist aggression with a minimum of cost," he told the press. He didn't think his "explanation will change anyone's mind," but he hoped it clarified what he was doing and what he intended to do "down the road."[76]

Though he made light of changing anyone's mind, the President, in fact hoped that he could weaken opponents of his policy by fair means and foul. One side of him saw the need for a thoughtful, reasoned appeal to Americans to understand and support what he believed was in the best interest of the United States. Another side encouraged him to view opponents as Communists or at least sympathizers who had few qualms about undermining the well-being of the country and against whom he should pull out all stops.

A number of Johnson's advisers believed that a series of well-timed and well-crafted public appeals could increase public understanding and support for the war. As they saw it, the administration had a communications problem. If they got out the right message in the right way, the country would stand fast until U.S. power forced a favorable outcome in Vietnam.

In April, Bill Moyers urged the President to give a televised talk "to a proper gathering of young people, stressing your desire for a humble peace, [and] internal and worldwide social progress." Walt Rostow also thought it was time for the President to confront his critics. "The Viet Nam debate is about over," he told Johnson in May; "it is time to rally the 60% of the country to sweat out the next stage with confidence."[77]

Former Johnson aide Horace Busby urged the President to understand that "until the people have a sense of participation and sacrifice [in the war]—confusion will increase, frustration will spread, irritation will rise hazardously." Busby recommended "a fireside setting, you alone with America," in which the President talked "philosophy" not programs and manifested "*self-confidence, natural ebullience and buoyancy.*" Lodge also thought a fireside chat was in order. He wanted Johnson to say: "We are involved in a vital struggle of great difficulty and complexity on which much depends. I need your help."[78]

In May, Johnson took his case to the country through speeches at Princeton University and at Democratic party dinners in Washington and Chicago. Speaking with "great feeling," he urged his audiences to understand that America's presence in Vietnam served no selfish gain. To the contrary, it involved the sacrifice of American lives to aid the cause of democracy and freedom. America's struggle in Vietnam was not an act of arrogance but an agony to deter aggression with limited means and for specific ends. He emphasized the need for American unity in this time of testing, for the only hope of success held by our adversaries rested on "a weakening of the fiber and the determination of the people of America."[79]

At a private meeting with members of the NSC staff in May, the President emotionally described our task in foreign policy as "to help bring peace to the world. The pursuit of peace requires strength and power; for we must never run from bullies. But in the pursuit of peace power counts for 10%, love for 90%. In all your waking hours you must carry in your minds the thought of the 5 or 6 billion human beings in the world.... The best recommendations I receive are prepared with a sense of obligation to humanity."[80]

Johnson couldn't understand how people saw him as a villain in the struggle. He sincerely believed that the war from the American side was a fight for people everywhere—not just in Vietnam—to enjoy freedom from political oppression and economic want. He was so convinced of the rectitude of fighting in Vietnam that he could only ascribe the worst motives to his antiwar opponents. On the plane to and from Princeton, for example, he spoke about "the concerted effort [in universities] to destroy the CIA." He "discussed FBI evidence of how the Communist sources stimulate propaganda lines on Vietnam."[81]

If he had used the theme of Communist subversion in March as essentially a political weapon against antiwar opponents, by May he seemed to have convinced himself that the danger was real. The proliferation of student protests against the war, including marches, rallies, picketing, and sit-ins on university campuses, the decision of professors around the country to deny information on students to the Selective Service without the student's permission, the tactic of civil rights leaders in trying "to drive a wedge between the poor and the rest of the country" by arguing that Vietnam meant taking money from the ghettos, and a media he saw giving one-sided "nation-wide publicity" to war opponents persuaded Johnson that sinister forces were behind the push to abandon Vietnam.[82]

Eric Goldman remembers that by this time "the domestic reformer of the Great Society days had become a war chief.... The ebullient leader given to moments of testiness and rage was now, day after day, bitter, truculent, peevish—and suspicious of the fundamental good sense and integrity of anyone who did not endorse the Vietnam War. This Lyndon Johnson was not only depressing; at times he could be downright frightening."

Goldman recalls an informal session at the White House with a Cabinet member and three aides over potato chips and soda. The mention of a liberal Senate war opponent brought a sneer to the President's face. These liberals were "crackpots," who had "just plain been taken in. . . . It's the Russians who are behind the whole thing," he declared. The FBI and the CIA "kept him informed about what was 'really going on.'" He described the Russians as "in constant touch with anti-war senators. . . . These senators ate lunch and went to parties at the Soviet embassy; children of their staff people dated Russians. 'The Russians think up things for the senators to say. I often know before they do what their speeches are going to say.'"[83]

J. Edgar Hoover was particularly active in feeding Johnson's suspicions. On May 13, Richard Russell participated in a two-and-a-half-hour discussion at the White House, which "mostly [focused on] Vietnam & CIA investigation. Talked to J E[dgar] H[oover] while I was there. [He] showed me visitors to S[oviet] Embassy & contacts."[84]

Animated by his suspicions, Johnson publicly belittled and privately harassed war critics. On May 12, in a speech to congressional Democrats at the National Guard Armory in Washington, D.C., Johnson snidely declared his pleasure at being here tonight, "with so many of my very old friends as well as some members of the Foreign Relations Committee. You can say one thing about those hearings," he added, "although I don't think this is the place to say it."[85]

The next day Harry McPherson told the President that he had been "disturbed by the speech," which he complained "was harsh, uncompromising, over-militant. It seemed you were trying to beat Fulbright's ears down before an audience of Democrats who . . . had earlier applauded him strongly. . . . The combination of tone, emphasis and frequent glances down at Fulbright made it (for me) wrong."[86]

McPherson's letter caused Johnson to dig in his heels. He gave McPherson the "freeze-out treatment" for several days, and used a dinner speech to Democrats in Chicago to hammer his opponents again. He urged against divisions over the war and suggested that Americans ask whether each public official and candidate for office was "trying to draw us together and unite our land or . . . trying to pull us apart to promote himself." He also warned against "Nervous Nellies" who under the strains of the war "will turn on their leaders, and on their country, and on our own fighting men." McPherson thought the "Nervous Nellie" remark "was a political disaster."[87]

Johnson was particularly keen on striking out against the media. Their occasional carelessness in inaccurately attributing to the "Johnson administration" a view or policy described by a junior official stirred him to complain privately. In April, when he caught the *New*

York Times in such an error, he instructed Rostow to bring it to Tom Wicker's attention. Though Wicker assured him that "this was a professional error of judgment" and not an indication of "ill will on the part of the *Times,* or an effort to do a hatchet job on our administration," the President was not appeased.[88]

He saw the television networks as even worse than the press. He believed they gladly showed pictures of atrocities by South Vietnamese or U.S. troops, but ignored a UPI story in May about the killing of twenty-seven women and children and the wounding of twenty-eight others by the Viet Cong. He pressed the networks to show pictures of this horror on the evening news, and asked the United States Information Service to distribute them in "this country." He also wanted to know why NBC undercut him by using a first-take of him speaking, in which his glasses glistened, rather than a third tape that made him look better.[89]

Johnson was convinced that the press hated him and wanted to bring him down. Newspaper, magazine, and television reporters complained to Robert Kintner in April, as he began working at the White House, that the President was overly sensitive about what "is printed about him." The journalists believed that Johnson would "not be able to work most effectively as President because of this concern. A great many of the people talked about how they were cut off from White House offices if they disagreed with administration policy." The reporters also complained about the President's tendency to mislead them.

By early June, Moyers was reporting that "the White House Press Corps has come to believe that we antagonize them deliberately, keep them as uninformed as possible, make their personal lives as difficult as we can, play games with them, are unduly secretive, massage them when we need them and kick them when we don't and generally 'downgrade the profession.' "[90]

If these complaints were suppose to cure Johnson of retaliatory impulses, they failed badly. In May, when he reviewed a White House guest list for a Presidential Scholars' ceremony, he approved everyone invited "except in category 17, newspapermen." He added the names of eleven journalists he considered friendly to him and deleted six he viewed as hostile: Russell Baker, Art Buchwald, Robert Donovan, Walter Lippmann, Peter Lisagor, and James Reston.[91]

Lisagor, the Washington bureau chief of the *Chicago Daily News,* particularly irritated LBJ. In June 1965 Lisagor published an article revealing that the Russians had sent Ilyushin-28 medium jet bombers to Hanoi. Johnson told J. Edgar Hoover that the article "was most disturbing." Since only Secretaries Rusk and McNamara, Under

Secretary of State Mann, and the Joint Chiefs knew about this, the President wanted the FBI "to find out how this information was leaked ... and from what source." The bureau learned that Lisagor had gotten his information from a friend who was married to an air force general.[92]

The following February Marvin Watson complained to Deke DeLoach that "the President feels Lisagor [who was very critical of the war] is tearing him apart and getting information from some place and thought we ought to put a surveillance on him to find out what he is doing and where he is getting his information." Since Watson did not allege that Lisagor was doing anything illegal, DeLoach replied, "We could not do that; if it were found out it would bring considerable discredit not only on the FBI, but the President himself." Though DeLoach told Hoover that "the White House understands this," it nevertheless pressed for "something substantive" on Lisagor.

Hoover and DeLoach agreed not to put "any positive emphasis on investigating Lisagor," but to leave the matter hanging by telling Watson that "we have various lines out to get a line on Lisagor." Though an FBI follow-up a week later noted that "Lisagor constantly attacks the President," it could report only that he was a very skilled reporter who worked extremely hard, was "one of the most able 'diggers' in the Washington press corps," had "many sources," "a knack for picking out significant remarks" made at briefings, and held the trust and respect of prominent officials, including the Vice President and Bobby Kennedy.[93]

No critic bothered Johnson more than Fulbright. They were old friends with mutual regard for each other's talents. But they were at dagger points over the war. Fulbright simply couldn't believe that "white men of Western stock can ever build a decent order in South Vietnam. We just don't belong there," he said; "we are alien to their culture, and where the French failed, we will fail." He appreciated that the United States simply could not pull out, but he thought that a secret emissary could convince Ho Chi Minh that we wanted compromise, not victory, and that this would get us to the negotiating table and out of Vietnam. Fulbright feared that an expanded conflict risked a confrontation with China and/or Russia that would be disastrous. His concerns about the war were so strong that Bill Moyers, who spoke with him privately in February, believed he had passed "beyond the pale of reasoning."[94]

Whatever his emotions about the conflict, Fulbright believed it essential to make a reasoned case against the war, which he did in a series of lectures at the end of April on "The Arrogance of Power."

He warned America against seeing its power as "a sign of God's favor, conferring upon it a special responsibility for other nations—to make them richer and happier and wiser, to remake them ... in its own shining image. Power confuses itself with virtue and tends also to take itself for omnipotence."[95]

Johnson took Fulbright's attack personally. He could not understand how someone who had supported the Tonkin Gulf Resolution so warmly could now be so critical of its implementation. He was furious at Fulbright's decision to hold open hearings attacking the administration's war policy. In March, after they had ended, the President called in the national commander of the American Legion and asked him to "take the initiative in having thousands of letters supporting the war sent to Fulbright." He asked that their discussion "be kept in strict confidence" and be viewed as "very definitely top secret."[96]

Believing that Fulbright's "arrogance of power" lectures were personally directed against him, Johnson used a White House reception attended by Fulbright to object to the characterization of himself as "arrogant." Fulbright, who believed it essential to keep lines open to the President, wrote Johnson a conciliatory note on May 9, saying that "never at *any* time have I spoken, or even thought, of *you* in connection with arrogance." He explained that he was referring to nations and hoped that "*this* country, presently the greatest and the most powerful in the world, may learn by the mistakes of its predecessors. I believe that under your leadership we will avoid similar mistakes." Fulbright concluded by expressing the hope that his viewpoint, which differed from that of "some of your advisers, ... can be of help to you."[97]

Johnson was not appeased. His Washington and Chicago speeches expressing disdain for Fulbright's views followed on the 12th and 17th. Yet at the same time, he believed it essential to maintain a working relationship with Fulbright and his committee. Consequently, on April 27, he had invited Fulbright and his wife to fly with him to a Democratic fund-raising dinner in Houston, but a previous engagement kept the senator from attending.

On May 27, Johnson sent Fulbright a cordial reply to his note. Written by Moyers, the letter nevertheless reflected the President's view that the lesson, above all, we need to learn from recent history was what happened when "aggressive powers are freely permitted in areas where the peace of the world is delicately balanced, to use direct or indirect force against smaller and weaker states in their path." The letter also took exception to the suggestion that the President might have some differences with his advisers. He asserted that there was great harmony in his administration on Vietnam, but that even if there were differences, the policy was his and not that of "my 'advisers.'" Johnson closed with a warm personal expression of hope that "our differences of policy have [not] erased the friendship we have shared for so long. I have a fondness for Betty and you that is real."[98]

In this renewed spirit of cordiality, Johnson agreed to meet privately with Fulbright at the White House on June 1. In a conversation lasting nearly two hours, the President dominated the discussion, reviewing the options open to him in the war and explaining how he was acting in the national interest. Fulbright made clear that he still did not have confidence in the administration's policy, but intended to "keep in touch" with the President. During the next two weeks, the senator attended three White House ceremonies, including one on June 15, where "the President greeted him warmly as an old friend, put his arm around the senator and talked animatedly for several seconds."[99]

In a fifty-minute private discussion with Fulbright following the public session greeting a goodwill delegation from Austria, Johnson reverted to what Fulbright characterized as "a highly emotional harangue." Emphasizing his determination to apply enough military might to force the Communists into a settlement, the President seemed more "insecure" and "frenetic" than Fulbright had ever seen him. "Fulbright went back to Capitol Hill very troubled. He told members of his staff he was afraid the President was beyond a rational discussion of Vietnam. The senator feared that while Johnson was in this mood, he was capable of almost any recklessness, including the bombing of China." Johnson's behavior was another demonstration of the "paranoia" that Moyers and Goodwin had seen in 1965 and others had remarked on in subsequent months.[100]

The Illusion of Omnipotence

In 1952, D. W. Brogan, a British historian and commentator on American affairs, described U.S. foreign policy as suffering from the "illusion of American omnipotence": the belief "that any situation which distresses or endangers the United States can only exist because some Americans have been fools or knaves." In Vietnam, as the limits of American power in a jungle war against a determined enemy became clear, policymakers in Washington succumbed to false convictions that our real enemy was the "fools and knaves" at home who gave encouragement to Hanoi and sapped our will to fight.[101]

Johnson, impelled by the same grandiosity and energy that encouraged him to think he could conquer poverty and build a Great Society, gave himself over to breaking the will of North Vietnam. He simply couldn't believe that they could sustain indefinitely American military punishment. Nevertheless, he also worried that further escalation might bring domestic riots, a draining war against China, and a dire confrontation with Moscow. For all his bravado with Fulbright about using American power to break Hanoi, Johnson had his doubts. The agitation that Fulbright witnessed from the President on June 15 reflected these concerns. As he moved toward a renewed emphasis on military actions in the air and on the ground, he worried whether he was doing the right thing. Was he now taking steps that would finally bring the war to a close or was he rushing headlong toward some disaster?

His first order of business in June was to decide on an escalation of the air war. He and his advisers had been talking about this since early in the year. Though there was no persuasive evidence to show that more bombing would compel Hanoi to negotiate, Johnson and his advisers convinced themselves that attacks on petroleum, oil, and lubrication (POL) facilities and transportation lines would disrupt North Vietnam's communications system and reduce its capacity to move men and supplies South.

At the end of May, Johnson told British Prime Minister Harold Wilson that it was becoming "essential" to "reduce their [North Vietnam's] oil supply in light of the radical increase in the flow of men and materiel by truck to South Vietnam. For me the calculus is, simply, whether they shall have less oil or I shall have more casualties."[102]

During the first two weeks of June, the President largely decided to expand the air war. Partly spurred by Lodge in Saigon, who asserted that Hanoi was "disturbed by the vigor of our bombing" and "feeling real pain," Johnson told Prime Minister Wilson that he saw "no way of avoiding such action, given the expansion of the illegal corridor through Laos, the continuing buildup of North Vietnamese forces in South Viet Nam, the growing abuse of Cambodian neutrality, and the absence of any indication in Hanoi of a serious interest in peace."[103]

On June 15, Rostow reported hopeful signs of "a change or the beginnings of change" in Hanoi's attitude toward negotiations. He thought that the casualty rate in the South and "the cumulative weight of the bombing in the North" were having their desired effects. But he counseled against becoming too optimistic or letting up our military pressure at this critical stage of the war. Johnson agreed. The next day he sent Rostow to press the case for more bombing with U.N. Ambassador Arthur Goldberg, who believed escalation might force a confrontation with the Russians without much impact on Hanoi. Nevertheless, Goldberg promised that he would be "a good soldier" and would follow the President's lead.[104]

At an NSC meeting on June 17, the President declared that he would hold off on a decision to strike POL targets until Rusk returned from a NATO meeting, a Canadian diplomat reported on a visit to Hanoi, and the State Department could inform allies. Because the choice, as Johnson described it, was between higher U.S. casualties and escalation, because there was "no uncertainty" about his authority to increase the bombing, and because the American people wanted "a quick end to the war," he had essentially decided to expand the air attacks.

Only Goldberg objected. He disputed the claim that bombing POL targets would save American lives. Since the attacks would have to include Hanoi and Haiphong, the Chinese and Russians would see this as a direct challenge. They would not let North Vietnam "go down the drain."

Goldberg convinced no one. Humphrey, Rusk, and McNamara, all of whom had previously raised questions about hitting POL facilities, now believed it essential to defeat the North Vietnamese. CIA Director Raborn saw no chance that China would send troops into Vietnam, and USIA Director Leonard Marks urged a decision based on military considerations rather than concerns about world opinion. "In order not to be lobbied on the decision," the President said, "not another soul should be informed of this discussion."[105]

On June 22, an NSC meeting discussed the issue again. Why hit POL now? McNamara asked. Because "this is now an important target. Tonnage to the South is increasing; truck traffic is up 100%, personnel infiltration 120%."

The President asked what results the Joint Chiefs expected. Wheeler predicted that in 60 to 90 days it would " 'affect the total infiltration effort.' " Johnson wanted to know " 'what might I be asked next? Destroy industry, disregard human life? Suppose I say no, what else would you recommend?' 'Mining Haiphong,' " Wheeler answered. "Do you think this will involve the Chinese Communists and the Soviets?" the President asked. "No, sir," Wheeler replied. "Are you more sure than MacArthur was?" Johnson said, recalling the failure to anticipate Chinese intervention in Korea. "This is different," Wheeler assured him. "We had ground forces moving to the Yalu."

After the President expressed his concern that public approval was deteriorating and would "continue to go down," he asked everyone around the table how they stood. Only Goldberg opposed. He still did not think more bombing would bring Hanoi to the peace table. To the contrary, he believed it would lead to a greater North Vietnamese presence in the South as well as more involvement by China and the Soviets. It would also increase criticism of U.S. policy at home and abroad. "Any warnings you want to give me before I go to commune with myself and my God?" Johnson asked. George Ball endorsed more bombing, but he thought the disadvantages would equal the advantages.[106]

Johnson did not wait long to make up his mind. A few hours after the NSC meeting, he discussed Vietnam with thirty-two members of Congress who had visited the country. The President, who looked very tired and had to keep himself from nodding off when others spoke, nevertheless gave a spirited defense of administration policy, predicting that "we are going to win!" He based his judgment on the heavy casualties suffered by the Communists, the reestablishment of Saigon's political control, prospects for national elections, and steps to bring inflation down and stabilize the economy.

"If some people thought he was going to waver because they didn't like this policy, they didn't know him," Rostow said of Johnson. ". . . He [LBJ] referred sneeringly to the actions of 'some senators' and said that Hanoi read their remarks more carefully than we did." As with civil rights, the war had become an extension of himself—of his presidency, of his place in history—and he would never give in, or so he believed in his optimistic or upbeat moments when he reassured himself that America would stand behind him and that we would force Hanoi into settling the war.[107]

Additional assurances in late June that he was on a proper course cinched his decision to expand the bombing. On the 21st, he received a report from Paris that Vietnamese Communists in France had begun to doubt the likelihood of a Viet Cong victory and would sue for peace after one last try at weakening U.S. morale. "Here is some more noise indicating a wobbling mood in Hanoi," Rostow wrote the President. "It also reinforces our instinct that they are waiting to assess our political strength, as well as the outcome of the rainy season operations." Four days later, Rostow told Johnson, "Mr. President, you can smell it all over: Hanoi's operation, backed by the Chi[nese] Com[munist]s, is no longer being regarded as the wave of the future out there. U.S. power is beginning to be felt. We're not in; but we're moving."

"Good," Johnson wrote on the bottom of the memo, "See me." On June 29 U.S. air forces began bombing POL targets. The day before Johnson had asked McNamara to accelerate the movement of

U.S. ground troops to Vietnam "so that General Westmoreland can feel assured that he has all the men he needs as soon as possible."[108]

The expanded bombing was partly aimed at Americans who hoped that it might force Hanoi to negotiate. On June 4, Johnson gave Rusk the bad news that "those approving my conduct of the presidency have fallen to 46%. Those who believe it was a mistake to send troops to fight in Vietnam have risen from 25% in March to 36%. Only 49% now believe it was not a mistake." The mounting criticism in the country that the administration was not "properly or comprehensively explaining our plans," especially for Vietnam, also troubled Johnson. "We may not agree with the criticism," he told the Cabinet in mid-June, "but it does exist." Moreover, by the end of the month, only 40 percent of the country approved of the President's "handling" of Vietnam, with 42 percent disapproving.[109]

Johnson was now so apprehensive about facing hostile audiences during domestic appearances that he asked the FBI to "send 'an advance man' along with Secret Service to survey the situation" in Des Moines, Iowa, and Omaha, Nebraska. He "wanted the FBI's opinion as to whether or not it would be safe for him to go." Although the bureau and Secret Service saw no danger from visiting these two midwestern cities, the White House held off announcing the trip until the morning of his departure on June 30. Aside from picketing by a few dozen anti-Vietnam demonstrators, the crowds were friendly and enthusiastic, and "there were no security problems of any sort."[110]

The best answer Johnson saw to the growing opposition was not only to increase military pressure on Hanoi but also to lobby Americans to "get with the program" or back their President and the "boys" in the field.

During June, memos flew back and forth at the White House on how to orchestrate this latest campaign for the country's hearts and minds. Bob Kintner took the lead on how to make the President more appealing to the "people" and more persuasive on Vietnam. But most everyone on Johnson's staff got into the act. Kintner urged him to hold "informal" discussions with the press; Rostow suggested a speech at Notre Dame University on reconciliation. "It would be, in effect, your Gettysburg Address of the Cold War."[111]

Johnson himself wanted to leak supporting data to a friendly columnist, and directed Califano to work with the National Security staff in preparing a brief defending the administration's "credibility" on Vietnam. Larry O'Brien suggested a meeting with nine House members with outstanding war records who, after visiting Vietnam, would give the President "a solid report in full support of you." Komer wanted Lodge to take "a more active role in 'guiding' the Saigon

press corps on what's really going on out there. It's the Saigon date-
lines that cause most of the trouble," he told LBJ. "Bill M. and I are
as one on this."[112]

Most of all, Johnson wanted critics to understand that dissent
and division were hurting the war effort and needed to be curbed.
After Kenneth Galbraith gave a critical commencement speech on
Vietnam, LBJ answered him in a letter: "And did I misread your
admonition to quit talking about Viet Nam and discuss the gains of
the Great Society?" he asked. "Then why don't *we*?"

He delivered the same message to Mansfield. Johnson urged him
to understand that the Communists were "watching us very closely
here to see how we react and whether or not we are a divided people.
Once they become convinced that we are not weak; that we are not
impatient; that we are not going to falter; that they cannot win . . .
then peace will come."[113]

The expanded bombing produced expected results only in its
impact on U.S. public opinion. During the first half of July, as Americans learned about the stepped-up air war, their hopes for a quick
end to the fighting soared and their support of the President's Vietnam policy jumped 12 points from 42 percent to 54 percent. Eighty-
six percent of the country believed the bombing would "get it over
with" in Vietnam "fairly soon, either by military victory or by negotiations." By a 5 to 1 margin Americans backed the bombing of oil
depots near Hanoi and Haiphong. Even if this meant causing civilian
casualties, 61 percent of the poll still thought such air attacks justified.[114]

Hopes for an end to the conflict were quickly disappointed. Two
months after the POL strikes began, military planners described the
bombing as having no significant impact on Hanoi's economy, will
to fight, or capacity to move men and supplies to the South. An
analysis of the fighting by the U.S. mission in Saigon in mid-July
painted a bleak picture: It concluded that a *"decisive military victory
for either side is not likely."* On August 8, the *New York Times*
reported that a Pentagon study predicted it would take eight years to
win the war unless U.S. forces were increased to 750,000, and then
it would take five.[115]

In August, a Defense Department study by four former science
advisers to the government said the bombing had had little impact
on North Vietnam; nor was there reason to believe that expanding
the air war or mining Hanoi's harbors would bring better results.
Attacks on transportation lines had done little to slow infiltration, and
raids against the limited number of industrial targets available had
small impact on a largely agricultural society. Worse yet, the scientists

"concluded that with very few exceptions our information on communist logistics and manpower was so inexact that it was difficult to come to any conclusions as to the effectiveness of our military policy. It is not an exaggeration to say that the data is so soft that we cannot state with confidence whether we have been doing better or worse militarily over the past year."[116]

Johnson refused to concede these realities. To be sure, he kept saying that no one should assume that the conflict will end soon, but he held to the conviction that American power was hurting Hanoi and that we were moving forward. On July 11, he met with fourteen congressmen who had come directly to the White House after a trip to Vietnam. Their report from the fighting front was everything Johnson wished to hear: We were winning, and it was the "Peaceniks" in the House and the Senate who "caused the Viet Cong to fight harder and gave them cause to hold out."[117]

A week later, when he met with congressional leaders, Johnson reported that "Viet Cong morale had been lowered by U.S. successes. The Viet Cong are recruiting teenagers 12 to 16. There have been reductions in food rations in each unit. U.S. forces have broken their transportation system. The Viet Cong have lost popular support. The Viet Cong exploit dissension in the United States." He had some hope that the war might be over by June 1967. "We see a slackening off" of Communist attacks, he said. "Our intelligence is encouraging but we dare not be too optimistic. We are putting on all the pressure that we can put on. General Westmoreland will get all he needs."[118]

In public Johnson was as upbeat and optimistic. At a press conference on July 20 he pointed to an improved economy, steps toward an orderly democratic election, and ten-fold enemy losses compared with America's in South Vietnam. "We have ceased speculating a long time ago on how long this situation would endure," he declared. "But I have said to you and to the American people time and again, and I repeat it today, that we shall persist." On July 23, during a visit to Indiana, Kentucky, and Illinois, he catalogued "discouraging setbacks for the militant Communists." He promised not "to run out on South Vietnam," not to break America's word. "However long it takes, we will persist until the Communists end the fighting or until we negotiate an honorable peace."[119]

At a Cabinet meeting on the 26th, the President recounted his reception in the Midwest. He described the crowds as "large, interested, and approving," and said: "Don't believe our newspapers and Republican critics—the country is for our Vietnam policy; the country approves the accomplishments of the Great Society."[120]

Johnson's pronouncements were more the product of wishful

thinking than realistic assessments. By saying repeatedly that we were making progress in Vietnam and that we would not give in to aggression, it seemed to make it so. In July he instructed all Cabinet members to talk to congressmen and senators, to public groups, and to appear on television in behalf of our Vietnam policy. "We need this widespread explanation not only so that the public may be informed but so we may obtain a more united public support of our efforts."

He said he was mystified by accusations of a credibility gap. "In my thirty some years in Washington, I know of no administration that has informed Congress better. I know of no administration that has taken the public more in its confidence, even sometimes at the risk of security. . . . But this information operation cannot be spasmodic—it must be continuous . . . Whatever trouble we may have in public support—and it is much less than our critics advise—it can be quickly reduced by more information and more explanation."[121]

Johnson was right if he and his spokesmen were indeed presenting honest, realistic assessments of developments in Vietnam. But what Johnson described as "information" was really advocacy or statements of belief that did not always conform to objective realities in the war. The President seemed to think that if he and his aides spoke long enough and loud enough about Vietnam, he could bend the American public and the North Vietnamese to his will. Because so much of what he hoped for in the war was at variance with the realities of the conflict, his expressions of faith, which rested on sincere convictions about what the U.S. military could achieve in Vietnam, made him seem devious.

Time-Life journalist Robert Sherrod described Johnson's problems with the war in a memo of a confidential conversation with the President on August 1. As Sherrod waited in an outer office, he discussed the war with Lieutenant General "Brute" Krulak, who had been McNamara's counterinsurgency chief and had made more than forty trips to South Vietnam since 1961. Krulak described himself as "quite optimistic," and "half of the things he told" Sherrod "were to be repeated by Johnson as his own opinions." Sherrod thought this "somewhat alarming" because Krulak "had a poor record as a soothsayer," having "guessed wrong many times" on Vietnam in the last five years.

Johnson gave Sherrod forty minutes. Seated in a rocker, the President "squirmed and scrunched as he talked, and wound up his legs and torso, corkscrew fashion." In reply to Sherrod's question about how the war was going, Johnson replied: " 'It looks pretty good, improving all the time, but we've got a long way to go. We clean up these villages, we fill in the tunnels, we feed the people, we doctor them, we rebuild their houses and dig them wells. We start teaching them.' He leaned forward in his rocker, pulled up his pant leg, pulled down his sock and scratched his bare leg, and said, "But there are 14,000 of these villages and we've taken care of maybe a hundred of them. . . . A long way to go."

When Sherrod asked what the President thought of a prediction from "military sources" that it would take 700,000 men to win the war, Johnson bristled: " 'Nobody mentioned that figure to me, I haven't heard it before.' He paused for a few minutes. 'Whether it takes 700,000 or a million, we are going to do the job. . . . ' He said this with that unfortunate smirk that betrays him so badly on television—a sort of gloating smile that comes out as something he doesn't intend at all. Throughout the interview Johnson was almost belligerently defensive."

The President devoted about half the interview to attacking the press, particularly the *New York Times*, which he "obviously felt was persecuting him. . . . He sneered at Walter Lippmann. He referred several times to Scotty Reston in uncomplimentary terms." He said: " 'David Halberstam killed Diem. He made us assassinate him. That man is a traitor—so they give him a Pulitzer Prize. They give Pulitzer Prizes to traitors nowadays.' "

As the interview ended, Johnson said, " 'I appreciate your friendship.' " He told Sherrod, who was leaving for Vietnam, " 'If you can just go out there and write something constructive, you'll be doing a fine thing for us.' His tone was almost plaintive."[122]

A week after Johnson saw Sherrod, the *New York Times* published the Pentagon estimate that 750,000 troops would be needed in Vietnam and the President would have to call up the Reserves. Learning that Marine Commandant General Wallace Greene was the source of this assertion, the President read Greene the riot act. The following week, when Westmoreland met with LBJ at his Texas ranch, he assured the President that "we're going to win this war for you without mobilization."[123]

Negotiations and Pacification

During the summer and fall, Johnson heard continuing predictions of Communist faltering and growing eagerness for peace. Lodge was confident that the war was now moving in the right direction and that Hanoi saw itself as unable to win. The Viet Cong were also showing "a progressive decline in morale and fighting capacity."

There is "a smell of victory" in the air, Lodge cabled the President on August 10. "We are not losing; we cannot lose in the normal sense of the word; never have things been going so well."[124]

Johnson received encouragement from other sources and other developments. At the beginning of September, Jim Lucas, a UPI journalist who had spent two and a half years in Vietnam, gave a congressional briefing at the White House. Though the President introduced him as "not a propagandist of mine, and not a spokesman for the administration," the reporter left no doubt that he was a "hawk" who believed U.S. forces were turning the tide in Vietnam. He conceded that "this is going to be a long war," but he had every confidence that "we can reduce them [the Viet Cong] to bandit status" by pushing them up into the hills.[125]

In September, the Agence France Presse reported from Hanoi that air raids were causing a "food squeeze," with "an acute food shortage" in the cities. At the same time, internal upheavals in China caused by the Cultural Revolution eased Johnson's fears of Peking's intervention in response to expanded U.S. military actions. An 80 percent turnout in the election of a constituent assembly in South Vietnam on September 11 also heartened LBJ. One U.S. senator called the results "a shattering blow to the Viet Cong." The President took special satisfaction from American primary results two days later: thirty out of thirty-one Democratic and four out of five Republican antiwar candidates were defeated. A CIA report later in the month confirmed Johnson's hope that Americans had the "will to persist" in the war and would not succumb to antiwar arguments. No one objected to the CIA's unauthorized focus on U.S. domestic politics.[126]

Despite all the good news, abundant evidence of a likely stalemate in Vietnam prodded Johnson to remain alert to any signs of Hanoi's interest in talks. Though nothing seemed in the offing, it allowed him to answer critics that he was eager to negotiate. He was under constant pressure to begin talking. Journalists, academics, members of Congress, protestors, and foreign leaders continually urged the White House to start discussions. The English philosopher Bertrand Russell, for example, attacked Johnson's Vietnam policy as "a barbaric ... aggressive war of conquest," and in June 1966 he initiated the establishment of an International War Crimes Tribunal to condemn the actions of America's leaders.[127]

Johnson took pains to let the world know that the Communists, not the American government, blocked the path to a settlement. "I am ready to go anywhere, anytime," he told congressmen and senators. "Mr. Rusk will be there tomorrow morning to talk instead of fight, and to reason the thing out. We are willing to go ... but it takes two to make a contract." The President told Lodge: "I should like you, General Westmoreland, and Ambassador [William] Porter to know how greatly I appreciate the backgrounding you are doing in Saigon. One can see and feel their constructive impact on the press and television reports now coming from Saigon." When Leonard Marks asked USIA posts for "ideas to improve understanding of the United States' position in Vietnam," Johnson pronounced it "Excellent—I want more of this and I want to see response summarized."[128]

But trying to find an end to the war was not simply a case of public relations. Johnson was eager to throw off the burden of Vietnam as quickly as possible, though, of course, only on acceptable terms. "It's like a prizefight," he said in July 1965. "Our right is our military power, but our left must be our peace proposals. Every time you move troops forward, you move diplomats forward."[129]

Johnson didn't want for peace initiatives. Not a month went by in 1966 without some new proposal for discussions. United Nations, African, and Asian leaders urged talks and offered to mediate differences.[130]

But the gap between the two sides was unbridgeable. Hanoi insisted that the United States stop bombing, withdraw its forces, and include the Viet Cong in peace talks; Washington demanded that North Vietnam reciprocate a bombing halt with a cessation of infiltration. Despite the impasse, Johnson accepted the need for continuing efforts to begin negotiations. In the summer of 1966, the White House kept close track of every initiative and made "preparations for a 'cessation of hostilities.' "[131]

At the beginning of August, Johnson appointed Averell Harriman "ambassador for peace" to promote negotiations. The President told him to explore all possibilities "no matter how dubious or unpromising—in every corner of the world." Harriman set up an interdepartmental Negotiations Committee to discuss peace initiatives. He traveled 26,000 miles in one month, talking to world leaders in Asia, the Middle East, and Europe. He sent Johnson and Rusk weekly reports on the work of his "peace shop," as critics called his committee. But there was more show than substance to the operation. Harriman had no freedom to depart from administration pre-conditions, and he was not included in high-level discussions of war policies.[132]

Nevertheless, Johnson was serious about finding some basis for negotiations. At the beginning of August, for example, when he heard that a South Vietnamese official had "talked to Lodge about possible contacts with VC," the President instructed Lodge "to encourage SVN to begin to see what contacts [they] can make covertly with VC." Johnson wanted Ky, who at a July 27 press conference had called for an invasion of North Vietnam, to quit sounding off about going North and instead "launch [a] peace campaign based on Honolulu where he said, 'come on over.' "[133]

The President also saw these peace activities as good politics. One member of Harriman's group said that the committee had been "set up with part public relations in mind and more than a casual relation with the 1966 [congressional] elections." Jack Valenti saw negotiations as closely linked to political developments in the United States. He urged Johnson to tell the press: "The Viet Cong is watching the elections in November. If the President suffers defeat, they will *not* agree to sit down and talk for they will believe the country has deserted the President. If, however, the President wins in November, they *will* agree to ... talk for it will be clear the country is with the President."[134]

Bill Moyers had another idea. As November approached, he thought it "would have a greater impact on the election [than domestic travel] ... if you were to take a successful trip in October (10 to 14 days) to visit our allies in Asia. ... You could limit it strictly to countries with troops in South Vietnam. The right kind of trip would be a tonic for the country." Johnson told Moyers to check with Rostow, McNamara, and Rusk.[135]

Johnson hoped that "pacification" in South Vietnam might be an alternative to peace talks. If programs of "revolutionary development" could improve living standards in the countryside and tie rural villages to Saigon, the Communists would lose their base of support and be compelled to fade away or reach a settlement with the South Vietnamese government.

But hopes for pacification generated at the Honolulu meeting were not being realized. In June the President pressed Westmoreland to get behind the effort. "I've put the best man on my own staff to work on getting the civil side rolling, and am solidly behind [Ambassadors Robert] Komer and [William] Porter in this. I know you will give them your fullest support and cooperation. They need all the help you can spare." After a second trip to Vietnam in June, Komer told the President that our "other war" did not yet match our military effort. He was more candid with Bill Porter, whom he told that pacification was a "mess" and "farcical" compared with military actions.[136]

In August, as Communist main forces avoided direct battles with American troops, the U.S. military gave higher priority to pacification. At the end of the month, Westmoreland submitted a "concept of military operations" for the coming year that gave "direct military support of revolutionary development" in coordination with South Vietnamese forces and U.S. civilian agencies. Westmoreland's plan of action, Rostow told LBJ, moves "towards pacification, without reducing the heat on the VC or NVN main force units." Johnson replied: "Let's get Komer to pick up & spark the inspiration." The proposal pleased Komer, but he acknowledged that "keeping up the momentum won't be easy."[137]

Komer was right. A report coming to Johnson in mid-September from another pacification official said: "We are not organized, not mobilized, not staffed in Vietnam to do the job that must be done." Though Komer and McNamara tried to address "management" problems retarding pacification, they ran into a buzz saw of debate. As Komer told Bill Moyers when he taped a television interview on Vietnam, "Pray for me." Predictably, a compromise was worked out between military and civilian authorities. But McNamara, who now saw pacification as critical to American success in Vietnam, said the program to date was a "basic disappointment." Johnson agreed, and at an NSC meeting on October 15 he gave the administrative compromise 90 to 120 days to work before he put the program fully under military control.[138]

The debate about pacification added to Johnson's frustration over Vietnam. It was clear to him that U.S. forces were not losing in Vietnam, but it was also evident that negotiations to end the fighting were nowhere in sight. He felt trapped and besieged by an increasingly unpopular war. Speeches in the U.N. attacking American policy, coordinated nationwide antiwar demonstrations, and threats to his personal safety during public appearances disturbed him. Yet however much he wished to throw off the burden, he believed it wrong to let go, back away, or abandon the cause: It would be a betrayal of America's national self-interest, of the fighting men who had lost their lives and the hundreds of thousands more now at risk.[139]

To reassure himself that he had made the right choice and should persevere, he decided to meet with America's allies—the South Vietnamese, Thais, South Koreans, Filipinos, Australians, and New Zealanders—at a three-day conference in Manila from October 23 to 25. Moyers, who had proposed the idea, saw the meeting as a demonstration of solidarity with our friends rather than an effort to "accomplish substantive policy gains." The President privately acknowledged that "the conference will probably accomplish little so we must consider how to keep the initiative in the period ahead."[140]

The principal purposes of the trip were to bolster Johnson's morale about Vietnam and to sell American voters on the war. The President and Bill Moyers micromanaged every public relations aspect of the journey. Moyers believed the trip would be "a great big plus— if done properly." The most important thing was to turn out "good crowds . . . at the time of day that we can get the best possible coverage back in the States. . . . The success of this trip depends so much on press arrangements made well in advance." Johnson agreed to have Moyers head "a full advance team . . . , with people being left in each spot to get ready for your arrival." Johnson also asked Bob Kintner to look into network plans for television coverage of the trip, and to offer help transmitting pictures back to the States.[141]

Johnson told reporters that the conference would review military progress, but would focus on South Vietnamese evolution toward representative government and economic development, prospects for a peaceful settlement, and regional development for Asia, where "two-thirds of humankind live." Johnson directed aides to tell the press that the meeting was neither a war nor a peace conference but a get-together "to produce a unified statement of determination, of pursuit for an honorable peace and broader objectives in the Asian Pacific area."[142]

After the meeting, a Defense Department official told McNamara: "The conference went well. I think we got what we wanted: Display of not-U.S. aloneness, of resolve, of beginnings of an awakening responsible Asia, and of concern for the miseries of the Asian billions." Johnson took away a sense of exhilaration at the conference's pronouncements recommitting the allies to stand fast against aggression and fulfill the ideals of democracy and revolutionary development in Vietnam and across Asia.[143]

As Johnson had anticipated, no substantive gains came out of the meeting. Participants shared a new sense of resolve by reinforcing each other's commitments to the war. But Johnson saw the conference as largely a public relations coup. He inserted into the final communique a commitment to remove U.S. forces from Vietnam within six months of a settlement, which was also to require North Vietnamese withdrawal from the South. The provision was partly a response to a Soviet suggestion that such a statement might help foster peace negotiations. For Johnson, however, it was also a way to answer critics, who described U.S. involvement in the fighting as a new expression of Western imperialism in Southeast Asia.[144]

Part of Johnson's public relations campaign was a triumphal return to the United States. First in Anchorage on November 1 and then at Dulles Airport in Washington the next day, "throngs of well-wishers" greeted the President to hail his return from the longest presidential journey ever—seventeen days to seven countries covering 31,500 miles. South Vietnamese promises of quicker military, political, social, and economic progress and allied commitments to withdraw from Vietnam after an honorable peace were hailed as the principal achievements of the journey.

The presence of Fulbright at the airport, which was arranged by Hubert Humphrey, allowed Johnson to see a renewed political unity in the United States for a war the country "could not afford to quit." A poll on November 2 showing a 63 percent approval rating for his handling of Vietnam confirmed LBJ's wish to believe that the Asian trip had rekindled American determination to stay the course in Vietnam.[145]

The Search for a Winning Strategy

Whatever Johnson's satisfaction at the results of his trip, his return to Washington forced him once more to face hard questions about Vietnam. Should he increase the military pressure on Hanoi? Should he gamble that pacification or revolutionary development would overcome the Viet Cong? Should he try another bombing pause to stimulate negotiations? Everyone he spoke to had opinions on these issues, but who was right? "During the past ten days I have heard a hundred diagnoses of our problems and about as many prescriptions for solving them," Harry McPherson told LBJ in December. Johnson had limited confidence in the calculations put before him by the military chiefs or the CIA or his own National Security advisers.[146]

His only certainty now was that he had to see the job through. He believed it vital to stop "a vicious and illegal aggression" and to honor the fallen Americans in the war by a victory that gave meaning to their sacrifice. In an emotional speech to U.S. servicemen at Camranh Bay on October 26, he had pledged: "We shall never let you down, nor your fighting comrades, nor the 15 million people of Vietnam, nor the hundreds of millions of Asians who are counting on us to show here—here in Vietnam—that aggression doesn't pay, and that aggression can't succeed." He urged the troops, in an injunction that later subjected him to much ridicule, to "nail that coonskin to the wall." He said of his visit to the troops: "I have never been more moved by any group I have ever talked to, never in my life."[147]

He was impatient to get on with the struggle. In a letter to Henry Cabot Lodge in November, he wrote: "When this reaches you it will be about a month since Manila and perhaps 500 of our boys are gone. Make them all follow your orders and let's get going."[148]

Johnson knew that the longer the war went on the more difficult it would become to sustain domestic support, whatever faith he or anyone else might have in the country's "will to persist." At the end of November, Missouri Senator Stuart Symington told Rostow that "you and I have been hawks since 1961. I am thinking of getting off the train soon. . . . We are getting in deeper and deeper with no end in sight. In 1968 Nixon will murder us. He will become the biggest dove of all times. There never has been a man in American public life that could turn so fast on a dime." The President replied: "I know at least one more fellow who can turn faster on a dime than Nixon. Guess who!"

A Gallup poll at the beginning of December illustrated the limits of Johnson's support. His overall approval rating had fallen back to 48 percent; on Vietnam, it was down again to 43 percent, with 40 percent disapproving. "It is going to be hard work in the months ahead to hold the Congress and the country together," LBJ told Rostow on December 9.[149]

The columnist Drew Pearson echoed the opinion survey in a letter describing a drastic change in public feeling toward the President. Pearson was convinced "that in any vote right now the odds would be against your reelection." Mid-term attrition, Vietnam, and inflation were all working against him. But "an alarming amount is personal." Part of the reason "people don't like you" was "overexposure" and an unflattering portrait of him as "a powerful, physically, domineering Texan" who came across as "omnipotent."

Yet these personality traits had not deterred LBJ from winning a landslide in 1964 and sustaining high approval ratings until 1966. It was principally the war that was eroding his hold on the public. A successful conclusion to the fighting would go a long way to restore his public standing. But how could he bring the conflict to a close?[150]

In mid-October, after returning from a trip to Vietnam, McNamara had put an eight-page memo before the President proposing a solution to his dilemma. He saw "no reasonable way to bring the war to an end soon." Despite some improvement in the military situation, the Communists were not about to crack. They had "adopted a strategy of keeping us busy and waiting us out (a strategy of attriting our national will)." Pacification was "a bad disappointment." So was the air campaign, which had neither "significantly affected infiltration [n]or cracked the morale of Hanoi."

McNamara recommended that we "continue to press the enemy militarily; . . . make demonstrable progress in pacification"; and "add a new ingredient forced on us by the facts." He urged a "military posture that we credibly would maintain indefinitely—a posture that makes trying to 'wait us out' less attractive." He suggested adding 70,000 troops in 1967 to the 400,000 already committed and holding at that level. It would be ample to "punish the enemy" and keep him "from interrupting pacification." It would remove "the specter of apparently endless escalation of US deployments."

He also urged the construction of an infiltration barrier near the

17th parallel running from the South China Sea across the neck of Vietnam and the trails in Laos. He recommended stabilizing the air attacks with no increases in the level of bombing or changes in the areas or kinds of targets being struck. A vigorous pacification program principally involving the South Vietnamese was crucial to persuading the enemy "to negotiate or withdraw." Finally, we needed to make our negotiating efforts more credible by promising to withdraw from Vietnam at the end of the fighting, quietly trying another bombing pause, and developing a realistic plan for including the Viet Cong in the negotiations and a postwar government.[151]

Military and civilian advisers disputed much of what McNamara recommended. They saw a need for between 530,000 and 750,000 troops, more bombing of old and new targets, and an expanded pacification effort under U.S. military control. Rostow urged the need "now to lean more heavily on the North." He had reviewed all the bombing reports and concluded that Hanoi and Moscow and the Eastern European countries as well were paying a significant military and economic cost for the air war. They didn't like it and "that increased burden may add to their interest in a negotiated settlement."

Likewise, a CIA report challenged McNamara's conclusions about bombing and pacification, arguing that attacks on Haiphong and rail lines to China could have an impact on Hanoi and that pacification was doing better than the Defense Secretary believed and seemed likely to do even better in the next two years.[152]

The President agreed to most of what McNamara recommended. On November 11 he committed himself to stabilizing troop deployments to South Vietnam and bombing in the North. He endorsed McNamara's view that pacification was "critical to the success of our effort in South Vietnam," and he agreed to press the case for negotiations by appointing Nicholas Katzenbach, who had become Under Secretary of State, Komer, Rostow, Vance, and a "good military man" to a committee that was to "meet three times a week on Vietnam and all its dimensions."[153]

But Johnson found it difficult to stick to McNamara's formula. He was especially ambivalent about inhibiting the use of air power. The reports from the Joint Chiefs and CIA saying that bombing was achieving more than McNamara believed and that it was a U.S. trump card in forcing Hanoi to the peace table made the President reluctant to veto more aggressive air action. On October 15, he had told McNamara and Wheeler that he would hold to the limitations in place on bombing around Hanoi and Haiphong, but would agree to striking new targets.[154]

Johnson's willingness to broaden the air war reflected a larger conviction that there was some progress in the fighting and that 1967 could be a decisive year in compelling the Communists to begin peace talks. "By early 1967 most of my advisers and I felt confident that the tide of war was moving strongly in favor of the South Vietnamese and their allies and against the Communists," he later wrote in his memoirs. In December 1966, however, he was less certain than this. McNamara's assessment alone was enough to make him harbor substantial doubts about what the coming year would bring. But given his determination to stay the course, he welcomed every scintilla of good news and expression of optimism.[155]

And most of his advisers who, like him, felt compelled to see the bright side, to believe that somehow or other American power had to prevail over so weak an enemy, gave him words of constant encouragement about the likely outcome in Vietnam. "*You* are still dead right on all the big issues & you still know more about how to make them come out right than any man in America," Mac Bundy told him in November. "For the first time since 1961 the U.S. military in Saigon and Washington estimate a net decline in VC/NVN forces in South Viet Nam," Rostow wrote him two days later.[156]

Rostow and Komer sent him a series of papers in December laying out strategic guidelines for 1967. They brimmed with optimism. Despite "the immensity of the task," Komer was "convinced that if we can jack up our management in Washington and especially Saigon, and press the GVN a lot harder than we have, we'll be able to see daylight by the end of 1967." Besides, Komer asked, "Do we have a better option?" He knew his "recipe does not guarantee success but . . . does anyone have a better one?" Johnson thought not. When Rostow told him that Komer's 1967 plan for Vietnam made "a good start," the President replied: "I agree—it's good. Come in with Bob on Monday."[157]

No one beat the drum louder for positive developments in Vietnam than Lodge. "In the 'military' war, our capacity to defeat the big Communist units and destroy redoubts is so well demonstrated that I would expect a very different military situation indeed here by next year," he cabled Johnson on December 11. As for the political situation, "one need not be an expert to see the difference between . . . today and that which existed in November 1963. . . . Vietnam is moving towards constitutional democracy."

In a meeting with LBJ at his ranch eight days later, Lodge stated that many worries of a year ago in Vietnam had disappeared: "They no longer feared that the Viet Cong could cut the country in half," or "that regionalism backed by the Buddhists might tear the country apart. They no longer feared a Communist coup from within." As for future military developments, "The Ambassador 'expects brilliant results in 1967.' " Pentagon claims that comparative military casualties in Vietnam had increased from 2.2 to 1 in 1965 to 3.3 to 1 in 1966 made Lodge's estimate seem compelling.[158]

In the context of so much optimism, Johnson believed it essential to maintain pressure on Hanoi. In November, he agreed to attacks on new targets around Hanoi. Having largely committed himself to McNamara's strategy of restraint, he felt compelled to give military chiefs, who were pressing for more aggressive action, the freedom to step up the air war.

Secret talks in Saigon, Hanoi, and Warsaw, Poland, about negotiations gave Johnson little reason to hold his hand. On November 11, a cable from Warsaw indicated that Hanoi would not bend on its demands for an unconditional halt to American bombing, a withdrawal of allied forces from South Vietnam, and a place for the National Liberation Front at the peace table. Six days later, Rostow told the President: "It is certain that the men in Hanoi have not yet decided that their best option is to negotiate." Rostow also thought it may "be important to communicate to them soon that we do not intend to let the war drag on; that we plan to up the ante; and our present offers to them may not hold indefinitely."[159]

At the same time, the State Department sent word to Hanoi through a Polish diplomat that the United States would stop bombing unconditionally if North Vietnam would agree soon after to take mutual steps of deescalation. The diplomat reported that the North Vietnamese had now agreed to secret discussions in early December in Warsaw. On December 2, Rostow told Johnson that Rusk saw this message as "of importance," and Rostow himself believed that an emphasis on secrecy and speed voiced by Hanoi made the initiative, code named MARIGOLD, seem genuine.[160]

The same day that word reached Washington of North Vietnamese interest in talks, American planes, under the President's authorization of additional bombing targets, struck military installations around Hanoi, the first attacks near the city since the POL raids in June. On December 4, U.S. planes hit the North Vietnamese capital again. More attacks were scheduled for mid-December, but McNamara, Katzenbach, and Lodge urged Johnson to hold off until they could see if MARIGOLD was leading anywhere.

But the President believed that Hanoi might see this as a sign of weakness. Besides, he was just then rejecting a Joint Chiefs demand for stronger air action, and scheduled attacks on Hanoi was a concession to military brass convinced that the White House was being too timid in fighting the war. "The President considered the problem of next steps in hitting targets in North Vietnam," Rostow summarized a meeting of December 9. "Broadly speaking, the decision was made to carry forward with what was necessary but at this particular moment not to expand our targeting." On December 13 and 14 U.S. planes staged even larger raids against Hanoi.[161]

The attacks now seemed to kill off the talks. There is good reason to think that Hanoi was not serious about these discussions anyway. But currently there is no way of knowing exactly what the North Vietnamese intended. It is certain, though, that the Johnson administration took a public relations beating over the bombing. During the last week in December, Harrison E. Salisbury, assistant managing editor of the New York Times, began publishing a series of articles on the air raids, asserting, in contradiction of Pentagon assertions, that the attacks had killed civilians. The reports embarrassed the White House and further called into question the credibility of the American government.[162]

As 1966 came to a close, Johnson's frustration with trying to defeat the Communists in Vietnam, hold the economy together, sustain Great Society programs, and position himself and the Democrats for another successful election campaign in 1968 became almost more than he could bear. He was livid at Salisbury and the press for challenging him over Vietnam. Moyers told James Reston that the President wouldn't allow him to raise any questions about the bombing. All the press wanted to talk about, Johnson complained, was "Veetnam, Veetnam, Veetnam, Veetnam." But it was constantly on his mind as well. Whenever he found himself with the President, Admiral Thomas Moorer, Chief of Naval operations, remembered, "you always discussed Vietnam, no matter where you were."[163]

And one result was that Great Society programs were "falling far short of the contributions they could make.... This is a problem," one White House aide asserted, "that can be solved only by the more direct exercise of presidential authority, direction, and muscle."

Democratic governors meeting in West Virginia in December vented their anger at the President for neglecting them, administration programs, and domestic politics. It incensed Johnson, who in "heated" remarks to them during a meeting at his ranch "said that he resented very deeply the remarks by the governors, publicly at the Greenbrier, and personally to him at the Ranch." He described it as "unfair to say because of my image, my popularity—that this caused us to lose these [congressional seats]. I do not like to hear this."[164]

"A pall seemed to have settled over the nation as a result of Johnson's continued escalation of the war in Vietnam," a White House chronology of events noted for December 31, 1966. It was a prelude for worse to come.

8

A Sea of Troubles

B Y the beginning of 1967, the dissent over Vietnam, urban riots, political reverses, and doubts about administration programs to elevate poor folks into the middle class and transform America into a Great Society made Johnson wonder why he had ever wanted to be President. He took some solace from the knowledge that all his predecessors had shouldered heavy burdens. "Men of ordinary physique and discretion cannot be Presidents and live, if the strain be not somehow relieved," Woodrow Wilson had complained. Herbert Hoover had called the office "a compound hell."[1]

During 1967 continuing and intensifying problems subjected Johnson to an ordeal that, in the words of one sympathetic columnist, "seems more than a man should have to bear." In the winter of 1966–67, even before a host of new difficulties appeared, he found himself defending his administration from attacks by friends and foes alike. Governor Warren Hearnes of Missouri told Johnson that if he were running in his state now he would lose by 100,000 votes, despite a half-million margin in 1964. "Frustration over Vietnam; too much federal spending and ... taxation; no great public support for your Great Society programs; and ... public disenchantment with the civil rights programs" had eroded the President's standing. Democratic senators echoed the same complaints at a White House meeting in January.

However much the criticism hurt and agitated him, he refused to show his true feelings in public. Any confirmation of dismay would encourage opponents at home and abroad. The attacks on him were "unfair," Johnson had told the governors in December, and he cautioned them "to wash our dirty linen outside of the newspapers." The columnist said: Johnson "loathes with all the fury of his giant physique, hyperactive mentality and volcanic temper" pictures of him "as downcast in spirit." He put the best possible face on everything.[2]

The economy was a case in point. During the first half of the 1960s an amazing 96 percent of Americans believed that their standard of living would improve. In January 1967, when Johnson told the country that wages were the highest in history, unemployment was at a thirteen-year low, and corporate profits and farm incomes were greater than ever, Americans nodded in agreement. True, a 4.5 percent jump in consumer prices over the previous eighteen months and an "excessive rise" in interest rates were disturbing elements in the national economic picture. But, the President reassured the country, "as 1966 ended, price stability was seemingly being restored," while interest rates were retreating from their earlier peaks.[3]

Johnson knew, however, that his public rhetoric masked potential budget deficits. Additional defense outlays and cost-of-living increases might lead to a recession and political defeat in 1968. But no one in the administration was sure. Their watchwords on the economy in early 1967 were: "Where are we headed?"

Mixed advice and confusing statistics were the answers given Johnson. The economist Paul Samuelson publicly warned that doing too much or too little could produce dire results. The additional bad news was that economists sharply disagreed on which way to turn. How can you guard against the "grave evils" of inflation or recession? Samuelson asked. "Certainly not by expecting a consensus from economic experts."[4]

The debate swirled around the 6 percent, one-year tax surcharge Johnson requested in his State of the Union speech and spending on domestic programs. Developments in the first quarter of 1967 gave ammunition to both pro- and antitax advocates as well as to proponents and opponents of Great Society spending. On one hand, rising defense costs and higher interest rates were increasing the budget deficit to $11 billion for fiscal 1967. And if congressional Republicans were to be believed, the shortfall would go as high as $18 billion, which they wanted to reduce not with new taxes but less spending. An inflationary price report in early January bolstered Republican demands for cuts and the administration's case for a tax hike.

At the same time, however, evidence of a slowdown in capital investment, less residential construction, flat industrial production, disappointing retail sales, and lower corporate profits raised concerns that a tax increase and cuts in federal outlays would precipitate a recession.[5]

The economic reports between February and April gave additional mixed signals. Wholesale prices jumped 0.3 percent in January, the first increase in four months. But the Consumer Price Index told a different story, increasing only a scant 0.1 percent in February, marking four straight months in which it had shown little change. Further, the gross national product in the first quarter was surprisingly weak, its poorest performance since the 1960 recession.

The CEA warned the President against reading long-term trends into current numbers. True, inventory levels and consumer buying were declining, but, they cautioned, these economic measures "are highly erratic. . . . The mixture of news makes the economic situation unusually puzzling." Besides, Gardner Ackley, the Chairman of the CEA, said: "Our social statistics are a mess. Trying to run down some of these numbers was terribly frustrating. I still can't guarantee their accuracy."[6]

The uncertainty frustrated and agitated Johnson. He complained that trying to manage fiscal policy in current circumstances was like driving a car with the gas pedal tied down.[7]

But his greatest complaint was against Congress, which showed little sympathy for his dilemma and, worse, used the uncertainty to beat up on him. Republicans and Democrats alike seized upon the President's problems to score political points. The "GOP is trying to have its cake and eat it," Fred Panzer, the White House pollster, declared. "If the tax increase is needed, they will demand that domestic spending be first 'cut to the bone.' If the tax increase is not needed for economic reasons, they will take credit for having stopped it."

Congressmen and governors lobbied against spending cuts affecting their constituents, but were eager for reductions and limitations serving their interests or those of "the nation." For example, Georgia's segregationist governor Lester Maddox, who wanted no part of federal reductions in highway funds, urged the President to restrain his office of education and leave schools under local control.[8]

Liberal Democrats were no more helpful to the President. They increased a number of his budget requests for social programs, which added to Republican pressure to reduce spending. Johnson complained to Nick Katzenbach that in 1966 he had sent up a request for $1.75 billion for his war on poverty, but Bobby Kennedy, Wayne Morse, and Joe Clark, "these wild men," added $750 million, which Dirksen eliminated along with another $150 million from the $1.75 billion request. The liberals, Johnson declared, "just will not follow the leader. There will not be any coordination. They are just going in opposite directions."[9]

Yet however uncertain the economic data and divided the Congress, Johnson did not have the luxury of waiting for clarity and unity before acting. In March, he asked Congress to restore the 7 percent investment tax credit he had persuaded it to suspend the previous October. He asserted that the suspension had achieved in six months what the administration thought might take a year. The *Washington Post* disagreed. It urged Congress to meet the President's request, but disputed the wisdom of having suspended the credit in the first place.[10]

The uncertainties, when added to frustration over Vietnam, kept Johnson's approval ratings below 50 percent. A late January survey showed that "strong approval" of the President's leadership had fallen from 23 percent in September 1966 to 16 percent in January 1967. A February poll on the tax increase and spending cuts placed the public on the anti-Johnson side. Only 24 percent favored the surcharge, with 65 percent opposed. If something was needed to hold down inflation, 75 percent of the public preferred less spending. In March and April, 45 percent of Americans approved of Johnson's overall job rating and 42 percent disapproved. The results were decidedly worse on Vietnam, with only 37 percent approving and 49 percent disapproving—an all-time low. A trial election matchup between LBJ and Michigan Governor George Romney gave Romney a nine-point—52 percent to 43 percent—lead.[11]

Though Johnson was unhappy about the downturn in his political fortunes, he believed that he could make a quick comeback if he held to a consistent line about the economy and Vietnam. The statistics from April to June were not very cooperative, showing strong movements in different directions that continued to confuse the CEA. "Our economic statistics have wriggled around in recent months without establishing a clear pattern," Ackley wrote LBJ in late May. "The record has shifted from seemingly *disastrous* reports on performance in February to *delightful* news about March, to *disappointing* results for April." The CEA declared that "to the reader of the financial press, the economy in recent months has at times appeared schizophrenic—a case for psychiatric rather than fiscal or monetary help."

In mid-June, when the President's advisers divided over the question of whether and when the tax increase was appropriate, Johnson sent Joe Califano a heartfelt plea: "For God's sake get agreement." Because reports in the second half of June provided mounting evidence that the economy was "renewing its forward advance," Johnson restated his call for the tax increase and limited spending cuts.[12]

His strategy now was to go back to basics—to do what he saw as right for the country without focusing on the personal political results. In a conversation with *Time*'s Hugh Sidey in May, he took the high ground, recalling that the press vilified other Presidents, who had more serious problems than he faced. "The things said about Roosevelt were more vicious," while Truman and Eisenhower also suffered terrible attacks. Johnson acknowledged that "every day is a difficult day" and that it was "tough to carry the burdens of being President."

Yet he refused to be anything but optimistic. The nation's economic growth had raised six million people above the poverty line, education was receiving $12 billion a year compared with $3 billion a few years ago, and his administration had produced a health care "revolution." If he was "so unpopular, why have I been so successful in winning so many elections?" he asked Sidey. And why did people accept him with open arms in so many places he went?[13]

Johnson's bravado hid a self-serving conviction that his rhetoric would serve his public standing, as indeed it did. His greater consistency on the economy and declarations of selfless politics helped improve his poll numbers in the spring. A May survey showed an improvement in his approval rating to 48 percent, with his disapproval index falling to 37 percent. A fresh sounding on a Johnson-Romney contest showed LBJ with a one-point advantage, 45 percent to 44 percent.[14]

But the uptick was short-lived. Developments in the summer shook public confidence in the administration's ability to stabilize the economy. Ironically, it was not a business slowdown and growing joblessness that undermined Johnson's credibility as a promoter of prosperity. Quite the opposite: The economy boomed between June and October—a solid 2.5 percent increase in gross national product and a decline in unemployment to 3.9 percent in the second quarter became a "whopping" 4.5 percent GNP expansion and 3.8 percent joblessness in the July to October period.[15]

The problem now was inflation and a potential runaway budget shortfall. Consumer prices jumped one point between June and August. At the same time, the federal budget deficit was threatening to reach $29 billion for the 1968 fiscal year that had begun on July 1, 1967. Higher spending and a drop in anticipated revenues accounted for the unwelcome budget run-up.[16]

In August, Johnson felt compelled publicly to describe the current economic problem facing the country and the austerity measures needed to solve it. He promised restraints on federal spending wherever possible, but the costs of Vietnam and mandated civilian programs limited what he could do. The only remedy he saw were temporary surcharges on corporate and personal income taxes of 10 percent beginning July 1 and October 1, 1967, respectively. They would expire on June 30, 1969, "or continue for so long as the unusual expenditures associated with our efforts in Vietnam require higher revenues."

His recommendation was now 4 percent more than the 6 percent proposal made in January. And he saw a failure to act on it as leading to inflation that would rob millions of people on fixed incomes of economic security. Higher interest rates and tight money would occur with devastating consequences for the housing industry. General prosperity would be endangered with results that "would haunt America and its people for years to come."[17]

Yet Congress and most people in the country were not persuaded. Wilbur Mills believed that a tax hike might precipitate rather than head off a recession, and he thought the Congress would reject Johnson's recommendation. Senator Russell Long also disputed the need for additional taxes, but was pleased to leave the issue to the House, where money bills had to originate. Businessmen and congressmen who showed some sympathy for Johnson's recommendation hedged their support with demands for "much larger" cuts in nondefense spending than LBJ wanted.[18]

Despite a campaign of public education, the President made little headway in convincing either reluctant House members or the mass of Americans that he was right. By September, the dispute over taxes and the future of the economy had contributed to a renewed downturn in Johnson's standing that left him "brooding" and snappish. In August and September his approval ratings fell to new lows of 39 and 40 percent, with disapproval numbers reaching highs of 47 and 48 percent.[19]

"Why do people dislike you?" Max Frankel of the *New York Times* asked the President. "I am a dominating personality, and when I get things done I don't always please all the people," Johnson replied. "Why is there so much hate talk about the President?" Frankel persisted. "I think it is because of Texas, because of the label of professional politician, and a good deal [of] my own impatience," Johnson answered.

Johnson also blamed the press, saying they operate without license, show "complete irresponsibility and lie and misstate facts and have no one to be answerable to." He also pointed to "the preachers, liberals and professors who are the first to cry discrimination if anybody says anything about them." They attacked him as "that lying SOB." But they couldn't explain his "popularity record." There was no one in U.S. history who had served for thirty-seven years in every important legislative and executive office with "a record of elections comparable to his," Johnson asserted. Could he win again in 1968, Frankel wondered. "I sure as hell can if I decide to run for office, I will win and be right here," Johnson asserted.[20]

Though Johnson declared himself "not unhappy and not bitter" toward his critics, the opposition made him furious. It is understandable that he considered opponents of the tax increase as advocates ready to sacrifice the national well-being for personal or political advantage. He was on the mark in believing that a prosperous America should not defer paying for a costly war or transfer the cost to the least advantaged members of the society by reducing social programs.

But the attacks on him were largely of his own making. If he had informed the country in 1965 what Vietnam might mean for the economy, he would have been justified in feeling that his critics had no reason to complain about costs they had agreed to bear. Part of the problem was his optimism in thinking that the war would be over by June 1967 or even sooner. But these estimates were dead wrong and left Johnson with commitments he had not prepared the public to make. His candor in 1967 about war costs, therefore, was too late to ward off reasonable complaints from a national majority, which had never been informed that Vietnam might be a long conflict requiring personal and financial sacrifices like every other war in U.S. history.[21]

Although it was too late to do anything about current commitments in Vietnam or to repair the damage to his credibility, Johnson saw no choice but to fight for a tax increase that economic news in the third and fourth quarters of 1967 seemed to make more essential every day. Higher interest rates, the fifth largest GNP gain on record in the July to October period, and an increase of $900 million in "uncontrollable" current expenditures made Johnson sputter. The economic advance since 1961 compared with the previous six years was "truly fantastic": A 19 percent growth in GNP during the Eisenhower years paled alongside the 39 percent in the Kennedy-Johnson terms.

It was too much of a good thing: Without his tax bill Johnson anticipated "a new depression in housing" precipitated by high loan costs and 5 percent inflation. He viewed congressional inaction as politics at its worse: "The Republicans would like to create a financial calamity," he told two *Washington Star* journalists on October 13. "Jerry Ford and his group, including [Melvin] Laird, are not going to lose any sleep if we have a $40 billion deficit."[22]

Johnson's concern had registered on the public. In mid-October, 60 percent of Americans saw the high cost of living as their number one problem; only 5 percent cited Vietnam. But they still wanted nothing to do with the President's remedy. Just 15 percent favored his 10 percent tax surcharge; 73 percent said it was best to cut federal spending.[23]

Even with the economy showing the same pace of advance in the last months of the year, Johnson could not sell his policy to Congress. But it was not for want of trying. In public and private he pressed the case for the tax increase, describing it in news conferences as "very necessary," "very essential," and an act of "wisdom." He was even more emphatic in his meetings with congressional leaders, but, as he said at one of these gatherings, his proposal had remained "unacted upon—while the storm clouds of inflation gather, while interest rates begin to soar, while international money markets are disrupted, while uncertainty hangs over our economy."[24]

Johnson understood that the tax fight had provoked a confrontation about fundamentals between himself and various factions in Congress. It was clear to him that conservatives—Democrats like Mills as well as Republicans—saw the country's economic problems as a chance not to raise taxes or even make temporary cuts in social programs but rather to force the President into retreating from the unprecedented expansion of federal actions fostered by the Great Society. Mills "wants to cut 5 to 10 billion dollars in expenditures and then in programs," Johnson told Democratic leaders. "This would be very difficult to do. Can you imagine our going back and cutting our programs we have passed in the last three years?" he asked rhetorically.

In a November address to labor leaders honoring George Meany, Johnson was more blunt: "The struggle for progress and reform in America has never been easy," he declared. "On the one hand is the old coalition of standpatters and nay-sayers. They never wanted to do anything. But this year they say they can't do it because of Vietnam. That is just pure bunk. This crowd was against progress before Vietnam. They are against progress tonight and they will be against progress tomorrow. And they will be against it when the war is over and when it is nothing but a dim memory."[25]

Johnson found it more difficult to "understand why some of the doves and super-liberals" were against the tax bill. But there was no real mystery. It was their way of forcing the President's hand on Vietnam. The more his Great Society programs were starved the more likely he would be to reduce commitments to the war. "You cannot vote against appropriations for the Vietnam war without arousing the wrath of super patriots and the families who have boys over there," a liberal Democrat wrote Texas Senator Ralph Yarborough, "but you can close down on the government's purse strings in domestic affairs and that will bring the President around faster than open defiance of his war effort."[26]

Conservatives and liberals understood that they were forcing Johnson into openly choosing between guns and butter. He had known since the end of 1965 that the war meant temporarily putting the Great Society on hold. But he had managed to mute the issue with a few significant reform gains and much flamboyant talk about continuing domestic advance. "For the first time in a decade the GOP leads the Democrats as the party best able to deal with the most important problems facing the nation," Johnson's pollster told him in November. The issue had been coming to a head for over two years.[27]

Farewell to Reform

It is a given of U.S. history that war kills reform. Populism could not outlive the Spanish-American clash; progressivism largely succumbed to World War I; "Dr. New Deal" gave way to "Dr. Win-the-War," in FDR's memorable phrase; Korea overwhelmed Truman's Fair Deal; and Vietnam largely stalled the War on Poverty and blocked Johnson's reach for the Great Society. The country had never had the psychological and fiscal wherewithal to back reform and war at the same time.

Johnson didn't need a war to limit his reform plans. As he understood, there was plenty of hostility to his social engineering from conservatives convinced that traditional laissez-faire—not government-sponsored efforts—was the best means to national prosperity and wider distribution of wealth. Even without Vietnam, LBJ and other reformers believed that their hold on the popular imagination would be fleeting.

Iowa Republican Senator Bourke B. Hickenlooper complained that Johnson really didn't care about the country's economic future. LBJ was a tax-and-spend Democrat who was content to let "the borrowed money" flow in so that he could "spend it for bread and circuses." One Alabama conservative satirized Johnson's reformism as a version of National Socialism.[28] By 1967 the resistance to liberal reform came not only from conservative ideologues but also from a growing feeling among middle-class Americans that the country had all the social programs it needed or that, as nineteenth-century British Prime Minister Benjamin Disraeli said of his countrymen, they were "tired of being improved." What the country wanted now, Harry McPherson told the President in December 1966, were not more reforms but evidence that the programs in place could work. All the noise in the country about the War on Poverty and the Great Society, senators told Johnson in January, was "about the way the programs were being administered."[29]

But whether ideologically or pragmatically inspired, attacks on administration reforms impressed Johnson as the predictable out-growth of a public shift back to traditional verities about the limited role of government, especially federal authority, in the country's life. Once the war took center stage in his administration, however, he saw it as largely hopeless to expect much domestic advance. To be sure, he spoke repeatedly of the country's capacity to fight a war and change its domestic life, but this was essentially "window dressing" or "brave words," Gardner Ackley says, that masked Johnson's con-viction that he had to cut reform programs to the bone. "During the acceleration of the Vietnam war," an interviewer asked Budget Di-rector Charles Schultze, "did you get any memos from Johnson saying something to the effect, 'Cut down on these other programs . . . ?' Oh, God, all the time," Schultze replied. "At least once a week."[30]

As in 1966, Johnson had no intention of acknowledging that he saw distinct limits to what we could spend on domestic reform or how far they could carry us toward a better world. To concede such limits would be to accept Richard Nixon's description of the poverty war as a "cruel hoax." Accepting this proposition, Johnson said, would have meant turning "the American dream into a nightmare."[31]

Johnson's strategy was to pump as hard as ever for antipoverty and Great Society programs. He still believed that strong expressions of support would have the advantage of holding at bay conservatives eager to scrap the whole thing and primarily devote national re-sources to fighting in Vietnam. Pressing the case for domestic reforms would also have the advantage of keeping most liberals on his side, or at least enough in his camp to give him some prospect of running successfully again in 1968.

But speaking out for domestic advance wasn't simply good pol-itics. It was also Johnson's way of keeping reformers engaged and social programs going until the war ended and opened the way to a fresh surge of activism. Johnson's rhetoric in 1966–67 far outran his substantive support of the great domestic changes he still envisioned. As a keen student of American government and public affairs, John-son understood that rhetoric and gestures or symbols carried signifi-cant consequences. Hence, whatever the realities—and they were increasingly at odds with the words and deeds of his administration— Johnson wanted no letup in the call to fulfill the promise of American life.

In public and private, the year 1967 was as much a summons

to domestic advance as the preceding three years. His January State of the Union speech was a new call to action: Reciting the litany of achievements, he declared the moment ripe for renewed commitments to improving the quality of life and enlarging the meaning of justice for all. It was a message "filled with high hope and clear purpose," UAW President Walter P. Reuther wired him.[32]

Specific recommendations followed Johnson's general appeal. In the course of the year he called for: a renewed attack on Appalachian poverty; a 20 percent increase in Social Security payments, wider availability of Medicare, and an end to age discrimination in hiring; expanded Head Start programs; a new national policy against housing discrimination; consumer protections against hidden lending costs, unsound investments, and unsafe products; more and better housing, especially for the poor; more effective community action, expanded legal services, and a wider attack on inner city blight, including a rat extermination program; and an air quality act.[33]

Johnson's support for a continuing reform surge resonated through Hubert Humphrey. During 1967 the Vice President was in constant motion promoting antipoverty, civil rights, and Great Society programs. In the first six weeks of the year he crisscrossed the United States. His objective, he told LBJ, was "to mobilize support for our urban, education, and War on Poverty programs" by speaking not only to the targeted groups but also the "publishers, editors and chief editorial writers of the major local dailies, plus the owners and managers of the local television stations."[34]

The garrulous Vice President was an administration evangelist bringing the word to everyone everywhere—governors, mayors, state legislators, minorities, chambers of commerce, regional councils of local governments, unions, boards of trade, corporate CEOs, bankers, university faculties and students, and community action leaders across the country. The administration remained determined to help the poor and advance America's quality of life. It was a crusade to assure safety from dangers abroad and reduce suffering, domestic divisions, and injustices at home.[35]

Behind the scenes, Johnson and Humphrey were as aggressive in pumping for the President's programs. At a Cabinet meeting in January, Johnson challenged his department chiefs to do their best for new antipoverty and Great Society measures. "I want draft messages of the *highest quality* and legislation that is *letter perfect*," he told them. "It's all up to you—so get going, write your messages, make your contacts, explain your programs, and get the votes. There is nothing more important you have to do."

At the same time, Humphrey pressed antipoverty officials "to take the offensive in getting from the Congress the full amount of appropriations you requested." In March, when "congressional relations" staff met at the White House, LBJ gave them a one-hour pep talk: "He discussed the problems of slanted newspaper coverage and partisan criticism; he scolded them; he entertained them hugely." He had a hundred bills he wanted passed, he said, and nothing had happened so far. Though he described them as the most effective organized pressure group ever, he gave them only "a C minus" to date for their work.[36]

No one tracing the Johnson-Humphrey lobbying efforts would see them as anything but commitments to more reform laws and bigger programs. In May, LBJ told business leaders that antipoverty programs were "much misunderstood"; they were neither "handouts" nor "impractical giveaways" but essential measures for turning tax eaters into tax payers. In July, he hectored Cabinet members for not being more effective with congressional subcommittees. "It is a disgrace that all the appropriations bills haven't passed by now," he declared.

In August, he complained to news commentators about congressional foot-dragging on urban programs needed to prevent riots. "It is of critical importance that the programs for the cities ... be enacted with the funding we have requested," Johnson told Humphrey. "I want you to intensify your efforts ... in obtaining prompt consideration and action on this legislation." In September, he told newspaper publishers that $6.8 billion in pending urban programs represented "the most comprehensive package on cities ever presented to Congress."[37]

Much of what Johnson and Humphrey said and did in behalf of domestic advance masked a less ambitious agenda—a commitment to reform programs that could fit into a war economy and would more or less stay in place until an end to the fighting freed resources for a renewed crusade against domestic evils.

Johnson was careful not to reveal this strategy. But in December 1967, when HEW Secretary John Gardner came to the ranch to plead for larger appropriations for social programs, Johnson had to turn him down and cut even more than Gardner assumed HEW would get. Gardner, a quiet man, who never "had an easy conversational relationship with the President," responded with a muted anguish that pained Johnson. As Gardner was about to get out of Johnson's car for a plane taking him back to Washington, the President put his arm around him and said: "Don't worry, John. We're going to end this damned war and then you'll have all the money you want for education, and health, and everything else." Doug Cater remembered it as "a poignant moment" in which LBJ, who had "his back to the wall" on the surtax and deficits, acknowledged the gap between what he wanted and what he felt he could do.[38]

Johnson was usually less direct about his intentions. In the summer of 1967, for example, the President's task force on education recommended stepped-up efforts to help poor urban and rural students. Johnson feared that the report might create pressures for greater spending. Normally, he wanted task force recommendations held in strict confidence until he decided their fate. Premature leaks would alert opponents to administration thinking and help them prepare the ground for effective counter action. On this occasion, however, Johnson instructed Califano to leak the report without any clue that the story had come from the White House. After the *New York Times* published a front-page article, Johnson gave Douglass Cater a tongue-lashing for the leak, which reduced him "almost to trembling."

Johnson's action mystified Cater, who learned of the leak from Califano. Johnson's deviousness served two purposes. The story allowed him to scrap the recommendations and blame the failed hopes for more education spending on Cater and liberals, or those who would complain most loudly about cutbacks in education programs. He was not proud of what he had done. When Califano showed the *Times* story to the President, asking if he had seen it, Johnson "grunted yes, and never mentioned it again to me, or Cater, or anyone else."[39]

Johnson also reined in liberal impulses to respond aggressively to urban riots and the "crisis in the cities." In July, after Newark and Detroit exploded over rumors of police brutality against inner-city blacks, Johnson asked Humphrey to chair a Cabinet working group on the crisis.

He made clear to Humphrey that proposed remedies should not include new legislation or new funding. But Humphrey, who saw the riots as a demonstration of "widespread rejection of our social system," urged the President to announce his determination to avoid cuts in existing programs affecting the cities. Moreover, despite the President's admonitions, the Vice President asked the secretaries of labor and commerce to work on a major new job program that, Califano warned Johnson, would entail "significant spending." Califano recommended that the President follow Budget Director Schultze's suggestion that they "tactfully disband the Vice President's group." After Humphrey issued a final report on August 23, Johnson put his committee "on ice."[40]

During 1967, as Johnson worked to limit spending on domestic programs, he kept emphasizing how much he had done to help the disadvantaged. "I want a chart of every President this century and how much . . . he has increased domestic spending . . . during his administration," he told Califano.

Look, he told the columnist Joseph Kraft in September, he had started with $800 million to fight poverty and now he was up to $1.6 billion. Never mind that antipoverty spending was no longer going up. Johnson stressed the importance of considering how far we had come in so short a time. Similarly, one could look at domestic laws enacted. Where FDR had passed only fifteen major bills in 1933, and JFK had gotten less than 50 percent of his proposed measures in 1961–63, LBJ had averaged about 60 percent in the following three years.[41]

Johnson wished to mute the fact that current budgets neither matched past gains nor even kept funding abreast of inflation. But he couldn't hide the fact that Vietnam spending now made him an ally of domestic budget-cutters in Congress. In May, for example, when Henry H. Wilson, Jr., a principal White House congressional liaison, tried to inform Johnson that the House was reducing model cities money to $12 million for planning and was deleting all funds for rent supplements, the President wouldn't take his call. It was a far cry from Johnson's involvement of just two years before.

In August, as the reality of a potential $30 billion deficit and no tax increase became a distinct possibility, Johnson's budget office laid plans to cut "heavily into Space, HEW, Agriculture, HUD, and OEO." The plan was to reduce civilian programs by a minimum of $1.5 billion and possibly as much as $2.5 billion. The Teacher Corps, for example, one of LBJ's prize ideas, suffered a nearly two-thirds reduction in funding. HUD took a 25 percent hit, while rent supplements received only a quarter of its proposed monies. In November, when Johnson accepted the need for across-the-board cuts of 2 percent in personnel and 10 percent in controllable domestic programs, Califano warned that Cabinet officials "will take cuts of this nature . . . very hard." But with no tax increase and ever more spending on Vietnam on tap, Johnson saw no escape from "substantial cuts in Great Society programs."[42]

Nowhere was the issue more clearly evident than in funding for OEO, the central antipoverty agency. In fiscal 1967, the OEO had received $1.612 billion, $138 million less than Johnson had asked and only 45 percent of the $3.5 billion the OEO had requested. Shriver and antipoverty officials saw the appropriation as the "irreducible minimum" needed to keep the program "moving forward." Though Johnson asked for an expanded national attack on poverty in his 1967

State of the Union speech, his words and actions demonstrated a new note of caution. Liberal critics complained that Vietnam made it impossible to fight an "unconditional war on poverty." *The Boston Globe* pointed out that the President now spoke of a "strategy against poverty" rather than a "war on poverty."[43]

Though Califano called descriptions of Johnson's waning efforts for the poverty fight "hogwash and trash" and though Johnson himself said that he was not backing off and had just begun to fight, his actions suggested otherwise. True, he asked for a 25 percent increase in OEO funding to $2.06 billion, with half of the additional $460 million slated for new programs. But he insisted that elected local officials play a significant part in community action programs, which suggested to liberal critics that the poor themselves would now have to cede power over the poverty war to mayors and city councils or established political authorities. Moreover, when House conservatives proposed a "bosses and boll weevil" amendment, giving local officials greater control over community action boards than the administration had proposed, the White House did nothing to prevent its adoption.[44]

Similarly, by the fall of 1967 Johnson readily accepted the need to reduce OEO funding below the proposed $2.06 billion. In July, he told Senate Democrats, "You can cut them [my appropriations bills] if you want." Then, in September, when Senator Joe Clark of Pennsylvania pressed a case for increased poverty funding of some $2.8 billion, especially for public service jobs, Johnson urged Senate Democratic leaders to "kill this bill in committee. The time to kill a snake is when you have a hoe in your hand," he said. Clark's proposal failed on the Senate floor.

In December, after the White House encouraged "orderly cuts" in OEO funding and Sargent Shriver agreed that an appropriation of $1.78 billion would keep the agency "at an even keel," Congress appropriated $1.77 billion. Though Shriver anticipated painful consequences from the funding limitations, the White House put out an upbeat statement, reaffirming "new hope for the poor; brighter opportunities for the deprived; and a stronger nation for all." The rhetoric was meant as much to buoy the sagging spirits of the administration as to convince the public in a time of growing troubles.[45]

Crime and Politics

Nothing signaled the waning of liberal influence and freedom to carry forward the reform agenda of 1964–65 more clearly than the emergence of crime as a major domestic issue in 1966. By March Johnson had felt compelled to send Congress a special message on the rise in murders, rapes, aggravated assaults, robberies, burglaries, and car thefts that had sparked an epidemic of fear in the nation and was costing the country some $27 billion a year. A law enforcement assistance act in 1965 had established a federal program to help local police agencies combat crime. But it was time now, Johnson said, for a coordinated campaign by local, state, and federal authorities to reverse the trend and strike at the roots of the problem. Though Johnson's call to action produced four minor bills, they did little to satisfy the national desire for substantive and symbolic responses to the country's growing lawlessness.[46]

Johnson's administration was seen as more the cause than the solution to the problem. Crime increased six times faster than population during the Kennedy-Johnson presidencies, Richard Nixon asserted in 1966. In the sixties, Supreme Court decisions widening the legal definition of obscenity, barring required prayer in schools, guaranteeing accused lawbreakers a right to an attorney, and compelling police to inform criminal suspects of their rights provoked complaints that liberal justices were more intent on protecting criminals than victims and were subverting the American way of life. "They've put the Negroes in the schools," an Alabama congressman complained, "and now they've driven God out." "Impeach Earl Warren" became a rallying cry of American conservatives.

Though the Court's decisions were not Johnson's responsibility, the country, especially after the Fortas appointment, identified the President with the Court's "bleeding heart" liberalism. The inner city riots of 1965–66, which many saw as a result of indulgent policies toward blacks, added to the feeling that Johnson's liberal excesses had undermined traditional restraints and given license to criminal behavior.

Johnson's decision in November 1966 to veto a tough D.C. crime bill, which he believed unconstitutional, encouraged the view that this President was a hopeless romantic incapable of bringing law and order to the country's mean streets. Nor did it help in February 1967 when he appointed Ramsey Clark as Attorney General and Tom Clark, his father, left the Supreme Court to avoid possible conflicts of interest. Losing "Dad" from the Court "would hurt you," Ramsey told Johnson. "He more than any other member of the Court stands for . . . tough law enforcement." The people who were incensed at your veto of the D.C. crime bill, Ramsey added, are the same folks who "see in Dad the strength of the Court."[47]

By the beginning of 1967 Johnson felt compelled to identify

himself with an anticrime crusade. Whatever its merits as social policy, it was essential politics. "By early 1967," Califano says, "crime had burst out of the closet as a national issue.... As citizen concern and political pressures closed in on him, he [LBJ] concluded that the federal government had to stake out a larger role in fighting crime."

In January, Johnson asked Congress to pass a Safe Streets and Crime Control Act. Califano, eager to convince people that the administration was determined to restore public and private safety, wanted to call the bill the Safe Streets Act. Ramsey Clark, fearful that the President would be attacked for promoting a utopian goal, urged Johnson to describe the bill as increasing crime control. Seeing political gain in both terms, Johnson embraced safety and control as coequal aims of the law.[48]

Quoting Lincoln, Johnson asked that " 'reverence for the law ... become the political religion of the Nation.' " He intended to "support—with all the constitutional powers the President possesses—our nation's law enforcement officials in their attempt to control the crime and violence that tear the fabric of our communities." The crime bill he put before Congress in February provided planning grants to state and local governments to improve their police, courts, and correctional systems. The means for doing this was left to the localities to determine.

To his credit, Johnson promised no quick fix. There will be no "sudden decline in the reported crime rate," he predicted. On the contrary, the immediate future was likely to see a continuing rise in criminal acts. But if the country moved "boldly, now, to treat ancient evils and to insure the public safety," it would pay off in greater crime control, or so Johnson said.[49]

Perhaps the most surprising part of Johnson's anticrime message was a recommendation that the Congress enact a Right of Privacy Act, which outlawed all public and private wiretapping. The only exceptions were to be for the sake of national security—"and then only under the strictest safeguards."[50]

The record of Johnson's presidency hardly suggests a man who was fastidious about constitutional guarantees of privacy or excessive government intrusion into private conversations and behavior. During his five-plus years in office Johnson secretly recorded over 10,000 conversations without the knowledge of other parties on the telephone or in his White House offices. Moreover, he had little hesitation about using the FBI to make secret recordings of actual and potential political opponents during the 1964 Democratic party convention; about planting bugs in embassies and private residences to monitor Nixon campaign activities in 1968; or about reading FBI and foreign intelligence reports obtained by electronic means.

Yet at the same time, his memos and private conversations on tapping and bugging bristle with indignation about such information-gathering. In February 1966, for example, when Califano asked Johnson's preference on wiretap legislation, he favored "a *complete ban* on all taps, even in national security cases." He also wanted a law banning "the use of non-telephone electronic 'bugging' devices." In May, when IRS Commissioner Sheldon Cohen justified his agency's use of eavesdropping and wiretapping, Johnson emphatically told him: "Sheldon—stop it all at once—and this is final—no microphones—taps or any other hidden devices, legal or illegal if you are going to work for me." Ramsey Clark remembers the President as "outraged" by "any wiretap, any bugging in the domestic area. 'I don't want to live in a country where they do that sort of thing,'" he told Clark.[51]

Was Johnson against taps, bugs, and everything else "Big Brother" might use to intrude on individual privacy except for himself? Was the right to monitor private conversations and activities to be reserved for him as the only one to be trusted with such information?

Johnson had a genuine aversion to the wiretapping and ugly invasions of privacy that the FBI had been committing for a long time. True, the FBI tapes of Martin Luther King's extramarital sexual activities amused LBJ. But he assumed that J. Edgar Hoover had similar, if not so explicit, files on his acts of self-indulgence, and this greatly troubled him. On one hand, he had no wish to hide his sexual conquests. "Why, I had more women by accident than he ever had by design," Johnson liked to say when people spoke of Kennedy's philandering. Womanizing partly satisfied Johnson's competitive urge to outdo political and personal rivals. On the other hand, Johnson, who so despised criticism, must have cringed at the thought of Hoover and others laughing at what they had on him in their files. More important, Hoover's files gave him power over Johnson that LBJ understandably feared.[52]

To say Johnson was ambivalent about tapping and bugs is only the first word on the subject. Johnson disliked the idea of anyone having the kind of control over political leaders Hoover and the FBI obtained through secret listening devices. But he also saw this technology as a political reality to which he accommodated himself. He rationalized his tapings and FBI tappings and bugs as necessary evils in the political and national security wars that he assumed were an inescapable part of contemporary public life.

Politics also partly made Johnson an advocate of privacy rights. In the summer of 1966, a war of words erupted between Hoover and Bobby Kennedy over FBI wiretaps in criminal investigations. Kennedy denied that he had authorized such taps during his time as Attorney General, and Hoover countered that he had acted with authorization from the Department of Justice prior to and during Kennedy's tenure. Johnson refused to get involved directly, checking "yes" on a memo when asked if we should "avoid this mess like The Plague." But he saw the controversy as a chance to trumpet his own purity on the issue alongside Bobby's allegedly questionable behavior. "Against this background," Califano says, "it was not surprising that Johnson took delight in drafting the section on privacy in his crime message and insisted that I point up his position in all my press briefings."[53]

During 1967 anticrime declarations aimed more to advance the political fortunes of the White House and the Republicans than to offer realistic plans for reducing lawlessness. In mid-February, a national crime commission Johnson had created in 1965 reported that the U.S. could bring crime "within manageable bounds" if it made intelligent use of substantially increased spending on law enforcement. Anticipating "tremendous press coverage," Johnson agreed to a public receipt of the report accompanied by "a call to urgent action" on the part of Congress, the states, and local governments. Later in the month Johnson came back to the issue in a special message to Congress on conditions in the nation's capital; eight pages of his thirteen-page report focused on the "plague" of lawlessness sweeping the city and the need for an all-out war to combat it.[54]

Against the backdrop of an FBI announcement that serious crime in the country increased by 11 percent in 1966, the White House in March convened a national conference of 500 state, city, and private authorities on law enforcement and criminal justice. "Let us make clear beyond the possibility of doubt or disbelief," Johnson told the gathering, "that ... our war on crime ... from this hour on with this little guard of courageous and enlightened leaders ... will be unremitting."

Similarly, in May, when the American Bar Association convened a conference on crime control, Johnson took time from "a rather busy day" to ask for help with the issue that next to peace was troubling Americans more than anything else. With the FBI announcing a 20 percent jump in serious crime during the first quarter of 1967, Johnson met in June with the National Council on Crime and Delinquency at the White House, where he lamented the tragic fact of 400,000 boys and girls behind bars awaiting trial, sitting in "jailhouses instead of schoolhouses—where they should have been," and implored the committee to join him in trying to do something about this national disgrace.[55]

Republicans would not let Johnson run away with an issue they had helped make a national concern. During the spring and summer of 1967, joined by southern Democrats, they made the President's Safe Streets and Crime Control Act a tougher law, for which they hoped to take credit. In the House they changed the name to the "Law Enforcement and Criminal Justice Assistance Act," while in the Senate John McClellan called the bill the "Law Enforcement Assistance Act." The name changes gave congressional conservatives claims to the law, which the administration wished to resist. More important, they altered the bill so that state governors rather than the federal government or Attorney General would control the distribution and use of funds; they added wording to give highest priority to combating riots, civil disorders, and organized crime; they deleted provisions against electronic eavesdropping; and they largely gutted a gun control law Johnson recommended as another essential element of any war on crime.[56]

Johnson and the Democrats fought back with attacks on Republican posturing and promises of action. In August, Deputy Attorney General Warren Christopher publicly complained that the Republicans were "cutting out [Johnson's anticrime] bill's heart" by limiting Washington's ability to make "direct grants which would enable local police departments to expand and modernize."

Humphrey weighed in with a declaration that America's "ill-equipped, ill-paid and unappreciated" police lacked the wherewithal to stem the 17 percent increase in crime during the first half of 1967. While there were "no panacea[s], . . . some answers are clear. . . . There is no substitute for action. More talk will not suffice." The answer was prompt enactment of the administration's safe streets bill.[57]

Johnson echoed the point in speeches and press releases during the last four months of the year. We cannot just preach sermons, write editorials, make speeches, and get our pictures taken talking about crime, he said. "We have to pay for it. We have to desire it. We have to be willing to sacrifice in order to get it."[58]

He believed it so important for the administration to make progress on crime control that he offered to compromise with Republicans and southern Democrats. "I'd rather have some compromise than no bill at all," he told congressional leaders in September. He was ready to weaken his gun control bill so that states could exempt themselves from a ban on mail order sales of rifles and shotguns but not handguns. Moreover, he gave McClellan the impression that he could have domestic wiretapping if the administration got the financing for its Safe Streets bill.[59]

Congressional liberals were not so pliant. They believed it premature for the White House to weaken the gun control bill before it got to the Senate floor, and they threatened a filibuster if the Senate judiciary committee tried to vote out McClellan's amended Safe Streets Act preserving federal wiretapping. The liberals "would just as soon see no crime bill even next year as to have wiretap in any form," Johnson was told. McClellan was so incensed at the liberals that he refused to allow a committee vote, effectively killing Safe Streets in the current session. Johnson's only measurable attack on crime took the form of a revised D.C. bill, which satisfied most, but not all, of the objections he had voiced a year before.

As 1967 came to a close, the surtax, Safe Streets, and gun control topped Johnson's list of unfinished congressional business. On what he considered the most urgent items Congress needed to enact, it had not been a good year.[60]

Newark and Detroit: A Nation Divided Against Itself

The lawlessness troubling the public and undermining confidence in the Johnson administration consisted of not only crimes against individuals but also the inner city riots that by 1967 had become an annual summer event. In May the FBI gave the White House "an intelligence survey of this summer's [potential] racial violence." The report noted that, in spite of social, economic, and political gains by black Americans, the continuing misery of ghetto life during oppressive summer weather seemed likely to produce new convulsions, which might spread into white neighborhoods. The bureau was convinced that agitation and propaganda by Communists and other subversives exploiting antiwar sentiments were fueling the explosions.[61]

Whatever Johnson might think of the bureau's assumption about subversives, he was convinced that inner-city poverty and despair were the principal ingredients behind the summer upheavals. In private and public, he made repeated references to the comparative deprivation afflicting African Americans. Where 7.8 percent of white families lived below the poverty line, 29.1 percent of black households were impoverished. Eighteen percent of white families occupied substandard housing, while almost 50 percent of nonwhites were trapped in such dwellings. Despite a drop in the number of Americans living in poverty from 38.9 million in 1959 to 32.7 million in 1965, the percentage of poor blacks had increased from 27.5 percent to 31 percent. Seven percent unemployment among blacks was more than twice the percentage of joblessness among whites; 23 percent black teenage unemployment compared with 10.8 percent for whites.[62]

In the spring of 1967, the White House fretted over dangers to the national well-being and the administration from another round of urban riots. The backlash against rioters, pollster Fred Panzer told LBJ's principal aides, included a readiness of white Americans to sacrifice liberty for the sake of order. Newspaper editors also saw inner-city troubles as near the top of everyone's concerns: If it were not for Vietnam, they told the White House, "race and city problems could well be the #1 issue of the 1968 campaign."

Johnson aides, anticipating that the coming violence would "have broad political as well as social effects," laid plans to minimize the white backlash against the administration and its legislative programs. They saw no way to alter fundamental attitudes, but they believed that an effort to encourage understanding among middle-class opinion leaders could go far to reduce anxieties or inhibit fears about blacks and the consequences of more riots.[63]

But the effort was too little and too late. In July, when rumors of police brutality against a black cab driver spread through Newark's ghetto, six days of rioting took twenty-six lives, injured 1500, and burned out much of the inner city. It was the worst urban violence since Watts in 1964. The *Boston Globe* called it "a revolution of black Americans against white Americans, a violent petition for the redress of long-standing grievances." The *Globe* asserted that the civil rights laws and antipoverty measures had done little to change fundamental conditions for blacks, who continued to live in slums, where poor housing, inferior schools, high unemployment, and pervasive hostility from the surrounding white community made their lives miserable.[64]

The riots threw Johnson into a mood of near despair. He did not want to send in federal troops and was eager for New Jersey's Governor Richard Hughes to handle the problem without direct intervention from Washington. When newspapers reported that Vice President Humphrey had offered the governor federal aid in a telephone conversation, Johnson told Califano to rein Humphrey in before he "brings down the administration." Johnson feared that federal help would be seen as a case of black rioters blackmailing the government into giving them more federal money.[65]

Johnson's complaint was against not Humphrey but really blacks and white liberals. He could not understand why the ghettos were exploding now. No administration had ever been as attentive to the problems and needs of African Americans as the current one, and

Johnson felt that they were paying him back with riots that embarrassed and undermined him.

And the liberals as well, with their incessant attacks on the war and "unrealistic" demands for more money for domestic programs, impressed him as intent on destroying him and, as he judged it, the most progressive presidency in American history. In July, when he met with Roy Wilkins and Whitney Young, both moderate black leaders and two of his strongest supporters, he complained about the ingratitude of the poor and how uncooperative congressional liberals were being. " 'You know the difference between cannibals and liberals?' " he asked in remarks now made repeatedly for liberal consumption. " 'Cannibals eat only their enemies.' "[66]

Johnson's frustration also stemmed from a sense of helplessness about how to ease poverty and prevent riots. He had no answers beyond what he had been doing, he told reporters. He had been trying to provide employment opportunities, better schools, better recreation areas, and better housing, but Congress, which was so intent on cutting programs, was now adding to the difficulty. His unspoken complaint was against a war in Vietnam that was eroding his freedom to mount a possibly more effective attack on poverty.

The answer he saw was to do more for the cities. And so he appointed the Humphrey Cabinet group to study the problem, but not to propose new programs costing additional monies. His objectives instead were to head off a congressional investigation, which could turn into an attack on the administration and the Democrats running the riot-scarred cities, and to get a report that would support the Administration's existing requests for urban programs.[67]

On July 23, as Humphrey's group began its work, Detroit erupted in the country's worst rioting since disturbances there in 1943. The civil disorders underscored Johnson's sense of immediate limits, but they also strengthened his resolve to do something for the long run about the problem.

The first order of business, though, was to minimize the loss of life and property and fend off a Republican attempt to exploit the tragedy for political gain. As with Newark, Johnson wanted to avoid federal intervention, which would identify the administration with the crisis and make him responsible for likely missteps by National Guardsmen, who were poorly trained to deal with urban riots. If the only way to halt the turmoil was with regular Army forces and federalized National Guardsmen, then Johnson was ready to act. But he cringed at the thought of seeing federal troops shooting women and children. He expressed concern "about the charge that we cannot kill

enough people in Vietnam, so we go out and shoot civilians in Detroit."[68]

Most of July 24, the first full day of the outbreak, was taken up
with crisis management and political maneuvering. In the early
morning hours, Republican Governor George Romney, a potential
rival for the presidency, vacillated between asking for federal troops
and relying exclusively on state and local law enforcement. Romney
aroused Johnson's suspicions by telling the press that he had asked
the White House for troops and then reversed course "because of the
situation in the rest of the country," suggesting the possibility of
insurrections across the United States. With Republican leaders declaring that "rioting and violent civil disorders have grown to a national crisis since the present administration took office," Johnson
could only assume that Romney and the Republicans were blaming
the turmoil on him.

At a meeting with Democratic congressional leaders that evening, Johnson read aloud from a UPI report of Republican party
leaders saying just that: " 'We are rapidly approaching a state of anarchy and the President has totally failed to recognize the problem.' "
Adding that mounting evidence indicated " 'organized planning and
execution on a national scale' " behind the Detroit outbreak, GOP
officials urged Johnson to support a Republican-sponsored antiriot
bill. " 'The nation is in a crisis and this administration has failed even
to make a proposal to protect our people on the streets and in their
homes from riots and violence,' " the Republicans declared.[69]

To counter the Republican attack, Johnson insisted that Romney
send a telegram saying he couldn't suppress the existing looting, ar-
son, and sniping without the assistance of federal troops. After Romney complied, Johnson announced that he was sending federal forces
"on the basis of your representation that that there is reasonable
doubt that you can maintain law and order in Detroit." Romney then
sent a telegram to Ramsey Clark saying that "time could be of the
essence" in providing federal help.[70]

Johnson replied with a nationally televised statement. He explained that within six minutes of receiving Romney's request for
federal troops he had ordered their deployment. Though he had been
reluctant to intervene, he had done so "only because of . . . the undis-
puted evidence that Governor Romney of Michigan and the local
officials in Detroit have been unable to bring the situation under
control." Johnson left no doubt that he would "not tolerate lawlessness" and that, if there were to be finger-pointing, the country should
look first at how Michigan authorities had failed to anticipate and
then deal with problems in their state.

During the reading of his statement, Johnson had J. Edgar Hoover, Clark, McNamara, and two Pentagon officials on camera behind him. The message couldn't have been clearer: Lyndon Johnson, backed by the highest authorities in Justice and Defense, was the country's strongest advocate of law and order. When CBS President Frank Stanton said that LBJ's performance was too contrived and too political, Johnson retorted, "I had the best damn constitutional lawyer in the country write that statement."[71]

Having given his political response to the Republicans, Johnson was eager to encourage hopes of relieving the ills that had provoked the crisis. On July 27, with Detroit beginning to calm down, Johnson gave a nationally televised address to reassure the country that he would not tolerate lawlessness and had a plan for meeting urban difficulties.

First, he announced the appointment of a bipartisan commission headed by Illinois's Democratic Governor Otto Kerner. The other members included Republican Mayor John Lindsay of New York as vice chairman, national and local government officials, business and labor leaders, and prominent blacks. The commission was to recommend means "to prevent or contain such disasters in the future."

But even before the commission reported, Johnson saw the need for "an attack—mounted at every level—upon the conditions that breed despair and violence." He chided those who decried the anti-poverty programs, and declared resistance to current congressional proposals to overcome urban misery as misguided and inhumane. He took particular exception to House members who poked fun at a rat extermination measure as a "civil rats bill," and suggested instead that the President unleash an army of federally supplied cats. Pointing out that helpless slum children suffered rat bites, Johnson asserted that a "government that has spent millions to protect baby calves from worms could surely afford to show as much concern for baby boys and girls."[72]

Califano warned Johnson that setting up the Kerner commission would be seen as a delayed and weak means of dealing with an immediate and severe problem. In addition, Califano predicted that the liberals Johnson had selected as commission members would recommend massive additional spending, which the administration would be unable to fund. But Johnson saw a commission as an effective means to head off a congressional investigation, which would produce attacks on him from the right for indulging rioters and from the left for not doing enough for the poor. A commission also seemed useful in underscoring the need for Congress to fund the administration's programs, especially Model Cities and rent supplements, which he viewed as the best potential means for dealing with inner-city suffering.[73]

But Johnson principally saw the commission as a way to buy time until he could shift money from Vietnam to the cities. In response, the *New York Times* urged Johnson not to use the commission as an excuse for delaying forceful leadership to initiate and enlarge programs that might ease urban ills. It was fine for the President to ask action on his urban proposals, the *Times* declared, but "the events of the past few weeks have demonstrated ... that they [alone] are not adequate" to the immediate or long-term challenge. The $662 million proposed for Model Cities and the $2.06 billion for the War on Poverty impressed the *Times* as "a mere drop in the bucket against the needs of 193 cities and counties that have applied for urban renewal."

A commission meeting in August on the problems of Newark echoed the *Times*'s view. The magnitude of the problem, the hearing showed, made it *"immensely difficult, if not impossible, to cut much ice with the strides made in the last few years."* And the administration's current plans amounted to *"a most modest effort."*[74]

The advice displeased Johnson. True, he publicly urged the commission to "let your search be free. Let it be untrammeled by what has been called the 'conventional wisdom.' As best you can, find the truth, the whole truth, and express it in your report." But privately he "left the impression ... that the administration wanted the commission's quick endorsement of hastily drawn reports and statements," which it refused to give.

The commission had no intention of "serving as a rubber stamp" or of succumbing to " 'railroading' by the administration," Johnson heard from Califano. Johnson's passion to do something about the cities was stronger than ever. But the war and the looming budget deficit convinced him that he could not go beyond what he had earmarked for urban advance at the start of the year. In a conversation with two journalists at the end of August he "went over his program for the cities, and pointed out the political practicality of trying to get programs passed before coming in with big new ideas with no chance of enactment."[75]

In addition, he understood that no one had a formula for an immediate substantive impact on the cities. When he told the commission to go beyond "the conventional wisdom," he meant it. But he heard nothing about managing the urban crisis that sounded at all unconventional. At the end of July, several of his aides advised against speaking to the League of Cities meeting, because "we have nothing to offer by way of a 'new' program." Moreover, he and others in the administration had begun to have doubts about some of the programs he had hoped could work a sea change in the lives of the poor and the inner cities.

In August, in a conversation with six journalists, for example, he said the assumption that lack of job opportunities partly accounted for the upheavals was not borne out by the evidence. "There *were* training vacancies open in *most* of the riot cities," Labor Secretary Wirtz told Johnson. People in the ghettos "*were not rioting for jobs.*" Wirtz saw a need "to find out why the on-the-job training programs aren't being more effectively used."

Johnson thought that "bad housing was more of a factor . . . and feeling against the police seemed to step up the tensions." He told labor leaders the same thing: "In Detroit, four out of five people arrested had jobs with salaries over $120 per week. So you see it is just not a matter of jobs. A lot of it is hate and bitterness which has been developing over many years. It is also a matter of rats and poor housing." He wanted the leaders to get behind the bills in Congress which he predicted "would alleviate these problems."[76]

A report from Harry McPherson in mid-August strengthened Johnson's belief that appropriate federal action to improve housing and ease tensions with the police could make a difference. Government money has been going into Harlem in substantial amounts, McPherson told him after a visit there. As a consequence, we "are making gains with a great many young people. Two people used the same metaphor: 'When the baby's got his mouth on the nipple he can't holler.' "

McPherson emphasized the "awful" housing conditions he saw in Harlem and Brooklyn's Bedford-Stuyvesant ghetto. "Ways have got to be found to do more about Harlem housing," McPherson said. "Kids being raised in the squalor of Harlem today really don't stand much of a chance." He also highlighted the absence of blacks on the police force and how the presence of white cops, who were seen as an "outside authority," added to ghetto tensions. It was not police brutality but the distance between the white cops and the black residents that made inner-city conditions more incendiary.[77]

Another report on "the condition of the Negro in America today" added to Johnson's conviction that his existing proposals for model cities, housing, and crime control bills could improve inner-city life and prevent riots. Great progress had been made but great problems remained, the report said. But everything was not getting worse and chaos was not "around the corner." Humphrey's Cabinet group stressed much the same thing: Housing and alienation were much more the problems than jobs. "It is of critical importance that the programs for the cities now pending before the Congress be enacted with the funding we have requested," LBJ wrote Humphrey on August 23.[78]

There was a quality of self-fulfilling prophecy in Johnson's push for his model cities, rent supplement, and crime control recommendations as sufficient to meet the current crisis. But there was more here than a cynical attempt to silence critics and paper over domestic problems until Vietnam stopped devouring federal resources. However constrained Johnson felt by spending limits, he genuinely believed that he could make significant gains with the programs he had proposed.

There was a measure of delusion in Johnson's thinking, but with his presidency now in a steep decline—at the beginning of June only 34 percent of Americans gave him a vote of confidence—he indulged in some wishful thinking. Unable to find many bright spots abroad or at home, he boosted himself with any ray of hope he could find.[79]

Setbacks in Space

The space program was not one of them. In 1964, Johnson had pushed hard to keep the space effort, in which he had so much pride of authorship, on track. Although determined to keep his first budget under $100 billion, he had agreed to increase NASA spending by $150 million to $5.25 billion. "Our plan to place a man on the moon in this decade remains unchanged," he had told Congress in January 1964. "It is an ambitious and important goal. In addition to providing great scientific benefits, it will demonstrate that our capability in space is second to no other nation's." But, he emphasized, "we cannot reach this goal without sufficient funds. There is no second-class ticket to space."[80]

Johnson's decision to press ahead with Apollo—the manned moon landing—rested less now on considerations of national security. In May 1963, he had declared: "I do not think this generation of Americans is willing to go to bed each night by the light of a Communist moon." But a U.S. missile buildup under JFK, the outcome of the Cuban missile crisis, and the Nuclear Test Ban Treaty in 1963 had eased concerns that we had fallen behind the Soviets in military might. On the day of his assassination, Kennedy himself had intended to say "that there was no longer any fear that a Communist lead in space would become the basis of military superiority."[81]

During the first half of 1964 Johnson had emphasized achieving outer space agreements with Moscow. "President Johnson has apparently lost his enthusiasm for the Soviet-American space race," the *New York Herald Tribune* reported in June. Earlier in the year, the President had sent the deputy administrator of NASA to Geneva "to seek agreements for a 'widening area' of cooperation in space with Moscow." As the astronaut and later Senator John Glenn saw it, Congress was no longer so easily moved to increase space spending by appeals to the Soviet threat. "The anti-Russian theme had worn out," Glenn says. Johnson, ever sensitive to congressional mood, had seen the need to press the case for space exploration on other grounds.[82]

He viewed immediate and long-term economic growth as irresistible arguments. Shortly after becoming President, he had pressed NASA to help Wisconsin and Minnesota expand "their research and engineering capabilities." NASA head James Webb, who was a good politician in his own right and understood the importance of tying NASA to economic benefits, laid plans to double NASA's "activity" in both states. More important, he kept close track of how NASA affected the nation's economy and took every opportunity to apprise Johnson of these gains.[83]

Johnson valued the political advantage coming to the White House principally from NASA spending in Florida, Alabama, Texas, Oklahoma, and California. But he was also mindful of the longer-term national advances NASA seemed likely to produce. As Webb told him, NASA's accomplishments were leading to the development of "new materials ... new structures" as well as "complex electronic, mechanical and chemical systems."[84]

Johnson himself had told a group of astronauts in 1965 that their missions not only increased "our knowledge of technology" but also promised "a better life for all." In a 1969 interview, Johnson said that plans to get to the moon inspired the country to do something about its national problems. In his 1971 memoirs he wrote: "Space was the platform from which the social revolution of the 1960s was launched. We broke out of far more than the atmosphere with our space program. ... If we could send a man to the moon, we knew we should be able to send a poor boy to school and to provide decent medical care for the aged. In hundreds of other forms the space program had an impact on our lives."[85]

In an expansive mood about space exploration in 1964, Johnson had asked Webb to plan post-Apollo projects. Webb had answered in May that new plans might include improved weather prediction and control; moon studies, which might tell us more about the origins of the solar system; the development of space stations, manned and un-manned; better weather, communications, and navigation satellites;

and exploration of the near planets and probes of more distant ones, partly in search of extraterrestrial life.

In February 1965 Webb had given Johnson a more precise statement of NASA's plans. Sensing that expanding commitments at home and abroad had made Johnson less eager for additional costly space projects, Webb had backed away from most of his earlier proposals. Instead, he had urged commitments to two modest programs: the exploration of Mars through an unmanned landing and further exploration of the moon with the technology developed for Apollo. The distinguishing features of the Webb proposals, an aide had told LBJ, were the absence of a request for any "major new launch vehicle systems" and a continuation of NASA funding at current levels.[86]

With Apollo still years away from fulfillment, Johnson had been unwilling to make new commitments. When Webb asked permission to give the chairmen of the House and Senate space committees copies of his February letter, Johnson had resisted. "Why do we need to do anything[?]" he had asked in a reply to Valenti, who was handling the matter. "I would think I would have more leeway & running room by saying nothing[,] which I would prefer."[87]

In 1965, Johnson had begun taking a two-track approach to NASA. His only priority was landing a man on the moon by the end of the decade, as Kennedy and he had promised. Beyond that, he had resisted significant commitments to post-Apollo planning that would cost billions of dollars. One of the striking features of Johnson's memoirs on his presidency is that he devotes only seventeen out of 600 pages to a discussion of space. And of those seventeen pages, only three describe space policy during his presidency. The rest focuses on his Senate and vice-presidential years, the period when he felt he had done his most important work for the space program.[88]

This is not to say that Johnson lost interest in space achievements. He closely attended to the various space missions between 1965 and 1968. Johnson watched each mission on television. He feted the astronauts at the White House and entertained them at the ranch. And as he told one NASA official, "he really in a sense flew with them on every flight from the beginning of the launch till they landed safely": "I've watched with eagerness, and pride, their every movement."[89]

Nevertheless, his interest didn't translate into support for post-Apollo projects. Everything that had initially spurred Johnson to back a major effort in space—fear of Soviet superiority and economic and political gains—now became reasons to avoid commitments to new big programs.

Johnson's concern, for example, that Soviet advances in space might undermine America's national security and prestige in the So-viet-American competition for global influence faded during his pres-idential years. In the spring of 1966, after the Soviets had landed an unmanned spaceship on the moon, Jim Webb pressed the President to use the Soviet feat to ask Congress for more NASA money. Webb told LBJ that he had done his best to "minimize the political risk to your administration from the fact that we are operating substantially under what would be the most efficient program." Webb's message was clear: If the Soviets beat the U.S. to the moon, Johnson would pay a high political price.[90]

But Johnson resisted Webb's pressure. He still hoped the U.S. would land men on the moon ahead of the Soviets, and he believed that Moscow was now more eager for cooperation than competition in space. Nine days before Webb's warning, LBJ had asked U.N. Am-bassador Goldberg to initiate discussions on a celestial bodies treaty. During the next three months, Soviet-American negotiators drafted an agreement. In December, Johnson publicly described the result as the "most important arms control development since the Limited Test Ban Treaty of 1963." The treaty, which was signed in January 1967, banned the placing of weapons of mass destruction in orbit, in outer space or on celestial bodies; established an unconditional commitment to assist and return astronauts who landed in another country; and forbid claims of sovereignty over celestial bodies.[91]

The treaty gave Johnson an advantage over Webb in a 1967 budget fight. After suffering a modest cut of about $75 million from 1965 to 1966, Webb was determined to increase NASA's funding in 1967. But Johnson wouldn't hear of it. Webb's request for $5.3 billion could not withstand a $300 million reduction. By August, moreover, it was clear that Congress and the President would drop NASA's funding below $5 billion for fiscal 1967. This would "leave no choice," Webb warned Johnson, "but to accelerate the rate at which we are carrying on the liquidation of some of the capabilities which we have built up." He predicted that options would now be foreclosed, and doubt and uncertainty would demoralize NASA.[92]

Johnson relied on his budget director to counter Webb's asser-tions. Schultze argued that NASA's funding was entirely adequate to meet the 1969 deadline for a moon landing and to work toward more distant goals like a Mars landing and/or earth orbital stations. After all, "the space program is not a WPA," Schultze declared. Nor did he or Johnson feel that NASA's budget was skimpy alongside $2 billion in spending on elementary and secondary education, $1.8 billion on the poverty program, $200 million on water pollution control, and $25 million for high-speed ground transportation.[93]

Johnson saw little political risk in turning aside Webb's demands. By the end of 1966, it was clear that NASA and space exploration beyond the Apollo landing had diminished popular appeal. In
the summer of 1965 a third of the nation had favored cutting the
space budget, while only 16 percent wanted an increase. Over the
next three and a half years the number for cutting space appropriations rose to 40 percent, with those preferring an increase dropping
to 14 percent.

At the end of 1967, the New York Times reported that a poll
conducted in six American cities showed five other public issues holding priority over efforts in outer space. Residents of these cities preferred doing something about air and water pollution, job training
for unskilled workers, national beautification, and poverty. The following year Newsweek said: "The U.S. space program is in decline.
The Viet Nam war and the desperate conditions of the nation's poor
and its cities—which make space flight seem, in comparison, like an
embarrassing national self-indulgence—have combined to drag down
a program where the sky was no longer the limit."[94]

The Congress as well strongly favored reducing NASA's budget.
A White House survey of congressional leaders at the end of 1966
had revealed pronounced sentiment for keeping Apollo on track but
for cutting NASA spending by skimping on post-Apollo outlays. In
this context, a Johnson request in January 1967 for a $5 billion NASA
budget, including $455 million for post-Apollo programs, was pretty
bold.[95]

Yet Johnson's inclination to be generous with NASA and provide
for a modest amount of post-Apollo spending could not withstand a
disastrous NASA accident and the growing budget deficit. On January
27, a fire destroyed an Apollo command module and killed astronauts
Roger B. Chafee, Edward H. White III, and Virgil I. Grissom during
a test at Cape Kennedy. In addition to the tragic loss of life, the fire
undermined national confidence in NASA, which was now accused of
carelessness in trying to move the Apollo project forward too quickly.
The fire, Johnson said later, represented "an all-time low" for the
space effort.

Senate hearings raised questions about defects in the spacecraft
and brought Webb into sharp conflict with three senators, who saw
him as whitewashing NASA's failings. The New York Times, which
was also highly critical of Webb, said that NASA stood for "Never a
Straight Answer." Though the hearings were "unpleasant and embarrassing for NASA," an administrative history of the agency asserts,
on the whole, "they gave NASA a sympathetic forum in which to
explain how a tragedy had come about, and show how it would serve

to correct deficiencies." NASA's forthrightness in responding to the failings that produced the fire restored a measure of confidence in the agency and decided the Senate committee to recommend continued backing of Apollo.[96]

But the federal budget crisis in the summer of 1967 dealt NASA another blow. Johnson targeted the agency for a $500 million reduction. Webb objected. But for Johnson, there was no choice, except where to apply the cuts. Despite recommendations to the contrary, he stuck to keeping Apollo on schedule, agreeing instead to cut post-Apollo applications and an unmanned landing on Mars. In spite of everything, Webb was still able to assure Johnson that "the goal of the manned lunar landing in this decade is preserved."[97]

The cuts genuinely troubled Johnson. Whenever there were reductions, he would tell Webb, "Next year I hope to make up for this." Johnson "had almost supreme confidence that at some point he could give us resources again and that we could catch up," Webb recalled. More specifically, in a message to Webb in September 1967, the President asked him to "be sure to make abundantly clear [to a congressional committee] that . . . Congress forced me to agree to effect some reductions or lose the tax bill." While Johnson's message was partly a case of political finger-pointing, he was truly uncomfortable reining in NASA or any government program he believed served the national well-being.[98]

Jim Webb also struggled against the reality of declining space commitments. In November 1967, he pressed Schultze to urge a strong statement by the President about NASA funding when signing its appropriation bill. NASA's congressional backers, Webb said, saw the President as having " 'knifed' the very activities he had previously been urging them to support."[99]

Yet nothing Johnson said could change the reality of shrinking budgets and enthusiasm for space exploration after Apollo. A *New York Times* story in April 1968 stated: "After a heady decade of uninterrupted hiring, building and dreaming great dreams of far-reaching exploration, the American space program is gearing down to a slower pace and a less certain future. . . . It is as if the astronauts are heading for a dead-end on the moon." By September, after the White House had proposed to reduce NASA spending another quarter of a billion dollars and congressional appropriations committees penciled in only $3.99 billion for NASA in fiscal 1969, James Webb resigned.[100]

There are conflicting accounts of the reasons behind Webb's departure. Webb himself claimed that he wanted to get out before the Apollo VII and VIII missions, the manned orbits of the earth and

the moon in the fall of 1968, so that he could respond to any failure
by going after critics in and out of Congress. Others say that Webb
was surprised when Johnson accepted his resignation. According to
these accounts, Webb had used the threat of resignation repeatedly
with the President as a way to press NASA's case. On September 16,
1968, however, Johnson, who had gotten "fed up with this same old
story," took Webb up on the offer, saying, "Let's call in the press."[101]

Whatever the realities behind the decision, Webb tried to turn
his resignation to NASA's advantage. At a press conference, he "bitterly" claimed that "congressional budget cuts had put the United
States second in the space race" behind the Russians. Though he
denied that he was leaving because of reductions totaling $1.4 billion
over the last four years, he nevertheless said that "the agency had
been used 'as a sort of whipping boy' by Congress and other agencies
competing for federal funds."[102]

Webb's public comments provoked an angry response in the administration. Donald F. Hornig, the President's Science Advisor, sent
Johnson a memo describing Webb's assertions as "unconscionable
statements," which "were undoubtedly motivated" by NASA's "budgetary problems." Hornig disputed assertions that the Soviets had " 'a
capability that could change the basic structure and balance of power
in the world,' that the U.S. was clearly second in space and that a
Soviet manned lunar landing could be achieved in the next year—a
time scale that is competitive with, or ahead of Apollo."[103]

Johnson sided with Webb, telling his aides to instruct Hornig
not to get into the NASA debate. Johnson told Hornig directly: "Drop
it!" Johnson defended Webb's concern that the Russians might
"achieve both the image and reality of power and forward motion."
Johnson warned Hornig that "even if your group should develop evidence to sustain their views, your report might be shortly followed
by some tragic occurrence in the U.S. program or a major triumph
in the Russian one. This would inevitably bring into question the
judgment of your group in a way that might impair its usefulness."[104]

Webb's concerns were greatly exaggerated, as demonstrated by
the successful Apollo VII and VIII missions in September and December 1968, respectively. But Johnson backed him nevertheless.
Partly, he had a warm feeling for Webb, who had served him so
loyally for almost five years and shown such staying power in the
face of adversity.[105]

But more than personal sentiment determined Johnson's support
of Webb. He felt that the historical reputation of his administration
was partly at stake. If Webb were right about the potential for renewed Soviet dominance in space and Moscow beat the U.S. in the

moon race, Johnson believed that he and Webb would be seen as having presided over a failed space program. By letting Webb beat up on Congress for shortchanging NASA, Johnson was preparing to point the finger at congressmen and senators for any retrospective weaknesses historians saw in his space effort. Shortly after the Apollo VII and VIII successes, when Johnson gave Webb NASA's Distinguished Service Medal and praised him as "the best administrator in the federal government," he was leaving no doubt that, unlike many in the Congress, he had been a staunch advocate of NASA generally and of Apollo in particular.

Lyndon Johnson wanted to be remembered as a President who made his mark in space. With the successful completion of Apollo in 1969 along with his earlier contributions to building NASA, he did. But in 1967–68 he had ample reason to believe that his presidency would be more notable for shortchanging space exploration than for effectively preparing a manned landing on the moon.[106]

The Six Days War

Middle East problems outdid Johnson's difficulties with space. For more than ten years since the Suez crisis of 1956, Israel and its Arab neighbors had fought a limited war. Attacks and counterattacks across the Israeli borders with Egypt, Jordan, Lebanon, and Syria had been commonplace. If this had been America's only problem in the Middle East, the Johnson administration would have been elated. The heavy dependence of Western Europe on Persian Gulf oil and aggressive Soviet efforts to expand Moscow's influence with radical Arab states led by Egypt, Syria, and Iraq gave Johnson constant concerns rivaling Vietnam. Though the struggle in Southeast Asia was at the center of Johnson's foreign problems, Middle East tensions, with the potential for a Soviet-American confrontation as dangerous as the Cuban missile crisis, was a constant concern.

During the first three years of his presidency Johnson had struggled to contain an Israeli nuclear program. Surrounded by well armed hostile neighbors with twenty times its population, Israel saw a nuclear capability as essential to its national survival. Fearful that Israel's acquisition of "the bomb" would encourage proliferation in the region and around the world, the Johnson administration discouraged Tel Aviv's nuclear plans with assurances about its security and military supplies.

At the same time, the Johnson State Department cultivated relations with Jordan, Iran, and Saudi Arabia, "moderate" Arab states frightened by Soviet support of "radicals" committed to overturning their governments. To implement its policies, in the summer of 1966 the administration began supplying Iran and Saudi Arabia with half a billion dollars in military equipment; providing an unprecedented flow of offensive weapons to Israel; shipping fighter planes to Jordan, where Palestinian radicals led by Yasir Arafat were destabilizing the country; reducing American economic aid to Gamal Nasser's Egypt; and isolating Hafez al-Assad's pro-Soviet Ba'athist regime in Damascus.[107]

Despite the administration's efforts to stabilize the region, by the spring of 1967 another Arab-Israeli war seemed in the offing. Increased Soviet support of Baghdad, Cairo, and Damascus had encouraged Palestinian guerrilla attacks on Israel from Syria, Jordan, and Lebanon. In April, after a Syrian artillery barrage triggered by a Palestinian incursion in northern Israel, Israeli jets bombed terrorist bases in the Golan heights and shot down six Syrian MIGs twenty miles from Damascus. In May, after Syria called on Cairo to discourage an Israeli military buildup on its borders, Nasser pressured Secretary-General U Thant into withdrawing U.N. observers in the Sinai and replaced them with Egyptian forces. On May 22, Nasser announced the closing of the Strait of Tiran and access to the Israeli port of Eilat from the Red Sea.[108]

The Israeli government pressed Johnson for a public statement on the extent of America's commitment to Israel's security. In a private response, the President sympathized with Israel's predicament, asked for patience while mediation efforts went forward, and warned that without prior consultation on unilateral actions Tel Aviv should not expect any commitment of support from the United States.

Johnson now came under "tremendous pressure" from American Jewish groups. According to White House aide John P. Roche, Johnson responded with a "little malicious game." He read a State Department statement to the pro-Israel lobbyists, which was so decidedly noncommittal it brought the Israeli ambassador to the verge of tears. " 'For God's sake, what is he doing?' " Roche asked Rostow. "Walt said, 'Oh, he's just getting a little therapy for all this pressure they put on him.' "

On May 23, the President issued a pro-Israel statement deploring the U.N. withdrawal, denouncing the closing of the Gulf of Aqaba as "illegal" and a potential threat to peace, backing Thant's efforts to alter Egypt's action, and reaffirming America's commitment to political independence and territorial integrity for all nations in the Middle East.[109]

Johnson's dilemma was how to prevent a war, or, if a war occurred, how to assure against a U.S. confrontation with the Soviet Union and heightened domestic opposition to Vietnam as a distraction from the "more important" Middle East conflict. When Israeli Foreign Minister Abba Eban came to Washington, Johnson wondered whether he could avoid a meeting that would include demands for support he was reluctant to give. Johnson was advised that having restrained the Israelis from an attack, he had no choice but to see Eban.

At their meeting on May 26, Eban outlined three possibilities: Israel could surrender to Egypt's action and face "strangulation"; it could fight and defeat Arab aggression; or it could hope for an international solution. Eban said he had come to see the President about the latter and in particular about a British proposal that "the principal maritime powers" declare their intention to keep the Strait of Tiran open. Johnson explained his preference for a U.N. settlement, and if that failed, he would press for the British plan. Eban reminded Johnson that the U.S. had commitments on the straits dating from 1957 and asked for assurances that the administration intended to honor them. Johnson said that he could not commit himself without congressional agreement. He also restated American opposition to an Israeli attack, saying "Israel need not be alone unless it chooses to go alone."[110]

The Israelis were willing to give Johnson's diplomacy a chance. But on May 30, when Jordan and the United Arab Republic, as Egypt called itself, announced a mutual defense pact, Tel Aviv saw almost no hope of an Arab retreat on Aqaba. Israeli Prime Minister Levi Eshkol pressed Johnson anew for a commitment to join in forcing open the gulf, but Johnson refused to go beyond what he had told Eban and counseled continued patience.

Because the Egyptians couldn't be moved, because he couldn't arrange a favorable response to the British proposal, and because Israel's civilian economy could sustain a full mobilization for only a limited time, Johnson expected Tel Aviv to launch an attack. In a conversation with John Roche at the beginning of June, Johnson vented his irritation with the Israelis by doing "a take-off on Eban, a little miniature Winston Churchill, and sort of did a little imitation of him," and asked: " 'Now, what do you think they're going to do?' " When someone said, " 'They'll wait,' " Johnson disagreed: " 'They're going to hit. There's nothing we can do about it.' He knew his customers—very, very penetrating intelligence," Roche says.[111]

On June 5 the Israelis began a six-day war in which they defeated Egyptian, Jordanian, and Syrian forces, taking the Sinai, the West bank of the Jordan, east Jerusalem, and the Golan Heights.

After the outbreak of hostilities, the White House immediately began trying to arrange a cease-fire and more extended agreements for a stable Middle East peace. But developments at home and in the region made it impossible for the United States to have a significant impact. "There's a picture of a sad man," Johnson said as he looked at a newspaper photo of himself on the first day of the war.[112]

His distress mounted over the next five days. On the afternoon of June 5, when a State Department spokesman declared the United States "neutral in thought, word and deed," it provoked a fire storm of criticism among American Jews. Since Washington was Israel's principal source of resupply, threats of withholding materiel was a means of restraining Tel Aviv from fully exploiting its war gains. But domestic complaints that Johnson was abandoning or reducing a nineteen-year commitment to Israel's survival stung him and limited his freedom to apply effective pressure to Tel Aviv.[113]

The President now found himself attacked by Arabs and Jews alike. With the Egyptians complaining that U.S. planes had supported initial Israeli ground actions, several Arab states broke relations with Washington. The State Department's declaration of neutrality had partly been an attempt to appease Arab sentiment. But its principal result was to leave the Arab governments unconvinced while angering the Israelis and their American supporters. Within hours of the State Department declaration, one of Johnson's principal Jewish friends complained that "neutrality" meant bans on fund-raising and arms shipments to Israel.[114]

But Johnson had no such policy. To repair the damage caused by the State Department, the President instructed Rusk and others to reiterate his announcement of May 23 about supporting territorial integrity and independence and his eagerness for a cease-fire and a long-term settlement. He also asked prominent Jewish friends to get the word out that he was working to assure Israel's security and that attacks on his administration were uncalled-for and unproductive.

Some in the Jewish community were not so sure. Mrs. Arthur Krim, the wife of one of the President's closest Jewish associates and principal fund raisers in 1964, sent word that American Jews couldn't easily forgive the "neutrality" statement. They took it "to mean that in an hour of gravest danger—before they knew the Israeli army would be victorious—that this country disengaged itself." Mrs. Krim urged a presidential statement to a scheduled rally in Washington's Lafayette Park. Without it, she feared the gathering might become "an anti-Johnson, rather than a pro-Israel—demonstration."[115]

Two White House Jewish aides, Larry Levinson and Ben Wattenberg, gave Johnson similar counsel. A statement to the rally, they advised, "would neutralize the 'neutrality' statement and could lead to a great domestic political bonus—and not only from Jews. . . . It would seem that the Mid-East crisis can turn around a lot of anti-Viet Nam anti-Johnson feeling, particularly if you use it as an opportunity." But Johnson now dug in his heels. He told Levinson on the phone how disappointed he was in his Jewish friends, who were showing so little trust in him. In fact, he was more than disappointed; he was furious. Liberal Jewish Americans, who had been among his sharpest critics on Vietnam, now wanted him to flex America's military might in the Middle East. He wouldn't give in to their "hypocrisy."

Shortly after their phone conversation, Johnson, on leaving the Oval Office, caught sight of Levinson down the hall. Waving a clenched fist, Johnson shouted at him, "You Zionist dupe! You and Wattenberg are Zionist dupes in the White House! Why can't you see I'm doing all I can for Israel. That's what you should be telling people when they ask for a message from the President for their rally."[116]

Johnson's diplomacy over the next several days repaired the political damage inflicted by the State Department. A significant element in the turnabout was the President's handling of the worst crisis in U.S.–Israeli relations since U.S. recognition of Israel in May 1948. On the afternoon of June 8, Israeli planes and torpedo boats attacked the USS *Liberty*, an electronic spy ship operating in international waters east-northeast of Port Said in the Mediterranean Sea. The assault killed thirty-four and wounded 171 American sailors.

Initially, the President thought Soviet forces had staged the attack, but a prompt signal from Tel Aviv that they had mistaken the *Liberty* for an Egyptian ship, which had allegedly been shelling the Israeli coast, identified the attacker as Israel.

The White House privately expressed shock and disbelief that the Israelis had committed such a gross error. "At the time of the attack," Rusk told Tel Aviv, the *Liberty* "was flying the American flag and its identification was clearly indicated in large white letters and numerals on its hull. It was broad daylight and the weather conditions were excellent." An hour and fifteen minutes before the attack, two Israeli aircraft circled the ship three times, with the evident purpose of identifying the vessel. "Accordingly there is every reason to believe that the USS *Liberty* was identified. . . . In these circumstances the later military attack . . . is quite literally incomprehensible. As a minimum, the [air] attack must be condemned as an act of military recklessness reflecting wanton disregard for human life." An assault by four torpedo boats twenty minutes later, "sub-

stantially after the vessel was or should have been identified by Israeli
military forces, manifests the same reckless disregard for human life.
The silhouette and conduct of the USS *Liberty* readily distinguished
it from any vessel that could have been considered as hostile."[117]

The Israelis insisted that the attack had been a mistake. The
presence of a U.S. ship in an area being used by Egypt for hostile
action caused the error. The Israelis expressed "deep regret" and offered "to make amends for the tragic loss of life and material damage."

The White House disputed Tel Aviv's version of events. To be
sure, the President's Foreign Intelligence Advisory Board (PFIAB)
placed the *Liberty* closer to the coast than initially thought, acknowledged that the Israelis had not been informed of the ship's presence
in a region of hostilities, and accepted that Israeli defense forces had
misinformation about a coastal attack. PFIAB also granted that Israel
forces had reason to think that the *Liberty* was an Egyptian supply
ship.

More important, the board concluded that available information
did not "reflect that the Israeli high command made a premeditated
attack on a ship known to be American." Nor did evidence "support
the theory that the highest echelons of the Israeli government were
aware of the *Liberty*'s true identity or of the fact that an attack on
her was taking place."[118]

So much for the official version of events, which was calculated
to avoid a crisis with Israel in the midst of an all-out war against
Arab states with ties to Moscow. Behind the scenes, the highest officials of the U.S. government, including the President, believed it
"inconceivable" that Israel's "skilled" defense forces could have committed such a gross error.

They assumed that the Israelis saw their attack on the *Liberty*
as an act of self-defense. Fearful that the American ship was monitoring and transmitting information about Israeli military preparations against Syria, the Israelis felt compelled to silence the *Liberty*:
If its intelligence inadvertently fell into the hands of the Arabs, they
could use it to inflict significant casualties on Israeli forces, and U.S.
government forewarnings of Israeli military plans might make it
more difficult for Tel Aviv to secure its war aims. The Israelis were
determined to avoid a repeat of 1956, when U.S., Soviet, and U.N.
pressure forced them into giving up the fruits of their victory against
Egypt.[119]

By June 8, Israeli-American differences over acceptable cease-
fire conditions had become a major concern. On the evening of June
6, after the U.S. government had persuaded the U.N. Security Council

not to insist on a cease-fire with a pullback to previous borders, Johnson announced American support of "a simple cease-fire" as a necessary first step toward a "settled peace" in the Middle East. Only after Israel had seized all Jordanian territory west of the Jordan River, however, did Tel Aviv take heed of Washington's warning that King Hussein might lose power and agree to a cease-fire with Amman on June 7. Moreover, Israel and Egypt continued fighting until Israeli forces had reached the Suez Canal and surrounded Egyptian units in the Sinai on June 8.

The fighting with Syria went on until June 10, despite Syrian agreement to call a halt on June 9. Eager to take advantage of Syrian weakness by seizing the Golan Heights on its Syrian border and, if possible, topple the Ba'athist regime, Tel Aviv would not stop fighting on the 9th. Israel ignored a warning from Secretary Rusk that it faced a Security Council condemnation unless it ended hostilities.

A Soviet threat carried more weight. On June 10, Moscow, which in Johnson's estimate "had lost their shirts" in the conflict, told the White House that unless Washington "made its influence with Israel felt and weighed in to stop this war ... the Soviet Union was going to have to take whatever actions it had within its capacities, including military actions." Unwilling to be bullied by Moscow, Johnson ordered the U.S. Sixth Fleet, "orbiting around Sicily," to head toward the eastern Mediterranean. Because Soviet naval forces were watching the Sixth Fleet "like a hawk," the message got "back to Moscow in a hurry." Nevertheless, the Soviet pressure disturbed Johnson, who "alarmed" Tel Aviv with a " 'clear signal' of American anxieties." With the Golan Heights already occupied, Israel agreed to a cease-fire on all fronts.[120]

The cease-fire concluded the immediate crisis, but left problems that could bring a renewed outbreak: Israel's occupation of Arab territories, militant Palestinian guerrillas threatening instability in Jordan, and Moscow's unprecedented opportunity to ally itself with anti-American Arab states were all predictable flashpoints. On June 16, the White House took note of Soviet arms shipments to the Middle East, which might lead to an Arab counterattack against Israel. On the 21st, Johnson privately described the region as "an explosive" area, where the United States had limited influence.

Johnson's frustrations and anxieties about the Middle East would last to the end of his term, despite U.N. Security Council Resolution 242 passed on November 22, 1967. Though the resolution struck a number of correct rhetorical chords about a "just and lasting peace," "secure and recognized boundaries," Israeli withdrawal "from territories occupied in the recent conflict," and the "sovereignty, territorial integrity and political independence of all states," the opposing sides refused to concede anything in practice that could advance the region toward a genuine peace. Though Johnson understood that "the basic problems have been there all the time," that "we can't solve the Middle East with two men in a room over a highball" and that people in the area would "have to talk to each other," the dilemma of the Middle East represented another of the intractable problems that besieged him during 1967.[121]

U.S.-Soviet Relations: Glassboro

The Six Days War had at least one salutary effect: It forced Soviet-American differences to the forefront of concerns in Washington and Moscow, propelling them into discussions that had been inhibited by Vietnam. Every President since FDR had held summit meetings with their Soviet counterparts. But three and a half years into his presidency, LBJ had had only written and electronic communications with officials in Moscow. More important, the White House had been unable to make any significant progress in major arms control discussions on nuclear proliferation and antiballistic missile systems. Likewise, the tensions between the two over the Middle East added to the dangers of a Soviet-American clash similar to the 1962 Cuban crisis. True, a consular treaty with the Soviets, a nearly completed agreement with Moscow on outer space, and an abortive attempt to join in preventing the Six Days War demonstrated that both sides were eager for improved relations. Nevertheless, the most important issues confronting the two remained to be addressed.[122]

An opportunity presented itself when Soviet Premier Aleksei Kosygin attended a special session of the U.N. General Assembly convened at Moscow's request to demand Israel's withdrawal from Arab territories. Kosygin, an understated bureaucrat who provided a sharp contrast to the flamboyant Khrushchev, came to New York for two apparent purposes. The Arab defeat required a show of support, which the presence of the Soviet leadership at the U.N. in behalf of an unrealizable goal largely fulfilled.

Kosygin also wanted to meet with Johnson. The Soviet leadership feared a Sino-American accommodation over Vietnam, which might force a U.S.-Soviet confrontation. A meeting with the President might ease some tensions and deter the White House from any arrangement with Peking. "Kosygin had an obsession about China," LBJ told Senator George Aiken on the eve of Kosygin's visit, "he was scared to death." Johnson told a Hearst newspaper man the same day:

"The Soviets seem to be terribly worried about China. Something odd is going on." The "something odd" was heightened Soviet fear of a China that in June 1967 detonated its first hydrogen bomb.[123]

Johnson's advisers urged him to allay Soviet suspicions about American intentions in the Middle East and Vietnam by meeting with the Premier. Zbigniew Brzezinski at the State Department's Policy Planning Council believed it "important that Kosygin emerge from any eventual meeting with the President disabused of the notion that the United States is out to humiliate the Soviet Union and is currently engaged in a broad political offensive directed against it. Some gesture may be in order." Fulbright thought there was a chance for genuine progress on the Middle East and Vietnam, and at the very least a meeting would advance the President's wish to build bridges that could lead to later progress. One of LBJ's principal aides believed that he could not avoid seeing Kosygin: If worsening relations followed a failure to meet, it would be blamed on the administration.[124]

Johnson foresaw no concrete agreements coming from a conference. And he worried that the only gains would go to the Soviets. "Kosygin had suffered a fiasco worse than the Bay of Pigs, and was struggling to recover," he told network bureau chiefs on June 19. Kosygin "came over here to try to get some of the polecat smell off of him," Johnson told another journalist. "His policies in the Middle East have been a flop and a failure. As far as I can tell, he has nothing constructive to offer toward solution."[125]

Nevertheless, Johnson felt compelled to meet the Kremlin's head man. He wanted to discuss the Middle East and Vietnam. He intended to emphasize that we had no foreknowledge of Israel's offensive, nor had we conspired with Israel or anyone to bring down the Egyptian and Syrian regimes. In addition, he hoped to persuade Kosygin that our only interest in Southeast Asia was the independence of South Vietnam, and he intended to sound him out about possible peace talks. He also had some hope that he could effectively advance the case for a nuclear nonproliferation treaty and an arms control agreement covering antiballistic missile systems.

"I do not think ... that a meeting will result in any specific agreement on any specific question," Ambassador Llewellyn Thompson in Moscow advised. But some direct questions about what might advance the possibility of peace talks with Hanoi might be useful. Also, "the effect of the President's personality on Kosygin would enable [him], when he goes back, to influence his colleagues in a better direction." And even if none of this came to pass, a meeting, Walt Rostow told Johnson, would "cover your flank to the left and among the columnists. If you don't do it, they will blame every difficulty that follows on the lack of a meeting. The Republicans will run on: I will go to Moscow."[126]

Problems finding a mutually agreeable site to meet foretold the difficulties of reaching substantive agreements. Johnson proposed the White House as a first choice or Camp David, a presidential retreat in Maryland, where security would present no problem. But being an official guest of the U.S. government would undermine Soviet relations with the Arabs and Hanoi and give Peking a propaganda advantage. Why not meet in New York? Kosygin asked. But a meeting in the city, and especially at the U.N., seemed certain to attract "a sea of pickets and protestors" from both sides of the political spectrum who would embarrass Johnson and Kosygin. The White House, which was now terribly apprehensive about any LBJ public appearance as a magnet to anti–Vietnam War opponents, suggested Maguire Air Force Base in New Jersey, where there could be no demonstrators. But Kosygin saw a military setting as an attempt to intimidate his government.

With the help of Governor Richard Hughes, the two sides settled on Glassboro, New Jersey, a small college town halfway between New York and Washington and easily accessible from the Philadelphia airport and the Jersey Turnpike. With the college out of session and the meeting convened overnight, the conference was insulated from hostile demonstrators.[127]

Johnson and Kosygin agreed to meet for four hours on June 23 beginning at 11 a.m. Hollybush, the home of Thomas Robinson, the president of Glassboro State College, became the conference site. The house was a simple two-story Victorian residence "topped by a belfry-like tower and faced with white, wrought-iron grillwork." The first floor consisted of two large rooms, a smaller, private study, and a dining area for twenty-four people. In the hours before the conference began, an air-conditioning system was installed and appropriate tables and chairs were provided for the larger rooms. Because no unobtrusive taping system could be set up on such short notice, a White House secretary recorded the conference proceedings by "eavesdropping from just outside the [meeting room] door and, after the door was closed, from a back stairway."[128]

As the host, Johnson arrived half an hour ahead of Kosygin, and then greeted him with "an elaborate negotiated handshake" as he left his car. On the walk to the house, the sixty-three-year-old Kosygin congratulated the fifty-eight-year-old President on the birth of his first grandchild two days before. Kosygin, vying to establish himself as the elder statesman, declared that he had been a grandfather

With Dwight Eisenhower, John Kennedy, Richard Nixon, and other notables looking on, Lyndon Johnson is sworn in as Vice President. LBJ Library Collection.

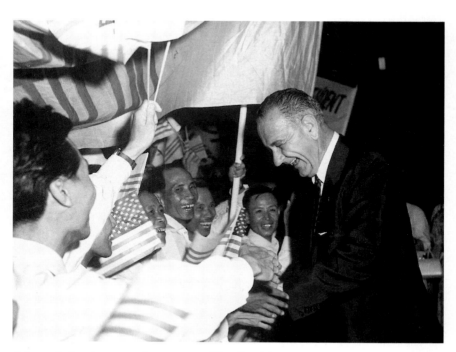

Johnson's few happy assignments as Vice President were trips abroad, where he was shown the deference he craved. On a trip to Asia in May 1961, he "pressed the flesh" of South Vietnamese civilians. LBJ Library Collection.

Kennedy, LBJ, and John Connally during President Kennedy's fatal visit to Dallas, Texas, November 21–22, 1963. LBJ Library Collection. Reprinted with permission of AP/Wide World Photos.

Johnson's grim swearing-in on Air Force One, with Jacqueline Kennedy in blood-stained clothes by his side and Lady Bird to his right. LBJ Library Collection.

A somber President speaks to Congress and the country, November 27, 1963, urging, "Let us continue." LBJ Library Collection.

At Ann Arbor, Michigan, in May 1964, Johnson asked the country to reach for a Great Society. LBJ Library Collection.

In January 1964, Johnson met with Martin Luther King, Jr., and other black leaders to plot legislative strategy for the most far-reaching civil rights law in American history. The law passed in July. LBJ Library Collection.

In August, a grim-faced Johnson described North Vietnamese torpedo boat attacks in the Gulf of Tonkin and a request to Congress for a resolution approving action to resist Communist aggression. LBJ Library Collection.

Johnson on the campaign trail in 1964. LBJ Library Collection.

The "Daisy Field" ad, which ran only once during the campaign, effectively portrayed Barry Goldwater as irresponsible. It launched the era of negative political advertising. LBJ Library Collection.

Johnson in a rare relaxed moment with his dog, December 1964. LBJ Library Collection.

Johnson, who said, "I never think about politics more than eighteen hours a day," micromanaged his administration. LBJ Library Collection.

1965 was the high point of Johnson's influence in passing major reforms. Here he is seen at a Medicare signing ceremony in July 1965 with former President Harry Truman, who had tried and failed to pass such a law in the 1940s. Vice President Hubert Humphrey, a forceful advocate for LBJ's reforms, looks on. LBJ Library Collection.

In August, Johnson, under pressure from King's voter registration campaign in Selma, Alabama, signed the Voting Rights Act. LBJ Library Collection.

By 1966, American demonstrations against the war and no discernible progress in the fighting convinced Johnson that his presidency was in jeopardy. LBJ Library Collection.

The march on the Pentagon in October 1967 enraged Johnson. LBJ Library Collection.

A conference in Honolulu with Vietnamese President Nguyen Van Thieu and Prime Minister Nguyen Cao Ky provided no solution to Johnson's difficulties with the war. LBJ speaks with Ky. LBJ Library Collection.

Johnson confers with General William Westmoreland. LBJ Library Collection.

Neither Secretary of State Dean Rusk, pictured to LBJ's right (top photo), nor Secretary of Defense Robert McNamara, the man Johnson considered the smartest member of his government, had a winning strategy. LBJ Library Collection.

In 1966, the war drove Senator J. William Fulbright, chairman of the Foreign Relations Committee, Robert F. Kennedy, and King into open opposition to LBJ. LBJ Library Collection.

Chairman of the Senate Armed Services Committee, Georgia Senator Richard Russell, Johnson's mentor, was unable to counsel him on how to find a successful end to the war. LBJ Library Collection.

Inner-city summer riots beginning with Watts in Los Angeles in 1965 culminated in the 1967 Detroit violence that led Johnson to set up the Kerner Commission to probe the causes and prevention of civil disorders. A burning building in Detroit's ghetto symbolized America's racial divide. LBJ Library Collection. Reprinted with permission of AP/Wide World Photos.

1968 was one of the worst years in American history. LBJ listens to a tape sent from Vietnam by Captain Charles Robb, his son-in-law. LBJ Library Collection.

On March 31, Johnson announced that he would not run again. LBJ Library Collection.

The Democratic convention in Chicago in August 1968 exploded in street violence. Policemen use their guns to push along youths arrested at Chicago's Lincoln Park. Hundreds of riot-helmeted, gas mask–clad policemen sprayed tear gas into thousands of Hippies, Yippies, and antiwar demonstrators to rout them into Lincoln Park and pursued the fleeing band through North Side streets. UPI/Corbis-Bettmann.

In retirement, Johnson found solace in the management of his Stonewall, Texas, ranch. LBJ Library Collection.

Johnson's last public appearance was at a civil rights symposium in December 1972, where he declared civil rights the greatest achievement of his thirty-seven-year political career. He is pictured with Barbara Jordan and Vernon Jordan. LBJ Library Collection.

Johnson died of a heart attack in January 1973. He was buried in a family cemetery at his ranch. LBJ Library Collection.

for eighteen years. Johnson, leaving no doubt who was in charge, led the Premier by the elbow into the house, where he introduced him to the supporting cast, posed for pictures, offered his guest a glass of ice water, and escorted him into Robinson's small study furnished with a rocking chair for the President, a three-seat sofa for Kosygin, and two large upholstered easy chairs for the translators.[129]

Kosygin impressed the President "as an extremely intelligent and competent person with a personal capacity for humor and human feeling." American accounts to the press of the meeting stressed the cordiality between the two sides. Reporters were told that Kosygin was "friendly, jolly, and warm" and that half the morning session was taken up with "folksy discussion" of the kind of world "in which their grandchildren could best grow and prosper." The Soviet press, by contrast, described the conference as initiated by Johnson and as an occasion for stern lectures to the Americans on "Israel, Vietnam, and other assorted American misdeeds."

Privately, Johnson did not discount the hard edge to the meeting. Afterward, he described Kosygin as "an extremely disciplined Communist leader" who presented "existing Soviet positions hard" and refused to make agreements. Quoting Averell Harriman, Johnson said: "With Russians it takes three meetings to make a deal: the first, courteous; the second, rough; the third, the deal is made. . . . The third session," Johnson added, "will not be a single session. It will consist in what unfolds in the weeks and months ahead on the specific issues and positions I took up with the Chairman."[130]

Johnson had it right. The two days of meetings on June 23 and 25 were largely an exercise in "cordial disagreement." But the subtext was a wish for better relations that would take months and years to blossom.

During the morning talks, both men outdid each other in professions of peaceful intentions. But, as Kosygin then put it, "we have the same goals, neither country wanted war. However, . . . when we began to discuss specific problems and practical steps for their solution, then a great many difficulties and differences arose."

The Middle East was Kosygin's first case in point. They could not agree on which of them bore responsibility for the recent fighting; nor could they agree that Israel would have to withdraw from conquered territories before peace talks could begin. Kosygin predicted renewed hostilities unless Israel withdrew. Johnson emphasized Israel's insistence on security as a prelude to any restoration of boundaries. When Kosygin replied that a war might provoke a Soviet-American confrontation, Johnson "leaned forward and said very slowly . . . , let us understand one another. I hope there will be no war. If there is a war, I hope it will not be a big war. . . . I hope you and we will keep out of this matter because, if we do get into it, it will be a 'most serious' matter." Both sides denied that they were giving ultimatums and turned to other problems.[131]

During an hour-and-a-half lunch session, the two sparred over antiballistic missile systems. Initial Soviet deployments of ABMS to counter America's advantage in offensive weapons stimulated a similar U.S. program and development of multiwarhead missiles.

Asked by Johnson to make the case against ABMS, McNamara described a vicious circle in which defensive missiles would beget offensive ones in ever larger numbers: An "insane" cycle of more weapons-building provoking a greater sense of insecurity and ever more defensive and offensive weapons. "It is our ability to destroy the attacker as a viable 20th-century nation that provides the deterrent," McNamara declared, "not the ability to limit damage to ourselves." Kosygin replied: "How well you speak," and dismissed McNamara's argument for building only less expensive offensive missiles as "a commercial approach to a moral problem." "When I have trouble sleeping," Kosygin added, "it's because of your offensive missiles, not your defensive missiles." McNamara denied Kosygin's assertion, but the Premier refused to see any merit in the secretary's argument.[132]

The afternoon session focused on Vietnam, with no indication that Soviet overtures to Hanoi would lead to peace talks. Johnson saw Kosygin as under instructions not to budge one inch: "His position was rigid and familiar: we should stop the bombing and get out of Vietnam."

Only on nonproliferation of nuclear weapons was there any sign of movement. Though no commitments were made, the American delegation saw "definite headway" on the subject. "It is perfectly clear that they want a non-proliferation treaty if they can get one," a U.S. summary of the talks stated. Despite the want of substantive gains, Johnson and Kosygin agreed to meet again two days later on Sunday. Kosygin emphasized "that there were forces in the world [China's Communists] which were interested in causing a clash between the United States and the USSR. He assured the President that such forces did exist." He was ready to meet again in the service of U.S.-Soviet peace.[133]

But having implied their eagerness for American support against China, the Soviets used the Sunday talks to underscore their independence and equality with the U.S. as a superpower. Kosygin began the meeting by trying to put Johnson on the defensive. The Premier declared himself "somewhat perplexed" by Johnson's published statement the previous day that competing socialist and capitalist systems would always provoke tensions. Johnson claimed he was misquoted, and declared his conviction that a new spirit of friendship was advancing them toward "mutually acceptable solutions to outstanding problems."

In particular, Johnson wanted discussions focused on reducing military budgets. Kosygin declared this an admirable but impractical idea as long as the United States spent $20 billion a year on fighting in Vietnam. Johnson countered that Soviet military supplies to Vietnam kept the war going. At the very least they should try for an agreement on limiting ABMS, Johnson said. But Kosygin saw no chance for disarmament gains without settlements in Vietnam and the Middle East. And the ensuing discussion of Middle East and Vietnam differences demonstrated that no agreements on these problems would emerge from the talks.

But Johnson was dogged about at least keeping the dialogue alive. Let us put aside a week every year to meet and talk, he proposed. Kosygin, who could not agree to anything without Kremlin approval, suggested that they stay in touch through the hot line, which, during the Middle East war, had allowed them to accomplish more in one day "than others could accomplish in three years."[134]

Johnson left Glassboro disappointed at his inability to coax Kosygin into anything concrete. But he had genuine hopes that agreements on major issues were within reach. These were boosted when Cyrus Eaton, a wealthy Ohio industrialist with special ties to the Soviets, reported in July that Kosygin described himself as "glad to meet again with President Johnson" and that Eaton considered it a "propitious" time for "a long-term arrangement with the Soviets." In August, after Eaton agreed to a proposal from Dmitri Polyansky, a Deputy Soviet Premier, to meet in Canada, Eaton urged Johnson to "move swiftly for a permanent accommodation with the Soviets."[135]

"You seem to be fairly sanguine about your relations with Russia," an English journalist told LBJ in a private conversation in October. Eager for both international and domestic purposes to put the best possible face on Soviet-American relations, Johnson said he didn't "know of any period in history when there have been more agreements between the U.S. and the USSR."

Possibly hoping that the military collaboration in World War II had faded from American minds, Johnson rested his case on a recent Soviet decision to work toward a nuclear nonproliferation treaty. He also believed that a McNamara speech in September announcing American intentions to go forward with a limited ABM deployment designed to meet a Chinese nuclear attack would push Moscow into serious discussions about limits on ABMS. Though it would take until the summer of 1968 before a nonproliferation agreement was concluded and commitments to begin ABM talks were announced, Johnson could see the glimmerings of what would become known in the 1970s as Soviet-American Détente.[136]

Thurgood Marshall

At the same time Johnson saw the potential for better Soviet-American relations as one bright spot in an otherwise gloomy world, he viewed an appointment to the Supreme Court as his principal chance in 1967 to make a major advance in domestic affairs. In its 178-year history Supreme Court justices had all been white males. No president had ever proposed appointing a person of color or a woman to the Court. Johnson believed that, as with desegregation of all public institutions, the Court should now reflect the shift in social and political mood toward fulfilling constitutional mandates on equal treatment under the law. And what better place to promote equality and justice for all than in the institution most responsible for defining the law of the land?

In February, when Tom Clark announced that he would resign from the Court at the close of its current term to assure against conflicts of interest with his son Ramsey, LBJ's choice for Attorney General, Johnson had a second chance to appoint an associate justice. Having convinced Abe Fortas to replace Arthur Goldberg on the bench, Johnson now wanted another liberal who would legitimize his Great Society reforms. But he also wanted someone who would underscore his administration's commitment to the civil rights revolution of 1964–65. In a discussion with advisers, he mentioned several black jurists but declared that he was also considering appointing the first woman to the Court. Lady Bird encouraged Lyndon to do just that.[137]

But Johnson concluded that a black had a prior claim on the position. Having made no major civil rights advances in almost two years and believing it impractical to expect any to pass Congress in the current or next session, Johnson saw a black appointment to the bench as a compelling alternative. Such a selection would have great symbolic as well as substantive significance. At a time when inner-city riots and black radicalism attached a stigma of lawlessness to black behavior, he wanted to reaffirm the commitment of blacks to American institutions and the rule of law.

No one promised to serve Johnson's purposes better than Thurgood Marshall. The fifty-eight-year-old Marshall was a seasoned jurist with a record of extraordinary accomplishment as an attorney and a judge. The son of a Pullman car steward and kindergarten teacher, Marshall grew up in Baltimore, as racially segregated as any Deep South city. "The only thing different between the South and Baltimore was trolley cars," Marshall said later. "They weren't segregated. Everything else was segregated." As a child and adolescent, Marshall had a comfortable existence with little impulse to rebel against the accepted social mores. During his years at Lincoln University in Pennsylvania, a black college with a white teaching staff, he was exposed to arguments about integrating the faculty that encouraged him to oppose separation of the races. Barred by the color line from attending the University of Maryland law school, he graduated first in his class from Washington, D.C.'s, Howard University with an LLB in 1933.

Under the tutelage of Charles H. Houston, the dean at Howard and later director of the NAACP's Legal Defense and Education Fund, Marshall launched a career as an advocate of black rights. Pressuring white store owners in Baltimore to hire blacks and the steel workers union to integrate, Marshall won a landmark case forcing the Maryland law school to accept a black applicant. Beginning in 1936, he joined the NAACP's legal office in New York, where he set legal precedents with cases ending restrictive covenants against selling homes to blacks, bars to black voting in Texas party primaries, and less pay to black school teachers for the same work done by whites. His successful advocacy in 1954 of school desegregation in *Brown v. Board of Education*, coupled with twenty-eight other winning pleas out of thirty-two made before the U.S. Supreme Court, secured Marshall's place as one of the greatest jurists in American history.[138]

In 1961 President Kennedy appointed Marshall to a lifetime position as a judge of the U.S. Court of Appeals for the Second Circuit, which handles appeals for New York, Connecticut, and Vermont. His confirmation was held up for twelve months by Senate Judiciary Committee Chairman James O. Eastland of Mississippi. In what may well be an apocryphal story, Eastland is supposed to have sent word to the President through his brother, the Attorney General, that he would "give him the nigger" if JFK would appoint conservative Mississippi judge Harold Cox to a district court seat. Whether Eastland made his wishes so explicit is unproven, but it seems likely that Kennedy's nomination of Cox facilitated Eastland's willingness to convert Marshall's recess appointment into a fixed one.[139]

In July 1965, Johnson nominated Marshall for appointment as Solicitor General, the U.S. government's top litigating lawyer. Marshall had understandable reservations. He had to give up a lifetime judgeship, take a pay cut, and risk losing his position should the President become dissatisfied with his performance or leave the presidency in 1969. Moreover, Johnson emphasized that the solicitor's job had "nothing to do with any Supreme Court appointment. I want that distinctly understood," he told Marshall. "There's no quid pro quo here at all." The President wanted a quick decision. Though he initially told Marshall that he could take all the time he wanted, Johnson called him the next day for an answer. "Well, Mr. President, you said I had all the time I needed," Marshall said. "You had it," Johnson replied.

Marshall saw compelling reasons to accept. As solicitor, he would have the power to influence what cases would come before the Supreme Court and how they would be framed; the job would assure him of "a powerful policy influence throughout the Executive Branch." In addition, as Johnson emphasized to him, he would become a standing example of what a black man could achieve—a powerful image for young people of all races that the "man up there with that swallow tail coat on arguing" before the Court was "a Negro" who had become Solicitor General of the United States.

Despite LBJ's injunctions about no "quid pro quo," Washington pundits predicted that the position was a way station for appointment to the Supreme Court. And Johnson himself said privately that if Marshall "proved himself outstanding as [solicitor] perhaps when a vacancy on the Supreme Court opened up, he might nominate him as a Justice—the first of his race." Johnson also said that Marshall's service as solicitor was a chance to assure that he wasn't "considered simply a one-issue lawyer concerned only with civil rights." When Johnson and Marshall walked into the White House press room to announce his appointment, "a murmur went around the press boys," Marshall recalled, "and I found out afterwards that the question they were asking was, 'Who has resigned from the Supreme Court?' "[140]

Twenty-three months later, Johnson gave Marshall the prize. But until the moment he offered him the seat, Johnson refused to acknowledge his appointment as a given. During Marshall's service as solicitor, Johnson kept reminding him that an opening on the high court would not necessarily lead to his appointment. At the same time he told Louis Martin, a well-to-do black newspaper publisher and Johnson spokesman to African-American leaders, that Marshall "wasn't worth a damn as an administrator, because [Archibald] Cox, who had preceded him, was a very efficient operator." Johnson complained to Martin that Marshall didn't " 'pay any attention to half the cases; he just gets those he likes.'" The President "really ripped him up."[141]

But Johnson's critical comments were meant to create suspense about whom he would select as his second appointment to the bench. Even Marshall didn't know he was being appointed until the day the President announced it. On June 13, Ramsey Clark advised Marshall that "the boss wants to see you" at 10:45 a.m. Marshall was to enter the White House without being seen by reporters. To escape detection, he joined a tour group and then made his way through a corridor to the Oval Office. After some pleasantries, Johnson told him: "'You know something, Thurgood, I'm going to put you on the Supreme Court.' I said, 'Well thank you, sir.' We talked a little while. We went out to the press and he announced it."

Despite the orchestrated dramatics, there was never any question but that Marshall was Johnson's choice for the job. On June 11, Johnson had met with Larry Temple, a young Texas attorney on Governor John Connally's staff whom the President was asking to become a special White House Counsel. "I have a Supreme Court appointment coming up," Johnson told Temple. "I'm thinking of appointing a black. Who would you recommend?" When Temple suggested Judge A. Leon Higginbotham, a Johnson appointee to the Federal District Court for Eastern Pennsylvania, the President leaned forward, fixing Temple in his gaze. "Larry," Johnson said, "the only two people who ever heard of Judge Higginbotham are you and his momma. When I appoint a nigger to the bench, I want everyone to know he's a nigger." Johnson's pejorative language was partly his way of intimidating a new staff member or of showing how tough and demanding he was.[142]

But it was also Johnson's crude way of saying that Marshall's appointment would resonate across the country and around the world. As he privately told a journalist two days later, Marshall's selection signaled that "'The old fences are coming down.' . . . Marshall's name is symbolic in America. There is probably not a Negro in America who did not know about the appointment." The President thought that Negro mothers would identify their children with Marshall. Johnson said: "It was worth more than all the gold in Fort Knox to know that there is an opportunity and that there is a sense of equality which has been generated." He believed this "the worse time to name a Negro. It would cost him some votes—probably more than would be gained by the appointment." But, he said, patting himself on the back, "any President who cares more about votes than about doing what is right shouldn't be President anyway."[143]

Marshall's appointment generated some predictable opposition.

His confirmation took two and a half months, which was an unusually long time for that era. Southern senators, led by Sam Ervin of North Carolina and John McClellan of Arkansas, were particularly outspoken. But the public opposition to Marshall was not overtly racial; by then, just three years after the 1964 civil rights bill condemned southern segregation, it was already impolitic to fight openly against someone of Marshall's exceptional competence on racial grounds. Instead, the southerners challenged his liberal views of the Constitution, particularly his reflection of the current impulse to assure alleged criminals their "constitutional rights." Richard Russell complained of Marshall's "extreme liberal views ... and his apparent agreement with [Chief Justice] Warren that the Constitution is to be twisted to suit the views of the Court" as ample reason to vote against his selection.

There were also telegrams from states as far apart as Massachusetts and California, Kansas, Michigan, and Arkansas, declaring Johnson's choice "appalling" and "completely insane." "You despicable bum. How do you have the guts to do it coming out of Texas," one man wired.

But the outcry was relatively muted and ineffective. Although the opposition delayed the confirmation until August 30, the vote was a decisive 69 to 11. The Marshall appointment was the high-water mark for Johnson in an otherwise miserable political year.[144]

9

Stalemate

IN February 1966 Chief Justice Earl Warren had told Drew Pearson that a seasoned politician like Lyndon Johnson would surely find his way through the maze of Vietnam. "This is going to last a long time, and the President will go through some rough sailing," Warren said. "But he's used to it. . . . LBJ has been at this game for years. . . . He knows where he's going. . . . He's working hard on Vietnam and has been for a long time, and he knows the answers for it. If this is submitted to arbitration and it goes against him, even so it will be a way out. He will find some way out."[1]

Warren's confidence in the President exceeded Johnson's capacity to set things right. Vietnam was a stalemate producing irreconcilable domestic divisions and a nightmare, to borrow from James Joyce, from which Johnson could not awake. More than ever in 1967 the war made him irrational and repressive toward opponents, provoking illusions about "winning" or negotiating our way out one moment and fears of losing the next. At a meeting with Senate leaders Mike Mansfield and Everett Dirksen in January, he "said he personally wished he had never heard of South Vietnam; [he] wishes we were not there but we are there." And the anguish was causing him indescribable grief.

"I just returned to the office from the Cabinet meeting," Agriculture Secretary Orville Freeman told him on February 1. "I would like very much to be more helpful to you in the Vietnam matter. I can only imagine how heavy a burden it is, how frustrating, how depressing, how it keeps jumping up." Dean Rusk told congressional leaders in mid-February: "the burdens that are put on the President . . . are beyond my description." When things go badly, Rusk added, the President bears the sole burden.[2]

With everyone "blaming the President for all of their troubles," with the likelihood that a continuation of the fighting into 1968 would be a political disaster for Johnson and the Democrats, he was almost desperate to end the war. But no one knew how to do it, at least on terms that Johnson believed acceptable. When Fulbright told him that "the President's first priority must be liquidation of the war—that the war poisons everything else—the President said he totally agreed." At the same time, Johnson told Ellsworth Bunker, who replaced Lodge as Ambassador to Saigon, that his "mission would be to wind up the war for American troops as quickly as possible."[3]

Yet however great the pressure to end the fighting before American civil strife became intolerable, Johnson wouldn't agree to military steps that might precipitate a larger conflict with China and/or Russia. A suggestion from Texas Governor John Connally that Johnson use tactical nuclear bombs to end a war that otherwise would destroy his administration nonplused LBJ.

Nor would he give into the doves: "We just have to save this country [South Vietnam]," he told Nicholas Katzenbach.—"We haven't got a cinch on winning out there at all, it is just the opposite[,] I am afraid." But it would be shattering to America's national security and international confidence in U.S. commitments if we cut and ran. At an NSC meeting in February, Johnson "made clear that the United States is going to continue its efforts to meet and stop the North Vietnamese aggression." At the same time, when during a ceremony in the Oval Office historian Fred L. Israel tried to make the case for peace in Vietnam, Johnson interrupted to say: "Professor, doves fly everywhere but see nothing! But hawks, hawks know their prey—they stalk it—swoop down—and woosh—the prey is gone."[4]

The best hope most Americans had in 1967 for an end to the conflict was a negotiated settlement that would preserve South Vietnamese independence and allow U.S. forces to go home. Every hint of Hanoi's willingness to talk became an occasion for inquiry and reiteration of American readiness to reach an agreement that promised the survival of Saigon's freedom from Communist control.

In December 1966, State Department analysts concluded that, since we could not possibly "win" the war by the summer of 1968, when the conflict would dominate electoral politics, the administration had no choice but to negotiate. And the only way to start peace talks was for the United States to convince Hanoi that we wanted discussions and that our only non-negotiable conditions were a "separate state in SVN, and a government which is not overtly Communist."[5]

Johnson would have been happy to settle for such arrangements, but he saw little prospect of a positive response from the Communists.

He wished to keep trying nevertheless, lest anyone say that he hadn't given peace every possible chance. Consequently, on December 19, Goldberg asked U Thant to initiate "discussions which could lead to a cease-fire." On the 23rd, after complaints that bombing raids of December 13 and 14 against Hanoi may have convinced North Vietnam to back away from potential talks being proposed by the Polish government, the President temporarily suspended such attacks in "hopes of reviving the Warsaw contact." The next day Johnson ordered a three-day Christmas truce and then repeated the suspension of hostilities for two days from December 30 to January 1 as additional demonstrations of U.S. goodwill.[6]

In January, Harrison Salisbury reported that Hanoi's Foreign Minister had signaled an interest in opening discussions, but wondered how to arrange them. Walt Rostow told Johnson that it was "conceivable, if not probable, that they are trying to get out of the war but don't know how." In Rostow's judgment, they needed to cut a deal that would spare them from embarrassment by the Chinese and the Viet Cong. Rostow didn't "give this very high odds," but he thought it "worth a try."[7]

So did Johnson. On January 9, he told Mike Mansfield that "it is not yet clear whether they are signalling us on their terms for negotiations rather than carrying forward their old campaign to get us unconditionally to stand down [from] bombing of the North." Was Hanoi ready "to accept honest self-determination by the people of South Vietnam?" The State Department told Hanoi that we wanted "a mutually agreeable, completely secure arrangement for exchanging communications . . . about the possibilities of achieving a peaceful settlement of the Vietnamese dispute." Hanoi asked for a clarification of what the U.S. meant by "completely secure arrangements" and a "settlement." Washington promptly replied: "Recognition of the independence and territorial integrity of North and South Vietnam, or of all Vietnam if the people should choose reunification."[8]

Hoping that U.S. military might was forcing Hanoi toward consideration of a settlement, Johnson urged Mansfield and Dirksen to prevent Senate doves from undermining prospects for talks. "There have been many plays, many feelers—These have all been our initiative. We now have a feeler back that seems reliable," he told them. He "mentioned that South Vietnamese morale is better than it has been" and declared that "we are doing better now than we have ever done in Vietnam if we just don't blow it."[9]

Johnson had little real hope that Hanoi was about to enter into meaningful discussions. His conversation with Mansfield and Dirksen, as most everything he did now about peace talks, was directed more toward U.S. congressional and public opinion than North Vietnam. He believed that the Communists were playing a public relations game and that his principal challenge was to hold Americans together while U.S. military pressure wore down Hanoi's resistance to negotiations, hopefully before the onset of the 1968 campaign.

It was no surprise to him, then, at the end of January, when Hanoi rejected talks unless the United States first stopped bombing and "all other acts of war" against North Vietnam. "They are either saying: no; or starting a negotiation from the very hard end," Rostow told the President. The State Department saw the response as part of Hanoi's "all-out efforts to build up public pressures on us to stop bombing in return for talks."

However eager Johnson was to end the war, he refused to make concessions to Hanoi. On the contrary, he was increasingly optimistic that, as South Vietnam President Ky put it on February 1, " 'We are getting stronger every day, and they are getting weaker every day—and they know it.' They are hurt by the bombing, and by the tremendous military 'meat-grinder' which devours the troops which they send into South Vietnam." At a Cabinet meeting on the same day, Johnson asked McNamara to explain "why we would not stop bombing on a nonreciprocal basis." Rostow and Komer said, "Whatever may be in the wind on the negotiating front, it is only prudent to keep up the pressure in the South."[10]

For the moment, Johnson saw peace efforts as sops to domestic and international opinion. At the beginning of February, when the British and Soviets offered to mediate, he reluctantly accepted. He saw nothing from North Vietnam that could be taken seriously, he told reporters. But he was "anxious for them [the Vietnamese] to make any proposal," which we will give "very prompt and serious consideration." Believing that the exchanges between the four capitals would become public knowledge, Johnson saw the discussions as an exercise in public relations. A bombing pause for the Tet holiday, February 6–13, fell into the same category.[11]

He coupled the pause with a direct appeal to Ho Chi Minh. The lives being lost, wounds being inflicted, and "simple human misery," he told Ho, put them under "a heavy obligation to seek earnestly the path to peace." History would judge them harshly if they failed to find "a just and peaceful solution" to the war. As a prelude to "serious and private discussions leading toward an early peace," Johnson asked assurances of an end to land and sea infiltration into South Vietnam. America would then cease bombing the North and increasing forces in the South.

Ho's reply on February 15 was a denunciation of U.S. actions as a ploy to deny the Vietnamese people their right to self-determination. "Our just cause," Ho declared, "enjoys strong sympathy and support from the peoples of the whole world, including broad sections of the American people." The only way out of the war for the United States was to "stop definitively and unconditionally its bombing raids and all other acts of war, withdraw from South Vietnam all U.S. and satellite troops, recognize the South Vietnam National Front for Liberation, and let the Vietnamese people settle themselves their own affairs." Ho concluded with a plea that the U.S. government "act in accordance with reason."[12]

Ho's response deepened Johnson's skepticism. At an NSC meeting on February 8, a week before Ho's letter, Rusk said: "We have undertaken dozens of probes. . . . All our efforts have encountered silence." Johnson echoed the point: "We have pursued every hint that the North Vietnamese were willing to give up something if we give up something. Hanoi is trying to force us to give up the bombing of North Vietnam. We will keep on until we get something from the North Vietnamese."[13]

Johnson's doubts about near-term prospects for talks reflected themselves in a fresh clash with Robert Kennedy. During a European trip in January and February, RFK met Etienne Manac'h, head of the French Foreign Ministry's Far East Office. Manac'h relayed a message from Hanoi saying negotiations would follow an unconditional bombing halt. Though a familiar proposal, *Newsweek* reported that the North Vietnamese had given Kennedy "a significant peace signal." Kennedy had not encouraged this unwarranted conclusion, but the story, which generated considerable publicity in the United States, angered the President. He assumed that a Kennedy supporter in the administration had leaked the story as a way to embarrass him and further undermine his Vietnam policy.

At a February 6 meeting with Kennedy in the Oval Office, Johnson gave full voice to his current thinking about Vietnam. Kennedy explained that the leak had come "from your State Department." "It's not *my* State Department, goddamnit," Johnson shot back. "It's *your* State Department." Johnson dismissed the negotiations as irrelevant.

Though he did not say so, the President had several reports predicting that American military progress would soon sink the North Vietnamese. Johnson predicted that the war would be over by summer. And further dove talk by Kennedy and his Senate friends—Fulbright and Frank Church, among others—would mean their political demise, Johnson warned. "I'll destroy you and every one of your dove friends in six months," he shouted. "You'll be dead politically in six months."

When Kennedy, who struggled to maintain his composure in the face of Johnson's assault, urged the President to stop bombing and follow a series of political steps to extricate U.S. forces from the conflict, Johnson exploded: "There just isn't a chance in hell that I will do that, not the slightest chance." He accused Kennedy and his friends of prolonging the war and having American blood on their hands. "I don't have to take that from you," Kennedy responded. After Katzenbach and Rostow, who were present, mediated, Kennedy agreed to tell reporters that he had not brought home any peace-feeler.

Johnson's intemperateness stunned Kennedy. "He was shouting and seemed very unstable," Kennedy told a friend. "I kept thinking that if he exploded like that with me, how could he ever negotiate with Hanoi." It was another instance of Johnson's erratic personal behavior over Vietnam. For all his hope and brave talk about progress in the fighting, he still feared that the war would destroy him politically and open the way to a successful Kennedy bid for the presidency.

Convinced that Kennedy would leak their confrontation, Johnson beat him to the punch. *Time* reported that Bobby had called Johnson a "sonofabitch." With the press making much of the nastiness between them, Kennedy made the best of a bad situation. At Washington's Gridiron dinner in March, he explained: "We had a long serious talk about the possibilities of a cease-fire, the dangers of escalation and the prospects for negotiation. And he promised me the next time we are going to talk about Vietnam."[14]

Johnson wasn't amused. The Kennedy episode increased public pressure on him to negotiate a settlement. But he saw it bringing Communism to South Vietnam. At the beginning of March, he declared himself "sick and tired of being afraid to blow a [diplomatic or negotiating] contact." His focus was fixed on keeping American opinion behind him rather than grabbing at proposals leading nowhere.[15]

The War at Home Continues

By the winter of 1966–67 public doubts about Johnson's war leadership had deepened and spread. "I have been distressed over the manner in which the public attitude toward you has so drastically changed," Drew Pearson told him in December. Pearson urged him to unleash the Cabinet against opponents "and deflect some of the criticism away from you."[16]

Johnson's failure to be more candid about expanding the fighting was eroding his credibility. Harrison Salisbury's articles in the *New York Times* in December and January that reported civilian casualties from air raids strengthened the feeling that the White House was hiding the truth about the war. A Defense Department spokesman saw Salisbury's revelations as a "national disaster."

The Economist described the administration as making "an ass of itself by not admitting much earlier what it knew perfectly well, that some of the bombs were missing their targets. It is not what he [LBJ] does," the magazine asserted, "it's the way he does it." Johnson's lack of openness was the root of the problem. Americans "want a President who will explain what he is up to, and why, as frankly as the national interest allows him to." Johnson's closest advisers told him the same thing. He needed to allow more debate before policy decisions were made; he needed to get out on the hustings and tell people how he was governing.[17]

But even if Johnson changed his "image" from a secretive manipulator, as his critics now described him, to a forthright educator, it could not eliminate or mute the problem that was diminishing his popularity. The country wanted him to end a war that was taking so many lives and costing so much money for a cause it didn't quite understand.

In December, when CBS conducted a "current events test" for a program titled "Vietnam—Where We Stand," less than half the country knew the answers to a majority of the questions about the conflict and about Vietnam. Only 28 percent could say how many servicemen were there, and only 48 percent knew that we had not blockaded Haiphong; by contrast, 62 percent wanted the U.S. to increase its bombing of the North.[18]

Johnson tried to rally the country to his standard with some straight talk. In his State of the Union speech on January 10, 1967, he wondered "whether we have the staying power to fight a very costly war, when the objective is limited and the danger to us is seemingly remote." Devoting nearly a quarter of his speech to explaining involvement in Vietnam, he quoted Thomas Jefferson's description of "the melancholy law of human societies to be compelled sometimes to choose a great evil in order to ward off a greater."

He saw the will of the American people being tested, and he predicted that it would take "a great deal of patience" before we could assure the independence of "all the small nations in Southeast Asia" as well as peace in the region and "perhaps the world." He wished he could report "that the conflict is almost over. This I cannot do. We face more cost, more loss, and more agony. For the end is not yet. I cannot promise you that it will come this year—or come next year." He only promised persistence, which would assure eventual success.[19]

At the same time, Johnson asked Bob Kintner to arrange for a weekly meeting among White House aides, who were to generate items "for planting with *Time, Newsweek*, etc." Kintner, Califano, Cater, press secretary George Christian, McPherson, and Rostow urged Johnson to supplement their efforts by seeing "key columnists," including unfriendly ones, "privately, for a maximum of a half-hour, on an off-the-record basis." They expected the President to "have a tremendous effect on them if the interviews are short and relatively spaced." Johnson agreed to see the journalists and also asked that the staff reinstitute a procedure of submitting daily reports on press contacts.[20]

But what could Johnson or anyone say that had not been said before? Repetition might make the case for Vietnam more convincing. But to whom? Certainly not doves, who saw the war as based on mistaken assumptions about American national security and Communist designs. In January, at a White House briefing, as Rusk offered familiar arguments for the war, Fulbright turned to Frank Church and Joe Clark and whispered: " 'I'm tired of listening to these prejudices and propaganda. . . . Let's get out of here.' Very shortly after, they left," an assistant secretary of state reported to LBJ.[21]

The mass public was becoming as skeptical. An opinion poll at the end of January showed only 41 percent approval for Vietnam policy. A poll in Minnesota was more revealing. Seventy-two percent were dissatisfied with progress in the war, with only 22 percent satisfied.

As telling, the President's overall approval rating in February stood at 46 percent, with 37 percent negative about his performance. By March, Johnson's general job rating had slipped another point, while his numbers on Vietnam fell to an all-time low: 49 percent disapproved of his war leadership and only 37 percent approved.

The one bright spot in the survey was that most Americans thought the President's potential rivals in 1968—Kennedy, Nixon, and Romney—would either do no better or might even be worse in dealing with Vietnam. A Harris poll showed a fund of sympathy for the President's plight. Seventy-four percent thought he was doing the best he could in a tough job, while 41 percent believed that critics were picking on him unfairly. But 34 percent saw him as untrustworthy, telling the press and people one thing and doing another.[22]

Senators echoed public doubts. In the first quarter of 1967, moderates and conservatives joined the doves, led by Fulbright, Morse, and Gruening, in urging an end to the war. It was "costing too much," Stuart Symington told the President, and counseled a greater, less restricted use of American air power. Russell of Georgia and Lister Hill of Alabama proposed a win or get out policy. People couldn't understand a conflict in which we held back from beating an avowed enemy of our institutions and national survival, they said. Moderates like Edmund Muskie of Maine and Joseph Pastore of Rhode Island emphasized the need to end a struggle that was spreading consternation across America and threatening Johnson's political life.

George Aiken of Vermont offered a more substantive proposal: We needed a radical change in strategy, he said. Instead of continuing with the "social reengineering" of South Vietnam, which we had been trying, he urged establishing enclaves: "a strong watch over that society, a watch maintained at strong points on the coast and at sea." Such a change in posture would allow us to escape the current choice between unthinkable withdrawal and escalation into a wider and more terrible war.[23]

No Senate critic troubled Johnson more than Robert Kennedy, who made a major speech on March 2 proposing a three-point program to end U.S. involvement. Acknowledging his personal responsibility along with other high officials for America's military presence in Vietnam and declaring his opposition to an unconditional withdrawal, he urged a fresh American initiative for negotiations. He suggested an unconditional bombing halt, followed by arrangements for reduced fighting in the South monitored by an international agency. The multinational force could then replace U.S. troops. National elections, including all political factions in South Vietnam, could be the basis for a political settlement.[24]

Opposition from senators, academics, and business and religious leaders incensed Johnson. He complained that petitions, letters, op-ed articles, and public demonstrations were giving aid and comfort to the enemy. He was particularly enraged at young people, who made life miserable for administration figures trying to convince college and university students that we were fighting a just war with no ulterior motives. In November 1966, when McNamara spoke at Harvard, a crowd of unruly students shouting obscenities mobbed his car and threatened his person. Hubert Humphrey suffered a similar experience at Stanford, while universities across the country became synonymous with antiwar demonstrations.[25]

No one was more the object of the antiwar anger than Johnson himself. Animated by an unshakable conviction that they held the moral high ground, some war opponents engaged in unrestrained attacks on LBJ as unworthy of the deference normally shown a President. In the spring of 1967, UPI journalist Merriman Smith decried the shameful attacks on the President and his family. He objected to demonstrators carrying signs asking, "Lee Harvey Oswald, where are you now?" and using "barnyard filth" to characterize Mr. Johnson. "LBJ's father should have pulled out" was one flagrant example.

The rage deepened the Secret Service's concerns about the President's safety at public gatherings. The FBI compiled thousands of pages on radical groups planning demonstrations wherever Johnson agreed to appear. The Students for a Democratic Society, the Committee to Stop the War in Vietnam, and the War Resisters League came under particular scrutiny as organizations under Communist influence that might try to harm the President.

But the bureau attended to more than presidential safety. In January 1967, when the movie actor Paul Newman suggested in a speech at Columbia University that LBJ be impeached for fighting a war without congressional authorization, the New York office of the FBI promised to keep track of any organized impeachment movement and post the bureau on its actions. A result of the organized opposition was that Johnson became a prisoner in the White House, largely losing his freedom to travel in the country. It added to the distance between himself and the public, exacerbating tensions and increasing the "credibility gap."[26]

Yet polls in the first quarter of 1967 showed Johnson how to fight back. The public strongly favored sustained bombing and intensified military pressure as the best way to end the conflict. A survey published on March 13, for example, cited a four-to-one margin against a halt in the bombing to test Hanoi's interest in peace talks. Between November 1966 and March 1967, the number of Americans favoring a "total military victory" rose from 31 percent to 43 percent.[27]

The polls strengthened Johnson's determination to give military action priority over negotiations. In private, he belittled those who thought Hanoi's demands for an unconditional bombing halt would bring talks and an end to Communist aggression against Saigon. We can't have peace "crawling on our stomachs," he told congressmen on February 15. "We can't have it with a cup in our hands. We can't have it begging. And we can't have it with enclaves," indicating that Aiken's proposal wouldn't work.[28]

Johnson refused to let war opponents dominate the media with "Communist" inspired accounts of the war. At the end of February, he told the president of NBC News that the networks were slanted against him. "He said he thought they were infiltrated, and said he watched the situation like a hawk. He had to do so ... to be ready to move on them if they move on us." During dinner at Senator Henry Jackson's house, he told NBC's Ray Scherer that "nothing good was ever written about his Vietnam policy."

On March 15, he restated the case for his Vietnam policy before the Tennessee state legislature. Howard K. Smith of ABC told him that he heard the reaction to the address was good, but the administration's greatest weakness was still "its inability to get over the complete story on its objectives in Vietnam." Johnson replied: "Our greatest weakness is our inability to communicate actions to the people so that they have been told. Nobody has tried as hard. I don't have an answer." Johnson refused to accept the possibility that it was the policy itself and not the means of communication that was flawed.[29]

No act of criticism bothered Johnson more than Robert Kennedy's speech. But his response was symptomatic of his deeper rage toward all his war opponents. He saw them as not simply disputing a policy or as men and women of goodwill committed to changing the national course in Vietnam but as personal enemies who above all were out to get him. He could not let go of the idea that this was his war being fought by his boys loyal to Lyndon Johnson's goals for Vietnam and the free world. "Don't refer to 'my' planes and 'my' troops," Drew Pearson advised him. "It gives people the feeling that it's your war and not theirs; and enough of your political enemies are already trying to make this point."

But Johnson couldn't act on Pearson's advice. He saw the war as a fight not only over a world view but also for the survival of Lyndon Johnson. It was a terrible mistake for him to so personalize the dispute. It crimped his capacity to make sensible, detached judgments on what now needed to be done. Advice from opponents could not get the sort of hearing it often deserved.

The vehemence of his response to Kennedy said it all. In February, when Bob Kintner advised him that RFK intended to make a speech critical of peace negotiations with Hanoi and China policy, Johnson asked Rostow for "comment & action" on the possibility of a preemptive "definitive" administration speech on foreign policy. Nothing was done.

On the day of Kennedy's speech in March, however, Johnson orchestrated a series of activities meant to deflect attention from Kennedy's peace proposal. Johnson held a press conference at which he announced Soviet agreement to discuss means of limiting the nuclear arms race; gave unscheduled talks at Howard University and the Office of Education; released a letter to Senator Henry Jackson restating the reasons for past and continued bombing of

North Vietnam; and confirmed rumors that his daughter Luci was
pregnant. He also asked Richard Russell to reply to Kennedy, but
the Georgia senator "saw nothing new in the speech or worthy of
my involvement."

Instead, Rusk spoke for the President, declaring that "proposals
substantially similar to those put forward by Senator Kennedy were
explored prior to, during, and since the Tet truce—all without result."
Westmoreland was also asked by "highest authority" to weigh in with
a defense of the bombing at a press conference held in time to make
newspapers on the same day that "highly placed opponents of bombing" issued public pronouncements.[30]

For days after Kennedy's speech, Johnson continued to obsess
about how to respond. At a Democratic National Committee dinner,
he declared the American people against "a dishonorable settlement
disguised as a bargain for popularity purposes." One national committeeman described Johnson's assault on Kennedy as "an unbelievable tirade."

Johnson's anger toward Kennedy and critics more generally was
irrepressible. On March 13, when he had an off-the-record talk with
Drew Pearson, he said that Bobby is "going to have twelve books
written about me and twelve books written about him before the
next election." Two of Bobby's journalists "are writing a book on my
foreign policy." Johnson had never met one of them, but, he said
sarcastically, "I guess he knows all about my foreign policy anyway."

On March 15, when *Time*'s Hugh Sidey sent word that a lengthy
conversation with Kennedy convinced him that Bobby was all but
"decided to get into the [1968 presidential] race," Johnson saw confirmation of his intention to use Vietnam to destroy him and reclaim
the White House for the Kennedy clan.[31]

Kennedy's peace proposal seemed bound to fall of its own
weight. There was little reason to think that an unconditional bombing halt for a week or two would bring Hanoi into talks. The North
Vietnamese agenda did not include compromise and outside supervision for country-wide elections but victory in a war of attrition and
unification of Vietnam on Hanoi's terms. Kennedy himself acknowledged that if nothing came of the bombing pause, we could "go back
to the war." But Johnson was unwilling to give Kennedy's approach
a try, whatever his confidence that it wouldn't work. He believed it
would only free the Communists to repair damaged facilities and
resupply themselves. Instead, he now wanted to act on the wider
American impulse to hit the enemy harder, though not so hard as to
draw the Chinese into the fighting or embarrass the Soviets, whom
he believed eager to help the United States end the war.

The Military Option

During the first quarter of 1967, almost everyone in the administration and the great majority of Americans agreed on the need for more effective action in Vietnam. But the goal remained as elusive as ever; no one had a surefire means of getting there. The prognosis for 1967 "was not comforting," Bill Bundy said at the end of 1966. "Even if the GVN and we both do the best we possibly can, the odds are on the whole against a major strengthening of the GVN position or a true crack in NVA/VC/NLF morale. . . . Its chances cannot be rated better than one in three for 1967."

The Joint Chiefs of Staff and the U.S. military command in Vietnam did not disagree. They would only say that "the war could be long and difficult, and the field commander should be granted the operational flexibility and resources he needed to do the job as he perceived it."[32]

As far as anyone could tell, the war was now stalemated. American military power was a standing assurance against South Vietnam's collapse, but it guaranteed nothing about North Vietnamese and Viet Cong defeat. Moreover, there was limited reason to believe that a Saigon government and independent South Vietnam would survive a U.S. withdrawal. A CIA report in January stated that the "chances that the Communists would win South Vietnam by a military victory had vanished, but everything else about the "course of the struggle" was "inconclusive." Evidence of diminished Communist capacity to continue the war was small to nonexistent.[33]

Despite difficulties assessing the impact of U.S. ground and air actions on opposing forces, Johnson and his advisers chose to put the best possible face on progress in the fighting. Walt Rostow told the President in January that "a debate continues on the absolute size of the enemy order of battle in Viet Nam." But whatever the size, the good news was that for the first time "official statistics" showed "a net decline in both VC main force and North Viet Nam army units for the fourth quarter of 1966. This is the first reversal of the upward trend since 1960."

Bob Komer and Lodge saw reason to be more optimistic. Komer told Johnson that "more and more people now tend to agree that we are doing a lot better in Vietnam. The trend line is up on the military, political evolution, and economic fronts. The VC/NVA are hurting, and it is beginning to show. Even pacification is beginning to move."[34]

Lodge was even more positive. He believed that the presence of U.S. forces during the last eighteen months had improved the

ARVN's performance, had contained the enemy main force threat, had allowed allied troops to enter former Communist sanctuaries in strength, had doubled Viet Cong defections, and had caused enemy battle field losses to be "punishingly one-sided." Bombing the North had increased enemy supply problems. The political, economic, and social sides of the equation were as noteworthy: Government stability in Saigon and development of democratic institutions were apparent; economic stability with diminished inflation and improved living standards were evident; and care of refugees, a stronger educational system, and greater press freedom were being achieved.[35]

These rosy assessments were largely wishful thinking by advocates convinced they were pursuing a just cause. In fact, no one could speak with certainty about conditions in Vietnam. A captured V.C. notebook, for example, indicated that they had lost control over a million people during 1966, and the U.S. mission in Saigon was glad to get out this news. But the notebook also claimed that the Viet Cong still controlled 5 million people, and this differed sharply from Lodge's estimate that only 20 percent of the population (3.3 million people) were under V.C. dominance.[36]

Other reports coming into the President suggested great doubts about everything from political and economic stability to military gains. The upcoming presidential contest between Thieu and Ky might turn bloody, Johnson heard at the end of January. Since "we have enormous stakes in the peaceful, political evolution of South Vietnam," John Roche told LBJ, "I strongly recommend that we take out coup insurance, that is, announce privately to the Vietnamese through the Ambassador and General Westmoreland, that we will not permit a coup to take place." In February, Komer reported rice shortages, a new spurt in inflation, and difficulties in making the Saigon government conform to sensible economic policies. At the same time, Ky complained to Lodge that "terror was increasing in South Viet-Nam. It exists now 'more than ever,' and will increase, notably at election time" in September.

Nevertheless, on February 7, the CIA concluded that North Vietnam's economy was being paralyzed by U.S. bombing, which was dealing "a severe blow" to its morale, and that the Viet Cong were "getting tired of this war faster than we are."[37]

Upbeat assessments continued to reach the White House during the rest of February and through March. The Soviets and East Europeans believed we were winning in Vietnam, Rostow told the President. We should hold to no less a judgment. When he had lunch with three network newsmen, Rostow advised, the President should say that "we are making progress in every part of the Viet Nam effort: We shall persist and we shall succeed." The defector rate among the Viet Cong was at its highest levels ever. It convinced Komer that they would "have a hard time maintaining their strength in 1967." As for bombing, the Pentagon saw it doing exactly what we wanted: It boosted South Vietnamese morale; forced half a million North Vietnamese troops into defensive and repair operations, and substantially raised the cost of bringing men and supplies into the South.

Despite the mixed reports, Johnson chose to accentuate the positive. At the end of February, he told NBC's president that he wasn't "sure that the North Vietnamese would not win, but thought it very unlikely.... He also could not be sure we'd win, but thought that quite likely. The President said he thought we could clean up Viet Nam, perhaps this year."[38]

There was little basis for Johnson's prediction. In early March, the U.S. military command in Saigon revised its estimates of battalion and larger size enemy-initiated actions for the twelve months between February 1966 and February 1967: There were many more attacks than previously thought. The implications of this data, Wheeler cabled Westmoreland, "are major and serious." "If these figures should reach the public domain," Wheeler declared, "they would, literally, blow the lid off of Washington."

Wheeler described an urgent need for an explanation of the discrepancy. "I cannot go to the President and tell him that, contrary to my reports and those of the other chiefs as to progress of the war in which we have laid great stress upon the thesis you have seized the initiative from the enemy, the situation is such that we are not sure who has the initiative in South Vietnam. Moreover, the effect of surfacing this major and significant discrepancy would be dynamite."[39]

There had been no attempt to "cook" the numbers; the discrepancies were the product of genuine uncertainty over how to measure enemy actions. When Lodge reflected this confusion in a cable which described "an average of last year's 'reasonable assumptions' reflecting contemporary 'monthly variations,'" Roche told Rostow that, if such a "formula got to the press, it would reinforce the 'credibility gap' and play right into the hands of those critics who assert that all statistics on Vietnam are cooked." Rostow replied: "You are correct. A number of us have been fighting this problem. The key is: MACV intelligence wants to keep every order of battle as high as possible" as a way to sell Washington on sending additional forces.

Westmoreland assured Wheeler that "no attempts have been made at this headquarters to use padded statistics to influence decisions concerning future strength levels. To the contrary, there is continuing effort to improve the accuracy of our data in order to permit sounder assessments and decisions at all levels."[40]

Similar problems existed with measuring infiltration of supplies and forces from North to South and in assessing Viet Cong manpower. "Anti-infiltration operations have severely complicated and slowed the infiltration of supplies into South Vietnam," an intelligence report confidently asserted. "There is, however, no evidence yet available which can substantiate any overall critical shortages of supply that would severely limit the VC/NVA force structure presently in SVN." Likewise, U.S. interdiction actions were impeding the movement of personnel from North to South, but there was "no good evidence that it is responsible for the drop-off in the infiltration of infantry regiments." Finally, captured enemy documents showed Viet Cong problems in maintaining force levels, but there was "as yet no indication that manpower problems will force the Viet Cong to curtail their combat operations."[41]

Did Johnson know about these uncertainties? Though the records do not indicate exactly which assessments reached him on these various matters, it is clear that he had substantial doubts. On March 24, Rostow told the President that he had briefed ABC's Howard K. Smith on progress in Vietnam. Smith counseled against saying "that we do not see a way out of the problem of Viet Nam. We should not say that we do not have the answer."

The doubts over Communist strength "became well known" to the President, McNamara said later. He also denied that Westmoreland, as some claimed after the war, had tried to hide such information from Johnson, and even if he had, which McNamara emphatically says he didn't, "he could not have succeeded because of the alternative information channels available to us."[42]

McNamara is surely right. No President who paid as close attention to Vietnam as Johnson would have been deceived for long about military conditions. McNamara himself assured that the President heard all estimates of what our military actions were achieving. On February 17, for example, when General Wheeler presented the case for increased bombing of the North, McNamara described the limits of what bombing had accomplished. He said that more attacks would not "affect the net flow of supplies into the South. The logistical capacity of the North was well beyond infiltration requirements." As for attacks on POL, which Johnson wanted evaluated, McNamara "said there was no obvious net reduction in consumption," and explained how Hanoi had managed to disperse their stocks and evade the loss of storage capacity.

In late March, when Walt Rostow briefed Johnson on infiltration rates, he candidly acknowledged that the figures were "uncertain—and subject to backward up-dating as evidence flows in."

Johnson's description of progress in the fighting and a possible
end to the war in 1967 rested more on a determination to boost
American morale rather than confront the reality of a stalemate. Because he saw little real military advance early in 1967 and had a
sense of urgency about ending the war, he decided to increase American military pressure on the Communists.

On February 17, he asked for "all the alternatives ... with respect to accelerating the effort in the North." He also wanted to hear
"every possibility for accelerating action in the South ...: more personnel, if necessary; more initiatives; more aggressiveness; additional
efforts in Laos. Our Viet Nam policy was operating on borrowed
time," he declared.[43]

On February 22, Johnson agreed to expanded military actions in
the North and the South and against infiltration routes in Laos. Fifty-
four additional targets were to be struck in the North, while selective
mining of inland waterways and estuaries, naval gunfire, and artillery
attacks across the DMZ (demilitarized zone at the 17th parallel) were
to complement the bombing. In the South, existing military actions
were increased and new initiatives were set in motion. Wheeler advised Westmoreland that he believed the President would now be
receptive to increasing U.S. ground forces from 470,000 to the 550,000
asked for in 1966. At another meeting on March 7, Johnson repeated
his desire "to put more pressure—every possible item of pressure in
Viet Nam."[44]

At a conference in Guam from March 20 to 22, where the President met with military commanders and Thieu and Ky, Westmoreland pressed the case for more men. Johnson intended to make no
major military decisions at the conference. He saw the meeting as a
chance publicly to reiterate American determination to stay the course
in Vietnam. But he was also eager to hear Westmoreland's estimate
of current conditions and future needs. Though Westmoreland saw
signs of V.C. crumbling partly caused by the bombing of the North,
which was interrupting the flow of supplies, he also warned that,
"unless our military pressure causes the Viet Cong to crumble, or
Hanoi withdraws her support, this war could go on indefinitely."[45]

In light of Westmoreland's prediction and evidence that the war
was stalemated, why did Johnson decide to expand military efforts
rather than conclude that the time had come to cut losses and plan
an early escape from a deepening morass? Johnson's motives are not
easy to discern. No doubt he believed that the Communists had a

breaking point, that if we could keep the military pressure on them long enough, they would give up the fight. But he also knew that they had great numbers of troops they could throw into the struggle, and he believed that they had few qualms about sacrificing lives for their ideological ends.

As far as he could tell, the Communists were unbending: They had "never picked up the phone and said to anyone that we know of, not any preacher, not any teacher, not any visitor, not any politician, not anyone, that they were willing to give up anything if we gave up bombing," Johnson told a group of congressmen in February. They were relying on our unwillingness to pay the price and make the sacrifices required in this war.[46]

It is surprising that Johnson did not make some contingency plan for a U.S. withdrawal before the country had lost patience with a lengthening war and the conduct of the struggle became a debating point in the 1968 campaign. It is clear that he was not going to let electoral politics stop a war he believed America needed to win or at least end with a peace that preserved South Vietnam. Still, he knew there was more at stake here than his reelection. The war was alienating the administration from many of the country's most thoughtful leaders; it was crippling Johnson's freedom to go forward with the Great Society and threatening to destroy programs that were already in place; it was casting a shadow over Johnson's presidency and changing the way in which history might judge him and his administration.

For a politician as resourceful as LBJ it was not beyond his capacity, as Senator Aiken had advised, to declare victory and leave. The South Vietnamese had been given ample opportunity to take up their own defense. After one more round of U.S. military escalation and a national election in the South in September 1967, Johnson could have declared South Vietnam reasonably safe and begun the withdrawal of American forces. He could have stifled possible Saigon objections with threats to cut off the U.S. aid needed to survive. And even if they lasted only a few more years and fell under North Vietnamese control, how many Americans would be ready to complain about how Vietnam was lost? Some would, of course; but, given U.S. sacrifices in the conflict and the growing mood of war weariness, most Americans were unlikely to oppose political leaders who saw the wisdom of ending a miserable drain on the country's blood and treasure.

But for Johnson most of this was muted or lost from view. The war had become a personal test of his judgment, of his wisdom in expanding the conflict in the first place. True, there was all the talk about avoiding a larger war by fighting a smaller one, and the fear that retreat would undermine international confidence in America's willingness to preserve its national interest in the face of a painful challenge. To leave Vietnam was tantamount to running up the white flag, as Johnson described it.

But so much of this was rhetoric. Who really believed that retreat from Vietnam would convince a divided China roiled by the cultural revolution or a cautious Soviet Union, ever concerned to avoid another massive conflict like World War II, to seize upon America's withdrawal from Vietnam as a reason to expand and risk a nuclear war?

The real issue now was Johnson's unrealistic optimism that we could still work our will in Vietnam and his stubborn unwillingness to admit that Vietnam was a "mistake." Having invested so much of his presidency in the conflict, having allowed the war to become the centerpiece of his four-year term, he would not acknowledge that his principal foreign policy initiative had largely failed.

The fact that Robert Kennedy was now making the case against Vietnam added to Johnson's determination to see the war through to a proper conclusion. Though no one can say with certainty what Johnson's fundamental motives were, including Johnson himself, it is not too much of a stretch to conclude that the Johnson personality was inhibiting him from a more realistic and sensible resolution of a war policy that seemed certain to lead to more losses, more domestic divisions, and greater limitations on his capacity to lead at home and abroad.

Between Hope and Illusion

Throughout the spring of 1967 public feeling about Vietnam could have convinced Johnson that it was time to prepare a U.S. withdrawal. Polling data indicated that the war was weakening support for Great Society programs. Where 72 percent of the country opposed cuts in domestic programs in 1966, the number had fallen to 54 percent by April 1967, and seemed certain to drop more as the cost of financing the war became more apparent. Defense expenditures for fiscal year 1968, Robert McNamara predicted in June 1967, would probably be $3 billion greater than anticipated the previous December. And this was assuming no major additional costs for Vietnam! "Clearly," McNamara declared, "this is intolerable," and $3 billion in temporary savings would have to be found.[47]

Surveys on Johnson's public standing and reelection prospects were also disquieting. In an April straw poll pairing him with George

Romney, the President commanded only 43 percent of the vote against Romney's 48 to 52 percent.

Vietnam was central to Johnson's decline: 45 percent of Americans gave him a negative rating on the war, while 65 percent complained that he was not fully informing the country about it. In May, Gallup found that the 26 percent of Americans who saw the war as immoral "could be a major obstacle to [Johnson's] reelection." Thirty-seven percent considered the involvement of U.S. troops a mistake, up from 32 percent in February.

In June, a decisive 66 percent of the country said they had lost confidence in the President's leadership. Half the country had no clear idea what the war was about; only 25 percent believed that South Vietnam could survive a U.S. withdrawal. A planned trip to Los Angeles by the President in late June promised to provoke the largest antiwar demonstration in the city's history.[48]

In May, Taylor told the President that he sensed "a new wave of pessimism regarding Viet-Nam pervading official circles in Washington, apparently arising from renewed doubts about the bombing of the North and increased concern over future troop requirements to carry on the war in the South." Taylor also had reports from some of the President's advisers that we were "dangerously close to a collision with Peking or Moscow or both as the result of the escalation of our bombing." The journalist Rowland Evans was more blunt about the President's problems. "What are you going to do now that your policy has failed?" Evans asked Walt Rostow. "What policy?" Rostow replied. "The policy of forcing Hanoi to negotiate by bombing. It's worse than the Bay of Pigs," Evans declared.[49]

In May and June the CIA echoed doubts about the value of bombing North Vietnam. The privations caused by the attacks were doing more to stiffen than undermine morale, the agency reported. Although the stepped-up bombing had "strongly shocked" Hanoi's leaders and made their vision of victory "less clear," it was consolidating their "determination ... to fight on." Indeed, the North Vietnamese people were "completely convinced that time is on their side." More important, the CIA concluded that the air raids were doing little to reduce "the flow of military and other essential goods sufficiently to affect the war in the South."[50]

Was there a way to surmount existing obstacles and bring the war to an end soon? McNamara saw none. He told the President in May that he saw "no attractive course of action. The probabilities are that Hanoi has decided not to negotiate until the American electorate has been heard in November 1968. Continuation of our present moderate policy ... will not change Hanoi's mind."

U.S. military Chiefs also saw no light at the end of the tunnel unless we resorted to greater force. The present "bombing campaign in the North," Wheeler said, "has not and cannot succeed in coercing the North Vietnamese into a settlement or reduce the flow of men and materiel to the South to the extent that victory is possible. The main-force war in the South is stalemated. . . . Pacification efforts have failed to achieve significant results and there is no evidence that pacification will ever succeed."[51]

Prospects for negotiation were no better. In June, Senator Claiborne Pell of Rhode Island, an outspoken advocate of deescalation without withdrawal, went to Paris at the invitation of a senior North Vietnamese diplomat. The envoy reiterated Hanoi's insistence on an unconditional U.S. bombing halt as a prelude to talks. Since Johnson believed it essential to get some commitment of restraint on infiltration across the DMZ before a bombing pause, nothing came of this discussion.

When Kosygin passed along the same suggestion from Hanoi at the Glassboro meeting, Johnson replied that a bombing halt would enable the North Vietnamese to send five additional divisions south, where they could inflict a "great many casualties among our boys," and he "would be crucified in this country." In his answer to Hanoi through Kosygin, Johnson asked that it not use the cessation of bombing to send additional forces South. Though Kosygin promised prompt action on the President's reply, nothing more was heard from Hanoi about this initiative.[52]

If Johnson wanted a way out of the war, McNamara offered him a plan on May 19. The administration would declare that its objective in the war—South Vietnam's self-determination—was being achieved. We had "already either denied or offset the North Vietnamese intervention." Moreover, September elections in the South would provide the chance for a coalition government, including the V.C. If this government collapsed under the weight of continuing Communist attacks, we could encourage the creation of a non-Communist regime, which would bear responsibility for maintaining internal stability. For this government to go Communist, it would take three to five years, and whether this "would appear to be a 'defeat' for the US in, say, 1970 would depend on many factors not now foreseeable."[53]

But Johnson remained as reluctant as ever to cut losses and accept a fig leaf for American defeat. Moreover, in the spring of 1967, he had enough good news to keep hope alive that all might turn out well yet. Though there was more illusion than sensible judgment in what Johnson now did, he had some reason to think that he was acting on developments that could change the course of the war.

Between April and July, a steady stream of optimistic reports more than matched negative assessments about the conflict. On April 3, the CIA reported that Moscow saw food shortages and problems "coping with modern weapons of war" impeding Hanoi's capacity to continue fighting. Hanoi itself was fearful that attacks on power plants and water works would reduce "vital electric power" and cause "widespread epidemics." Its greatest hope for victory lay in U.S. "war weariness" and desertions from the South Vietnamese Army.

Another CIA assessment painted a gloomy picture of North Vietnamese military manpower. Army morale was poor, and desertion rates were becoming unmanageable. Rural areas "have been drained of healthy young men," and mobilization of veterans between the ages of thirty-seven and fifty and of men with chronic illnesses indicated "that North Vietnam is exhausting its manpower." The same day, Walt Rostow sent Johnson a report from a North Vietnamese prisoner of war showing "a radically worse manpower position than our intelligence authorities would suggest." Though Rostow saw reason to be skeptical, he thought "we should keep our minds open to the possibility he [the prisoner] is right."[54]

On April 5 Rostow gave Johnson information from a Soviet official indicating that "bombing of the North is having its effect; and the Soviet Union may be reducing its aid to Hanoi." The North Vietnamese economy was described as "destroyed, and the help from Socialist countries is poor." Hanoi had "used up all the old stocks of war materiel," and Moscow was reluctant to supply newer materiel and equipment on "the pretext that the North Vietnamese do not know how to handle and use them."

Rostow also provided a positive picture of developments in the South. Though the South Vietnamese military could not function effectively without direct U.S. help, the trends were all positive. There was a "drastic drop" in South Vietnamese desertions, and good "progress toward revamping" ARVN forces. Captured V.C. documents sent to Johnson on April 19 "underline the progress we have made from 1965—when we were on the defensive; to 1966, when the main force offensive was defeated; to 1967, where they [the Communists] are in a defensive posture strategically and trying to buy time while preventing the collapse of the VC infrastructure."[55]

At the end of April, during briefings in Washington, Westmoreland declared himself "very optimistic" about progress in the war. If the American public backed our troops, he assured everyone that "our struggle will succeed." Did Westmoreland's emphasis on

greater force, one skeptical journalist asked Bob Komer, mean that
we were unable to reform the South Vietnamese military and would
be compelled to fight for a long time? No, Komer emphasized, Washington and Saigon were increasingly optimistic about South Vietnam's
efforts on the "civilian and military sides. . . . 'The political process
was going better than we dared hope.' "[56]

Komer was an inveterate optimist: "I believe that *Westy takes
much too cautious a view of the momentum we have already
achieved in Vietnam*," he wrote Johnson on April 28. "I believe that
by this time next year we can break the back of the VC in South
Vietnam."[57]

In May, the CIA described success in attracting non-Communist
members of the National Liberation Front into a coalition government that would come out of the September elections. "This program
has moved," Rostow told the President, "and next steps are under
active consideration."

Max Taylor urged Johnson to sustain the bombing as a way to
move toward peace. "We must pass this test of persistence. . . . If we
yield on the bombing issue, we can be quite sure of no future 'give'
by Hanoi on any important point."

V.C. and North Vietnamese strength had shown "rapid erosion"
since September 1966, a drop of 10 percent, Johnson heard on May
13. He was optimistic about the war, the President told Keyes Beech
of the *Chicago Daily News*. He saw domestic criticism of the war
abating, and believed that Moscow was eager to help end the fighting.
Did the President want continued funding of CIA Revolutionary Development Teams in Vietnam? an aide asked LBJ in mid-May. "By
all means," Johnson answered, signaling his undiminished faith in
pacification as a weapon against the Viet Cong.[58]

In a conversation with Ky on May 30, Ambassador Ellsworth
Bunker emphasized "the great importance we attached to the evolution of the constitutional process and the forthcoming elections
through which we hoped and expected the free will of the people
would be expressed. . . . 'Don't worry,' " Ky assured Bunker, " 'I know
how to handle the situation. It is like a western movie, it will come
out all right in the end.' " Bunker hoped that "the happy ending of
the western movie which he [Ky] envisages will not be preceded by
the gun play which is a normal part of every western."[59]

Whatever doubts Johnson had about the war and Saigon's readiness for self-government gave additional ground in June to fresh
"evidence" of advances in the fighting. Viet Cong and North Vietnamese casualties seemed to be mounting. Where the Communists in
the five years from 1961 to 1966 suffered about 100,000 battlefield

deaths, the number had doubled in 1966 and was running at a similar level through the first half of 1967.

Likewise, according to latest estimates, the bombing was beginning to inflict serious losses on the North Vietnamese. According to the U.S. military command in the Pacific, "there is an upward trend of strategic impact against North Vietnam. It is most significant that these changes are recent and have occurred since early May when we stepped up our air operations in the North and made our presence felt on a much more continuous basis in the enemy's rear support area."[60]

By the end of June, the White House was convinced that it was only a matter of time before Hanoi agreed to talk. "Hanoi is moving towards negotiations," Rostow told the President on June 28. "Just as we never had to conduct the great offensive of 1919 or actually invade Japan in 1945," so we might be able to end this war without further escalation. The Communists cannot win in South Vietnam, Johnson told Virginia Senator Harry F. Byrd, Jr., the next day. "That is, they cannot if we stand firm and if our Vietnamese allies continue to move forward on their urgent internal political and economic and social tasks."[61]

Johnson was convinced that winning the struggle at home against antiwar opponents was now as crucial as the continuing "progress" in Vietnam. Administration leaders told him that as Hanoi paid a heavier price for the war, it invested more hope in American unwillingness to sustain the costs of the struggle. More peace moves would be counterproductive, Ambassador Llewellyn Thompson advised from Moscow. "We have made it abundantly clear that at any time they [the Communists] are ready to move toward either settlement or de-escalation we will agree to almost any time, place or channel."

Thompson was preaching to the converted. The Communists " 'think we won't go the route,' " Johnson told Hugh Sidey of *Time* in May. "They want South Vietnam. They will persist as long as they think we won't stick it out, as long as they think we won't go the route."[62]

By the spring of 1967 the antiwar movement in America was at fever pitch. Students, faculty, clergymen, professional and business leaders, and numerous mainstream politicians were convinced that the war was a great mistake and must be ended as soon as possible.

In response, the administration gave increasing attention to combating antiwar opponents. Johnson saw their agitation sapping the will of ordinary Americans to sustain the war effort and giving the Communists emotional strength to continue the struggle.

Though Johnson saw the antiwar movement eroding his free-dom to fight a long war, he couldn't come to terms with its appeal—the growing skepticism that the price of fighting in Vietnam was worth paying. Johnson preferred to believe that antiwar critics were mainly radical intellectuals and misfits incapable of shaping majority sentiment. In April 1967, for example, when Martin Luther King joined the ranks of war opponents with a speech condemning the U.S. government as "the greatest purveyor of violence in the world today," Johnson took comfort from editorials in the *New York Times* and *Washington Post* condemning King's address as injurious to peace and the cause of civil rights.[63]

John Roche gave Johnson other reasons to dismiss King's speech as the ramblings of a "loser." Roche thought that "King—in desper-ate search of a constituency—has thrown in with the commies.... The Communist-oriented 'peace' types have played him."[64]

Johnson believed that King had joined the ranks of the crack-pots, whom he saw at the center of the antiwar movement. It was one thing to have dissent, the President told Stuart Loory of the *Los Angeles Times*. America had never had unanimity; "this is a feature of an open society." But he saw a difference between "vocal critics" and "draft-card burners." The White House welcomed the possibility that Ben Bradlee might run a *Washington Post* series on "the type of people who throw eggs and appear outside of meetings—both here and in Europe." Anything publicizing the FBI's findings that "the Communist party and other organizations" were using the "peace" movement "to force the United States to change its present policy toward Vietnam" impressed LBJ as a good thing.

"Do you have any doubts about the strength of our country—meaning the flag?" Hugh Sidey asked Johnson. "Youth doesn't bother me," he replied. "I am worried about attempts to subvert the country. I am not a McCarthy, but I am concerned. I am concerned about [Ambassador Anatoly] Dobrynin when he gets back from Moscow. Most of the protests are Communist-led. (The President cited the one at the University of Texas.) I read one hour of reports on it every night."[65]

Bob Kintner asked Ramsey Clark to see whether "a report could be authentically prepared that would show that there was common planning throughout the United States of public demonstrations, riots in colleges, and similar types of activity." Kintner wasn't sure exactly how they would publicize the findings, but he told Clark that "the President is interested in this and asked me to explore it with you."[66]

Yet however much Johnson and others saw war opponents as extremists with limited appeal, they felt compelled to counter the effects they saw from unanswered criticism and demonstrations. Bill Moyers wanted the President to get out from behind a teleprompter and the setting of a press conference to talk things over with the country in more informal settings. "There is an uneasiness in the land that could be arrested to a considerable degree by a reassuring talk from you," Moyers wrote him on May 1. "I believe a clear majority are behind you on the basic issues of Vietnam and on the question of bombing, too. But for a long time now they have been hearing from Martin Luther King and Stokely Carmichael and men like Walter Lippmann and others, and I sense an erosion of their certainty. . . . The dissenters will not retreat," Moyers concluded, "but the great majority of the middle will be reassured that the dark road ahead can be safely traversed."[67]

Jim Rowe also urged a counterattack against dissenters. "It is elementary that this is an unpopular war," he wrote Johnson on May 17. The bulk of the country supported LBJ's policies, but it was "restless" in the face of the opposition. These "opinion makers" may eventually "convert the people, particularly if unopposed."[68]

Johnson didn't wish to get out front in this campaign, believing that he was already something of a redundancy in arguing the case for Vietnam. He was comfortable speaking to journalists off the record, but he was eager for "prompt counter attack[s]" from administration leaders "against widely exaggerated media criticism" and for "plenty of backgrounders" from embassy and military staff in Vietnam. A Rusk meeting with forty-three university student leaders and a series of Westmoreland briefings on a visit to the United States in April appealed to Johnson. In May, when John Roche proposed establishing a National Committee for Peace with Freedom in Vietnam, Johnson agreed, but told Roche: "Don't get surfaced." The objective was to convince the country that such a committee had spontaneous beginnings and was independent of the administration.[69]

During the spring, Johnson convinced himself that he was winning both wars—at home as well as in Vietnam. According to the polls, the majority of Americans wanted no halt to the bombing; in May, public approval of Vietnam policy exceeded disapproval for the first time in five months; Robert Kennedy's dissent on Vietnam made him less popular than LBJ; while straw votes on Johnson against Romney and Nixon gave him reason to think he could be reelected. "If the election were held today [May 12]," Panzer wrote him, "and decided on the war alone, Harris says, you would be re-elected."[70]

In a conversation with Hugh Sidey on May 16, Johnson exalted in the expressions of support. " 'If I am so unpopular, why have I been so successful in winning so many elections?' " he asked Sidey.

" 'Look at those people a few minutes ago. (The President had stopped at the Southeast Gate and talked and shook hands with some passers-by.) Did you see the excitement in their eyes as they saw me. They were so kind. Their remarks were of praise.' "[71]

At the same time Johnson assessed his standing at home, he was trying to decide on additional air and ground actions. Westmoreland and the Joint Chiefs recommended a "relentless application of force." They urged expanded strikes against North Vietnam to eliminate military and industrial facilities in the Hanoi-Haiphong area, destroy crops by hitting dams and dikes, and disrupt freedom of movement by bombing ports and rail lines to China. They also wanted a U.S. reserve call-up, which would give Westmoreland 200,000 more troops to attack North Vietnamese main units in the South, support pacification, and expand the war to Cambodia, Laos, and southern North Vietnam, just above the 17th parallel, to counter infiltration.[72]

McNamara and civilian aides in the Defense Department opposed the JCS proposals as likely to provoke China and Russia and increase domestic divisions over the war. They suggested instead that the President "limit force increases to no more than 30,000; avoid extending the ground conflict beyond the borders of South Vietnam; and concentrate the bombing on the infiltration routes south of 20 degrees." This would limit U.S. troop strength to 500,000, halt the bombing around Hanoi and Haiphong, and concentrate air attacks in the southern neck of the country between the 17th and 20th parallels.[73]

Johnson was reluctant to do anything that might provoke the Soviets and Chinese. In a conversation with Richard Russell on May 12, he described the three choices open to him on bombing as (1) moving "further in the North—but they tell me that moving further in the north with the bombing will result in only killing civilians and will not accomplish anything that we've not already accomplished. (2) I can concentrate completely on the DMZ. (3) I can concentrate on the areas between the seventeenth and twentieth parallels and make my planes make that a desert. Just destroy anything that moves."

Russell's advice was for a quick end to the fighting. The longer the war went on, the greater the chance for a bigger conflict. "We've just got to finish it soon," Russell said, "because time is working against you both here and there." Russell wanted the President to blockade North Vietnamese ports and deny them supplies. But Johnson thought this would be more likely to provoke a larger conflict than end the current one. He also believed that hitting more targets around Hanoi and Haiphong would have the same result. "The only thing left to take out there is a power plant which is located ½ mile from Ho's headquarters. Suppose we miss," he said.[74]

As always, Johnson's impulse was to find some middle ground between competing recommendations. Above all, he didn't wish to rush into anything. Before he decided on future military actions, he wanted another close appraisal of existing conditions. At the beginning of July he sent McNamara, Wheeler, and other Defense, State, and White House officials to reach an agreement with Westmoreland on how to proceed. The only certainty in the picture as the mission went forward was that the war would go on.

"There Is No Stalemate"

By early July the word most often used to describe the war was "stalemate." The war was deadlocked—American ground forces in South Vietnam made it impossible for the Communists to win, but Viet Cong–North Vietnamese tactics and greater manpower made it unlikely that they would lose.

The suggestion that the United States was on a treadmill in Vietnam frustrated and angered Johnson. Americans were growing impatient with a war costing so much blood and showing few signs of a discernible end. By the middle of 1967, nearly 70,000 Americans had been killed or wounded. But, to give up now—to declare victory and leave—was unacceptable. To declare war on Hanoi and risk a larger conflict with China and Russia was also out of the question. Keep going, muddle through, and hope that Hanoi would cave in before we did seemed the only alternative. But to reach this goal required a steady commitment from the American people. By the summer of 1967, holding the country on course seemed as uncertain as knowing when Hanoi might give up the fight.

If his military gave him assurances that American firepower was working—that the ground war in the South and the air war in the North were grinding down the enemy—Johnson would keep the country on course at home. When McNamara returned from Vietnam on July 11, the President asked: "Are we going to be able to win this goddamned war?"[75]

Johnson wanted to hear only one answer: It may take additional time and more men and more bombing, but *we will win*. Everyone high in the administration and military chiefs in Vietnam knew what the President wanted them to say. And like Johnson they had invested their reputations in the war. They could not tell him that the war was a lost cause or an open-ended struggle that could go on for years. Like the President they wanted to believe that they had acted wisely—that their decisions had been sound and the lives lost were in the service of a realizable goal.

Consequently, Johnson's principal aides told themselves and him what they all wanted to believe: We are going to "win." During McNamara's visit to Vietnam, Westmoreland said, "The situation is not a stalemate. We are winning slowly but steadily, and the pace can accelerate if we reinforce our successes." Bunker echoed Westmoreland's optimism.

Hubert Humphrey returned from a trip to Korea, where he discussed Vietnam with Korean, Japanese, and Vietnamese leaders. They were all optimistic about the future of East Asia, and believed "that the military defeat of the United States/South Vietnam forces is no longer a possibility."

The following day Rostow gave Johnson a memo he had requested: "The Viet-Nam situation is not a stalemate," Rostow declared. "We are moving uphill—slowly but steadily. The enemy is moving downhill, paying an increasingly heavy price for his aggression." Richard Helms of the CIA, the government agency most skeptical about progress in Vietnam, weighed in with a positive report about recent bombing results. Though Hanoi's situation was "not yet ... unmanageable, they have something to think about as they look ahead over the next year," Helms declared.[76]

At a White House meeting on July 12, Johnson heard more of the same. "The optimistic briefings I had received in Saigon had momentarily eased my long-standing doubts about the war's progress in the South," McNamara recalls. "On the *economic front* ... Progress was measurable since his last trip." While Saigon politics presented the "greatest danger," most everything else looked good.

General Wheeler also emphasized the absence of a military stalemate, saying, "There has been an unbroken series of military successes"; he saw "no great military problems in sight." Nicholas Katzenbach declared "that if the American people gave us a chance here at home, ... we could win the war in the field."

Johnson's aides were echoing his hopes. At the July 12 meeting he "said the U.S. people do think, perhaps, that the war cannot be won." He described himself as "more frightened by this than by the Thieu-Ky difficulties." He said the American people do not think "we are doing ... all we should to get the war over as quickly as it should be." He acknowledged that 10,000 American troops had been killed in Vietnam, but he was "constantly reminded that the North Vietnamese have lost more in 60 days than we have lost in the past 6 years. The President said we cannot get it over in 60 days but we must make every effort to try to do what we can."[77]

At a news conference the next day, the President, Wheeler, and Westmoreland put the best possible face on the war. The objective was simply to give U.S. military power more time to work. Johnson declared himself happier than ever with U.S. military and civilian leadership in Vietnam. He was "generally pleased with the progress we have made militarily. We are very sure that we are on the right track."

Johnson announced that some additional troops would be sent to Vietnam, but he saw no need to call up reserves. When a reporter asked the President to comment on what military developments might look like in the coming year, Johnson asked Westmoreland to "touch on this 'stalemate' creature." Westmoreland called it a "complete fiction. It is completely unrealistic." He said that "tremendous progress" had been made in the past year, and ticked off enemy losses and South Vietnamese gains.[78]

Johnson's greatest worry was the U.S. press corps in Saigon; its reporting could sap American domestic morale and force an unsatisfactory end to the war. USIA Director Leonard Marks returned from Vietnam in early July with a discouraging report about the journalists. They were more pessimistic and critical than at any time in the past two years. They doubted our ability to defeat the Communists, saw the South Vietnamese government as hopelessly corrupt, and refused to believe that the September election would be anything but a mockery of democratic procedures. Marks ascribed their cynicism to youth and inexperience. "Many of these correspondents . . . are here on their first 'big assignment,' " he told Johnson, "and have a tendency to search for the critical story which might lead to a Pulitzer Prize."[79]

Johnson asked McNamara, Wheeler, Westmoreland, and press secretary George Christian what they thought of censoring U.S. correspondents in Vietnam. All agreed that the price of censorship would be "too great." Christian said it would create a "morass. We cannot do it."[80]

Neither Johnson nor any of his advisers gave public credence to the journalists' judgments. They accepted Marks's conclusion that inexperience and personal gain motivated them. And though LBJ's advisers didn't recommend censorship, they saw the need to muzzle press critics as best they could. Despite brave talk about no stalemate and winning, they feared that the journalists might be accurately describing conditions in Vietnam.

The unacknowledged doubts about U.S. effectiveness in Vietnam moved Johnson and his aides to mislead the press and the public.

They didn't want the country to know, for example, that Westmoreland wanted another 200,000 troops above the 470,000 already committed to the fighting. Since a force of 670,000 would require a reserve call-up and provoke additional domestic divisions, Johnson wanted nothing said about so large an increase. In fact, he would give Westmoreland only another 55,000 troops for a total of 525,000. And Westmoreland was expected to describe the increase as entirely sufficient.

Johnson also said nothing about a Clark Clifford–Maxwell Taylor mission to ask U.S. allies for additional troops, an indication that Westmoreland was getting fewer American men than he wanted. When Johnson, McNamara, and Westmoreland spoke to the press about increased forces in Vietnam, they described themselves as in complete agreement. Westmoreland said he was getting everything he needed.[81]

Johnson's doubts about American effectiveness in Vietnam surfaced in a discussion with Clifford before he went on his Asian trip. The President wanted advice from Clifford and Taylor on how to increase pressure on Hanoi. He wasn't confident that the additional 55,000 troops or current bombing campaign would force the North Vietnamese to talk. He believed, however, that additional military force, which could mute American doubts about winning and might help end the conflict, was necessary. Johnson hoped that their Asian visit could instruct him on what to do.

Clifford returned from his trip with no good advice for the President. Instead, he was "puzzled and troubled, dismayed by our failure to get more support from our allies." Clifford says that he "could only hint" at his level of concern in a joint report to the President, because Taylor did not share it. In private, however, he told Johnson of his shock at "the failure of the countries whose security we believed we were defending to do more for themselves."[82]

Faced with so many questions about progress in the fighting, the administration saw every negative Vietnam story as a blow to America's war morale. "A report from Vietnam on [the] Huntley-Brinkley [News Hour] tonight was devastating," Harry McPherson told George Christian on July 18. It described U.S. Marines being sent to the DMZ, where, "if the present rate of fighting continues, more than half . . . will be wounded or killed." It was another in a series of "stories about bewildered, depressed men. It was really bad news," McPherson said.

Dean Rusk told the Cabinet the next day that "there is no evidence of a stalemate in Vietnam." The assumption was the product of a press corps, that "are more antagonistic now than they ever have been." We had stopped all "major enemy offensives," and "roads have been opened where they were not before." The President cited a confidential report showing increased effectiveness in bombing the North; there was "no question about progress."[83]

All the positive talk, however, couldn't dispel increasing doubts. At a meeting of Senate leaders with the President on July 25, Fulbright frankly declared the war "a hopeless venture." He thought it was "ruining our domestic and our foreign policy. I will not support it any longer," he said. Johnson told him he had "a blind spot" on Vietnam, and challenged the senators to repeal the Gulf of Tonkin Resolution. "You can tell the troops to come home. You can tell General Westmoreland that he doesn't know what he is doing."

Senator Fritz Hollings of South Carolina sent word to Johnson through Rostow the following week that he was "very worried about the mood on Viet Nam among the men whose support you really need in the Senate." There was "a general feeling that we are on a treadmill." Rostow responded that "never had the Saigon and Washington teams so completely agreed that in military terms we were making good progress; we could see a process under way that really gave light at the end of the tunnel." Hollings said, "It was extremely important that we conveyed all the evidence for this view to these key senators."[84]

But the administration simply lacked compelling information to convince most Americans that the war was going well. A Gallup poll at the end of July showed 52 percent of the country disapproving the President's handling of the war, his highest negative rating to date. Only 34 percent thought we were making progress in the fighting. Westmoreland and Wheeler responded with a stepped-up effort to convince newsmen and the American public that "nothing could be farther from the truth" than descriptions of the war as either a stalemate or a struggle in which we had lost the initiative.[85]

But military and civilian proponents of the war had lost public trust. The journalists in Vietnam seemed more reliable. Despite what Johnson and others in the administration might think, the press's critical view of the war seemed to come not from youthful inexperience or personal ambition or any lack of patriotism but from information and detached analysis showing the war at a standstill and unlikely to change.

New York Times Saigon bureau chief R. W. (Johnnie) Apple, Jr., for example, was a man of unquestionable integrity who honestly reported military and political realities in Vietnam. On August 7, he published a front-page account in the *Times*, which in retrospect was one of the seminal stories on the war. He described a war that "is not going well. Victory is not close at hand. It may be beyond reach," he asserted. "It is clearly unlikely in the next year or even the next two years, and American officers talk somberly about fighting here for decades. . . . 'Stalemate' is a fighting word in Washington. President Johnson rejects it as a description of the situation in Vietnam. But it is the word used by almost all Americans here, except the top officials, to characterize what is happening."

Critics in Vietnam told Apple that 200,000 enemy troops may have been killed but that Communist forces now numbered nearly 300,000; that despite U.S. air strikes, the V.C. and North Vietnamese were better supplied with modern weapons than ever; that 1.2 million allied troops had control of only a fraction of a country less than one and a half times the size of New York State; that the North Vietnamese had committed only one-fifth of their regular Army to the fighting, while the allies were struggling to find additional forces; and that the Saigon government, for all the talk of free elections, was an unstable regime, which would crumble once the American military prop was removed.[86]

The story "sent Lyndon Johnson into orbit," CBS-TV correspondent Murray Fromson recalls. After Apple's story appeared, Johnson called Barry Zorthian, the embassy public affairs officer in Saigon. Apple, who was at Zorthian's home when the President called, was the object of Johnson's anger. He demanded that Zorthian get Apple out of Vietnam and get other journalists "in line" or "on the team." He told Zorthian that Apple was "a Communist," and he disapproved of him seeing Apple. Jim Jones, an aide at the White House, also told Apple that LBJ thought he was "a Communist, a threat to national security."

But LBJ was mistaken: It was not the reporters who were describing the sorry state of the U.S. war effort in Vietnam, but rather American officers, including a senior general, who told Fromson and Apple that the war "was unwinnable, that we had reached a stalemate and should find a dignified way of getting out."

If Johnson had a quarrel with anyone, it was with U.S. military men on the ground in Vietnam who faithfully told Fromson and Apple what they saw and knew. But in response to unrelenting pressure for good news, reports from the field were made as upbeat as possible. Company commanders pressed for body counts gave what Apple describes as "WAGs—wild-ass guesses," or in their cleaned-up version in the New York Times, "WEGs—wild-eyed guesses." Apple remembers spending a night with an American provincial adviser. When he showed him a printout of secure provincial hamlets he had obtained in Saigon and asked to visit one, the adviser exclaimed: "You can't go there. We'll get killed if we try to go there." The adviser explained that he had reported those hamlets as "insecure," but "when it got up to corps level or to country level, they had to make a quota; they felt they had to show those hamlets secure."

Johnson's real quarrel should have been with himself and advisers whose errors of judgment had drawn the United States into a quagmire from which they could not extricate themselves. His quarrel should have been with a mindset that insisted on hopeful assessments—with an outlook demanding that the military give "the old man [LBJ] good news." Acknowledging a failed policy that had cost so many lives was more than someone with so fragile an ego as Johnson's could manage. Losing was never a word in Lyndon Johnson's vocabulary.[87]

The Search for a Magic Bullet

In the summer of 1967 Johnson hoped that a combination of heavier bombing and the election of a popular government in Saigon would prod Hanoi into peace talks. He saw these two conditions as making it so difficult for the Communists to seize power that they would negotiate a settlement. "The problem is how to get free and honest elections and not have a coup," Johnson told Peter Lisagor in August. "When they have that election, that's when South Vietnam stops crawling and begins to walk—when they get a democratic government."[88]

In July and August U.S. military chiefs urged the President to believe that American bombing against the North was beginning to have the desired effects. "As you know," Walt Rostow told the President on July 17, "our military feel that they have achieved real momentum in their attack on the northern part of North Vietnam."

Johnson didn't need convincing. He was eager to believe these reports. At a Cabinet meeting on July 19, he read aloud a confidential memorandum from an air force general asserting that "the effectiveness of the air bombing in North Vietnam has increased." He believed it essential that we now "increase our pressure." U.S. military chiefs agreed: They described bombing as "the only offensive element of our strategy" and the only means by which we could win the war.[89]

Johnson wanted to give the military more latitude. On July 15, he asked Rostow: "How could our bombing of the North Vietnamese transport system be intensified without excessive public clamor here and abroad?" McNamara cautioned against unrestricted or "free bombing," which military commanders in Vietnam wanted. He predicted civilian casualties, greater U.S. plane losses, and heightened tensions with China and Russia. But sensing Johnson's desire for increased bombing, McNamara declared: "Mr. President, your responsibility is to the people of this country. Whatever you feel we must do, let's do it." It was a good example of the President's advisers telling him what he and they wanted to hear rather than the unwelcome truth about their war strategy.

Johnson ordered "a limited extension of previous targets." It was not as much as the military wanted, but it demonstrated that the President would not reduce bombing. He told Fulbright: "General Westmoreland told me . . . that the bombing is our offensive weapon. And it will be just like tieing his right hand behind him if we were to stop it."[90]

During the first week of August Johnson received fresh indications that the bombing had reduced infiltration by forcing between 500,000 and 700,000 North Vietnamese into repair work. Clark Clifford and Maxwell Taylor urged him to expand the target list and move the "margins" closer to China. They predicted that unless we increased the bombing to reduce the flow of men and supplies south, we would find ourselves no further along toward winning the war a year from now.[91]

Clifford and Taylor were only reflecting what Johnson had already stated to them as his preference. Johnson had told Clifford that "the time has come to exert maximum pressure on the enemy." And when Clifford saw Westmoreland in Vietnam at the end of July, he had told him that there was "great interest . . . in targets that had not been struck in North Vietnam."[92]

In a White House meeting on August 8, Johnson left no question about his preference for increased bombing. He wanted to expand the target list and make Hanoi pay a greater price for its aggression. When McNamara and Rusk questioned the value and dangers of an escalating air war, Johnson said, "It doesn't look as though we have escalated enough to win." McNamara's response that "hitting these targets would not necessarily mean that we would win" did not deter Johnson. He stated his intention to "authorize all targets except the cities [Hanoi and Haiphong] and the buffer zone [with China]. He concluded: "We have got to do something to win. We aren't doing much now." It was as close as Johnson came to acknowledging that the war was stalemated and that we could not end the fighting without some additional use of force.[93]

On August 16, Johnson met again with his national security team, which asked him to clarify his strategy on bombing. "Our strategy, as I see it, is that we destroy all we can without involving China

and Russia between now and September 1 [two days before elections
in South Vietnam]. I do not believe that China and Russia will come
in. The [American] people will not stay with us if we do not get
destroyed all we can. . . . Let us find the least dangerous and the most
productive targets."[94]

Part of Johnson's expanded bombing campaign was directed at
a Senate subcommittee holding hearings on the air war. He did not
want the hearings to portray the White House as restraining the
military from actions that might end the fighting. Therefore, when
McNamara told the subcommittee on August 25 that bombing by
itself would not bring Hanoi to the peace table, it enraged the Joint
Chiefs, who considered a mass resignation in protest against a defense
secretary with whom they disagreed. Johnson was also incensed at
McNamara for his candor. On his way back to the Pentagon from
the hearings, McNamara received a summons from the President,
who spent three hours upbraiding and roaring at him.[95]

But McNamara was simply telling what he knew to be the case.
Though a CIA report four days later described the "increased effectiveness" of the bombing, the conclusion remained that "despite increasing hardships . . . caused by the air war, Hanoi continues to meet
its own needs and to support its aggression in South Vietnam. Essential military and economic traffic continues to move." More important, a secret memo Helms gave only to the President on September
12 argued that the United States could withdraw from Vietnam without lasting injury to our national security.[96]

Johnson knew that the air war was insufficient to break Hanoi's
will to fight. As long as the North Vietnamese believed that American
resolve was likely to collapse before theirs and that South Vietnam
lacked the political stability to remain a viable country without U.S.
power, they saw every reason to fight on. If he could convince them,
however, that America would not relent in its military campaign and
that South Vietnam was evolving into a durable national state, he
saw hope for some kind of settlement. Moreover, withdrawal from
Vietnam in 1967 or 1968, especially when so many of his principal
advisers foresaw eventual success in the fighting, was unacceptable to
him.

An election establishing a legitimate constitutional government
in the South was an essential counterpart to increased bombing. With
Ky agreeing to accept the vice presidency in a newly elected government, a Thieu-Ky conflict for political control largely ended and, in
LBJ's view, opened the way to fair and honest elections on September
3. Twenty-two U.S. observers Johnson sent to oversee the elections
reported that they were "clean" and a demonstration of democracy

THE SEARCH FOR A MAGIC BULLET

in action. Fifty-six percent of the electorate went to the polls and gave South Vietnam its first taste of what Johnson described as self-determination. The result, one historian says, was "rightly hailed as a sign of progress, but the government, however chosen, remained incompetent and riddled with corruption."[97]

The elections were not as "clean" as Johnson wanted to believe. Eugene C. Patterson, the editor of the *Atlanta Constitution* and one of the observers, described their meeting with LBJ as "a performance and not a report." Patterson separated himself from his twenty-one colleagues by declaring that the Saigon government "had barred several popular candidates from entering the race." When Patterson spoke, Johnson, who had been nodding in response to the encouraging talk from the other observers, "glared at me with obvious anger as if I were doing an unfair thing." The President wanted to hear only positive comments about the elections.[98]

Whatever the political realities in Saigon, Johnson and Rusk took the elections as a reason to hope that Hanoi might now be more receptive to talks. Rusk saw the beginnings of a "new chapter in Vietnam." He cautioned the Cabinet to "be careful about thinking that the election results will produce an immediate peace move." But he believed the "chances are certainly better—Saigon is now better equipped 'to probe Hanoi.' "

The President saw the election outcome as a reason "now to probe in every way to find some way to get Ho Chi Minh to talk, even as they continue to fight if necessary." He wanted the new government to declare its readiness for all sorts of reforms and to be as forthcoming as possible in trying to bring "the NLF into the constitutional political process." He asked Bunker to "explore with Thieu and Ky as soon as possible . . . some possible offer to the Viet Cong relating to their entering into political life in SVN under the constitution."[99]

Current U.S. opinion polls gave Johnson added reason to seize any possible initiative for peace talks. Fifty-six percent of Americans did not think the Vietnamese elections would lead to a stable government in Saigon; 54 percent were skeptical that the voting would reflect "the true wishes of the South Vietnamese people." A Harris poll at the end of August gave Johnson a new sense of urgency about ending the war. Sixty-seven percent of Americans disapproved of the President's handling of Vietnam; 61 percent opposed sending more troops; while 71 percent favored a negotiated peace "as quickly as possible."[100]

Shaky domestic support and Johnson's doubts about military progress made him eager for a prompt settlement. Consequently, at the end of July, when Ho Chi Minh and North Vietnamese Premier Pham Van Dong agreed to see two Frenchmen proposing to mediate the conflict, the White House saw new hope for negotiations. At a meeting with LBJ on August 8, McNamara declared the news "the most interesting message on the matter of negotiations which we have ever had."

Johnson was not so sure. He "saw no need until the facts became clearer to slow up the bombing.... We will discontinue all bombing north of the 17th parallel if we know they will not take advantage of it. But we will not quit until we have their assurance they will not take advantage of the bombing halt."[101]

On August 11, the White House gave Harvard political scientist Henry Kissinger, who was the U.S. contact with the French messengers, a statement for delivery to Pham Van Dong. "The United States is willing to stop the aerial and naval bombardment of North Vietnam if this will lead promptly to productive discussions.... We would assume that, while discussions proceed..., the DRV would not take advantage of the bombing cessation or limitation." When Kissinger presented the statement to the Frenchmen for transmittal to Hanoi, they urged a reduction in bombing during their next visit as a signal of U.S. intentions. During a White House discussion of bombing targets on August 18, Johnson agreed to a temporary cessation of bombing inside a ten-mile zone around Hanoi. Both Rusk and McNamara saw greatly improved chances of "secret contacts" resulting from this initiative. Johnson made no predictions.[102]

In fact, he remained highly skeptical. On September 5, he told a group of American correspondents that "the new South Vietnamese government would seek peace ... and that we would encourage them. We would stop bombing tomorrow if that could lead to productive talks, ... but he said North Vietnam would offer no assurances that they won't use a pause to their military advantage." On September 11, when Hanoi responded to Johnson's August 11 statement, it complained about continuing heavy raids against North Vietnam, despite reduced attacks on Hanoi, and restated its refusal to talk until there was an unconditional halt to all acts of war. Kissinger suggested that Washington "treat the message as a first step in a complicated bargaining process" and favored "going along a little further."[103]

Johnson accepted Kissinger's advice. On September 12, at a Tuesday lunch meeting, which had become a White House fixture in the ongoing discussions about Vietnam, Johnson suggested simplifying our message to Hanoi: "Why shouldn't we quit explaining so much," he said, "and just say we will stop bombing, if a conference is arranged and if it will lead to fruitful discussions"?[104]

A message to the North Vietnamese on September 13 declared that the U.S. "proposal contained neither conditions nor threats and should not be rejected on these grounds." The U.S. government assumed that the DRV "would be willing promptly to engage in productive discussions leading to peace when there was a cessation of aerial and naval bombardment."

The President underscored his shift toward a more flexible position at a luncheon with U.S. labor leaders two days later. "We are offering to negotiate with Ho Chi Minh," he said. "Our position is clear. We will stop the bombing if he will launch productive and meaningful discussions. We are not asking, as most people think, that stopping the infiltration is a condition of a bombing pause."[105]

Getting no meaningful response from Hanoi during the next two weeks, Johnson vented his anger toward Ho and U.S. dissenters. In a conversation with Australian broadcasters on September 20, he described the restraint with which U.S. forces were conducting the war. "But the television doesn't want that story," he said. "I can prove that Ho is a son-of-a-bitch if you let me put it on the screen—but they [the TV networks] want me to be the son-of-a-bitch. Press coverage of Vietnam is a reflection of broader and deeper public attitudes, a refusal by many Americans 'to see the enemy as the enemy'. ...NBC and the *New York Times* 'are committed to an editorial policy of making us surrender.' "[106]

At a meeting with advisers on September 26, Johnson complained that the North Vietnamese "are playing us for suckers. They have no more intention of talking than we have of surrendering." He now wanted the bombing to continue until it forced Hanoi into talks. He asked Katzenbach for a memo on "wrapping it [the peace initiative] up, because we have been met twice with a firm no." The same day, at a meeting with college and university educators, Johnson declared: "The problem is not one of communication. The problem is that Ho wants South Vietnam. He isn't going to give it up. He doesn't want to talk about it." Johnson was, of course, correct. But he was unable to act upon his understanding that Ho would not give in and we lacked the wherewithal to change his mind.[107]

To win the public relations war in this latest round of abortive exchanges, Johnson gave a speech on September 29 in San Antonio, Texas. He emphasized his readiness "to send a trusted representative of America to any spot on this earth to talk in public or private with a spokesman of Hanoi. ... The United States is willing to stop all aerial and naval bombardment of North Vietnam when this will lead promptly to productive discussions," he said. "We, of course, assume that while discussions proceed, North Vietnam would not take advantage of the bombing cessation or limitation." In what came to be called the San Antonio formula, Johnson returned to the qualification that Hanoi not seek an advantage from the bombing halt. He believed that if he omitted this condition, he would subject himself to attacks from hawks complaining that he was risking American lives to appease Ho. The speech signaled once again that neither side was ready to come to the table.[108]

Despite an unqualified rejection of his latest call for discussions, Johnson spent most of October ruminating over how to start talks. This impulse to see ongoing hints of interest in discussions had become a form of rationalization for continued bombing. If Hanoi seemed unreceptive to negotiations, it suggested that the bombing was having no effect. If the North Vietnamese showed some inclination to negotiate, or, more to the point, if the administration could see them as having such an inclination, it legitimized the bombing and even encouraged discussions of heavier bombing.

Johnson now believed that the bombing served three functions: It protected U.S. troops from stronger North Vietnamese attacks; it showed Hanoi that we would not give up the fight; and it compelled them to pay a price for their aggression. Since Hanoi's attitude depended on the determination of the American public and since continued bombing showed our resolve to stay the course, the President told Clark Clifford, Dean Acheson, and other "wise men" on October 2 that a bombing halt would demonstrate our "frustration & failure" and would only encourage North Vietnam.[109]

Though he had little or no reason to be optimistic about talks, Johnson continued to make negotiations a regular topic of his discussions about Vietnam. At a White House meeting on October 3, he asked about the status of the Paris talks, code-named "Pennsylvania," an initiative by the Shah of Iran to start peace talks, and Soviet Foreign Secretary Andrei Gromyko's views on Hanoi's response to a bombing halt. Johnson also asked his advisers to say what effect a decision by him not to run again for President might have on the war. Rusk urged him not to stand down, saying it "would have a very serious effect on the country. . . . Hanoi would think they have got it made." Johnson replied: "Our people will not hold out for four more years. I want to get rid of every major target. Between now and election, I am going to work my guts out. I would be 61 when I came back in, and I just don't know if I want four more years of this. . . . But I am afraid it would be interpreted as walking out on our men." He described congressional opinion as convinced "we will lose the election if we do not do something about Vietnam quick."[110]

The next day Johnson again discussed bombing and negotiations.

He wanted to know about new messages from Paris. Rusk recommended that we "keep this dialogue going and not let the matter come to a head quickly." When Rusk described the North Vietnamese as "still weaseling on us," Johnson suggested that we "clear up everything short of Hanoi. . . . I know this bombing must be hurting them," he said. "Despite any reports to the contrary, I can feel it in my bones. . . . Let's hit them every day and go every place except Hanoi." Wishful thinking had replaced rational assessment as the basis for decision-making. Only on negotiations did he remain realistic. When McNamara discussed possible negotiations, Johnson replied, "I'm not as encouraged by all of this as you all are."[111]

During the next week, plans for increased bombing were interspersed with discussions of how peace talks might occur. The White House studied messages from Paris, picking over the meaning of every word and phrase for signs that the North Vietnamese were preparing to talk. On October 16, however, Rusk acknowledged that "we haven't seen any serious response from Hanoi." Still, everyone at the White House did not want to break off the Paris contact.[112]

Instead, they began a fresh discussion of whether a bombing halt was now in order. Johnson wanted to know what damage we might suffer from a pause. McNamara saw no damage: "We could develop our own talk-and-fight strategy." He thought a halt would be a "domestic plus." Rusk worried about the length of a pause. Johnson did not think we could get into a long one. He also feared the consequences of Communist military operations during a pause.[113]

On October 17, with Hanoi still unresponsive to inquiries about talks, Johnson discussed leaking the initiative to the press for whatever public relations gains he could get. "We have to have something to carry us in this country," he said. "Every hawk and every dove and every general seems to be against us." He remained determined to give "Pennsylvania" every conceivable chance. At the same time, he asked Rostow for a paper making the strongest possible case for continued bombing.[114]

CIA reports coming to Johnson on the 18th confirmed his skepticism about Hanoi's intentions. Even if there were a U.S. bombing halt, the agency predicted, it guaranteed nothing. The North Vietnamese would probably then demand that the negotiations include expressions of U.S. willingness to withdraw troops from the South. Rostow believed that Hanoi's intention now was to trade an end to its "no-bombing campaign," which was undermining American support of the war and hurting the President, for a halt to the bombing. "The only way we can get something solid for a cessation of bombing," Rostow concluded, "is to prove that we can manage—or live with—the pressures at home and abroad."[115]

On the evening of October 18, the President had a full-dress discussion of negotiations and a bombing pause. He described three options: "An early bombing pause; close out the [Pennsylvania] channel and resume activity; or wait for [a] further response." His advisers divided sharply on what to do. Rusk urged direct official talks rather than more of the same through Kissinger. Katzenbach suggested leaving all options open on negotiations and initiating a thirty- to forty-day pause in November or December. McNamara also favored a pause. Clifford and Taylor saw nothing coming from the Kissinger channel and believed a bombing halt would only signal weakness and would make "*the possibility of peace much more remote.*"

Johnson said almost nothing except to express the view that Hanoi wanted the Paris channel kept open as a way to keep the U.S. from bombing Hanoi. "I know if they were bombing Washington, hitting my bridges and railroads and highways, I would be delighted to trade off discussions through an intermediary for a restriction on the bombing. It hasn't cost him [Ho] one bit. The net of it is that he has a sanctuary in Hanoi in return for having his Consul talk with two scientists who talked with an American citizen." As for a pause, the President asked Clifford and Rostow to set up a ten-man committee to consider the idea.[116]

On October 23, the President conceded that the current effort to open negotiations through the Paris contacts had failed. He said: "I am unable to find any evidence—apart from hope or wishful thinking—which indicates that Hanoi is ready at this time to talk seriously." His "best judgment and advice" was that current policies—bombing the North and ground fighting in the South—"are best to bring us to an honorable peace."[117]

However reluctant Johnson was to see any immediate hope for negotiations, he could not resist exploring fresh hints of possible talks. On October 28, for example, Rostow brought him news of an NLF contact, who described three potential negotiations: one on "the political settlement within South Vietnam"; a second on U.S.-Hanoi relations; and a third between the North and the South. Rostow described the contact as "the first piece of paper we have received from the other side which goes directly to the heart of the matter which is political settlement in South Vietnam. It comes, as we always thought a truly serious probe would come, while the war proceeds, including a full-scale bombing of North Vietnam." Rostow's response to the contact told more about administration hopes than about real possibilities for a settlement. Such a "probe" reconfirmed White

House convictions that U.S. policy was on the right track and would eventually force Hanoi to agree to end the war.[118]

The Year-End Strategy: Words and Bullets

Johnson had no intention of giving up on negotiations, but with nothing concrete to go on in late October he felt compelled to focus once again on combating the antiwar movement by convincing Americans that we were making progress and would eventually get a settlement. In a discussion with McNamara, Rusk, and Wheeler on the 23rd, he declared: "We are back to where we started. We've tried all your suggestions. We've almost lost the war in the last two months in the court of public opinion. These demonstrators and others are trying to show that we need somebody else to take over this country. . . . The hawks are throwing in the towel. Everybody is hitting you. San Antonio did not get through. I cannot mount a better explanation. . . . We've got to do something about public opinion."

He saw his only option as more military pressure. He wanted to "hit all the military targets short of provoking Russia and China." He asked, "What about the reserves?"—indicating that he was considering a call-up, which would allow him to expand the number of U.S. troops fighting in the South. McNamara and Wheeler saw no need for them at the current level of operations.[119]

Mounting expressions of opposition to the war in the second half of 1967 deepened Johnson's frustration with public opinion and Hanoi. Growing dissent in the Congress from hawks, doves, and moderates eager for an end to the fighting particularly troubled him. In early October, he complained that 95 percent of the Congress believed that U.S. public opinion was turning against the war.[120]

The loss of moderate Massachusetts Representative Tip O'Neill, a prominent House Democrat, to the ranks of the dissenters especially upset Johnson. In 1966, after a White House briefing on the war by Rusk, O'Neill led his fellow congressmen in "a rousing vote of confidence." A few hours later Johnson called O'Neill to express his appreciation. By September 1967, however, conversations with military and CIA officials had convinced O'Neill that the war was unwinnable "and that our involvement there was wrong." As a result, he sent a newsletter to his constituents explaining his change of opinion.

In mid-September, when the *Washington Star* printed a front-page story headlined, "O'Neill splits with LBJ Over Vietnam Policy," Johnson, O'Neill says, was "angry and hurt at what he saw as my betrayal. 'Tip, what kind of a son of a bitch are you?' " Johnson asked him during a one-on-one meeting. " 'I expect something like this from those assholes like [liberal New York Congressman] Bill Ryan. ... But you? You're one of my own.' " When O'Neill explained that his opposition was not for political gain but out of conviction that the war couldn't be won, Johnson "calmed down." O'Neill then urged him either to escalate the bombing enough to win or get out. Johnson said that he couldn't risk war with China and Russia by unrestrained bombing. Nor did he intend to abandon the war. Instead, he asked O'Neill to give him " 'time on this thing. Don't go running to the press or telling everybody your views on the war. You're the first member of the Democratic establishment to oppose me on this, and I don't want you to start the snowball rolling.' "[121]

Johnson wanted time to combat the downturn in public support for the war. The polling data in October added to his sense of urgency about boosting national sentiment. A Gallup survey released on the 4th showed a decided advantage for a Rockefeller-Reagan ticket in 1968. The source of Johnson's decline was frustration over Vietnam. At the start of October only 28 percent approved of his "handling of the war," with 57 percent disapproving. People were fed up with a conflict that seemed open-ended. Of those who disapproved, 48 percent wanted the U.S. to scale down the fighting or simply get out and 37 percent favored increased use of military power. When the 28 percent who approved of Johnson's leadership were added to the group favoring greater military power, support for the war measured 49 percent.[122]

Nevertheless, Johnson could not take comfort from the numbers. Gallup surveys toward the end of the month showed 70 percent of Americans eager to have the U.N. take over the war or have South Vietnamese forces gradually replace Americans. When Gallup asked whether it was a mistake to have become involved in Vietnam, 46 percent said, "yes."[123]

On October 19, Johnson told Robert Manning of *The Atlantic* that he had "never thought there shouldn't have been intervention or bombing. If history indicts us for Vietnam," Johnson said, "it will be for fighting a war without trying to stir up patriotism." Nothing could have been further from the truth. From day one of the escalation in 1965 Johnson had doubted the wisdom of a wider war. Moreover, a two-pronged strategy for combating public demoralization gave the lie to his assertion about shaping potional opinion: On one hand, he approved a campaign to discredit antiwar demonstrators, and on the other, he tried to convince the country that the war was being won.[124]

Johnson agreed to have every government intelligence agency

investigate, monitor, and undermine antiwar activists. Under its anti-subversion or Communist Infiltration and Counterintelligence programs, the FBI assigned thousands of agents to these tasks. In response to urban riots and antiwar rallies, the army set up an Intelligence Command unit that infiltrated and reported on the work of peace and civil rights groups. Despite bars on domestic spying, the CIA created a Special Operations Group to look for connections between American dissenters and foreign operatives. The Justice Department and the National Security Agency also joined in the surveillance of radicals who were seen as disrupting domestic tranquility and undermining the war effort.[125]

The administration's response to an antiwar march on the Pentagon during the weekend of October 21 was a microcosm of Johnson's efforts to control and limit domestic dissent. Information that antiwar groups would send 200,000 protestors to Washington stimulated a White House counterattack. At a meeting with McNamara, Katzenbach, Attorney General Clark, and Interior Secretary Stewart Udall, Johnson agreed to a central command post, which was to urge bus companies to withhold buses from marchers to "discourage attendance"; to monitor protest activities; and to plan troop deployments where needed. Despite an FBI report that only 40,000 to 50,000 protestors would come to Washington and that limits on available transportation would further reduce that number, Johnson saw the march as confirming Hanoi's belief that America was too divided to sustain the war.[126]

During the first week in October, with the conviction that at least 100,000 protestors would show up, the White House stepped up plans to make matters as uncomfortable for them as possible. "We will not supply any amenities to them, e.g., electricity, speaker stands, water, toilets, first aid.... The idea is to keep the pressure on them," an aide told Joe Califano.

During a meeting with national security advisers the next day, Johnson told McNamara to get going on plans to protect the White House, Pentagon, and Capitol. The task force set up to deal with the march wondered whether the President should stay in Washington. "Yes, I will be here," Johnson declared, "they are not going to run me out of town." McNamara anticipated that thousands might have to be arrested. Johnson wanted daily reports on counterdemonstration plans, "together with any new FBI information."[127]

At a Cabinet meeting on October 4, Clark reported that the Justice Department was "working with interest groups here to create other diversionary events on day and night of March." Johnson wanted to know whether the sponsoring groups were "Pacifists? Com-

munists?" Though supporting evidence of significant Communist involvement was thin to nonexistent, Clark described them as "a
combination of both. There is a heavy representation of 'extreme left-
wing groups with long lines of Communist affiliations.' 'Is that a
secret?' " Johnson asked. " 'No,' " Clark replied. " 'Wouldn't it help to
leak that?' " Rusk asked. John Gardner declared: " 'The people have
got to know that.... They must know that!' " Clark reported that
" 'the fact of Communist involvement and encouragement has been
given to some columnists.' 'Let's see it some more,' " Johnson responded.[128]

On October 10, Califano told the President how the task force
planned to arrest "unlawful demonstrators efficiently and quietly,"
and how it hoped to get marchers out of town as quickly as possible.
On the 16th, Califano reported that White House planners would try
to reduce the number of "less extreme antiwar sympathizers from
attending" by leaking "FBI material showing the very heavy Communist involvement in the demonstration."[129]

During the two-day demonstration, Johnson kept close tabs on
developments. He was worried that " 'Communist elements' would
take advantage of the situation to 'make sure that there will be big
trouble in the Negro ghetto.' " He had troops on the alert and deployed "to protect the Pentagon, the Capitol, and the White House.
Army troops were even secretly stationed in the basement of the
Commerce Department, so they could rapidly assume positions surrounding the White House if such action became necessary." George
Christian remembers a tense White House fearful of a siege.[130]

Though the demonstration was relatively peaceful, with only
some 650 people arrested out of a crowd of nearly 100,000, Johnson
wanted to tar the protestors as deviants and subversives. When Califano gave him reports of demonstrators urinating on the Pentagon
lawns and 15 to 20 "hippie" girls taunting troops by asking,
"Wouldn't you rather fuck than fight?," Johnson ordered the information leaked to prowar columnist Joseph Alsop. He told congressional Democrats that a substantial number of the 256 protestors who
burned draft cards "were crazy people who had previous history in
mental institutions, according to FBI reports." He also "noted that he
did not want to be like a McCarthyite, but this country is in a little
more danger than we think and someone has to uncover this information."[131]

Two weeks after the march, Johnson said to aides: " 'I'm not
going to let the Communists take this government and they're doing
it right now.' The President pointed out that he has been protecting
civil liberties since he was nine years old, but 'I told the Attorney

General that I am not going to let 200,000 of these people ruin everything for the 200 million Americans.' "[132]

Johnson and Rusk were convinced that foreign, "Communist" sources were behind the Pentagon demonstration. The President asked Helms to unearth the "international connections of the U.S. peace movement." In a report on November 15, which drew on NSA, FBI, CIA, and military sources, Helms said: "We found little or no information on the financing of the principal peace movement groups. Specifically, we were unable to uncover any source of funds for the costly travel schedules of prominent peace movement coordinators. . . . We could find no evidence of any contact between the most prominent peace movement leaders and foreign embassies, either in the U.S. or abroad." The peace movement was described as being so diverse that it was "impossible to attach specific political or ideological labels" to it. Many of the movement's leaders had "close Communist associations *but they do not appear to be under Communist direction. . . . Covert or overt connections between these US activists and foreign governments are limited.* . . . On the basis of what we now know," the report concluded, "we see no significant evidence that would prove Communist control or direction of the US peace movement or its leaders."[133]

After Helms read the CIA's findings to the Cabinet, Johnson and Rusk "vigorously disputed" them. Rusk said: "It was naive to think the Communists weren't behind it somewhere; the CIA just hadn't looked hard enough." Ramsey Clark remembers Helms trying to defend the agency's study, but, in response to pressure from the President and Rusk, he agreed to review the matter again. A December 21 follow-up report echoed earlier conclusions.[134]

But Johnson was not interested in the judicious analysis provided by the CIA; he had to believe that the Communists were behind the antiwar movement. He could not accept that millions of patriotic Americans opposed the war because it did not serve the national well-being.

Johnson was not alone in his view of war protestors as Communist-controlled. The FBI and others encouraged his suspicions. On October 23, Rostow gave Johnson "evidence on [march organizer David] Dellinger's direct ties to Hanoi." The "evidence" and agency providing it are still classified information, and so it is impossible to assess it, but Rostow was sure it would "interest" LBJ. After a "dump Johnson" meeting of West Side New York liberals met on November 1, Ed Weisl, Johnson's old friend, described the meeting as "shocking. . . . The charges made against our President were similar to the charges made by the Russians and the Arabs at the U.N. It was an audience of Communists, Left-wingers and beatniks." Two weeks later, White House advisers, reflecting the President's suspicions, asked the FBI to determine "how and why demonstrators are so well organized and so efficient in getting to locations where the President is speaking and whether there is any proof that there is a prearranged policy to prevent the President from speaking."

Leonard Marks documented for the White House the value Hanoi placed on U.S. antiwar protests and demonstrations, as if favoring them also proved that they controlled them. An intelligence report from Vietnam in December describing the creation of a "VC Intelligence Organization" consisting of "Vietnamese students and under-cover agents of the Soviet and other Communist embassies in the US" to exploit American divisions over the war was, Rostow told the President, "as blunt a link between [the] Viet Cong . . . and U.S. politics as we're likely to find."[135]

Despite the CIA's inability to demonstrate Communist control of the peace movement, Johnson fanned suspicions by telling Minority Leader Gerald Ford and other House Republicans that the October 21 march was "basically organized by international Communism." When Ford announced this on the floor of the House on November 22 and called on the President to release supporting information, Johnson refused. Preferring to keep suspicions of Communist influence on the demonstrations alive, he did not want the CIA findings to become public. Instead, he sent Clark to make the case to Ford against releasing information, and he allowed Rusk to tell a national news magazine that such a release "would trigger a new wave of McCarthyism in this country."[136]

For Johnson, the question at the end of 1967 was not whether U.S. war protests were Communist-inspired but how to convince Americans that the war was going well and would be won if only they continued to back the boys in the field. At a late September meeting with college and university educators "troubled about Vietnam," Johnson declared that "many people are being used in this country and are hurting the country perhaps without even knowing it." He urged the educators to understand that North Vietnamese "losses have been very heavy. We are trying to hold them there. . . . We believe the time will come when their power to make war will no longer be there. The price will be enough to make them talk."[137]

Johnson's statements to the educators reflected the concerted effort he now thought necessary "to sell our product to the American people. I want to counter these arguments" in the press, he told McNamara, Rusk, Rostow, and Christian on October 4, "about the South Vietnamese not fighting, about the value of an enclave theory, [which he saw as a prelude to getting out] and about the pay-off to stopping the bombing."[138]

Johnson knew that it wasn't enough to fight back; there also had to be a convincing argument made by persuasive people. Finding Vietnam advocates was no problem. Johnson himself made the case to journalists, congressmen, interest groups, and the mass public. "Do you think that you, personally, can help to alleviate some of the uncertainty in the country over Vietnam?" a journalist asked him at a November 1 press conference. "I am doing my best to do that every day," he replied.

In private conversations with reporters, he described "phenomenal progress in the last two years in building a democratic government in South Vietnam and in the conduct of the war." He said that "North Vietnam hasn't won a single victory" during this time. "We are making steady progress," he advised one journalist. Saigon was "in a constitutional process." Your speech to the international labor group was "great," a congressman told him in late October. "You put Viet Nam in just the proper perspective."

But Johnson found it difficult to sustain his rationality in dealing with war critics. During a private conversation with some reporters who pressed him to explain why we were in Vietnam, Johnson lost his patience. According to Arthur Goldberg, "LBJ unzipped his fly, drew out his substantial organ, and declared, 'This is why!' "[139]

Johnson took special pains to keep Congress behind the war. In a briefing of House members on November 2, he emphasized that the rapport between him and military advisers had never been better. They were in full agreement on all the "basic decisions." Their policies had assured against a war with Russia or China by convincing them that Ho was not going to win, that the U.S. would not abandon the struggle, that we had no designs on North Vietnam or China, and that we would leave South Vietnam when the violence stopped. The air war was the product of the shared judgments of himself and air commanders, and, where there was some disagreement on targets, hitting them would reduce Communist supply shipments by only 1 percent. Most important, the Communists were now "suffering terribly": they were losing 1500 men a day to our 15.[140]

Two weeks later, he asked Westmoreland to give a congressional briefing. The general couldn't have been more upbeat. "We have got our opponent almost on the ropes," he declared. "We are confident that we are winning this war. . . . We are grinding this enemy down. And at the same time, we are building up the South Vietnamese to the point where they will be able to progressively take over the greater part of the load."[141]

Johnson wanted all the help he could get in making the case for Vietnam. On November 1, he told Rostow, "I can't clean up all the mess the *New York Times* leaves behind while these old pros and intellectuals [at Radio Free Europe] sit silent." At a White House meeting with Acheson and other "wise men" on November 2, he pressed the case for "far more vigorous action to stabilize public support for our policy in Vietnam." Everyone from Supreme Court Justice Abe Fortas to old political friend Jim Rowe, columnist Joe Alsop, former President Eisenhower, former conservative Congressman Walter Judd, a White House–inspired National Citizens Committee for Peace with Freedom in Vietnam, the American Legion, the Veterans of Foreign Wars, Senators Paul Douglas of Illinois and Gale McGee of Wyoming, and the U.S. Embassy staff in Vietnam were enlisted in the effort.[142]

But Johnson knew that statements about progress in the war needed to have the ring of truth. Harry McPherson brilliantly made the point in a letter to him on October 27. The air war, he said, "has just about become *the war* in the eyes of the press and the minds of the public." And with so many middle-road Democratic supporters growing "edgy about the bombing program," it was time to make clear "what we hope to gain from it." More important, the President needed to describe progress in the South, where the war was going to be won or lost. He needed to show "whether the [Saigon] government works, whether ARVN improves, whether substantial areas are and will remain pacified, whether corruption and inefficiency are reduced, whether people start to trust their leaders, whether the VC is losing support, whether we are licking them on the ground in all four Corps areas."[143]

Johnson had anticipated McPherson's suggestion. On October 25, Walt Rostow told McNamara, Rusk, and Helms that "the President has an urgent need for reliable, usable data on Vietnam and ways of measuring the evolution of the conflict." Rostow asked "that a special interagency task force be established to develop further ways of measuring the progress of the war in all its facets." The "process" was to "be started immediately so that reporting" on this more convincing basis could begin on January 1, 1968.[144]

Twelve U.S. government experts on Vietnam began meeting at a CIA facility in Virginia, where they were isolated and told not to come back until they had developed an effective formula for measuring war gains. One participant, an army colonel, remembers that the group met for over two and a half weeks without success. "We argued and we fought and we screamed," the colonel says, "and we wrote on blackboards and we finally prayed, and then asked permission to please come back to our homes and regular jobs." They couldn't come up with an equation or formula for measuring progress; they couldn't agree on the validity of the data about body counts, weapons captured, small or large unit Communist operations, or what could be considered pacified and unpacified areas.[145]

At the end of the year, *New York Times* correspondent R. W. Apple reported that U.S. officials at every level in Vietnam were under increasing pressure from Washington to provide convincing evidence of advances in the war, especially by the South Vietnamese. But the problem with doing so, one American in Saigon complained, was the "difficulty of getting anything done quickly."[146]

When David Halberstam, former *Times* correspondent in Vietnam, revisited the country in December 1967, he rediscovered a world of illusions. Light at the end of the tunnel, corners being turned, victory in a matter of months were some of the upbeat descriptions on the lips of U.S. officials. But Halberstam came away doubting "our capacity to win." It was not that U.S. military power lacked victories. They were real, but ephemeral. American military successes had done little, if anything, to help the South Vietnamese to help themselves. Their society was "rotten, tired, and numb" after twenty-one years of war. The government of South Vietnam was "largely meaningless to its citizens," and U.S. programs and wishes could not change that.

"I do not think we are winning in any true sense," Halberstam concluded, "nor do I see any signs we are about to win. . . . I do not think our Vietnamese can win their half of the war, nor do I think we can win it for them." Even if we stayed for another five years, we could achieve no more than a settlement the Vietnamese would have to make themselves. The best we could hope for in an unwinnable war was the stalemate that had taken hold in 1967 and seemed all too likely to continue for the foreseeable future. No amount of number juggling or posturing about significant gains could change the harsh realities of Vietnam.[147]

10

Last Hurrahs

IN the fall of 1967, more than anything, Johnson wanted to end the uncertainty over Vietnam. The "most important decision" we now have, the President told Rostow in October, was a "strategy for the next 12 months on Vietnam—military, political, negotiating." There had been "too much vague talk," Johnson complained.[1]

It was clear to Johnson that the North Vietnamese "simply are not yet ready to quit," and a fresh look at the war was now in order. He asked the "Wise Men"—Dean Acheson, General Omar Bradley, George Ball, Mac Bundy, Arthur Dean, Douglas Dillon, Abe Fortas, Averell Harriman, Henry Cabot Lodge, Robert Murphy, and Max Taylor—to meet with him on November 2. As a prelude, the President asked McNamara, Buzz Wheeler, and George Carver, the CIA's expert on Vietnam, to brief them.

At lunch with the "Wise Men" on October 31, McNamara gave vent to his growing doubts about the war. "Perhaps everything I and Dean Rusk have tried to do since 1961 has been a failure," McNamara said. He also declared that "continuation of our present course of action in Southeast Asia would be dangerous, costly in lives, and unsatisfactory to the American people."[2]

McNamara's anguish over the war found fuller expression in a memo he gave the President on November 1. Because he was proposing a change of course on Vietnam, which might be "incompatible with" LBJ's view, McNamara withheld the paper from other administration officials. He foresaw our present course as leading to U.S. troop increases in 1968 and a doubling of casualties, which would further erode popular support. Instead, McNamara urged Johnson to announce "a policy of stabilization": a cap on U.S. ground forces at 525,000; a unilateral and indefinite halt to bombing the North, which was gaining us little, if anything; and a transfer of greater responsibility for ground operations to the South Vietnamese, which would reduce U.S. casualties.[3]

McNamara's recommendations agitated Johnson. The Secretary, who had been so committed to escalating the war, was now all but conceding defeat. McNamara's change of view left Johnson feeling abandoned and angry. McNamara says, "It raised the tension between two men who loved and respected each other—Lyndon Johnson and me—to the breaking point."

Johnson now described McNamara to several people as in a state of near collapse. He worried that McNamara might "pull a Forrestal," meaning he might take his own life as the former Defense Secretary had in 1949. McNamara, in fact, manifested considerable strain. His haggard appearance—glazed eyes and jowly face—was accompanied by erratic behavior. He would speak with "terrible emotion" about the war, with tears "in his eyes and in his voice." At one meeting he went on for a full five minutes "in rage and grief and almost disorientation." During conversations in his office, he would turn away from his visitors and cry into the curtain.

McNamara denies that he was "near emotional and physical collapse. I was not. I was indeed feeling stress. I was at loggerheads with the President of the United States; I was not getting answers to my questions; and I was tense as hell. But I was not under medical care, not taking drugs except for an occasional sleeping pill, and never contemplated suicide."[4]

Nevertheless, given McNamara's characteristically contained, even stoic, behavior, it is understandable that Johnson now saw him as near collapse. Yet Johnson's hostility toward him for abandoning the war may partly account for the Forrestal analogy. More important, suspecting that McNamara and some of his aides were secretly encouraging Robert Kennedy to run for President, which they were, Johnson now pushed McNamara out of the administration.

On November 27, the London *Financial Times* reported that McNamara would become president of the World Bank. The appointment had been in the works since the spring, when McNamara had disclosed interest in the post to Johnson. But it was only after the November 1 memo that the President had decided to let him go. Johnson rationalized the decision by seeing it as the best way to save McNamara from himself. But there was as much animus in the action as kindness toward an anguished colleague begging release from unbearable burdens. During a conversation with *Washington Post* reporter Chalmers Roberts about McNamara's resignation, the Secretary called. " 'Yes, Bob,' " Johnson said, " 'I'm sitting here with tears in my eyes, too.' LBJ was as dry-eyed as any human being could be," Roberts says.[5]

By dropping McNamara, Johnson was signaling that he would not follow his lead; at least, not now. He shared the Secretary's memo with Rusk and Rostow, the two men closest to the President's conviction that the administration needed to sustain the war effort. Johnson instructed Rostow to show the memo to several others in the administration and to some of the "Wise Men" without identifying its author. It was Johnson's way of avoiding a full and open debate or risking additional advice that he shift ground and begin withdrawing from Vietnam.

To Johnson's satisfaction, his advisers uniformly argued for continued firmness in the fight against a Communist South Vietnam. After briefings describing "a good chance of success," they all agreed that there was "great improvement and progress" in Vietnam, and that the administration should "press forward" with its program. Told that enemy losses totaled 46,145 in the first six months of 1967, a 288 percent increase since 1965, and that "GVN-aligned" population had increased 45 percent from 8.3 to 12.1 million in two and a half years, while "VC-aligned" had dropped 25 percent from 6.3 to 4.7 million, the Wise Men were programmed to endorse current policy.

Only George Ball dissented. But he saved his most forceful objection for a private aside to Acheson, McCloy, and John Cowles, publisher of the *Minneapolis Tribune*. As they left the Cabinet room, he said: "I've been watching across the table. You're like a flock of old buzzards sitting on a fence, sending the young men off to be killed. You ought to be ashamed of yourselves."[6]

Johnson wanted no dissent from positive assessments of the fighting. When Hubert Humphrey, for example, visited Saigon from October 30 to November 1, he told Johnson what he wanted to hear. "We are winning—steady progress is everywhere evident.... More than ever, I am convinced that what we are doing here is right and that we have no choice but to persevere and see it through to success," he cabled LBJ.

However, Dr. Edgar Berman, a close friend who accompanied Humphrey, remembers him as decidedly pessimistic. He believed that we were "throwing lives and money down a corrupt rat hole." When Berman asked him what he would tell Johnson in private, Humphrey replied: "As of right now I'm damn sure we're not doing the Vietnamese or ourselves any good. We're murdering civilians by the thousands and our boys are dying in rotten jungles—for what? A corrupt, selfish government that has no feeling and no morality. I'm going to tell Johnson exactly what I think, and I just hope and pray he'll take it like I give it."

If Humphrey told Johnson any of this, he forbid Hubert to repeat it. On November 8, when Humphrey reported on his trip to the National Security Council, Johnson pushed a note across the table ordering him "to make it short, make it sweet, and then shut up and sit down." Humphrey complied, giving an upbeat assessment describing progress in the war and Saigon's advance toward political democracy.[7]

Johnson himself took the unusual step of drafting a memo for the record on how he viewed McNamara's proposals. He said that he had "read it, and studied it, with the utmost care." He understood that it "raises fundamental questions of policy with reference to the conduct of the war in Vietnam."

His conclusions were: "with respect to bombing North Vietnam," he wished "to strike those remaining targets which ... we judge to have significant military content but which would not involve excessive civilian casualties; excessive U.S. losses; or substantial increased risk of engaging the USSR or Communist China in the war;—maintain on a routine basis a restrike program for major targets throughout North Vietnam." He also wanted to "remove ... the public attention given to our North Vietnamese bombing operations." An "unrequited bombing stand-down" would be misread at home and in Hanoi as a weakening of our will. He also opposed announcement of a stabilization policy on U.S. ground operations; it would have the same effect as a bombing halt. Nevertheless, he saw no reason to increase the number of U.S. troops above 525,000. He also saw merit in McNamara's recommendation that we review U.S. ground operations, "accelerating the turnover of responsibility to the GVN, and working toward less destructive and fewer casualties in South Vietnam."[8]

However strong Johnson's resistance to McNamara's change of course, it heightened his sense of urgency about bringing America's military involvement in South Vietnam to a speedy and successful conclusion. At a Tuesday lunch meeting on November 4, Johnson wondered "how we are going to do a better job of winning the war in the South. We've been on dead center for the last year," he said, acknowledging a stalemate in the fighting he had been denying so vehemently in public. Two days later, he asked for a military plan bringing faster results. "Highest authority is now thinking in terms of assigning top priority to those programs which would have a maximum impact on progress in South Vietnam during the next six months," Wheeler cabled Westmoreland on November 8. "A major purpose for Ambassador Bunker's, Komer's and your trip back to Washington is to attempt to achieve agreement on these programs."[9]

At every meeting on Vietnam during the rest of November,

Johnson pressed the case for quick results. On the 15th, he asked
Bunker "what more he would do to bring the war to a conclusion if
he were President." Bunker answered: "I would do exactly what we
are doing." Johnson wasn't satisfied. "What about pushing up the
arrival time of more units?" he asked. He also ordered his advisers
"to do two things. First, get the number of [bombing] targets down
to the absolute minimum. Second, get the troops out there as rapidly
as possible."[10]

Johnson's priority was clear to anyone attentive to his comments.
He wanted to find ways in which the South Vietnamese could take
over the fighting from American forces. He also wanted to hit all
remaining targets in the North on the Pentagon's list. During a November 21 discussion he asked about schedules for getting additional
allied and U.S. troops to Vietnam. "The clock is ticking," he said.
"We need to get all the additional troops as fast as we can." He also
"stressed the need to bring the South Vietnamese government to the
center of the stage stressing tax needs, anti-corruption measures and
a need for a reform image." Johnson's greatest concern was to assure
that "the Vietnamese, by what they do—even if it is limited—must
gradually emerge towards the center of the stage."[11]

When Rostow told Johnson about a suggestion from the physi-
cist Edward Teller that South Vietnamese autonomy could be speeded
by training more Vietnamese-speaking Americans, who would then
facilitate post-military social and economic development, Johnson replied: "Hurry! Staff it out."[12]

Westmoreland had no doubt what Johnson wanted. During his
visit to Washington in November, he began discussing his "withdrawal strategy." In congressional testimony, on *Meet the Press*, and
in meetings with LBJ, McNamara, and the Joint Chiefs, he foresaw
a larger role for South Vietnamese forces in the fighting during the
next two years and the beginnings of a phased withdrawal by U.S.
forces. "The concept is compatible with the evolution of the war since
our initial commitment and portrays to the American people 'some
light at the end of the tunnel,'" Westmoreland said.[13]

Johnson was never more mindful of how much Americans
wanted to end the war. To win time for the "withdrawal strategy,"
he launched a fresh campaign to rekindle public hope that an honorable peace was within reach. On November 16, Rostow reported on
"my first week's execution of your instruction with respect to the
press." Rostow described extensive contacts with American and foreign journalists in which he emphasized confidence in our basic strategy and depicted "not stalemate but progress" in the fighting,

"although we cannot set a date for victory." When the Washington *Evening Star* carried a story about "slow, steady" progress in Vietnam, Rostow wrote the President: "I can't—or wouldn't—claim it all; but my first identifiable salesman's return is attached." After Johnson saw several Washington correspondents off the record, a USIA official called it "a masterful public relations stroke," which did "much to clear the atmosphere."[14]

During a discussion on November 21 of battlefield casualties, Johnson proposed an end to the reporting of such statistics. He wanted to know why "we continue to release these statistics, especially since they make it appear that U.S. troops are suffering more casualties than South Vietnamese troops." Although our "regular Army losses are higher than the South Vietnamese regular army losses," to include "popular and regional losses" would demonstrate that "their losses are higher than ours."[15]

The following month the *New York Times* reported growing pressure from Washington on U.S. Embassy officials "to produce convincing evidence of progress, especially by the South Vietnamese. . . . Washington's latest campaign for 'results,' " the report continued, "appears to differ from some in the past in that it is directed more toward the South Vietnamese, military and civilian, than the Americans." The White House wanted to hear that GVN forces were fighting well, that corruption was on the decline, and that the South Vietnamese cared as much, if not more, about winning the war than the United States.[16]

In December, partly in response to the "withdrawal strategy," which the public favored by a 66 to 15 percent count, Johnson's approval ratings on his handling of Vietnam increased from an August low of 33 percent to 40 percent. Lou Harris reported that the public now heavily favored "escalation over deescalation," and supported "the administration position that the war is preventing further Communist aggression in Southeast Asia." Harris believed that the upturn in public support resulted from assurances that we were doing better in the war and that antiwar protestors had no convincing alternate strategy to recommend. Fred Panzer concluded that "all in all it looks like the public has greater understanding of what the administration is trying to do in Vietnam—and accepts it."[17]

Johnson had no illusions about the upturn in public support. As long as Americans saw him moving toward an honorable withdrawal from Vietnam, the public would remain more supportive of his leadership. Should it begin to see him again as stubbornly committed to an inconclusive struggle, his approval ratings were certain to tumble.

As much as anyone, he wanted to end America's involvement in the
war. But he refused to go without believing that a non-Communist
South Vietnam would survive American departure. When the journalist David Brinkley asked him why he simply didn't give up on
Vietnam and save American lives that Brinkley thought were being
needlessly lost, Johnson replied: "I'm not going to be the first American President to lose a war."[18]

Johnson didn't know how long it would take to secure his goal,
but he hoped, given all the talk of progress, that we might get there
in 1968 or 1969. In the meantime, he intended to facilitate American
military advance in Vietnam while he encouraged domestic opinion
to believe that we would stop fighting before too long.

Between December 20 and the 24th Johnson traveled to Austra-
lia, Vietnam, and Italy. The drowning death of Australian Prime
Minister Harold Holt triggered Johnson's decision to make this whirlwind journey. Genuine affection for Holt and the Australians, who
were a reliable ally, were principal motives for the trip. But it was
also another opportunity to build domestic support and advance toward peace.

Johnson's public comments during the five days stressed military
gains. "We are not going to yield. We are not going to shimmy," he
declared with Hanoi principally in mind. "We are going to wind up
with a peace with honor which all Americans seek," he said, mainly
for U.S. public consumption. At Cam Ranh Bay in Vietnam, where
he urged American troops to nail "that coonskin to the wall," he
described "how far we had come from the valleys and the depths of
despondency to the heights and the cliffs, where we know now that
the enemy can never win." The enemy may not have been beaten,
but he knew that he had met his master in the field and was holding
on desperately.[19]

The President also used the trip to pressure South Vietnam's
President Thieu to open talks with the National Liberation Front.
Johnson hoped that a coalition government or a chance to share
power might persuade the NLF to separate itself from Hanoi and
cease fighting. Thieu publicly promised "to grant full rights of citizenship to those now fighting against the government who are prepared to accept constitutional processes and to live at peace under the
constitutionally elected government." But he would not recognize the
NLF "as an independent organization in any sense." Johnson scored
points with the American public through news stories describing his
endorsement of reconciliation talks in South Vietnam. But he understood that such publicity would be ephemeral without real progress.[20]

To that end, he flew from Vietnam to Rome for a meeting with Pope Paul VI. He pressed the Holy Father to persuade Thieu, a Catholic, "to begin informal talks with some of those associated with the NLF." Since Hanoi would not negotiate, the President hoped "that South Vietnam and representatives of the NLF can talk and settle their differences locally. . . . If South Vietnam's government would more or less leave us and talk informally with the NLF—and thereby the NLF leave Hanoi—this could be a way for South Vietnam to settle its own fate and have Hanoi and the U.S. pull away. . . . This would be one effective way of disengaging the NLF from Hanoi— and South Vietnam from us."

When the Pope replied evasively to the request, Johnson pressed harder for a commitment. "My motto now," he said, "is 'Peace in South Vietnam for South Vietnam and by South Vietnamese.' " He urged the Pope to tell Thieu to talk to the NLF. "I strongly believe it would offer some chance of peace." The Pope thought he could do something.[21]

On December 29, after Ted Sorensen had suggested that the administration submit a document to the United Nations demonstrating that differences between the NLF and Saigon were not enough to justify "continued Communist resistance to a negotiated settlement," Rostow told LBJ that this "idea had already occurred to us, and we are far down the road with it. . . . The major difference between what we are doing and what Sorensen suggests is to have the document go to the United Nations from the government of Vietnam, rather than from the U.S. government."[22]

The following week Rostow told Rusk and McNamara that "we must now face two issues [with Saigon] which we have for long postponed: Truly candid discussions with the South Vietnamese . . . on negotiation strategy and tactics; [and] a top-priority effort to begin to pull the South Vietnamese non-Communist factions together into a big national party to cope with the inevitable VC-managed popular front which is bound to emerge."[23]

Johnson had no illusion that peace was at hand. There was an almost universal feeling, Johnson told New Hampshire's Senator Tom McIntyre on December 28, "that Hanoi will not negotiate until they see the outcome of the election of November 1968 here." In the meantime, though, Johnson promised to use every resource at his command to advance the goal of peace, especially through efforts in South Vietnam rather than against the North. Whether it would be sufficient to end the war in 1968 was a prediction Johnson refused to make.[24]

Vietnam: Tet

At the beginning of 1968 Johnson genuinely hoped that a settlement in Vietnam was within reach. However difficult to describe with precision, he believed that slow, steady progress in the fighting and toward a stable South Vietnamese government were forcing the NLF and Hanoi toward an inevitable settlement. His upbeat mood, which polling data in December indicated had impressed itself on the public, found fresh expression in his State of the Union message on January 17.

Acknowledging that the country was still being challenged in Vietnam and that the enemy was not yet ready to make peace, he nevertheless saw an America having "the will to meet the trials that these times impose." Democratic elections, coupled with enemy defeats "in battle after battle" and a widening hold by Saigon on the people of the country convinced him that the Communists faced growing frustration in trying to impose their will on South Vietnam. The enemy hoped "that America's will to persevere can be broken. Well—he is wrong," Johnson said. "America will persevere." He concluded with renewed pledges of America's readiness to halt its bombing and begin peace talks if Hanoi agreed. Only acceptance of their inability to make aggression work stood in the way.[25]

A belief that a Communist "general counteroffensive and general uprising" would occur in January or February fueled Johnson's optimism. Recent defeats and hopes that it could spark the military and political collapse of South Vietnam's army and government moved Hanoi to plan a widespread assault. Johnson was confident that American military power would prevail in this coming clash and would force the Communists to negotiate.[26]

The focus of the North Vietnamese offensive seemed to be Khe Sanh, a U.S. Marine base in northwest South Vietnam, just south of the DMZ near the Laos border. Johnson, believing that Hanoi saw Khe Sahn as America's Dien Bien Phu, took every precaution against a defeat.

On January 10, Rostow assured the President that he had "for some time been asking questions about Khe Sahn." It was clear "that Westmoreland has it very much on his mind." Nevertheless, Rostow intended to "look further into our contingency planning." On the 22nd, Westmoreland reported that he anticipated "a country-wide show of strength just prior to Tet, with Khe Sahn being the main event."[27]

Johnson assured himself that Khe Sahn would not turn into a disaster. At a meeting with the Joint Chiefs on January 29, he pressed for confirmation that Westmoreland would be able to "take care of the expected enemy offensive against Khe Sahn." They described themselves as confident that Westmoreland and his troops could "cope with any contingency." The next day Johnson told congressional Democrats that he had received assurances from the Chiefs that we had adequate forces to resist a Khe Sahn assault. "I went around the table and got their answers to these questions," Johnson said. "In addition, I have it in writing that they are prepared." Johnson left no doubt about who would be blamed for a failure, should it occur. But he shared Westmoreland's confidence that no defeat was in the offing; quite the contrary, they saw the battle as a chance to inflict heavy casualties on the enemy and force the war to a conclusion.[28]

The focus on Khe Sanh was misplaced. "There was simply no comparison between the two cases," Dien Bien Phu and Khe Sanh, General Bruce Palmer, Jr., says.[29]

The "main event" was not at Khe Sanh but at a time and in places U.S. analysts hadn't anticipated. Because Tet was seen as a kind of inviolable period throughout Vietnam, an annual event "cherished by every religious group and social class," neither South Vietnam's leaders nor America's military and civilian officials foresaw the timing of the attack. When the Viet Cong and North Vietnamese struck on January 30–31, GVN and American forces were surprised. And not simply by the timing, but also the extent and ferocity of the offensive.

The Communists assaulted thirty-six of South Vietnam's provincial capitals, five of its six largest cities, and almost one-third of the country's district centers. In Saigon itself, they struck the U.S. Embassy compound, Tan San Nhut Air Base, the Presidential Palace, South Vietnam's Joint General Staff headquarters, and other government installations. Effective resistance blunted their attacks in Saigon, but most of Hue, the country's ancient capital and site of the symbolically important Imperial Citadel, fell under Communist control. Except for Hue, where the enemy held out for twenty-six days against a massive counterattack, the fighting slowed after two weeks.[30]

Johnson later regretted that he had not publicly gone "into details concerning the buildup of enemy forces or warned of the early major combat I believed was in the offing." Though he and others in the administration had repeatedly given "background" briefings to journalists about the "heavy action ... expected soon," a reluctance to alert "the enemy to our knowledge of its plans" persuaded him to refrain from saying too much.

But this is retrospective thinking. Johnson's failure to reveal more about Communist plans had largely to do with a failure to

anticipate them. Though he and his advisers knew that an uncommonly big attack was in the making, they did not foresee its dimensions. When Rostow gave him news of the attacks on Saigon, Johnson
responded: "This could be very bad. What can we do to shake them
from this?"[31]

Much would be made later of Westmoreland's alleged willingness to deceive the President about Communist strength as a reason
for Johnson's failure to foresee what was coming. But the problem
was not with Johnson's knowledge of enemy strength. Rather, it resulted from a kind of auto-intoxication or self-deception as to allied
progress in the fighting and limited enemy capacity. After three years
of bombing that had unleashed more tonnage on Vietnam than in
all of World War II, and after so many ground actions in which Viet
Cong and North Vietnamese forces had supposedly suffered demor-
alizing losses, it was difficult, if not impossible, for Johnson and most
of his advisers to imagine the sort of offensive mounted during Tet.[32]

Tet was a major military defeat for the Viet Cong and North
Vietnamese. Estimates of Communist losses range between 33,000 and
58,000, with thousands more wounded and captured. Many of the
Viet Cong's and Hanoi's best troops were lost in the fighting. By
contrast, between 1,100 and 4,000 U.S. troops were killed, depending
on whether one counts losses for two weeks or two months. During
February and March about 5,000 South Vietnamese soldiers died in
action. The Communists achieved neither of their immediate objectives: to cripple the South Vietnamese military or topple the government in Saigon. Nevertheless, the Tet attacks succeeded in forcing
the American government to retreat from an expansion and even
continuation of the war as it had been fought.[33]

The principal casualty of the Tet offensive was U.S. public opinion. Johnson had been saying for months that the Communists hoped
to win the war not on the battlefields in Vietnam but by sapping the
American will to fight. His first response to the expanded fighting
was to assure the public that the offensive was not what it appeared
to be—a demonstration of Communist capacity to sustain the conflict
despite the alleged losses described in recent months by the U.S.
government. At a press conference on February 2, he repeatedly stated
that the offensive was no surprise and that as a military campaign it
was "a complete failure." Moreover, he warned that the Communists
would try to substitute "a psychological victory" for a military victory.
But "when the American people know the facts ... and when the
results are laid out for them to examine, I do not believe that they
[the Communists] will achieve a psychological victory."[34]

Johnson mounted a public relations campaign to counter any

advantage Hanoi would try to gain from Tet. On January 31, he sent word to Westmoreland and Bunker that he wanted them to give daily press briefings that would "convey to the American public your confidence in our capability to blunt these enemy moves, and to reassure the public here that you have the situation under control." Seeing "a critical phase in the American public's understanding and confidence toward our effort in Vietnam," he believed that "nothing can more dramatically counter scenes of VC destructiveness than the confident professionalism of the Commanding General . . . and [the] wisdom of our Ambassador."

At a meeting with congressional leaders on January 31, Johnson warned that " 'agents of the enemy' in this country [are] working against us." He saw them trying "to destroy confidence in your leaders and in the South Vietnamese government." He asked the legislators to measure their statements. "The greatest source of Communist propaganda statements is our own statements," he said. To counter a rising tide of negativism, Johnson directed Cabinet and sub-Cabinet officials to make the case for the war on television and in the newspapers through interviews with journalists.[35]

Initially, Johnson took heart from polling data showing an upsurge of public support in response to Tet. On January 31, Panzer sent him "evidence that the people's commitment to the Vietnam war is 'real and abiding.' " By a 64 to 24 percent vote the public said that, despite the war, the Johnson domestic program does not have to be reduced. But if a choice had to be made between guns and butter, the public gave priority to the war by 52 percent to 30 percent. Moreover, in mid-February, Gallup and Harris found a surge in "hawk" opinion, with 61 percent, a five-point increase from January, saying they favored stronger military measures to end the conflict.

Tet produced a "rally" effect, with 70 percent of Americans— up from 63 percent in December—saying they wanted the U.S. to continue the bombing of North Vietnam, and 53 percent favoring either a gradual broadening and intensifying of military operations or "an all-out crash effort in the hope of winning the war quickly even at the risk of China or Russia entering the war."[36]

The increased support was temporary. By March the public impulse to back the troops and sustain U.S. involvement until the North Vietnamese made peace fell victim to doubts about the war. News stories on American television were particularly instrumental in strengthening public reluctance to "stay the course" in Vietnam. When newsmen reported that a U.S. major had said it was necessary to destroy a village to save it from the Viet Cong, and when television broadcast images of South Vietnam's national police chief executing a bound V.C. prisoner, it intensified feelings that neither we nor the Vietnamese were winning anything in a conflict that seemed principally to produce brutal actions and endless casualties.

On February 27, Walter Cronkite of CBS, whom opinion surveys described as "the nation's most trusted person," expressed the view on television that the conflict was deadlocked and that additional fighting would change nothing. No less an authority than General Creighton W. Abrams, Jr., Westmoreland's principal deputy, privately told Cronkite that the war was stalemated. "To say we are closer to victory today," he announced on his evening news show, "is to believe, in the face of the evidence, the optimists who have been wrong in the past. To suggest we are on the edge of defeat is to yield to unreasonable pessimism. To say that we are mired in stalemate seems the only realistic, yet unsatisfactory, conclusion." After hearing Cronkite's assessment, Johnson reportedly said, "If I've lost Cronkite, I've lost Middle America."[37]

Demoralization about the war was everywhere. Administration talks with U.S. governors revealed a mood of impatience reflective of constituent feelings. "Let's go in and win or else get out," the governors said. "We can't let this go on for another four or five years." Douglass Cater told the President that during a meeting with four prominent university presidents he "detected a feeling of concern amounting almost to fear that he had never seen before." They "were almost of a mood to sign a public petition against another step-up of the war."

In February, when Califano and McPherson met with foreign policy officials to discuss a speech the President planned for the end of March, the advisers, in Califano's words, "were beyond pessimism. They sounded a chorus of despair. Rusk appeared exhausted and worn down." Bill Bundy described South Vietnam as "very weak" and said, "our position may be truly untenable." He suggested withdrawal "with the best possible face." On the way back to the White House "in a state of depression," Califano said: " 'This is crazy.' McPherson nodded. 'It really is all over, isn't it?' " Califano asked. " 'You bet it is,' " McPherson replied.[38]

The polling numbers showed a "new wave of pessimism on Vietnam." In early March, 49 percent of Americans thought it was a mistake to have sent troops to fight. Forty-one percent believed it was right. Only 35 percent of the country saw the conflict ending in less than two years. Sixty-nine percent of Americans approved of a "phase-out plan" to replace U.S. troops with South Vietnamese.

The President's job ratings now reached new lows: 26 percent approved of his handling of Vietnam; 63 percent disapproved. Thirty-six percent gave him overall approval, but 52 percent were negative. On March 22, Johnson told a group of advisers that there had been "a dramatic shift in public opinion on the war, that a lot of people are really ready to surrender without knowing they are following a party line."[39]

Despite a growing "cut and run" attitude, Johnson assumed that most Americans still preferred to hold out against defeat. Since he initially feared additional Communist attacks, which might destroy the South Vietnamese Army and compel a coalition government asking U.S. withdrawal, the President sent word to Westmoreland on February 8 that "the United States government is not prepared to accept a defeat in South Vietnam. In summary, if you need more troops, ask for them." Westmoreland responded, "I would welcome reinforcements at any time they can be made available."[40]

Johnson agreed to send an additional 10,500 troops. He also discussed the possibility of taking stronger action. At a meeting on February 9 with the Joint Chiefs, Rusk, McNamara, and Clark Clifford, who was to become Secretary of Defense at the end of the month, he directed them "to hope for the best and plan for the worst. Let's consider the extensions, call-ups, and use of specialists," he said. "Dean," he asked Rusk, "should we have more than the Tonkin Gulf resolution in going into this? Should we ask for a declaration of war?" Rusk thought not, but the President wanted to know what the international impact of a declaration might be. Rusk saw severe effects, including "a direct challenge to Moscow and Peking in a way we have never challenged them before."

Clifford saw "a very strange contradiction in what we are saying and doing. We have publicly told the American people that the communist offensive was: (a) not a victory, (b) produced no uprising among the Vietnamese in support of the enemy, and (c) cost the enemy between 20,000 and 25,000 of his combat troops. Now our reaction to all of that is to say that the situation is more dangerous today than it was before all of this. We are saying that we need more troops and possibly an emergency call-up." Johnson replied: "The only explanation I can see is that the enemy has changed its tactics. They are putting all of their stack in now. We have to be prepared for all that we might face." Because the Communists had added about 15,000 troops, the President thought that we needed to match their escalation.[41]

The Joint Chiefs saw the President's worries as an opportunity to press for a large call-up of reserves. When Clifford questioned the sudden sense of urgency about getting all these additional forces, Westmoreland and the Chiefs described the request as a chance to seize the initiative and decisively defeat the enemy. With neither McNamara nor Clifford convinced, Johnson asked for written recommendations on troop increases from both sides in the debate.[42]

The Chiefs now asked for a reserve call-up of 206,000 troops, half to go to Vietnam and the rest to form a backstop for possible use in other hot spots around the globe. Wheeler gave a gloomy report about conditions in South Vietnam, describing the Tet offensive as "a very near thing" and the additional troops as allowing the U.S, first, "to counter the enemy offensive and ... eject the NVA invasion force in the north. Second, to restore security in the cities and towns. Third, to restore security in the heavily populated areas of the countryside. Fourth, to regain the initiative through offensive operations."[43]

The size of the Chiefs' request, Clifford says, "astonished Washington, and triggered the first fundamental debate over the course of the war since the decisions of 1965." Recognizing that he was faced with a major decision that contained "military, diplomatic, economic, congressional, and public opinion problems," the President asked Rusk and Clifford to consider every alternative in recommending what should be done. A commitment of this size would mean a further Americanization of the war, a substantial new strain on the budget, and a challenge to U.S. public opinion, which would want assurances that such an increased commitment would bring a quick end to the war.

At a review meeting on February 28, Wheeler described the margin of victory as "very thin in a number of battles." He predicted that 1968 "will be a critical year in the war. There is heavy fighting ahead. The losses will be high in men. The losses will be high in equipment." The only alternative he saw to putting in the additional forces was to give up the two northern provinces of South Vietnam, which he thought would "cause the collapse of the ARVN."

McNamara, during his last full day in office, challenged Wheeler's conclusions. He did not think adding 200,000 men would change anything, since North Vietnam would match our increase. He urged instead an emphasis on getting the South Vietnamese to fight their war. Johnson refused to be rushed into a decision. Instead, he asked Clifford to begin his term as Defense Secretary by considering "these demanding problems. He had not been living with Vietnam day in and day out as the others had, and I thought that a new pair of eyes and a fresh outlook should guide this study," Johnson said later. The President ended the discussion by telling Clifford: "Give me the lesser of evils. Give me your recommendations."[44]

In asking Clifford to assess Vietnam policy, Johnson was getting exactly what he wanted. At sixty-one years of age with a track record dating from the Truman administration of distinguished service as a White House counsel, an expert on national security affairs, and a Washington insider, Clifford had a commanding presence and independence that assured he would not be intimidated by admirals, generals, and Presidents. Having met with Clifford thirty-four times during 1967 and twenty-eight times in January and February 1968, Johnson knew that Clifford was skeptical of further escalation. As a prelude to appointing Clifford, Johnson had reviewed his remarks in July 1965 when he had expressed doubts about the wisdom of expanding U.S. involvement in the fighting.[45]

Five days after Johnson directed him to assess the Chiefs' troop request, Clifford recommended against it. True, he proposed 22,000 more men for Vietnam and "a Reserve call-up . . . adequate to meet the balance of the Westmoreland request." But a "decision to meet the Westmoreland request in full" was to be contingent on a week-by-week examination of "the desirability of further deployments," the "improved political performance of the GVN and increased contribution in effective military action by the ARVN," and "a complete review of our political and strategic options in Vietnam."

Clifford said later that the conditions were meant to prevent another disastrous escalation and to lay the groundwork for an honorable end to American involvement. His remarks at a White House meeting on March 4 left little doubt where he stood. "Do you continue down that same road of more troops, more guns, more planes, more ships?" he asked. "As we build up our forces, they build up theirs. The result is simply that we are fighting now at a higher level of intensity." He was willing to meet the exigencies of only the next three or four months. "We are not sure that a conventional military victory, as commonly defined, can be achieved. . . . We seem to have gotten caught in a sinkhole. We put in more, they match it. . . . I see more and more fighting with more and more casualties on the U.S. side, and no end in sight."[46]

Johnson readily accepted Clifford's recommendations. An increase in U.S. force levels proposed by the Chiefs seemed likely to produce a fiscal-economic crisis and a renewed assault on Johnson's credibility, which would further weaken his political hold on the country. Clifford summed up the potential public opinion disaster from a troop call-up in a memo to LBJ: "We were not stretched too thin. Suddenly we have no Strategic Reserve and the nation is in danger. . . . We were winning the war. Now we need emergency help. . . . We won the Tet Offensive. Now we haven't."

With the Tet fighting largely over and the diminished likelihood of a defeat, which Johnson had feared at the start of the offensive, he reverted to his end-of-year strategy for a reduced American role in the war coinciding with increased South Vietnamese action. The need, in short, was not for more U.S. troops but greater efforts by Saigon to assure its security and independence. President Thieu's announcement that he would increase draft calls and raise ARVN troop strength by 135,000 men gave Johnson the freedom to reject the Westmoreland-Wheeler call-up. He also now promoted Westmoreland to Chief of Staff of the Army. It was a way to shield Westmoreland from public attacks for disappointments over Vietnam, but it also signaled that Johnson would take a different tack from the one he and Westmoreland had been following.[47]

By March 1968 Johnson was desperately eager for an honorable way out of the war. He would not commit himself to a straightforward plan for ending U.S. involvement lest it look too much like an acknowledgment of defeat. Nor would he say anything in public that suggested he was giving up on the possibility of an American victory.

In speeches to the National Alliance of Businessmen on March 16 and the National Farmer's Union on March 18, he took a hard line. The contest in Southeast Asia, he said, was between Communist aggression and the forces of freedom trying to preserve the independence of South Vietnam. "We must meet our commitments in the world and in Vietnam," he declared. "We shall and we are going to win.... Make no mistake about it—I don't want a man in here to go back home thinking otherwise—we are going to win." It was time for all Americans "to unite ... to stand up and be counted."[48]

Johnson's speeches were largely meant to intimidate Hanoi. Convinced that the Communists had taken a beating in the Tet offensive and might now be ready to talk, he wanted them to think that, despite growing domestic opposition to war costs, there was no likelihood of a U.S. pullback. He wished Hanoi to believe that its only hope for a settlement was through negotiations.

To give Hanoi an added incentive to talk, Johnson now agreed to a Rusk proposal for reduced bombing. On March 4, when Rusk suggested that we could stop bombing most of North Vietnam during the coming rainy season, a time of diminished air raids anyway, Johnson jumped at the proposal. "Dean," he responded, "I want you to *really* get on your horse on that one—right away." At a meeting the next day, Rusk urged the President to include a statement in a forthcoming speech on Vietnam directing "that U.S. bombing attacks on North Vietnam [would] be limited to those areas which are integrally related to the battlefield. No reasonable person could expect us to fail to provide maximum support to our men in combat. Whether this step I have taken can be a step toward peace is for Hanoi to determine. We shall watch the situation carefully."[49]

Johnson was eager to accept Rusk's suggestion. But he believed it could succeed only if Hanoi saw a new peace overture coming not from weakness but strength. During the second half of March, as he moved toward a major speech on Vietnam, Johnson played a double game. While he consulted and developed ideas about another try at negotiations, he did all he could to encourage the belief that the United States remained committed to South Vietnam's independence, even if it meant a long war.

To advance along the peace track, the President agreed to further discussions with the Wise Men, several of whom, including, most prominently, Dean Acheson, now saw the war as unwinnable and urged a withdrawal strategy. Clifford himself described the war as "a loser" and proposed to "cut losses & get out." The "ground war [was] wrong for us militarily," while the "air strikes [were] wrong politically."

Additional evidence of Johnson's plans were in conversations Rostow, Rusk, and Clifford now had with South Vietnam Ambassador Bui Diem. They all emphasized that Americans were "sick and tired of this war" and that Saigon faced "the loss of American support" unless it "broaden[ed] the government, clean[ed] up the corruption," and demonstrated a capacity to fight more effectively.[50]

At the same time, Johnson tried to hide his interest in deescalation and a rising sense of urgency about peace talks. On March 14, he told Clifford that he believed in consultation but feared bringing too many people into the discussion for fear that Hanoi would learn about his "new policy." Johnson also worried that the head of the group studying Acheson's idea not reveal that he was "doing a Vietnam review job."

During the two weeks before his speech on Vietnam, Johnson emphasized that he intended to make his talk a justification for sending more troops and calling up the reserves. On March 20, eleven days before he was to speak, he told Harry McPherson to "get 'peace' out of the speech except [to say] that we're ready to talk. We are mixing up two different things when we include peace initiatives in this speech. Let's just make it troops and war. . . . Later on we can revive and extend our peace initiative."[51]

But Johnson's hard-line talk was a smokescreen for the peace initiative he was about to make. There has been much discussion of the idea that a Johnson meeting with the Wise Men on March 26 turned him away from escalation toward deescalation. Though the majority of the advisers in that meeting expressed disillusionment and counseled a measured withdrawal from the war, several of them continued to urge a sustained commitment to the fighting.

Johnson himself encouraged the picture of a President startled by what the briefers had told the Wise Men and their change in perspective. He angrily asked Clifford and Rusk, "Who poisoned the well with these guys? I want to hear those briefings myself." But it is inconceivable that Johnson had casually allowed the Wise Men to receive objectionable briefings. Johnson, the master manipulator who never left preparations to chance, knew that the Wise Men would receive mixed messages from any honest briefing. As Mac Bundy told him after the meeting, "We did *not* receive an unduly gloomy briefing. . . . I think your people gave us a clear, fair picture, and one which matched with what many of us have learned from all sources over recent weeks." Johnson's "outrage" over the briefings was feigned; it was part of his continuing effort to present himself as an unreformed hawk.[52]

The President's shift to a slow withdrawal strategy came not from what the briefers said and argued or what some of the Wise Men counseled, but from a recognition of the reality that the war was stalemated and unwinnable without an escalation that would risk a domestic and international crisis unwarranted by the country's national security.

On March 20, he told his closest White House advisers, "I want war like I want polio. What you want and what your image is are two different things." As for his forthcoming speech, he wanted it to "meet emergency needs in strength" and to make "a reasonable offer on peace." On the 22nd, he told most of the same group that, when the weather turned bad, "we should take advantage of possibilities for changes in bombing." Clifford endorsed the need for a change. The people "do not see victory ahead. . . . The military has not come up with a plan for victory. . . . The people were discouraged as more men go in and are chewed up in a bottomless pit. . . . The President asked for opinions on how to proceed on more peace moves."

At a meeting with the Chiefs on the 26th, Johnson gave what Clifford saw as a "painfully sad speech about his own difficulties." Johnson said: "We need more money in an election year, more taxes in an election year, more troops in an election year and more [budget] cuts in an election year. As yet I cannot tell them [the people] what they expect to get in return. We have no support for the war." The President's comments suggested to Clifford that Johnson "understood the need for a dramatic change in policy."[53]

When Johnson finally spoke to the nation on March 31, his speech was not a discussion of escalation or troop additions but of "Steps to Limit the War in Vietnam." The address began: "Tonight I want to speak to you of peace in Vietnam and Southeast Asia." He then reminded Americans that for years representatives of the U.S. government had unsuccessfully traveled the world seeking a basis for talks. His latest attempt at San Antonio last September to launch discussions had been rejected, and the Tet offensive, which had "failed," had produced only more suffering in a country already burdened by twenty years of war. Now he wanted to renew the offer to stop bombing North Vietnam as a spur to negotiations, during which he assumed Hanoi would not take advantage of our restraint.

He then announced an immediate unilateral halt to the bombing of North Vietnam, except in the area north of the DMZ, where a continuing buildup threatened "allied forward positions." He named Averell Harriman as his personal representative who would go anywhere, any time to talk peace. Reviewing the growing effectiveness of the South Vietnamese in their own defense and the need for a tax increase in the United States to meet expenditures in the war and at home, Johnson expressed the "fervent hope" that North Vietnam would cease its efforts to achieve a military victory and agree to join us at the peace table.[54]

The Unhappy State of the Union

On January 17, 1968, Johnson gave his fifth State of the Union address. It was the least hopeful and most constrained of his messages. Gone were the optimistic forecasts of 1964 and 1965 about conquering poverty and building a Great Society; gone were the emphases on advances toward a Brave New World in the 1966 and 1967 speeches. The tone in 1968 was defensive—the acceptance implicitly, if not explicitly, that America was "challenged, at home and abroad."

He saw the country's "will . . . being tried" and the need to remind Americans that they had the wherewithal to meet current trials. True, his address made much of recent accomplishments in Vietnam, the Americas, across Asia, and with the Soviet Union; it celebrated America's unprecedented prosperity. But he also acknowledged a "restlessness," as the ship of state moved through "troubled and new waters," and he described the domestic problems facing the country, particularly in its cities, where violence and joblessness, slums and poverty blighted the lives of millions of citizens. He warned of the precarious state of the economy, which, without a tax increase to slow inflation, sustain home-building, and support the dollar, could become "a tragedy for every American family."[55]

The most striking feature of Johnson's address was his sense of constraint: the implicit message that Vietnam had put limits on what the country could now do at home and abroad. He never believed that this was a permanent state of affairs, but only a consequence of his depleted political influence, which an end to the war could replenish. And given his evangelism—his undiminished passion for grand designs, for history-making deeds— he faced 1968 with half a mind to reach for large goals anyway. But economic and political realities dictated otherwise. Indeed, Johnson later said that he experienced so much "frustration and genuine anguish" during that year, he "sometimes felt" as if he were "living in a continuous nightmare."[56]

A crisis with North Korea in January was one instance. At two o'clock in the morning on January 23, Johnson received news that the North Koreans had seized the USS *Pueblo*, an intelligence ship stationed three and a half miles beyond territorial waters in the Sea of Japan gathering electronic information. Though the ship was virtually unarmed, crew members resisted and sustained injuries, including one fatality. The North Korean action was subsequently seen as tied to Hanoi's Tet offensive. The White House believed that the Communists hoped to divert U.S. military resources to Korea and to compel the South Koreans to bring home two divisions from Vietnam. In response, the U.S. strengthened its air forces in South Korea and called up air units to maintain needed levels of strategic reserves in the United States.

A North Korean declaration of intent to punish the crew as criminals provoked American demands for actions that would free the sailors and teach Pyongyang a lesson. Reluctant to expand U.S. military responsibilities abroad and provoke additional recriminations at home, Johnson refused to use force. He rejected suggestions for mining Wonsan Harbor, seizing North Korean ships, blockading ports, bombing military targets, and sending troops across the DMZ. Such actions seemed likely to cost crew members their lives, and provoke a crisis with China and/or Russia, which had defensive alliances with North Korea.

He couldn't say when the men would get home, the President privately told reporters. But he was "sure . . . that we can't get them back by military force." Instead, Johnson took his case to Kosygin, the U.N., neutral capitals, and Panmunjom. It produced no immediate result. "Eleven miserable months went by before the men of the *Pueblo* were given their freedom," Johnson recalled. "Every day that passed during those eleven months, the plight of those men obsessed and haunted me."[57]

Johnson's economic problems at the start of 1968 were another source of anguish. The costs of Vietnam and the Great Society were producing an estimated 1968 budget deficit of $19.8 billion. The Republicans predicted that the deficit would run between $25 and $30 billion. Johnson himself, trying unsuccessfully to frighten the Congress into passing his tax surcharge, had warned the previous November that the deficit might reach $35 billion. Without additional taxes, the administration saw an $8 billion deficit for fiscal 1969 growing to $20 billion. Though Johnson's January budget message pegged the 1968 imbalance at slightly under $20 billion, his remarks had contributed to international fears that the U.S. economy now faced runaway inflation and a recession, if not a depression.

A widening imbalance in America's international trade accounts, a run on the country's gold supplies, and continuing poor prospects for a tax increase gave financial markets everywhere a case of New Year's jitters. For seventeen of the previous eighteen years the United States had run trade deficits. A 1967 imbalance of between $3.5 and $4 billion, almost three times the amount in the previous year, coupled with a drop in U.S. gold reserves to $12.4 billion, the lowest since 1937, excited concerns about the value of the dollar. When opinion surveys indicated that 79 percent of Americans opposed a tax increase, financial analysts began talking about the dangers of an economic collapse. On January 24, Gardner Ackley told Johnson that there was a sure "*risk* of a critical deterioration of the world economic situation—one that could even lead to a world depression if prompt action were not taken to reverse it."[58]

Johnson renewed calls for the 10 percent tax surcharge and announced steps to reduce the balance of payments and federal deficits and curb inflation. Once again, he felt compelled to inhibit domestic spending. Though reducing poverty and raising living standards remained abiding aims, he refused to consider launching new domestic programs. He rejected Humphrey's plea that the State of the Union address include a jobs program, expanded aid to education, and a general assault on urban blight and poverty through "a reactivated, visible, low and moderate income housing program."[59]

Johnson's resistance to new domestic crusades, or even expanded old ones, surfaced in response to the Kerner Commission's report. At the end of February, the White House received an advance copy of the commission's recommendations. Led by New York's Mayor John Lindsay, the commission argued that racism dividing America into black and white societies was central to inner-city problems. A national commitment to spend large amounts of money on job training, education, welfare, housing, and anticrime programs was the commission's answer to urban-minority problems. In fiscal 1969 alone, its recommendations seemed likely to cost $11.9 billion, with the amount rising to $24.5 billion in 1971. Johnson thought the cost could run as high as $75 to $100 billion over several years.[60]

The commission's conclusions and proposals incensed him—a combination of personal pique and political realism. After all his efforts to combat racism and poverty, Johnson saw the report as suggesting that his administration had been deficient in meeting both problems. Privately, he sent word to the commission that it needed to include some suggestions on how to pay for its recommendations. And when they offered no answer, he initially refused to receive a copy of the report or publicly acknowledge its appearance. When one businessman on the commission sent word that he thought some of the proposals unrealistic and might raise public questions about them, Johnson scribbled on his letter: "I agree."

But his response to Kerner's report was more ambivalent than simply hostile. He privately told a group of black editors and publishers in March that this was "the most important report made to me since I have been President." When several of his aides urged him publicly to acknowledge and partly endorse the report, he told a press conference in late March that the commission had "made many good recommendations." He declared himself only partly in agreement with its proposals but emphasized his shared wish to achieve most of its goals. The problem was finding resources.[61]

The challenge now was to make social gains without spending much money. His frustration with the commission was partly due to its failure to recognize the political resourcefulness he was bringing to bear on the problem. Before the report appeared, Johnson had taken four initiatives that spoke to the commission's concerns with crime, racism, jobs, and housing but without costing billions of federal dollars.

Fighting the rising epidemic of crime in the country's cities was a high Johnson priority. It not only promised to improve the lives of inner-city minorities but also resonated with middle-class Americans who, by the end of 1967, saw lawlessness as the nation's greatest domestic problem. Because crime control was chiefly in the hands of state and local agencies, federal involvement could be high-profile and low-cost. After the failure to win congressional passage of an Omnibus Crime Control and Safe Streets Act in 1967, Johnson resurrected the bill at the beginning of 1968 and doubled its funding from $50 to $100 million. "There is no more urgent business before this Congress than to pass the Safe Streets Act this year," the President declared in his State of the Union message.

Johnson believed that an anticrime program costing $100 million was excellent politics and sensible economics. But he also understood that it served the well-being of impoverished slum dwellers who were the most frequent victims of violent crimes. The Kerner Commission's description of the insecurity and misery visited upon blacks by the highest crime rates in the country was a focus of presidential concern dating back several years.[62]

Similarly, Johnson fought hard for a 1968 civil rights law guaranteeing open housing to all Americans. In reviewing the state of civil rights in a congressional message at the end of January, Johnson described "a spirit of restlessness," saying that "this feeling of disquiet is more pronounced in race relations than in any other area of domestic concern." He worried about the fact that one out of three nonwhite families still lived below the poverty line; that the infant mortality rate for nonwhite children was nearly double that of whites; that the percentage of black high school graduates remained well below that of whites; and that minority unemployment was still twice the rate of whites. But he offered no major legislative initiative to address these issues, because doing so would have required substantial financial commitments.

Instead, he focused on discrimination in housing. If America was ever to become a truly integrated society, it would have to eliminate racial apartheid in neighborhoods. Studies in some cities indicated that residential segregation was increasing, Johnson said. It was time to remedy the problem through a federal law prohibiting discrimination in the sale and rental of all housing in the United States.

Housing segregation, Johnson declared, had compounded the country's urban problems. "Minorities have been artificially compressed into ghettoes where unemployment and ignorance are rampant, where human tragedies and crime abound, and where city administrations are burdened with rising social costs and falling tax revenues. Fair housing practices," he asserted, "—backed by meaningful federal laws that apply to every section of the country—are essential if we are to relieve the crisis in our cities."

The unspoken side of Johnson's message was that fair housing would be a major advance in civil rights at little financial cost. In a time of great federal stringency, Johnson saw fair housing as an ideal program. "He was relentless," Califano says. "I mean there was no give. We were pushing, pushing, pushing. This was going to be done."[63]

Job training for minorities and low-income housing were other initiatives Johnson thought he could pursue without significant impact on the federal budget. His idea was to create a partnership between the federal government and private sector in developing jobs and building homes. In a conversation with television journalists in December 1967, Johnson said there are half a million "hard-core unemployed in our principal cities and we've just got to go find jobs for them." He declared his intention to call in the businessmen of America and press them to help develop jobs for the chronically unemployed. The alternative would be an expensive government program. Likewise, he saw a compelling need to rescue people living in "filth and dilapidated houses" through a public-private program.[64]

Johnson invited business leaders around the country to forge a National Alliance of Businessmen to address the job problem and an alliance of industrialists, bankers, and labor chiefs to establish a commission to study the housing problem. At a meeting with the National Alliance in January, the President promised to contribute $350 million over the next eighteen months to help prepare 500,000 hard-core unemployed workers for private-sector jobs by June 1971. Johnson acknowledged that "this is a tall order for American business," but he was convinced that "the special talents of American business can make this program work."

Moreover, he pressed American entrepreneurs to meet the challenge of rebuilding the country's inner cities. Every citizen should be decently housed, he told Congress in February. The federal government could help, but "the real job belongs to local government and the private sector—the homebuilder, the mortgage banker, the contractor, the nonprofit sponsor, the industrialist who now sees in the challenge of the cities a new opportunity for American business." The involvement of U.S. business now needed to "match the massive dimension of the urban problem."[65]

Many liberals were not happy with Johnson's refusal to commit himself to new or expanded programs for social advance. HEW Secretary John Gardner resigned partly in protest against domestic budget cuts. And Bobby Kennedy "will sharply attack the administration's new housing program" as inadequate to the task, an aide warned Johnson. But LBJ had no patience with such complaints. He might not be able to focus the attention and resources on domestic difficulties as earlier in his term, but he believed that his administration had "*presided over the most remarkable period of economic and social progress in the Nation's history.*" Besides, he took pride in the fresh ways he saw to continue the good fight. The principal question before him at the start of 1968 was whether he should seek another term in which he could implement his evolving plans for domestic change.[66]

"I shall not seek, and I will not accept . . ."

By January 1968 Johnson had been struggling for more than a year with a decision about running again. After the Democrats lost forty-seven House seats, three Senate seats, and eight governorships in November 1966, the President began giving continuous thought to the question. In and of itself there was nothing surprising about in-cumbent party losses in a mid-term election; it was predictable, es-pecially given the large Democratic majorities in 1964. But other influences were at work that made Johnson think he might not win again. The inner-city riots had produced a backlash against his sup-port of minority programs that seemed unlikely to soften in the next two years. Having assumed that the South would shift toward the Republicans in response to the civil rights and voting rights acts, Johnson now saw northern blue-collar whites also turning against him and the Democrats.[67]

At the same time, Johnson's personal style or character had eroded his popularity. In December 1966, historian Arthur Schlesin-ger told a Washington gathering that he saw " 'diffuse discontent and disquietude' in the country, not particularly because of the Viet Nam war but more as a result of 'the picture—true or false—which people have about President Johnson's character.' " In 1967, *Newsweek* made the same point when it quoted an Idaho Democrat, who said: "I'm beginning to hate that man." Minnesota's Republican Governor Har-old LeVander said that faith in the government had "all but perished in the wake of a ruthless President who manipulates the rights of American citizens to know the truth about their government."

In January 1968, *Avant-Garde*, a small radical magazine, asked psychiatrists to say whether they considered "Lyndon B. Johnson psy-chologically fit to be President of the United States." Allied to the "Dump Johnson" movement and citing the opinion of 206 clinical psychologists that LBJ's conduct of the Vietnam War was not "rea-sonable," the magazine added to concerns about the President's emo-tional fitness for the country's highest office. In March, *New York Times* columnist James Reston decried "The Perils of Personal Gov-ernment" in which an egotistical President personalized all problems and made decisions not on the basis of objective data but in terms of what served his personal advantage. The result was a "poisonous mood" in Washington that worked against effective governance.[68]

Though Johnson found it difficult, if not impossible, to admit, his behavior was largely responsible for the complaints about his offensive personal style. It wasn't simply that he was overbearing or that people didn't like him, as he complained in moments of self-pity, but his grandiosity, explosiveness, and deviousness raised questions about his fitness to be President. If Johnson feared that some people might now vote against him because he had been abrasive and intemperate, he was acknowledging a personal flaw that was as much a part of the man as his passion to help the disadvantaged and serve the national well-being.

In deciding whether to run, Johnson also considered the possibility that Robert Kennedy might take the nomination from him. In July 1966, Bill Moyers privately reported from New York that Bobby's Senate staff was promoting the tale that Johnson would settle the Vietnam War by 1968 and then retire for health reasons. They were urging people "to get on the Kennedy bandwagon . . . now." In November, Marvin Watson told LBJ that Arthur Krim, the president of United Artists, a close Johnson friend and principal fundraiser, said that Kennedy was discouraging party donors from giving money to LBJ and suggested instead that donations go to the New York State Democratic committee.[69]

The preoccupation with a Kennedy campaign became an almost daily absorption for LBJ in the winter of 1966–67. Press stories about William Manchester's authorized book on JFK's assassination were everywhere in December. Most of these focused on the negative portrait Manchester had drawn of Lyndon Johnson during JFK's trip to Texas in November 1963 and in the hours and days immediately following Kennedy's death. Manchester privately acknowledged that he saw LBJ as "somebody in a grade D movie on the late show." The original manuscript of Manchester's *Death of a President* painted an ugly picture of Johnson as a boorish, uncouth Texan lacking even minimal sensitivity toward Jackie and Robert Kennedy in the aftermath of JFK's killing.[70]

The public controversy about Manchester's forthcoming book convinced Johnson that it was part of a concerted Kennedy effort to oust him from the White House. To Johnson, Manchester was a "fraud" whose objective was not an unbiased reconstruction of JFK's murder, but a sensational account that would undermine him and promote Robert Kennedy's political fortunes.

In a series of telephone conversations with aides and friends, Johnson complained that the book "makes Bobby look like a great hero and makes me look like a son-of-a-bitch, and 95 percent of it is completely fabricated." Johnson told Moyers: "Any difference I have with Bobby, Bill, I think this has been carefully constructed through the months to prove that I cannot be believed." He told Abe Fortas: "I believe that Bobby is having his governors jump on me, and he's having his mayors, and he's having his nigras, and he's having his Catholics."[71]

Although there was considerable exaggeration in Johnson's view of Kennedy's campaign to get him, many agreed that the Manchester book was a heavy-handed attack on LBJ. Schlesinger complained to Manchester that an opening scene in the book depicted "a boorish Johnson" pressing a reluctant John Kennedy into killing a deer on LBJ's ranch. It had the effect, Schlesinger told him, "of defining the book as a conflict between New England and Texas, decency and vulgarity, Kennedy and Johnson." The publisher thought the manuscript "gratuitously and tastelessly insulting to Johnson."

Johnson's friends agreed, but they also shared his conviction that the objective here was, as one put it, to "gut Johnson." The Governor of Louisiana declared that "Kennedy is trying to destroy Johnson, and that's what Manchester's book is all about." If the Kennedys allowed Manchester to publish in 1967, another LBJ friend told *U.S. News & World Report*, "it will be a clear signal that Robert Kennedy intends to challenge Lyndon Johnson for the 1968 Democratic presidential nomination."[72]

Johnson set aides to work refuting Manchester's anti-Johnson allegations. But he instructed them to avoid public involvement in the controversy. It left him feeling helpless against the "Kennedy machine." He told Moyers: "I do not believe that we are equipped by experience, by tradition, by personality or financially to cope with this. I just do not believe that we know how to handle public relations and how to handle advertising agencies and how to handle manuscripts and how to handle book writers."[73]

Yet at the beginning of 1967 Johnson's political prospects were not all bleak. In January, Jim Rowe sent him encouraging comments from numerous Democrats. Despite congressional losses, they remained hopeful. "*It is impossible to document the thesis that there was a national vote against President Johnson or the administration, even against the Vietnam situation,*" the analysts declared. "*There is no need to panic and retreat from the Great Society.*" If the President and the party attended to fund raising challenges, if the administration explained more clearly what we were doing in Vietnam, and if it dealt firmly with violence in the streets and found some dramatic way to address "*the Negro Ghetto problem,*" there was every reason to think that the Democrats could recoup their congressional losses in 1968.[74]

Johnson also learned that his worries about Kennedy were over-drawn. Where a straw poll showed Kennedy ahead of the President by a 48 percent to 39 percent margin early in the year, the Man-chester controversy reversed the trend, boosting Johnson to a 54 per-cent to 46 percent advantage. "If you have seen the new . . . Harris—it just reverses it [the RFK–LBJ rating]. God, it murders Bobby and Jackie both," Johnson told Katzenbach at the end of January.[75]

Yet Johnson knew that Kennedy's decline did not necessarily translate into "a spectacular comeback for the President. To the con-trary," Harris stated, "a just completed survey shows Johnson's own rating still reads out at only 43 percent positive, exactly where it was in December . . . the low point in his standing." Moreover, opinion surveys during the first three months of the year made clear that Johnson was in trouble with the public over Vietnam. By mid-March public approval of his handling of the war had dropped to 40 percent, its lowest point to date. Moreover, a Gallup presidential trial heat pitting him against George Romney showed the Michigan governor ahead by a 50 percent to 42 percent count; Johnson against Nixon produced a tie. Yet Johnson wasn't ready to give up on 1968. To the contrary, between January and June there is considerable evidence that he was working to assure party support for his renomination should he decide to run again.[76]

But the more he thought about running, the more hesitant he became. True, by the beginning of May his approval rating was up to 48 percent, and he beat Kennedy in a trial heat by 49 percent to 37 percent. But only 43 percent approved of his handling of Vietnam, and a straw poll against Romney in June showed him trailing by three points.[77]

More important, health concerns made him reluctant to serve another four years. In January 1965, he had been rushed to the hos-pital with chest pains, which turned out to be a serious respiratory infection causing a temperature of 104.4 degrees. In October, he had surgery to remove his gall bladder and a kidney stone. Given his medical history, the surgery raised concerns about a cardiac episode. There were also fears that he might have pancreatic cancer. Though neither of these problems occurred, his recovery from the surgery was more painful and slower than anticipated. In addition, when attempts to defuse rumors that he had had a heart attack by showing his surgical scar to reporters provoked attacks on his crudeness, he became depressed and discussed resigning. In late December, he returned to the hospital for throat surgery on a benign polyp and a repair on his gall bladder incision, which had never fully healed.

In 1967 he had a secret actuarial study prepared on his life expectancy. He wished an assessment of his own belief that his family history made it unlikely that he'd survive a second term. "The American people had enough of Presidents dying in office," he said.[78]

Lady Bird was eager for Lyndon to step aside at the end of 1968. In May 1967, she spoke to Abe Fortas for an hour and a half "on the subject that has engaged so much of my thinking ever since Lyndon got into this job—how to get out and when." Remembering the example of Harry Truman, she had set March 1968 as the time when Lyndon should announce his decision to step down. For the first time in her life, she was convinced that he could be "a happy man retired." He could find enough to do at the ranch and could "pour himself into some sort of teaching work at the University of Texas," where they planned to set up a Johnson school of public service. She thought of "another campaign like an open-ended stay in a concentration camp."[79]

If health worries weren't enough to drive Johnson out of the race, additional bad news in the summer of 1967 brought him closer to such a decision. Senator Daniel Inouye of Hawaii told an LBJ aide that if the Republicans had a chief of staff with "the power and the authority to dream up and impose upon the President the most burdensome problems the mind of man is capable of conceiving, the President would not have any more problems cast upon him than he now has." Poll numbers were depressing: Seven out of ten Republicans thought their chances in 1968 were good and four out of ten Democrats agreed. Johnson's job rating was down to 39 percent favorable, the lowest since he had taken office.[80]

The war had become an unshakable burden. He had "explained Vietnam fifty times," he told a journalist. But to no effect. "It is hell," he said, "when a President has to spend half his time keeping his own people juiced up." Democratic senators complained to him that people everywhere were "frustrated and negative" about the war, and that they could save themselves only by attacking the President. Senators Birch Bayh of Indiana, Fred Harris of Oklahoma, Edmund Muskie of Maine, and Philip Hart of Michigan "all have the same story to tell about their states," Harry McPherson told Johnson. "It is Vietnam, Vietnam."[81]

September polls showed Johnson's approval and disapproval ratings holding steady at 40 percent and 48 percent. The numbers on Vietnam were even worse, with only 28 percent positive and 57 percent negative. In early September, the *Christian Science Monitor* published a map of the states showing Johnson's widespread vulnerability to defeat in 1968.[82]

That month Johnson reached a tentative decision not to run

again. During an eight-hour conversation at his ranch on September 8 with Texas Governor John Connally, Congressman Jake Pickle, and Lady Bird, LBJ reviewed his options. Connally told him he didn't think he could get reelected. Johnson himself saw withdrawal as an opportunity to make peace without abandoning Vietnam. Pickle agreed with the President's reasoning, but worried that Johnson's retirement would make it difficult for Democrats to hold their congressional seats. Lady Bird expressed fears that bad health might overtake him in another term: something not incapacitating but enough to put a distinct limit on his capacity "to be the sort of a President he wanted to be—to put in the eighteen hours a day—and unable to draw enough vitality from the once bottomless well of his energy. A physical or mental incapacitation would be unbearably painful for him to recognize, and for me to watch," she believed.[83]

Johnson considered announcing his retirement at a Democratic party dinner in October or at a political function in December. Connally advised an early declaration, which would leave Johnson free to work exclusively on national problems, including Vietnam, and give other potential candidates a chance to prepare their campaigns. But Johnson did nothing in October, and though he asked George Christian and Connally to write a withdrawal statement for December, he still held back from acting. Remembering how many times before Lyndon had threatened not to run, Lady Bird was skeptical of his intentions. When Pickle told her in September that Lyndon would not run, she replied, "Good, get him to write it down." She noted in her diary: "I think we all knew that we would only really know what was going to happen when we heard it happen."[84]

Lady Bird's skepticism was well advised. While he made plans to retire, he encouraged discussions about a 1968 campaign. In the fall of 1967, he gave Larry O'Brien, John Roche, Jim Rowe, and Marvin Watson reason to think he would run again. At the end of September, O'Brien completed a forty-four-page campaign strategy paper describing how to return LBJ to the presidency. When Rowe responded to O'Brien's paper by asking Johnson whether he would devote one or two evenings a week to campaign issues with "a number of people in whom he has confidence," Johnson checked the "yes" box.[85]

In January 1968 Johnson again considered withdrawing. In December, after *U.S. News & World Report* had predicted that Johnson would win only twelve states with 110 electoral votes, he had told Tom Johnson and Horace Busby that he would step aside, and asked Busby to draft a withdrawal statement. He again consulted Connally, who said that the State of the Union would be an excellent nonpartisan vehicle for announcing his plans. Connally also advised that the longer the President waited the more it would help Bob Kennedy, "who is already free to operate while others are not." At the last minute Johnson decided against using the statement. He handed the text to Mrs. Johnson before leaving for the Capitol and did not have it with him during his speech. He said later that a withdrawal now would make him a lame duck and cripple chances of passing his legislative program. He kept delaying an announcement, Lady Bird recalls, because he thought another few months or even weeks could make a difference in getting "three or four cliff hangers" approved. "If I can stay in there," he told her, "and put in all my chips and whatever prestige I have left, [I might be able to] get these things pinned down."[86]

But more was at work here than Johnson's concern with bending Congress to his will. He was ambivalent about leaving the presidency while the war continued. Mrs. Johnson remembers how much he worried about the impact of his decision on the troops in Vietnam. "What if," they and their families would say, "you can get out but we can't?" Besides, in December and January, as impressions grew that he was heading toward a settlement in Vietnam, his political fortunes turned up. His approval-disapproval ratings reversed themselves. In December, he had a 46 percent to 41 percent positive margin, which improved in January to 48 percent to 39 percent.[87]

However great his reluctance to bear the demands of another national campaign, he also relished the thought of beating liberal opponents, especially Kennedy, and winning vindication from voters. In late November, he had told ABC's Howard K. Smith that Robert Kennedy's strategy "is to win the nomination this year if possible." But he took satisfaction from the fact that Kennedy was torn about running. Seeing himself as unlikely to wrest the nomination from the President, Kennedy thought he shouldn't run. On January 30, he told reporters off the record that he "would not oppose Lyndon Johnson under any conceivable circumstances."

The only candidate liberals seemed able to run against LBJ was Senator Eugene McCarthy of Minnesota, whose emergence as the point man in a "dump Johnson" movement at the end of November indicated that Johnson could be renominated. Johnson's supporters saw McCarthy as "more of a diversion than a serious threat." He was a one-issue candidate—Vietnam—with little public visibility. Polls in early December showed that only four out of ten Americans had heard of him, and these voters favored LBJ over McCarthy by a two-to-one margin. Among rank-and-file Democrats, Johnson led by three to one. "McCarthy is doing so badly," John Roche told Johnson in mid-December, "that I am tempted to float a rumor that he is actually working for you to dispirit the 'peace movement.' " One Washington commentator was convinced that McCarthy was causing Robert Kennedy more problems than Johnson by making Kennedy look weak and opportunistic, should he decide to run.[88]

Though Johnson's "vulnerability" was widely discussed, in December and January he also heard much that encouraged him. Democratic party officials began organizing against McCarthy, while straw polls pitting the President against Nixon, Romney, and Rockefeller gave Johnson hope of winning again. More immediately, McCarthy's challenge to the President in the March New Hampshire primary seemed unlikely to be a problem. Evans and Novak predicted that McCarthy would face "a defeat close to annihilation"; one state poll showed Johnson ahead of McCarthy among Democrats by 76 percent to 6 percent.[89]

The upturn in Johnson's political fortunes was short-lived. The Tet offensive sent his approval ratings into a tailspin. In February, his positive standing with the public fell back to 41 percent, with 47 percent negative. On Vietnam, public confidence in his policy stood at only 35 percent, with 50 percent expressing disapproval; Lou Harris said the negative rating was at 62 percent. In late February, Panzer reported that a trial run against Nixon produced a deadlock. A New Jersey Democratic leader described the party as in "deep trouble" in his home state and New York. Bob Kintner predicted that the Republicans would score points by saying they could run the war better, raise America's international prestige, handle city riots more effectively, and rein in inflation.[90]

The polling numbers were not decisive in reviving Johnson's impulse to step down. He understood that public mood shifted all the time and could as easily turn in his favor over the next nine months as become more negative. More important, the demands of the office and especially of managing the war were wearing him down. The previous October, Dr. Willis Hurst, the President's physician, had confided concern to Lady Bird about Johnson's physical and emotional condition. "He did not see the bounce, the laughter, the teasing quality in Lyndon that he has watched over these twelve years. He thought he was running on marginal energy—that he was bone tired."[91]

Tet drained Johnson's resources beyond endurance. Senator John Stennis of Mississippi told Richard Russell that "the war situation . . . looks mighty bad and is really making my hair gray. The President is really under a great strain." Stennis knew only half of it. During the week after Tet began, Johnson got almost no sleep. He spent his nights distracting himself from the anxieties of the war by shuffling between the Situation Room, the Oval Office, and his living quarters, where he played dominoes with his brother Sam Houston and old Texas friends. Sam remembers him as "very tired and deeply worried." He was "tormented" by Vietnam. Sam watched him in bathrobe and slippers shuffle "down the hall toward the elevator on his way to the Situation Room in the basement to get the 3 o'clock report from Saigon. He looked tired and lonely as he pushed the down button." When Richard Russell met with him alone at the White House, Johnson cried uncontrollably.[92]

As the Tet offensive became a military defeat for the Communists, Johnson's thoughts of staying in the race revived. A March 4 poll showed him winning almost two-thirds of Democratic votes in New Hampshire against McCarthy's 11 percent. The fact that all the President's vote would be write-in ballots made it particularly impressive. The following day a U.S. News & World Report reporter predicted that Nixon would win the Republican nomination and lose to Johnson in a close race. But in order to win, a number of aides now told the President, he needed to take the political offensive and set organizing efforts in motion to assure primary victories and delegate support at the August convention. On March 8, Johnson told them to go ahead. He was also receptive to seeing Ted Sorensen, who was counseling Bobby Kennedy not to enter the race. Johnson was especially pleased to hear that Senator George McGovern of South Dakota, a leading dove, predicted uniform support for Johnson from antiwar opponents if Nixon were the Republican nominee.[93]

Johnson's thoughts of running received a fresh blow on March 12 when McCarthy shocked the country by winning 42 percent of the primary vote in New Hampshire. Though Johnson received 49 percent, it was well below the two-thirds predicted for him and suggested that his candidacy faced greater difficulties than most analysts had anticipated. Some of McCarthy's votes were from hawks fed up with Johnson's failure to win the war. Johnson supporters had underestimated the extent to which voters saw Tet as an American defeat, and overestimated gains to be made from describing a vote for McCarthy as a vote for Ho Chi Minh.[94]

For almost another three weeks, Johnson refused to give up the conviction that he could still be renominated and reelected. Political roundups from nineteen states suggested that he could win enough delegates to regain the nomination. Moreover, on March 14, when Kennedy told Clark Clifford that he would not enter the presidential race if Johnson agreed to a reevaluation of his policy in Vietnam and set up a board of Kennedy-designated advisers, Johnson refused.

He was willing to risk Kennedy's challenge. Indeed, in the two weeks after Kennedy announced his candidacy on March 16, Johnson continued to promote his own candidacy, instructing aides to organize campus youth groups, to round up one prominent Democrat in each state for his nomination, to discuss party unity with Mike Mansfield, to advance his candidacy in the Wisconsin primary scheduled for April 2, and to keep a count on convention delegates. The *New York Times* reported on March 24 that LBJ seemed likely to get more than 65 percent of the votes at the Democratic convention.[95]

But all the activity and positive speculation on his chances could not withstand the reality of Johnson's fall from political grace. The polling numbers in March told the story: 36 percent approval and 52 percent disapproval for his overall performance, and a meager 26 percent approval and a decisive 63 percent disapproval on Vietnam. Democratic caucuses around the country were showing sharp divisions, which threatened to tear the party apart at its summer convention. After announcing his candidacy, Kennedy surged to a 54 to 41 percent lead over Johnson among Democrats. Journalists and political insiders predicted that Johnson would lose in Wisconsin and then the nomination. But even if he managed to survive that test, Johnson would be an easy mark for a Republican nominee promising a change in current policies.[96]

During the last days of March, Johnson decided not to run. Pessimistic assessments of his chances and sheer exhaustion strongly influenced his decision. When his old friend Elizabeth Wickenden saw him at the White House in early March, "he looked absolutely terrible . . . so tired, exhausted. . . . He felt betrayed by his friends. He never said exactly that, but Lady Bird did; she said, 'It was our friends that destroyed us.' " To former aides, he now appeared to be "old," "weathered," "battered," "drained," "pallid," and "aged." Johnson himself later said that it had become "a question of how much the physical constitution could take. I frankly did not believe in 1968 that I could survive another four years of the long hours and unremitting tensions I had just gone through."[97]

He feared a stroke or some other debilitating disease that would incapacitate him. He kept thinking of Woodrow Wilson's last year and a half in office, when he was "stretched out upstairs in the White House, powerless to move, with the machinery of the American government in disarray around him." He later recounted a dream to Doris Kearns that haunted him during this time of "being chased on all sides by a giant stampede. . . . I was being forced over the edge by rioting blacks, demonstrating students, marching welfare mothers, squawking professors, and hysterical reporters. And then the final straw. The thing I feared from the first day of my presidency was actually coming true. Robert Kennedy had openly announced his intention to reclaim the throne in the memory of his brother. And the American people, swayed by the magic of the name, were dancing in the streets."[98]

But as much as anything, Vietnam shaped his judgment to leave office. He saw the war as "a blot on his administration he wanted to remove." If he were running for reelection, he "might miss or postpone an opportunity to achieve peace. 'What if we were late in the campaign and I have to make a decision that might result in a peace settlement but will be politically risky,' he mused one night in March. 'I want my hands free to do what's necessary to end this thing.' " His actions beginning in late 1967 give the ring of truth to his statement. He wanted to end the war in 1968 without regard for domestic political considerations. The issue now, as he saw it, was the historical reputation of his five-year administration.[99]

Even with all the many reasons he saw for stepping aside, he clung to thoughts that he should run again. Only on the afternoon of March 31 did he convince himself to quit. But even then he showed some hesitation. During the morning, he showed Hubert Humphrey two endings to his speech, one with and one without a withdrawal statement. During that afternoon he told aides he wanted them to inform Cabinet officers and congressional leaders about his decision not to run. But he did not want the aides to begin calling until he started giving his speech. He wanted to hold open the option that he might change his mind at the last minute. Only after he had gone on the air could his messengers assume that he would follow through on a decision not to run. The Vice President learned of Johnson's decision from Marvin Watson, who telephoned him in Mexico City, where Humphrey had gone to sign a nuclear nonproliferation treaty for the Western Hemisphere.[100]

On Sunday evening, March 31, at the close of his speech on Vietnam, he declared that he did not want "the presidency to become involved in the partisan divisions that are developing in this political year. . . . With our hopes and the world's hopes for peace in the balance every day, I do not believe that I should devote an hour or a day of my time to any personal partisan causes or to any duties other than the awesome duties of this office—the presidency of your country. Accordingly, I shall not seek, and I will not accept, the nomination of my party for another term as your President." After his speech, one aide remembers that he "bounded from his chair in the Oval Office to join his family in watching the television reviews. His shoulders temporarily lost their stoop. His air was that of a prisoner let free." Mrs. Johnson recalls, "We were all fifty pounds lighter and ever so much more lookin' forward to the future."[101]

The Statesman

The response to Johnson's announcement was the most positive expression of national support since his landslide election in 1964. Democrats and Republicans alike described his decision as an act of selfless patriotism. Some of his most vocal critics, like William Fulbright, said this was "an act of a very great patriot." New York Republican Senator Jacob Javits declared that "in a grave hour of war and national doubt, the President has lifted the office of the presidency to its proper place, far above politics." U.N. Ambassador Arthur Goldberg told him: "You looked 10 feet high when you stood there not thinking of any other consideration but what would serve the country best."

A number of Democrats thought Johnson's action would lead to a draft at the party's convention, and they hoped he would accept. But Bill Moyers said no one should read political motives into the President's decision. His withdrawal should "prove to friend and foe alike that he believes in what he has been doing." Johnson himself declared that "I never was any surer of any decision I ever made in my life, and I never made any more unselfish one. I have 525,000 men whose very lives depend on what I do, and I can't worry about the primaries."

The change in Johnson's mood and toward him was reflected in the tone of a White House correspondents dinner in May, where the journalists saw the President as "in rare and splendid form, brilliantly funny." Since his March 31 speech, he said, he had to wear a White House pass to gain access to the building. "One day, as I was walking over for my nap," Johnson related, "a guard stopped me in the hall and looked at me very carefully and said, 'Excuse me, buddy, but do you work here?'" Poking fun at his calls for unity, he counseled the reporters "to end the partisanship, between wires and weeklies, between the reels and the stills, between the black and the white and the color."

He urged the president of the White House Correspondents Association to achieve unity by standing aside. "And you'll find out that once you step aside, things start happening: Mary McGrory [of the *Washington Post*] may even call you a statesman. Walter Lippmann may think so, but can't quite bring himself to say so. College students do their 'thing' somewhere else, or against another President, and a different 'Dean.'" Johnson reminded the audience that he had promised not to seek the nomination of "*my* party.... And ever since that night, I have been waiting for Everett Dirksen to drop by." Opinion polls confirmed the change in sentiment: 57 percent of the country now approved of Johnson as President.[102]

He even found common ground with Kennedy in the tide of good feeling that followed his announcement. Kennedy described his decision not to run as "truly magnanimous," and asked for an opportunity to see him as soon as possible "to discuss how we might work together in the interest of national unity during the coming months."[103]

They met for an hour and a half in the White House Cabinet room on the morning of April 3. In addition to the two principals, Ted Sorensen, Walt Rostow, and Charles S. Murphy, a former Under Secretary of Agriculture and Chairman of the Civil Aeronautics Board, who was to work on transition matters, as he had for Truman and JFK, also attended the meeting.

Johnson began by discussing Vietnam, the bombing halt, and his hopes for peace. Kennedy and Sorensen remarked on how helpful such a briefing was and hoped there would be others. Johnson promised to make Cabinet officers available in the future and to invite McCarthy and Nixon to speak with them as well.

Johnson said he would be glad for Kennedy "to make suggestions. I feel no bitterness or vindictiveness," he declared. "I want everybody to get together to find a way to stop the killing." He also discussed the need for the tax surcharge and said the earlier tax cut "perhaps should be a lesson to all of us—never repeal another tax. It's too hard to put it back when you need it." He believed passing a tax bill was "absolutely critical." He listed his key concerns for the nation as Vietnam, the Middle East, the tax bill and the deficit, and the question of the cities and race tensions.

Kennedy turned the discussion to politics. "Where do I stand in the campaign?" he asked Johnson. "Are you opposed to my effort and will you marshall forces against me?" Johnson declared his intention to stand aside and keep the presidency out of the campaign. "I'm not that pure," he acknowledged, "but I am that scared. The situation in the country is critical." He intended to tell Hubert the same thing. He won't help any candidate. "If I had thought I could get into the campaign and hold the country together, I would have run myself. If I campaign for someone else, it will defeat what I am trying to do." His plans to stay aloof could change, he candidly said, but for the time being he would be neutral. He promised to let Kennedy know in advance if he decided to declare his support of a candidate.[104]

Later that day Johnson discussed his decision and the presidential campaign with Humphrey. He repeated what he had told Kennedy about shunning involvement in the contest. But his partiality to Hubert over Kennedy kept poking through. However cordial the discussion with Kennedy that morning, it wasn't enough to wash away Johnson's animus toward him. Johnson said that he would be happy to see Humphrey as President, and that "some of the President's friends would probably be willing to help the Vice President. Vast sums are now required to run in American politics," Johnson said, "notably in the face of the great expenditures now being made by the Kennedy camp." Johnson pointed to "examples of large sums being used to induce the support of students."

Johnson also advised Humphrey that he would have no problem with "the President, if he chose to run; nor with his staff. His problem was money and organization." He urged Humphrey to remember how the Kennedys had beaten him "in the West Virginia primary in 1960 because that is the kind of thing he would be up against. He thought the Vice President had always been more charitable about those events than himself." He also counseled Hubert to "make his decision soon and bear in mind that the heart of the matter lay not with the Southerners who, in the end, might well support him, but with the following 6 states: New Jersey, Pennsylvania, Illinois, Michigan, Ohio, and Indiana." Johnson believed it "critical" for Humphrey "to get to those who wanted him to run and tell them that they, in turn, would have to bring around the leaders in the 6 critical states."[105]

Johnson's advice to Humphrey was a lapse in his self-denying proposition about involvement in the campaign. His focus during the three months after his withdrawal was largely on making final gains at home and abroad. At the end of April, when asked how he was likely to feel out of power, he acknowledged that he would miss having "the machinery . . . the power . . . the leadership . . . the forum" to achieve big things for the country. He still believed that "there is a national answer for every national problem," and regretted that there were still so many problems of poverty, disease, education, discrimination, and conservation to be solved.[106]

But as long as he remained in office, he intended to do what he could to ease national difficulties. A fair housing law was a case in point. The 1964 Civil Rights Act had prohibited discrimination in all housing receiving federal assistance. But the law, supported by Executive Orders, affected only 4 percent of the country's dwellings and only 15 percent of new housing. In 1966 and 1967 Johnson had unsuccessfully asked congressional action on a comprehensive bar to racial discrimination in the sale and rental of properties. Johnson's proposed law would have applied to an additional 80 percent of American residences. But Congress refused to act.

Opinion surveys showed 70 percent of Americans opposed to substantial numbers of blacks moving into their neighborhoods and "open housing" proposals as unpopular with a majority of those who knew about them. Joe Califano remembers that the President's fair-housing request in 1966 "prompted some of the most vicious mail LBJ received on any subject," and the only death threat Califano ever received as a White House assistant.[107]

At the beginning of 1968, Johnson renewed his appeal for a fair housing bill. In January, he told Congress that, despite local and state laws barring racial discrimination in housing, residential segregation was increasing in some cities, adding to national tensions over race relations. In February and March, he successfully pressured the Senate into passing a bill.

The House was more of a problem. The results of the 1966 elections had produced a twenty-two-vote loss in representatives favorable to a fair housing law. As Johnson aide "Barefoot" Sanders told him in February, "In order to command a House majority we must get a number of the new Republicans and try to change some of the Democrats who opposed us in 1966." Sanders was not optimistic. On March 19, the House Rules Committee voted 8 to 7 to delay floor action until April 9. Supporters of the measure feared that the start of a Poor People's Campaign in April would arouse opposition to the bill and that the delay was aimed at killing an open housing law. "There had been little hope of getting the House to pass the Senate bill," Califano recalls. "Urban representatives, normally civil rights supporters, were besieged by middle-class white constituents who wanted to keep blacks out of their neighborhoods."[108]

But on April 4 Martin Luther King, Jr., was assassinated by a sniper, James Earl Ray, who escaped and would not be apprehended until June. Mrs. Johnson remembers the news of King's death as "one of those frozen moments, as though the bomb had fallen on us." King's death both demoralized and energized the President. LBJ's response to King's death refutes accusations made twenty-nine years later by King's son Dexter that Johnson had a part in plotting the assassination. "Everything we've gained in the last few days we're going to lose tonight," he said on hearing about King's murder. Though he accurately foresaw that the country's inner cities would explode again in rioting, he seized the occasion to press the case for the fair housing bill.

His first reaction to the killing was to arrange for black leaders

to help stop or limit the anticipated rioting. On April 5, as he pro-
claimed a day of mourning for King, he announced his wish to go
before Congress to recommend "constructive action instead of destructive action—in this hour of national need." The same day he sent
McCormack and Ford a letter urging "all good men" to ask: "What
more can I do to achieve brotherhood and equality among all Americans?" Johnson's answer was passage of the Fair Housing law as a
renewed commitment to "the great promise of opportunity and justice
under law."

On April 10, the House passed the bill. Johnson signed it the
following day with an appeal for an end to violence and support for
legal processes like the enactment of open housing and other social
justice measures that were the work of democracy.[109]

Califano now urged Johnson to build on the fair housing victory
with a "basic reassessment" of domestic programs. He wanted the
President to ask for additional taxes to address critical domestic problems. He requested Johnson's permission to ask Cabinet officers for
confidential memos "on what should now be done at home." Johnson
told him to "forget it." With the tax bill still stalled in Congress, he
believed it unrealistic to press the case for anything new.

When Ben Wattenberg, another White House aide, suggested
that Johnson give a series of speeches on major domestic issues, he
also put him off. By contrast, Johnson approved of a Wattenberg
proposal for the Census Bureau and Bureau of Labor Statistics to
publish a pamphlet describing both Negro progress and the "grim
problems" remaining to be addressed. "Hurry!" he told Wattenberg.
"Go strong!"[110]

For Johnson, the key to doing more in domestic affairs was
House action on his tax surcharge. Wilbur Mills was willing to support the bill if Johnson agreed to cut domestic spending, or so he
said. The congressional pressure to reduce Great Society programs to
finance the war was intense. At the end of March, the President's
economic advisers calculated that even with a tax increase there
would have to be a $5 billion cut in domestic outlays to balance an
additional $5 billion for Vietnam. Budget Director Charles Zwick told
the President that, while fifty senators were ready to cut back Great
Society spending but spare military and space appropriations, only
five favored cutting all three. Johnson was ready to combine the tax
surcharge with $10 billion in reduced appropriations, which would
cut expenditures by $4 billion. But Mills didn't think it was enough,
and Barefoot Sanders advised Johnson to find a way "to blast the Tax
Increase out of Ways and Means."[111]

Johnson believed the tax bill vital to the national well-being.

He needed it for spending on Vietnam. To cut war funds would reduce pressure on Hanoi to negotiate. He also saw a crisis in the cities, which the latest rioting made essential to address with federal monies. Domestic budget and international balance-of-payment deficits threatened a crisis that a tax increase could partly relieve. Yet Mills would not agree to one without domestic cuts Johnson considered dangerous to national stability. In meeting after meeting during April he searched for ways to resolve the tax-budget stalemate with Mills and the Congress.[112]

The President summed up the dilemma on April 26 when he met with the board of the new Urban Institute, which had been set up to find solutions to city problems. Setting aside his prepared remarks, he said: "Let me tell you what's on my mind. Your job is to worry about the future. Well, here's the number one problem for anyone that wants to help their country and the people in it. You've got to figure out how to raise the taxes to pay for these social programs our people need and to rebuild our cities and educate our children.... What we need is someone smart enough to tell us how to convince the American people that they should ante up."[113]

Johnson's remarks were rhetorical. He knew that he would have to extract a tax bill from Congress. And it would have to be over Mills's objections; he "*belittled*" compromise proposals and seemed determined to dismantle the President's domestic reforms. Califano warned that "if you get stuck either with no tax bill or with provisions of the kind Mills is now peddling, I think the ball game may well be over on the Hill for the rest of the year. Indeed, you may have an increasingly difficult time running the Executive Branch of the government and leading the country."[114]

Johnson now brought all possible pressure to bear on Mills and Congress. At a May 3 press conference, he emphasized the need to fund the war and meet the "very serious problems in the cities" and of the poor. He described his $186 billion budget as "very lean." But if we were to avoid large deficits, stem inflation, win the confidence of world financial leaders, and "best serve our own people," there would have to be a tax increase. Though Congress talked about it, there was too little action. In addition, the proposed restrictions as the price of passing a bill would "bring chaos to the government.... We are courting danger by this ... continued delay," Johnson said.

If Congress didn't like his budget, then they should "stand up like men and answer the roll call and cut what they think ought to be cut." It was time "to pass a tax bill without any 'ands,' 'buts,' or 'ors.' "[115]

Armed with a memo from the Council of Economic Advisers

warning of dire consequences from inaction, Johnson now sent written messages to Everett Dirksen and House Speaker John McCormack
and phoned other members of Congress to say: "That's the risk Wilbur Mills is taking with our country because his momma doesn't like
the welfare program."

On May 21, the council gave him yet another memo predicting
a "possible world financial crisis." Defeat of the tax surcharge, the
council warned, could mean "a *major world political defeat for the
United States*," a kind of symbolic bankruptcy. It could also cause
paralysis of world trade, cutbacks in hiring with a "severe economic
downturn," shaken financial markets around the world, an international power vacuum, and the collapse of peace talks with Hanoi,
which would see America as unable to remain in Vietnam.

Even if congressmen and senators discounted such warnings as
political arm-twisting, they didn't wish to risk such a collapse. Understanding that the CEA had given him the needed leverage to win
the tax fight, Johnson kept public pressure on Congress through May
and June. His May 3 press conference was the first in a series of
public statements urging passage of the tax law. When the House
finally acted at the end of June, it tied the bill to a $6 billion cut in
domestic spending. Johnson reluctantly accepted the cuts, but in the
belief that Congress would reduce outlays "by considerably less than
$6 billion."

He was right about the need for the tax rise and Congress's
inability to cut more than half the slated reductions. Getting the tax
bill through Congress was a triumph of economic sense and political
astuteness by a lame-duck President.[116]

The Peacemaker

But could he talk the Vietnamese into making peace? It was a formidable challenge. And he attacked it with the same determination
and manipulativeness that had produced his greatest legislative successes. Clark Clifford later said that, "despite his overwhelming personality and unique understanding of political power, Lyndon
Johnson during this period often acted more like a legislative leader,
seeking a consensus among people who were often irreconcilably opposed to each other, rather than a decisive Commander in Chief giving his subordinates orders." Clifford doubts that Johnson had a clear
idea of his objective in Vietnam after his March 31 speech. He sees
Johnson as "torn between an honorable exit and his desire not to be
the first President to lose a foreign war."[117]

To Johnson, these were not mutually exclusive goals. Indeed, the key to his peacemaking was to arrange a settlement that both preserved South Vietnam as an independent state and sped America's exit from a war the country no longer wished to fight. Contrary to Clifford's belief, Johnson knew what he wanted. His problem was finding the means to get there, including the means to satisfy competing domestic factions urging different strategies for ending the war and the means to reach a settlement with Hanoi and an accommodation with Saigon.

The first challenge to his purpose came the day after his speech. When U.S. planes bombed Than Hoa, a junction 205 miles north of the DMZ and just south of the 20th parallel, critics complained that reduced bombing was an empty promise. Since many people had the impression that his March 31 announcement meant limiting the bombing to the area immediately above the DMZ, Johnson now agreed to confine the attacks to the area between the zone and the 19th parallel, meaning that 90 percent of North Vietnam's population and 75 percent of its territory would be off-limits. Despite concerns that Hanoi would take advantage of the reduced bombing to pour supplies into South Vietnam through Laos and would show the U.S. as overly eager for peace, Johnson felt compelled to accept the limits.[118]

During the next two months, as he struggled to begin negotiations with Hanoi, arguments erupted between Clifford and Rusk over bombing targets. On May 8 and again on the 15th and 21st, Rusk pressed the case for resumption of air attacks in the area between the 19th and 20th parallels. Though Johnson described himself as "nervous about the infiltration and this MIG activity" possibly from a base six miles south of the 20th parallel, and though Wheeler sided with Rusk, the President refused to jeopardize the negotiations by expanding the air raids. He was worried that "North Vietnam may misread this as a voluntary act of foolishness" and that our restraint was letting "more men and ammunition get through. . . . [But] I will put it [expanded bombing] off again against my better judgment," he said. "You're just carrying me along week-to-week on this one," he told Clifford. His comments were meant to placate Rusk, Rostow, and the military chiefs. But he would not agree to alter bombing limits.[119]

On the issues of a site and an agenda for negotiations, Johnson showed himself as firm but eager to start talks. On April 3, the North Vietnamese announced an interest in "contact with U.S. representatives to decide . . . the unconditional cessation of bombing and all other war acts against the DRV so that talks can begin." A dispute among the President's advisers on whether to publicly reiterate his readiness for discussions or to step up the military pressure on the Communists moved Johnson to say, "It's easier to satisfy Ho Chi Minh than Bill Fulbright." Johnson was not going to let this chance for talks go unanswered. He issued a public statement repeating his willingness to send representatives "to any forum, at any time."[120]

Despite the rhetoric, Johnson bargained over the forum. He wanted a neutral site, where both sides would have "good communications," which would allow them to send and receive messages promptly. When Hanoi suggested Phnom Penh, Cambodia's capital, and then Warsaw, Poland, Johnson refused. Instead, he proposed Vientiane, Laos; Rangoon, Burma; Djakarta, Indonesia; and New Delhi—believing an Asian capital the best site for talks. If Hanoi preferred a European setting, Johnson was ready to accept Berne, Copenhagen, Helsinki, or Vatican City. When Hanoi rejected these proposals, Johnson added six Asian and two European capitals to the list. The meeting site now became a preliminary, month-long tug-of-war in the struggle over advantages in the negotiations. As Rostow told Rusk, the President "regards site as matter of substance and test of will which could foreshadow character of negotiation."[121]

By April 18, Hanoi's resistance to Johnson's choices moved him to announce, "It is time for a serious and responsive answer." His eagerness for talks reflected itself in a request to Horace Busby for a speech based on "some radical new ideas" for moving "our military out of Vietnam." He wanted the proposal to include supervised U.N. elections—"one man, one vote," with everybody withdrawing their forces and the cost of the fighting now going to Vietnam's economic development.

Johnson was so eager to find a way through the deadlock that he accepted the possibility of going to Bucharest, the capital of a dissident Communist country. But Rusk thought Paris would be a better venue. The President was reluctant, believing that DeGaulle, who had removed France from NATO and been hostile to U.S. actions in Vietnam, would be friendly to Hanoi during the talks. But Johnson's determination to gain something from his March 31 initiative persuaded him to accept Paris as an alternative. On May 3, when Hanoi offered to meet in Paris the following week, Johnson announced American agreement.[122]

The struggle over a meeting place was relatively minor compared with the debate over defining an agenda. During April, while discussion of a site proceeded, hawks and doves battled over what to offer the North Vietnamese. Rusk, Rostow, Bunker, Max Taylor, Fortas, and the military chiefs favored a tough declaration of terms:

a cessation of bombing on condition that Hanoi did not then improve its military position, the onset of substantive talks within a week of reaching agreement, a willingness to discuss everything relevant to peace, and a place for South Vietnam at the peace table.

The hawks also believed that we needed to act in concert with Saigon, even if it were not to have "a veto over our positions." Led by Rusk and Bunker, this group urged a slow pace in any negotiations lest we undermine South Vietnamese stability. Their objective was to force Hanoi into concessions or to compel them to take responsibility for breaking off the talks.[123]

The doves—Clifford, Harriman, Cyrus Vance, Katzenbach, and Goldberg—wanted the American delegation to enter negotiations with the freedom to respond flexibly to the North Vietnamese. The hawks, by contrast, wanted to hold U.S. negotiators to a strict agenda dictated from Washington. Because they feared that Harriman would follow his own lead, they proposed reining him in with a deputy sympathetic to the hawks. Since Ambassador Llewellyn Thompson, whom LBJ had initially announced as co-chair of the delegation, could not spare time from arms control talks with the Russians, the hawks wanted the President to replace him with someone reflecting their viewpoint. Instead, Johnson chose Deputy Defense Secretary Cyrus Vance, who was more sympathetic to Harriman's flexible approach than the hawk position.[124]

Once both sides agreed to meet in Paris, Clifford says the hawks intensified their efforts to control the agenda. At a meeting on May 6, the President declared himself pessimistic but urged his advisers to be optimistic. Rusk saw no reason to be all that hopeful. He expected Hanoi to demand an unconditional bombing halt before substantive talks began, predicting that "they'll come in with a roar" and seek a propaganda advantage by publishing their position. Harriman, by contrast, took hope from the fact that "they're willing to hear our conditions for stopping the bombing." He also saw their forty-three-member delegation and request for a villa as signs that they were planning to stay for a period of time and were ready for "phase I and phase II" of negotiations. Clifford urged the group to face the "very real problem" that Hanoi would refuse to negotiate without an agreement on a bombing halt. Rusk countered: They then "have to take the burden of breaking off the talks."

Johnson wanted an answer to Clifford's concern. "Assume they do say what Clark says, what do we say?" Johnson asked. "Should we propose mutual withdrawal, reinstitute DMZ, supervised election?" as possible suggestions for breaking a stalemate. Reverting to the proposal he had made to the Pope in December, he wondered: "Shouldn't

Bunker be getting Thieu to go ahead on talking with the NLF?" But
Johnson came back to the central question: "What would you do
about stopping the bombing?" Nothing was resolved, except to meet
again before the delegation left for Paris on May 9.[125]

At a meeting on May 7, Johnson took a hard line. Rusk urged
that we "not pull our punches" and "not understate our own case."
He wanted to make the North Vietnamese "face up to hard issues,
including the no advantage formula." Johnson wanted the American
negotiators "to be tough traders. Let's not put our minimum condition
on the table first," he said. "It is easier to retreat than move forward."
In short, if he needed to compromise to get peace, he would. When
Fulbright asked Clifford whether Johnson was serious about wanting
peace, Clifford replied, "about 50 times as much as you do."[126]

Though estimates that Hanoi had sent between 80,000 and
100,000 men into South Vietnam in the previous four months greatly
troubled him, Johnson remained determined to advance toward peace.
On May 7, when he spoke with Thai leaders at the White House, he
declared his intention to take "a firm position" in the discussions. But
he also planned to "press quite hard for clear indications of what
Hanoi would do.... If Hanoi did not give us such indications," he
said, "we might at some point face the question of stopping the bombing on a trial basis to see what happened."[127]

More immediately, he agreed to an initial statement by the U.S.
delegation that opened the way to a compromise formula on bombing.
Instead of insisting on a North Vietnamese promise not to take advantage of a bombing halt, Harriman was to propose "prompt and
serious substantive talks looking toward peace in Vietnam, in the
course of which an understanding may be reached on a cessation of
bombing in the North under circumstances which would not be militarily disadvantageous." Johnson also wanted Harriman to "talk
about the new Marshall Plan for that area." He thought "the statement doesn't give 'effective pitch.' We need something a truck driver
can understand."[128]

The talks beginning on May 13 proved to be as difficult as
everyone had imagined. "The opening statement by the chief North
Vietnamese delegate could have been an editorial in Hanoi's Communist party newspaper," Johnson said. "Their solution was for us to
stop the bombing and pull all our forces out.... As these denuncia-
tions and demands were repeated, meeting after meeting, week after
week, our hopes for a fair compromise and an early settlement grew
dimmer." Adding to the problem was a series of attacks across South
Vietnam and the aggressive use of the talks as a forum for public
appeals to the American antiwar movement. One National Security

adviser believed that Hanoi simply viewed the "negotiations as a device for improving its chances of achieving its objectives." Rusk saw the Communists as "pretty well fixed on a new propaganda offensive now. They will be trying very hard to force the President's hand."[129]

But Johnson refused to be discouraged or break off contact. Instead, he accepted Senator Mike Mansfield's suggestion that we continue "the negotiations in Paris in a low, patient, and determined key; we have tried to end this war by military means for about three years, at great cost and without success," he told LBJ on May 16, "and the negotiators have been at it for not much more than three sessions." Rostow agreed: "There is no basis yet for optimism," he told the President the following day, "but—equally—there is no reason to draw the conclusion that the negotiations will have no substance. We need a bit more time."[130]

As weeks passed with no discernible movement on Hanoi's part and the hawks pressed for military actions, which might force the Communists into substantive discussions, Johnson accepted the need for more patience. On May 21, Clifford told LBJ that there was no military solution to the war by either side and that something would eventually come out of the negotiations. "Our hopes must go with Paris," he said. He was convinced that Hanoi had "turned to Paris hoping for a political deal." Though Johnson refused to acknowledge that we couldn't win a military victory, he wouldn't jettison the talks.

The following day Clifford asserted that Paris was "a propaganda-plus for us. The North Vietnamese public posture is suffering. Ambassador Harriman is taking a reasonable and positive position, resulting in public opinion gains for us. The absurd position taken by the North Vietnamese concerning their refusal to acknowledge that their troops are in South Vietnam is hurting them."[131]

Johnson was skeptical. He saw "no evidence that the North Vietnamese will negotiate seriously. They will do no more than remain in Paris to talk rather than negotiate until the next administration takes over." Rusk supported Johnson's assumption, saying he didn't think anything would happen until at least July or possibly the August Democratic convention. Johnson had unhappy thoughts of a Kennedy, McCarthy, or Humphrey administration negotiating a quick end to the war for which one of them would get the credit. Johnson also had his doubts about propaganda gains. "Why do you think we are getting the best of them in propaganda"? he asked his foreign policy advisers on May 28. "I am not quite as optimistic as Clark and Cy [Vance] about our position in world opinion," he said. "We have such a good case. Look at what Ho is doing. Hitler in his prime day didn't do this."[132]

Johnson's skepticism now colored his response to an initiative from Moscow. On June 4, two weeks after Harriman had told Soviet Ambassador Valerian Zorin that Johnson was under great pressure to resume bombing unless there were some sign of progress in Paris, Soviet Premier Aleksei Kosygin sent Johnson a letter. He assured him that he and his "colleagues believe—and we have grounds for this— that a full cessation by the United States of bombardments and other acts of war against the DRV could promote a breakthrough in the situation that would open perspectives for peaceful settlement" without "adverse consequences whatever for the United States." Kosygin also suggested that there be "unofficial contacts between the delegations" in Paris.

Clifford urged the President to take Kosygin at his word. He believed that only the Soviets, who were providing 80 percent of North Vietnam's supplies, had the leverage to force Hanoi into a settlement. Johnson thought we should first get clarification of what the Soviets were telling us. "I feel," he said, "we should say we will stop all bombing when we are sure of restraint by them. . . . I am not willing to take their assurance and rely on it on face value." Johnson recalled Soviet assurances in late 1965 that "something good" would come from a bombing halt. The thirty-seven-day pause in 1966 had netted no gain. When Clifford continued to press for a bombing halt, Johnson said: "I don't think being soft will get us peace."[133]

Johnson sent Kosygin what Clifford describes as a "noncommittal message asking what would happen if we stopped the bombing." The reply essentially killed the opportunity, in Clifford's words, for "a true test" of what the Soviet initiative meant. The President's reply put Clifford in "a gloomy mood" and made him doubtful that Johnson was ready to take the sort of chances that might be needed to end the war.[134]

The President was not happy about his cautious response to Moscow, but he believed that a positive reply would have trapped him into an unreciprocated bombing halt and deprived the United States of leverage in the talks. On June 10, when a senior member of the North Vietnamese negotiating team publicly told CBS news that American insistence on "reciprocity" was absurd and unacceptable, Johnson felt vindicated in responding to Kosygin's initiative as he had. Rostow described Lay Duc Tho's statement "as rigid . . . as one could produce."[135]

Yet Johnson's interest in advancing the talks was as keen as ever. On June 14, he swore George Ball in to replace Arthur Goldberg as U.N. Ambassador. The appointment of someone so consistently opposed to the war was both a symbolic and a substantive expression of the President's commitment to ending the conflict.[136]

Johnson and his advisers believed that the best way now to advance the negotiations was through private discussions. On June 12, Harriman and Vance broached the subject with the North Vietnamese. Though saying that they doubted whether anything could be achieved when our differences were so great, they agreed to take the suggestion under consideration. In fact, the North Vietnamese were fully receptive to the idea. That day, one of their lower-level delegates agreed to have dinner with his U.S. counterpart soon. "We have not been able to get private talks going yet," Rusk told a Cabinet meeting on the afternoon of the 12th, "but we have some hopes. There is some reason to think that the coffee break intervals have become of larger significance."[137]

Two weeks later, the first private meeting between Vance and Hanoi's second-ranking delegate occurred in a suburban Paris "safe house." Though the exchange of comments was familiar and gave no indication of a change in position on either side, Harriman was hopeful that private talks would shield the North Vietnamese from having to acknowledge that they had agreed to any conditions for a U.S. bombing halt. Nevertheless, Harriman anticipated no "miracles. We need patience above all." The coming months testified to the wisdom of his advice.[138]

Politics: The Nonpartisan as Partisan

Johnson's withdrawal from the presidential race, coupled with a declaration of noninvolvement in "any personal partisan causes" during the rest of his term, did not mean he would stay clear of politics. Whatever his public pronouncements, he could not abruptly end lifelong habits. As he freely admitted, he was a political animal who loved the machinations, the give and take, the brokering and deal-making that had always energized him.

Did he really intend to retire from the presidency? Some of the old pols like House Speaker John McCormack refused to take Johnson at his word. In mid-April he called Marvin Watson to say that "people at home . . . are behind the President. . . . The country is really behind the President and they are not confused by the few intellectuals who make all the news. . . . I haven't given up hope on the President," McCormack concluded. "I believe he will still be my candidate."[139]

In the weeks after his announcement, Johnson had no intention of running again. This did not preclude a continuing interest in the emerging campaign or, more to the point, in trying to shape its outcome. Fred Panzer continued to give him detailed reports on the presidential race, describing last-minute shifts in the Wisconsin primary and the current findings on various Democratic-Republican matchups in November as a result of the President's withdrawal. Johnson also kept close tabs on the Indiana primary scheduled for early May. He was especially interested in Robert Kennedy's poll numbers. Johnson now also reluctantly agreed to release his convention delegates. White House counsel Larry Temple told LBJ that he had no alternative; "those pledged cannot be transferred anyway." Johnson's initial response was to discuss the situation with Temple to see whether he actually had no choice.[140]

In April, Johnson maintained a strong private interest in both the Democratic and Republican nomination fights. On balance, he favored Humphrey among the Democrats. His cordial meeting with Kennedy did little to soften Johnson's antagonism. He did not think McCarthy had a chance to win.

As for Humphrey, Johnson was ambivalent about his fitness for the presidency. He liked Hubert and believed he would be a staunch advocate of the domestic programs they favored. But he also considered him too soft or too much of a bleeding-heart liberal who would have trouble making tough decisions. He was a nonstop talker who wore his heart on his sleeve. "Maybe he doesn't have enough reserve because he feels very deeply about human problems," Johnson privately told a reporter in May. "I have noticed that people from Minnesota have a propensity for talking." After a meeting in which Goldberg and Humphrey did most of the talking, Johnson said to an aide, "Goldberg and Humphrey, my two silent partners."

Johnson was especially suspicious of Hubert's resolve to forge a proper peace in Vietnam. After McCarthy declared that Humphrey did not believe in his public position on Vietnam, Hubert told Johnson that McCarthy admits never hearing "me say anything on Vietnam privately that he had not heard me say publicly." Johnson had his doubts.[141]

Johnson's choice as his successor was New York's Republican Governor Nelson Rockefeller. The two men had a high regard for each other. Johnson saw Rockefeller as a sensible moderate who, in Lady Bird's words, "was a good human being, a person who was for the disadvantaged, who was a man of compassion, with a capable and effective mind, and capable of being effective, getting things done." He also believed that Rockefeller was the one man who could beat Bobby Kennedy, no small asset in Johnson's mind.

Rockefeller reciprocated Johnson's feelings. He saw the President as "a great statesman and a great American patriot." Rockefeller said later: "He was a tremendous guy." They and their wives enjoyed a warm personal relationship. Nelson recalled how frank his wife Happy could be with Lyndon, telling him at the ranch not to drive so fast or drink so much. "She was successful in getting him to slow down, which I don't think most people were."

Rockefeller also felt that they shared common political ground. "No President that I have known showed greater awareness, sensitivity to, or respect for the role of governors than he did," Rockefeller said. "Whenever there was a major problem he'd call us down and consult with us about it." Rockefeller thought him "very generous, and my work with him and with the governors conference was not on a partisan basis, but was on a bipartisan basis." Rockefeller sympathized with "the problems that he had in the Vietnam situation. So I felt badly for this man, I really did, because he was a tremendous patriot."

Toward the end of April, Johnson invited the Rockefellers to the White House for dinner, where he urged the governor to declare for the Republican nomination. "He was very friendly about '68, and very supportive of me for '68," Rockefeller said. Johnson also told him that he would never campaign against him. "You've been a longtime friend." Happy Rockefeller remembered how during that evening Johnson urged Rockefeller to run. "He did want Nelson to be President," she said. Johnson encouraged others to back Rockefeller as well. On April 7, after Irwin Miller, a prominent member of "Republicans for Johnson" in 1964 had asked whether the President would object to his chairing a Draft Rockefeller Committee, LBJ gave Miller "a full-speed go-ahead."

Rockefeller didn't need much prodding. On April 10, following a brief conversation with Johnson at New York's St. Patrick's Cathedral, where they attended Archbishop Terence Cooke's installation, Rockefeller announced his "availability" for the Republican nomination. On April 30, after the White House evening, Rockefeller declared himself a candidate for the presidency.[142]

Partly to help Rockefeller and partly to keep focused on advancing peace talks and making domestic gains, Johnson insisted on political neutrality by everyone in his administration. It was very difficult. Cabinet secretaries and White House aides were eager to line up behind preferred candidates. Some like Douglass Cater asked Johnson whether he minded a personal endorsement by him for Humphrey. Others like Wilbur Cohen, who had succeeded John Gardner as HEW secretary, simply announced his backing for Hubert.

When Humphrey decided to announce his candidacy at a luncheon on April 27, several Cabinet members, eager to demonstrate their support, planned to attend. Johnson ordered Califano to stop them: "I can't have the government torn apart by Cabinet officers and presidential appointees fighting among themselves about Kennedy, McCarthy, and Humphrey," Johnson said. Califano was to tell everyone in the Cabinet "to stay out of the race or get out of the government."[143]

Most of Johnson's subordinates agreed to follow his lead. But a number refused. Agriculture Secretary Orville Freeman, who was a Minnesotan and committed Humphrey backer, believed it impossible for him to stand back. If he didn't attend Humphrey's luncheon, Freeman told LBJ, it would be seen as a denial of support for Humphrey by the President. Would his attendance compel his resignation? Freeman asked Califano. Califano thought not. Labor Secretary Bill Wirtz promised to make no further public statements backing Humphrey, but he was already " 'pretty extensively' involved in doing staff work for the Vice President" and didn't see how he could simply abandon his campaign. Johnson also wanted the wives of his aides to remain neutral, but none of them thought it likely.[144]

Predictably, Johnson's greatest tensions were with the administration's Kennedy supporters. When Agriculture Under Secretary John Schnittker came out for RFK, Johnson himself called to set him straight. Ted Sorensen then complained that Johnson seemed to be applying different standards when people came out for Humphrey as opposed to Kennedy. While the White House made no objection to endorsements for Humphrey by Wirtz, Freeman, and Cohen, Sorensen said, it immediately moved to muzzle Schnittker. Johnson angrily told Califano to make clear to Sorensen that "in no way does the President owe anything to Bobby Kennedy," but that nevertheless he intended to stay away from "supporting, refraining from supporting or opposing anyone."[145]

It was difficult for Johnson to punish aides for favoring a candidate when he himself was partisan. At the same time he encouraged Rockefeller's candidacy, Johnson made clear that he preferred Humphrey over Kennedy and McCarthy. During a conversation with UAW President Walter Reuther, both men danced around the nomination question. Before they met, Califano reported that Reuther implied his support for Humphrey, but seemed likely to endorse the President's insistence on neutrality. Though Johnson refused openly to back Humphrey and Reuther avoided pressing the point during their talk, Johnson said: "Do whatever you are going to do and put it on the line. I don't have the slightest doubt where your best interest lies," implying that labor would want to back Humphrey.

When a reporter writing a piece for *Look* magazine about Humphrey asked to talk to Johnson off the record, LBJ agreed. He gave Hubert an "A" or "A plus" rating, describing him as "the man of all the people I know in either party that I thought in 1964 was best equipped to be President.... I'd be happy to have him run my affairs," Johnson declared. "He is very courageous and cautious about big things. The tougher it gets, the better he is."[146]

The anti-Kennedy bias was publicly muted but as strong as ever in private. During May, Fred Panzer kept Johnson abreast of how many delegates Humphrey seemed likely to get at the convention and how Kennedy fared in the national straw polls against Nixon and George Wallace. A memo to Johnson on May 9 predicted that Kennedy would try to seize the "law and order" issue. "*It seems obvious that this area should be occupied continually by the President and the Vice-President so as not to leave a void for Kennedy,*" the adviser recommended.[147]

Johnson couldn't keep his partisanship entirely hidden. On May 16, syndicated columnist Victor Riesel published an "almost verbatim report" of an off-the-record White House meeting with the AFL-CIO Executive Council. He described LBJ as understanding "that George Meany was right when ... [he] warned that a cut in welfare and new era monies would be used by his political enemies to attack the President and his 'friends.' The political enemies are Bob Kennedy and Gene McCarthy. The friends mostly are Hubert Humphrey."

Four days later, Merriman Smith published a story saying that LBJ had discussed and approved plans for the Democratic Convention in Chicago with Mayor Richard Daley. White House aide Tom Johnson tried to convince Smith that it wasn't true, but Smith said he had a reliable source, which he did. "It looks as though somebody has filled Smitty in very well," Tom Johnson told the President.[148]

Despite his desire quietly to shape political developments, Johnson was without significant impact on either the Democratic or Republican campaigns. When Robert Kennedy won the California primary on June 5, he became the odds-on favorite to win the nomination. By then, it was also clear that Rockefeller had little chance of defeating Nixon's bid to be the Republican nominee.

Robert Kennedy's assassination by Sirhan B. Sirhan at the victory celebration in Los Angeles on the night of June 5 stunned Johnson. It was "too horrible for words," the President said on being awakened to hear the news. "Since he was well aware of his own psychological baggage," Califano says, "in no situation did Lyndon Johnson try harder to do the right thing—for the country, the Kennedy family, and himself—than in the hours and days following the shooting." Appreciating how antagonistic many of those closest to Kennedy would feel toward him, he tried not to intrude on their grief. He took a low profile at St. Patrick's Cathedral, where there was a funeral mass on June 8, and again at the funeral itself at Arlington National Cemetery, where Kennedy was laid to rest 100 feet from his brother's grave.[149]

Johnson had a genuine sense of anguish over this latest act of senseless violence, which had not only taken the life of another popular public figure but raised questions about whether America was "a sick society." The journalist Hugh Sidey described the President's response to the replay of a radio report on Kennedy's death. He "stopped work. His head slumped way down between his knees as he listened, so low that those in front of the desk could barely see him. When it was over, he snapped the radio off, rose from his chair a stricken man, walked out of the French doors into the Rose Garden and stood there alone, silent."[150]

Kennedy's death revived Johnson's interest in a possible reelection campaign. One former national security adviser sent word to the President that he should consider running. "Many young people throughout the Washington area . . . are convinced that the President is the only man who can keep the country on the move after January." He didn't think Humphrey could beat Nixon, but he believed LBJ could.[151]

A consideration in mulling over the possibility was whether he could be effective. In mid-March he had told Harry McPherson that he thought Nixon, Kennedy, or McCarthy "could get a program through next year better than I could. . . . Congress and I are like an old man and woman who've lived together for a hundred years. . . . We're tired of each other." Shortly after, when Califano told Johnson that he thought Bob Kennedy would get the nomination, LBJ replied: "What's wrong with Bobby? He's made some nasty speeches about me, but he's never had to sit here. . . . Bobby would keep fighting for the Great Society programs. And when he sat in this chair he might have a different view on the war."[152]

His efforts in the aftermath of Kennedy's death to set up a Commission on the Causes and Prevention of Violence, pass his Safe Streets law, and win gun control did not give him reason to think that his March assessment was much off the mark. Though the commission became a reality, it was not going to produce anything meaningful in the short term, or possibly at all.

The crime and gun control measures Johnson got from Congress only approximated what he wanted and left him frustrated and dejected. Minnesota Senator Walter Mondale urged the President to veto the crime bill, saying it was especially deficient in its wiretap provisions. The AFL-CIO called the Safe Streets Act "legislation so destructive of constitutional rights [that] the welfare of the nation would best be served by vetoing it." Harry McPherson told the President that the Crime Control and Safe Streets law was "the worst bill you have signed since you took office." Similarly, the elimination of owner licensing and gun registration in the gun control law moved Johnson to declare the "voices that blocked these safeguards were not the voices of an aroused nation. They were the voices of a powerful lobby, a gun lobby, that has prevailed for the moment in an election year."[153]

Johnson also doubted that the nomination would be worth much in what seemed to be shaping up as a Republican season. Panzer told him that "political creatures are sniffing the air and scenting a GOP year." Panzer wasn't so sure, predicting that Humphrey or Johnson could beat Nixon. Johnson doubted Panzer's conclusion, telling congressional Democrats that he saw "dissatisfaction with the 'ins' and thus the climate favors the Republicans." New York Times columnist Tom Wicker believed that "the thread" running "through the primary elections this year . . . is the rejection of the Johnson administration and its policies."[154]

Still, Johnson could not quite let go of the thought that he might yet rescue the country from itself. Polls at the end of June showed Humphrey and McCarthy in a virtual deadlock with Nixon. But if Massachusetts Senator Edward Kennedy was the vice-presidential nominee, it decisively tipped the scale to the Democratic candidate. Panzer believed that "adding Teddy Kennedy to the ticket would result in a Democratic landslide." According to one Washington columnist, Kennedy was considering the possibility of running with Humphrey. Johnson had a good relationship with Ted Kennedy. Nothing was said or done even to hint at a Johnson-Kennedy ticket. But, as events in the summer would make clear, Johnson had not yet definitively abandoned thoughts of another term.[155]

11

Unfinished Business

JOHNSON knew that exercising power in the waning months of a presidential term defied the laws of political gravity. But he had no intention of letting his time in office simply run out. As long as he held power, he was determined to use it. His diminishing capacity to make things happen stimulated not acceptance of the inevitable but vigorous efforts to dramatize the unfinished business he saw in domestic and foreign affairs.

In the last months of his presidency he never tired of telling his favorite Winston Churchill story. "It is so apropos of conditions in our country and in the world where people are trying to stay resigned to the status quo," Johnson said. A group of elderly temperance ladies called on the Prime Minister near the end of World War II to complain about his drinking habits. They told him that if all the alcohol he had consumed during the war were emptied into his office, it would reach halfway to the ceiling. "My dear ladies," Churchill replied, "so little have I done, so much have I yet to do."[1]

At a staff meeting on June 25 the President complained of "recent press reports that the White House staff is tired . . . that many officials are soon leaving . . . and that the machinery of government is grinding to a halt." He hoped the entire staff would stay until January, but he would accommodate those who felt compelled to go earlier. In the meantime, however, "there's lots of work to do and no room for a letdown."

He wanted fresh proposals for what they should do between now and January. But not because he was short on ideas; he knew what he wanted to accomplish. He hoped staff initiatives might generate renewed enthusiasm among aides focused on post–White House careers. Lest the staff doubt his determination to take on additional challenges, he announced that he had asked Joe Califano to oversee the preparation of "specialized speeches on major subjects," describing what had "been done in a particular area—education, for example—during the past 180 years. What we have accomplished during the past eight years. [And] the unfinished problems; what needs to be done in the next eight years, between now and the [200th] anniversary of our independence." He also asked the staff to think about ways "to get our legislation moving."[2]

It was typical Johnson. Not a major problem would remain unaddressed, even if he saw little likelihood of getting much done. By describing the country's ongoing difficulties, he hoped to prod his successor, Congress, and the public into keeping the focus on its greatest challenges. "A substantial number of the legislation [sic] passed during his administration," wrote New York Times reporter David Wise in the fall, "originated with President Truman, and he wants to take a long look ahead on what else the country needs. He plans no wild dreams, but wants to give his views on the years ahead."[3]

In May, for example, when the House appropriation for HUD fell "far short" of what LBJ had asked for "programs so essential to ease the crisis in our cities," he publicly urged the Senate to restore the funds "so that we can move forward with the urgent task of rebuilding the American city."

At the end of June, after Califano told him that he had made his mark in the fields of education, health, jobs, poverty, and housing but needed, despite food stamps, to launch "a major [food] program" to assist America's hungry, LBJ proposed a "meeting to see where and how this should be developed." Toward the end of the year he publicly described "hunger and malnutrition as intolerable," and urged a 140 percent increase in food assistance programs between 1968 and 1970. "The Nation," he declared, "cannot be satisfied until no man, woman, or child in it is hungry or undernourished because of poverty beyond his control."[4]

In the second half of 1968 he was like a whirling dervish in behalf of domestic advance. Early in the summer, he pressed Congress for natural gas pipeline safety, the eighteen-year-old vote, an end to discrimination in hiring, more effective urban mass transit, a tenfold increase in low- and middle-income public housing, family planning and population control, stronger air pollution controls, more aggressive conservation of natural resources, expanded protections for security holders, a fresh attack on juvenile delinquency, and additional support for black economic progress.[5]

At the end of July, he told the national governors' conference that he saw fifty major bills in Congress that he considered "essential to the well-being of all of the American people." He counted among these teenage protection from dangerous drugs, keeping guns from criminals, job security and safety, decent universal housing, and preservation of forests, scenic trails, and rivers.[6]

As his presidency moved toward a close, his efforts for domestic advance quickened. On August 1, he hailed the passage of the HUD Act of 1968 as "the Magna Carta to liberate our cities." The law created "new means to win new rights ... the fundamental and very precious American right to a roof over your head—a decent home." However hyperbolic, however unlikely that the law would assure his goal, he saw the occasion as a chance to challenge the country and— as additional remarks eight days later made clear—other nations around the world to reach for a lofty goal on a scale with Woodrow Wilson's vision of ending war.[7]

During the next four weeks, he celebrated laws eliminating barriers to the handicapped in public buildings and protecting Americans from flammable, toxic, and corrosive gases. On August 14, in a speech to the annual convention of the National Medical Association, a group of black physicians, he pled the case for assuring that "every boy and girl born into this land has a chance to start life with good health. ... Medicare is a triumph of rightness," he said. "Now we must seek new ways to improve and to expand medical care." It was not only health but a chance at jobs, education, and homes that he declared the birthright of every American citizen.

On August 17, he announced the establishment of a National Eye Institute to prevent blindness, which afflicted 400,000 Americans, and the enactment of a Health Manpower Act to aid medical, dental, public health, and nursing schools to train health professionals, who were in short supply. Two days later, he signed the Wholesale Poultry Products Act, reminding the country of the poem: "Mary had a little lamb, and when she saw it sicken, she shipped it off to packing town, and now it's labeled chicken."[8]

In the midst of the presidential campaign, he believed it essential that the country remember its "unfinished business," and that somehow the campaign might "lift the national spirit; ... [and] make our people eager to get on with the business of the next four years." On Labor Day, he emphasized the need for individual dignity and economic justice and urged all Americans to "open their hearts and work with a new sense of purpose to help the disadvantaged enter the mainstream of our society." He declared himself confident "that America will continue its march toward universal human decency."[9]

At a press conference on September 6, he reminded Congress

that "we are paid on a year-round basis, and even while the campaign is on, we have business to do." He saw thirty or forty bills that needed action before the end of the year.

And where he could act on his own, he did. On September 9, he announced the creation of the National Housing Partnership and the appointment of industrialist Edgar F. Kaiser to head it. It was to begin a cooperative effort of government and the private sector to build 600,000 low- and middle-income housing units Johnson saw putting roofs over the heads of disadvantaged and middle-class Americans. On the 11th, he asked Congress to pass a coal mine health and safety act before adjournment. On the 12th, he publicly instructed HEW Secretary Wilbur Cohen to consider Social Security benefits "for not only next year, but for the decade ahead." On the 16th, he reported to Congress on adult basic education, calling attention to "the challenges ahead." On the 24th, he commended the President's Committee on Mental Retardation for its impressive achievement and urged no letdown in its efforts.[10]

During the next ten days, he preached the virtues of conservation to Congress and the country, and took special pleasure in signing a Handicapped Children's Early Education Assistance Act. On September 26, he asked Wilbur Cohen to brief White House aides on future social challenges and the reforms needed to meet them. He had heard Cohen give this talk in another forum several days before. "I got so excited about it the other day," the President said, "I had to take sleeping pills at night."

As Cohen described the great reforms going back to the New Deal, Johnson asked his staff to "pick out the ten most comprehensive, far-reaching, beneficial, constructive pieces of legislation—the top ten—of the last 30 years. Let's see if we can't get an article written on that." People don't know about the programs available to them, Johnson said. He wanted to educate the public to the value of government services.

Between October 2 and election day, November 5, he signed bills extending the food stamp program and the Food and Agriculture Act of 1965, which had contributed to a resurgence of farm prosperity. He also approved the amended Merchant Marine Act of 1936, "a temporary palliative" toward revitalizing U.S. maritime capacities, and Public Health Service amendments, which increased the likelihood of better health for all Americans. Three education bills, affecting higher and vocational education and extending veterans benefits, a radiation control act, the 20th consumer protection measure of his presidency, a conservation statute making Florida's Biscayne National Monument into a national park, and a bill creating a

Woodrow Wilson International Center for Scholars at the Smithson-ian Institution concluded this burst of preelection reform activism.[11]

Liberals were not uniformly happy with Johnson's performance. So much of what he supported was more symbolic than substantive. Still concerned to hold down federal spending, he did not suggest immediate increases in domestic outlays. His proposals and declarations were aimed more at future administrations than his own. Understanding what Johnson was doing, Drew Pearson complained at the end of September that LBJ had "been too kind to Congress lately. You have argued, persuaded, cajoled, almost got down on your knees to Congress," Pearson wrote him. "It's time you took off the gloves and really whaled them."[12]

Johnson spurned Pearson's advice. He remained concerned that the government lacked the funds to mount the large-scale attack on domestic problems Pearson favored. In July, the Budget Bureau accurately calculated the 1968 deficit at $25 billion. And though the tax surcharge had dramatically improved prospects for fiscal 1969, in August the Council of Economic Advisers still anticipated a shortfall of between $1.8 and $5.1 billion.[13]

By the beginning of 1969, however, Johnson predicted that for the first time since the 1950s the country could expect to have a federal budget surplus. Though only $2.4 billion in fiscal 1969, he believed it would increase to $3.4 billion in 1970. More important, he thought it would facilitate "some necessary increases" in domestic programs. He would now be able to leave town on January 20 "a happy man and a thankful man."[14]

Some of his satisfaction came from having carried forward international advances as well in the last eight months of his term. In June 1968 he returned to the Glassboro campus for a commencement address. In spite of predictions "that the war in Vietnam would prevent any progress" in Soviet-American relations, he said, the current period had been as productive in promoting cooperation as any in our history, except for World War II. He pointed to the treaty outlawing armaments in space, the negotiation of a consular agreement, which was the first bilateral accord in Soviet-American relations, a civil air convention allowing both sides to fly commercial planes to each other's countries, and ongoing efforts to advance a Nuclear Nonproliferation Treaty (NPT).[15]

In July Johnson signed the agreement banning the spread of nuclear weapons. With fifty-six countries agreeing to the limitation, he declared it "a very reassuring and hopeful moment in the relations among nations." The provisions of the treaty committed the non-nuclear signatories to forego the production of such weapons, to receive "the full peaceful benefits of the atom," and committed the nuclear powers to work toward arms control and disarmament. At the same time, he announced an agreement with Moscow "to enter in the nearest future into discussions on the limitation and reduction of both offensive strategic nuclear weapons delivery systems and systems of defense against ballistic missiles."

When he asked the Senate to ratify the NPT, Johnson declared it "the most important international agreement limiting nuclear arms since the nuclear age began. It is a triumph of sanity and of man's will to survive." With the promise of strategic arms limitation talks also to hand, he declared himself hopeful that "this treaty will mark the beginning of a new phase in the quest for order and moderation in international affairs."[16]

In July, Johnson proposed to the Soviets that he come to Moscow to discuss ongoing points of difference. He saw the visit as an opportunity to press the case for arms limitation. An exchange of technical papers on strategic arms was to precede the meeting. At the conference, he hoped they could reach agreement on broad principles to guide future negotiations. Rusk told Soviet Ambassador Dobrynin that he considered such discussions possibly "the most important talks between our two countries since World War II." Dobrynin agreed, and on August 19 Moscow cabled its agreement to have President Johnson visit the Soviet Union in early October for "the exchange of opinions with the leading figures of the USSR on the questions of mutual interest."[17]

Johnson was eager to go, and he planned to announce the news of his trip on August 21. But on the evening of the 20th Dobrynin informed Johnson that Soviet forces had invaded Czechoslovakia to repress "a conspiracy of the external and internal forces of aggression against the existing social order." After much anxiety that the liberalizing policies of a popular government under Alexander Dubcek might unsettle other Communist regimes in Eastern Europe, Moscow had decided to enforce a return to orthodoxy with Soviet troops. Understanding that it would be seen as condoning the invasion if he now agreed to meet in Moscow, Johnson instructed Rusk to inform Dobrynin of his decision not to announce anything about a visit or talks.

"The Czechoslovakia situation has made problems in Europe more acute," Johnson told David Wise several weeks later. Angry and frustrated by the Soviet action, which also delayed Senate action on the NPT, he added: "You live in one of the most dangerous periods in history. It would be easy for the Russians to take further moves. They got away with Czechoslovakia. If they thought this government was prostrate till January 19, I don't know what they would do. You cannot trust a totalitarian country."

Although convinced that he should wait until the Czech crisis receded and the November election decided who would succeed him, Johnson wished to end his term with a Soviet-American summit. In the summer of 1968, Johnson shelved but did not abandon hopes of arms talks that might mark his presidency as an important milestone on the road to Soviet-American détente.[18]

Courtpacking: "The Fortas Fiasco"

In the closing months of his term, Lyndon Johnson thought not only about setting an agenda for future advances at home and abroad but also about how to assure that a next, possibly more conservative administration would not overturn or reduce the accomplishments of the last five years. He was particularly concerned that a Republican President not use appointments to the Supreme Court to promote judicial review of Great Society reforms. Though he would acknowledge it only as an afterthought in his memoirs, Johnson said he feared that "a conservative Court" would lead to "a reversal of the philosophy of the Warren Court, and a dissipation of the forward legislative momentum we had achieved during the previous eight years."

Califano believes that "Johnson saw the Court as a means of perpetuating his social reform, particularly racial justice. He also wanted the Court to uphold the compromise he had reached with Catholics on funds for parochial schools, as well as his consumer, health, and environmental legislation." Johnson had won the congressional fights over these measures, but he expected disputes about them "inevitably [to] play out in the courts long after he left the White House, and he intended to win them as well after he had gone."[19]

The opportunity to counter such a development emerged in June 1968 when Chief Justice Warren advised Johnson that he wished to resign. Warren was in good health and seemed capable of continuing on the Court. But at seventy-seven he feared this might change at any time. Moreover, he was concerned that 1968 would bring a Republican victory and possibly a Richard Nixon presidency. Seeing Nixon as unethical, Warren couldn't stand the thought of Nixon choosing his successor. Warren said "he wanted President Johnson to appoint his successor, someone who felt as Justice Warren did." To guard against the possibility that a lame-duck President couldn't do it, Warren's letter of resignation to Johnson said that his departure would be "effective at your pleasure." Johnson's reply made the hedge explicit: "With your agreement, I will accept your decision to retire effective at such time as a successor is qualified."[20]

Johnson conferred with Clark Clifford about Warren's replacement. The President explained that he wanted to elevate Abe Fortas to the Chief Justiceship and replace him with a Texas jurist and old friend Homer Thornberry. Though a progressive Democrat, Thornberry was a southerner who had served in the House, been a federal circuit judge, and was currently on the federal court of appeals. Johnson believed that Richard Russell and other southern senators would be enthusiastic enough about Thornberry to accept Fortas, whose liberal opinions and Jewish identity seemed certain to arouse opposition. Without this inducement, Johnson thought the southerners would resort to a filibuster and kill off both appointments, declaring their intention to leave matters to a new President.

Clifford was not convinced and predicted that Johnson would never get the appointments approved. The Republicans, expecting to win the presidency in 1968, would resist, and would win enough Senate support by complaining that Thornberry was a Johnson crony. Clifford suggested that Johnson name a moderate nonpolitical Republican instead of Thornberry as a way to win GOP support. White House Counsel Larry Temple agreed. But Johnson refused to listen. He argued with Clifford and Temple, saying he understood the politics of the situation much better then they did. "What office did you ever get elected to?" he asked Temple. He believed that he had enough Senate votes to confirm Fortas and Thornberry, and Fortas, who shortly participated in the discussion, agreed that Johnson's strategy promised the best results.[21]

There were warnings signs that Johnson's nomination of Thornberry would not stop southern opposition to Fortas. On June 25, Mike Manatos, Johnson's Senate liaison, reported that Robert Byrd of West Virginia "would do 'everything in [his] power' to oppose Abe Fortas, to whom he refers as that 'leftist' member of the Court ... Russell Long [of Louisiana] classifies Fortas as 'one of the dirty five' who sides with the criminal against the victims of crime. He believes that ... Fortas-Thornberry package would be real trouble."

Mississippi Senator James Eastland, the Judiciary Committee chairman, warned that Fortas could not be confirmed and that there would be a filibuster. Eastland also reported that he "had never seen so much feeling against a man as against Fortas." John McClellan of Arkansas described himself as eager to do battle against Fortas on the Senate floor. He urged Eastland "not to raise any block against sending up Fortas because he was looking forward to having 'that SOB formally submitted to the Senate' so that he could fight his nomination." Sam Ervin of North Carolina said: "Considering what the Supreme Court has done to the Constitution, I'll have to read Fortas's decisions before I can decide."[22]

Yet Johnson had some reason for optimism. After he announced the nominations on June 26, Manatos reported that they were "generally well received. The only soft areas are among certain Southern Democrats, and a small Republican group." A Senate head count showed sixty-two supporters and five probable backers—a total of sixty-seven, which could defeat a filibuster. Yet three of the five probables were really question marks, and three of six probable votes against seemed opened to conversion. When Johnson spoke privately with a reporter on July 1, he put the best possible face on Fortas's chances. Based on an additional head count of sixty-one "solid right votes" and nine "probably right," he saw "about 70 votes favorable and added that those in the remaining 30 are going to have to live with a bad vote."[23]

Johnson's impulse to go ahead rested partly on his belief that he would win enough Republican support through Everett Dirksen's backing and enough southern votes through Richard Russell's enthusiasm for Thornberry. Discussions with Dirksen had yielded a Johnson promise to sustain the existence of the Subversive Activities Control Board beyond June 30, 1968, an institution Dirksen's conservative friends pressed him to save. In return, Dirksen, who admired Fortas's brilliance as a lawyer, agreed to back his appointment as Chief Justice.

Similarly, during a family dinner at the White House, Johnson won Russell's commitment to Fortas. Russell did not regard Fortas "as an ideal appointment," though he considered him "an extremely able man" and "more stable and conservative than the man [Goldberg] he succeeded on the bench. . . . When I knew Fortas," Russell told a constituent, "he was an extreme liberal, but I do not believe that he was a member of the Communist Party." As Johnson had anticipated, Russell was ready to take Fortas to get Thornberry, who had been a hunting partner. Russell characterized Thornberry as "a good man, an able man, and a fair man."[24]

Even with Dirksen and Russell supporting Johnson's recommendations, LBJ knew that the outcome was too close to call. But he decided to go ahead anyway. He saw the potential gain as considerable and the possible loss as minimal. If he couldn't get Fortas and Thornberry approved, it would have little impact on the last months of his presidency. But if he could make Fortas Chief Justice and Thornberry an Associate Justice, it would strengthen the likelihood that the Court would sustain Great Society programs for the foreseeable future.

Johnson also felt a debt of gratitude to Fortas and wanted to reward one of his oldest and most loyal political friends. Fortas had not only made a large difference in the 1948 contested Senate race, which opened the way to Johnson's Senate, vice presidential, and presidential careers, but he had also been a principal and valued adviser on everything from the Dominican invasion to Great Society programs, labor disputes, the Detroit riots, anticrime legislation, and Vietnam. As Fortas biographer Laura Kalman puts it, "during the Johnson years, Fortas was part of the judicial branch and, as well, an unofficial member of the executive branch." According to a White House record, there were 145 LBJ-Fortas meetings between November 23, 1963, and July 2, 1968, and this did not include telephone calls.[25]

There was apparently nothing Fortas wouldn't do for Johnson, including crossing ethical lines. In 1966, after becoming a Justice, Fortas passed along Court deliberations about an illegal eavesdropping case, which might discredit Robert Kennedy. J. Edgar Hoover falsely claimed that in 1963, as Attorney General, Kennedy had authorized an electronic surveillance of a Washington lobbyist who was later convicted of fraud. When his appeal reached the High Court, the illegal wiretap was revealed, raising the possibility that Kennedy might have broken a law. According to an FBI memo, Fortas said that "the entire matter boiled down to a continuing fight for the presidency."

Though Fortas knew that revealing private discussions among the Court's members was a violation of judicial ethics, his loyalty to Johnson over that to his Court colleagues persuaded him to send the information to the White House. "If facts, as possessed by the FBI, concerning Kennedy's approval of wiretapping were made known to the general public it would serve to completely destroy Kennedy," Fortas said. Fortas, Kalman states, "would not pass up the opportunity to make Johnson's enemies his own."[26]

Because Johnson anticipated a tough Senate fight over Fortas and Thornberry, he immediately followed their nominations with a behind-the-scenes confirmation campaign. Califano says that, within three days of announcing his Court nominees, Johnson "assumed personal direction of every detail of the effort to secure confirmation of his friend Fortas." Seeing anti-Semitism behind much of the opposition, Johnson declared it bad for the country to have the first Jewish Chief Justice turned down. He predicted that the campaign against Fortas would unleash powerful anti-Semitic forces. He wanted someone to speak to Albert Jenner, the chair of the American Bar Association's committee on federal judicial nominations, to enlist his support against anti-Semitic influences.[27]

At the President's direction, White House aides lobbied everyone they could identify with any influence on the 100 members of the Upper House. Joe Califano, for example, talked to Henry Ford, who promised to "get to work on [Robert] Griffin" of Michigan, a principal organizer of the anti-Fortas forces. Ford also intended to talk to Governor George Romney about a statement of support. Paul J. Austin, the president of Coca Cola, thought he could deliver several senators.

Ed Weisl, Sr., was at work getting favorable newspaper editorials, while Washington attorney Lloyd Cutler had "numerous people talking to [Louisiana Congressman Hale] Boggs, [Senator Allen J.] Ellender [of Louisiana], Fulbright and Hill." Clark Clifford hoped to turn the DuPonts loose on the two Delaware senators. White House aide Ernest Goldstein had persuaded prominent Illinois Jews to thank Dirksen "for his support and keep him lined up on your side."[28]

Johnson also instructed Califano to line up black support for Fortas. Prominent black Republican attorney William Coleman was asked to assure that Massachusetts Republican Senator Edward Brooke would vote right. And Philadelphia federal judge Leon Higginbotham was contacted about getting black Pennsylvania attorneys to pressure Hugh Scott, their state's Republican senator.

Johnson's efforts were not enough to overcome a rising tide of opposition. Led by Griffin, eighteen senators responded to Johnson's nomination with a statement that the next President should appoint the next Chief Justice. Griffin now found a silent partner in Richard Russell, who promised that he and other southern Democrats would quietly work with the Republicans to block Fortas's appointment.[29]

On July 1, Russell had given Johnson direct notice that he no longer saw his commitment on Fortas and Thornberry as binding. Johnson's failure to act on the appointment of Alexander Lawrence as U.S. District Judge for the Southern District of Georgia provoked Russell's change. Though Johnson had explained the delay in the appointment, which had been pending since February, by saying that opposition to him made a thorough investigation of his qualifications advisable, Russell had concluded that Johnson intended to make Lawrence's appointment a condition of Fortas's confirmation.

"To be perfectly frank," he told the President, "even after so many years in the Senate, I was so naive I had not even suspected that this man's nomination was being withheld from the Senate due to the changes expected on the Supreme Court of the United States until after you sent in the nominations of Fortas and Thornberry. . . . This places me in the position, where, if I support your nominees for the Supreme Court, it will appear that I have done so out of my fears that you would not nominate Mr. Lawrence." He now considered himself "released from any statements that I may have made to you with respect to your nominations."[30]

Johnson was furious at Ramsey Clark for having held up Lawrence's appointment and having " 'destroyed one of the great friendships I've had with one of the great men that has ever served this country. I'm unhappy about it.' He said it much stronger than that, as a matter of fact," Larry Temple recalls.

Temple also says that Russell's premise "was just false. It was just a lie. . . . Russell was way off base. He was wrong. He was completely wrong." Johnson believed that an anti-Fortas southern senator or somebody else had sold Russell on the false connection. And though Johnson tried to assuage Russell by promptly moving on Lawrence's appointment and sending intermediaries to repair the damage, it was too late. Even a call from the President himself was not enough to change Russell's mind. In their telephone conversation, Johnson informed him of Lawrence's appointment and said that he would not lobby him or assume any commitment on his part to Fortas or Thornberry. Russell gave no indication that he would change his mind, and the long-standing Johnson-Russell friendship now largely came to an end.[31]

With Russell's departure from the Fortas-Thornberry camp, Johnson believed that his only hope of winning was to have quick hearings and a prompt vote on the nominations. He told Larry Temple: " 'We're going to be in trouble on this. . . . We've got to get this thing through, and we've got to get it through early, because if it drags out we're going to get beat. Dirksen will leave us.' " After Dirksen spoke out for the nominees, Califano was reassured. But Johnson thought it counted for little. " 'Just take my word for it,' " he said. " 'I know him. I know that Senate. If they get this thing drug out very long, we're going to get beat. . . . Ev Dirksen will leave us if we get this thing strung out very long.' " When the Committee purposely slowed the process, Johnson complained: " 'They're whipsawing us to death because they're dragging their feet. We've got to do something." But he was powerless to force a speedup.[32]

Fortas's decision to testify served the Committee's purposes. Precedent suggested that a sitting Justice nominated for the Chief's job not appear before the committee. It was "inappropriate" for him to discuss past Court decisions. But Fortas, who had considerable experience at congressional hearings and had performed "superbly well" in his 1965 appearance, thought it would be advantageous. Though he stated his intention to avoid discussing the Court's opinions or his votes, he nevertheless declared his pleasure at being able to appear and his readiness to address any concerns senators had.[33]

The committee hammered at Fortas on two themes. First, they wanted to know about his ties to the President, which may have compromised the independence of the Court or undermined the separation of the judicial and executive branches. Senator Griffin had preceded Fortas before the committee, where he recounted newspaper stories of Fortas's work for LBJ and called him a Johnson "crony." Fortas responded to specific questions about his role in recommending judges and making domestic and foreign policies by describing only a minor part in White House deliberations. Aside from Vietnam and limited work on the Detroit riots, he untruthfully asserted that he had no involvement in executive decisions.[34]

His active part in numerous White House discussions was an open secret. Fortas had boasted of knowing the secret entrances to the White House from the Executive Office Building and the Treasury, passages that shielded him from the eyes of the media. Colleagues and aides at the Court knew that Fortas had a special White House telephone line and that when the red light on his secretary's phone was lit, he was not to be interrupted.

Johnson and Fortas rationalized their collaboration by saying that "the history of this Republic is replete with shining examples of a close relationship between a President and a Justice of the Supreme Court—and the Republic has been the beneficiary." The White House compiled a list of fifteen Justices from John Jay, who had "offered George Washington the benefit of his wisdom on a variety of political problems," to Chief Justice Fred Vinson and Associate Justice Sherman Minton, advisers to Truman, as evidence that Fortas's actions were nothing new.

Yet Califano says that "Fortas's testimony was so misleading and deceptive that those of us who were aware of his relationship with Johnson winced with each news report of his appearance before the Senate committee. . . . Fortas was so consistently present," Califano adds, "and Johnson so often directed me to consult him that the Supreme Court Justice became part of the staff and his involvement so routine that early shock and concern over time faded, like Fortas himself, into the woodwork of the White House." Fortas's willingness in 1967–68 to discuss a pending case before the Court about the Pennsylvania Railroad merger and then write the Court's final opinion especially troubled Califano.[35]

Califano believes that liberal Senate supporters of Fortas did not realize until later just how vulnerable he was to the charge of cronyism. But in the summer of 1968 Texas Senator Ralph Yarborough and Alaska's Ernest Gruening agreed that Fortas's attempts to talk Gruening out of opposition to the Vietnam War "violated the separation of powers and the judicial code of ethics." A sitting Justice, Yarborough told a friend, had no "business phoning senators and trying to change their votes, statements, or positions on matters of great national policy." In addition, Griffin was able to score points against Fortas by pointing out that his statement on "full disclosure" of White House ties did not include his work on the State of the Union message and a legislative amendment.[36]

The committee also pressed the case against Fortas as a member of the "activist" Warren Court, which had been a judicial legislator on criminal and obscenity questions. Committee conservatives complained that the Court had coddled criminals, encouraged lawlessness, and destroyed community morals. Though Fortas's role in the obscenity decisions was anything but clear and the Court's judgments on the rights of criminals had strong defensible grounds, a self-imposed restriction against discussing Court decisions inhibited Fortas from any effective defense.

Larry Temple recalled that Fortas "was a very tormented man throughout this whole nomination process because he could not fight back." Fortas saw the committee's actions as an expression of "bitter, corrosive opposition to all that has been happening in the Court and the country: the racial progress, and the insistence upon increased regard for human rights and dignity in the field of criminal law."[37]

At the beginning of August, when Eastland told Johnson that Fortas would not be confirmed, the President considered withdrawing the nomination. But he felt that Abe would be able to emerge from the contest with his head high and a firmer hold on his Court seat if they forced a Senate vote against a southern filibuster in which Fortas at least won a majority.[38]

But the decision to continue the battle opened the way to more damaging attacks. After a summer recess, when the hearings resumed in September, the committee revealed that Fortas was teaching a seminar at American University and that his salary was being paid not by the University but wealthy former clients and other businessmen who might be interested parties in matters coming before the Court. Though Fortas had the freedom to recuse himself from such cases, his critics made much of the assertion that the arrangement at A.U. allowed wealthy supporters to subsidize Fortas's income. A $15,000 payment for nine weeks of teaching, which was about 40 percent of a Justice's salary, seemed excessive, especially since it was seven times the amount paid to any other summer seminar teacher at the University.[39]

Though he had quietly joined the Griffin opposition in July, Richard Russell now used the A.U. revelation to justify his vote against Fortas. The information that Fortas had accepted $15,000 for his teaching, and "the manner in which it was handled," Russell wrote the President, "make it impossible for me to support Justice Fortas." The matter raised "a very grave question of ethics and propriety."[40]

Though the Judiciary Committee endorsed Fortas's nomination by 11 to 6, his supporters could not break a filibuster on the Senate floor. As Johnson had predicted, Dirksen now abandoned Fortas to join his Republican colleagues in opposition. A vote to bring cloture on the filibuster failed by 45 to 43, well short of the required two-thirds. Having the small satisfaction of majority support Johnson wanted for him, Fortas asked the President to withdraw his nomination, which he did on October 1. If he had another four-year term, Johnson privately told a journalist, "the Fortas appointment would have been different." It was not the only time during the presidential campaign that Johnson had reflected on the advantages of another term.[41]

Vietnam: More Frustration

The start of secret talks in Paris at the end of June had sparked some hope that Hanoi might be willing to make peace. "Something is stirring on the other side," Rusk told the President on July 2. Johnson approved a fresh inquiry in a private meeting on what Hanoi "would do if we stop bombing." But the private discussions proved to be no more productive than the public ones. In mid-July, Rostow told the President that the negotiators were "absolutely hung up on the issue of a total bombing cessation; that is, the other side has refused to commit itself in any way to military de-escalation either to match our present bombing cutback or a total bombing cessation."

Rostow opposed a bombing halt without some promise of reciprocal deescalation. The level of infiltration and evidence of a planned major offensive in the weeks ahead foreclosed a gamble on an unreciprocated commitment to stop bombing. Such a move would forego "the 20% or so attrition we now impose on men and supplies moving south."

Despite the impasse, the Paris negotiators and Washington observers were not without hope. The North Vietnamese seemed eager to maintain contact, and during tea breaks there had been "some feeling out of general positions," which made it conceivable that Hanoi was now conferring "on next steps. In short," Rostow told Johnson, "while there is absolutely no solid progress to report, it still seems worthwhile to persist in the Paris effort."[42]

Maxwell Taylor thought such optimism misplaced. He accurately described Hanoi's preference for a stalemate. "It gives them time to rebuild and refit their forces in South Viet-Nam and to chip away at the GVN," Taylor told the President. "Likewise, it gives them time to study the reactions of the U.S. domestic front and to reflect on the probable consequences of presidential alternatives."[43]

Johnson now asked Clifford to visit Vietnam to find out whether a renewed offensive was imminent and whether U.S. forces would be better prepared than during Tet. More important, he wanted to know the current state of South Vietnam's military. "Could more of the ARVN be brought into I Corps so that the burden of conflict there could be more evenly shared?" he asked Clifford. He also gave renewed expression to the hope that "the ARVN effort can be better dramatized and their contribution to the war kept in the headlines." In short, if we could not reach a settlement with Hanoi, he had thoughts of getting out of the war anyway by shifting military responsibilities to Saigon.

Former Colonel John Paul Vann, currently a top civilian adviser on pacification, encouraged Johnson's hope with a report that where we had been "ridiculously optimistic in the past, we may be dangerously pessimistic now." Vann believed that we could "start to withdraw some U.S. forces in the reasonably near future 'without loss of overall military effectiveness—indeed, with some gain.' The Vietnamese are getting much better," Vann said, "and they will get better still if we start to reduce the size of our presence in Vietnam." Johnson's greatest hope in the closing phase of his presidency, he told Deputy Press Secretary Tom Johnson, was "to bring about a successful resolution of the conflict in Southeast Asia."[44]

During his trip to Vietnam, Clifford made Johnson's intention clear to Thieu and Ky. He "told the Vietnamese leaders that in the absence of visible progress the American public would simply not support the war effort much longer. If we could not achieve a settlement in Paris, we expected the South Vietnamese gradually to take over the war. Bunker was shocked at my bluntness," Clifford recalls, "but I was convinced that our gentle and dignified Ambassador had not made Thieu and Ky sufficiently aware of the degree of impatience and frustration felt by both the President and the American public.

Saigon's weakness was the major cause of our dilemma, and I saw no reason to indulge it."[45]

Between July 18 and 20, the President conferred with Clifford, Rusk, Bunker, Rostow, Thieu, and Ky in Honolulu. Clifford's assessment of conditions in Vietnam was discouraging. He believed it unlikely that the South Vietnamese could take over the fighting. They were poorly led, inadequately trained, and under-equipped. He declared it "impractical to replace any U.S. forces now in I Corps with further ARVN forces." Instead, he suggested equipping, training, and manning Regional Vietnamese army forces "as priority items so that U.S. forces may be gradually withdrawn from Vietnam." It would be a "long-range development." None of this would allow Washington to dramatize an increased ARVN role. Only an actual replacement of U.S. forces by South Vietnamese troops would solve the problem.[46]

During a private meeting with LBJ, Rusk, and Rostow, Clifford made his concerns more explicit. First, he emphasized that "we could not win the war." Second, he declared himself " 'absolutely certain' that the South Vietnamese did not want the war to end—not while they were protected by over 500,000 American troops and a 'golden flow of money.' . . . Thieu and Ky clearly feared the loss of American support the moment the war ended. The entire American-Vietnamese relationship was riddled with corruption." Third, Clifford urged Johnson to tell the Vietnamese that "we were going to make an all-out effort to settle the war in the next six months," and that whoever the next President might be, he would have a strong mandate to end American involvement in the fighting.

Though Rusk disagreed with Clifford's assessment and recommendations, Johnson, according to Clifford, was convinced. After the President had a private meeting with Thieu and Ky, he pulled Clifford aside to say that, "impressed with my three points, he had raised all of them with Thieu."

But Johnson's candor with the Vietnamese resolved nothing. Though Thieu stated a conviction that U.S. forces could begin a withdrawal by mid-1969, he made no actual commitment to replace U.S. forces with South Vietnamese units. Moreover, he pressed for an American promise not to stop bombing the North until all of Hanoi's troops had left the South. Nor would he agree to send a delegation to Paris as long as Hanoi insisted on having the NLF there as an equal partner. Clifford left the conference depressed, believing that we had gained nothing, "not even a vague acceptance of the need for greater flexibility in Paris."[47]

In a public communique and statement to the press, Johnson put the best possible face on the discussions. Washington and Saigon mutually deplored Hanoi's failure to respond meaningfully to peace overtures. They anticipated another North Vietnamese offensive and stood ready to combat it. The U.S. government had no intention of imposing a "coalition government" or any other form of government on South Vietnam. Saigon was eager for national reconciliation, with political participation open to anyone renouncing force and abiding by the country's new constitution.

Johnson emphasized the expanding role of the South Vietnamese in the fighting and declared it "pure, absolute tommyrot and fiction" that the United States was about to stop the bombing or pull out of Vietnam. Though both possibilities were very much on his agenda, Johnson, as he later acknowledged in his memoirs, believed that any indication of his inclination to quit bombing or bring the boys home "would give Hanoi the wrong signal." After their Tet defeat, it "would give them new encouragement."[48]

When he returned to Washington from the Honolulu meeting, Johnson was frustrated and angry. The North Vietnamese were showing no give; the South Vietnamese were little better; and the administration's principal foreign policymakers, Clifford and Rusk, couldn't agree on how to break the deadlock and achieve the goal Johnson wanted most for the end of his term: an acceptable peace agreement.

A number of administration officials, led by Clifford, thought the key to breaking the logjam was to stop bombing and see whether Hanoi responded. In June and July, assessments of bombing results strengthened the case for a unilateral halt. On June 21, Johnson received a memo from the "President's Science Advisory Committee on the Effectiveness of Air Strikes in North Vietnam and Laos." The panel concluded that the bombing "can only temporarily disrupt North Vietnam's and its communist suppliers' ability to maintain the flow of combat materiel necessary to support the war in South Vietnam."

Despite Wheeler's disagreement with the conclusion and "shortcomings in the available data," Clifford "believe[d] that the panel's general conclusion is probably valid. This finding is consistent with other bombing studies which have been made from time to time." Clifford shared the committee's view that " 'factors other than our air campaign in North Vietnam will largely determine the scale of the war in South Vietnam in the future.' "[49]

At the end of July, Assistant Secretary of Defense Paul Warnke echoed the point. In response to the report, Johnson had defended the bombing as an effective instrument for reducing the flow of supplies and men into South Vietnam by 25 percent. Warnke disputed the conclusion. He said that "all the evidence" showed that the bombing before March 31 and the more concentrated campaign since had not "been able significantly to reduce the infiltration of men and supplies from North Vietnam to South Vietnam." Infiltration levels depended not on bombing but on "the amount of effort exerted by the North Vietnamese." Infiltration in the first quarter of 1968 was estimated at more than twice what it had been in the first three months of 1967.[50]

Against this backdrop, Harriman, Vance, and Clifford urged the President to announce a bombing halt on the assumption that Hanoi would not take advantage of it. If this proved to be wrong, "we would resume the bombing." Johnson rejected the proposal as "mush" and said that "the enemy is using my own people as dupes." He wanted a report on "this new wave of demands to stop the bombing." He believed "the International Communists have a movement under way to get me to stop the bombing." He also complained that Rusk and Clifford were not making an effective case for the bombing in press conferences, telling Clifford that a description of the concentrated post–March 31 air raids as more effective than the earlier attacks was "a damned lie."[51]

On August 4, in a private meeting with the President, Clifford described the military realities and restated the wisdom of a bombing halt. It took only thirty tons a day for the North Vietnamese to supply the South. If they moved a hundred tons and we got twenty-five, they were still amply supplied. V.C. monthly recruitment was continuing at the same level as in 1967. Even with 7500 a month losses, enemy forces were continuing to increase. We "have tried for 3½ years to win militarily. [It] cannot be done," Clifford said. Because we were fighting a limited war, we could not get results "like W.W. I or II." The South Vietnamese had no interest in ending the war now. We needed to reduce the level of fighting through the Paris talks and to press Saigon into negotiations with Hanoi.[52]

Johnson rejected Clifford's recommendations. "I don't agree with a word that you have said," he replied. The latest reports from Paris stiffened his resolve to make a bombing halt dependent on North Vietnamese commitments to deescalate. During their third private meeting on August 4, Cyrus Vance reported, Hanoi's delegate demanded U.S. withdrawal from South Vietnam and recognition of the NLF as the "determining voice in the settlement of South Vietnamese affairs." On August 9, the Pentagon predicted "stepped-up Communist military activity" as a means of extracting concessions from the United States in the talks.

Despite Johnson's skepticism about the value of a bombing halt, he asked Clifford to discuss his ideas with Rusk and put them on paper. Like the President, Rusk saw no merit in Clifford's proposal. When the New York Times published a story about the Clifford-Rusk differences, Johnson told Clifford: "Every day I read something in the papers about deep policy differences between you and Dean. I am telling both of you that I want it stopped."[53]

As Clifford sensed, Johnson's differences with him were less than his comments suggested. But however strong his desire to stop the bombing and end the war, Johnson believed it a mistake to make this unreciprocated concession to the North Vietnamese. He feared it would do more to prolong than shorten the fighting.[54]

Mac Bundy now weighed in with the argument that the time to stop bombing had come, despite many years of thinking otherwise. His reasons were: the limited military value of the air attacks, the increased political pressure a bombing halt would put on Hanoi and Saigon to reach a settlement, the extent to which it would mirror American public sentiment, and the degree to which it would make it easier for the United States "to do those other things which are still necessary to protect our real achievements in Vietnam and in Southeast Asia."[55]

Johnson's reply, which Rostow drafted, categorically rejected Bundy's arguments. Johnson didn't think a bombing pause would affect Hanoi's decision for peace. He didn't think their stepped-up infiltration should be rewarded with a bombing halt. Besides, with the North Vietnamese apparently poised to launch a new offensive, he was convinced that a pause would increase U.S. losses. He could not "casually write off at this time as a minor matter the attrition we are imposing on the other side through our bombing." He told the Cabinet on August 22: "We want peace now worse than anyone in the world—but with honor, without retreat." Moreover, "61% of the people don't want to halt the bombing."[56]

LBJ's Last Campaign

After Robert Kennedy died, Johnson began thinking about whether he should reverse course and run again. Part of his decision to step down rested on the conviction that Kennedy would either take the nomination from him or would so badly damage him in an intraparty fight that he would lose the fall election. As Hubert Humphrey put it, Johnson had decided against running because "he knew he couldn't make it." Vietnam had been central to these developments, and so even with Kennedy's death, another LBJ bid for the presidency would still face public tensions over the war. If, of course, he managed to end the fighting before November or if it was sufficiently clear that peace was in the offing, a Johnson reelection was not farfetched. In fact, a Johnson candidacy might convince Hanoi to move sooner on negotiations rather than wait to see who the Democratic or Republican alternative would be.[57]

An initial spur to another Johnson bid came from the spring and early summer polling numbers. In April, 49 percent approved and only 40 percent now disapproved of Johnson's presidential performance. A 64 percent majority endorsed his March 31 decision to cut back on the bombing. In May, for the first time in five months, Johnson's job rating on Vietnam showed more Americans approving than disapproving—43 percent to 42 percent. Moreover, 59 percent of the country now saw the war as "morally justified."

Though presidential trial heats in June showed Humphrey with a small edge over Nixon, by July and August Nixon had taken a substantial lead. An August 21 poll put Nixon ahead of Humphrey by 16 points. Johnson, by contrast, beat Nixon by six points in a mid-July straw poll. If the Democrats were to hold on to the White House and sustain administration policies, Johnson seemed more likely than Humphrey to achieve this. One political newsletter predicted that Johnson, the "sole Democratic candidate able to beat Nixon," would win nomination in Chicago "by acclamation." Lou Harris believed that "while it would be a mistake to take his [LBJ's] current standing against Nixon as indicative of what would happen in the event of a draft at the Democratic National Convention, it is also a mistake to conclude that Lyndon Johnson has no political following in America."[58]

During July, Johnson acted as if he might run. He was concerned that the White House plan his public announcements more carefully and that the press office put out "two good news stories daily." Johnson wanted to structure his "weekly schedule for maximum press advantage."

Johnson was always eager to get the best possible publicity for himself, but this surge of pressure on his aides to burnish his image was partly a response to his doubts about Humphrey's candidacy. Newspaper columnists and Humphrey supporters were urging him to break with the President over the war, if he were to have any hope of being elected. It enraged Johnson. He also thought Hubert was being too soft in his bid for the nomination. To offset charges that he was steamrolling the convention, Humphrey agreed to concede some delegates to Gene McCarthy. Johnson told him: "The trouble with you, Hubert, is that you're just too damn good. Somebody comes along and kicks you in the face, and you pat their leg. I give them nothing."[59]

Humphrey wanted to give a speech in which he put some daylight between himself and Johnson on Vietnam. He hoped to convince "the large number of antiwar voters that he would somehow be more ready to compromise on Vietnam than the President." Humphrey hinted at the possibility that he would include the NLF in peace talks, a policy publicly opposed by the White House and the Saigon government. Clifford recalls hearing at this time that Humphrey "was considering a limited declaration of independence from the administration on the war."

Humphrey's proposed speech angered Johnson. In a conversation with the Vice President on July 25, after Hubert showed him a draft, Johnson said he "would be jeopardizing the lives of his sons-in-law and endangering the chances of peace. If I announced this, he'd destroy me for the presidency," Humphrey told an aide. Clifford says that Johnson now "branded Humphrey weak and 'disloyal.' "[60]

On July 24, Johnson told Clifford, Rusk, and Rostow that he wanted to discuss world affairs with Nixon. "When he gets the nomination he may prove to be more responsible than the Democrats. He says he is for our position in Vietnam. . . . The GOP may be of more help to us than the Democrats in the next few months," Johnson said.

When he met with Nixon on July 26, Nixon promised not to criticize Johnson as long as he did not "soften" his position on Vietnam or, in short, make concessions for peace that might give the election to the Democrats. Nixon said he "admired [the] way all of you have stood up through great fire. *This is a hard time.*" He compared Congress to a bowl of jelly, and vowed not "to advocate a bombing pause." Clifford summed up Nixon's response as offering "us his support in return for inflexibility in our negotiating position, and thereby freeze poor Hubert out in the cold. Humphrey wants to change the policy, but the President won't let him say so."[61]

Johnson's discomfort with Humphrey on Vietnam strengthened his impulse to run again. Humphrey tried to blunt Johnson's antagonism with assurances that he was solid on Vietnam. But Johnson didn't trust him, and laid plans to become the nominee. In August, he gave serious thought to attending the Democratic Convention. The ostensible reason was to be honored by his fellow Democrats on his sixtieth birthday, August 27. Numerous party leaders, including Democratic National Committee Chairman John Bailey, Convention Chairman Carl Albert, New Jersey Governor Richard Hughes, and Chicago Mayor Richard Daley, and members of the arrangements committee all urged him to attend. In the days before and at the start of the convention, Johnson had his speech writers preparing an address for delivery in Chicago.

It was to be a triumphant moment, but Mayor Daley and White House aide Jake Jacobsen believed it would be more than that. They foresaw a draft nomination if the President would just give the word. "That's what I am for," Daley said. "I'm for a draft, and I'll start it if there is any chance he will do it." White House aide Jim Jones reported: "Jake says this convention is going to draft the President if there is the slightest indication the draft will be accepted."[62]

Johnson found the possibility compelling. He sent White House aides Harry McPherson and Larry Levinson to Hollywood to help script a film about his presidency, and he insisted that a movie about Bobby Kennedy be shown on August 29, the day after the nominations, when Senator Ted Kennedy, who was giving indications of running, couldn't stampede the convention. Several of Johnson's principal aides—George Christian, Harry Middleton, and Larry Temple—acknowledge that he was interested in being drafted. Califano says that as the convention began, it was "apparent to Temple at the ranch and me back at the West Wing of the White House that LBJ hoped, and probably anticipated, that the convention delegates in Chicago would offer to draft him to be their party's candidate, a draft," Califano believes, "he intended to turn down but one that validated his presidency in the eyes of fellow Democrats."[63]

John Connally was Johnson's point man in Chicago. "What will throw a new wrinkle into history," Connally said in 1990, "is that I could make a very strong case that, notwithstanding his statement of withdrawal, he very much hoped he would be drafted by the convention in 1968." Connally and Warren Woodward, LBJ's former Senate aide, who was with Johnson during this time, say that he sent Marvin Watson to Chicago to "assess the possibility of that convention drafting LBJ.... I want to get it on the record," Connally said, "that even though there had been a withdrawal, Marvin Watson was up there for the specific purpose of talking to delegates at Mr. Johnson's [direction]."

"I personally was asked to go to meet with the governors of the southern delegations, with Buford Ellington, Farris Bryant, and that group, to see if they would support President Johnson in a draft movement in 1968," Connally adds. "Whether or not he really intended there to be a draft, who knows? Maybe it was a ploy to force Hubert Humphrey to support his Vietnam policy. But I believed it strongly enough that I went before all those southern governors and asked them if they would support Johnson in a draft, and they said, 'No way.'"[64]

Johnson's unpopularity also worked against him. On August 23, a Baltimore television station asked people to telephone with their opinions of whether Johnson should run again. Though hardly a scientific sample, as the station manager acknowledged, 63 percent of the 2300 calls were against another Johnson presidential campaign. Moreover, with the negotiations in Paris deadlocked, Johnson's approval rating plunged to 35 percent. As before his March 31 speech, 52 percent now disapproved of his performance.[65]

If the poll numbers weren't enough to discourage Johnson, events in Chicago destroyed all hope of a draft. On August 23, three days before the convention began, an advance guard of "Yippie" protestors convened at the Chicago civic center to nominate their candidate, a pig named "Pigasus." The next day, the Women's Strike for Peace picketed at the Hilton Hotel, Democratic party headquarters, without incident. That night a hippie bonfire demonstration in Lincoln Park provoked a clash with police. A larger gathering in the park the next day produced more violence punctuated by verbal abuse, stone throwing, and police charges with batons. On convention eve, the 25th, the violence escalated, with protestors hurling rocks and bottles at police cars and the cops indiscriminately attacking demonstrators. By the 28th and 29th, the third and fourth days of the convention, melees between police and demonstrators stretched from Grant Park to the Amphitheater, where the Democrats were meeting. The worst violence occurred at the Hilton, when enraged police beat protestors in front of and then inside the hotel. Though the public generally blamed the violence on radicals, later assessments described a police riot sanctioned by Mayor Daley's refusal to grant demonstration permits and instructions to police to protect the convention from "extremists."

The riots foreclosed a presidential visit, which seemed certain to provoke more violence and might jeopardize Johnson's safety. Until the evening of the 27th, George Christian says, Johnson "fantasiz[ed] that the convention would be such a mess that he would go in on a flying carpet and be acclaimed as the nominee." When he met with the press at 5:45 p.m. on the 27th, he described himself as undecided about going to Chicago. By later that evening, however, he had given up hope of attending and being drafted. Instead, he sent a message to the delegates, which Carl Albert read on the 28th, asking that his "name not be considered by the convention."[66]

Though unable to get the nomination, Johnson assured himself of party support on Vietnam. Publicly, he insisted that he had done nothing. In his press conference on the 27th, he emphasized his detachment from convention proceedings. In a post-convention conver-

sation with *Chicago Daily News* reporter Peter Lisagor, who asked
Johnson whether he had "rejected the first draft of the platform and
made them rewrite it," LBJ declared: "Nobody ever submitted to me
either the dove platform or the pro-administration platform. I think
it is obvious that Hanoi thought the course of the war could be
influenced by the platform. . . . Nobody showed me the platform," he
reiterated.[67]

It was an open secret that Johnson had fought for a platform
plank on Vietnam to his liking. On August 27 and September 2, the
New York Times and Drew Pearson, respectively, published accurate
accounts of how Johnson had influenced the platform committee to
do what he asked.

Johnson, in fact, micromanaged convention arrangements. He
vetoed a suggestion from Humphrey that the convention be moved
from Chicago to Miami, and he rejected all Humphrey's recommendations for convention officers. Johnson's control was so great, Humphrey biographer Carl Solberg says, he "dictated the city, the date,
the officers, the program of the convention. His control of its arrangements was so complete that Humphrey's son-in-law had to line up
every morning for tickets for members of the Humphrey family."
Johnson's denial of these facts strengthened public belief in a credibility gap.[68]

His active control of convention deliberations is a matter of record. On July 9, Hale Boggs, the platform committee's chairman, called
the White House to say that no liaison "has been set up for him to
work with on the Platform Committee." He wondered "if the President will visit with him on this to give him some direction. Shall I
set up appointment for Boggs later this week?" Jim Jones asked LBJ.
Johnson said, "Yes." Four days later, when Califano told Johnson that
he had talked to Wirtz and Humphrey about the platform and
planned to put together an initial draft, "unless you object," Johnson
replied: "Do nothing for God's sake on this." On July 29, after DNC
chairman Bailey asked to see Johnson about "several points concerning the Convention," including who would be co-chairmen of various
committees and candidate speaking appearances, someone scribbled
on the memo: "Better not get involved." Johnson's involvement was
to be as well hidden as possible.[69]

Johnson's control of the convention's platform committee began
when he assured that Boggs rather than Ed Muskie, Humphrey's
choice, become its chairman. Humphrey wanted a compromise plank
on Vietnam neither calling for an unreciprocated bombing halt nor
insisting on guarantees that Hanoi not take advantage of an end to
air raids. Humphrey proposed an endorsement of a bombing halt that

took "into account, most importantly, the risk to American troops as well as the response from Hanoi." There was a thin wisp of daylight between Johnson's hard line and Humphrey's so-called compromise.

But Johnson wanted no part of it. He had Rostow send a back-channel message to General Creighton Abrams in Saigon asking an assessment of the bombing and in particular whether it was a hedge against larger American losses. Abrams's reply on August 23 stressed the damage done to enemy trucks and supplies crossing into South Vietnam. As for an estimate of "additional casualties we would take if we stopped the bombing of North Vietnam," Abrams predicted "a several-fold increase in U.S. and allied casualties in the First Corps."[70]

Johnson called Boggs in Chicago to come to the White House on August 24 to confer on the Czech crisis. But it was really to arrange a briefing by Westmoreland, who read excerpts of Abrams's message to him. Boggs returned to Chicago armed with Abrams's assessment to counter the doves in what Jake Jacobsen said was going to be "the big fight—Vietnam." Humphrey's representatives persuaded the committee to accept the modest changes he suggested from what LBJ wanted in the plank. When Johnson saw the result he "hit the ceiling" and forced a fight that produced a plank to his liking by a 1,567 to 1,041 vote.

Clifford says that Johnson's victory "was a disaster for Humphrey. At a moment when he should have been pulling the party back together to prepare for the battle against Nixon, Humphrey had been bludgeoned into a position that had further split the party and given more evidence of his own weakness." It was the prelude to a fall campaign that would produce as much skulduggery and hidden actions as any in American history.[71]

The Fall Campaign: Who Was LBJ's Candidate?

As the fall campaign began, Johnson privately declared his backing for Humphrey. "I would like to see Humphrey elected and a Democratic Congress elected," he told Peter Lisagor on September 5. " 'Not all the Democrats have been supporters of mine, but it has been my experience that Democratic Congresses are better than Republican Congresses. I am going to keep my nose to the grindstone.' 'Any politicking?' " Lisagor asked. " 'Of course, I want to see Humphrey elected,' " Johnson replied. " 'I frankly don't know whether I would do him good or harm—that is his judgment. If he loses, we will get blamed for losing the election, you press fellows will see to that.' "[72]

On September 12, after Humphrey had announced his intention

to start bringing troops home in 1969, Johnson complained to his foreign policy advisers about Hubert's independence. When Clifford tried "to calm him down," Johnson declared: " 'Look, I *want* the Vice President to win.' ... I want the Democratic party to win. They are better for the country.' He paused, then added: 'Humphrey wants space. In his heart he is with us, but he thinks it is politically wise to keep space.' " Clifford was "encouraged" by Johnson's comments, but he "knew that, in fact, in his heart, Humphrey was against the war, but thought it still *necessary* to stick with the President."

Johnson was much more antagonistic to Humphrey than his remarks to Clifford indicated. He understood that Humphrey was under great pressure to break with him. To keep close tabs on the inner workings of Hubert's campaign, Johnson had the FBI tap Humphrey's phones. If Humphrey were going to come out against the war, Johnson wanted advance notice and a chance to dissuade him.[73]

Johnson was of two minds about Humphrey and Nixon. He understood that if Humphrey lost, it would largely be blamed on him and historians would interpret it as a repudiation of his administration. He pressed administration officials to defend his achievements during the campaign, as a way to make a record for historians. Johnson saw the up side of a Nixon victory as a Vietnam policy that would save him from the historical complaint that he was the only President to have lost a war. Whatever Johnson might say about Humphrey's political need for space and heartfelt commitment to his policy, he knew that Clifford was right: Humphrey would abandon the war the minute he took the oath of office.[74]

Developments during the rest of September deepened Johnson's ambivalence about both candidates. The election contest revolved around the war and who would be able to end American involvement. Johnson wanted Humphrey and Nixon to follow his lead. He saw any dissent from his position, especially on the bombing, as an inducement to Hanoi to concede nothing in the negotiations. He told Lisagor that "we are ... going to be trying to get Hanoi to move. If we can quiet down McCarthy and the others for a while, maybe we can have some moves."

To keep critics from challenging his bombing policy, Johnson asked Wheeler for a critical assessment of the Democratic party's minority plank against continued bombing. Wheeler replied that an unconditional end to bombing "would result in greatly increased casualties to American and free world forces." He also opposed reducing offensive operations in South Vietnam and the early withdrawal of U.S. troops as an invitation to the enemy to seize the initiative and increase American and South Vietnamese casualties.[75]

On September 15, though the North Vietnamese delegates in Paris privately agreed to negotiate after a bombing halt, Johnson refused to see this as a reliable commitment. Ambassador Chester Bowles in India, Mac Bundy, Clifford, Harriman, and George Ball urged Johnson to test their sincerity, but he refused. He cited the military's warnings about greater casualties and depicted an unconditional end to the attacks as a sign of weakness that would embolden Hanoi and lead to American defeat.

To discourage Humphrey from siding with anti-bombing proponents, Johnson gave an uncompromising defense of his Vietnam policy on September 10 before the annual American Legion convention in New Orleans. Harry McPherson told him that everyone he spoke to took his remarks "as a 'real blast at Humphrey.'" It was what Johnson wanted. He told Clifford on September 24 that he doubted Humphrey's ability to be President. He lacked the guts for the job. He would have respected him more if he "showed he had some balls."[76]

More than ever, Johnson believed it essential for the United States to maintain a hard line in Paris. "If we can stay for a few weeks with our present posture in Vietnam," he told an NSC meeting on September 4, "we can convince the North Vietnamese that they won't get a better deal if they wait. If we can hold where we are, a break will come from their side." He was certain that the domestic opposition to his policy came not from the bulk of the public but from radical groups that were "Communist infiltrated, Communist supported and aggravated."

He would not bend until and unless Hanoi agreed to respect the DMZ, quit its attacks on South Vietnamese cities, and welcome the Saigon government to the peace talks. Though the last was the most important, "all three [conditions] had to be satisfied" for a sustained bombing halt. Since we were unlikely to get a formal commitment to the first two conditions, Johnson wanted his foreign policy advisers to agree to resume bombing if the North Vietnamese violated either of these two provisions.[77]

Nixon's public stance on the war also troubled Johnson. In a series of sixty-second television spots, he did "a brilliant job," using "war footage in the best antiwar new-wave style. Punctuating the visual shock," Fred Panzer told the President, "was Nixon's calm voice promising to end the war and correct the mistakes of the old set of leaders who were responsible. Because this message was *not* part of a news show ... but *was* dropped into the regular entertainment schedule, [and] will be repeated and repeated—it is devastatingly effective. Like arsenic in small doses, you never know what hit you until you're dead." Panzer suggested that "Nixon be attacked for twisting to partisan purposes the sacrifices of American troops."[78]

Despite his clever attack on Johnson's war policy, Nixon took pains to neutralize him in the campaign. In August, after getting the nomination, he made informal remarks to a group of reporters, which got back to Johnson. He "hoped he shared with everybody in the room the view that the President and Vice President of the United States should have the respect of all citizens and he would do nothing to destroy that respect. He said anyone speaking on public policy in this country must be aware that he is being heard in Hanoi, and that voices heard in Hanoi are of major importance to our country. He said he thought the first priority of the Vietnam War now was not to stop the bombing, as some had suggested, but to stop the killing of American boys. This, he said, was the goal of all Americans."[79]

On September 15, the Reverend Billy Graham carried word to LBJ from Nixon that he would "1. . . . never embarrass him (President Johnson) after the election. I respect him as a man and as the President. He is the hardest working and most dedicated President in 140 years. 2. I want a working relationship with him. . . . And will seek his advice continually. 3. Want you (President Johnson) to go on special assignments after the election, perhaps to foreign countries. 4. I must point out some of the weaknesses and failures of the administration. But will never reflect on Mr. Johnson personally. 5. When Vietnam is settled he (Nixon) will give you (President Johnson) a major share of credit—because you . . . deserve it. 6. Will do everything to make you . . . a place in history because you deserve it."

Graham went over Nixon's comments point by point. Johnson "was not only appreciative but I sensed that he was touched by this gesture on Mr. Nixon's part. . . . The President asked me to read him these points twice. Then he took the paper from my hand and studied it for a moment but I could see he was having difficulty reading my writing. He then said, 'Let me give you answers point by point.' The substance of his answers were warm appreciation. He said, 'I intend to loyally support Mr. Humphrey but if Mr. Nixon becomes the President-elect, I will do all in my power to cooperate with him.' " When Nixon called Graham to learn LBJ's response, Graham reported "that the President was deeply appreciative of his generous gesture."[80]

Nixon's initiative influenced Johnson's view of him. During an NSC meeting on September 25, when an argument erupted between Clifford and Rusk over bombing and Rusk said, "if we stop the bombing with no conditions, many Democrats would vote for Nixon," Johnson sharply replied: "Mr. Nixon shouldn't enter into this in any way. The North Vietnamese feel the same about all of us." The problem, Johnson implied, was not with Nixon, who, like him, didn't want to give in to Hanoi, but with the doves, who were too ready to make unreciprocated concessions.[81]

A Humphrey decision to separate himself further from the President in a September 30 speech strengthened Johnson's reluctance to help him. With the polls showing Humphrey trailing Nixon by between eight and fifteen points, Hubert publicly declared on September 20 and 21, "I'm going to seek peace in every way possible, but only the President can do it now. Come January, it's a new ball game. Then I will make peace." In his speech, Humphrey promised that "as President, I would stop the bombing of North Vietnam as an acceptable risk for peace." Humphrey hedged his commitment by saying that before he acted he would expect Hanoi to restore the DMZ, and, if the North Vietnamese showed bad faith, he reserved the right to resume bombing.

Humphrey's qualifying phrases did not appease Johnson. When Hubert called to tell him he was giving the speech, Johnson said: "I gather you're not asking my advice." Humphrey said that was true, but explained that the speech would neither embarrass Johnson nor jeopardize the peace talks. Johnson replied "tartly and finally, 'Well, you're going to give the speech anyway. Thanks for calling, Hubert.' "

Johnson later made the dubious claim that the speech cost Humphrey the presidency. It made the South Vietnamese "extremely nervous and distrustful of the Johnson-Humphrey administration and of the entire Democratic party," Johnson asserted. It persuaded Saigon to do all it could to thwart the negotiations in Paris in the hope that Nixon would succeed Johnson and maintain a tough policy toward North Vietnam.[82]

Publicly, Johnson avoided indications of tensions between himself and Humphrey. Rostow recommended to the President that he respond to Humphrey's speech with a statement by George Christian that "as you know, we are keeping away from comments on statements made by the presidential candidates." Charles Murphy suggested that Christian tell the press that the White House sees Hubert's "speech as consistent with the administration's position." The conciliatory public posture belied Johnson's antagonism to Humphrey, whom he refused to help by taking advantage of an opportunity to hurt Nixon in the campaign.[83]

At this time, Elias P. Demetracopoulos, a Greek journalist, who had fled Athens in 1967 after a colonels' coup, provided the President with a chance to damage, if not sink, Nixon's campaign. Demetracopoulos had information that Greece's military dictators had funneled more than half a million dollars into the Nixon-Agnew campaign. He gave this information to Larry O'Brien, who had been head of the DNC and had become Humphrey's campaign manager. Demetracopoulos urged O'Brien to put this before Johnson and to tell him that CIA Director Richard Helms could confirm its accuracy. O'Brien took the story to the President, but Johnson, according to what O'Brien told Demetracopoulos, refused to act upon it. He would neither ask Helms to investigate the report nor consider leaking it to the press, should it prove to be true.

Johnson had not developed a sudden fastidiousness about leaking stories that could not be traced to the White House. He was a master of this game. Rather, three other considerations held him back from acting on the report. First, he had little use for Demetracopoulos. The administration, which was comfortable with Greece's anti-Communist military regime, viewed Demetracopoulos as a troublemaker, who stirred opposition to its foreign policy. The State Department had tried to bar him from the United States, but he had won political refuge from a regime that had him marked out as a public enemy.[84]

Second, Johnson was reluctant to do anything that might help Humphrey win. Nixon's approach to him through Graham had, at least for the moment, neutralized LBJ in the campaign. In addition, Humphrey's speech had so irritated Johnson that he refused to talk to him. When Jim Rowe asked the President to campaign in October for Humphrey in New Jersey, Texas, and key border states, Johnson refused. "You know that Nixon is following my policies more closely than Humphrey," he told Rowe.

Humphrey requested a meeting with LBJ to mend fences. Johnson agreed. But when Humphrey showed up a little late from a Maryland campaign rally, Johnson refused to see him. Humphrey was furious. He told his aide Ted Van Dyk: "That bastard Johnson. . . . I saw him sitting in his office. Jim Jones was standing across the doorway, and I said to him: 'You tell the President he can cram it up his ass.' I know Johnson heard me."[85]

Third and ironically, Johnson's distrust of Nixon made him reluctant to use Demetracopoulos's information now. Johnson feared that a Nixon presidency might bring efforts to indict him and his principal aides. Johnson kept saying to Larry Temple at this time that if Nixon becomes President, "he will indict all of us." Temple asked: "For what?" But Johnson would never say. Though Johnson refused to use Nixon's Greek connection against him during the campaign, he filed it away for possible future use. Four years later, after Nixon's second presidential campaign, Johnson found himself confronted by just such circumstances.[86]

During the first ten days of October, Johnson came under increasing pressure to help Humphrey. An analysis of eighteen southern, midwestern, and western states showed Nixon ahead in ten of them with 129 electoral votes, Humphrey favored in five with 76 electoral votes, and Alabama Governor George Wallace running as an independent leading in three states with 33 electors.

Lou Harris traced Humphrey's problems to the turmoil at the Democratic convention and questioned whether he could recover before Election Day. Nixon had "a well-oiled campaign going," Harris said. "By contrast, Humphrey is down in the polls, is 'plagued by disorder' on the road and seems to be unable to get his campaign rolling." Former California Governor Pat Brown, who was defeated by Ronald Reagan, said: "Hubert is making all the same mistakes I did in 1966. Too many cliches. Too much crap. He talks too long. When he opens up for questions, he gets in trouble." The Republicans also scored points against Humphrey by "charging him with 'hide-and-seek' " statements on Vietnam. Nixon refused to comment on the war, saying that he did not want to do anything that might "prejudice the Paris negotiations."[87]

In response to the bad news, O'Brien and Rowe urged the President to help Humphrey during the last critical weeks of the campaign. O'Brien wanted Johnson to remind voters of the progress made under his leadership and to help "bring together the disparate elements" that had supported his candidacy in 1964. He urged Johnson "to undertake an extensive speaking (with some fund-raising) tour in 14 cities around the country as well as all the major cities in Texas."

Rowe told Johnson that he "should be working harder" in the campaign. He wanted him to speak in Kentucky, Tennessee, and especially Texas. Johnson agreed to give a radio talk, but he used the precedent of Eisenhower's limited role in the 1960 campaign to avoid larger commitments. Ike had campaigned for only five days during the 1960 election, and that wasn't until the last twelve days of the contest.[88]

In addition to his reservations about helping Humphrey win, Johnson did not want to take time away from consideration of the Paris peace talks. Though the negotiations remained deadlocked at the beginning of October, every day brought additional developments, and he had some hope of a breakthrough before the election on November 5.

On October 2, Rusk discussed Vietnam with Gromyko, emphasizing the three conditions that the President saw as essential to a bombing halt and serious talks. "Under no circumstances must Harriman know of these exchanges," Rusk told Johnson; "he would resign." Rusk believed that the administration's unbending stance and willingness to negotiate through the Russians rather than in Paris would enrage the ambassador. In a conversation with Johnson at the White House on the following day, Vance described himself as optimistic that Hanoi's deteriorating military position and Saigon's improving military and political conditions would compel the North Vietnamese to settle the war sooner rather than later.[89]

On October 9, the White House received indications of a major shift by Hanoi. Early that morning, Rostow reported a talk between Lou Harris and a U.N. Soviet diplomat, Mikhail Kosharyan. The diplomat described Moscow as "now in a much better position to put pressure on North Vietnam." Kosharyan expressed fear of "a Nixon–Wallace–LeMay deal," which would expand the influence of "the military-industrial complex" in America and heighten international tensions. By contrast, he said the Soviets believed that Johnson wanted "rapprochement and peace."[90]

That afternoon, the North Vietnamese delegates said they were ready to discuss the presence of the GVN at the talks in a private conversation later that week. When they met on the 11th, the North Vietnamese wanted to know whether we would quit bombing in return for including Saigon at the peace table. The North Vietnamese are "hurting and thwarted as never before and might be ready for real give-and-take peace negotiations," Rostow told the President. Believing that Hanoi was militarily in retreat, that it had at least temporarily given up trying to topple Thieu's government, and that it preferred to negotiate with Johnson rather than Nixon, who they saw winning the presidency, Johnson and his advisers seized upon the chance to advance the talks.[91]

Before he would signal U.S. acceptance of the North Vietnamese proposal, however, Johnson assured that all his advisers and President Thieu agreed to support his response. In a series of cables and White House discussions between October 11 and 14, Johnson asked Bunker, Abrams, Rusk, Clifford, Helms, Wheeler, Taylor, the Joint Chiefs, and Thieu to review the North Vietnamese proposal from every possible angle. "He did not wish our understanding to be 'fuzzy,'" Johnson declared at one meeting. "It was necessary that there be clarity among us. If they [the North Vietnamese] take advantage and violate the 'facts of life' [the agreements on the DMZ and attacking cities] as we have stated them, what do we do?" he asked. "We resume bombing" was the response.

Johnson was assuring himself that if we tested Hanoi's "good faith" by a bombing halt and they then violated it, he would have everyone's backing to "resume [bombing] *without any limitations.*"

He also said: "I do not want to be the one to have it said about [me] that one man died tomorrow who could have been saved because of this plan." Though he was "scared" that nothing positive might come from a bombing halt, he said, "Let's try it." He believed this was his last chance to make peace.[92]

He also worried that he would "be charged with politics" or accused of trying "to influence the election. Nixon will be disappointed," he said. "Many people will call it a cheap political trick." Johnson quoted Senator George Smathers, who "said the word is out that we are making an effort to throw the election to Humphrey. He said Nixon had been told of it." Clifford doubted that it would influence the campaign and cited Mark Twain's comment: " 'When in doubt, do *right*.' " Johnson agreed with Twain's adage, but he was confident that Republicans and Democrats alike would see the start of serious peace talks as partly a political ploy to assure a Humphrey victory.[93]

Johnson didn't yet know the half of it. Bryce Harlow, a former member of Eisenhower's White House staff and a Nixon campaign adviser, had, in his words, "a double agent working in the White House. I knew about every meeting they held," Harlow said. "I knew who attended the meetings. I knew what their next move was going to be. I kept Nixon informed."

When White House discussions about a bombing halt began in October, Harlow warned Nixon, Johnson's "going to dump on you." Nixon at first refused to believe it, saying, "He promised me he would not. He has sworn he would not." But Harlow insisted it was about to happen. As soon as Johnson had the Joint Chiefs on board, he would announce a bombing halt that could throw the election to Humphrey. If it happened, Nixon asked what Harlow thought they should do. Harlow had no good response. He could only warn that "it could be disaster, total. But at any rate, be prepared," he urged Nixon. "It's going to happen."[94]

On October 16, Johnson used a conference call to inform Humphrey, Nixon, and Wallace of the developments in Paris. Johnson emphasized to Nixon that he was not being political—that he was ready to stop bombing because the North Vietnamese were agreeing to the conditions he had described to Nixon in earlier briefings. "Nixon," Bill Bundy says, "reaffirmed his support for a deal on that basis, and Mr. Johnson took him at his word." Yet the same day, as a demonstration of how little Nixon trusted Johnson, Dirksen declared in a speech that the "President will play politics with peace before [the] election."[95]

When the Paris negotiators disagreed over how quickly discussions would begin after the bombing halt, Nixon saw it as a way to counter Johnson's "political maneuver." The United States wanted the talks to start within twenty-four hours, but the North Vietnamese held out for a substantially longer delay. These differences lasted until October 27, when both sides agreed that the President would announce a bombing halt on October 31 and the talks would start on November 2.[96]

In the meantime, Nixon had begun a secret campaign to sidetrack the negotiations by discouraging South Vietnamese participation. Most everyone in the Johnson administration agreed that Saigon's presence was essential for any progress in the talks. If Nixon could convince Thieu that a Nixon peace arrangement would be better for South Vietnam than one made by Johnson, Saigon would undoubtedly wait until January 1969 before coming to the peace table.

Johnson got wind of this development on October 17. Leaks out of Saigon about the prospective bombing halt began, in Johnson's words, to "generate in the United States enormous confusion and pressure. They may very well interfere with the possibility of carrying forward a successful negotiation at a critical stage," LBJ asked Bunker to tell Thieu. Believing, however, that this was more the result of intrigue in South Vietnam than anything the Nixon campaign was doing, Johnson also advised Thieu that "we may not be able to give him as much notice should the negotiating process bring us to a moment of decision unless better communications security prevails."[97]

During the next ten days, Washington received growing evidence of Saigon's resistance to prompt involvement in the peace talks. On October 18, South Vietnamese Ambassador Bui Diem told Rostow that Thieu feared "that disastrous consequences would flow to the morale of the ARVN and South Vietnamese population if the NLF participates in the conference—especially if this participation is in the form of the NLF being a distinct entity from the DRV." Diem warned that such a development would destabilize South Vietnam, and Thieu believed "it would be very difficult for the GVN to participate in the conference under those circumstances." The following day, Rusk cabled Paris and Saigon: "We are deeply concerned about the rapid buildup in Saigon to the course of action we are following in Paris, which we thought we were taking with the agreement of the GVN."[98]

On October 22, Rostow advised Johnson that the South Vietnamese Ambassador in Paris was raising new concerns. He urged an agreement between the U.S. and Hanoi on all procedural points before negotiations began, and, in particular, he asked that there be two flags on our side of the table but only one on theirs. Thieu, Rostow added, was worried "that Hanoi won't talk to Saigon, only to the U.S." When Thieu publicly stated four conditions for entering into the Paris talks, Johnson instructed Bunker to tell Thieu that "it is impossible for the U.S. government to consult in confidence and security if the South Vietnamese government is going to conduct the discussions with us via the press." Business needed to proceed through "established channels."[99]

On October 23, a Soviet diplomat raised warning signals about the South Vietnamese. Moscow's U.N. Ambassador told Lou Harris that he could speak for "*our* side" and promise that there would be no rejection of the arrangement to talk, "but I can't say that we feel the same for *your* side. . . . We do not know that the government of South Vietnam will go *along* with any agreement. . . . We have done our work with North Vietnam. We're not sure you've done your work in *South Vietnam*."

CIA reports to Rusk and Rostow echoed the Soviet concern. They described Thieu as "worried and uncertain" about the peace talks. In conversations with visitors, he spoke repeatedly of Johnson's determination to use the Paris discussions to aid Humphrey's candidacy. Thieu said "that Johnson and Humphrey will be replaced and then Nixon could change the U.S. position."[100]

On October 25, Nixon assured Johnson that he saw the peace talks as untainted by domestic politics. In a public statement, Nixon rejected press speculation that this was "a cynical last-minute attempt by President Johnson to salvage the candidacy of Mr. Humphrey. This I do not believe." He described the President as dealing impartially with the candidates on Vietnam. Johnson had repeatedly made it clear to him "that he will not play politics with this war" and American lives. Nixon concluded by pledging his continuing support of the President and his Vietnam policy.

Nixon's public statement was also a way of drawing voter attention to rumors and speculation that the peace talks had become an extension of the presidential campaign. Nixon's statement enraged Johnson, who said it contained "ugly and unfair charges." Nixon was "a man who distorts the history of his time," Johnson said.[101]

It was not until October 29 that Nixon's interference in the negotiations registered fully on Johnson. That morning, Rostow told him about a conversation his brother Eugene Rostow had with Alexander Sachs, a New York banker. Someone "very close to Nixon" had told Sachs that Nixon would block the negotiations by inciting "Saigon to be difficult." The Rostows considered the information "explosive . . . on how certain Republicans may have inflamed the South

Vietnamese to behave as they have been behaving." Walt Rostow saw "no hard evidence that Mr. Nixon himself is involved," and it was unclear exactly what the Republicans were telling Bui Diem and what he was "drawing from what they have said."[102]

At an early morning meeting on October 29 with military and diplomatic advisers, Johnson reviewed developments in Paris since October 11 and confirmed his intention to stop the bombing. At 6:04 a.m. Rusk called to say that Thieu saw three days as too short a time for him to get a delegation to Paris. Johnson described Thieu's response as a delay spurred by Nixon. It "would rock the world if it were said [that] he [Thieu] was conniving with Republicans. Can you imagine what people would say if it were to be known that Hanoi has met all these conditions and then Nixon's conniving with them [the South Vietnamese] kept us from getting it?" Rostow then reported to the group on the information provided by his brother. "It all adds up," Johnson said. "Thieu delayed seeing Bunker."

Johnson ordered that the greatest possible pressure be applied to Thieu, but stated his determination to go ahead with the bombing halt regardless of Thieu's response. "We can't walk out, quit, split," the President said. "We have got to hold together. We must tell them [the South Vietnamese] we won't stand for them vetoing this. . . . We have attained what we worked for. We must not let this get away from us." Johnson believed that when Thieu realized what a mistake he was making, he would come around.[103]

Because it was unclear how explicit the Republicans were being in their advice to Saigon, Johnson instructed the FBI to use wiretaps and other surveillance means to ascertain the facts. Since this was a national security matter involving possible violations of the Neutrality Act and Foreign Agents Registration Act, no questions of illegal bugging arose.

Nevertheless, there were reasons for concern. Johnson asked that Anna Chennault, the widow of General Claire Chennault, a member of the China Lobby, and a co-chair of Republican Women for Nixon, be put under surveillance. She was carrying messages to the South Vietnamese, and Johnson wanted her watched and a tap put on her telephone. A White House aide warned of "real difficulties. She lives at Water Gate—a huge apartment," the aide advised. "She is constantly seeing Republicans—the risk of discovery is high." The White House should have passed the memo along to Nixon and John Mitchell for future reference.[104]

Johnson was convinced that Nixon knew and had even ordered the initiative to discourage Saigon from coming to the peace talks. He had good reason for his suspicions. In July 1968, John Mitchell,

Nixon's campaign manager, Bui Diem, and Anna Chennault had discussed Vietnam with Nixon in his New York apartment. Nixon had asked Chennault to be "his channel to Mr. Thieu via Bui Diem." On October 27, Chennault conveyed "via Bui Diem apparently authoritative Republican messages urging Mr. Thieu to abort or cripple the [Paris] deal by refusing to participate." Johnson learned about these messages on the 29th when U.S. intelligence passed intercepted South Vietnamese Embassy cables to the White House.[105]

Because he had some hope that Thieu could be brought to recognize his error, Johnson was willing to have Bunker take a final run at him on October 30–31. A strong message to Thieu "shook" but did not bend him. Thieu refused to participate in the Paris talks before the U.S. election.

Thieu's response incensed Clark Clifford, who declared at a White House meeting on the 30th that it was a "calculated, planned program to delay, to get through November 5.... This message is 'horseshit,'" Clifford said. "This message is thoroughly insulting." "After my outburst," as Clifford described it, the President instructed Rusk to tell Bunker that "we are ready to go tonight. We would stop the bombing on the following day, October 31, and schedule the first plenary meeting for Wednesday, November 6, the day after the election." Johnson said we would then have "a hundred and sixty-eight hours" before November 6 to persuade Saigon to send someone to Paris.[106]

On the 31st, Bunker spent nine hours in three meetings pressuring Thieu to send a delegation to the opening of the talks on the 6th. While Johnson waited on the Bunker-Thieu discussions, he held a final meeting with his foreign policy advisers before announcing the bombing halt. He said he would go on the air that evening at 8 p.m. and that bombing would stop the following morning at 8 a.m. "Negotiations will resume on November 6," he stated. If they [the South Vietnamese] are there, fine. If not, we will go on anyway.... Bunker and Thieu are meeting. We hope to issue a joint statement. But if not, we will go ahead with our own."

At 6:05 p.m. Johnson made a conference call to Humphrey, Nixon, and Wallace to inform them of his decision. He pointedly said: "Some old China hands are going around and implying to some of the embassies and some others that they might get a better deal out of somebody that was not involved in this. Now that's made it difficult and it's held up things a bit, and *I know that none of you candidates are aware of it or responsible for it.*"[107]

In his national address on the evening of the 31st, Johnson gave no hint of any political problem. He reaffirmed his nonpartisanship in taking this step and said that throughout the campaign "generally speaking . . . we have been able to present a united voice supporting our government and supporting our men in Vietnam."

Johnson, however, now had ample proof from taps, intercepted messages, and FBI observations of Chennault's movements that the Nixon campaign had discouraged Saigon from immediate participation in the talks. Moreover, it was clear from Thieu's actions in Saigon that he wished to do everything possible to help Nixon win. On November 1, after announcing a major speech to his Parliament, he refused to see Bunker. In his public address on November 2, Thieu stated his unwillingness to send anyone to Paris to begin negotiations with the NLF on November 6.[108]

The issue for Johnson in the second half of October was how far he should go to help Humphrey in the campaign and, more specifically, whether he should publicize Nixon's interference in the negotiations.

For all his irritation with Humphrey and doubts about his likely strength as a Chief Executive, Johnson was now even more antagonistic to Nixon. "I just remember a lot of talk about Anna Chennault and the machinations of . . . Machiavellian folks," Mrs. Johnson says, "and his [Lyndon's] very severe disappointment that any American should impede . . . any peace process." LBJ was in fact furious at Nixon for undermining the peace talks and prospects for a settlement before he ended his term in January. He told aides that Nixon was guilty of "treason." American boys were dying in the service of Nixon's political ambition. The fact that he would have to leave office with the war unsettled also greatly frustrated him.

Johnson's anger at Nixon partly stemmed from the belief that Thieu's refusal to participate at Paris raised public doubts about the negotiations. The White House thought that Thieu's action made Johnson's decision to halt bombing seem "dubious. . . . The political effect of the bombing halt has been reduced by 25 to 33 percent," an aide concluded.

Johnson's anger also extended to Thieu and Ky for believing that impeding the peace talks now would get South Vietnam a better deal from Nixon later. On November 5, when Thieu and Ky asked Johnson for reassurances about the talks, he sent word that he was "in no mood for reassurances to them." He wanted them to know that his "confidence in them is deeply shaken—very deeply shaken. If a viable relation is to be reestablished," Bunker was told, "it is their task—and they should set about it promptly—very promptly."[109]

Johnson's anger toward Nixon drew him back into the campaign.

Moreover, because a Humphrey victory would refute talk about a repudiation of Johnson, he warmed to the idea of helping beat Nixon. In the last three weeks of the campaign, Johnson aides encouraged him to see Humphrey's election serving his historical reputation. A Nixon presidency, Panzer told LBJ on October 17, would signal public eagerness for a change from Johnson and the Democrats. A vote for Nixon would express the belief that he and the Republicans could do better coping with or even possibly resolving current difficulties over Vietnam, lawlessness, and inflation.

With Humphrey gaining ground in the last days of the campaign, Johnson thought a push for him might make a difference. Ben Wattenberg urged the President to "go out and 'press the flesh'.... You would vastly outdraw either Nixon or Humphrey, the crowds would be more enthusiastic and it would graphically give the lie to the canard that Johnson and the Johnson record are a drag on Democrats." The Humphrey image is improving, Panzer told the President on October 23. "Fewer people now disqualify him because 'he was too close to LBJ.' "[110]

With his approval rating up to 45 percent and the prospect of helping Humphrey, Johnson now agreed to do some campaigning. On the two Sundays before the election he gave radio and television talks. Assured by the FBI that he would face no disruptive demonstrations, he campaigned in Kentucky and West Virginia on October 26. The following day he attended a DNC luncheon in New York, where he gave what columnist Jimmy Breslin described as "probably the best speech anybody in the room can remember him making. He waved his fist, his voice thundered and he said he did not like Richard Nixon and he really did not like George Wallace.... He had the audience standing and cheering a couple of times.... In New York, on his way to retirement," Breslin said, "Lyndon Johnson still was the best looking campaigner we've seen all fall."

On November 3, he joined Humphrey at a rally in the Houston Astrodome and broadcast a taped television talk from the White House. His Astrodome speech was a valedictory on his own career. He described the stakes in the election as nothing less than the fundamental way the country goes about doing its public business. He reminded the Texas audience of the Democratic party's role in bringing the South into the mainstream of the country's economic and political life. Leaders like Sam Rayburn, Franklin Roosevelt, and now Hubert Humphrey understood that "only with union—only with real union—could the South 'rise again'—as a vigorous, progressive part of America." Humphrey, Johnson asserted, was the one best able to carry forward this tradition. So, "for the sake of our American union, this man—Hubert Humphrey—should, and must, become the 37th President of the United States."[111]

Nixon's cynical manipulation of the peace talks gave LBJ ammunition to shift the balance to Hubert's side. Appreciating that such a revelation could precipitate a constitutional crisis, Johnson consulted Rusk, Clifford, and Rostow. Because there was no direct evidence of Nixon's involvement and because they hoped it might be possible to convince Thieu to join the talks on November 6, Johnson called Everett Dirksen on the evening of November 2 to say that "we don't want this thing to blow up."[112]

Bryce Harlow remembers Johnson's remarks to Dirksen as more threatening. He said that "Nixon and/or his troops were in direct dealings with the South Vietnamese government, and were telling them not to go along with the Johnson peace deal for political reasons, and that if you didn't cease and desist instantly or do something, that he was going to dump all over him [Nixon]. . . . He was mad as all get-out."

Harlow passed the message from Dirksen to Nixon. He told him: "You've got to talk to LBJ. Someone has told him that you're dumping all over the South Vietnamese to keep them from doing something about peace and he's just about to believe it. If you don't let him know quickly that it's not so, then he's going to dump. . . . Ev is just beside himself. He says that Lyndon is simply enraged and we ought to do something." Nixon called George Smathers to say that "he understands the President is ready to blast him for allegedly collaborating with [Texas Republican Senator John] Tower and Chennault to slow the peace talks. Nixon says there is not any truth at all in this allegation. Nixon says there has been no contact at all," Smathers reported to LBJ.

On November 3, Nixon called Johnson directly and said: "There was absolutely no truth in it, as far as he knew." According to a later story in the *Sunday (London) Times*, "Nixon was able to convince him [LBJ] that her [Chennault's] activities had not been licensed by him or his staff. . . . When he finally hung up, Mr. Nixon and his friends collapsed with laugher. It was partly in sheer relief that their victory had not been taken from them at the eleventh hour." Asked whether he was convinced that Nixon's involvement "was not true," Harlow replied: "No, I'm not convinced that it was not true. It was too tempting a target. I wouldn't be a bit surprised if there were some shenanigans going on. . . . But at any rate, Nixon told him no and Johnson put down his pistol, except Johnson probably didn't believe it." Nixon "categorically denied any connection or knowledge," Bill Bundy says, but it is "almost certainly a lie in light of later disclosures." In 1997, Chennault acknowledged that Nixon, Mitchell, and Tower knew everything. "I was constantly in touch with Mitchell and Nixon," she said.[113]

On November 4, Johnson had an opportunity to publicize Nixon's unseemly part in the Paris talks. Saville Davis, a reporter for the *Christian Science Monitor*, asked Rostow to comment on a dispatch from the paper's Saigon correspondent about "political encouragement from the Richard Nixon camp" as "a significant factor in the last-minute decision of President Thieu's refusal to send a delegation to the Paris Peace talks—at least until the American presidential election is over." LBJ instructed a spokesman to say: "I'm not going to get into this kind of thing in any way, shape or form." Since they were unable to get confirmation of the allegations, Davis said they would not print the story in the form in which it was filed, but would report that Thieu had decided to hold out on his own until after the election.[114]

Johnson saw several reasons to shield the story from public view. Should Nixon win the election, accusations that he had manipulated foreign negotiations as a private citizen would have opened him to possible indictment and prosecution. Such charges against a President-elect would have precipitated an unprecedented constitutional crisis. A Nixon presidency would have begun under a terrible cloud and made it unlikely that he could function effectively in office. And even if he were exonerated, it would have left him as a weakened Chief with diminished capacity to end the Vietnam War and make foreign policy. Another consideration for LBJ was the certainty that Nixon would have seen the press story as originating at the White House. As President, he would have done all he could to make life difficult for Johnson and administration officials after January 1969.[115]

On November 1, Johnson instructed Bill Bundy to brief Humphrey on the Nixon-Chennault pressure on Thieu. Since there was no direct evidence of Nixon's involvement, Humphrey believed it unwise to leak the story or take it directly to the press. Besides, Humphrey told his aides, it would be "difficult to explain how we knew about what she had done." On November 3, when he received news that Thieu would not bend to White House pressure, Humphrey pounded a table and shouted: "I'll be damned if I'm going to let the China Lobby of all people steal the election from me." In the heat of the moment he dictated a press statement declaring that "As President I would sever all relations with the South Vietnamese and leave them on their own." After he cooled down, he decided to say that "if the Vietnamese do not come to the conference table as promised, the United States should go on without them."[116]

Some aides now pressed Humphrey to publicize the story as a way to gain an edge on Nixon in the last hours of an evenly divided campaign. Others warned that such a last-minute revelation would be seen as cynical politics and would produce a backlash that could cost Humphrey the election. With still no firm evidence to link Nixon to Chennault's actions, Humphrey decided against provoking a national crisis for the sake of an electoral gain. Humphrey aide Ted Van Dyk later said: " "Ninety-nine out of a hundred men with the presidency at stake would have had no inhibitions—they would have demagogued it." Writing about the election a year later, the journalist Theodore White described Humphrey's restraint as an uncommon act of political decency.[117]

On Election Day Humphrey fell short of Nixon by less than .01 percent of the popular vote, though he lost the electoral college by 301 to 191. As he himself said later, his defeat was not the result of any specific action but the loss of "some of my personal identity and personal forcefulness. . . . It would have been better that I stood my ground and remembered that I was fighting for the highest office in the land. I ought not to have let a man who was going to be a former President dictate my future." It was a sound assessment. The defeat belonged as much to Lyndon Johnson as it did to Hubert Humphrey.[118]

Final Days

On November 22, UPI journalist Helen Thomas interviewed the President about his achievements, remaining days in office, and postpresidential plans. He spoke enthusiastically about the domestic and international accomplishments of his administration but spent more time describing his frustrations and regrets—particularly having had to fight in Vietnam, not having been able to do as much as he would have liked for the cities and the poor, and the terrible problems he had had with the media, newspapers, and television. He thought he might have "made a mistake of trying to go too far too fast, trying to do too much too soon, trying to correct the evils that have grown up over a century and to remake America overnight."

He thought "our most tragic error was our inability to establish a rapport and a confidence with press and television, the communication media." He attributed some of these problems to the bias of easterners against Texans, "toward anyone that comes from my area." He said he "never really could visualize the intensity of it, the duration of it, and the complete unanimity of it." He acknowledged some failure on his part to be an effective communicator, but he was unrelenting about press bias against him. He didn't think the *New York Times* and *Washington Post* had been objective, and the news magazines and television networks had been no better. He complained of the "ugly things" said about him and his family. It was as if the media felt they had "a privilege ... to abuse and harass and really handicap our leaders, our Presidents."

It was a surprising complaint from someone who had cut as many corners as LBJ. He knew that exposing political manipulation was part of the media's work, and given his manipulativeness, which he saw as the successful politician's stock in trade, he was fair game. He also understood that tension between Presidents and the press was a traditional aspect of the country's governmental system. But three weeks after Humphrey's defeat, which he saw as a repudiation of himself, he was venting his anger against journalists whom he thought had been principal contributors to his political demise.

The interview with Thomas suggests that he saw himself as a misunderstood and rejected leader who was given little credit for presidential gains. "I know we're leaving office pretty well repudiated," speech-writer Bob Hardesty remembers him telling aides. Johnson told Thomas: "I was talking to a group of leading educators last night. We were discussing the Housing Act of this year, which I think was one of the ten greatest bills that the Congress has passed in 188 years. I found that none of them really knew anything about it. Even the people in my own household didn't know it had passed.... That bill involved 26 million homes. There is nothing like it in our history of housing. But I didn't get it over."[119]

Characteristically, his response to feeling defeated and ignored was to work harder to succeed—to try in the last weeks of his term to make some striking gains. He saw a key to this in good relations with Nixon's new administration. He intended to do all he could to help his successor, he told Thomas.[120]

Johnson meant what he said. A White House meeting with Nixon on November 11 had been entirely cordial. Rusk, Clifford, and Wheeler briefed the President-elect on Vietnam and the Nuclear Nonproliferation Treaty (NPT). Nixon said he would do nothing on Vietnam unless "the President and Secretary of State thought it would be helpful.... We must be a united front," Nixon declared. "There must be a conviction there will be a continuation of policy after January 20 in both Saigon and Hanoi." Clifford pressed the case for "South Vietnam to appear in Paris. We need to resolve this uncertainty," he said. "We need to do everything we can do to get South Vietnam to the table." When Rusk urged Senate action on NPT,

Nixon declared himself "for the treaty, and willing to support it if Johnson called a special congressional session." That evening, Bryce Harlow called LBJ aide Jim Jones to say "how 'desperately nice all of us were and how helpful' we were to the Nixon staff. Bryce also mentioned that Nixon had commented how very helpful and forthright the President was to Nixon."[121]

Clifford remembers the contrasting styles of the two men. Nixon was cautious, polite, deferential, measuring every phrase, calculating every sentence. "Where Johnson liked to obscure his strategy with a stream of Texas stories and rhetoric, Nixon was self-controlled, and conveyed the impression of a man weighing every word. But one could easily overlook Nixon's skill with words, because he left such a strong impression of physical awkwardness."[122]

Johnson and Nixon spoke and met again before the transition on January 20. And though relations between the staffs remained correct, and even cordial between the President and the President-elect, Nixon proved much less forthcoming than Johnson hoped he would be. On November 11, for example, after their private meeting, Nixon told the press that current administration policies toward Vietnam, the Middle East, and the Soviet Union would "be carried forward by the next administration." But Nixon soon had second thoughts and announced that there would have to be "prior consultation and prior agreement" if there were to be continuity in policy. "Surprised" by Nixon's declaration, Johnson told the press that until January 20 only he and his advisers would make foreign policy.[123]

Johnson had some hope that Nixon might let him reappoint Arthur Goldberg to the Court to succeed Warren as Chief Justice. Drew Pearson and LBJ discussed this possibility after Nixon's election. "While you can't say so," Pearson wrote Johnson on November 18, referring to the Chennault issue, "you have been extremely cooperative with the incoming President-elect—more so than any previous that I know of—and he owes you more than any previous President-elect." Without "disclosing anything about our personal talk," Pearson said he was "trying to get some of the big Jewish contributors to Nixon to do a little plowing of the political soil for Arthur." Pearson said his action was "prompted by my fervent desire to see the great accomplishments of your administration continued."

In his conversation with Thomas on the 22nd, Johnson expressed some hope that he might yet be able to name Warren's replacement. There is no evidence that LBJ raised the matter with Nixon, but, however warm the relationship, it is inconceivable that Nixon would have given away the chance to appoint a new Chief Justice to the Court.[124]

Nixon also equivocated about supporting Johnson's recommendations on extending the tax surcharge or calling a special session to ratify the NPT. Johnson believed that a year's extension on the 10 percent tax rise would assure a credible budget for fiscal 1970 and a small budget surplus that was "needed for a stable economy." During the campaign, Nixon had stated his opposition to keeping the tax surcharge, "once the war is ended." Despite pressure from Johnson after November 5 to endorse a one-year surcharge extension, Nixon refused to make a commitment. As a consequence, Johnson hesitated to include such a request in his final budget recommendations. Only when Nixon gave him a private commitment to make the surtax part of his budget did Johnson recommend a year's extension. He now felt free to describe "an immediate lowering of taxes . . . [as] irresponsible." All the experts agreed, Johnson said, "that this fiscal restraint is essential to safeguard the purchasing power of the dollar and its strength throughout the world."[125]

Though Nixon had promised in their November 11 conversation to help Johnson with the NPT, he reneged at the end of the month. Informed that Republican senators were unenthusiastic about ratifying the treaty so soon after the Soviets had invaded Czechoslovakia, Nixon refused to endorse a special congressional session. On November 27, when reporters asked Ron Ziegler, Nixon's press secretary, whether Nixon considered it "an inopportune time to ratify the treaty," Ziegler said that nothing had occurred to change that position. Privately, Nixon sent word to Johnson that "he could do no more than leave responsibility with the President." He "will not express hope of ratification in a special session."[126]

Johnson saw Nixon's refusal to commit himself to NPT approval as a blow to making some last-minute gains in Soviet-American relations. In September, after the aborted announcement of a U.S.-Soviet summit, the two sides began talking about a presidential visit to Moscow before the end of 1968. Moscow seemed eager "to revive the 'rapprochement' track," Rostow told Johnson in October, "because they feel that if there is no continuity it will get closed down for a whole year."

Johnson and Kosygin were both eager to discuss a strategic arms limitation agreement. In mid-November, during a lunch Dobrynin initiated with Rostow, he said, "Moscow is clearly ready to go—and eager—if you can work it out. Their reasons are quite similar to our own: to create a good backdrop for the NPT in January; to keep the momentum of the work on missiles going into the next administration; and, therefore, to avoid a long delay in both the NPT and the missile affairs.... The heart of the matter," Rostow said, "is ... in persuading Nixon that this is the right course."[127]

At the end of November, Johnson still wanted a meeting but worried that strategic arms talks would stall without ratification of the NPT. At the beginning of December, ABC news reported that Johnson would be the first President to confer in the Kremlin. The report was premature. On December 9, a back-channel message from the President to the U.S. Embassy in Moscow described "the whole government" as in favor of missile talks. The failure to meet could mean a loss of "time, momentum, and unity" toward an arms control agreement. But on the 11th, Ambassador Thompson reported Dobrynin's observation "that if the President decided not to go ahead with the meeting, that would be understood in Moscow and there would be no hard feelings." Johnson scribbled on the bottom of the message: "I'm ready—are they?" Later that day Rostow told the President that "every normal argument is for leaving it to Nixon. And that may be the correct course. But it may also be a decision we shall regret more than any other in the years ahead." Rostow urged a last assessment "before abandoning the concept finally." Johnson noted on Rostow's memo: "I agree."[128]

The meeting never occurred. "Everything we learned," Johnson later said, "indicated that they [the Soviets] were not" ready to meet. "I believed the Soviet leaders had been persuaded that it made more sense for them to deal with the incoming administration. I had a strong feeling that they were encouraged in that view by people who were very close to the Nixon camp." Clifford says that "near the end of December, President Johnson learned, rather bitterly, that Nixon had secretly told the Russians he was opposed to a Johnson-Kosygin meeting." Johnson believed that the failure to meet delayed the onset of strategic arms talks by a year.[129]

Johnson's growing irritation with Nixon registered in an exchange over a task force report on government reorganization. When the Nixon transition team asked for a copy of the report at the end of November, Johnson said in response: "Hell no. And tell him [Frank Lincoln, Nixon's transition representative] I'm not going to publish my wife's love letters either."[130]

Though Nixon's uncooperativeness crimped foreign policy advances, Johnson had the satisfaction of seeing the North Koreans free the *Pueblo* crew in December, and the Apollo moon program make notable gains in October and December: Astronauts successfully tested Apollos VII and VIII in flights that seemed to assure the decade-long goal of landing a man on the moon.[131]

Vietnam, above all, consumed the energies of Johnson during

the final days. It was the focus of his November 11 discussions with Nixon and was at the center of most other postelection meetings. The goal was to get Saigon to the Paris talks. The South Vietnamese were warned that Americans opposed a delay in negotiations. But Johnson believed that without pressure from Nixon the South Vietnamese would stay on the sidelines until January.

Rostow and Rusk drafted a Nixon letter to Thieu, which urged him "quickly to resolve whatever problems may remain in getting your delegation to Paris and finding ways, in collaboration with the United States, to come to grips promptly with the substantive issues on which a peace settlement depends." Joe Alsop was enlisted in the cause, telling Bui Diem "that a failure to get a Saigon delegation to Paris promptly will blow all Saigon's supporters out of the water— including himself." Clifford held a press conference in which he denounced Saigon's foot-dragging and urged the President to proceed with the talks regardless of what the South Vietnamese did.[132]

By the middle of November, there were signs that Thieu would soon send a delegation to Paris. But as late as November 19, LBJ described Thieu as "intransigent" and told him that "he was dealing with a more friendly President now than he would be in the future." Clifford complained the following day that "we are getting a runaround in Saigon. . . . We cannot agree to what they are insisting on. We have a perfect right to go on with the talks." Only on November 26, after Nixon sent what LBJ privately called "a strong word" to Saigon, did they publicly agree to go to Paris.

But even then, Thieu delayed sending representatives until December 8, and, when they got there, they argued about procedural questions, which delayed the start of substantive discussions until Nixon took office. On January 7, LBJ warned Thieu of "the dangerous implications that I see developing from the situation in Paris. . . . A continued stalemate on present lines can only have most serious effects on basic American public support for our whole effort to assist your country to preserve its independence." Johnson's pressure, in one of his favorite adages, was a case of "pissing into the wind." His inability to influence the outcome of the talks in the last days of his administration was a metaphor for the frustration he had suffered over Vietnam throughout the five years and two months of his presidential term.[133]

Despite the disappointments over Vietnam and the outcome in the November election, Johnson had no intention of leaving office with any sign of defeat. Though he had considered making his last State of the Union message only a written document, he decided instead to adhere to recent custom and deliver it in person as a fare-

well address. The speech was a celebration of not simply his administration with its landmark domestic reforms and eight years of
economic growth but a paean to the compassion and decency of a
great nation devoted to eliminating poverty and assuring equal justice
and opportunity for all.

He freely admitted that his decision to come in person before
Congress was partly sentimental, partly a chance to bid farewell to
people and an institution he loved. The representatives and senators
reciprocated the feeling with five minutes of applause as he entered
the House Chamber and shouts, handshakes, tears, and a rendering
of "Auld Lang Syne" as he left.

"Now, it is time to leave," Lyndon Johnson ended his address.
"I hope it may be said a hundred years from now, that by working
together we helped to make our country more just, more just for all
of its people, as well as to insure and guarantee the blessings of liberty
for all of our posterity.

"That is what I hope. But I believe that at least it will be said
that we tried."[134]

Johnson's last day in the White House is indelibly printed on
the memories of his aides. The last evening the President and Mrs.
Johnson hosted a party for their staffs. "I would think that the last
night they were going to spend in the White House would be of such
significance to them that they might want to have the Cabinet in—
key leaders of Congress, or just have their family," Larry Temple
says. Instead, they had "a relatively small, very, very nice buffet–
cocktail party for the staff" in the mansion on the second floor of the
White House.

Temple recalls that Johnson that night "was kind of like a yo-
yo, kind of back and forth. He was in great form, and then he'd be
quiet awhile—and he'd look very sad and very unhappy; and then
he'd get back into it with his loud, booming voice, telling some story
with all the motions that he puts into a story. . . . The only sad thing
was they struck up 'Hello Dolly,' and everybody on the staff sang the
'Hello Lyndon' song that brought lots of tears to lots of eyes, not the
least of whom was the President."[135]

"The final evening party was a happy event," Joe Califano says.
"We shared a sense of relief that it was over and a sense of achievement. . . . All of us knew that we'd been part of a monumental social
revolution." Califano remembers the President as "in good spirits,
relieved, mingling happily with his staff, teasing many of us, recalling
the good times, the funny gaffes, eating in his favorite chair near the
dining-room entrance."

Amid the reminiscences and jovial teasing Johnson "had some

rueful comments" and gave Califano some personal advice. The President, who had repeatedly said unkind things about William Fulbright for his opposition on civil rights and Vietnam, had second thoughts about their relationship. Maybe he had personalized their differences too much, Johnson told Califano. Instead of complaining that he was a "revolving son-of-a-bitch," that is, "someone who is a son-of-a-bitch any way you look at him," LBJ thought we should have "talked to him more, had him over here more, found some things to agree with him on. We never should have let the fight become so personal."

Johnson also counseled Califano to watch out for Nixon. "It's not enough for Nixon to win," Johnson said. "He's going to have to put some people in jail." Johnson suggested that Califano pay an additional five hundred dollars above what he owed in federal taxes each year as insurance against an investigation from Nixon's IRS. He also warned Califano against jealous people. "Jealousy and sex drive people to do more damn mean and crazy things than anything else," he said.[136]

January 20 was a whirlwind of activity. "You wouldn't have known that the President was behaving any differently that day than almost any other day," Tom Johnson says. "He picks up the phone and expects the staff to be there." He gave medals of freedom to Clark Clifford, Dean Rusk, Walt Rostow, Arthur Krim, and the journalist William S. White. And in his last official act before attending Nixon's inaugural, he signed five proclamations adding lands to the national park system. The last of these, which was a kind of valedictory on the arc of his whole public career, established a "Franklin Delano Roosevelt Memorial Park."[137]

After the transfer of power at the Capitol, the Cliffords hosted a lunch for the Johnsons at their Georgetown home. To Lyndon's satisfaction, the front lawn "was jam-packed with people—little boys up the apple trees, babies in arms, high school and college youngsters carrying signs—'WE'LL NEVER FORGET YOU, LBJ,' 'YOU DID A GOOD JOB,' 'WE STILL LOVE YOU, LYNDON,' 'LBJ, YOU WERE GOOD FOR THE U.S.A.'" Lady Bird remembered the occasion as "one of the most significant and dear parties we shall ever attend." Most of the Cabinet and many old friends crowded into the Cliffords' home for the farewell, which was punctuated by warm words of praise and tears of relief and sadness.

And then there was the drive and helicopter ride to Andrews Air Force Base for the trip home to Texas. Many of the people who had served the Johnsons over the years were there to say goodbye. And to Johnson's surprise the Texas Republican Congressman George

Bush and his wife Barbara were in the crowd. Asked why he was there to see the President off, Bush replied: "He has been a fine President and invariably courteous and fair to me and my people, and I thought that I belonged here to show in a small way how much I have appreciated him." The Bushes' presence touched Johnson. It gave him solace to believe that as he ended his thirty-two-year career he was being honored not as a partisan but a statesman who had struggled to do his best for all Americans in tumultuous times.[138]

12

After the Fall

I T is no exaggeration to say that the return to Texas and a bucolic life on the banks of the Pedernales appealed to and troubled Johnson. For thirty-two years he had primarily lived in Washington, D.C., where he had observed and exercised political power every day of his life. His identity, his very being was bound up with his work. "My daddy committed political suicide for that war in Vietnam," younger daughter Luci told me. "And since politics was his life, it was like committing actual suicide."[1]

Despite his love affair with politics and power, by 1969 one side of Johnson was ready to go home. He was exhausted and looked forward to escaping the hurly-burly of the presidency—the endless pressures over Vietnam, managing domestic and international crises, meeting deadlines, balancing budgets, stroking supporters, combating opponents, working sixteen- and eighteen-hour days in behalf of policies and programs that misfired as often as they succeeded. He was dead tired by the time he turned over the government to Nixon and boarded Air Force One for the trip back to Texas. "He returned to the Texas Hill Country so exhausted by his presidency that it took him nearly a full year to shed the fatigue in his bones," *Time* reporter Leo Janos said.[2]

As a private citizen, he intended to indulge himself—to do whatever made him happy. He was tired of being cooped up in the White House, he told George Christian. " 'By God, I'm going to do what I want to do. If I want to drink a glass of whiskey, I'm going to drink a glass of whiskey. And if I want to have some bad manners, I'm going to have bad manners. I've got to have some freedom to do what I want to do.' "

In November, he told Helen Thomas: " 'The first thing I want to do is to go home and relieve myself of the weight I have been carrying around, all the problems. . . . I will have a chance to spend a little more time with my kin folks. My family means a lot to me. I want to see people who want . . . to see me. I want to walk miles and miles and miles. I want to breathe pure air and drink pure water and take a long sleep in the morning if I want to. . . . I just want to be lazy for awhile.' " A needlepoint pillow on a living room sofa in Stonewall, Texas, said it all: "This is my ranch and I do as I damn well please."[3]

He no longer planned to worry about his relations with the press and all those people a politician, and especially a President, has to suffer for reasons of state and politics. He told his staff to keep reporters away from him. He wanted no more of their inquisitions, their probes and innuendos. "I've served my time with that bunch," he said, "and I give up on them. There's no objectivity left anymore. The new style is advocacy reporting—send some snotty-nosed reporter down here to act like a district attorney and ask me where I was on the night of the twenty-third. I'm always guilty unless I can prove otherwise. So to hell with it."[4]

He was tired of indulging people he didn't care about, of going through the motions of politeness and social formalities expected of a public figure. When Texas Governor Preston Smith asked to visit him at the ranch, Johnson felt compelled to invite him. He called aide Harry Middleton in Austin to find out what Smith wanted. Middleton had no idea. The next day Middleton called back to ask about the visit. "Well, he came down here, brought his wife and momma and sat around my living room for three hours," LBJ said. "The son of a bitch never said what he wanted. Maybe he wanted me to kiss his ass. If so, he should have just said so. After all that's the business I've been in for the last forty years."[5]

Few things appealed to Johnson more in this post-presidential period than the freedom to indulge his appetites. Out of a concern that he not suffer another heart attack or some other debilitating disease as President, he had limited his drinking, avoided cigarettes, kept his weight down, and maintained a regimen of exercise and rest that relieved the strains of his job. But once back in Texas, he largely abandoned all these self-denying habits. He drank more freely; smoked two and three packs of cigarettes a day, as he had before his first heart attack; ate rich foods, which drove his weight back above 200 pounds; and mainly counted work around the ranch as exercise.

"He took up smoking again," one friend recalls, "he smoked like a fiend." Tom Johnson says: "He loved hamburgers." They would go to the Night Hawk restaurant on South Congress in Austin or he'd have hamburgers sent to his ninth-floor office in the Federal Building. By the summer of 1972, Wilbur Mills remembers that Johnson "was way overweight then. . . . I was worried about him because he was so excessively fat."[6]

He found pleasure in driving around his ranch and on adjacent country roads at breakneck speeds. Wilbur Mills recalls how he'd insist you "get in that danged convertible Lincoln, with the top down, take off at seventy miles an hour across the field, with no road or nothing to show me something. Finally, ended up he had to take me by and show me the graves of his mother and father." There was often talk of how he planned to be buried, "laid to rest," in the same plot of ground, in native soil, next to his parents.[7]

He wanted to reconnect with people he cared about. He planned to see Walter Jenkins and "just throw his arms around him and hug him. . . . Jenkins had been as dear a friend working for him as he ever had, and had been as loyal a servant as he ever had," Johnson said. Jenkins had been put in the public spotlight because he had worked for me, Johnson added.[8]

It was a kinship, one may speculate, born of shared public rejection. He was now joining Jenkins as a kind of spurned public figure. Besides, in all the years since 1964, when Jenkins left Washington in disgrace, Johnson, the President, could not afford to embrace his aide and friend. But now they could once more come together in a sort of shared exile. And Johnson, the liberated private citizen, could act upon his better instincts rather than the inhibiting political motives that for so long had shaped his every move.

The chance to spend more time with Lady Bird, his daughters, and his two grandchildren was a source of comfort and pleasure. Doris Kearns, who moved to Austin to help with his memoirs, remembers the "outward signs of deep affection and love" for Mrs. Johnson: "the gentle touch of his hand on her knee as they rode in the car, in the kidding jests about her financial management as they entertained at dinner, in the warm, crinkly smile with which he greeted her after being separated for less than a day."

More than ever, Lady Bird, who had helped him manage the inner storms that afflicted him throughout his adult years, was an anchor in his daily life, bringing him a measure of serenity in a period of difficult adjustment. "She mellowed him," Bob Hardesty says. "She softened him. She slowed him down. She placated him. She tempered his rashness with a sense of calm, penetrating judgment that he had long since come to depend on." When exasperated friends and aides would complain to Mrs. Johnson about Lyndon's insistent demands, she usually replied: "My dear, just look on it all as one great adventure," which is surely what she must have told herself in her struggles to rein in this troubled, difficult, well-meaning man.

Time spent with his daughters and especially his grandchildren made the transition from President to private citizen all the more palatable to him. "In his play with his grandchildren," Doris Kearns observed, "Johnson exhibited the wonderful childlike qualities he himself had never lost. He could entertain them for hours with the same repetitive game long after most adults would have lost their patience."[9]

And he began to have fun. After thirty-five years in public service, daughter Luci says, she thought his return to Texas and the ranch "would be like putting him in a tomb. But he discovered play. That was a word that was not in his vocabulary." He started going to quarterhorse races in Fredericksburg and making trips to Acapulco, Mexico, in February. They stayed in an elegant waterfront villa owned by former Mexican President Miguel Aleman and invited friends to join them for a winter vacation. Meals could last for hours, with Johnson telling stories, doing imitations, regaling guests with Washington war tales. He was the center of attention, which he loved, and all the guests had to follow his agenda. "If he wanted to sit on the beach in the morning, we all sat on the beach in the morning because it never occurred to him that that wasn't what everybody would want to do," one guest recalled.

"Johnson was just having a hell of a good time," Bob Hardesty says. "He'd go up to New York to see [Arthur] Krim, [Bob] McNamara, and Henry Ford, and go partying. He had fits of depression, of course," Hardesty adds, "but he was enjoying himself and doing things he wanted to do, for the first time."[10]

Nothing signaled Johnson's post-presidential sense of freedom as clearly as his personal appearance. "His craggy face was kind and mellow in those days," Warren Woodward recalls. "His hair was long; it swept back and curled on the ends like that of an elder statesman in the Andy Jackson vein. The lines in his face were deep, but in all, Lyndon Johnson appeared less strange than in those horrendous days at the end of his term. Outside the gaze of the public eye, he aged gracefully."[11]

The most startling demonstration of his liberation from White House formalities was his long silver hair. Like the rebellious students who had done so much to bring him down, Johnson now defied the conventionalities by refusing to have his hair cut. For someone who had spent a lifetime upbraiding aides and secretaries for the smallest departure from proper, formal dress, Johnson now announced his retirement from Washington's sartorial rules by sporting shoulder length curls. His appearance formed a striking contrast with Nixon's White House staff, whose crew-cuts set them off from "long-hair" radicals.[12]

But the return to the Hill Country wasn't strictly pleasurable. Mood swings were a common occurrence. "He was probably the most moody person I've ever known," Jewell Malechek, the wife of ranch manager Dale Malechek, says. "I guess working for him, that was one of the hardest things to adjust to. Some days you had to be quiet, and some days you could talk." He was his "normal manic-depressive self," Bob Hardesty says. Along with the sense of liberation and good times came feelings of diminished stature, of grief at losing his place of centrality in the country and the world.

In July 1969, he attended the launching of Apollo XI, which was to fulfill the goal of landing a man on the moon. He described the occasion to Doris Kearns as a misery he should not have exposed himself to. He remembered being one of thousands of people in the bleachers under a glaring sun, which left his clothes soaked and his stomach upset. The spotlight was on Vice President Spiro Agnew, who stood in for Nixon at the ceremony. The whole experience was a metaphor for Johnson's lost standing. As an ex-President he even had to take a back seat to a sitting Vice President.[13]

By the spring of 1969, Johnson was terribly withdrawn and morose. When Elizabeth Wickenden and Tex Goldschmidt called Lady Bird from Houston, where they were attending a convention, Mrs. Johnson insisted that they come to the ranch. When they arrived, Elizabeth realized that Lady Bird hoped their visit might help lift Johnson out of a deep depression. "Bird was obviously frantic about his state of mind," Wickenden says. But the visit had no salutary effect. Lady Bird tried to boost him with positive talk about White House achievements. But Lyndon wanted no part of it. He talked only about "the early days—about the WPA or the LCRA [Lower Colorado River Authority]. He wouldn't speak about anything in between; he just had it completely blotted out of his mind."[14]

Two other visitors to the ranch at that time also saw him as painfully remote and maybe even "crazy." Shortly after the Wickenden visit, Oklahoma Senator Fred Harris went to ask his counsel on some congressional business. Harris described him as "so odd." He wouldn't discuss the matters Harris raised. "He was totally withdrawn."[15]

Henry Kissinger, Nixon's National Security Adviser, briefed Johnson at the ranch on foreign policy issues in the fall and came away convinced Johnson had lost his moorings. Johnson thought Kissinger "was the Prime Minister of Germany. . . . And then he got me all mixed up and called me Dr. Schles-ing-er. He didn't know who I was." When someone told Kissinger that Johnson was putting him on, Kissinger refused to believe it. " 'No,' " Kissinger replied, " 'he's crazy.' "[16]

Others in the Nixon White House shared Kissinger's opinion. When Johnson visited Nixon at his San Clemente, California, home in August 1969, H. R. Bob Haldeman, Nixon's domestic affairs chief, thought LBJ was off the deep end. During a discussion in Nixon's office, LBJ "launched immediately into a discussion of his problems with adequate staff, funds, G[eneral] S[ervices] A[dministration] snooping and press leaks, etc. He's really psychopathic," Haldeman recorded in a diary.[17]

Johnson's unhappiness and hypersensitivity to criticism made him at times extremely difficult to work for. George Christian, Walter Jenkins, and Bill Moyers had warned W. Tom Johnson, LBJ's twenty-seven-year-old deputy press secretary, against staying with LBJ after he left the White House. "Tom," they said, "this is the worst thing in the world you could ever do. Go back to Georgia. Go back to the newspaper business. He's going to be a bitter, frustrated, hard man to do business with. It's going to be unbelievable. . . . He'll drive you crazy."

Though Tom Johnson remembers his time in Texas with the President as a chance to watch fascinating people, including LBJ, John Connally, Henry Ford, Arthur Krim, and Lew Wasserman, and be "exposed to a world of ideas and issues and people that I otherwise would have never been," he also recalls some painful clashes. When Johnson asked Jim Jones and Walter Jenkins to evaluate Tom Johnson's office arrangements, Tom asked whether the President had lost confidence in his management skills. LBJ didn't like that and "sort of went quiet for a few days." When Tom arranged a book party for Bill Moyers in Austin and asked the President to come, LBJ, who had fallen out with Moyers over suspicions that he had gone over to Bobby Kennedy, was furious with Tom for what he saw as divided loyalties. He hung up on Tom and wouldn't speak to him for weeks.[18]

Productive Work

Johnson's emotional downs were not much different from or much more severe than what he had struggled against throughout his life. All his aides who came with him to Texas expected the worst. He would "be impossible to live with . . . a caged tiger with all that pent-up energy, alternately roaring at those around him, out of frustration, and then sulking in a corner out of self-pity," Hardesty predicted. There were those moments and even days, but his antidote for the blues, for feeling ignored, diminished, and sorry for himself, was what it had always been, the healing force of work.

As he moved toward the end of his presidency, he mapped out a plan for keeping himself busy. For all his talk of relaxing, sleeping late, taking things easy, he also aimed to use his post-presidential time for productive ends. "He approached his life in retirement much as he had approached life in the White House," Tom Johnson says. "There was an urgency to everything he undertook."

He had five major projects he aimed to complete in the next few years: write his memoirs, set up his presidential library in Austin, establish a Lyndon B. Johnson School of Public Affairs at the University of Texas, complete seven one-hour television interviews with CBS's Walter Cronkite, and put his ranch and business affairs in order against the day he died and Lady Bird would have to live off their estate.[19]

Because he knew that writing a book and creating a library and a school were challenges he could not meet on his own, he wanted a first-rate staff to help him. He saw Tom Johnson as someone who could fill the bill. And so he convinced him not to go back to a newspaper job in his native Georgia but instead become a chief of staff or coordinator of post-presidential appointments and activities. He persuaded Walt and Elspeth Rostow to teach at the University of Texas, where, as seasoned faculty members, they could guide him in developing the library and the LBJ School. He recruited speech-writers Harry Middleton and Bob Hardesty to help him write the memoirs.[20]

He also pressed Doris Kearns, a Harvard Ph.D. in political science and White House fellow, to join his writing team. She was initially reluctant, and his promises of everything from a high salary and millionaire suitors to exotic travel did not turn her head. On the next to last day of his presidency, however, when he called her to the Oval Office, she could not turn him down. " 'I need help,' he said gently, the voice barely audible above the steady clicking of news tickers, 'part-time as you wish, on weekends, during vacations, whatever you can give.' ... This time he made no fancy promises," and the sincerity of the plea moved Kearns to say yes. " 'It's not so easy to get the help you need when you're no longer on top of the world,' " he told her. "Even at this moment of helplessness," Kearns commented later, "the greatest political bargainer of them all had not wholly lost his touch."[21]

Even with a fine staff, Johnson found the transition from President to author and part-time organizer and promoter of personal projects a painful process. The idea of sitting by himself for long stretches of time writing a book was repugnant to him. True, he saw the memoirs as "the last chance I've got with the history books, and I've got to do it right," he told Kearns. But writing for an unseen, remote audience was an accommodation he couldn't make. It was too much like being alone, which he hated, or feeling cut off from immediate contact with people he could see and hear and from whom he could evoke a response.[22]

Because he couldn't write even a draft of the book, which Hardesty, Kearns, and Middleton could then rewrite, Johnson began recording interviews for his ghostwriters to use in drafting chapters. But he found it almost as difficult as trying to write. Whenever he "sat down to talk in front of the tape machine, he froze," Kearns recounts; "his language became artificial and he insisted on having sheaves of memos on his lap before he'd say a word. The audience was too far away, too abstract, too unknown." He took to holding chapter conferences during which Hardesty, Kearns, and Middleton would review the documentary record with him as a prelude to writing. Hardesty remembers sitting in Johnson's convertible with an archives box in his lap while Johnson sped around the ranch barking orders on a two-way radio to his foreman and intermittently discussing the details of his presidency.[23]

Chapter drafts were sent to administration officials, who invariably counseled against saying anything that offended anyone. The result was a sanitized book drained of the real LBJ. He was determined not to let factual errors slip into the narrative or to say anything controversial. He excluded all of the anecdotes he told so avidly about the high and the mighty he had known over the years in Washington. He insisted that the book be "presidential," a statesman-like reconstruction of events with the human comedy omitted.[24]

Kearns recalls that the two chapters she drafted were not very good, except in places where she had defied LBJ's orders and put in "the anecdotes and stories I had heard him tell informally about his dealings with men like Russell, Dirksen, Mills, King, Young, Mitchell, and others." Instead of seeing how this material made the story come alive, Johnson insisted on their excision. " 'God damn it,' " he told Kearns, " 'I can't say this'—pointing to a barbed comment on Wilbur Mills—'get it out right now, why he may be the Speaker of the House someday. And for Christ's sake get that vulgar language of mine out of there. What do you think this is, the tale of an uneducated cowboy? It's a presidential memoir, damn it, and I've got to come out looking like a statesman, not some back-woods politician.' "[25]

Hardesty also wanted to liven up the book with the real LBJ: the humorist, the storyteller, the mimic, the raconteur. Johnson and the friends and associates he showed draft chapters "cut out all the color." Though Hardesty thought the final product accurate, truthful, and significant enough as a history of the Johnson administration, he objected to its muted description of LBJ, the book's leading man. It was a shadow portrait that gave readers little sense of the real Lyndon Johnson.[26]

Johnson's hope that establishing the LBJ Library and Public Affairs School would be satisfying alternatives to sitting in the White House also fell short of expectations. Successful fund-raising for both institutions and an LBJ Foundation was gratifying. The $1.2 million dollars he and Lady Bird received in advances for his memoirs and a White House diary she published, as well as lecture fees and $300,000 for the CBS interviews, were given to the library, the school, and the foundation. Johnson also enjoyed reviewing the architectural details of the library and consulting about the recruitment of a library staff and a faculty for the school.[27]

The library's dedication on May 22, 1971, was a moment of reflected glory that he greatly enjoyed. Much of the Washington establishment showed up, including Nixon, Barry Goldwater, Humphrey, Muskie, most of the Johnson Cabinet, and congressmen and senators. Senator Philip Hart of Michigan "never thought he'd come to Austin, Texas, and know half the people I saw." One Texas political friend says that for Lyndon "that was the greatest day in the world. He was in hog-heaven that day. He had them all there—Goldwater and all the bunch. Nixon came."

Johnson told the assembled dignitaries: "It's all here, the story of our time—with the bark off. There is no record of a mistake, nothing critical, ugly or unpleasant that is not included in the files here. We have papers from my four years of public service in one place for friend and foe to judge, to approve or disapprove." It was actually the record of Johnson's whole career, 31 million pages stretching from background and birth to post-presidential activities and some 10,000 taped conversations, which the library, faithful to Johnson's wish for openness, began releasing in the 1990s.[28]

Yet the library and the LBJ School produced their share of frustrations. Johnson was unhappy with the library's first director. Chester Newland "was almost too much of a librarian and a professional," Tom Johnson says, "and there just wasn't the personal connection between the two men." They "just never hit it off personally at all."

The problem was settled when Harry Middleton, who "had the magic touch with President and Mrs. Johnson" and enjoyed the respect and confidence of the Johnson associates, replaced Newland. Nevertheless, the transfer of power, in Tom Johnson's words, "was not a pleasant undertaking."[29]

Middleton's tenure was not without its stresses as well. After agreeing that the library should sponsor a series of symposia on major Johnson administration programs, Middleton ran into difficulties with LBJ over what constituted appropriate disclosure of archival materials. Johnson, undoubtedly believing that his reputation had nowhere to go but up, wanted the fullest possible release of documents. In 1972, when the library prepared to open materials on education policy to mark a conference on the subject, Johnson wanted to know why Middleton was not opening the full record to researchers. Middleton reminded him that "papers injurious or embarrassing to living persons should be closed for a while." But Johnson wanted no part of it. "Good men have been trying to save my reputation for forty years," he declared, "and not a damn one succeeded. What makes you think you can?"[30]

There was more here than bravado on Johnson's part. The distant chants of 2000 antiwar demonstrators at the opening of the library gave Johnson a renewed sense of urgency about establishing his place in history. Because he believed that the good in his administration's record outweighed the complaints against him, he was eager to have the story told. Moreover, he wanted to repair the damage done by the "credibility gap." He knew biographers and historians would find unpleasant revelations in the record, but he also took pleasure from the thought that it would demonstrate his political shrewdness and, in the final analysis, endear him to researchers for letting them see the real LBJ at work.

The LBJ School also became a disappointing project for Johnson. He was keenly interested in its development and took much satisfaction from the appointment of John Gronouski as its first dean. Gronouski combined the academic and practical political credentials LBJ thought should be the distinguishing feature of the school's faculty. But he worried that the school would neglect the hands-on side of public affairs for the theoretical. Nevertheless, he knew and accepted the reality that his influence on building the faculty and choosing students would be distinctly limited by university rules of self-governance. Whatever his investment in the institution, it was not something he considered a major part of his daily post-presidential activities.[31]

The Cronkite interviews produced more frustration. Hoping they would become largely a televised record of his administration's achievements, Johnson put great energy into preparing himself to discuss the seven prearranged topics—JFK's assassination and the transition, civil rights, space, Vietnam, the major decisions of 1968, Harry Truman, and politics. But instead of a pro-LBJ showcase, the documentary became a recounting of successes and failures. With CBS deciding what it would use from the interviews, Johnson, or more precisely his aides and lawyers, fell into a sharp struggle with the network over how it "cut and spliced" them. Compromises were reached, but only after much acrimony that left both sides partly discontented about the final product.[32]

More satisfying to Johnson were business dealings by which he consolidated his holdings and turned much of his estate into cash. By 1969, he and Lady Bird had multimillion-dollar investments in radio-television properties, land holdings, and bank stocks. He had been very careful not to violate any conflict-of-interest laws as President. His assets had been put in a blind trust by Abe Fortas and were managed by Donald S. Thomas, an Austin attorney and business associate, and Jesse Kellam, the executive director of the Johnsons' broadcasting stations.

Don Thomas and Tom Johnson are convinced that LBJ avoided improprieties; they remember his business dealings as strictly above-board. Thomas says that because the press distorted "the business affairs that pertained to the Johnson family," he took pains after LBJ's death to demonstrate through full disclosure that the President had built a "modest fortune" through wise investment and management.

Likewise, Tom Johnson confronted "this whole question of ethics and morality" in his oral history interviews with the LBJ Library. "I've searched my mind, and I've searched my notes," Tom Johnson says. "I've really searched my heart on this a whole lot, and I don't believe that there is any evidence to conclude that it was that way"—that is, anything like Watergate or "shuffling around" on business affairs. Johnson is convinced that LBJ practiced what he preached: Several times he told Tom that when in doubt about either government or business matters, "Do what's right."[33]

During his presidency LBJ had been concerned to assure that not a whiff of scandal sidetrack his administration from the public's business. He told people in his government that if they were caught in any wrongdoing, "I'll cut your balls off." The only scandal embarrassing Johnson was the Walter Jenkins episode during the 1964 election, though the revelations about Abe Fortas during his 1968 confirmation hearings also distressed him.

It is difficult to believe, despite the blind trust, that Johnson did not keep tabs on his financial holdings while President. Nevertheless, there is nothing to refute the Thomas and Tom Johnson assertions about his fastidiousness toward personal business affairs during his presidency.

But this says nothing about Johnson's pre-presidential behavior when he accumulated much of his wealth. The story of the radio and television assets, as recounted in my first volume, is a tale of using influence at the Federal Communications Commission (FCC) to assure the financial success of his broadcast stations. His land and bank holdings were the products partly of shrewd calculation and partly of his Texas connections to cut favorable deals.

By the time he had become Vice President the radio and television properties were generating considerable returns—about $1 million a year in net profits. "Don, what in hell are we going to do with this money?" he asked Thomas after being elected Vice President. Thomas urged him to invest in ranch and farm land, which would be owned and operated in partnership with Thomas and A. W. Moursund, another old Texas friend and associate, and folded into a Thomas-owned company in Austin, Brazos Tenth Street.

Johnson found the advice irresistible. On one visit back to Austin, Thomas pointed to a three bedroom, two-bath house with about 1600 feet of frontage on the highway he and a partner were buying for $63,000. " 'Hell, that's just the way you are,' " Johnson complained to him. " 'Goddamn, I'm up there in Washington. I'm working twenty hours a day. I'm trying to save this country and I'm trying to make you rich, make this area bloom, and, by God, every time a good deal comes along, you want it.' So I said, 'Hold up. You want it?' 'Yes, I want it,' " LBJ replied. " 'Okay,' " Thomas said. " 'You're going to get it.' " Thomas arranged the sale to LBJ for $58,000. In March of 1987 he was not sure how much Johnson ultimately made on the deal; but it was a profitable venture, which resulted not from his friendship with Thomas but his willingness to use his status as Vice President of the United States.

Believing that interest rates would go up in the immediate future, LBJ took 4 percent loans in 1960, which he used for land investments and to buy bank stocks. He urged Thomas to "borrow all the money you can borrow . . . because interest rates are going to go out the top. And so he [LBJ] did. He went around and arranged to borrow money that he didn't need." They made a lot of money by buying land at $65 and $100 an acre and selling it after Johnson's presidency at $500, and occasionally as much as $1500, an acre. Johnson then put a lot of money into tax-free bonds or what he called "walking-around-money," because he didn't have to report it to the FCC, as part of his broadcast profits, or to the IRS.[34]

After Johnson left the White House he was free to resume control of his holdings. In 1972, an FCC ruling against owning a television station and a cable company in the same market compelled Johnson to sell one of these properties. He chose to sell the station to the Times-Mirror corporation for $9 million. It was an act of great shrewdness. "Who do you know that would have sold his television station and kept a half interest in a cable system that was just a source of . . . losses rather than profits?" Don Thomas wondered. "Who could have seen over the hill that way?" When the cable property was sold in 1979, it netted $23 million in cash and another $23 million in tax write-offs from debts owed by the company. "He was an extremely smart man in business," Thomas adds. "If he hadn't been President, I don't know how rich he would have gotten." Leonard Marks echoes the point: "God—if he hadn't been president, he would have been the biggest tycoon this world has ever seen. He'd have rivaled the head of the largest corporation. He'd have made the largest fortune."[35]

Lyndon Johnson saw the sale of family holdings as a way to provide for Mrs. Johnson and his daughters after he died. He told Tom Johnson several times: "You know, you can divide up stock or you can divide up cash between your children, but you can't very well divide up companies. You can't decide who gets the photo processing plant and who gets the radio plant and this kind of thing." To assure that much of the profits from his land and television deals did not go to the IRS, he balanced his capital gains with donations to the National Park Service of his ranch home and surrounding property on the condition that he and Lady Bird would have the use of them for the rest of their lives.[36]

Nothing engaged LBJ more in his post-presidential years than the management of his ranch. While he had lived in Washington and was in office, the Stonewall ranch was a satisfying diversion or hobby. But beginning in 1969, it became a full-time avocation. Eighty percent of his time was spent on ranch business. "He went to work on the ranch," Tom Johnson says. "He started running that ranch the way he had the presidency—involved in every piece of it." And, Tom Johnson adds: "In a sense, rather than running the government he was running another little set of responsibilities—not little, they were big responsibilities." A friend who visited LBJ at the ranch complained: "He's become a goddamn farmer. I want to talk Democratic politics, he only talks hog prices."[37]

The ranch became a cloistered world in which he controlled

everything or tried to assure a kind of order and predictability he never found in the White House. Quickly, after coming to Stonewall, he fell into a comfortable routine, which made life on the Pedernales seem preferable to the strains of his tumultuous presidency. Up and out by six most mornings, he dogged the steps of ranch manager Dale Malechek and the several ranch hands who worked under him. He installed two-way radios in all the ranch vehicles and the rooms of his residence, so that he could reach them at any time during the work day. The only one who regretted Johnson's return to Stonewall was manager Malechek. He said: "I never worked for a harder man in my life." Malechek hoped Johnson would run again for the presidency.[38]

Nothing in the daily routine at the ranch escaped Johnson's attention. The number of eggs laid by the hens, the state of fence repairs, the health of the cattle, the irrigation of fields—all were part of his everyday concerns. Memos to the staff, morning meetings to review ranch conditions, night reading to plan for the next day's work were miniature replicas of White House procedures. During lunch at his residence with visitors, he liked to have Dale Malechek show up in his work clothes to brief Johnson on the day's developments. "He would sort of give them a lesson in how to run a ranch," Jewell says.

But even in this small agricultural world light years away from Washington and momentous crises, Johnson found that he couldn't bend everything to his will. "He tried, I think, to incorporate a lot of things that he had used in his office in Washington here at the ranch that really didn't work too well, like memos," Jewell Malechek recalls. "Cowboys aren't very good at writing memos. . . . When you're really busy it's kind of hard to come in at night . . . and write out a memo to President Johnson about what you're going to do the next day when sometimes the weather [dictates what you do]."[39]

The ranch became an extension of LBJ, and everything about it had to be not adequate or good but the best—a model of what other ranchers would try to emulate, a remarkable achievement that would command attention and demonstrate Lyndon Johnson's mastery. "I want each of you to make a solemn pledge that you will not go to bed tonight until you are sure that every steer has everything he needs," he told ranch hands at a morning meeting. "We've got a chance of producing some of the finest beef in this country if we work at it, if we dedicate ourselves to the job. And if we treat those hens with loving care, we should be able to produce the finest eggs in the country. Really fresh. But it will mean working every minute of every day."[40]

And the reward for all their hard work, for their conformity to

Johnson's wishes, was outlandishly expensive gifts. State-of-the-art calculators and Polaroid cameras, clothing, and new cars—Lincolns and Corvettes—the likes of which ranch hands had never imagined owning became one year's Christmas presents. "He gave people things as if he were giving part of himself," Jewell Malechek explains. And he loved to see them open the gifts, try on the clothes, drive the cars, and show gratitude for the largesse their benefactor had provided. As with so many others who had worked for him through the years, he demanded much—some said the impossible—and he gave lavishly in return. Life on the ranch was a miniature of his whole career.[41]

Politics

Although he shunned reporters and largely closed himself off from national and international affairs, Johnson could not entirely escape domestic politics. During his presidency he had launched the building of a nursing home facility in Austin, which he hoped would be a model for giving care to the elderly. A visit to former Austin Mayor Tom Miller in a shabby old-age home had sparked his interest in the project. He had arranged for HEW, the University of Texas, and the local Catholic Diocese to finance the center, where seniors could get adequate housing and health care. He monitored every detail of the project's development down to where bathtub handrails and toilet-paper rollers would be located.

Joe Califano, whom LBJ had charged with responsibility for the plan, remembers the President telling him and a task force developing proposals on nursing homes that he didn't want "good taxpayer dollars spent to keep people in ratholes." He described existing facilities as "fire traps, rat traps, a disgrace . . . no one of you would let your mother near one." He urged the group to plan homes that addressed the "special care" of the elderly. He suggested "flat floors, and grades, so that wheelchairs can easily be used," and bathrooms with handles on tubs and showers for safety and accessible toilet paper racks. To make his last point, he acted the part of an aged person straining to reach toilet tissue, ending with the injunction: "Stick it right there alongside them or in front of them so it's easy to reach."[42]

After Johnson left the White House, Nixon's Justice Department began investigating the project. Sensitive to any suggestion that he and his friends might profit in some way from the plan, LBJ had vetoed a suggestion from Frank Erwin, chairman of the University of Texas Trustees, that the center be named after his mother. " 'Goddamn you,' " he told Larry Temple, who had passed the idea along to the President, " 'Frank's got no judgment, no sense. Why should you tie my poor mother into that? Somebody will catch this. The *New York Times* will write it up that I was spending a bunch of federal money for a memorial to my mother. You tell Frank that we're going to do the project, but to forget that he ever mentioned my mother in connection with it.' "

Johnson went directly to Nixon about the investigation. " 'Somebody is screwing with my program,' " Johnson said. " 'I haven't asked for much, but this is something that I started, something that's good, that's worthwhile, and I won't benefit from it except for the enjoyment of seeing something worthwhile done. You tell your folks there isn't any stealing; nobody's getting anything out of this except old folks.' " Nixon called off the probe. On December 11, 1969, Johnson had breakfast with Nixon at the White House. The two-hour meeting "apparently went pretty well," H. R. Haldeman recorded, "mainly because we've more or less ironed out his problems about pilot project for reviewing his papers and getting the geriatrics home back on track."

The project reached completion with a plan to name it after the Texas Archbishop supporting it. But with the heat off, LBJ insisted that it be called the Rebekah Baines Johnson Retirement Center. " 'Larry, what are they doing to me?' " he told Temple in a phone call. " 'You and Frank Erwin promised me that they would name it after my mother.' " The mystified Temple replied: " 'Mr. President, I thought you didn't want it named after your mother.' He said, 'Where did you get a silly idea like that? Why sure, I want it named after my mother. It would be a great honor to have it named after her.' " And so it was.[43]

In pressing Nixon for some consideration, Johnson knew he had earned it. In March 1969, he refused to support public attacks by Clark Clifford on Nixon's Vietnam policy. That spring, he gave indirect support to Congressman George Bush, who had declared himself a Republican candidate for Ralph Yarborough's U.S. Senate seat. In February 1970, he had Tom Johnson inform Haldeman that he had refused to discuss the Anna Chennault issue with a *St. Louis Post-Dispatch* reporter and that "all our people in Austin had been directed not to say anything on the matter." Haldeman "was most appreciative" and "seemed genuinely pleased and surprised that we would call on such a matter and expressed his thanks again for the attitude we have been taking toward President Nixon."

In May 1970, when domestic demonstrations resulting in deaths on the Kent State and Jackson State University campuses followed a U.S. ground attack on North Vietnamese supply routes in Cambodia,

Johnson refused to criticize Nixon. Instead, in a Democratic party unity speech in Chicago, he blamed Hanoi for the continuing problems in Southeast Asia and urged all Americans to lend their backing to "our President." Nixon wrote him: "I deeply appreciate your support and understanding." He also conferred with LBJ at the White House, who described their private meeting as "very beneficial. You know in these times of difficulty, I stand ready to be helpful whenever possible," Johnson wrote him.[44]

Johnson also largely stayed out of the 1972 presidential campaign. The Democratic convention in Miami in July depressed him. The party leaders did not invite him, and, except for Ted Kennedy, party officials made no mention of him, even omitting his photograph from the customary picture display of former Democratic Presidents. After Maine Senator Ed Muskie, LBJ's choice, lost the nomination to South Dakota Senator George McGovern, a vocal Johnson critic, Johnson refused to issue a statement or give an interview about his candidacy.

In August, when he announced his support of McGovern and agreed to receive him at the ranch, it was about as low-key an endorsement as Johnson could give. He described their differences on foreign affairs and made clear that he was acting more out of loyalty to the Democratic party than out of any enthusiasm for McGovern. Their discussion at the ranch included "a lacing" from LBJ on the war, and a statement that "I've always supported the Democratic nominee and I'm going to support you." He told McGovern that he thought him "crazy as hell" on the war and suggested they not talk about it. He urged him to run a "homespun, down-to-earth" campaign with an emphasis on how "the Republicans always sell you out to Wall Street."[45]

Behind the scenes he did what he could to promote Nixon's reelection. He declared McGovern "the most inept politician, inept presidential candidate ... in all of history. ... I didn't know they *made* presidential candidates that dumb," he said privately. In July, before he went on record in support of McGovern, he told Nixon in a phone conversation that he would "encourage his people to support us behind the scenes. Although he will not come out himself, of course." Texas Democrats for Nixon, led by John Connally, George Christian, and Larry Temple, was the principal result of Johnson's promise.

Billy Graham quietly encouraged LBJ to work for Nixon's reelection. He "helped Johnson modify his endorsement [of McGovern] to make it as cool as possible." Johnson advised Nixon through Graham "to ignore McGovern. ... He thinks the McGovern people will defeat themselves. He feels very strongly anti-McGovern," Graham reported. "Says the P[resident] should not do too much campaigning, stay above it, as Johnson did with Goldwater." When Graham discussed the bugging of Nixon's campaign in 1968 and Vietnam, Johnson said that he didn't "think bugging is going to hurt us. . . . said it won't hurt a bit," meaning he had no intention of leaking anything to the press about the Chennault affair.

In August, as Johnson was about to see McGovern, John Connally told Haldeman that LBJ was "mad as hell, furious about the whole McGovern approach to things. He told McGovern that he'll meet with him for one hour, that there's to be no press and no pictures. Then McGovern will have a press conference afterward." After the meeting, Johnson reported on the conversation to Graham: He had told McGovern he wouldn't campaign for him, "cited all the good things" Nixon had done for him, warned McGovern that he was "associating with amateurs," and advised him to stand up for America.[46]

For his troubles, Johnson got a symbolic slap in the face from Nixon. In October, Nixon told the press that he had no intention of making "the wrong kind of settlement [in Vietnam] before the election. We were around that track in 1968 when well-intentioned men made a very, very great mistake in stopping the bombing without adequate agreements from the other side."[47]

More important, in January 1973, after Nixon had won a landslide victory and the Democratic-controlled Senate threatened an investigation of the Republican break-in of Democratic headquarters at the Watergate, Nixon tried to intimidate Johnson into having the inquiry called off. On January 9, Nixon asked that Attorney General John Mitchell talk to Deke "De Loach to see what he can get out of him on the LBJ thing, because if he can get that cranked up," Haldeman recorded in his diary, "LBJ could turn off the whole congressional investigation." Nixon hoped that the threat of a press leak about FBI bugs ordered by LBJ on his and Agnew's 1968 campaign planes would persuade Johnson to pressure congressional Democrats into dropping a Watergate probe.

When Johnson got wind of what Nixon was proposing, he called De Loach "and said to him that if the Nixon people are going to play with this, that he would release (deleted material—national security)," Haldeman's published diary reads, "saying that our side was asking that certain things be done. By our side, I assume he means the [1968] Nixon campaign organization," Haldeman said. "De Loach took this as a direct threat from Johnson. . . . As he recalls it, bugging was requested on the [Nixon-Agnew campaign] planes [in 1968], but was turned down, and all they did was check the phone calls, and put a tap on the Dragon Lady (Mrs. Anna Chennault)."[48]

The deleted material from Haldeman's diary was Johnson's threat that if the Nixon White House released information about LBJ's alleged bugging of their campaign in 1968, he would retaliate with material from National Security Administration files demonstrating that Nixon's campaign had illegally interfered with the Paris peace talks by convincing Saigon to stay away until after Nixon came to office. Johnson may also have considered releasing material about the secret Greek money funneled into the Nixon campaign in 1968, but this was probably a backup piece of information that Johnson would use only if the Chennault material was not enough to blunt Nixon's threat, which, of course, it did.[49]

Last Days

Johnson's concern that he might not live out another presidential term was well-grounded. In March 1970, fourteen months after leaving office, he was hospitalized at Brooke Army Medical Center in San Antonio because of severe chest pains. Since his serious heart attack in 1955, he had had a number of medical problems, but there had been no other significant cardiological episode. The problem now, doctors told him, was not a heart attack but angina, a hardening of the arteries supplying blood to the heart. Heart specialists in Atlanta and Houston concluded that he was not a good candidate for bypass surgery. They recommended nitroglycerin to control the pain, weight loss, and a regimen of nonsmoking and less tension.[50]

Though he relied on the nitroglycerine tablets for pain control and made some effort to change his diet, he resigned himself to the inevitable. "He decided that you could have quality or quantity in your life and he decided to live and to do whatever he wanted to do because he didn't think he had that much time left," Jewell Malechek says.[51]

In April, he came back to Washington, where he met with editors and reporters from the *Washington Post*. Richard Harwood remembers him "looking less tall, less bulky.... His hair was almost completely white, and was growing long in the back." LBJ said that he was on a daily 850-calorie diet and that he had suffered quite a bit of pain before being hospitalized.

Harwood recalls that as he spoke, he took on "another appearance: The pallor and signs of sickness went away and all of a sudden you were sitting with a vigorous, commanding, strong man whose mind was so clear, so well organized, so quick that you suddenly became aware of the power of that personality, of the ability to dominate and persuade and overwhelm." Harwood adds, "There were some bitter-end Johnson critics around that table," but they kept their peace. "They sat there, drinking it all in, and when it was over some had tears in their eyes and they all stood up and gave him their applause."[52]

In June 1972, while visiting his older daughter Lynda and her husband, Charles Robb, in Charlottesville, Virginia, he suffered a severe heart attack. Believing that he was now dying and determined to be home when he did, he insisted on being flown to San Antonio. He survived the journey, and, after a two-week hospital stay, he recovered sufficiently to return to the ranch. There he moved and spoke more slowly, climbed no stairs, almost never drove, and vacillated between hope and resignation. His mornings were pretty good, he told friends, but by the afternoon he was drained of energy, suffered a lot of pain, had to lie down, and took oxygen from a portable tank next to his bed.[53]

Yet he was not ready to see himself as an invalid passively waiting for the end. In September, he went to Temple, Texas, to help the Scott and White Clinic celebrate its 75th anniversary. Reflecting as much on his own condition as the state of national affairs, he declared: "With the coming of September each year, we are reminded, as the song says, that the days are dwindling down to a precious few. By the calendar, we know that soon the green leaves of summer will begin to brown; the chill winds of winter will begin to blow; and— before we are ready for the end to come—the year will be gone. If we permit our thoughts to dwell upon this perspective, these days can become a melancholy season. . . . Yet melancholy is not a mood which I have ever allowed to weigh for long upon my spirits." His message was one of hope and promise: "that this land and its people are quickening with new life and new potential of what will become the springtime of a new America."[54]

His fall schedule was full of activities, mainly at the ranch, with lots of interesting guests coming to visit. In December, he called Horace Busby to say that he wanted " 'to get really active this year.' " He planned to " 'speak up a little more . . . go more places and see more people again.' "[55]

His attendance at a civil rights conference at the LBJ Library earlier in the month had stimulated his interest in once more influencing public issues. On December 11 and 12, all the notable civil rights activists of the fifties and sixties gathered in Austin: Associate Justice Thurgood Marshall, Roy Wilkins, Clarence Mitchell, Whitney

Young, Hubert Humphrey, Chief Justice Earl Warren, and Burke Marshall. Younger, newer activists, who were less well known to LBJ came, too: Barbara Jordan, Julian Bond, Vernon E. Jordan, Jr., Reynaldo G. Garza, and Henry Gonzalez. And an anti-Nixon contingent led by the Reverend Kendall Smith of the Council of Churches in New York and Roy Innes, chairman of CORE, attended with the intention of denouncing the indifference of the current administration to advancing equal rights.

Johnson looked forward to the symposium with pleasure; it was a chance to remember the greatest moments of his presidency. But he was awfully sick by then, and his doctors urged him not to attend, and especially not to exert himself by giving a scheduled talk. He put aside their objections to drive the seventy miles from his ranch through an ice storm. The only concession to his pain and weakness was to watch the proceedings from a back room with a television monitor. But he was still in charge. When conference organizers wanted to deny Smith and Innes a chance to speak against Nixon, LBJ vetoed their decision and promised to give them some time.

It was evident to everyone who watched Johnson come to the podium for his talk that he was not well. He walked slowly and spoke in a low but steady voice. His message was inspiring: "Of all the records that are housed in this Library—31,000,000 papers accumulated over a forty-year period of public life—" he said, "it is the record of this work which has brought us here that holds the most of myself within it and holds for me the most intimate meanings.... I do not want to say that I've always seen this matter, in terms of the special plight of the black man, as clearly as I came to see it in the course of my life and experience and responsibility." But he had come to understand the urgency of equal rights in America, and he briefly cataloged the advances of the last ten years.

His concern now, he declared, was not to have this symposium "spend two days talking about what we have done. The progress has been much too small; we haven't done nearly enough. I am sort of ashamed of myself, that I had six years and couldn't do more than I did.... So let no one delude themselves that our work is done. By unconcern, by neglect, by complacent beliefs that our labors in the fields of human rights are completed, we of today can seed our future with storms that would rage over the lives of our children and our children's children.... The black problem today, as it was yesterday, is not a problem of region or states or cities or neighborhoods. It is a problem, a concern and responsibility of this whole nation.... To be black in a white society is not to stand on level and equal ground. While the races may stand side by side, whites stand on history's mountain and blacks stand in history's hollow. Until we overcome unequal history, we cannot overcome unequal opportunity."

"While I can't provide much go-go at this period of my life," he said in subsequent remarks, "I can provide a lot of hope and dream and encouragement and I'll sell a few wormy cows now and then and contribute."[56]

But the time left to him was brief. After his trip to Austin for the symposium in December, he spent two days in bed recovering. During the next six weeks, he continued to feel poorly. He had a lot of pain and could relieve it only by lying in bed taking oxygen. Tom Johnson remembers thinking that "he was really getting close to his time."

On the morning of January 22, he discussed plans to go to Acapulco in February and went over a list of "action" items on the phone with Tom Johnson. He wanted to know about a visit of Israeli Premier Golda Meir to Austin and about a *Los Angeles Times* investigation of a state park being set up at his boyhood home in Johnson City. He urged Tom to encourage Pat Nugent, LBJ's son-in-law, to rejoin the Johnson radio company. With Tom planning to become editor of the *Dallas Times Herald* and Jesse Kellam past seventy-three, LBJ was eager to have Nugent become the station's chief executive. He discussed a visit to the ranch that afternoon of J. B. Fuqua, a Georgia industrialist. It evoked comments from him about distinguished Georgians, including Walter George, Richard Russell, and Carl Vinson. "Well, Tom, anything else?" he concluded their discussion.

Phone calls from and to his physicians, business associates, secretaries, and a staff aide dealing with matters at the library and LBJ School filled the rest of his morning. At 11:20 a.m., Jewell Malechek drove him around the ranch to check on some deer fencing. After a light lunch, he lay down for a nap.

At 3:49 p.m. LBJ called Secret Service agent Mike Howard, who was out of his ranch office. Johnson said, "Well send over whatever agent is on duty." Two other agents, alarmed by the President's tone, ran to his bedroom with a small oxygen tank. They found LBJ lying unconscious on the floor and began administering CPR. They called the President's physician in San Antonio, but it was apparent to them that Johnson was dead. A physician from Johnson City arrived as the agents were carrying the President on his plane to fly him to San Antonio. The eighteen-minute flight brought them to San Antonio at 4:35. But it was already too late. The physician on board pronounced him dead before removing his body from the plane. Mrs. Johnson, who had been in Austin, had been flown to San Antonio by helicopter. She arrived at 5:54 and was told by Agent Howard, "This time we didn't make it." She said, "Well, we expected it."

When Lady Bird called Tom Johnson to ask him to coordinate funeral arrangements, Tom remembered thinking: "Well, that rascal. He left on this trip just like he would have wished, without any advance notice to the press. He never wanted to go anywhere on a trip and let us tell the press about it beforehand.... He didn't do it like Harry Truman; lie around several days and have the press gather outside."[57]

Johnson's body lay in state in his Austin library from the afternoon of January 23 until 9 a.m. the following morning. According to the library's count, 32,000 people paid their respects. When Library Director Harry Middleton assigned an assistant to keep track of how many people viewed the President's remains, an associate asked Middleton why he wanted that information. "Because," Middleton replied, "I know that somewhere, sometime, President Johnson's going to ask me."

From the 24th to the 25th, Johnson's remains lay in state at the Capitol Rotunda in Washington. One observer of the mourners paying their respects guessed that 60 percent were African Americans. He overheard one black woman say to her little girl: " 'People don't know it, but he did more for us than anybody, any President, ever did.' ... That was his epitaph as far as I was concerned," this observer said. After Leonard Marks reported Lady Bird's comment "that the thing Lyndon hated most was to be by himself," a group of Johnson's friends decided to keep watch at the casket all night.

On the morning of the 25th the casket was moved to the National City Christian Church. Leontyne Price sang "Onward Christian Soldiers," and Marvin Watson delivered the eulogy: "He was ours," Watson declared, "and we loved him beyond all telling of it." That afternoon the President's body was flown back to Texas, where it was carried to the family cemetery at the Stonewall ranch. Anita Bryant sang the "Battle Hymn of the Republic." General Westmoreland placed a wreath sent by President Nixon at the foot of the coffin. John Connally spoke the last words: "Along this stream and under these trees he loved he will now rest. He first saw light here. He last felt life here. May he now find peace here."[58]

"But John," one can imagine him replying, "there's still so much more to be done."

Afterword

A long biography deserves a short afterword. Besides, I see little to add to the detailed descriptions and efforts at explanation of Lyndon Johnson's behavior. It may be, as Russell Baker said, that Johnson was "a human puzzle so complicated that nobody could ever understand it." But I think my two volumes bring us closer to some explanation of what drove this outsized man. Like the climber who ascends the mountain because it is there, knowing Johnson better can simply satisfy our curiosity. But his substantial impact on all our lives has made searching out his motives all the more compelling.

It may be that future biographers will have superior methods for deciphering a man of such uncommon ambition, capacity, and energy. But whether they do or not, it is difficult to believe that they will ever fully agree on how to assess this larger-than-life figure. There were enough surprises in what he did to rule out uncontested explanations of his actions. Johnson was one of those great success stories posing the question: Did he reach such great heights and ultimately fall so far because of or despite his inner demons?

More in order are a final few words about Johnson's antipoverty crusade, Great Society, and war in Vietnam. More than thirty years after LBJ's great assault on domestic problems, it is possible to make assessments of the many programs he put in place to change race relations, ease the suffering of underprivileged Americans, and improve the national quality of life. As the text of the book makes clear, Johnson had his hits and misses. Civil rights and voting rights corrected long-standing wrongs and opened the way to the rise of a larger, more affluent black middle class. Affirmative action, however, as developments in the late 1990s make clear, proved to be a disappointing method for solving racial tensions. Likewise, Medicare, Medicaid, urban renewal, aid to education, immigration reform, and safety and consumer regulations have their defenders and detractors.

Debates about the sort of social engineering Johnson sponsored will not disappear. Nevertheless, there is at least one side of Johnson's reformism that the great majority of Americans have embraced and seem unlikely to abandon for the foreseeable future. There is a striking analogy here between Johnson and FDR. Roosevelt's New Deal never brought full recovery from the Depression. But it put in place a series of measures that humanized the American industrial system. Social Security, unemployment insurance, public power, and regulatory protections for consumers command the allegiance of most citizens, many of whom may have no idea or even interest in knowing the origins of laws that seem essential in a civilized democratic society.

Similarly, many of the laws spawned by Lyndon Johnson's war on poverty and Great Society have either fallen into disrepute or command little support from most Americans. But the spirit and some of the substance behind Johnson's reform programs maintain a hold on the public imagination that endures. Who among us would agree to return to the segregated world of the 1950s and early 1960s? How many in America are prepared to dispense with Medicare and Medicaid? Few are willing to abandon federal aid to education or environmental protections, even if the details of those programs seem highly imperfect. For all the recent recrimination over more controversial initiatives from the sixties like national public broadcasting, legal services, the national endowments for the arts and the humanities, conservatives have found it impossible to repeal them. Like FDR's New Deal, Johnson's poverty war and reach for a Great Society may seem somewhat outdated or inadequate to current challenges, but the humanizing force behind them abides and gives both men historical standing as visionaries who helped advance the national well-being and fulfill the promise of American life.

Johnson had at least one indisputable triumph in domestic affairs for which he deserves credit. He played a large part in bringing the South into the mainstream of the country's economic and political life. Beginning in the 1930s he saw New Deal federal programs as a means to raise the southern standard of living. As a senator in the fifties and then as president, he understood that civil rights would do more than assure equal treatment for African Americans. It would also help make the South a more equal member of American society. Johnson recognized that segregation not only separated the races in the South, it also set the region apart from the rest of America. An end to southern apartheid meant the reintegration of the South into the nation. The prosperity enjoyed by the region since the 1960s and three southerners in the White House—Jimmy Carter, George Bush, and Bill Clinton—out of the last six presidents demonstrate the point.

Johnson's domestic record is ultimately a study in paradox. His strength as a President partly rested on his affinity for doing big things: taking on the largest problems others have been either too timid or too politically opposed to federal activism to address. But in doing so, he overreached himself. His grandiosity led him to promise more than he could ever possibly deliver: An end to poverty, a Great Society of contented citizens largely free of racial tensions were false hopes that did more to spawn national cynicism than turn America into a perfect Union. Johnson would have done better to have remembered Theodore Roosevelt's admonition: "Speak softly and carry a big stick."

Vietnam was a larger mistake. It was the worst foreign policy disaster in the country's history. Aside from the sacrifice of the many brave men and women who lost their lives or suffered because of the conflict, there seems nothing heroic about the struggle. Where World Wars I and II and even Korea had set-piece battles that seemed to lead somewhere, where high level meetings engaged thoughtful civilian and military chiefs in difficult decisions that demonstrated the general wisdom of the country's leaders, Vietnam was a morass. The battlefield clashes and constant discussions in Washington and Saigon about the war were a confusion leading nowhere. For all the determination and dedication to duty of the decision makers, the planning for Vietnam led to unproductive commitments in what came to seem like an open-ended conflict.

Defenders of the war believe that America's ten-year presence in Vietnam spared Southeast Asia from Communism, giving the region time to develop and resist subversion from socialist neighbors. The assertion is impossible to prove. Moreover, it leaves out of the equation the likelihood that a Communist takeover in Vietnam would have spurred a U.S. effort in Thailand, a more congenial place to make a stand against falling dominoes.

The principal products of administration discussions about the fighting were false hopes, self-generated illusions, and paranoid fears of domestic opponents, who were not the Communist dupes Johnson believed them to be but men and women as devoted to the national security and well-being as anyone in the government and military.

Johnson knew from the first that he might be pursuing a losing cause in Vietnam. Why then didn't he cut his losses in 1967 or 1968 by declaring victory and getting out? Domestic sentiment coupled with developments in Vietnam made this possible beginning in September 1967. Richard Nixon's later fig leaf for ending a fruitless commitment, Vietnamization, was available to Johnson. But he chose to continue and escalate U.S. involvement until the Tet offensive clearly demonstrated that Americans had lost patience with a costly struggle leading only to more losses.

Johnson's reasons for "staying the course," as he described it, were a combination of noble and ignoble motives that little serve his historical reputation. To the end of his presidency, LBJ believed his own rhetoric about dominoes and Munich and right-wing domestic control compelling him to fight the war. Though Johnson, in the words of his younger daughter, may have committed political suicide or courageously fallen on his own sword for Vietnam, it still does not speak especially well of his judgment. None of Johnson's fears have come to pass despite U.S. defeat in Vietnam. The dominoes in Southeast Asia never toppled; Russia and China took no greater risks in the Cold War, which could have heightened the likelihood of an East-West confrontation; conservative critics made no direct political gains from the outcome in Vietnam; and Communist victory in the war did nothing to prop up socialism in Russia, Eastern Europe, or even China.

Even less flattering to LBJ is the reality that he also pursued the war for selfish motives. To admit failure on so big an issue as Vietnam would have been too jarring to Johnson's self-image as a can-do leader. Moreover, realizing by 1966–67 that defeat in Vietnam would blight his reputation as the only President in American history to have lost a war and intent on proving his critics wrong, especially Robert Kennedy, whose emergence as a political opponent revolved around differences over Vietnam, Johnson refused to acknowledge that he had led the country into a stalemate, which would require large additional commitments to break.

Plaguing Johnson as well was an irrational conviction that his domestic opponents were subversives or the dupes of subversives intent on undermining national institutions. Johnson's paranoia raises questions about his judgment and capacity to make rational life and death decisions. I do not raise this matter casually. It is a frighteningly difficult issue, which the country has never seriously addressed. And for good reason. It is one thing if a President is seriously incapacitated by some physical malady that bars him from performing his duties. And even then, as in the case of Woodrow Wilson, few, if any, were ready to demand that the Vice President assume the responsibilities of office.

Determining psychological incapacity may be impossible. We have never had a President who was so demonstrably depressed or unstable that he had to temporarily or permanently give up governing. Richard Nixon's decision to resign was a rational response to legal and political circumstances beyond his control.

Who then is to say when a President has passed the bounds of rational good sense? Certainly in Johnson's case, for all the cranky nonsense he espoused about his enemies, he remained largely in control of his faculties and more than capable of functioning as President.

Still, no one should make light of how much his suspicions and anger toward his domestic critics distorted his judgments in dealing with Vietnam. It may be that he would have pursued the war as avidly even without his personal antagonisms. But it is clear that his personal quirks in dealing with war opponents contributed nothing constructive to the national dialogue on a failing war.

How then to sum up Johnson's nearly four decades in politics? He stands in the front ranks of those who served as congressional aides, NYA directors, congressmen, and senators. His vice presidency was no more nor less than what others had suffered through in that office.

His presidency was a story of great achievement and terrible failure, of lasting gains and unforgettable losses. Whatever impulse future historians may have to pigeonhole Johnson as a near great, average, or failed President, I am confident that a close review of his time in office will leave them reluctant to put any single stamp on his term. Some people loved the man and some despised him. Some remember him for great works and others for a legacy of excessive governance at home and defeat abroad. In a not so distant future, when coming generations have no direct experience of the man and the passions of the sixties are muted, Johnson will probably be remembered as a President who faithfully reflected the country's greatness and limitations—a man notable for his successes and failures, for his triumphs and tragedy.

Only one thing seems certain: Lyndon Johnson will not join the many obscure—almost nameless, faceless—Presidents whose terms of office register on most Americans as blank slates. He will not be forgotten.

Sources

MANUSCRIPTS

Barker Texas History Center, Austin, Texas
  Ralph Yarborough Papers
Bates College Library
  Edmund Muskie Papers
Boston University, Boston, Massachusetts
  John W. McCormack Papers
Everett Dirksen Library, Pekin, Illinois
  Everett Dirksen Papers
Federal Bureau of Investigation
  J. Edgar Hoover Official and Confidential Files
  Lyndon B. Johnson
    Main Files
    Cross-Reference Files
  Robert F. Kennedy Microfilm File
Lyndon B. Johnson Library, Austin, Texas
  George W. Ball Papers
  McGeorge Bundy Papers
  William P. Bundy Papers
    MS History of the Vietnam War
  Joseph A. Califano, Jr., Papers
  Ramsey Clark Papers
  Clark Clifford Papers
  LBJ Archives: Subject File
  W. Thomas Johnson Papers
    Meeting Notes
  Drew Pearson Papers
  Post-Presidential Papers
    Name File
    Reference Files
  Pre-Presidential Confidential File
  Pre-Presidential Daily Diary
  Presidential Papers
    Administrative Histories
    Cabinet Papers
    Conference on Vietnam, March 9–10, 1991
    Congressional Briefings on Vietnam
    Declassified and Desanitized Documents from Unprocessed Files

Diaries and Appointment Logs
  Diary Backup
Handwriting File
Legislative Background
Meeting Notes File
National Security File
  Country Files
  Intelligence File
  International Meetings and Travel Notes
  McGeorge Bundy File
  Robert W. Komer File
  Memos to the President
  Name Files
  National Security Action Memorandums
  National Security Council Histories
  National Security Council Meetings
  John P. Roche File
  Subject Files
  Walt W. Rostow File
Office of the President File
Reference File: Anna Chennault
Reference File: Vietnam
Reference File: Westmoreland vs. CBS
Reference File: Wiretaps
Reports on Pending Legislation
Special File on the Assassination of John F. Kennedy
Special File Pertaining to Abe Fortas and Homer Thornberry
Statements of LBJ
Task Force Reports
Telephone Tapes
White House Central Files: Aides
  Horace Busby, Jr.
  Joseph A. Califano, Jr.
  Douglass Cater
  George E. Christian
  James C. Gaither
  Robert E. Kintner
  Harry C. McPherson
  John W. Macy, Jr.
  Charles Maguire
  Mike Manatos
  Bill Moyers
  Charles S. Murphy
  Matthew Nimetz
  Frederick Panzer
  George Reedy
  Willie Day Taylor
  Larry Temple
  Jack Valenti

Marvin W. Watson
Ben Wattenberg
Lee C. White
Henry H. Wilson
White House Central Files
Confidential File
Executive Series
General Series
Name File
White House Famous Names
Harold (Barefoot) Sanders, Jr. Papers
Vice Presidential Papers
Civil Rights Files
Security Files
Space Files
Subject Files: Congress 1962
John F. Kennedy Library, Boston, Massachusetts
Ralph A. Dungan Papers
Walter Heller Papers
John F. Kennedy Presidential Papers
National Security Action Memorandums
Pre-Presidential Papers
President's Office Files
JFK Correspondence
LBJ File
White House Central Files
Committee on Equal Employment Opportunity
Robert F. Kennedy Papers
Attorney General's Files
Theodore Sorensen Papers
Lee C. White Papers
Library of Congress, Washington, D.C.
Association of Former Members of Congress Papers
J. William Fulbright Oral History
Gale W. McGee Oral History
Minnesota Historical Society, St. Paul, Minnesota
Hubert H. Humphrey Papers
National Aeronautics and Space Administration Archives, Washington, D.C.
Lyndon B. Johnson Files
Robert Sherrod Apollo Collection
James E. Webb Papers
Princeton University Library
Arthur Krock Papers
Harry S. Truman Library, Independence, Missouri
Charles S. Murphy Papers
University of Alabama, Montgomery, Alabama
Lister Hill Papers
University of Arkansas, Fayetteville, Arkansas
J. William Fulbright Papers

University of Georgia, Richard Russell Library, Athens, Georgia
  Dean Rusk Oral History, Tapes AAAA, NN, XXX
  Richard Russell Papers
Wayne State University, Detroit, Michigan
  Walter Reuther Papers
Wisconsin State Historical Society, Madison, Wisconsin
  Wilbur J. Cohen Papers

ORAL HISTORIES

Lyndon B. Johnson Library, Austin, Texas
  (Dates are listed when there are multiple oral histories)
  Gardner Ackley, April 13, 1973, March 7, 1974
  Samuel A. Adams
  George W. Ball, July 9, 1971
  Charles L. Bartlett
  Charles Boatner
  William P. Bundy
  Cecil E. Burney
  Joseph A. Califano, Jr., October 17, 1968, August 21, September 12, 1969,
      October 29, December 15, 1987, January 27, March 16, November 15,
      December 21, 1988, January 18, June 13, 1989
  Elizabeth Carpenter, May 15, 1969
  Leslie Carpenter
  Clifton C. Carter, October 30, 1968
  Douglass Cater, April 29, May 8, 1969, May 26, 1974, April 24, 1981
  Ramsey Clark, March 21, June 3, 1969
  Wilbur J. Cohen, May 10, 1969
  John Corson
  C. Douglas Dillon
  Ralph Dungan
  James Farmer
  Michael V. Forrestal
  Abe Fortas
  Orville L. Freeman
  James C. Gaither, November 19, 1968, January 17, 1969
  John W. Gardner
  Arthur J. Goldberg
  Arthur E. Goldschmidt
  Andrew J. Goodpaster
  Ashton Gonella
  Kermit Gordon, January 9, March 21, 1969
  D. B. Hardeman, April 22, 1969
  Bryce N. Harlow, May 6, 1979
  Walter W. Heller, December 21, 1971
  Richard R. Helms
  Bourke B. Hickenlooper

Jerry Holleman
Walter Jenkins, August 24, 1971
W. Thomas Johnson, June 19, 1973, April 11, 1974, Feb. 22, 1989
Nicholas Katzenbach, November 12, 1968
Francis Keppel, April 21, 1969
Leon Keyserling
Carroll Kilpatrick
Harry C. McPherson, Jr., December 5, 19, 1968, January 16, 1969
Robert S. McNamara
Mike Manatos
Frank F. Mankiewicz
Thomas C. Mann
Burke Marshall
Thurgood Marshall
John Bartlow Martin
Louis Martin
George Meany
Wilbur Mills
Newton Minow
Clarence Mitchell
Powell Moore
Thomas H. Moorer
Richard H. Nelson
David G. Nes
Lawrence F. O'Brien, September 18, October 29, 30, 1985, February 11, 12,
      April 8, 9, June 25, July 24, September 10, 1986
Kenneth P. O'Donnell
Arthur M. Okun, April 15, 1969
Frank "Posh" Oltorf
Thomas O. Paine, March 25, 1969
Carl D. Perkins
J. J. (Jake) Pickle, Aug. 17, 1992
A. Philip Randolph
George E. Reedy, December 12, December 19, 20, 1968, June 7, 1975
Charles Roberts
John P. Roche
Nelson Rockefeller
Dean Rusk, July 28, 1969, January 2, March 8, 1970
Harold (Barefoot) Sanders, Jr., November 3, 1969
Arthur M. Schlesinger, Jr.
Charles L. Schultze, March 28, April 10, 1969
Jewell Malechek Scott, December 20, 1978, May 30, 1990
Sargent Shriver, August 20, 1980, July 1, 1982
Hugh Sidey
John V. Singleton, Jr.
Byron G. Skelton
Hobart Taylor, Jr.
Larry Temple, June 12, 26, August 11, 13, 1970

J. William Theis
Donald S. Thomas, March 13, 1987
Jack Valenti, June 14, October 18, 1969, February 19, March 3, 1971, July
    12, 1972
Paul C. Warnke
Earl Warren
Robert C. Weaver, Nov. 19, 1968
James E. Webb
Edward C. Welsh
June White
Lee C. White, February 18, 1971
Thomas G. Wicker
Roy Wilkins
Adam Yarmolinsky, July 13, 1970
John F. Kennedy Library, Boston, Massachusetts
  Joseph Alsop
  Jack Conway
  Elizabeth Gatov
  Averell Harriman
  Nicholas Katzenbach
  Peter Lisagor
  John Macy
  Burke Marshall
  Joseph L. Rauh
  Edwin L. Weisl, Sr.
  Harris Wofford
Senate Historical Office
  Stuart E. McClure
  Roy L. McGhee
  Carl Marcy
  George A. Smathers

INTERVIEWS AND CORRESPONDENCE WITH AUTHOR

R. W. Apple, June 18, 1997, Washington, D.C.
Robert G. Baker, no date, telephone interview with John Brice
Francis Bator, Jan. 28, 1997, Cambridge, Massachusetts
Alan Brinkley, no date, Washington, D.C.
McGeorge Bundy, March 30, Sept. 25, 1993, New York, New York
William P. Bundy, May 17, 1992, Princeton, New Jersey
Horace Busby, July 16, 1988, Washington, D.C.
George E. Christian, June 23, 1992, April 2, 1994, March 14, 1996, Austin,
    Texas
John Culver, July 2, 1996, Washington, D.C.
Thomas Curtis to Author, Sept. 24, 1986
Elias P. Demetracopoulos, May 18, 1992
Robert Fratkin, Telephone Conversation, June 10, 1993, Washington, D.C.
Murray Fromson, May 2, 1992, Aug. 21, 1993, Los Angeles, California; tele-
    phone conversation, Sept. 8, 1997

Daniel M. Giat to R.D., June 10, 1967
Robert L. Hardesty, Nov. 4, 1996, Washington, D.C.
Richard R. Helms, May 18, 1992
Max Holland, Dec. 14, 1992, Los Angeles, California
Lady Bird Johnson, July 13–18, 1983, with John and Sandra Brice, Austin, Texas
Lady Bird Johnson, Oct. 6, 1997, Austin, Texas
Lyndon B. Johnson, Aug. 12, 1969, with William J. Jorden, Austin, Texas
Lyndon B. Johnson, Dec. 19, 1968, Sept. 23, 1969, with Walter Cronkite, Austin, Texas
Nicholas Katzenbach, May 17, 1992, Princeton, New Jersey
Robert S. McNamara, March 26, 1993
Harry Middleton, March 14, 1996
Bill Moyers in *Modern Maturity*, Oct.–Nov. 1993
Bill Moyers, Jan. 26, 1994, New York City; May 14, 1997, Washington, D.C.
J. J. Jake Pickle, April 10, 1996, Austin, Texas
George Reedy to R.D., Nov. 20, 1991
Walt W. Rostow, July 27, 1992, Austin, Texas
Sheldon Stern, March 27, 1992, Boston, Massachusetts
Jane Sumner, Sept. 11, 1991, Dallas, Texas
Larry Temple, March 29, 1989, Aug. 2, 1993, April 2, 1994, March 14, 1996, Austin, Texas; telephone convention, Sept. 21, 1997
Luci Johnson Turpin, Feb. 25, 1996, Austin, Texas
Ted Van Dyk, March 14, 1996, Feb. 28, 1997, Washington, D.C.
Elizabeth Wickenden, Dec. 20, 1986

UNPUBLISHED BOOKS, PAPERS, AND THESES AND FILMS

Stephen Ansolabehere et al., "Does Attack Advertising Demobilize the Electorate?," unpublished paper, Department of Political Science, University of California, Los Angeles, California.
Donald R. Burkholder, "The Caretakers of the Presidential Image," Ph.D. Thesis, Wayne State University, Detroit, Michigan.
Matthew J. Dallek, "Young Americans for Freedom, 1960–1964," M.A. Thesis, Columbia University, New York, New York, 1993.
Lawrence R. Jacobs and Robert Y. Shapiro, "Leadership and Responsiveness: Some New Evidence on the Johnson Presidency," unpublished paper, American Political Science Association, Sept. 1992.
Michael E. Latham, "Panama Crisis: The Johnson Administration and 'The Chiari Problem,' January–April 1964," unpublished seminar paper, History Department, University of California, Los Angeles, California.
"Political Activities of the Johnson White House, 1963–1969," Microfilm, University Publications of America.
Phillip Charles Saunders, "War with Numbers: Politics and SNIE 14.3–67," Senior Thesis, History Department, Harvard University, Cambridge, Massachusetts, 1988.
David Grubin, TV Documentary: "LBJ," 1991.
"Lady Bird Johnson," TV Documentary, 1993.
Oliver Stone, director, *JFK*, film, 1991.

NEWSPAPERS AND PERIODICALS

American Heritage
Athens Daily Post
Atlantic Monthly
Baltimore Sun
Boston Globe
Chicago Daily News
The China Quarterly
Christian Science Monitor
Congressional Quarterly
Congressional Record
Des Moines Register
Diplomatic History
The Economist
Harper's Magazine
Journal of American History
LC Information Bulletin
Life
Los Angeles Times
Miami Herald
Minneapolis Tribune
Mother Jones
Naval War College: *Proceedings*
The New Republic
New York Herald Tribune
New York Post
New York Review of Books
New York Times
New Yorker
Newsweek
Political Psychology
Political Science Quarterly
Public Opinion Quarterly
Presidential Studies Quarterly
Reviews in American History
Review of Politics
Saturday Evening Post
Saturday Review
SHAFR Newsletter
Texas Observer
Time
U.S. News & World Report
USA Today
Vanity Fair
Wall Street Journal
Washington Post
Washington Star
Wichita Falls Record News

BOOKS

Adams, Samuel A. *War of Numbers: An Intelligence Memoir.* South Royalton, Vt., 1994.

Ambrose, Stephen E. *Nixon: The Triumph of a Politician, 1962–1972.* New York, 1989.

Bailyn, Bernard, et al. *The Great Republic: A History of the American People.* Lexington, Mass., 1992 ed.

Baker, Leonard. *The Johnson Eclipse.* New York, 1966.

Ball, George W. *The Past Has Another Pattern.* New York, 1982.

Berkowitz, Edward D. *Mr. Social Security: The Life of Wilbur J. Cohen.* Lawrence, Kans., 1995.

Berman, Edgar. *Hubert.* New York, 1979.

Berman, Larry. *Planning a Tragedy: The Americanization of the War in Vietnam.* New York, 1982.

———. *Lyndon Johnson's War: The Road to Stalemate in Vietnam.* New York, 1989.

Bernstein, Irving. *Promises Kept: John F. Kennedy's New Frontier.* New York, 1991.

———. *Guns or Butter: The Presidency of Lyndon Johnson.* New York, 1994.

Beschloss, Michael R. *Taking Charge: The Johnson White House Tapes, 1963–1964.* New York, 1997.

Bibby, John, and Roger Davidson. *On Capitol Hill: Studies in the Legislative Process.* New York, 1967.

Bill, James A. *George Ball: Behind the Scenes in U.S. Foreign Policy.* New Haven, Conn., 1997.

Blight, James G., and David A. Welch. *On the Brink: Americans and Soviets Examine the Cuban Missile Crisis.* New York, 1989.

Blum, John Morton. *Years of Discord: American Politics and Society, 1961–1974.* New York, 1991.

Bornet, Vaughn Davis. *The Presidency of Lyndon B. Johnson.* Lawrence, Kans., 1983.

Brands, H. W. *The Wages of Globalism: Lyndon Johnson and the Limits of American Power.* New York, 1995.

Burke, John P., and Fred I. Greenstein. *How Presidents Test Reality: Decisions on Vietnam, 1954 and 1965.* New York, 1989.

Califano, Joseph A., Jr. *Governing America: An Insider's Report from the White House and the Cabinet.* New York, 1981.

———. *The Triumph & Tragedy of Lyndon Johnson.* New York, 1991.

Chomsky, Noam. *Rethinking Camelot: JFK, the Vietnam War, and U.S. Political Culture.* Boston, 1993.

Clifford, Clark. *Counsel to the President: A Memoir.* New York, 1991.

Coffin, Tristam. *Senator Fulbright: Portrait of a Public Philosopher.* New York, 1966.

Cohen, Warren, and Nancy Tucker, eds. *Lyndon Johnson Confronts the World.* New York, 1994.

Cooper, Chester. *The Lost Crusade: America in Vietnam.* New York, 1970.

Cronkite, Walter. *A Reporter's Life.* New York, 1996.

Dallek, Robert. *Lone Star Rising: Lyndon Johnson and His Times, 1908–1960.* New York, 1991.

———. *Hail to the Chief: The Making and Unmaking of American Presidents.* New York, 1996.

Davies, Gareth. *From Opportunity to Entitlement: The Transformation and Decline of Great Society Liberalism.* Lawrence, Kans., 1996.

Diamond, Edwin, and Stephen Bates. *The Spot: The Rise of Political Advertising on Television.* Cambridge, Mass., 1984.

Dietz, Terry. *Republicans and Vietnam, 1961–1968.* New York, 1986.

Divine, Robert A., ed. *The Johnson Years.* Vol. 1: *Foreign Policy, the Great Society and the White House.* Austin, Tex., 1981.

———, ed. *The Johnson Years.* Vol. 2: *Vietnam, the Environment, and Science.* Lawrence, Kans., 1987.

———, ed. *The Johnson Years.* Vol. 3: *LBJ at Home and Abroad.* Lawrence, Kans., 1994.

Donovan, John. *The Politics of Poverty.* Indianapolis, Ind., 1973 ed.

Ennes, James M., Jr., *Assault on the Liberty.* New York, 1980.

Evans, Rowland, and Robert Novak. *Lyndon B. Johnson: The Exercise of Power.* New York, 1968.

Firestone, Bernard J., and Robert C. Vogt. *Lyndon Baines Johnson and the Uses of Power.* New York, 1988.

Fite, Gilbert C. *Richard B. Russell, Jr.: Senator from Georgia.* Chapel Hill, N.C., 1991.

Fulbright, J. William. *The Arrogance of Power.* New York, 1966.

Gallup, George H. *The Gallup Poll: Public Opinion, 1935–1971*, volume 3: *1959–1971.* New York, 1972.

Gardner, Lloyd C. *Pay Any Price: Lyndon Johnson and the Wars for Vietnam.* Chicago, 1995.

Garrow, David J. *Protest at Selma: Martin Luther King, Jr., and the Voting Rights Act of 1965.* New Haven, Conn., 1968.

———. *The FBI and Martin Luther King, Jr.* New York, 1983 ed.

Gentry, Curt. *J. Edgar Hoover: The Man and the Secrets.* New York, 1991.

Gibbons, William C. *The U.S. Government and the Vietnam War. Part 2: 1961–1964.* Washington, D.C., 1986.

———. *The U.S. Government and the Vietnam War. Part 3: January–July 1965.* Princeton, N.J., 1989.

———. *The U.S. Government and the Vietnam War. Part 4: July 1965–January 1968.* Washington, D.C., 1994.

Gittinger, Ted, ed. *The Johnson Years: A Vietnam Roundtable.* Austin, Tex., 1993.

Gleijeses, Piero. *The Dominican Crisis: The 1965 Constitutionalist Revolt and American Intervention.* Baltimore, Md., 1978.

Goldman, Eric F. *The Tragedy of Lyndon Johnson.* New York, 1969.

Goodwin, Doris Kearns. *The Fitzgeralds and the Kennedys: An American Saga.* New York, 1987.

Goodwin, Richard. *Remembering America: A Voice from the Sixties.* Boston, 1988.

Gould, Lewis L. *Lady Bird Johnson and the Environment.* Lawrence, Kans., 1988.

Goulding, Phil G. *Confirm or Deny: Informing the People on National Security.* New York, 1970.

Graff, Henry F. *The Tuesday Cabinet: Deliberation and Decision on Peace and War Under Lyndon B. Johnson.* Englewood Cliffs, N.J., 1970

Graham, Hugh Davis. *The Uncertain Triumph: Federal Education Policy in the Kennedy and Johnson Years.* Chapel Hill, N.C., 1984.

———. *The Civil Rights Era: Origins and Development of National Policy, 1960–1972.* New York, 1990.

Gravel, Mike, ed. *The Pentagon Papers: The Defense Department History of United States Decisionmaking on Vietnam.* 5 vols. Boston, 1971.

Guthman, Edwin O. and Jeffrey Shulman. *Robert Kennedy: In His Own Words.* New York, 1988.

Haar, Charles M. *Between the Idea and the Reality: A Study in the Origin, Fate, and Legacy of the Model Cities Program.* Boston, 1975.

Halberstam, David. *The Best and the Brightest.* Greenwich, Conn., 1973 ed.

———. *The Powers That Be.* New York, 1979.

Haldeman, H. R. *The Haldeman Diaries: Inside the Nixon White House.* New York, 1994.

Hallin, Daniel C. *The "Uncensored" War: The Media and Vietnam.* New York, 1986.

Hardesty, Robert L., ed. *The Johnson Years: The Difference He Made.* Austin, Tex., 1993.

Herring, George C. *The Secret Diplomacy of the Vietnam War: The "Negotiating Volumes" of the Pentagon Papers.* Austin, Tex., 1983.

———. *America's Longest War: The United States and Vietnam, 1950–1975.* New York, 1986 ed.

———. *LBJ and Vietnam: A Different Kind of War.* Austin, Tex., 1994.

Hersh, Seymour M. *The Price of Power: Kissinger in the Nixon White House.* New York, 1983.

Hofstadter, Richard. *The Paranoid Style in American Politics.* New York, 1964

Hoopes, Townsend. *The Limits of Intervention.* New York, 1973.

Humphrey, Hubert H. *The Education of a Public Man.* Garden City, N.Y., 1976.

Janeway, Eliot. *Prescriptions for Prosperity.* New York, 1983.

Johnson, Lady Bird. *A White House Diary.* New York, 1970.

Johnson, Lyndon B. *The Vantage Point: Perspectives on the Presidency, 1963–1969.* New York, 1971.

Johnson, Sam Houston. *My Brother Lyndon.* New York, 1969.

Kahin, George McT. *Intervention: How America Became Involved in Vietnam.* New York, 1986.

Kalman, Laura. *Abe Fortas: A Biography.* New Haven, Conn., 1990.

Karnow, Stanley. *Vietnam: A History.* New York, 1984.

Kearns, Doris. *Lyndon Johnson and the American Dream.* New York, 1976.

Kissinger, Henry. *White House Years.* Boston, 1979.

Krepinevich, Andrew F. *The Army and Vietnam.* Baltimore, 1986.

Kutler, Stanley I. *The Wars of Watergate: The Last Crisis of Richard Nixon.* New York, 1991.

LaFeber, Walter. *The Panama Canal: The Crisis in Perspective.* New York, 1978.

————. *Inevitable Revolutions: The United States in Central America*. New York, 1984 ed.

Lamont, Lansing, and J. Duncan Edmonds. *Friends So Different: Essays on Canada and the United States in the 1980s*. Ottawa, Canada, 1990.

Leacock, Ruth. *Requiem for Revolution: The United States and Brazil, 1961–1969*. Kent, Ohio, 1990.

Lemann, Nicholas. *The Promised Land: The Great Black Migration and How It Changed America*. New York, 1991.

Lichtenstein, Nelson, ed. *Political Profiles: The Johnson Years*. New York, 1976.

Lincoln, Evelyn. *Kennedy and Johnson*. New York, 1968.

Link, Arthur S. *Woodrow Wilson and the Progressive Era, 1910–1917*. New York, 1963 ed.

McAuliffe, Mary S. *CIA Documents on the Cuban Missile Crisis, 1962*. Washington, D.C., 1992.

McDougall, Walter A. *The Heavens and the Earth: A Political History of the Space Age*. New York, 1985.

McNamara, Robert S. *In Retrospect: The Tragedy and Lessons of Vietnam*. New York, 1995.

McPherson, Harry. *A Political Education: A Washington Memoir*. Austin, Tex., 1995 ed.

Manchester, William. *The Death of a President*. New York, 1967.

Mann, Robert. *The Walls of Jericho: Lyndon Johnson, Hubert Humphrey, Richard Russell, and the Struggle for Civil Rights*. New York, 1996.

Matusow, Allen J. *The Unravelling of America: A History of Liberalism in the 1960s*. New York, 1984.

May, Ernest R. *"Lessons" of the Past: The Use and Misuse of History in American Foreign Policy*. New York, 1973.

May, Ernest R., and Philip Zelikow. *The Kennedy Tapes: Inside the White House During the Cuban Missile Crisis*. Cambridge, Mass., 1997.

Miller, Merle. *Lyndon: An Oral Biography*. New York, 1980.

Mueller, John E. *War, Presidents and Public Opinion*. New York, 1973.

Murphy, Bruce Allen. *The Brandeis-Frankfurter Connection: The Secret Political Activities of Two Supreme Court Justices*. New York, 1982.

————. *Fortas: The Rise and Ruin of a Supreme Court Justice*. New York, 1988.

Neustadt, Richard, and Ernest R. May. *Thinking in Time: The Use of History for Decision Makers*. New York, 1986.

Newman, John M. *JFK and Vietnam*. New York, 1992.

Oberdorfer, Don. *Tet!*. New York, 1971.

O'Brien, David M. *Storm Center: The Supreme Court in American Politics*. New York, 1986.

O'Donnell, Kenneth P., and David F. Powers. *Johnny, We Hardly Knew Ye*. Boston, 1972.

O'Neill, Thomas P. *Man of the House: The Life and Political Memoirs of Speaker Tip O'Neill*. New York, 1987.

Palmer, Bruce, Jr., *The 25-Year War: America's Military Role in Vietnam*. Lexington, Ky., 1984.

Parmet, Herbert S. *JFK: The Presidency of John F. Kennedy*. New York, 1984 ed.

Patterson, James T. *America's Struggle Against Poverty, 1900–1980*. New York, 1981.

Pearson, Lester B. *Memoirs*. Toronto, Canada, 1975.

Piven, Frances Fox, and Richard A. Cloward. *Regulating the Poor: The Functions of Public Welfare*. New York, 1971.

Powers, Richard Gid. *Secrecy and Power: The Life of J. Edgar Hoover*. New York, 1987.

Powers, Thomas. *The Man Who Kept the Secrets: Richard Helms and the CIA*. New York, 1979.

Public Papers of the Presidents of the United States: Lyndon B. Johnson. 10 vols. Washington, D.C., 1965–70.

Rainwater, Lee, and William L. Yancey, *The Moynihan Report and the Politics of Controversy*. Cambridge, Mass., 1967.

Redford, Emmette S., and Marlan Blissett. *Organizing the Executive Branch: The Johnson Presidency*. Chicago, 1981.

Report of the National Advisory Commission on Civil Disorders. New York, 1968.

Roberts, Chalmers M. *First Rough Draft: A Journalist's Journal of Our Times*. New York, 1973.

Roosevelt & Frankfurter: Their Correspondence, 1928–1945. London, England, 1968.

Safer, Morley. *Flashbacks*. New York, 1990.

Salisbury, Harrison E. *Behind the Lines—Hanoi, December 23, 1966–January 7, 1967*. New York, 1967.

———. *A Time of Change: A Reporter's Tale of Our Time*. New York, 1988.

Schlesinger, Arthur M., Jr., *A Thousand Days: John F. Kennedy in the White House*. Boston, 1965.

———. *Robert Kennedy and His Times*. Boston, 1978.

———. *The Cycles of American History*. New York, 1986.

Seaborg, Glenn T., and Benjamin S. Loeb. *Stemming the Tide: Arms Control in the Johnson Years*. Lexington, Mass., 1987.

Schandler, Herbert Y. *The Unmaking of a President: Lyndon Johnson and Vietnam*. Princeton, N.J., 1977.

Shapley, Debroah. *Promise and Power: The Life and Times of Robert McNamara*. Boston, 1993.

Sheehan, Neil. *A Bright Shining Lie: John Paul Vann and America in Vietnam*. New York, 1988.

Shesol, Jeff. *Mutual Contempt: Lyndon Johnson, Robert Kennedy, and the Feud That Shaped a Decade*. New York, 1997.

Small, Melvin. *Johnson, Nixon and the Doves*. New Brunswick, N.J., 1989.

Smith, Richard Norton, and Timothy Walch, eds. *Farewell to the Chief: Former Presidents in American Public Life*. Worland, Wy., 1990.

Solberg, Carl. *Hubert Humphrey: A Biography*. New York, 1984.

Sorensen, Theodore C. *Kennedy*. New York, 1966.

Sorian, Richard. *The Bitter Pill: Tough Choices in America's Health Policy*. New York, 1990.

Spector, Ronald. *After Tet: The Bloodiest Year of the Vietnam War*. New York, 1985.

Starr, Paul. *The Social Transformation of American Medicine*. New York, 1982.

Steel, Ronald. *Walter Lippmann and the American Century.* Boston, 1980.

Steinberg, Arthur. *Sam Johnson's Boy.* New York, 1968.

Sulzberger, C. L. *Seven Continents and Forty Years.* New York, 1977.

Sundquist, James L., ed. *On Fighting Poverty.* New York, 1969.

Theoharis, Athen G., and John Stuart Cox. *The Boss: J. Edgar Hoover and the Great American Inquisition.* Philadelphia, Pa., 1988.

Thomas, Helen. *Deadline: White House.* New York, 1975.

Turner, Kathleen J. *Lyndon Johnson's Dual War.* Chicago, 1985.

Ulam, Adam B. *Expansion & Coexistence: The History of Soviet Foreign Policy, 1917–1967.* New York, 1968.

United States Congress. *Hearings: Select Senate Committee to Study Governmental Operations with Respect to Intelligence.* Vol. 6. Washington, D.C., 1975.

———. *Final Report of the Senate Select Committee to Study Governmental Operations with Respect to Intelligence Activities.* Books 2 and 3. Washington, D.C., 1976.

———. House Committee on Ways and Means. *Overview of Entitlement Programs: 1993 Green Book.* Washington, D.C., 1993.

United States Department of State. *Foreign Relations of the United States, 1961–1963: Vietnam, 1961.* Washington, D.C., 1988.

———. *Foreign Relations of the United States, 1961–1963: Vietnam, August–December, 1963.* Washington, D.C., 1991.

———. *Foreign Relations of the United States, 1964–1968: Vietnam, 1964.* Washington, D.C., 1992.

Valenti, Jack. *A Very Human President.* New York, 1975.

VanDeMark, Brian. *Into the Quagmire: Lyndon Johnson and the Escalation of the Vietnam War.* New York, 1991.

Vandiver, Frank E. *Shadows of Vietnam: Lyndon Johnson's Wars.* College Station, Tex., 1997.

Wells, Tom. *The War Within: America's Battle Over Vietnam.* New York, 1996 ed.

Westmoreland, William C. *A Soldier Reports.* New York, 1976.

White, Theodore H. *The Making of the President, 1964.* New York, 1965.

———. *The Making of the President, 1968.* New York, 1969.

Wicker, Tom. *JFK and LBJ: The Influence of Personality upon Politics.* Baltimore, 1969 ed.

Wise, David. *The Politics of Lying: Government Deception, Secrecy, and Power.* New York, 1973.

Witcover, Jules. *The Year the Dream Died: Revisiting 1968 in America.* New York, 1997.

Woods, Randall B. *Fulbright: A Biography.* Cambridge, England, 1995.

Zarefsky, David. *President Johnson's War on Poverty.* Birmingham, Ala. 1986.

Zirbel, Craig I. *The Texas Connection.* Scottsdale, Ariz., 1991.

ARTICLES

Adler, Bill. "The Killing of Henry Marshall," *Texas Observer* (Nov. 7, 1986).

Alsop, Stewart. "LBJ and RFK," *Saturday Evening Post* (Feb. 22, 1964).

Altschuler, Bruce E. "Lyndon Johnson and the Public Polls," *Public Opinion Quarterly* (Fall 1986).

Ambrose, Stephen E. "Writers on the Grassy Knoll," *New York Times Book Review* (Feb. 2, 1992).

Barrett, David M. "The Mythology Surrounding Lyndon Johnson, His Advisers, and the 1965 Decision to Escalate the Vietnam War," *Political Science Quarterly* (Winter 1988–89).

————. "Secrecy and Openness in Lyndon Johnson's White House: Political Style, Pluralism, and the Presidency," *Review of Politics* (Winter 1992).

Barron, John. "The Johnson Money," *Washington Star* (June 9, 1964).

Blonsky, Marshall. "Bill Moyers Acts Up," *Los Angeles Times Magazine*, March 27, 1994.

Brauer, Carl M. "Kennedy, Johnson and the War on Poverty," *Journal of American History* (June 1982).

Brenner, Marie. "Mr. Ambassador!: Bob Strauss Comes Home," *New Yorker* (Dec. 28, 1992).

Brogan, D. W. "The Illusion of American Omnipotence," *Harper's Magazine* (Dec. 1952).

Chen, Jian. "China's Involvement in the Vietnam War, 1964–1969," *China Quarterly* (June 1995).

"Controversy in Congress Over 'Medicare,'" *Congressional Quarterly Fact Sheet* (March 1965).

Cooper, Lieut. Gen. Charles G. "The Day It Became the Longest War," (Naval War College) *Proceedings* (May 1996).

Dallek, Robert. "Lyndon Johnson and Vietnam: The Making of a Tragedy," *Diplomatic History* (Spring 1996).

Ferguson, Andrew. "The Power of Myth: Bill Moyers, Liberal Fraud," *New Republic* (Aug. 19 and 26, 1991).

Gilbert, Robert E. "The Political Effects of Presidential Illness: The Case of Lyndon Johnson," *Political Psychology* (Fall 1995).

Graff, Henry F. "How Johnson Makes Foreign Policy," *New York Times Magazine* (July 4, 1965).

Halberstam, David. "Return to Vietnam," *Harper's* (Dec. 1967).

Holland, Max. "After 30 Years: Making Sense of the Assassination," *Reviews in American History* (June 1994).

————. "The Key to the Warren Report," *American Heritage* (Nov. 1995).

Humphrey, David C. "Searching for LBJ at the Johnson Library," *SHAFR Newsletter* (June 20, 1989).

Janos, Leo. "The Last Days of the President: LBJ in Retirement," *Atlantic* (July 1973).

Jones, James R. "Behind LBJ's Decision Not to Run in '68," *New York Times* (April 16, 1988).

Kiker, Douglas. "Johnson Shakedown in Crises," *New York Herald Tribune* (Jan. 31, 1964).

Kohlmeier, Louis. "The Johnson Wealth," *Wall Street Journal* (March 23, 1964).

Lacoutre, Jean. "Vietnam: The Turning Point," *New York Review of Books* (May 12, 1966).

"LBJ Reminisces: The Fatal Trip to Dallas,"*Among Friends of LBJ* (Jan. 1, 1983).

Lewis, Anthony. "Shriver Moves into the Front Rank," *New York Times Magazine* (March 15, 1964).

Leuchtenburg, William E. "The Genesis of the Great Society," *The Reporter* (April 21, 1966).

————. "A Visit with LBJ," *American Heritage* (May/June 1990).

————. "The Old Cowhand from Dixie," *Atlantic Monthly* (Dec. 1992).

Marmor, Theodore R., and Lawrence R. Jacobs. "Don't Settle for Crumbs on Health Reform," *Los Angeles Times* (Nov. 16, 1992).

Middleton, Harry. "Speech That Halted a Great Society," *Los Angeles Times* (March 31, 1988).

Moyers, Bill. "Flashback," *Newsweek* (Feb. 10, 1975).

Osborne, David. "The Great Society Revisited," *Mother Jones* (June 1986).

Presley, James. "What Is an LBJ?," *Texas Observer* (Oct. 18, 1963).

Raskin, A. H. "Generalissimo of the War on Poverty," *New York Times Magazine* (Nov. 22, 1964).

Roper, Elmo. "After the Election," *Saturday Review* (Nov. 28, 1964).

Sidey, Hugh. "Some Pages Not in L.B.J.'s Book," *Life* (Nov. 5, 1971).

————. "One More Call to Reason Together," *Life* (Dec. 29, 1972).

Sloan, John W. "President Johnson, the Council of Economic Advisers, and the Failure to Raise Taxes in 1966 and 1967," *Presidential Studies Quarterly* (Winter 1985).

Smith, Nancy Kegan. "Presidential Task Force Operation During the Johnson Administration," *Presidential Studies Quarterly* (Spring 1985).

Suddreth, Lucy D. "Thurgood Marshall," *LC Information Bulletin* (Feb. 22, 1993).

Weber, Eugen. "Schooling for Whom? Education for What?," *Explorations: The Twentieth Century*, Special Series, VI (1992).

Wheeler, Keith, and William Lambert. "The Man Who Is the President," *Life* (Aug. 14 and 21, 1964).

————. "How L.B.J.'s Family Amassed Its Fortune," *Life* (Aug. 21, 1964).

Wicker, Tom. "Johnson's Men: 'Valuable Hunks of Humanity,'" *New York Times Magazine* (May 3, 1964).

Williams, T. Harry. "Huey, Lyndon, and Southern Radicalism," *Journal of American History* (Sept. 1973).

Abbreviations Used in Notes

AP Associated Press
CIA Central Intelligence Agency
CF Confidential File
CF Country File (in National Security File)
CEA Council of Economic Advisers
DSDUF Declassified and Desanitized Documents from Unprocessed Files
EEOC Equal Employment Opportunity Committee
EX Executive File
FBI Federal Bureau of Investigation
FRUS Foreign Relations of the United States
GEN General File
HHH Hubert H. Humphrey
JEH J. Edgar Hoover
JFKL John F. Kennedy Library
LBJA Lyndon B. Johnson Archive
LC Library of Congress
LBJL Lyndon B. Johnson Library
MF Microfilm
MFDP Mississippi Freedom Democratic Party
NASA National Aeronautics and Space Administration
NSAM National Security Action Memorandum
NSC National Security Council
NSF National Security File
O&C Official and Confidential File
OEO Office of Economic Opportunity
OFP Office Files of the President
OH Oral History
POF President's Office File
PPCF Pre-Presidential Confidential File
PPF Post-Presidential File
PPP Pre-Presidential Papers
PPP *Public Papers of the Presidents*
RFK Robert F. Kennedy
RSAC Robert Sherrod Apollo Collection

SAC Special Agent in Charge
SF Subject File
SHO Senate Historical Office
TELCONS Telephone Conversations
TT Telephone Tape
UPI United Press International
VPP Vice Presidential Papers
VPSF Vice Presidential Security File
WHCF White House Central File
WHFN White House Famous Names

Notes

CHAPTER 1: "THE MOST INSIGNIFICANT OFFICE"

1. Leonard Baker, *The Johnson Eclipse* (New York, 1966), 3–9; Theodore C. Sorensen, *Kennedy* (New York, 1966 ed.), 273–75.

2. The account of LBJ's behavior during the 1960 campaign is in George Reedy to Author, Nov. 20, 1991.

3. Rowland Evans and Robert Novak, *Lyndon B. Johnson: The Exercise of Power* (New York, 1968 ed.), 115–16; Merle Miller, *Lyndon: An Oral Biography* (New York, 1980), 212–14.

4. Gardner Ackley Oral History, April 13, 1973, Lyndon B. Johnson Library (hereafter cited as OH, LBJL). Unless otherwise noted, all oral histories cited are from the LBJL. Dates of the oral history interviews are cited only when there are two or more interviews on different dates.

5. Marie Brenner, "Mr. Ambassador!: Bob Strauss Comes Home," *New Yorker*, Dec. 28, 1992, pp. 148, 150.

6. Robert Dallek, *Lone Star Rising: Lyndon Johnson and His Times, 1908–1960* (New York, 1991), passim.

7. Doris Kearns, *Lyndon Johnson and the American Dream* (New York, 1976), 53–54.

8. See Dallek, *Lone Star Rising*, passim.

9. Evans and Novak, *LBJ: Exercise of Power*, 323; Arthur M. Schlesinger, Jr., *Robert Kennedy and His Times* (Boston, 1978), 625, 621. The title of this chapter is taken from John Adams's observation that the vice presidency is "the most insignificant office that ever the invention of man contrived or his imagination conceived." For an excellent discussion of the vice presidency, see chap. 12, "The Future of the Vice Presidency," in Arthur M. Schlesinger, Jr., *The Cycles of American History* (New York, 1986).

10. Doris Kearns Goodwin, *The Fitzgeralds and the Kennedys: An American Saga* (New York, 1987), 780; Dallek, *Lone Star Rising*, 559, 565, 569.

11. Arthur Steinberg, *Sam Johnson's Boy* (New York, 1968), 530; LBJ to George E. Reedy, n.d., with memo attached, White House Central Files: Aides: George E. Reedy (hereafter cited as WHCF: Aides: Reedy), LBJL. Unless otherwise noted, all manuscript materials are from the LBJL.

12. Evans and Novak, *LBJ: Exercise of Power*, 323–26; Steinberg, *Sam Johnson's Boy*, 547–48; Miller, *Lyndon*, 337.

13. Evans and Novak, *LBJ: Exercise of Power*, 326–27; Steinberg, *Sam Johnson's Boy*, 551, 558.

14. Kenneth P. O'Donnell OH; Dallek, *Lone Star Rising*, 540; Steinberg, *Sam Johnson's Boy*, 552; Schlesinger, *Cycles of American History*, 146, 150.

15. Evans and Novak, *LBJ: Exercise of Power*, 327–28; O'Donnell OH;

Miller, *Lyndon*, 340–42; Schlesinger, *Robert Kennedy*, 621–22; Ralph A. Dungan to JFK, Oct. 3, 1962, President's Office Files, John F. Kennedy Library (hereafter cited as POF, JFKL).

16. Arthur M. Schlesinger, OH; O'Donnell OH; Evans and Novak, *LBJ: Exercise of Power*, 334–35.

17. Harris Wofford to JFK, Dec. 30, 1960, Pre–Presidential Papers (hereafter cited as PPP), JFKL; "Vice President's Views of the Vice Presidency," Nov. 22, 1963, WHCF: Aides: Reedy.

18. George A. Smathers OH, Senate Historical Office (hereafter cited as SHO), Washington, D.C.

19. Walter Jenkins OH, Aug. 24, 1971.

20. Elizabeth Carpenter OH, May 15, 1969; Steinberg, *Sam Johnson's Boy*, 565; Kearns, *Lyndon Johnson*, 167–68; Miller, *Lyndon*, 343–45.

21. Steinberg, *Sam Johnson's Boy*, 566–67; J. William Theis OH; Ashton Gonella OH.

22. Carroll Kilpatrick OH; Steinberg, *Sam Johnson's Boy*, 567; Murray Fromson interview, May 2, 1992; he recounted the episode about patting the children. Cf. Miller, *Lyndon*, 345. Amb. Young to Sec. of State, May 20, 1961, Vice-Presidential Security File (hereafter cited as VPSF).

23. J. K. Galbraith to JFK, May 10, Aug. 15, 1961, POF, JFKL; Miller, *Lyndon*, 348; Evans and Novak, *LBJ: Exercise of Power*, 341–42.

24. Ibid., 342; Miller, *Lyndon*, 343, 348–49; Steinberg, *Sam Johnson's Boy*, 568; Galbraith to Sec. of State, May 20, 1961, VPSF; J. William Theis OH.

25. Walter Jenkins OH, Aug. 24, 1971; George Reedy OH, Dec. 12, 1968; Steinberg, *Sam Johnson's Boy*, 568–69.

26. When President Ayub Khan of Pakistan visited the United States, Johnson entertained him at his ranch, where he described the standard of living thirty years ago in central Texas as much like that of Pakistan now. In what then Defense Department official William P. Bundy called a "deeply moving," "spontaneous" speech, Johnson explained improved conditions for Texans as the result of rural electrification. Saying you can do it too, Johnson made "a tremendous impression on Ayub." William P. Bundy interview, May 17, 1992. Elizabeth Carpenter OH, May 15, 1969; Arthur Schlesinger, Jr., *A Thousand Days: John F. Kennedy in the White House* (Boston, 1965), 705, relates the anecdote about the diplomat. I have followed the version in Kearns, *Lyndon Johnson*, 411 n 14.

27. Thomas G. Wicker OH; Carroll Kilpatrick OH; Steinberg, *Sam Johnson's Boy*, 578–80.

28. Charles L. Bartlett OH.

29. George C. Herring, *America's Longest War: The United States and Vietnam, 1950–1975*, 2nd ed. (New York, 1986), 73–78.

30. JFK to Diem, n.d. (May 8, 1961); LBJ to JFK, May 23, 1961, VPSF. Also see *Foreign Relations of the United States, 1961–1963: Vietnam, 1961* (Washington, D.C., 1988), 135–78.

31. Galbraith to JFK, March 2, 1961, POF, JFKL.

32. Herring, *America's Longest War*, chap. 3; Brian VanDeMark, *Into the Quagmire: Lyndon Johnson and the Escalation of the Vietnam War* (New York, 1991), 6–10; LBJ interview, Aug. 12, 1969, with William J. Jorden; Richard H. Nelson OH. For the deliberations on Cuba, see Ernest R. May and Philip

Zelikow, *The Kennedy Tapes: Inside the White House During the Cuban Missile Crisis* (Cambridge, Mass., 1997).

33. Schlesinger, *A Thousand Days*, 394–97; Evans and Novak, *LBJ: Exercise of Power*, 343–44.

34. See the Pre-Presidential Daily Diary, Aug. 18–21, 1961; VPSF: Berlin, Aug. 1961; Baker, *Johnson Eclipse*, 67–77; Miller, *Lyndon*, 350–54.

35. See Walter A. McDougall, *The Heavens and the Earth: A Political History of the Space Age* (New York, 1985), 301–5; Robert A. Divine, ed., *The Johnson Years*, vol. II: *Vietnam, the Environment, and Science* (Austin, Tex., 1987), 228–33.

36. JFK to LBJ, April 20, 1961; LBJ to JFK, April 28, 1961, POF, JFKL; Richard H. Nelson OH; Memorandum, n.d., (1961), beginning: "Despite all the heated public discussion," WHCF: Aides: Reedy: McDougall, *The Heavens and the Earth*, 320; Edward C. Welsh OH.

37. McDougall, *The Heavens and the Earth*, 302–3.

38. Ibid., 308–10; Newton Minow OH.

39. JFK to LBJ, July 29, 1963; LBJ to JFK, July 31, 1963, White House Famous Names (hereafter cited as WHFN): JFK; Newton Minow OH; McDougall, *The Heavens and the Earth*, 322–23, 376, 389–96.

40. LBJ to Ed Welsh, July 26, 29, 1961; LBJ to Walter Jenkins, Aug. 2, 1961; Welsh to LBJ, Aug. 11, Sept. 8, 13, 14, 1961; Welsh to Henson, Oct. 9, 1961, Vice Presidential Papers (hereafter cited as VPP): Space.

41. George Smathers OH, SHO; McDougall, *The Heavens and the Earth*, 361–63, 373–76.

42. Robert Sherrod telephone conversation with Richard L. Callaghan, Jan. 28, 1971; Sherrod telephone conversation with Kenneth O'Donnell, May 13, 1971, Robert Sherrod Apollo Collection, National Aeronautics and Space Administration Archives (hereafter cited as RSAC, NASA Archives).

43. James Burke interview with Webb, May 23, 1979, James Webb Papers, NASA Archives.

44. See Dallek, *Lone Star Rising*, esp. 83–84; Nicholas Lemann, *The Promised Land: The Great Black Migration and How It Changed America* (New York, 1991), 136–37.

45. Ibid., 137.

46. "You will become the target of the ADA and the 'advanced liberals' because you are not doing anything and also the target of the southerners every time you try to do something even minor. . . . It will be impossible to satisfy either group no matter what you do," James Rowe to LBJ, Dec. 22, 1960, VPP: Civil Rights. Also see Wofford to JFK, Dec. 30, 1960, PPP, JFKL; Press Release, March 6, 1961, WHCF, JFKL; Reedy to LBJ, Feb. 10, 1961, WHCF: Aides: Reedy; Hobart Taylor, Jr. OH; Hugh Davis Graham, *The Civil Rights Era: Origins and Development of National Policy, 1960–1972* (New York, 1990), 27–40.

47. Harris Wofford OH, JFKL; James Farmer OH.

48. Charles Boatner OH; Elizabeth Gatov OH, JFKL.

49. Abe Fortas OH; Nicholas Katzenbach OH, JFKL; LBJ telephone conversation with Richard Goodwin, Mar. 4, 1961, VPP: Civil Rights; Steinberg, *Sam Johnson's Boy*, 561.

50. Dr. Jack E. White to LBJ, March 16, 1961; LBJ to Conrad Hilton,

March 21, 1961; LBJ telephone conversation with White, March 26, 1961; LBJ telephone conversation with Porter Parrish, June 15, 1961; messages for LBJ, June 15, 19, 1961; Angier Biddle Duke to LBJ, June 19, 1961, VPP: Civil Rights.

51. "Vice President's Views of the Vice Presidency," Nov. 22, 1963, WHCF: Aides: Reedy; Statement used by LBJ, May 2, 1961, VPP: Civil Rights.

52. Davis, *Civil Rights Era*, 47–52.

53. Robert Troutman, Jr., to LBJ, Dec. 5, 6, 1961; LBJ to Troutman, Jr., Dec. 13, 1961, VPP: Civil Rights; LBJ, Press Conference, April 3, 1962, WHCF: Aides: Reedy; Harris Wofford OH, JFKL; Jerry Holleman OH; Graham, *Civil Rights Era*, 48, 52–53.

54. *New York Times*, July 12, Nov. 25, 1961; John Feild Memo for Holleman, n.d., WHCF: Aides: Willie Day Taylor; Lee C. White OH; Graham, *Civil Rights Era*, 52–53.

55. Hobart Taylor, Jr., OH; Burke Marshall OH, JFKL; LBJ, Press Release, March 28, 1962, WHCF: Aides: Reedy; Robert Troutman, Jr., to JFK, June 28, 1962; JFK to Troutman, Aug. 22, 1962, WHCF: CEEO; Lee C. White to Robert Troutman, Jr., Aug. 17, 1962, Lee C. White Papers, JFKL; Graham, *Civil Rights Era*, 54–58.

56. Theodore Kheel to LBJ, n.d., 1962, WHCF: Aides: Taylor; Hobart Taylor, Jr., OH; Graham, *Civil Rights Era*, 57–59.

57. Ibid., 59–63

58. Herbert S. Parmet, *JFK: The Presidency of John F. Kennedy* (New York, 1984 ed.), 249–62.

59. Ibid., 256–57.

60. Ibid., 257–59, 262–63.

61. Ibid., 260, 263; Ralph A. Dungan to JFK, Oct. 3, 1962, POF: LBJ; Joseph L. Rauh OH, JFKL; see folder titled "Senate—Rules of—Rule XXII (1963)" in *Lyndon* B. Johnson Archive: Subject File (hereafter cited as LBJA: SF); and a folder titled "Congress: Senate: Rule XXII" in VPP: Subject File: Congress 1962.

62. Parmet, *Presidency of JFK*, 263–68, 271.

63. Ibid., 267–68, 272–76.

64. Averell Harriman OH, JFKL; Joseph Alsop OH, JFKL; Parmet, *Presidency of JFK*, 20–21; Schlesinger, *Robert Kennedy*, 193; Lee C. White OH.

65. Burke Marshall OH, JFKL.

66. Dallek, *Lone Star Rising*, 490, 559; Peter Lisagor OH, JFKL.

67. Schlesinger, *Robert Kennedy*, 623.

68. Edwin O. Guthman and Jeffrey Shulman, *Robert Kennedy: In His Own Words* (New York, 1988), 407, 26; Schlesinger, *Robert Kennedy*, 623–24.

69. LBJ's comment to RFK was told to me, July 27, 1992, by Walt W. Rostow, who was present at an April 3, 1968, meeting between them.

70. JFK to LBJ, Feb. 21, May 7, 1963, WHCF: EEOC, JFKL; JFK to LBJ, April 17, 1963; LBJ to JFK, Feb. 25, April 22, 1963, WHFN: JFK; Guthman and Shulman, eds., *Robert Kennedy*, 150–54; Graham, *Civil Rights Era*, 67–73.

71. Lemann, *Promised Land*, 137–38; Burke Marshall OH; John Macy OH, JFKL; Minutes of CEEO Meetings, May 29, July 18, 1963; telephone conversation LBJ with Theodore Sorensen, June 3, 1963, VPP: Civil Rights; Jack Conway OH, JFKL; Schlesinger, *Robert Kennedy*, 335–36; Graham, *Civil Rights Era*, 71–73.

72. Lee C. White OH; Johnson's speeches are in VPP: Civil Rights.

73. Lee C. White OH; LBJ telephone conversation with Sorensen, June 3, 1963, VPP: Civil Rights.

74. Ibid.; Norbert Schlei to *Robert Kennedy*, June 4, 1963, Attorney General's Papers, JFKL; Guthman and Shulman, eds., *Robert Kennedy*, 177–78; LBJ to Sorensen, June 10, 1963, Theodore Sorensen Papers, JFKL.

75. John Macy OH, JFKL; Arthur Schlesinger, OH.

76. Guthman and Shulman, *Robert Kennedy*, 177–78, 410–11.

77. See my discussion of Johnson's election campaigns, his involvements with George and Herman Brown and their firm Brown and Root, and his acquisition of radio and television properties in *Lone Star Rising*. Also see Keith Wheeler and William Lambert, "How L. B. J.'s Family Amassed Its Fortune," *Life*, Aug. 21, 1964, pp. 62–72. Lady Bird Johnson described "The Elms" as "The most beautiful house we were ever to know." Interview by John and Sandra Brice, July 13–18, 1983.

78. See the folders on the Estes case in Boxes 1 and 2 of LBJ's Pre-Presidential Confidential File (hereafter cited as PPCF), LBJL. The pertinent FBI materials demonstrating the Kennedys' concern and the bureau's investigation of the charges against LBJ are in an FBI LBJ cross-reference file on Estes I obtained in 1991 under a Freedom of Information request. The most important documents are dated April 3, 18, 19, May 26, June 1, and Aug. 10 and 23, 1962. The documents dated May 23 and June 13, 22, 27, and 28, 1962, in J. Edgar Hoover's Official and Confidential File (hereafter cited as O&C, JEH), FBI, are also of interest. Also see Orville Freeman to JFK, April 16, 1962; RFK to JFK, May 4, 1962; Herbert J. Miller to Director, FBI, May 10, 1962; and Miller to Freeman, May 22, 1962, in RFK's Attorney General's Papers, JFKL.

79. *Los Angeles Times*, Aug. 14, 1985, p. 8; *New York Times*, Aug. 14, 1985, p. 13; Bill Adler, "The Killing of Henry Marshall," *Texas Observer*, Nov. 7, 1986, pp. 7–19; Leo Janos, "The Last Days of the President: LBJ in Retirement," *The Atlantic*, July 1973. "Was there any direct connection between Mr. Johnson and Billy Sol Estes?" an interviewer asked Secretary of Agriculture Orville Freeman in 1969. "No, I don't think there was any at all," Freeman replied. Orville L. Freeman OH.

80. My research in three other collections with substantial Estes materials also revealed nothing about LBJ: the papers of liberal Texas Senator Ralph Yarborough, a Johnson antagonist, in the Barker Texas History Center, Austin, Texas; of Charles S. Murphy, the Under Secretary of Agriculture, in the Harry S Truman Library, Independence, Missouri; and of Senator Edmund Muskie of Maine, a member of the Permanent Subcommittee on Investigations, which held hearings on the Estes case. The Muskie papers are in the Library of Bates College, Lewiston, Maine.

81. *Time*, Oct. 18, 1963, pp. 29–30; LBJ to Bobby Baker, Jan. 5, 1962, PPCF; Harry McPherson OH, Dec. 5, 1968; Dallek, *Lone Star Rising*, 477–78.

82. *Time*, Oct. 18, 1963, pp. 29–30; Special Agent in Charge (SAC), Baltimore, to JEH, July 27, 1962; JEH to SAC, Baltimore, Aug. 2, 1962; C. D. DeLoach to JEH, Jan. 20, 1964, O&C File, JEH, FBI; Steinberg, *Sam Johnson's Boy*, 595–99.

83. Lawrence F. O'Brien OH, Feb. 11, 1986; Charles L. Bartlett OH. Also

see Bill Geoghegan to RFK, Oct. 4, 1963, RFK: Attorney General's Papers, JFKL. After LBJ became Vice President, he was sensitive to anything that might involve him or any friend in Baker's illegal activities. See Gale W. McGee OH, Association of Former Members of Congress Papers, Library of Congress (hereafter cited as LC), Washington, D.C.; and Gale W. McGee OH. Also see George Reedy's astute comments on LBJ and Baker, OH, Dec. 12, 1968. "Johnson literally did not know a damned thing about the operations that Bobby [Baker] got himself tied up in and I know that to be the case." Harry McPherson OH, Jan. 16, 1969.

84. John V. Singleton, Jr., OH.

85. John Brice telephone interview with Robert G. Baker, n.d., in which Baker said: "Bobby [Kennedy] had ream after ream of wire taps on every conversation that Johnson ever had [as Vice President]. And Johnson knew that." LBJ told Hugh Sidey of *Time* that RFK "bugged him all during the time he was Vice President." *Time*, Feb. 10, 1975. Elias P. Demetracopoulos, a Greek journalist, recounted LBJ's conversation with the ambassador to me. Interview, May 18, 1992. He also gave me a copy of his published interview with Edward Kennedy in the *Athens Daily Post*, Aug. 29, 1962. Harry McPherson to LBJ, Jan. 24, 1963, LBJA: SF; Charles Boatner OH; Leslie Carpenter OH; Helen Thomas, *Deadline: White House* (New York, 1975), 121.

86. Schlesinger, *Robert Kennedy*, 604–5, 624; Kenneth O'Donnell OH; Evans and Novak, *LBJ: Exercise of Power*, 352; Miller, *Lyndon*, 365, 377–78.

87. For the Clark investigation, see a clipping of a Drew Pearson column, "Who's Telling Truth on RFK Feud?," Feb. 16, 1968, the RFK File, FBI Microfilm.

88. Richard G. Held to JEH, Feb. 10, 1964; C. D. DeLoach to JEH, March 6, 1964, O&C, JEH, FBI; Miller, *Lyndon*, 377–78.

89. Evelyn Lincoln, *Kennedy and Johnson* (New York, 1968), 205; Schlesinger, *Robert Kennedy*, 605; Miller, *Lyndon*, 377; Thomas G. Wicker OH.

90. Schlesinger, *Robert Kennedy*, 607.

91. James Presley, "What Is An LBJ?," *Texas Observer*, Oct. 18, 1963, p. 8.

92. Schlesinger, OH; Schlesinger, *A Thousand Days*, 706–7; Harry McPherson OH; Frank "Posh" Oltorf OH; Elizabeth Wickenden interview, Dec. 20, 1986; Schlesinger, *Robert Kennedy*, 622–23; Kearns, *Johnson*, 162–64.

93. Steinberg, *Sam Johnson's Boy*, 552; Kearns, *Lyndon Johnson*, 164–65.

94. LBJ to JFK, Jan. 7, 1962, POF, JFKL; Kearns, *Lyndon Johnson*, 162–63; Schlesinger, *A Thousand Days*, 704–5; Mrs. William S. White OH; Miller, *Lyndon*, 341.

95. George Reedy to LBJ, July 20, Nov. 22, 1961, VPP; Evans and Novak, *LBJ: Exercise of Power*, 328–29.

96. Drew Pearson, "LBJ Urging for Texas Trip Disputed," clipping of an undated 1967 column in Special Assassination File on JFK in LBJL; Kenneth O'Donnell OH, July 23, 1969; Clifton C. Carter OH; Ralph A. Dungan to JFK, Oct. 28, 1963, with Jerry R. Holleman to Dungan, Oct. 18, 1963, attached, Dungan Papers, JFKL; Schlesinger, *A Thousand Days* 1019.

97. Pearson, "LBJ Urging for Texas Trip Disputed"; two clippings, one by Evans and Novak, n.d., 1963, and the other by Margaret Mayer, Jan. 13,

1967, in Special Assassination File on JFK; Walter Jenkins OH, Aug. 24, 1971; George Reedy OH, Dec. 19, 1968; Byron T. Skelton OH; Cecil E. Burney OH; John V. Singleton, Jr., OH and Memorandum: RE: President Kennedy's Visit to Houston, Nov. 21, 1963, attached; Walter Jenkins to LBJ, Feb. 2, 1963, VPP; "LBJ Reminisces: The Fatal Trip to Dallas," *Among Friends of LBJ*, Jan. 1, 1983, LBJL.

98. William Manchester, *The Death of a President* (New York, 1967), 6–7.

99. Ibid., 73–74, 79, 114, 121–24; Kenneth O'Donnell OH; Lawrence O'Brien OH, Sept. 18, 1985.

100. Transcript from Mrs. Johnson's tapes relating to Nov. 22, 1963; and notes taken during interview with Mrs. Johnson, June 15, 1964, Special Assassination File on JFK; Manchester, *Death of a President*, 134, 154–56; Lyndon B. Johnson, *The Vantage Point: Perspectives on the Presidency, 1963–1969* (New York, 1971), 8; Miller, *Lyndon*, 382–83.

101. Transcript from Mrs. Johnson, and notes during interview, Special Assassination File; LBJ, *Vantage Point*, 9–10; Miller, *Lyndon*, 383–85.

102. Schlesinger, *A Thousand Days*, 1029–31.

103. LBJ, *Vantage Point*, 9–10.

104. Schlesinger, *Robert Kennedy*, 626; LBJ, *Vantage Point*, 10–12; Miller, *Lyndon*, 385–86.

105. Schlesinger, *Robert Kennedy*, 609; LBJ, *Vantage Point*, 13–15; Miller, *Lyndon*, 386–87, 389–90; Kenneth O'Donnell OH; Manchester, *Death of a President*, 318–23.

106. Elizabeth Carpenter Recollection, Dec. 1963, Special Assassination File; Schlesinger, *Robert Kennedy*, 625–28; Kearns, *Lyndon Johnson*, 170.

107. LBJ, *Vantage Point*, 25–27.

108. See two memos, Jenkins to LBJ, Nov. 24, 1963, and "shorthand note says:" n.d., Special Assassination File; Miller, *Lyndon*, 423–24; Schlesinger, *Robert Kennedy*, 614–15. Max Holland, who is writing a book on the Warren Commission, has seen a diary by a staff attorney on the Warren Commission describing pressure from LBJ for a report before the 1964 election. Interview Dec. 14, 1992.

109. For public skepticism about the Warren Commission findings, see the *New York Times* article about conspiracy theories on JFK's death, Jan. 5, 1992, p. 12, which cites a poll showing that fewer than one-third of the American people accepted the findings of the Warren Commission that Oswald acted alone. On Feb. 2, 1992, *New York Times Book Review* listed one hardback and three paperback best-sellers describing different conspiracies behind JFK's death; also see Stephen E. Ambrose, "Writers on the Grassy Knoll," in the same issue of the *Review*.

On the FBI and CIA, see JEH, Memo, Nov. 29, 1963, O&C, JEH, FBI; and Schlesinger, *Robert Kennedy*, 614–15. On LBJ's concern about discouraging speculation on a Soviet or Cuban role, see Earl Warren OH; and LBJ telephone tapes of conversations with Thomas Kuchel, Nov. 29, 1963, 8:30 p.m., and Richard Russell, Nov. 29, 1963, 8:55 p.m., in the LBJL (hereafter cited as TT).

On the Warren Commission, see two excellent essays by Max Holland, "After 30 Years: Making Sense of the Assassination," *Reviews in American*

History, June 1994, pp. 191–204; and "The Key to the Warren Report," *American Heritage*, Nov. 1995, pp. 50–64.

On allegations against LBJ coming to the FBI, see Pre-Processed Docs. from HQ Files: Serials 105–82555 and 62–109060, which I received in response to an FOIA request to the FBI. In the 1960s an off-Broadway play, *MacBird*, depicted LBJ as the culprit in Kennedy's murder. Oliver Stone's 1991 film, *J.F.K.* and a 1992 best-seller by Craig I. Zirbel, *The Texas Connection* (Scottsdale, Aniz., 1991) also alleged an involvement by LBJ.

110. LBJ's press secretary George Christian told me: "Whenever anything went wrong, Johnson suspected a conspiracy," June 23, 1992; Nicholas Katzenbach described LBJ to me as a man with a suspicious turn of mind, May 17, 1992. *Washington Post*, Dec. 13, 1977; JEH, Memo, Nov. 29, 1963, O&C, JEH, FBI; and LBJ telephone conversation with JEH, Nov. 29, 1963, 1:40 p.m., TT.

111. Miller, *Lyndon*, 424–25; Thomas Powers, *The Man Who Kept the Secrets: Richard Helms and the CIA* (New York, 1979), 121.

112. *Time*, Feb. 10, 1975; Joseph A. Califano, Jr., *The Triumph and Tragedy of Lyndon Johnson* (New York, 1991), 295; Leo Janos, *The Atlantic*, July 1973, p. 39; LBJ interview with Walter Cronkite, Sept. 23, 1969; *New York Times*, June 25, 1976; Powers, *Man Who Kept the Secrets*, 157; memos in JEH O&C for Jan. 21, 31, Feb. 20 and esp. Feb. 26, 1964, describing the White House meeting. LBJ's suspicions about a conspiracy and fear that he would be its next victim are a demonstration that he had nothing to do with killing JFK.

113. Bill Moyers interview, May 14, 1997.

114. *New York Times*, Sept. 25, 1975.

CHAPTER 2: FROM JFK TO LBJ

1. Miller, *Lyndon*, 410; for the opinion surveys, see Kearns, *Lyndon Johnson*, 412 n. 3; Vaughn Davis Bornet, *The Presidency of Lyndon B. Johnson* (Lawrence, Kans., 1983), 8.

2. Kearns, *Lyndon Johnson*, 171–72; LBJ, *Vantage Point*, 12, 18.

3. Ibid., 12; Evans and Novak, *LBJ: Exercise of Power*, 363–64.

4. Notes on Meeting with LBJ, Nov. 23, 1963, Walter H. Heller Papers, JFKL.

5. *Public Papers of the Presidents of the United States: Lyndon B. Johnson 1963–1964* (hereafter cited as *PPP: LBJ, 1963–64*), vol. I (Washington, D.C., 1965), 2, 4–7.

6. *PPP: LBJ, 1963–64*, I, 8–10. Jack Valenti to LBJ, Nov. 27, 1963, WHCF: Executive/SP 2-3\Spec. Message (hereafter cited as WHCF: EX), LBJL.

7. Cabinet Meeting, Nov. 23, 1963, Cabinet Papers, LBJL.

8. Schlesinger, *Robert Kennedy*, 626–28, 647; George Reedy to LBJ, Nov. 27, 1963, WHCF: Aides: Reedy.

9. C. D. DeLoach to JEH, Jan. 15, 1964, O&C, JEH, FBI.

10. C. D. DeLoach to JEH, March 6 and 9, 1964; DeLoach to Mohr, March 20, 1964, ibid.; Athen G. Theoharis and John Stuart Cox, *The Boss* (Philadelphia, 1988), 349–53; Kearns, *Lyndon Johnson*, 200; Schlesinger, *Robert Kennedy*, 628–32, 650–52; Kenneth P. O'Donnell OH; Richard Goodwin, *Remembering America: A Voice from the Sixties* (Boston, 1988), 247–48, who relates the conversation between LBJ and RFK. Also see LBJ telephone con-

versations with Ed Weisl, Sr., Feb. 5, 1964; Cliff Carter, Feb. 10, 8:15 p.m.; Feb. 11, 5:21 p.m.; and Feb. 12, 1964, 9:52 a.m., TT.

11. *PPP: LBJ, 1963–64*, I, 11ff.; Reedy to LBJ, Nov. 27, 1963, Hand-writing File, LBJL; *The Gallup Poll: 1935–1971*, III: *1959–1971* (New York, 1972), 1855–56.

12. *PPP: LBJ, 1963–64*, I, 9–10.

13. Elizabeth Wickenden interview, Dec. 20, 1986; Gardner Ackley, Notes on Meeting with LBJ, Nov. 25, 1963, Diary Backup.

14. Lemann, *Promised Land*, 130–31, 140–41; Notes on Meeting with LBJ, Nov. 23, 1963, Heller Papers, JFKL.

15. Elizabeth Wickenden interview; Lemann, *Promised Land*, 142.

16. Miller, *Lyndon*, 440–41; Lemann, *Promised Land*, 141–42.

17. Administrative History: Office of Economic Opportunity, pp. 1–21; Walter Heller to Ted Sorensen, Dec. 20, 1963, Special File: Legis. Bkground; Horace Busby to LBJ, Dec. 30, 1963, WHCF: EX/FG1, LBJL; Miller, *Lyndon*, 441–42; Bornet, *Presidency of LBJ*, 52–54; Lemann, *Promised Land*, 142–44.

18. LBJ, *Vantage Point*, 69–75.

19. *PPP: LBJ 1963–64*, I, 112–15, 117–18. The Michigan experts are discussed in Edward D. Berkowitz, *Mr. Social Security: The Life of Wilbur J. Cohen* (Lawrence, Kans., 1995), 191–98.

20. For the congressional response, see State of the Union message, Jan. 8, 1964, noting that LBJ was applauded 80 times for 9 minutes and 33 seconds, Statements of LBJ, LBJL; for public sentiment, see *Gallup Poll*, III, 1859–60; LBJ's comment about what was on his desk was to Horace Busby, Interview, July 16, 1988. LBJ-HHH, Jan. 28, 1964, 6:15 p.m., TT. For the "martyr's cause," see Kearns, *Lyndon Johnson*, 178. Michael R. Beschloss, *Taking Charge: The Johnson White House Tapes, 1963–1964* (New York, 1997), 25.

21. On LBJ's Senate leadership, see Dallek, *Lone Star Rising*, 470–78; on his management of Congress as President, see Kearns, *Lyndon Johnson*, 178–86, 221–27, the quote is on p. 226.

22. Jack Valenti OH, March 3, 1971; Drew Pearson Memo, April 1965, LBJ Files, Drew Pearson Papers, LBJL; LBJ-Larry O'Brien, March 11, 1964, 2:20 p.m., TT; George Meany OH; Charles L. Schultze OH, March 28, 1969.

23. Kermit Gordon OH, March 21, 1969.

24. Lawrence F. O'Brien OH, Oct. 29, 1985. White House aide Henry H. Wilson worried that LBJ's intense lobbying would lead "the pundits ... to append the label 'Majority Leader of the Congress'" to him, which would lay the blame at his doorstep for anything in the Congress that failed: Wilson to LBJ, Jan. 10, 1964, WHCF: Aides: H. H. Wilson.

25. Schlesinger, *A Thousand Days*, 93; Kearns, *Lyndon Johnson*, 225–26; Lawrence F. O'Brien OH, Oct. 29, 1985; LBJ-O'Brien, April 9, 1964, 5:21 p.m., TT.

26. Ibid.; Tom Wicker, "Johnson's Men: 'Valuable Hunks of Humanity,'" *New York Times Magazine*, May 3, 1964.

27. Eric F. Goldman, *The Tragedy of Lyndon Johnson* (New York, 1969 ed.), 119, 123–27; Wicker, "*Johnson's Men*."

28. Goldman, *Tragedy of LBJ*, 139–43.

29. Ibid., 143–47.

30. Ibid., 127–35.

31. Wicker, *"Johnson's Men"*; Jack Valenti OH, June 14, Oct. 18, 1969; Goldman, *Tragedy of LBJ*, 135–39.

32. Kearns, *Lyndon Johnson*, 178; Goldman, *Tragedy of LBJ*, 22–23.

33. LBJ, *Vantage Point*, 33–34.

34. Miller, *Lyndon*, 416.

35. LBJ, *Vantage Point*, 39; Evans and Novak, *LBJ: Exercise of Power*, 380–86.

36. Notes on Leadership Breakfast, Dec. 3, 1963, Diary Backup.

37. Lawrence O'Brien to LBJ, Dec. 10, 1963, Office Files of the President (hereafter cited as OFP); Reedy to LBJ, Dec. 16, 1963; Notes on Leadership Breakfast, Dec. 17, 1963, Diary Backup; Arthur Goldschmidt OH; *PPP: LBJ, 1963–64*, I, 84–85; Evans and Novak, *LBJ: Exercise of Power*, 385–89; LBJ, *Vantage Point*, 39–41.

38. Evans and Novak, *LBJ: Exercise of Power*, 389; Allen J. Matusow, *The Unraveling of America: A History of Liberalism in the 1960s* (New York, 1984), chap. 2, includes an excellent discussion of the debate over the tax cut. Also see the recollections of C. Douglas Dillon in OH; and Leon Keyserling OH, who believed the tax cut was a mistake because it starved public investment.

39. Dwight D. Eisenhower to LBJ, Nov. 23, 1963; Seymour Harris to LBJ, Dec. 4, 1963, WHCF: Confidential File (hereafter cited as WHCF: CF); Douglas Dillon to LBJ, Nov. 25, 1963, WHCF: EX/SP2–3\Spec. Mess.; Robert Anderson to LBJ, n.d. but probably Nov. 25 or 26, 1963, Statements of LBJ, LBJL; Walter Heller to LBJ, Nov. 23, 1963, Heller Papers, JFKL; Evans and Novak, *LBJ: Exercise of Power*, 390.

40. Troika Meeting with President Johnson, Nov. 25, 1963, Walter Heller Papers, JFKL; Gardner Ackley OH.

41. See "Tax Bill—Expediting Procedures," Dec. 3, 1963; Memorandum for the President, Dec. 13, 1963; H. H. Fowler to Jenkins, Dec. 21, 1963; Jack Valenti to LBJ, Jan. 9, 1964; Memorandum to the President, Jan. 21, 1964, WHCF: EX/FI11\Taxation; *PPP: LBJ, 1963–64*, I, 22–25, 119–20.

42. Jack Valenti OH, Oct. 18, 1969; Kermit Gordon OH, March 21, 1969; LBJ-Douglas Dillon, Jan. 8, 1964, 4:42 p.m.; LBJ-Vance Hartke, Jan. 23, 1964, 1:11 p.m.; LBJ-Abe Ribicoff, Jan. 23, 1964, 1:14 p.m.; LBJ-Harry Byrd, Sr., Jan. 23, 1964, 5:40 p.m., TT; "Reminder Sheet for tel. convers.," Jan. 30, 1964, WHCF: EX/FG1, advising LBJ on what he might say to eleven Democratic senators about advancing the tax-cut bill. Evans and Novak, *LBJ: Exercise of Power*, 394–96; Goodwin, *Remembering America*, 261–65.

43. *PPP: LBJ, 1963–64*, I, 311–14.

44. *PPP: LBJ, 1963–64*, I, 114, 247, 367; Administrative History: Office of Economic Opportunity, pp. 21–22, LBJL; Miller, *Lyndon*, 442; Lehmann, *Promised Land*, 151; Walter Lippmann, "Today and Tomorrow," *New York Herald Tribune*, March 17, 1964.

45. LBJ-Roy Wilkins, Jan. 6, 1964, 5:12 p.m., TT.

46. John K. Galbraith to LBJ, Jan. 31, 1964; Robert Kennedy to LBJ, Jan. 16, 1964, WHCF: Aides: Moyers, LBJL; Bornet, *Presidency of LBJ*, 56; Lemann, *Promised Land*, 146.

47. A four-page memo, "Anti-Poverty Program," which is part of a document, "The 1964 Johnson Legislative Program," Jan. 20, 1964, WHCF: EX/ FG1, contains explicit mention of RFK as chairman of a Cabinet-level council, and a handwritten note: "LBJ . . . doesn't like the Council idea." LBJ's affinity for FDR's approach is described in Sargent Shriver OH, Aug. 20, 1980. On Shriver, see interview with Bill Moyers, May 14, 1997; Anthony Lewis, "Shriver Moves into the Front Rank," *New York Times Magazine*, March 15, 1964; A. H. Raskin, "Generalissimo of the War on Poverty," *New York Times Magazine*, Nov. 22, 1964; Lehmann, *Promised Land*, 145–47. Also see LBJ-J.K. Galbraith, Jan. 29, 1964, 11:55 a.m.; LBJ-Kermit Gordon, Jan. 29, 1964, 12:20 p.m., TT.

48. David Grubin interview with Sargent Shriver, American Experience television documentary, "LBJ," PBS, 1991. Also see Shriver OH, Aug. 20, 1980; and four LBJ-Shriver telephone conversations on Feb. 1, 1964, TT.

49. LBJ to Shriver, Feb. 11, 1964, WHCF: EX/WE9.

50. Carl M. Brauer, "Kennedy, Johnson and the War on Poverty," *Journal of American History*, June 1982, p. 115; Raskin, "Generalissimo."

51. Administrative History: Office of Economic Opportunity, pp. 27–33; Frank Mankiewicz OH; Adam Yarmolinsky OH, July 13, 1970; Schlesinger, *Robert Kennedy*, 637–38; Raskin, "Generalissimo."

52. Frank Mankiewicz OH; Bill Moyers to Shriver, Feb. 20, 1964, WHCF: EX/WE9; Moyers to Adam Yarmolinsky, Feb. 28, 1964, WHCF: Aides: Moyers. Also see Adam Yarmolinsky OH, July 13, 1970, who describes LBJ as playing a very limited role in the work of Shriver's task force.

53. Lemann, *Promised Land*, 153–54; James T. Patterson, *America's Struggle Against Poverty, 1900–1980* (New York, 1981), chap. 8, is an excellent summary of the origins of the war on poverty; p. 141 describes LBJ's response to Shriver.

54. *PPP: LBJ, 1963–64*, I, 375–80.

55. See Schlesinger, *Robert Kennedy*, 638–39, who says that RFK sold Shriver on community action; and Lehmann, *Promised Land*, 147–55, who says that the experts did it. Adam Yarmolinsky remembers that some "analysts" described the poverty bill as "hasty and jerrybuilt" and suggested a "study commission." Yarmolinsky says this came from political opponents who wanted to kill the program: "We knew enough to mount a program which we could reasonably expect would have some useful effect. . . . The way to begin was to begin, and that was a typical Kennedy as well as Johnson approach." OH, July 13, 1970.

56. *PPP: LBJ, 1963–64*, I, 367–68.

57. Evans and Novak, *LBJ: Exercise of Power*, 448; Goodwin, *Remembering America*, chap. 15, esp. pp. 267–71, 275, 277–78; Goldman, *Tragedy of LBJ*, chap. 1, 193–95.

58. Jack Valenti OH, July 12, 1972; Goodwin and Moyers to LBJ, May 18, 1964; Moyers to Valenti, May 18, 1964; Moyers to Allen Duckworth, Aug. 11, 1965, WHCF: EX/SP3-20; Evans and Novak, *LBJ: Exercise of Power*, 448–49.

59. *PPP: LBJ, 1963–64*, I, 704–707.

60. Miller, *Lyndon*, 458–59.

61. Bill Moyers interview, May 14, 1997.

62. See *Gallup Poll: 1935–1971*, III, 1870.

63. Ibid., 1865–67, 1869, 1874, 1880, 1885, 1887.

64. See LBJ-Edwin Weisl, Sr., Jan. 25, 1964, 12:00 p.m., TT; Douglas Kiker, "Johnson Shakedown in Crises," *New York Herald Tribune*, Jan. 31, 1964; Reston quoted in Goodwin, *Remembering America*, 282; Bill Moyers to LBJ, May 15, 1964, WHCF: Aides: Moyers. Also see Evans and Novak, *LBJ: The Exercise of Power*, 412–13.

65. See Dallek, *Lone Star Rising*, passim, for LBJ's foreign and national security affairs experience up to 1960. The vice presidency is covered in Chapter One of this volume.

66. Arthur Krock memorandum, July 7, 1960, Arthur Krock Papers, Princeton University; Walt W. Rostow OH, March 21, 1969; Bundy is quoted in Joseph S. Tulchin, "The Promise of Progress: U.S. Relations with Latin America During the Administration of Lyndon B. Johnson," in *Lyndon Johnson Confronts the World*, edited by Warren Cohen and Nancy Tucker (New York 1994), 225. Also see Dean Rusk OH, July 28, 1969, who says: "I found him [LBJ] extraordinarily well-informed about foreign affairs. . . . He came into the [presidential] office well-informed about most of the key issues of foreign policy."

67. See Busby's undated memos: "Background Release Series: Review of Erhart's Visit" and "Future Diplomatic Visits," WHCF: EX/FG1; Bromley Smith to LBJ, Jan. 31, 1964, National Security Files (hereafter cited as NSF): Memos to the President: McGeorge Bundy; Memo: Mr. Moyers: Meeting with Canadian Prime Minister, and attachment: "General," Jan. 1964; LBJ-Dean Rusk, Jan. 31, 1964, 3:11 p.m.; LBJ-Marshall McNeil, Jan. 31, 1964, 9:00 p.m., TT; McGeorge Bundy to Jack Valenti, April 10, 1964; Memo: "for use at luncheon w Wash Post people," April 15, 1964, Diary Backup.

68. LBJ-Reedy, April 8, 1964, 11:45 a.m., TT.

69. Arthur S. Link, *Woodrow Wilson and the Progressive Era, 1910–1917* (New York, 1963 ed.), 81; Goldman, *Tragedy of LBJ*, 447–48.

70. William P. Bundy and Nicholas Katzenbach emphasized this difference between JFK and LBJ to me. Interview, May 17, 1992.

71. Goodwin, *Remembering America*, 283.

72. McCone, Memorandum, Meeting with LBJ, Oct. 21, 1962, in *CIA Documents on the Cuban Missile Crisis, 1962*, edited by Mary S. McAuliffe (Washington, D.C., 1992), 245. What LBJ did not know was that the Soviet military chief on Cuba had the freedom to use nuclear weapons against the United States if an invasion had occurred. See James G. Blight and David A. Welch, *On the Brink: Americans and Soviets Reexamine the Cuban Missile Crisis* (New York, 1989). By the close of the crisis LBJ had backed away from bombing and signed on to JFK's blockade and the removal of Soviet missiles from Cuba and American Jupiter missiles from Turkey. But he could not ignore the fact that his principal impulse had been to bomb the Soviet installations, and that he had come back to this idea on the final day of the crisis. See Jeff Shesol, *Mutual Contempt: Lyndon Johnson, Robert Kennedy, and the Feud That Shaped a Decade* (New York, 1997), 93–99.

73. Schlesinger, *A Thousand Days*, 432–36; Evans and Novak, *LBJ: Exercise of Power*, 414; Goldman, *Tragedy of LBJ*, 93–94; David Halberstam, The Best and the Brightest (Greenwich, Conn., 1973 ed.), 376–402; McGeorge Bundy interview, March 30, 1993; Bill Moyers interview, May 14, 1997.

74. Halberstam, *Best and the Brightest*, 263–303; Evans and Novak, *LBJ: Exercise of Power*, 461; the fullest description of McNamara is Deborah Shapley, *Promise and Power: The Life and Times of Robert McNamara* (Boston, 1993).

75. The quote "enormously energetic" is from McGeorge Bundy interview, March 30, 1993; the rest is in Kearns, *Lyndon Johnson*, 177.

76. Halberstam, *Best and the Brightest*, 56–81.

77. Ibid., 372–73, and 53, where Rayburn is quoted; Schlesinger, *A Thousand Days*, 208–9. For the memos, see Bundy to LBJ, Dec. 2 and 7, 1963, and to Jack Valenti, April 10, 1964, in Diary Backup; to LBJ, Nov. 23, Dec. 2, 1963, in NSF: Bundy; to LBJ, Jan. 16, 17, Feb. 4, 10, 11, 17, 24, 25, 28, 29, 1964, NSF: Memos to the President; and to LBJ, April 3, 1964, NSF: Country File: Panama; the Stevenson-Harriman advice is in: Walter Jenkins to LBJ, Dec. 8, 1963, WHCF: EX/FG1.

78. McGeorge Bundy interview, March 30, 1993.

79. H. W. Brands, *The Wages of Globalism: Lyndon Johnson and the Limits of American Power* (New York, 1995), 41–42; LBJ, *Vantage Point*, 187.

80. See Ruth Leacock, *Requiem for Revolution: The United States and Brazil, 1961–1969* (Kent, Ohio, 1990), 198–99, for LBJ's view of JFK's policy; and Tom Wicker, *JFK and LBJ: The Influence of Personality upon Politics* (Baltimore, 1969 ed.), 196, for the LBJ quote. Also see Ralph Dungan, who had some responsibility for Latin America under JFK, and thought LBJ "had kind of a romantic, Tex-Mex view of Latin America...." OH.

81. Evans and Novak, *LBJ: Exercise of Power*, 415–17; Walter LaFeber, *Inevitable Revolutions: The United States in Central America* (New York, 1984 ed.), 148–55; Ralph Dungan OH.

82. Evans and Novak, *LBJ: Exercise of Power*, 417–19; LaFeber, *Inevitable Revolutions*, 156–57; Leacock, *Requiem for Revolution*, 199; LBJ-Richard Russell, Jan. 10, 1964, 1:25 p.m., TT; Harry McPherson OH, Jan. 16, 1969.

83. Evans and Novak, *LBJ: Exercise of Power*, 419–20; Schlesinger, *Robert Kennedy*, 630–32.

84. *PPP: LBJ, 1963–1964*, I, 325.

85. Walter LaFeber, *The Panama Canal: The Crisis in Perspective* (New York, 1978), 132–40.

86. Thomas C. Mann OH.

87. McGeorge Bundy to LBJ, Jan. 12, 17, 1964, NSF: Memos to the President; LBJ-Richard Russell, Jan. 22, 1964, 6:55 p.m., TT; *The Gallup Poll, 1959–1971*, 1864; LaFeber, *Panama Canal*, 142–43; Brands, *Wages of Globalism*, 36–37.

88. LaFeber, *Panama Canal*, 141–42; Brands, *Wages of Globalism*, 30–33; Michael E. Latham, "Panama Crisis: The Johnson Administration and 'The Chiari Problem,' January-April 1964," unpublished seminar paper, UCLA, May 1992; LBJ-Mike Mansfield, Jan. 10, 1964, 10:25 p.m., TT; Bundy to LBJ, Jan. 10, 1964; Memorandum of Conference with LBJ, Jan. 13, 1964, NSF: Bundy; Mann to Martin, Jan. 14, 1964, NSF: Country: Panama; LBJ, *Vantage Point*, 180.

89. LBJ-George Brown, Jan. 13, 1964, 4:10 p.m.; LBJ-Roberto Chiari, Jan. 10, 1964, 11:40 a.m.; LBJ-Thomas Mann, Jan. 14, 1964, 1:03 p.m., TT; NSC History: Panama Crisis, 1964; Administrative History of the Panama Canal Co.

and Canal Zone, LBJL; LBJ, *Vantage Point*, 181–84; Brands, *Wages of Globalism*, 35–41.

90. Fulbright is quoted in Tristram Coffin to Drew Pearson, May 7, 1965, Drew Pearson Papers. For the rest, see Evans and Novak, *LBJ: Exercise of Power*, 423–27; Goldman, *Tragedy of LBJ*, 86–91, 452; *PPP: LBJ, 1963–1964*, I, 383–84; LBJ-Richard Russell, Feb. 26, 1964, 12:10 p.m.; LBJ-Adlai Stevenson, Feb. 26, 1964, 12:31 p.m.; LBJ-Mac Bundy, March 16, 1964, 4:40 p.m. and 5: 57 p.m.; March 18, 1964, 4:20 p.m.; LBJ-Chiari, April 3, 1964, 3:35 p.m., TT; *Robert Kennedy: In His Own Words*, 249, 354, 416; Schlesinger, *Robert Kennedy*, 635.

91. Leacock, *Requiem for Revolution*, 200.

92. See chap. 10 of Leacock, *Requiem for Revolution*, esp. 200–201. The abundant materials on Brazil demonstrating American support for the Brazilian coup is in NSF: Country: Brazil; WHCF: EX/CO37; and NSF: NSC Meeting File. Also see LBJ's telephone conversations with Ball, April 2, 1964, 10:40 a.m.; Mann, April 3, 1964, 12:06 p.m.; Bundy, April 14, 1964, 12:50 p.m., TT.

93. John Connor to LBJ, April 9, 1964, WHCF: EX/CO37; LBJ-Mann, Feb. 19, 1964, 11:32 a.m., TT; Goodwin, *Remembering America*, 282–83.

94. George Ball OH, July 9, 1971.

95. The argument that Kennedy would have withdrawn from Vietnam is made most fully in: John M. Newman, *JFK and Vietnam* (New York, 1992). Also see Arthur Schlesinger's judicious but generally favorable review of the book in the *New York Times Book Review*, March 29, 1992. For the contrary view, see Leslie Gelb, "Kennedy and Vietnam," *New York Times*, Jan. 6, 1992; Walt W. Rostow to Editor, *New York Times*, Feb. 15, 1992; Leonard Bushkoff's review of Newman in *Los Angeles Times Book Review*, Feb. 23, 1992; Bornet, *Presidency of LBJ*, 70–71; Noam Chomsky, *Rethinking Camelot: JFK, the Vietnam War, and U.S. Political Culture* (Boston, 1993); and Robert Dallek, "Lyndon Johnson and Vietnam: The Making of a Tragedy," *Diplomatic History* (Spring 1996), 147–49. See *Foreign Relations of the United States (hereafter cited as FRUS)*, vol. IV: *Vietnam, August-December 1963* (Washington, D.C., 1991), 640–41, for the Vietnamese view of the troop reduction announcement. William Bundy and Dean Rusk see the change in policy on troop withdrawal as resulting from a more realistic appraisal of conditions in Vietnam than had been made earlier in 1963. Dean Rusk OH, Tape NN, Richard Russell Library, University of Georgia, Athens.

96. McGeorge Bundy interview, March 30, 1993; Lawrence F. O'Brien OH.

97. Robert S. McNamara interview, March 26, 1993

98. The memo of this conversation is in *FRUS*, vol. IV: *Vietnam, Aug.–Dec. 1963*, 635–37.

99. See Wicker, *JFK and LBJ*, 205; and William Bundy's comment on p. 10 of "Conference on Vietnam," March 9–10, 1991, transcript at the LBJL.

100. McGeorge Bundy interview, March 30, 1993.

101. Bill Moyers, "Flashback," *Newsweek*, Feb. 10, 1975.

102. Ibid.

103. See the Nov. 21 NSAM 273 in the JFKL and the Nov. 26 version in the NSF: NSAM, LBJL. Also, *FRUS*, IV: *Vietnam, Aug.-Dec. 1963*, 650–51. Newman, *JFK and Vietnam*, 445–49, sees some significant differences in the

Nov. 21 and 26 versions, but I think he exaggerates the importance of these distinctions.

104. Bundy to LBJ, Dec. 5, 1963, NSF: Memos to Pres.; McNamara to LBJ, Dec. 21, 1963, NSF: Country: Vietnam. McNamara told Lodge on Dec. 12: We should "make clear to the North Vietnamese that the U.S. will not accept a Communist victory in South Vietnam and that we will escalate the conflict to whatever level is required to insure their defeat." William C. Gibbons, *The U.S. Government and the Vietnam War*, Part III: *January-July 1965* (Princeton, N.J., 1989), 3.

105. LBJ-John Knight, Feb. 3, 1964, 5:45 p.m., TT.

106. Gibbons, *U.S. Government and Vietnam*, III, 4–5; Gilbert C. Fite, *Richard B. Russell, Jr.: Senator from Georgia* (Chapel Hill, N.C., 1991), 435–37, 440–41; LBJ-Russell, March 9, 1964, 9:45 p.m.; June 11, 1964, 12:26 p.m., TT; Mansfield to LBJ, Dec. 7, 1963, Jan. 6, 1964, NSF: Memos to the Pres.; Bundy to LBJ, Jan. 6 and 9, 1964; McNamara to LBJ, Jan. 7, 1964; Rusk to LBJ, Jan. 8, 1964, NSF: Country: Vietnam.

107. Sorensen to LBJ, Jan. 14, 1964, NSF: Country: Vietnam.

108. LBJ's view of Lodge is in McGeorge Bundy interview, March 30, 1993; for the rest, see *FRUS*, IV: *Vietnam, Aug.-Dec. 1963*, 690, 744–47.

109. See Michael Forrestal to LBJ, Jan. 30, 31, 1964, NSF: Country: Vietnam; Ball-Moyers telephone conversation, Jan. 30, 1964, George Ball Papers; Moyers to LBJ, Feb. 1, 1964; LBJ to General Khanh, WHCF: EX/CO 312.

110. Bundy to LBJ, Feb. 4, 1964, NSF: Bundy; William P. Bundy MS History of the Vietnam War, chap. 12, pp. 15–19; *PPP: LBJ, 1963–64*, I, 304. Also see LBJ-McNamara, March 2, 1964, 11:00 a.m.; LBJ-Rusk, March 2, 1964, 11:35 a.m., TT.

111. LBJ-Mac Bundy, March 2, 1964, 12:35 p.m.; LBJ-Fulbright, March 2, 1964, 8:50 p.m., TT; William Bundy MS History, pp. 20–30B; *PPP: LBJ, 1963–64*, I, 387–88; NSC Meeting, April 3, 1964, NSF: NSC Meetings.

112. Randall B. Woods, *Fulbright: A Biography* (Cambridge, U.K., 1995), 334–36.

113. LBJ-McNamara, April 30, 1964, 7:50 p.m., TT.

114. See McGeorge Bundy to LBJ, April 29, May 22, 1964, NSF: Memos to Pres.; LBJ-Mac Bundy, May 13, 1964, 5:35 p.m., TT; Bundy to LBJ, May 25, 1964, NSF: Bundy; Bundy to LBJ, May 26, 1964, Diary Backup; William Bundy MS History of Vietnam, chap. 13; *PPP: LBJ, 1963–64*, I, 692–94; *FRUS, 1964–1968: Vietnam: 1964*, V 346ff.; Gibbons, *U.S. Government and Vietnam*, III, 7–8.

115. Conference on Vietnam, March 9–10, 1991, pp. 22–23, LBJL.

116. William Bundy MS History of Vietnam, chap. 13, pp. 18ff.; John E. Mueller, *War, Presidents and Public Opinion* (New York, 1973), 35, 81; *Gallup Poll*, III, 1882.

117. William Bundy MS History of Vietnam, chap. 12, pp. 30C–E; Ball-Fulbright telephone conversation, May 28, 1964, George Ball Papers.

118. See McGeorge Bundy memoranda for discussion and to LBJ for June 10, 15, 25, 1964, NSF: Memos to the Pres.; Questions the "public" is asking, June 2, 1964, WHCF: EX/CO 312; NASM 308, June 22, 1964, NSF: NSAM; Frank E. Vandiver, *Shadows of Vietnam: Lyndon Johnson's Wars* (College Station, Tex., 1997), for Bundy quote "not so stupid," p. 18.

119. John Bibby and Roger Davidson, *On Capitol Hill: Studies in the Legislative Process* (New York, 1967), 234–35.

120. Ibid., 238–40; David Zarefsky, *President Johnson's War on Poverty* (Birmingham, Ala., 1986), 51–53.

121. The quote about LBJ is in Administrative History of OEO, chap. 1, p. 41, LBJL; the quote by him is in *PPP: LBJ, 1963–64*, I, 483. Also see Lawrence O'Brien OH, April 8, 1986, on LBJ's role in passing the law.

122. *PPP: LBJ, 1963–64*, I, pp. 544, 627–28. Also see Box 130 of WHCF: Aides: Moyers.

123. Administrative History of OEO, chap. 1, pp. 41–42, LBJL.

124. The Republican is quoted in James L. Sundquist, ed., *On Fighting Poverty* (New York, 1969), 28. On Landrum, see O'Brien to LBJ, Jan. 31, 1964; Wilson to O'Brien, Feb, 4, 1964; O'Brien to Wilson, Feb. 5, 1964, WHCF: Aides: H. H. Wilson; O'Brien OH, April 8, 1986.

125. Administrative History of OEO, chap. 1, p. 47; Lehmann, *Promised Land*, 156–57; John W. Carley to Adam Yarmolinsky, July 30, 1964, WHCF: Aides: Moyers.

126. LBJ-John McCormack, May 13, 1964, 3:55 p.m.; LBJ-Carl Albert, May 13, 1964, 4:21 p.m., TT.

127. Wickenden to Jenkins, May 4, 1964, WHCF: Aides: Moyers.

128. See LBJ-Charles Halleck, June 22, 1964, 6:24 p.m., TT, in which LBJ pressed Halleck to get the poverty bill reported out of the Rules Committee. It is a priceless example of Johnson's legislative leadership. LBJ's note to O'Brien is on O'Brien to LBJ, July 9, 1964, WHCF: EX/LE\WE; O'Brien OH, Oct. 30, 1985, April 8, 1986; Frank Mankiewicz OH; Bibby and Davidson, *On Capitol Hill*, 241.

129. Ibid., 242–44, 246; Lemann, *Promised Land*, 157; Adam Yarmolinsky OH.

130. Donovan, *The Politics of Poverty*, (Indianapolis, Ind., 1973 ed.), 36; *PPP: LBJ, 1963–64*, II, 988–90; the quotes by commentators are in Administrative History of OEO, chap. 1, p. 52; for LBJ's statement, see Lemann, *Promised Land*, 158.

131. Matusow, *Unraveling of America*, 126–27.

132. See LBJ-Walker Stone, Jan. 6, 1964, 3:30 p.m., TT; the documentary "LBJ" broadcast on public television, Sept. 30-Oct.1, 1991; *New York Times*, July 2, 1989; *PPP: LBJ, 1963–64*, I, 22. For the meeting with black leaders, see the oral histories at the LBJL of James Farmer, Burke Marshall, Clarence Mitchell, A. Philip Randolph, and Roy Wilkins. Lee C. White OH, Feb. 18, 1971. Also see Robert Mann, *The Walls of Jericho: Lyndon Johnson, Hubert Humphrey, Richard Russell, and the Struggle for Civil Rights* (New York, 1996), chap. 19.

133. Roy Wilkins OH.

134. Harry McPherson OH, Dec. 5, 1968; Robert S. McNamara interview.

135. LBJ to Hoover, April 8, 1964; Hoover to LBJ, April 10, 1964, WHCF: CF: EX/HU2\ST Equality of Races.

136. Roy Wilkins interview on the TV documentary "LBJ," PBS. Also see LBJ-Whitney Young, Jan. 6, 1964, 3:55 p.m., TT.

137. See Dallek, *Lone Star Rising*, for LBJ's understanding of the problem before 1961. Also see T. Harry Williams, "Huey, Lyndon, and Southern Radicalism," *Journal of American History*, Sept. 1973.

138. *Gallup Poll*, III, 1844, 1852, 1867, 1881; Kearns, *Lyndon Johnson*, 191; Mann, *Walls of Jericho*, 393. Also see LBJ-Whitney Young, Jan. 6, 1964, 3:55 p.m., TT.

139. See the TV documentary: "LBJ," PBS.

140. Hubert H. Humphrey, *The Education of a Public Man* (New York, 1976), 274–75.

141. Carl Solberg, *Hubert Humphrey: A Biography* (New York, 1984), 221–22; *Robert Kennedy: In His Own Words*, 211–12.

142. Nicholas Katzenbach OH, Nov. 12, 1968; Lawrence O'Brien OH, April 8, 1986: McNamara interview.

143. Graham, *Civil Rights Era*, 125–34.

144. LBJ remarks to Governors, Nov. 25, 1963; notes on first congressional leadership breakfast, Dec. 3, 1963; Lee White memo, Dec. 4, 1963; notes on leadership breakfast, Dec. 17, 1963, Backup Diary; Robert D. Loevy, " 'To Write It in the Books of Law: President Lyndon B. Johnson and the Civil Rights Act of 1964," in *Lyndon Baines Johnson and the Uses of Power*, edited by Bernard J. Firestone and Robert C. Vogt (New York, 1988), 109–11.

145. See Roy Wilkins, Valenti, and Pickle comments in TV documentary "LBJ," PBS; Lawrence O'Brien OH, April 8, 1986; Valenti to LBJ, Jan. 21, 1964, WHCF: EX/LE\HU2; LBJ-Eugene Keogh, Feb. 10, 1964, 8:49 p.m.; LBJ-Frank Thompson, Feb. 10, 1964, 8:52 p.m., TT; Loevy, "LBJ and the Civil Rights Act," 111–13; Graham, *Civil Rights Era*, 138–39; Clarence Mitchell OH, April 30, 1969.

146. LBJ, *Vantage Point*, 158–59; LBJ-Robert Kennedy, Feb. 10, 1964, 9:07 p.m.; LBJ-Katzenbach, Feb. 10, 1964, 9:45 p.m.; LBJ-Mansfield, Feb. 11, 1964, 5:32 p.m.; Feb. 20, 1964, 5:28 p.m., TT.

147. *PPP: LBJ, 1963–64*, I, 259; Lee C. White to LBJ, April 15, 1964, WHCF: EX/HU2; Loevy, "LBJ and the Civil Rights Act," 113–15; "LBJ" TV documentary.

148. Lee C. White OH, Feb. 18, 1971, LBJL.

149. LBJ-Roy Wilkins, Jan. 6, 1964, 5:12 p.m., TT; Kenneth P. O'Donnell OH.

150. Clarence Mitchell OH; Miller, *Lyndon*, 450.

151. Jack Valenti OH, Oct. 18, 1969; LBJ-Roy Wilkins, Jan. 6, 1964, 5:12 p.m., TT; Miller, *Lyndon*, 449.

152. Humphrey, *Education of a Public Man*, 276–77; Solberg, *Humphrey*, 223–24; Miller, *Lyndon*, 449.

153. Humphrey, *Education of a Public Man*, 277–82; Solberg, *Humphrey*, 223–26; Loevy, "LBJ and the Civil Rights Act," 118–20.

154. Loevy, "LBJ and the Civil Rights Act," 121–22; Humphrey, *Education of a Public Man*, 282, 478–79 n. 9; Stewart Udall to LBJ, May 7, 1964; Mike Manatos to Larry O'Brien, May 11, 1964, WHCF: EX/LE\HU2.

155. Humphrey, *Education of a Public Man*, 276, 282–83; Mann, *Walls of Jericho*, 426.

156. LBJ-Lee White, June 16, 1964, 10:13 a.m., TT. The photo hangs in the research room at the LBJ Library. *PPP: LBJ, 1963–64*, II, 842–44.

157. LBJ-HHH, May 13, 1964, 7:25 p.m., TT.

158. Moyers, "What a Real President Was Like," *Washington Post*, Nov. 13, 1988. In 1990, an opinion poll showed that only 31 percent of southerners identified themselves as Democrats. *New York Times*, June 3, 1991, p. A10.

159. For administration anxiety about what the law might produce, see Attorney General to LBJ, June 18, 1964, WHCF: EX/LE\HU2; LBJ-George Taylor, June 19, 1964, 2:15 p.m.; LBJ-Roy Wilkins, June 19, 1964, 5:20 p.m.; LBJ-Luther Hodges, June 23, 1964, 2:59 p.m., TT; Russell's view is in Humphrey, *Education of a Public Man*, 284 and 479 n. 12.

CHAPTER 3: "LANDSLIDE LYNDON"

1. Goldman, *Tragedy of LBJ*, 21.

2. Miller, *Lyndon*, 475–76.

3. LBJ, *Vantage Point*, 95–97.

4. George E. Reedy OH, June 7, 1975.

5. Ibid.; Lady Bird Johnson, *A White House Diary* (New York, 1970), 210; notes of Russell telephone conversation with LBJ, Aug. 25, 1964, Richard Russell papers.

6. Edwin Weisl, Sr., OH.

7. Matusow, *Unraveling of America*, 132; Stewart Alsop, "Only Johnson Can Beat Johnson," n.d., "Affairs of State" column; Survey of Public Opinion, April 1964, WHCF: CF: EX/PR 16.

8. Busby to LBJ, Jan. 23, 1964, WHCF: EX/FG1.

9. See Evans and Novak, *LBJ: Exercise of Power*, 429–38; "Reedy Denies Speeding by President in Texas," *New York Times*, April 2, 1964; and Theodore H. White, *The Making of the President, 1964* (New York, 1965), 247.

10. LBJ-Mike Mansfield, April 29, 1964, 11:32 a.m., TT.

11. The memo on Williams is: To: W. C. Sullivan, Feb. 26, 1964, in LBJ, Cross-Refs No. 2; the material on the Klan dated Jan. 21-April 13, 1964, is in LBJ, Cross-Refs. No. 3. For LBJ's remarks, see ? to J. Edgar Hoover, May 28, 1964, LBJ, Cross-Refs. No. 5, FBI Files. On Hoover's retirement, see Richard Gid Powers, *Secrecy and Power: The Life of J. Edgar Hoover* (New York, 1987), 393–96; Theoharis and Cox, *The Boss*, 353, 357; Curt Gentry, *J. Edgar Hoover: The Man and the Secrets* (New York, 1991), 560–61.

12. LBJ-Richard Russell, Jan. 22, 1964, 6:55 p.m., TT; Dick Nelson to LBJ, March 26, 1964; Abe Fortas to LBJ, March 26, 1964; Horace Busby to LBJ, April 16, 1964; *Minneapolis Tribune* clipping, March 10, 1964, WHCF: GEN/PR16; LBJ-Bundy, April 14, 1964, 12:50 p.m., TT.

13. See William J. Hopkins to Willard Wirtz, March 17, 1964; LBJ-Arthur Goldberg, April 9, 1964, 4:34 p.m.; Mike Mansfield, 7:46 p.m.; John McCormack, 7:50 p.m.; McNeil, April 10, 1964, 6:40 p.m., for LBJ's description of the negotiations, TT; three memos of Walter Heller to LBJ, April 10, 1964, WHCF: GEN/LA6; Evans and Novak, *LBJ: Exercise of Power*, 438–41; Miller, *Lyndon*, 453–55.

14. Walter Heller to LBJ, April 15, 1964; Willard Wirtz to LBJ, April 15, 1964; Statement of Railroad Operating Unions, April 22, 1964; Charles Luna to LBJ, April 28, 1964; Al Chesser to LBJ, May 1, 1964; UPI release, April 23, 1964, WHCF: GEN/LA6; Evans and Novak, *LBJ: Exercise of Power*, 441–43; Miller, *Lyndon*, 455–56; *PPP: LBJ, 1963–64*, I, 517–19.

15. *Wichita Falls Record News*, May 4, 1964.

16. Averell Harriman to Bill Moyers, Jan. 27, 1964, WHCF: EX/PL.

17. Unsigned Memo for the President, Jan. 2, 1964; Wayne Phillips to

Jack Valenti, March 4, 1964, WHCF: EX/PL 6–3; Averell Harriman to Moyers, Jan. 27, 1964; Daniel P. Moynihan to Ken O'Donnell, Feb. 14, 1964, WHCF: EX/PL.

18. Daniel Patrick Moynihan to Kenneth O'Donnell, Feb. 14, 1964, WHCF: EX/PL; George Reedy to LBJ, Feb. 22, 1964, with Clayton Fritchey to Reedy, Feb. 21, 1964, attached, WHCF: CF: EX/PL.

19. George Reedy to LBJ, Feb. 22, 1964, with Clayton Fritchey to Reedy, Feb. 21, 1964, attached, WHCF: CF: EX/PL; White, *Making of the President, 1964*, 72–111.

20. LBJ-HHH, Jan. 28, 1964, 6:15 p.m., TT.

21. Oliver Quayle Survey of Public Opinion 154, April 1964, WHCF: CF: EX/PL.

22. Between Jan. 1 and May 31, 1964, LBJ had 88 conversations about the Baker case, many of them with Walter Jenkins, George Reedy, and Abe Fortas. But he spoke with a number of congressional Democrats as well. See the index of conversations to the LBJ telephone tapes.

23. See Busby Memo, "Guidelines Not-for-Attribution Backgrounder," April (?) 1964, WHCF: Aides: Busby; *PPP: LBJ, 1963–64*, I, 152–53, 211, 286–88, 366; Reedy News Conference July 14, 1964, Diary Backup.

24. Busby, "Guidelines Not-for-Attribution Backgrounder," April (?) 1964, WHCF: Aides: Busby.

25. See White, *Making of the President, 1964*, 90–98, 115, 128, 130–32, 137–38.

26. Ibid., 103–7, 207–12.

27. Moyers to LBJ, n.d., with attached Roche to Moyers, June 12, 1964, WHCF: Aides: Moyers; The Harris Survey, July 13, 1964, WHCF: Name: Goldwater.

28. White, *Making of the President, 1964*, 199–200.

29. Ibid., 200–201.

30. Ibid., 214–17.

31. See Busby to LBJ, July 16, 1964, Diary Backup; Douglass Cater to LBJ, July 10, 1964, WHCF: EX/PL6-3; Henry H. Wilson, Jr., to Larry O'Brien, July 8, 1964, WHCF: Name: Goldwater; White, *Making of the President, 1964*, 233–34.

32. See Talking Points, Lunch with Arthur Krock, July 8, 1964; and point seven of the Moyers, Goodwin, Valenti memo to LBJ, July 21, 1964, Diary Backup; Paul Southwick to George Reedy, July 14, 1964; Moyers to LBJ, July 17, 1964; LBJ to Moyers, July 17, 1964, WHCF: EX/PL6-3; James Rowe to LBJ, July 19, 1964, WHCF: Aides: Moyers; Goldman, *Tragedy of LBJ*, 226.

33. Busby to LBJ, July 21, 1964; Moyers, Goodwin, Valenti to LBJ, July 21, 1964, Diary Backup.

34. See *PPP: LBJ, 1963–64*, II, 890–91; Moyers, Goodwin, Valenti to LBJ, July 21, 1964; Moyers to LBJ, July 24, 1964; Lee White etc. to LBJ, July 24, 1964, Diary Backup; White, *Making of the President, 1964*, 235–36.

35. "The Race for Vice President," a poll of all voters, n.d., WHCF: Aides: Moyers; *Gallup Poll*, III, 1874–75, asked only Democrats to state their preference in late March, and they favored RFK by almost three to one over Stevenson and nearly five to one over Humphrey; Stewart Alsop, "LBJ and RFK," *Saturday Evening Post*, Feb. 22, 1964.

36. Schlesinger, *Robert Kennedy*, 650–52.

37. Alsop, "LBJ and RFK"; Kenneth P. O'Donnell and David F. Powers, *Johnny, We Hardly Knew Ye* (Boston, 1972), 391; Kenneth P. O'Donnell OH.

38. Goldman, *Tragedy of LBJ*, 92–93; Kenneth P. O'Donnell OH; Schlesinger, *Robert Kennedy*, 651–52; Guthman and Shulman, *RFK: In His Own Words*, 406–7; Evans and Novak, *LBJ: Exercise of Power*, 463–65.

39. Lawrence O'Brien OH, Feb. 12, 1986.

40. Guthman and Shulman, *RFK: In His Own Words*, 326–27; Schlesinger, *Robert Kennedy*, 649.

41. Bill Moyers interview, May 14, 1997.

42. Ibid.; Kenneth P. O'Donnell OH; Evans and Novak, *LBJ: Exercise of Power*, 460–61; Miller, *Lyndon*, 471.

43. Kenneth P. O'Donnell OH; Miller, *Lyndon*, 471–72.

44. Bill Moyers interview, May 14, 1997.

45. Evans and Novak, *LBJ: Exercise of Power*, 461–63; Robert McNamara interview, March 26, 1993.

46. Schlesinger, *Robert Kennedy*, 652–53.

47. Guthman and Shulman, *RFK: In His Own Words*, 413–17.

48. See White, *Making of the President, 1964*, 262; Goldman, *Tragedy of LBJ*, 232–33; Miller, *Lyndon*, 730–31 n. 2; Lawrence O'Brien OH, Feb. 12, 1986; Sam Houston Johnson, *My Brother Lyndon* (New York, 1969), 165.

49. Elizabeth F. Harris to Moyers, June 19, 1964, WHCF: Aides: Moyers; Clifton C. Carter to LBJ, July 22, 1964, WHCF: EX/PL1; Evans and Novak, *LBJ: Exercise of Power*, 468; Goldman, *Tragedy of LBJ*, 233–34; Schlesinger, *Robert Kennedy*, 658.

50. Lawrence O'Brien OH, Feb. 12, 1986.

51. See Goldman, *Tragedy of LBJ*, 234–35; LBJ, *Vantage Point*, 99–100; Schlesinger, *Robert Kennedy*, 659; LBJ-Clark Clifford, July 29, 1964, 11:45 a.m., TT.

52. LBJ, *Vantage Point*, 99–100, 576–77; LBJ-Clark Clifford, July 29, 1964, 2:17 p.m., TT.

53. Schlesinger, *Robert Kennedy*, 659–61.

54. Goldman, *Tragedy of LBJ*, 235–36; Evans and Novak, *LBJ: Exercise of Power*, 469–70; Schlesinger, *Robert Kennedy*, 661–62.

55. Ibid.; Lawrence O'Brien OH, Feb. 12, 1986; Kenneth O'Donnell OH.

56. White, *Making of the President, 1964*, 263–65; Evans and Novak, *LBJ: Exercise of Power*, 471; Goldman, *Tragedy of LBJ*, 236–37; Miller, *Lyndon*, 474.

57. Goldman, *Tragedy of LBJ*, 236; Miller, *Lyndon*, 474.

58. See "Alternative public positions," June 10, 1964, NSF: Country: Vietnam; Record of Meeting on SE Asia, June 10, 1964, NSF: Bundy File; Material Concerning Southeast Asia, June 13, 1964, WHCF: CF: EX/ND19\CO312; William C. Gibbons, *The U.S. Government and Vietnam War*, Part II: *1961–1964* (Washington, D.C., 1986), 266–75.

59. Michael V. Forrestal OH.

60. LBJ, May 26, 1964, Handwriting File.

61. LBJ-Stevenson, May 27, 1964, 10:50 a.m., TT.

62. LBJ-Russell, May 27, 1964, 10:55 a.m., TT; Bill Moyers interview, May 14, 1997.

63. LBJ-Bundy, May 27, 1964, 11:24 a.m., TT.

64. *PPP: LBJ, 1963–64*, I, 772, 803–4; Gibbons, *U.S. Government and Vietnam War*, II, 278–79; LBJ-James Reston, June 17, 1964, 6:58 p.m., TT; Douglass Cater to LBJ, June 23, 29, 1964, with LBJ notes handwritten on both memos, Reference File: Vietnam. Also see LBJ-Robert McNamara, June 16, 1964, 9:55 a.m., TT.

65. Moyers to LBJ, July 3, 1964, WHCF: Country: Vietnam; Bundy-Ball TELCON, July 9, 1964, 1 p.m., George Ball Papers.

66. McGeorge Bundy to LBJ, July 24, 1964; Michael Forrestal to Bundy, July 22, 1964, NSF: Country: Vietnam; Gibbons, *U.S. Government and Vietnam War*, II, 280–82.

67. *Gallup Poll*, III, 1896–97; Harris Survey, Aug. 10, 1964, WHCF: EX/ PR16.

68. Gibbons, *U.S. Government and Vietnam War*, II, 282–84.

69. Ibid., 284–85.

70. Ibid., 285; Shapley, *Promise and Power*, 304; Ball-Fulbright TEL-CON, Aug. 3, 1964, George Ball Papers.

71. Shapley, *Promise and Power*, 304–5; Vietnam Conference, March 9– 10, 1991, pp. 29–30; William Bundy, MS History of the Vietnam War, chap. 14, pp. 10, 14. Also see Dean Rusk OH, Tape NN, University of Georgia, Athens; and an interview with Bill Moyers, who said of the Tonkin Gulf Resolution: "Johnson did not want to go to war in Vietnam. He did not want to set up a situation that would force him to take irretrievable steps. *It was not a set up.*" *Modern Maturity*, Oct.–Nov. 1993, p. 86.

72. Vietnam Conference, March 9–10, 1991, pp. 40–41.

73. Ibid., 44.

74. William Bundy, MS History of the Vietnam War, chap. 14, pp. 19– 22; Mac Bundy to Reedy, Aug. 7, 1964: A brief chronology of events—Aug. 3–7, NSF: Memos to the Pres.; Chronology on Vietnam, Nov. 1965, NSF: Bundy File; TELCONS: Ball-McNamara, 9:55 a.m., 10:40 a.m.; Ball-Bundy, 10:15 a.m., 10:40 a.m., 4:30 p.m.; all Aug. 3, 1964, George Ball Papers; George Ball OH.

75. Chronology of Second Attack, n.d., NSF: Country: Vietnam; LBJ-McNamara, Aug. 4, 1964, 9:43 a.m. and 10:53 a.m., TT; Gibbons, *U.S. Government and Vietnam War*, II, 288–89.

76. Interview with McGeorge Bundy, March 30, 1993; Conference, Vietnam War, March 9–10, 1991; Gibbons, *U.S. Government and Vietnam War*, II, 301.

77. Mac Bundy to Reedy, Aug. 7, 1964, A brief chronology of events— Aug. 3–7, NSF: Memos to the Pres.; Ball-Reston, TELCON, Aug. 5, 1964, 6:00 p.m., Ball Papers; Gibbons, *U.S. Government and Vietnam War*, II, 290.

78. *FRUS: Vietnam, 1964*, V, 607–9.

79. Gibbons, *U.S. Government and Vietnam War*, II, 290–91; *FRUS: Vietnam, 1964*, V, 631, 639; Reston-Ball TELCON, Aug. 5, 1964, 6:00 p.m., George Ball Papers.

80. McNamara-Sharp TELCON, Aug. 4, 1964, 4:08 p.m.; chronology of events, Aug. 4–5, 1964, NSF: Country: Vietnam.

81. NSC Meeting, Aug. 4, 1964, 6:15–6:45 p.m., NSF: NSC Meetings.

82. Leadership Meeting, Aug. 4, 1964, Meeting Notes File.

83. *PPP: LBJ, 1963–64*, II, 927–28.

84. Gibbons, *U.S. Government and Vietnam War*, II, 302–30.

85. Ibid., 304–5.

86. Stanley Karnow, *Vietnam: A History* (New York, 1984), 374; Goldman, *Tragedy of LBJ*, 210; Gibbons, *U.S. Government and Vietnam War*, II, 295.

87. *PPP: LBJ, 1963–64*, II, 1164, 1390–91; Bill Moyers interview, May 14, 1997.

88. George W. Ball, *The Past Has Another Pattern* (New York, 1982), 379.

89. For the argument that the incident didn't occur, see Karnow, *Vietnam*, 369–74. For the counter argument based on materials released in 1991, see the comments of Larry Levinson, deputy counsel to the President, 1965–69, and others in Vietnam Conference, March 9–10, 1991, pp. 30–35. Also see Dean Rusk OH, Tape NN, University of Georgia, Athens.

90. Vietnam Conference, March 9–10, 1991, pp. 38–40.

91. Ibid., 42–43.

92. Harris Survey, Aug. 10, 1964, WHCF: EX/PR16; *Gallup Poll*, III, 1899.

93. White, *Making of the President, 1964*, 266.

94. Solberg, *Hubert Humphrey*, 240–44.

95. Goldman, *Tragedy of Lyndon Johnson*, 239–40.

96. Humphrey, *Education of a Public Man*, 298.

97. Solberg, *Humphrey*, 246, 254.

98. Humphrey, *Education of a Public Man*, 300–301; Solberg, *Humphrey*, 254–55.

99. Humphrey, *Education of a Public Man*, 303–4; Solberg, *Humphrey*, 255–56; Jack Valenti OH, Feb. 19, 1971; *PPP: LBJ, 1963–64*, II, 1008–9.

100. Solberg, *Humphrey*, 255.

101. See Elizabeth Harris to Bill Moyers, June 19, 1964; and to Walter Jenkins, June 19, 1964, WHCF: Aides: Moyers; Harris to Jenkins, Aug. 8, 1964; and Bob Hunter to Doug Cater, Sept. 3, 1964, WHCF: EX/PL1; Jack Valenti OH, Feb. 19, 1971; Goldman, *Tragedy of Lyndon Johnson*, 225–26; Humphrey, *Education of a Public Man*, 305.

102. Schlesinger, *Robert Kennedy*, 662–63; Kenneth O'Donnell OH; *Final Report of the Senate Select Committee to Study Governmental Operations with Respect to Intelligence Activities* (Washington, D.C., 1976), Bk. III, 346.

103. See Elizabeth Harris to Walter Jenkins, May 25, 1964; and Dick Nelson to Jenkins, June 2, 1964, WHCF: EX\PL1, demonstrating initial concerns about civil rights demonstrations. On the MFDP, see Valenti to LBJ, July 20, 1964; Paul Popple to LBJ, Aug. 24, with telegram from Martin Luther King attached, WHCF: EX/PL\ST22–24; and *Hearings: Select Senate Committee to Study Governmental Operations with Respect to Intelligence*, 94th Cong., 1st Sess., Vol. 6, 713–17.

A report from Jim Rowe about Communist party influence at the Convention fueled Johnson's anxiety about disrupting forces. See Rowe to Ken O'Donnell, July 16, 1964, WHCF: Name: Rowe.

104. Notes of Russell telephone conversation, Aug. 20, 1964, Richard Rus-

sell papers; *Final Report of the Senate Select Committee*, Bk. III, 346–49; *Hearings: Select Senate Committee*, 94th Cong., 1st Sess., Vol. 6, 495–507.

105. *Hearings: Select Senate Committee*, Vol. 6, 508–10; LBJ to J. Edgar Hoover, Aug. 31, 1964, Handwriting File. For a debate about Bill Moyers's role in this and other questionable practices during LBJ's presidency, see Andrew Ferguson, "The Power of Myth: Bill Moyers, Liberal Fraud," *New Republic*, Aug. 19 and 26, 1991; and the exchange between Moyers and Ferguson in *New Republic*, Oct. 7, 1991.

106. *Final Report of the Select Senate Committee*, Bk. III, 347–48.

107. Solberg, *Humphrey*, 245; Miller, *Lyndon*, 477–78.

108. Solberg, *Humphrey*, 245; mjdr to Dorothy, March 1, 1965, with mjdr to LBJ, Aug. 24, 1964, attached, WHCF: EX/PL1.

109. *Final Report of the Senate Select Committee*, Book III, 347–49; White, *Making of the President, 1964*, 277–80; David J. Garrow, *The FBI and Martin Luther King, Jr.* (New York, 1981), 118–19.

110. Schlesinger, *Robert Kennedy*, 664–65.

111. Goldman, *Tragedy of Lyndon Johnson*, 255–58; Robert Bower, Reactions to LBJ's Speech, Sept. 1, 1964, WHCF: EX/PR16; Miller, *Lyndon*, 479–80.

112. *Gallup Poll*, III, 1894, 1896, 1898–99, 1901–3.

113. Jack Valenti OH, March 3, 1971.

114. Vanderbilt to Valenti, July 15, 1964, WHCF: EX/PL 6–3; Tristram Coffin to George Reedy, July 24, 1964, WHCF: Name: Goldwater. Rovere is quoted in Richard Hofstadter, *The Paranoid Style in American Politics and Other Essays* (New York, 1964), 112.

115. Norman Maher to Valenti, July 20, 1964; Valenti to Maher, July 22, 1964; and to Moyers, July 23, 1964, WHCF: Gen/PL 6–3.

116. Weisl to Walter Jenkins, Sept. 15, 1964, WHCF: EX\PR16; an advanced copy of the survey for *Fact* magazine, Sept. 30, 1964, WHCF: Name: Goldwater; Hofstadter's comment is in a Young Americans for Freedom *Newsletter* at the University of Kansas Lawrence, cited in Matthew J. Dallek, "Young Americans for Freedom, 1960–1964," M.A. thesis, Columbia University, 1993, p. 19. Hofstadter's view of the Goldwaterites as "pseudo-conservatives" animated by nonrational concerns reflected the views of most intellectuals in the country in 1964. See Hofstadter's *Paranoid Style*.

117. See Busby to Jenkins, Aug. 11, 1964, with Harry McPherson to Busby, Aug. 7, 1964, and Leonard Scruggs to McPherson, n.d. attached, WHCF: Aides: Moyers.

118. See Report of the Public Opinion Index: Voters Appraise the Johnson Administration, Sept. 1964. Johnson was also warned that safety on the streets or crime in the cities "could turn out to be the Republican candidate's secret weapon." Dick Nelson to LBJ, Aug. 31, 1964, providing an advance look at a Louis Harris survey, WHCF: Gen/PR16.

119. Valenti to LBJ, Sept. 7, 1964, WHCF: EX/PL2.

120. White, *Making of the President, 1964*, 315.

121. The quotes are in Hofstadter, *Paranoid Style*, 117; White, *Making of the President, 1964*, 326.

122. See Hofstadter, *Paranoid Style*, 115–37; and White, *Making of the President, 1964*, 325, 328–29.

123. Statement to be released by Jim Farley in behalf of the President, July 20, 1964, WHCF: EX/PL6–3; Joseph English to Moyers, July 28, 1964, WHCF: Aides: Moyers.

124. See Paul Southwick to Moyers, Aug. 3, 1964; the 112-page report of the confidential meeting, Aug. 12, 1964, WHCF: EX/PL6–3; Frank Stanton to Moyers, Aug. 14, 1964; Guidelines, Aug. 25, 1964, WHCF: Aides: Moyers.

125. Bob Hunter to Douglass Cater, Sept. 3, 1964, WHCF: EX/PL1.

126. Lawrence O'Brien OH, April 9, June 25, 1986; Rowe to LBJ, RE: The Schedule, Aug. 3, 1964, Diary Backup; Moyers to LBJ, Aug. 29, Sept. 1, 28, 1964; Stewart Udall to LBJ, Oct. 6, 1964, WHCF: Aides: Moyers; Valenti to LBJ, Sept. 2, 1964; Cliff Carter to LBJ, Sept. 12, Oct. 7, 1964; James Teague to LBJ, Sept. 25, 1964; Paul Popple to Cliff Carter, Oct. 10, 1964, WHCF: EX/PL6–3; Leonard Marks to LBJ, Sept. 18, 1964, WHCF: EX/PL2; Robert Kintner to LBJ, Sept. 30, Oct. 6, 1964, WHCF: Aides: Charles Maguire; Larry O'Brien to LBJ, Oct. 8, 9, 1964; Kenneth O'Donnell to LBJ, Oct. 13, 20, 21, 1964, WHCF: EX/PL2. Robert Fratkin of Washington, D.C., told me about the buttons and gave me copies of them. Kenneth O'Donnell OH.

127. See Chester L. Cooper to Moyers, Sept. 2, 1964, WHCF: Aides: Moyers.

128. Moyers to LBJ, Sept. 2, 1964, WHCF: EX/PL6–3.

129. Kearns, *Lyndon Johnson*, 246–47.

130. Moyers to LBJ, Sept. 5, 1964, WHCF: Aides: Moyers; Heller to LBJ, Sept. 10, 1964; Carter to Valenti, Sept. 16, 1964, WHCF: EX/PL6–3.

131. Leonard Marks to LBJ, Sept. 18, 1964; Tom Finney to LBJ, Oct. 31, 1964, WHCF: EX/PL2; Clifton C. Carter OH, Oct. 30, 1968, the two pages following Carter's remarks about reporters' calls during the night are omitted from the transcript because of "restricted material"; Douglass Cater to LBJ, Oct. 1, 1964, Diary Backup.

132. Valenti to Moyers, Meyer Feldman, Fred Dutton, Sept. 14, 1964, WHCF: EX/PL2.

133. Myer Feldman to Moyers, Sept. 10, 1964, ibid. The memo lists all the members of the committee.

134. Evans and Novak, *LBJ: Exercise of Power*, 492–93. At least two of its members didn't think the committee was doing anything untoward. See D. B. Hardeman OH, April 22, 1969; and Adam Yarmolinsky OH, July 13, 1970.

135. See Moyers to LBJ, Sept. 1, 1964, WHCF: Aides: Moyers; Valenti to LBJ, Sept. 2, 1964; Moyers to Lloyd Wright, Sept. 14, 1964, WHCF: EX/PL 6–3. Also see Edwin Diamond and Stephen Bates, *The Spot: The Rise of Political Advertising on Television* (Cambridge, Mass, 1984), 127, 146.

136. Ibid., 127–29.

137. Ibid., 129; Miller, *Lyndon*, 488–89; Bill Moyers interview, May 14, 1997.

138. Diamond and Bates, *The Spot*, 132–36.

139. Ibid., 136–37.

140. Public Opinion News Service, Sept. 24, 1964, WHCF: EX/PR16; Udall to LBJ, Oct. 6, 1964, WHCF: Aides: Moyers; Austin Ranney to John Stillman, Oct. 29, 1964; Tom Finney to LBJ, Oct. 30, 1964, WHCF: CF: EX/PR16.

141. See Louis Kohlmeier, "The Johnson Wealth," *Wall Street Journal*, March 23, 1964; John Barron, "The Johnson Money," *Washington Star*, June 9, 1964; Keith Wheeler and William Lambert, "The Man Who Is the President," *Life*, Aug. 14, 21, 1964; a copy of the editorial-ad, "LBJ Gets Rich in Office," was in the *Des Moines Register*, Oct. 7, 1964, clipping in the Drew Pearson Papers.

142. See Drew Pearson, "Books Smearing Johnson Outsell Lurid Novels," clipping of his Aug. 25, 1964 column in Pearson Papers; also see his letter to LBJ, Oct. 8, 1964. Lawrence O'Brien OH, April 9, 1986; Gifford Phillips to Walter Jenkins, Oct. 9, 1964; Kenneth O'Donnell to LBJ, Oct. 20, 1964; Tom Finney to LBJ, Oct. 31, 1964, WHCF: EX/PL2; John Cowles to LBJ, Oct. 10, 1964, WHCF: GEN/PL6–3.

143. Under Sec. of State Crockett to Amb. Gilstrap, Oct. 17, 1964; Gilstrap to Crockett, Oct. 19, 1964; Crockett to Consul Gen. Rice, Oct. 17, 1964; Rice to Crockett, Oct. 18, 1964, Hoover O&C File, FBI.

144. Memo: "Call from Mrs. Connor," dlf, Oct. 5, 1964, Drew Pearson Papers; Memo from News and Information, DNC, Oct. 25, 1964, WHCF: Aides: Moyers; C. A. Evans to Mr. Belmont, Oct. 17, 1964; DeLoach to Mohr, Oct. 30, 1964, LBJ File 94–4–3830, FBI.

145. Rowe to LBJ, Oct. 20, 1964, WHCF: CF: EX/PR16.

146. Diamond and Bates, *The Spot*, 144–45.

147. Ibid., 144; Kenneth O'Donnell to LBJ, Oct. 21, 1964, WHCF: EX/PL2.

148. Miller, *Lyndon*, 486–87, 731 n. 6; George Reedy OH, Dec. 20, 1968; Jack Valenti OH, Feb. 19, 1971.

149. George Reedy OH, Dec. 20, 1968; FBI interviews in LBJ, Cross-Refs. Only 1; the specific interview is dated Oct. 16, 1964, and is on p. 47 of this material, FBI.

150. Reedy OH, Dec. 20, 1968; Kenneth O'Donnell OH; Jack Valenti OH, Feb. 19, 1971.

151. Kearns, *Lyndon Johnson*, 207–8.

152. On the earlier arrest, see C. Douglas Dillon to Nicholas Katzenbach, Oct. 16, 1964, NSF: McGeorge Bundy File.

153. White, *Making of the President, 1964*, 369–71.

154. Murray Fromson interview, August 21, 1993.

155. See Stephen Ansolabehere et al., "Does Attack Advertising Demobilize the Electorate?," unpub. paper, Dept. of Political Science, UCLA, which argues that negative TV ads do more to discourage people from voting than to win them to the attacking politician's side.

156. John B. Martin to Moyers, Oct. 1, 1964, WHCF: Aides: Moyers; Lawrence O'Brien OH, April 9, 1986; Kenneth O'Donnell to LBJ, Oct. 20, 1964, WHCF: EX/PL2.

157. The trip is described in White, *Making of the President, 1964*, 364–67; and Jack Valenti OH, Feb. 19, 1971.

158. Frank Gibney Memo, and Moyers to Valenti, Oct. 9, 1964, WHCF: Aides: Moyers; *PPP: LBJ, 1963–64*, II, 1279, 1283, 1285–86; White, *Making of the President, 1964*, 363–64; Miller, *Lyndon*, 484–85.

159. Busby to LBJ, n.d. [Oct. 12, 1964], WHCF: Aides: Moyers.

160. See White, *Making of the President, 1964*, 380; and Bernard Bailyn

et al., *The Great Republic: A History of the American People*, II, 4th ed. (Lexington, Mass, 1992), app. xxiii, for a more accurate popular vote.

161. White, *Making of the President, 1964*, 381.

CHAPTER 4: KING OF THE HILL

1. Bill Moyers interview, Jan. 26, 1994; Humphrey, *Education of a Public Man*, 306.

2. Ibid., 305–6.

3. Miller, *Lyndon*, 480–81; Humphrey, *Education of a Public Man*, 305.

4. Ibid., 307–8; Miller, *Lyndon*, 481; Roy L. McGhee OH, SHO.

5. McGhee OH; LBJ's relationships with the "queens" were described by a confidential source; LBJ-Macy, Jan. 6, 1964, 3:30 p.m., TT; the historian Alan Brinkley, David's son, described his mother's experience to me; LBJ-Marshall McNeil, Jan. 31, 1964, 9:00 p.m., TT.

6. Mrs. Johnson commented on her husband's behavior in a 1993 TV documentary about her public career. A confidential source related the Alice Glass story to me. Jane Sumner of the *Dallas Morning News*, who covered LBJ at the White House, described his reaction to Lady Bird's absence to me, Sept. 11, 1991. Memo, May 5, 1965, Krock Papers; conversation with George Christian and Larry Temple, April 2, 1994; McGeorge Bundy interview, March 30, 1993.

7. Conversation with George Christian and Larry Temple, April 2, 1994.

8. Jack Valenti to LBJ, Nov. 11, 1964, Handwriting File.

9. President's Remarks at Cabinet, July 2, 1964, attached to Bill Moyers to Ackley, etc., July 6, 1964, Four-Year Farm Program, Legislative Background Papers; Draft of Speech: "Policy Formulation," n.d., WHCF: Aides: James C. Gaither; James C. Gaither OH, Nov. 19, 1968, Jan. 17, 1969; William E. Leuchtenburg, "The Genesis of the Great Society," *The Reporter*, April 21, 1966; Nancy Kegan Smith, "Presidential Task Force Operation During the Johnson Administration," *Presidential Studies Quarterly* (Spring 1985), 320–22.

10. David M. Barrett, "Secrecy and Openness in Lyndon Johnson's White House: Political Style, Pluralism, and the Presidency," *Review of Politics* (Winter 1992), 98–101. Also see Henry Wilson to Larry O'Brien, Nov. 25, 1964, describing in detail meetings on Task Force reports, WHCF: Aides: H. H. Wilson.

11. Clark Clifford to LBJ, Nov. 5, 1964, WHCF: Name: Clifford.

12. Douglass Cater to LBJ, Jan. 13, 1965, Diary Backup; Goldman, *Tragedy of LBJ*, 306–9, 326–27.

13. Goldman, *Tragedy of LBJ*, 307; Elmo Roper, "After the Election," *Saturday Review*, Nov. 28, 1964, with Jack Valenti to LBJ, n.d., and LBJ's comment on it attached, Handwriting File.

14. Stewart E. McClure OH, SHO.

15. Jack Valenti, *A Very Human President* (New York, 1975), 178; J. J. (Jake) Pickle OH, Aug. 17, 1972.

16. McCormack to LBJ, Aug. 20, 1964, WHCF: GEN/FG412 Speaker of the House; Valenti, *A Very Human President*, 193–94; LBJ to O'Brien, Jan. 13, 1965; LBJ to Eastland, Jan. 13, 1965, Handwriting File.

17. Thomas Curtis to Author, Sept. 24, 1986.

18. Goldman, *Tragedy of LBJ*, 307–9; LBJ conversation with Catledge, Dec. 15, 1964, Arthur Krock Papers, Princeton University.

19. See Perry Barber to Jack Valenti, Nov. 16, 1964; and the AP press release, "Johnson-Program," Nov. 18, 1964, WHCF: GEN\FG412 Speaker of the House. Also, Kearns, *Lyndon Johnson*, 222.

20. *PPP: LBJ, 1963–64*, II, 1604–5; *PPP: LBJ, 1965*, I, 1.

21. William E. Leuchtenburg, "A Visit with LBJ," *American Heritage*, May/June 1990, pp. 52, 54.

22. Cabinet Meeting, Oct. 5, 1965, Cabinet Papers.

23. *PPP: LBJ, 1965*, I, 1–9.

24. This material is drawn from Goldman, *Tragedy of LBJ*, 336–37; and Bibby and Davidson, *On Capitol Hill*, 144–69.

25. Kearns, *Lyndon Johnson*, 222–24; Larry O'Brien to mjdr, Jan. 22, 1965; Ramsey Clark to mjdr, Jan. 22, 1965, Diary Backup.

26. Kearns, *Lyndon Johnson*, 232–37; also see boxes 4, 5, 7, 9, and 19 of the Harold (Barefoot) Sanders Papers, LBJL, which include Larry O'Brien's work in keeping track of congressional votes and "Daily Congressional Contact Reports"; and Mike Manatos OH.

27. See Valenti to LBJ, April 1, and June 18, 1965, and Valenti to Dirksen, July 31, 1965, WHCF: Name: Dirksen; Marvin Watson to LBJ, March 29, 1965, on LBJ's contacts with Dirksen during the first three months of 1965, Handwriting File; and Dirksen to LBJ, Jan. 11, 12, April 1, 30, July 22, Aug. 18, Sept. 15, 1965, Alphabetical File, f, Everett Dirksen Papers, Pekin, Ill. Valenti, *A Very Human President*, 182–84. For the Church story, see *Los Angeles Times*, Nov. 22, 1993, p. 18. On punishing uncooperative Congressmen, see memo of Larry O'Brien's call to LBJ, Dec. 31, 1964, WHCF: Name: John Mc-Cormack; and Bibby and Davidson, *On Capitol Hill*, 160, 162–65.

28. Miller, *Lyndon*, 496.

29. See Richard Goodwin to LBJ, July 19, 1964, Diary Backup; and *PPP: LBJ, 1963–64*, II, 1563–64.

30. Hugh Davis Graham, "The Transformation of Federal Education Policy," in *The Johnson Years*, I, edited by Robert Divine, (Austin, Tex., 1981), 155–57, 177 n. 10. Also see Irving Bernstein, *Promises Kept* (New York, 1991), chap. 7, on JFK's unsuccessful efforts to pass federal support of elementary and secondary education.

31. Graham, "Transformation of Federal Education," 161–63; Michael R. Reopel and Lance W. Bardsley, "Strategies for Governance: Domestic Policy-making in the Johnson Administration," in Firestone and Vogt, *LBJ and Uses of Power*, 15–16.

32. Wilbur Cohen OH, May 10, 1969.

33. Anthony Celebrezze to Bill Moyers, Dec. 1, 1964, with Keppel memo attached, WHCF: EX/ED. Also see To the President, Dec. 1, 1964, WHCF: EX/LE\FA2; Keppel to Richard Goodwin, Dec. 2, 1964; Keppel to Douglass Cater, Dec. 3, 1964, WHCF: CF: EX/FG165; Cater to LBJ, Dec. 19, 1964, WHCF: GEN/FG165\A-Z; Keppel to Cater, Dec. 21, 1964, WHCF: EX/LE\FA2. And Hugh Davis Graham, *The Uncertain Triumph: Federal Education Policy in the Kennedy and Johnson Years* (Chapel Hill, N.C., 1984), 70–76.

34. See Graham, "Transformation of Federal Education Policy," 161–63; Graham, *Uncertain Triumph*, 76–78; Francis Keppel OH, April 21, 1969. Also

see Wilbur J. Cohen OH, May 10, 1969; Douglass Cater OH, April 29, 1969; John W. Gardner OH, Dec. 20, 1971; Carl D. Perkins OH, May 12, 1983.

35. LBJ is quoted in Reopel and Bardsley, "Strategies for Governance," 18.

36. *PPP: LBJ, 1965*, I, 25–34.

37. Francis Keppel OH, April 21, 1969.

38. Wilbur J. Cohen to Bill Moyers, Jan. 14, 1965, giving a round up of newspaper opinion on the bill, WHCF: Aides: Cater.

39. Moyers to O'Brien, Jan. 13, 1965, WHCF: Aides: Moyers; Cater to Juanita Roberts, Jan. 15, 1965, Diary Backup.

40. O'Brien to Moyers, Jan. 14, 1965, WHCF: Aides: Moyers.

41. Wilson to O'Brien, Jan. 26, 1965, WHCF: EX/LE\FA2.

42. All these developments are described in O'Brien to LBJ, March 8, 1965, WHCF: EX/LE\FA2.

43. See Douglass Cater to LBJ, Feb. 15, 1965, WHCF: EX/LE\FA2; Keppel to Valenti, Feb. 26, 1965, WHCF: Gen/FG165\A-Z; *PPP: LBJ, 1965*, I, 226–31.

44. See Cater to LBJ, March 24, 1965; Larry O'Brien to LBJ, March 27, 1965, WHCF: Name: John McCormack; Valenti to LBJ, March 23, 24, 1965; Cater to LBJ, March 26, 30, 31, 1965, WHCF: EX/LE\FA2; Cater to LBJ, March 30, 1965, Handwriting File; Graham, *Uncertain Trumpet*, 78; Goldman, *Tragedy of LBJ*, 363–64.

45. *PPP: LBJ, 1965*, I, 407–8, 412–14, 415–19; Goldman, *Tragedy of LBJ*, 363–65.

46. *PPP: LBJ,1965*, I, 414,416.

47. Graham, *Uncertain Triumph*, 203–16; Matusow, *Unraveling of America*, 223–26; "After 20 Years, Education Programs Are a Solid Legacy of Great Society," *New York Times*, Sept. 30, 1985, p. 11.

48. *New York Times*, Sept. 30, 1985.

49. Outline of the Higher Education Act of 1965, Aug. 30, 1965, WHCF: EX/ED; Graham, *Uncertain Triumph*, xiv, 80–83; Eugen Weber, "Schooling for Whom? Education for What?," *Explorations: The Twentieth Century*, Special Series, VI, 1992.

50. *New York Times*, Dec. 9, 1993.

51. Califano, *Triumph and Tragedy*, 29–30. LBJ wasn't the only one who had compelling personal reasons to support medical research and health care reform. According to Larry O'Brien, JFK and he partly backed Medicare in 1961–63 because of personal unhappiness with the cost of medical care for the elderly. Lawrence O'Brien OH, Oct. 30, 1985.

52. Dallek, *Lone Star Rising*, 274–75, 495–96; Paul Starr, *The Social Transformation of American Medicine* (New York, 1982), 342–43; Clarence G. Lasby, "The War on Disease," in *The Johnson Years*, II, 186–88.

53. *PPP: LBJ, 1963–64*, I, 275–84.

54. On the history of Medicare, see "Controversy in Congress Over 'Medicare,'" *Congressional Quarterly Fact Sheet*, March 1965; on the commission, see *PPP: LBJ, 1963–64*, I, 282.

55. Ibid., 478–79.

56. Lasby, "The War on Disease," 191–94; *PPP: LBJ, 1963–64*, II, 1650–51.

57. Lasby, "The War on Disease," 194–98. Henry Wilson told Larry

O'Brien in November 1964 that AMA opposition to RMP "will be last-ditch and unyielding.... The issue of socialized medicine can truthfully be raised here. It [RMP] would be a good one to win, but it would really be tough." Nov. 25, 1964, WHCF: Aides: H. H. Wilson. Likewise, Assistant Secretary of HEW Wilbur Cohen saw the HDCS bill as "more radical" than Medicare and the medical community as fearful that RMP "would completely reorganize medical care in the United States." Memo, Aug. 30, 1965, Wilbur J. Cohen Papers, State Historical Society of Wisconsin, Madison.

58. Lawrence R. Jacobs and Robert Y. Shapiro, "Leadership and Responsiveness: Some New Evidence on the Johnson Presidency," unpub. paper, American Political Science Association, Sept, 1992, pp. 17–18, 21–22. Memos, Nov. 15, 17, 18, 1964, Cohen Papers; Berkowitz, *Mr. Social Security*, 222–23.

59. Lawrence O'Brien OH, Oct. 30, 1985; Celebrezze to LBJ, Nov. 25, 1964; O'Brien to LBJ, Dec. 9, 1964, with Mike Manatos to O'Brien, Dec. 8, 1964, attached, WHCF: EX/IS1.

60. Sheri I. David, "Medicare: Hallmark of the Great Society," in Firestone and Vogt, eds., *LBJ and the Uses of Power*, 42; Memo, July 16, 1964, Cohen Papers; Kearns, *Lyndon Johnson*, 301–2.

61. Lawrence O'Brien OH, Sept. 18, 1985.

62. LBJ, *Vantage Point*, 214; Berkowitz, *Mr. Social Security*, 225–27.

63. *PPP: LBJ, 1965*, I, 6, 13–14.

64. Theodore R. Marmor and Lawrence R. Jacobs, "Don't Settle for Crumbs on Health Reform," *Los Angeles Times*, Nov. 16, 1992; Celebrezze to LBJ, Nov. 25, 1964, WHCF: EX/LE\IS1; Wilbur Cohen to Claude DeSautels, Jan. 11, 1965, Reports on Legislation; McCormack to Larry O'Brien, Jan. 14, 1965, WHCF: Name: John McCormack; LBJ, *Vantage Point*, 215; Berkowitz, *Mr. Social Security*, 212–27.

65. David, "Medicare," 45; Berkowitz, *Mr. Social Security*, 227–31.

66. Wilbur Cohen to LBJ, March 2, 1965, WHCF: EX/LE\IS1; LBJ, *Vantage Point*, 215–16.

67. Ibid., 216; Joseph A. Califano, Jr., *Governing America: An Insider's Report from the White House and the Cabinet* (New York, 1981), 140.

68. Lawrence O'Brien OH, July 24, 1986; LBJ, *Vantage Point*, 216–17.

69. See Wilbur Cohen to Larry O'Brien, May 6, 1965; Elizabeth Wickenden to Jack Valenti, May 28, 1965; Cohen to LBJ, June 17; to O'Brien, July 20, 1965, WHCF: EX/FG165; Mike Manatos to Larry O'Brien, June 21, 1965, WHCF: Aides: Manatos; Cohen to Claude DeSautels, June 7, 14, 18, 28, July 6, 12, 26, 1965, Reports on Legislation; David, "Medicare," 46; Berkowitz, *Mr. Social Security*, 233–34.

70. LBJ, *Vantage Point*, 217–18; the Reagan quote is in Richard Sorian, *The Bitter Pill: Tough Choices in America's Health Policy* (New York, 1990), 93.

71. Berkowitz, *Mr. Social Security*, 236; Cohen to Douglass Cater, July 26, 1965, WHCF: Aides: Cater; Cater to LBJ, July 28, 1965, WHCF: EX/HE; LBJ, *Vantage Point*, 217–18.

72. Wilbur Cohen told this story to Sheldon Stern of the John F. Kennedy Library, who told it to me, March 27, 1992.

73. Diary Backup, July 29, 1965; LBJ, *Vantage Point*, 217–18; Califano, *Governing America*, 140–41; Califano, *Triumph and Tragedy*, 50–51.

74. Sorian, *Bitter Pill*, chap. 1, and 89–90.

75. Matusow, *Unraveling of America*, 226–32; Sorian, *Bitter Pill*, chap. 6; *Overview of Entitlement Programs: 1993 Green Book*, House Committee on Ways and Means, 103rd Cong., 1st Sess.

76. LBJ conversation, Dec. 15, 1964, Krock Papers.

77. *PPP: LBJ, 1965*, I, 5–6; David J. Garrow, *Protest at Selma: Martin Luther King, Jr., and the Voting Rights Act of 1965* (New Haven, Conn., 1978), 35–39; Graham, *Civil Rights Era*, 162–64.

78. For LBJ's interest in pushing a bill, see Lee White to Bill Moyers, Dec. 30, 1964, WHCF: Aides: White; for his reluctance, see LBJ, *Vantage Point*, 160–61; and the Turner Catledge memo of Dec. 15, 1964, in the Krock Papers.

79. Garrow, *The FBI and King*, chaps. 3–4; Bill Moyers interview, May 14, 1997.

80. Garrow, *Protest at Selma*, 39–40; Miller, *Lyndon*, 522; Matusow, *Unraveling of America*, 181–82; Graham, *Civil Rights Era*, 163–65.

81. Garrow, *Protest at Selma*, 40–50; Lee White to LBJ, Feb. 3, 1965, WHCF: Name: M. L. King, Jr.

82. *PPP: LBJ, 1965*, I, 132–33, 138–39.

83. Garrow, *Protest at Selma*, 52–56.

84. Lee White to LBJ, Feb. 5, 1965; Valenti to LBJ, Feb. 9, 1965; Points That King Might Make upon Leaving White House, n.d., Diary Backup; White to LBJ, Feb. 8, 1965, WHCF: EX/HU2.

85. See Bill Moyers to LBJ, with Horace Busby to Moyers and White attached, Feb. 27, 1965; Katzenbach to Moyers and White, March 1, 1965, WHCF: Aides: Busby; White to LBJ, March 4, 1965, WHCF: EX/HU2.

86. Garrow, *Protest at Selma*, 73–81; Matusow, *Unraveling of America*, 182–83.

87. Garrow, *Protest at Selma*, 78–82; *PPP: LBJ, 1965*, I, 272–73.

88. Louis Martin to Marvin Watson, March 8, 1965, WHCF: Name: M. L. King, Jr.; Memo: Selma, listing meetings and phone calls on March 8, 9, 1965, Legislative Background: Voting Rights Act, 1965; Garrow, *Protest at Selma*, 82–87, 91, 97; Matusow, *Unraveling of America*, 183–84.

89. UPI-90, March 12, 1965, Diary Backup; LBJ, *Vantage Point*, 162; Garrow, *Protest at Selma*, 89, 91, 93; Goldman, *Tragedy of LBJ*, 369.

90. See "Fauntroy Said," n.d. [March 12, 1965], Diary Backup; Norbert Schlei to Lee White, March 11, 1965, WHCF: Aides: White; LBJ, *Vantage Point*, 162; Garrow, *Protest at Selma*, 92–93, 276 nn. 20, 21.

91. George Wallace to LBJ, March 12, 1965; Lee White to LBJ, March 13, 1965, WHCF: EX/HU2\ST1; Memo, Selma, March 13, 1965, Legislative Background: Voting Rights Act, 1965; Douglass Cater to LBJ, n.d., but March 12 or 13, 1965; Katzenbach to LBJ, March 13, 1965; Talking Points, n.d. [March 12 or 13, 1965], Diary Backup; Goodwin, *Remembering America*, 319–21.

92. Ibid., 320–24; Miller, *Lyndon*, 524–25.

93. *PPP: LBJ, 1965*, I, 274–77; Goodwin, *Remembering America*, 323; Jack Valenti's Notes, March 18, 1965, Diary Backup; Wallace to LBJ, March 19, 1965; Bill Moyers to LBJ, March 19, 1965; LBJ to Wallace, March 20, 1965, Legislative Background: Voting Rights Act, 1965; Garrow, *Protest at Selma*, 112, 114–15.

94. See Jack Valenti Notes, March 14, 1965, Backup Diary; LBJ, *Vantage*

Point, 163–65; Goodwin, *Remembering America*, 324–29; Goldman, *Tragedy of LBJ*, 378. Also see Valenti to LBJ, March 16, 1965, describing efforts to convince the press that LBJ "wrote the speech," WHCF: EX/SP23\1965\ HU2-7.

95. *PPP: LBJ, 1965*, I, 281–87; Goldman, *Tragedy of LBJ*, 378–82; Goodwin, *Remembering America*, 331–38.

96. Matusow, *Unraveling of America*, 185–87; Graham, *Civil Rights Era*, 166–70.

97. For the progress of the bill, see Jim Jones to Marvin Watson, March 17, 1965, WHCF: EX/HU2-7; the memos in WHCF: EX/LE\HU2-7 for March-Aug. 1965; Legislative Background: Voting Rights Act, 1965, March 17-Aug. 5, 1965; and the weekly Reports on Pending Legislation for March-Aug. 1965 in LBJL. Graham, *Civil Rights Era*, 171–73; *PPP: LBJ, 1965*, II, 840–43.

98. Garrow, *Protest at Selma*, 189; Matusow, *Unraveling of America*, 188; Goodwin, *Remembering America*, 339; "Civil Rights Act Has Shaped Nation's Politics for 25 Years," *New York Times*, July 2, 1989.

99. On the shift in the South, see "Civil Rights Act Has Shaped Nation's Politics for 25 Years," *New York Times*, July 2, 1989: 57 percent of southern whites identified themselves as Democrats in 1960; in 1964 the number had dropped to 51 percent, and by 1988, it was down to only 32 percent. The quote is in William E. Leuchtenburg, "The Old Cowhand from Dixie," *Atlantic Monthly*, Dec. 1992, p. 97.

100. See Lee Rainwater and William L. Yancey, *The Moynihan Report and the Politics of Controversy* (Cambridge, Mass., 1967), 38–124; Graham, *Civil Rights Era*, 209–10; Moynihan to Bill Moyers, Jan. 21, 1965, WHCF: EX/ HU2-1.

101. Goodwin, *Remembering America*, 342–48; Graham, *Civil Rights Era*, 174; *PPP: LBJ, 1965*, II, 635–40. Also see M. L. King, Jr., to LBJ, June 7, 1965, WHCF: Name: King, Jr.

102. John Morton Blum, *Years of Discord: American Politics and Society, 1961–1974* (New York, 1991), 252–54; Ramsey Clark's remarks in "Lyndon Johnson and the Civil Rights Revolution: A Panel Discussion," in Firestone and Vogt, eds., *LBJ and the Uses of Power*, 175. LBJ is quoted in Kearns, *LBJ*, 305. Ramsey Clark OH, March 21, 1969.

103. Califano, *Triumph and Tragedy*, 59–63.

104. For the administration's efforts in Watts, see Adam Yarmolinsky to Bill Moyers, Aug. 16, 1965, WHCF: CF: EX/LG; Nicholas Katzenbach to LBJ, Aug. 17, 1965, WHCF: EX/FG135; the numerous memos in Aug., Sept., and Oct. 1965 in WHCF: EX/LG\Los Angeles, especially Ernest Friesen, Jr., to Lawrence Levinson, Oct. 26, 1965; "L.A. Riots: Ramsey Clark Report" file in WHCF: Aides: Califano; and material in boxes 76 and 109 of Ramsey Clark's Papers, LBJL.

105. See Graham, *Civil Rights Era*, 161–62; Califano, *Triumph and Tragedy*, 64–65; LBJ to HHH, Dec. 2, 1964, and Humphrey's 33-page undated response to LBJ as well as several Humphrey memos to the President between March and Sept. 1965 on civil rights issues, Memos to the President, Hubert H. Humphrey Papers, Minnesota Historical Society, St. Paul.

106. See Graham, *Civil Rights Era*, 180–89; Califano, *Triumph and Tragedy*, 65–66.

107. See HHH to LBJ, Sept. 24, 1965, and the attached White House Press Release, Humphrey Papers; Califano, *Triumph and Tragedy*, 66–69; *PPP: LBJ, 1965*, II, 1017–19; Humphrey, *Education of a Public Man*, 407–9; Solberg, *Humphrey*, 276–78.

108. See HHH to LBJ, Aug. 17, 1965, Hubert Humphrey Papers; Lee C. White to LBJ, July 23, 1965, WHCF: Name: M. L. King, Jr.; White to LBJ, Aug. 4, 10, 1965, Diary Backup; Califano to LBJ, Sept. 24, 1965, WHCF: EX/ HU2; Rainwater and Yancey, *The Moynihan Report*, 409–11, 457–66, 474–78; Matusow, *Unraveling of America*, 197–98.

109. *PPP: LBJ, 1965*, I, 199–202; Patterson, *America's Struggle Against Poverty*, 171, for the numbers on AFDC.

110. On Project Head Start, see Sargent Shriver OH, July 1, 1982; for the rest, see *PPP: LBJ, 1965*, I, 199–202; II, 930–33. For the poverty programs in March and then at the end of 1965, see "Catalog of Federal Improvement Programs," March 1965, and "Poverty Program Information," Jan. 1, 1966, WHCF: Aides: Moyers.

111. *PPP: LBJ, 1965*, II, 823, 923, 927, 1037–40. Also see Hayes Redmon to Bill Moyers, July 21, 1965, WHCF: Aides: Moyers; and Henry Wilson to Larry O'Brien, July 23, 1965, WHCF: Aides: H. H. Wilson. For administration work on the bill, see additional memos in the Moyers and Wilson files and WHCF: EX/IM; LE/IM; and Legislative Background: Immigration Law, 1965.

112. *PPP: LBJ, 1965*, I, 114–15, 231–40; II, 985–86.

113. See Emmette S. Redford and Marlan Blissett, *Organizing the Executive Branch: The Johnson Presidency* (Chicago, 1981), chap. 2: "HUD: A New Commitment to Urban Problems."

114. See Larry O'Brien to LBJ, July 30, 1965; Califano to LBJ, Sept. 23, Oct. 31, 1965; Lee C. White to LBJ, Oct. 22, 1965; Harry McPherson to LBJ, Oct. 29, 1965; White House Press Release, Oct. 31, 1965, WHCF: EX/FG 170; Lawrence O'Brien OH, Oct. 30, 1985; Sept. 10, 1986; Califano, *Triumph and Tragedy*, 126–28.

115. Bill Moyers to LBJ, Dec. 11, 1965; LBJ note, Dec. 11, 1965, Legislative Background: HUD; Robert C. Weaver OH, Nov. 19, 1968; Califano, *Triumph and Tragedy*, 128–30.

116. See LBJ, *Vantage Point*, 336; "Report of the Task Force on Environmental Pollution," Nov. 9, 1964, Task Force Reports, LBJL; *PPP: LBJ, 1965*, I, 8, 115, 155–65, 576–81; II, 774–76, 867–72,-1036–37, 1066–67, 1072–75.

117. Lawrence O'Brien OH, Sept. 10, 1986; LBJ, *Vantage Point*, 337.

118. For the legislative battles, see Legislative Background: Water Pollution Control; Clean Air; Reports on Legislation; WHCF: EX/HE8-1; EX/ LE\HE8-4; GEN/LE\HE8-1; GEN/HE8-4; CF: EX/LE\HE8-4; Aides: Califano; Manatos; H. H. Wilson; Califano, *Triumph and Tragedy*, 81–85; Lewis L. Gould, *Lady Bird Johnson and the Environment* (Lawrence, Kans., 1988). For LBJ's remarks, see *PPP: LBJ, 1965*, II, 1034–35, 1066–67, 1072–75.

119. See Legislative Background: Arts and Humanities Foundation, 1965; WHCF: EX/FG266; EX/LE\AR; *PPP: LBJ, 1965*, I, 273–74; II, 832–34, 1022–23.

120. Leuchtenburg, *American Heritage*, May/June 1990, pp. 49–50.

121. Califano, *Triumph and Tragedy*, 151–52.

122. Leuchtenburg, *American Heritage*, 51–52.

123. Cabinet Meeting, Sept. 13, 1965, Cabinet Papers.

124. Califano, *Triumph and Tragedy*, 152; Lawrence O'Brien OH, Sept. 10, 1986.

125. *PPP: LBJ, 1965*, II, 930; Bill Moyers interview, May 14, 1997.

126. For political activities by some justices, see *Roosevelt and Frankfurter: Their Correspondence, 1928–1945* (London, 1968); Bruce Allen Murphy, *The Brandeis-Frankfurter Connection: The Secret Political Activities of Two Supreme Court Justices* (New York, 1982); *New York Times*, April 10, 1989, describing the lobbying activities of Thomas Corcoran at the Supreme Court; and Dallek, *Lone Star Rising*, 339–42. LBJ to Hugo Black, Feb. 27, 1965, Handwriting File. Also see David M. O'Brien, *Storm Center: The Supreme Court in American Politics* (New York, 1986); and Bruce Allen Murphy, *Fortas: The Rise and Ruin of a Supreme Court Justice* (New York, 1988), 165–66, and 623 n. 11, which says that "very few" justices strictly observed the separation-of-powers stricture.

For additional evidence of Johnson's use of "insiders" to get advance information on what opponents were thinking, see Terry Dietz, *Republicans and Vietnam, 1961–1968* (New York, 1986), 150, who discusses LBJ's infiltration of "the Republican decision-making process on Capitol Hill."

127. For the LBJ-Fortas relationship, see Dallek, *Lone Star Rising*; and Bruce Allen Murphy, *Fortas*, chaps. 5–6. William O. Douglas to LBJ, July 21, 1965, WHCF: EX/FG535A.

128. Laura Kalman, *Abe Fortas: A Biography* (New Haven, Conn., 1990), 230–32; Murphy, *Fortas*, 158–59.

129. Steve Young to LBJ, Nov. 6, 1964; John B. Clinton to Ralph A. Dungan, Nov. 10, 1964; Ramsey Clark to LBJ, Feb. 3, 1965; *Wall Street Journal*, clipping, April 23, 1965; Press Release, July 27, 1965, Celebrezze folder; Mildred Stegall to Cartha DeLoach, May 10, 1965, Goldberg and Fortas folders, WHCF: Aides: Macy; Valenti to LBJ, June 11, 1965, Diary Backup; LBJ Memo, June 24, 1968; Jack Valenti, Summary of Conversation with Arthur Goldberg, n.d., Goldberg Folder, WHCF: Aides: Valenti; Arthur Goldberg OH; Murphy, *Fortas*, 169.

130. Lady Bird Johnson, *A White House Diary* (New York, 1970), 299; Douglass Cater to LBJ, July 26, 1965, Handwriting File; Arthur Goldberg OH; Murphy, *Fortas*, 167–71; Kalman, *Fortas*, 240–41.

131. I have largely followed Kalman here, who argues that despite what Fortas said then and later, he badly wanted the appointment. *Fortas*, 240–45. Lady Bird Johnson interview, Oct. 6, 1997. Bill Moyers told me that he heard Mrs. Johnson say, " 'Abe wants to go on the Court.' " Interview, May 14, 1997.

132. Fortas to LBJ, July 19, 1965, WHCF: CF: EX/FG535; LBJ, *Vantage Point*, 545; Abe Fortas OH; Kalman, *Fortas*, 242.

133. Murphy, *Fortas*, 182–84; Kalman, *Fortas*, 245.

134. Ibid., 246–48; Murphy, *Fortas*, 184–85.

CHAPTER 5: FOREIGN POLICY DILEMMAS

1. Memorandum for the Record, Aug. 13, 1964, NSF: Files of McGeorge Bundy.

2. *PPP: LBJ, 1963–64,* II, 1126–27, 1164–65, 1267, 1390–91. Also see transcript of Vietnam Round Table, March 9–10, 1991, pp. 48–51, which describes LBJ's remarks as spontaneous.

3. Telcon: Ball and Reston, Aug. 29, 1964, Ball Papers; Chronology on Vietnam, pp. 58–59, NSF: Files of McG. Bundy; Bundy to LBJ, Aug. 31, 1964, NSF: Memos to the President.

4. Gibbons, *U.S. Government and Vietnam,* II, 350–52.

5. Meeting on South Vietnam, Sept. 9, 1964, NSF: Meeting Notes File.

6. Bundy to LBJ, Sept. 14, 1964, NSF: Memos to the President.

7. Bundy to LBJ, Sept. 20, 1964, NSF: Memos to the President; DeSoto Patrol, Sept. 21, 1964, Handwriting File; Shapley, *Promise and Power,* 309; Ball, *Past Has Another Pattern,* 379–80; Gibbons, *U.S. Government and Vietnam,* II, 354–57.

8. For conditions in Vietnam, see *FRUS: Vietnam, 1964,* 787ff. Bundy to LBJ, Oct. 1 and 6, 1964, NSF: Memos to the President. For LBJ's public statements, see *PPP: LBJ, 1963–64,* II, 1181ff.

9. The Bien Hoa episode is well summarized in Gibbons, *U.S. Government and Vietnam,* II, 363–65; and William P. Bundy, MS History of the Vietnam War, chap. 17, pp. 26–28. Also see, *FRUS: Vietnam, 1964,* 873–84.

10. Ibid., 881–82, 886–87; Mike Gravel, ed., *The Pentagon Papers: The Defense Department History of United States Decisionmaking on Vietnam,* 5 vols. (Boston, 1971), III, 206–7; Gibbons, *U.S. Government and Vietnam,* II, 366.

11. *FRUS: Vietnam, 1964,* 914–16; Jack Valenti to LBJ, Nov. 14, 1964, WHCF: CF: CO312.

12. Gravel, ed., *Pentagon Papers,* III, 245–61; *FRUS: Vietnam, 1964,* 965–69.

13. Ibid., 974–78, 984.

14. Ibid., 966; David Wise, *The Politics of Lying: Government Deception, Secrecy, and Power* (New York, 1973), 295. Also see George McT. Kahin, *Intervention: How America Became Involved in Vietnam* (New York, 1986), 251–54, which contrasts LBJ's caution with the intemperateness of his advisers.

15. *FRUS: Vietnam, 1964,* 1031–32, 1043–44, 1049, 1051–53, 1057–59; Bill Moyers interview, May 14, 1997. Also see Kahin, *Intervention,* 260–61.

16. Mansfield to LBJ, Dec. 9, 1964; LBJ to Mansfield, Dec. 17, 1964, with Bundy to LBJ, Dec. 16, 1964, attached, NSF: Names: Mansfield; Ronald Steel, *Walter Lippmann and the American Century* (Boston, 1980), 556.

17. Halberstam, *Best and Brightest,* 614; James L. Greenfield to Rusk, Nov. 19, Dec. 18, 1964, with American Opinion Survey: Vietnam attached, NSF: Country File: Vietnam; John E. Mueller, *War, Presidents and Public Opinion* 54; Bruce E. Altschuler, "Lyndon Johnson and the Public Polls," *Public Opinion Quarterly,* Fall 1986, p. 296.

18. Halberstam, *Best and Brightest,* 605–6, 614–15.

19. On the last point, see Kearns, *LBJ,* 251–52; and VanDeMark, *Into the Quagmire,* 67–8.

20. John Corson OH, July 17, 1978.

21. Conversation between LBJ and Catledge, Dec. 15, 1964, Krock Papers.

22. Kearns, *LBJ,* 251–52.

23. William Bundy to Rusk, Jan. 6, 1965, NSF: Country File: Vietnam.

24. Bundy MS History of the Vietnam War, chap. 20, pp. 24–27; LBJ Meeting with Congressional Leaders, Jan. 22, 1965, NSF: McG. Bundy Files; Gibbons, *U.S. Government and Vietnam*, II, 391–92; Gibbons, *The U.S. Government and the Vietnam War*, Part III (Princeton, N.J., 1989), 33–36.

25. Cater to LBJ, Jan. 26, 1965, NSF: Country: Vietnam; Bundy to LBJ, Jan. 27, 1965, NSF: Memos to the President. This memo is known as the "Fork in the Y Memo," Gibbons, *U.S. Government and Vietnam*, III, 47.

26. Gibbons, *U.S. Government and Vietnam*, III, 50–52.

27. Bundy to LBJ, Feb. 7, 1965, NSF: NSC History: Deployment of U.S. Forces to Vietnam, July 1965.

28. NSF: NSC Meeting, Feb. 6, 1965; Bundy MS History of the Vietnam War, chap. 22B, pp. 5–6; Mansfield to LBJ, Feb. 8, 1965, NSF: Name File: Mansfield; LBJ, *Vantage Point*, 125.

29. NSF: NSC Meeting, Feb. 7, 1965.

30. Gibbons, *U.S. Government and Vietnam*, III, 65.

31. NSF: NSC Meeting, Feb. 8, 1965.

32. LBJ to Maxwell Taylor, Feb. 8, 1965, NSF: Memos to the President.

33. NSF: NSC Meeting, Feb. 10, 1965.

34. Gibbons, *U.S. Government and Vietnam*, III, 85–86; *New York Times*, Feb. 14, 1965. Lady Bird Johnson interview, Oct. 6, 1997.

35. Gibbons, *U.S. Government and Vietnam*, III, 83–85; and Gen. Bruce Palmer, Jr., *The 25–Year War: America's Military Role in Vietnam* (Lexington, Ky., 1984), 33–35.

36. Ibid., 34–35; Ball, *Past Has Another Pattern*, 380–83, 389–92. For an analysis of why strategic bombing couldn't work against North Vietnam, see Ernest R. May, *"Lessons" of the Past: The Use and Misuse of History in American Foreign Policy* (New York, 1973), chap. 5.

37. Ball, *Past Has Another Pattern*, 504–5 n. 8; Ball is quoted in Gibbons, *U.S. Government and Vietnam*, III, 88.

38. Ball, *Past Has Another Pattern*, 391–92.

39. Ibid., 380–83, 392.

40. Bundy to LBJ, Feb. 16, 1965, NSF: Memos to the President.

41. VanDeMark, *Into the Quagmire*, 76–84.

42. Notes on J. W. Fulbright luncheon, Feb. 11, 1965, Krock Papers.

43. Bundy to LBJ, Feb. 7, 13, 16, 1965, NSF: Memos to the President.

44. Humphrey, *Education of a Public Man*, 320–24; also see the handwritten and typed drafts of this letter in Humphrey's vice-presidential files, HHH Papers.

45. Notes on J. W. Fulbright luncheon, Feb. 11, 1965, Krock Papers; Humphrey, *Education of a Public Man*, 327.

46. See Bill Moyers to LBJ, Feb. 16, 1965, WHCF: CF: PR16; Gibbons, *U.S. Government and Vietnam*, III, 72–77.

47. *New York Times*, Feb. 27, 1965.

48. Carl Rowan to LBJ, Feb. 24, 1965, WHCF: CF: CO312; Congressional Briefings on Vietnam, Feb. 25, March 2, 1965; Halberstam, *Best and Brightest*, 683–84; Gibbons, *U.S. Government and Vietnam*, III, 148–49.

49. Bill Moyers interview, May 14, 1997.

50. Bundy to LBJ, March 6, 1965, NSF: Country File: Vietnam; Bundy

notes, March 9, 1965, meeting, McGeorge Bundy Papers; Lady Bird Johnson, *White House Diary* 247–48.

51. Gibbons, *U.S. Government and Vietnam*, III, 161–69, 179–80; VanDeMark, *Into the Quagmire*, 97–98.

52. Gibbons, *U.S. Government and Vietnam*, III, 161–62, 166; Van-DeMark, *Into the Quagmire*, 92–94; Andrew F. Krepinevich, *The Army and Vietnam* (Baltimore, 1986), 140.

53. See McGeorge Bundy handwritten notes of meetings, March 16, April 1, 1965, Bundy Papers; NSF: McG. Bundy Files, March 23, 1965; NSF: NSAM, April 5, 1965; *PPP: LBJ, 1965*, I, 370–71; Gibbons, *U.S. Government and Vietnam*, III, 168–205; VanDeMark, *Into the Quagmire*, 102–13.

54. Goldman, *Tragedy of LBJ*, 477–78.

55. See Walter Reuther to LBJ, March 30, 1965, Walter P. Reuther Papers, Wayne State University, Detroit; Chester L. Cooper to McGeorge Bundy, April 6, 1965, NSF: Country: Vietnam; Kathleen J. Turner, *Lyndon Johnson's Dual War* (Chicago, 1985), 115–18, 122; Gibbons, *U.S. Government and Vietnam*, III, 127–48.

56. Bundy is quoted in ibid., 148.

57. Coffin to Pearson, March 26, 1965, Drew Pearson Papers.

58. Lester B. Pearson, *Memoirs* (Toronto, 1975), III, 138–41. For Pearson's account to his Cabinet, see Anthony Westell, "A Farewell to Quiet Diplomacy," in Lansing Lamont and J. Duncan Edmonds, *Friends So Different: Essays on Canada and the United States in the 1980s* (Ottawa, 1990).

59. Ibid., 140–41.

60. Lou Harris Poll, April 6, 1965, WHCF: CF: PR16.

61. For the evolution of the speech, see Jack Valenti's "notes on the Johns Hopkins speech," April 7, 1965, LBJ Statements, LBJL; Moyers to LBJ, March 25, 1965, Office Files of the Pres.; Valenti to LBJ, March 29, 1965, Handwriting File; Ginny Thrift to Juanita, April 1, 1965, with "Statement of Sen. George McGovern to Pres. Johnson," March 26, 1965, attached; and McG. Bundy to LBJ, April 6, 1965, Diary Backup; for the speech, see *PPP: LBJ, 1965*, I, 394–99.

62. Bill Moyers interview, Jan. 26, 1994; McG. Bundy to LBJ, April 10, 1965; Memo for Bundy, April 20, 1965, NSF: Country: Vietnam; VanDeMark, *Into the Quagmire*, 123–24.

63. See James L. Greenfield to Sec. Rusk, April 15, 1965, NSF: Country: Vietnam; Turner, *Johnson's Dual War*, 129–33.

64. Piero Gleijeses, *The Dominican Crisis: The 1965 Constitutionalist Revolt and American Intervention* (Baltimore, 1978), chaps. 1–4, esp. pp. 124–26. Also see John Bartlow Martin OH, Jan. 30, 1971.

65. Gleijeses, *Dominican Crisis*, 175–82.

66. Ibid., 217–18, chaps. 8–9, esp. pp. 240–44, 248–55.

67. John Bartlow Martin to Dean Rusk, May 26, 1965, briefing paper attached, p. 22, NSF: NSC History; Martin OH; Gen. Andrew J. Goodpaster OH; Dominican Crisis: CIA reports, April 24–28, 1965, NSF: NSC History; William G. Bowdler to W. W. Rostow, Oct. 23, 1968: The Dominican Conflict, NSF: NSC History; Dean Rusk OH, Jan. 2, 1970, LBJL.

68. Meeting with Congressional Leadership, April 28, 1965, Meeting Notes File; *PPP: LBJ, 1965*, I, 461.

69. LBJ conversations, April 29–May 5, 1965, Krock Papers.

70. John B. Martin OH.

71. Meeting in Cabinet Room, April 30, 1965, Jack Valenti Notes, Office of the Pres.

72. *PPP: LBJ, 1965*, I, 465–66.

73. Congressional Briefing, May 2, 1965, Valenti Notes, Office of the Pres. File.

74. *PPP: LBJ, 1965*, I, 469–74.

75. Turner, *Johnson's Dual War*, 135–37.

76. Congressional Briefing, May 2, 1965, Office of the Pres. File; *Time*, May 14, 1965, p. 23. Also see Dean Rusk OH, Jan. 2, 1970.

77. See "Press Contacts, April 28–May 9, 1965," WHCF: EX/PR18; Goldman, *Tragedy of LBJ*, 467–70; Turner, *Johnson's Dual War*, 136–37; *PPP: LBJ, 1965*, II, 678–79.

78. For criticism of LBJ, see "The President's Man Views Dominicans: War Without Ideas," *Washington Post*, May 12, 1965; Jack Valenti and Douglass Cater to LBJ, May 12, 1965; Valenti to LBJ, May 18, 19, June 17, 1965; Bill Moyers to LBJ, Sept. 16, 1965, WHCF: EX/ND19\CO62; briefing on situation in the Dominican Republic, July 14, 1965, before U.S. Senate Committee on Foreign Relations, NSF: NSC History. For the administration's response, see Valenti to LBJ, May 3, 14, 1965, WHCF: EX/ND19\CO62; F. Bradford Morse to Thomas Mann, May 25, 1965; Valenti to LBJ, June 16, 1965, with LBJ's handwritten comment, Diary Backup; Mann-Ball TELCON, July 29, 1965, George Ball Papers; W. T. Bennett to Mac Bundy, July 31, 1965: Bundy to LBJ, Aug. 12, 1965, WHCF: CF: CO62.

For LBJ's comments, see Dean Rusk OH AAAA, University of Georgia, Athens; Douglass Cater to LBJ, June 10, 1965; Richard Goodwin to LBJ, May 14, 1965, with LBJ's notes on the memos, Handwriting File. On the White Paper, see Turner, *LBJ's Dual War*, 136–37.

79. See "The Dominican Conflict," Oct. 23, 1968, NSF: NSC History; Gleijeses, *Dominican Crisis*, chap. 10.

80. Quayle Poll, Aug. 9, 1965, WHCF: CF: PR16.

81. "Lyndon Johnson's Time of Trial," *Newsweek*, May 3, 1965.

82. Briefings, April 12, 13, 14, 1965, Congressional Briefings on Vietnam; Gibbons, *U.S. Government and Vietnam*, III, 221.

83. Amb. Taylor, Telegram, April 14, 1965; Mac Bundy to LBJ, April 14, 1965; McNamara to LBJ, April 21, 1965; Rusk to Taylor, April 22, 1965, NSF: Memos to the Pres.; George Ball to LBJ, April 21, 1965, NSF: Country: Vietnam; VanDeMark, *Into the Quagmire*, 124–31; Ball, *Past Has Another Pattern*, 392–95; Gibbons, *U.S. Government and Vietnam*, III, 225–34.

84. *Washington Post*, May 3, 1965; *PPP: LBJ, 1965*, I, 484–94.

85. Ibid., 494–98.

86. Gibbons, *U.S. Government and Vietnam*, III, 242–50; Bundy MS History of the Vietnam War, chap. 25, pp. 18–19.

87. See Max Taylor to LBJ, June 1, 1965, NSF: Country: Vietnam; VanDeMark, *Into the Quagmire*, 144–50.

88. VanDeMark, *Into the Quagmire*, 150–51; Bundy, MS History of Vietnam War, chap. 25, pp. 20–24.

89. Gibbons, *U.S. Government and Vietnam*, III, 276.

90. Bundy MS History of the Vietnam War, chap. 26, pp. 3–6.

91. Gibbons, *U.S. Government and Vietnam*, III, 277–78; William C. Westmoreland, *A Soldier Reports*, (New York, 1976), 140.

92. Bundy MS History of Vietnam War, chap. 26, pp. 6–15A; NSC Meeting, June 11, 1965, NSF: NSC Meetings.

93. Henry F. Graff, "How Johnson Makes Foreign Policy," *New York Times Magazine*, July 4, 1965.

94. LBJ interview, June 24, 1965, Arthur Krock Papers. The interviewer is unidentified.

95. George Ball to LBJ, June 18, 1965, NSF: NSC History: Deployment of Forces.

96. Ball, *Past Has Another Pattern*, 395–96; Bundy MS History of Vietnam War, chap. 26, pp. 22–23.

97. Bundy MS History of Vietnam War, chap. 27, pp. 1–14; VanDeMark, *Into the Quagmire*, 167–73.

98. Bundy MS History of Vietnam War, chap. 27, pp. 15–21; Van DeMark, *Into the Quagmire*, 173–76.

99. Bundy MS History, chap. 27, p. 20; George Ball OH, July 9, 1971.

100. *PPP: LBJ, 1965*, II, 725–26, 735–36, 751–52.

101. VanDeMark, *Into the Quagmire*, 180–81; Mac Bundy to LBJ, July 19, 1965, NSF: NSC History: Deployment of Forces.

102. Chester L. Cooper Notes of Meetings on Vietnam, July 21, 1965; and Cabinet Room Meeting: Vietnam, July 21, 1965, both in Meeting Notes File; Ball, *Past Has Another Pattern*, 399–402; Califano, *Triumph and Tragedy of LBJ*, 124; Bundy MS History, Chap. 27, pp. 25–33.

103. Cabinet Room, noon, July 22, 1965, Meeting Notes File.

104. Cabinet Room, 3:00 p.m., July 22, 1965, Meeting Notes File.

105. Kearns, *LBJ and the American Dream*, 282–83.

106. NSC Meeting, July 27, 1965; congressional leadership meeting, July 27, 1965, Meeting Notes File.

107. *PPP: LBJ, 1965*, II, 794–803.

108. LBJ quoted in VanDeMark, *Into the Quagmire*, 213. For conflicting views of LBJ's decision-making on Vietnam in the summer of 1965, see Larry Berman, *Planning a Tragedy: The Americanization of the War in Vietnam* (New York, 1982); Kahin, *Intervention: How America Became Involved in Vietnam*; David M. Barrett, "The Mythology Surrounding Lyndon Johnson, His Advisers, and the 1965 Decision to Escalate the Vietnam War," *Political Science Quarterly*, no. 4 (1988–89), 637–63; John P. Burke and Fred I. Greenstein, *How President's Test Reality: Decisions on Vietnam, 1954 and 1965* (New York, 1989), Parts III and IV; and William C. Gibbons, *The U.S. Government and the Vietnam War, August 1965–January 1968*, Part IV (Washington, D.C., 1994), 19 n. 57.

109. Kearns, *LBJ and the American Dream*, 282; Leuchtenburg, *American Heritage*, May/June 1990, p. 52.

110. Kearns, *LBJ and the American Dream*, 259–60.

111. "The Johnson Years: A Vietnam Roundtable," LBJL Conference March 9, 1991, pp. 70–71.

112. Clark Clifford, *Counsel to the President: A Memoir* (New York, 1991), 417.

113. Gibbons, *U.S. Government and Vietnam*, III, 142–46, 277–73, 351–54.

114. Valenti to LBJ, April 23, 1965, WHCF: EX/HU4; Valenti and Cater to LBJ, May 12, 1965, WHCF: EX/HU2–7; Turner, *Johnson's Dual War*, 134–51, esp. 140–41; Goldman, *Tragedy of LBJ*, 484–85; Hugh Sidey OH.

115. Goldman, *Tragedy of LBJ*, chap. 16, the quotes are on 418, 420, and 450–51. LBJ handwritten note to Moyers and Valenti on Dick Goodwin to LBJ, June 1, 1965, Handwriting File.

116. Goodwin, *Remembering America*, 392.

117. Ibid., 395, 400, 402–6.

118. See Cartha DeLoach to Clyde Tolson, June 17, 1965, JEH, O&C File, FBI.

119. For congressional attitudes, see Gibbons, *U.S. Government and Vietnam*, IV, 89–91.

120. Larry Temple interview, Sept. 21, 1997; Lady Bird, Johnson interview, Oct. 6, 1997; Bill Moyers interview, May 14, 1997.

121. On strategic planning at this time, see Gibbons, *U.S. Government and Vietnam*, IV, 43–55. Moyers's comment is in "An Interview" he gave to the *Atlantic*, July 1968. For Taylor's comment, see NSF: NSC Meeting, Aug. 5, 1965. Also see Henry Cabot Lodge to LBJ, Oct. 13, Nov. 3, 1965; Mac Bundy to LBJ, Nov. 16, 1965, NSF: Memos to the President.

122. Gibbons, *U.S. Government and Vietnam*, IV, 56–57.

123. Ibid., 58–67. On Vann, see Neil Sheehan, *A Bright Shining Lie: John Paul Vann and America in Vietnam* (New York, 1988), 532–59. Also see William Bundy's thoughtful comments on the limits of this operation, MS History of the Vietnam War, chap. 31, pp. 3–8.

124. See Valenti to Bundy, April 23, 1965, WHCF: CF: Country/312; Chester L. Cooper, April 24, 1965; Carl Rowan to LBJ, April 26, 1965; Cooper to Doug Cater, July 12, 1965, NSF: Country: Vietnam; Valenti to LBJ, April 24, 1965; Marvin Watson to LBJ, May 7, 14, 1965, WHCF: EX ND19/CO312; James C. Thomson, Jr., to Mac Bundy, May 14, 1965; Cooper to Bundy, May 15, 1965; W. W. Rostow to Rusk, May 17, 1965; Cooper to Valenti, May 17, 1965; Gordon Chase to Mac Bundy, June 14, 1965, NSF: McG. Bundy Files; Watson to LBJ, June 4, 1965; Cliff Carter to Watson, June 9, 1965; Bill Moyers to LBJ, June 10, 1965; Moyers to Cater, July 28, 1965; Cater to LBJ, July 29, 1965, Diary Backup; Averell Harriman to LBJ, April 29, 1965; Cater to LBJ, July 10, 13, 14, 19, 20, 22, 1965; Watson to LBJ, July 28, 1965, Handwriting File; HHH to LBJ, May 4, 13, 1965, Humphrey Papers; Mac Bundy to LBJ, July 14, 1965, NSF: Memos to the President; Cater to LBJ, July 15, 16, 24, 1965, WHCF: Aides: Cater.

125. NSF: NSC Meeting, Aug. 5, 1965.

126. Morley Safer, *Flashbacks* (New York, 1990), 88–97; David Halberstam, *The Powers That Be* (New York, 1979), 488–90; Daniel C. Hallin, *The "Uncensored War": The Media and Vietnam* (New York, 1986), 132; Murray Fromson interview, Aug. 21, 1993; Moyers to LBJ, n.d., Handwriting File. LBJ wasn't the only one incensed by the CBS report. See Sen. George Smathers to LBJ, Aug. 6, 1965, WHCF: EX/PR18, who saw Safer's report as an example of "irresponsible coverage," or the media "going out of their way to put our participation in the Vietnam situation in the worst possible light."

127. Moyers to LBJ, Sept. 21, 1965, Office of the Pres. File; James Rowe to LBJ, July 21, 1965, WHCF: EX/PR18.

128. Pearson to Moyers, July 9, 1965, Drew Pearson Papers; Alsop quote is in Donald R. Burkholder, "The Caretakers of the Presidential Image," Ph.D. thesis, Wayne State University, 1973, p. 89.

129. Doug Cater to LBJ, Aug. 14, 1965, Handwriting File; Cater to LBJ, Aug. 5, 1965, WHCF: EX/PR18; Cabinet Room Meeting, Dec. 17, 1965, Meeting Notes File; Harry McPherson, Jr., to LBJ, Sept. 22, 1965, WHCF: EX/ND19\CO312.

130. Leuchtenburg, *American Heritage*, May/June 1990, p. 62.

131. See Moyers to LBJ, July 27 and Nov. 1, 1965, Office of the Pres. File; Valenti to LBJ, Aug. 2, 1965; Moyers to LBJ, Oct. 7, 1965; and Merriman Smith to Moyers, Oct. 21, 1965, WHCF: EX/PR18; Burkholder, "Caretakers of Presidential Image," 93–95.

132. On qualified congressional support, see Gibbons, *U.S. Government and Vietnam*, IV, 22–23. Richard Russell to Harvey Kennedy, Aug. 13, 1965, and other letters in the series "Dictation: Political" in the Richard Russell Papers, University of Georgia, Athens.

133. J. William Fulbright to LBJ, Oct. 7, 1965, Series 87, Fulbright Papers, University of Arkansas, Fayetteville; Fulbright OH, March 5, 1979, Association of Former Members of Congress Papers, Library of Congress; Doug Cater to LBJ, Feb. 8, 1965, with LBJ's comment, Handwriting File; Carl Marcy OH, Oct. 5, 1983, SHO. For efforts to refute Fulbright, see Marvin Watson to LBJ, Sept. 15, 1965, Handwriting File; McGeorge Bundy to LBJ, Sept. 17, 1965, NSF: Memos to the President; and Fulbright Folders in WHCF: Aides: Panzer.

134. DeLoach to Tolson, March 7, 1966, JEH O&C File, FBI.

135. See the meetings of the Public Affairs Policy Committee for Aug. 4, 10, 23, and 30, 1965; and Chester L. Cooper to Bundy, Aug. 18, 1965; and Gordon Chase to Cater, Aug. 23, 1965, as well as other notes of meetings and memos on the subject in 1965 in NSF: Country: Vietnam. For the campaign to promote the war, see materials for the second half of 1965 in the WHCF: EX/ND19\CO312; EX/PR16; EX/PR18; Name File: Cartha DeLoach; EX/HU4; Diary Backup; and the Handwriting File. The Goldman letter, Nov. 3, 1965, is in WHCF: EX/ND19\CO312.

136. Lou Harris to Hayes Redmon, June 17, 1965; Aug. 9, 1965, WHCF: CF: PR16; Marvin Watson to LBJ, Aug. 28, 1965, WHCF: EX/PR16; Lou Harris stories in *Washington Post*, Sept. 12, 13, Oct. 11, 1965; Redmon to Marie Fehmer, Nov. 19, 1965; and to Moyers, Nov. 26, Dec. 9, 1965, WHCF: EX/PR16.

137. Chester L. Cooper to Bundy, Moyers, Valenti, and Cater, Dec. 14, 1965, WHCF: CF: ND19/CO312.

138. Richard E. Neustadt and Ernest R. May, *Thinking in Time: The Uses of History for Decision Makers* (New York, 1986), 88–89.

CHAPTER 6: RETREAT FROM THE GREAT SOCIETY

1. See Joe Califano to LBJ, Oct. 21, 1965, WHCF: EX/FG11–8–1; "Working for Johnson Is Hard But Rewarding," *New York Times*, May 1, 1966.

2. "Broadcast," *Vanity Fair*, April 1991, p. 116; *Congressional Quarterly Fact Sheet*, Feb. 25, 1966.

3. See George Reedy OH, Dec. 20, 1968; Larry Berman, "Johnson and the White House Staff," in Divine, ed., *Johnson Years*, I, 192–93; the sketch of Moyers in Nelson Lichtenstein, ed., *Political Profiles: The Johnson Years* (New York, 1976), 441–43; Marshall Blonsky, "Bill Moyers Acts Up," *Los Angeles Times Magazine*, March 27, 1994, with Moyers's remark; Moyers to LBJ, n.d., with a note from LBJ, "Forget it [the press coverage of Moyers]—I'm not concerned one moment"; and Moyers to LBJ, Sept. 1, 1966, about his ulcers, WHCF: Aides: Moyers.

4. See the sketch of Califano in Lichtenstein, ed., *Political Profiles*, 88–89. Also see Harry McPherson OH, Dec. 19, 1968.

5. Califano, *Triumph and Tragedy*, 9, 20.

6. Califano OH, Jan. 18, 1989.

7. See the sketches of Watson in the WHCF: Aides: Watson; and Lichtenstein, *Political Profiles*, 635–36.

8. See Lewis L. Gould's description of Watson in "Political Activities of the Johnson White House, 1963–1969," which is part of the microfilm project of University Publications of America. Also see C. D. DeLoach to Tolson, Jan. 15, 1966, JEH, O&C, FBI.

9. McGeorge Bundy interview, Sept. 25, 1993.

10. See the sketch of Rostow in Lichtenstein, ed., *Political Profiles*, 527–30.

11. Valenti OH, March 3, 1971.

12. The story was told to me by Rostow.

13. Califano OH, Sept. 12, 1969.

14. See the sketch of Cater in Lichtenstein, ed., *Political Profiles*, 95.

15. Ibid., 396–97; Douglass Cater OH, May 8, 1969.

16. See the biographical sketch in WHCF: Aides: Kintner.

17. The quotes are in Berman, "Johnson and the White House Staff," 195–96.

18. Ibid., 196–97.

19. Califano OH, Dec. 21, 1988; Irving Bernstein, *Guns or Butter: The Presidency of Lyndon Johnson* (New York, 1994), 531.

20. *PPP: LBJ, 1966*, I, 3.

21. Ibid., 3–4.

22. Ibid., 4–7; *Washington Post*, Jan. 13, 1966.

23. See Califano OH, March 16, 1988; Dec. 21, 1988; June 13, 1989; "Legislative Program Outline for 1966," WHCF: Aides: Califano; Califano, *Triumph and Tragedy*, 117–18; Goodwin, *Remembering America*, 423–24; "Chronology: 1966–1968" in Box 47 of Joseph A. Califano, Jr.'s Papers, LBJL, includes his comment about the speech; Bernstein, *Guns or Butter*, 319–23; *PPP: LBJ, 1966*, I, 4, 8.

24. See Heller to LBJ, June 2, 1964, WHCF: EX/FI 11–4; Ackley to LBJ, July 30, 1965 in Administrative History: Council of Economic Advisers, Vol. 2, Pt. 1, LBJL; Gardner Ackley OH, April 13, 1973, March 7, 1974; also see Ackley to the Editor, *Newsweek*, Nov. 6, 1978, and Ackley to Harvey Mansfield, Feb. 23, 1979, attached to the OH; and Donald F. Kettl, "The Economic Education of Lyndon Johnson: Guns, Butter, and Taxes," in Divine, ed., *Johnson Years*, II, 57–9.

25. See W. Willard Wirtz to LBJ, Aug. 24 and 25, 1965; John T. Connor

to LBJ, Aug. 25, 1965; Califano to LBJ, with Connor to LBJ attached, Aug. 26, 1965, WHCF: CF: LA6.

26. Califano, *Triumph and Tragedy,* 86–87.

27. Ibid., 87–90.

28. See handwritten notes of Aug. 30, 1965, meeting, Diary Backup; also see Califano, *Triumph and Tragedy,* 90.

29. Ibid., 90–93.

30. Ibid., 94; Walter Heller to LBJ, Sept. 5, 1965.

31. See "President Johnson's Recent Statements on the Need to Exercise Restraint in Prices and Wages," n.d., Box 57, WHCF: Aides: Califano.

32. The quote is from Califano to Moyers, May 16, 1966, Chron Files, Califano Papers. For the rest, see Califano's Chron files for 1966, which are full of materials describing the efforts to maintain the wage and price guidelines.

33. Bernstein, *Guns or Butter,* chap. 14; "Pres. Johnson's Recent Statements," n.d., WHCF: Aides: Califano.

34. *PPP: LBJ, 1966,* II, 804–5; Califano to LBJ, Aug. 9, 1966, Chron Files, Califano Papers.

35. "Talking Points for President's Joint Meeting with Airlines and Union," July 29, 1966, Diary Backup; Ackley to Califano, "Retreat from Guideposts," Aug. 9, 1966, WHCF: Aides: Califano; "Presidential Remarks to Introduce Chairman Ackley," Agenda, Aug. 10, 1966, Cabinet Papers; Califano to LBJ, Aug. 13, 1966, WHCF: CF: LA6; Califano, *Triumph and Tragedy* of LBJ, 144–46.

36. Califano to LBJ, Dec. 21, 1965, WHCF: EX/WE9; Georgia Legislature, Jan. 17, 1966, Speech/Media Series III, Richard Russell Papers.

37. Califano to LBJ, Dec. 21, 1965, WHCF: EX/WE9.

38. See LBJ, *Vantage Point,* 325.

39. *PPP: LBJ, 1966,* I, 47–68.

40. Ackley to LBJ, Dec. 17, 1965; Califano to LBJ, Dec. 17, 1965, WHCF: EX/FI4.

41. Califano to LBJ, Dec. 23, 1965, Chron Files, Califano Papers; Ackley to LBJ, Dec. 27, 1965; Schultze to LBJ, Dec. 27, 1965; Larry Levinson to LBJ, Dec. 29, 1965, WHCF: CF: FI4; *PPP: LBJ, 1966,* I, 49.

42. Schultze to LBJ, Feb. 14, 1966; LBJ to Cabinet Officers and Heads of Major Agencies, Feb. 23, 1966; Schultze to John McCormack and Carl Albert, March 10, 1966, WHCF: EX/FI4.

43. See Franklin Dryden to LBJ, Jan. 26, 1966; W. Willard Wirtz to LBJ, March 17, 1966, WHCF: CF: BE5; Gardner Ackley to LBJ, Feb. 22, March 1, 1966, WHCF: EX/FI; CEA to LBJ, March 12, 1966, WHCF: CF: FI11; LBJ, *Vantage Point,* 444–45.

44. See transcript, "Tax Increase," pp. 9–11, Box 133, Califano Papers; Ackley to LBJ, March 16, 1966, WHCF: EX/FI11.

45. *PPP: LBJ, 1966,* I, 321–22.

46. Ibid., 373–81. For conflicting advice LBJ was receiving on what to do about the economy, see Califano to LBJ, March 25, 1966, Chron Files, Califano Papers. Also see Hubert Humphrey to LBJ, April 5, 1966, WHCF: EX/BE4

47. Ackley to LBJ, April 9, 1966, WHCF: EX/FI; Jake Jacobsen to LBJ,

with AP release attached, April 19, 1966, Office of the Pres. File: Memoranda for the Pres.; Henry Fowler to LBJ, May 10, 1966, WHCF: Aides: Califano; Califano to LBJ, May 7, 1966, WHCF: CF: BE5; Califano to LBJ, May 20, 1966, WHCF: EX/FI; Robert Kintner to LBJ, June 9, 1966, WHCF: CF: BE5-2; Califano to LBJ, June 11, 1966, Chron Files, Califano Papers; Califano to LBJ, June 14, 1966, with draft memo attached, and June 22, 1966, Diary Backup; Kintner to LBJ, June 28, 1966, WHCF: CF: BE5; and Kintner to Fowler et al., June 29, 1966, WHCF: EX/FI11.

48. Ackley to LBJ, July 30, Aug. 17, 26; Fowler et al. to LBJ, Sept. 2, 1966, WHCF: EX/FI; Califano to LBJ, Aug. 16, 1966, WHCF: Aides: Califano; Sen. George Smathers to LBJ, Sept. 1, 1966, WHCF: EX/E5.

49. *PPP: LBJ, 1966*, II, 985–91. Also see Smathers to LBJ, Sept. 1, 1966, reporting conversations with Wilbur Mills and Russell Long, who had little sympathy for a tax-increase proposal before the elections, WHCF: EX: BE5. For an analysis of LBJ's hesitation in raising taxes, see John W. Sloan, "President Johnson, the Council of Economic Advisers, and the Failure to Raise Taxes in 1966 and 1967," *Presidential Studies Quarterly* (Winter 1985), 91–92.

50. Henry Fowler to LBJ, Sept. 16, 1966, Diary Backup; Ackley to LBJ, Sept. 22, 1966, WHCF: EX/FI; Califano to LBJ, Oct. 14, 1966, Chron Files, Califano Papers.

51. Califano to LBJ, Nov. 5, 1966; Ackley to LBJ, Nov. 8, 1966, WHCF: EX/BE5.

52. Califano to LBJ, Dec. 8, 1966, WHCF: CF: FI4; Heller to LBJ, Dec. 23, 1966, WHCF: EX/FI 11; Ackley to LBJ, Dec. 30, 1966, WHCF: EX/BE5.

53. *PPP: LBJ, 1967*, I, 39–43, 72–77.

54. Califano, *Triumph and Tragedy*, 113, 149–50; Califano to Robert Kintner, May 24, 1966; Remarks of LBJ at the meeting of Under Secretaries, May 25, 1966, Cabinet Papers; Travel of Cabinet Officers, n.d., Chron Files, Califano Papers; list of "Landmark Laws" for 1966 inside the front cover of LBJ, *Vantage Point*.

55. Califano, *Triumph and Tragedy*, 113–14.

56. Ibid., 140–42, 148.

57. Cater to LBJ, Aug. 4, 1966, WHCF: EX/PL2; Fred Panzer to LBJ, Oct. 5, 1966, with a page from the *Congressional Record*, Sept. 6, 1966, attached, Diary Backup.

58. Lee White to Bill Moyers, Nov. 20, 1965, WHCF: Aides: White; Califano to Moyers, Dec. 15. 1965, Chron Files, Califano Papers; New Programs: "Operation 'Trim,' " Part One—Govt. Reorganization, n.d., WHCF: Aides: Califano; Califano to LBJ, Sept. 22, 1965, WHCF: EX/FG175; Califano, *Triumph and Tragedy*, 123–24.

59. See the numerous memos to LBJ for Dec. 1965 and Jan. and Feb. 1966 on contacts with government and industry leaders about a department in WHCF: EX/FG175; and in Legislative Background: Dept. of Transportation; Califano, *Triumph and Tragedy*, 124.

60. *PPP: LBJ, 1966*, I, 250–63.

61. Henry Wilson to LBJ, March 21, 1966; Mike Manatos to LBJ, April 29, 1966; Califano to LBJ, May 24, June 9 and 13, 1966; and Califano, Memo

for the Record, June 21, 1966, WHCF: EX/FG175; Alan Boyd to John Connor, May 11, 1966, Legislative Background: Dept. of Transportation; Califano to LBJ, June 10, 29, 1966, Chron Files, Califano Papers.

62. Califano to LBJ, June 13, 1966, Handwriting File; Califano to LBJ, July 13, 1966, Diary Backup; Califano, *Triumph and Tragedy*, 125.

63. Ibid., 126.

64. See Califano to LBJ, Aug. 2, 1966, Diary Backup; and William Cassidy to Stanley Resor, Oct. 5, 1966, WHCF: EX/FG175. On the struggle over an independent maritime agency, see Henry Wilson to LBJ, June 21, 1966; John Connor to Califano, July 29, 1966, WHCF: EX/FG175; "One Shipping Bill Moved," *Baltimore Sun*, Aug. 11, 1966; George Meany telegram, Oct. 10, 1966, Diary Backup; Chronology of 1966 Legislation, Califano Papers.

65. Schultze to LBJ, Aug. 10, 1966, WHCF: EX/FG175; Califano to Moyers, Aug. 19, 1966, Legislative Background: Transportation Department.

66. Willard Wirtz to LBJ, Aug. 25, 1966; Milton Semer to LBJ, Sept. 13, 1966; Califano to LBJ, Oct. 5, 1966, WHCF: EX/FG175; Califano to LBJ, Aug. 31, 1966, Diary Backup; Henry Wilson to LBJ, Oct. 1, 1966, Legislative Background: Transportation Dept.; Chronology of 1966 Legislation, Califano Papers.

67. *PPP: LBJ, 1966*, II, 1188–89; Califano, *Triumph and Tragedy*, 126.

68. *PPP: LBJ, 1966*, II, 1002–4, 1189.

69. On safety gains, see Califano OH, Oct. 17, 1968; and "Two Groups See Auto Safety Efforts as Waning After 20 Years of Gain," *New York Times*, Sept. 10, 1986.

70. Charles M. Haar, *Between the Idea and the Reality: A Study in the Origin, Fate, and Legacy of the Model Cities Program* (Boston, 1975), chap. 1.

71. Reuther to LBJ, May 15, 1965 in Haar, *Between Idea and Reality*, 289–91, and chap 2; Notes on Model Cities, Oct. 14, 1968, Legislative Background: Model Cities; Califano, *Triumph and Tragedy*, 130–31.

72. *PPP: LBJ, 1966*, I, 82–91.

73. Harry McPherson to LBJ, Jan. 27, 1966; Califano to LBJ, Jan. 27, 1966; Robert Weaver to LBJ, Feb. 7, 1966, WHCF: EX/LG; Haar, *Between Idea and Reality*, 61–64.

74. Robert Weaver to LBJ, May 22, 1966; Weaver to Califano, May 24, 1966; Milton Semer to LBJ, May 25, 31, 1966; Henry Wilson to LBJ, May 30, 1966, Legislative Background: Model Cities; Ashley Foard to Weaver, May 25, 1966, WHCF: CF: LE/HS; Haar, *Between Idea and Reality*, 64–67; Califano, *Triumph and Tragedy*, 131.

75. Califano to LBJ, June 6, 1966, WHCF: EX/LG; Califano to LBJ, June 28, 1966, Chron Files, Califano Papers; HHH to LBJ, Oct. 16, 1966, Humphrey Papers; Haar, *Between Idea and Reality*, 67–71; Califano, *Triumph and Tragedy*, 131–32.

76. Califano to LBJ, June 6, 1966, WHCF: EX/LG; Demonstration Cities Act: A Chronology, n.d., Califano Papers; Haar, *Between Idea and Reality*, 71–73; Califano, *Triumph and Tragedy*, 132–33.

77. Larry Levinson to Larry O'Brien, July 5, 1966; Levinson to Califano, July 20, 1966; Califano to LBJ, July 26, 1966; Robert Weaver to Califano, Aug. 9, 1966; Califano to LBJ, Aug. 10, 1966, Chron Files, Califano Papers; Califano

to LBJ, July 18, 1966; Mike Manatos to LBJ, July 19, 1966, Diary Backup; Demonstration Cities Act: A Chronology, Califano Papers; Haar, *Between Idea and Reality*, 74–75; Califano, *Triumph and Tragedy*, 133.

78. Haar, *Between Idea and Reality*, 76–85; Califano, *Triumph and Tragedy*, 134; *PPP: LBJ, 1966*, II, 844–49; Califano to LBJ, Sept. 30, 1966, WHCF: EX/LE\LG; "Housing, Demonstration Cities Bill Enacted," 1966 Legislation, Califano Papers.

79. Robert Weaver to Califano, Sept. 13, 1966; JCG to Califano, Sept. 29, 1966; Califano to LBJ, Oct. 10, 1966, Legislative Background: Model Cities; Demonstration Cities: Status Report, n.d., Model Cities Folder, Califano Papers; O'Brien and Califano to LBJ, Oct. 5, 1966; Califano to LBJ, Oct. 6, 1966, Chron Files, Califano Papers; *PPP: LBJ, 1966*, II, 1119–20.

80. Haar, *Between Idea and Reality*, 87–89.

81. Califano, *Triumph and Tragedy*, 135; *New York Times*, July 3, 1992.

82. Haar, *Between Idea and Reality*, 212–14.

83. On the riots, see Haar, *Between Idea and Reality*, 76–77. *U.S. News & World Report*, Dec. 13, 1965; for the surveys, see Olin E. Teague to Friend, July 1966, WHCF: CF: PR16; *Gallup Poll, 1935–1971*, III, 2030–31.

84. Califano, *Triumph and Tragedy*, 69–70, 72–74; *PPP: LBJ, 1965*, II, 1116–17.

85. Nicholas Katzenbach to LBJ, Dec. 1966, WHCF: EX/HU2; *PPP: LBJ, 1966*, I, 5.

86. Califano to LBJ, Oct. 28, 1965, Chron Files, Califano Papers.

87. Califano to LBJ, March 8 and 15, 1966, Chron Files; "Civil Rights Bill," 1966 Legislation, Califano Papers; Steven F. Lawson, "Civil Rights," in Divine, ed., *Johnson Years*, I, 105.

88. *PPP: LBJ, 1966*, I, 461–69.

89. Jack Valenti to LBJ, April 2, 1966; Califano to LBJ, April 13, 1966, Chron Files, Califano Papers; Califano to LBJ, April 27, 1966, Diary Backup; *PPP: LBJ, 1966*, I, 469.

90. Califano to LBJ, April 23, 1966, Diary Backup.

91. Bill Moyers to LBJ, June 10, 1966, WHCF: EX/PR 16; "Civil Rights: House Action," 1966 Legislation, Califano Papers; Henry Wilson to LBJ, July 24, Aug. 5, 1966; Katzenbach to LBJ, July 24 and 28, 1966, WHCF: EX/ LE\HU2; *PPP: LBJ, 1966*, II, 814–15.

92. "Civil Rights: Senate Action," 1966 Legislation, Califano Papers; Katzenbach to LBJ, Sept. 9, 1966, Diary Backup.

93. See Steven F. Lawson, "Mixing Moderation with Militancy: Lyndon Johnson and African American Leadership," in Divine, ed., *Johnson Years*, III, chap. 4.

94. McPherson to LBJ, Sept. 12, 1966, WHCF: Aides: McPherson.

95. Gallup Poll, Sept. 1966, WHCF: EX/PR 16; Rowland Evans and Robert Novak, "LBJ and the Cities," *Washington Post*, Aug. 10, 1966; Califano to Katzenbach, Sept. 5, 1966, Civil Rights Files, Califano Papers.

96. See Hayes Redmon to Bill Moyers, Dec. 1, 1965; Harry McPherson to Moyers, Dec. 10, 1965; Cliff Alexander to LBJ, May 5, 1966, with attached *Wall Street Journal* clipping, WHCF: EX/HU2\MC; Califano to LBJ, Feb. 3, 1966, Chron Files, Califano Papers; Berl I. Bernhard to the Council, May 7, 1966, Diary Backup.

97. See Califano to LBJ, Jan. 27, Feb. 3, 1966; McPherson to LBJ, May 18, 1966, WHCF: Aides: McPherson; Louis Martin to Marvin Watson, May 20, 1966; Cliff Carter to LBJ, June 3, 1966, WHCF: Aides: Watson; McPherson to Robert Kintner, May 25, 1966, Cabinet Papers; Lawson, "Civil Rights," 110–11.

98. *PPP: LBJ, 1966*, I, 571–75.

99. Cliff Alexander to LBJ, June 22, 1966, WHCF: CF: HU2\MC; and Alexander to LBJ, Aug. 24, 1966, Cabinet Papers.

100. McPherson to LBJ, June 10, 1966, WHCF: CF: HU2/MC; Robert Kintner to LBJ, Aug. 23, 1966, Diary Backup; Kintner to LBJ, Aug. 24, 1966, Cabinet Papers; *PPP: LBJ, 1966*, II, 894–95; Lawson, "Civil Rights," 110; Lawson, "Mixing Moderation with Militancy," 110 n. 43, 114 n. 90.

101. McPherson to LBJ, Dec. 19, 1966, WHCF: Aides: McPherson.

102. Kearns, *LBJ*, 291.

103. Heller to LBJ, Dec. 21, 1966, WHCF: CF: WE9.

104. See Califano to LBJ, Dec. 20, 1966, Chron Files, Califano Papers; "The War on Poverty: An Overall View," n.d., WHCF: EX/WE9; Cabinet Presentation: The War Against Poverty, 1968, Cabinet Papers.

105. See Johnson's many references to antipoverty efforts in *PPP: LBJ, 1966*, I and II. Also see Fred Panzer to LBJ, Oct. 5, 1966, Diary Backup.

106. Schultze to LBJ, Nov. 7, 1966, WHCF: EX/FG 170.

107. Moyers to LBJ, Sept. 30, 1966, Diary Backup; Mark I. Gelfand, "The War on Poverty," in Divine, ed., *Johnson Years*, I, 134–37; David Osborne, "The Great Society Revisited," *Mother Jones*, June 1986, pp. 14–17.

108. Gelfand, "War on Poverty," 136–37. Califano, *Triumph and Tragedy*, 77–79. For a different interpretation of how LBJ viewed CAP, see Frances Fox Piven and Richard A. Cloward, *Regulating the Poor: The Functions of Public Welfare* (New York, 1971), 250–63.

109. Osborne, "The Great Society Revisited," p. 16; Lawson, "Mixing Moderation with Militancy," 93–95.

110. Osborne, "The Great Society Revisited," 16.

111. Califano to LBJ, Dec. 18, 1966, Chron Files, Califano Papers; Califano, *Triumph and Tragedy*, 80.

112. Califano to LBJ, Dec. 15, 1966, Chron Files, Califano Papers; Wilbur J. Cohen OH; Gelfand, "The War on Poverty," 138–39.

113. See Schultze to LBJ, Jan. 24, Aug. 10, Dec. 8, 1966; Califano to LBJ, March 22, Nov. 21, 1966, WHCF: EX/FI4; Douglass Cater to LBJ, March 4, 1966, Handwriting File; Cater to LBJ, July 15, 1966, Diary Backup; Moyers to LBJ, Dec. 11, 1966, WHCF: EX/WE 9–1.

114. Califano to LBJ, March 16, 1966, Handwriting File; Lee to Califano, Nov. 16, 1966; Califano to Weaver, Nov. 19, 1966, Chron Files, Califano Papers; Weaver to Califano, Nov. 23, 1966, WHCF: EX/FG 170; Robert Kintner to Marvin Watson, Dec. 20, 1966, WHCF: CF: HU4.

115. See Robert Pear, "Poverty 1993: Bigger, Deeper, Younger, Getting Worse," *New York Times*, Oct. 10, 1993.

116. Osborne, "The Great Society Revisited," 17–18.

117. See HHH to LBJ, Aug. 23, 1965, Humphrey Papers; Gallup Polls, Nov. 14, 1965, March 9, 1966; Hayes Redmon to Moyers, Feb. 28, 1966; to LBJ,

March 21, 1966, WHCF: CF: PR16; Douglass Cater to LBJ, Nov. 29, 1965; Charles Roche to Marvin Watson, Jan. 27, 1966, WHCF: EX/PL2.

118. Lewis L. Gould, "Never a Deep Partisan: Lyndon Johnson and the Democratic Party, 1963–1969," in Divine, ed., *Johnson Years*, III, 21–24.

119. Marvin Watson to John Gonella, April 22, 1966; Bill Moyers to LBJ, May 2, 1966, reporting what Cliff Carter advised, WHCF: EX/PL2; Busby to LBJ, May 23, 1966, WHCF: EX/PL.

120. Fred Panzer to Hayes Redmon, May 4, 1966; Senate Races, May 10, 1966; Moyers to LBJ, May 19, 1966, WHCF: EX/PL2; Harris Survey, May 16, 1966, WHCF: CF: PR16; Gallup Poll, May 26, 1966; Marianne Means column, May 26, 1966, WHCF: EX/PR16.

121. Gallup Poll, June 1966, WHCF: EX/PR16; Moyers to LBJ, June 9, 1966, WHCF: CF: PR16; Kintner to Moyers, June 16, 1966; Kintner to LBJ, June 22, 1966, WHCF: CF: PL2; Kintner to LBJ, May 4, 1966, with LBJ's notation on it, Cabinet Papers; Carter to LBJ, June 3, 1966, Diary Backup.

122. Watson to LBJ, Feb. 15, 1966, Handwriting File; Kintner to LBJ, June 9, 1966, WHCF: CF: PR16; June 22, 24, 1966, WHCF: CF: PR18; Tom Johnson Meeting Notes, June 1966, Tom Johnson Papers, LBJL.

123. Kintner to LBJ, July 1, 6, 1966, WHCF: CF: PR18; Califano to Moyers, July 12, 1966, Chron Files, Califano Papers; Hayes Redmon to Kintner, July 13, 1966, Cabinet Papers; Gallup Poll, July 24, 1966; Redmon to Charles Roche, July 26, 1966, WHCF: EX/PR16; Frank Coniff to Moyers, with Means column attached, July 26, 1966, Diary Backup; *PPP: LBJ, 1966*, I, 679–95; II, 760–84.

124. Kintner to LBJ, July 9, 1966, WHCF: CF: PL2; Moyers to LBJ, July 17, 1966, WHCF: EX/PL2; Sherwin Markman to Watson, July 18, 1966; Mike Manatos to LBJ, July 28, 1966, Diary Backup.

125. See *PPP: LBJ, 1966*, II, 838–76, 896–920; Harris Survey, Sept. 12, 15, and 19, 1966; Gallup Poll, Sept. 18, 1966 WHCF: CF: PR16; Hayes Redmon to Moyers, Sept. 26, 1966; Kintner to LBJ, Sept. 29, Oct. 13, 1966; Watson to LBJ, Oct. 14, 1966, Diary Backup; Kintner to LBJ, Oct. 6, 1966, WHCF: Aides: Maguire; Kintner to LBJ, Nov. 5, 1966, WHCF: CF: PL2.

126. *PPP: LBJ, 1966*, II, 1046–47, 869, 1117–18, 1169; Gould, "Never a Deep Partisan," 30–32.

127. Means, Oct. 23, 1966, WHCF: EX: PL2.

128. Watson to LBJ, March 21, Oct. 3, 1966, WHCF: Aides: Watson; Memo on Democratic primaries, Oct. 5, 1966, WHCF: CF: PL2.

129. Califano, *Triumph and Tragedy*, 151–52.

130. Watson to LBJ, Oct. 11, 1966, WHCF: Aides: Watson; Watson to LBJ, Oct. 20, 1966, WHCF: EX/PL; Califano, *Triumph and Tragedy*, 151–52.

131. Ibid.; Henry Wilson to LBJ, Nov. 9, 1966, WHCF: EX/PL2; Jake Jacobson to LBJ, Nov. 10, 1966, Diary Backup.

CHAPTER 7: "LYNDON JOHNSON'S WAR"

1. Hayes Redmon to Jake Jacobsen, Nov. 30, 1965; Valenti to LBJ, Dec. 14, 1965, WHCF: EX/PR16.

2. Hayes Redmon to Bill Moyers, Nov. 24, 1965, Jan. 2, 1966; Valenti to LBJ, Dec. 14, 1965; Moyers to LBJ, Dec. 27, 1965, ibid.

694 NOTES (PAGES 341–348)

3. Lodge to LBJ, Nov. 3, 1965, NSF: Memos to the President.

4. LBJ, *Vantage Point*, 234; Handwritten Notes, Oct. 18, Nov. 11, 12, 13, 1965, McGeorge Bundy Papers; Gibbons, *The U.S. Government and Vietnam*, IV, 77–89.

5. Ball-LBJ, Nov. 16, 1965, TELCON, Ball Papers; American Opinion Survey, Nov. 18–24, 1965; Hayes Redmon to Bill Moyers, Dec. 27, 1965, who passed it on to LBJ, "right away," WHCF: EX/PR16. Also see George C. Herring, *LBJ and Vietnam: A Different Kind of War* (Austin, Tex. 1994), 93–94.

6. Gibbons, *U.S. Government and Vietnam*, IV, 103–6; Mac Bundy Notes, Nov. 22 and 23, 1965, McG. Bundy Papers; Lt. Gen. Charles G. Cooper, "The Day It Became the Longest War," *Proceedings*, May 1996, pp. 77–80; Chen Jian, "China's Involvement in the Vietnam War, 1964–1969," *China Quarterly*, June 1995, pp. 356–80.

7. Shapely, *Promise and Power*, 355–62.

8. Moyers to LBJ, July 27, 1965, with LBJ's handwritten note on it, Handwriting File; Bundy notes, Nov. 30, 1965, McG. Bundy Papers.

9. Mac Bundy to LBJ, Nov. 27, 1965, NSF: Memos to the President.

10. Mac Bundy notes, Dec. 3, 1965, McG. Bundy Papers; Bundy to LBJ, Dec. 3, 1965, NSF: Memos to the President.

11. Mac Bundy notes, Dec. 7, 1965, McG. Bundy Papers.

12. Meeting of Dec. 17, 1965, Meeting Notes File.

13. Meeting Notes, Dec. 18, 1965, Meeting Notes File; Valenti, *A Very Human President*, 240; Gibbons, *U.S. Government and Vietnam*, IV, 121–23.

14. Meeting Notes, Dec. 21, 1965, Meeting Notes File.

15. William Bundy, MS History of the Vietnam War, chap. 33, pp. 31–32, 35–38.

16. Califano OH, Jan. 27, 1988.

17. Mac Bundy to LBJ, two memos of Dec. 27, 1965, NSF: Memos to the President; Valenti to LBJ, Dec. 24, 1965, WHCF: EX/CO312; Redmon to Jacobson, Dec. 23, 1965; Moyers to LBJ, Dec. 27, 1965, WHCF: EX/PR16; Robert McNamara OH; Shapley, *Promise and Power*, 364.

18. Gibbons, *U.S. Government and Vietnam*, IV, 127–29.

19. LBJ-Ball TELCON, Dec. 28, 1965, Ball Papers.

20. William J. Jorden, "The Thirty-Seven Day Pause," n.d., NSF: Country: Vietnam; HHH to LBJ, Memos of Jan. 5, 1966, Humphrey Papers; Gibbons, *U.S. Government and Vietnam*, IV, 129; Herring, *LBJ and Vietnam*, 99–100.

21. LBJ-Ball TELCON, Dec. 30, 1965, Ball Papers.

22. Meeting Notes, Jan. 3, 1966, Meeting Notes File; NSF: NSC Meeting, Jan. 5, 1966; Arthur McCafferty to LBJ, Jan. 5 and 7, 1966, NSF: Country: Vietnam; Gibbons, *U.S. Government and Vietnam*, IV, 133–35.

23. See Symington to LBJ, Jan. 2, 1966, NSF: Country: Vietnam; Russell to Symington, Jan. 6, 1966, Richard Russell Papers; Valenti to LBJ, Jan. 27, 1966, Handwriting File; Meeting Notes, Jan. 10 and 11, 1966, Meeting Notes File; G. Mennen Williams to Rusk, Jan. 8, 1966, describing a conversation with LBJ, NSF: Country: Vietnam.

24. LBJ-Ball, Jan. 12, 1966, 9:30 a.m, 2:10 p.m., TELCON, Ball Papers; Gibbons, *U.S. Government and Vietnam*, IV, 136–37.

25. Rusk to LBJ, Jan. 24, 25, 1966, NSF: Country: Vietnam; Meeting Notes, Jan. 24, 1966, McG. Bundy Papers; Meeting Notes, Jan. 24, 1966, WHCF: Aides: Valenti; Meeting Notes, Jan. 25, 1966, Diary Backup; Gibbons, *U.S. Government and Vietnam*, IV, 143–47.

26. See Henry Wilson, to LBJ, Jan. 21, 1966; Mike Manatos to LBJ, Jan. 25, 1966, Diary Backup; "Public Opinion Regarding Bombing of North Vietnam," Jan. 22, 1966, WHCF: Aides: Panzer.

27. Meeting Notes, Jan. 22, 1966, WHCF: Aides: Valenti.

28. Califano and Reedy told him that no one had explained how the bombing would help end the war: Califano to LBJ, Jan. 29, 1966; Reedy to LBJ, Jan. 31, 1966, WHCF: ND19/CO312; Meeting Notes, Jan. 26, 1966, Meeting Notes File.

29. Meeting Notes, Jan. 27, 1966, ibid.

30. Meeting Notes, Jan. 28, 1966, ibid.

31. *PPP: LBJ, 1966*, I, 114–15; Meeting Notes, Jan. 29, 1966, 11:35 a.m. and 12:45 p.m., Meeting Notes File.

32. Gibbons, *U.S. Government and Vietnam*, IV, 164–70, 213–14, 220–28.

33. See *PPP: LBJ, 1966*, I, 144–46, 148–49. Also see Jack Valenti to LBJ, Jan. 31, 1966, NSF: NSC History of the Vietnam War; and Mac Bundy to LBJ, Feb. 3, 1966, NSF: Memos to the President.

34. *PPP: LBJ, 1966*, I, 146–48.

35. Theoharis and Cox, *The Boss*, 397–98.

36. Valenti to LBJ, Jan. 31, 1966, NSF: NSC History of the Vietnam War; NSF: NSC History: Honolulu Conference, Feb. 6–8, 1966; Moyers to LBJ, Jan. 25, 1966, Handwriting File; Comments of Senator Robert F. Kennedy, Jan. 31, 1966, NSF: Country: Vietnam.

37. Rusk to U.S. Embassy, Saigon, Feb. 4, 1966, NSF: International Meetings and Travel Notes; Possible Questions for General Westmoreland, Feb. 6, 1966, Diary Backup.

38. "Demonstrations Protesting U.S. Intervention in Vietnam," Feb. 7, 1966, File 62-109119, FBI; Talking Points for the President, Feb. 7, 1966, NSF: International Meetings and Travel Notes.

39. LBJ Notes, Feb. 7, 1966, Handwriting File.

40. Transcript of Remarks, Feb. 7, 1966, International Meetings and Travel Notes.

41. Talking Points for the President, Feb. 7, 1966, ibid.; LBJ's private conversation is recorded in a State Dept. memo, Moyers to U. Alexis Johnson, Feb. 16, 1966, quoted in Gibbons, *U.S. Government and Vietnam*, IV, 230–31 n. 52.

42. Transcript, Feb. 8, 1966, International Meetings and Travel Notes.

43. *PPP: LBJ, 1966*, I, 152–55.

44. NSF: NSC History: Honolulu Conference, Feb. 6–8, 1966.

45. LBJ to Lodge, n.d. [February 1966]; Rusk's remarks are in "Honolulu Conference," n.d., NSF: International Meetings and Travel Notes; Bundy to LBJ, Feb. 11, 1966; Valenti to LBJ, Feb. 11, 1966; Valenti to LBJ, Feb. 11, 1966, NSF: Memos to the President; Notes, Feb. 15, 1966, McG. Bundy Papers.

46. *PPP: LBJ, 1966*, I, 155–57.

47. Humphrey, *Education of a Public Man*, 329–30; Gibbons, *U.S. Gov-

ernment and Vietnam, IV, 233–34; HHH to LBJ, March 3, 1966, Memos to President, Humphrey Papers.

48. Meeting Notes, Feb. 24, 1966, WHCF: Aides: Valenti. There is a fuller transcript of this meeting in Congressional Briefings on Vietnam.

49. HHH to LBJ, March 3, 1966, Humphrey Papers.

50. Gibbons, *U.S. Government and Vietnam,* IV, 236–37, 243–48.

51. See ibid., 237–42, 249–51; Mike Manatos to LBJ, Feb. 10, 17, 1966; WHCF: EX/ND19\CO312; Califano to LBJ, Feb. 19, 1966; Marvin Watson to LBJ, Feb. 21, 1966, Handwriting File; Meeting Notes, Feb. 19, 1966, McG. Bundy Papers; Richard Helms to Bill Moyers, Feb. 23, 1966; Valenti to Henry Cabot Lodge, March 24, 1966, WHCF: CF: ND19/CO312.

52. Jean Lacoutre, "Vietnam: The Turning Point," *New York Review of Books,* May 12, 1966.

53. Gibbons, *U.S. Government and Vietnam,* IV, 267–70.

54. Ibid., 270–71; Bromley Smith to LBJ, March 9, 1966, NSF: Country: Vietnam.

55. Meeting Notes, March 12, 1966, Office of the Pres. File: Valenti.

56. Bromley Smith to LBJ, March 16, 1966, with attached cable, NSF: Country: Vietnam.

57. See Chester L. Cooper to Komer, March 15, 1966; Henry H. Fowler to LBJ, March 23, 1966; R. W. Komer to LBJ, March 25, 1966; Robert McNamara to LBJ, March 28, 1966, NSF: Country: Vietnam; NSAM No. 343, March 28, 1966, NSF: Memos to the President; Jack Valenti to LBJ, March 12, 1966; Leonard H. Marks to LBJ, March 28, 1966, Handwriting File; HHH to LBJ, March 30, 1966, Humphrey Papers.

58. Meetings, April 2 and 4, 1966, Meeting Notes File.

59. Hayes Redmon to Bill Moyers, Feb. 27, March 7, 1966, WHCF: EX/ PR16; Gallup Poll, March 9, 1966, WHCF: CF: PR16.

60. Douglas MacArthur II to Rusk, March 8, 1966, Handwriting File.

61. Fulbright to LBJ, March 19, 1966, Fulbright Papers; LBJ to Fulbright, March 22, 1966; Galbraith to LBJ, April 3, 1966, WHCF: EX/ ND19\CO312; Valenti to LBJ, April 3, 1966, WHCF: Aides: Valenti.

62. The quotes are all from cables cited in Gibbons, *U.S. Government and Vietnam,* IV, 280–81.

63. Comparative Military Casualties Vietnam, March 31, 1966; Vance to LBJ, April 8, 1966; Taylor to LBJ, March 29, 1966, NSF: Country: Vietnam.

64. Rostow to LBJ, two memos on April 5, 1966, NSF: Memos to the President.

65. Gibbons, *U.S. Government and Vietnam,* IV, 283–86.

66. Moyers to LBJ, April 11, 12, 1966; Marvin Watson to LBJ, April 12, 1966, WHCF: CF: ND19\CO312.

67. Maxwell Taylor to LBJ, April 12, 1966; LBJ to Rostow, April 13, 1966; Col. Robert N. Ginsburgh to Rostow, April 20, 1966; Memo on Casualties, April 25, 1966; Rostow to LBJ, May 9, 1966, NSF: Country: Vietnam; Komer to LBJ, April 19, 1966, NSF: Files of Robert Komer. NSF: NSC Meeting, May 10, 1966. Also see Rostow to LBJ, April 21, 1966, NSF: Memos to the President.

68. R. C. Bowman to Rostow, April 25, 1966; Col. Robert N. Ginsburgh to Rostow, May 10, 1966, NSF: Country: Vietnam.

69. Vietnam Meeting, Agenda, April 25, 1966; Rostow, Memo for the Record, April 26, 1966, NSF: Country: Vietnam; Gibbons, *U.S. Government and Vietnam*, IV, 286–301.

70. Ibid., 301–3; NSF: NSC Meeting, May 10, 1966.

71. Gibbons, *U.S. Government and Vietnam*, IV, 315–16.

72. Lodge is quoted by William Bundy in "The Johnson Years: A Vietnam Roundtable," Conference March 9, 1991, pp. 108–9; *PPP: LBJ, 1966*, I, 531–32.

73. For the resolution of the crisis, see Gibbons, *U.S. Government and Vietnam*, IV, 316–34. Wheeler is quoted on pp. 320–21.

74. Mueller, *War, Presidents and Public Opinion*, 52–54, 56; *Gallup Poll*, III, 1998–99, 2001, 2007–11, 2013–14; Gibbons, *U.S. Government and Vietnam*, IV, 334–40; Russell's comment is quoted in Moyers to LBJ, May 3, 1966; also see Moyers to LBJ, June 9, 1966, Reference File: Vietnam.

75. *PPP: LBJ, 1966*, I, 535.

76. Ibid.

77. Moyers to LBJ, April 25, 1966, WHCF: CF: PR18; Bob Fleming to LBJ, May 16, 1966, WHCF: EX/PL; Rostow to LBJ, May 1, 1966, NSF: Memos to the President.

78. Busby to LBJ, May 23, 1966, WHCF: EX/ND19\CO312; Lodge to LBJ, May 25, 1966, NSF: Memos to the President.

79. *PPP: LBJ, 1966*, I, 493–98, 504–5, 517–20.

80. Memo of talk to NSC Staff, May 27, 1966, made by Walt W. Rostow, and given to me by him, Jan. 24, 1992.

81. See "*Princeton Speech*," May 11, 1966; Eric Goldman to Marie Fehmer, May 13, 1966, Diary Backup.

82. See D. W. Ropa to Moyers, March 25, 1966, NSF: Country: Vietnam; HHH to LBJ, April 27, May 19, 1966, Humphrey Papers; Califano to LBJ, May 13, 1966, WHCF: EX/HU4; McPherson to LBJ, May 18, 1966, WHCF: Aides: McPherson.

83. Goldman, *Tragedy of LBJ*, 590–93.

84. See MGW to Russell, May 13, 1966, with Russell's handwritten notes on the memo, Interoffice Communications, Russell Papers.

85. *PPP: LBJ, 1966*, I, 502.

86. McPherson to LBJ, May 13, 1966, WHCF: Aides: McPherson.

87. *PPP: LBJ, 1966*, I, 517, 519; McPherson interview, Feb. 28, 1979, Congressional Research Service, quoted in Gibbons, *U.S. Government and Vietnam*, IV, 311.

88. Rostow to LBJ, April 27, 1966, NSF: Memos to the President.

89. Kintner to LBJ, May 26, 1966, WHCF: CF: PR18.

90. See Charles Bartlett to LBJ, May 12, 1966; LBJ to Bartlett, May 13, 1966; "The President and the News," April 19, 1966, WHCF: EX/PR18; Kintner to Moyers, April 30, 1966, WHCF: CF: PR18; Moyers to LBJ, June 6, 1966, WHCF: Aides: Moyers.

91. Memo for the File, Peter Siemien, May 17, 1966, WHCF: EX/PR18.

92. *Chicago Daily News*, June 3, 1965; C. D. DeLoach to E. D. Mohr, June 4, 1965; Hoover to Tolson et al., June 4, 1965, JEH O&C File, FBI.

93. Hoover Memo for File, Feb. 25, 1966; R. E. Wick to DeLoach, March 3, 1966, ibid.

94. Moyers to LBJ, Feb. 21, 1966, WHCF: Aides: Moyers.

95. J. William Fulbright, *The Arrogance of Power* (New York, 1966).

96. DeLoach to Tolson, March 3, 1966, JEH, O&C, FBI.

97. Fulbright to LBJ, May 9, 1966, LBJ File, Fulbright Papers.

98. Lee Williams to Fulbright, April 25, 1966, ibid.; LBJ to Fulbright, May 27, 1966, NSF: Memos to the President.

99. Diary Backup, June 1, 15; Gibbons, *U.S. Government and Vietnam*, IV, 343–44.

100. Tristam Coffin, *Senator Fulbright: Portrait of a Public Philosopher* (New York, 1966), 313.

101. D. W. Brogan, "The Illusion of American Omnipotence," *Harper's Magazine*, Dec. 1952, pp. 21–28.

102. See Rostow to LBJ, May 6 and 10, 1966; LBJ to Wilson, May 27, 1966, NSF: Memos to the President; Gibbons, *U.S. Government and Vietnam*, IV, 360–67.

103. Lodge to LBJ, June 8, 10, 1966; also two memos of Rostow to LBJ, June 8, 1966; LBJ to Wilson, June 14, 1966, NSF: Memos to the President.

104. Rostow to LBJ, June 15, 16, 1966, ibid.

105. NSF: NSC Meeting, June 17, 1966.

106. Ibid., June 22, 1966.

107. Rostow to LBJ, June 22, 1966, NSF: Country: Vietnam; Gibbons, *U.S. Government and Vietnam*, IV, 376–77.

108. Bohlen cable and Rostow to LBJ, June 21, 1966; LBJ to McNamara, June 28, 1966, NSF: Memos to the President; Rostow to LBJ, June 25, 1966, Handwriting File.

109. LBJ to Rusk, June 4, 1966, NSF: Memos to the President; Presidential Opening Remarks, Cabinet Luncheon, June 16, 1966, Cabinet Papers; Gallup Political Index, June 1966, WHCF: EX/PR16.

110. DeLoach to Tolson, June 20, 21, 28, 1966; D. J. Brennan to Sullivan, June 23, 29, July 1, 1966; Sizoo to Sullivan, June 30, 1966; SAC, Omaha to Director, July 1, 1966, Cross References No. 3, LBJ, FBI.

111. Kinter to LBJ, June 3, 1966; Kintner to Moyers, June 8, 1966, WHCF: CF: PR18; Rostow to LBJ, June 3 and 15, 1966, NSF: Memos to the President.

112. See Kintner to Rostow, June 6, 1966, WHCF: CF: PR18; Califano to LBJ, June 10, 1966, three memos, Chron Files, Califano Papers; William J. Jorden to Rostow, June 10, 1966, NSF: Memos to the President; O'Brien to LBJ, June 8, 1966, WHCF: EX/PR16; Komer to LBJ, June 18, 1966, NSF: Komer File.

113. LBJ to Galbraith, June 20, 1966; Memo of LBJ's talk to "Gentlemen," n.d., on NATO and Vietnam, NSF: Memos to the President; LBJ to Mansfield, June 22, 1966, WHCF: EX/ND19\CO312. Also see Moyers to LBJ, June 28, 1966, Reference File: Vietnam, who urged reporters seeking more "information on the Hanoi-Haiphong situation . . . to put the nation's security above the natural desire to dig out a story."

114. See Jake Jacobsen to Hayes Redmon, July 9, 1966; Redmon to Moyers, July 14, 1966; Gallup Poll, July 24, 1966, WHCF: EX/PR16.

115. Gibbons, *U.S. Government and Vietnam*, IV, 379–81.

116. Ibid., 382–83.

117. Notes by Marvin Watson of Meeting, July 11, 1966, Diary Backup.

118. Meeting Notes, July 18, 19, 1966, Tom Johnson Papers.

119. *PPP: LBJ, 1966*, II, 750–51, 760–62.

120. Cabinet Meeting, July 26, 1966, Cabinet Papers.

121. Ibid., July 15, 1966.

122. Sherrod to George P. Hunt, Oct. 1, 1966, LBJ Files, Robert Sherrod Papers, NASA Archives.

123. Herring, *LBJ and Vietnam*, 50; Meeting Notes, Aug. 13, 1966, Tom Johnson Papers.

124. See Lodge to LBJ, July 22, Aug. 9, 10, 1966, NSF: Memos to the President; Comparative Military Casualties, July 29, 1966; Rostow to LBJ, Aug. 2, 1966, NSF: Country: Vietnam.

125. Congressional Briefing, Sept. 6, 1966, Congressional Briefings on Vietnam.

126. Agence France Presse, Sept. 13, 1966; South Vietnamese Elections, Sept. 12, 1966; Remarks by Senator Ralph Yarborough, n.d.; Arthur McCafferty to LBJ, Sept. 12, 1966; William Jorden to Rostow, Sept. 12, 1966; Richard Helms to Rostow, Sept. 2, 1966, NSF: Country: Vietnam; Rostow to LBJ, Sept. 16, with cable of Sept 15, 1966, attached, NSF: Memos to the President; Fred Panzer to Moyers, Anti-Vietnam Candidates, Sept. 14, 1966, WHCF: EX/PR16.

127. For the pressures, see Rostow to LBJ, July 1, 7, 21, 1966, NSF: Memos to the President; John K. Galbraith to LBJ, June 16; LBJ to Galbraith, July 13, 1966, WHCF: CF: ND19/CO312; Norman H. Brooks to Califano, Aug. 2, 1966, WHCF: Aides: Califano; HHH to LBJ, Aug. 13, 1966, Humphrey Papers; Gallup Poll, Aug. 21, 1966, WHCF: EX/PR16. On Russell, see Gibbons, *U.S. Government and Vietnam*, IV, 431–34.

128. Congressional Briefing, Sept. 6, 1966, Congressional Briefings on Vietnam; LBJ to Lodge, July 12, 1966, NSF: Memos to the President; Robert Kintner to LBJ, July 26, 1966; Kintner to Marks, July 28, 1966, WHCF: CF: ND19/CO312.

129. VanDeMark, *Into the Quagmire*, 202; Herring, *LBJ and Vietnam*, 102.

130. See "Negotiating Attempts on Vietnam," n.d., NSF: Country: Vietnam.

131. See "Potential Peace Initiatives," n.d.; Maxwell D. Taylor to LBJ, June 13, July 11, 1966; Rostow to LBJ, July 8, 16, 31, 1966 NSF: Memos to the President; Agenda, Meeting with the President, July 15, 1966, NSF: Rostow Files.

132. Herring, *LBJ and Vietnam*, 102–4.

133. Rostow notes of lunch meeting with LBJ, Aug. 2, 1966, NSF: Rostow Files.

134. Gibbons, *U.S. Government and Vietnam*, IV, 388–89; Valenti to LBJ, Aug. 29, 1966, WHCF: EX/ND19\CO312.

135. Moyers to LBJ, Aug. 31, 1966, Reference File: Vietnam.

136. Gibbons, *U.S. Government and Vietnam*, IV, 387–88; LBJ to Westmoreland, and to Lodge, June 18, 1966, WHCF: EX/CO312; Komer to LBJ, July 1, 1966, NSF: Country: Vietnam; Herring, *LBJ and Vietnam*, 73.

137. Westmoreland Cable, Aug. 26, 1966; Rostow to LBJ, Aug. 29, 1966, NSF: Country: Vietnam; Komer to LBJ, Aug. 30, 1966, NSF: Rostow Files.

138. HHH to LBJ, Sept. 16, 1966, memo of conversation with Robert Nathan, Sept. 13, 1966, attached, Humphrey Papers; Komer to LBJ, Sept. 13,

20, 1966, NSF: Rostow Files; McNamara to LBJ, Sept. 30, 1966; Rusk to LBJ, Oct. 18, 1966, NSF: Memos to the President; Komer to Moyers, Sept. 16, 1966, WHCF: EX/ND19\CO312; Herring, *LBJ and Vietnam*, 74–77; Gibbons, *U.S. Government and Vietnam*, IV, 468–71.

139. See Rostow to LBJ, Oct. 6, 1966, on the U.N., NSF: Memos to the President; Califano to LBJ, Oct. 14, 1966, on demonstrations, Chron Files, Califano Papers; and the LBJ Main File HQ62-111200 for Oct. 1966, FBI, on LBJ's concern to have FBI as well as Secret Service protection on his trip to the Pacific and Asia.

140. NSC Meeting, Oct. 15, 1966, Meeting Notes File.

141. Moyers to LBJ, Sept. 28, 1966, Diary Backup; Kintner to LBJ, Oct. 7, 1966, WHCF: CF: PR18.

142. *PPP: LBJ, 1966*, II, 1117–18, 1122–23, 1155–56, 1162–64; Draft Statement, Oct. 23, 1966, NSF: Rostow Files.

143. The memo to McNamara is quoted in Gibbons, *U.S. Government and Vietnam*, IV, 444. For public statements on Conference achievements, see *PPP: LBJ, 1966*, II, 1256–65.

144. *PPP: LBJ, 1966*, II, 1263; Harriman to LBJ, Oct. 3, 7, 1966; Memorandum for the President, Oct. 10, 1966; Rostow to LBJ, Nov. 3, 1966, especially Tab A describing the withdrawal commitment as a response to a suggestion from Gromyko, NSF: Memos to the President; NSF: NSC History: Manila Conference and President's Asian Trip, Oct. 17–Nov. 2, 1966, pp. G5-G7; Gibbons, *U.S. Government and Vietnam*, IV, 442–44.

145. See NSF: NSC History of the Manila Conf., pp. H-7–H-8; Kintner to LBJ, Nov. 2, 1966, WHCF: CF: ND19/CO312; Gibbons, *U.S. Government and Vietnam*, IV, 446.

146. McPherson to LBJ, Dec. 19, 1966, WHCF: Aides: McPherson.

147. *PPP: LBJ, 1966*, II, 1269–70; Herring, *LBJ and Vietnam*, 18–19.

148. LBJ to Lodge, Nov. 16, 1966, NSF: Country: Vietnam.

149. Rostow to LBJ, Nov. 28, 1966; LBJ to Rostow, Nov. 30, 1966, WHCF: CF: ND19/CO312; Gallup Political Index, Nov.–Dec. 1966, WHCF: EX/PR16; Rostow to Lodge, Dec. 9, 1966, NSF: Memos to the President.

150. Pearson to LBJ, Dec. 5, 1966, WHCF: EX/PR18.

151. McNamara to LBJ, Oct. 14, 1966, NSF: Country: Vietnam.

152. Gibbons, *U.S. Government and Vietnam*, IV, 457, 461–62; Westmoreland to Rostow, Oct. 24, 1966; Rostow to LBJ, Nov. 9, 1966, NSF: Memos to the President.

153. Gibbons, *U.S. Government and Vietnam*, IV, 462–68; on the committee, see Lunch Meeting with the President, Nov. 15, 1966; and Rostow to LBJ, Nov. 30, 1966, NSF: Rostow Files.

154. Gibbons, *U.S. Government and Vietnam*, IV, 462–63.

155. LBJ, *Vantage Point*, 257–58.

156. Bundy to LBJ, Nov. 17, 1966, NSF: McG. Bundy Files; Agenda for the President, Nov. 19, 1966, NSF: Rostow Files.

157. Komer to LBJ, Nov. 28, Dec. 10, 1966, NSF: Country: Vietnam; Strategic Guidelines for 1967 in Vietnam, Dec. 10, 1966, NSF: Rostow Files; Komer to LBJ, Dec. 1, 1966, NSF: Komer Files; Rostow to LBJ, Dec. 10, 1966, with LBJ's reply, Handwriting File.

158. Lodge to LBJ, Dec. 11, 1966, NSF: Memos to the President; Meeting

with the President, Dec. 19, 1966, NSF: Rostow Files; Comparative Military Casualties, Dec. 13, 1966, NSF: Country: Vietnam; LBJ, *Vantage Point*, 258.

159. Nod's-Aspen, Nov. 11, 1966; Suggested Agenda, Nov. 15, 1966, NSF: Rostow Files; Rostow to LBJ, Nov. 17, 1966, NSF: Memos to the President.

160. Chester Cooper, *The Lost Crusade: America in Vietnam* (New York, 1970), 334; William Bundy OH; Rostow to LBJ, preliminary agenda, Dec. 2, 1966, NSF: Rostow Files; Rostow to LBJ, Dec. 2, 1966, handwritten note, NSF: Memos to the President.

161. Herring, *LBJ and Vietnam*, 104–6, 205–6 n.5; for the President's Diary, Dec. 9, 1966, Meeting Notes File.

162. See William J. Jorden to Rostow, n.d. [apparently Feb. 1967], NSF: Memos to the Pres.; Harrison E. Salisbury, *Behind the Lines—Hanoi, December 23, 1966–January 7, 1967* (New York, 1967); Gibbons, *U.S. Government and Vietnam*, IV, 499–500; Herring, *LBJ and Vietnam*, 106–7.

163. Harrison E. Salisbury, *A Time of Change: A Reporter's Tale of Our Time* (New York, 1988), 160; C. L. Sulzberger, *Seven Continents and Forty Years* (New York, 1977), 443; Admiral Thomas Moorer OH.

164. Memo for the President, Subject: Eric Goldman Memo, Aug. 10, 1966, WHCF: EX/FG11-8-1\Goldman, Eric; *Miami Herald*, Dec. 17, 1966; *Baltimore Sun*, Dec. 18, 1966; *New York Times*, Dec. 18, 1966; Notes on Dec. 21, 1966, Meeting with Governors at LBJ Ranch, Dec. 28, 1966, Diary Backup.

CHAPTER 8: A SEA OF TROUBLES

1. For these quotes, see Robert Dallek, *Hail to the Chief: The Making and Unmaking of American Presidents* (New York, 1996).

2. See three columns by Holmes Alexander, Jan. 20, 23, 24, 1967, in Diary Backup. For the meetings, see meeting with governors, Dec. 22, 1966, Tom Johnson Papers; and meeting with senators, Jan. 9, 1967, Diary Backup.

3. See Louis Uchitelle, "Three Decades of Dwindling Hope for Prosperity," *New York Times*, Sec. 4, May 9, 1993; *PPP: LBJ, 1967*, I, 7–8. For internal administration expressions of optimism about the economy, see Ben Wattenberg to Douglass Cater, Dec. 30, 1966; Gardner Ackley to LBJ, Dec. 30, 1966, WHCF: EX/BE5.

4. *Newsweek*, Jan. 2, 1967.

5. Gardner Ackley to LBJ, Jan. 4, 1967, WHCF: CF: EX/BE; Ackley to LBJ, Jan. 7, 1967, WHCF: EX/BE5-2; UPI 126, Jan. 12, 1967, WHCF: EX/FI4; Joe Califano to LBJ, Dec. 26, 1966, WHCF: EX/BE; Henry H. Fowler to LBJ, Jan. 11, 1967, Diary Backup; UPI 155, 157, Jan. 11, 1967 WHCF: EX/BE5; UPI 32, Jan. 11, 1967, WHCF: EX/BE5-3; Willard Wirtz to LBJ, Jan. 18, 1967, WHCF: CF: EX/BE5-2; "LBJ's Budget Plans," *Washington Post*, Jan. 22, 1967; Marvin Watson to LBJ, Jan. 24, 1967, with UPI 67 attached, WHCF: EX/FI4.

6. Willard Wirtz to LBJ, Feb. 2, March 15, 1967; Califano to LBJ, April 19, 1967, WHCF: EX/BE5-2; Comments on Economic Outlook, Feb. 21, 1967, attached to Tom Johnson to LBJ, Feb. 18, 1967; Ackley to LBJ, March 29, 1967, Diary Backup; Ackley to LBJ, March 15, 1967, WHCF: CF: EX/BE5-4; Arthur Okun to LBJ, Feb. 18, 1967, WHCF: EX/BE5; Ackley to LBJ, Feb. 27, 1967, Handwriting File.

7. Memo of LBJ meeting with Edwin D. Etherington, Jan. 12, 1967, Diary Backup.

8. Fred Panzer to Robert Kintner, Jan. 26, 1967, WHCF: CF: EX/FI11-4; UPI 99, Jan. 30, 1967; Henry H. Wilson, Jr., to LBJ, Jan. 31, 1967, WHCF: EX/FG11-1; Ackley to LBJ, Feb. 25, 1967, WHCF: EX/BE5; LBJ-Maddox Meeting, Feb. 2, 1967, Diary Backup.

9. LBJ-Katzenbach, Jan. 25, 1967, TT.

10. Califano to LBJ, Mar. 8, 1967, WHCF: EX/BE5; *PPP: LBJ, 1967*, I, 301–4; *Washington Post*, March 11, 1967.

11. Polls dated Feb. 19, 24, March 11, and April 7, 1967, WHCF: EX/PR16.

12. Arthur Okun to LBJ, April 18, 1967; Ackley to LBJ, May 22, 1967, WHCF: EX/BE5; Ackley to LBJ, May 5, 1967, WHCF: EX/BE5-4; Wirtz to LBJ, May 17, 1967, WHCF: EX/BE5-2; CEA, "Tax Policy and the Economy," attached to Administrative Budget, May 23, 1967, WHCF: Aides: Califano; Califano to LBJ, June 12, 1967; Ackley to LBJ, June 19, 1967, Handwriting File; Califano to LBJ, June 26, 1967, WHCF: EX/FI.

13. Sidey-LBJ interview, May 16, 1967, Diary Backup.

14. Panzer to LBJ, May 5, 1967, June 30, 1967, WHCF: EX/PR16.

15. Ackley to LBJ, Aug. 25, Sept. 1, 1967, WHCF: EX/BE5; Wirtz to LBJ, Aug. 31, 1967, WHCF: CF: EX/LA2; Okun to LBJ, Sept. 13, 1967, WHCF: CF: EX/BE5-4; Cabinet Meeting, Sept. 20, 1967, Cabinet Papers.

16. Wirtz to LBJ, July 20, Aug. 21, 1967, Sept. 21, 1967, WHCF: EX/BE5-1 and BE5-2; LBJ meeting with businessmen, July 14, 1967; with Senate Committee chairmen, July 25, 1967; with Democratic congressional leadership, July 31, 1967; with Democratic congressmen, Aug. 8, 1967, Tom Johnson Papers; *PPP: LBJ, 1967*, II, 733–38.

17. *PPP: LBJ, 1967*, II, 737–46.

18. Califano to LBJ, July 14, 1967, WHCF: EX/FI11-4; Barefoot Sanders to LBJ, July 20, 1967, Diary Backup; Henry Fowler to LBJ, July 26, 1967, WHCF: CF: EX/FI11-4; A. B. Trowbridge to LBJ, July 27, 1967, WHCF: CF: EX/LE\FI11-4; LBJ meeting with Democratic congressmen, Aug. 8, 1967, Tom Johnson Papers; Charles Schultze to LBJ, Sept. 16, 1967, WHCF: Aides: Califano.

19. *PPP: LBJ, 1967*, II, 795–96, 885–86; LBJ meeting with Bureau Chiefs, Aug. ?, 1967, Tom Johnson Papers; Bob Fleming to LBJ, Aug. 7, 1967, WHCF: EX/PR18; Barefoot Sanders to LBJ, Aug. 7, 1967; LBJ meeting with Business Leaders, Aug. 10, 1967, Diary Backup; Fowler to LBJ, Aug. 17, 1967, Handwriting File; HHH to LBJ, Aug. 25, 1967, Humphrey Papers; Ackley to LBJ, Aug. 29, 1967, WHCF: EX/FI; Lloyd Hackler to George Christian, Aug. 17, 1967, WHCF: EX/PR18; B. Marvel to Panzer, Sept. 12, 1967, WHCF: Aides: Panzer.

20. LBJ meeting with Max Frankel, Sept. 15, 1967, Diary Backup.

21. For LBJ's uncertainty about what the war would cost or how long it would last, see Kermit Gordon OH, II, Jan. 9, 1969: "Certainly nobody in 1966—nobody in authority—thought we would still be fighting an apparently unsuccessful war in Vietnam in January 1969." Also see Charles L. Schultze OH, April 10, 1969; Arthur Okun OH, April 15, 1969; and Joseph A. Califano, Jr., OH, Dec. 15, 1987.

22. Ackley to LBJ, Oct. 10, 1967, WHCF: EX/FI; Schultze to LBJ, Oct.

12, 1967, WHCF: CF: EX/FI4; Califano to LBJ, Nov. 8, 1967, WHCF: Aides: Califano; LBJ meeting with Jack Horner and Lee Cohn, Oct. 13, 1967, Tom Johnson Papers.

23. Panzer to LBJ, Oct. 13, 17, 1967, WHCF: EX/BE5-3.

24. Ackley to LBJ, Dec. 12, 14, 29, 1967, WHCF: CF: EX/BE5 and BE5-4; *PPP: LBJ, 1967*, II, 969, 1091–2; LBJ meeting with Bipartisan Leadership, Nov. 20, 1967, Tom Johnson Papers.

25. Statement of Wilbur Mills, Oct. 6, 1967; Mills OH, May 15, 1987; Califano to LBJ, Oct. 7, 1967, describing Mills's insistence on "no new programs in 1969 before we can get action on a tax bill"; and Nov. 21, 1967, WHCF: Aides: Califano; LBJ meeting with congressional leaders, Oct. 17, 1967, Tom Johnson Papers; *PPP: LBJ, 1967*, II, 1009. For opposition from the *New York Times* and *Washington Post*, see Walter Heller OH, Dec. 21, 1971.

26. LBJ meeting with Hobart Rowen, Oct. 17, 1967, Diary Backup; Fagan Dickson to Yarborough, Oct. 19, 1967, Ralph Yarborough Papers.

27. Panzer to LBJ, Nov. 9, 1967, WHCF: EX/PR16.

28. Bourke B. Hickenlooper OH; anon., "Unter Der Lyndon," Senator Lister Hill Papers, University of Alabama Archives, Montgomery.

29. See the Spivack Report, Nov. 14, 1966, in Diary Backup; McPherson to LBJ, Dec. 19, 1966; Jan. 9, 1967, WHCF: Aides: McPherson; LBJ meeting with senators, Jan. 9, 1967, Diary Backup.

30. Gardner Ackley OH, March 7, 1974; Charles L. Schultze OH, April 10, 1969.

31. Administrative History: Office of Economic Opportunity, chap. 1, p. 43.

32. *PPP: LBJ, 1967*, I, 2–9; Reuther to LBJ, Jan. 11, 1967, Walter P. Reuther Papers.

33. See Califano to LBJ, Nov. 7, 1966, WHCF: Aides: Califano; Douglass Cater to LBJ, March 17, 1967, WHCF: EX/FG11-15; *PPP: LBJ,1967*, I, 31–39, 150–61, 184–206, 244–58, 273–74, 331–46, 710–11, 1067–70.

34. HHH to LBJ, Feb. 13 and 23, 1967, Humphrey Papers.

35. See Humphrey's many memos to LBJ for 1967 in Memos to the President, Humphrey Papers.

36. Memos of LBJ's introductory and concluding remarks, Cabinet meeting, Jan. 18, 1967, Cabinet Papers; HHH to LBJ, Jan. 25, April 22, 1967, Humphrey Papers; Meeting of congressional relations officers, March 10, 1967, Diary Backup.

37. Lloyd Hackler, Memorandum for the Diary, May 10, 1967, Diary Backup; LBJ meeting with Cabinet, July 19, 1967, Cabinet Papers; LBJ conversation with six commentators, Aug. 11, 1967; LBJ to HHH, Aug. 23, 1967, Humphrey Papers; Larry Levinson summary of LBJ meeting with publishers, Sept. 6, 1967, Diary Backup; LBJ Cabinet meeting, Nov. 15, 1967, Cabinet Papers; Douglass Cater and Charles Maguire to LBJ, Nov. 21, 1967, Diary Backup.

38. Douglass Cater OH, May 26, 1974, April 24, 1981.

39. Califano, *Triumph and Tragedy*, 172.

40. See HHH to LBJ, July 27, Aug. 12 and 23, 1967; LBJ to HHH, Aug. 23, 1967; HHH to Ken Gray, Aug. 31, 1967, Humphrey Papers; Califano to LBJ, Aug. 16, 1967, WHCF: EX/FG11-1.

41. LBJ to Califano, March 28, Aug. 31, 1967; LBJ meeting with Kraft, Sept. 27, Diary Backup; LBJ meeting with Democratic Leaders, Nov. 7, 1967, Tom Johnson Papers.

42. Wilson, Jr., to LBJ, May 17, 1967, Diary Backup; Schultze to LBJ, Aug. 4 and 11, 1967, WHCF: EX/FG11-1; Wilbur J. Cohen to Mike Manatos, July 31, 1967, WHCF: CF: EX/FG165; LBJ Cabinet meeting, Aug. 2, 1967, Cabinet Papers; *PPP: LBJ, 1967*, II, 989–90, 1002–3; Califano to LBJ, Nov. 16, 1967, WHCF: Aides: Califano; Califano to LBJ, Dec. 4, 1967, WHCF: EX/FI4.

43. Administrative History: Office of Economic Opportunity, 559–63.

44. Ibid., 563–64, 566–69, 598–604; Barefoot Sanders to LBJ, Nov. 6, 1967, WHCF: EX/FG11-15.

45. LBJ meeting with Democratic congressional leadership, July 31, 1967, Tom Johnson Papers; Administrative History: Office of Economic Opportunity, 592–94, 604–7; LBJ meeting with congressional leadership, Sept. 19, 1967, Diary Backup; Marvin Watson to LBJ, Oct. 4, 1967; Barefoot Sanders, Nov. 3, 1967, WHCF: EX/FG11-15; Sanders to LBJ, Dec. 14, 1967, Diary Backup; Shriver to LBJ, Dec. 22, 1967, WHCF: Aides: Califano; Califano to LBJ, Dec. 22, 1967; Jan. 9, 1968, WHCF: CF: EX/FI4\FG11-15.

46. *PPP: LBJ, 1966*, I, 291–99, 644–45, 1356–57.

47. Bill Moyers to the Attorney General, Sept. 9, 1966, WHCF: CF: EX/JL3; Califano, *Triumph and Tragedy*, 153–4; *PPP: LBJ, 1966*, II, 1381–83; *PPP: LBJ, 1967*, I, 258–59; LBJ-Ramsey Clark, Jan. 25, 1967, TT.

48. Califano, *Triumph and Tragedy*, 185–86; *PPP: LBJ, 1967*, I, 6–7.

49. *PPP: LBJ, 1967*, I, 134–45.

50. Ibid., 144.

51. Califano, *Triumph and Tragedy*, 186–88; Califano and Lee White to LBJ, Feb. 9, 1966, WHCF: EX/LE\JL; Charles Maguire to Jake Jacobsen, Dec. 5, 1966, WHCF: CF: EX/JL; Cohen to Marvin Watson, May 27, 1966, attached to Watson to LBJ, May 28, 1966, Handwriting File; Ramsey Clark OH, June 3, 1969.

52. See Garrow, *The FBI and King*, chap. 4.

53. M. A. Jones to Wick, June 28, July 19, Dec. 12 and 13, 1966, FBI File on Robert F. Kennedy, MF, Scholarly Resources; the most authoritative account of the RFK–Hoover controversy is in Schlesinger, *Robert Kennedy*, 250ff.; for LBJ's response, see Robert Kintner to LBJ, Dec. 12, 1966, with Robert Hardesty to Kintner, Dec. 12, 1966, attached, WHCF: CF: EX/JL; Carol to Watson, March 14, 1967, WHCF: EX: LE/JL; Califano, *Triumph and Tragedy*, 188.

54. Califano to LBJ, Feb. 13, 1967, WHCF: EX/FG763; *Washington Post*, Feb. 19, 1967; *PPP: LBJ, 1967*, I, 208–9; *PPP: LBJ, 1967*, I, 226–39.

55. Barefoot Sanders to Marvin Watson, Feb. 21, 1967; Ramsey Clark to LBJ, Feb. 27, March 15, 1967; Cliff Sessions to Robert Fleming, March 10 and 17, 1967; to Loyd Hackler, June 15, 1967, WHCF: EX/FG135; *PPP: LBJ, 1967*, I, 400–403, 528–30, 637–40.

56. Wilfred Rommel to Califano, Aug. 3, 1967; Flug to Califano, Nov. 21, 1967, Legislative Bkground: Safe Streets and Crime Control Act; Barefoot Sanders, Aug. 7, 1967; Califano to LBJ, Sept. 18 and 19, 1967, Diary Backup; *Christian Science Monitor*, Aug. 10, 1967; Califano to LBJ, Aug. 29, 1967, WHCF: EX/JL; *New York Times*, Sept. 29, 1967; *PPP: LBJ, 1967*, II, 839–41.

57. Califano to LBJ, Aug. 29, 1967, with Christopher statement attached, WHCF: EX/JL; HHH to LBJ, Sept. 14, 1967; Larry Levinson to LBJ, Sept. 14, 1967, Legislative Background: Safe Streets and Crime Control Act.

58. *PPP: LBJ, 1967*, II, 831–36, 839–41, 990–91, 1005–7, 1116, 1177–78, 1192–93.

59. LBJ meeting with congressional leaders, Sept. 19, 1967, Diary Backup; *New York Times*, Sept. 29, 1967; Ramsey Clark OH, June 3, 1969; on the financing, see James Gaither OH, Nov. 19, 1968.

60. *New York Times*, Sept. 29, 1967; Jim Flug to Califano, Nov. 21, 1967, with attachment; Mike Manatos to LBJ, Dec. 7, 1967, Legislative Background: Safe Streets and Crime Control Act; *PPP: LBJ, 1967*, II, 1192–95.

61. FBI, "Racial Violence Potential in the U.S. This Summer," May 23, 1967, WHCF: CF: EX/HU2.

62. Doug Cater to Bill Moyers, March 31, 1967, WHCF: EX/HU2.

63. Panzer to Kintner et al., April 6, 1967; to LBJ, June 2, 1967, WHCF: EX/HU2; Albert Mark to Sherman Markman, June 5, 1967; Charles Maguire to LBJ, April 22, 1967, Diary Backup.

64. Califano, *Triumph and Tragedy*, 209–12; *Boston Globe*, July 18, 1967.

65. Califano, *Triumph and Tragedy*, 209–10; HHH to LBJ, July 17, 1967, Humphrey Papers.

66. Califano, *Triumph and Tragedy*, 210–11.

67. *PPP: LBJ, 1967*, II, 701–2; LBJ meeting with Cabinet, July 19, 1967, Cabinet Papers; LBJ meeting with Kenneth Crawford of *Newsweek*, July 19, 1967, Tom Johnson Papers; Mike Manatos to LBJ, July 20, 1967, WHCF: EX/HU2, warning against the dangers of a congressional investigation; HHH to LBJ, Aug. 12, 1967, Humphrey Papers.

68. See the Detroit Riots: Chronology, Diary Backup; Notes of the President's Activities during the Detroit Crisis, July 24, 1967, 10 p.m.–12:30 a.m., Tom Johnson Papers; Note on conversation with LBJ, July 24, 1967, Walter P. Reuther Papers; Califano, *Triumph and Tragedy*, 213–17.

69. See the Detroit Riots: Chronology, Diary Backup; Final Report of Cyrus R. Vance Concerning the Detroit Riots, July 23–Aug. 2, 1967; Notes from the President's Meeting with the congressional leadership, July 24, 1967, Tom Johnson Papers; "GOP Blames President for Racial Riots," *Washington Post*, July 25, 1967.

70. LBJ meeting with McNamara, Fortas, Christian, July 24, 1967, 10:35–11:12 a.m.; LBJ meeting with Clark, McNamara, and Others, July 24, 1967, 11:15 a.m.–12:20 p.m., Diary Backup; *PPP: LBJ, 1967*, II, 714–15; Califano, *Triumph and Tragedy*, 214–15.

71. *PPP: LBJ, 1967*, II, 715–17; Califano, *Triumph and Tragedy*, 217–18.

72. See Tom Johnson to LBJ, July 26, 1967, WHCF: EX/HU2; HHH to LBJ, July 27, 1967, Humphrey Papers; *PPP: LBJ, 1967*, II, 721–24.

73. Califano, *Triumph and Tragedy*, 219–20; Doug Cater to LBJ, July 26 and 28, 1967, WHCF: EX/HU2; LBJ meeting with Mel Elfin et al., July 28, 1967, Diary Backup; *PPP: LBJ, 1967*, II, 724–26. Also see Walter Reuther's notes on his conversations with LBJ on July 24–25, 1967, urging passage of his urban programs, Reuther Papers.

74. *New York Times*, July 29, 1967; Califano to LBJ, Aug. 24, 1967, with report attached Fred Bohen to Califano, WHCF: EX/FG690.

75. *PPP: LBJ, 1967*, II, 726; Califano to LBJ, Aug. 24, 1967, WHCF: EX/ FG690; LBJ meeting with Chuck Roberts and Mel Elfin, Aug. 24, 1967, WHCF: Aides: Christian.

76. McPherson to LBJ, July 31, 1967, WHCF: Aides: McPherson; Wirtz to LBJ, Aug. 10, 1967, WHCF: CF: EX/LA2; LBJ conversation with six commentators, Aug. 11, 1967, Diary Backup; LBJ meeting with labor leaders, Aug. 9, 1967, Tom Johnson Papers. Also see James Q. Wilson, "Letter from America," attached to Wilson to Califano, Aug. 8, 1967, and Califano to Wilson, Aug. 14, 1967, WHCF: EX/HU2. Wilson's "Letter" discussed, among other things, the growing skepticism about liberal social programs or social engineering. Johnson did not dismiss the need for job training, but he now believed that it could be done better by private industry: see Califano to LBJ, Aug. 1, Sept. 19, 1967, WHCF: EX/FG160; HHH to LBJ, Sept. 15 and 26, 1967, Humphrey Papers; Califano, *Triumph and Tragedy*, 223–26.

77. McPherson to LBJ, Aug. 14, 1967, WHCF: Aides: McPherson.

78. Wattenberg to McPherson, Aug. 19, 1967, with Cater to LBJ, Aug. 11, 1967, attached, and LBJ's approving comment written at the top, WHCF: EX/HU2; HHH to LBJ, Aug. 11 and 23, 1967; LBJ to HHH, Aug. 23, 1967, Humphrey Papers; also see *PPP: LBJ, 1967*, II, 782–83, 790–91, 809–10.

79. For LBJ's standing, see Panzer to LBJ, June 1, 1967, Diary Backup.

80. "Questions from Everett Collier re President Johnson's Attitude on Space," Feb. 8, 1964, WHCF: EX/OS; Administrative History of NASA, chap. 2, pp. 1–9; Robert A. Divine, "Lyndon B. Johnson and the Politics of Space," in Divine, ed., *Johnson Years*, II, 233–34.

81. See ibid., 234; and Administrative History of NASA, chap. 7, p. 3.

82. "U.S. Talking Down the Space Race," *New York Herald Tribune*, June 9, 1964; Charles Johnson to McG. Bundy, Feb. 4, 1964; Bundy to LBJ, Feb. 29, 1964; James Webb to LBJ, April 30, June 29, 1964; NSAM 285 and 288, NSF: NSAM; interview with John Glenn, Oct. 18, 1968, RSAC, NASA Archives.

83. James Webb to LBJ, Dec. 20, 1963, WHCF: GEN/FG260\NASA; and Webb to LBJ, Oct. 29, 1965, WHCF: EX/FG260.

84. See the weekly NASA reports to LBJ from Edward C. Welsh for 1964 in WHCF: EX/OS; and the Webb-LBJ Briefing, Oct. 14, 1968, from which the quotes are drawn, Webb Papers, NASA Archives.

85. Divine, "Lyndon B. Johnson and Space," 235; Walter Cronkite interview with LBJ, July 5, 1969, LBJ Files, NASA Archives; LBJ, *Vantage Point*, 285–86.

86. LBJ to Webb, Jan. 30, 1964; Webb to LBJ, Feb. 16, 1965; Jack Valenti to LBJ, Feb. 17, 1965, WHCF: EX/OS; Webb to LBJ, May 20, 1964; Charles S. Sheldon II to George Reedy, May 26, 1964, WHCF: Aides: Moyers.

87. Webb to Jack Valenti, March 30, 1965; Valenti to LBJ, March 30, April 1, 1965; LBJ's handwritten note is on Valenti's March 30 memo, WHCF: EX/OS.

88. LBJ, *Vantage Point*, 270–86; also see Cronkite interview with LBJ, July 5, 1969, NASA Archives.

89. Edward C. Welsh OH; Cronkite interview with LBJ, July 5, 1969, NASA Archives.

90. James Webb to LBJ, April 1, May 16, 1966, WHCF: CF: OS.

91. See "Outer Space Treaty Chronology," WHCF: Aides: Califano; WHCF: Legislative Background: Outer Space History; and Henry Owen to Walt W. Rostow, Dec. 9, 1966; "Space Goals After Lunar Landing," Oct. 1966, NSF: Subject Files.

92. See Divine, "Lyndon B. Johnson and Space," 238–40; Webb to LBJ, May 16, 1966, WHCF: CF: OS; Webb to LBJ, Aug. 26, 1966, WHCF: EX/OS.

93. Schultze to LBJ, Sept. 1 and 20, 1966, WHCF: EX/OS; Webb to LBJ, Dec. 17, 1966, WHCF: EX/FI4\FG260; Divine, "Lyndon B. Johnson and Space," 240–42.

94. *The Gallup Poll: Public Opinion, 1935–1971*, III, 1952, 2183–84, 2209; *New York Times*, Dec. 3, 1967; *Newsweek* is quoted in Administrative History of NASA, chap. 2, p. 48.

95. For congressional opinion, see the survey made by Charles Schultze in Box 23 of WHCF: EX/FI4; LBJ's budget is described in Administrative History of NASA, chap. 2, pp. 17–19.

96. Administrative History of NASA, chap. 2, pp. 47–52; Cronkite interview with LBJ, July 5, 1969; Robert Sherrod interview with Senator Clinton P. Anderson, July 25, 1968; Sherrod to John B. Oakes, May 24, 1972, RSAC; Eugene M. Emme interview with Edward C. Welsh, Feb. 20, 1969, all in NASA Archives.

97. Webb to LBJ, July 10, 1967, WHCF: CF: Agency Reports/NASA; Webb to LBJ, Aug. 10, 1967, WHCF: EX/FI4\FG200; Divine, "Lyndon B. Johnson and Space," 243–45.

98. James Webb OH; LBJ's message to Webb is in Divine, "Lyndon B. Johnson and Space," 244–45.

99. Webb to Schultze, Nov. 6, 1967, WHCF: EX/FI4\FG260.

100. *New York Times*, April 16, 1968; Divine, "Lyndon B. Johnson and Space," 238, 245.

101. James E. Webb OH; Thomas O. Paine OH, March 25, 1969; Memo on Thomas O. Paine by Robert Sherrod, Aug. 25, 1970; Sherrod interview with David Williamson, Jr., April 10, 1972, RSAC, NASA Archives.

102. Administrative History of NASA, chap. 2, pp. 34–37, 53–55; *Washington Post*, Sept. 17, 1968.

103. Donald Hornig to LBJ, Sept. 26, 1968; Edward C. Welsh to LBJ, Sept. 30, 1968, WHCF: EX/OS.

104. James Webb to LBJ, Oct. 1, 2, 5, 1968, answering Welsh; LBJ memo, n.d.; and LBJ memo to Donald Hornig, n.d., both attached to Larry E. Temple Memorandum for the Files, Oct. 10, 1968, WHCF: EX/OS.

105. Thomas O. Paine OH, March 25, 1969; Cronkite interview with LBJ, July 5, 1969, NASA Archives.

106. LBJ's awards to and praise for Webb are described in Divine, "Lyndon B. Johnson and Space," 246–47.

107. See Douglas Little, "Choosing Sides: Lyndon Johnson and the Middle East," in Divine, ed., *Johnson Years*, III, 150–71.

108. Ibid., 171–75.

109. See "U.S. Policy and Diplomacy in the Middle East Crisis, May 15–

June 10, 1967: Summary," NSF: NSC History; John P. Roche OH; *PPP: LBJ, 1967*, I, 561–63.

110. NSF: NSC Meeting, May 24, 1967; Memorandum of LBJ Conversation with Eban, May 26, 1967, Diary Backup; Arthur Goldberg OH; Dean Rusk OH, XXX, University of Georgia, Athens.

111. NSF: NSC Histories: "Mid-East Crisis: Summary" and "The President in the Middle East Crisis, May 12–June 19, 1967"; Rostow to LBJ, May 31, 1967, Diary Backup; John P. Roche OH.

112. See LBJ to Harold Wilson, June 5, 1967; Rostow to LBJ, June 5, 5: 45 p.m., NSF: Memos to the Pres.; and the entry for 6:58 p.m., June 5, 1967, in the NSF: NSC History: "Pres. in Mid-East Crisis," for LBJ's reference to himself.

113. See both NSC Histories on the Mid-East Crisis: NSF; Califano to LBJ, June 5, 1967, 5:10 p.m., Diary Backup.

114. See NSF: NSC History: "Mid-East Crisis: Summary"; and the entry for 6:55 p.m., June 5, 1967, for a complaint from Arthur Krim about military shipments to Israel, NSC History: "The Pres. in Mid-East Crisis." Also see John Roche to LBJ, June 6, 1967, NSF: Country File: Middle East; and Califano, *Triumph and Tragedy*, 204–5.

115. Ibid.; and Califano to LBJ, June 5, 1967, 5:10 p.m.; Watson, Rostow, and Califano to LBJ, all June 7, 1967, Diary Backup; Rostow to LBJ, June 7, with memo of Mrs. Krim to Rostow attached; and Katzenbach to LBJ, June 6, 1967, NSF: Country File: Middle East.

116. Levinson and Wattenberg to LBJ, June 7, 1967, Diary Backup; Califano, *Triumph and Tragedy*, 205.

117. Memorandum for the Record of Preliminary Information, June 8, 1967, 1530 EDT; "Diplomatic Activity in Connection with S.S. Liberty Incident," June 8–14, 1967; Rusk statement to Israeli Ambassador, June 10, 1967, NSF: Country File: Middle East.

118. Statement of Israeli Ambassador to Rusk, June 12, 1967; Rostow to LBJ, June 26, 1967, NSF: Country File: Middle East; Clark Clifford to Rostow, July 18, 1967, with PFIAB report attached, NSF: Memos to the Pres.

119. See Paul Warnke OH; David G. Nes OH; Richard Helms interview, May 18, 1992; NSF: NSC Special Committee Meeting, June 9, 1967; James M. Ennes, Jr., *Assault on the Liberty* (New York, 1980); Clifford, *Counsel to the President*, 445–47; A. M. Rosenthal's column of Nov. 8, 1991; and letters to the editor, Nov. 20, 1991, *New York Times*.

120. NSF: NSC Meeting, June 7, 1967; Rostow to LBJ, June 7, 1967, Files of the Special Middle East Committee; NSC Histories: Mid-East Crisis, Summary; "Pres. in Mid-East Crisis"; HHH to LBJ, June 8, 1967, Humphrey Papers; *PPP: LBJ, 1967*, I, 598–99, 602; LBJ meeting with Bob Baskin, June 14, 1967, Diary Backup; Richard Helms OH, who relates the events of June 10.

121. NSF: NSC History: "Pres. in Mid-East Crisis"; Rostow, Agenda for meeting with LBJ, June 16, 1967, NSF: Rostow Files; LBJ meeting with Bob Thompson, June 21, 1967, WHCF: Aides: Christian; TASS News Release, June 21, 1967; Rusk to LBJ, June 22, 1967; McG. Bundy to LBJ, June 22, 1967, NSF: Memos to the Pres; LBJ meeting with Rusk et al., July 12 and 18, 1967; LBJ meeting with Special Committee on Mid-East, July 14, 1967; LBJ meeting with Cabinet, July 19, 1967, Tom Johnson Papers; NSF: NSC Meetings, Sept. 13,

Oct. 26, 1967. Also see Henry Kissinger, *White House Years* (New York, 1979), 343–47.

122. See Rostow to LBJ, Feb. 18, 1967; Aleksei Kosygin to LBJ, Feb. 28, 1967; LBJ to Kosygin, May 19, June 4, 1967, NSF: Rostow File; Francis Bator to LBJ, March 9, 1967, Diary Backup; LBJ meeting with Stu Loory, May 1, 1967, WHCF: Aides: Christian; Dean Rusk OH, March 8, 1970; *PPP: LBJ, 1967,* I, 356, 545–46, 1097; Glenn T. Seaborg and Benjamin S. Loeb, *Stemming the Tide: Arms Control in the Johnson Years* (Lexington, Mass., 1987).

123. See Adam B. Ulam, *Expansion and Coexistence: The History of Soviet Foreign Policy, 1917–1967* (New York, 1968), 747–49; Rostow to LBJ, Feb. 18, 1967, describing Ambassador Llewellyn Thompson's conversation with Kosygin, NSF: Memos to the Pres.; Notes on telephone call from Aiken, June 21, 1967; LBJ Meeting with Bob Thompson, June 21, 1967, Diary Backup.

124. Brzezinski Memo, June 16, 1967, NSF: Country File: USSR; Fulbright to LBJ, June 17 and 19, 1967, Fulbright Papers; Tom Johnson to LBJ, June 20, 1967, Diary Backup.

125. LBJ Lunch with Bureau Chiefs, June 19, 1967; LBJ meeting with Bob Thompson, June 21, 1967, Diary Backup.

126. Thompson messages, June 21 and 22, 1967; Rostow to LBJ, June 21, 1967, 6:15 p.m., June 22, 1967, 8:10 p.m.; Mac Bundy to LBJ, June 22, 1967; Rusk to LBJ, June 22, 1967, NSF: Memos to the Pres.

127. LBJ, *Vantage Point*, 481–82.

128. Rostow to LBJ, June 23, 1967, 7:05 a.m.; Sherwin Markman to Marvin Watson, June 23, 1967, Diary Backup; *New York Times*, June 24, 1967; David C. Humphrey, "Searching for LBJ at the Johnson Library," *SHAFR Newsletter*, June 20, 1989, p. 11.

129. *New York Times*, June 24, 1967.

130. See Debriefing by the President, June 23, 1967, NSF: Rostow File; Talking Points for Leadership Meeting, June 26, 1967, NSF: Country File: USSR; *New York Times*, June 24, 1967; Ulam, *Expansion and Coexistence*, 749.

131. Debriefing of the President, June 23, 1967, NSF: Rostow File; Memo of conversation, LBJ and Kosygin, June 23, 1967, 11:15 a.m.–1:30 p.m., NSF: Country: USSR: Glassboro.

132. LBJ and Kosygin Lunch, June 23, 1967, 1:30–3:00 p.m., NSF: Country: USSR: Glassboro; Seaborg and Loeb, *Stemming the Tide*; Tom Wicker, "The Great Turnabout," *New York Times*, Nov. 11, 1985; Robert A. Divine, "Lyndon Johnson and Strategic Arms Limitation," in Divine, ed., *Johnson Years*, III, 245–46, 254.

133. Talking Points for Leadership Meeting, June 26, 1967, NSF: Country: USSR; pool report of talk with LBJ, June 23, 1967, Diary Backup; Memo of LBJ and Kosygin conversation, June 23, 1967, 3:15 p.m.–4:30 p.m., NSF: Country: USSR: Glassboro.

134. Memos of LBJ-Kosygin conversations, June 25, 1967, 1:30–2:45 p.m., and 1:30–6:30 p.m.. NSF: Country: USSR: Glassboro; *New York Times*, June 26, 1967.

135. HHH to LBJ, July 31, 1967, with memo of Eaton-Kosygin conversation on June 30 attached; HHH to LBJ, Sept. 6, 1967, with Eaton to HHH, Aug. 21, 1967, attached, Humphrey Papers.

136. LBJ interview with Nicholas Carroll, Oct. 5, 1967, Diary Backup; LBJ,

Vantage Point, 484–86; Rostow to LBJ, Aug. 2 and 28, 1967, NSF: Country: USSR; Wicker, "The Great Turnabout"; Seaborg and Loeb, *Stemming the Tide*.

137. Califano, *Triumph and Tragedy*, 208.

138. *New York Times*, June 14, 1967; Juan Williams, "One Man vs. Racial Injustice," *Los Angeles Times*, Jan. 14, 1990; Lucy D. Suddreth, "Thurgood Marshall," *LC Information Bulletin*, Feb. 22, 1993, pp. 75–80.

139. Ibid.; Schlesinger, *Robert Kennedy*, 307–8.

140. Thurgood Marshall OH; *Washington Post*, July 14, 1965; *New York Times*, July 14, 1965; Lady Bird Johnson, *White House Diary*, 294; Louis Martin OH.

141. See the Marshall and Martin oral histories.

142. Ibid.; Larry Temple interview, March 29, 1989.

143. LBJ interview with Wallace Terry, June 15, 1967, WHCF: Aides: Christian.

144. *New York Times*, July 14, 1967; Williams, *Los Angeles Times*, Jan. 14, 1990; Russell Robo letter, June 27, 1967, Richard Russell Papers; Califano, *Triumph and Tragedy*, 208–9; telegrams, June 14–16, 1967, WHCF: EX/FG535\A.

CHAPTER 9: STALEMATE

1. Pearson Diary Notes, Feb. 7, 1966, Pearson Papers.

2. LBJ meeting with Mansfield, Dirksen, Jan. 17, 1967, Diary Backup; Freeman to LBJ, Feb. 1, 1967, WHCF: CF: ND19/CO312; NSF: Congressional Briefings on Vietnam, Feb. 15, 1967.

3. LBJ meeting with senators, Jan. 9, 1967, Diary Backup; Palmer, *25-Year War*, 47–48.

4. See Connally comments in David Grubin's TV documentary "LBJ"; LBJ-Katzenbach, Jan. 25, 1967, TT; Bromley Smith to Rostow, Feb. 8, 1967, NSF: Country: Vietnam; Fred L. Israel to Lewis L. Gould, Jan. 15, 1993.

5. Gibbons, *U.S. Government and Vietnam*, IV, 492 n. 28.

6. See "Some U.S. Efforts to Achieve Peace in Vietnam," 1961–1968; "Chronology" for 1966; and "Bombing Pauses," 1965–67, NSF: Country: Vietnam; George C. Herring, *The Secret Diplomacy of the Vietnam War: The "Negotiating Volumes" of the Pentagon Papers* (Austin, Tex., 1983), 233.

7. Rostow to LBJ, Jan. 3, 1967, NSF: Rostow Files.

8. LBJ to Mansfield, Jan. 9, 1967, with Mansfield to LBJ, Jan. 6, 1967, attached, WHCF: EX/ND19/CO312; Gibbons, *U.S. Government and Vietnam*, IV, 500–504.

9. Ibid., 504–6; LBJ meeting with Mansfield, Dirksen, et al., Jan. 17, 1967, Diary Backup.

10. Gibbons, *U.S. Government and Vietnam*, IV, 506–7; Rostow to LBJ, Jan. 27, 1967, NSF: Rostow Files; Lodge to State Dept., Feb. 1, 1967; Rostow to LBJ, Feb. 4, 1967, NSF: Country: Vietnam; Kintner to Roberts, Cabinet Meeting Notes, Feb. 1, 1967, Diary Backup.

11. *PPP: LBJ, 1967*, I, 133; see Rostow's summary of the exchanges on "Project Sunflower," Feb. 13, 1967, Diary Backup.

12. Gibbons, *U.S. Government and Vietnam*, IV, 511–20.

13. NSC Meeting, Feb. 8, 1967.

14. See Schlesinger, *Robert Kennedy*, 767–69; and Jeff Shesol, *Mutual Contempt*. For information encouraging LBJ's positive view of the fighting, see Schlesinger, *Robert Kennedy*, 767, but also a CIA cable, Feb. 7, 1967, on the military situation in Vietnam, NSF: Country: Vietnam.

15. LBJ lunch meeting, March 7, 1967, NSF: Rostow Files.

16. Pearson to LBJ, Dec. 5 and 23, 1966, Pearson Papers.

17. Phil G. Goulding, *Confirm or Deny: Informing the People on National Security* (New York 1970), 54; "The Man with the Whaam," *The Economist*, Jan. 7, 1967; McPherson to LBJ, Jan. 3, 1967, WHCF: Aides: McPherson; Ben Wattenberg to LBJ, two memos of Jan. 6, 1967, WHCF: Aides: Wattenberg.

18. "For CBS News," polling data dated December 1966, WHCF: Aides: McPherson; "What the People Say," Dec. 1966, attached to Califano to LBJ, Jan. 20, 1967, WHCF: EX/PR16.

19. *PPP: LBJ, 1967*, I, 2, 11-14.

20. Kintner to LBJ, Jan. 12 and 18, 1967; Tom Johnson to Staff, Jan. 13, 1967, WHCF: EX/PR18.

21. John Gonella to LBJ, Jan. 19 and 23, 1967, WHCF: EX/ND19/CO312.

22. Gallup Report, March 10, 1968, which includes the data for Feb. 1967; Panzer to LBJ, Feb. 17, March 11 and 13, 1967; HHH to LBJ, Feb. 10, 1967; Panzer to Kintner, March 13, 1967, WHCF: EX/PR16; Harris Survey, *Washington Post*, March 13, 1967.

23. Gibbons, *U.S. Government and Vietnam*, IV, 547–51, also see 579–603.

24. Ibid., 593–94; Schlesinger, *Robert Kennedy*, 769–74.

25. Gibbons, *U.S. Government and Vietnam*, IV, 553–55; Robert S. McNamara, *In Retrospect: The Tragedy and Lessons of Vietnam* (New York, 1995), 252–59.

26. "President Called Target of Smears," *New York Times*, April 30, 1967; and see the thousands of pages in the LBJ Main Files, FBI, for the period October 1966 to June 1967, and in particular memos of Jan. 9 and March 14, 1967.

27. Harris Survey, *Washington Post*, March 13, 1967; Gibbons, *U.S. Government and Vietnam*, IV, 555–56; McNamara, *In Retrospect*, 252–53.

28. LBJ, Congressional Briefing, Feb. 15, 1967; cf. Feb. 23, 1967, NSF: Congressional Briefings on Vietnam.

29. LBJ meeting with William McAndrew, Feb. 27, 1967; LBJ meeting with Smith, March 31, 1967, Diary Backup; Scherer to George Christian, March 25, 1967, WHCF: EX/ND19\CO312; Pearson Diary, March 13, 1967, Pearson Papers; *PPP: LBJ, 1967*, I, 348–54.

30. Pearson to LBJ, May 11, 1967, Pearson Papers; Kintner to LBJ, Feb. 17, 1967, NSF: Name: Kintner; *PPP: LBJ, 1967*, I, 259–69; Schlesinger, *Robert Kennedy*, 771–72; Russell Diary entry, March 2, 1967, Richard Russell Papers; Rusk Statement, March 2, 1967, NSF: Rostow Files; Gen. Earle Wheeler to Westmoreland, March 2, 1967, Declassified and Desanitized Docs. from Unprocessed Files: Vietnam (hereafter cited as DSDUF).

31. Schlesinger, *Robert Kennedy*, 774; UPI-49, March 7, 1967; Rostow to LBJ, March 3, 1967; Watson to LBJ, March 7, 1967; McNamara to LBJ, March 9, 1967; Rusk to LBJ, March 10, 1967, NSF: Rostow Files; Pearson Diary,

March 13, 1967, Pearson Papers; Lloyd Hackler to Jim Jones, March 15, 1967, Diary Backup.

32. Gibbons, *U.S. Government and Vietnam*, IV, 491–93.

33. Ibid., 525–26.

34. Rostow to LBJ, Jan. 20, 1967, NSF: Country: Vietnam; Komer to LBJ, Jan. 23, 1967, NSF: Komer File.

35. Lodge to LBJ, Jan. 25, 1967, NSF: Memos to the Pres.

36. Komer to LBJ, Jan. 27, 1967, NSF: Country: Vietnam.

37. Roche to LBJ, Jan. 30, 1967; Komer to LBJ, Feb. 1, 1967, NSF: Komer File; Lodge cable, Feb. 1, 1967; CIA cable, Feb. 7, 1967; Komer to LBJ, Feb. 3 and 11, 1967, NSF: Country: Vietnam.

38. Rostow to LBJ, Feb. 18, 1967, NSF: Country: Vietnam; Feb. 21, March 8, 1967, NSF: Memos to the Pres.; Komer to LBJ, March 3 and 6, 1967, NSF: Komer Files; LBJ, Congressional Briefing, Feb. 23, 1967, NSF: Congressional Briefings; *PPP: LBJ, 1967*, I, 267–69; LBJ meeting with William R. McAndrew, Feb. 27, 1967, Diary Backup.

39. Wheeler to Westmoreland, March 9 and 11, 1967; Westmoreland to Wheeler, March 14, 1967, DSDUF: Vietnam.

40. Roche to Rostow, with Rostow's handwritten reply, March 16, 1967, NSF: Roche File; Westmoreland to Wheeler, March 14, 1967, DSDUF: Vietnam.

41. OASD/ISA, March 17, 1967; CIA Memo, March 9, 1967; CIA Memo, Morell to Smith, March 27, 1967, NSF: Country: Vietnam.

42. Rostow to LBJ, March 24, 1967, NSF: Memos to the Pres.; McNamara, *In Retrospect*, 237–42.

43. LBJ meeting with McNamara, Wheeler, et al., Feb. 17, 1967, NSF: Rostow Files. For more on McNamara's doubts and advice to LBJ, see Rostow to LBJ, March 10, 1967, ibid. Also see Rostow to LBJ, March 22, 1967, NSF: Memos to the Pres. And see Gibbons, *U.S. Government and Vietnam*, IV, 609, who says that in early 1967, "it would appear that he [Johnson] knew the war was not going well and that it could be 'won' only by a political settlement."

44. Gibbons, *U.S. Government and Vietnam*, IV, 557–72; LBJ meeting with Rusk et al., March 7, 1967, NSF: Rostow Files.

45. See Rostow to LBJ, March 8, 1967; Memos of March 20 and 21 on the conference discussions, NSF: International Meetings and Travel File; Rostow to LBJ, March 17, 1967, Diary Backup; and Gibbons, *U.S. Government and Vietnam*, IV, 609–612.

46. LBJ, congressional briefings, Feb. 15 and 23, 1967, NSF: Congressional Briefings on Vietnam.

47. Jacobsen to Kintner, April 1, 1967, WHCF: EX/PR16; McNamara to LBJ, June 8, 1967, WHCF: CF: FI4.

48. Panzer to LBJ, two memos of April 7, summarizing Gallup and Harris polls, and one of June 1, 1967, WHCF: Aides: Panzer; and Panzer to LBJ, May 13 and June 16, 1967, WHCF: EX/PR16. *Gallup Poll*, III, 2052, 2063. Peace Action Council press release, May 13, 1967, Diary Backup.

49. Maxwell Taylor to LBJ, May 11, 1967; Rostow to LBJ, May 15, 1967, NSF: Memos to the Pres.

50. See CIA reports, May 23, 1967, NSF: Country: Vietnam; May 25, 1967, NSF: Rostow Files; June 21, 1967, NSF: Memos to the Pres.; Gibbons, *U.S. Government. and Vietnam*, IV, 653–55.

51. Ibid., 640–41, 705–6.

52. Pell Memorandum of conversation with Bo, June 19, 1967; Rostow to LBJ, June 20, 1967, NSF: Memos to the Pres.; Manatos to LBJ, June 20, 1967, WHCF: EX/ND19\CO312; Gibbons, *U.S. Government and Vietnam*, IV, 687–92, 722–24.

53. Ibid., 646–48. Also see McNamara to LBJ, May 20, 1967, NSF: Rostow Files.

54. CIA Report, April 3, 1967, NSF: Country: USSR; CIA Report, April 3, 1967; Rostow to LBJ, April 3, 1967, NSF: Memos to the Pres.

55. Rostow to LBJ, April 5, 17, 19, 1967, NSF: Memos to the Pres.; Komer to LBJ, April 19, 1967, NSF: Komer File.

56. Komer to George Christian, April 26, 1967, NSF: Komer Files; Sen. Ralph Yarborough to Staff, April 28, 1967, describing a Westmoreland briefing at the White House, Yarborough Papers; Rostow to LBJ, April 28, 1967, NSF: Memos to the Pres.

57. See Watson to LBJ, April 21, 1967, with Komer to LBJ, April 28, 1967, attached, Dairy Backup.

58. Rostow to LBJ, May 9 and 13, 1967; Maxwell Taylor to LBJ, May 11, 1967, NSF: Memos to the Pres.; McNamara to LBJ, May 20, 1967, NSF: Rostow Files; Memo of LBJ conversation, May 13, 1967, Diary Backup.

59. Rostow to LBJ, attaching Bunker's dispatch, May 30, 1967, NSF: Country: Vietnam.

60. Comparative Military Casualties, June 2 and 17, 1967, NSF: Country: Vietnam; Rostow to LBJ, June 1, 1967; Text of Cable from CINCPAC, June 22, 1967, NSF: Memos to the Pres.

61. Rostow to LBJ, June 28, 1967, NSF: Memos to the Pres.; LBJ to Byrd, Jr., June 29, 1967, WHCF: EX/ND19\CO312.

62. Dispatch of April 19, 1967, NSF: Country: USSR; Komer to LBJ, April 21, 1967, NSF: Country: Vietnam; Sidey interview with LBJ, May 16, 1967, Diary Backup.

63. Tom Wells, *The War Within: America's Battle Over Vietnam* (New York, 1996 ed.), 115–35.

64. Roche to LBJ, April 5, 1967, WHCF: CF: HU2.

65. Loory meeting with LBJ, May 1, 1967; Hugh Sidey meeting with LBJ, May 16, 1967, Diary Backup; Kintner to LBJ, May 8, 1967, WHCF: EX/PR18; Watson to LBJ, May 16, 1967, WHCF: CF: EX/HU4. For examples of the reports reaching LBJ, see Memorandum for the Record, n.d. [probably May 1967], WHCF: Aides: Watson; and Thomas L. Johns, U.S. Secret Service, to Watson, June 19, 1967, Diary Backup.

66. Kintner to Clark, May 19, 1967, WHCF: CF: EX/HU4.

67. Moyers to LBJ, May 1, 1967, WHCF: Aides: McPherson.

68. Rowe to McPherson, May 17, 1967, with Rowe to LBJ, May 17, 19567, attached, WHCF: CF: EX/ND19\CO312.

69. See Notes on LBJ's meeting with reporters, April 5, 1967; Bob Fleming, for Diary, n.d.; LBJ meeting with Kansas City Star journalists, May 3, 1967; Diary Memorandum, May 22, 1967, Diary Backup; Komer to Christian, April 8, 1967, NSF: Komer Files; Watson to LBJ, May 1, 1967, with Komer to LBJ, May 1, 1967, attached, Diary Backup. For the Rusk meeting and Roche proposal, see Ropa to Hawks, March 1, 1967; and Roche to LBJ, May 26, 1967, WHCF:

CF: EX/ND19\CO312; for Westmoreland's tour, Rostow to LBJ, April 21, 1967, NSF: Country: Vietnam. Also see Wells, *War Within*, 143–50.

70. HHH to LBJ, April 12, 1967, with poll attached, Humphrey Papers; Panzer to LBJ, May 5, 8, June 29, 1967, WHCF: Aides: Panzer; Panzer to LBJ, May 12, 1967, WHCF: EX/PR16.

71. LBJ interview with Hugh Sidey, May 16, 1967, Diary Backup.

72. See Gibbons, *U.S. Government and Vietnam*, IV, chap. 15.

73. Gen. Wheeler to Adm. Sharp, May 26, 1967, DSDUF. Also see Rostow to LBJ, June 15, 1967, who leaned toward the JCS recommendations, NSF: Memos to the Pres.

74. See the notes typed on LBJ's Daily Dairy for May 12, 1967.

75. McNamara, *In Retrospect*, 283.

76. Ibid.; HHH to LBJ, July 6, 1967, Humphrey Papers; Rostow to LBJ, July 7 and 8, 1967, the second memo summarizes Helms's report, NSF: Memos to the Pres.

77. Memo of LBJ meeting with Rusk, McNamara, et al., July 12, 1967, Tom Johnson Papers.

78. See Notes of LBJ meeting with Rusk et al., July 12, 2:45 p.m., Tom Johnson Papers; *PPP: LBJ, 1967*, II, 690–96; meeting between LBJ and Scali, July 12, 1967, Diary Backup.

79. Marks to LBJ, July 13, 1967, NSF: Memos to the Pres.

80. LBJ meeting with McNamara et al., July 13, 1967, Tom Johnson Papers.

81. Ibid.; *PPP: LBJ, 1967*, II, 690–96; LBJ meeting with Clifford and Taylor, July 14, 1967, Tom Johnson Papers; Gibbons, *U.S. Government and Vietnam*, IV, 731–35.

82. LBJ meeting with Rusk et al., Aug. 5, 1967, Tom Johnson Papers; Clifford-Taylor report, Aug. 5, 1967, NSF: Country: Vietnam; Clifford, *Counsel to the President*, 449–51; Gibbons, *U.S. Government and Vietnam*, IV, 736–38.

83. McPherson to Christian, July 18, 1967, WHCF: EX/PR18; Notes of Cabinet meeting, July 19, 1967, Tom Johnson Papers.

84. LBJ meeting with senators, July 25, 1967, Tom Johnson Papers; Rostow to LBJ, Aug. 1, 1967, DSDUF.

85. Panzer to LBJ, July 28, 1967, WHCF: Aides: Panzer; Westmoreland to Wheeler, Aug. 2, 1967, NSF: Memos to the Pres.

86. *New York Times*, Aug. 7, 1967.

87. Murray Fromson, summary of remembrances from August 1967, which he shared with me; LBJ meeting with Bureau Chiefs, n.d. [clearly August], Tom Johnson Papers. R. W. Apple interview, June 18, 1997.

88. LBJ meeting with Lisagor, Aug. 4, 1967, Tom Johnson Papers.

89. Rostow to LBJ, July 17, 1967, NSF: Memos to the Pres.; LBJ meeting with the Cabinet, July 19, 1967, Tom Johnson Papers; Gibbons, *U.S. Government and Vietnam*, IV, 728, 731–32.

90. Rostow to LBJ, July 15, 1967, NSF: Memos to the Pres.; LBJ meeting with Rusk et al., July 18, 1967; meeting with senators, July 25, 1967, Tom Johnson Papers; Gibbons, *U.S. Government and Vietnam*, IV, 735–36.

91. Rostow to LBJ, Aug. 7, 1967, NSF: Memos to the Pres.; LBJ meeting with Clifford and Taylor, Aug. 5, 1967, Tom Johnson Papers.

92. Clark Clifford Notes, n.d., but clearly the notes related to Clifford's trip to Asia in July 1967, Clifford Papers; Gibbons, *U.S. Government and Vietnam*, IV, 738–40.

93. LBJ meeting with McNamara et al., Aug. 8, 1967, Tom Johnson Papers; LBJ meeting with six commentators, Aug. 11, 1967, Diary Backup; LBJ meeting with Bob Lucas, Aug. 14, 1967, WHCF: Aides: Christian.

94. LBJ meeting with Rusk et al., Aug. 16, 1967, Tom Johnson Papers.

95. Gibbons, *U.S. Government and Vietnam*, IV, 750–52; McNamara doubts that the Chiefs ever considered resigning: *In Retrospect*, 284–91.

96. Richard Helms to LBJ, Aug. 29, 1967, NSF: Memos to the Pres.; McNamara, *In Retrospect*, 291–95.

97. LBJ, *Vantage Point*, 263–65; Herring, *LBJ and Vietnam*, 115.

98. Gibbons, *U.S. Government and Vietnam*, IV, 773–74.

99. Minutes of Meeting, Sept. 6, 1967, Cabinet Meetings; Christian to Dick Berlin, Sept. 13, 1967, WHCF: EX/PR18; LBJ meeting with Rusk, McNamara, et al., Sept. 5, 1967, NSF: Meeting Notes; for Ambassador from Sec., Sept. ?, 1967, NSF: Memos to the Pres.; telephone conversation. W. W. Rostow and Ben Read, Sept. 5, 1967, NSF: Rostow Files.

100. Panzer to LBJ, Aug. 25, Sept. 1, 1967, WHCF: EX/PR6.

101. For background on this initiative called "Pennsylvania," see Rostow to LBJ, Sept. 9, 1967, NSF: Rostow Files; Gibbons, *U.S. Government and Vietnam*, IV, 776–78. LBJ meeting with McNamara et al., Aug. 8, 1967, Tom Johnson Papers; Rostow to LBJ, NSF: Memos to the Pres.

102. Memorandum for Dr. Kissinger, n.d. [Aug. 11, 1967], NSF: Memos to the Pres.; LBJ meeting with Rusk, McNamara, Wheeler, and Rostow, Aug. 18, 1967, NSF: Meeting Notes File; Cooper, *Lost Crusade*, 379.

103. LBJ meeting with Eric Sevareid et al., Sept. 5, 1967; also see LBJ meeting with publishers and election observers, Sept. 6, 1967, NSF: Meeting Notes File. Message from Kissinger, Sept. 11, 1967, NSF: Country: Vietnam.

104. LBJ meeting with Rusk, McNamara, et al., Sept. 12, 1967, NSF: Meeting Notes File.

105. See four State Dept. cables to Kissinger, Sept. 13, 1967, NSF: Rostow Files; LBJ meeting with AFL-CIO Executive Council, Sept. 15, 1967, NSF: Meeting Notes File.

106. LBJ meeting with Australian Broadcast Group, Sept. 20, 1967, Diary Backup.

107. LBJ meetings with McNamara et al. and educators, Sept. 26, 1967, Tom Johnson Papers.

108. *PPP: LBJ, 1967*, II, 876–81.

109. LBJ meeting with Col. Robin Olds, Oct. 2, 1967, Tom Johnson Papers; Clifford Notes on meeting with LBJ, Oct. 2, 1967, Clifford Papers.

110. LBJ meeting with McNamara et al., Oct. 3, 1967, Tom Johnson Papers.

111. LBJ meeting with McNamara et al., Oct. 4, 1967, Tom Johnson Papers.

112. McNamara to LBJ, Oct. 4, 1967, CF: EX/ND19\CO312; "Pennsylvania," Oct. 5, 7, 8, 1967, NSF: Rostow Files; LBJ meeting with McNamara, Rusk, Rostow, Oct. 5, 1967; Rusk et al., Oct. 16, 1967, Tom Johnson Papers; Rostow to LBJ, Oct. 6, 7, 9, 1967, NSF: Memos to the Pres.

113. LBJ meeting with Rusk et al., Oct. 16, 1967, Tom Johnson Papers.

114. LBJ meeting with McNamara et al., Oct. 17, 1967, Tom Johnson Papers; Rostow to LBJ, Oct. 18, 1967, NSF: Rostow Files.

115. See Rostow to LBJ, Oct. 19, 1967, with two CIA reports of Oct. 18, 1967, attached; also Rostow to LBJ, Oct. 20, 1967, NSF: Memos to the Pres.

116. LBJ meeting with Rusk et al., Oct. 18, 1967, Tom Johnson Papers; Rostow to LBJ, Oct. 20, 1967, NSF: Memos to the Pres.

117. LBJ meeting with members of Congress, Oct. 23, 1967, Tom Johnson Papers. Also see Rostow to LBJ, Oct. 27, 1967, with "Pennsylvania Channel" attached, NSF: Memos to the Pres.

118. Rostow to LBJ, Oct. 28, 1967, NSF: Memos to the Pres.

119. LBJ meeting with Rusk, McNamara, and Wheeler, Oct. 23, 1967, Tom Johnson Papers.

120. For growing congressional opposition, see Gibbons, *U.S. Government and Vietnam*, IV, chap. 19; LBJ meeting with McNamara, et al., Oct. 3, 1967, Tom Johnson Papers.

121. Tip O'Neill, *Man of the House: The Life and Political Memoirs of Speaker Tip O'Neill* (New York, 1987), 189–99.

122. Panzer to LBJ, Oct. 3, 1967; Gallup Report, Oct. 7, 1967, WHCF: Aides: Panzer; Gibbons, *U.S. Government and Vietnam*, IV, 841.

123. Panzer to LBJ, Oct. 20, 1967; Gallup Report, Oct. 25, 1967, WHCF: EX/PR16.

124. LBJ meeting with Manning, Oct. 19, 1967, Diary Backup.

125. See Books Two and Three of the U.S. Senate Select Committee to Study Governmental Operations with Respect to Intelligence Activities and the Rights of Americans, April 1976. Also see the excellent summary of government spying in Gibbons, *U.S. Government and Vietnam*, IV, 853–59.

126. LBJ meeting with McNamara et al., Sept. 20, 1967, Tom Johnson Papers.

127. Matt Nimetz to Califano, Oct. 2, 1967, WHCF: Aides: Nimetz; LBJ meeting with McNamara et al., Oct. 3, 1967, Tom Johnson Papers; LBJ memo for Ramsey Clark, Oct. 3, 1967, Diary Backup.

128. Cabinet meeting, Oct. 4, 1967, Cabinet Meeting Papers.

129. Califano to LBJ, Oct. 10, 16, 19, 1967, WHCF: Aides: Nimitz. Also Cabinet meeting, Oct. 19, 1967, Cabinet Meeting Papers.

130. See Califano to LBJ, Oct. 21 and 22, 1967, WHCF: Aides: Califano; Califano, *Triumph and Tragedy*, 198–200; Melvin Small, *Johnson, Nixon and the Doves* (New Brunswick, N.J., 1989), 116–18.

131. Califano to LBJ, Oct. 26, 1967, WHCF: CF: EX/HU4; Califano, *Triumph and Tragedy*, 200; LBJ meeting with Democratic leaders, Oct. 31, 1967, Diary Backup.

132. LBJ meeting with Rusk et al., Nov. 4, 1967, NSF: Meeting Notes File.

133. Helms to LBJ, Nov. 15, 1967, NSF: Intelligence File.

134. Powers, *Man Who Kept the Secrets*, 246.

135. Rostow to LBJ, Oct. 23, Nov. 17, 1967, with Marks's report attached, NSF: Country: Vietnam; LBJ to Watson, Nov. 3, 1967, with Weisl's letter of Nov. 1 attached, Handwriting File; Califano to LBJ, Nov. 15, 1967, WHCF: EX/HU4; Rostow to LBJ, Dec. 13, 1967, WHCF: EX/ND19\CO312.

136. See Gerald R. Ford News Release, Nov. 22, 1967, in WHCF: Aides: Nimitz.

137. LBJ meeting with Educators, Sept. 26, 1967, Tom Johnson Papers.

138. LBJ meeting with McNamara, et al., Oct. 4, 1967, Tom Johnson Papers; Cabinet Meeting, Oct. 4, 1967, Cabinet Meeting Papers; LBJ meeting with Rusk, et al., Nov. 4, 1967, NSF: Meeting Notes File.

139. *PPP: LBJ, 1967*, II, 975; LBJ meeting with Nicholas Carroll, Oct. 5, 1967; LBJ meeting with Mr. and Mrs. Jack Zaiman, Oct. 6, 1967, Diary Backup; Rostow to LBJ, Oct. 25, 1967, NSF: Country: Vietnam. The Goldberg quote is in Daniel M. Giat to author, June 10, 1997.

140. LBJ meeting with House members, Nov. 2, 1967, NSF: Congressional Briefings on Vietnam.

141. Congressional Briefing, Nov. 16, 1967, NSF: Congressional Briefings on Vietnam.

142. LBJ to Rostow, Nov. 1, 1967, Handwriting File; Rostow to LBJ, Nov. 3, 1967; and Max Taylor to LBJ, Nov. 17, 1967, NSF: Memos to the Pres.; Abe Fortas, Comments, Nov. 5, 1967; Rostow to LBJ, Nov. 8, 1967, NSF: Rostow Files; LBJ meeting with Walter Judd, Oct. 16, 1967; Rostow to LBJ, Oct. 7 and 20, 1967, NSF: Country: Vietnam; John P. Roche to LBJ, Oct. 7, 1967; Nov. 13, 1967, and subsequent memo of June 5, 1968; W. J. Driver to Watson, Oct. 20 and 27, 1967, WHCF: CF: EX/ND19\CO312; Memos on the Legion, Oct. 12, Nov. 15, 1967, WHCF: Name: DeLoach; HHH to LBJ, Dec. 6, 1967, Humphrey Papers.

143. McPherson to LBJ, Oct. 27, 1967, WHCF: Aides: McPherson.

144. Rostow to McNamara et al., Oct. 25, 1967, NSF: Country: Vietnam.

145. Gibbons, *U.S. Government and Vietnam*, IV, 842.

146. *New York Times*, Dec. 31, 1968.

147. David Halberstam, "Return to Vietnam," *Harper's*, Dec. 1967.

CHAPTER 10: LAST HURRAHS

1. Memo, Oct. 11, 1967, NSF: Rostow Files.

2. Rostow to LBJ, Oct. 26, 1967, NSF: Memos to the Pres.; McNamara to LBJ, Nov. 1, 1967, NSF: Meeting Notes File; Shapley, *Promise and Power*, 436.

3. McNamara, *In Retrospect*, 307–9.

4. Ibid., 311, 313; Shapley, *Promise and Power*, 443–44.

5. Kearns, *LBJ*, 320–21; Clifford, *Counsel to the President*, 456–59; McNamara, *In Retrospect*, 312–13; Califano, *Triumph and Tragedy*, 249, 264; John P. Roche OH, July 16, 1970; Chalmers M. Roberts, *First Rough Draft: A Journalist's Journal of Our Times* (New York, 1973), 264.

6. See Rostow to LBJ, Nov. 2, 20, 21, 1967; Clifford, Memorandum, n.d.; Max Taylor to LBJ, Nov. 3, 1967; Fortas to LBJ, Nov. 5, 1967; Katzenbach to LBJ, Nov. 16, 1967; Rusk to LBJ, Nov. 20, 1967, NSF: Rostow Files; C. Douglas Dillon OH, June 29, 1969; Rostow to LBJ, Sept. 18 and 27, 1967, NSF: Memos to the Pres. Cf. Jim Jones to LBJ, Nov. 2, 1967, NSF: Meeting Notes; Ball, *Past Has Another Pattern*, 407. Also see James A. Bill, *George Ball: Behind the Scenes in U.S. Foreign Policy* (New Haven, Conn., 1997).

7. Edgar Berman, *Hubert* (New York, 1979), 115; Humphrey, *Educa-*

tion of a Public Man, 348–49; Gibbons, *U.S. Government and Vietnam*, IV, 894–95; conversation with Ted Van Dyke, March 14, 1996, who described the contents of the note; NSF: NSC Meeting, Nov. 8, 1967.

8. Memorandum of President for the File, Dec. 18, 1967, NSF: Rostow Files.

9. Meeting Notes File, Nov. 4, 1967; Rostow to LBJ, Nov. 6, 1967, NSF: Memos to the Pres.; Wheeler to Westmoreland, Nov. 8, 1967, DSDUF.

10. Meeting Notes, Nov. 15, 1967, Tom Johnson Papers.

11. Agenda, Meeting with the Pres., Nov. 21, 1967, NSF: Rostow Files; Meeting Notes, Nov. 21, 1967, Tom Johnson Papers.

12. Rostow to LBJ, Dec. 12, 1967, NSF: Country: Vietnam.

13. Gibbons, *U.S. Government and Vietnam*, IV, 896–97, 931–32.

14. Rostow to LBJ, Nov. 16, 1967, NSF: Memos to the Pres.; Larry LeSueur to Marvin Watson, Dec. 1, 1967, WHCF: EX/PR18.

15. Meeting Notes, Nov. 21, 1967, Tom Johnson Papers.

16. "U.S. Said to Press Sharply for Good Vietnam Reports," *New York Times*, Dec. 31, 1967.

17. Gibbons, *U.S. Government and Vietnam*, IV, 900–902; Panzer to LBJ, Dec. 28, 1967, Jan. 4, 1968, WHCF: CF: EX/PR16.

18. Brinkley recounted this anecdote on "Larry King Live," Dec. 2, 1996. LBJ's comment is a repetition of what he said to others, including Henry Cabot Lodge in November 1963. But see Panzer to Marvin Watson, March 19, 1968, for a White House effort to deny Johnson's authorship of the comment. WHCF: Aides: Panzer.

19. *PPP: LBJ, 1967*, II, 1179–86. Also see LBJ meeting with Australian Cabinet, Dec. 21, 1967, NSF: Meeting Notes File.

20. *PPP: LBJ, 1967*, II, 1180–81; John Roche to LBJ, Dec. 20, 1967, WHCF: CF: EX/PR18; WHCF: Transcript of LBJ interview with CBS, Dec. 19, 1968.

21. Meeting of the Pope and the President, Dec. 23, 1967, NSF: Meeting Notes File.

22. Rostow to LBJ, Dec. 29, 1967; LBJ to Sorensen, Jan. 2, 1968, WHCF: EX/ND19\CO312.

23. Rostow to Rusk and McNamara, Jan. 6, 1968, NSF: Rostow Files.

24. LBJ to Sen. Thomas J. McIntyre, Dec. 28, 1967, WHCF: EX/ND19\CO312.

25. Congressional Briefing, Jan. 17, 1968, NSF: Congressional Briefings on Vietnam; *PPP: LBJ, 1968*, I, 25–26.

26. LBJ, *Vantage Point*, 380–82; Herbert Y. Schandler, *The Unmaking of a President: Lyndon Johnson and Vietnam* (Princeton, N.J., 1977), chap. 3.

27. Ibid., 68–69; Palmer, *25-Year War*, 77, 80; Rostow to LBJ, Jan. 10, 1968; Westmoreland Cable, Jan. 22, 1968, NSF: Rostow Files; LBJ meeting with Democratic leadership, Jan. 23, 1968, Tom Johnson Papers.

28. LBJ meeting with Joint Chiefs, Jan. 29, 1968; LBJ meeting with Democratic leadership, Jan. 30, 1968, Tom Johnson Papers.

29. Palmer, *25-Year War*, 80.

30. LBJ, *Vantage Point*, 382; Schandler, *Unmaking of a President*, 74–80.

31. LBJ meeting, Jan. 30, 1968, Tom Johnson Papers; LBJ, *Vantage*

Point, 380; Palmer, *25-Year War*, 79; Clifford, *Counsel to the President*, 467–69.

32. For the debate about Westmoreland's "manipulation" of the enemy's "order of battle," see Samuel A. Adams OH, Sept. 20, 1984; Sam Adams, *War of Numbers: An Intelligence Memoir* (South Royalton, Vt., 1994); and the accounts of the Westmoreland–CBS law suit in Reference File: Westmoreland vs. CBS: Clippings; and in DSDUF: Vietnam. Also see Phillip Charles Saunders, "War with Numbers: Politics and SNIE 14.3–67," Senior Thesis, Harvard University, 1988.

33. LBJ, *Vantage Point*, 382–83; Townsend Hoopes, *The Limits of Intervention*, (New York, 1973), 142; Herring, *America's Longest War*, 190–91; Clifford, *Counsel to the President*, 473.

34. *PPP: LBJ, 1968*, I, 155–57.

35. Schandler, *Unmaking of a President*, 83–84; LBJ meeting with congressional leaders, Jan. 31, 1968, Tom Johnson Papers; George Christian to LBJ, Feb. 16, 1968, Handwriting File; Rostow to LBJ, Feb. 7 and 17, 1968, NSF: Memos to the Pres.; and Country: Vietnam.

36. Panzer to LBJ, Jan. 31, Feb. 12 and 15, 1968, WHCF: EX/PR16; Mueller, War, *Presidents and Public Opinion*, 56, 72, 90, 106–7.

37. Schandler, *Unmaking of a President*, 80–81, 194–99; Oberdorfer, *Tet!*, chap. 7; Walter Cronkite, *A Reporter's Life* (New York, 1996), 257–58. Cronkite's producer at CBS told Murray Fromson that Abrams was Cronkite's principal source for the "stalemate" conclusion. Fromson interview, Sept. 8, 1997. For questions about the impact of TV on public attitudes toward the war, see Herring, *America's Longest War*, 202–203.

38. Rusk to LBJ, Feb. 20, 1968, NSF: Country: Vietnam; Cater to LBJ, March 8, 1968, WHCF: EX/ND19\CO 312; Califano, *Triumph and Tragedy*, 262–64.

39. Panzer to LBJ, March 8, 12, 29, 1968, WHCF: EX/ND19\CO312; LBJ luncheon meeting, March 22, 1968, Diary Backup.

40. See Maj. Gen. W. E. DePuy to Chairman, Joint Chiefs, Feb. 7, 1968, NSF: Memos to the Pres.; LBJ meeting with Advisers, Feb. 9, 1968, Tom Johnson Papers; Schandler, *Unmaking of a President*, 85–101.

41. LBJ meeting with Joint Chiefs, Feb. 9, 1968, and Foreign Policy Advisers, Feb. 12, 1968, Tom Johnson Papers.

42. LBJ meeting with Foreign Policy Advisers, Feb. 12, 1968, Tom Johnson Papers; Wheeler to LBJ, Feb. 12, 1968; Westmoreland to Wheeler, Feb. 13, 1968, NSF: Memos to the Pres.; LBJ, *Vantage Point*, 386–87; Schandler, *Unmaking of a President*, 98–109.

43. Rostow to LBJ, Feb. 25 and 27, 1968, NSF: Memos to the Pres.; Schandler, *Unmaking of a President*, 109–16; Herring, *America's Longest War*, 193–95.

44. Clifford, *Counsel to the President*, 481; LBJ to Secs. of State and Defense, Feb. 28, 1968, NSF: Memos to the Pres.; Schandler, *Unmaking of a President*, 116–20; LBJ meeting to discuss Wheeler's trip, Feb. 28, 1968, Tom Johnson Papers; LBJ, *Vantage Point*, 389–93.

45. For a biographical sketch of Clifford and a list of his meetings with LBJ dating from Nov. 1965, see the Clark Clifford Papers. Also see Richard Russell's handwritten note, Jan. 19, 1968, about his discussion with LBJ on

Clifford's appointment, Russell Papers. For Clifford's opposition to the 1965 escalation, see Clifford, *Counsel to the President*, 411–22.

46. See Draft Memorandum to the Pres., March 4, 1968, Clifford Papers; Rostow to LBJ, Clifford Committee, March 4, 1968, NSF: Memos to the Pres.; LBJ meeting with Foreign Policy Advisers, March 4, 1968, Tom Johnson Papers; Clifford, *Counsel to the President*, 492–95.

47. See Clifford, *Counsel to the President*, 495; Tab H: "Problems We Can Anticipate in U.S. Public Opinion," Draft Memorandum to the Pres., March 4, 1968, Clifford Papers; Herring, *America's Longest War*, 198–99, 203–4.

48. *PPP: LBJ, 1968*, I, 404, 409–13.

49. LBJ, *Vantage Point*, 398–402; Clifford, *Counsel to the President*, 496–97.

50. Undated 1968 Clifford Memo, "S.V.N.," Clifford Papers; Rostow to LBJ, "Summary of Dean Acheson's Proposal," March 14, 1968; and "Draft Directive," March 16, 1968, NSF: Memos to the Pres.; Clifford, *Counsel to the President*, 507–9.

51. Memo, March 14, 1968, Clifford Papers; Rostow to LBJ, Draft Directive, March 16, 1968, NSF: Memos to the Pres.; Clifford, *Counsel to the President*, 509–10.

52. See Clifford, *Counsel to the President*, 511–19; McGeorge Bundy to LBJ, March 27, 1968, WHCF: EX/ND19\CO312. Also see Rostow to LBJ, Feb. 1, 1968, describing Gen. Ridgeway's growing skepticism about the war, Diary Backup; and Mac Bundy's "Summary of Notes," March 26, 1968; and "Summary," March 26, 1968, NSF: Meeting Notes.

53. Notes of meeting, March 20, 1968; LBJ meeting with Wheeler, JCS, and Gen. Creighton Abrams, March 26, 1968, Tom Johnson Papers; luncheon meeting, March 22, 1968, Diary Backup; Clifford, *Counsel to the President*, 515–16.

54. *PPP: LBJ, 1968*, I, 469–76. For a review of how the speech evolved into a peace address, see Rostow to LBJ, March 19, 1970, NSF: Country: Vietnam.

55. *PPP: LBJ, 1968*, I, 25–33.

56. LBJ, *Vantage Point*, 532–33.

57. See State Dept. Meeting on the Pueblo, Jan. 24, 1968; LBJ meeting with Democratic congressional leadership, Feb. 6, 1968; Notes on Prime Minister Wilson's visit, Feb. 8–9, 1968, Diary Backup; NSF: NSC Meeting, Jan. 24, 1968; Rostow to LBJ, Jan. 25, 1968; LBJ to Kosygin, Jan. 25, 1968, NSF: Memos to the Pres.; LBJ meeting with businessmen, Jan. 27, 1968, Tom Johnson Papers; Congressional leadership briefing, Jan. 30, 1968, NSF: Congressional briefings on Vietnam; Charles Roberts OH, Jan. 14, 1970; LBJ, *Vantage Point*, 533–37.

58. See *PPP: LBJ, 1967*, II, 1049–50; *PPP: LBJ, 1968*, I, 83–86, 8–13; Republican Coordinating Committee, "Let's Stop Creating Financial Chaos," Dec. 11, 1967, WHCF: EX/FO4–1; LBJ meeting with National Alliance of Businessmen, Jan. 27, 1968, Tom Johnson Papers; Henry H. Fowler to LBJ, Jan. 30, 1968, WHCF: Aides: Califano; Panzer to LBJ, Jan. 23, 1968, WHCF: EX/FI11–4; Ackley to LBJ, Jan. 24, 1968, Diary Backup.

59. *PPP: LBJ, 1968*, I, 1–13, 22–23, 31–35, 124–40, 227–28. HHH to LBJ, Dec. 28, 1967, Humphrey Papers.

60. See *Report of the National Advisory Commission on Civil Disorders* (New York, 1968); Irv Sprague to Barefoot Sanders, Jan. 15, 1968; "Tentative Pricing of Recommendations," Feb. 29, 1968; James R. Jones to Watson, March 15, 1968, notes of LBJ's comments on the Report, WHCF: EX/FG690.

61. LBJ to Califano, Feb. 26, 1968; Larry Temple to LBJ, Feb. 26, 1968; Califano to LBJ, Feb. 28, March 2, 5, 8, 1968; McPherson to Califano, March 1, 1968; Louis Martin to Califano, March 5, 1968; Robert C. Weaver to LBJ, March 7, 1968; Liz Carpenter to LBJ, March 19, 1968; Doug Cater to LBJ, March 22, 1968; Notes on LBJ meeting with Negro editors, March 15, 1968, WHCF: EX/FG690; HHH to LBJ, March 26, 1968, Humphrey Papers; *PPP: LBJ, 1968*, I, 434–36; Califano OH, Aug. 21, 1969; Califano, *Triumph and Tragedy*, 260–62.

62. For Johnson's preoccupation with the crime issue, see WHCF: EX/FG135, JL, JL3, and Legislative Background: Safe Streets and Crime Control Act for 1967–1968. Also see *PPP: LBJ, 1968*, I, 30–31, 179–96. *Report of the National Advisory Commission on Civil Disorders*, 266–69.

63. See *PPP: LBJ, 1968*, I, 55–62, 243; Califano OH, Oct. 29, 1987.

64. LBJ conversation with CBS News, Dec. 19, 1967. Also see LBJ's comments at Cabinet meeting, Jan. 17, 1968, Cabinet Papers.

65. *PPP: LBJ, 1968*, I, 46–54, 78–80, 248–63, esp. 257–58.

66. Tom Johnson to LBJ, clipping on Gardner resignation, Jan. 24, 1968; Economic and Social Gains Under Pres. Johnson, Feb. 26, 1968, WHCF: EX/FG1; Bob Fleming to LBJ, Jan. 25, 1968, WHCF: EX/PR18; Larry Levinson to LBJ, March 19, 1968, WHCF: Aides: Califano.

67. See *New York Times*, June 3, 1991, p. A10, for a discussion of the shift away from the Democrats dating from the mid-sixties.

68. UPI release of Schlesinger's speech, Dec. 1, 1966, Diary Backup; the Democrat is quoted in Lewis L. Gould, "Never a Deep Partisan," 35; *Minneapolis Tribune*, Sept. 17, 1967; Vera Williams to "Dear Doctor," n.d. [Jan. 1968]; Panzer to Watson, Feb. 1, 1968; Dr. Walter Barton to Doug Cater, Feb. 13, 1968, WHCF: EX/FG1; *New York Times*, March 8, 1968.

69. Moyers for Pres.'s night reading, July 11, 1966, WHCF: Aides: Watson; Watson to LBJ, Nov. 17, 1966, WHNF: Arthur Krim.

70. For a fine summary of this episode, see Shesol, *Mutual Contempt*, 356–65.

71. See LBJ-Bill Moyers, Dec. 26, 1966, 10:17 a.m.; LBJ-Nicholas Katzenbach, Dec. 6, 1966, 10:46 a.m.; LBJ-Fortas, Dec. 17, 1966, 10:45 a.m., TT.

72. Schlesinger, *Robert Kennedy*, 760–62; Robert Kintner to LBJ, Dec. 16, 1966, Special File on Assassination of JFK; *U.S. News & World Report*, April 1, 1968.

73. See Special File on Assassination of JFK; and LBJ-Moyers, Dec. 26, 1966, 10:17 a.m., TT.

74. Rowe to LBJ, Jan. 6, 1967, WHCF: Aides: Watson. Also see Henry H. Wilson to LBJ, Jan. 21, 1967, Diary Backup.

75. See Robert Kintner to Drew Pearson, Feb. 17, 1967, for this polling data, Pearson Papers; LBJ-Katzenbach, Jan. 25, 1967, 7:45 p.m.; LBJ-Ramsey-Clark, Jan. 25, 1967, 8:22 p.m., TT; cf. Gallup's analysis in the *Washington Post*, March 26, 1967, p. A6.

76. LBJ-Ramsey Clark, Jan. 25, 1967, 8:22 p.m., TT; Harris Survey, March 13, 1967, WHCF: EX/PR16; *Gallup Poll, 1935–1971*, III, 2049, 2055. On LBJ's political efforts, see Watson to LBJ, Feb. 18, 1967, WHCF: Aides: Watson; Kintner to LBJ, Feb. 20, 1967; Ben Wattenberg, March 25, 1967; Watson to LBJ, May 31, 1967, Handwriting File; Valenti to LBJ, n.d. [probably March 8, 1967]; Watson to LBJ, March 20, 1967, June 10, 1967; LBJ conversation with Charles Bailey, April 7, 1967; Kintner to Mrs. Roberts, May 19, 1967, Diary Backup.

77. *Gallup Poll, 1935–1971*, III, 2062–63, 2067.

78. Robert E. Gilbert, "The Political Effects of Presidential Illness: The Case of Lyndon Johnson," *Political Psychology* (Fall 1995), 761–69.

79. Lady Bird Johnson, *White House Diary*, 518.

80. Mike Manatos to LBJ, Aug. 10, 1967, WHCF: EX/ND19\CO312; Panzer to LBJ, Aug. 8 and 11, 1967, WHCF: EX/PR16; Panzer to LBJ, Aug. 17 and 18, 1967, WHCF: Aides: Panzer.

81. LBJ conversation with Bob Thompson, Aug. 21, 1967, WHCF: Aides: Christian; Manatos to LBJ, Aug. 22, 1967, WHCF: EXD/ND19\CO312; McPherson to LBJ, Aug. 25, 1967, WHCF: Aides: McPherson.

82. B. Marvel to Panzer listing Gallup polls, Sept. 12 and 14, 1967; Gallup Report, Sept. 30, 1967, WHCF: Aides: Panzer; Underwood to Jim Jones, Sept. 6, 1967, with the *Monitor* article attached, WHCF: EX/PR16.

83. Lady Bird Johnson, *White House Diary*, 565–67; Jake Pickle interview, April 10, 1996; Larry Temple OH, Aug. 13, 1970.

84. Drew Pearson to George Christian, May 15, 1968; Christian to Pearson, May 15, 1968, WHCF: SP3–236; conversation between Christian and Dorothy Territo, March 19, 1969, Diary Backup; Pickle interview, April 10, 1996; Lady Bird Johnson, *White House Diary*, 567.

85. See Roche to LBJ, Sept. 8, 1967; Larry O'Brien, "A White Paper for the President on the 1968 Presidential Campaign," Sept. 29, 1967; Rowe, Notes and Comments on O'Brien White Paper, n.d., WHCF: Aides: Watson; Roche phone message, Sept. 23, 1967, Diary Backup.

86. *U.S. News & World Report*, Nov. 27, 1967; Christian to LBJ, Jan. 17, 1968, LBJ Statements; Christian to Pearson, May 15, 1968, WHCF: SP3-236; conversation between Christian and Territo, March 19, 1969, Diary Backup; James R. Jones, "Behind LBJ's Decision Not to Run in '68," *New York Times*, April 16, 1988; Lady Bird Johnson interview, Oct. 6, 1997.

87. Lady Bird Johnson interview, Oct. 6, 1997; Gallup Poll, 1935–1971, III, 2096, 2099, 2103; Panzer to LBJ, Nov. 27, Dec. 29, 1967, WHCF: EX/PR16; and Harris survey, Dec. 4, 1967, in WHCF: Aides: Panzer.

88. LBJ meeting with Smith, Nov. 21, 1967, Tom Johnson Papers; Schlesinger, *Robert Kennedy*, 824–41. Watson to LBJ, Dec. 15, 1967; Roche to LBJ, Dec. 18, 1967, Jan. 26, 1968; Robert G. Spivak, "Watch on the Potomac," Jan. 12, 1968; Jim Rowe to LBJ, Jan. 16, 1968, WHCF: Aides: Watson; Panzer to LBJ, Dec. 5, 1967, WHCF: Aides: Panzer.

89. On LBJ's vulnerability, see Tom Johnson to LBJ, Nov. 27, 1967, WHCF: EX/PL2, reporting on the *New York Times*'s Max Frankel's fifteen-day tour of the United States. On support, see Watson to LBJ, Dec. 5, 1967, WHCF: Aides: Watson; Panzer to LBJ, Dec. 8, 1967, Jan. 5, 9, 19, 1968, WHCF: EX/PR16. On New Hampshire, see Roche to LBJ, Nov. 25, 1967, WHCF: Aides:

Watson; LBJ conversation with Gov. John W. King, Dec. 5, 1967, Diary Backup; *Washington Post*, Jan. 25, 1968; Panzer to LBJ, Jan. 18, 1967, WHCF: EX/ PR16.

90. Panzer to LBJ, Feb. 15, 16, 22, 23, 1968, WHCF: EX/PR16; *Gallup Poll, 1935–1971*, III, 2105–6; Califano to LBJ, Feb. 28, 1968, with Bohen to Califano attached, WHCF: Aides: Califano; Kintner to Watson, Feb. 5, 1968, WHCF: CF: EX/PL2.

91. Lady Bird Johnson, *White House Diary*, 573.

92. Stennis to Russell, Feb. 8, 1968, Richard Russell Papers; Jake Pickle OH; Johnson, *My Brother Lyndon*, 4; Gilbert, "Political effects of Presidential Illness," 769–70.

93. Panzer to LBJ, March 4, 1968, WHCF: EX/PR16; De Vier Pierson to LBJ, March 5, 1968; Califano to LBJ, March 8, 1968, WHCF: EX/FG1; meeting, Rowe et al., March, 5, 1968; LBJ to Watson, March 8, 1968, with Roche memo attached, WHCF: Aides: Watson; Pierson to LBJ, March 4 and 9, 1968, Diary Backup; Lloyd Hackler to Mike Manatos, March 12, 1968, WHCF: EX/PL\Nixon, Richard.

94. Panzer to LBJ, March 13, 1968, WHCF: EX/PR16; Gould, "Never a Deep Partisan," 38–39.

95. Mike Manatos, memo, March 16, 1968; William Connell to HHH, March 19, 1968, WHCF: Aides: Watson. On the exchange with RFK, see Clifford memo of conference with Kennedy and Sorensen, March 14, 1968; De Vier Pierson to LBJ, March 14, 1968; Juanita Roberts to Clifford, March 18, 1968, with transcript of Pierson-Sorensen conversation, March 14, 1968, WHFN: Robert F. Kennedy; Schlesinger, *Robert Kennedy*, 851–54. Rostow to LBJ, March 22, 1968; Doug Cater to LBJ, March 25, 1968; Watson to LBJ, March 26, 1968, with Jim J to LBJ, March 25, 1968 attached; Charles D. Roche to LBJ, March 27, 1968, Handwriting File; Panzer to LBJ, March 28, 1968, WHCF: EX/PR16; Delegates, March 29, 1968, WHCF: EX/PL1; John Gonella to LBJ, March 22, 1968, WHCF: EX/PL\Kennedy, Robert; *NYT*, March 24, 1968.

96. Panzer to LBJ, March 22, 27, 29, 1968, WHCF: EX/PR16; Califano to LBJ, March 8 and 27, 1968, WHCF: Aides: Califano; Rowe to LBJ, March 19, 1968, WHCF: Aides: Watson; Rostow to LBJ, March 20, 1968, NSF: Rostow Files; Christian to LBJ, March 22, 1968, WHCF: Aides: Christian; Doug Cater to LBJ, March 28, 1968, WHCF: EX/FG1.

97. Elizabeth Wickenden interview, Dec. 20, 1986; Gilbert, "Political effects of Presidential Illness," 770–71; LBJ, *Vantage Point*, 425–26.

98. Kearns, *Lyndon Johnson*, 28–29, 32, 342–43.

99. See James R. Jones, "Behind L.B.J.'s Decision Not to Run in '68," *New York Times*, April 16, 1988.

100. See Larry Temple OH, June 26, 1970, who describes LBJ's wish to keep his options open until the very last minute. Humphrey, *Education of a Public Man*, 358–59.

101. *PPP: LBJ, 1968*, I, 476; Jones, *New York Times*, April 16, 1988; Lady Bird Johnson interview, Oct. 6, 1997.

102. See *New York Times*, April 2, 1968; memo from mf to Dorothy, describing calls and comments to LBJ after his speech, July 30, 1968; Jack Valenti to LBJ, May 13, 1968, Diary Backup; Minutes of Cabinet Meeting, April 3, 1968, Cabinet Papers; Harry Middleton, "Speech That Halted a Great Soci-

ety," *Los Angeles Times*, March 31, 1988; *PPP: LBJ, 1968*, I, 598–600; Panzer to LBJ, April 5, 1968, WHCF: EX/PR16.

103. RFK to LBJ, April 1, 1968, WHFN: Robert F. Kennedy.

104. Daily Diary, April 3, 1968, WHFN: RFK; Notes on meeting of LBJ with Sen. Robert Kennedy, April 3, 1968, Murphy's notes and Rostow's, both in Diary Backup. Also see Minutes of Cabinet Meeting, April 3, 1968, Cabinet Papers.

105. LBJ conversation with HHH, April 3, 1968, Diary Backup.

106. "On-Camera Interview with Pres. Johnson," April 27, 1968, Diary Backup.

107. Administrative History: Housing and Urban Development, Nov. 1963–Jan. 1969, chap. 8: "Equal Opportunity"; *Gallup Poll, 1935–1971*, III, 1941–42, 2022, 2057, 2076; Califano, *Triumph and Tragedy*, 276.

108. *PPP: LBJ, 1968*, I, 55–56, 61–62, 243, 374, 445–46; also see Manatos to LBJ, Feb. 2 and 13, March 5, 1968; Califano to LBJ, Feb. 17, 1968; Ramsey Clark to LBJ, Feb. 20, 1968; Larry Temple to LBJ, Feb. 23, 1968; mr to LBJ, Feb. 26, 1968; Sanders to LBJ, Feb. 29, March 9, 11, 12, 13 (two memos), 19, 21, 25, 1968, Legislative Background: 1968 Civil Rights Law; Louis Martin to Califano, Mar. 1, 1968, EX/HU2; *Congress and the Nation, 1965–1968*, II, 378–83; Califano, *Triumph and Tragedy*, 276.

109. Lady Bird Johnson interview, Oct. 6, 1997; Califano OH, Oct. 29, 1987; Califano, *Triumph and Tragedy*, 273–76; H. "Barefoot" Sanders OH, Nov. 3, 1969; LBJ meeting with Negro Leaders, April 5, 1968, Tom Johnson Papers; *PPP: LBJ, 1968*, I, 493–94, 496–97, 509–10.

110. Califano to LBJ, April 10, 1968; Wattenberg to LBJ, April 26, May 23, 1968, Handwriting File.

111. Arthur Okun to LBJ, March 27, 1968; Zwick to LBJ, March 30, 1968, WHCF: EX/FG 11–1; Sanders to LBJ, April 1, 1968, Diary Backup; Congressional Leadership Breakfast, April 2, 1968, NSF: Meeting Notes File.

112. See Minutes of Cabinet Meeting, April 3, 1968, Cabinet Papers; LBJ meeting with congressional leaders, April 3, 1968, Tom Johnson Papers; Henry H. Fowler to LBJ, April 10, 1968; Okun to LBJ, April 27, 1968; Sanders to LBJ, April 29, 1968, Diary Backup; Sanders to LBJ, April 22, 1968, WHCF: EX/FG 11–1; Jim Jones to LBJ, April 26, 1968, Handwriting File; Sanders to LBJ, April 27, 1968, WHCF: EX/FI 11–2.

113. Califano, *Triumph and Tragedy*, 284. Johnson's prepared remarks are in *PPP: LBJ, 1968*, I, 542–43.

114. See Charles Zwick to LBJ, May 2, 1968; Califano to LBJ, May 2, 1968, WHCF: EX/FI 11–4.

115. *PPP: LBJ, 1968*, I, 560–62.

116. See LBJ to Dirksen, May 4, 1968, Everett Dirksen Papers, Pekin, Ill.; LBJ to John W. McCormack, May 4, 1968, McCormack Papers, Boston University; Arthur Okun to LBJ, May 21, 1968, WHCF: CF: EX/BE 5; Califano, *Triumph and Tragedy*, 285–88; *PPP: LBJ, 1968*, 574–78, 593–97, 651, 654–55, 674–75, 729, 754–56.

117. Clifford, *Counsel to the President*, 527–28.

118. See Rostow to LBJ, March 30, 31, April 3, 1968, NSF: Rostow Files; April 2 and 3, 1968, NSF: Memos to the Pres.; Harriman to LBJ, April 2, 1968, NSF: Country: Vietnam; LBJ meeting with Clifford, Katzenbach, Rostow, Chris-

tian, April 2, 1968, Tom Johnson Papers; Clifford, *Counsel to the President*, 528–29.

119. LBJ meeting with Clifford, Rusk, et al., May 8 and 21, 1968, Tom Johnson Papers; lunch meeting with LBJ, Agenda, May 14, 1968, NSF: Memos to the Pres.; lunch with LBJ, Agenda, May 21, 1968, NSF: Rostow File; Clifford, *Counsel to the President*, 538–41.

120. See the Record of Vietnam Peace Bids, April 3, 1968, NSF: Country: Vietnam; Cabinet Meeting, April 3, 1968, Cabinet Papers; LBJ meeting with Sec. Gen. U Thant, April 4, 1968, NSF: Meeting Notes; Clifford, *Counsel to the President*, 529–30; *PPP: LBJ, 1968*, I, 492.

121. See "Aboard Air Force One," n.d., NSF: Rostow Files; LBJ meeting with U Thant, April 4, 1968, NSF: Meeting Notes; Rostow to LBJ, April 5 and 13, 1968, NSF: Memos to the Pres.; Rostow to Bromley Smith, April 15, 1968; Smith to Rostow, April 15, 1968; Rostow to Rusk, April 18, 1968, NSF: Country: Vietnam; LBJ, *Vantage Point*, 501–3.

122. Rostow to Rusk, April 18, 20, 22, 1968; Larry Temple to LBJ, April 21, 1968, NSF: Country: Vietnam; From Jim Jones, April 19, 1968, WHCF: EX/ND19\CO312; LBJ meeting with Rusk, Clifford, Rostow, April 22, 1968; Meeting in Cabinet Room, May 4, 1968; LBJ meeting with congressional leaders, May 7, 1968, NSF: Meeting Notes; *PPP: LBJ, 1968*, I, 556.

123. See Rostow to LBJ, April 4, 1968, 2:05 p.m. and 5:50 p.m., Diary Backup; Instructions for Governor Harriman, April 6, 1968; Ellsworth Bunker, Viet-Nam Negotiations, April 8, 1968, NSF: Country: Vietnam; LBJ meeting at Camp David, April 9, 1968, NSF: Meeting Notes; Clifford, *Counsel to the President*, 528, 531–33.

124. See Joseph Kraft, "Talks Start on Wrong Foot; Rostow Steps Questioned," *Washington Post*, April 16, 1968; Clifford, *Counsel to the President*, 528, 530.

125. LBJ meeting with foreign policy advisers, May 6, 1968, NSF: Meeting Notes; Clifford, *Counsel to the President*, 536.

126. LBJ Tuesday Lunch Meeting, May 7, 1968; LBJ meeting with negotiating team, May 8, 1968, Tom Johnson Papers.

127. See LBJ meeting with congressional leaders, May 7, 1968, NSF: Meeting Notes; Rostow to LBJ, May 7, 1968, NSF: Memos to the Pres.; LBJ meeting with Thanom, May 8, 1968, NSF: Rostow Files.

128. Clifford, *Counsel to the President*, 537–38; LBJ meeting with negotiating team, May 8, 1968, Tom Johnson Papers; Rostow to LBJ, May 9, 1968, WHCF: CF: EX/ND19\CO312.

129. LBJ, *Vantage Point*, 507–8; Robert N. Ginsburgh to Rostow, May 14, 1968, NSF: Memos to the Pres.; Cabinet Meeting, May 14, 1968, Cabinet Papers.

130. Mansfield to LBJ, May 16, 1968, WHCF: EX/ND19\CO312; Rostow to LBJ, May 17, 1968, NSF: Memos to the Pres.

131. LBJ meeting with foreign policy advisers, May 21, 1968, Tom Johnson Papers; Notes of NSC Meeting, May 22, 1968, NSF: NSC Meetings.

132. Ibid.; LBJ meeting with foreign policy advisers, May 25, 1968, NSF: Meeting Notes; LBJ meeting with foreign policy advisers, May 28, 1968, Tom Johnson Papers.

133. See Lloyd Gardner, "Lyndon Johnson and Vietnam: The Final Months," in Divine, ed., *Johnson Years*, III, 217–20; Kosygin to LBJ, June 5,

1968; LBJ to Kosygin, June 9, 1968, draft letter, NSF: Rostow Files; LBJ meeting with foreign policy advisers, June 9, 1968, Tom Johnson Papers; LBJ, *Vantage Point*, 510.

134. Clifford, *Counsel to the President*, 546–48.

135. Rostow to LBJ, June 11, 1968, with statement attached, NSF: Memos to the Pres.

136. See *PPP: LBJ, 1968*, I, 537–38; LBJ lunch meeting, Agenda, June 4, 1968, NSF: Rostow Files.

137. Harriman to Rusk, June 12, 1968, NSF: Memos to the Pres.; Cabinet Meeting, June 12, 1968, Cabinet Papers.

138. Cabinet Meeting, June 26, 1968, Cabinet Papers; Rostow to LBJ, June 29, 1968; Gen. Maxwell Taylor to LBJ, June 29, 1968, NSF: Memos to the Pres.; Clifford, *Counsel to the President*, 549.

139. Watson to LBJ, April 17, 1968, WHCF: EX/FG1.

140. See FBI memo, April 15, 1968, LBJ Main File, describing Drew Pearson's assessment that LBJ would not consent to be drafted by the Democratic Convention. Panzer to Watson, April 2, 1968; to LBJ, April 12, 1968, WHCF: Aides: Panzer; Memo of Eugene Pulliam phone call about Indiana, April 23, 1968, WHCF: EX/PL\Kennedy, Robert; Temple to LBJ, April 2, 1968, Handwriting File.

141. LBJ meeting with Richard Wilson, May 20, 1968, WHCF: Aides: Christian; Francis Bator interview, Jan. 28, 1997; HHH to LBJ, June 9, 1968, Humphrey Papers.

142. Califano, *Triumph and Tragedy*, 289–90; Califano to LBJ, April 7, 1968, with Fred Bohen to Califano, April 5, 1968, attached, WHCF: Aides: Califano; Nelson Rockefeller OH.

143. See Cater to LBJ, April 10, 1968; UPI-112, April 24, 1968, for Cohen's announcement, WHCF: EX/PL\Humphrey, Hubert; Califano, *Triumph and Tragedy*, 291–92.

144. Califano to LBJ, April 24, 1968, WHCF: EX/PL\Humphrey, Hubert; Califano to LBJ, April 25, 1968, WHCF: EX/FG1.

145. See Schnittker to LBJ, April 25, 1968, with notation that LBJ had talked to him on the phone; Califano to LBJ, April 25, 1968, relaying Sorensen's comments, WHCF: EX/PL\Kennedy, Robert; Murphy to LBJ, April 26, 1968, WHCF: Aides: Charles S. Murphy; Califano, *Triumph and Tragedy*, 292–93.

146. Califano to LBJ, April 29, 1968; George Christian to LBJ, May 16, 1968, Diary Backup; LBJ meeting with Richard Wilson, May 20, 1968, WHCF: Aides: Christian; Califano, *Triumph and Tragedy*, 293.

147. Panzer to LBJ, May 4, 1968, WHCF: EX/PL\Humphrey, Hubert; May 4 and 14, 1968, PL\Kennedy, Robert; May 13, 1968, PL1; unsigned memo, May 9, 1968, in RFK's PL file.

148. Califano to LBJ, May 17, 1968, with Riesel article attached, WHCF: Aides: Califano; Larry Temple to LBJ, May 20, 1968, with Tom Johnson to LBJ, May 20, 1968, attached, WHCF: EX/PL1.

149. Califano, *Triumph and Tragedy*, chap. 19.

150. Hugh Sidey, "Some Pages Not in L.B.J.'s Book," *Life*, Nov. 5, 1971.

151. Tom Johnson to LBJ, June 11, 1968, WHCF: EX/PL2.

152. McPherson, *A Political Education: A Washington Memoir* (Austin, Tex., 1995 ed.), 428; Schlesinger, *Robert Kennedy*, 866.

153. See Legislative Background Files for Gun Control and Safe Streets; Califano, *Triumph and Tragedy*, chap. 19, esp. p. 304 for LBJ's public comment on gun control; Califano to LBJ, June 7, 1968; McPherson to LBJ, June 17, 1968, WHCF: EX/JL3; Walter Reuther to LBJ, June 13, 1968, Reuther Papers, Wayne State Univ.; McPherson to LBJ, June 14, 1968, Reference File: Wiretaps.

154. Panzer to LBJ, June 9, 1968, WHCF: EX/PR16; LBJ meeting with congressional leadership, June 11, 968, NSF: Meeting Notes; Dick Darling to Doug Nobles, June 20, 1968, WHCF: CF: EX/PL2; *New York Times*, June 20, 1968.

155. "Marianne Means' Washington," June 18, 1968, WHCF: Aides: McPherson; Panzer to LBJ, June 21 and 22, 1968, WHCF: EX/PL\Humphrey, Hubert.

CHAPTER 11: UNFINISHED BUSINESS

1. *PPP: LBJ, 1968*, II, 873–74, 1203.

2. LBJ meeting with staff, June 25, 1968, NSF: Meeting Notes. Cf. Califano to Derek Bok, June 6, 1968, WHCF: EX/FG1.

3. LBJ meeting with David Wise, Oct. 1, 1968, WHCF: Aides: Christian.

4. *PPP: LBJ, 1968*, I, 585, 1297; Califano to LBJ, June 25 and 28, 1968, Diary Backup.

5. *PPP: LBJ, 1968*, I, 745, 751–53; II, 763, 767–68, 804–805, 817, 840, 842–44, 846–49, 854–55.

6. *PPP: LBJ, 1968*, II, 833–38.

7. *PPP: LBJ, 1968*, II, 865–67, 876–77.

8. Ibid., 882–89, 891–93, 895–96.

9. Ibid., 911, 921–22.

10. Ibid., 924–25, 935–36, 950–51, 958–59, 961–62, 972–74, 991–96.

11. Ibid., 1000–1003, 1012, 1032–36, 1038–39, 1050–54, 1069–70; HEW, Off-the-Record Review, HEW, Sept. 26, 1968, Diary Backup.

12. Pearson to LBJ, Sept. 30, 1968, Drew Pearson Papers.

13. Charles Zwick to LBJ, July 3 and 23, 1968, WHCF: EX/FG11-1; Arthur Okun to LBJ, Aug. 6, 1968, WHCF: CF: EX/FG11-1.

14. *PPP: LBJ, 1968*, II, 1270–73.

15. *PPP: LBJ, 1968*, I, 679–84, 715–16.

16. Ibid., II, 763–65, 801–3.

17. LBJ and Kosygin, July 29, 1968, Clark Clifford Papers; LBJ to Kosygin, July 30, 1968, NSF: Memos to the Pres.; Memo of conversation between Rusk and Dobrynin, Aug. 16, 1968; Rostow to LBJ, Aug. 19, 1968, NSF: Rostow Files.

18. LBJ, *Vantage Point*, 487–90; LBJ meeting with David Wise, Oct. 1, 1968, WHCF: Aides: Christian.

19. LBJ, *Vantage Point*, 547; Califano, *Triumph and Tragedy*, 307.

20. See Murphy, *Fortas*, 269–73. James Jones, Memorandum for the Record, June 13, 1968, WHCF: EX/FG535\A.

21. Kalman, *Abe Fortas*, 327–28; Larry Temple OH, Aug. 11, 1970.

22. Manatos to LBJ, June 25, 1968, memos of 3:00 p.m. and 4:15 p.m.; June 26, 1968, 5:30 p.m., Special File: Fortas and Thornberry; Kalman, *Abe Fortas*, 329.

23. Barefoot Sanders to LBJ, June 28, 1968, 8:50 p.m.; Manatos to LBJ, June 29, 1968, Special File: Fortas and Thornberry; LBJ meeting with Bill Theis, July 1, 1968, WHCF: Aides: Christian. Larry Temple says that he had "hard and fast commitments of some seventy-three people." OH, Aug. 11, 1970.

24. Kalman, *Abe Fortas*, 329–31; Murphy, *Fortas*, 292–300; Memo, July 2, 1968, 6:40 p.m., Special File: Fortas and Thornberry; Russell to J. Owen Forrester, Aug. 12, 1968, Richard Russell Papers; W. Thomas Johnson OH, Feb. 22, 1989; LBJ, *Vantage Point*, 545–46.

25. Kalman, *Abe Fortas*, chap. 14, and p. 310 for the quote. The record of contacts is in Special File: Fortas and Thornberry.

26. See *New York Times*, Jan. 22, 1990; *USA Today*, Jan. 22, 1990, p. 4A; Theoharis and Cox, *The Boss*, 368–93; Kalman, *Abe Fortas*, 314–17.

27. Califano, *Triumph and Tragedy*, 309–10.

28. Califano to LBJ, June 29, 1968, Special File: Fortas and Thornberry. Also see Steven Gerstel, "Court" (UPI), July 2, 1968, WHCF: Name: Fortas.

29. Murphy, *Fortas*, 274–76, 282–83, 302; Kalman, *Abe Fortas*, 331–32.

30. See Tom Johnson to Jim, May 22, 1968; Russell to LBJ, July 1, 1968; LBJ to Russell, July 2, 1968, WHCF: Aides: Temple; Powell Moore OH; Larry Temple OH, Aug. 11, 1970; W. Thomas Johnson OH, Feb. 22, 1989.

31. Temple OH, Aug. 11, 1970.

32. Ibid.; Califano, *Triumph and Tragedy*, 308.

33. Kalman, *Abe Fortas*, 335–37.

34. Ibid., 337–40.

35. Ibid., 311–12; unsigned, undated memo beginning, "During these past few days some distinguished senators would have us believe that a new crime has been added to the statute books," Special File: Fortas and Thornberry; "Supreme Court Justices as Presidential Advisors," WHCF: Aides: Califano. Califano, *Triumph and Tragedy*, 312–15; Califano OH, Nov. 15, 1988.

36. Yarborough to John D. Cofer, Aug. 28, 1968, Ralph Yarborough Papers; Larry Temple to LBJ, Sept. 9, 1968, Special File: Fortas and Thornberry.

37. Kalman, *Abe Fortas*, 340–42, 348; Temple OH, Aug. 11, 1970.

38. Kalman, *Abe Fortas*, 349–50.

39. Ibid., 351–53.

40. Temple OH, Aug. 11, 1970; Russell to LBJ, Sept. 26, 1968, Richard Russell Papers.

41. Kalman, *Fortas*, 354–55; LBJ meeting with David Wise, Oct. 1, 1968, WHCF: Aides: Christian.

42. LBJ meeting with foreign policy advisers, July 2, 1968, Tom Johnson Papers; Rostow to LBJ, July 13, 1968, NSF: Memos to the Pres.

43. Gen. Maxwell Taylor to LBJ, July 17, 1968, Clark Clifford Papers.

44. LBJ to Clifford, July 10, 1968, Clark Clifford Papers; McPherson to LBJ, July 3, 1968, with a summary of Vann's views, WHCF: EX/ND19\CO312; LBJ read McPherson's report from Vann to the Cabinet on July 10, 1968, Cabinet Papers; W. Thomas Johnson OH, June 19, 1973.

45. Clifford, *Counsel to the President*, 550–51. Also see Rostow to LBJ, July 17 and 18, 1968, Dairy Backup, demonstrating that Clifford accurately represented LBJ's views.

46. Clifford to LBJ, July 18, 1968, Clark Clifford Papers.

47. Clifford, *Counsel to the President*, 551–53; Notes for U.S. Briefing on Honolulu meetings, July 19, 1968, NSF: Rostow Files.

48. *PPP: LBJ, 1968*, II, 823–30; LBJ, *Vantage Point*, 510–12.

49. Clifford to LBJ, June 21, 1968, Clark Clifford Papers.

50. Paul Warnke to Clifford, July 29, 1968, Clifford Papers.

51. LBJ meeting with foreign policy advisers, July 30, 1968, Tom Johnson Papers; Clifford, *Counsel to the President*, 567–68.

52. "Talks with LBJ," Aug. 4, 1968, Clifford Papers; Clifford, *Counsel to the President*, 568.

53. Ibid., 569; Bromley Smith to LBJ, Aug. 5, 1968; White House Situation Room to LBJ, Aug. 9, 1968, Diary Backup.

54. Max Taylor to LBJ, Aug. 5, 1968, NSF: Memos to the Pres.; *PPP: LBJ, 1968*, II, 896–903.

55. McGeorge Bundy to LBJ, Aug. 15, 1968, WHCF: CF: EX/ND19\ CO312.

56. LBJ meeting with foreign policy advisers, Aug. 20, 1968, Tom Johnson Papers; Cabinet Meeting, Aug. 22, 1968, Cabinet Papers; Rostow to LBJ, Aug. 22 and 23, 1968, NSF: Memos to the Pres.; Rostow to LBJ, Aug. 23, 1968, NSF: Meeting Notes; LBJ to Mac Bundy, Aug. 25, 1968, NSF: Country: Vietnam; *PPP: LBJ, 1968*, II, 916.

57. The Humphrey quote is in Solberg, *Hubert Humphrey*, 345.

58. *Gallup Poll, 1935–1971*, III, 2121, 2134, 2139, 2150, 2154–55; Panzer to LBJ, May 5, 13, July 10, 11, 27, Aug. 20, 1968, WHCF: EX/PR16.

59. Califano to LBJ, July 15, 1968; Charles Maguire to Jim Jones et al., July 26, 1968, WHCF: EX/PR18. Solberg, *Hubert Humphrey*, 345–46. For Humphrey's effort to appease Johnson, see Bill Connell to HHH, July 18, 1968, Humphrey Papers.

60. UPI-61, Humphrey, July 31, 1968, NSF: Country: Vietnam; former Iowa Senator John Culver related the Humphrey-LBJ conversation to me, July 2, 1996. Humphrey told it to Culver. Humphrey aide Ted Van Dyk said Humphrey told him the same thing. Van Dyk interview, Feb. 28, 1997. Solberg, *Hubert Humphrey*, 347–49; Clifford, *Counsel to the President*, 562–63.

61. LBJ meeting with foreign policy advisers, July 24, 1968; meeting with Nixon, July 26, 1968, Tom Johnson Papers; Clifford, *Counsel to the President*, 563; Stephen E. Ambrose, *Nixon: The Triumph of a Politician, 1962–1972* (New York, 1989), 166.

62. HHH to Jim Jones, Aug. 5, 1968; Jones Memo, Aug. 21, 1968, WHCF: EX/ND19\CO312; Bert to Jim Jones, Aug. 9, 1968, WHCF: CF: EX/PL1; Don Furtado to Harry McPherson, Jr., Aug. 15, 1968; Jim Jones to LBJ, Aug. 25, 1968; Califano to LBJ, Aug. 27, 1968; Jim Jones Memo, Aug. 24, 1968, 1:10 p.m., WHCF: EX/PL1; Califano, *Triumph and Tragedy*, 318–20.

63. Ibid.; Larry Temple OH, Aug. 13, 1970; Christian, Middleton, and Temple told me this in Austin, in March 1996.

64. Robert L. Hardesty, ed., *The Johnson Years: The Difference He Made* (Austin, Tex., 1993), 156–58.

65. Robert B. Cochrane to John M. Bailey, Aug. 23, 1968, WHCF: Aides: Panzer; *Gallup Poll, 1935–1971*, III, 2158.

66. See J. Edgar Hoover to Clifford, Sept. 17, 1968, alleging that the violence was "the direct result of deliberate and long-planned provocations by

a hard core of subversive agitators," Clark Clifford Papers; Wells, *The War Within*, 276–81; Larry Temple OH, Aug. 13, 1970; Califano, *Triumph and Tragedy*, 321–22; *PPP: LBJ, 1968*, II, 914–17.

67. *PPP: LBJ, 1968*, II, 914–17; LBJ meeting with Peter Lisagor, Sept. 5, 1968, WHCF: Aides: Christian. Also see Califano to LBJ, July 15, 1968, Diary Backup.

68. *New York Times*, Aug. 27, 1968; Tom Johnson to LBJ, with Pearson column of Sept. 2, 1968, WHCF: EX/PL1; Solberg, *Hubert Humphrey*, 341, 357. Also see Memo, July 10, 1968, 9:30 p.m., with John Criswell to Jim Jones attached, July 10, 1968, Diary Backup.

69. Jim Jones memo, July 9, 1968; John Criswell to Jim Jones, July 29, 1968, WHCF: EX/PL1; Califano to LBJ, July 11, 1968, Handwriting File.

70. Summary of General Abrams' View, Aug. 23, 1968, NSF: Country: Vietnam; Clifford, *Counsel to the President*, 564–65.

71. Jim Jones Memo, Aug. 24, 1968; Tom Johnson to LBJ, Pearson column of Sept. 2, 1968, WHCF: EX/PL1; Bromley Smith to LBJ, "Situation Report on Vietnam Plank," n.d., NSF: Country: Vietnam; Clifford, *Counsel to the President*, 564–65.

72. LBJ meeting with Lisagor, Sept. 5, 1968, WHCF: Aides: Christian; Cabinet Meeting, Sept. 5, 1968, Cabinet Papers.

73. UPI-123, Sept. 10, 1968; L. T. to Walt, n.d. [clearly Sept. 10, 1968], NSF: Country Vietnam; LBJ meeting with foreign policy advisers, Sept. 12, 1968, Tom Johnson Papers; Clifford, *Counsel to the President*, 569–70. Van Dyk interview, Feb. 28, 1997. Van Dyk described how the White House had instantaneous information about Humphrey's campaign decisions that could have come only from wiretaps.

74. Charles S. Murphy to LBJ, Sept. 4 and 12, 1968, WHCF: EX/PL2.

75. LBJ meeting with Lisagor, Sept. 5, 1968, WHCF: Aides: Christian; Bromley Smith to LBJ, Aug. 28, 1968, WHCF: CF: EX/PL1.

76. Chester Bowles to LBJ, Sept. 21, 1968, NSF: Country: Vietnam; Mac Bundy to LBJ, Sept. 23, 1968, WHCF: CF: EX/ND19\C032; *PPP: LBJ, 1968*, II, 936–43; McPherson to LBJ, Sept. 13, 1968, WHCF: Aides: McPherson; Clifford, *Counsel to the President*, 570–72.

77. NSF: NSC Meeting, Sept. 4, 1968; Cabinet Meeting, Sept. 18, Cabinet Papers; LBJ pre-lunch meeting with Harriman, Sept. 17, 1968, NSF: Rostow Files.

78. Panzer to LBJ, Sept. 19, 1968, WHCF: CF: EX/ND19\C0312.

79. Bob Fleming to LBJ, Aug. 19, 1968, WHFN: Richard Nixon.

80. Billy Graham Memo, n.d., WHFN: Richard Nixon.

81. NSF: NSC Meeting, Sept. 25, 1968; Clifford, *Counsel to the President*, 571–72.

82. Panzer to LBJ, Sept. 13, 21, 24, 27, 1968, WHCF: EX/PL2; Clifford, *Counsel to the President*, 572–73; Humphrey, *Education of a Public Man*, 403, 493; Solberg, *Hubert Humphrey*, 378–79; LBJ, *Vantage Point*, 548–49.

83. Rostow to LBJ, Sept. 30, 1968, NSF: Country: Vietnam; Murphy to LBJ, Oct. 1, 1968, WHCF: EX/ND19\C0312.

84. See Rowland Evans and Robert Novak, *Washington Post*, Nov. 2, 1967; Jack Anderson's Washington Merry-Go-Round columns for *Washington Post*, June 24, 1975, June 16, 1993, December 24, 1995, Nov. 7, 1996; "Military

Aid to Greece," *Congressional Record: Senate*, Oct. 9, 1968; Eliot Janeway, *Prescriptions for Prosperity* (New York, 1983), 42–43; Seymour M. Hersh, *The Price of Power: Kissinger in the Nixon White House* (New York, 1983), 136–38; Stanley I. Kutler, *The Wars of Watergate: The Last Crisis of Richard Nixon* (New York, 1991), 205–8.

85. Ted Van Dyk interview, Feb. 28, 1997; Solberg, *Hubert Humphrey*, 391–92.

86. Larry Temple interview, Aug. 2, 1993. See Chapter 12 for how Johnson may have used this material to protect himself in 1972.

87. Panzer to LBJ, Oct. 1 and 2, 1968, WHCF: EX/PR16; Irv Sprague to Jim Jones, Sept. 13, 1968, Diary Backup; AP "Senate-Vietnam," Oct. 3, 1968, NSF: Country: Vietnam.

88. Califano to LBJ, Oct. 9, 1968, with O'Brien to LBJ, Oct. 8, 1968, attached, WHCF: EX/PL2; Rowe to LBJ, Oct. 10, 1968; Panzer to LBJ, Oct. 10, with Jones to McPherson, Oct. 11, 1968, attached, Handwriting File; *PPP: LBJ, 1968*, II, 1026–29.

89. Rostow to LBJ, Oct. 2, 1968; LBJ meeting with Vance, Oct. 3, 1968, NSF: Rostow Files.

90. Memo, Oct. 9, 1968, 8:10 a.m., NSF: Rostow Files.

91. Harriman-Vance Cable, Oct. 9, 1968; Rostow to LBJ, Oct. 12, 1968, NSF: Memos to the Pres.; Key Chronology of Total Bombing Cessation, June 5–Oct. 31, 1968, Meeting Notes File; Cable to Bunker, Oct. 11, 1968; Rostow to LBJ, Oct. 11, 1968, NSF: Country: Vietnam; William P. Bundy, letter to the *New York Times*, June 13, 1991.

92. Cable to Bunker and Abrams, Oct. 11, 1968, NSF: Country: File; LBJ meeting with foreign policy advisers, Oct. 14, 1968, 9:40 a.m.; Key Chronology of Total Bombing Cessation, Meeting Notes Files; LBJ meeting with Joint Chiefs, Oct. 14, 1968, 1:40 p.m.; LBJ meeting with Rusk et al., Oct. 14, 1968, 7:20 p.m., Tom Johnson Papers.

93. LBJ meeting with Joint Chiefs, Oct. 14, 1968, 1:40 p.m.; LBJ meeting with Rusk et al., Oct. 14, 1968, 7:20 p.m., Tom Johnson Papers.

94. Bryce Harlow OH, May 6, 1979. Harlow would never say who his source in the White House was. He himself wasn't sure. He had someone on the outside who got the information from a White House aide, who thought his outside contact was passing it on not to Nixon's but to Humphrey's campaign.

95. Dorothy Territo to LBJ, Nov. 3, 1968, listing calls on Oct. 16, 1968, Reference File: Anna Chennault. William Bundy, letter to the *New York Times*, June 13, 1991.

96. There are a substantial number of documents tracing these exchanges over the timing of the talks in the LBJ National Security Files and in the Tom Johnson meeting notes. In particular, see Rostow memos to LBJ, Oct. 28, 1968, 1:40 a.m., NSF: Rostow Files; 2:00 p.m., NSF: Memos to the Pres.; Cable to Harriman and Vance, Oct. 28, 12:15 p.m., NSF: Country: Vietnam; LBJ meeting with foreign policy advisers, Oct. 28, 1968, 6:30 p.m., Tom Johnson Papers.

97. LBJ to Bunker, Oct. 17, 1968, NSF: Rostow Files.

98. Rostow, Memorandum of Conversation, Oct. 18, 1968; Rusk to U.S. Embassys, Paris, Saigon, Oct. 19, 1968, NSF: Country: Vietnam.

99. Rostow to LBJ, Oct. 22, 1968, two memos, NSF: Memos to the Pres.;

Cable to Harriman and Vance, Oct. 22, 1968; AP News Release, Oct. 22, 1968; Rostow to Bunker, Oct. 22, 1968, NSF: Country: Vietnam.

100. Lou Harris and JRJ, Oct. 23, 1968, NSF: Rostow Files; see three CIA memos to Rusk and Rostow, Oct. 1968, Reference File: Anna Chennault.

101. Christian to LBJ, with Nixon statement attached, Oct. 25, 1968, WHCF: EX/PL\Nixon, Richard; Ambrose, *Nixon,* 209–10.

102. Rostow to LBJ, Oct. 29, 1968, 6:00 a.m., NSF: Memos to the Pres.; and 12:50 p.m., Reference File: Anna Chennault; Rostow to LBJ, Oct. 29, 1968, 8:50 a.m., NSF: Rostow Files.

103. See notes in the Tom Johnson Papers for four LBJ meetings on October 29, 1968. Also Clifford, *Counsel to the President,* 586–88.

104. See Rostow memo, May 14, 1973, with a blacked-out paragraph following a summary of the information received from Eugene Rostow. Rostow then wrote, referring to the blacked-out surveillance order, "This was done, yielding the FBI evidence the folder contains." Reference File: Anna Chennault. Bundy, letter to the *New York Times,* June 13, 1991; Rostow to LBJ, Oct. 30, 1968, 6:50 p.m., contains the warning on the Watergate, NSF: Memos to the Pres.

105. Bundy, letter to the *New York Times,* June 13, 1991; Clifford, *Counsel to the President,* 590.

106. Rostow to LBJ, Oct. 30, 1968, 7:30 a.m., NSF: Memos to the Pres.; LBJ meeting with Rusk, Clifford, et al., Oct. 30, 1968, Tom Johnson Papers; Clifford, *Counsel to the President,* 590–92.

107. Benjamin H. Read Memo, Oct. 31, 1968, NSF: Country: Vietnam; Rostow to LBJ, Nov. 3, 1968, summarizing Bunker-Thieu talks of Oct. 31, NSF: Memos to the Pres.; LBJ meeting in the Cabinet Room, Oct. 31, 1968; mjdr to Harry, Oct. 31, 1968, Diary Backup; Dorothy Territo to LBJ, Nov. 3, 1972, Reference File: Chennault; Clifford, *Counsel to the President,* 502–3.

108. *PPP: LBJ, 1968,* II, 1099–103. See Memo, n.d., 1968, "2 The President believes that they [So. Vietnamese] have lost some of their interest in a meeting because of impressions from Nixon associates," NSF: Rostow Files; see the numerous FBI memos of Oct. 31–Nov. 3, 1968, to Bromley Smith at the White House about Chennault, Reference File: Chennault; Clifford, *Counsel to the President,* 504.

109. Lady Bird Johnson interview, Oct. 6, 1997. George Christian quoted Johnson's "treason" remark to me. Johnson Memo, Nov. 4, 1968, describing the political impact of Thieu's actions, Reference File: Chennault; and Rostow to LBJ, Nov. 5, 1968, on Thieu and Ky, NSF: Country: Vietnam.

110. Panzer to LBJ, Oct. 17, 1968, memos of 3:30 and 5:35 p.m.; Oct. 29 and 31, 1968, WHCF: EX/PL2; Oct. 23, 24, Nov. 4, 5, 1968, WHCF: EX/PR16; Wattenberg to LBJ, Oct. 21, 1968, Handwriting File.

111. Panzer to LBJ, Oct. 25, 1968, WHCF: EX/PL2; Oct. 26, 1968, WHCF: EX/PR16; Barefoot Sanders to Jim Jones, Oct. 23, 1968; two Jim Jones memos, Oct. 24, 1968, Diary Backup; Jimmy Breslin, "LBJ on the Stump," *New York Post,* Oct. 28, 1968; *PPP: LBJ, 1968,* II, 1073–96, 1107–13.

112. Rostow, Memorandum for the Record, May 14, 1973; Territo to LBJ, Nov. 3, 1972, Reference File: Chennault; "Walt Reports," Nov. 2, 1968, Diary Backup.

113. Jim Jones memo, Nov. 3, 1968, 11:25 a.m.; the *Times* story was in

the Spectrum section, n.d., Reference File: Chennault; Bryce Harlow OH, May 6, 1979; *New York Times*, June 13, 1991; Clifford, *Counsel to the President*, 594–96; Jules Witcover, *The Year the Dream Died: Revisiting 1968 in America* (New York, 1997).

114. Memo, Nov. 4, 1968; Rostow to LBJ, Nov. 4, 1968, Reference File: Chennault.

115. Rostow to LBJ, Nov. 4, 1969, Reference File: Chennault.

116. Solberg, *Humphrey*, 398–400.

117. Ibid., 401–2; *(Washington) Evening Star*, July 9, 1969; Theodore H. White, *The Making of the President, 1968* (New York, 1969), 445.

118. Solberg, *Humphrey*, 407.

119. Robert L. Hardesty, "With Lyndon Johnson in Texas: A Memoir of the Post-Presidential Years," in *Farewell to the Chief: Former Presidents in American Public Life*, edited by Richard Norton Smith and Timothy Walch (Worland, Wy., 1990), 95; LBJ meeting with Helen Thomas, Nov. 22, 1968, Diary Backup.

120. Ibid.

121. LBJ meeting with Nixon, Nov. 11, 1968, Tom Johnson Papers; Jim Jones memo, Nov. 11, 1968, Diary Backup.

122. Clifford, *Counsel to the President*, 599–600.

123. Territo to LBJ, Nov. 3, 1972, Reference File: Chennault, for LBJ-RN telephone conversations of Nov. 14, 1968; Jim Jones to LBJ, Dec. 10, 1968, memos of 11:12 a.m. and 2 p.m., Diary Backup; LBJ, *Vantage Point*, 555–57.

124. Pearson to LBJ, Nov. 18, 1968, Drew Pearson Papers; LBJ meeting with Helen Thomas, Nov. 22, 1968, Diary Backup.

125. Califano to LBJ, Nov. 19 and 21, 1968, WHCF: EX/PL\Nixon, Richard; Glen Phillips to LBJ, Dec. 4, 1968; Okun et al. to LBJ, Dec. 10, 1968; Charles Zwick to LBJ, Dec. 30, 1968; Califano to LBJ, Dec. 30, 1968, Diary Backup; *PPP: LBJ, 1968*, II, 1311–15; Califano, *Triumph and Tragedy*, 330–33.

126. Rostow phone conversations with Robert Murphy, Nov. 24, 1968; Rostow to LBJ, Nov. 29, 1968, NSF: Rostow Files; Jim Jones Memo, Nov. 27, 1968; Press Release, Nov. 27, 1968; UPI-5, Nov. 30, 1968; WHCF: EX/PL\Nixon, Richard; LBJ meeting with foreign policy advisers, Nov. 26, 1968, Tom Johnson Papers; Rostow to LBJ, Nov. 29, 1968; LBJ meeting with Frank Reynolds, Dec. 17, 1968, Diary Backup.

127. Rostow to LBJ, Sept. 1, 1968, NSF: Memos to the Pres.; Memo, Sept. 7, 1968; Rostow to LBJ, Sept. 10, Oct. 4, 17, 25, Nov. 14, 3:30 and 5:30 p.m., 1968; Memo, Sept. 16, 1968, NSF: Rostow Files.

128. NSF: NSC Meeting, Nov. 25, 1968; LBJ meeting with foreign policy advisers, Nov. 26, 1968, Tom Johnson Papers; Glen Phillips to LBJ, Dec. 6, 1968; LBJ meeting with Charles Bailey, Dec. 10, 1968, Diary Backup; Notes, Strategic Talks, Dec. 1968, Clark Clifford Papers; Message to Amb. Thompson, Dec. 9, 1968; Rostow to LBJ, Dec. 11, 1968, memos at 9:55 a.m. and 1:35 p.m., NSF: Rostow Files.

129. LBJ, *Vantage Point*, 490–91; LBJ meeting with Frank Reynolds, Dec. 17, 1968, Diary Backup; also the Chalmers Roberts story in the *Washington Post*, Jan. 12, 1969; and Clifford, *Counsel to the President*, 599.

130. Charles S. Murphy to LBJ, Nov. 22, 1968, WHCF: EX/FG11-8.

131. *PPP: LBJ, 1968*, II, 1058, 1103–7, 1173–77, 1208–9, 1210–11; E. C. Welsh to LBJ, Sept. 30, 1968; Califano to LBJ, Dec. 26, 1968, WHCF: Aides: Califano.

132. Rostow to LBJ, Nov. 4, 1968; cable to Harriman and Vance, Nov. 10, 1968; Draft letter, Nov. 10, 1968; Rostow to LBJ, Nov. 11, 1968, 10:30 and 10:40 a.m., NSF: Country: Vietnam; Rostow to LBJ, Nov. 11, 1968, Diary Backup; Clifford, *Counsel to the President*, 600–601.

133. Rostow to LBJ, Nov. 12, 1968; UPI-109, Nov. 15, 1968; cable from U.S. Embassy, Saigon to State Dept., Nov. 15, 1968, NSF: Country: Vietnam; LBJ meeting with Rusk et al., Nov. 19, 1968, NSF: Meeting Notes; LBJ meeting with foreign policy advisers, Nov. 20, 1968, Tom Johnson Papers; UPI-8, Nov. 27, 1968, WHCF: EX/PL\Nixon, Richard; LBJ meeting with Frank Reynolds, Dec. 17, 1968, WHCF: Aides: Christian; Cable to Saigon and Paris, Jan. 7, 1969, DSDUF; LBJ, *Vantage Point*, 529; Clifford, *Counsel to the President*, 604–606.

134. Califano, *Triumph and Tragedy*, 333–34; *PPP: LBJ, 1968*, II, 1263–70.

135. Larry Temple OH, Aug. 13, 1970.

136. Califano, *Triumph and Tragedy*, 335–38.

137. Tom Johnson OH, Feb. 22, 1989; *PPP: LBJ, 1968*, II, 1369.

138. Lady Bird Johnson, *White House Diary*, 779–81; Joe B. Frantz to LBJ, Jan. 23, 1969; LBJ to George Bush, Jan. 31, 1969, Post-Presidential: Name File: George Bush; Tom Johnson OH, Feb. 22, 1989.

CHAPTER 12: AFTER THE FALL

1. Luci Johnson Turpin told me this at a dinner at the LBJ Library, Feb. 25, 1996.

2. Leo Janos, "The Last Days of the President: LBJ in Retirement," *The Atlantic*, July 1973.

3. Miller, *Lyndon*, 661; LBJ interview with Helen Thomas, Nov. 22, 1968, Diary Backup; Robert L. Hardesty, "With LBJ in Texas," in *Farewell to the Chiefs*, 97.

4. Ibid.

5. The story was told to me by Harry Middleton.

6. Miller, *Lyndon*, 664; W. Tom Johnson OH, April 11, 1974; Wilbur Mills OH, Mar. 25, 1987.

7. Ibid., Larry Temple OH, June 12, 1970.

8. Ibid., Aug. 11, 1970.

9. Kearns, *Lyndon Johnson*, 356–57; Hardesty, "With LBJ in Texas," 99.

10. Miller, *Lyndon*, 663–64, 667–68; Hardesty, "With LBJ in Texas," 101–2.

11. Miller, *Lyndon*, 671.

12. Hardesty, "With LBJ in Texas," 100–101.

13. Jewell Malechek OH, Dec. 20, 1978; Robert Hardesty interview, Nov. 4, 1996; Kearns, *Lyndon Johnson*, 358–59.

14. Robert Hardesty interview, Nov. 4, 1996; Elizabeth Wickenden interview, Dec. 20, 1986; Miller, *Lyndon*, 662.

15. Wickenden interview.

16. Miller, *Lyndon*, 664–65.

17. H. R. Haldeman, *The Haldeman Diaries: Inside the Nixon White House* (New York, 1994), 82–83.

18. W. Tom Johnson OH, April 11, 1974, Feb. 22, 1989.

19. Hardesty, "With LBJ in Texas," 96, 102; LBJ interview with Helen Thomas, Nov. 22, 1968, Diary Backup; W. Tom Johnson OH, April 11, 1974, Feb. 22, 1989.

20. W. Tom Johnson OH, April 11, 1974.

21. Kearns, *Lyndon Johnson*, 11–14.

22. Ibid., 13, 353–54.

23. Ibid., 353–54; Hardesty, "With LBJ in Texas," 97–98.

24. W. Tom Johnson OH, April 11, 1974.

25. Ibid., 355.

26. Hardesty, "With LBJ in Texas," 104–5.

27. W. Tom Johnson OH, April 11, 1974, Feb. 22, 1989; Hardesty, "With LBJ in Texas," 105; Miller, *Lyndon*, 663; *New York Times*, Jan. 27, Dec. 27, 1969.

28. Miller, *Lyndon*, 669–70.

29. W. Tom Johnson OH, Feb. 22, 1989.

30. Harry Middleton, "A President and His Library: My Recollections of Working with Lyndon Johnson," *Farewell to the Chiefs*, 109–111.

31. LBJ interview with Helen Thomas, Nov. 22, 1968, Diary Backup; W. Tom Johnson OH, Feb. 22, 1989.

32. Ibid.; Hardesty, "With LBJ in Texas," 102–3.

33. Donald S. Thomas OH, March 13, 1987; W. Tom Johnson OH, April 11, 1974.

34. Donald S. Thomas OH, March 13, 1987.

35. Ibid.; Miller, *Lyndon*, 674–75.

36. W. Tom Johnson OH, April 11, 1974; Miller, *Lyndon*, 663.

37. Jewell Malechek Scott OH, May 30, 1990; Miller, *Lyndon*, 663; W. Tom Johnson OH, April 11, 1974; Janos, "Last Days of the President."

38. Jewell Malechek OH, Dec. 20, 1978; Miller, *Lyndon*, 665–66; Hardesty, "With LBJ in Texas," 97.

39. Kearns, *Lyndon Johnson*, 358–62; Jewell Malechek Scott OH, May 30, 1990.

40. Kearns, *Lyndon Johnson*, 360.

41. Jewell Malechek OH, Dec. 20, 1978, May 30, 1990.

42. Miller, *Lyndon*, 666; W. Tom Johnson OH, Feb. 22, 1989; Califano, *Triumph and Tragedy*, 178–79.

43. Miller, *Lyndon*, 666–67; W. Tom Johnson OH, Feb. 22, 1989; H. R. Haldeman, *Haldeman Diaries*, 114.

44. Rostow to LBJ, March 19, 1969; Tom Johnson to LBJ, Feb. 27, 1970; William J. Jorden, May 1, 1970; RN to LBJ, May 22, 1970; LBJ to RN, May 28, 1970, Post-Presidential: Name: Nixon; Tom Johnson to LBJ, May 28, 1969; George Bush to LBJ, May 29, 1969, Post-Presidential: Name: Bush; LBJ Speech, May 1, 1970, Reference File: Post-Presidential: Speeches.

45. Miller, *Lyndon*, 671–73; Harry Middleton to LBJ, July 13, 1972; LBJ Statement and UPI Press Release, Aug. 16, 1972; Robert Healy article, "M'Govern Trips on Credibility," Sept. 1, 1972; William S. White article, "McGovern's Lunch at LBJ Ranch an Irony of Race," Sept. 11, 1972; Tom Braden

article, "McGovern's Letter to Johnson," Oct. 3, 1972, Post-Presidential: Name: McGovern.

46. Miller, *Lyndon*, 673; Haldeman, *Haldeman Diaries*, 485, 494–97.

47. Memorandum, Oct. 5, 1972, Post-Presidential: Name: Nixon.

48. Haldeman, *Haldeman Diaries*, 565–67.

49. See Daniel Schorr, "The Secret Nixon-LBJ War," *Washington Post*, May 28, 1995. The speculation about the Greek money is mine.

50. Janos, "Last Days of the President"; W. Tom Johnson OH, Feb. 22, 1989; Miller, *Lyndon*, 668–69.

51. Jewell Malechek Scott OH, May 30, 1990.

52. Miller, *Lyndon*, 668–69.

53. Jewell Malechek OH, Dec. 20, 1978, Malechek Scott OH, May 30, 1990; Janos, "Last Days of the President"; Miller, *Lyndon*, 671–72.

54. For the background to the speech, see ibid., 673–74; the speech given on Sept. 16, 1972, is in Reference File: Post-Presidential: Speeches.

55. Reference File: Post-Presidential; Schedule, 1972–73, Miller, *Lyndon*, 675.

56. Hugh Sidey, "One More Call to Reason Together," Dec. 29, 1972, *Life*; LBJ, Speech, Dec. 12, 1972, Reference File: Post-Presidential: Civil Rights Symposium; Miller, *Lyndon*, 680–85.

57. Janos, "The Last Days of the President"; Jewell Malechek Scott OH, May 30, 1990; W. Tom Johnson OH, June 19, 1973, April 11, 1974, Feb. 22, 1989.

58. See Post-Presidential: Reference File: LBJ Funeral; Middleton told me the anecdote; Miller, *Lyndon*, 676–79.

Index